Caribbean

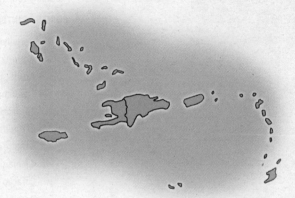

Published by AAA Publishing

1000 AAA Drive, Heathrow, FL 32746-5063
Copyright AAA 2011, All rights reserved

Advertising Rate and Circulation Information: (407) 444-8280

Printed in the USA by Quad/Graphics

Photo Credit: (Cover & Title Page)
Marigot Bay, Saint Lucia
© Michael Lawrence / Lonely Planet Images

Printed on recyclable paper.
Please recycle whenever possible.

This book is printed on paper certified by third-party standards for sustainably-managed forestry and production.

Caribbean

HOTELS & RESTAURANTS 249-523

MAPS

Featured Information

The Playful Side of Paradise

Breezes Resorts & Spas, the Playful Side of Paradise, where virtually everything you can eat, drink and do is included in one simple, up front price with no tipping allowed. That's the Super-Inclusive® difference!

Everything from award-winning cuisine, premium brand beverages, fabulous rooms & suites, every land and water sport imaginable - even golf* - and so much more. All included in some of the most stunningly beautiful locations.

Breezes Resorts & Spas are exactly what you should expect in a true tropical retreat - and so much more! Our smaller, boutique-like resorts mean fewer steps to the beach. With fewer rooms and guests than you would find at many other large all-inclusive resort chains, you can spend more time actually vacationing and less time queuing in long buffet lines. You'll spend less time claiming beach chairs and more time actually sunbathing. It means you get more square feet of beach and more vacationing per minute than you'll find elsewhere. Plus, our higher staff to guest ratio means you'll get the attention you deserve.

Choose more. Choose Super-Inclusive®.

To learn more about the Super-Inclusive®
Breezes Resorts & Spas, call your favorite AAA Travel Agent,
visit breezes.com or call us toll free at 877-Breezes (273-3937)

A tropical escape made just for you.

Fun. Romantic. Active. And, best of all, Super-Inclusive®. So, leave your wallet behind and bring a healthy appetite for great food and endless fun. All on some of the best beaches anywhere.

At Breezes, even your Dream Wedding is complimentary. It's our wedding gift to you and includes everything from the wedding planner, choice of location, marriage officiant (minister), marriage license, champagne, wedding cake, flowers, music and more.

To make your big day even more special, we offer upgraded Dream Wedding packages at an additional charge.

JAMAICA / BAHAMAS / CURAÇAO / PANAMA / BRAZIL

Using Your Guide

How the Guide is Organized

The guide is organized into three distinct sections.

The **Points of Interest** section helps you plan daily activities and sightseeing excursions and provides details about the city or attraction you are visiting.

The **Hotels and Restaurants** section helps you select AAA Approved accommodations and dining facilities meeting your specific needs and expectations.

The **Reference** section provides indexes for locating information within this guide and items to aid the trip planning process.

Locating the Attractions, Hotels and Restaurants

Attractions, hotels and restaurants are listed under the city in which they physically are located — or in some cases under the nearest recognized city. Most listings are alphabetically organized by state, region or island, then by city and establishment name.

A color is assigned to each state, region or island so you can match the color bars at the tops of pages to switch from the Points of Interest section to the corresponding Hotels and Restaurants section.

Spotting maps help you physically locate points of interest, hotels and restaurants in the major destinations.

The Comprehensive City Index located in the Reference section contains an A-to-Z list of cities.

Destination Cities and Destination Areas

Destination cities, established based on government models and local expertise, include metropolitan areas. Destination areas are regions with broad tourist appeal made up of several cities.

If a city falls within a destination's vicinity, the city name will appear at its alphabetical location in the book, and a cross reference will give you the exact page on which listings for that city begin.

An Orientation map appears at the beginning of each destination section to familiarize you with that destination.

About Listed Establishments

AAA Approved attractions, hotels and restaurants are listed on the basis of merit alone after careful evaluation and approval by full-time, professionally trained AAA inspectors. An establishment's decision to advertise in the guide has no bearing on its evaluation or rating; nor does inclusion of advertising imply AAA/CAA endorsement of products and services.

Information in this guide was believed accurate at the time of publication. However, since changes inevitably occur between annual editions, please contact your AAA/CAA travel professional or visit AAA.com to confirm prices and schedules.

Location Abbreviations

Directions are from the center of town unless otherwise specified, using these highway abbreviations:

Bus. Rte.=business route

CR=county road

FM=farm to market

FR=forest road

Hwy.=Canadian or Caribbean highway

I=interstate highway

LR=legislative route

Mex.=Mexican highway

R.R.=rural route

SR/PR=state or provincial route

US=federal highway

Understanding the Diamond Ratings

Hotel and restaurant evaluations are unscheduled to ensure our professionally trained inspectors encounter the same experience members do.

- When an establishment is Diamond Rated, it means members can expect a good fit with their needs. The inspector assigns a rating that indicates the type of experience to expect.

- While establishments at high levels must offer increasingly complex personalized services, establishments at every level are subject to the same basic requirements for cleanliness, comfort and hospitality. Learn more at AAA.com/Diamonds.

Hotels

Budget-oriented, offering basic comfort and hospitality.

Affordable, with modestly enhanced facilities, decor and amenities.

Distinguished, multi-faceted with enhanced physical attributes, amenities and guest comforts.

Refined, stylish with upscale physical attributes, extensive amenities and high degree of hospitality, service and attention to detail.

Ultimate luxury, sophistication and comfort with extraordinary physical attributes, meticulous personalized service, extensive amenities and impeccable standards of excellence.

Restaurants

Simple, familiar specialty food at an economical price. Often self-service, basic surroundings.

Familiar, family-oriented experience. Home-style foods and family favorites, often cooked to order, modestly enhanced and reasonably priced. Relaxed service, casual surroundings.

Fine dining, often adult-oriented. Latest cooking trends and/or traditional cuisine, expanded beverage offerings. Professional service staff and comfortable, well-coordinated ambience.

Distinctive fine-dining, typically expensive. Highly creative chefs, imaginative presentations and fresh, top-quality ingredients. Proficient service staff, upscale surroundings. Wine steward may offer menu-specific knowledge.

Luxurious and consistently world-class. Highly acclaimed chefs, artistic and imaginative menu selections using the finest ingredients. Maitre d' and unobtrusive, expert service staff.

What's the difference?

Red Diamonds mark establishments that participate in the AAA logo licensing program for increased visibility to members.

Black Diamonds identify all other AAA Approved and Diamond Rated establishments.

Attraction Listings

ATTRACTION NAME, 3 mi. n. off SR 20A (Main Ave.), consists of 250 acres with Olmsted-designed gardens, a 205-foot marble and coquina bell tower and a Mediterranean-style mansion. One of the state's oldest attractions, the tower and gardens were dedicated to the American people in 1929 by President Calvin Coolidge on behalf of their founder, a Dutch immigrant.

Other features include daily concerts from the 60-bell carillon, a nature observatory and Nature Preserve Trail. The visitor center presents art exhibits, an orientation film and exhibits about the family legacy, the carillon and endangered plants and animals found on the property.

Hours: Gardens daily 8-6. Last admission 1 hour before closing. Visitor center daily 9-5. Estate tours are given at noon and 2. Carillon concerts are given at 1 and 3. Phone ahead to confirm schedule. **Cost:** $10; $3 (ages 5-12). Gardens and estate $16; $8 (ages 5-12). **Phone:** (555) 555-5555. 〖Ⅱ〗 〖A〗

AAA inspectors may designate an attraction of exceptional interest and quality as a GEM — a *Great Experience for Members*®.

Adventure Travel

Activities such as air tours, hiking, skiing and white-water rafting are listed to provide member information and do not imply AAA/CAA endorsement. For your safety, be aware of inherent risks and adhere to all safety instructions.

Cost

Prices are quoted without sales tax in U.S. dollars or in local currency as an approximate U.S. dollar equivalent. Children under the lowest age specified are admitted free when accompanied by an adult. Most establishments accept credit cards, but a small number require cash, so please call ahead to verify.

Icons

SAVE   Show Your Card & Save member discount

A   Camping facilities

Ⅱ   Food on premises

X   Recreational activities

🐕   Pets on leash allowed

A   Picnicking allowed

© Monashee Frantz / age fotostock

Information-Only Attraction Listings

Bulleted listings, which include the following categories, are listed for informational purposes as a service to members:

- **Gambling establishments** (even if located in a AAA Approved hotel)
- **Participatory recreational activities** (those requiring physical exertion or special skills)
- **Wineries** that offer tours and tastings

Hotel and Restaurant Listings

1 Diamond Rating – AAA Approved hotels and restaurants are assigned a rating of one to five Diamonds. Red Diamonds distinguish establishments that participate in the AAA logo licensing program. For details, see p. 8 or AAA.com/Diamonds.

[fyi] indicates hotels and restaurants that are not AAA Approved and Diamond Rated but are listed to provide additional choices for members:

- **Hotels** may be unrated if they are: too new to rate, under construction, under major renovation, not evaluated, do not meet all AAA requirements. Hotels that do not meet all AAA requirements may be included if they offer member value or are the only option; details are noted in the listing.
- **Restaurants** may be unrated if they have not yet been evaluated by AAA.

2 Classification or Cuisine Type – Noted immediately below the Diamond Rating.

- **Hotel Classifications** indicate the style of operation, overall concept and service level. Subclassifications may also be added. (See p. 12 list.)
- **Restaurant Cuisine Types** identify the food concept from more than 100 categories. If applicable, a classification may also be added. (See p. 13 list.)

3 Dollar Amounts – Quoted without sales tax in U.S. dollars, rounded up to the nearest dollar. Most establishments accept credit cards, but a small number require cash, so please call ahead to verify.

- **Hotel Rates** indicate the publicly available two-person rate or rate range for a standard room, applicable all year unless effective dates are indicated.
- **Restaurant Prices** represent the minimum and maximum entree cost per person. Exceptions may include one-of-a-kind or special market priced items.

4 Spotting Symbol – Ovals containing numbers correspond with numbered location markings on hotel and restaurant spotting maps.

5 Parking – Unless otherwise noted, parking is free, on-site self parking.

6 Hotel Value Nationwide – Blue boxes highlight everyday member benefits available at all AAA Approved locations across a hotel chain. (See p. 17 for details.)

7 Hotel Unit Limited Availability – Unit types, amenities and room features preceded by "some" are available on a limited basis, potentially as few as one.

8 Hotel Terms – Cancellation and minimum stay policies are listed. Unless otherwise noted, most properties offer a full deposit refund with cancellations received at least 48 hours before standard check-in. Properties that require advance payment may not refund the difference for early departures.

9 Hotel Check-in/Check-out – Unless otherwise noted, check-in is after 3 p.m. and check-out is before 10 a.m.

10 Restaurant Dress Code – Unless otherwise noted, dress is casual or dressy casual.

11 Restaurant Menu – Where indicated, menus may be viewed in a secure online environment at AAA.com or, if a mobile tag is provided, via the restaurant's website.

12 Hotel Icons – May be preceded by CALL, FEE and/or SOME UNITS.

Member Information:

[SAVE] Rate guarantee: discounted standard room rate or lowest public rate available at time of booking for dates of stay.

[ECO] Eco-certified by government or private organization. Visit AAA.com/eco for details.

[X] Smoke-free premises

Services:

[wifi] Wireless Internet service on premises

[+] Airport transportation

[pets] Pets allowed (Call property for restrictions and fees.)

[fork] Restaurant on premises

[fork+] Restaurant off premises (walking distance)

[room service] Room service for 2 or more meals

HOTEL LISTING

RESTAURANT LISTING

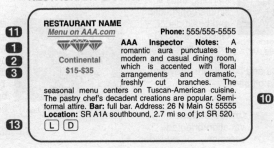

🍸 Full bar

🛝 Child care

BIZ Business services

♿M Accessible features (Call property for available services and amenities.)

Activities:

🎰 Full-service casino

🏊 Pool

🏋 Health club on premises

🏋 Health club off premises

In-Room Amenities:

🎥 Pay movies

🧊 Refrigerator

🍱 Microwave

☕ Coffee maker

🆉 No air conditioning

📺 No TV

📺 No cable TV

☎ No telephones

Safety Features:

S Sprinklers

SD Smoke detectors

13 **Restaurant Icons**

SAVE Show Your Card & Save member discount

🆉 No air conditioning

♿M Accessible features (Call property for available services and amenities.)

🚭 Designated smoking section

B Breakfast

L Lunch

D Dinner

24 Open 24 hours

LATE Open after 11 p.m.

Hotel Classifications

Quality and comfort are usually consistent across each Diamond Rating level, but decor, facilities and service levels vary by classification.

1884 Paxton House Inn
Thomasville, GA

Bed & Breakfast – Typically small-scale, emphasizing personal touches. Individually decorated units may not include televisions, telephones or private bathrooms. Usually a common room and continental or full, hot breakfast.

Greenbrier Valley Resorts at
Cobbly Nob, Gatlinburg, TN

Cabin – Vacation-oriented, typically small-scale, free-standing units with simple construction and basic decor. Often in wooded, rural or waterfront location. Cleaning supplies, utensils and bath linens provided. Check-in may be off site.

Camelot by the Sea
Myrtle Beach, SC

Condominium – Vacation-oriented, commonly for extended stays. Routinely rented through a management company. Generally one or more bedrooms, living room, full kitchen and eating area. Studio units combine sleeping and living areas. Cleaning supplies, utensils and linens provided. Check-in may be off site.

The Dunes on the Waterfront
Ogunquit, ME

Cottage – Vacation-oriented, typically small-scale, freestanding units with homey design and decor. Often in wooded, rural or waterfront location. Cleaning supplies, utensils and linens provided. Check-in may be off site.

The Lodge at Moosehead
Lake, Greenville, ME

Country Inn – Similar to bed and breakfasts but larger scale with spacious public areas and dining facility that serves, at a minimum, breakfast and dinner.

The Grand America Hotel
Salt Lake City, UT

Hotel – Commonly multistory with interior room entrances. Unit styles vary. Public areas determined by overall theme, location and service level, but may include restaurant, shops, fitness center, spa, business center and meeting rooms.

Best Western Plus Sea Island
Inn, Beaufort, SC

Motel – Commonly one- or two-story with exterior room entrances and drive-up parking. Typically one bedroom with bathroom. Limited public areas and facilities.

Lost Valley Ranch
Deckers, CO

Ranch – Typically a working ranch with rustic, Western theme, equestrian activities and various unit styles.

Indian Creek-Alexander
Holiday Homes
Kissimmee, FL

Vacation Rental House – Commonly for extended stays. Typically large scale, freestanding and of varying design. Routinely rented through a management company. Often two or more bedrooms, living room, full kitchen, dining room and multiple bathrooms. Cleaning supplies, utensils and linens supplied. Check-in may be off site.

© Adivin / iStockphoto

Hotel Subclassifications

These additional descriptives may be added to the classification for more information:

- **Boutique** – Often thematic and informal, highly personalized experience. May have fashionable, luxurious or quirky style.
- **Casino** – (Identified by listing icon) Extensive gambling facilities such as blackjack, craps, keno and slot machines.
- **Classic** – Landmark property, older than 50 years, renowned style and ambience.
- **Contemporary** – Design and theme reflective of current mainstream tastes and style.
- **Extended Stay** – Predominantly long-term units with full-service kitchens.
- **Historic** – Typically 75 years or older with historic architecture, design, furnishings, public record or acclaim and at least one of the following: maintains integrity of the historical nature, listed on the National Register of Historic Places, designated a National Historic Landmark or located in a National Register Historic District.
- **Resort** – Recreation-oriented, geared to a specific destination experience. Typically offer travel packages, meal plans, themed entertainment and social and recreational programs. Extensive recreational facilities may include spa treatments, golf, tennis, skiing, fishing or water sports. Larger resorts may offer a variety of unit types.
- **Retro** – Contemporary design and theme that reinterpret styles of a bygone era.

- **Vacation Rental** – Typically a house, condo, cottage or cabin offering space, value and conveniences such as full kitchens and washers/dryers. Located in a resort or popular destination area near major points of interest. May require reservations and off-site check-in. Limited housekeeping services.
- **Vintage** – Design and theme reflective of a bygone era.

Restaurant Classifications

If applicable, in addition to the cuisine type noted under the Diamond Rating, restaurant listings may also include one or both classifications:

- **Classic** – Renowned and landmark operation in business for 25 plus years; unique style and ambience.
- **Historic** – Meets one of the following: Listed on National Register of Historic Places, designated a National Historic Landmark or located in a National Register Historic District.

Mobile Tags

Look for codes like this Microsoft Tag in the ads and restaurant listings to access special online offers, menus, videos and more.

To use Microsoft Tags:

- Download the free Tag Reader app to your smartphone at http://gettag.mobi.
- Start scanning Tags.
- Link to featured content.

Some advertisers use codes other than Microsoft Tags. In those cases, please note any accompanying text that indicates where to download the required reader.

The urge
to tear up
your return
ticket
runs just
as deep.

You think it can't get any better. And then a ripe mango falls in your lap.

JAMAICA

Call 1-800-JAMAICA or
LOG ON TO visitjamaica.com

Once you go, you know.

Just For Members

Show Your Card & Save® Member Discounts

Before you go, contact your local AAA/CAA club for locations, reservations and other details regarding the following Show Your Card & Save member discounts. Gray Line and Hard Rock Café savings may be used for up to six patrons. Other restrictions may apply.

DINING

Hard Rock Cafe
- Save 10% on food, nonalcoholic beverages and merchandise at all U.S., Canadian and select international locations.

TOURS

Gray Line
- Save 10% on sightseeing tours of 1 day or less worldwide at AAA.com/GrayLine.

TRANSPORTATION

Hertz
- Save on daily, weekend, weekly and monthly rentals at AAA.com/hertz, hertz.com or 1-800-654-3080.

AAA Approved Hotels

For members, AAA Approved means quality assured.

- Only properties that meet basic requirements for cleanliness, comfort and hospitality pass inspection.
- Approved hotels receive a Diamond Rating that tells members the type of experience to expect.

Guest Safety

Inspectors view a sampling of rooms during evaluations and, therefore, AAA cannot guarantee the presence of working locks and operational fire safety equipment in every guest unit.

If a hotel met AAA's security requirements at the time of inspection, the listing denotes "Meets AAA guest room security requirements" and includes icons for sprinklers and/or smoke detectors.

Member Rates

AAA/CAA members can generally expect to pay no more than the maximum listed rate for a standard room. Member discounts apply to rates quoted within the rate range and are applicable at the time of booking. Listed rates are usually based on last standard room availability. Within the range, rates may vary by season and room type. Obtain current AAA/CAA member rates and make reservations at AAA.com.

Exceptions

- Rates in the Mexico Guide are not guaranteed and may fluctuate based on the currency exchange rate.
- Rates for properties operating as concessionaires for the U.S. National Park Service are not guaranteed due to governing regulations.
- Special advertised rates and short-term promotional rates below the rate range are not subject to additional member discounts.
- During special events, hotels may temporarily increase room rates, not recognize discounts or modify pricing policies. Special events may include holidays, holiday periods and festivals. Although some special events are listed in this guide and on AAA.com, it's always wise to check in advance with AAA/CAA travel professionals for specific dates.

If you are charged more than the maximum listed rate, question the additional charge. If an exception is not in effect and management refuses to adhere to the published rate, pay for the room and contact AAA/CAA. The amount paid above the stated maximum will be refunded if our investigation indicates an unjustified charge.

Reservations and Cancellations

When making your reservation, identify yourself as a AAA/CAA member and request written confirmation of your room type, rate, dates of stay, and cancellation and refund policies. At registration, show your membership card.

To cancel, contact the hotel or your AAA/CAA club office, depending on how you booked your reservation. Request a cancellation number or proof of cancellation.

If your room is not as specified and you have written confirmation of your reservation for a specific room type, you should be given the option of choosing a different room or receiving a refund. If management refuses to issue a refund, contact AAA/CAA.

Contacting AAA/CAA About Approved Properties

If your visit to a AAA Approved attraction, hotel or restaurant doesn't meet your expectations, please tell us about it — *during your visit or within 30 days*.

Please send us the details, and save your receipts and other documentation for reference.

- **E-mail:**
  memberrelations@national.aaa.com
- **Mail:**
  AAA Member Comments, 1000 AAA Dr., Heathrow, FL 32746.

AAA Preferred Hotels

All AAA Approved hotels are committed to providing quality, value and member service. Those also designated as AAA Preferred Hotels offer these extra values at Approved locations. Valid AAA/CAA membership required.

- **Best AAA/CAA member rates for your dates of stay.**
- **Seasonal promotions and special member offers.** Visit AAA.com to view current offers.
- **Everyday member benefit.** Look for the blue boxes in the hotel listings to find everyday values offered at all AAA Approved locations. Chains and offers valid at time of publication may change without notice.

- **Total satisfaction guarantee.** If you book your stay with AAA/CAA Travel and your stay fails to meet your expectations, you can apply for a full refund. Bring the complaint to the hotel's attention during the stay and request resolution; if the complaint is not resolved by the hotel, ask your AAA/CAA travel agent to request resolution through the AAA/CAA Assured Stay program.

Preferred Hotels

Best Western, Best Western Plus and Best Western Premier

Conrad Hotels & Resorts, DoubleTree by Hilton, Embassy Suites, Hampton Inns & Suites, Hilton Hotels & Resorts, Hilton Garden Inns, Hilton Grand Vacations, Home2 Suites, Homewood Suites and Waldorf Astoria Collection

ANdAZ, Grand Hyatt, Hyatt Place, Hyatt Regency, Hyatt Summerfield Suites and Park Hyatt

Autograph Collection by Marriott, Courtyard, EDITION Hotels by Marriott, Fairfield Inn, JW Marriott, Marriott Hotels & Resorts, Renaissance Hotels, Residence Inn, Ritz-Carlton Hotels & Resorts, SpringHill Suites and TownePlace Suites

Aloft, Element, Four Points, Le Meridien, Sheraton, St. Regis Hotels & Resorts, The Luxury Collection, Westin and W Hotels

Vacation with Peace of Mind

perience an incredible vacation with amazing value on select *AAA Vacations®* tour and cruise departures. Includes our **Best Price Guarantee** and **24/7 Member Care** for a worry-free vacation.

Contact your local AAA Travel Professional or visit **AAA.com/Travel** for full details on these exclusive *AAA Vacations®* benefits.

Terms and conditions apply

Caribbean

English Forts & Spanish Castles

Ruins and restored landmarks offer a glimpse of colonial history

Underwater Treasures

Coral reefs, shipwrecks and shimmering fish are jewels of the sea

Tropical Eden

Botanical gardens and national parks preserve the islands' natural beauty

Shoppers' Paradise

Designer goods and local crafts make perfect souvenirs

Hot Pot and a Bottle of Rum

Try a spicy taste of island cooking— but don't forget the local drink

Elbow Cay, Hope Town,
Great Abaco Island,
The Bahamas
© Larry Ulrich

Nelson's Dockyard National Park, English Harbour, Antigua / © SIME / eStock Photo

Like beads in a coral necklace strung between the Atlantic Ocean and the Caribbean Sea, the islands of the West Indies stretch east and south from the Gulf of Mexico and Florida to the northern coast of South America—a span of more than 2,000 miles.

The Caribbean islands' diversity of races and traditions generates an aura of romance and mystery. The Arawak, Taíno and Carib Indians were the first to arrive, migrating to the Antilles some 2,000 years before Columbus landed in 1492. Spanish, French, Dutch and American settlers would follow, bringing with them African slaves to work the gold mines and sugar mills that flourished on the islands until the late 19th century.

Explorers, pirates, settlers and slaves—all would carry their own customs to the archipelago Columbus called "the most beautiful land that human eyes have seen."

Today, tourism is the lifeblood of the islands, bringing a new influx of travelers from across the seas. Cruise ships have replaced three-masted schooners as the best way to get there, and lying in the sun with an umbrella drink may be all some visitors do once they arrive. For the more energetic, there's sightseeing, shopping, fishing, sailing, scuba diving, horseback riding, tennis and golf.

The lush islands of the Caribbean, The Bahamas and Bermuda offer enough natural beauty and cultural variety to please any visitor's tastes.

The hundreds of islands in the Caribbean archipelago are divided into The Bahamas and the Greater and Lesser Antilles. The Antilles were named after *Antillia,* a mythical island sought by Spanish explorers. The Greater Antilles include the largest islands: Cuba, Jamaica, Puerto Rico and the island of Hispaniola, which contains Haiti and the Dominican Republic.

The Lesser Antilles encompass the remaining arc of smaller isles as well as several islands off the coast of Venezuela. Major groupings within the Lesser Antilles include the Virgin Islands and the Windward and Leeward Islands. Bermuda is not a Caribbean island at all, but is located in the Atlantic Ocean, 650 miles due east of Cape Hatteras, N.C.

According to geologists the Caribbean archipelago is a portion of a once unbroken bridge that joined North and South America. Through unknown events some of the land sank, and what remains are the peaks of a submarine volcanic mountain range. A few of the Caribbean islands, as well as Bermuda, are coral formations.

The easterly trade winds that maintain the region's even temperatures were responsible for depositing Columbus at what he thought was the "back door" to India—probably San Salvador in The Bahamas. Columbus continued onward to Cuba and Hispaniola. Although the great golden treasures he envisioned never fully materialized, he did meet the Arawaks and the Caribs, whom he mistook for East Indians. His return to Spain with charts, a small amount of gold and tales of great fortune gained him financing for three more visits.

On the heels of Columbus came such *conquistadores* as Hernando Cortés and Francisco Pizarro seeking their share of land and gold. European investors built mining operations and sugar plantations, using native Indians as laborers. As the local work force declined, a license was arranged permitting the importation of African slaves—an agreement that was to have far-reaching effects on the New World.

Ships with holds laden with the produce of the Caribbean opened the door on yet another occupation. Buccaneers, pirates, smugglers and freebooters proliferated, using the islands' numerous caves and inlets for shelter and ambush. The result was many years of terror, bloodshed and territorial feuding. As Spanish supremacy in the region weakened, England, France, the Netherlands and the United States all added their cultural marks to the Caribbean.

In his first of three voyages to find a westward route to China, Christopher Columbus lands in the Bahamas.

1492

Library of Congress

Hernando Cortés sails to Hispaniola, the base for Spanish exploration in the Caribbean.

1504

The Dutch West India Company gains control of Curaçao.

1634

1510
The first African slaves in the New World are brought to Santo Domingo.

1623
England establishes its first permanent colony in the West Indies on St. Kitts.

Caribbean Historical Timeline

Today's island groups reflect this heritage among sovereign states, overseas departments and dependencies. The French West Indies include Guadeloupe, Martinique, St. Barthélemy and St. Martin. The Dutch islands of the Kingdom of the Netherlands are Aruba, Bonaire, Curaçao, St. Eustatius and Saba and St. Maarten. The British West Indies encompass Anguilla, the Cayman Islands, the British Virgin Islands and Turks and Caicos Islands. The American flag flies over the U.S. Virgin Islands and Puerto Rico.

Hundreds of Hideaways

With so many islands to visit, choosing one can be a daunting task. If language barriers are a concern, keep in mind that English is spoken at most large resorts and in most shops and restaurants.

Consider your priorities and interests: If you do not care for water sports, sunbathing or having lots of time on your hands, choose one of the more developed islands that offers plenty of shopping, sightseeing, dining and nightlife. On the other hand, if you want to "get away from it all," there are still some islands that have yet to be "discovered" and commercialized. On such islands modern conveniences might be rather sparse but privacy is abundant.

The local currency exchange rate also might influence your decision. Check Fast Facts for the governing rates at press time. Exchange rates can fluctuate significantly, so you should always check them with a financial institution prior to departure.

Because of the varying economic conditions on most islands, the contrast between luxury resorts and poverty-ridden villages can be a harsh reality. You might want to investigate the political and social climate of an island before planning your trip.

Tropical Seasons

Much of The Bahamas and all of the Caribbean islands lie below the Tropic of Cancer, the northern limit of the tropics, and therefore enjoy a mild climate year round. The main season varies from island to island and hotel to hotel but generally runs from mid-December to mid-April. The off-season is late spring, summer and fall, except in Bermuda, which is much farther north, where the off-season spans November to mid-March. Most islands are subject to a rainy season between June and November, which coincides with hurricane season.

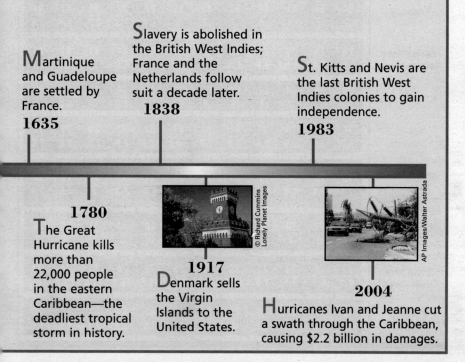

Martinique and Guadeloupe are settled by France.
1635

Slavery is abolished in the British West Indies; France and the Netherlands follow suit a decade later.
1838

St. Kitts and Nevis are the last British West Indies colonies to gain independence.
1983

1780
The Great Hurricane kills more than 22,000 people in the eastern Caribbean—the deadliest tropical storm in history.

1917
Denmark sells the Virgin Islands to the United States.

© Richard Cummins Lonely Planet Images

AP Images/Walter Astrada

2004
Hurricanes Ivan and Jeanne cut a swath through the Caribbean, causing $2.2 billion in damages.

Temperature Averages / Rainfall
(Temperatures are in Fahrenheit, rainfall in inches)

	JAN	FEB	MAR	APR	MAY	JUNE	JULY	AUG	SEPT	OCT	NOV	DEC
The Valley, Anguilla	78 / 1.8	76 / 1	78 / 1.8	78 / 5	78 / 4.8	78 / 1	78 / 4	80 / 2	80 / 2	80 / .8	78 / 10	78 / 2.6
St. John's, Antigua	78 / 1.8	76 / 1	78 / 1.8	78 / 5	78 / 4.8	78 / 1	78 / 4	80 / 2	80 / 2	80 / .8	78 / 10	78 / 2.6
Oranjestad, Aruba	80 / 1.9	80 / .7	81 / .4	82 / .5	83 / .5	83 / .6	83 / .8	84 / .7	84 / 1.1	84 / 2.6	83 / 3.8	80 / 3.2
Nassau, Bahamas	71 / 1.4	71 / 1.5	73 / 1.4	75 / 2.5	78 / 4.6	81 / 6.4	82 / 5.8	83 / 5.3	82 / 6.9	79 / 6.5	76 / 2.8	73 / 1.3
Bridgetown, Barbados	77 / 2.6	76 / 1.1	78 / 1.3	79 / 1.4	80 / 2.3	81 / 4.4	80 / 5.8	81 / 5.8	81 / 6.7	80 / 7	79 / 8.1	77 / 3.8
Hamilton, Bermuda	63 / 4.4	63 / 4.7	63 / 4.8	65 / 4.1	70 / 4.6	75 / 4.4	79 / 4.5	80 / 5.4	78 / 5.2	74 / 5.8	69 / 5	65 / 4.7
Kralendijk, Bonaire	80 / 2	80 / 1	81 / .8	81 / .6	82 / .7	82 / .7	82 / 1	83 / 1.1	83 / 1.3	83 / 2.7	82 / 4.7	81 / 3.5
George Town, Cayman Islands	78 / 1.8	78 / 1.4	79 / 1.0	80 / 1.6	83 / 7.4	85 / 9.6	85 / 7.0	85 / 6.4	84 / 8.8	83 / 11	82 / 5	81 / 2.8
Hato, Curaçao	79 / 2.3	79 / 1.2	80 / .7	81 / .8	82 / .8	82 / .9	82 / 1.2	83 / 1.4	84 / 1.4	83 / 3.4	82 / 4.8	80 / 4
Roseau, Dominica	76 / 5.2	76 / 2.9	78 / 2.9	79 / 2.4	81 / 3.8	82 / 7.7	81 / 10.8	81 / 10.3	82 / 8.9	80 / 7.8	79 / 8.8	78 / 7.8
Santo Domingo, Dominican Republic	75 / 2.4	76 / 1.4	76 / 1.9	77 / 3.9	79 / 6.8	80 / 6.2	80 / 6.4	81 / 6.3	80 / 7.3	80 / 6	78 / 4.8	76 / 2.4
St. George's, Grenada	77 / 3	78 / 3	78 / 1	80 / 2	81 / 6	80 / 12	80 / 10	80 / 10	81 / 6	81 / 6	80 / 8	78 / 7
Basse-Terre, Guadeloupe	71 / 9.2	70 / 6.1	70 / 8.1	72 / 7.3	74 / 11.5	75 / 14.1	75 / 17.6	76 / 15.3	76 / 16.4	75 / 12.4	74 / 12.3	72 / 10.1
Kingston, Jamaica	77 / .9	77 / .6	77 / .9	79 / 1.2	80 / 4	82 / 3.5	82 / 1.5	82 / 3.6	81 / 3.9	81 / 7.1	79 / 2.9	78 / 1.4

Temperature Averages / Rainfall
(Temperatures are in Fahrenheit, rainfall in inches)

	JAN	FEB	MAR	APR	MAY	JUNE	JULY	AUG	SEPT	OCT	NOV	DEC
Fort-de-France, Martinique	76 / 4.7	77 / 4.3	77 / 2.9	79 / 3.9	80 / 4.7	80 / 7.4	80 / 9.4	81 / 10.3	81 / 9.3	80 / 9.7	79 / 7.9	78 / 5.9
San Juan, Puerto Rico	75 / 4.3	75 / 2.7	76 / 2.9	77 / 4.1	79 / 5.9	80 / 5.4	80 / 5.7	81 / 6.3	81 / 6.2	80 / 5.6	79 / 6.3	77 / 5.4
Gustavia, St. Barthélemy	73 / 9.6	72 / 6	71 / 8.4	72 / 7	73 / 11.2	75 / 10.2	75 / 18	76 / 15	75 / 16	75 / 12.8	74 / 12.8	73 / 10.2
Oranjestad, St. Eustatius	77 / 2.7	78 / 1.8	78 / 1.9	80 / 2.1	81 / 3.6	82 / 3.4	82 / 4	82 / 4.6	82 / 5.3	81 / 4.8	80 / 5.2	78 / 3.5
Basseterre, St. Kitts	76 / 4.1	76 / 2	77 / 2.3	78 / 2.3	80 / 3.8	81 / 3.6	81 / 4.4	81 / 5.2	81 / 6	80 / 5.4	79 / 7.3	78 / 4.5
Soufrière, St. Lucia	76 / 5.3	76 / 3.6	77 / 3.8	79 / 3.4	81 / 5.9	81 / 8.6	81 / 9.3	81 / 10.6	81 / 9.9	80 / 9.3	78 / 9.1	77 / 7.8
Philipsburg, St. Maarten	77 / 2.6	77 / 1.8	78 / 1.6	79 / 2.4	81 / 4	83 / 3.1	83 / 3.2	83 / 4.3	82 / 5.5	82 / 5	80 / 5.5	78 / 3.3
Kingstown, St. Vincent	76 / 5	77 / 4	78 / 4	78 / 3	78 / .6	78 / 9	78 / 9	78 / 11	78 / 10	77 / 9	76 / 9	76 / 8
Port of Spain, Trinidad	76 / 2.3	77 / 1.2	77 / 1.4	79 / 1.3	80 / 2.8	79 / 6.4	79 / 7.8	79 / 7.6	80 / 6.9	80 / 5.6	79 / 6.5	78 / 4.7
Grand Turk, Turks and Caicos Islands	77 / 2.2	77 / 1.6	78 / 1.0	78 / 1.6	80 / 2.8	81 / 1.8	82 / 1.8	84 / 2	83 / 3.2	82 / 4	82 / 4.6	81 / 2.8
Road Town, Virgin Islands, British	78 / 4	78 / 3	78 / 3	80 / 4	82 / 6	82 / 5.2	82 / 6	82 / 6	82 / 6	82 / 6	80 / 6	78 / 5
Charlotte Amalie, Virgin Islands, U.S.	76 / 1.5	77 / 1.9	77 / 2.2	78 / 2.6	80 / 4.1	82 / 2.8	82 / 3.2	82 / 5.5	81 / 7.6	81 / 7.1	79 / 7.5	77 / 2.9

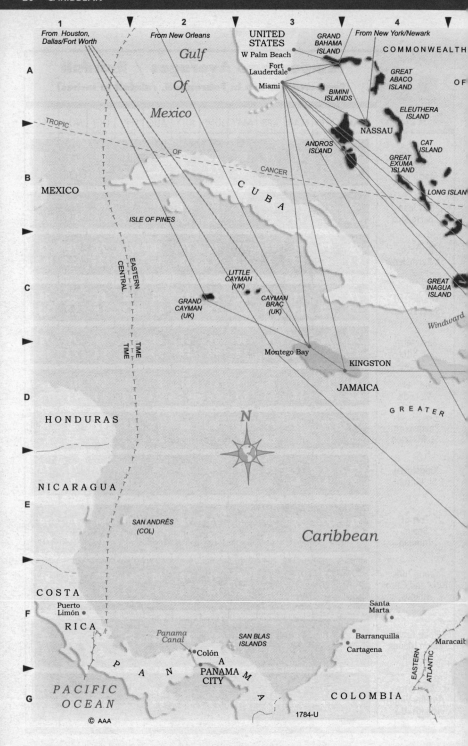

1   2   3   4

From Houston,
Dallas/Fort Worth

From New Orleans

Gulf

UNITED
STATES

W Palm Beach

Fort
Lauderdale

Miami

GRAND
BAHAMA
ISLAND

From New York/Newark

COMMONWEALTH

Of

GREAT
ABACO
ISLAND

OF

Mexico

BIMINI
ISLANDS

ELEUTHERA
ISLAND

TROPIC

OF

NASSAU

CAT
ISLAND

A

CANCER

ANDROS
ISLAND

GREAT
EXUMA
ISLAND

B

MEXICO

C U B A

LONG ISLAN

ISLE OF PINES

EASTERN
CENTRAL

LITTLE
CAYMAN
(UK)

C

GREAT
INAGUA
ISLAND

GRAND
CAYMAN
(UK)

CAYMAN
BRAC
(UK)

Windward

TIME
TIME

TIME

Montego Bay

KINGSTON

D

HONDURAS

JAMAICA

GREATER

N

NICARAGUA

E

SAN ANDRÉS
(COL)

Caribbean

COSTA

F

Puerto
Limón

Santa
Marta

RICA

Panama
Canal

SAN BLAS
ISLANDS

Colón

Barranquilla

Maracaib

EASTERN
ATLANTIC

Cartagena

PANAMA
CITY

PACIFIC

COLOMBIA

G

OCEAN

© AAA

1784-U

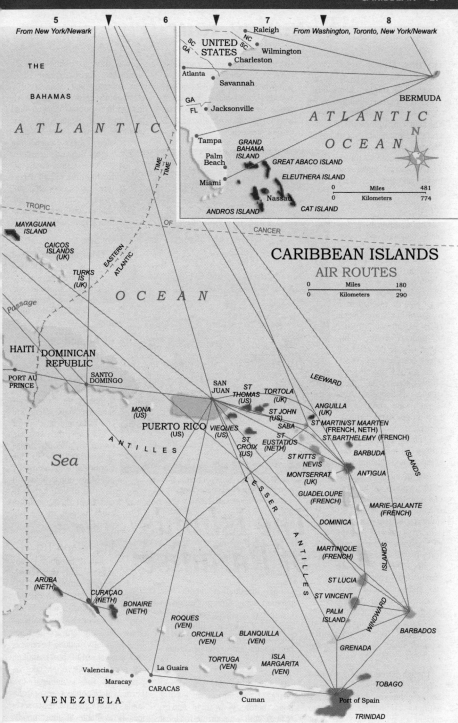

From New York/Newark

From Washington, Toronto, New York/Newark

THE
BAHAMAS

A T L A N T I C

UNITED
STATES

SC
NC
GA

Raleigh

NC
SC
Wilmington

Charleston

Atlanta

Savannah

GA
FL
Jacksonville

A T L A N T I C

O C E A N

BERMUDA

N

Tampa

GRAND
BAHAMA
ISLAND

Palm
Beach

Miami

GREAT ABACO ISLAND

ELEUTHERA ISLAND

Nassau

ANDROS ISLAND

CAT ISLAND

Miles   481
Kilometers   774

TROPIC

MAYAGUANA
ISLAND

CAICOS
ISLANDS
(UK)

TURKS
IS
(UK)

EASTERN

TIME
TIME

OF

CANCER

CARIBBEAN ISLANDS
AIR ROUTES

Miles   180
Kilometers   290

ATLANTIC

O C E A N

Passage

HAITI

DOMINICAN
REPUBLIC

PORT AU
PRINCE

SANTO
DOMINGO

SAN
JUAN

ST
THOMAS
(US)

TORTOLA
(UK)

LEEWARD

ANGUILLA
(UK)

MONA
(US)

PUERTO RICO
(US)

VIEQUES
(US)

ST JOHN
(US)

ST MARTIN/ST MAARTEN
(FRENCH, NETH)

SABA

ST BARTHELEMY (FRENCH)

A N T I L L E S

ST
CROIX
(US)

ST
EUSTATIUS
(NETH)

BARBUDA

ISLANDS

Sea

ST KITTS
NEVIS

MONTSERRAT
(UK)

ANTIGUA

L E S S E R

GUADELOUPE
(FRENCH)

MARIE-GALANTE
(FRENCH)

DOMINICA

A N T I L L E S

MARTINIQUE
(FRENCH)

ISLANDS

ARUBA
(NETH)

CURAÇAO
(NETH)

BONAIRE
(NETH)

ROQUES
(VEN)

ORCHILLA
(VEN)

BLANQUILLA
(VEN)

ST LUCIA

ST VINCENT

PALM
ISLAND

WINDWARD

BARBADOS

GRENADA

Valencia

Maracay

La Guaira

TORTUGA
(VEN)

ISLA
MARGARITA
(VEN)

CARACAS

Cuman

TOBAGO

VENEZUELA

Port of Spain

TRINIDAD

Planning Your Trip

Getting There

Travel to the islands is by plane, cruise ship or charter boat. Planned excursions tailored to fit your schedule and pocketbook are abundant; the mode of transportation you select is a matter of personal preference. However you choose to travel, a AAA travel agent can make all the necessary arrangements.

By Air

Air transportation has made the weekend, 1- or 2-week vacation as practical as it is delightful. Many excursion fares, some with stopovers, are available. Most Caribbean destinations can be reached in a matter of hours from major cities and often in a matter of minutes from Miami. Some islands do not have direct air service; check with a AAA travel agent about access to these smaller destinations. Also consult your travel agent for group fares, special packages, seasonal rates and current schedules. Most offices can make plane reservations and obtain tickets.

Air travel in the Caribbean requires some special considerations. Many island governments require visitors to complete a tourist card and perhaps a customs declaration form before entering their country. These forms are provided by your air carrier and should be completed while en route. Allow about an hour to clear customs and immigration upon arrival. *Keep your copy of the tourist card; it must be returned when you depart.*

Though island travel laws may vary, the U.S. Dept. of Homeland Security requires that all citizens returning from the Caribbean present a valid passport. See your destination's *Fast Facts* box for

specific immigration requirements. AAA recommends carrying a passport when traveling anywhere outside the United States, both to expedite your way through customs and to provide identification in case of emergency.

Statue of Noel Coward, Port Maria, Jamaica
© Anthony Pidgeon / Lonely Planet Images

The Islands of Paradise

For information about the passport application process or an emergency passport, contact the National Passport Information Center at (877) 487-2778. Passport photos are available through your AAA travel office.

On departure day you should arrive at the airport at least 2 hours before your flight leaves. (Check with your airline for local requirements.) This will ensure

enough time to obtain seat assignments, check luggage, convert currency and clear security checkpoints before boarding. Allow another hour when you land to claim your luggage and clear customs. Allow at least 90 minutes to make a connecting flight. Schedule similarly for your return home, allowing time to pay departure taxes, convert unspent currency and submit customs declaration forms.

By Sea

Other than owning and operating your own vessel, there are two ways to visit the Caribbean via the bounding main: by charter boat and by cruise ship.

By Air and Sea

Try a combination air *and* sea vacation. Some cruise lines will fly you from their departure point to one of the balmy Caribbean islands where you can relax and unwind for a few days; then you can return by luxury cruise ship—or cruise to the Caribbean and return by air. Many cruise lines will pay part of your airfare to and from their departure point as part of the full cruise package.

Interisland Travel

Island hopping is enjoyable and simple. Although almost all of the Caribbean islands are accessible by air or seaplane, a more exotic way to travel is by sailboat. These leisurely cruises to other islands usually include beverages and a meal. Mail boats, though not as glamorous, often take on passengers for a nominal fee. Ferries also connect several islands. Information on these services is available at most hotels, tourist bureaus and shops.

Intraisland Travel

Driving conditions on the islands range from good to poor. Most roads are not as well maintained as in the United States, and some are narrow and meandering, making it difficult to stay to one side. As well, in some areas domestic animals are known to roam the roads freely. Where road signs exist they are usually in the native tongue, so studying a phrase book or translation dictionary in advance is helpful. On most of the islands driving is on the left side of the road.

Given the confusion of other tourists and the independent driving nature of some locals, defensive driving is a must. It might be best to first monitor the driving conditions on the island before going out on your own. You might decide to leave the driving to the cabbies and bus operators.

Sightseeing Tours

Sunning, swimming, surfing and skin diving are all part of a Caribbean vacation, but to make your pleasure complete add another "S"—sightseeing. Each island has its own scenic attractions, quaint villages and exotic countryside. To miss them is to miss some of the islands' charm and history. For information on self-guiding or guided tours, see *Sightseeing* under the individual islands.

Car rentals are available on the major islands; rental information is listed under *Transportation*. To avoid disappointment, make reservations well in advance through a local AAA club. Arrangements for guided tours can be made through a AAA travel agency, your hotel activities desk or your ship's cruise director.

Climate and Clothing

The best rule to follow when packing for any trip, whether by plane or ship, is to first include everything that seems absolutely indispensable and then repack, taking only half as much as you would have originally planned. Another rule is to not take anything you would hate to lose, such as expensive jewelry or unneeded credit cards. Remember to pack toiletries and extra sunglasses, as they are often more expensive on the islands. Be sure to pack prescription medicines, in their original containers, and other essentials in your carry-on luggage.

Keep in mind the climate, the islands you will visit and where you plan to stay. Clothing made from artificial fibers can be uncomfortable in the heat. A good compromise is a cotton-synthetic blend that is both cool and wrinkle free.

In general, colorful, lightweight sport and resort-style clothes are appropriate all year throughout the islands. A lightweight wrap for cool evenings should be added for The Bahamas, Bermuda, the Cayman Islands, the Dominican Republic and Jamaica. In fact, it is always wise to pack a sweater, no matter how tropical the climate. In Bermuda, silks and lightweight woolens are comfortable during the day from mid-December to late March. For the most part, cocktail dresses and jackets and ties are not required for evening wear in the Caribbean except at resorts and large hotels on some of the more developed islands.

When packing for a cruise follow the same general rules. Formal clothes—dinner jackets and long dresses—are suitable for such highlights as the captain's dinner or the captain's cocktail parties. For regular dinners, most passengers change from their daytime attire to more sophisticated garb.

For shore visits or strolling around the deck, any type of vacation or outdoor clothing is appropriate. Swimwear, however, should be worn only at the beach or pool, not in public areas. Bathing *au naturel* or topless is fashionable at some beaches in the French West Indies, but is still an unwelcome trend on most of the other islands. Some of the people in the more conservative countries are offended by revealing clothes, especially if they are worn in the daytime.

Electricity

Typical U.S. electric shavers, hair dryers and travel irons operate on 110- to 120-volt, 60-cycle alternating current. However, some islands use 210-230 volt, 50-cycle AC electricity, which will burn out most U.S. appliances. On other islands, 110- to 127-volt, 50-cycle AC current is used. At 50 cycles U.S. electric appliances operate at

Dominican Republic, Punta Cana Beach / © Cosmo Condina Caribbean / Alamy

slower than normal speeds and damage to an appliance can occur. A converter plug is necessary in the French West Indies, where European plugs are used. Check the *Fast Facts* boxes for the electric current used locally.

While some U.S. department stores do sell electric items for use overseas, be sure to check the voltage requirements before you purchase; do not be misled by a salesperson who offers you an "adapter" that only enables you to plug the appliance into the wall socket. A transformer is needed to convert high-voltage current for use with U.S. appliances.

Health and Safety

The sun's rays are intense in the Caribbean. Just an hour in the Caribbean sun can result in a painful sunburn and even illness to the unwary visitor. Be sure to bring plenty of suntan lotion or sunscreen; the higher the sunscreen rating the more it protects the skin from the most harmful rays. A good pair of sunglasses and a lightweight hat give added protection.

Some other commonsense precautions include taking an extra pair of glasses or contact lenses and extra quantities of prescription medicines, along with a letter from your physician stating the nature of your ailment and the recommended dosage. Keep prescription medicines in their original containers. Persons with physical conditions that might require emergency care should carry a card or tag identifying the condition.

Even the strongest constitution can sometimes be caught off guard by the excitement of travel or by culinary exploration. Reasonable precautions will usually eliminate serious risks, but should they fail, see a doctor. Medical services are generally excellent on the more developed islands, and your hotel desk or travel agent can refer you to a reliable physician or clinic. Emergency medical treatment also is available on cruise ships.

Rain is the main source of fresh water on many islands; sparse rainfall means scarce water. Even on islands where water is distilled from the sea, the supply is limited and should be used sparingly. Tap water and water served in restaurants and bars is generally safe; if in doubt, abstain or drink bottled water, beverages made with boiled water, canned or bottled carbonated beverages, beer or wine. If the water quality is unknown, avoid ice, containers that have held water, and such foods as fruit or vegetables that might have been rinsed in contaminated water.

Where mosquitoes abound, use a repellent, wear clothing that covers your arms and legs and stay in well-screened areas. Mosquitoes bearing malaria, yellow fever and other infections exist in very limited regions. In the Caribbean the risk of malaria is present in Haiti and in rural areas of the Dominican Republic bordering Haiti. Travelers to any of these areas are urged to check with their physician or local health department to determine the advisability of taking a preventative drug.

Cases of dengue (breakbone) fever, also a mosquito-borne infection, have been reported on most Caribbean Islands and throughout northern South America, Central America and Mexico. There are no preventative medical measures other than

Carnival, Trinidad and Tobago / © Angelo Cavalli / age fotostock

wearing insect repellent, and treatment is limited to relieving the symptoms. A few cases of yellow fever have occurred in Trinidad and Tobago. Inoculations for yellow fever are available; most of the islands require vaccination certificates for yellow fever *only* of those travelers arriving from endemic countries.

Hepatitis B is highly prevalent in the Dominican Republic and Haiti. A hepatitis B vaccination is recommended for those traveling to these areas. Hepatitis A is found in rural areas. Schistosomiasis is a parasitic infection contracted in Antigua, the Dominican Republic, Guadeloupe, Martinique, Puerto Rico and St. Lucia. A few cases of poliomyelitis have been reported in the Dominican Republic and Haiti; visitors should consult a physician about the need for immunization.

The Centers for Disease Control and Prevention in Atlanta recommends that before traveling, visitors should make sure that all immunizations are current (the tetanus/diphtheria vaccine should be boosted as needed). It also is recommended that travelers receive either an immune serum globulin or the hepatitis A vaccine if they are planning to visit an area of questionable sanitation. The center's hot line, offering international health requirements and recommendations for foreign travelers, is available daily 24 hours; phone (800) 232-4636.

Carefully assess the risk potential of recreational activities on the islands. Sports equipment that you rent or buy might not meet U.S. safety standards. Unless you are certain that scuba diving equipment, for example, is safe, do not use it. Be especially careful when out on excursions: Should you need it, help might not be readily available.

Many pools and beaches on the islands do not have lifeguards, so take heed when swimming. Undertows can be treacherous; be sure to inquire about such

New Providence, Bahamas
© Stephen Frink Collection / Alamy

conditions before entering the water. Do not dive into unknown waters; hidden rocks, coral formations and shallow depths can cause serious injury or death.

Familiarize yourself with the local laws and customs of the islands you are visiting; remember, you are subject to *their* laws. It is wise to leave a copy of your travel itinerary with family or friends at home and to phone or register in person with the U.S. embassy or consulate upon your arrival. If you get in trouble, contact the U.S. consulate.

You can take various precautions to avoid being victimized by thieves. Travel light and do not leave luggage unattended in public places. It also is a good idea to leave expensive jewelry, clothing and unnecessary credit cards at home. Be sure not to travel with all of your money, credit cards and travelers checks in one place. Consider leaving valuables in your hotel safe or safe deposit box.

You should be alert at all times, especially in crowds. Secure your wallet carefully, perhaps in a front pocket, or wear a money belt; carry your purse diagonally across your chest. When shopping, keep just a small amount of spending money readily available; do not display the entire contents of your wallet. Try to conceal your camera when

not in use. Do not venture into unfamiliar areas, especially when you are alone and certainly not at night.

Visitors are often approached on the street by locals offering a variety of products and services that are best obtained through more reputable outlets. In most cases a polite "No, thank you" will suffice, but the more persistent vendor will require several similar responses. It is best to display a pleasant but assertive manner in such situations. Avoid prolonged discussions and do not answer questions that might reveal where you are staying or what your plans are. Accept rides from only licensed taxi or tour operators.

Travel Advisories

The U.S. Department of State issues Consular Information Sheets, Travel Warnings and Public Announcements concerning serious health or security conditions that might affect U.S. citizens. They can be obtained at U.S. embassies and consulates abroad, regional passport agencies in the United States and from the Overseas Citizens Services; phone (202) 647-5225. The Bureau maintains a Web site at http://travel.state.gov.

Consular Information Sheets provide information about entry requirements, currency regulations, health conditions, security, political disturbances, areas of instability and drug penalties. A Travel Warning is issued when the situation in a country is dangerous enough for the Department of State to recommend that Americans not travel there. Public Announcements are a means of releasing information to travelers about short-term conditions that might pose security risks to Americans traveling abroad.

In addition, travelers are urged to remain abreast of regional events and to contact their AAA travel agent or air or sea carrier for the latest updates.

Sandy Ground / © Angelo Cavalli / Photolibrary

Anguilla

L ong and narrow Anguilla (An-GWIL-ah) takes its name from the Spanish word for eel. The island lies about 9 miles (14 km) north of St. Martin and 60 miles (97 km) north of St. Kitts. Unlike the other Leeward Islands, low-lying Anguilla is of coral limestone rather than volcanic formation. Cottages and houses are sprinkled across the island, with concentrations around the capital of The Valley and the villages of South Hill, Stoney Ground, Blowing Point and Island Harbour. Accommodations on Anguilla range from charming cottages to world-class hotel and villa resort properties.

History

Christopher Columbus sighted Anguilla during his second voyage in 1493; it is not known whether he actually visited the island. English settlers from St. Kitts colonized Anguilla in 1650, and the island has remained a British territory ever since. In 1688 the island was attacked by a party of Irishmen who eventually settled there, and such surnames as Smith and Webster are evident among their descendants, particularly around Island Harbour. Anguilla repelled two attacks by the French in the 18th century. The island declared its independence from the Associated State of St. Kitts and Nevis and became a self-governing territory of the British Commonwealth in 1967. After several years of negotiations, Anguilla became a separate British dependent territory on Dec. 19, 1980.

It is said that the first seeds of the highly prized sea island cotton came from Anguilla. Today the island's economy is based on tourism and financial services.

Shopping

Visitors to Anguilla won't find the duty-free shops and open markets common on other islands, but browsing at a resort boutique, an art gallery or a craft shop is still a popular pastime. Local shopping favorites include the Anguilla

Arts and Crafts Center in the Brooks Complex in The Valley; Irie Life, overlooking the scenic Road Bay and Sandy Ground; Cheddie's Carving Studio, on the island's west end, containing sculptures and carvings; Linde Gallery, at Malliouhana Hotel & Spa, presenting an extensive selection of fine clothing and jewelry; Micasa Ltd.; Devonish Art Gallery, on West End Road; Le Petit Gift Shop; World Art and Antiques; and La Galleria. Boutiques such as Caribbean Fancy, Janvel's, Kimmy's, Liacia's, Shoes Plus and Something Special feature elegant resort wear, casual summer fashions, shoes and accessories.

Fresh fruits and vegetables are available from the People's Market in The Valley and at roadside stands throughout the island. Shopping hours are generally Mon.-Sat. 8-4, with supermarkets usually open until 8:30 p.m.; some stores are open on Sundays. Banking hours are Mon.-Thurs. 8-2, Fri. 8-4.

Food and Drink

Fine dining is a specialty in Anguilla, which calls itself the "cuisine capital of the Caribbean." Local restaurants—from casual beachside eateries to elegant establishments—serve sumptuous dishes that reflect the ancestry of island residents: European, African and Caribbean.

Freshly caught lobster, crayfish, whelk, and red and yellowtail snapper are several of the seafood delights that appear on tables in Anguilla. The tantalizing fare includes stuffed crab, conch salad, grilled crayfish and Creole soups.

Sports and Amusements

Nightlife of the classic variety is somewhat limited on Anguilla. Most hotels offer nightly music, and several beach bistros can be found at Sandy Ground and Shoal Bay. Most recreation, however, is related to the island's white coral sand beaches, which offer many opportunities for swimming and shell collecting; swimming and sunbathing *au naturel* are prohibited.

Some of the island's 33 beaches are accessible only by rough dirt roads or paths. The secluded atmosphere of these beaches, however, makes the visit worth the trouble. Popular beaches include those at Meads Bay, Rendezvous Bay and Shoal Bay East. Visitors should note that wearing swimsuits in public places other than the beach is considered inappropriate.

The crystal-clear waters surrounding Anguilla are excellent for snorkeling, scuba diving and fishing. Favorite snorkeling and diving spots are Little Bay, Cove Bay and Shoal Bay, the last distinguished by its undersea garden trail. Experienced divers can reach seven shipwreck sites. Shoal Bay Scuba rents snorkeling

equipment, while Anguillian Divers can take you to the hottest dive spots on the eastern part of the island. Most hotels rent water sports equipment. Tennis also is popular on the island; most hotels and villas have courts. The Ronald Webster Park Complex in The Valley offers two public courts.

Boats and guides for fishing trips are available for hire at Sandy Ground and Island Harbour. Many islanders are anglers by trade, and you can sample their succulent bounty at any local café or restaurant. Fish soup, sweet and sour conch, and lobster with lime butter are some of the primary delicacies.

Special events are held on Anguilla Day, May 30, and in August during the annual Summer Festival. On both occasions, sailors race boats made in Anguilla. Summer Festival, which begins on the last Friday in July and ends on the first Sunday in August, features calypso contests, street dancing, the coronation of Miss Anguilla (the carnival queen), sailboat races, beach barbecues and the Prince and Princess Show.

Sightseeing

Sightseeing tours can be arranged through Bennie's Travel & Tours at Blowing Point and Malliouhana Travel & Tours, in The Valley. Bennie's offers tours of the island and half- and full-day trips to Prickly Pear; Marigot, St. Martin; and Philipsburg, St. Maarten; phone (264) 497-2788.

The Anguilla National Trust offers guided tours of the island, including stops at Fort Hill, the East End Pond Bird Sanctuary and the Big

Spring Heritage Site; phone (264) 497-5297 for information and reservations.

Fountain Cavern in Shoal Bay, considered the most significant archeological site on the island, is being developed as a national park and is currently closed to the public. The Arawaks used this cave for ritual purposes, carving a 12-foot stalagmite statue of the Taíno god Jocahu beside a freshwater pool. Other petroglyphs depict the solar chieftain and the rainbow god, Juluca.

Transportation

Connections to Clayton J. Lloyd International Airport are through San Juan, St. Thomas, Antigua, St. Kitts and St. Maarten. Rental cars or taxis are necessary to get around the island, as beaches, stores and various accommodations are not within reasonable walking distance. Taxi rates are fixed, but agree on the fare in advance.

The Blowing Point Ferry runs to Marigot, St. Martin, about every half hour from 7 a.m. to 6:15 p.m. The final return from Marigot leaves at 7 p.m. The ferry trip takes about 25 minutes. Travel documents are required, and a $20 U.S. departure tax is collected upon departure from Anguilla (day trippers from Anguilla pay a departure tax of $5 U.S.); departure tax from St. Martin is $3 U.S. One-way fare is $12-$15 U.S. depending on departure time. A ferry also runs infrequently to Philipsburg, St. Maarten; phone (264) 497-6665.

Fast Facts

POPULATION: 14,254.

AREA: 91 sq km (35 sq mi.).

CAPITAL: The Valley.

HIGHEST POINT: 65 m (213 ft.), Crocus Hill.

LOWEST POINT: Sea level, Caribbean Sea.

TIME ZONE(S): Atlantic Standard.

LANGUAGE: English.

GOVERNMENT: British Overseas Territory.

UNIT OF CURRENCY: Eastern Caribbean (E.C.) dollar. $1 U.S. = 2.7 E.C. dollars. U.S. currency is widely accepted.

ELECTRICITY: 110 volts, 60 cycles AC.

MINIMUM AGE FOR DRIVERS: 21-25, depending on the rental car agency. Temporary local license ($20 U.S.) required, available at rental agencies or the Inland Revenue government office in The Valley and issued on presentation of current license from home country; valid for 6 months; drive on left.

SEAT BELT/CHILD RESTRAINT LAWS: Seat belts are not required by law, but are recommended for all passengers.

HELMETS FOR MOTORCYCLISTS: Required.

HOLIDAYS: Jan. 1; Good Friday; Easter Monday; Labour Day, May (1st Mon.); Whit Monday, May or June (8th Mon. after Easter); Anguilla Day, May 30; Queen's Birthday, June (2nd Mon.); August Monday, August Thursday and Constitution Day, (1st Mon. and following Thurs. and Fri.); Separation Day, Dec. 19; Hero and Heroines Day, Dec. 21; Christmas, Dec. 25; Boxing Day, Dec. 26.

TAXES: A 10 percent room tax and 10 percent service charge are added to most hotel bills, plus $1 U.S. per room, per night. A 15 percent service charge is also added to restaurant bills. Departure tax is $20 U.S. ($10 U.S. ages 5-12) by air, or by sea at Blowing Point Ferry Port. Departure tax for day trips leaving Blowing Point Ferry Port is $5 U.S.

IMMIGRATION REQUIREMENTS: A valid passport and return or onward ticket are required. No visa needed for stays up to 3 months. The U.S. Dept. of Homeland Security requires all U.S. citizens returning from the Caribbean to present a valid passport.

PHONING THE ISLANDS: To call Anguilla from the U.S. or Canada, dial 1 + 264 + the 7-digit local number.

FURTHER INFORMATION FOR VISITORS:

Anguilla Tourist Board New York
246 Central Ave.
White Plains, NY 10606
(914) 287-2400
(877) 426-4845

Anguilla Tourist Board
Coronation Avenue
The Valley, Anguilla AI-2640
(264) 497-2759
(800) 553-4939

Anguilla Hotel and Tourism Association
Coronation Avenue
The Valley, Anguilla AI-2640
(264) 497-2944

Points of Interest

See map page 33.

EAST END (A-2) pop. 614

The tombstone of Gov. John Richardson, who was buried in the Sandy Hill Cemetery in 1742, is thought to be the oldest on the island. Southwest along the coast are the ruins of Sandy Hill Fort. Here the Anguilla militia held off the second French invasion in 1796.

HERITAGE COLLECTION MUSEUM is next to East End Pond Bird Sanctuary. Artifacts, photographs and archeological relics span the island's history from the Arawak culture to the 1967 revolution. Exhibits highlight Anguilla's fishing and boatbuilding trades, as well as the salt industry that collapsed in the 1980s. **Time:** Allow 1 hour minimum. **Hours:** Mon.-Sat. 10-4:30. Closed major holidays. **Cost:** $5; $3 (ages 5-11). **Phone:** (264) 497-4092 or (264) 235-7440.

THE VALLEY (B-2) pop. 1,169

Anguilla's tiny capital sits at the center of the coral limestone island. The Valley's oldest building is Wallblake House, the only surviving plantation manor from the 18th century. Other historic structures are found on the road to Crocus Hill, including Ebenezer Methodist Church, built by slaves in 1830. The Warden's Place, former quarters of the magistrate, is now home to the KoalKeel Restaurant. The limestone blocks used to build its high foundation were carved from the cliffs of nearby Crocus Bay.

Farther west at Sandy Ground is the Manse, a three-gabled house recently restored as a center for art studios and shops. The Old Salt Factory and Pumphouse preserves the history of the once-thriving salt industry in Anguilla.

WALLBLAKE HOUSE is on Carter Rey Blvd. next to St. Gerard's Catholic Church. Thought to have been built by sugar planter William Blake in the 1780s, this is the oldest house on the island and one of the last survivors of 18th-century plantation life. The mansion was set ablaze by French soldiers during the 1796 invasion, but the stone walls withstood the fire. Later used as a Catholic rectory, the plantation complex was restored in 2004. It is one of few in the Caribbean to retain all of its original outbuildings, including a bakery, a stone cistern, stables and workers' quarters. **Hours:** Guided tours are offered Mon., Wed. and Fri. 10-2. **Cost:** $5.

Devil's Bridge, Pares, Antigua / © Heeb Photos / eStock Photo

Antigua and Barbuda

A t the northeastern curve of the West Indies, Antigua (an-TEE-ga) is one of 11 links in the chain of Leeward Islands. Christopher Columbus' first impression adequately describes this tropical paradise: "What beautiful lands the sun lights up in the distance." The seascape alternates rocky coves with white sunny beaches punctuated by gentle salt breezes. Thirty miles (48 km) north is the tiny coral island of Barbuda (bar-BEW-da), a haven for seabirds. The rocky volcanic islet of Redonda is an uninhabited dependency.

Antiguans are charming people, reserved but cordial. Their expressive English *patois* with its musical intonation enchants visitors. While engaged in daily affairs, the locals form a vivid tableau. Sitting around a *warri* board, taxi drivers play an ancient game while waiting for a fare. Dressed for school in distinctive uniforms that vary according to school and grade, Antiguan children add their smiles and colors to the scene. In equally vivid dress, members of Antigua's many steel bands parade during Carnival in St. John's, where the colorful activities contrast with the more traditionalist English atmosphere of the island's capital.

History

Christopher Columbus sighted Antigua in 1493, naming it after Santa Maria de la Antigua, a church in Seville, Spain. An attempt to colonize the island was not made until almost a century and a half later, perhaps due to the unwelcoming population of Carib Indians.

Antigua became a British possession in 1632, when English planters from nearby St Kitts successfully settled the area despite Carib resistance. African slaves were imported to clear forests for the planting of tobacco, ginger, cotton and indigo. In 1666 French raiders claimed the island, but the Treaty of Breda in 1667 restored the land to the British.

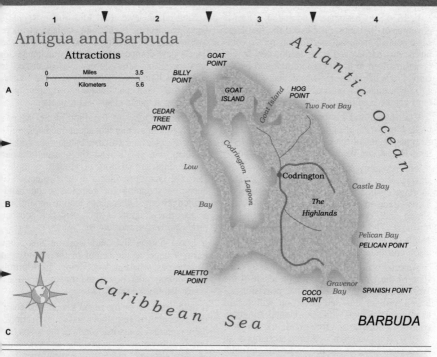

Antigua and Barbuda
Attractions

Miles 3.5
Kilometers 5.6

GOAT POINT

BILLY POINT

GOAT ISLAND

HOG POINT

Goat Island

Atlantic Ocean

Two Foot Bay

CEDAR TREE POINT

Codrington Lagoon

Low

Codrington

Castle Bay

Bay

The Highlands

Pelican Bay
PELICAN POINT

PALMETTO POINT

Gravenor Bay

COCO POINT

SPANISH POINT

BARBUDA

Caribbean Sea

N

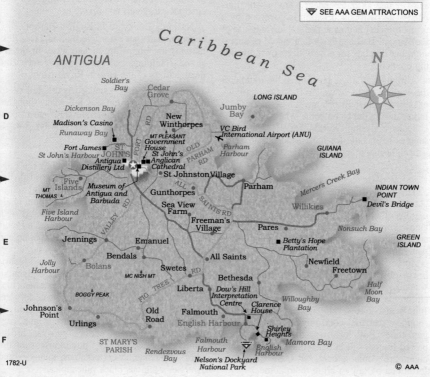

SEE AAA GEM ATTRACTIONS

Caribbean Sea

ANTIGUA

N

Soldier's Bay

Cedar Grove

Dickenson Bay

LONG ISLAND

Jumby Bay

Madison's Casino

New Winthorpes

Runaway Bay

MT PLEASANT

VC Bird International Airport (ANU)

Fort James
St John's Harbour

ST JOHN'S

Government House

St John's Anglican Cathedral

Parham Harbour

GUIANA ISLAND

Antigua Distillery Ltd

St Johnston Village

Museum of Antigua and Barbuda

Gunthorpes

Parham

Mercers Creek Bay

INDIAN TOWN POINT
Devil's Bridge

MT THOMAS

Five Islands

Sea View Farm

Willikies

Five Island Harbour

Freeman's Village

Pares

Nonsuch Bay

GREEN ISLAND

Jennings

Emanuel

Betty's Hope Plantation

Bendals

All Saints

Newfield

Jolly Harbour

Bolans

Swetes

Freetown

MC NISH MT

Bethesda

Half Moon Bay

BOGGY PEAK

Liberta

Dow's Hill Interpretation Centre

Willoughby Bay

Johnson's Point

Old Road

Falmouth

Clarence House

Urlings

English Harbour

Shirley Heights

Falmouth Harbour

English Harbour

Mamora Bay

ST MARY'S PARISH

Rendezvous Bay

Nelson's Dockyard National Park

© AAA

In 1674 Sir Christopher Codrington, a former governor of Barbados, established the first large sugar plantation on Antigua. Codrington's accomplishments encouraged other landowners to become involved in the sugar industry, and by the early 1700s the landscape was dotted with some 170 sugar mills; the ruins of many of these structures can be seen throughout the island.

Codrington and his brother settled on Barbuda four years prior to cultivating sugar on Antigua. Ruins of the Codrington estate, Highland House, are on the island's highest point.

The economy suffered a severe blow when slavery was abolished in 1834, and a labor shortage ensued. Due to mounting pressure for a free trade market, sugar prices steadily declined and forced several plantations out of business. Three natural disasters in the mid-1800s—a hurricane, a fire and an earthquake—also contributed to the economic decline.

Antigua was granted status as an associated state of the United Kingdom as a result of the West Indies Act of 1967. This provision allowed Antigua to be self-governing with regard to internal matters, while the United Kingdom controlled defense and foreign affairs. On Nov. 1, 1981, Antigua graduated from its status as an Associated State of the British Commonwealth and became an independent country with Barbuda. The twin-island nation is governed by a prime minister and an upper and lower house of Parliament. Barbuda has often talked of secession, but remains for now with its own governing council.

Antigua's strategic position in the middle of the Antilles chain, as well as its natural harbors, made it the chief British naval base in the West Indies during the Napoleonic Wars and a prime U.S. base during World War II. The main sources of income for most islanders are tourism, light manufacturing and agriculture.

Shopping

The main shopping district is in St. John's between Redcliffe and Newgate streets, but numerous other shops are concealed in alleys and lanes. Popular buys are imports, straw handicrafts and sea island and silk-screened cottons. Antigua's duty-free shopping includes French perfumes, cashmeres, English tweeds, Irish linen, tobacco, pipes, English bone china, Swiss watches, jewelry, crystal and cameras as well as children's clothing, accessories and toys. St. John's also has several jewelry stores where shoppers can find good buys on their favorite gemstones. Both locally produced rum and imported liquors sell at discounted prices. Cuban cigars are available here, but U.S. citizens are forbidden by law to bring them home.

Situated on lower Redcliffe Street, Redcliffe Quay consists of a charming collage of shops overlooking the waterfront. The area, which was once a slave compound, harbored warehouses for area merchants after slavery was abolished in 1834. Traditional architecture is accented by narrow alleys and picturesque courtyards interspersed with quaint shops and restaurants.

Heritage Quay, at the foot of St. Mary's Street, contains a pier that accommodates cruise ships. Reggae and calypso bands occasionally perform at a small band shell, usually when cruise ships are in port. A modern complex, Heritage Quay provides a diverse selection of duty-free shopping for gemstones and handcrafted jewelry. Other shops feature apparel and accessories, fragrances and cosmetics, tobacco products, liquor and linens.

Local potters live and work at Sea View Farm Village, at the center of the island near Gunthorpes, where products range from primitive cooking pots, bowls and trays to figurines, vases, lamps and mugs.

Jolly Harbour, on the island's southwest coast, boasts an array of restaurants and shops overlooking a picturesque marina. Many of the shops feature beachwear, jewelry, perfume and souvenirs. Visitors also can make arrangements for boat charters, car rentals and diving excursions.

Nelson's Dockyard in English Harbour also accommodates an extensive marketplace. Restaurants and shops are tucked away in the restored buildings of what was once the headquarters of the British Royal Navy.

Some shops have extended hours, but stores are generally open Mon.-Sat. 8-5. Many shops are open on Sundays when cruise ships are in port. Banking hours are Mon.-Thurs. 8-2, Fri. 8-4.

Food and Drink

West Indian cookery, influenced by the English, graces most tables. Favorite local dishes include salted codfish, curry conch and souse, or pickled pork. *Fungi,* a type of polenta made with cornmeal and okra, is often served with pepperpot stew. Ducana dumplings are a favorite dessert, a mixture of grated sweet potato and coconut steamed in a banana leaf. A large portion of Antiguan food is imported, and resort-area restaurants feature American, Continental, French and Italian cuisine. Many eateries close during the summer months. In season, lobsters are caught daily off the coast of both Antigua and Barbuda. Locally grown fruits and vegetables include herbs, eddoes, papayas, breadfruit, coconuts, ginger, pumpkins, soursop, okra, sugarcane, sweet potatoes, mangoes and Antigua's famous black pineapples.

Sports and Amusements

Antigua is known as a sailor's paradise, and is a popular mooring spot for a variety of vessels, including luxury yachts. At most hotels and at English Harbour, you can charter yachts and other types of sailing vessels with trained crews for an afternoon or for longer island-hopping excursions. Smaller vessels also are available for rent.

Yachts, schooners and gaffers converge on English Harbour in mid-April for the Antigua Classic Yacht Regatta, a celebration of traditional artisanship. Events include races, a heritage festival and the Concours d'Elegance show and competition. Antigua Sailing Week, considered by some to be *the* world's warm-water sailing regatta, generally is held the last Sunday in April through the first Saturday in May. The island also hosts the 9-day Antigua Charter Yacht Show in early December.

The coastline of Antigua is indented with beautiful bays and some 365 coral beaches, many accessible only by boat. Swimmers, shell collectors and sunbathers need never visit the same beach more than once in a year. Those planning beach outings are advised to carry insect repellent; no-see-ums can be a nuisance on the leeward side of the island, especially at dusk.

The beaches on the northwest coast are frequented by tourists due to the high concentration of resorts in the area. Popular northwest coast beaches include Dickenson Bay, a pretty white-sand beach bordered by several hotels and restaurants. Water sports enthusiasts will appreciate the multitude of operators offering rental equipment for windsurfing. The bay also is a departure point for glass-bottom boat and catamaran excursions.

The gentle surf at Runaway Beach also is perfect for water sports, especially children's activities. Visitors can rent floats, kayaks, windsurfers and sailboats. Water skiing also can be arranged. Landlubbers can explore the area on horseback.

The coral reefs and the remains of shipwrecks, where many multicolored fish gather, make snorkeling and scuba diving popular; many dive operators on the island provide equipment and lessons. In Deep Bay, snorkelers and divers can explore a sunken ship, *The Andes*. The stately ruins of Fort Barrington rise high above the picturesque beach area bordering the bay. A path leads to the top of the fort; the hike can be strenuous, and only those in good physical condition should attempt it. Hikers who make the trek to the top will be rewarded with striking views of St. John's Harbour.

Half Moon Bay, in Half Moon Bay National Park on Antigua's southeast coast, derives its name from the coastline's shape. The crescent-shaped beach, enhanced by azure waters and cool breezes, is perfect for a pleasant stroll. Visitors like to climb the rocks at the north end of the shore. Surf conditions vary due to the bay's shape; visitors can experience crashing waves that present excellent opportunities for body surfing or gentle ripples ideal for swimming.

Darkwood Beach is situated on the island's southwest coast. The white-sand beach, surrounded by a hilly landscape, is punctuated by sailboats docked in crystal-blue water. Beach chairs can be rented at a small snack area, and shelters covered with palm fronds provide respite from the sun. On a clear day, visitors can see the island of Montserrat looming on the horizon. Morris Bay, off Antigua's south coast, is the site of the Curtain Bluff Resort. In this tranquil, secluded setting adorned by sweeping palms, a prominent bluff rises majestically from the sea.

Deep-sea fishing trips for marlin, wahoo, kingfish, shark and barracuda may be chartered out of Falmouth Harbour. Fishing tournaments are held every Labour Day and Whit Monday.

Golf enthusiasts have two 18-hole courses on which to chase birdies: Cedar Valley Golf Club, (268) 462-0161; and Jolly Harbour Golf Course, (268) 462-7771. Tennis courts are available at most hotels, and tournaments held throughout the year attract many professionals. Men's and women's singles and doubles matches take place along with matches that pit amateurs against the pros. Antigua Tennis Week is held at Curtain Bluff Resort in early May and mid-November.

As in other English West Indian islands, cricket is the national obsession, and Antigua is home to some of the world's best cricketers. A stadium for World Cup Cricket is named for one of the island's cricket legends, Sir Vivian Richards. Tournaments between local district teams can be seen across the island on weekends. Spectators also enjoy netball (a women's game similar to basketball, only the hoop has no backboard), basketball, soccer and Thoroughbred racing in season.

Carnival is the island's most spectacular event. Inspired by the splendor of Queen Elizabeth's coronation and the desire for a yearly festival symbolizing freedom, the Antigua and Barbuda Tourist Board instituted the Antigua Carnival. Beginning the last week in July, Carnival commemorates the Antiguan people's emancipation in 1834.

For 10 days, culminating the first Monday and Tuesday in August, Carnival throngs revel from early evening until dawn to the pulsating strains of steel and brass band music. Holiday visitors join the community in the traditional "jump up," a kaleidoscope of singing, dancing and laughter from the early morning hours until the sun is high in the sky. Carnival City, in the Recreation Grounds at St. John's, presents talented entertainers amid magnificent sets.

Shirley Heights Lookout, which offers a spectacular view of English Harbour, is the site of 6 hours of nonstop entertainment on Sunday beginning at 4 p.m. Visitors have the opportunity to mingle with residents, enjoy succulent barbecue and dance to the beat of reggae and steel bands. The island has a few small nightclubs, and year-round nightlife opportunities range from an evening at the theater to gambling in a casino or strolling on a beach.

Sightseeing

Three-hour and all-day sightseeing cruises along Antigua's coast depart from Dickenson Bay and Heritage Quay. Catamaran cruises and eco-tours often include stops for snorkeling and swimming. Many other types of boat trips are available, including cocktail, barbecue and glass-bottom boat cruises. For more information inquire at your hotel, the Antigua and Barbuda Department of Tourism in St. John's at the Government Complex on Queen Elizabeth Highway, or the information booths at V.C. Bird International Airport, St. John's Harbor and Heritage Quay pier.

Fig Tree Drive in southwestern Antigua winds inland through terrain similar to a rain forest and takes about 1 hour to explore by private car. Although this scenic drive is a bit bumpy, visitors are rewarded with views of old sugar mills and lush vegetation. Such tropical fruits as mangoes, oranges, guavas, pineapples, bananas and soursop grow alongside the road. Don't expect to see any figs—in Antigua, fig is the word for banana. Fig Tree Drive residents sell fruits and vegetables from stands in front of their homes. The road leading to Fig Tree Hill provides breathtaking views of fertile valleys and magnificent 1,320-foot (402-m) Mount Obama.

From Green Castle Hill, south of St. John's between Jennings and Emanuel, visitors can survey the island's interior plain and a volcanic formation.

Allow about a day to drive the coastal routes, taking time along the way to explore Nelson's Dockyard in English Harbour, the small fishing villages and such coastal archeological sites as Indian Creek and Mill Reef.

An excellent opportunity to mingle with Antiguans is at Heritage Market near "The Bridge" on Market Street in southern St. John's. At this open-air market, you can bargain for fresh fish, fruits, vegetables and spices or simply enjoy the stimulating, colorful atmosphere. Local arts and crafts are featured in an adjacent complex. The market is open daily.

Another way to grasp the nature of the island and its people is to watch a game of *warri*. This ancient betting game is played on a board with 14 holes and a handful of seeds. Originally brought from Africa with the slave trade, it has remained a favorite pastime.

Air and sea excursions travel north to Barbuda, a sparsely populated coral island lined with white and pink sand beaches that run for miles. Reefs harbor tropical fish and lobster while hiding nearly 100 sunken wrecks. Barbuda's interior, notable for its wildlife, includes a large natural frigate bird sanctuary, said to be the largest in the Western Hemisphere.

The only monument on Barbuda is the Martello Tower; although its origins are unknown, its design and location suggest that it was a lighthouse. Caves near Two Foot Bay have sheltered Barbudans for centuries—even during the 2004 hurricanes. Dark Cave is home to a species of blind shrimp found in only two places in the world. There are a few guest houses in the main village of Codrington, which is named for the family who leased the island from the British Crown for "one fat pig per year if asked." Today most of the population lives here, leaving the rest of the island unspoiled.

A full-day excursion to Barbuda by air includes a tour of the Frigate Bird Sanctuary and Codrington as well as a picnic lunch with rum punch. Most hotels will make arrangements for the Barbuda day tour, which should be planned at least 24 hours in advance.

Eco-tours to Long Island and the Jumby Bay resort offer a rare glimpse of the hawksbill turtle, one of the most endangered sea turtles in the Caribbean. A stretch of sand known as Hawksbill Beach is one of the largest breeding grounds. Turtle watches are organized during nesting season from May to December.

Flights to Montserrat, the island paradise devastated by volcanic eruptions since 1995, depart four times daily from V.C. Bird International Airport via FlyMontserrat.

Transportation

Direct service to V.C. Bird International Airport, 6 miles (10 km) from St. John's, is provided from Atlanta, Charlotte, Miami, New York City and Newark; carriers include American Airlines, Caribbean Airlines, Continental Airlines, Delta and US Airways. LIAT offers nonstop flights to Antigua from San Juan, Puerto Rico. LIAT and Winair service other island destinations, with connections to Barbuda's Codrington Airport. Many cruise ships include Antigua on their regular itineraries.

You can drive rented cars over most of Antigua's roads; however, use caution due to left-hand driving. Be on the lookout for the occasional goat wandering across the road. The primary roads are navigable, but potholes are common—and so are "sleeping policemen" (the Antiguan nickname for speed bumps). Although most of the island's roads are not marked, most hotels and the Antigua and Barbuda Department of Tourism provide a map that is easy to follow.

Signs throughout Antigua show arrows pointing toward major resorts and attractions: These can assist in determining direction. If you are planning to drive through St. John's, be sure to obtain a good map; even though most of the streets are well-marked, many of them are one-way.

Presentation of a valid U.S. license and $20 entitles you to a driver's license good for 90 days. Hertz in St. John's offers rental car discounts to AAA members; phone the head office on Carlisle Estate Airport Road, (268) 481-4440; or branch offices at the Jolly Harbour Hotel, (268) 481-4456; the Royal Antiguan Hotel, (268) 481-4457; and the airport, (268) 481-4455. Other car rental agencies and scooter rental agencies are listed in the telephone directory. Taxis are readily available at major resorts and are plentiful throughout St. John's. Fares from the airport to hotels are listed at the airport, and range from $5 to $34 for four passengers and their luggage, depending upon the destination; for all other excursions round-trip fares are charged. Be sure to ask if fares are quoted in U.S. dollars or the local E.C. currency.

Fast Facts

POPULATION: 69,481.

AREA: 280 sq km (108 sq mi.).

CAPITAL: St. John's.

HIGHEST POINT: 405 m (1,320 ft.), Mount Obama.

LOWEST POINT: Sea level, Caribbean Sea.

TIME ZONE(S): Atlantic Standard.

LANGUAGE: English and an English patois.

GOVERNMENT: Independent. Member of the British Commonwealth of Nations.

UNIT OF CURRENCY: Eastern Caribbean (E.C.) dollar. $1 U.S. = 2.7 E.C. dollars. U.S. currency is widely accepted.

ELECTRICITY: 110 volts AC and 220 volts AC, 60 cycles; voltage and current vary with location.

MINIMUM AGE FOR DRIVERS: 21-25, depending on the rental car agency. Local license ($20 U.S.) required, valid for 90 days; drive on left.

MINIMUM AGE FOR GAMBLING: 18.

SEAT BELT/CHILD RESTRAINT LAWS: Seat belts are required for all passengers. Children under 10 must ride in the back seat.

HOLIDAYS: Jan. 1; Good Friday; Easter Monday; Labour Day, May (1st Mon.); Whit Monday, May or June (8th Mon. after Easter); Caricom Day, July (1st Mon.); Carnival, Aug. (1st Mon. and Tues.); Independence Day, Nov. 1; V.C. Bird Day, Dec. 9; Christmas, Dec. 25; Boxing Day, Dec. 26.

TAXES: An 8.5 percent room tax and 10-15 percent service charge are added to most hotel bills. Departure tax is $28 U.S. and is usually included in airline ticket prices.

IMMIGRATION REQUIREMENTS: Passport or proof of U.S. citizenship and a return or onward ticket are required. No visa needed for stays up to 6 months. The U.S. Dept. of Homeland Security requires all U.S. citizens returning from the Caribbean to present a valid passport.

PHONING THE ISLANDS: To call Antigua and Barbuda from the U.S. or Canada, dial 1 + 268 + the 7-digit local number.

FURTHER INFORMATION FOR VISITORS:

Antigua and Barbuda Department of Tourism
3 Dag Hammarskjold Plaza
305 E. 47th St., Suite 6A
New York, NY 10017
(646) 215-6035
(888) 268-4227

Antigua and Barbuda Department of Tourism, St. John's
Government Complex
Queen Elizabeth Highway
St. John's, Antigua
Antigua and Barbuda
(268) 462-0480

Points of Interest

See map page 37.

ENGLISH HARBOUR (F-2) pop. 614

English Harbour is 15 miles (24 km) from St. John's on the south side of the island. Once an outfitting center for British warships, this harbor played host to the ships of Horatio Nelson, Sir Francis Drake and Walter Rodney. It suffered from neglect for many years until yachtsmen rediscovered its charm and natural beauty. Restored to its 18th-century appearance, the town is now one of the island's most popular tourist destinations.

DOW'S HILL INTERPRETATION CENTRE is near Shirley Heights. "Reflections of the Sun" is a multimedia show tracing Antigua's history, heritage and culture. Displays include a shell collection and 18th-century artifacts. A guided tour includes a visit to the Belvedere, an observation area that provides a 360-degree panorama of Nelson's Dockyard National Park. In the distance, the islands of Guadeloupe and Martinique are often visible. The remains of a 1780s house and a gun platform also are on the grounds. **Time:** Allow 30 minutes minimum. **Hours:** Daily 9-5. **Cost:** (includes Nelson's Dockyard National Park and Nelson's Dockyard Museum) $7; free (ages 0-11). **Phone:** (268) 481-5022.

NELSON'S DOCKYARD NATIONAL PARK extends inland from a line along the southern coastline from Mamora Bay to Carlisle Bay. Built 1743-94, the site is reputed to be the only existing Georgian dockyard. It was used by a number of British admirals, including Horatio Nelson, as the home port of the British Fleet during the Napoleonic Wars. The dockyard also was used as a repair and maintenance station for ships. Several buildings have been restored. Fort Berkeley, the original British garrison, was built in 1704 and manned by more than 3,000 troops. Also noteworthy is the dockyard's marketplace.

The park, which covers 15 square miles (39 sq km) of rolling hills, affords memorable views of the dockyard and surrounding countryside. **Tours:** Guided tours are available. **Time:** Allow 1 hour minimum. **Hours:** Daily 9-6. Last admission is at 4:30. **Cost:** (includes Dow's Hill Interpretation Centre and Nelson's Dockyard Museum) $7; free (ages 0-11). **Phone:** (268) 481-5022. [⊓]

Nelson's Dockyard Museum is on the ground floor of the Admiral's House in Nelson's Dockyard National Park. Displays in the 1855 Victorian building include naval buttons, maps, coins from the 1800s, telescopes, muskets, cannon balls, clay pipes, ships models and belongings of Horatio Nelson. A late 1700s sandbox tree next to the museum produces pods which once were used as ink blotters. **Hours:** Daily 8-5. **Cost:** (includes Dow's Hill Interpretation Centre and Nelson's Dockyard National Park) $7; free (ages 0-11). **Phone:** (268) 481-5037.

SHIRLEY HEIGHTS is across the bay from Nelson's Dockyard. This lovely rise, which affords a view of Antigua's southern coast, was named for Gen. Thomas Shirley, who became governor in 1781. Clarence House, the Georgian villa on the road to the Heights, was built 1804-1806 as the residence of the commissioner of the Royal Navy's dockyard. The Heights served as the main lookout post in the days of Nelson. Approximately 60 structures were built here 1781-1825, and visitors can see the remains of Fort Shirley's barracks, officers' quarters and powder magazines.

The Shirley Heights Barbecue, popular with tourists and locals alike, starts every Sunday at 4 and runs late into the night with live music and dancing. **Hours:** Heights open Mon. 9-4, Tues.-Sat. 9-dusk (also Fri.-Sat. dusk-10), Sun. 4-10. **Cost:** Free. Sunday event $8. [⊓]

PARES (E-3)

BETTY'S HOPE PLANTATION is in the rural limestone district. Once the largest sugar plantation on Antigua, the site served as the seat of government 1689-1704. Sir Christopher Codrington assumed ownership in 1674, naming the plantation for his daughter. The estate remained in the Codrington family for nearly 300 years. Most of the buildings lie in ruin, but one of the windmill towers has been restored. Museum exhibits illustrate the history of sugar in the West Indies, and interpretive markers describe the site. **Hours:** Tues.-Sat. 10-4. **Cost:** $2. **Phone:** (268) 462-4930 or (268) 462-1469.

DEVIL'S BRIDGE is about 5 mi. (8 km) e. at Indian Town Point. This natural limestone arch was created by the erosive force of the Atlantic Ocean. Water rushes through crevices in the rock and spouts through blowholes in dramatic bursts. Archeologists have uncovered artifacts at nearby Indian Town, one of the earliest Arawak settlements on the island. **Cost:** Free.

ST. JOHN'S (D-2) pop. 22,342

Antigua's capital, St. John's has quaint shops and colonial homes above a landlocked harbor. Tempering St. John's 19th-century English atmosphere is a progressive spirit symbolized by modern architecture. The man-made harbor, completed in 1968, has made the island an important port of call for passenger and commercial vessels; cruise ships dock at Heritage Quay.

Shops, banks and other businesses line High Street, which runs through the center of the city to the pier. The produce market in the southern part of town is divided into sections for fruits and vegetables, meat and fish. Vendors pay weekly or monthly rent for stalls, except on Saturdays when they pay according to the number of bundles they carry through the gates. Visitors enjoy watching this "weighing-in" process.

St. John's Botanical Garden is near the intersection of Factory Road and Independence Avenue, behind the National Archives building. This small park's shaded benches and gazebo provide a quiet refuge from the bustle of activity in St. John's.

Antigua and Barbuda Department of Tourism: Government Complex, Queen Elizabeth Highway, St. John's, Antigua. **Phone:** (268) 462-0480.

ANTIGUA DISTILLERY LTD. is on Friars Hill Road. The only distillery on the island produces nearly 400,000 gallons of rum each year, bottling under two labels, Cavalier and English Harbour. The company was formed in 1934 with the purchase of several old sugar estates and a muscovado molasses factory; copper stills are still used. **Hours:** Daily 8-4. **Cost:** Free. **Phone:** (268) 480-3200.

FORT JAMES is at the northern entrance to St. John's harbor. Built in 1739 to guard the port, Fort James is one of the many installations built by the British in the 18th century. Fear of French invasion prompted its construction. A powder magazine, several cannons and the foundation of the fort's walls remain. **Hours:** Daily 24 hours. **Cost:** Free.

GOVERNMENT HOUSE is on Independence Drive. Originally known as "The Parsonage," the official residence and office of the governor-general of Antigua has dignified colonial lines and is surrounded by beautiful grounds. The grounds are open to the public; the house is closed for ongoing restoration. **Phone:** (268) 462-0003.

MUSEUM OF ANTIGUA & BARBUDA is at Long and Market sts. The Old Court House, built in 1750, contains exhibits tracing the history of early inhabitants, colonists and slaves. **Time:** Allow 30 minutes minimum. **Hours:** Mon.-Thurs. 8:30-4, Fri. 8:30-3, Sat. 10-2. Closed major holidays. **Cost:** $3. **Phone:** (268) 462-1469.

ST. JOHN'S ANGLICAN CATHEDRAL is at the intersection of Newgate St. and Church Ln. The Church of St. John the Divine was originally built in 1683 and redone in stone in 1745. An earthquake destroyed it nearly 100 years later, and it had to be reconstructed yet again. Island legend holds that the figures of St. John the Baptist and St. John the Divine at the south gate were taken from the masts of one of Napoleon's ships. **Hours:** The cathedral is open to the public for tours, except during religious services; renovations are ongoing. **Cost:** Donations. **Phone:** (268) 462-0820.

GAMBLING ESTABLISHMENTS

- **King's Casino** is at Heritage Quay. **Hours:** Daily 10 a.m.-4 a.m. **Phone:** (268) 462-1727.
- **Madison's Casino** is at Runaway Bay in the Rush Entertainment Complex. **Hours:** Daily 10 a.m.-3 a.m. **Phone:** (268) 562-7874.

Bushiribana Gold Mine Ruins, Bushiribana / © Gabriel Jaime Jimenez / eStock Photo

Aruba

A ruba is the smallest and most westerly of the "ABC" (Aruba, Bonaire and Curaçao) islands. Just 15 miles (24 km) north of Venezuela, it has an exceptionally dry climate that is considered one of the most desirable in the Caribbean. Aruba's arid interior, marked by surreal, wind-bent divi-divi trees, sprawling stands of cactus and aloe vera, and huge boulders strewn like marbles contrasts sharply with the more tropical, palm-lined southwest coast. It is perhaps as much the desert landscape as the active nightlife that gives Aruba the reputation as the Las Vegas of the Caribbean.

History

Assessments of Aruba's worth have varied since 1499, when Alonso de Ojeda claimed the island for Spain. Because the Spaniards considered Aruba worthless, the native Arawak Indians were spared the annihilation their kinfolk faced on islands thought more valuable. The Dutch, who hardly considered the island prime real estate, took over in 1636.

During the Napoleonic Wars the British settled Aruba for a few years, but by 1816 the Dutch had returned to stay. Compared with other Caribbean islands, Aruba had a rather quiet history; the island was fought over only twice and suffered few pirate attacks.

Gold discovered on Aruba in 1824 attracted considerable investment, but a century later the mine was exhausted. A different sort of gold renewed interest in the island in 1924, when the Lago Oil and Transport Co. built a large refinery that brought one of the highest standards of living in the Caribbean.

This prosperity was furthered by the development of tourism, which became Aruba's primary industry when the refinery closed in 1985. (It reopened in 1991.) Because of the focus on tourism and the number of resorts on the island,

Arubans enjoy a very low unemployment rate. A moratorium on building new hotels or time-share resorts contributes to sustainable development and a high standard of living on the island. Arubans are proud of their heritage and are concerned that with the importation of additional workers the island's local flavor might be lost.

Aruba's location outside the hurricane belt, its near constant 82 F (28 C) temperature, the ever-present trade winds (which, at times, can be quite gusty) that cool off even the hottest days, its comparatively low humidity and infrequent rainy days combine to make the island a favorite for visitors year-round.

Practically all Arubans are fluent in four languages: English, Dutch and Spanish and Papiamento, the native language of the three "ABC" islands. A mélange of Dutch, Spanish, Portuguese, African, English and French, Papiamento is a lilting, melodic language spoken by locals at home and with friends. Arubans, known for their hospitality and their friendly, outgoing nature, treat visitors as important guests and extend a sincere *Bon Bini* ("welcome"). This conviviality can be traced to a line from the country's national anthem: "The greatness of our people is their great cordiality."

Aruba became a separate entity within the Kingdom of the Netherlands on Jan. 1, 1986; prior to that date it was a member of the Netherlands Antilles, which was dissolved in October 2010. The Kingdom of the Netherlands, which also includes the Netherlands, Bonaire, Curaçao, St. Eustatius, St. Maarten and Saba, is responsible for the entire kingdom's defense and foreign affairs while the government of each country performs autonomously.

Shopping

Aruba offers the finest in European luxury items, but it is always wise to check prices before leaving home, as not everything sells at a discount. Shops in Aruba charge percent sales tax on purchases. U.S. dollars are as readily accepted as Aruban florins, and prices are frequently shown in dollars as well as the local currency. Credit cards are accepted at most stores. The main shopping areas are Royal Plaza Mall, Renaissance Mall, Renaissance Marketplace, Aventura Mall, Plaza Daniel Leo and the shops along Caya Betico Croes (Main Street) in cosmopolitan Oranjestad. In addition to these downtown shopping areas, many of the larger hotels have shopping arcades that feature branches of the downtown shops.

Paseo Herencia Mall, opposite the Holiday Inn Sunspree Resort Aruba, features designer shops, restaurants and a cinema. In front of Occidental Grand Aruba is Arawak Garden, featuring souvenir shops and restaurants, while the Village and South Beach shopping complexes are adjacent to the Radisson Aruba Resort.

Royal Plaza Mall on L.G. Smith Boulevard features designer clothing, jewelry and watches. Souvenirs, beachwear and local and foreign music also can be found at the colorful mall built in the Dutch Caribbean style of architecture. Though Cuban cigars are available here, U.S. citizens are expressly forbidden from bringing them home.

Behind the Royal Plaza Mall are a post office and Botica Kibrahacha, a drugstore and pharmacy. Two ATMs inside the mall offer local currency and U.S. dollars. The Renaissance Mall adjoining the Renaissance Aruba Resort has entrances on Havenstraat and L.G. Smith Boulevard. The mall, where visitors can see the hotel's indoor boat lagoon, contains more than 60 shops and designer boutiques.

On Plaza Daniel Leo across from the Seaport Mall are European boutiques, perfumeries and cosmetics shops. The square is recognized by its Dutch Colonial architecture painted in pastels.

Shops along Caya Betico Croes, which starts at Plaza Daniel Leo, offer clothing, perfume and cosmetics, sunglasses, souvenirs and imported items such as Dutch pewter, Delftware and Hummel figurines.

Renaissance Marketplace is on L.G. Smith Boulevard across from the Parliament building. Situated on the waterfront next to a marina and

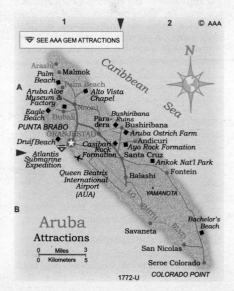

© AAA

SEE AAA GEM ATTRACTIONS

Caribbean Sea

N

Arashi
Palm Beach ◆ Malmok
Palm Beach
Aruba Aloe
Museum & ◆ Alto Vista
Factory Chapel
Eagle ◆ Noord
Beach Bubali Bushiribana
PUNTA BRABO Para- ◆ Ruins
ORANJESTAD dera ◆ Bushiribana
Druif Beach ◆ Aruba Ostrich Farm
Casibari ◆ Andicuri
Atlantis Rock ◆ Ayo Rock Formation
Submarine Formation Santa Cruz
Expedition ★ ◆ Arikok Nat'l Park
Queen Beatrix Balashi ◆ Fontein
International
Airport YAMANOTA
(AUA)

B

Aruba
Attractions
0   Miles   3
0 Kilometers 5

Bachelor's
Beach

Savaneta

San Nicolas

Seroe Colorado
COLORADO POINT

1772-U

the Seaport Casino, the market contains a movie theater, restaurants and souvenir shops.

Most Oranjestad stores are open Mon.-Sat. 9-6. Some stores also are open Sunday mornings and holidays when cruise ships are in port. The port, which can handle up to four ships, is near downtown Oranjestad and convenient to the main shopping areas. Banking hours are Mon.-Fri. 8-4. The Caribbean Mercantile Bank at the airport is open Mon.-Thurs. 8-4, Fri. 8-5.

Food and Drink

Menus catering to all tastes and budgets can be found in Oranjestad. Signs reading *Aki ta bende kuminda krioyo* mean "local food sold here." Island specialties include *funchi,* a polenta-like cornmeal staple served with meat or fish; *pan bati,* a somewhat sweet Aruban pancake made of cornmeal; and *keri keri,* a mixture of tomatoes, peppers, shredded fish and herbs.

Other popular Aruban dishes include *keshi yena,* a Dutch cheese stuffed with meat, chicken or fish that is seasoned with raisins, olives, onions and tomatoes; and *pastechi,* pastries filled with cheese, meat, seafood or other ingredients. *Erwten soep* is a thick pea soup cooked with pork, ham and sausage; *stoba* is a stew of vegetables and meat (usually goat); and *soppi di pisca* is fish soup seasoned with *yerbi hole,* a local variety of basil. *Robo porco,* salted pig's tail, is often added to traditional dishes.

Island flavors are evident in fresh caught fish such as wahoo, snapper or grouper simply prepared and served with a *Criollo* (Creole) sauce of tomatoes, onions, garlic and bell peppers. The proximity of the island to South America accounts for the popularity of Argentinian *churrasco* steaks and *churrascarias,* Brazilian steak houses. A popular accompaniment to any Aruban meal is the locally produced Balashi beer, a pilsner-style brew.

Most restaurants automatically add a service charge of 15 percent to the bill, not all of which goes to the server. An additional tip is appreciated, especially when service is exceptional. Dinner reservations are recommended at the island's better restaurants, and the majority accept credit cards.

As for liquid refreshment, sparse rainfall used to make drinking water scarce, but modern technology allows fresh water to be distilled from the sea. In fact, Aruba boasts one of the world's largest desalinization plants; drinking tap water is safe and refreshing.

Sports and Amusements

As on its sister islands, vegetation on Aruba is sparse. The dusty interior contains huge boulders and wind-bent *divi-divi* (watapana) trees.

Recreational activities include hiking through Arikok National Park; cave exploring at Fontein, Huliba and Quadirikiri; and horseback riding through the outback.

There is plenty to do along the coast, with beach-related and water activities at the top of the list. Although all of Aruba's beaches are public, beach chairs are reserved for hotel guests. *Palapas,* or thatch-covered beach huts, are so coveted for shade that guests line up early in the morning for reservations.

Seven miles (11 km) of uninterrupted beach stretch from Druif Beach to Eagle Beach and from Palm Beach to Malmok. The best swimming spots are Eagle and Palm beaches, due to the fact that the water is the calmest off the island's southwest coast. These beaches also are where the majority of the island's hotels are concentrated. Banana boats and parasailers being towed behind speed boats are a common sight along Palm Beach. For those in search of expansive stretches of sand, Eagle Beach and nearby Manchebo Beach offer wider strips than can be found at Palm Beach.

Druif Beach, south of Eagle Beach, also is a pleasant place to swim for those not averse to some slight wave action. There are small beach coves on the north coast—Boca Prins, Boca Grandi and Dos Playa. Although the scenery is beautiful, the north coast is not recommended for swimming, due to strong currents and large waves.

The beaches in the southeast section of the island just beyond the oil refinery tend to be less populated than the southwest beaches. Baby Beach, a large, secluded inlet at the island's southeast tip, is so named because it is perfect for small children and inexperienced swimmers. This is because the water remains shallow quite a distance from the shore, achieving depths no greater than 5 feet (1.5 m). It also is a popular beach among the locals for relaxing and picnicking.

At Rodgers Beach, next to Baby Beach, swimmers can enjoy a little more surf and find good swimming and snorkeling opportunities. And although it can be somewhat disconcerting to see the large refinery looming so close by, the water and air at Baby and Rodgers beaches are crystal clear, and the beaches are ideal for a family outing.

Trade winds that blow at a maximum speed of 27 knots (31 mph, 50 km/h) daily, with an average speed of 18 knots (21 mph, 34 km/h), make conditions perfect for windsurfing; the Aruba Hi-Winds Tournament takes place in June. The entire area of coast between Hadicurari and Malmok beaches provides excellent windsurfing opportunities. Hadicurari, locally referred to as "Fishermen's Huts," is one of the most popular spots.

North of Fishermen's Huts, the Malmok Beach area is a great place to learn how to windsurf since the water is only between 2 and 3 feet (.6 and .9 m) deep. There are many small guest houses and day-rental apartments in this area which cater to windsurfers, and windsurfing lessons and equipment rental are readily available. Boca Grandi, just north of Seroe Colorado Point, is an area famous for professional windsurfing.

Visibility in Aruba's clear waters can extend as far as 90 feet (27 m) and the water temperature is never under 70 F (21 C), making the area very desirable for snorkeling and scuba diving. A vessel often explored by divers is the *Antilla,* the wreckage of a World War II German freighter off the coast midway between Arashi and Malmok. One of the largest wrecks in the Caribbean, the ship was purposefully sunk in 1941 in order to avoid capture by Allied forces. Another cement cargo ship, the *Jane Sea,* lies near the Barcadera Reefs.

Arashi Beach, north of Malmok on the southwest coast, is frequented by both scuba divers and snorkelers. Mangel Halto, a reef off the southeast coast halfway between Oranjestad and San Nicolas, is a favorite with divers; snorkeling also is possible in this area. Isla d'Oro, about 1 mile (1.6 km) east of Spanish Lagoon, is another popular dive site. Barcadera Reef is especially recommended for scuba diving.

Snorkeling is a featured activity at De Palm Island, and a beautiful reef is easily accessible off the shallow channel of Baby Beach. Berth Reef, off Rodgers Beach, and the reefs off Bachelor's Beach, on the northeast coast, are favored snorkeling spots for advanced swimmers. Rental equipment for diving, windsurfing and water skiing is available throughout the island.

Fishing for blue and white marlin, kingfish, tuna, bonito and other game fish is best July through October. Also in abundant supply are sailfish, mahi mahi, amberjack, wahoo and barracuda. Boats for deep-sea fishing can be chartered at the Seaport Marina and Oranjestad piers. Some yachts and catamarans offer 2-hour coastal cruises, complete with snacks and beverages. Motorboats, small sailboats, pedalboats and sea jeeps (wave runners) can be rented for shorter periods of time at diverse aquatic facilities.

As for non-aquatic recreation, most hotels and private clubs provide tennis courts and information about horseback riding. Tierra del Sol, (297) 586-0978 or (866) 978-5158, features an 18-hole golf course designed by Robert Trent Jones Jr. A nine-hole course is available at The Links at Divi Aruba, (297) 581-4653.

Regardless which outdoor activity you choose—whether languidly soaking up some sun on the beach or energetically hiking or bicycling through the island's interior—always remember that you are in the tropical Caribbean, and the effects of the sun can be devastating. Keep hydrated, use plenty of high-octane sunscreen and wear a head covering.

In addition to the many activities available during the day, Aruba also has an active nightlife: Hotel casinos and various nightclubs and restaurants offer dancing and after-dinner entertainment. The island's resorts sponsor more than 50 themed events that occur on a weekly basis, including folkloric, limbo and steel-band shows.

Casino gambling is a popular pastime in Aruba, with 11 casinos offering blackjack, roulette, baccarat, craps and slot machines. One of the most common games is Caribbean stud poker, which can be played by table or machine. Visitors to the casinos must be at least 18. Aruba's casinos are not as formal as those in Atlantic City or Las Vegas, and casual attire is acceptable.

Some of the best local entertainment takes place at the Bon Bini Festival, held every Tuesday evening at Fort Zoutman in Oranjestad at 6:30 p.m. Offerings include food, music and crafts. Concerts and folkloric shows also are performed at the Cultural Center (Cas di Cultura) at Vondellaan 2 in Oranjestad. Movies, usually American, are shown at the cinema at the Renaissance Marketplace.

The island version of New Orleans' Mardi Gras, Aruba's Carnival is celebrated during January and February and enlists locals and tourists alike in parades, dances, contests and parties; the Grand Parade takes place the Sunday before Ash Wednesday.

Aruba Today, Aruba's English newspaper, is available free of charge at most hotels.

Sightseeing

Aruba has good roads, though many are unmarked. However, the government has marked the roads to point the way to the resort areas and specific attractions. You might have to rely on word of mouth or try navigating by the divi-divi trees which always point southwest away from the trade winds; if you are lost, just remember that these trees blow in the direction of the resorts. The island is about 19.6 miles (32 km) long and 6 miles (10 km) wide at its broadest point and most of it can be toured by car.

Jeep tours are a popular way to experience the otherworldly rock-strewn, almost moon-like landscape common to Aruba's interior, and caravans of four-wheel-drive vehicles are a familiar sight along the hilly, bumpy dirt roads of such spots as Arikok National Park. A guide, who rides in the lead vehicle, provides a narration, which can be heard through speakers mounted in each visitor-driven jeep.

For an adventurous excursion, drive into Aruba's *cunucu*, or countryside, where fields of cactuses and aloe vera are punctuated by wandering goats and colorful cottages. Old-style cunucu houses, which appear throughout the island, are characterized by such features as rain tanks, a necessity in the days before desalinization, wooden windows and doors, and chimneys once used for cooking.

Chances are you will find your own Kodak moment—perhaps one of the huge rock formations that mark the area around Casibari and Ayo, from which a road continues northeast to Andicuri. Here was the famed Natural Bridge, a coral limestone formation that collapsed into the sea in 2005. A smaller "daughter" bridge is nearby. With a little further exploration you might discover secluded inlets where crashing waves leap upward above the cliffs.

On J.E. Irausquin Boulevard, the main road leading to the high-rise hotels at Palm Beach, is an Aruban landmark, the Old Dutch Windmill. Built in the Netherlands in 1804, it was moved to Aruba and reconstructed at its present site in 1974. It currently houses a restaurant.

Directly across the road from the windmill is the Bubali Bird Sanctuary. An anomaly in semiarid Aruba, the lush refuge is a resting and breeding grounds for more than 80 species of migrating waterfowls, including herons, egrets, cormorants, ducks and gulls. There is no charge to walk through the marsh grasses or birdwatch from the observation tower.

Visitors can view the entire island at Hooiberg, also nicknamed Haystack Mountain, between Santa Cruz and Ayo. Athletically inclined individuals may choose to climb the more than 600 steps that ascend to the mountain's top, which at 541 feet (165 m) is the island's second highest elevation. Mount Jamanota, to the southeast at the center of the island, is Aruba's highest point at 617 feet (188 m). The panorama from its summit includes Frenchman's Pass on the south coast, where Indians defended their island against the French.

At the island's northern tip, the California Lighthouse, named for the wreck of the cargo ship *California* just offshore, is on a cliff that offers a panorama of Arashi, Malmok, Palm and Eagle beaches. At this point, the difference can be observed between the calm southern coast and the northern coast with waves crashing against the shoreline.

Glass-bottom boats provide views of colorful fish, coral formations and shipwrecks during 90-minute trips to the California Lighthouse. Trimaran and catamaran sailing excursions, which offer snorkeling trips and sunset cocktail cruises, also are available.

Reputable ticket booking establishments include *Atlantis* Submarine, De Palm Tours, Pelican Adventures, Red Sail Sports and Unique Sports of Aruba. Both half-day and full-day tours, in various combinations, are available; check with your hotel for details.

Some companies offer tours that cater to such specialized interests as wildlife or history. Information about excursions can be obtained at the Aruba Tourism Authority Public Relations Department at L.G. Smith Boulevard #8 or at most hotels; phone (297) 582-3777.

Transportation

Queen Beatrix International Airport has direct flights from Atlanta, Boston, Charlotte, Chicago, Houston, Miami, Newark, New York, Philadelphia, Puerto Rico and Tampa; interisland flights to the other "ABC" islands are available on Tiara Air, Insel Air and the Dutch Antilles Express. Direct flights from Aruba to Colombia and Venezuela also are available. In addition, Aruba is a popular port of call for cruise ships.

Hotels, by law, are not allowed to provide transportation to and from the airport for their guests. Taxis, however, are readily available at the airport. Cabs are not metered, but fares are set by the government and are based on destination rather than mileage. The fare (per taxi, not per person) from the airport to the downtown area is $18; the fee to the Eagle Beach hotel area is $22; and to the Palm Beach hotel area the cost is $25.

Most American car rental firms have branches on the island, and there also are several local companies. Many rental agencies have outlets across from the main terminal at Queen Beatrix International Airport, though if you prefer to rent a car for just a few days, the larger hotels have rentals available on-site. Hertz—with outlets at the airport, the cruise terminal and at several major hotels—offers discounts to AAA members; phone (297) 588-7570 or (800) 654-3080.

Speed limits in Aruba are generally 30 mph (50 km/h) in town and 50 mph (80 km/h) on out-of-town roads. Drivers should be aware that most of the traffic in Oranjestad is one-way, and vehicles approaching from the right have the right of way when there is no road sign posted. Driving is on the right side of the road, and right turns on red are not permitted. "Roundabouts," traffic circles common in Europe, also can be found at major intersections in Aruba.

Traffic in the heart of Oranjestad can be quite congested during peak hours, and parking spaces are often at a premium. The free parking lot near Royal Plaza Mall, adjacent to the main bus station, is a good alternative; from there it's only a short walk to the main shopping areas.

Due to Aruba's European heritage, speed limits and distances on road signs are presented in kilometers, and the international symbols used on the signs may be unfamiliar to drivers accustomed to U.S. signage. Not all of these symbols are self-explanatory; be sure and familiarize yourself with their meanings before setting out.

Part of L.G. Smith Boulevard, which runs in front of the Palm Beach hotels, is known as J.E. Irausquin Boulevard. Some street signs in the stretch of road between the Divi Tamarijn and the Aruba Marriott Resort & Stellaris Casino reflect this name.

Although maps might show street names and highway numbers, once you leave the downtown area in Oranjestad road signs and street markers are few and far between. Also, outside the main commercial and residential areas, and especially if you venture into the countryside (*cunucu*), roads are not likely to be paved. Even so, it's a small island and not difficult to navigate as long as you remember to ask for directions before heading out.

Use caution when traveling on wet roads; dirt and oil accumulate due to scarce rainfall,

Fast Facts

POPULATION: 100,018.

AREA: 181 sq km (70 sq mi.).

CAPITAL: Oranjestad.

HIGHEST POINT: 188 m (617 ft.), Mount Jamanota.

LOWEST POINT: Sea level, Caribbean Sea.

TIME ZONE(S): Atlantic Standard.

LANGUAGE: Dutch and Papiamento are the official languages, but Spanish and English are widely spoken.

GOVERNMENT: Autonomous member of the Kingdom of the Netherlands.

UNIT OF CURRENCY: Aruba florin divided into 100 cents. $1 U.S. = approx. 1.8 Aruba florin. U.S. currency is widely accepted.

ELECTRICITY: 110-120 volts, 60 cycles AC.

MINIMUM AGE FOR DRIVERS: 21-25, depending on the rental car agency; maximum age 65-70. U.S. license valid; drive on right.

MINIMUM AGE FOR GAMBLING: 18.

SEAT BELT/CHILD RESTRAINT LAWS: Seat belts are required for all passengers. Children under 12 must ride in the back seat. Child restraints are required for under age 5.

HELMETS FOR MOTORCYCLISTS: Required.

HOLIDAYS: Jan. 1; G.F. "Betico" Croes' Day, Jan. 25; Carnival Monday, Feb. (Mon. before Ash Wednesday); National Anthem and Flag Day, Mar. 18; Good Friday; Easter; Easter Monday; Queen's Birthday, Apr. 30; Labour Day, May 1; Ascension Day, May (6th Thurs. after Easter); Christmas, Dec. 25; Boxing Day, Dec. 26.

TAXES: Shops charge 1.5 percent sales tax on purchases. A 7.5 percent room tax and 10-12 percent service charge are added to most hotel and restaurant bills. For flights to the United States, a departure tax of $36.75 U.S. and a special facility charge of $3.25 are usually included in airline ticket prices.

IMMIGRATION REQUIREMENTS: Passport or proof of U.S. citizenship and return or onward ticket are required. No visa needed for stays up to 3 months. The U.S. Dept. of Homeland Security requires all U.S. citizens returning from the Caribbean to present a valid passport.

PHONING THE ISLANDS: To call Aruba from the U.S. or Canada, dial 011 + 297 + the 7-digit local number beginning with "5."

FURTHER INFORMATION FOR VISITORS:
Aruba Tourism Authority
100 Plaza Drive, First Floor
Secaucus, NJ 07094
(201) 558-1110
(800) 862-7822
Aruba Tourism Authority, Oranjestad
L.G. Smith Blvd. 8
Oranjestad, Aruba
(297) 582-3777

resulting in slippery conditions in the rain. If you are planning an excursion through Aruba's interior, a car with four-wheel-drive is a good idea. Make sure your vehicle is in good working order, since repair facilities are not always available.

Scooters and motorcycles also can be rented, but keep in mind that the island is deserted in certain areas and the terrain can be rough and hilly. Taxis also can be hired for sightseeing. If you choose to take a cab, check the fixed taxi rates beforehand. To order a cab phone (297) 582-2116.

An inexpensive transportation option to Oranjestad from the hotels at Eagle and Palm beaches is the regular bus service provided by Arubus. Stops are conveniently located in front of most major lodgings along the road to the downtown area. The main bus terminal is on L.G. Smith Boulevard, exit to Royal Plaza in downtown Oranjestad.

Buses run daily 5:40 a.m.-11:40 p.m. From Monday through Saturday the buses make scheduled stops 20 minutes before the hour, 10 minutes before the hour, on the hour and 25 minutes after the hour; after 7 p.m. buses only stop 20 minutes before the hour. On Sunday buses run on a reduced schedule, stopping 20 minutes before the hour. The fare is $1.25, or $2.25 for a round-trip.

Since the U.S. Dept. of Homeland Security has officers stationed at Queen Beatrix International Airport, U.S. visitors save time by clearing customs in Aruba before departure rather than at their destination.

Points of Interest

See map page 45.

BUSHIRIBANA (A-2)

The castle-like ruins of an old pirate stronghold still stand at Bushiribana, perhaps dating to the 15th century. Here too are the abandoned gold mines that once produced some three million pounds of gold. The rugged north coast is known for its crashing waves and unusual rock formations.

The island's most famous tourist attraction, the Natural Bridge, fell into the sea in 2005. The 100-foot-long coral span, which had survived centuries of the ocean's pounding, was the largest of its kind in the Caribbean.

ARUBA OSTRICH FARM is on Natural Bridge Road at Matividiri 57. Guided tours of the 12-acre (5-hectare) farm provide information about these long-necked birds, raised solely for breeding and educational purposes. Aruba's climate is too humid for eggs to mature on their own; visitors see the incubators where the huge eggs are kept until they hatch. Chicks frequently can be seen and held, and the older birds can be fed.

The birds' life cycle is explained as visitors are led around the complex. Emus, an Australian relative of the ostrich, also are on the premises. **Time:** Allow 30 minutes minimum. **Hours:** Tours depart on the half hour daily 9-4. **Cost:** $12; $6 (ages 3-12). **Phone:** (297) 585-9630. ⑪

AYO ROCK FORMATION is 1.9 mi. (3 km) s. of Bushiribana. The origin of this geological mystery has never been determined. Diorite boulders, each weighing several thousand tons, balance precariously on edge or on each other. Indian paintings can be seen on some of the rocks. **Hours:** Daily dawn-dusk. **Cost:** Free.

BUSHIRIBANA GOLD MINE RUINS is at Boca Mahos inlet. Remains of the Aruba Island Gold Mining Company's smelting works, built in 1872 and used for only a decade, stand in a barren area with desertlike terrain. Some 3 million pounds of gold were produced here. Striking views of the north coast can be seen from the ruins. **Hours:** Daily dawn-dusk. **Cost:** Free.

CASIBARI ROCK FORMATION is just s. of Paradera. Diorite boulders weighing thousands of tons make up this stone summit. A climb to the top, made possible by ascending steps that wind through the boulders, is rewarded by a panorama of the southwest portion of the island. A rock garden at the base of the formation is accented by beachgrape trees and contains boulders said to resemble certain animals. Only those in good physical condition should attempt the climb. **Hours:** Daily dawn-dusk. **Cost:** Free.

FONTEIN (B-2)

Aruba's caves first provided shelter to Arawak Indians who left their paintings on the cave walls. According to legend, pirates later stashed their gold in these grottoes along the north coast. Now preserved within Arikok National Park, the caves have become a popular tourist destination.

ARIKOK NATIONAL PARK is w. on Hwy. 7A near San Fuego. The park, which covers nearly 20 percent of the island, abounds with such wildlife as parakeets, goats, donkeys, iguanas and the warawara, a red-beaked eagle. Flora includes such rare species of trees as brazilwood, lignum vitae, kibrahacha and the only divi-divi tree that doesn't grow in a characteristically bent shape. Indian symbols can be seen on some of the boulders at Cunucu Arikok. The summit of Mount Jamanota, the island's highest point, offers a sweeping view of the northeast coast and Boca Prins. Because of its rugged landscape, the park is best experienced in a jeep. **Tours:** Guided tours are available. **Hours:** Daily 8-5. Last admission 2 hours before closing. **Cost:** $8; free (ages 0-17). A $15 park guide with driving and hiking maps is available at the park office at Piedra Plat 42 in Paradera. **Phone:** (297) 585-1234. (A)

Fontein Cave is s. of Boca Prins in Arikok National Park. Once used by Arawak Indians, this limestone hollow contain pre-Columbian petroglyphs. A ranger is present at the cave entrance to point out important markings. Paths and steps are rocky and uneven; handrails may not be present. **Hours:** Daily 8-5. Last admission 2 hours before closing. **Cost:** Free with park admission. **Phone:** (297) 585-1234.

Quadirikiri Cave is s. of Fontein along the coast in Arikok National Park. Sunlight filters into two chambers in this 100-foot tunnel, which features impressive stalagmites and stalactites. Farther south is the Huliba Cave or Tunnel of Love, named for its heart-shaped entrance rather than its romantic atmosphere; paths are cramped and hot, and the smell of guano can be overpowering. Bats in both caves are harmless. **Hours:** Daily 8-5. Last admission 2 hours before closing. **Cost:** Free with park admission. Flashlight and helmet rental $10. **Phone:** (297) 585-1234.

ORANJESTAD (A-1) pop. 26,355

Oranjestad, which translates to "Orange City," derived its name from the House of Orange, the ruling family of the Netherlands. Dutch architecture in Oranjestad blends nicely with Caribbean colors: Dutch colonial houses are painted green, blue, yellow and brown. This profusion of color is maintained by a local tenet that warns against coveting the color of a neighbor's house. Modern residences, broad boulevards and a park complement the city's charm.

Aruba Tourism Authority: L.G. Smith Blvd. 8, Oranjestad, Aruba. **Phone:** (297) 582-3777. *(See ad p. 262.)*

ALTO VISTA CHAPEL is e. of Noord on a paved road to the coast. Arawak Indians and Spanish missionaries built the first Catholic church on this site in 1750. A priest came to the island several times a year to perform masses, baptisms and marriages. The tiny yellow chapel that stands at the edge of a cliff above the sea was built in 1952 and features a hand-carved altar. Stations of the cross mark the road leading to the chapel, often called the Pilgrim's Church, a peaceful spot for contemplation. **Hours:**

Open daily. **Cost:** Free.

ARUBA ALOE MUSEUM & FACTORY is .6 mi. (1 km) e. on Rte. 4A from the Eagle Beach traffic circle, then .2 mi. (.5 km) s. to Pitastraat 115. Since 1890, the aloe vera plant has influenced everything on Aruba from art and architecture to health and healing—at one point it covered almost two-thirds of the island's surface. Guided tours of the factory demonstrate how aloe vera leaves are transformed into finished lotions. Museum exhibits reflect aloe's importance to Aruba's history and economy. **Time:** Allow 30 minutes minimum. **Hours:** Tours are given Mon.-Fri. 8:30-4, Sat. 9-noon. **Cost:** Free. **Phone:** (297) 588-3222.

ARUBA BUTTERFLY FARM is on J.E. Irausquin Blvd. More than 35 species from around the world are housed in a tropical garden. Tours trace the four stages of the butterfly life cycle. **Time:** Allow 30 minutes minimum. **Hours:** Daily 8:30-4:30. Last admission 30 minutes before closing. **Cost:** (good for 7 days) $15; $8 (ages 4-16). **Phone:** (297) 586-3656.

ARUBA NUMISMATIC MUSEUM is on Weststraat across from the cruise ship terminals next to Royal Plaza. Various forms of currency from more than 400 countries date from 221 B.C. to the present. The 40,000-piece display, amassed by collector Mario Odor and maintained by his family, includes Aruban Indian shell artifacts used for barter; wampum beads used as money by North American Indians; currency from World Wars I and II, including inflation and occupation money and money used in concentration camps; and bills made of linen and silk. **Hours:** Mon.-Thurs. 9-4, Fri. 9-1 (also Sat. 9-noon, when cruise ships are in port). **Cost:** (includes a 30-minute guided tour and a commemorative medal for each family) $5. **Phone:** (297) 582-8831 or (297) 965-6969.

(GEM) *ATLANTIS* SUBMARINE EXPEDITION departs from the Seaport Village Marina at L.G. Smith Blvd. 82. This 65-foot-long (20 m), 48-passenger submarine cruises at a maximum depth of 130 feet (43 m), offering excellent views of Barcadera Reef, marine life and coral formations. **Time:** Allow 2 hours minimum. **Hours:** Trips depart daily at 11 and noon. A 20-minute ferry ride transports passengers between the dock and the submarine for the 50-minute tour. **Cost:** Fare $99; $49 (ages 4-11). Children under 36 inches tall are not permitted. Reservations are required. **Phone:** (297) 588-6881.

BALASHI GOLD MILL RUINS is 3 mi. (5 km) s.e. of the airport. Balashi was the site of Aruba's early gold mining industry. Ruins of gold smelters are visible at Frenchman's Pass. Aruba's drinking water is produced at the nearby desalination plant, one of the largest in the world. The water's purity gives it the nickname "Balashi cocktail," and the island brewery uses the same source. **Hours:** Daily dawn-dusk. **Cost:** Free.

FORT ZOUTMAN AND THE WILLEM III TOWER is on Zoutmanstraat. Dominating the city's skyline, the fort was built in 1798 to protect the island from pirates, while the tower was added in 1868 to serve as a lighthouse. It was named in honor of the reigning Dutch king. Historical displays at the Museo Arubano include weights and measures, coins, historic documents, furniture and antique tools. The Bon Bini Festival is held every Tuesday evening on the patio of the fort from 6:30-8:30; visitors can sample Aruban cuisine, crafts, music and dancing. **Hours:** Museum open Mon.-Fri. 8:30-3:30. **Cost:** Fort (includes guided tour and refreshments) $5. Festival $3. **Phone:** (297) 588-5199.

NATIONAL ARCHAEOLOGICAL MUSEUM OF ARUBA is at Schelpstraat 42. Artifacts representing Aruba's cultural heritage include the remains of stone tools dating from 2000 B.C., known as the pre-ceramic period. Items dating from 1000 A.D., the ceramic period, include pottery, sling stones used for hunting and burial artifacts of the Debajuroid Aruban Indians. Also displayed are skeletal remains excavated from an Indian burial site. **Hours:** Tues.-Fri. 10-5 (also Sat.-Sun. 10-2, Sept.-July). **Cost:** Free. **Phone:** (297) 582-8979.

ST. ANNA CHURCH is on Caya F. D. Figueroa in Noord. The first Catholic church on this site was constructed in 1776; the current building dates to 1914. The neo-Gothic altar was intended for a Dutch chapel in Noord-Brabant but shipped to

Aruba by accident; the ceiling had to be cut to accommodate the intricate hand-carved piece. Adjoining the church is a cemetery with tomb "houses" painted in pastel colors and adorned with flowers and various mementos. Sunday mass is given in Papiamento and Latin, with a special English service at 11. **Cost:** Donations. **Phone:** (297) 587-1409.

WILHELMINA PARK is off L.G. Smith Blvd. The park was created in 1955 in honor of the visit of Queen Juliana and Prince Bernhard of the Netherlands. A statue of Queen Mother Wilhelmina of the Netherlands, sculpted of white marble in Italy by Arnoldo Lualdi, dominates the plaza. The park is particularly beautiful when the tropical foliage is blooming in June, September and October. Visitors can rest on benches shaded by palm trees. **Hours:** Daily 24 hours. **Cost:** Free.

GAMBLING ESTABLISHMENTS

- **Alhambra Casino** is at J.E. Irausquin Boulevard 47 at Manchebo Beach. **Hours:** Daily 10 a.m.-4 a.m. **Phone:** (297) 583-5000.
- **Crystal Casino at Renaissance Aruba Resort & Casino** is at L.G. Smith Blvd. 82 in Seaport Village. **Hours:** Daily 24 hours. **Phone:** (297) 583-6000 or (800) 421-8188.
- **Seaport Casino at Renaissance Aruba Resort & Casino** is at L.G. Smith Blvd. 9 in Seaport Village. **Hours:** Daily 10 a.m.-4 a.m. **Phone:** (297) 583-5027.

PALM BEACH (A-1)

GAMBLING ESTABLISHMENTS

- **Allegro Casino at the Occidental Grand Aruba** is at J.E. Irausquin Blvd. 83. **Hours:** Daily noon-4 a.m. **Phone:** (297) 586-9039 or (297) 586-4500.
- **The Casino at the Radisson Aruba Resort, Casino & Spa** is at J.E. Irausquin Blvd. 81. **Hours:** Daily 2 p.m.-3 a.m. **Phone:** (297) 586-4045.
- **Cool Casino at Riu Palace Aruba Resort** is at J.E. Irausquin Blvd. 79. **Hours:** Daily 10 a.m.-3 a.m. **Phone:** (297) 586-3900 or (297) 528-0993.
- **Copacabana Casino at the Hyatt Regency Aruba Resort & Casino** is at J.E. Irausquin

Blvd. 85. **Hours:** Daily 10 a.m.-4 a.m. **Phone:** (297) 586-1234 or (800) 233-1234.

- **Excelsior Casino at Holiday Inn Sunspree Resort Aruba** is at J.E. Irausquin Blvd. 230. **Hours:** Daily 8 a.m.-4 a.m. **Phone:** (297) 586-7777 or (866) 358-6518.
- **Palm Beach Casino at The Westin Resort, Aruba** is at J.E. Irausquin Blvd. 77. **Hours:** Daily noon-4 a.m. **Phone:** (297) 586-2283 or (297) 586-4466.
- **Stellaris Casino at Aruba Marriott Resort** is at L.G. Smith Boulevard 101. **Hours:** Daily 24 hours. **Phone:** (297) 586-9000 or (800) 223-6388.

SAN NICOLAS (B-2) pop. 15,848

San Nicolas, 12 miles (19 km) southeast of Oranjestad, is Aruba's second largest city. Known as the island's Sunrise Side, San Nicolas was once a bustling company town when Lago Oil and Transport operated 1924-85. The refining of oil is again playing a part in Aruba's economy: Coastal Corp. reopened the oil refinery in 1991, and Valero took ownership in 2004. A Dutch marine camp is off Commanders Bay near the fishing village of Savaneta.

Charlie's Bar and Restaurant, in operation since 1941, once had a colorful reputation as a hangout for rowdy sailors and oil refinery workers. The establishment is known for its amazing variety of bric-a-brac. Pictures, business cards and license plates grace the walls of the bar while the hundreds of items hanging from the ceiling include hats, Frisbees, an inner tube, a life jacket and even shirts from the Boston Braves and Brooklyn Dodgers.

There is a small natural bridge east of Seroe Colorado at the island's southern tip near Colorado Point. Along the road at Seroe Preto is the Lourdes Grotto, a shrine to the Virgin Mary built into the limestone rock by a Catholic priest in the 1950s.

Hermitage of Father Jerome, Cat Island / © Heeb Photos / eStock Photo

The Bahamas

The subtropical Bahamas, where turquoise waters flow along miles of white sand beaches, include more than 2,000 cays, islets and rocks. Of the approximately 700 islands, 30 of the largest ones are inhabited. Beginning 50 miles (80 km) from the Florida coast, The Bahamas form a 760-mile (1,223-km) arc through the Atlantic, creating a natural barrier across the eastern gateway to the Gulf of Mexico. The island of Bimini is closest to Florida, while the southernmost island, Inagua, is 60 miles (97 km) from Haiti. Spaniards named this archipelago *baja mar*, or "shallow sea."

The two most popular tourist destinations in The Bahamas are the city of Nassau/Paradise Island and Grand Bahama Island. The islands' capital, Nassau, on New Providence Island, is rich in colonial history and charm and offers varied opportunities for sports activities, shopping and sightseeing. Prestigious Paradise Island, linked by entry and exit bridges to Nassau, is a playground of the rich. Freeport, the modern resort-residential complex on Grand Bahama Island, is more cosmopolitan and sports oriented than Nassau. Grand Bahama was developed more recently than Nassau and has become a favored resort, due in part to its nearness to Florida. About 80 percent of the people vacationing in The Bahamas are from the United States.

The Out Islands, known the world over for game fishing, scuba diving, sailing, pristine beaches and emerald-blue seas, extend as far as you can see. There are resorts in areas noted for their lack of commercial development, and where only the silver-top thatch palms and flamingoes claim residence. The principal Out Islands are Abaco, Andros, Bimini, Cat Island, Eleuthera, Exuma and Long Island. Abaco has naturally protected waters and dozens of offshore cays (pronounced *keys*) that make them a favorite with yachting and fishing enthusiasts.

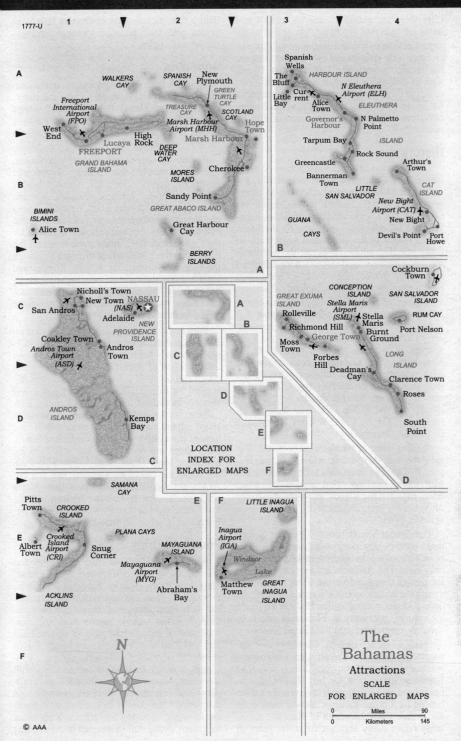

1777-U

The
Bahamas

Attractions

SCALE
FOR ENLARGED MAPS

© AAA

Here there are excellent marinas, guides and boats for hire, and championship golf courses.

Just off the island of Eleuthera, with its picturesque little villages and exclusive resorts, are the charming settlements of Harbour Island, with its pink sandy beaches, and Spanish Wells, which in the old days served as a watering hole for Spanish galleons. The Exumas have many cays, most of which can be reached only by boat.

History

The Bahamas claim the distinction of being Christopher Columbus' first New World discovery. In 1492 he stepped ashore on an island originally called *Guanahani* and renamed it San Salvador. The Lucayan Indians, who then populated the islands, were soon sent by the Spaniards to labor in the mines and sugar mills of Cuba and Hispaniola. However, the Spaniards did not settle here, and in 1629 King Charles I of England granted the islands to Sir Robert Heath, attorney general of England.

A group of English merchants and pioneers from Bermuda, known as the Eleutherian Adventurers, then came seeking religious freedom. They colonized Eleuthera in 1648 and attempted to establish the first republic in the New World. This attempt at colonization and other settlements which followed were, for the most part, unsuccessful. As a result, The Bahamas were soon overrun by pirates such as Blackbeard and Calico Jack, who were finally routed in 1718 by Capt. Woodes Rogers, the first royal governor.

Another wave of immigration occurred after the American Revolution, when Loyalist refugees fled to The Bahamas, taking their slaves with them. England ruled until 1782, when Spain captured the islands; however, the Treaty of Versailles returned them to England once again in 1783.

Throughout The Bahamas' turbulent history their strategically positioned cays and islets played a vital role in international intrigues. Not only were The Bahamas a formidable hideout for pirates, but Confederate blockade runners during the American Civil War and bootleggers during America's Prohibition Era also exploited the islands' proximity to Florida in efforts to smuggle contraband into the United States.

From 1718 to 1969 a governor was appointed by the British Crown; after 1969 the appointment was made in consultation with The Bahamas Government. On July 10, 1973, the islands became an independent sovereign nation headed by a prime minister. Now a member of the British Commonwealth of Nations, the islands retain many legacies from the years of British rule, including the distinctive Bahamian accent and two popular spectator sports— cricket and rugby.

Shopping

Shoppers have a field day exploring the multitude of stores and boutiques lining the streets of Nassau and Grand Bahama Island. Shops also are found just over the bridge on Paradise Island, at Cable Beach and at shopping malls in the outlying areas.

Bay Street is the center of activity in Nassau, where the merchandise consists of imported European goods: perfumes, brass, leather goods, cameras, cashmere, candies, jewelry, china, porcelain, crystal, glass, figurines, linens and designer and sportswear fashions to name just a few. Duty-free prices, made available for the first time in 1992, make these items all the more attractive. Available at discount prices are the island's own liqueur, Nassau Royale, and local banana rums and coconut liqueurs. Festival Place, on Prince George Wharf, features local crafts, food and music in an atmosphere reminiscent of a Bahamian village.

Built in the 1930s, Nassau's Straw Market on Bay Street was famed for its island handicrafts made not only from straw but also from wood and a variety of shells, including coconut and conch (pronounced *konk*). The market was destroyed by fire in 2001, displacing some 500 vendors to smaller booths a block away. Bargaining is expected here, but not in Nassau's shops. Items made from tortoiseshell are banned from importation into the United States. Most shops are open Mon.-Sat. 9-5. Banking hours are Mon.-Thurs. 9:30-3, Fri. 9:30-4:30. All banks are closed on Saturday and Sunday. ATMs are available 24 hours a day. Major credit cards, such as Visa and MasterCard, are widely accepted in New Providence, Grand Bahama and in most out islands.

Food and Drink

With the exception of fruit, vegetables and seafood, most food is imported. Many restaurants and hotels feature European, Chinese, Polynesian, Japanese and American cuisines. But Bahamian specialties should not be overlooked: dishes include pigeon peas and rice, rock lobster, baked crab, grouper cutlets, fried jack and fried snapper. Souse is a hearty dish of simmered vegetables and chicken or pig's feet. Conch, a meaty mollusk, is served raw—with fresh lime juice, onions, tomatoes and peppers—and can also be steamed, pounded and deep-fried ("cracked"), or used as an ingredient in soups, chowders and fritters. Rum-raisin ice cream, guava duff (a steamed bread pudding topped with guava sauce) or a coconut tart round off the meal. Tap water is usually safe to drink; bottled water is widely available. Milk is pasteurized.

Graycliff Manor in Nassau, reputedly built by a successful pirate, is currently as renowned for its jet-set clientele as for its cuisine. The resort has its own cigar factory and a wine cellar with more than 250,000 vintage bottles. The Bahamian Club on Paradise Island is one of the most popular restaurants in The Bahamas.

Vendors at the "Fish Fry" on Arawak Cay, just west of Bay Street, provide an array of local specialties, including conch salad and fried fish. The Bamboo Shack and Dirty's on Nassau Street are two of the many take-out restaurants that serve such Bahamian specialties as cracked conch with hot sauce.

Prices for meals in hotels are slightly higher during the winter season, but most lodgings in Nassau offer a modified American plan, which includes breakfast and dinner as an additional option. On the whole, native dishes are usually the least expensive. Most restaurants add a 15-percent service charge to the bill.

Sports and Amusements

Local and international yachting and sailing regattas, golf and tennis tournaments, cricket, rugby and squash are only a few of the activities available in The Bahamas. That golf ranks high in popularity is verified by the number of 18-hole public golf courses on New Providence Island, including the Cable Beach and Ocean Club golf courses. The PGA-rated Ocean Club Golf Course on Paradise Island is exclusively for the guests of Atlantis properties.

Grand Bahama Island offers two championship 18-hole courses at Radisson Our Lucaya Resort: the Reef Course, designed by Robert Trent Jones, Jr., and the Lucayan Course by Dick Wilson. Great Abaco Island boasts two more 18-hole courses, the Treasure Cay Golf Club and the Scottish-style Abaco Club on Winding Bay.

Most hotels have tennis courts and information about horseback riding, which is available in Nassau, Freeport and Abaco.

Though landlubbers enjoy their share of activities, water sports captivate the majority of island travelers. The numerous coves along the beaches of New Providence Island create natural pools ideal for swimming and snorkeling. The 142-mile (228-km) underwater coral reef known for its "blue holes," freshwater springs that well to the surface, offers excellent scuba diving. Paradise Island boasts one of the finest beaches in The Bahamas. Fishing in The Bahamas is good, and light-tackle anglers are amply rewarded.

Peterson Cay National Park, some 15 miles (24 km) east of Freeport, offers excellent opportunities for snorkeling and diving in a pristine setting and is accessible by boat only.

The trade winds ensure fine sailing conditions all year; boats and equipment for sailing, parasailing, fishing, water skiing, windsurfing, snorkeling, scuba diving and spear fishing can be rented from charter firms at the major marinas and from the docks of many waterfront hotels. Hotels that offer parasailing are found in Nassau and Paradise Island; Freeport and Lucaya, Grand Bahama Island; and Cockburn Town, San Salvador Island.

An informative publication for those interested in bareboat charters is the "Yachtsman's Guide to The Bahamas," available at many yachting supply stores, marinas and bookstores in The Bahamas. The 1- or 2-hour scuba diving lessons offered throughout the islands are usually not enough preparation for the sport; you should take a complete course in advance. One of the best places to learn diving is at the Underwater Explorers Society (UNEXSO), in the Grand Bahama's Port Lucaya area, home base of a prominent society of diving experts.

Those who prefer indoor recreation will find nightclubs and casinos on New Providence, Paradise Island and Grand Bahama. Hotel nightclubs and restaurants usually sponsor dancing and after-dinner entertainment. The Out Island hotels occasionally feature calypso and steel-drum bands. First-run American movies are shown in New Providence, Grand Bahama and Eleuthera theaters.

Lively festivals and tournaments are offered throughout the year. Junkanoo, the Bahamian national festival, is held on December 26 (Boxing Day) and January 1. Across the islands, competing groups in costumes and playing music parade through the streets from 1 a.m. to dawn vying for prizes. The most spectacular parade takes place on Bay Street in Nassau, where the sounds of cowbells, goatskin drums and whistles can be heard in the distance. Visitors are free to join in the revelry as part of a "scrap" group.

Smaller versions of Junkanoo are held at various hotels year-round. The Junkanoo Summer Festival is held at Arawak Cay Heritage Park every Saturday in July from 2-10 p.m. Featured are Bahamian food, craft demonstrations, story telling, special children's activities, live entertainment and parades. For additional information, contact the Ministry of Tourism's Events and Entertainment Department; phone (242) 302-2000.

Sightseeing

Popular excursions include glass-bottom boat trips, which depart from the Prince George Dock in Nassau and the Port Lucaya Marketplace on Grand Bahama Island, or swimming and snorkeling cruises around Nassau and to Blackbeard's Cay on the catamarans *Coral I* and *Coral II*. Several yacht trips depart from the Nassau Yacht Haven for excursions to nearby cays.

Views of the underwater world around Nassau are offered daily aboard the *Seaworld Explorer*, a semi-submarine that operates out of New Mermaid Marina. Glass-bottom boats depart from Prince George Wharf for 90-minute tours of the Sea Gardens, with views of colorful tropical fish and coral formations.

East End Adventures offers all-day tours which include a 54-mile (87-km) drive through pine forests and along deserted beaches with a hike to an inland blue hole and caverns and ending with a 6-mile (9.7-km) speed boat ride to Sweeting's Cay; phone (242) 373-6662.

The tour buses that leave from the major hotels and Festival Place (the cruise ship port) are convenient and economical ways to tour Nassau. A pleasant 2-hour drive might include stops at such sites as the Queen's Staircase, Government House, Ardastra Gardens and forts Fincastle, Montagu and Charlotte.

Fast Facts

POPULATION: 303,611.

AREA: 13,934 sq km (5,380 sq mi.).

CAPITAL: Nassau.

HIGHEST POINT: 63 m (206 ft.), Mount Alvernia, Cat Island.

LOWEST POINT: Sea level, Atlantic Ocean.

TIME ZONE(S): Eastern Standard. DST.

LANGUAGE: English (Creole among Haitian immigrants).

GOVERNMENT: Independent. Member of the British Commonwealth of Nations.

UNIT OF CURRENCY: Bahamian dollar. $1 U.S. = 1 Bahamian dollar. U.S. currency is widely accepted.

ELECTRICITY: 110-220 volts, 60 cycles AC; voltage varies with location.

MINIMUM AGE FOR DRIVERS: 21-25, depending on the rental car agency; maximum age 65 without medical certificate. U.S. license valid for 3 months; drive on left.

MINIMUM AGE FOR GAMBLING: 18.

SEAT BELT/CHILD RESTRAINT LAWS: Seat belts are required for all adult passengers. Children are to be secured in seating apparatus fitted to the rear seat; those less than 20 pounds require an infant car seat that should face the vehicle's rear, those between 20 and less than 40 pounds require a convertible car seat, and those over 40 pounds or up to 4 feet, 9 inches tall require a booster car seat. Seating apparatus may be fitted to the front seat if the vehicle has no rear seat.

HELMETS FOR MOTORCYCLISTS: Required.

HOLIDAYS: Jan. 1; Good Friday; Easter Monday; Whit Monday, May or June (8th Mon. after Easter); Labour Day, June (1st Fri.); Independence Day, July 10; Emancipation Day, Aug. (1st Mon.); Discovery Day, Oct. 12; Christmas, Dec. 25; Boxing Day, Dec. 26.

TAXES: A 6 percent mandatory hotel guest tax and 10-15 percent service charge is added to most hotel bills. On Grand Bahama Island, a $5 airport security fee is assessed for all ticketed passengers. Departure tax is $15 U.S. from all islands except Grand Bahama, which charges $18 U.S. Departure tax is included in the airline ticket cost.

IMMIGRATION REQUIREMENTS: Passport and a return or onward ticket are required. No visa needed for stays up to 8 months for U.S. citizens. The U.S. Dept. of Homeland Security requires all U.S. citizens returning from the Caribbean to present a valid passport.

PHONING THE ISLANDS: To call The Bahamas from the U.S. or Canada, dial 1 + 242 + the 7-digit local number.

FURTHER INFORMATION FOR VISITORS:

The Bahamas Tourist Office, Florida
1200 South Pine Island Rd., Suite 750
Plantation, FL 33324
(954) 236-9292
(800) 422-4262
The Bahamas Ministry of Tourism
King and George Sts.
Nassau, New Providence Island
The Bahamas
(242) 302-2000
(800) 224-2627

Transportation

Air service from the East Coast and the Midwest is available aboard many major carriers to Lynden Pindling International Airport and Grand Bahama International Airport. US Airways provides nonstop scheduled flights from its Charlotte hub, Philadelphia, Washington, D.C., New York (La Guardia) and Boston. Delta provides nonstop service from its Atlanta hub to Nassau/Paradise Island and Grand Bahama Island; daily service from New York (La Guardia) to Nassau/Paradise Island; and seasonal service from Cincinnati to Nassau/Paradise Island. JetBlue offers up to three nonstop departures per day (during peak periods) from JFK to Nassau/Paradise Island and daily service from Boston to Nassau/Paradise Island, while Continental Airlines offers daily scheduled service from Newark to Nassau/Paradise Island and seasonal service from Houston to Nassau/Paradise Island. American Eagle, Spirit, JetBlue and Gulfstream International Airlines (Continental Connection) provide direct service from such Florida cities as Fort Lauderdale, Miami, Orlando, Palm Beach and Melbourne to several points in The Bahamas.

Some of the large islands have bus service. Bicycles and motor scooters rent by the hour, day or longer. For more luxurious transportation, chauffeur-driven limousines can be hired in Nassau and Freeport. A quaint way to see the sites in Nassau is by horse-drawn carriage, called a "surrey tour." Metered taxis are a convenient way to get around, and the rates are regulated. There are major car rental agencies in Nassau and on Grand Bahama Island; rentals also are available on most of the Out Islands. Driving is on the left side of the road.

More than 145 miles (230 km) of good roads make for pleasant motoring from downtown Nassau to almost all parts of New Providence Island; road conditions on the Out Islands have improved since 1992. Automobiles can be taken duty free to Nassau for up to 6 months. A deposit covering duty charges (50 percent of the car's value plus 4 percent stamp tax), in the form of a customs bond executed by a local bank, is refunded if the vehicle is removed from the Commonwealth before the end of this period. A U.S. driver's license is valid for 3 months.

Island-hopping is possible by both plane and boat. Bahamasair has regularly scheduled interisland flights from Nassau. If there is not a direct flight to the island of your choice, check with the charter companies listed in the telephone directory; information also is available at hotels on the Out Islands.

Many cruise services travel from Miami, Port Everglades and Port Canaveral to Nassau and Grand Bahama Island on a once- or twice-weekly basis. There also is a day cruise from Fort Lauderdale to Freeport on Discovery cruise lines, which sails every day except Wednesday. Traveling by mail boat, though it might be slow and lacking in some comforts, is an inexpensive way to island hop. Since departures are subject to change without notice, advance arrangements with the captain are recommended.

Bahamas Ferries offers a 2-hour ferry ride to Harbour Island, Spanish Wells or mainland Eleuthera. The ferry departs Nassau at 8 a.m. and returns at 6:25 p.m.; phone (242) 323-2166.

Points of Interest

See maps on pages 55 and 63.

Andros Island (D-1)

The largest island in The Bahamas but one of the least populous, Andros covers 2,300 square miles (5,957 sq km) replete with stands of virgin pine that often soar to more than 70 feet (21 m). During the early 1840s a group of Seminole Indians and runaway slaves settled at Red Bays, where some of their descendants remain to this day. Legend has it that miniature red-eyed creatures called chickcharnies—a kind of subtropical leprechaun, half man and half bird—nest in the trees and exert both good and bad influence over daily events.

The spectacular reef that borders the island's eastern coast is the world's third-largest barrier reef.

Five national parks have been established on Andros and in its surrounding waters to protect 286,080 acres (115,774 hectares) of forest, wetlands and marine ecosystems. Blue holes, many of which have never been explored, abound in the sea floor and offer plentiful opportunities for divers. The Tongue of the Ocean, a canyon in the ocean floor between Andros and Nassau, is the site of oceanographic research. Freshwater lakes harbor waterfowl and provide hunting in season.

Anglers also are drawn to Andros, as the surrounding waters provide many varieties of sea life. The island claims to be the world's premier spot for bonefishing. The 1892 Andros Lighthouse stands at the southern entrance to Fresh Creek Channel. The Androsia Factory at Fresh Creek produces colorful batik with exquisite designs.

Bimini Islands (B-1)

Westernmost of The Bahamas, North and South Bimini and Cat Cay lie on the northwestern edge of the Grand Bahama Bank. With record catches of bonefish, marlin, dolphin, wahoo and tuna, this region is considered one of the world's fishing capitals. Ernest Hemingway's fishing trips in the Biminis in the 1930s inspired him to write his classic story "The Old Man and the Sea." Fishing guides and accommodations are available on both islands. Offshore waters beckon scuba divers with underwater caves, reefs and sunken ships.

Cat Island (B-4)

The pirate Arthur Catt is said to have given his name to this island, one of the least inhabited Out Islands. The main road traverses 50 miles (80 km) of rolling hills and secluded beaches from Arthur's Town in the north to Port Howe in the south. The aptly named Fine Beach is noted for its pristine pink sands. Among many 18th-century plantation ruins that dot the island is Deveaux Mansion, once the home of Col. Andrew Deveaux of the U.S. Navy, who received 1,000 acres (400 hectares) on the island as reward for ousting the Spanish from Nassau in 1783.

At the summit of Mount Alvernia, the highest point in The Bahamas, is the Hermitage of Father Jerome, a stone monastery built by the Jesuit missionary in the 1940s. St. Francis of Assisi Catholic Church in Old Bight is one of several other religious structures built by Father Jerome in the Bahamian islands.

Eleuthera Island

Eleuthera has been a refuge for several groups seeking religious freedom since 1648, when the Eleutherian Adventurers established the first settlement here. These settlers gave the island its name, which is derived from the Greek word *eleutheros,* meaning "free."

Settlements at Governor's Harbour and Rock Sound have contributed to Eleuthera's development as a leading family-oriented resort destination. Its miles of secluded beaches and quiet atmosphere are its most appealing features. The main road runs the 110-mile (177-km) length of the island. A marina and a safe harbor are on the ocean side of Rock Sound. Worth seeing are the pineapple fields in Gregory Town and Ocean Hole Park in Rock Sound. Ferries connect Eleuthera with Harbour Island and Spanish Wells.

Grand Bahama Island (B-1)

Only 55 miles (89 km) east of Florida, Grand Bahama Island is a major tourist destination. The fourth largest island of the group, it covers more than 530 square miles (1,373 sq km) and is known for excellent bonefishing, reef and deep-sea fishing. Grand Bahama Island's hotels and nightspots have earned it the title of "New World Riviera."

The community of West End gained notoriety during America's Prohibition Era as a jumping-off place for rum runners to the United States. Public beaches include Barbary, Churchill, Fortune, Gold Rock Creek, Paradise Cove and Taíno beaches. The Underwater Explorers Society adjacent to the Port Lucaya Marketplace has a diver-training pool and rental equipment. "The Dolphin Experience," a program offered by UNEXSO, enables visitors to swim and interact with these marine mammals; phone (242) 373-1244 or (800) 992-3483.

FREEPORT (B-1) pop. 26,910

The resort center of the island, Freeport lures outdoor enthusiasts with its many opportunities for fishing, sailing, snorkeling, swimming, golf and tennis.

The Bahamas Ministry of Tourism: Poinciana Drive, Grand Bahama Island, The Bahamas. **Phone:** (242) 302-2000 or (800) 224-2627.

RAND NATURE CENTRE is 3 mi. (5 km) n.e. of the International Bazaar on E. Settler's Way. A nature trail winds through this 100-acre (40-hectare) sanctuary, which preserves the native flora and fauna of Grand Bahama Island. An ideal spot for bird-watching, especially October through May, the area is home to more than 120 species. Exhibits at the education center reflect the island's ecology, culture and natural history. The Gloria Banks Art Gallery features the work of local artists. **Hours:** Mon.-Fri. 9-4:30. Guided tours depart Tues. and Thurs. at 10:30. **Cost:** $5; $3 (ages 5-12). **Phone:** (242) 352-5438.

RECREATIONAL ACTIVITIES

Horseback Riding

- **Pinetree Stables** is off East Sunrise Hwy. Guided 2-hour trail rides are offered. Weight limit is 200 pounds and children under 8 years are not permitted. **Phone:** (242) 373-3600, or (305) 433-4809 outside The Bahamas.

- **Trikk Pony Adventures** provides transportation from local hotels. Guided 90-minute beach rides are offered. **Phone:** (242) 727-0131.

Kayaking

- **Grand Bahama Nature Tours** offers transportation from local hotels. Guided tours include a 6-hour kayak trip through Lucayan National Park and a 5-hour kayak/snorkel excursion at Peterson Cay National Park; both tours include lunch. Snorkeling, bicycling, hiking, bird-watching and jeep driving tours also are offered. **Hours:** Tours depart daily. **Phone:** (242) 373-2485 or (866) 440-4542.

LUCAYA (B-1) pop. 9,924

Twenty miles east of Freeport along the southern coast of Grand Bahama Island is Our Lucayan

Beach and Golf Resort. The 6-acre Port Lucaya Marketplace and Marina features shops, restaurants, and live entertainment centered around Count Basie Square, named for the jazz artist who wintered on the island.

LUCAYAN NATIONAL PARK is on Grand Bahama Hwy. The 40-acre (16-hectare) park contains one of the largest explored underwater cave systems in the world. Ecological zones in the park include pineland with hardwood hammocks, rocky coppice, whiteland coppice, mangrove marshes and sand dunes. A 1-mile trail and boardwalk leads to Ben's Cave, Burial Ground Cave, Gold Rock Creek and Gold Rock Beach.

Swimming in the caves is prohibited; diving requires special permits. **Hours:** Daily 8-4. Ben's Cave is closed during the summer to protect the fruit bat nurseries. **Cost:** Park $3; free (ages 0-12). Tickets must be purchased in advance at the Rand Nature Center in Freeport *(see attraction listing)*. Cash only. **Phone:** (242) 352-5438. ⏴

GAMBLING ESTABLISHMENTS

- **Treasure Bay Casino at Our Lucaya** is on Sea Horse Lane at the Radisson Our Lucaya Resort. **Hours:** Daily 24 hours. **Phone:** (242) 350-2000.

Great Abaco Island (B-2)

Great Abaco is more than 100 miles (160 km) long with a chain of offshore barrier cays lying east of Grand Bahama Island. Its tourism-based economy is supplemented by agriculture and fishing.

Reports of sunken treasure have brought Great Abaco fame and modern-day explorers. In the 1950s, two Nassau businessmen discovered several 17th-century Spanish coins and a 72-pound silver bar that was identified as the personal property of King Philip IV of Spain and valued at $20,000. Shipwrecks and reefs abound in the waters off Abaco's east coast, making it a popular dive center. A Civil War warship with a huge Dahlgren cannon lies in 30 feet (9 m) of water off Man-O-War Cay.

Many residents, descendants of Loyalists who fled the American Colonies after the Revolution, have carried on the art of boat building, which was introduced here centuries ago. However, local artisans have substituted the use of fine Abaco pine with imported wood and fiberglass to construct the boats. The sailmaker's loft of the Alburys is worth a visit; bags, hats and other canvas items are made here. Marsh Harbour is the commercial center of the island as well as the bareboat charter center of the northern Bahamas.

Abaco's resort potential is enhanced by many secluded, safe harbors along the cays. Such activities as sailing, bonefishing and bird-watching can be arranged. Among the leading vacation spots are Treasure Cay, known for one of the world's top ten beaches and home of endangered wild horses; Elbow Cay, known for its candy-striped lighthouse;

the northernmost island of Walker's Cay, a sport-fishing resort; Green Turtle Cay, which exudes an early New England atmosphere; Man-O-War Cay, known for the art of boatbuilding; and Guana Cay, site of a Sunday pig roast and live entertainment at Nipper's Beach Bar & Grill.

HOPE TOWN (B-2)

Elbow Cay's famous landmark, the red-and-white-striped Hope Town Lighthouse, was built in 1863. The mechanically-operated beacon is powered by kerosene; its Fresnel lens floats in a bed of mercury. Cars are not permitted in the harbor village.

WYANNIE MALONE HISTORICAL MUSEUM is on Gillam Street. Wyannie Malone, the widow of a British Loyalist who fled America during the Revolutionary War, was one of the founders of the settlement of Hope Town in 1783. The museum, in a replica of her century-old white clapboard house, displays historical maps, ships models and items of everyday life. The Balcony House contains historical displays, artifacts and flora and fauna from across the region.

Guided tours of the museum may be arranged by appointment. **Time:** Allow 30 minutes minimum. **Hours:** Mon.-Sat. 10-3, Nov.-Aug. **Cost:** $3; $5 (family). **Phone:** (242) 366-0293 to schedule a tour.

NEW PLYMOUTH (B-2)

In downtown New Plymouth on Green Turtle Cay, the Loyalist Memorial Sculpture Garden displays 30 bronze busts of famous Bahamian citizens; phone (242) 367-3067. Green Turtle Cay is a sister city to Key West, Florida, where many Abaco residents moved in the 1800s.

ALBERT LOWE MUSEUM is 1 blk. from the docks on Parliament St. Named for a master builder of model boats, this museum features photographs, antiques and artifacts tracing Abaco's history and development. The restored Loyalist home also houses a display of paintings by Lowe's son Alton, whose work is featured on Bahamian postage stamps; and a fine collection of carved ship models by Vertrum Lowe, who carries on his father's tradition. **Hours:** Mon.-Sat. 9-11:45 and 1-4. Closed major holidays. **Cost:** $5; $2.50 (ages 7-12); free (ages 0-6 with adult). **Phone:** (242) 367-4094.

Great Exuma Island (C-3)

The Exumas consist of 365 islands, ranging from small, uninhabited dots on the map to the two largest islands, Great Exuma and Little Exuma. At the southernmost tip of the Exuma Cays, Great Exuma is 40 miles (64 km) long.

A popular excursion follows the slave route from George Town to Rolleville, a village once owned by

Loyalist Lord Rolle, who, upon his death, gave freedom, the land and the name of Rolle to all the tenants. The land may never be sold, but is passed down to each succeeding generation.

Visitors will enjoy touring Elizabeth Harbour and the pristine hidden coves and inlets throughout the 365 cays. Sailing tours often stop to feed swimming pigs at Big Major Cay, iguanas on Allan Cay and nurse sharks at Compass Cay.

Thunderball Grotto is site of colorful underwater reefs, while Dog Rocks is one of the best dive spots in the Bahamas—it starts at 35 feet and slopes off to approximately 50 feet before dropping off into the Exuma Sound. The Exuma Wall, off Highbourne Cay, is a 75-foot sloping wall dive offering views of such tropical creatures as angel fish, grouper, turtles, horse-eye jacks and the occasional shark, billfish and tuna.

Sixty miles of flats on the island's west side offer excellent bonefishing in knee-deep turquoise waters. Sheltered coves and hidden inlets make kayaking in the Exumas ideal for the whole family.

GEORGE TOWN (C-3)

The administrative capital of Exuma, George Town is on Lake Victoria. Several popular festivals entertain visitors. In March, the Bahamian Music and Heritage Festival features popular musicians as well as arts and crafts, Bahamian foods, storytelling, singing, poetry reading and a sloop and Junkanoo exhibition. More than 60 native sloops race at the National Family Island Regatta during the last full week in April. George Town also hosts its own Junkanoo festival on Saturdays in July and August.

EXUMA CAYS LAND AND SEA PARK stretches 22 mi. (35 km) from Wax Cay Cut in the north to Conch Cut in the south and is accessible only by boat. Said to be the first national park of its kind, this marine preserve was established in 1958. The park is made up of 15 major cays and many smaller islands in a pristine area encompassing 176 square miles (456 sq km). The vast underwater park attracts snorkeling and scuba enthusiasts from around the world. The bird and marine life sanctuary is home to sea turtles, rock iguanas and the Bahamas Hutia, a small rodent once thought to be extinct. **Hours:** The park headquarters at Warderick Wells is open Mon.-Sat. 9-noon and 1-4, Sun. 9-noon. **Cost:** Free. **Phone:** (242) 357-8344.

Harbour Island (A-3)

Harbour Island almost encloses the northeast tip of Eleuthera, forming a harbor 6 miles (10 km) long and 3 miles (5 km) wide. The island boasts 3 miles (5 km) of pink sand beach, the color provided by particles of shell ground against the outer reefs by the force of the sea.

Harbour Island also claims one of the oldest settlements in The Bahamas, Dunmore Town. At the northern end of the island, the town retains an Old World charm through its many restored, brightly colored homes, whose carved shutters and verandas outlined in white create a gingerbread-cottage atmosphere. Many colonial houses were built during the latter part of the 19th century; Loyalist Cottage on Bay Street dates from 1790. Other historic points of interest include a shipyard, sugar mill, jailhouse, fort and the Higgs family tomb. A pink municipal building adds the finishing touch to this picturesque town. Snorkeling, scuba diving and bonefishing are popular.

Long Island (C-4)

Long Island is almost wholly within the Tropic of Cancer zone. The island is approximately 80 miles in length and covers 230 square miles (596 sq km), with a width of only a half-mile (.8 km) in some places. It also is one of The Bahamas' chief agricultural islands. According to legend, when Christopher Columbus landed here he found the inhabitants living in tent-shaped buildings and sleeping in nets stretched between posts. The latter idea, adopted by his sailors, evolved into the hammock.

Interesting sites include the Adderley Plantation ruins in Stella Maris, the Long Island Museum and Library in Buckleys, Hamilton's Caves located in Hamilton, the ruins of Gray's Plantation in Grays, the Columbus Monument in Seymour's and Dean's Blue Hole in Turtle Cove. Clarence Town has beautiful twin churches on two hilltops: St. Paul's Anglican Church and St. Peter's & St. Paul's Catholic Church. The Stella Maris Inn stands on the island's highest point and affords superb views. The waters off the coast of Long Island are ideal for scuba diving and fishing. There are daily flight services to two airports on the island by Bahamasair as well as other carriers from Nassau.

New Providence Island (C-2)

Home to a majority of the country's population, New Providence Island is the domain of the capital city, Nassau. A prime tourist destination, the island features all the amenities associated with The Bahamas-an array of water sports, golf, tennis, nightlife, casinos, international shopping and a colorful history.

The 21-mile-long (34-km), 7-mile-wide (11-km) island also is home to the popular resort areas of Cable Beach and Paradise Island, linked to Nassau by entry and exit bridges. The tiny island was privately owned for many years until Huntington Hartford, whose fortune came from the A&P supermarket chain, developed it as a resort. In the 1960s, Hartford purchased a ruined 14th-century monastery from William Randolph Hearst, who had imported it piece by piece from France. The stone ruins, known as the Cloisters, overlook Nassau Harbor, surrounded by the Versailles Gardens. A popular wedding site, the gardens are open to the public.

Boasting one of the finest beaches in the Caribbean, Paradise Island offers tennis, golf and parasailing for the sports minded; the "strip" features a casino and other entertainment. Bridge toll is $2 per vehicle; 25c per pedestrian.

NASSAU (C-2) pop. 210,832

Capital and principal city of The Bahamas, Nassau is on the northeast coast of New Providence Island. This resort was a battleground for Spanish, British and French colonization efforts and a haven for buccaneers. It was here that the infamous pirate Blackbeard posted a lookout in his tower while he caroused around the islands. In 1718, a century after the first British colony was established, the British sent the first

royal governor to The Bahamas. Nassau was named in 1729 for King William III of the House of Orange-Nassau. Residents call themselves "Nassuvians."

There is always plenty to do in downtown Nassau: touring by surrey (a horse-drawn carriage), photographing the colorful buildings, dining, dancing, duty-free shopping or enjoying native entertainment during the holiday season. The focal point of Nassau is Bay Street, which runs along the water from Prince George Wharf. Directly across from the cruise ship docks is Rawson Square, anchored by the Churchill Building. Across from Rawson Square is Parliament Square. Here are the two chambers of Parliament and the Supreme Court. Visitors can watch the proceedings of the House of Assembly when it is in session by making arrangements with the Chief Clerk; to find out when the House will be in session, phone (242) 322-2041. Not far from the

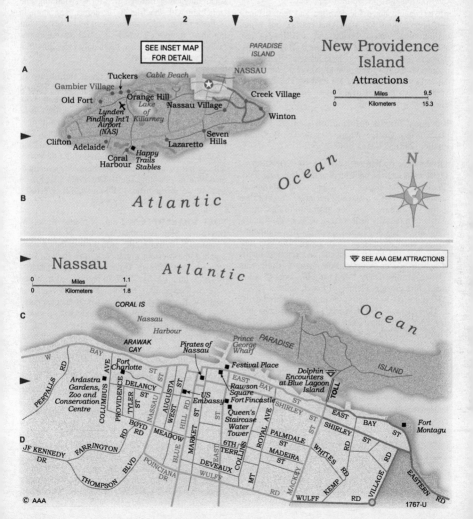

square is the Garden of Remembrance, with its cenotaph honoring Bahamians who died in World Wars I and II; nearby is the octagonal Nassau Public Library and Museum, once a jail.

Nassau's 18th-century forts also are worth visiting. Of the three forts, only Fort Montagu at the eastern entrance to the harbor was confronted by invaders. High above the city, Government House is host to tea parties held the last Friday of each month; shorts and jeans are not permitted. A colorful 45-minute changing of the guard ceremony takes place every other Saturday at 11 a.m.

Vibrant, sociable Nassau possesses almost every conceivable sports facility. Tennis courts and golf courses abound, as do local entrepreneurs marketing rentals or lessons for snorkeling, scuba diving, fishing and sailing. Nassau's many fine beaches include Cabbage, Goodman's Bay, Saunders, Delaport, Caves, Montagu and Western Esplanade.

The waters, noted for deep-sea and reef fishing, are most famous for giant blue marlin, but white marlin, tuna, wahoo, bonito and sailfish also are abundant. Nassau Yacht Haven on E. Bay Street is the charter and fishing headquarters. Sailing is popular in the bays and around the coral islands; local and international races are held by The Bahamas Sailing Association, Royal Nassau Sailing Club and The Nassau Yacht Club.

Bahamas Tourist Information Center: Festival Place, Prince George Wharf, Nassau, The Bahamas. **Phone:** (242) 323-3182 or (242) 502-9150.

ARDASTRA GARDENS, ZOO AND CONSERVATION CENTRE is on Chippingham Rd. near Fort Charlotte. More than 4,000 tropical and subtropical plants flourish on 5.5 acres (2 hectares). Against this setting, a flamingo platoon marches to the commands of a friendly drill sergeant. The birds, usually a shy and easily frightened species, will stand while visitors snap pictures at close range. The zoo has more than 200 birds, mammals and reptiles, many of which are endangered Bahamian or Caribbean species. **Hours:** Daily 9-5. Last admission 45 minutes before closing. Flamingos march daily at 10:30, 2:10 and 4:10. Lory parrot feedings are offered daily at 11, 1:30 and 3:30. Closed Jan. 1, Christmas and day after Christmas. **Cost:** $15; $7.50 (ages 4-12). **Phone:** (242) 323-5806. [T]

DISCOVER ATLANTIS is at the Atlantis Resort on Paradise Island. This 1-hour guided tour includes a 14-acre waterscape and "The Dig," a walk-through aquarium displaying more than 50,000 exotic fish and sea animals among the ruins of the fabled Atlantean civilization. Surrounding water slides and pools are open only to resort guests. **Hours:** Tours depart every 40 minutes daily 9-4. **Cost:** $39; $29 (ages 4-12). **Phone:** (242) 363-3000.

DOLPHIN ENCOUNTERS AT BLUE LAGOON ISLAND departs from the Paradise Island Ferry Terminal at 1 Marina Dr. between the bridges. Visitors board a high-speed catamaran which transports them to this pretty saltwater lagoon, where they have an opportunity to mingle with highly intelligent bottlenose dolphins. Participants receive an orientation prior to meeting the dolphins, so they know what to expect; observers are welcome to watch from nearby. Professional trainers are on hand to ensure guests enjoy as much hands-on time as possible with the dolphins, and photographers stand by to record the moment.

During the Dolphin Encounter, exposure to the dolphins is obtained by standing on a submerged platform in shallow water—these sociable animals will allow participants to pet, hug and kiss them. Children are very comfortable in this more controlled setting. In a similar environment, guests choosing the Sea Lion Encounter interact instead with California sea lions.

With the Dolphin Swim, there's even more personal interaction through free-form swimming and frolicking with the friendly creatures. The strength of these remarkable mammals can be witnessed during the "footpush," which involves two dolphins pushing a volunteer's feet, ultimately propelling him or her across the lagoon.

Participants should bring a towel and change of clothes. **Time:** Allow 3 hours minimum. **Hours:** Boats depart daily at 8:30, 10:30, 1:30 and 3:30. **Cost:** Swim with the Dolphins $185. Ages 6-12 must be accompanied by a participating adult, ages 13-17 by an observing adult. Close Encounter $98; free (ages 0-3 with participating adult). Sea Lion Encounter $80 (ages 0-7 or children under 48 inches tall are not permitted; ages 8-12 must be accompanied by a participating adult). Observers $25. Reservations are recommended. **Phone:** (242) 363-1003, (242) 363-7171 or (866) 918-9932.

FORT CHARLOTTE is 1 mi. (1.6 km) w. on W. Bay St. at Marcus Bethel Way. One of the largest forts in The Bahamas, the military installation commanded the western entrance to the harbor. Lord Dunmore, the British Governor of The Bahamas 1787-96, built the fort 1787-89 and named it for the wife of George III. The fort never fired a shot in hostility. Tours of the dungeon, which features corridors cut out of solid rock, are conducted by guides who provide historical information about the fort. To the east of Fort Charlotte is the original guardhouse. **Hours:** Daily 8-4. **Cost:** $5; $3 (ages 65+); $2 (ages 6-12). **Phone:** (242) 325-9186 or (242) 326-4872.

FORT FINCASTLE stands atop Bennet's Hill. Builders named this 1793 fort in honor of Lord Dunmore, Viscount of Fincastle. The stone structure resembles a paddlewheel steamer. The 65 steps of the Queen's Staircase leading up to the fort from Elizabeth Avenue were cut from solid rock. The summit of the 126-foot Water Tower, reached by elevator, is the highest point on the island. The tower has cannon facings and a viewing deck overlooking Nassau and New Providence. Tours of the fort are offered by local guides. **Hours:** Daily 8-4. **Cost:** Free. Tipping for tours is recommended. **Phone:** (242) 356-9085.

AAA Travel Information
In Print, Online and On The Go

Get AAA's reliable travel information just the way you want it.

 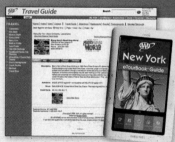

- **TourBook® Guides** - Printed guidebooks available at AAA/CAA offices
- **Travel Guides** - Online destination content available at AAA.com and CAA.ca
- **eTourBook℠ Guides** - eReader travel guides available at AAA.com/ebooks

Create and save trips online with TripTik® Travel Planner and use them on the go with the TripTik Mobile app.

- **TripTik Travel Planner** - Online trip planning at AAA.com and CAA.ca
- **TripTik Mobile** - Travel app details at AAA.com/mobile

NASSAU BOTANICAL GARDENS is bounded by W. Bay St., N. Dunmore and Infant View rds., Marcus Bethel Dr. and Fort Charlotte. Hundreds of native and exotic plant species, including orchids, are showcased on 20 acres (8 hectares). The British military occupied this site in the 1800s, and according to folklore, slaves who died in the construction of Fort Charlotte were buried in the gardens. Originally designed to introduce new species to the Bahamas from around the world, the gardens have been ravaged by hurricanes many times over the years; restoration is ongoing. **Hours:** Mon.-Fri. 7-2. **Cost:** $2; $1 (ages 5-12). **Phone:** (242) 356-6475 or (242) 356-6477.

THE NATIONAL ART GALLERY OF THE BAHAMAS is at West and West Hill sts. across from St. Francis Xavier Cathedral. Housed in a stately villa, the gallery collects, exhibits, preserves and promotes the country's national collection of art. Themed exhibits rotate every 6 months, with the emphasis on contemporary art. An art library also is on the premises. **Tours:** Guided tours are available. **Time:** Allow 45 minutes minimum. **Hours:** Tues.-Sat. 10-4. Closed major holidays. **Cost:** $5; $3 (ages 13-18 and 65+); free (ages 0-12). **Phone:** (242) 328-5800 or (242) 328-5801.

PIRATES OF NASSAU is near the corner of Marlborough and George sts. The history of local pirate activity 1690-1720 is related through taped commentaries, sound effects and wall plaques. Visitors can experience a pirate's life at sea aboard *Revenge*, a replica pirate ship. Exhibits about female pirates and the pirate's code of conduct also are offered. **Time:** Allow 1 hour minimum. **Hours:** Mon.-Sat. 9-6, Sun. 9-noon. Closed major holidays. **Cost:** $12; $6 (ages 4-17). **Phone:** (242) 356-3759.

RECREATIONAL ACTIVITIES

Horseback Riding

- **Happy Trails Stables** provides transportation from downtown hotels, cruise ships and Paradise Island. Guided trail rides explore the beaches of Coral Harbour and Adelaide, a nearby village. No riding experience is necessary. Riders must be 12 or older and weigh 200 lb. (90kg) or less. **Hours:**

Rides are offered Mon.-Sat. early and late morning. **Phone:** (242) 362-1820.

GAMBLING ESTABLISHMENTS

- **Atlantis Casino at Paradise Island Resort** is on Casino Drive. **Hours:** Daily 24 hours. **Phone:** (242) 363-3000 or (800) 722-7466.

- **Crystal Palace Casino at Wyndham Nassau Resort** is on West Bay Street at Cable Beach. **Hours:** Daily 24 hours. **Phone:** (242) 327-6200 or (242) 677-4100.

Spanish Wells Island (A-3)

Spanish Wells, covering half a square mile (1.3 sq km), is one of the smallest inhabited islands in The Bahamas. At the end of St. George's Cay near the northern tip of Eleuthera, it derived its name from the Spanish ships that once stopped here to replenish their water supply from the island's wells.

Several years after the Eleutherian Adventurers established a settlement a half-mile (.8 km) east on the island of Eleuthera, they moved to Spanish Wells because it was smaller and easier to defend. Loyalists fleeing the results of the American Revolution also settled here. Some of them attempted to establish a plantation economy. However, the original settlers would not tolerate slavery, so the idea was squelched. This attitude earned the Spanish Wellsians the hatred of their slave-trading sister islands. Relics of that era include some colorful New England-style homes and traces of the English dialect spoken by early settlers.

The lobster industry is the most important factor in an economy that depends primarily on the sea. Tomatoes, cucumbers, onions and pineapples provide supplemental income. Sailing and fishing are among the main attractions for tourists. Offshore a wide variety of shipwrecks and coral reefs provide scuba divers and snorkelers with a wealth of underwater adventures.

Soup Bowl, Bathsheba, St. Joseph Parish / © SIME / eStock Photo

Barbados

Easternmost of the Caribbean islands, Barbados is the "Little England of Eternal Summer." Meaning "the bearded ones," its name is said to have been given by a Portuguese discoverer because of the beardlike vines on the fig trees. With nearly 1,600 inhabitants per square mile, Barbados is one of the most densely populated countries in the Caribbean; the friendliness of its people is its foremost charm.

The silver sand beaches on the Caribbean side of the island contrast with the rugged Atlantic coastline. Roads are bordered by fields of cane, royal palms and rolling hills and terraces. Vivid tropical flowers, including fragrant oleander, frangipani, jasmine, cassia, bougainvillea, hibiscus and lady-of-the-night, lie in profusion along neat hedgerows. Scarlet flame trees and coral walls shelter the well-tended lawns of color-washed houses, and windmills of former sugar plantations dot the land, though the Morgan Lewis Sugar Mill is the only one with its arms and wheelhouses still intact.

Bridgetown, the capital, is representative of the island's heritage. Its typically English atmosphere is enhanced by names like Yorkshire and Windsor and by the ritual of afternoon tea, which occurs at "half past four."

History

Once inhabited only by Arawak Indians, Barbados was discovered by the Portuguese in the 16th century. The English claimed it in 1625, and 2 years later the first settlers arrived. The island's population increased significantly during the mid-1600s as English immigrants fled the political unrest in their homeland and slaves were brought from Africa to work the sugar crops. The colony thrived early on as a result of the tobacco and cotton trade and became a prosperous sugar producer in the 17th and 18th centuries. During the struggle for European supremacy in the Caribbean, 35 forts were built along 25 miles (40 km) of coastline. The ruins of many are still visible.

Of all the islands in the West Indies, Barbados is the only one to have remained solely in the hands of its original settlers. This fact helps explain the island's stability and the British flavor that has remained constant over the centuries.

Since 1954 Barbados has had a ministerial system of government with a governor general appointed by the Queen of Great Britain on recommendation of the prime minister, who heads the island's government. Barbados became an independent nation on Nov. 30, 1966. A coat of arms bearing the motto "Pride and Industry" speaks for the high literacy rate and prosperous economy; Barbados is one of the most economically stable Caribbean islands, with tourism, sugar production, financial services and light industry forming the basis of the economy.

Shopping

High-quality English clothing and Scottish and English fabrics are excellent buys in Barbados. Bridgetown tailor shops on Prince Alfred and Tudor streets offer made-to-measure clothing in a variety of materials ranging from Sea Island cotton to imported tweeds. Baskets, seashell trinkets, pottery, English china and silver, silks and Oriental objects and antiques also are popular purchases. Another leading commodity available at a very low price is Barbados rum, said to be the world's oldest. By shopping in the afternoon you can avoid the morning rush.

Most of the duty-free shopping in Bridgetown is concentrated on Broad Street. Cave Shepherd, Bridgetown's largest department store, features Waterford, Wedgwood, Royal Doulton and Swarovski china and crystal, an extensive selection of cosmetics and fragrances, leather goods, jewelry, electronics, fashions and a liquor department. Harrison's is a department

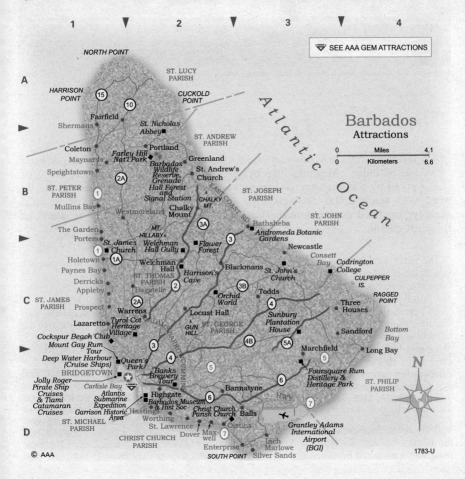

Barbados Attractions

© AAA

1783-U

store containing a vast assortment of luxury items including Lladró figurines, designer sweaters, jewelry and watches by Cartier, Fendi and Gucci.

DaCostas' Mall, also on Broad Street, houses several interesting boutiques. Just opposite is Mall 34, with shops displaying high quality merchandise from India and Europe, and the Royal Shop, with a wide selection of watches.

Malls in the Hastings and Worthing area of Christ Church include Hastings Plaza, Sandy Bank, Skyway Plaza and Quayside Centre. Sheraton Mall, said to be the island's largest shopping establishment, is in Christ Church at Sargeants' Village, less than 20 minutes from the airport.

Chattel House Village, a shopping area in Holetown, St. James, consists of a medley of actual chattel houses, all colorfully painted. The village contains a variety of boutiques, including a Best of Barbados gift shop. Also situated in Holetown is the West Coast Mall, a marketplace popular with locals containing a small Cave Shepherd store, a supermarket and various shops.

Barbados is said to have some of the finest antiques in the West Indies. Reputable dealers include Antiquaria II in Holetown, St. James, and Greenwich House Antiques at Greenwich Village, St. James.

Medford Craft World, on White Hall Main Road, specializes in such local handicrafts as pottery, wood carvings, and batik and woven baskets. Shells, metal art, leather, coral and other island-made articles can be found at Pelican Village, on Princess Alice Highway near Deep Water Harbour. Clothing, jewelry and mahogany pieces are among the items crafted by artisans at Heritage Park in St. Philip.

The Best of Barbados Shops, with several locations throughout the island, sell only products made or designed in Barbados. The shops have a wide assortment of local handicrafts and souvenirs including hand-painted tile, kitchen items, local prints, pottery and T-shirts. Earthworks Pottery atop Shop Hill in St. Thomas offers handmade pottery.

Some stores feature in-bond departments, where certain merchandise has been set aside and marked with two prices. The higher price applies to buy-and-take purchases. The second in-bond price, usually considerably lower, once applied only to merchandise purchased in the store and delivered to the airport or pier. However, most in-bond shops now allow tourists with proper ID (passport and travel ticket) to take their duty-free items from the store. Shopping hours for most stores in Barbados are Mon.-Fri. 8-4, Sat. 8-noon. Banks are open Mon.-Thurs. 9-3, Fri. 9-4.

Food and Drink

In addition to fine Continental and curried dishes, Barbados has many island specialties. These include *bonavist,* small white beans often seasoned with pumpkin and herbs; *jug-jug,* a molded dish of chopped ham and salt beef or pork combined with green peas; *cou-cou,* a savory pudding made with cornmeal and okra; and Barbadian black pudding, similar to a sausage stuffed with seasoned grated sweet potatoes.

Other local foods include pepperpot, a spicy stew made with selected meats; and *conkies,* a steamed concoction of sweet potatoes, cornmeal, pumpkin, coconut, raisins and spices served in a banana leaf. Roast suckling pig and native "flying fish" are favorite specialties. Fresh lobster and seafood are available. The fruits of Barbados are avocados, mangoes, guavas, bananas, breadfruit, golden apples, hog plums, gooseberries, cherries, pears, oranges, limes and grapefruit.

The name "rum" may have originated in Barbados, where a 17th-century observer wrote, "The chief fuddling they make in the Island is Rum Bullion, alias Kill-Devil, and is made of sugarcane distilled, a hot, hellish and terrible liquor." Today, the island rum is known for its smooth, refined taste.

Most hotels and resorts on Barbados include a 10-percent service charge on the guest's bill to cover gratuities. However, in nightclubs and restaurants, tipping is at the discretion of the guest.

Sports and Amusements

Most major hotels have a beach or are near one, and all types of aquatic gear can be rented. Motorboats (for water skiing) and sailboats are available for hire at beach club resorts. Conditions are excellent for skiing in the tranquil waters off the west coast, while sailing is favorable on both the west and south coasts. In the path of the trade winds, the east coast beaches are considered dangerous for swimming but ideal for surfing, with the Soup Bowl at Bathsheba being the best area for this sport.

Popular west coast beaches include Mullins Beach near Speightstown, which features a good snorkeling reef just offshore as well as shaded areas, shower facilities and an open-air restaurant providing a view of the bay. Paynes Bay, recognizable by the neighboring fish market, is a site where numerous water sports are indulged in. Visitors will enjoy the picturesque bay at Sandy Lane, with public access available on either side of the hotel.

Southeast coast beaches are not known for swimming amenities, but rather for their rugged beauty. Bottom Bay is a delightful cove with a white sand beach surrounded by cliffs and a coconut grove. At Crane Beach, pounding waves crash against the rocky shore. The Crane, reputedly the Caribbean's oldest operating hotel, rests atop a dramatic cliff surrounding the beach; parking is available at the beach or hotel. Foul Bay Beach is accessible by a road that travels downward to a paved parking area. This long stretch of beach, nestled between two cliffs, has a wide expanse of seagrape trees.

Popular beaches on the south coast of Barbados include Accra, where water-sports equipment is available for rental and opportunities are good for body surfing. Casuarina Beach is frequented by windsurfers due to large waves and abundant winds. Sandy Beach is preferred by families because of its shallow lagoon and calm seas.

Conditions for windsurfing are excellent on the south coast, due to constant trade winds and year-round water temperatures of about 78 degrees Fahrenheit.

At the Folkestone Marine Park off Holetown on the St. James coast, snorkelers and divers can follow an underwater trail along a coral reef where fish, sea anemones and sea fans can be seen.

Scuba diving lessons lasting about 2.5 hours are taught at several dive shops; reputable establishments include Lorenzo's Scuba Dreams and Underwater Barbados. Scuba gear rentals and dives can be arranged through some hotels.

Numerous shipwrecks in the waters around Barbados provide excellent diving opportunities. A large number of these wrecks are concentrated in Carlisle Bay, including *Sea Trek,* deliberately sunk in about 40 feet (12 m) of water; *The Berwyn,* an old tugboat brimming with sea life less than 10 feet (3 m) from the surface; and *The Fox,* a 120-foot schooner approximately 40 feet (12 m) from the surface that is home to numerous crustaceans. *Friar's Craig* is a small vessel in the area of coast just east of Aquatic Gap. The *Stavronikita,* a Greek freighter, was deliberately sunk by the Park and Beaches Commission in Folkestone Underwater Park.

January through June are the best fishing months; dolphin fish, kingfish, snapper, yellowfin tuna, shark and barracuda are plentiful. Fishing boats and guides can be hired for fishing excursions at most hotels or through the Barbados Game Fishing Association. The association also sponsors an annual fishing contest the last week in March, and visitors may enter the international competition.

Though Barbados calls itself the "Land of the Flying Fish," the national symbol has become scarce in recent years. Schools of the small, leaping fish have migrated south to warmer waters off Trinidad and Tobago, leaving the Bajan fishing fleet without its signature catch.

Check at your hotel's activities desk for information about snorkeling, scuba diving, deep-sea fishing and charter boats. Carlisle Bay is the island's sailing headquarters.

There are tennis courts at many hotels; reservations are recommended. Squash enthusiasts can play at the Almond Beach Village and the Barbados Squash Club.

Golfers also can enjoy their sport at several courses on the island. The 18-hole Barbados Golf Club in Christ Church is open to the public. Renowned golf course architect Tom Fazio has designed two 18-hole courses at the Sandy Lane Golf Club; the "Old Nine" also is available for play. Eighteen holes of a 27-hole championship golf course at Royal Westmoreland in St. James are open to resort guests. Temporary memberships are available for nine-hole courses at Almond Beach Village and Rockley Golf & Country Club.

Horseback riding inland is offered at Caribbean International Riding Centre at the Cleland Plantation in St. Andrew, (246) 422-7433. Beau Geste Farm & Stable in St. George, (246) 429-0139, offers riding lessons for new equestrians and trails for experienced riders.

Cricket is the chief spectator sport in Barbados. Visitors can watch matches at the national level at several sports clubs May through December, and at the international level January through March. Queens Park and Kensington Oval, both in Bridgetown, regularly hold matches. Soccer is popular January through April. Polo is played July through February at Holder's in St. James.

The Garrison Savannah has a horse-racing track with races held every other Saturday, except during the month of September. The Sandy Lane Gold Cup, the biggest race in the Caribbean, usually takes place in March; festivities and a parade accompany this exciting event. The Barbados Turf Club's race meetings, held five times a year, are joyous occasions with music, food booths and a general carnival atmosphere.

Many discos, nightclubs and restaurants provide after-dinner entertainment. The limbo and calypso, danced to the haunting rhythm of steel bands, entertain spectators and participants alike. For those who would rather look at the stars than dance beneath them, the Barbados

Astronomical Society offers a night of stargazing at the Harry Bayley Observatory in nearby Clapham every Friday from 8:30 to 10:30 (weather permitting); phone (246) 426-1317. Although there are no casinos in Barbados, slot machines are permitted; there are arcades in Bridgetown and at some resorts. The Plantation Restaurant stages a dinner show, "Bajan Roots and Rhythms," on Wednesday and Friday at 6:30 p.m.; phone (246) 428-5048.

Annual events include the Barbados Horticulture Society's Flower and Garden Show, an event in late January showcasing local plants, crafts and pottery. The Holetown Festival in February commemorates the arrival of English settlers in 1627. Activities include a parade of vintage cars, a street fair and arts and crafts.

The month of March is Holders Season, a celebration of opera, music and theater. In April, the Oistins Fish Festival pays tribute to Barbados' fishing industry; a Coast Guard exhibition, boat races and a fish-boning contest are among the events. Barbados Gospelfest brings top performers to Bridgetown on Whitsuntide weekend at the end of May.

Barbadians eagerly anticipate the nonstop revelry of the Crop-Over Festival, which occurs from late May to early August. The event, an island-wide folk celebration in honor of the completion of the sugar cane harvest, is considered one of the Caribbean's most popular. It features calypso competitions, art shows, food, music, crafts, a costume parade and fireworks on Kadooment Day (a national holiday) and other entertainment. Bajan music, singing, drama, dance and writing are celebrated every year at the National Independence Festival of Creative Arts in November.

The *Barbados Advocate* and *The Nation-News* are Bridgetown's daily newspapers. *The Nation* also produces *The Weekend Nation, The Sun on Saturday, The Sunday Sun, Better Health Magazine* and *Friends Magazine,* a weekly tourist publication containing entertainment information.

Sightseeing

From January through April the Barbados National Trust offers its Open House Programme, allowing the public to visit some of Barbados' most attractive and interesting private homes and gardens. Tours are offered every Wednesday from 2:30-5:30. Admission is $15.25; $7.75 (ages 5-12). A different house is featured each week, with past highlights including Cluffs Plantation House, Hopefield Manor, Forster Lodge and Sunbury Plantation House; phone the National Trust at (246) 426-2421 for the weekly program. Boyce's Tours provides

round-trip transportation from local hotels; tour rates include the house entrance fee; phone (246) 435-7811.

The National Trust also sponsors guided hikes on the Arbib Nature and Heritage Trail, starting at St. Peter's Church in Speightstown. These free informative walks range from 3 miles (4.8 km) to 10 miles (16.1 km) and offer insight into Barbados' history, environment and culture. Tours are offered daily at 9:30 and 2:30. Reservations must be made a day in advance; phone (246) 234-9010.

Barbados has four lighthouses positioned on strategic areas of coastline. Ragged Point Lighthouse, in St. Philip at the island's eastern tip, is constructed of coral limestone and provides an outstanding view of the east coast and Pico Tenerife. South Point Lighthouse, at the island's southernmost point in Christ Church, is a cast-iron structure made in England and shipped to Barbados in 1851. Other lighthouses are at Harrison Point in St. Lucy and Needham's Point in St. Michael.

You can arrange to tour some of the large sugar factories, such as Portvale and Andrews. The Sir Frank Hutson Sugar Museum and Factory, next to the Portvale factory yard near Holetown, is open during the sugar-grinding season from February through May. Visits should be arranged in advance; phone (246) 426-2421 or (246) 432-0100.

Tours and tastings also are available at Mount Gay Rum Distillery in Bridgetown on Spring Garden Highway; the Corkspur Beach Club (formerly known as Malibu Visitor Centre) on Brighton Beach, where Malibu and Cockspur rums are made; and Banks Breweries, producers of the award-winning Banks beer.

Glass-bottom boats afford a fascinating view of sea life among the coral reefs of the west coast; the Folkestone Marine Park and the old shipwrecks in Carlisle Bay are popular attractions. Lunch cruises aboard the *Jolly Roger* depart from Pirate's Pier in Bridgetown. Music and swimming are featured on four-hour cruises that take passengers along the coast in a replica of a pirate ship. Snorkeling stops are offered on catamaran cruises, which often include a buffet lunch. The MV *Harbour Master* offers a variety of cruises aboard the 4-deck boat complete with a ramp for beach landings and a semi-submersible chamber to view the underwater life; phone (246) 430-0900.

Cruises to neighboring islands can be arranged through Caribbean Safari Tours, (246) 420-7600; Chantours Caribbean, (246) 432-5591; Grenadine Travel, (784) 458-3795; and St. James Travel and Tours, (246) 432-0774.

Tour operators offering a wide variety of land excursions include Boyce's Tours, (246) 435-7811, and Island Safari, (246) 429-5337.

One of the most popular sightseeing drives follows the rugged Atlantic coast past such points of interest as Codrington College, St. John's Church and the pottery works at Chalky Mount. Those touring Barbados will notice numerous chattel houses made of wood, historically built up on rocks so they could be dismantled easily and moved to another location. Rum shops also contribute to the local flavor, serving as village meeting places where locals can exchange news.

The East Coast Road, traversing the rolling hills and greenery of the Scotland district and the rocky east coast, provides spectacular sightseeing opportunities. The road travels past Bathsheba, a haven for surfers and identified by the huge boulders protruding from the water; a small park area provides picnic tables and restroom facilities.

Cattlewash, a scenic stretch of coast punctuated by beach houses, took its name from the cattle that occasionally wander through the area. North of Cattlewash, Barclays Park is a popular spot for picnicking and recreation. The park overlooks a scenic stretch of coast lined with seagrape, hog plum and Casuarina trees. Swimming is not recommended due to the strong undercurrent. Visitors have access to a facility with changing rooms, showers and restrooms. A small restaurant in the 50-acre (20-hectare) park serves good Barbadian food on a seasonal basis.

Fast Facts

POPULATION: 273,000.

AREA: 430 sq km (166 sq mi.).

CAPITAL: Bridgetown.

HIGHEST POINT: 332 m (1,089 ft.), Mount Hillaby.

LOWEST POINT: Sea level, Atlantic Ocean.

TIME ZONE(S): Atlantic Standard.

LANGUAGE: English.

GOVERNMENT: Independent. Member of the British Commonwealth of Nations.

UNIT OF CURRENCY: Barbados dollar. $1 U.S. = 2 Barbados dollars. U.S. bills and travelers checks are accepted by most hotels.

ELECTRICITY: 110 volts, 50 cycles AC.

MINIMUM AGE FOR DRIVERS: 21-25, depending on the rental car agency. Local license ($5 U.S.) required, valid for 60 days; drive on left.

SEAT BELT/CHILD RESTRAINT LAWS: Seat belts are required for all passengers.

HOLIDAYS: Jan. 1; Errol Barrow Day, Jan. 21; Good Friday; Easter; Easter Monday; National Heroes Day, Apr. 28, Labour Day, May 1; Whit Monday, May or June (8th Mon. after Easter); Emancipation Day, Aug. 1; Kadooment Day, Aug. (1st Mon.); Independence Day, Nov. 30; Christmas, Dec. 25; Boxing Day, Dec. 26.

TAXES: A 8.75 percent room tax and 10 percent service charge are added to most hotel bills. A 15 percent VAT (value-added tax) is charged for food and beverages. Airport passenger service charge and security fee $30, usually included in airline ticket price.

IMMIGRATION REQUIREMENTS: A valid passport and a return or onward ticket are required. No visa required for U.S. and Canadian citizens for stays up to 6 months. The U.S. Dept. of Homeland Security requires all U.S. citizens returning from the Caribbean to present a valid passport.

PHONING THE ISLANDS: To call Barbados from the U.S. or Canada, dial 1 + 246 + the 7-digit local number.

FURTHER INFORMATION FOR VISITORS:

Barbados Tourism Authority, United States
820 Second Ave., 5th Floor
New York, NY 10017
(212) 551-4350
(800) 221-9831
(212) 986-6516

Barbados Tourism Authority, Canada
105 Adelaide St. W.
Suite 1010
Toronto, ON, Canada M5H 1P9
(416) 214-9880
(800) 268-9122

Barbados Tourism Authority, Bridgetown
Harbour Road
Bridgetown, Barbados
(246) 427-2623
(800) 744-6244
(246) 427-2624

Barbados' famed "Platinum Coast" along the Caribbean is lined with luxury hotels boasting tranquil beaches of powdery sand. A tour through St. Thomas Parish in the center of the island usually includes the botanical garden at Welchman Hall Gully and Harrison's Cave. St. Thomas and neighboring St. George are the only parishes without any coastal area.

Oistins is a picturesque fishing village in Christ Church Parish at the south end of the island. Several restored historic rum shops are in the area and can be visited. Visitors and locals can partake in freshly-cooked fish at the Oistins Fish Fry.

Transportation

Daily nonstop flights from New York and Miami touch down at Barbados' Grantley Adams International Airport. Interisland flights connect Barbados with Trinidad, Grenada, St. Vincent, St. Lucia, Martinique, Jamaica and the islands to the north. Barbados also is a port of call for many cruise ships.

The roads from Bridgetown to the popular districts are good, and the Adams-Barrow-Cummins (ABC) Highway from the airport to Highway 2A at Warrens enables traffic to bypass Bridgetown, reducing travel time by about 50 percent. You can rent cars, minimokes (resembling small jeeps), scooters, bicycles, chauffeur-driven cars and limousines. You must present a valid U.S. driver's license to obtain a Barbados permit.

Driving is on the left side of the road. Speed limits are 35 mph (60 km/h) in most areas of the island, with the exception being 25 mph (40 km/h) in town and 50 mph (80 km/h) on the Spring Garden and ABC highways. No car may be driven in Barbados without third-party insurance coverage. Slow-moving vehicles should travel on the left side of all double-lane highways.

Frequent bus service connects the parishes with Bridgetown. Transport Board buses, painted blue and trimmed in yellow, depart every half-hour from the three main terminals in Bridgetown: The Lower Green and Princess Alice Highway terminals provide transportation to destinations in the north part of the island and along the west coast, while the Fairchild Street terminal is for southbound travelers. There also is a Transport Board terminal in the north in Speightstown.

Privately owned minibuses, yellow with blue trim, travel shorter distances and therefore have faster turnaround times. The main minibus terminals are in Bridgetown at Probyn Street, River Road and Cheapside. Even when at a designated stop, you must wave at the minibuses to get the driver to come to a halt. Buses run daily 6 a.m.-midnight; fare is $.75 U.S. and exact change is required for the Transport Board buses.

Taxis are readily available in the National Heroes' Square area of Bridgetown; a taxi stand is next to a fountain adorned with dolphins. Check the fixed rates before taking a cab.

Points of Interest

See map page 68.

Christ Church Parish (D-2)

One of 11 parishes defining Barbados, Christ Church is at the southern end of the island. Visitors arriving by air see this parish first; it's the home of Grantley Adams International Airport. East of Oistins are Silver Sands and Enterprise beaches, both popular with sunbathers and windsurfers.

St. Lawrence Gap is the parish's hub for dining and entertainment opportunities. The area is punctuated with nightclubs, bistros and upscale restaurants, many with views of the water. A small beach area dotted with fishing boats provides a pedestrian-friendly atmosphere ideal for a daytime or evening stroll.

OISTINS (D-2)

The fishing community of Oistins hosts the island's annual fish festival in April and a fish fry every Friday and Saturday night. The local catch is prepared by street vendors for all to enjoy.

CHRIST CHURCH PARISH CHURCH is on Church Hill Road. This Anglican church was the scene of considerable excitement during the 19th-century "Restless Coffins Mystery." Coffins in the sealed Chase Vault were reportedly found in different positions each time the vault was opened. To stem the hysteria provoked by the strange incidents, the governor finally had the coffins buried elsewhere. **Hours:** Daily dawn-dusk. **Cost:** Donations. **Phone:** (246) 428-8087 or (246) 428-2319.

St. Andrew Parish (B-2)

About 850 feet (259 m) above sea level, Cherry Tree Hill offers an excellent view of the hilly Scotland District, where cane fields stretch toward the coast. Mahogany trees on the hill's summit are a playground for monkeys, usually visible in the evening. St. Andrew also is home to Mount Hillaby, the highest point on the island at 1,089 feet (332 m); a narrow, winding road leads from the town of Hillaby to the summit. Nearby Turner's Hall Woods, a 50-acre (20-hectare) ecosystem containing many indigenous plant and animal species, is what remains of a dense tropical forest that once covered the island.

St. Andrew's Parish Church dates from 1846. The previous building withstood the 1780 and 1831 hurricanes. The wooden altar, with stained-glass windows at its center, is surrounded by colorful floor tiles.

CHALKY MOUNT POTTERY is e. of Hwy. 2. Formed by a deposit of clay that looks like a reclining man with hands folded over his chest, Chalky Mount has been nicknamed "Napoleon" by local residents. Only a few pottery businesses continue to operate, several of them located in private homes. Visitors can watch potters form their clay shapes on a kick wheel. A variety of articles are for sale, including plant pots, tableware, pitchers, jugs and cooking utensils. **Hours:** Daily 8:30-5. **Cost:** Free.

MORGAN LEWIS SUGAR MILL is about 1 mi. (1.6 km) s.e. of Cherry Tree Hill. The last working example of some 500 sugar mills that once dotted the island, this massive windmill has been restored by the Barbados National Trust. Stones in the conical tower were cemented together with a mixture of egg whites and coral dust. Visitors can enter the 18th-century mill and observe the machinery used to grind sugar cane until the 1940s; exhibits include historic photographs and plantation artifacts. The window on the top level provides a striking view of the surrounding Scotland District. **Hours:** Mon.-Fri. 9-5. **Cost:** $10; $5 (children). **Phone:** (246) 422-7429 or (246) 426-2421.

St. George Parish (C-2)

Built in 1784 after a hurricane destroyed the first structure on the site, St. George Parish Church is noted for its altarpiece, "The Resurrection," by American painter Benjamin West.

GUN HILL SIGNAL STATION is off Hwy. 3 on Fusilier Rd. During British occupation of the island, this 700-foot (213-m) rise was one of several points used to relay messages. A monument to Britain's supremacy is the lion carved on the side of a limestone cliff by British soldiers in 1868. The restored 19th-century station contains a collection of military memorabilia. **Hours:** Mon.-Sat. 9-5. Closed major holidays. **Cost:** $5; $2.50 (ages 0-11). **Phone:** (246) 429-1358.

ORCHID WORLD is off Hwy. 3B between Gun Hill and St. John's Church. This 6-acre (2-hectare) site in the high rainfall sector of Barbados is said to contain more than 20,000 orchids. Paths wind through a lush tropical setting accented by vibrantly colored orchids, most of which are labeled. A number of varieties are displayed in greenhouses, depending on growing conditions. Views of the surrounding countryside are punctuated by sugarcane fields. **Time:** Allow 1 hour minimum. **Hours:** Daily 9-5. Closed Good Friday and Christmas. **Cost:** $10; $5 (ages 5-13). **Phone:** (246) 433-0306. 🍴

St. James Parish (C-1)

The island's first English settlement was established in St. James Parish in 1627, two years after Captain John Powell claimed the island in the name of King James I. Originally named Jamestown, the village came to be called Holetown for the narrow offshore channel where ships were serviced.

North of Holetown, the Folkestone Marine Park is an underwater park and sanctuary where snorkelers and divers can follow an underwater trail along a coral reef. The park includes a beach and the Folkestone Marine Museum, which displays live and mounted fish native to local waters.

HOLETOWN (C-1)

Opening celebrations of the week-long Holetown Festival are held in February at the Holetown Monument, which commemorates the first British landing on Barbados in 1625. Now a major tourist area, this area of upscale resorts, shops and shimmering beaches is called the "Platinum Coast."

Vestiges of the island's sugar industry are preserved at the Sir Frank Hutson Sugar Museum and Factory in the yard of the Portvale sugar factory. Antique and modern machines are displayed February through May during the harvest season; phone (246) 432-0100 or (246) 426-2421.

ST. JAMES' PARISH CHURCH is on Hwy. 1. Most of the present church was built in 1874. Hurricanes destroyed the first wooden structure, erected in 1628, and its stone replacement. The original church bell is inscribed "God Bless King William 1696." Other relics include hand-beaten silver pieces that date from the late 17th century and the original baptismal font with its mahogany cover. A graveyard where many of Barbados' early settlers are interred adjoins the church. **Hours:** Daily dawn-dusk. **Cost:** Donations. **Phone:** (246) 422-4117.

St. John Parish (B-3)

One of the highest points on the island, Hackleton's Cliff rises 1,000 feet (305 m) above sea level. A steep, winding drive rewards visitors with a panoramic view of the east coast and the Scotland district.

CODRINGTON COLLEGE is on Sargeant St. overlooking Consett Bay. The site of the college originally was a plantation owned by Sir Christopher Codrington, former governor general of the Leeward

Islands. Founded in 1745, this is one of the oldest seminaries in the Western Hemisphere. The wooded grounds offer a spectacular view of Consett Bay on the east coast. **Hours:** Daily dawn-dusk. **Cost:** Donations. **Phone:** (246) 423-1140.

ST. JOHN'S PARISH CHURCH is n.e. on Hwy. 3B. The 1836 Gothic chapel perches on the edge of Hackleton's Cliff, affording a spectacular view of the Atlantic coast. The floor is paved with memorial tablets rescued from earlier churches, all destroyed by hurricane or fire. Ferdinando Paleologus, an alleged descendant of Constantine the Great, was buried in the churchyard in 1678. **Hours:** Daily dawn-dusk. **Cost:** Donations. **Phone:** (246) 433-5599.

St. Joseph Parish (B-3)

St. Joseph, on the northeastern shore, is in the heart of the Scotland District, a rugged vista that reminded homesick settlers of their native hills. Near the top of Horse Hill is the Cotton Tower, one of six signal stations built across Barbados by the British as part of the island's defense.

BATHSHEBA (B-3)

A resort 14 miles (23 km) from Bridgetown, Bathsheba has been called a miniature Cornish coast. The Flying Fish Fleet, purveyors of Barbados' national dish, arrives daily at Tent Bay. The outside verandah of the Atlantis Hotel is a popular spot for a typical Barbadian lunch, with Tent Bay and Bathsheba providing a scenic backdrop.

ANDROMEDA BOTANIC GARDENS, .2 mi. (.3 km) off Hwy. 3 following signs, clings to a rocky hillside overlooking the Atlantic coastline. Founded in 1954 by world-renowned horticulturist Iris Bannochie, Andromeda's lush gardens span 6.5 acres and host a collection containing some 650 species from the Caribbean, tropical Americas, Africa, Asia, Australia and the Pacific Islands. Visitors wind their way past flowering trees, palms and orchids, enjoying sea breezes in a tranquil setting. **Time:** Allow 1 hour minimum. **Hours:** Daily 9-5. Closed Good Friday, Easter and Christmas. **Cost:** $10.10; $5.05 (ages 0-12). **Phone:** (246) 433-9384.

FLOWER FOREST is on Hwy. 2 at Richmond Plantation, following signs. Well-marked, easy to navigate hillside trails wind among tropical trees and plants, including bamboo, banana, avocado, breadfruit, coconut, coffee, cocoa and Barbados cherry. Relics of the sugar industry can be seen on the 50-acre (20-hectare) Richmond Plantation site. **Time:** Allow 1 hour minimum. **Hours:** Daily 9-5. Last ticket sold at 4. Closed Good Friday and Christmas. **Cost:** $10; $5 (ages 5-13). **Phone:** (246) 433-8152.

St. Lucy Parish (A-2)

The Animal Flower Cave in St. Lucy is one of the most scenic coastal areas in Barbados. Steps descend into a coral limestone cave containing three rooms. This sea-sculptured formation obtains its name from the sea anemones that exist in the pools, one of which is deep enough to swim in. Sneakers or reef shoes are recommended since the steps are steep and the rocks can be slippery. A guide leads the way into the cave, which is sometimes closed due to rough seas; phone (246) 439-8797.

From the cliffs surrounding Cove Bay, visitors can watch the tumultuous waves of the Atlantic Ocean crashing against the shore. Towering above the cove is Pico Tenerife, a jagged rock formation rising from the ocean to a height of 269 feet (82 m).

St. Michael Parish (D-1)

With its first English camp in 1628, St. Michael Parish soon gained prominence over earlier settlements in St. James and St. Peter due to its sheltered bay and freshwater access. The area later named Bridgetown would become one of the most important commercial ports in the West Indies.

BRIDGETOWN (D-1) pop. 7,500

Barbados' capital, Bridgetown was founded in 1629 and was the chief residential section during the island's settlement. The exuberance of its people and customs blend with a Victorian austerity typified by the public buildings that house parliament.

A statue of Lord Nelson in National Heroes' Square (formerly Trafalgar Square) was erected by planters in recognition of the British admiral, who saved their sugar profits from the French. St. Michael's Cathedral, on St. Michael's Row, was rebuilt in 1831 of coral rock after the original was destroyed by hurricanes. George Washington is recorded as having attended services in the original cathedral in 1751; it is now one of the town's main attractions.

The parliamentary buildings are on Broad Street facing National Heroes' Square. The House of Assembly meetings, held in the east building's Public Gallery, usually can be observed Tuesday at noon; visitors must be appropriately dressed and cameras are not permitted. The gallery contains stained-glass windows representing the sovereigns of England and a speaker's chair with intricate carvings.

The Careenage, in central Bridgetown alongside Wharf Street, is a picturesque harbor where pleasure craft are docked. Chamberlain Bridge, one of two spans over the Careenage, contains the Independence Arch, originally erected in 1987 and later rebuilt; it commemorates the island's 21st anniversary as a self-governing nation. Next to the arch is an area of shops, craft vendors and restaurants overlooking the water. Fishing and sailing charters as well as scuba diving excursions can be arranged at the waterfront shops.

Off Broad Street, visitors can find duty-free shops offering china, crystal, leather and fine jewelry. A colorful market can be found on Cheapside Street.

The Bridgetown Synagogue, on Magazine Lane, dates from 1654. Said to be one of the oldest Jewish synagogues in the Western Hemisphere, the structure was destroyed by a hurricane in 1933 and has been restored. The adjoining cemetery has tombstones dating from the 1630s.

Situated on Bay Street, opposite the Prime Minister's office and next to Bayshore Beach, the Esplanade offers a nice view of Bridgetown's harbor area and Carlisle Bay. The small park, which was once a village of wooden houses, contains benches shaded by trees and a lovely gazebo. St. Patrick's Roman Catholic Cathedral, also on Bay Street, dates from 1839.

East of Bridgetown, in a residential area at the northern end of St. Barnabas Highway, is the Emancipation Statue of Bussa, a national hero. Commemorating the abolition of slavery in 1834, the statue depicts a slave standing with his chains broken and his hands to the sky in triumph. In 1816, Bussa purportedly led a revolt at Bayley's Plantation in St. Philip Parish that was to be the largest revolt on the island.

Barbados Tourism Authority: Harbour Road, P.O. Box 242, Bridgetown, Barbados. **Phone:** (246) 427-2623, (246) 427-2624 or (800) 744-6244.

GEM *ATLANTIS* **SUBMARINE EXPEDITION** departs from the Shallow Draft in Deep Water Harbour. The 65-foot-long, 48-passenger submarine cruises at a maximum depth of 150 feet (45 m), offering excellent views of reefs, coral formations, marine life and a sunken ship. **Time:** Allow 3 hours minimum. **Hours:** Trips depart daily on the hour 9-4; closed 1 week in Sept. A 15-minute ferry ride transports passengers between the dock and the submarine for the 50-minute tour. **Cost:** Fare $104; $52 (36 inches-age 17). Round-trip transportation to harbor/hotels $7.50. Children under 36 inches tall are not permitted on the submarine. Reservations are recommended. **Phone:** (246) 436-8929 or (866) 546-7820.

BANKS BREWERY TOUR is in the Wildey area. The guided tour begins with a brief orientation video depicting the beer brewing process. Visitors are then led through the plant where they see milling equipment in the Brew House, the fermentation tanks and the Bottling Hall, where bottles are washed, filled, pasteurized and labeled. After the tour, guests are treated to complimentary samples of the various products produced on site. **Time:** Allow 1 hour minimum. **Hours:** Tours Mon.-Fri. at 10, noon and 2. Under 10 are not permitted. Closed major holidays. **Cost:** $6; $3 (ages 10-15). Reservations are recommended. **Phone:** (246) 227-6782.

BARBADOS MUSEUM AND HISTORICAL SOCIETY is 2.5 mi. (4 km) s.e. on Bay St. at the Garrison. Exhibits in the 1817 British military prison depict the natural history of the Caribbean, Amerindian prehistory and the history of Barbados. The museum also has collections of ceramics, silver, maps and prints; period rooms from a Barbadian plantation house; an African gallery; a military gallery; a children's gallery; and a prisoner's cell as well as changing exhibits. **Hours:** Mon.-Sat. 9-5, Sun. 2-6. Closed major holidays. **Cost:** $7.50; $3.75 (children). **Phone:** (246) 427-0201 or (246) 436-1956.

COCKSPUR BEACH CLUB is off Spring Garden Hwy. on Brighton Beach. A guided tour begins with a 10-minute videotape highlighting the plant's signature products, Malibu and Cockspur rum. Participants view the aging and filling rooms where the rum is blended and bottled. The guide provides a detailed explanation of the fermentation and distillation processes. Tour fee includes beach chair rental and complimentary drink. **Time:** Allow 1 hour minimum. **Hours:** Visitor center Mon.-Fri. 9-4:30. Tours on the half-hour except 11-noon. Last tour at 3:45. **Cost:** Tour $15; $8 (ages 0-11). **Phone:** (246) 425-9393. [¶]

GARRISON HISTORIC AREA is 2.5 mi. (4 km) s.e. on Bay St. at the outskirts of Bridgetown. This military site began with construction of Charles Fort by the Barbados Militia in 1650. British troops were garrisoned here 1780-1905. The West India Regiment was the first British unit of black soldiers; their distinctive Zouave uniforms are still worn by the Barbados Defence Force Band.

The community surrounding the Garrison Savannah racetrack features some 70 buildings of historical and architectural interest, including the 1705 St. Ann's Fort and the 1804 Main Guard House with its prominent clock tower. Bush Hill House (known locally as George Washington House), where George Washington and his ailing brother lived for three months in 1751, has been restored; tours are available by appointment. The National Cannon Collection displays several dozen of the more than 400 iron guns that have been excavated on the island, including an Elizabethan cannon forged in 1600. **Phone:** (246) 436-9033, or (246) 228-5461 for Bush Hill House tour reservations.

MOUNT GAY RUM TOUR is on Spring Garden Hwy. near Bridgetown's deep water port. The guided 45-minute tour begins with an audiovisual presentation in a theater resembling a rum shop. A knowledgeable guide then offers an in-depth explanation of all aspects of rum production, focusing on the aging process involved in producing a mature rum. The tour also includes a look at the blending and bottling areas of the plant. Afterward, visitors may participate in a tasting. A buffet lunch tour is available. **Hours:** Traditional tours depart every hour Mon.-Fri. 9:30-3:30; Sat. 10:30-2:30. Lunch tour departs Tues. and Thurs. at noon. Cocktail tour departs Wed. at 2:30. Closed major holidays. **Cost:** Traditional tour $7; free (ages 0-11). Lunch tour including transportation $40; $20 (ages 4-11). Cocktail tour including transportation $30; children not permitted. Reservations are required for lunch and cocktail tours. **Phone:** (246) 425-8757 or (246) 425-9066. [¶]

QUEEN'S PARK is off Constitution Rd. The British government purchased this area in the 1780s as a residence for the general commanding the British troops. The building, formerly known as "King's House," was later changed to "Queen's House" when Queen Victoria came to power. On the grounds are a playground, a bandstand, a fountain and lush gardens that create an escape from the bustle of Bridgetown. A 1,000-year-old baobab tree stands some 90 feet high and measures more than 81 feet around its trunk.

An art gallery in Queen's Park House features local works, and a theater presents local productions. **Hours:** Daily dawn-dusk. Gallery Mon.-Sat. 10-6. **Cost:** Free. **Phone:** (246) 425-1200 or (246) 426-2555.

TIAMI **CATAMARAN CRUISES** departs from the Shallow Draught harbor of Bridgetown port. Lunch and sunset cruises are offered, both of which include snorkeling stops; sites may vary due to weather conditions. Passengers enjoy views of the island's southwest coast. Food, beverages and hotel transfers are included. Allow a half day. Snorkeling equipment is provided. Bring a swimsuit, towel and sunscreen. **Tours:** Guided tours are available. **Hours:** Five-hour lunch cruises depart daily at 10. Sunset cruise departs Sun. at 4. Closed Christmas. **Cost:** Lunch cruise $90; $45 (ages 4-12). Sunset cruise $60; $45 (ages 4-12). **Phone:** (246) 430-0900.

TYROL COT HERITAGE VILLAGE is at Codrington Hill. The home of Sir Grantley Adams, who led the struggle for democracy in Barbados, contains family photographs and articles, as well as antique mahogany pieces. Reproductions of chattel houses in the surrounding four-acre village include a replica of an 1820s slave hut, a working blacksmith's shop and a home depicting the domestic life of Barbadians in the 1920s. Artisans are on site displaying their crafts. **Time:** Allow 1 hour, 30 minutes minimum. **Hours:** Mon.-Fri. 9-5. Closed major holidays. **Cost:** Free. House $11.50; $5.75 (ages 0-12). **Phone:** (246) 424-2074.

St. Peter Parish (B-1)

St. Peter and St. Lucy, which share the northern end of the island, are the only two parishes in Barbados with shorelines on both the Atlantic Ocean and Caribbean Sea. The port of Speightstown was once a vital trading link with England, and British landowners established several large estates here in the 17th century, including Saint Nicholas Abbey and Farley Hill.

Wild green monkeys frolic in their natural habitat at the Barbados Wildlife Reserve, which protects 4 acres (1.6 hectares) of mahogany forest.

SPEIGHTSTOWN (B-1)

This fishing village was once a shipping center known as Little Bristol. In 1663 Sir John Yeamans

sailed from Speightstown (pronounced *Spites-town*) on an expedition to colonize South Carolina; he later became the third governor of that colony. His house, St. Nicholas Abbey, is one of the oldest sugar plantation great houses still standing in the Caribbean. Also in the area are the remains of the Old Denmark, Orange and Dover forts. Six Men's Bay north of town is lined with cannons and old buildings once used for drying whale blubber.

FARLEY HILL NATIONAL PARK borders the Barbados Wildlife Reserve. On a cliff 900 feet (275 m) above sea level, the park provides sweeping views of the coast amid gardens and the ruins of a sugar planter's estate. The earliest part of the house, known originally as Grenade Hall, is thought to have been built in 1818. In 1856, original owner Joseph Lyder Briggs gave the property to his son, Thomas Graham Briggs. Thomas spent large sums developing Farley Hill into one of the finest country residences in the West Indies and entertained distinguished guests there. The park also is the site of concerts and festivals. **Hours:** Daily 8:30-4:30. **Cost:** $3.45 per private vehicle. **Phone:** (246) 422-6700. 🅰

GRENADE HALL FOREST AND SIGNAL STATION borders the Barbados Wildlife Reserve and Farley Hill National Park. The 1819 station commands a panorama of the island and offers insight into its original role as part of a communications network that was unique in the Caribbean. The site was originally used by the Royal Artillery to communicate between island signal stations and the capital of Bridgetown. Visitors can explore a mile (1.6 km) of coral pathways winding through trees, shrubs, vines and herbs.

Hours: Daily 10-5. Last admission 1 hour, 30 minutes before closing. Closed Jan. 1 and Christmas. **Cost:** (includes the Barbados Wildlife Reserve) $12; $6 (ages 3-12). **Phone:** (246) 422-8826.

ST. NICHOLAS ABBEY is 5.5 mi. (9 km) n.e. via Hwy. 1 following signs. Built about 1658 for a sugar planter, the Jacobean mansion had as its second resident Sir John Yeamans, commissioned by King Charles II as lieutenant general and governor of South Carolina. This functioning sugar plantation, which never actually served as an abbey, has well manicured grounds and gardens. Visitors tour the ground floor, which is decorated with antique English and Barbadian furniture. An 1890 steam mill grinds sugar cane bi-weekly December through June for the on-site distillery; sugar and rum products can be sampled. An 18-minute home movie filmed in 1935 depicts the sugar-making process and other island scenes. **Time:** Allow 1 hour minimum. **Hours:** Sun.-Fri. 10-3:30. Closed major holidays. Phone ahead to confirm schedule. **Cost:** $35; $20 (ages 1-12). **Phone:** (246) 422-8725 or (246) 432-6392.

St. Philip Parish (D-4)

The rugged coastline on the southeast edge of the island is famous for its waves. Crane Beach, with its dramatic limestone cliffs, is considered one of the most beautiful beaches on the island. The area is named for a large winch that was once used to unload ships.

FOURSQUARE RUM DISTILLERY AND HERITAGE PARK is s. of Six Cross Roads on Hwy. 6. The Foursquare Plantation's 19th-century sugar factory has been modified to produce rum. Self-guiding tours of the underground furnace room offer insight about early sugar boiling methods; rum production, from barreling to aging, is explained through displays in the distillery. The 8-acre (3-hectare) landscaped park contains a folk museum, craft shops, an outdoor sugar museum, an amphitheater and a children's play park. **Time:** Allow 1 hour minimum. **Hours:** Mon.-Fri. 9-5. Closed major holidays. **Cost:** Free. **Phone:** (246) 420-1977 or (246) 423-5630. ⑪

SUNBURY PLANTATION HOUSE is .7 mi. (1.1 km) w. of Six Cross Roads on Hwy. 5. Built in 1660, Sunbury is one of the oldest plantation houses on the island. Guides lead 30-minute tours of the house, which is furnished with period pieces and antiques. The yam cellars contain collections of horse-drawn vehicles and an optometrist's artifacts. The surrounding plantation is still being worked. A candlelight dinner is offered Tuesday and Thursday; reservations are required. **Hours:** Tours are offered daily 9-4:30. Closed Christmas. **Cost:** $10; $5 (ages 5-12). **Phone:** (246) 423-6270. ⑪

St. Thomas Parish

St. Thomas is one of two land-bound parishes on Barbados; the other is St. George to the south. The 1799 Sharon Moravian Church is one of the few unaltered 18th-century structures on the island.

HARRISON'S CAVE is on Hwy. 2 at the southern end of Welchman Hall Gully. Narrated 45-minute tram rides travel through subterranean stream passages. An introductory slide show at the visitor center depicts the discovery and development of the cave. Comfortable shoes are recommended. **Hours:** Trams depart every 15 minutes daily 8:45-3:45. Closed Jan. 1, Good Friday, Easter, first Mon. in Aug. and Christmas. **Cost:** $30; $15 (ages 3-12). Reservations are recommended. **Phone:** (246) 438-6640 or (246) 417-3700. ⑪

WELCHMAN HALL GULLY is on Hwy. 2. A ravine created by collapsed limestone caverns contains a 13-acre (5-hectare) tropical garden of fruit and spice trees. The gully is rimmed by cave-pocked cliffs inhabited by monkeys. A massive pillar formed by the joining of stalactites and stalagmites seems to support the rock cliff. With a diameter of more than 4 feet (1.2 m), the limestone pillar is one of the largest of its kind in the world. **Tours:** Guided tours are available. **Hours:** Daily 9-4:30, Nov.-Aug.; Mon.-Sat. 9-4:30, rest of year. Closed Jan. 1, Good Friday, first Mon. in Aug. and Christmas. **Cost:** $10; $5 (ages 5-12). **Phone:** (246) 438-6671.

Horseshoe Bay, Southampton Parish / © Jim Schwabel / age fotostock

Bermuda

Viewed from the air, Bermuda presents a kaleidoscope of pink beaches, blue-green ocean and patchwork isles. The mainland is a graceful chain of eight islands joined by roads and bridges; in all, Bermuda consists of 181 islands and islets. A closer view reveals well-ordered homes with white roofs and a profusion of flowers—Easter lilies, amaryllis, oleander, gladioli, hibiscus and poinsettias. Because Bermuda is the northernmost of the coral islands, limestone, the residual product of coral, is seen everywhere. The island is 650 miles (1,046 km) east of Cape Hatteras, N.C., and about a 2-hour flight from New York, Atlanta and other East Coast gateway cities.

Thanks to a mild climate and beautiful beaches, Bermuda's main business is tourism. However, Bermuda is a subtropical island—the weather during December, January and February can be brisk enough to keep most people out of the water. The peak tourist season runs from spring until fall.

History

Bermuda's discoverer and namesake, Juan de Bermúdez of Spain, is thought to have anchored off the islands as early as 1505. The first settlers, however, were Virginia-bound British colonists who were shipwrecked off St. George's Island in 1609. Some historians credit the event with providing Shakespeare with background for "The Tempest."

Although tourism, banking and international business are today's primary industries, Bermuda relied on shipbuilding as the mainstay of its economy about 70 years after its founding as a colony. Vessels constructed of cedar were the basis of the island's flourishing economy until wooden ships were replaced by those made of steel during the late 1800s and tourism began to take on economic importance.

As a British colony Bermuda is administered by a governor appointed by the reigning British

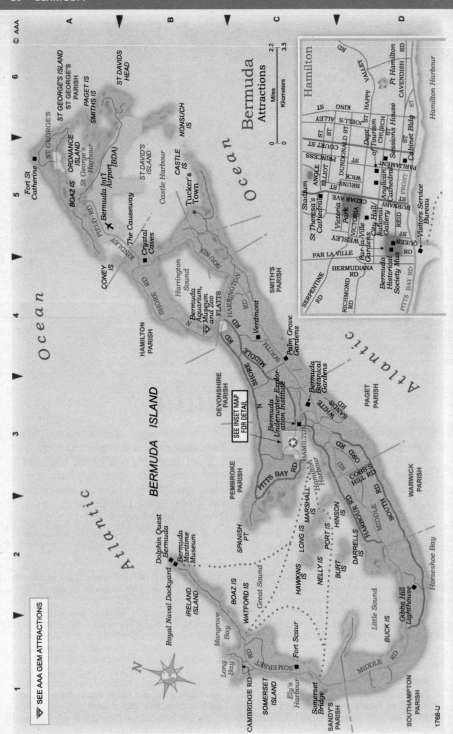

© AAA

SEE AAA GEM ATTRACTIONS

Bermuda Attractions

Miles 2.2 3.5
Kilometers

Hamilton

Ft Hamilton

Hamilton Harbour

Dept. of Tourism
Sessions House
Cabinet Bldg

St Theresa's Cathedral
Stadium
Victoria Park
City Hall/ National Gallery
Anglican Cathedral
Par-la-Ville Gardens
Visitors Service Bureau
Bermuda Historical Society Mus

CAVENDISH RD
HAPPY VALLEY RD
KING ST
CHURCH ST
S.JOELL'S ST
COURT ST
DUNDONALD ST
PRINCESS ST
ELLIOT ST
ANGLE ST
BRUNSWICK ST
CEDAR AVE
WESLEY ST
REID ST
FRONT ST
QUEEN ST
VICTORIA ST
PAR-LA-VILLE RD
BERMUDIANA RD
RICHMOND RD
SERPENTINE RD
PITTS BAY RD

SEE INSET MAP FOR DETAIL

BERMUDA ISLAND

Ocean

Atlantic Ocean

Atlantic

Ocean

ST GEORGE'S ISLAND
ST GEORGE'S PARISH
PAGET IS
SMITHS IS
ST DAVIDS HEAD
NONSUCH IS
ST GEORGE'S
ORDNANCE ISLAND
Fort St Catherine
BOAZ IS
St George's Harbour
FIELD RD
KINDLEY
CONEY IS
The Causeway
Bermuda Int'l Airport (BDA)
ST DAVID'S ISLAND
Castle Harbour
CASTLE IS
Tucker's Town
Crystal Caves
SHORE RD
Harrington Sound
HAMILTON PARISH
SOUND RD
Bermuda Aquarium, Museum and Zoo
FLATTS
HARRINGTON RD
Verdmont
SMITH'S PARISH
Palm Grove Gardens
MIDDLE RD
SOUTH RD
DEVONSHIRE PARISH
SHORE RD
Bermuda Botanical Gardens
Bermuda Underwater Exploration Institute
WHITE SANDS RD
PAGET PARISH
PEMBROKE PARISH
PITTS BAY RD
Hamilton
Hamilton Harbour
MARSHALL IS
SPANISH PT
COBB'S HILL RD
HARBOUR RD
ORD RD
MIDDLE RD
SOUTH RD
WARWICK PARISH
Dolphin Quest Bermuda
Bermuda Maritime Museum
Royal Naval Dockyard
IRELAND ISLAND
Mangrove Bay
BOAZ IS
WATFORD IS
Great Sound
LONG IS
HAWKINS IS
NELLY IS
PORT IS
BURT IS
DARRELL'S IS
HINSON IS
Little Sound
BUCK IS
Gibbs Hill Lighthouse
Horseshoe Bay
Long Bay
CAMBRIDGE RD
SOMERSET ISLAND
SOMERSET RD
Ely's Harbour
Fort Scaur
Somerset Bridge
SANDY'S PARISH
MIDDLE RD
SOUTHAMPTON PARISH

N

1768-U

monarch; a cabinet appointed by the premier; a senate jointly formed by the governor, the premier and the opposition party; and a house of assembly elected by the citizens. The country's nine parishes are governed by separate advisory councils. The islands hold the distinction of being the oldest self-governing colony in the British Commonwealth. Bermuda's constitution, adopted in June 1967, provides for a large measure of self-government.

Shopping

Browsing for antiques and bric-a-brac is entertaining in itself. Shops in Hamilton have given Bermuda its reputation as the "Showcase of the British Commonwealth." Choice woolens, cashmeres, silver, English china, leather gloves and slacks, French perfumes, German cameras, Swiss watches, Swedish crystal and Italian leather can be purchased at great savings.

On Front Street, A.S. Cooper & Sons Ltd. sells Wedgwood china and William Bluck & Co. Ltd. deals in fine china and crystal. The Calypso Shop on Front Street and the Irish Linen Shop feature linens from Ireland, Italy and Switzerland. Perfumes can be found at Peniston Brown & Company.

Fine selections of jewelry are displayed at Astwood Dickenson on Front Street and at Crisson on Queen, Reid and Front streets in Hamilton and Water Street in St. George's. The specialty shops composing The Emporium, entered from Front Street, allow visitors with limited time to purchase an array of interesting Bermudian items in one stop. Bermuda Perfumery, at 5 Queen St. in Stewart Hall, St. George's, preserves the traditional creative processes of this native industry.

Branch stores and specialty shops are tucked away in St. George's and Somerset as well as in several of the larger resort hotels throughout the island. Most stores are open Mon.-Sat. 9-5, and some have extended hours during the Christmas holidays and summer months. Banking hours generally are Mon.-Fri. 9-4:30.

Food and Drink

In Bermuda the lobster season extends from September through March. The delicacy is served steaming with melted butter or one of several rich sauces. Cassava pie filled with chicken and pork is a popular treat during the Christmas season. The secret of its unique flavor is the grated and baked root of the cassava plant. Favorite desserts are sweet potato pudding and *syllabub*, a guava jelly-cream-wine concoction.

Fruits and vegetables are grown locally, but meat is imported from the United States and Canada. Drinking water is distilled from sea water for hotels or collected on rooftops, and milk is pasteurized. All popular American drinks are available; meals in hotels are similar to those served in the United States. Reservations are suggested for lunch and dinner at the best restaurants. A tip of 15 percent, with extra allowance for special service, is customary. However, most hotels, restaurants, cottage colonies and guesthouses add a 15-percent gratuity to the accommodation or food bill. Most hotels and restaurants accept credit cards.

Sports and Amusements

Part of Bermuda's appeal is that it has something for everyone. Golf, tennis, horseback riding, fishing and water sports lure the athletically inclined, while shoppers can enjoy Hamilton's exclusive stores and civic activities. St. George's, the former capital, provides a journey into the past with its 17th-century architecture and narrow lanes. Lazy days are filled by sunning, sightseeing or browsing in out-of-the-way shops.

Bermuda ranks among the most sports-conscious countries of the world: More than 30 sporting clubs are found in an area of 21 square miles (54 sq km). The island's diverse activities include bowling, bridge, cricket, cycling, dog and horse shows, fishing, golfing, parasailing, sailing, swimming, scuba diving, tennis, racquetball, squash, table tennis, horseback riding, water skiing and windsurfing.

Soccer and cricket are the national sports—soccer matches are scheduled September through April, and cricket matches are held May through September. The Annual Cup Match, a national holiday, is a cricket match played between teams representing the island's east and west ends on the Thursday and Friday before the first Monday in August; most shops and eateries close during the event. Rugby also is popular; one major international tournament, the World Rugby Classic, is played in mid-November.

Other sporting events include golf and tennis tournaments; yacht races on Saturday and Sunday; the Bermuda Game Fishing Association Tournament, held throughout the year; and the Bermuda Triple Crown Billfish Championship in July. Summer is celebrated on Bermuda Day, the fourth Monday in May, with dinghy races in St. George's Harbour and cycling and inline skating races in Hamilton.

The beaches on the south shore are wild stretches of sand and surf. Horseshoe Bay is one of the most popular. Because Bermuda is not subject to strong ocean currents that stir up sediment, the waters are usually clear and excellent for snorkeling. In addition, more than 600 species of fish live in the surrounding waters. One of the most unusual underwater sports

Bermuda offers is bell diving, or underwater walking. Bermuda Bell Diving offers an opportunity for nonswimmers and people who wear glasses or contacts to see the incredible variety of marine life in Bermuda's waters. Anyone from 5 to 85 can participate in the guided 30-minute tours departing from Flatts Village in Smith's Parish, daily April through November, weather permitting; phone (441) 535-8707.

You can rent boats and equipment for snorkeling, scuba diving and spear fishing at many places on the island; spear fishing is not permitted within 1 mile (1.6 km) of the shore, and the importation and use of a spear gun in Bermuda is illegal. Since 1- or 2-hour scuba diving lessons are usually insufficient preparation for a novice, you should take a complete course in advance. Several operators offer snorkeling and scuba diving lessons on trips aboard glass-bottom boats.

Information on trips for deep-sea, reef or shore fishing is available from Visitor Service Bureaus on Front Street in Hamilton, King's Square in St. George's and the Royal Naval Dockyard in Sandy's Parish. Boats with tackle and bait can be chartered for both half- and full-day excursions; no license is required. Rentals and lessons for sailing vessels and windsurfing are abundant. Water skiing is best May through September and is permitted in Hamilton Harbour, the Great Sound, Castle Harbour, Mangrove Bay, Spanish Point, Ferry Reach, Ely's Harbour, Riddells Bay and Harrington Sound; the law requires that skiers be towed by a licensed skipper.

If you prefer to play on land, you can choose among golf, tennis, squash, bicycling or horse-back riding. Public golf courses include the Belmont Hills Golf Club, Warwick Parish; Fairmont Southampton Golf Club, Southampton Parish; Ocean View Golf Course, Devonshire Parish; and Port Royal Golf Course, Southampton Parish.

Many large hotels have tennis courts. The Bermuda Squash Racquets Club in Devonshire Parish is available by advance reservation to visitors for a fee of $10 plus a $6-$8 court fee; phone (441) 292-6881. Bowlers can pursue their sport at the Warwick Lanes on Middle Road in Warwick Parish.

Bicycling is an engaging pastime, particularly on the Railway Trail, which runs along an old railroad line. The nature trail runs the entire length of Bermuda, St. George to Somerset, except for a 3-mile (4.8-km) section in and around Hamilton. The 21 miles (34 km) of trails are divided into seven sections, each with its own flavor and character. The trail also is a fine walking and equestrian path. A free, 18-page trail guide is published by the Bermuda Department of Tourism (see Fast Facts box). The guide includes a history of the trail, maps, descriptions of various sections of the path and historical photos; phone (441) 236-4201.

The self-guiding African Diaspora Heritage Trail crisscrosses the island and provides glimpses into Bermuda's role in black history. The trail includes such sights as the slave graveyard at St. Peter's, Crow Lane and the slave exhibit at Commissioner's House in the Bermuda Maritime Museum.

The Spicelands Equestrian Centre in Warwick Parish offers a variety of programs, including trail rides, evening rides and lessons; phone (441) 238-8212.

Several publications listing weekly events and entertainment are distributed at hotels and other establishments. Dancing and after-dinner entertainment are nightly fare at hotels and large cottage colonies. Calypso bands and local talent fill Hamilton nightclubs, some of which stay open until 3 a.m.

Sightseeing

Excursions can be taken to almost any point on Bermuda by cycle, taxi, boat or bus. A blue flag on a taxi signifies that the driver has been approved as a qualified tour guide by the government. Excellent maps are available at Visitor Service Bureaus on Front Street in Hamilton, King's Square in St. George's and the Royal Naval Dockyard in Sandy's Parish. Some hotels will arrange escorted excursions.

Popular cruises include a 2-hour cruise aboard a glass-bottom boat to the sea gardens and a 3-hour catamaran cruise of Great Sound. Reservations can be made directly through the operator or arranged through a hotel activities desk. Ferries operate daily from Hamilton to the Bermuda Maritime Museum, Royal Naval Dockyard, in Sandy's Parish.

DID YOU KNOW

Native Bermudians refer to themselves as "Onions."

Transportation

Several air carriers provide service to L.F. Wade International Airport from Atlanta, Baltimore, Washington D.C., Miami, New York, Philadelphia, Newark, London and Toronto. Flights last from 1 hour, 50 minutes to 2.5 hours.

Because law forbids the use of automobiles by nonresidents, car-rental services are not available. Perhaps the most common and economical means of transportation in Bermuda is cycling. Mopeds can be rented for about $50 a day for a single or $75 a day for a double. For the hardier visitor, bicycles (known as "pedal bikes") can be rented for about $35 for a full day; weekly rates also are available. Cycle rental operations are found throughout the island and at many of the large hotels. Riders should use caution, as roads in Bermuda are narrow, hilly, curving and banked in many spots by coral walls. Carriages with fringed tops also can be hired.

Bus service, priced by zone, is available throughout the island; the central bus terminal is on Church Street in Hamilton. Exact change, tokens or tickets are required; books of 15 tickets are available at substantial savings at the central terminal or at most sub-post offices throughout the island. Adult fare for up to three zones is $3 cash, $12 for a day covering all zones.

Bermuda Ferry Service runs daily between Hamilton, Paget, Warwick, Somerset, Dockyard and Rockaway. An additional route to St. George's operates May to early November. The Hamilton-Paget-Warwick fare is $2.50 one way; the Hamilton-Somerset fare is $4 one way. The flat fare for ages 5 to 16 is $2, $4 to St. George. Cash is no longer accepted on the ferries; tickets must be purchased before boarding. Motor-assisted cycles and pedal bikes on the Hamilton-Somerset or Hamilton-Dockyard ferry cost $4 extra one way and are not permitted on other routes. Bus and ferry combination day passes are available. Bus and ferry schedules, which include maps of routes and fare zones and sample fares, can be obtained at the bus and ferry terminals, visitor's service bureaus and most hotels.

Fast Facts

POPULATION: 64,500.

AREA: 54 sq km (21 sq mi.).

CAPITAL: Hamilton.

HIGHEST POINT: 76 m (250 ft.), Town Hill.

LOWEST POINT: Sea level, Atlantic Ocean.

TIME ZONE(S): Atlantic Standard. DST.

LANGUAGE: English.

GOVERNMENT: British Overseas Territory.

UNIT OF CURRENCY: Bermudian dollar, divided into 100 cents. $1 U.S. = 1 Bermudian dollar. Most shops, restaurants and hotels accept U.S. currency.

ELECTRICITY: 110 volt, 60 cycles AC.

MINIMUM AGE FOR DRIVERS: Nonresidents may not drive cars on Bermuda; rental cars are not available. Driving is on the left.

HELMETS FOR MOTORCYCLISTS: Required.

HOLIDAYS: Jan. 1; Good Friday; Bermuda Day, May (4th Mon.); Queen's Birthday, June (1st or 2nd Mon.); Cup Match and Somers Day, Thurs. and Fri. before 1st Mon. in Aug.; Labour Day, Sept. (1st Mon.); Remembrance Day, Nov. 11; Christmas, Dec. 25; Boxing Day, Dec. 26.

TAXES: A 9.5 percent room tax and 10-15 percent service charge are added to most hotel bills. Most restaurants include a 10-15 percent service charge. There is no sales tax on the island. Departure tax and airport security fee is $35 U.S. by air, $60 by sea.

IMMIGRATION REQUIREMENTS: Passport and a return or onward ticket are required. No visa needed for stays up to 21 days.

PHONING THE ISLANDS: To call Bermuda from the U.S. or Canada, dial 1 + 441 + the 7-digit local number.

FURTHER INFORMATION FOR VISITORS:

Bermuda Department of Tourism
675 Third Ave., 20th Floor
New York, NY 10017
(212) 818-9800
(800) 223-6106

Visitors Service Bureau
The Royal Naval Dockyard
Pier 41
Sandy's Parish, Bermuda MA01
(441) 799-4842
(800) 237-6832

Points of Interest

See map page 80.

Devonshire Parish (C-3)

One of nine Bermudian parishes, each comprising 1,250 acres (500 hectares), Devonshire is at the geographical center of the island. The area is named for William Cavendish, the first Earl of Devonshire. The Old Devonshire Parish Church on Middle Road dates to 1716, though it has been destroyed and rebuilt at least twice.

PALM GROVE GARDENS is at 38 South Shore Rd. The private estate contains tropical birds and native and exotic trees and flowers. A pond has a relief map of Bermuda. **Hours:** Mon.-Thurs. 9-5. Closed major holidays. **Cost:** Free.

Hamilton Parish (B-4)

Hamilton Parish, wrapped like a semicircle around Harrington Sound, is known for its labyrinth of caves. Though it shares the same name, this parish does not contain the island's capital; the city of Hamilton is in Pembroke Parish. The Bermuda Railway Museum, 37 North Shore Rd., contains memorabilia from the days of the Bermuda Railway and is open by appointment; phone (441) 293-1774.

BERMUDA AQUARIUM, MUSEUM AND ZOO is at 40 North Shore Rd. in Flatts Village. Most species of fish found in Bermuda waters are represented, along with tropical birds, lemurs, golden lion tamarins, turtles, seals and binturongs. The 140,000-gallon North Rock Exhibit has two viewing tanks showcasing Bermuda's ocean resources and the underwater environment of the nearby North Rock coral reef. A touch pool and Discovery Cove also are on site.

The Australasia Exhibit features the wildlife of Australia, New Guinea, Borneo and Malaysia. The museum highlights the unique geological development of Bermuda. A full-sized whale skeleton also is displayed. Self-guiding audio tours are available, and videotapes about Bermuda's marine life run continuously. **Time:** Allow 1 hour minimum. **Hours:** Daily 9-5. Last admission 1 hour before closing. An interpretive tour is offered daily at 1:10, Apr.-Sept; Sat.-Sun. at 1:10, rest of year. Closed Christmas. **Cost:** $10; $5 (ages 5-12 and 65+). **Phone:** (441) 293-2727.

THE CRYSTAL & FANTASY CAVES OF BERMUDA is at 8 Crystal Caves Rd. off Wilkinson Ave. on Bailey's Bay. Folklore says that two boys discovered the first cavern in 1905 while searching for a lost cricket ball. The main cave takes its name from the crystal-clear waters of its underground lake, which is 55 feet (17 m) deep. A second passage in the underground network, Fantasy Cave, features rare chandelier clusters of soda straw formations and calcite mineral deposits resembling frozen waterfalls. The 81 steps in Crystal Cave might be difficult for some; benches are available for resting. **Time:** Allow 1 hour minimum. **Hours:** Guided tours daily 9:30-4:30. Last admission 30 minute before closing. Closed Jan. 1, Good Friday, Christmas Eve, Christmas and day after Christmas. **Cost:** One cave $20; $8 (ages 5-12). Combination $27; $10 (ages 5-12). **Phone:** (441) 293-0640.

Paget Parish (D-3)

Across the harbor from the capital city of Hamilton, Paget Parish includes the resort area of Elbow Beach.

BERMUDA BOTANICAL GARDENS is at 169 South Rd. via Berry Hill and Point Finger rds. On the property of Camden, the official residence of Bermuda's premier, the 37-acre (15-hectare) gardens display native and introduced flora and feature several display houses and a garden for the blind. A visitor center at the Berry Hill entrance offers educational displays and a videotape presentation. **Time:** Allow 1 hour, 30 minutes minimum. **Hours:** Gardens open daily dawn-dusk. Visitor center open Mon.-Fri. 9:30-3:30. Display houses open Tues.-Sat. 10-4. Free tours depart from the visitor center Tues.-Wed. and Fri. at 10:30 (weather permitting). The premier's residence is open, except during official functions, Tues. and Fri. noon-2. **Cost:** Free. A fee is charged during the Agricultural Exhibition in April. **Phone:** (441) 236-4201.

Pembroke Parish (C-3)

Once known as Spanish Point, Pembroke Parish is home to the island's capital. Bermuda's most populous parish covers a peninsula between the Atlantic Ocean and Hamilton Harbour.

HAMILTON (C-3) pop. 969

Incorporated in 1793, Hamilton succeeded St. George's as capital in 1815. The city, overlooking Hamilton Harbour, is a latticework of pastel houses surrounded by tropical flowers. Whitewashed roofs, shuttered windows, arched doorways, Old World carriages and clusters of shops all enhance Hamilton's charm.

The sparkling white tower of City Hall rises 90 feet above Church Street. Its bronze weather vane depicts Sir George Somers' shipwrecked *Sea Venture*. A first floor gallery displays a stamp collection and oil portraits of Queen Victoria and Prince Albert. Upstairs is the Bermuda National Gallery *(see attraction listing)*. Behind the building is Victoria Park with its 19th-century gazebo, built in honor of Queen Victoria's golden jubilee.

Visitors Service Bureau, Hamilton: Front St. near ferry terminal, Hamilton, Bermuda. **Phone:** (441) 295-1480.

BERMUDA HISTORICAL SOCIETY MUSEUM is next to the public library at 13 Queen St. Displayed are china, silver, antique furniture, Bermudian coins, cedar carvings, personal belongings of Adm. Sir George Somers and sketches and models of early Bermuda ships. Somers was commander of the fleet carrying settlers to Virginia when it was shipwrecked off St. George's Island in 1609. Also featured is a collection of blue and white Canton porcelain and locally made silver spoons from 1727. The Benbow Gallery contains a fine collection of artifacts made by prisoners of war held in Bermuda. **Hours:** Mon.-Fri. 10-2, June-Sept.; 10:30-1, rest of year. Closed major holidays. **Cost:** Free. **Phone:** (441) 295-2487.

BERMUDA NATIONAL GALLERY occupies the second floor of City Hall at 17 Church St. The country's art museum showcases fine and decorative arts from around the world. The permanent collection features Bermudian works, 15th- through 19th-century European art, African sculpture and contemporary pieces. Highlights include paintings by Thomas Gainsborough, Sir Joshua Reynolds and George Romney; photographs by Richard Saunders; and prints by Hale Woodruff. **Time:** Allow 1 hour minimum. **Hours:** Mon.-Fri. 10-4, Sat. 10-2. Guided tours are offered Thurs. at 10:30. Closed major holidays. **Cost:** Free. **Phone:** (441) 295-9428.

BERMUDA UNDERWATER EXPLORATION INSTITUTE (BUEI) is just outside Hamilton on E. Broadway at 40 Crow Lane. Designed to foster an understanding and appreciation of the world's oceans, the BUEI features two floors of interactive exhibits. Through simulator modules, visitors can dive 12,000 feet in a deep-sea submersible or survive an attack in a shark cage. Highlights include the Jack Lightbourne Shell Collection and a display of artifacts discovered by diver and explorer Teddy Tucker. Marine exhibits include diving bells, a bathysphere and the space-like Exosuit, an atmospheric diving suit. **Hours:** Mon.-Fri. 9-5, Sat.-Sun. 10-5. Last admission 1 hour before closing. Closed Christmas. **Cost:** $12.50; $10 (ages 66+); $6 (ages 6-17). **Phone:** (441) 292-7219. 🍴

THE CABINET BUILDING is at 105 Front St. Known as the Secretariat, the 1841 building houses several government offices and the council chamber of the Senate, the upper house of the legislature. **Hours:** Mon.-Fri. 9-5. Open Senate sessions held Wed. beginning at 10, Nov.-July. Closed major holidays. **Cost:** Free. **Phone:** (441) 292-5501.

CATHEDRAL OF THE MOST HOLY TRINITY is on Church St. Built of native limestone and stones from around the world, the Anglican cathedral was consecrated in 1911. Special features include a marble altar, mosaics and stained-glass windows. The 155 steps to the top of the cathedral's tower lead to a panoramic view of Hamilton. **Hours:** Cathedral open daily 8-5. Tower Mon.-Fri. 10-4 (weather permitting). Services are held Mon.-Fri. at 8 (also Wed. at 12:15), Sun. at 8 and 10. Closed major holidays. **Cost:** Free. Tower $3; $2 (ages 65+ and students with ID). **Phone:** (441) 292-4033.

FORT HAMILTON is e. on Happy Valley Rd. This well-preserved coral fortress was built during the American Civil War to prevent blockade running; the underground passageways and large cannons are noteworthy. A semitropical garden occupies the moat. Picnicking is permitted on the lawn, which offers a fine view of Hamilton, Paget and Warwick parishes and the harbor. **Hours:** Daily 9:30-5. **Cost:** Free. 🍴

PAR-LA-VILLE GARDENS is on Queen St. just off Front St. Native flowers and plants are presented in a formal arrangement. The Perot Post Office is on the grounds. **Hours:** Gardens open daily 8 a.m.-dusk. Post office open Mon.-Fri. 9-5; closed major holidays. **Cost:** Free. **Phone:** (441) 292-9052 for the post office.

ST. THERESA'S CATHEDRAL is on Elliot St. Stained-glass windows from Munich, Germany, enhance the Spanish-style architecture of this Roman Catholic church, which was built in 1932. **Hours:** Mon.-Fri. 7 a.m.-8:30 a.m., Sat.-Sun. 8 a.m.-7:30 p.m. Closed major holidays. **Cost:** Donations. **Phone:** (441) 292-0607.

SESSIONS HOUSE (PARLIAMENT BUILDING) is at 21 Parliament St. Completed in 1819, this building accommodates the Supreme Court and the House of Assembly, which meets from November to May. **Hours:** Building open Mon.-Fri. 9-12:30 and 2-5. Closed major holidays. **Cost:** Public gallery free. **Phone:** (441) 292-7408.

St. George's Parish (A-6)

At the eastern end of Bermuda, St. George's Parish comprises several islands, the largest of which is St. George's Island. During World War II, when Bermuda became an important base for Atlantic military operations, four U.S. posts were built here.

ST. DAVID'S ISLAND (A-6)

The 650-acre St. David's Island is connected to the mainland by a bridge on St. George's Harbor. Its U.S. naval air station remained active until 1995. The picturesque St. David's Lighthouse has been in continuous use since 1879.

CARTER HOUSE is off Southside Rd. on the former U.S. Navy base. One of the vicinity's oldest buildings, the former dwelling features original cedar beams and two limestone-flanked open fireplaces. Two floors display various items relating to the history of whaling, boat building and farming, while native trees and plants surround the restored 17th-century stone structure. **Time:** Allow 30 minutes minimum. **Hours:** Tues.-Thurs. and Sat. 10-4, Feb.-Nov.; Sat. 10-4, rest of year. Phone ahead to confirm schedule. **Cost:** Donations. **Phone:** (441) 293-5960.

ST. GEORGE'S (A-6) pop. 1,752

The town of St. George's is about 12 miles (19 km) northeast of Hamilton and is connected with the mainland by causeway. St. George's was once the seat of Bermuda's government, which was organized in 1612. It would be difficult to find a more delightful storybook town. The quaintness of St. George's is reflected in the names of its narrow, twisting lanes: Old Maids Lane, Shinbone Alley, Featherbed Alley and One Gun Alley.

The Old State House on the town square dates to 1620. In April the governor of Bermuda makes his formal call on the Freemasons to collect the annual rent of one peppercorn for their use of the Old State House.

At the head of Duke of Kent Street stand the stone arches and columns of the Unfinished Church, which was intended as a replacement for St. Peter's Church. Politics, budget problems and storm damage caused the roofless cathedral to be abandoned in the 1870s; the mossy ruins are open to the public.

Visitors Service Bureau, St. George's: King's Square, St. George's, Bermuda. **Phone:** (441) 297-1642.

BERMUDA NATIONAL TRUST MUSEUM is at 32 Duke of York St. on King's Square. Housed in the old Globe Hotel, built 1698-1700 and used as a Confederate headquarters during the American Civil War, the museum chronicles the boom era of blockade running, when small steamships ran goods from St. George's to Confederate ports in the United States. A 12-minute videotape presentation gives an overview of Bermuda's history. **Hours:** Mon.-Sat. 10-4, May-Oct.; Wed. and Fri.-Sat. 10-4, rest of year. Closed major holidays. **Cost:** $5; $2 (ages 6-18); free (on Fri.). Combination ticket with Tucker House and Verdmont $10. **Phone:** (441) 297-1423.

BERMUDIAN HERITAGE MUSEUM is on the corner of Duke of York and Water sts. Artifacts, memorabilia and photographs relating to the cultural history of black Bermudians are displayed in a historic building. The highlight of the two-story museum is a model replica of the slave ship *Enterprise*. **Time:** Allow 30 minutes minimum. **Hours:** Tues.-Sat. 10-3. **Cost:** $4; $2 (ages 65+); free (ages 0-5). **Phone:** (441) 297-4126.

THE DELIVERANCE is on Ordnance Island at King's Square. The ship is a full-size replica of the vessel built to carry the shipwrecked company of the *Sea Venture* to Jamestown, Va., in 1609. This saga of shipwreck and survival on Bermuda is thought to have been the basis of Shakespeare's play "The Tempest." A bronze sculpture of British admiral Sir George Somers also is here. A taped narration is given. **Hours:** Daily 9-5, Apr.-Oct. Closed Good Friday and Easter. **Cost:** $3; $1 (ages 0-11).

FORT ST. CATHERINE is at 15 Coot Pond Rd. Development of the fort began virtually from the moment Sir George Somers and the original settlers washed ashore at adjacent Gates Bay in 1609. The fort would be remodeled several times over the following centuries, growing in both size and armament. Today it stands virtually as it did in the late 19th century, with massive 18-ton rifled muzzle loader guns. Exhibits explain the life and times of the Victorian-era soldiers who stood vigil against any attack from the sea. **Time:** Allow 30 minutes minimum. **Hours:** Daily 10-4. Closed Christmas. **Cost:** $7; $5 (ages 65+); $3 (ages 0-11). **Phone:** (441) 297-1920.

KING'S SQUARE is in the heart of town. In front of the 1782 Town Hall are replicas of stocks, a pillory, a whipping post and a ducking stool, once used to punish gossiping and other 18th-century offenses. Several times a week at noon, St. George's town crier appears in period costume to convene a mock tribunal. Market Night, a local street fair, is held on Tuesday evenings in the summer. **Hours:** Daily 24 hours. **Cost:** Free. **Phone:** (441) 297-1532.

ST. GEORGE'S HISTORICAL SOCIETY MUSEUM is on Featherbed Alley at Duke of Kent St. The 18th-century building of Bermuda limestone contains exhibits of Bermuda furniture, documents and pictures. Behind the museum is the Featherbed Alley Printery, which features a working replica of a Gutenberg-style printing press. **Hours:** Museum open Mon.-Wed. and Fri.-Sat. 10-4, Apr.-Nov.; Wed. and Sat. 10-4, Jan.-Mar. Closed major holidays. **Cost:** $5; $2 (ages 0-12). **Phone:** (441) 297-0423.

ST. PETER'S CHURCH is at 33 York St. Founded in 1612, this is the oldest Protestant church site in continuous use in the New World. The original cedar-frame structure was erected by Bermuda's first governor, Richard Moore. After a hurricane in 1712, parishioners salvaged the altar, pulpit and beams and rebuilt in stone. The silver Communion set displayed in the vestry was a gift from King William III in 1697. Another silver chalice dates from 1625. **Hours:** Mon.-Sat. 10-4. **Cost:** Donations. **Phone:** (441) 297-2459.

SOMERS GARDEN is on Duke of York St. Two memorials are dedicated to Adm. Sir George Somers, who established the first British settlement in

1609. **Hours:** Daily dawn-dusk. **Cost:** Free. **Phone:** (441) 297-1532.

TUCKER HOUSE MUSEUM is at 5 Water St. The 1775 residence of Henry Tucker, president of Bermuda's Governor's Council, contains a collection of family silver, china and antiques. During the American Civil War, Joseph Rainey, a former slave from South Carolina and later the first black member of the U.S. House of Representatives, operated a barbershop at the house. **Time:** Allow 30 minutes minimum. **Hours:** Mon.-Fri. 10-2, May-Oct.; Wed.-Fri. 10-2, rest of year. Closed major holidays. **Cost:** $5; $2 (ages 6-18). Combination ticket with Bermuda National Trust Museum and Verdmont $10. **Phone:** (441) 297-0545.

Sandy's Parish (C-1)

Sandy's Parish is a popular picnicking area in rural Bermuda. Sightseers often arrive by ferry from Hamilton and return by bicycle via the Railway Trail. A visitor's bureau on Somerset Road offers maps and brochures describing the Somerset area; it is open Mon.-Fri. 10-3.

Somerset Bridge on Middle Road is believed to be the world's smallest hand-operated drawbridge. The 13-inch gap allows the masts of sailboats to pass.

THE ROYAL NAVAL DOCKYARD is at the n. end of Ireland Island. The dockyard supported British naval operations from the War of 1812 through World War II. Major construction of this "Gibraltar of the West" began in 1809, involving large land reclamations and the labor of slaves and thousands of British convicts. The dockyard's great warehouses and fortifications now house shops and restaurants. The 1823 Commissioner's House, one of the oldest surviving examples of prefabricated cast iron construction, has been restored as a museum. Spectacular views are offered at the 10-acre (4-hectare) citadel keep, which features ramparts, underground magazines, dolphin encounters and exhibits.

Hours: Dockyard open daily 24 hours; closing times vary for shops and restaurants. Cruise ships dock Apr.-Nov. Visitors can reach the island via a fast ferry or bus from Hamilton. Buses leave Hamilton and the dockyard every 15 minutes. **Cost:** Free. **Phone:** (441) 234-1333.

Dolphin Quest Bermuda is located at the National Museum of Bermuda at the Royal Naval Dockyard. Visitors of all ages can play and swim with dolphins in a variety of fun and educational encounter programs ranging from 20 minutes to 1 hour long. Train the Trainer programs also are available. Swimsuits and towels are required; water footwear is recommended. **Hours:** Programs are offered daily 9:30-4:30. Closed Christmas. Phone ahead to confirm schedule. **Cost:** Discover Dolphins $160. Encounter $245. Ultimate Adventure $310. Reservations are required. **Phone:** (441) 234-4464, or (800) 248-3316 Mon.-Fri. 8 a.m.-9 p.m.

National Museum of Bermuda is inside the fortress keep of the Royal Naval Dockyard. Among eight historic exhibit halls is the Commissioner's House, which showcases local heritage and military history. Bermuda's maritime history—including shipwrecks, shipbuilding, ocean commerce, transport and the dockyard—is chronicled in converted ammunition storehouses on the lower grounds. Boats, ship models, shipwreck artifacts and artillery also are displayed. **Time:** Allow 1 hour minimum. **Hours:** Daily 9:30-5; 10-4 in winter. Last admission 2 hours before closing. Closed Christmas. **Cost:** $10; $8 (ages 61+); free (ages 0-12). **Phone:** (441) 234-1418.

SCAUR HILL FORT PARK is off Somerset Rd. on Somerset Island. Built in the 19th century to protect the Royal Naval Dockyard from possible American invasion after the Civil War, the fort was never tested. Its polygonal shape, based on a Prussian design, makes it nearly invisible from land or sea. The view is exceptional. **Hours:** Daily dawn-dusk. **Cost:** Free. **Phone:** (441) 236-5902.

Smith's Parish (C-4)

Bermuda's largest nature and wildlife reserve, Spittal Pond, is in Smith's Parish on South Road. The 59-acre (24-hectare) sanctuary harbors many species of waterfowl and plant life. The best season for bird-watching is September through April. The North Nature Reserve at Mangrove Lake across from Pink Beach also preserves various examples of the island's fauna and flora. Both reserves are open daily.

VERDMONT is at 6 Verdmont Ln. This restored mansion, circa 1710, blends Bermudian and New England design elements and is furnished with period antiques. The three-story house remains virtually unchanged, standing as it did some 300 years ago. The grounds offer ocean views and gardens of herbs, old roses and fruit trees typical of the 18th century. **Time:** Allow 30 minutes minimum. **Hours:** Tues.-Thurs. and Sat. 10-4, May-Oct.; Wed. and Sat. 10-4, rest of year. Closed major holidays. **Cost:** $5; $2 (ages 6-18). Combination ticket with Bermuda National Trust Museum and Tucker House $10. **Phone:** (441) 236-7369.

Southampton Parish (D-1)

On the southwest end of the island, Southampton Parish was originally known as Port Royal, perhaps preceding the town of the same name in Jamaica. The area offers a nature reserve and dramatic coastal views.

GIBBS' HILL LIGHTHOUSE is on Lighthouse Rd. This cast-iron lighthouse was built in 1846 and is believed to be the oldest of its kind in the world. The observation platform, reached by a 185-step climb, affords a magnificent view. **Hours:** Daily 9-5, Mar.-Jan. Closed Christmas and day after Christmas. **Cost:** $2.50; free (ages 0-4). **Phone:** (441) 238-8069. ⚑

© Reinhard Dirscherl / Photolibrary

Bonaire

Bonaire is the least populated and developed of the "ABC" (Aruba, Bonaire and Curaçao) islands. Pink is the island's official color—flamingos congregate here by the thousands—but a dive into Bonaire's turquoise waters reveals a world of rainbow hues. Not only is Bonaire surrounded by coral reefs, it *is* a reef, harboring an incredible variety of sea life. This, coupled with excellent underwater visibility, makes Bonaire one of the foremost diving and snorkeling spots in the world. Strict laws prohibiting spear fishing and the gathering of shells and coral protect the delicate ecological balance of marine life in Bonaire's waters.

History

When discovered by Amerigo Vespucci, sailing for Spain in 1499, Bonaire was the home of the Arawak Indians. Vespucci named the island after the Arawak word *boynare,* which means "low country." The Spaniards sent some of the natives to Spain and others to Hispaniola to work the copper mines; as a result, within 20 years no Arawak Indians were left on Bonaire. Several caves around the island, particularly those at Boca Onima, bear Indian inscriptions that have never been deciphered.

In 1816 control passed to the Dutch, who realized that the abundant sunshine and scant rainfall created ideal conditions for the manufacture of salt through evaporation. It was the Netherlanders who first brought slaves to work the saltpans at the southern end of the island, an endeavor that thrived until abolition curtailed the labor supply and caused production to cease. The area, already agreeable to flamingos, became even more attractive, and the colorful, exotic birds moved into the deserted saltpans to build thousands of nests.

The Cargill Company has revived the practice using an updated version of the old methods. Thanks to a sanctuary set aside from a portion of the old saltpans, the flamingos continue to exist in harmony with people. Bonaire's other industry—in addition to its main staple of tourism—is an oil storage terminal.

An autonomous special municipality of the Kingdom of the Netherlands, Bonaire is administered by an island council and has its own representative to the Crown. Though Dutch is the official language, the majority of islanders prefer the colloquial tongue of Papiamentu. Spanish and English also are widely spoken.

Shopping

Shopping is not Bonaire's main attraction; even so, the island has many good buys. Most of the shops in Kralendijk are on Kaya Grandi, J.A. Abraham Boulevard and Kaya Simon Bolivar. Such stores as Littmans, Atlantis and Island Fashions & Gifts offer a wide selection of jewelry, watches, clothing and gifts. Shopping opportunities also are available at Les Galeries, a mall in downtown Kralendijk.

The Divi Flamingo Beach Resort & Casino and Plaza Resort Bonaire have shops that offer fashions, jewelry and perfumes. Sand Dollar Plaza near the hotels on the island's north end features shops and an Internet cafe. The Harbourside Mall in Kralendijk has several shops and restaurants. Store hours are Mon.-Sat. 9-noon and 2-6; some stores remain open during lunch when cruise ships are in port. Banking hours are Mon.-Fri. 8-3:30.

Food and Drink

Most of the best restaurants can be found in Kralendijk or in area hotels. Menus vary from fresh seafood and steaks to Chinese, Tex-Mex, Indonesian and Continental cuisine. Waterfront restaurants specialize in lobster, fresh fish, shrimp and, best of all, wonderful views of the sea, sailboats and sunsets. A number of restaurants serve such local specialties as goat stew, iguana, gumbo and a stuffed cheese known as *keshi yena*. Beer, wine and rum drinks complement meals. There is no lack of fresh drinking water since it is distilled from the sea.

Sports and Amusements

Most visitors come to Bonaire for outdoor recreation: Water sports, including scuba diving, snorkeling, kayaking, kiteboarding and windsurfing, head the list of popular activities, along with bird-watching and mountain biking. The island is home to thousands of tropical birds, including parrots, parakeets, pelicans, pearly-eyed thrashers, mangrove cuckoos and hummingbirds. The flamingo colonies are particularly colorful March through May, when the deep-pink parents raise their gray hatchlings. To photograph or observe these shy birds, approach them slowly and quietly. If you come upon any nest areas, do not disturb them. The best bird-watching places are at Pekelmeer in the southern part of the island and Goto Meer Lake in the northwest (the actual flamingo sanctuary is off-limits to visitors).

Diving is popular in Bonaire; the island and its reef are said to be among the top five dive destinations in the world. Of the more than 80 diving locations around the island, more than half are accessible from the shore. The best spots for diving are off the leeward side of the island. Klein Bonaire, an offshore uninhabited island, is an excellent location for underwater exploring. You can make arrangements for snorkeling, scuba diving, kayaking, sailing or deep-sea fishing for marlin, tuna or bonito at several hotels or at the various commercial establishments on the island. Guided snorkeling programs also are available.

Although diving is what Bonaire is primarily known for, the island also offers opportunities for windsurfing, kiteboarding, sea and mangrove kayaking, hiking, mountain biking, landsailing and horseback riding, all of which provide alternative methods of exploring the island's natural beauty. The Riding Academy Club at Kunuku Warahama features a beach trail where riders can swim with their horses; phone (599) 560-7949.

Nightlife in Bonaire is mainly centered at the island's hotels, many of which offer theme dinners and live entertainment. Free slide shows are presented weekly at several establishments; more information is available in *The Bonaire*

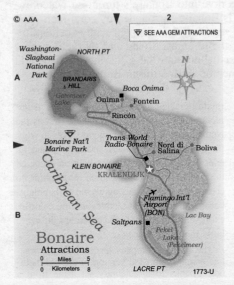

© AAA   1   ▼   2

▽ SEE AAA GEM ATTRACTIONS

Washington-
Slagbaai
National
Park

NORTH PT

A

BRANDARIS
HILL

Boca Onima

Gotomeer
Lake

Onima   Fontein

Rincón

Bonaire Nat'l
Marine Park

Trans World
Radio-Bonaire

Nord di
Salina   Boliva

KLEIN BONAIRE

KRALENDIJK

Caribbean Sea

Flamingo Int'l
Airport
(BON)

Lac Bay

B   Saltpans

Pekel
Lake
(Pekelmeer)

Bonaire

Attractions

0   Miles   5

0   Kilometers   8

LACRE PT

1773-U

Reporter, a free bi-monthly newspaper available at most hotels. Dancing and live music venues include Karel's Beach Bar and City Café in Kralendijk.

Sightseeing

Guided walking tours of Bonaire's outback, or "kunuku," are available at Rooi Lamoenchi Kunuku, a 138-acre (56-hectare) site highlighting the island's cultural history, flora and fauna. Rooi Lamoenchi, or Lime River, features a restored plantation house, aloe fields, a 1908 dam and marked trails showing such plant varieties as cactus, divi-divi and mesquite. For tour reservations, phone (599) 717-8489 or (599) 540-9800.

Bonaire Tours & Vacations features bus tours to destinations across the island, including Washington-Slagbaai National Park, which covers nearly one-fifth of the island; phone (599) 717-8778. Soldachi Tours offers bus and walking tours of Rincon, Bonaire's oldest village, departing on Monday mornings, market days (the first Saturday of the month) and by request; phone (599) 717-6435 or (599) 790-5657.

Full- or half-day sailing excursions and cocktail cruises are the perfect way to experience Bonaire's charms and climate; information about charters is available at the Harbour Village, Bonaire Nautico and Plaza marinas.

Transportation

Flights are available to Kralendijk's Flamingo Airport via Curaçao on InselAir from Miami. Continental Airlines offers non-stop service from Houston on weekends and Delta offers regular service from Atlanta. Dutch Antilles Express, the island airline, provides daily service between Aruba, Bonaire, Curaçao, Dominican Republic and St. Maarten, while Divi Divi provides daily flights between Curacao and Bonaire. There is no regular ferry service between Bonaire and Aruba or Curaçao, but the island is a port of call for cruise ships.

Fast Facts

POPULATION: 14,203.

AREA: 290 sq km (112 sq mi.).

CAPITAL: Kralendijk.

HIGHEST POINT: 238 m (784 ft.), Mount Brandaris.

LOWEST POINT: Sea level, Caribbean Sea.

TIME ZONE(S): Atlantic Standard.

LANGUAGE: Dutch, Spanish, English and Papiamentu.

GOVERNMENT: Autonomous special municipality of the Kingdom of the Netherlands.

UNIT OF CURRENCY: U.S. dollar.

ELECTRICITY: 127/220 volts, 50 cycles AC; voltage varies with location.

MINIMUM AGE FOR DRIVERS: 21-25, depending on the rental car agency. U.S. license valid; drive on right.

MINIMUM AGE FOR GAMBLING: 21.

SEAT BELT/CHILD RESTRAINT LAWS: Seat belts and child restraints are required.

HELMETS FOR MOTORCYCLISTS: Required.

HOLIDAYS: Jan. 1; Carnival Rest Day (Jan. or Feb.); Good Friday; Easter; Easter Monday; Queen's Birthday and Rincón Day, Apr. 30; Labor Day, May 1; Ascension Day, May (6th Thurs. after Easter); Bonaire Day, Sept. 6; Christmas, Dec. 25; Boxing Day, Dec. 26.

TAXES: A per-day room tax of $6.50 per person and a 10-15 percent service charge are added to most hotel and restaurant bills. A 8 percent sales tax (NAOB) is assessed on most goods and services. The airport departure tax and security fee is $35 U.S. per person over age 2; interisland tax is $9, $4.50 ages 2 to 12 and over 60. A per-day tax of $3.50 is added to rental car bills.

IMMIGRATION REQUIREMENTS: Passport and a return or onward ticket are required. No visa needed for stays up to 2 weeks. The U.S. Dept. of Homeland Security requires all U.S. citizens returning from the Caribbean to present a valid passport.

PHONING THE ISLANDS: To call Bonaire from the U.S. or Canada, dial 011 + 599 + 7-digit local number.

FURTHER INFORMATION FOR VISITORS:

Tourism Corporation Bonaire
80 Broad Street, Suite 3202
New York, NY 10004
(212) 956-5912
(800) 266-2473

Tourism Corporation Bonaire, Kralendijk
Kaya Grandi 2
Kralendijk, Bonaire
(599) 717-8322

You can tour Bonaire in a day on the island's excellent roads. Several car rental agencies serve the island. Double-cab pickup trucks are ideal for shore diving and tours across Bonaire's desert interior. Taxi rates are fixed, and you should check them before taking a cab.

Points of Interest

See map page 90.

KRALENDIJK (B-1) pop. 2,000

Kralendijk (crawl-en-dike) is the capital of Bonaire. The tropics and the Netherlands meet in this pink and orange town, whose name means "coral dike." North of town along the coast is Boca Onima, a grotto inscribed with Indian drawings. At the northern end of the island is Bonaire's inland lake, Goto Meer, home to great numbers of flamingos. The best time to view these colorful birds is early morning. The chief breeding ground is south at Pekelmeer *(see attraction listing).*

Bonaire Government Tourist Office: Kaya Grandi 2, Kralendijk, Bonaire, Netherlands Antilles. **Phone:** (599) 717-8322.

BONAIRE NATIONAL MARINE PARK extends around the coast and coral reefs of Bonaire and Klein Bonaire. This unique environment can be explored by scuba diving, snorkeling and kayaking. The park protects the waters around the island from the high-water mark to a depth of 200 feet (60 m); its restrictions and regulations preserve and allow best use of the island's coastline. Obtain a diving guide at dive operations or in local bookstores for a complete list of park guidelines. Guide service is available. **Cost:** Nature fee tag (good for the calendar year) $25 (diving); $10 (swimming and other watersports). **Phone:** (599) 717-8444.

DONKEY SANCTUARY-PARADISE SAFARI PARK is off Kaya Randolph Statius van Eps, following signs. These pack animals were brought to Bonaire in the 17th century to work the saltpans, and hundreds of their descendants roamed wild, falling prey to disease and car accidents. The sanctuary cares for sick and orphaned donkeys and provides a home for healthy donkeys.

Visitors are encouraged to bring fruit and bread snacks to hand-feed the residents. The park also contains an iguana and tortoise garden, watchtower and pond area with pink flamingos. **Time:** Allow 30 minutes minimum. **Hours:** Daily 10-5. Last admission 1 hour before closing. **Cost:** $6; $3 (ages 0-12). **Phone:** (599) 560-7607.

PEKELMEER SANCTUARY is on the s.w. end of the island. This vast stretch of salt flats is the chief breeding ground for flamingos. As seawater evaporates, the beds turn various shades of pink, matching these birds that choose to nest near towering stacks of salt crystals. The flamingos skillfully construct nests of mud in which they hatch their young during March and April; the birds must be watched from a distance.

Three 30-foot obelisks used as navigational aids by the salt ships of the 1800s still stand, and primitive stone huts of the slaves who once worked the saltpans have been restored. The majority of salt produced in Bonaire today is used in water softeners. **Hours:** Daily dawn-dusk. **Cost:** Free.

TRANS WORLD RADIO-BONAIRE is n. of Kralendijk at Blvd. G.N. Debrot 64. Once reputed to be the most powerful privately-owned transmitter in the Western Hemisphere, the Christian station now reaches all of the Caribbean and northern South America. TWR broadcasts on 800 AM with programming in Spanish, Portuguese, English, Baniua and Maxuci. The local broadcast on 89.5 FM is carried in English, Dutch, Spanish and Papiamentu. **Tours:** Guided tours are available. **Phone:** (599) 717-8800.

WASHINGTON-SLAGBAAI NATIONAL PARK covers the northwest end of the island. The 13,500-acre (5,463-hectare) wildlife sanctuary—a tropical desert landscape of scrub plains, salt flats, beaches and caves—protects many bird and lizard species unique to Bonaire. Two rugged driving trails lead through the former Washington and Slagbaai plantations, which exported goats, cattle, aloe extract, charcoal, salt and divi-divi pods (used in leather tanning).

A hiking trail leads to the top of Mount Brandaris, and other options include the Kasikunda climbing trail and Lagadishi walking trail. Free maps are available at the park entrance. A visitor center features exhibits about the park's flora and fauna, plantation history, geology and archeology. Mountain biking, kayaking, swimming, snorkeling and scuba diving are popular activities; several companies on the island offer transportation and guided tours. Allow at least 5 hours for the 22-mile (35-km) driving tour, 3 hours for the 15-mile (24-km) tour. Vehicles should have high ground clearance and a spare tire; motorcycles are not allowed. During rain, the dirt roads may become impassable (four-wheel drive vehicles are recommended). Food is available on weekends. **Hours:** Daily 8-5. Last admission is at 2:45. Closed Jan. 1 and Christmas. **Cost:** Land access only $15; free (ages 0-11). Water access $25 (per scuba diver); $10 (per non-scuba diver). All admissions good for one calendar year. **Phone:** (599) 788 9015 or (599) 717-8444.

GAMBLING ESTABLISHMENTS

• **Divi Flamingo Beach Resort & Casino** is at J.A. Abraham Blvd. 40. **Hours:** Mon.-Sat. 8 p.m.-2 a.m. **Phone:** (599) 717-8285.

Rum Point, Grand Cayman / © SuperStock / age fotostock

Cayman Islands

S urrounded by sapphire waters and coral reefs, the Cayman Islands is an outdoor-lover's paradise. Neither a sleepy, secluded destination nor a luxury resort area, the Cayman Islands is the best of both worlds. Its reputation as one of the top diving spots in the Caribbean coupled with its proximity to Florida—the islands are about 480 miles (772 km) due south of Miami—also account for its increasing popularity.

Of the three islands—Grand Cayman, Cayman Brac and Little Cayman—Grand Cayman, 22 miles (35 km) long and 8 miles (13 km) wide, is the largest and the best equipped to handle tourism. Most of the islands' inhabitants live on Grand Cayman near the capital city of George Town.

History

The Cayman Islands were sighted in 1503 by Christopher Columbus while on his fourth and last voyage to the New World. It was Columbus who named them *Las Tortugas* for the large number of turtles in the waters. The present name comes from *caymanas,* a derivation of the Carib Indian name for the crocodile.

Although the islands were ceded to the British by the Treaty of Madrid in 1670, there was no serious attempt to settle them until the early 18th century, when a group from Jamaica moved in; they were recalled 3 years later over problems in protecting them from Spanish pirates. The earliest settlers, however, were believed to be from Oliver Cromwell's army, shipwrecked sailors and refugees fleeing religious persecution in Britain.

With the passing of the days of sail, the Cayman Islands lapsed into isolation until the 1950s, when air travel was introduced. Flights now serve all three islands, making them a readily accessible vacation spot.

Despite independence movements among its neighbors, the Cayman Islands is content with

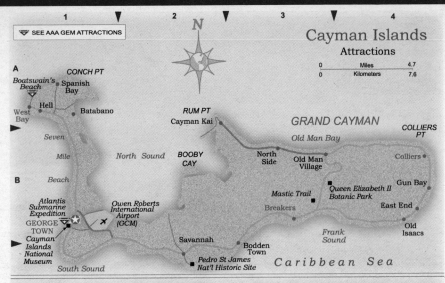

Cayman Islands
Attractions

	Miles	
0		4.7
0	Kilometers	7.6

CONCH PT

Boatswain's Beach

Spanish Bay

West Bay

Hell

Batabano

Seven

Mile

Beach

North Sound

RUM PT
Cayman Kai

BOOBY CAY

North Side

Old Man Bay

GRAND CAYMAN

COLLIERS PT

Colliers

Old Man Village

Gun Bay

Queen Elizabeth II Botanic Park

East End

Mastic Trail

Breakers

Old Isaacs

Atlantis Submarine Expedition

GEORGE TOWN

Cayman Islands National Museum

Owen Roberts International Airport (GCM)

Savannah

Bodden Town

Frank Sound

Pedro St James Nat'l Historic Site

South Sound

Caribbean Sea

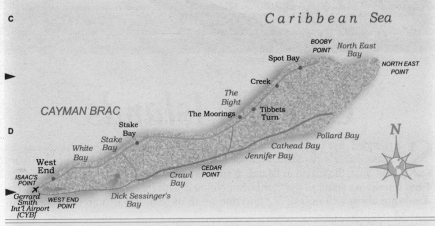

Caribbean Sea

BOOBY POINT

North East Bay

Spot Bay

NORTH EAST POINT

Creek

The Bight

CAYMAN BRAC

The Moorings

Tibbets Turn

Stake Bay

Pollard Bay

White Bay

Stake Bay

Cathead Bay

Jennifer Bay

West End

Crawl Bay

CEDAR POINT

ISAAC'S POINT

Gerrard Smith Int'l Airport (CYB)

WEST END POINT

Dick Sessinger's Bay

SNIPE POINT

EAST POINT

LITTLE CAYMAN

Mary's Bay

SANDY POINT

Bloody Bay

Wearis Bay

Spot Bay

Tarpon Lake

Edward Bodden Airfield (LYB)

The Bight

WEST END POINT

South Town

Caribbean Sea

1781-U

its status as a United Kingdom Overseas Territory. Formerly governed by Jamaica, Cayman is now administered by a governor appointed by the queen.

The governor is president of the Legislative Assembly and chairman of the Cabinet. Electoral districts in the Cayman Islands are George Town, West Bay, Bodden Town, North Side, East End, Cayman Brac and Little Cayman. Every 4 years elections are held to select 15 representatives from these districts, based on each area's population. These representatives form the Legislative Assembly, which is responsible for enacting laws.

The Cabinet consists of five elected ministers, while three members are appointed by the governor—the chief secretary, attorney general and financial secretary. Council ministers are responsible for the administration of the country, advising the governor on policy issues and instituting programs.

Political and economic stability—and tax neutrality—has helped make the Cayman Islands one of the largest financial centers in the world. Laws passed by the Legislative Assembly in the 1960s paved the way for international banking, investments, trusts, insurance, corporate registries and the Cayman Islands Stock Exchange (CSX). The country has no income, corporation, capital gains, estate or gift taxes.

Though the biggest moneymakers are financial services and tourism, some Caymanians still depend upon the sea and soil for their livelihood. Relatively flat with no rivers, the Cayman Islands is covered by the tropical vegetation of mangroves, mangoes and palms. Trade is conducted mainly with Jamaica, the United States and Costa Rica.

Grand Cayman has one of the highest standards of living in the Caribbean. Visitors can explore the island without fear of being approached by street and beach vendors or beggars; the law prohibits such activity.

Shopping

Free-port shopping is plentiful on Cardinal Avenue in George Town. Cameras, perfumes, watches, linens, china and British woolens are sold at reduced prices. Kirk Freeport Plaza contains La Parfumerie, Kirk Freeport, Swatch and the Waterford/Wedgwood Shop. Treasure Cove, affiliated with Kirk Freeport, is on the opposite side of the street and consists of Fossil, Kirk Leather, Cartier and La Parfumerie II.

Island Plaza, between the shops on Harbour Drive, surrounds an open-air courtyard with a snack area. The mall contains Tropical Traders, with an array of island souvenirs, and jewelry stores Grand Switzerland Diamonds Direct, Landmark Jewellers and Island Jewellers.

The English Shoppe, at the intersection of Cardinal Avenue and Harbour Drive, has jewelry and souvenirs among its merchandise. Caymania Freeport, located on Shedden Road, has a vast selection of perfumes and some jewelry. Easily recognized by its flying flags and attractive blue and white buildings, Elizabethan Square is situated on Shedden Road. This complex contains an American Express office and boutiques that offer children's clothing, leather goods, jewelry, sportswear and gift items. Caymania Jewelers is on Edward Street. Bayshore Mall is opposite the cruise ship terminal on South Church Street at Goring Avenue.

The Seven Mile Beach area has several shopping plazas with a wide assortment of goods. These plazas, all on West Bay Road, include Coconut Place, The Falls Shopping Centre, Galleria Plaza, Queen's Court, Seven Mile Shops, West Shore Centre and The Marquee.

Island products make meaningful souvenirs: coral or conch-shell jewelry and sculpture, hammocks, and woven baskets. Antique gold and silver coins and coin jewelry are of high quality and good value in the Cayman Islands. Many shops in Grand Cayman and Cayman Brac offer local arts and crafts. For handicrafts with a unique touch, try Pure Art Gallery & Gifts on South Church Street or the Craft Market on Harbour Drive. The products of the local artistic community can be seen at several galleries, including the National Gallery in Harbour Place, Kennedy Gallery Cayman Fine Art in West Shore and Morgan's Gallery in Galleria Plaza.

Shopping hours are generally Mon.-Sat. 9-5; some hotel shops are open on Sunday. Banking hours are Mon.-Thurs. 9-4, Fri. 9-4:30. Cayman Islands Dollars are available in denominations of $1, $5, $10, $25, $50 and $100.

Food and Drink

Although 90 percent of the islands' food is imported from Florida, noteworthy local dishes include turtle steak, conch, lobster and chowders. Locally grown vegetables and fruit—bananas, plantains, cassava and breadfruit—complement any meal.

Caymanians also enjoy their deep-fried or baked johnny cake, a doughy unseasoned concoction that resembles a heavy dough ball, and patties, pastry stuffed with beef, chicken or vegetables. "Bread Kind" refers to local vegetables such as yams, cassava, breadfruit and potatoes. Pepperpot is a hearty soup that contains *callaloo*, a leafy, spinach-like vegetable, and potatoes seasoned with hot peppers and spices.

Ackee and saltfish, a dish adopted from Jamaica, is another local favorite. In addition to native fare, there are also restaurants devoted to Chinese, Italian, German, Continental and Thai cuisine. Most dining establishments are in George Town, along Seven Mile Beach or in the hotels.

The National Trust for the Cayman Islands offers a cooking class the second Wednesday of each month October through May with a focus on such traditional Caymanian dishes as stewed conch, cassava cake and fried fish and fritters; phone (345) 749-1121.

Desalination provides adequate drinking water, and water is safe in restaurants and hotels. Pasteurized milk is imported from the United States.

Sports and Amusements

Vacationers come to the Cayman Islands to escape the pressures of the outside world; fishing and scuba diving are two means to this end. Rich catches of dolphin, blue marlin, wahoo and yellowfin tuna reward fishing enthusiasts. Little Cayman has bottom fishing outside the reef, bone fishing and fly fishing close to shore and tarpon fishing in a landlocked lake. Half- and full-day deep-sea charters are available. The Cayman Islands International Fishing Tournament takes place in May. For entry information write to the Cayman Islands Angling Club, P.O. Box 30280 SMB, Grand Cayman, Cayman Islands KY1-1202; phone (345) 945-3131.

Due to favorable currents and the proximity of deep open water to the shore, Northwest Point, Rum Point, Southwest Point, South Coast Drop Off and 12-Mile Bank are prime fishing destinations in Grand Cayman. Charter Boat Headquarters, (345) 945-4340, and Bayside Watersports, (345) 949-3200, serve as centralized booking agencies for charter boats in Grand Cayman; trips can be arranged for deep-sea, bottom, reef, bone and tarpon fishing. Marinas that are available to visiting yachtsmen include Cayman Islands Yacht Club and Harbour House Marina, both in the North Sound, and Morgan's Harbour Marina in West Bay.

Grand Cayman's trade winds coupled with water temperatures that average in the 80s provide excellent opportunities for windsurfing. Morritt's Tortuga Club & Resort at East End boasts good winds and calm waters inside the reef area. Winds blow 15-25 knots (17-29 mph) in the winter and 10-20 knots (12-23 mph) in the summer; lessons and rentals are available from Tortuga Divers/Red Sail Sports at the resort. A windsurfing regatta is held at the Tortuga Club every January. With constant breezes blowing 6-12 knots (7-14 mph), Grand Cayman is a prime place to learn how to windsurf.

Parasailing is available on Grand Cayman; inquire at Red Sail Sports (located within most hotels) for information on equipment rentals; phone (877) 506-6368. A few operators offer water skiing. Sunfish, Hobie Cat and Jet Ski rentals are available at many hotels. Sailing regattas are scheduled by the local sailing club throughout the year, generally in conjunction with public holidays.

Landlubber activities range from cave exploring to sunbathing. Most of the caves that can be explored are on Cayman Brac. The only caves accessible on Grand Cayman are the Pirate's Caves in Bodden Town.

Bird-watching opportunities abound on all three islands. The Grand Cayman and Cayman Brac parrots are found only in these islands, which also are home to more than 180 other resident and migratory species.

Seven Mile Beach, where 90 percent of the resorts and water sports operations are found, lures swimmers and sun worshipers to the west coast of Grand Cayman. One of the longest unbroken white sand beaches in the Caribbean, Seven Mile Beach is actually about 5.5 miles (9 km) long. The beach received its name from the fact that it is 7 miles (11 km) from the northwest to the southwest point of Grand Cayman.

Colliers Point on the east end of the island also has a lovely beach. Old Man Bay and Cayman Kai, on the north coast of Grand Cayman, are secluded beaches with golden sands that are occasionally punctuated by exquisite beach houses. Smith Cove, on the south coast off South Church Street, is known for swimming and snorkeling rather than for a beach. Picnic tables are available, and shaded areas provide respite from the sun.

Rum Point, on the north central tip of the island, is a park area that overlooks the North Sound. Visitors can relax on the beach, swim or snorkel in the shallow waters and rest in hammocks shaded by casuarina trees, also known as Australian pines. Red Sail Sports operates a full-service water sports and dive facility; activities include diving, jet skiing, snorkeling, sailing, windsurfing and water skiing. A restaurant, snack bar, changing facilities, hammocks, picnic tables and showers also are available.

Hikers are attracted to the eastern tip of the island. Also popular with hikers is Cayman Brac, where a trek along the Bluff is rewarded with a view of the tropical wilderness where 150 species of resident and migratory birds can be spotted. A trail used primarily as a cow path leads to the caves that honeycomb the Bluff.

Many hotels on Grand Cayman and Cayman Brac are equipped with tennis courts. Temporary health club memberships are offered by World Gym, (345) 949-5132, off West Bay Road; The Fitness Connection, (345) 949-8485, just south of George Town on Glen Eden Road; and Powerhouse Gym at Kings Sports Centre on Crew Road, (345) 946-5464 or (345) 949-0555, which also features squash courts and a rock-climbing wall.

Two types of golf can be played at the Jack Nicklaus designed Britannia Golf Course—regulation play on a nine-hole course and a Caymanian version on an 18-hole course. The Ritz-Carlton at Seven Mile Beach has a challenging nine-hole course for the exclusive use of its guests; designed by Greg Norman, the course is situated along a scenic saltwater lagoon.

The Truman Bodden Sports Complex and Stadium in George Town features a variety of amateur and professional sporting events.

While water sports dominate the action in the Cayman Islands, most hotels offer some form of evening entertainment. Ports of Call, the bar at The Wharf Restaurant at the south end of Seven Mile Beach, is known for its spectacular ocean view. The Next Level, Obar and District 6 are popular discos/nightclubs.

The Cayman National Cultural Foundation presents a variety of events from October to June, and the Cayman Drama Society stages productions at the Prospect Playhouse on Shamrock Road year-round. Top-name entertainers perform at the Lion's Centre on Crewe Road in the Red Bay area. Movies are shown regularly at Hollywood Theatres in Camana Bay; phone (345) 640-3456.

Island festivities peak when the Cayman Islands honors its earliest settlers during Pirates Week in November. Celebrations include colorful costumes, parades, treasure hunts and a lively reenactment, when a group of Cayman residents costumed as rogues and wenches board a replica of a pirate ship and approach the harbor. The landing turns into a mock battle with those who ruled the sea lanes more than 200 years ago.

Other island events include Carnival Batabano, a festival with costume parades and street dances held during the first week of May. An open house and garden party at Government House and a parade are highlights of the Queen's Birthday celebration in mid-June.

Several publications provide information about local events, activities and points of interest. Two island newspapers, *The Caymanian Compass* and *Cayman Net News,* are published Monday through Friday. *Key to Cayman,* a complimentary magazine distributed at hotels, contains a wide assortment of visitor information. *Horizons,* a free magazine published bimonthly by Cayman Airways, can be found at retail establishments and other points throughout Grand Cayman. *What's Hot* is a monthly feature magazine filled with an up-to-date listing of activities; it is available free of charge at many stores.

Scuba Diving

Scuba diving is the Cayman Islands' claim to fame: It is said that these islands are the most popular diving destination in the world. The three islands that make up the Cayman Islands are actually the tips of three undersea mountains surrounded by vertical drop-offs that plunge thousands of fathoms to the bottom of the sea. The Cayman Trench drops to a depth of 25,216 feet.

The Cayman walls encircle the Cayman Islands. The drop-offs begin at 55-60 feet and provide spectacular underwater scenery. A barrier reef encircles Grand Cayman in the shallower depths preceding the walls. Visibility can range from 125 to 200 feet, and conditions for underwater photography are excellent. Surrounded by colorful corals and sponges, the wall at Bloody Bay on Little Cayman begins its drop-off at 18 feet, then plunges to a reported 6,000 feet.

Diving close to the shore often eliminates the need for boats. Sometimes only a mask, snorkel and fins are needed to explore shallow-water reefs. An even more intensive diving experience is available on live-aboard dive boats, which offer divers access to the best sites around the islands. A guided trip with a qualified dive master is recommended. Among the many reputable dive operators are Divetech, (345) 946-5658 or (888) 946-5656; Don Foster's Dive Cayman, (345) 945-5132; Ocean Frontiers, (345) 947-0000 or (800) 348-6096; Red Sail Sports, (345) 623-5965 or (877) 506-6368; and Sunset Divers, (345) 949-7111.

All divers must possess a certification card from one of the international diving schools before any island dive shop will rent scuba gear. Most dive operations offer beginning divers a short "resort course" that provides enough familiarity with the equipment to allow them to take supervised, shallow diving trips. Harming or collecting coral or other marine life is illegal, as is spear fishing. A recompression chamber at George Town Hospital is staffed daily 24 hours; for emergencies phone 911.

The Cayman Islands has numerous recorded shipwrecks but divers are only able to see about a dozen. With more than 240 known diving locations it is impossible to list each one, but following are some of the most popular dive sites surrounding Grand Cayman.

The waters off the north side of the island include Eagle Ray Pass, an area of narrow canyons inhabited by eagle rays, barracudas, tarpons and sometimes sharks. For experienced divers only, Grand Canyon consists of giant canyons up to 150 feet wide that were formed by collapsed reefs. Hepp's Pipeline, with depths ranging from 20 to 60 feet, has two mini-walls that provide a home for stingrays and tropical fish. Divers can feed and pet friendly stingrays in 12 feet of water at Stingray City, considered one of the world's best shallow dive sites.

The west side of Grand Cayman also contains several renowned underwater sites. Aquarium, a shallow dive considered ideal for beginners, has tame parrotfish and angelfish that provide excellent photographic opportunities. Experienced divers will want to visit Big Tunnels, where two tunnels lead downward through a reef to open up on the Cayman Wall; one tunnel can be entered at 80 feet, while the other can be entered at 160 feet. At Bonnie's Arch, extraordinary marine life and spectacular arch formations can be viewed. Trinity Caves, a wall dive with dramatic caves and arches, features such sea life as sponges, black coral, sea turtles and eagle rays.

East coast spots favored by divers include Grouper Grotto, situated just before the 6,000 foot drop-off at the Cayman Trench. The Maze is a series of caverns, tunnels and archways that twist through an elaborate coral formation extending 500 feet along the East End Wall. Three Sisters is composed of three massive pinnacles of coral named Agnes, Bertha and Claire; each measures about 70 feet in diameter.

The south side of Grand Cayman also has many underwater wonders. Among them are Japanese Gardens, a series of narrow passages containing beautiful elkhorn coral formations and tropical fish, and Red Bay Gardens, known for striking elkhorn and antler coral, colorful caves and wide areas of sand.

Devil's Grotto has numerous caverns and grottoes as well as a long tunnel that leads to a room. Eden Rock, a good spot for inexperienced divers, consists of a coral cliff inhabited by tropical fish. Parrot's Reef, only 30 yards off the park's dock, contains the wreck of the *Anna Marie* and teems with parrotfish that swim among coral heads and sponges. About 150 yards from the dock, Polly's Perch is a wall dive that starts at 70 feet.

Many shipwrecks lay in the waters off the islands, such as the *Balboa,* a Norwegian freighter that sank off the George Town shore in the 1932 hurricane. The *Cali* is a sunken cargo freighter near George Town harbor that houses such marine life as barracudas, parrotfish and lobsters.

Oro Verde, off the coast of Seven Mile Beach, is the wreckage of an old cargo vessel sunk purposely in 1980 for the enjoyment of underwater explorers. Off Cayman Brac in 1996, the Russian frigate *Capt. Keith Tibbetts* was sunk to form an artificial reef. The MV *Ridgefield,* which ran aground on the coral reef off Gun Bay, attracts divers and snorkelers. Other shipwrecks include the *Doc Polson* wreck, a barge off Grand Cayman's northwest corner, and the wreck of the *David Nicholson,* a vessel in 65 feet of water deliberately sunk offshore from the Sunset House Dive Resort.

Sightseeing

A driving tour of Grand Cayman runs south from George Town along the South Sound coastal road that merges with the Bodden Town Road. Lined with tall casuarina trees, the route travels through the historic outer districts, which were the heart of the island in the 17th and 18thf centuries. Once a thriving settlement, Prospect was destroyed by a hurricane in 1846, leaving only a monument erected on the site of an 18th-century fort that was built to protect against Spanish pirates.

About 3 miles (5 km) east of Prospect in Savannah, the Old Savannah Schoolhouse has been restored to reflect a typical 1950s Caymanian school; phone (345) 749-1121.

Two cannons guard the entrance to Bodden Town, the first capital of the Cayman Islands, where you can explore Gun Square, the Slave Wall and the Pirates' Caves. It is believed that pirates once hid in the caves, an extensive maze of tunnels that eventually connects with underwater caves. Across the street is a cemetery where pirates are supposedly buried. Queen Victoria's Monument, erected by residents to commemorate the queen, is in the center of Bodden Town. Also along the way is caymanite, a multicolored rock found only in these islands.

The road traveling east out of Bodden Town is bordered on the left by a bird sanctuary, where such species as heron, snowy egret and black-necked stilt can be viewed at dawn and dusk. About a mile (1.6 km) before East End are the Blowholes: As the incoming surf surges against the shore, water is forced through crevices in the coral rock, shooting more than 60 feet into the air to create a geyser effect.

Just northeast of the village of East End is Gun Bay, the scene of the "Wreck of the Ten Sails" in 1794. British sailors from the *Cordelia* tried to warn their merchant fleet after running aground; however, the other nine ships misinterpreted their warning and followed onto the reef. Islanders were recognized by King George III for saving all lives aboard. Folk stories claim that the islands were granted freedom from taxation as a reward. The two cannons in Bodden Town are from the wreck, and an anchor that protrudes from the water off East End's shore is believed to be from one of the ships. A monument and scenic overlook commemorating this maritime disaster was unveiled by Queen Elizabeth II in 1994. The coastal road continues through Old Man Bay Village and ends at Rum Point.

You also can drive to Boatswain's Beach on the rugged northwest coast. The forbidding "Hell" coral formations are near West Bay. The coral, which is more than 1.5 million years old, is colored by black algae and caymanite. Even though the coral limestone resembles charred ruins, folklore claims that the spot received its name in the 1930s when a visiting official from England fired at a bird near the formations, missed, and said "Oh, hell." Tourists have made the post office of this tiny town popular by getting their postcards and letters canceled with the stamp of "Hell, Grand Cayman."

Sightseeing tour buses depart from hotels on Seven Mile Beach and head to George Town. The 2-hour tours include stops at Hell and Boatswain's Beach, Tortuga Rum Company bakery and store, and a conch-shell house; the full-day tours also include stops at Cayman Kai and the Pirate's Caves. Cruises along Seven Mile Beach also are available. The National Trust conducts walking tours of George Town every Thursday at 9 a.m., visiting such historic sites as the Fort George site, the Legislative Assembly building and Elmslie Memorial Church; phone (345) 749-1123. A self-guiding walking tour booklet of the historical districts of West Bay and George Town can be purchased from the National Trust office at Dart Park, 558 S. Church St. in South Sound; phone (345) 749-1121.

Several boats offer afternoon and dinner cruises, and glass-bottom boat rides can be arranged at many resorts and water sports outlets. Picnicking, shelling, snorkeling and swimming are other popular activities.

A popular way to spend a day and to experience the Cayman Islands is to participate in a North Sound Beach lunch/snorkeling trip. The all-day boat excursion features a native-style lunch prepared by the captain; diving for a conch (except during off-season, May through October) to be used later as part of the meal; and three snorkeling stops, including Stingray City. These trips, available from more than 20 captains, can be booked through Bayside Watersports at Morgan's Harbour, (345) 949-3200; Charter Boat Headquarters on Birchtree Hill Road in West Bay, (345) 945-4340; and through Captain Marvin's, (345) 945-6975. Half-day excursions without lunch also are offered.

The smaller islands are less developed than Grand Cayman, but they provide a welcome change of pace and an opportunity to see the islands in a more natural state. The dramatic limestone cliffs of Cayman Brac, 89 miles (143 km) east of Grand Cayman, are a popular destination for hikers and bird-watchers. A 2-mile nature trail offers glimpses of frigate birds, red-footed boobies and the rare Cayman Brac parrot. The island also offers many opportunities for fishing, scuba diving and exploring, with many hidden caverns reputed to have once been the hideouts of pirates and their treasures.

Snorkeling, scuba diving and deep-sea fishing also are excellent on Little Cayman, 5 miles (8 km) northwest of Cayman Brac. The diving at Bloody Bay Wall has been described as spectacular. A haven for bird-watchers, the island is home to one of the largest breeding colonies of red-footed boobies in the Caribbean. Road signs advise: "Iguanas Have the Right of Way; Drive Slowly."

Transportation

Cayman Airways, the national flag carrier, provides daily direct flights from Miami to Grand Cayman's Owen Roberts International Airport, as well as regular service from Chicago, Tampa, Washington-Dulles and New York (JFK). American Airlines offers daily flights from Miami, US Airways has flights from Charlotte and Delta Air Lines provides daily service from Atlanta. Saturday flights are available on Continental Airlines from Newark.

Cayman Airways regularly flies between Grand Cayman and Kingston, Jamaica. Grand Cayman also is a leading port of call for cruise ships, serving an average of 13 vessels per week.

Interisland service to Cayman Brac's Gerrard Smith International Airport is provided by Cayman Airways. Island Air provides charter flights between the Sister Islands. Cayman

Airways Express provides day trips to Cayman Brac and Little Cayman leaving from Grand Cayman. Flights from Grand Cayman to Little Cayman take approximately 40 minutes. Service from Grand Cayman to Cayman Brac is 18 minutes by jet, and 45 minutes by propeller plane. There is no jet service to Little Cayman.

It is best to rent a car if your accommodations are not in the Seven Mile Beach area. Major and local car rental agencies serve the island. Hertz, (345) 949-2280 or (800) 654-3080, offers discounts to AAA members. Driving permits are issued upon presentation of a valid driver's license and cost $8. Speed limits are 40 mph on West Bay Road in the Seven Mile Beach area and 25 mph in George Town; in other parts of the island, speed limits range from 25 to 50 mph. Driving is on the left side of the road. A seat belt law is in effect.

Independent, privately-owned minibuses run between West Bay Road and George Town; buses stop at the side of the road by white circular bus stop signs. Roughly, buses run about every half-hour between 7 a.m. and 9 or 10 p.m.

Taxis, motor scooters and bicycles are available on both Grand Cayman and Cayman Brac. Taxis, often driven by islanders versed in local folklore and history, can be chartered for island tours. Jeeps are available on Little Cayman, where bicycling also is very popular. Taxis do not have meters, as rates are fixed by the government. Visitors must be at least 17 to rent a scooter, and a scooter permit is required. The permit, which can be purchased for $10, does not entitle you to drive a car; if you plan to do both, two permits are necessary. Use caution when renting scooters or bicycles; although the island is relatively flat, traffic can be heavy in George Town and on portions of West Bay Road.

Fast Facts

POPULATION: 53,172.

AREA: 259 sq km (100 sq mi.).

CAPITAL: George Town, Grand Cayman.

HIGHEST POINT: 43 m (141 ft.), The Bluff.

LOWEST POINT: Sea level, Caribbean Sea.

TIME ZONE(S): Eastern Standard.

LANGUAGE: English.

GOVERNMENT: British Overseas Territory.

UNIT OF CURRENCY: Caymanian dollar, divided into 100 cents. $1 U.S. = approx. .8 Cayman Islands dollar. U.S. currency is widely accepted.

ELECTRICITY: 110 volts, 60 cycles AC.

MINIMUM AGE FOR DRIVERS: 21-25, depending on the rental car agency. Local license ($8 U.S.) required; drive on left.

SEAT BELT/CHILD RESTRAINT LAWS: Seat belts are required for all passengers.

HELMETS FOR MOTORCYCLISTS: Required.

HOLIDAYS: Jan. 1; National Heroes' Day, Jan. (4th Mon.); Ash Wednesday; Good Friday; Easter Monday; Discovery Day, May (3rd Mon.); Queen's Birthday, June (2nd Mon.); Constitution Day, July (1st Mon.); Remembrance Day, Nov. (closest Mon. to Nov. 11); Christmas, Dec. 25; Boxing Day, Dec. 26. Cayman holidays falling on a weekend are legally observed the following Monday.

TAXES: A 10 percent room tax and 10-15 percent service charge are added to most hotel bills.

IMMIGRATION REQUIREMENTS: Passport and a return or onward ticket are required. No visa needed for stays up to 6 months. The U.S. Dept. of Homeland Security requires all U.S. citizens returning from the Caribbean to present a valid passport.

PHONING THE ISLANDS: To call the Cayman Islands from the U.S. or Canada, dial 1 + 345 + the 7-digit local number.

FURTHER INFORMATION FOR VISITORS:
Cayman Islands Department of Tourism, United States
Empire State Building
350 5th Ave.
Suite 1801
New York, NY 10118
(212) 889-9009

Cayman Islands Department of Tourism, George Town
Windward 3, West Bay Rd.
George Town, Grand Cayman KY1-1102
Cayman Islands
(345) 949-0623
(877) 422-9626

Points of Interest

See map page 94.

Cayman Brac

Cayman Brac (brac means "bluff" in Gaelic) is named for the limestone ridge running the length of the island, rising to a height of 140 feet (43 m). The 3,500 residents of this 14-square-mile (36 sq-km) island call themselves "Brackers."

The 180-acre (73-hectare) Brac Parrot Reserve is a protected breeding area of the native Cayman Brac parrot.

CAYMAN BRAC MUSEUM is at Stake Bay on Stake Bay Road. This small museum in a former government building displays artifacts pertaining to the island's seafaring history, cultural heritage and Brackers' past ways of life. **Hours:** Mon.-Fri. 9-noon and 1-4, Sat. 9-noon. **Cost:** Free. **Phone:** (345) 948-2622 or (345) 244-4446.

Grand Cayman

Covering about 76 square miles (197 sq km), Grand Cayman is the most developed of the island group. The majority of resorts and diving facilities are found along Seven Mile Beach, where portions of the movie "The Firm" were filmed.

GEORGE TOWN (B-1) pop. 20,626

Named for King George III of England, George Town is the capital of the Cayman Islands. It is a bustling city that serves as a center for shopping, banking, tourism and other businesses.

The post office on Cardinal Avenue is a busy meeting place where locals exchange news; the hundreds of boxes on the outside of the building reflect the fact that there is no home or office mail delivery in Grand Cayman. Just 2 miles (3.2 km) from the airport, George Town is the gateway to Seven Mile Beach, which stretches north to West Bay. The Royal Watler Cruise Terminal opened to passengers in 2006.

Distinctive Caymanian architecture, with its ornate hand-carved trim and zinc roofs, adds a gingerbread character that can be seen in Pantonville, where three original houses have been restored.

George Town's architectural landmarks include the Elmslie Memorial United Church, built by Captain Rayal Bodden, a skilled shipbuilder whose signature timber roof framing is a structural highlight; the Peace Memorial, which once served as a town hall; the Clock Tower, built in honor of King George V; and the George Town Public Library,

which has elaborate ceilings and houses an assortment of English novels.

A plaque on the corner of Fort Street and North Church Street commemorates the area where Fort George once stood. Just a small portion of the wall remains. The coral-rock fort, which guarded the harbor's entrance, was constructed in the late 1700s to defend the island against the Spanish.

When the legislature is not in session, the sergeant-at-arms is frequently available to provide tours through the Legislative Assembly building on Fort Street. Visitors are permitted to observe the legislature in session from the upstairs gallery; appropriate dress is required.

Cayman Islands Department of Tourism: Regatta Office Park, Windward 3, West Bay Rd., George Town, Grand Cayman, Cayman Islands. **Phone:** (345) 949-0623 or (877) 422-9626.

Tourist information is available at all cruise ship terminals and at Owen Roberts International Airport.

Self-guiding tours: A pamphlet describing a self-guiding historic walking tour of central George Town is available at The National Trust office at Dart Park in South Sound and at the gift shop in the Cayman Islands National Museum.

ATLANTIS SUBMARINE EXPEDITION departs from 30 S. Church St. at the George Town harbor. This 65-foot-long, 48-passenger underwater vessel cruises along the Cayman Wall at a maximum depth of 100 feet (30 m), offering excellent views of coral formations and sea creatures.

Other tours include a shallow water experience aboard the semi-submarine *Seaworld Explorer*. Passengers sit 5 feet below the surface in an air-conditioned glass observatory to view the *Cali* shipwreck, coral reefs and abundant marine life. The 1-hour tour includes a diver fish-feeding show at Cheeseburger Reef. *Atlantis* night trips also are available. **Time:** Allow 1 hour, 30 minutes minimum. **Hours:** Morning and afternoon trips depart Mon.-Sat. A 10-minute ferry ride transports passengers between the dock and the submarine for the 45-minute tour. **Cost:** *Atlantis* fare $99; $59 (ages 4-12). *Seaworld Explorer* fare $49; $24 (ages 2-12). Children under 36 inches tall are not permitted on *Atlantis*. Reservations are required. **Phone:** (345) 949-7700.

BOATSWAIN'S BEACH is 8 mi. (13 km) n. via Seven Mile Beach Rd. to 786 North West Point Rd. in West Bay. Green sea turtles once were a mainstay of the Cayman economy, but their numbers in the wild dwindled toward extinction. This 23-acre adventure marine park is home to some 7,300 turtles representing five of the seven known species, including the endangered Ridley turtle.

The park also includes an interactive turtle touch tank area—the site is an actual working farm, both educational and entertaining, and turtles are available for guests to hold for photographs. In addition, visitors have an opportunity to swim and snorkel with fish and other marine life in the 1.3-million-gallon saltwater lagoon, or enjoy a refreshing dip in the Breaker's freshwater tidal lagoon. The predator tank offers close-up views of sharks and eels. Feedings are conducted throughout the day.

Visitors also can wander through a free-flight bird aviary or stroll down a historic Caymanian street with craft vendors and local food. A nature trail allows guests to experience the rich history of Caymanian life in a fun and safe environment, while providing opportunities to observe and interact with native flora and fauna. The park's research and educational facility focuses on the conservation of green sea turtles.

Visitors should be aware that sea turtle products purchased in the Cayman Islands cannot be taken home; U.S. customs officials will confiscate any items brought into the country. **Time:** Allow 2 hours minimum. **Hours:** Mon.-Sat. 8-5; last admission 30 minutes before closing. Lagoons Mon.-Sat. 8-2. Closed Good Friday and Christmas. **Cost:** $45; $25 (ages 4-12). Turtle farm tour only $30; $20 (ages 4-12). **Phone:** (345) 949-3894. ⓘ

CAYMAN ISLANDS NATIONAL MUSEUM is on Harbour Dr. at the waterfront. Cultural and historic exhibits are displayed in the 19th-century Old Courts Building. Highlights of the 4,000-item collection include natural history specimens, coins, rare documents and a traditional catboat. A children's gallery offers interactive exhibits. **Time:** Allow 30 minutes minimum. **Hours:** Mon.-Fri. 9-5, Sat. 10-2. Last admission 30 minutes before closing. Closed Good Friday, Christmas and first Mon. of the month. **Cost:** $5; $2.50 (ages 7-17 and 65+). **Phone:** (345) 949-8368. ⓘ

NORTH SIDE (B-3) pop. 1,079

Once the most remote area of Grand Cayman, the North Side district preserves an ancient forest and a footpath used by islanders for two centuries. On the northern coast is Rum Point, named for the cargo barrels that floated ashore after a shipwreck. Nearby is Stingray City, where divers can swim with hundreds of docile stingrays.

MASTIC TRAIL is s. of Old Man Bay, paralleling Frank Sound Rd. A 200-year-old footpath winds through this 2 million-year-old woodland reserve in the dense interior of the island. The National Trust offers 3-hour hiking tours of the 2-mile (3-km) trail where visitors can view native flora and fauna, including the Grand Cayman parrot and other unique bird species. An ancient yellow mastic tree stands at the midpoint of the trail, which traverses rocks, swamps, high woods and farmland.

Comfortable hiking shoes, drinking water, insect repellent and sunscreen are advised. Hiking tours are not recommended for senior citizens or children under 6. **Hours:** Guided hikes depart Tues.-Fri. at 8:30 a.m. (8 a.m. during the summer) and are limited to 9 persons. **Cost:** $24. Reservations are required. **Phone:** (345) 749-1121.

QUEEN ELIZABETH II BOTANIC PARK is off Frank Sound Rd. at 367 Botanic Rd. The 65-acre (26-hectare) park is dedicated to preserving the island's native plants and animals. Along the Woodland Trail, visitors can view labeled trees and plants representing 55 percent of the island's native flora. The Floral Colour Garden displays flowering plants from around the world. The Heritage Garden features a traditional wooden cottage, sand garden, fruit trees and crops. Palm and orchid gardens also are offered. Aquatic birds including the West Indian whistling duck reside at the lake, and blue iguanas roam the park.

Time: Allow 1 hour, 30 minutes minimum. **Hours:** Daily 9-6:30, Apr.-Sept.; 9-5:30, rest of year. Last admission 1 hour before closing. Closed Good Friday and Christmas. **Cost:** $10; free (ages 0-12). **Phone:** (345) 947-9462.

RECREATIONAL ACTIVITIES

Kayaking

- **Cayman Kayaks** departs from Safehaven Drive adjacent to North Sound Club. Guided 1.5 to 2-hour eco-adventure tours explore the mangroves, bird-nesting areas and coral reefs of the Cayman coastline. **Hours:** Tours are offered daily. **Phone:** (345) 926-4467 or (345) 746-3249.

SAVANNAH (C-2)

Savannah was settled in the 18th century by William Eden, who built a stone meeting house and residence named Pedro St. James. The "Pedro Castle" was the only building on the island to survive the hurricane of 1785. The house stood through two centuries of Caribbean storms; it was destroyed by fire in 1967. Pedro St. James has been restored as a national historic site.

PEDRO ST. JAMES NATIONAL HISTORIC SITE is off the South Sound coastal road following signs. The 8-acre (3-hectare) site contains a restoration of one of the island's oldest structures, a 1780 plantation house built by English settler William Eden. Revered as the "Birthplace of Democracy in the Cayman Islands," the house was the 1831 meeting site of residents who established government by representation. The three-story manor features period Caribbean furniture. A multimedia theater offers a 20-minute film about the "Pedro Castle."

Time: Allow 1 hour minimum. **Hours:** Daily 9-5. Films are shown on the hour from 10-4. Closed Good Friday and Christmas. **Cost:** $10; free (ages 0-12). **Phone:** (345) 947-3329.

Little Cayman

Ten miles (16 km) long and two miles (3 km) at its widest point, Little Cayman is the smallest and flattest of the island group. Game fishing, scuba diving and bird-watching attract thousands of visitors, but Little Cayman boasts fewer than 170 permanent residents. Most live near Blossom Village on the island's southernmost tip, where turtle fisherman first settled in the 1600s. The 334-acre Booby Pond Nature Reserve is home to 20,000 red-footed boobies, considered the largest breeding colony in the Caribbean. More than 200 other species of resident and migratory birds may be sighted on the island.

The National Trust House in Blossom Village offers information about Little Cayman's natural and historic sites.

Willemstad / © Henry Beeker / age fotostock

Curaçao

C uraçao lies 35 miles (61 km) off the coast of Venezuela. Small hills throughout the island offer a variety of scenery, but vegetation is sparse because of
slight rainfall. Willemstad, the capital, is a bright mosaic of narrow streets
lined with 18th-century Dutch-Caribbean houses topped with red tile roofs. Each
house is painted a pastel shade, which lends a storybook Dutch charm.

History

Curaçao shares much of its history with the
other Dutch islands. Discovered in 1499 by
Alonso de Ojeda, a lieutenant of Christopher
Columbus, the island was named for the tribe of
Caiquetios, an Arawak-speaking group which
lived here. A more popular legend claims that
Curaçao's name was derived from the Spanish
word *curación,* meaning "cure," when several
malarial sailors miraculously recovered from
scurvy after an extended visit to the island. It is
pronounced *cure-a-sow.*

The initial Spanish colonizers were displaced
early in the 17th century by Dutch settlers, who
made the islands flourishing centers of trade.
One of the first governors was Peter Stuyvesant, later governor of another island colony:
New   Amsterdam   on   Manhattan   Island.

Sephardic Jews fleeing the Spanish Inquisition
sought refuge on the island among the tolerant
Dutch and would make up half of the white
population by the 18th century. The Netherlands Antilles changed hands several times in
the early 19th century, but by 1815 the Dutch
were here to stay. In October 2010, the Netherlands Antilles was dissolved and Curaçao became an autonomous country within the
Kingdom of the Netherlands.

Except for a brisk slave trade that ended in
1863, the 19th century was less than prosperous
for Curaçao and its sister islands. Then the discovery in 1914 of oil in Venezuela made their
position astride the trade routes important.
Curaçao's economic mainstays today are banking, tourism and refinery facilities. It also has
several large local industries, including Senior

& Co. Curaçao Liqueur; a battery manufacturer; the largest nonmilitary drydock in the hemisphere; and cigarette, soap and paint factories.

One of the languages spoken on Curaçao is Papiamentu, a blend of Portuguese, Dutch, Spanish and English with African dialects. In this colorful language, *Dushi Kòrsou* means "Beloved Curaçao."

Shopping

Because of the low import duty on most goods, Curaçao is an excellent shopping center; prices are often lower than in the products' countries of origin. Duty free shops sell perfume, electronics and jewelry. Local handicrafts also make popular souvenirs.

Curaçao's foremost shopping promenades are the Gomezplein and the Heerenstraat in Willemstad. Designed for pedestrians, they are closed to traffic and their roadbeds have been raised to sidewalk level and covered with European bricks.

Smart offerings combined with the excitement of a Middle Eastern bazaar are found on the estraat and Madurostraat in Punda, the oldest section of Willemstad. Mini-malls on the outskirts of Willemstad worth visiting include Salinja Galleries and Bloempot Shopping Center.

Lining the Waaigat Canal is the "Floating Market," a string of schooners from Venezuela, Colombia and other West Indian islands. Alive with color and buzzing with voices haggling over the prices of fresh fish, tropical fruit, vegetables and handicrafts, this seafaring market is a photographer's delight.

Shops in Curaçao are generally open Mon.-Sat. 8:30-noon and 2-6 and when ships are in port. Banking hours are Mon.-Fri. 8-3:30. The bank at the airport is open Mon.-Sat. 8-8 and Sun. 9-4 for currency exchange.

Food and Drink

Like those on the other Dutch islands, restaurants on Curaçao set an international table, often combining Dutch, Spanish, American, Creole, Italian, Indonesian, French and Chinese cuisine on one board. Other specialties include *erwten soep*, a thick pea soup cooked with pork, ham and sausage, and *funchi*, a cornmeal-like dish served steamed or fried.

Local specialties include *keshi yena*, a baked Edam cheese stuffed with chicken or fish; *sopito*, a fish soup flavored with coconut; and *sopi juana*, otherwise known as iguana soup. Another local specialty is *rijsttafel* ("rice table"). This Dutch-Indonesian banquet consists of rice served with up to 20 side dishes. Local tap water distilled from the sea is so pure that minerals must be added for taste. Curaçao produces Curaçao Liqueur made from the *laraha*, a local variety of orange.

Sports and Amusements

With 38 miles (61 km) of shoreline and 12.5 miles (20 km) of protected coral reef, recreation on Curaçao centers on the sea. The clear water draws swimmers, snorkelers, skiers, anglers, sailors, windsurfers and scuba divers, and the

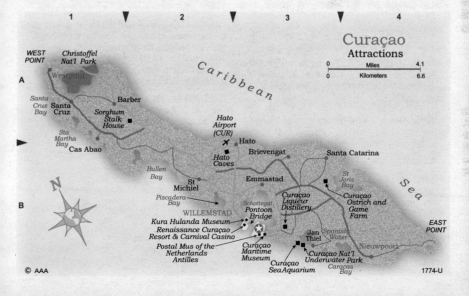

secluded coves and beaches at Blauw Bay, Cas Abao, Santa Barbara, Santa Cruz, Westpunt, Jan Thiel, Knip Bay and the Curaçao Sea Aquarium are favorites for lounging. Game fishing for marlin, wahoo, kingfish and dolphin is best July through October. Fishing boats can be chartered for a half-day or a full day, and sailboats and speedboats can be rented by the hour. The Curaçao Yacht Club is in Spanish Water east of Willemstad. Windsurfing and scuba diving lessons also are available; check with your hotel for information.

Caracas Bay Island, on a scenic peninsula south of Willemstad, offers a wide variety of land and water activities, including bicycling, diving, windsurfing, jet skiing and snorkeling. Operators include Windsurfing Curacao, (599) 9-738-0883 or (599) 9-524-4974 and WannaBike, (599) 9-527-3720.

With 68 diverse dive sites, Curaçao is known for its scuba diving opportunities. In 1983, 12.5 miles (20 km) of Curaçao's waters were designated a national marine park. The park features coral beds, steep walls and several shipwrecks. The Total Submersion Curaçao Dive Festival, beginning in early July, is a weeklong event featuring guided dives, seminars, workshops, live entertainment and other activities.

Sports include tennis and basketball, played at the Curaçao Sport Club; golf at the Curaçao Golf and Squash Club and the Blue Bay Golf Resort, an 18-hole course; and baseball and soccer at S.D.K. Stadium, Antoin Maduro Stadium and smaller fields. Horseback riding and bowling also are available. Schooner races between Curaçao and Bonaire are occasionally held.

Written in the native Papiamentu, Curaçao's *tumba* furnishes a lively and interesting musical comment on island politics and gossip. Spirited visitors can enjoy gambling at island casinos or joining in the songs and dances at discos,

Fast Facts

POPULATION: 130,000.

AREA: 471 sq km (182 sq mi.).

CAPITAL: Willemstad.

HIGHEST POINT: 372 m (1,221 ft.), Mount Christoffel.

LOWEST POINT: Sea level, Caribbean Sea.

TIME ZONE(S): Atlantic Standard.

LANGUAGE: Dutch, Papiamentu, Spanish and English.

GOVERNMENT: Autonomous country within the Kingdom of the Netherlands.

UNIT OF CURRENCY: Guilder (also called the florin), divided into 100 cents. $1 U.S. = 1.6 guilders. U.S. currency is widely accepted.

ELECTRICITY: 110-130 volts, 50 cycles AC.

MINIMUM AGE FOR DRIVERS: 21-25, depending on the rental car agency. U.S. license valid; drive on right.

MINIMUM AGE FOR GAMBLING: 18.

SEAT BELT/CHILD RESTRAINT LAWS: Seat belts are required for all passengers. Child restraints required for under age 4; children under 12 must ride in the back seat.

HELMETS FOR MOTORCYCLISTS: Required.

HOLIDAYS: Jan. 1; Carnival Monday, Feb. (Mon. before Ash Wednesday); Good Friday; Easter Monday; Queen's Birthday, Apr. 30; Labour Day, May 1; Ascension Day, May (6th Thurs. after Easter); Flag Day, July 2; Antillean Day, Oct. 21; Christmas, Dec. 25; Boxing Day, Dec. 26.

TAXES: A 7 percent room tax and 12 percent service charge are added to most hotel bills. Most restaurants include a 10 percent service charge. Departure tax $22 U.S.; interisland tax $10.

IMMIGRATION REQUIREMENTS: A passport and a return or onward ticket are required. No visa needed for stays of up to 2 weeks. The U.S. Dept. of Homeland Security requires all U.S. citizens returning from the Caribbean to present a valid passport.

PHONING THE ISLANDS: To call Curaçao from the U.S. or Canada, dial 011 + 599 + 9 + the 7-digit local number.

FURTHER INFORMATION FOR VISITORS:

Curaçao Tourism Corp.
One Gateway Center, Suite 2600
Newark, NJ 07102
(973) 353-6200
(800) 328-7222

Curaçao Tourist Board
Pietermaai 19
Willemstad, Curaçao
(599) 9-434-8200

beachfront clubs and during the island's many festivals. *Island Tours* or *K-PASA*, available at hotel desks, lists weekly events and entertainment.

Sightseeing

You can tour the island by car in about a day. The western tour along the main road from Piscadera Bay includes most of the island's beaches and plantation houses. Christoffel National Park, at the northwestern end of the island, encompasses a wildlife preserve, gardens, caves, plantation ruins and Mount Christoffel, the highest point on the island.

A shorter trip to Bullen Bay might include a stop at the fishing village of St. Michael. Interesting destinations east of Willemstad are Caracas Bay, site of Fort Beekenburg, and Spanish Water, home of the Curaçao Yacht Club. A popular 45-minute drive northwest from Willemstad heads through Curaçao's *cunucu*, or countryside, punctuated by wind-bent divi-divi trees, cactuses and other drought-resistant plants.

Not far from Willemstad is Parke Tropical Zoo, a botanical garden and zoo open daily 9:30-5:30. Glass-bottom boat tours depart daily from Cabana Beach, Hyatt Regency Resort and Curaçao Sea Aquarium.

North of Santa Barbara is Den Paradera, a historic botanical garden containing herbs and plants that have traditionally been used for the treatment of various ailments. A reconstructed settlement contains small huts with scenes depicting rural life. Tours are offered by appointment; phone (599) 9-767-5608.

Transportation

Two daily nonstop flights to Curaçao are available on American Airlines from Miami, with connections from all major U.S. gateways. Weekly Saturday service direct to Curaçao from Newark is available on Continental Airlines. Dutch Antilles Express and Inselair provide daily service between Aruba, Bonaire, St. Maarten and Curaçao. American Eagle provides connecting flights from San Juan. Hato Airport boasts one of the longest jet landing strips in the West Indies. Many of the major cruise lines visit Curaçao, docking at Willemstad.

There are taxi stands at the airport, major hotels and in Willemstad; check the fixed fares before you ride. Car rentals are available from major U.S. companies and several local firms; a U.S. driver's license is acceptable. Driving is on the right side of the road. Hourly buses connect Willemstad with the airport.

Points of Interest

See map page 105.

WILLEMSTAD (B-2) pop. 43,550

Often called "Little Amsterdam," Willemstad is the capital of Curaçao. Its architecture is a tropical adaptation of the traditional Dutch style. The pastel colors characterizing government buildings and private homes alike are a legacy from a governor-general who complained in 1817 that the tropical sun's glare on the white-painted buildings caused his blinding headaches. To ease his discomfort, he decreed that thereafter only other colors would be used.

Curaçao's trademark, Queen Emma Bridge spans Santa Anna Bay. Originally, pedestrians wearing shoes paid a toll of 2c to cross the swinging pontoon bridge; the barefooted walked free. The toll was eventually eliminated after the wealthy routinely discarded their shoes before crossing. Today the bridge links the city's two sections—Punda and Otrobanda—along with the four-lane Queen Juliana Bridge, which arcs nearly 200 feet (60 m) above the bay. Otrobanda means, literally, "the other side." West of the Queen Emma Bridge in Brionplein

Square is the Pedro Luis Brion Statue commemorating a local hero who served under Simón Bolívar and pursued the hostile British in 1805.

With its narrow streets and shopping promenade, Punda recalls old Holland. Architectural tours of the city include the classic colonial-style governor's mansion and Department of Finance building on Pietermaai, the Georgian-style Masonic Temple and the stately homes of the merchant princes in Scharloo. A collection of Dutch coins is displayed at the Numismatic Museum at the Centrale Bank van Curaçao en Sint Maarten at Simón Bolivar Plein 1; phone (599) 9-462-5913 or (599) 9-434-5500.

Northeast of Punda atop Ararrat Hill is the Franklin D. Roosevelt House, constructed by islanders in 1950 as a symbol of the friendship between the Netherlands and the United States during World War II. It now serves as the residence of the U.S. Consulate General.

Willemstad and Schottegat Harbor, the island's natural harbor, are designated as UNESCO's (United Nations Education, Scientific and Cultural Organization) World Heritage places.

Curaçao Tourism Development Bureau: Pietermaai 19, P.O. Box 3266, Willemstad, Curaçao, Netherlands Antilles. **Phone:** (599) 9-434-8200.

ATLANTIS SUBMARINE SEAWORLD EXPLORER departs from the Hilton hotel pier on Piscadera Bay. This semi-submarine travels just below the surface of the water, providing dramatic views of Curaçao's shipwrecks and coral reefs through large glass windows. **Hours:** Sightseeing trips depart daily at 10, based upon cruise ship demand. Buses provide transportation to the dive site. Closed holidays. **Cost:** Fare $39; $19 (36 inches tall-age 11). Children under 36 inches are not permitted. Reservations are required. **Phone:** (599) 9-461-0011 or (599) 9-690-6054.

BETH HAIM JEWISH CEMETERY is n.w. on Schottegatweg West. Consecrated in 1659, the burial ground was one of the first Hebrew cemeteries in the New World. Tombstones marking some 2,500 graves feature ornate sculptures and inscriptions in Portuguese, Spanish, Hebrew, Dutch, English and French. **Tours:** Guided tours are available. **Hours:** Open Sun.-Fri. dawn-dusk. **Cost:** Donations.

CHRISTOFFEL NATIONAL PARK is 38 mi. (60 km) n. of Willemstad at the n.w. end of the island, entered at Landhuis Savonet. This 5,683-acre (2,300-hectare) wildlife preserve is the island's largest preserved area and encompasses three former plantations. Twenty miles (31 km) of driving trails offer glimpses of rare orchids, bromeliads, cacti, several bird species, iguanas, lizards and Curaçao's white-tailed deer. Several bat caves are adorned with Arawak petroglyphs. Well-marked hiking trails traverse the park and ascend Mount Christoffel, the highest point on the island. The Savonet Museum houses a whale exposition with skeletons found on the island's shores.

The 2-hour mountain hike from the visitor center should be planned for the cool morning hours. Safari, deer-spotting, bird-watching, mountain climbing, cave and guided walking tours are offered for an additional fee. Visitors should pack water, sunscreen and insect repellent. **Tours:** Guided tours are available. **Time:** Allow 2 hours minimum. **Hours:** Park open Mon.-Sat. and holidays 7:30-4, Sun. 6-3. Last admission 1 hour, 30 minutes before closing. Closed Christmas Eve, Christmas, day after Christmas and Dec. 31-Jan. 1. **Cost:** $10; $5 (ages 6-12). Deer-spotting tour $20; free (ages 0-6). Safari tour $30; $20 (ages 6-12). Reservations are required for all tours. **Phone:** (599) 9-864-0363. ▲ ⓘ ⊞

CURAÇAO LIQUEUR DISTILLERY is 3 mi. (5 km) e. at Schottegatweg Oost 129. Housed in the Chobolobo Mansion, the Senior & Co. Distillery produces genuine Curaçao Liqueur from the fruit of the laraha tree. The orange-flavored product, distilled 115 years in old copper stills, is offered for tastings and purchase. **Hours:** Self-guiding tours Mon.-Fri. 8-noon and 1-5, Sat.-Sun. when cruise ships are in port. **Cost:** Free. **Phone:** (599) 9-461-3526 or (599) 9-461-6946.

CURAÇAO MARITIME MUSEUM is at Van den Brandhofstraat 7 in Scharloo, across from the Floating Market. The island's maritime history is traced with such artifacts as antique ships models and maps. Special exhibits focus on the area's oil industry and such prominent area residents as American consul Leonard Smith, who brought electricity to the island. Videotape presentations detail the development of the harbor and offer a look at Curaçao's past role as one of the largest slave depots in the Caribbean.

Guided 2-hour tours of the harbor are offered aboard a ferry that also provides transportation to the museum from cruise ships. **Hours:** Museum open Tues.-Sat. 9-5. Harbor tours offered Wed. and Sat. at 2. **Cost:** Museum $6; $4.50 (ages 8-15). Harbor tour $15; $7.50 (ages 4-18); reservations required. **Phone:** (599) 9-465-2327. ⓘ

THE CURAÇAO MUSEUM is .5 mi. (.8 km) w. of the Queen Emma Bridge at Van Leeuwenhoekstraat and Donderstraat in Mundo Nobo. The 1853 military hospital building, a fine example of ornate Dutch architecture, houses historical exhibits, colonial antiques and an art gallery. The SnipGallery houses the cockpit of De Snip, the first KLM airliner to cross the Atlantic. On the grounds is a 47-bell carillon, a sculpture garden and a cultural children's village. **Hours:** Mon.-Fri. 8:30-4:30, Sat.-Sun. 10-4. Closed major holidays. **Cost:** $4; $2.50 (ages 0-12). **Phone:** (599) 9-462-3873.

CURAÇAO NATIONAL UNDERWATER PARK covers an area from the Curaçao Sea Aquarium to the s.e. tip of the island. Marked underwater trails and sunken ships can be explored by snorkelers and scuba divers. The park features 14 signed dive sites. **Cost:** Free. **Phone:** (599) 9-462-4242.

CURAÇAO OSTRICH & GAME FARM is 7 mi. (11 km) e. on Groot St. Joris. Visitors to this working farm can hold an egg or a day-old chick while they learn about the life cycle and lifestyle of this large, powerful, flightless bird. **Time:** Allow 2 hours, 30 minutes minimum. **Hours:** Daily 9-5. Tours depart on the hour. **Cost:** $15; $12 (ages 2-12). Ostrich ride $35. Reservations are required. **Phone:** (599) 9-747-2777. ⓘ

CURAÇAO SEA AQUARIUM is 4 mi. (6 km) e. on Martin Luther King Blvd. to Bapor Kibra. The facility displays more than 600 species of fish, crabs, lobsters, sea lions, dolphins, sharks, stingrays, sea turtles, anemones, colorful sponges and coral, all natives of the reefs surrounding Curaçao. A variety of diving, snorkeling and educational programs provide hands-on encounters with marine animals. The Seaquarium Beach is nearby.

Time: Allow 1 hour minimum. **Hours:** Daily 8-5. Last admission 1 hour before closing. Animal Encounter dives and snorkeling daily at 9, 11, 1 and 3. Sea Lion Training Experience and Kids Encounters daily at 8:30 and 1. **Cost:** Aquarium $18.50; $9.50 (ages 5-11). Animal Encounter $49 (snorkeling); $99 (scuba diving). Kids Encounter $45 (half-day); $100 (full-day). Dolphin Encounters $79-$300. Beach admission $3. Reservations are required for marine animal programs. **Phone:** (599) 9-461-6666. ⓘ

FORT AMSTERDAM is off Breedestraat in Punda, adjoining the waterfront. Built in 1769 to protect the island from invaders, the fort was once the living quarters of the directors of the West Indian Co. It now contains the official palace of the governor of the Netherlands Antilles, the Ministry and government offices.

The Fort Church Museum preserves the island's oldest Protestant church, completed in 1769. Lodged in the southwest wall is a cannonball fired by the British in 1804. A collection of artifacts from the Dutch Protestant congregation includes antique silver chalices, a mahogany and silver baptismal font, the original governor's bench and historic maps of the island. **Hours:** Museum open Mon.-Fri. 9:30-noon. **Cost:** Free. Church and museum $6; $3 (ages 6-14). **Phone:** (599) 9-461-1139.

HATO CAVES is .5 mi. (.8 km) n. of the Hato Airport on F. D. Rooseveltweg. Historical guided tours take visitors into more than 12 limestone chambers that were formed below sea level millions of years ago. A sloping trail leads past unusual formations, pools and a waterfall. Caquetio Indian carvings are visible on the outer walls. A colony of long-nose fruit bats lives inside the cave, and some 100 iguanas roam the surrounding park. **Time:** Allow 1 hour minimum. **Hours:** Tours depart daily on the hour 10-4. **Cost:** $8; $6 (ages 4-11). **Phone:** (599) 9-868-0379.

MIKVÉ ISRAEL-EMANUEL SYNAGOGUE is at Hanchi di Snoa 29 in Punda. Consecrated in 1732, the synagogue is the oldest active Jewish temple in continuous use in the Western Hemisphere. A thick layer of sand on the floor symbolizes the Israelites' wanderings in the desert before they reached the Promised Land. **Hours:** Mon.-Fri. 9-4:30. Services are held Fri. at 6:30 p.m., Sat. and Jewish holidays at 10 a.m. **Cost:** $6. **Phone:** (599) 9-461-1067.

Jewish Cultural Historical Museum is entered through the synagogue courtyard at Hanchi di Snoa 29. Dating from 1651, the collection includes Torah scrolls, Hanukkah lamps, antique personal and household belongings and a centuries-old ritual bath. **Hours:** Mon.-Fri. 9-4:30. Closed Jewish and public holidays. **Cost:** Synagogue and museum $10; free (ages 0-12). **Phone:** (599) 9-461-1633.

KAS DI PAL'I MAISHI MUSEUM is 8 mi. (13 km) w. of the airport at Dokterstuin 27 in Weg naar Westpunt. The Sorghum Stalk House, built in the late 19th century, is typical of the rural dwellings in which most of the island's Afro-Curaçaoan population lived until the 1950s. Walls are made of loam and branches, the floor of loam, cow dung and caustic lime; the roof is thatched with sorghum stalks. Period artifacts include furniture and cooking utensils. **Tours:** Guided tours are available. **Time:** Allow 30 minutes minimum. **Hours:** Tues.-Fri. 9-4, Sat.-Sun. 9-5. **Cost:** $2; 80c (ages 4-10). **Phone:** (599) 9-864-2742 or (599) 9-864-2497. ⓘ

KURÁ HULANDA MUSEUM is at Klipstraat 9 in Otrobanda. African culture and history is portrayed in reconstructed 19th-century buildings on the site of a former wharf and slave yard. Exhibits include a collection of original 19th- and 20th-century European prints and artifacts from ancient West African empires. The transatlantic slave trade is depicted through a full-size re-creation of the hold of a slave ship and a plantation worker's cabin. "The Living History," a play about the slave trade, is presented every Wednesday at 7:30. Audio tours are available in English and Dutch. **Hours:** Tues.-Sat. 10-5. Closed Christmas. **Cost:** $9; $6 (ages 0-11 and 65+); $7 (students with ID). **Phone:** (599) 9-434-7765.

POSTAL MUSEUM OF THE NETHERLANDS ANTILLES is at Kaya Toni Prince in Punda. The museum features a collection of stamps from the Netherlands Antilles and other countries as well as related artifacts, such as old post boxes and scales. Special exhibits of theme stamps from around the

world change quarterly. The museum is housed in Punda's oldest surviving building, which dates from 1693. **Time:** Allow 30 minutes minimum. **Hours:** Tues.-Fri. 10-4. **Cost:** $2; $1 (ages 6-15). **Phone:** (599) 9-465-8010.

WILLEMSTAD TROLLEY TRAIN TOUR departs from Fort Amsterdam near the Queen Emma Pontoon Bridge. This 1.5-hour narrated tour passes many historic Willemstad sights, including the Floating Market, Scharloo, Bolo di Bruid (the "Wedding Cake House"), Mikve Israel Synagogue, Pietermaai Cathedral, Queen Wilhelmina Park, Waterfort Arches and Fort Amsterdam. **Time:** Allow 2 hours minimum. **Hours:** Schedule varies, depending upon cruise ship demand. Closed major holidays. **Cost:** $25; $20 (children). Reservations are required. **Phone:** (599) 9-461-0011 or (599) 9-690-6054.

GAMBLING ESTABLISHMENTS

- **Breezes Curaçao Resort Spa & Casino** is at 8 Dr. Martin Luther King Blvd. **Hours:** Daily 10 a.m.-4 a.m. **Phone:** (599) 9-736-7888 or (877) 273-3937.

- **Curaçao Casino at Hilton Curaçao** is on John F. Kennedy Blvd. on Piscadera Bay. **Hours:** Daily 10 a.m.-3 a.m. **Phone:** (599) 9-462-5000.

- **Curaçao Howard Johnson Plaza Hotel & Casino** is at Brionplein z/n in Otrobanda. **Hours:** Daily 1 p.m.-4 a.m. **Phone:** (599) 9-462-7800.

- **Curaçao Marriott Beach Resort & Emerald Casino** is on John F. Kennedy Boulevard at Piscadera Bay. **Hours:** Daily 11 a.m.-3:30 a.m. **Phone:** (599) 9-736-8800 or (800) 223-6388.

- **Renaissance Curaçao Resort & Carnival Casino** is at Baden Powellweg 1. **Hours:** Daily 11 a.m.-2 a.m. **Phone:** (599) 9-435-5000.

- **Veneto Casino at The Holiday Beach Resort** is at Pater Euwensweg 31. **Hours:** Daily 11 a.m.-4 a.m. **Phone:** (599) 9-462-5400.

Roseau / © Terrence Klassen / age fotostock

Dominica

D eep tropical rain forests, mountains and isolation have preserved the wild beauty of Dominica (dom-in-EE-ka), reminding visitors of an earlier, less commercial Caribbean. What the island lacks in nightlife, duty-free shops and white sand beaches, it makes up for with the natural splendor of its volcanic mountain ranges swathed in the rich green of towering trees, exotic ferns and flowers. Fed by the ample rainfall in the island's interior, numerous rivers wind through Dominica's primordial forest, which is home to such endangered species as the imperial and red-necked parrots.

History

So named because Christopher Columbus discovered it on a Sunday, Dominica was a stronghold of the Carib Indians, who were the dominant indigenous group found on many of the Caribbean islands. Although the Carib population on many other islands was severely depleted, and in some instances wiped out, the Caribs on Dominica frustrated the efforts of the French and British to successfully colonize the island. In the 18th century the island became the scene of fierce battles between the French and the English for outright possession. The British prevailed in 1783 and remained in control until 1978, when Dominica became independent. Some 3,000 Carib Indians still live on the island.

Since gaining independence from Great Britain, Dominica has carefully nurtured its pristine resources. Rather than depending on high-rise resorts and glittering casinos for its economy, Dominica relies primarily on the export of produce. The island government also is encouraging tourism and light industry.

Shopping

Handcraft centers in the Old Market Plaza in Roseau and in the Carib Territory offer handmade items, including finely woven baskets and Dominica's unique grass mats; also in the marketplace is the Dominican Museum. There are several boutiques in Roseau and at some hotels throughout the island. Other buys include soaps made locally from fresh coconut oil, other toiletries, leather goods, cigars and cigarettes and cassette recordings of the traditional *jing-ping* folk music.

Duty-free shopping is available throughout Roseau. Pirates, on Long Lane, has a wide selection of cheeses and French wines. In the Fort Young Hotel on Victoria Street are Whitchurch Duty Free Shop and Jewellers International. Baroon International is at the Prevo Cinemall on Kennedy Avenue. Duty Free Emporium is on Dame Eugenia Boulevard. Limers Jeans Shop on Cork Street offers brand-name clothing and shoes. Among the duty-free items available at various shops are cosmetics, crystal ware, handicrafts, articles made from pearls, perfume, cigars, liquor, watches and cameras.

Banking hours are Mon.-Thurs. 8-2, Fri. 8-4. Business hours are Mon.-Fri. 8-4, Sat. 8-1.

Food and Drink

Traditional dishes include freshwater crayfish; *tee-tee-ree accras,* fried fish cakes; *callaloo* soup, made from dasheen leaves and coconut cream; and *crab backs,* black and red land crabs stuffed with spicy crab meat. Nectar, syrups, jams and sherbets are available as well as locally made rums and ginger beer. Sea moss is a seaweed shake made with milk, sugar and cinnamon spices.

Crapaud, the local delicacy known as "mountain chicken," has disappeared from restaurant tables. The national dish is not fowl but frog—*leptodactylus fallax*, one of the world's largest frogs. Found only on Dominica and Montserrat, this rare species may be on the brink of extinction.

Sports and Amusements

Dominica's many streams and rivers shaded by giant ferns attract both swimmers and canoeists. A few northern beaches offer swimming; Coconut Beach is the most appealing. About 25 miles (40 km) north of Roseau, it has silver volcanic sand and a mountain backdrop. Other options are Mero Beach, about 12 miles (19 km) north of Roseau, and Purple Turtle Beach Club in Portsmouth, which has restaurant facilities on the beach. Fishing on the island is good; Dive Dominica, (767) 448-2188, provides boats and equipment for deep-sea fishing. Spectators can enjoy cricket, soccer, netball, volleyball, tennis and basketball in season.

Scuba diving also is available and must be arranged through a local dive operator. Establishments include ALDive, (767) 440-3483 or (767) 275-3483; Anchorage Dive Center, (767) 448-2638 or (888) 790-5264; Cabrits Dive Centre, (767) 445-3010 or U.S. (347) 329-4256; Dive Dominica, (767) 448-2188; East Carib Dive, (767) 449-6575; Fort Young Hotel, (767) 448-5000; Irie Safari, (767) 440-5085 or (767) 275-7001; Nature Island Dive, (767) 449-8181; and SeaSide Dive at Sunset Bay Club, (767) 446-6522.

The island has several spectacular dive sites, including L'Abyme, or the Abyss. Champagne, outside Pointe Michel, has an incredible reef where divers swim through bubbling waters created by volcanic activity on the sea bed. On the north side of Cabrits National Park, the marine park at Douglas Bay contains a snorkeling trail. There are wrecks at nearby Toucarie and Capuchin.

Sea kayaking and mountain biking are two popular ways to discover Dominica. Nature Island Dive Center, on Soufrière Bay, offers hourly, half-day and full-day trips. In Portsmouth near

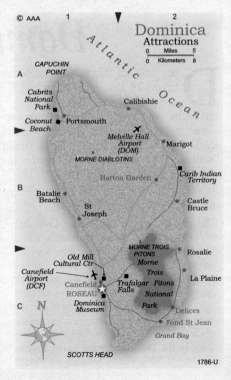

© AAA

Dominica
Attractions

0 Miles 5
0 Kilometers 8

1786-U

Coconut Bay kayaking, windsurfing, kneeboarding and snorkeling are just some of the water activities offered by Cabrits Dive Centre.

Dominica starts the new year with Mas Domnik (Carnival), in February and March. The arts are celebrated April through June during the Dominica Festival of Arts. Sports enthusiasts can partake in Dive Fest in early July. The World Creole Music Festival is held in late October. National Day and Independence festivities are held during the month of October and continue through early November.

Sightseeing

Dominica is famous for the exotic flora that grows wild around its river pools and rain forests. Morne Trois Pitons National Park, covering 17,000 acres (6,880 hectares) on the southern end of the island, is the first natural heritage site in the Eastern Caribbean to be listed as a UNESCO World Heritage Site. Its volcanic wonders include mud pots, hot springs, sulphur vents and the Boiling Lake.

Dominica's Carib Indians distinguished themselves from other Caribbean tribes by fighting so fiercely that in 1748 both the English and the French abandoned the island. Consequently, Carib descendants are among the island's inhabitants, and in 1903 the British set aside 3,700 acres (1,497 hectares) of land to establish the Carib Territory on the east coast, where the Indians can practice their own culture and continue the craft of basket making. Trips to the territory can be arranged through your hotel or a local tour operator.

Whale-watching in Dominica is a popular activity with sightings of sperm, pilot and melon-headed whales as well as bottlenose, Risso and spinner dolphins. Excursions can be arranged through Anchorage Dive Center and Dive Dominica.

Roseau, Dominica's capital, occupies a picturesque setting on the banks of the Roseau River. Saturday mornings come alive with the bustle of the colorful market, whose cinnamon scent fills the air. The grass rugs that are in demand throughout the Caribbean are woven at Tropicrafts, opposite the Woodbridge Bay port.

A site pass is required for visiting selected tourist sites. Site pass $5 per site, weekly pass

Fast Facts

POPULATION: 69, 625.

AREA: 749 sq km (289 sq mi.).

CAPITAL: Roseau.

HIGHEST POINT: 1,447 m (4,747 ft.), Morne Diablotins.

LOWEST POINT: Sea level, Caribbean Sea.

TIME ZONE(S): Atlantic Standard.

LANGUAGE: English, but a French patois (Creole) is widely spoken.

GOVERNMENT: Independent. Member of the British Commonwealth of Nations.

UNIT OF CURRENCY: Eastern Caribbean (E.C.) dollar. $1 U.S. = 2.7 E.C. dollars.

ELECTRICITY: 220-240 volts, 50 cycles AC.

MINIMUM AGE FOR DRIVERS: 25 to drive a rental car; maximum age 65. Local license ($12 U.S.) required, valid for 30 days; drive on left.

SEAT BELT/CHILD RESTRAINT LAWS: Seat belts are required for all passengers.

HELMETS FOR MOTORCYCLISTS: Required.

HOLIDAYS: Jan. 1; Merchants' Day, Jan. 2; Carnival Monday and Tuesday, Feb. 19-20; Good Friday; Easter Monday; Labour Day, May 5; Whit Monday, May or June (8th Mon. after Easter); August Monday, Aug. (1st Mon.); Independence Day, Nov. 3; Community Day of Service, Nov. 4; Christmas, Dec. 25; Boxing Day, Dec. 26.

TAXES: A 10 percent VAT (value-added tax) is charged at all hotels. A 15 percent VAT (value-added tax) and a 10 percent service charge are added to restaurant bills. Departure tax $22 U.S.

IMMIGRATION REQUIREMENTS: A passport and a return or onward ticket are required. The U.S. Dept. of Homeland Security requires all U.S. citizens returning from the Caribbean to present a valid passport.

PHONING THE ISLANDS: To call Dominica from the U.S. or Canada, dial 1 + 767 + the 7-digit local number.

FURTHER INFORMATION FOR VISITORS:

Discover Dominica Authority
1st Floor Financial Center
Roseau, Dominica
(767) 448-2045
(866) 522-4057

$12. Passes can be obtained from tour operators and at attractions.

Transportation

International access into Dominica is facilitated via airports of neighboring Caribbean islands with connections to the island's two small airports: Canefield Airport, 5 minutes from Roseau, and Melville Hall Airport, on the northeastern tip of the island about an hour from Roseau. Airlines servicing Dominica include American Eagle, Liat and Winair. Major gateway connections to Dominica are from Antigua, Barbados, Guadeloupe, Martinique, Puerto Rico, St. Lucia and St. Maarten.

Car rentals are available at the airports; taxis meet all flights. City and island sightseeing tours with a driver-guide are available. L'Express des Iles operates high-speed ferries that connect Dominica with Guadeloupe, Martinique and St. Lucia. A departure tax is charged; phone (767) 448-2181 for schedules and fares. Cruise ships call at the docks in Roseau and Woodbridge Bay.

Points of Interest

See map page 112.

PORTSMOUTH (A-1)

Portsmouth sits on the northwest coast at Prince Rupert Bay, where Christopher Columbus moored on his fourth voyage to the New World in 1504. It is said that the swampy terrain around the Indian River prevented Portsmouth from becoming the island's capital.

CABRITS NATIONAL PARK is 1.5 mi. n. of town between Douglas and Prince Rupert's bays. Perched on a forested, twin-peaked peninsula, Cabrits National Park contains the ruins of a military garrison used by British and French forces 1770-1854. Its centerpiece is Fort Shirley, which is surrounded by more than 50 major structures, including gun batteries, powder magazines, storehouses and barracks that housed up to 600 men.

Trails connecting the sites meander through thick tropical growth. Light clothing and comfortable shoes are recommended. **Time:** Allow 4 hours minimum. **Hours:** Daily 9-5. **Cost:** $5. **Phone:** (767) 448-2401, ext. 3277 or 3429 or (767) 266-3817.

ROSEAU (C-1) pop. 16,535

The island's capital, Roseau (Rōzō) was named by the French for the reeds that once grew at the mouth of the river. The busy wharf area north of town caters to large freighters as well as local wooden sloops. High stone walls surround the 19th-century Our Lady of Fair Haven Cathedral and the convent.

Within walking distance are the Government House and the 44-acre (18-hectare) Roseau Botanical Garden. Some heavy damage caused by Hurricane David in 1979 can still be seen.

Discover Dominica Authority: Valley Road, P.O. Box 293, Roseau, Commonwealth of Dominica, W.I. **Phone:** (767) 448-2045 or (866) 522-4057.

DOMINICA MUSEUM is on the bayfront across from the cruise ship port. Housed in the old post office, the museum offers a comprehensive introduction to Dominica and its history. The formation of the island is illustrated with volcanic ash and rocks. Other exhibits depict the first Amerindian settlement, colonial plantation life and Dominica's agricultural and political changes. **Hours:** Mon.-Fri. and major holidays 9-4, Sat. 9-noon. **Cost:** $3. **Phone:** (767) 448-8923.

MORNE TROIS PITONS NATIONAL PARK stretches across the southern half of the island. The visitor center is 14 mi. (23 km) n.e. on Canefield-Castle Bruce Rd. to Pond Casse-Rosalie Rd. Covering 17,000 acres (6,880 hectares), Morne Trois Pitons is the first natural heritage site in the Eastern Caribbean and only the second in the insular Caribbean to be listed as a UNESCO World Heritage Site.

The park centers around the volcanic "mountain of three peaks" with its steaming vents, fumaroles and hot springs. Boiling Lake is said to be the largest of its kind in the world. Bubbling mud pots and sulphur vents mark the barren Valley of Desolation.

The twin torrents at Trafalgar Falls in Roseau Valley offer an ideal setting for a picnic within reach of wild orchids and tropical rain forests. At 300 feet (91 m), Middleham Falls is the highest waterfall in the park. Emerald Pool, a short walk from the visitor center, is a popular destination for cruise ship excursions. A qualified guide must be hired for the 8-mile (13-km) hike to Boiling Lake. Hikers should wear sturdy shoes and raingear and protect cameras from moisture. **Hours:** Daily dawn-dusk. **Cost:** $5. **Phone:** (767) 448-2045 or (866) 522-4057. ⛺

OLD MILL CULTURAL CENTRE is .5 mi. (.8 km) s. of Canefield Airport. The boiling house of what was one of the largest sugar mills on the island is now the venue for training residents in the performing and visual arts, including steel band music, dance and painting. An art gallery presents changing exhibitions. **Hours:** Mon.-Fri. 8-4. Closed major holidays. **Cost:** Free. **Phone:** (767) 449-1804 or (767) 449 3075.

Columbus Castle Museum, Santo Domingo / © Angelo Cavalli / age fotostock

Dominican Republic

When Christopher Columbus came ashore in 1492, he wrote in his diary, "This is the most beautiful land that human eyes have seen." He would leave members of his family behind to colonize the island and would return to it after venturing throughout the Caribbean. In his will, he asked to be buried in Santo Domingo. It's no wonder the Dominican Republic calls itself "the land Columbus loved best."

A relaxed atmosphere is not just a promise here; it is a way of life. Old World charm lingers here in language, food, customs and thought. The emphasis placed on music, dance, history and art as well as the usual island activities of sunbathing and swimming make the Dominican Republic a popular Caribbean vacation destination.

Santo Domingo, capital and cultural center, preserves the Dominican Republic's rich history with its many churches, palaces, museums, forts, monuments and restored homes. Puerto Plata in the north, Punta Cana in the east and La Romana in the southeast are other major resort centers. Pico Duarte, at 10,128 feet (3,087 m), is the highest point in the Caribbean; just 50 miles (80 km) southwest, Lake Enriquillo, at 144 feet (44 m) below sea level, is the lowest point in addition to being the largest salt lake in the Caribbean.

History

The Dominican Republic occupies the eastern two-thirds of the island the Indians called *Quisqueya* and Christopher Columbus named Hispaniola; Haiti occupies the western third. When Columbus ran the *Santa María* aground on the northern coast on Dec. 25, 1492, he used the ship's salvaged lumber to build Fuerte de Navidad, or Fort Christmas. About a year later, Columbus returned to discover the settlement destroyed and 38 of his men massacred.

Columbus then founded La Isabela farther east in the present-day Dominican Republic.

Dominican Republic and Haiti
Attractions

A   B   C   D

Atlantic   Ocean

N

HAITI

St Nicholas
Voute i Englise
Port-de-Paix
Jean Rabel
151
Baie de Henne
Gonaives
St Marc
Montrouis
L'Arcahaie
150
100
Limbé
Le Borgne
Cap-Haïtien
Fort Liberté
Milot
Trou du Nord
St Raphael
Ennery
100
Artibonite
Rivière
Desarmes
Mirebalais
Cabaret
109
300
Pétion-ville
PORT-AU-PRINCE
Port-au-Prince Int'l Airport (PAP)
Petit-Goâve
Grand Goâve
Léogâne
Kenscoff
Jimani
Belle Anse
Marigot
Jacmel
209
209
Bainet
200
208
Mouillage Fouquet
St Louis du Sud
Aquin
Miragoâne
Anse-à-Veau
Pte à Raquette
Anse à Galet
ÎLE DE LA GONÂVE
Golfe de la Gonâve
ÎLE À VACHE
200
Les Cayes
Port Salut
Coteaux
213
Port-à-Piment
Anse-d'Hainault
Dame Marie
Jérémie
220
214
MASSIF DE LA HOTTE
Pointe-à-Gravois

DOMINICAN REPUBLIC

Monte Cristi
Copey
Dajabón
121
Mao
Villa Bisonó
San J de las Matas
Restauración
Bánica
Elías Piña
Hinche
300
Lascahobas
Las Matas
El Cercado
San Juan
Constanza
Jarabacoa
Jánico
Moca
La Vega
Bonao
Rincón
Cotui
Castillo
San Francisco de Macorís
SANTIAGO
Mt Isabela de Torres Cable Car
Puerto Plata
Amber Museum
Ocean World
Gregorio Luperón Int'l Airport (POP)
Outback Safari Tours
Luperón
Río Yaque del Norte
Sosúa
Cabarete
Cabrera
Río San Juan
Nagua
Baoba
Villa Riva
Rivas
Las Terrenas
Las Galeras
Samaná
Bahía de Samaná
Bahía Escocesa
Sánchez
Sabana De La Mar
Hato Mayor
El Seibo
Pintado
Higüey
Río Chavón
Uvero Alto
Bávaro
Punta Cana
San Rafael de Yuma
Boca de Yuma
Bayahibe
ISLA SAONA
Altos de Chavón
La Romana
ISLA CATALINA
San Pedro de Macorís
Boca Chica
Wildlife Refuge
Cave of the Three Eyes
La Isabela Int'l Airport (JBQ)
Los Llanos
Bayaguana
El Llano
Dolio
Amber World Museum
Parthenon Nat'l Museum
Larimar Museum
Fortress Ozama
Bellagua Park
Nat'l Zoological Park
SANTO DOMINGO
Columbus Lighthouse Monument (Faro A Colon) & Colonial Santo Domingo
Colonial Zone (Zona Colonial)
San Cristóbal
Palenque
Baní
Las Calderas
Azua
San José de Ocoa
Río Yaque del Sur
Barahona
Neiba
Lago Enriquillo
Étang Saumâtre
ISLA BEATA
ISLA CATALINA
Oviedo
Pedernales
Enriquillo
102
Duvergé

Caribbean   Sea

Bahía

Llano

O

L

A

N

P

S

I

H

0   Miles   65
0   Kilometers   105

Dominican Republic and Haiti
Attractions

© AAA

▽ SEE AAA GEM ATTRACTIONS

1778-U

The first European city in the New World, La Isabela was to become Columbus' base of operations for the next 2 years. In 1496 Bartolomeo Columbus, Christopher's brother, founded New Isabela on the southern coast—where the Republic's capital of Santo Domingo thrives today.

The only colony ever governed by its discoverer, Hispaniola was the base for excursions by many famous Spanish explorers, including Francisco Pizarro, Hernando Cortés, Hernando de Soto, Vasco de Balboa, Alonzo de Ojeda, Diego Velásquez and Juan Ponce de León. Considered the oldest university in the Americas, the University of Santo Domingo was founded in 1538.

The French settled in western Hispaniola in 1697, and within 100 years the entire island had come under French rule. Spain regained the eastern two-thirds in 1809. The Dominican Republic declared its independence in 1821 to prevent invasion from Haiti. Shortly thereafter, however, troops from newly independent Haiti overran the Republic and held it for another 22 years.

Led by national hero Juan Pablo Duarte, the Republic gained its independence once again in 1844, but it was to be lost and gained yet one more time: Spain reannexed the territory in 1861 and held it until 1865, when fierce fighting led to the Republic's restoration.

Foreign parties were not the sole source of aggravation; the country has experienced a turbulent internal history as well. Political instability had become the rule by 1904, when Theodore Roosevelt sent U.S. customs agents to oversee the Dominican Republic's finances and enforce payment of its foreign debt. U.S. Marines occupied the country 1916-24 until the installation of a constitutionally elected government. Democracy was restored but short-lived: The dictator Rafael Trujillo came to power in 1930 and held it until his assassination in 1961. U.S. troops intervened again in 1965 following another civil uprising. Democracy was restored the following year, and the nation has enjoyed free elections ever since.

For many years, agriculture was the backbone of the economy. Traditional exports—sugar, cocoa, coffee, bananas and tobacco—flourished in this land of fertile valleys and foliage-clad mountains. Today, tourism is one of the Dominican Republic's primary industries. Resorts have sprung up in the coastal beach towns and around the capital city of Santo Domingo. There also has been an increase of ecotourism in the interior, with hiking, caving, white-water rafting, cascading and biking tours through the mountains and countryside.

Shopping

In Santo Domingo one shopping area extends along Calle El Conde from El Conde Gate eastward to the colonial section; the long thoroughfare is closed to vehicular traffic. There are less expensive shops nearby—along avenidas Duarte and Mella, near Columbus Park and along Mercedes. Plaza Central, at the intersection of avenidas 27th of February and Winston Churchill is a popular shopping center. Mercado Modelo, the public crafts market, is at the corner of avenidas Mella and Santome. Santo Domingo also offers several modern shopping malls.

Shopping opportunities in Puerto Plata can be found around Central Park, the Plaza Turisol and a popular crafts center near Playa Dorada. In Santiago shoppers go to Calle El Sol and the Mercado crafts market. Haggling is expected in the crafts markets but not at the commercial shops.

There are free-port zones at Santo Domingo's Las Américas International Airport and at Puerto Plata's Gregorio Luperón International Airport. Duty-free purchases must be made in U.S. dollars and are delivered to your point of departure. Shopping hours are generally Mon.-Sat. 9-7:30. Banking hours are Mon.-Fri. 8:30-5.

One of the best buys is jewel-like amber—the Dominican Republic is one of the few spots in the Western Hemisphere where this fossilized resin is found. Larimar, a blue stone similar to turquoise, also is found in the Dominican Republic. Other good buys include embroidery, woven baskets, dolls, leather goods, art objects and handicrafts of local cedar and mahogany. Imported perfume and jewelry also are available. Local handicrafts made of tortoiseshell, such as combs or jewelry, may not be imported into the United States.

Food and Drink

The national dish, *sancocho,* is a hearty stew of vegetables and meats. The local staple is the plantain, served ripe or green in a variety of ways. *Fritos verdes* are plantain fritters; *mangú* is a puree of boiled plantains and onions. *La bandera*, which means "the flag," is a tricolored meal of white rice, red beans and meat. Dishes prepared *a la criolla* reflect the country's Creole heritage. Fish in coconut-milk sauce *(pescado con coco)* is a traditional favorite. Stewed goat *(chivo guisado)* is served in most restaurants; goats on the island are said to graze on wild oregano, which lends flavor to the meat. The locals are especially partial to a snack food of fried pork rinds, *chicharones.*

Numerous restaurants provide traditional and contemporary Caribbean specialties along with many Italian, French, Spanish, Indian, Japanese and Chinese dishes. A 10-percent service charge—in addition to a 15-percent value-added tax—is added to the bill in all restaurants and hotels; a tip of up to 10 percent more is customary for good service.

Dominican rum is the most popular drink, though imported brands claim a substantial following. Barcelo, Bermudez and Brugal are readily available. Dominican Republic beer rivals German brands for robust flavor. Presidente is the local favorite, but Bohemia also is popular.

If a milder form of refreshment is preferred, try a *batida,* or fruit shake. Dominican coffee is considered excellent, especially by those who like their coffee strong. Tap water is *not* considered safe to drink by visitors, even in the hotels. Water served in restaurants is generally safe, and bottled water is readily available.

Sports and Amusements

With nearly a thousand miles of coastline, the Dominican Republic offers a wide choice of unspoiled beaches for swimming and other water sports. Top destinations include the Amber Coast, near Puerto Plata on the northern shore, Boca Chica and La Romana on the southern shore, Punta Cana on the island's eastern tip and Samaná on the northeast coast.

Marlin, wahoo, kingfish and barracuda are the desired catches of deep-sea anglers. Samaná is noted for excellent bay fishing. Other prime fishing areas are Cumayasa, La Romana and Cabeza de Toro, east of the capital; and Puerto Plata on the north coast.

Charter boats for sailing and yachting can be rented at most resorts by the hour or day. Opportunities for snorkeling and scuba diving are not as widespread as on other Caribbean isles; however, the reefs around Catalina Island, accessible by boat from La Romana, are popular for underwater exploring. Windsurfing, kiteboarding, surfing, water skiing and other water sports can be arranged at the Puerto Plata and Cabarete resorts and at Casa de Campo near La Romana.

Facilities for such land sports as golf, tennis and horseback riding are excellent. With more than 21 golf courses, the island is becoming a popular year-round golf destination. Championship 18-hole courses are available at Playa Grande on the north coast, Punta Cana to the east, Playa Dorada at Puerto Plata, Casa de Campo near La Romana and Coral Costa Caribe near Juan Dolio. Tennis courts are found in the resort areas as well as in the city. Stables are in and around Santo Domingo, Puerto Plata and La Romana, where horseback riding proves to be a practical way to sightsee in the surrounding countryside.

Spectator sports in the Republic include horse racing, basketball, baseball, boxing and polo. Sports facilities built for the 2003 Pan-American games represented the largest public works project in the country's history. Nearby are the V Centenario Hipódromo, the horse racing track, and Quisqueya Stadium, where baseball—the national sport—is played.

The country has lent more than its share of baseball talent to U.S. teams. In fact, nearly 10 percent of American Major League baseball players come from the Dominican Republic. Notable names include Bartolo Colón, Vladamir Guerrero, Pedro Martinez, Manny Ramirez, Alex Rodriguez, Alfonso Soriano, Sammy Sosa and Miguel Tejada. Though baseball is played year-round, the more acclaimed winter league plays late October through January.

A country that gave the world dances like the *merengue* is bound to have a lively nightlife. African, Spanish and Indian influences have been sifted, filtered and then combined in a swirl of *Criollo* activity and Latin good times. *Bachata,* a soulful variation on the traditional merengue, has become a Dominican trademark. The nightclubs and casinos in Santo Domingo feature top-name entertainers; dance bands are featured at most restaurants and hotels.

The National Theater in Santo Domingo's Plaza de la Cultura regularly presents dramatic productions and orchestral performances. Plays also are staged at the Palace of Fine Arts (Palacio de Bellas Artes) and the Casa de Teatro in the capital.

Sightseeing

Major hotels and ground tour operators can arrange guided sightseeing tours. Tours away from the city visit coffee, sugar, banana, cocoa and pineapple plantations, rice paddies and tobacco farms. The drive along Duarte Highway, connecting Santo Domingo on the coast to Puerto Plata on the north coast, affords a glimpse of the country's diverse interior. The highway cuts through the mountainous region of the island, an area noted for its coffee plantations. Popular stops along the way are La Vega, a typical island mountain town, and Santiago, where Bermudez Rum is made. Both towns are known for their carnival celebrations, which are held every Sunday in February.

At Puerto Plata are opportunities to relax, swim or ride a cable car to the top of 2,565-foot (782-m) Mount Isabel de Torres, which offers a spectacular view of the countryside. At the top of the mountain is the statue of "Christ the Redeemer." East of town near Río San Juan is Laguna Gri Gri, where boats can be rented to explore the mangrove-lined lagoon and the island's north coast. The mountain town of Jarabacoa, 90 miles (145 km) south of Puerto Plata, is an ecotourism base for river rafting, hiking, horseback riding and mountain biking. About 50 miles (80 km) southeast of Río San Juan is the Samaná Peninsula, noted for its pristine white sand beaches and excellent sailing, diving, whale watching and fishing opportunities.

West of Santo Domingo are San Cristobal, where the dictator Rafael Trujillo built a fabulous palace and college; Barahona, with its miles of unspoiled beaches; and Lake Enriquillo, one of the largest lakes in the Caribbean, complete with flamingos and crocodiles. Another worthwhile excursion is a 2-hour drive east from Santo Domingo to La Romana. Here is Altos de Chavon, a replica of a 16th-century Mediterranean village, with an artists' colony on a cliff overlooking the Chavón River.

More than ten percent of the country's land area is set aside for national parks, natural monuments and scientific reserves. Though few sites offer tourist facilities, many are open to guided tours. In the north, Parque Nacional Monte Cristi covers 212 sq mi. (550 sq km) between the Haitian border and Punta Rucia. The coastal park features beaches, mangrove swamps and the limestone mesa of El Morro. Christopher Columbus's first home in the New World is among the archeological excavations at Parque Nacional La Isabela near Luperón.

At Cabarete, lagoons and underground pools characterize Parque Nacional El Choco. On Samaná Bay, Parque Nacional Los Haïtises is noted for its bird life, caves and rock formations.

In the central mountain region, Parque Nacional Armando Bermúdez and Parque Nacional José del Carmen Ramírez are home to the highest peaks in the Antilles, including 10,128-foot (3,087-m) Pico Duarte. The ruins of Old Vega, a fort town destroyed by an earthquake in 1562, are preserved at Parque Histórico La Vega Vieja, where Christopher Columbus is said to have erected a wooden cross during a battle with the Taíno Indians.

In the southeast, Parque Nacional del Este covers 166 sq mi. (430 sq km) on the peninsula between Bayahibe and Boca del Yuma, including the island of Saona. Manatees and bottlenose dolphins are among the endangered marine mammals found in the park, which is noted for its caves and coral formations.

Near San Cristóbal, Parque Nacional Cuevas de Bourbón o de El Pomier features a network of 54 caves marked by thousands of Taíno pictographs and petroglyphs.

In the southwest, Parque Nacional Isla Cabritos comprises three islands in Lake Enriquillo. The country's largest protected area, Parque Nacional Jaragua, covers 560 sq mi. (1,450 sq km) on the southern Pedernales Peninsula. The desertlike landscape is home to 130 bird species, including the region's largest flamingo population. Parque Nacional Sierra de Bahoruco, on the Haitian border, is an area of great ecological diversity; some 50 bird species and 166 orchid species are found here.

When visiting any major tourist area, be prepared for the approach of helpful—and sometimes aggressive—freelance tour guides. You may find yourself walking with a friendly stranger who gives directions and then charges for the information. Should you wish to take a guided tour, agree in advance upon a fee, but feel free to decline such services. Tours are optional, even within most attractions.

Transportation

American Airlines, Continental and Delta are among carriers offering regular flights and packages from New York, Newark and Miami to Puerto Plata's Gregorio Luperón International Airport and Santo Domingo's Las Américas International Airport. Connections also are available from San Juan, Puerto Rico and Bonaire. American Airlines and American Eagle also serve La Romana International Airport and Punta Cana International Airport.

Ferry transportation from Puerto Rico to the Dominican Republic is provided by America Cruise Ferries, which operates the *Caribbean Fantasy* between Mayagüez and Santo Domingo. The eight- to 12-hour overnight crossing departs Monday from Puerto Rico's Pan American terminal and Wednesday and Friday from Port of Mayagüez; phone (809) 688-4400.

The Dominican Republic has good highways, though the back roads are not as well maintained. The Duarte Highway (Autopista Duarte) bisects the country, connecting Santo Domingo with Santiago and Puerto Plata to the north. The Sanchez Highway stretches westward from Santo Domingo and the Mella Highway eastward. Rental cars are available. Unless otherwise posted, speed limits are 50 mph (80 km/h) on the highway, 35 mph (60 km/h) in suburban areas and 25 mph (40 km/h) in the city. On newer highways, the limit may be raised to 60 mph (100 km/h). A U.S. driver's license is valid in the Dominican Republic for 90 days.

Because Dominican law allows for detaining visitors who have become involved in accidents in which injuries are claimed, extreme caution is advised while driving. For some this possibility rules out driving altogether. Reasonable alternatives are available.

In the city most visitors prefer the convenience of taxis. There are four types. Regular taxis are government-regulated and rates are fixed; they are found at hotels and tourist spots. Radio taxis are dispatched and the rate is set over the phone. Public taxis, or *públicos,* are operated independently; they are available along established routes. Collective taxis, or *conchos,* also operate along major thoroughfares. Rates are fairly inexpensive. Regardless of the type of taxi used, the fare should be agreed upon before entering the vehicle.

Bus service is provided by Caribe Tours and Metro Bus between cities and from Santo Domingo to the airport. Comfortable, inexpensive buses operate several times daily between Santo Domingo and Puerto Plata, a 4-hour ride. Buses depart hourly; reservations are advised. Phone (809) 221-4422 or (809) 566-7123, respectively.

Note: Rented vehicles cannot cross the border between the Dominican Republic and Haiti.

Fast Facts

POPULATION: 8,950,034.

AREA: 48,443 sq km (18,704 sq mi.).

CAPITAL: Santo Domingo.

HIGHEST POINT: 3,087 m (10,128 ft.), Pico Duarte.

LOWEST POINT: -44 m (-144 ft.), Lago Enriquillo.

TIME ZONE(S): Atlantic Standard.

LANGUAGE: Spanish.

GOVERNMENT: Representative democracy.

UNIT OF CURRENCY: Dominican Republic Peso, divided into 100 centavos, also known as "chele." $1 U.S. = approx. 37 pesos. Keep all exchange receipts to reconvert to U.S. dollars. Only 30 percent of the original amount will be reconverted.

ELECTRICITY: 110 volts, 60 cycles AC.

MINIMUM AGE FOR DRIVERS: 25 to drive a rental car; maximum age 65. U.S. license valid; drive on left.

MINIMUM AGE FOR GAMBLING: 18.

SEAT BELT/CHILD RESTRAINT LAWS: Seat belts are required for all passengers.

HELMETS FOR MOTORCYCLISTS: Required.

HOLIDAYS: Jan. 1; Epiphany Day, closest Mon. to Jan. 6; Lady of Altagracia Day, Jan. 21; Juan Pablo Duarte Day, closest Mon. to Jan. 26; Carnival, Feb. 26; Independence Day, Feb. 27; Good Friday; Labour Day, closest Mon. to May 1; Corpus Christi Day, May or June (9th Thurs. after Easter); Restoration Day, closest Mon. to Aug. 16; Our Lady of Las Mercedes Day, Sept. 24; Constitution Day, Nov. (2nd Mon.); Christmas, Dec. 25.

TAXES: Taxes and service charges totaling 26 percent are added to all hotel and restaurant bills. This includes a 16 percent sales tax and a 10 percent service charge; in restaurants, an additional gratuity of up to 10 percent is customary. Departure tax $20 U.S.

IMMIGRATION REQUIREMENTS: A passport and a return or onward ticket are required. Tourists without a visa must pay $10 U.S. for a 30-day tourist card (available through air or sea carrier or upon arrival); the card must be surrendered upon arrival at the airport. The U.S. Dept. of Homeland Security requires all U.S. citizens returning from the Caribbean to present a valid passport.

PHONING THE ISLANDS: To call the Dominican Republic from the U.S. or Canada, dial 1 + 809 + the 7-digit local number.

FURTHER INFORMATION FOR VISITORS:

Dominican Republic Tourist Office
848 Brickell Ave., Suite 747
Miami, FL 33131
(305) 358-2899
(888) 358-9594

Ministry of Tourism, Government Offices
Calle Cayetano Germosen
Esquina avenida Gregorio Luperón
Santo Domingo, Dominican Republic
(809) 221-4660

Points of Interest

See map page 116.

BÁVARO (B-6)

Part of the Punta Cana destination area, Bávaro Beach stretches for 23 miles along the eastern edge of the island, protected by a coral reef. The first hotel was built here by a group of American investors in the 1970s; some two dozen resorts now line the shore.

MANATÍ PARK is n.w. of the Punta Cana resort district on Carretera Manatí; free bus service is provided from area hotels. This nature park features dolphin, sea lion, horse and parrot shows. Iguanas, exotic birds and reptiles are displayed in a tropical garden setting. An interactive program allows visitors to swim with dolphins. On the grounds is a Taíno village with a museum and demonstrations of native dancing.

Time: Allow 3 hours minimum. **Hours:** Daily 9-6. Swimming with Dolphins programs at 9, 2 and 5:15; reservations are required. Animal show times vary. **Cost:** $30; $15 (ages 2-12). Swimming with Dolphins (includes admission) $95. **Phone:** (809) 221-9444. 🍴

BOCA CHICA (C-5) pop. 46,385

About 20 miles (32 km) east of Santo Domingo, Boca Chica boasts a white sand beach and shallow, crystal-clear waters. The area has been a favorite vacation spot since being discovered by the Republic's elite in the late 1920s. Coral reefs provide a natural barrier, creating excellent conditions for water skiing, windsurfing, scuba diving and snorkeling. Modern accommodations are nearby.

CABARETE (A-5)

A fortuitous combination of wind and geography has created near ideal conditions for windsurfing at Cabarete, and since the 1980s the town has become an internationally renowned destination for the sports enthusiasts. Surfing and the newer sport of kite-boarding also are popular here.

RECREATIONAL ACTIVITIES
Mountain Biking

- **Iguana Mama** departs from Calle Principal No. 74. The outfitter offers half- and full-day biking trips into the Cordillera Septentrional mountain range. Other activities are offered. **Hours:** Daily 8-5. **Phone:** (809) 571-0908 or (809) 571-0228.

LA ROMANA (C-6) pop. 191,303

A sugar town on the southeast coast, La Romana means "the scales"; the cane growers brought their crops here to be weighed and bought. Most of its residents work at the sugar mill, which offers tours by appointment. Recreation includes tennis, polo, horseback riding and golf at three 18-hole courses, all at the nearby 7,000-acre (2,832-hectare) resort of Casa de Campo. An all-day boat excursion to Catalina Island, with its small offshore reef and powdery beaches, can be arranged at the harbor near town. The fishing village of Bayahibe, noted for its pristine beaches and diving sites, is a growing resort area.

Thousands of Dominicans make the yearly pilgrimage to the Basilica of Nuestra Señora de la Altagracia at Higüey (EE-gway), which is 23 mi. (37 km) northeast of La Romana. The large cathedral, built in honor of the country's patron saint, is considered one of the island's finest examples of modern architecture. West of La Romana are the beach resort towns of Juan Dolio, Guyacanes and San Pedro de Macorís, home of some of the country's—and America's—greatest baseball players.

⬥GEM **ALTOS DE CHAVÓN** is high above the Chavon River, 8 mi. (13 km) e. via Casa de Campo. Built in 1976 to resemble a 16th-century Renaissance village, this artistic community promotes Dominican and international culture. The self-contained campus is host to many Dominican and international writers, painters, musicians and artisans.

The Altos de Chavón Art Gallery displays monthly exhibits by Dominican and international painters, sculptors and photographers. The Regional Museum of Archeology interprets aboriginal evolution from the first pre-ceramic groups to the highly developed Taíno Indians. The museum's fine collection of some 3,000 Taíno art and artifacts was collected along the banks of the Chavon River.

Chavon Amphitheater, built in the classic Greek tradition, presents performances all year. The 5,000-seat theater was inaugurated by Frank Sinatra in 1982. St. Stanislaus Church was named after Poland's patron saint in honor of Pope John Paul II, who donated the saint's ashes to the community. The church is built entirely of hand-cut stone.

Spanish influences can be seen along the cobblestone streets with their limestone buildings and wrought-iron balconies. Within these buildings are craft workshops, artist studios, ethnic restaurants and fine shops. **Hours:** Art gallery open Tues.-Sun. 10-10. Museum open Tues.-Sun. 8-8. **Phone:** (809) 523-8011. 🍴

CAVE OF WONDERS (LA CUEVA DE LAS MARAVILLAS) is w. of La Romana between the Soco and Cumayasa rivers on San Pedro de Macoris Hwy. Guided 1-hour tours take visitors 80 feet (25 m) underground to the Cave of Wonders, which contains dramatic formations and some 500 pre-Columbian pictographs. Knowledgeable guides offer history and anecdotes; tours are available in English.

To protect rock formations, photography is prohibited. The cave is equipped with lighted pathways and an elevator; comfortable walking shoes are advised. **Time:** Allow 1 hour minimum. **Hours:** Tours depart on the hour Tues.-Sun. 10-5. **Cost:** $8; $4 (children). **Phone:** (809) 696-1797. 🕎

LUPERÓN (A-4)

On the northern coast of Hispaniola, the protected bay at Luperón has long provided shelter for seafaring travelers. Returning on his second voyage to the New World, Christopher Columbus moored near here with 17 ships and 1,500 men to establish the first European town in the Americas. The settlement of La Isabela, named after the queen of Spain, would be abandoned within 5 years.

PARQUE NACIONAL LA ISABELA is 8.5 mi. (14 km) w. of Luperón. In December 1493, Christopher Columbus established the first European settlement in the New World, building a walled city named La Isabela on the east bank of the Bajabonico River. The foundations of a fort, a sentry tower, a chapel and Columbus's limestone house are visible. A small museum features exhibits about Spanish and Taíno culture and artifacts excavated from the site; labels are in Spanish. **Hours:** Mon.-Sat. 9-5:30. **Cost:** $2. **Phone:** (809) 472-3717.

PUERTO PLATA (A-4) pop. 112,036

Puerto Plata, meaning "silver port," was named so by Christopher Columbus in 1493 because of the silver mist that hovers around the nearby mountains at sunset. Soon after its founding by Columbus' brother Bartolomeo in 1496, Puerto Plata began to flourish as a trade center for the Spanish colonies. Increasing competition from newer ports, however, led to its demise, and by 1520 Puerto Plata had become overrun by smugglers. Illegal trade continued well into the 17th century, despite the crown's decree that the town be destroyed and abandoned. Legitimate trade resumed in the mid-1700s, but it is tourism that fuels the local economy today.

Puerto Plata's charm lies in its cobblestone streets, Victorian homes and leisurely pace of life. Horse-drawn carriages are available for city tours. Central Park attracts sightseers; a large gazebo adorns the site. Puerto Plata's Brugal Rum is considered to be among the world's finest; the distillery on Avenida Luis Ginebra offers tours Mon.-Fri. 9-noon and 2-5.

Puerto Plata is the gateway to the 75 miles (120 km) of golden beach known as the Amber Coast. The many beaches along this beautiful strip include Sosúa, Long, Grande, Dorada, Cofresí and Cabarete. This glittering vista is best viewed from the top of Mount Isabel de Torres (see attraction listing). Most of the major resorts are east of town in Playa Dorada and Costa Dorada.

Other interesting local attractions include Laguna Gri Gri and the town of Sosúa, a refugee colony of European Jews during World War II and the site of the island's largest dairy industry.

AMBER MUSEUM (MUSEO DEL ÁMBAR DOMINICANO) is on the second floor of the Villa Bentz at the corner of Calle Duarte and Padre Castellanos. Housed in an early 20th-century mansion built by wealthy German merchants, the museum features a large collection of amber. One particularly rare specimen contains a small lizard. Exhibits describe how the gem is formed and how and where it is mined in the Dominican Republic. Visitors can also see samples of copal, which is relatively young resin that has not completely hardened into amber.

Time: Allow 30 minutes minimum. **Hours:** Mon.-Sat. 9-6. **Cost:** $1. **Phone:** (809) 586-2848 or (809) 320-2215.

MONSTER TRUCK SAFARIS provides shuttle service from area hotels. Narrated day-long tours aboard 8 x 8 all-terrain trucks depart from Puerto Plata and travel the back roads and rivers of the island. Stops include mingling with a local family at a typical Dominican home, visiting with children at a local schoolhouse and going for a river swim. A lunch stop features an island buffet.

Hours: English language tours depart from Puerto Plata Mon.-Sat. at 9, with hotel pick-up starting at 8. Guests are returned to their hotels by 5. **Cost:** $89-$95; $44.50-$47.50 (ages 2-12). Actual fare depends on hotel pick-up location. **Phone:** (809) 244-4060.

MOUNT ISABEL DE TORRES CABLE CAR (PICO ISABEL DE TORRES TELEFÉRICO) is s.w. of downtown near the jct. of Ave. Circunvalación Sur & Ave. Teleférico following signs. The cable car transports visitors to the top of 2,565-foot (782-meter) Mount Isabel de Torres for stunning views of the Cordillera Septentrional mountains, Puerto Plata and the Silver Coast. The statue "Christ the Redeemer" and a 35-acre botanical garden with tropical plants and winding paths crown the summit. Visitors should arrive in the morning to avoid view-obscuring clouds that often develop. Long waits can be expected on weekends.

Time: Allow 3 hours minimum. **Hours:** Thurs.-Tues. 9-6. Phone ahead to confirm schedule. **Cost:** $10; $6 (ages 0-12). **Phone:** (809) 970-0501. 🕎

OCEAN WORLD is 3 mi. (5 km) w. on the Carretera 5 (C-5) to Cofresí Beach following signs. Comprising a series of artificial lagoons and aquariums constructed along the Atlantic shore, the adventure park is home to bottlenose dolphins, sea lions, sharks, stingrays, tropical birds and other exotic animals. Park admission includes snorkeling in a tropical reef aquarium and swimming in Tiger Grotto, a pool where tigers are separated from guests by a glass wall.

The highlight of the park is its dolphin, sea lion, shark and stingray encounter programs, which allow guests to interact with these intelligent marine mammals. Visitors can also walk through bird aviaries and a rain forest and relax on a sandy beach.

Guests also can enjoy other forms of entertainment in the complex, including sunset dinners overlooking the Atlantic Ocean, a disco-lounge and casino. During "Bravissimo Show," a Las Vegas-style dance show, performers in vibrant costumes take the audience on an enchanted Caribbean journey through interpretive dance representing tropical destinations; reservations are required.

Guests should wear swimwear under clothes and bring a towel and sunscreen. **Time:** Allow 4 hours minimum. **Hours:** Daily 9-6. **Cost:** Park $55; $40 (ages 4-12 and 65+); free (ages 0-3). Fees charged for additional activities. **Phone:** (809) 291-1000. ⃞

OUTBACK SAFARI TOURS picks up passengers at area hotels. The tour company provides half- and full-day, narrated excursions into the countryside aboard four-wheel-drive vehicles. Guides acquaint passengers with the lifestyle of average Dominicans through visits to a typical home and a schoolhouse. The excursion features a stop at a petting zoo and a cruise down a tropical river. Activities include swimming in a stream and boogie boarding at a white-sand beach. Allow a full day. **Hours:** Full-day tour 9-4:30. Half-day tour 9-1. Hotel pick up starts at 8. **Cost:** Full-day tour $79; $39.50 (ages 3-12). Half-day tour $68; $34 (ages 3-12). **Phone:** (809) 244-4886 or (809) 320-2525. ⃞

SAN FELIPE FORT (EL MORRO DE SAN FELIPE) dominates the Puerto Plata waterfront. It was built in 1520 to protect the country from English pirates and Carib Indians. The fort was used as a prison for political dissidents during the Trujillo regime. **Hours:** Guides conduct narrated tours Mon.-Sat. 9-5, Sun. 9-noon. **Cost:** Tour $1.30; tipping is customary.

PUNTA CANA (B-6)

One of the country's fastest-growing destinations, Punta Cana is known for its quiet beaches and all-inclusive resorts. The silky sand beaches on this eastern tip of the island stretch for some 30 miles (50 km), and watersports offer the chief source of entertainment. A coral reef—the longest in the region—breaks the waves offshore, keeping the surf gentle. Local communities in the Punta Cana area include Arena Gorda, Bávaro *(see place listing p. 121)*, Cabeza de Toro, Cap Cana, El Cortecito, Macao and Uvero Alto.

Punta Cana International Airport, reputedly the world's first privately owned international airport, is located within the 15,000-acre Puntacana Resort and Club. The Punta Cana Ecological Reserve is a natural sanctuary for local flora and fauna.

MANATÍ PARK—*see Bávaro p. 121.*

MONSTER TRUCK SAFARIS provides shuttle service from area resorts. Narrated day-long tours aboard 8 x 8 all-terrain trucks travel the back roads

and rivers of the island. Passengers visit a local Dominican family, a river where they can swim, a fruit plantation, a schoolhouse and a voodoo doctor. A lunch stop features an island buffet.

Hours: English-language tours depart Mon.-Sat. at 9, with hotel pick-up starting at 8. Guests are returned to their hotels by 5. **Cost:** $89-$99; $44.50-$49.50 (ages 2-12). Actual fare depends on hotel pick-up location. **Phone:** (809) 244-4060. ⃞

SANTIAGO (B-4) pop. 507,418

Santiago is the Dominican Republic's industrial center and second largest city. In addition to being the home of the world-famous *merengue* music, Santiago specializes in fine restaurants, robust Dominican coffee, fine handmade cigars and Bermudez Rum. In February this otherwise conservative city enjoys the merrymaking of Carnival, when revelers don elaborate costumes and colorful horned masks.

Santiago actually had three beginnings. Bartolomeo Columbus founded Santiago de los Caballeros in 1495 after an inland settlement at La Vega was abandoned. The town was moved to present-day Jacagua a few years later, leveled by an earthquake in 1562, then rebuilt at its present site. The ruins at La Vega can still be seen. Just north at Santo Cerro, or Holy Hill, Christopher Columbus reputedly raised the first cross of Christianity in the New World. The hill affords a spectacular view of the valley below.

In Santiago's Duarte Park is the Catedral de Santiago Apostol. The Gothic and neoclassical cathedral was built 1868-95 and features a carved mahogany altar and stained-glass windows by Rincon Mora. Other points of interest are the Tobacco Museum (Museo del Tabaco), also in Duarte Park; the Museum of the City of Santiago, in the 19th-century town hall; and the Tomás Morel Museum of Folkloric Art (Museo Folklórico Yoryi Morel), featuring a display of prizewinning Carnival masks. A good way to take in some of Santiago's historical and architectural sights is by horse-drawn carriage.

MONUMENT TO THE HEROES OF THE RESTORATION OF THE REPUBLIC is in the s.e. section of the city. Constructed in the 1940s during the Trujillo era, the 200-foot column stands on a two-story base faced with native white marble. The monument offers an excellent view of the city. Murals by Spanish painter Vela Zanetti are displayed in an interior museum. **Hours:** Daily dawn-dusk. **Cost:** Free.

SANTO DOMINGO (C-5) pop. 1,887,586

Capital of the Dominican Republic, Santo Domingo was founded in 1496 by Bartolomeo Columbus. During the early 16th century, the city was the prize jewel of the Spanish colonies, enjoying great prosperity as the cultural center of the Caribbean and Spain's stepping stone to further explorations in the New World. It was during this period that many of the city's splendid palaces and churches were built.

However, when Spain turned its interests toward the gold fields of Mexico, Santo Domingo faced a sudden decline in prestige and wealth. The final blow occurred in 1586 when Sir Francis Drake of England pillaged and burned the city, which survived only to be invaded by the French and Haitians.

Many buildings and narrow streets reminiscent of the Old World have escaped the razing of expansive modernization projects. Ruins of city walls, ancient gates and crumbling fortresses in the colonial section (Zona Colonial) are vivid reminders of the city's history. Most notable are the ruins of San Nicolas de Bari Hospital and the Monastery of San Francisco, first of their kind in the New World.

The Atarazana, a restored 16th-century shipyard, covers a city block across from the Alcázar de Colón. Cafes, restaurants and boutiques as well as faithful restoration work make this a most interesting section to visit. A departure from the area's pervasive antiquity is the Mercado Modelo, the modern crafts market at avenidas Mella and Santome. On Calle Padre Billini is the Convent of the Dominicans, which dates from 1510. Inside the church is the Capilla del Rosario, or Chapel of the Rosary, a stone vault embellished with the signs of the Zodiac.

The western section of the city has benefited most from redevelopment. Of particular interest are the National Palace on Calle Moises Garcia and the Palace of Fine Arts (Palacio de Bellas Artes) at avenidas Independencia and Máximo Gómez. University City, site of the University of Santo Domingo, occupies several blocks west of Máximo Gómez. In the northwest section of the city are the Juan Pablo Duarte Olympic Center and Quisqueya Stadium.

BELLAPART MUSEUM (MUSEO BELLAPART) is on the fifth floor of the Honda Building at Ave. John F. Kennedy & Dr. Luis Lembert Peguero. This small private collection traces the evolution of more than 100 years of Dominican fine art. Divided into four sections corresponding to important artistic trends, the museum features works by native Dominicans as well as expatriates from abroad who were influenced by their years in the Dominican Republic. Artists represented include Yoryi Morel, Jamie Colson, Darío Suro and José Vela Zanetti.

Time: Allow 30 minutes minimum. **Hours:** Mon.-Fri. 10-6, Sat. 9-noon. **Cost:** Free. **Phone:** (809) 541-7721.

COLONIAL ZONE (ZONA COLONIAL) extends about 1 mi. (1.6 km) w. from the bank of the Ozama River, bounded on the north by Ave. Mella and on the south by the Caribbean Sea. The New World's first fortress, cathedral, monastery, hospital, palaces and government offices were built here after Christopher Columbus' arrival in 1492.

At the heart of this UNESCO World Heritage Site is Columbus Park. Two blocks east is the Ozama Fortress, within which stands the Tower of Homage (La Torre del Homenaje), built 1503-07. North along Calle de Las Damas is the National Pantheon, where the remains of some of the country's greatest heroes are enshrined.

Visitors to the colonial section are advised to wear comfortable shoes and light clothing, but not shorts; those wearing shorts can be denied admission to some attractions. Caution should be exercised in this area, especially after dark, as tourists are often approached by locals asking for money. Amiable freelance tour guides are eager to offer their services; it is wise to ask to see a government-issued identification card and to agree upon the guide's fee before taking a tour. Visitors should feel free to decline tours despite the insistence of overzealous guides; such tours are optional, even within most of the attractions.

Amber World Museum is at the center of the Colonial Zone between Calle Celestino and Restauración; the museum is on the second floor of a historical mansion. Formed over the course of millions of years from hardened tree resin, amber is found in abundance in the Dominican Republic. The museum's displays describe the semiprecious gem's origins, the variety of material often contained in amber (leaves, insects, spiders, small frogs, lizards, etc.), how it is mined and what distinguishes Dominican amber from that which is found elsewhere in the world. **Tours:** Guided tours are available. **Time:** Allow 30 minutes minimum. **Hours:** Mon.-Sat. 8-6, Sun. 8-1. Closed Christmas. **Cost:** $1.35. **Phone:** (809) 682-3309.

Cathedral Basilica Santa Maria (Cathedral Metropolitana Santa María de la Encarnación) is on Arzobispo Meriño next to Columbus Park in the Colonial Zone. Pope Paul III pronounced this the first cathedral in the New World in 1542. Sir Frances Drake reputedly lived in the cathedral for 25 days. With a Gothic vault, Spanish Renaissance facades, Romanesque arches and Baroque ornamentation, the cathedral is an architectural marvel. Exquisite stained-glass windows were crafted by Dominican artist Rincón Mora. Guide service of the cathedral is available. Appropriate attire is required; persons in shorts are not admitted. **Hours:** Mon.-Sat. 9-4. **Cost:** Donations. **Phone:** (809) 682-3848 or (809) 689-1920.

Columbus Castle Museum (Museo Alcázar de Colón) is at the n. end of Calle Las Damas next to the Gate of San Diego on the Plaza de España in the Colonial Zone. This 22-room palace overlooking the Ozama River was built 1510-14 for Columbus' son Diego, first viceroy of the West Indies. The coral-rock castle served as the seat of the Spanish court for 68 years. Colonial furniture and 16th-century works of art add to the elegance of the interior. Guided tours are available in English, French, Italian, German and Spanish. **Hours:** Thurs.-Sun. 9-5. **Cost:** $3. **Phone:** (809) 682-4750.

Cord House (Casa del Cordón) is at 214 Calle Isabel la Católica in the Colonial Zone. Diego Columbus lived here while the Alcázar was under construction. Built in 1503 and spared by earthquakes, hurricanes and Sir Francis Drake, it is said to be the oldest standing house in the Western Hemisphere. The stone cord carved above the door is the sign of a Franciscan order. The building now houses a bank and offices. **Hours:** Mon.-Fri. 8-4. **Cost:** Free.

Dominican Family Museum (Casa del Tostado) is on Calle Padre Billini and Arzobispo Meriño in the Colonial Zone. The 16th-century Tostado House, once used as the archbishop's palace, contains displays of 19th-century household effects and furnishings. The house's Gothic double window is architecturally unique. **Tours:** Guided tours are available. **Hours:** Mon.-Sat. 9-4. **Cost:** $3. **Phone:** (809) 689-5057.

Fortress of Santo Domingo (Fortaleza Ozama) is in the southeastern corner of the Colonial Zone at Calle Las Damas and Padre Billini. Begun in 1503 on the banks of the Ozama River, the fortress is said to be the oldest military complex in the New World. Dominating the open space within is the Tower of Homage (Torre del Homenaje), which was used as a prison until the 1960s and offers picturesque views from its battlements. A bronze statue of Gonzalo Fernández de Oviedo, the 16th-century Spanish historian and prison warden, looms nearby. **Tours:** Guided tours are available. **Time:** Allow 30 minutes minimum. **Hours:** Mon.-Sat. 9-5, Sun. 10-3. **Cost:** $1; fee higher during special exhibition in May. Guided tour $6. **Phone:** (809) 333-8672 or (809) 333-8673.

Juan Pablo Duarte Museum (Museo de Juan Pablo Duarte) is at 308 Calle Isabel la Católica between calles Restauración and Vicente Celestino Duarte in the Colonial Zone. The 1813 birthplace of Juan Pablo Duarte, father of the Dominican Republic, contains personal possessions and furniture of the patriot and the Duarte-Diez family, as well as portraits of Duarte, paintings with historical themes and artifacts and documents of the independence period. **Hours:** Tues.-Fri. 9-5, Sat. 9-noon. **Cost:** $1. **Phone:** (809) 687-1436 or (809) 687-1475.

Larimar Museum is on the second floor of a building at the corner of Isabel La Católica and Padre Billini in the Colonial Zone. While the mineral pectolite can be found all over the world, blue pectolite—also called larimar—has been found only in the Dominican Republic's Barahona province. The small museum features labeled displays describing the semiprecious stone's volcanic formation and how it is mined. **Time:** Allow 30 minutes minimum. **Hours:** Mon.-Sat. 8-6, Sun. 8-2. **Cost:** Free. **Phone:** (809) 689-6605 or (809) 686-5700.

Museum of the Royal Houses (Las Casas Reales) is on Calle de Las Damas at Mercedes in the Colonial Zone. This architecturally interesting and historically important complex includes two palaces built in the early 16th century. Various facets of Spanish colonial life are depicted through artifacts, tapestries, maps and a re-created courtroom. Recovered treasures from sunken Spanish galleons and a large collection of arms and armor from the first through the 18th centuries also are displayed. **Tours:** Guided tours are available. **Hours:** Daily 9-5. **Cost:** $2.40. **Phone:** (809) 682-4202.

National Pantheon (Panteón de la Patria) is near the corner of Las Damas and Las Mercedes in the Colonial Zone. Originally a Jesuit church completed in the 1740s, the building endured periods as a warehouse and a theater before it was converted to a mausoleum in 1956 for Dominican dictator Rafael Trujillo. Interred within its walls are the remains of many of the nation's most illustrious political figures. A large bronze chandelier, a gift from Spanish dictator Francisco Franco, hangs beneath the domed ceiling. Appropriate attire is required; persons in shorts are not admitted. Amiable freelance tour guides are eager to offer their services; it is wise to ask to see a government-issued identification card and to agree upon the guide's fee before taking a tour. Visitors should feel free to decline tours despite the insistence of overzealous guides; such tours are optional. **Time:** Allow 30 minutes minimum. **Hours:** Tues.-Sun. 9-6. **Cost:** Free. **Phone:** (809) 689-6010.

Naval Museum of the Atarazanas (Museo Naval de las Atarazanas) is at 4 Calle Colon at the corner of Vicente Celestino Duarte Ave. in the Colonial Zone. On the street of taverns and shops that once served Spanish sailors, this museum chronicles 17th-century maritime life. Exhibits include shipwreck artifacts from the galleon *Concepción,* which sank off the coast in 1641. The museum also chronicles the gold, silver and slave trades. Most exhibits are labeled in Spanish. **Time:** Allow 30 minutes minimum. **Hours:** Mon.-Tues. and Thurs.-Sat. 9-5, Sun. 9-1. **Cost:** $1; free (children and students). **Phone:** (809) 682-5834.

San Francisco Monastery Ruins (Ruinas del Monasterio de San Francisco) are on a hilltop n. of Ave. Mercedes at Calle Hostos in the Colonial Zone. The Franciscan monastery was thought to be the first in the Americas. Construction began around 1508, but a series of natural disasters, followed by Sir Francis Drake's 1586 rampage, thwarted its completion. **Hours:** Daily dawn-dusk. **Cost:** Free.

San Nicolás de Bari Hospital Ruins (Ruinas El Hospital San Nicolás) are on Ave. Mercedes in the Colonial Zone. Stone walls remain from the first hospital to be erected in the Americas. A wooden building that had housed the sick and injured since 1503 was replaced in 1530 by the stone structure; records contain accounts of facilities that included a number of wards, a chapel and a cemetery.

COLUMBUS LIGHTHOUSE MONUMENT (FARO A COLÓN) is on the east side of the Ozama River at Ave. España in Mirador del Este Park. The massive seven-story, cross-shaped edifice features 145 flood lamps that project a shining cross into the night sky. Displays in mahogany-trimmed rooms illustrate the discoveries of Christopher Columbus and how they changed the world.

Visitors also can see excellent scale models of the *Niña, Pinta* and *Santa María.* An entire hall is devoted to the construction of the monument, which was dedicated in 1992 to commemorate the 500th anniversary of Columbus' landing. Exhibits include photographs and drafts submitted by architects from around the world. An art gallery displays work from Santo Domingo.

The ornate bronze box suspended in a three-story marble monument—and guarded by militia—is said to contain a portion of the explorer's remains. **Time:** Allow 1 hour minimum. **Hours:** Tues.-Sun. 9-5:30. **Cost:** $1.25; 35c (ages 0-11). **Phone:** (809) 591-1492, ext. 238.

INDEPENDENCE PARK (PARQUE INDEPENDEN-CIA) is at the w. end of Calle El Conde at avs. Bolivar and Independencia. The park contains two national icons. At the east end is El Conde Gate, one of the city's original entranceways and the site of the nation's 1844 proclamation of independence. To the west is the Altar of the Nation, a white marble mausoleum containing the remains of founding fathers Juan Pablo Duarte, Francisco del Rosario Sánchez and Ramón Matías Mella. The images of both edifices can be seen on the Dominican 100-peso bill. **Hours:** Daily dawn-dusk. **Cost:** Free.

NATIONAL AQUARIUM (ACUARIO NACIONAL) is on Ave. España. A variety of marine and freshwater animals are displayed in tanks reflecting their natural habitats. A short film is presented. **Time:** Allow 30 minutes minimum. **Hours:** Tues.-Sun. 9:30-5:30. Film presented on the hour Tues.-Thurs. and every half-hour Fri.-Sun. **Cost:** $1. **Phone:** (809) 766-1709. ⛽

NATIONAL BOTANICAL GARDEN (JARDÍN BOTÁNICO NACIONAL) is n.w. of downtown on Av. Republica de Columbia in Altos de Galá. Highlights of the 400-acre (162-hectare) park include the Japanese Garden, the Great Ravine, Medicinal Garden, Aquatic Garden, the Floral Clock and the Orchid Pavilion. A passenger train transports visitors through the park. **Hours:** Daily 9-5. **Cost:** $1.50; 25c (children). Train $1.50; 35c (children). **Phone:** (809) 385-2611 or (809) 385-0774.

NATIONAL ZOOLOGICAL PARK (PARQUE ZOOLÓGICO NACIONAL) is at Ave. Vega Real and Ave. Los Arroyos Arroyo Hondo. The zoo preserves the natural environment of a wide variety of animals, which are allowed to roam freely. The park includes the African Plain, a children's zoo and one of the largest bird cages in the world. Five miles (8 km) of roads and walks traverse the park. Train tours also are available. **Time:** Allow 2 hours minimum. **Hours:** Tues.-Sun. 9-5. Closed Good Friday and Dec. 24-31. **Cost:** $5; $3 (children). Pony rides $1. **Phone:** (809) 378-2149. ⛽

PLAZA DE LA CULTURA is at avs. Mexico and Máximo Gómez. Representing the modern side of Santo Domingo, this cultural and educational center is distinguished by its progressive architecture. A park inside the plaza contains national cultural buildings, a theater and museums, set amid tropical gardens. **Hours:** Daily dawn-dusk. **Cost:** Free.

Museum of the Dominican Man (Museo del Hombre Dominicano) is on Calle Pedro Henríquez Ureña in the Plaza de la Cultura. The museum presents Dominican history and folklore from pre-Columbian times to the present. Exhibits include Indian artifacts excavated on the island and graphic displays charting migration in the Caribbean. **Hours:** Tues.-Sun. 10-5. **Cost:** $2; $1 (students with ID). **Phone:** (809) 687-3622.

Museum of Modern Art (Museo de Arte Moderno) is on Calle Pedro Henríquez Ureña in the Plaza de la Cultura. The museum displays a collection of contemporary paintings and sculpture by Dominican and foreign artists as well as changing displays by current artists. **Hours:** Tues.-Sun. 10-6. **Cost:** $4; $1.60 (ages 0-11). **Phone:** (809) 685-2153 or (809) 685-2154.

National Library (Biblioteca Nacional) is at Ave. César Nicolás Penson 91 in the Plaza de la Cultura. The library holds half a million books and magazines; its excellent research facilities require a good command of Spanish. **Hours:** Mon.-Fri. 8 a.m.-10 p.m., Sat.-Sun. 8-4. **Cost:** Free. **Phone:** (809) 688-4086 or (809) 688-4660.

National Museum of History and Geography (El Museo Nacional de Historia y Geografia) is on Ave. César Nicolás Penson in the Plaza de la Cultura. Devoted to Dominican history, the museum highlights the war against Haiti and the dictatorship of Rafael Trujillo. Photography is prohibited. **Hours:** Tues.-Sun. 9-4:30. **Cost:** $2; $1 (students with ID). **Phone:** (809) 686-6668 or (809) 689-9509.

National Museum of Natural History (Museo Nacional de Historia Natural) is on Ave. César Nicolás Penson in the Plaza de la Cultura. Exhibits focus on the natural characteristics and ecology of the island, from its creation to future developments. Of note is an extensive collection of mounted birds and fish. A planetarium offers simulated views of the stars and planets. A library houses materials covering biodiversity and natural resources. **Hours:** Tues.-Sun. 10-5. **Cost:** $3; $2 (ages 0-12 and students with ID). **Phone:** (809) 689-0106. ⛽

National Theater (Teatro Nacional) is on Ave. Máximo Gómez in the Plaza de la Cultura. Architect Teófilo Carbonell's imposing structure is home to ballets, operas, dramas and concerts by local and visiting artists. Changing exhibits and a permanent collection of artwork by Dominican artists are displayed in the third-floor exhibition rooms. **Hours:** Guided tours are offered Mon.-Sat. 9-1. **Cost:** Free. **Phone:** (809) 687-3191.

WILDLIFE REFUGE CAVE OF THE THREE EYES (REFUGIO DE VIDA SILVESTRE CUEVA LOS TRES OJOS) is s.e. via Las Americas Hwy. Three lagoons in 50-foot-deep caverns are accessible by limestone walkways; a fourth can be reached by water taxi. Stalactites, stalagmites and columns have created interesting formations. Several movies were filmed here. Swimming is not permitted. Wear comfortable, non-slip shoes and a light jacket. Guided tours are available in English. **Hours:** Daily 8-5:30. **Cost:** $1.50; 60c (children). **Phone:** (809) 788-7056.

Carenage, St. George's, St. George Parish / © Robert Harding Images / Masterfile

Grenada

Popularly known as "the Spice Island of the Caribbean," Grenada (gre-NAY-da) has a moderate tropical climate that ensures the success of spice production. The island is famous for its cocoa, mace, cloves, vanilla, cinnamon, ginger—and nutmeg. Grenada is the largest nutmeg producer in the Western Hemisphere.

Grenada's balmy climate lures travelers seeking an ideal Caribbean retreat. Its 133 square miles (344 sq km) of tropical landscape, encompassing volcanic mountains, lush valleys and pristine beaches, have distinguished it as one of the most beautiful West Indian islands. Ninety miles (145 km) north of Trinidad, Grenada is the southernmost of the Windward Islands and offers a remoteness that is the essence of its appeal.

History

Though Christopher Columbus discovered Grenada during his third voyage in 1498, the island was relatively neglected until 1650, when it was purchased by the governor of Martinique. The French began their colonization with a series of skirmishes that virtually exterminated

the island's native Carib population. The survivors were pushed north to Le Morne des Sauteurs, where rather than surrender they jumped off the cliff to the jagged rocks below. Today the site of the Carib defeat is known as Carib's Leap or Leapers' Hill.

After gaining complete control in 1714, the French introduced the cultivation of cocoa, coffee and cotton. During the wars between France and Great Britain, the island changed hands several times until the Treaty of Versailles finally ceded it to Britain in 1783. Slave labor and large plantation holdings brought prosperity to the island, which served as the headquarters of the British West Indies 1885-1958. After unsuccessful attempts to federate with other West Indian islands, Grenada assumed the status of an Associated State of Britain in 1967.

The island became independent from the United Kingdom in 1974 and obtained dominion status within the Commonwealth.

Following a revolution on March 13, 1979, a People's Revolutionary Government replaced the parliamentary system of democracy in Grenada. Revolutionary rumblings and ideological differences erupted into a coup d'etat against the presiding prime minister in October 1983, prompting U.S. and Eastern Caribbean military intervention. Political order in Grenada was reestablished with the election of a representative government on December 3, 1984.

Shopping

A Grenada spice basket—a handwoven pannier of palm leaf or straw filled with cinnamon, nutmeg, ginger, vanilla, cloves and other native spices—is an easy way to bring the aroma of Grenada back home. Spice necklaces also are popular souvenirs. Straw and sisal items are usually bargains, particularly at the Blind Handicraft Center and the Straw Mart on the Carenage in St. George's. Another good buy is woodcarvings.

The Yellow Poui Art Gallery on Young Street in St. George's sells paintings, sculpture, photography, print editions, antique maps and graphics by local artists. Art Fabrik, also on Young Street, offers a large selection of hand-painted batik art, clothing and accessories. Other popular shops are Tikal, Ganzee and Amba Kaila Spice Place.

More than 25 shops provide a wide range of quality items in Esplanade Mall at Melville Street Cruise Ship Terminal. Five shopping centers in the hotel area in Grand Anse contain fine shops, especially ones that sell china, crystal and other luxury items. With 82 booths, the Grand Anse Vendors' Market is an ideal place to purchase handcrafted jewelry, straw goods, clothing and spices. The market is open daily 9-6.

Shops are generally open Mon.-Fri. 8-4, Sat. 8-1. Banking hours are generally Mon.-Thurs. 8-2, Fri. 8-4.

Food and Drink

An almost endless list of seafood and home-grown fresh fruit is available at most island hotels and restaurants. *Callaloo* soup, crab backs, *lambi* (conch) dishes and avocado and nutmeg ice cream are local favorites. A liberal dose of Grenadian rum punch, made with lime juice, syrup, Angostura bitters, grated nutmeg and local rum, often helps encourage the visitor to experiment with the native cuisine. Gin and coconut water is another popular libation, as is the locally brewed Carib beer.

Sports and Amusements

Since much of the island nation is mountainous, it is easy to understand why hiking is a popular activity. Although guides may be necessary for some excursions, opportunities exist for hikes to waterfalls, historic sites, scenic views and nature study. Sailing the island's clear waters is another available form of outdoor recreation. Grand Anse, a dazzling 2-mile (3-km) stretch of sand on southwestern Grenada, is considered one of the world's finest beaches. Grenada's dependencies of Carriacou and Petite Martinique also have scenic coves with white sand beaches.

Scuba diving has become a major sport and is good off Point Salines and Molinere Point. Viewing the underwater sculptures at Molinere Marine Park also makes for an intriguing dive excursion. Experienced divers can reach the *Bianca C.,* a cruise ship that sank outside St. George's harbor in 1961; it is the largest shipwreck site in the Caribbean. Deep-sea vessels can be chartered for a half- or full-day. Arrangements for day sails and longer charters around Grenada and the Grenadines can be made at the marinas in St. George's, L'Anse aux Epines and True Blue Bay.

For an exotic Grenadian experience back on land, visit the 1,740-foot-high (530-m) Grand

1 ▼ 2 © AAA

Grenada
Attractions

0 Miles 5
0 Kilometers 8

A

N

Caribbean Sea

RONDE ISLAND

LEVERA ISLAND

ST MARK PARISH
Sauteurs
GREEN ISLAND

Victoria
ST PATRICK PARISH

B

Gouyave
ST JOHN PARISH
MT ST CATHERINE EL 840m
ST ANDREW PARISH
River Antoine Rum Distillery

Grand Roy
Grenada National Museum
Concord Falls
Grand Etang National Park
TELESCOPE PT

ST GEORGE PARISH
Annandale Falls
Grenville

ST GEORGE'S
Grand Anse Beach
ST DAVID PARISH
Bay Gardens
Great Bacolet Bay

C

Maurice Bishop International Airport (GND)
ST DAVID PT

POINT SALINES
L'Anse Aux Epines
Atlantic Ocean

1787-U

Etang Lake, a lake-filled crater of an extinct volcano within a tropical bird sanctuary and forest reserve; local guides are available for hiking. Annandale Falls, a mountain stream plunging 30 feet (9 m) into an adjacent pool surrounded by flowers and plants, also provides an ideal setting for an afternoon off the beaten path. To the north of St. George's are the three Concord Falls. The first is accessible by road; the second and third, known as Au Coin and Fontainbleu, are reached by foot through mountain terrain. La Sagesse Nature Center offers hiking trails, some 86 varieties of tropical birds, a plantation with guided tours and an extensive beach area.

Several spice and cocoa plantations welcome visitors. Gouyave, a small fishing village on the island's west coast, is a center of the nutmeg industry; its Dougaldston Estate and spice processing station are open to the public. Every Friday at 6 p.m., the village hosts a fish festival with a smorgasbord of freshly caught shrimp, lobster and other seafood cooked on open fires. Grenville's spice factory also is open for tours. Saturday in Grenville and St. George's is market day. Pastries, breads, fruits, spices, vegetables and handmade baskets, bags and hats are among the items for sale.

Some hotels have tennis courts, and two tennis clubs are near St. George's. The Grenada Golf Club has a nine-hole course. Cricket and soccer are the most popular spectator sports.

Because most visitors come to Grenada to soak up the sun, sail, snorkel or roam, the evenings tend to be much quieter than on some of the larger Caribbean islands. The hotels provide nightly entertainment in season, including dancing to popular music or calypso rhythms.

When the sun finally sets, however, the majority of people are content to sit back, sip a rum punch and listen to a steel band.

Sightseeing

Popular tours on Grenada include a 2.5-hour ridge tour past the 18th-century forts on Morne Jaloux Ridge above St. George's; the fishing village of Woburn, where parts of the movie "Island in the Sun" were filmed; a small rum factory at Woodlands; and the beaches at Lance Aux Epines. A city tour of St. George's, which includes the Market Square, the Grenada National Museum, churches and surrounding 18th-century forts, also lasts about 2.5 hours.

A 3-hour mountain tour explores the island's tropical interior and passes spice, cocoa and banana plantations en route to Grand Etang National Park and Annandale Falls. A full-day tour departs St. George's and leads to Dougaldston Estate and the Nutmeg Processing Station at Gouyave before continuing by way of Victoria, Sauteurs, Levera Beach, Tivoli, Grenville and Grand Etang.

Full-day tours usually last 7 hours (including lunch) and visit most of the island's points of interest as well as some beaches. A special photographer's tour, conducted for a minimum of eight people, leads participants past 40 miles (64 km) of landscapes, ruins, villages, wildlife and native vegetation. If you wish to brave Grenada's narrow roads and hairpin turns yourself, road maps are available at the Grenada Board of Tourism on the Carenage in St. George's. Most hotels provide information about guided tours.

Local hotels also can arrange all-day yacht cruises along the island's western and southern coasts. If your time on the island is short, you

may want to take a cruise of St. George's harbor and the surrounding area aboard the *Rhum Runner.* Moonlight cruises also are available. Phone (473) 440-4386.

Another popular excursion is a visit to the island of Carriacou (carry-a-KOO), 23 miles (37 km) northeast of Grenada. Noted for some of the best beaches in the Caribbean, the island also is famous for its small boatyards where villagers build wooden schooners using hand tools and centuries-old techniques. Good times to visit are in February during Carnival, in late April for the Carriacou Maroon & String Band Music Festival, late July to early August when the Carriacou Regatta takes place and in December for the Parang Festival on the weekend before Christmas.

Transportation

Flights to Maurice Bishop International Airport are offered by American Eagle from San Juan, Puerto Rico, and by Caribbean Airlines and Delta nonstop from New York, with connections from other cities. American Airlines flies from Miami to Grenada three times weekly. There also are air connections to Grenada via Barbados and Trinidad. Many cruise lines also call at Grenada's deep-water port.

Taxis provide transportation between the airport and island hotels. Rental cars equipped for the island's left-hand driving are available in St. George's; a 2-day minimum rental is required. Driving conditions can be treacherous on some shoulderless, one-lane roads. Minibuses provide alternative means of transportation. Buses regularly depart from the St. George's bus terminal and the Esplanade for all parts of the island. Inexpensive water taxis transport passengers across the harbor and to the Grand Anse and Morne Rouge beaches.

Daily 15-minute flights and interisland ferries travel to the island of Carriacou. Local boat service also reaches Grenada's satellite island of Petite Martinique. Several flights depart daily to and from Maurice Bishop International Airport. Boats depart daily from the Carenage.

Fast Facts

POPULATION: 108,132.

AREA: 344 sq km (133 sq mi.).

CAPITAL: St. George's.

HIGHEST POINT: 840 m (2,756 ft.), Mount Saint Catherine.

LOWEST POINT: Sea level, Caribbean Sea.

TIME ZONE(S): Atlantic Standard.

LANGUAGE: English and a French patois.

GOVERNMENT: Independent. Member of the British Commonwealth of Nations.

UNIT OF CURRENCY: Eastern Caribbean (E.C.) dollar. $1 U.S. = 2.7 E.C. dollars.

ELECTRICITY: 220 or 240 volts, 50 cycles AC.

MINIMUM AGE FOR DRIVERS: 21-25, depending on the rental car agency. Local license ($12 U.S.) required; drive on left.

SEAT BELT/CHILD RESTRAINT LAWS: Seat belts are required for front-seat passengers.

HOLIDAYS: Jan. 1; Independence Day, Feb. 7; Good Friday; Easter Monday; Labour Day, May 1; Whit Monday, May or June (8th Mon. after Easter); Feast of Corpus Christi, May or June (9th Thurs. after Easter); Emancipation Day, Aug. (1st Mon.); Carnival, Aug. (2nd Mon. and Tues.); Thanksgiving, Oct. 25; Christmas, Dec. 25; Boxing Day, Dec. 26.

TAXES: An 8 percent GCT (general consumption tax) and a 10 percent service charge are added to most hotel and restaurant bills. Departure tax $20 U.S.; $10 for ages 5-12.

IMMIGRATION REQUIREMENTS: Passport and a return or onward ticket are required. No visa is needed for stays up to 3 months. The U.S. Dept. of Homeland Security requires all U.S. citizens returning from the Caribbean to present a valid passport.

PHONING THE ISLANDS: To call Grenada from the U.S. or Canada, dial 1 + 473 + the 7-digit local number.

FURTHER INFORMATION FOR VISITORS:

Grenada Board of Tourism, United States
P.O. Box 1668
Lake Worth, FL 33460
(561) 588-8176
(800) 927-9554

Grenada Board of Tourism, St. George's
Burns Point
St. George's, Grenada
(473) 440-2279

Points of Interest

See map page 128.

St. Andrew Parish (B-2)

The largest of Grenada's six parishes, St. Andrew has the longest coastline and is the island's agricultural center. Mangos, pumpkins, yams, lemons and coconuts are just a few of the crops that supplement the region's nutmeg production.

GRAND ETANG NATIONAL PARK (B-2)

Grand Etang National Park is 9.3 mi. (15 km) n.e. of St. George's in St. Andrew Parish, following signs to Snug Corner and St. Margaret. The park preserves 3,816 acres (1,544 hectares) of rain forest in the central mountain range, 1,740 feet (530 m) above sea level. Grand Etang Lake fills the crater of an extinct volcano.

Marked trails include a 15-minute introduction to the rain forest, a 1-hour hike around the lake and a 2-hour climb to the top of Mt. Qua Qua. Trail maps are usually available at the Grand Etang Forest Center, which offers exhibits and videotape presentations about the park's diverse flora and fauna.

Trails are often muddy; waterproof hiking boots are recommended. Allow 1 hour minimum. Mon.-Fri. 8-4, Sat.-Sun. 9-5. Admission $2. Phone (473) 440-6160.

GRENVILLE (B-2)

Grenada's second largest town is home to one of the island's largest nutmeg factories. The Grenville Nutmeg Processing Station offers guided tours and demonstrations. Saturday morning is market day, when local farmers, anglers and merchants bring their wares to town. Culture, music and exotic foods are all part of the Rainbow City Festival on the first weekend in August.

St. George Parish (C-1)

Home to Grenada's capital city, St. George Parish encompasses the southwest corner of the island. A number of historic forts crown the hilltops above St. George's Harbour; the best restored of these is the Fort George, built by the French in 1705.

ST. GEORGE'S (C-1) pop. 37,000

The streets of St. George's wind in a medieval tangle up several steep hillsides. One hill is so steep that it divides St. George's, but a tunnel through the hill connects the two sections. These terraced ways, the red- and white-gabled houses and the lively Saturday morning market lend an Old World charm to the town, considered by many travelers to be among the most picturesque in the Caribbean.

Grenada Board of Tourism: Burns Point, P.O. Box 293, St. George's, Grenada. **Phone:** (473) 440-2279.

BAY GARDENS is 4 mi. (6 km) n.e. in the suburb of St. Paul's. On the slope of an old sugar mill, the 20-acre walkthrough tropical garden is landscaped with fish pools, fruit and spice trees and more than 3,000 species of plants and flowers in tropical bloom. Guides explain the growing and processing of spice plants; tours are available by appointment. **Hours:** Open Mon.-Sat. at 8; closing times vary. Closed Jan. 1, Easter and Christmas. **Cost:** $4. **Phone:** (473) 435-4544 or (473) 404-6266.

GRENADA NATIONAL MUSEUM is on Young St. in the Antilles Bldg. Housed in a former French army barracks and prison built in 1704, the museum traces the island's history with pictorial displays and artifacts from the Indian period, the colonial period, the 1979 revolution and the 1983 intervention. Art galleries and a children's play center also are featured. **Hours:** Mon.-Fri. 9-5, Sat. 10-1, Sun. by appointment. **Cost:** $4; $1 (ages 3-12). **Phone:** (473) 440-3725.

St. Patrick Parish (B-2)

The northernmost parish on the island, St. Patrick encompasses the 16-acre (6-hectare) Lake Antoine, a shallow crater lake formed by an extinct volcano. Leapers Hill, a cliff near the fishing village of Sauteurs, marks the spot where some 40 Carib Indians jumped to their death in 1651 rather than submit to French colonists who were battling for possession of the island.

The 450-acre (180-hectare) Levera National Park protects mangrove swamps, another volcanic crater lake and a scenic beach. Hiking, swimming and bird-watching are popular activities.

RIVER ANTOINE RUM DISTILLERY is 6 mi. (10 km) n. of Grenville near Lake Antoine. One of the oldest water-driven distilleries still in operation in the Caribbean, the mill was built in 1785. Its signature product is the overproof Rivers Rum, a high-octane drink with an alcohol volume of more than 75 percent, or 151 proof. Guided tours of the distillery's operation include sugar cane crushing, extraction, fermentation and bottling. **Time:** Allow 30 minutes minimum. **Hours:** Self-guiding tours are offered Mon.-Fri. 8-4, Sat.-Sun. by appointment. **Cost:** $2. **Phone:** (473) 442-7109.

Parc National de la Guadeloupe, Basse-Terre / © Christian Heeb

Guadeloupe

K nown as "the Emerald Isle," Guadeloupe (gwa-da-LOOP) lies midway between Puerto Rico and Venezuela. The "island" is really two smaller land
masses joined by two bridges over a narrow channel called Rivière-Salée.
Grande-Terre to the east typifies the French Antilles with rolling hills and sugarcane
fields; Basse-Terre to the west is a rugged, mountainous island dominated by the
volcano of La Soufrière. Its hills and ravines are lush with hardwood forests, ferns,
bamboo, bananas, hibiscus, bougainvillea and guava. One road follows the coast
while another crosses the highlands, providing a spectacular drive.

Pointe-à-Pitre, Guadeloupe's commercial
center on Grande-Terre, and Basse-Terre, the
capital, contrast busy port life with a French
provincial atmosphere. This Gallic ambiance
also is evident in Guadeloupe's island dependencies. The closest of these are Marie-Galante;
La Désirade; and Les Saintes, where Norman-
French speech and customs prevail. Farther
north are Guadeloupe's two other island dependencies: St. Barthélémy, once a Swedish
colony; and Saint Martin, where French and
Dutch influences mingle.

History
Called "the island of beautiful waters" by
the Carib Indians, Guadeloupe was discovered
by Christopher Columbus in 1493, on his second voyage. He named the island for the Spanish monastery of Santa Maria de Guadalupe de
Estremadura, but Spain established no colonies
due to fierce opposition from the Caribs.
Guadeloupe and her sister island Martinique
were settled by French colonists in 1635 and
soon became important centers of sugar
production.

Both islands were incorporated as departments of France in 1946 and elevated to regions
in 1974, with each island holding representation
in the French Parliament by two senators, four
deputies and two members of the Economic
Council. The local government consists of

elected General and Regional Councils as well as a prefect, or governor; the island's inhabitants are French citizens.

Shopping

The French islands are excellent shopping centers, where perfumes and other luxury made-in-France products are sold at or below Paris, New York or St. Thomas prices. Au Bonheur des Dames and Passion Beauté on the Rue Frébault are among the most popular places to shop for perfumes. Rues de Nozières and Schoelcher also have shops carrying French imports as well as madras cottons, watches, silver and china. The local outdoor market, Marché d'Epices, and the Place de la Victoire are worth visiting.

Most shops are open Mon.-Fri. 8-noon and 2-6, Sat. 9-1, and are closed holidays. Banking hours are Mon.-Fri. 8-noon and 2-4; summer hours are Mon.-Fri. 8-3. Stores can give up to 20-percent discounts on some luxury goods purchased with travelers checks or certain credit cards.

Food and Drink

Guadeloupe shares its cuisine with France. Delicacies like *escargots* are on the menus of many restaurants and can be savored with excellent French wines. Traditional Creole dishes available in most restaurants lend added zest to dining. *Colombo,* a spicy Indian dish of curry-like seeds cooked with either beef, pork, chicken, mutton, conch or goat, is eaten with rice; stuffed crab and crayfish are prepared in a variety of ways; *calalou* soup is made from greens, West Indian herbs and bacon; *court bouillon* combines a thick fish stew with rice; gumbos are eaten with rice and fried codfish; and yams are cooked in their skins and seasoned with butter and cheese. Gourmet menus list roasted wild goat, duckling and a salad of coconut and hearts of palm.

Meals taste best preceded by Punch Guadeloupéen, or "Ti Punch," a delicious and quite potent rum potion. Rum is bottled locally, as is mineral water. Local milk and water are safe. At the airport and around the dock at Terre-de-Haut, one of the Saintes islands, barefoot children sell a delicious coconut pastry called *tourment d'amour,* or "torment of love."

Guadeloupe boasts more than 200 restaurants, often modest in appearance but superior in cuisine. Served after noon, lunch is a big meal in Guadeloupe, as evidenced by

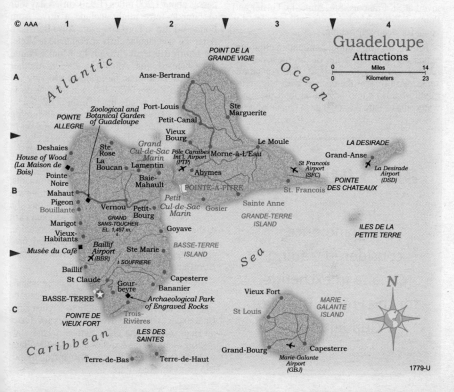

multicourse Creole lunches. Most hotels and restaurants include a 10- to 15-percent service charge in their prices. If not, this charge will be added to the final bill.

Sports and Amusements

Beaches of white, ochre and black volcanic sand offer almost unlimited opportunities for swimming, snorkeling, scuba diving, water skiing, windsurfing and other aquatic sports. Grande-Terre's southern coast boasts several good public beaches, including those at Ste. Anne, St. François and Gosier as well as tiny coves of white powdery sands only a hike away from the main beach road. Favorable trade winds called *les alizés* create conditions ideal for sailing, water skiing and windsurfing between Grande-Terre and the islet of Gosier, just offshore from Gosier.

Beginning scuba divers can enroll in several diving schools based at local hotels. Several water sports concessions are congregated on the beach at Gosier. Yacht chartering has become increasingly popular in recent years; arrangements can be made at Port de Plaisance in Bas du Fort; at Nautica in Gourbeyre; or through any of the island's hotels.

Sailing, cruising and jet skiing can be enjoyed at St. François, Ste. Anne, Le Gosier and Pointe-à-Pitre. Most resorts will arrange for boats for deep-sea fishing.

Riding, hiking, camping, mountain climbing, tennis and golf are some of the most popular recreational pursuits on land. The adventuresome, wise to arm themselves with bug spray, might wish to camp or hike around the many waterfalls of Parc National de la Guadeloupe on

---

DID YOU KNOW

England once considered trading Canada in exchange for the French island of Guadeloupe.

Basse-Terre; the tourism office at 5 Square de la Banque in Pointe-à-Pitre publishes *Walks and Hikes*. St. François boasts a championship golf course, and several of the larger hotels throughout the island have their own tennis courts, lighted for night playing. Cockfighting is in season from November through April, and horse racing takes place periodically at Baie-Mahault, Bellecourt and the St. Jacques Hippodrome at Anse Bertrand.

Guadeloupe has two seasonal festivals that captivate islanders and visitors alike. The first is the pre-Lenten Carnival in February or March, which includes masked revelers and costumed dancers winding through the streets, parades with elaborate floats and street parties. The second, on the Saturday closest to August 10, is called the Fête des Cuisinières, or the Women Cooks' Festival. The celebration begins with a religious service in the cathedral in Pointe-à-Pitre. Then there is a procession of women in Creole dress carrying exotic island specialties through the capital, followed by a 5-hour feast with much singing and dancing.

Sightseeing

Guadeloupe's major road system encompasses about 1,200 miles (1,930 km). A day tour of Grande-Terre might include a drive from Pointe-à-Pitre to Port-Louis and Anse Bertrand. After the spectacular cliffs at Pointe de la Vigie, the return trip leads through Le Moule, Pointe des Châteaux, Ste. Anne and Gosier. Another all-day excursion can be made by crossing the channel to Basse-Terre, following Route de la Traversèe as it winds through the 73,240-acre (29,640-hectare) Parc National, then turning south along the coast to Basse-Terre and on to the archeological park at Trois-Rivières, and returning to Pointe-à-Pitre via the coast road.

Other excursions include a drive from Pointe-à-Pitre to the village of St. François, then east to Pointe des Châteaux, returning via Ste. Anne or Le Moule; and a drive along the Route de la Traversèe through the national park to the white and golden beaches near Deshaies, returning through Ste. Rose. A detailed brochure on these drives is available from the tourist office in Pointe-à-Pitre.

Excursions to Guadeloupe's offshore islands of Les Saintes, Marie-Galante and La Désirade offer an alternative approach to sightseeing. Boat excursions leave Trois-Rivières for Terre-de-Haut, one of the eight Saintes islands, affording visits to fine beaches and a small village with quaint bistros. Ferries also travel round-trip from Pointe-à-Pitre.

Ninety-minute minibus tours of Terre-de-Haut (narrated in French) include a visit to the island bastion Le Fort Napoléon. Round trips are available via Air Caraïbes. The island of Marie-Galante, dotted with sugar factories and century-old windmills, can be reached by air in 15 minutes or by ferry in 35 minutes. Another scenic excursion cruises along the Rivière-Salée from La Darse (the harbor) in Pointe-à-Pitre to one of the small islands just north.

Transportation

Pôle Caraïbes International Airport, just north of Pointe-à-Pitre, services flights from New York, Newark, Miami, San Juan and other U.S. cities and Caribbean islands. Air Caraïbes makes frequent flights to Guadeloupe's island dependencies and to the other islands of the French West Indies. Charter flights can be arranged at the small airports at St. François on Grande-Terre and Baillif on Basse-Terre. Pointe-à-Pitre is a port of call for many cruise ships.

Taxi fare from the airport to Pointe-à-Pitre is approximately $18; from 9 p.m. to 7 a.m., all day Sunday and on holidays the fare increases by 40 percent. Crowded buses used largely by islanders also are available. Car rental plans should be made in advance; a valid U.S. driver's license is required. Rates are approximately $50 a day plus a kilometer charge; gas is not included. Camper-car rentals are available at Abymes.

Daily ferry transportation to the islands of Marie-Galante and Les Saintes is offered by Brudey Frères and TMC Archipel. These island routes also are serviced by Caribbean Express and L'Express des Iles, high-speed passenger ferries that connect Guadeloupe with Dominica, Martinique and St. Lucia.

Fast Facts

POPULATION: 431,170.

AREA: 1,373 sq km (530 sq mi.).

CAPITAL: Basse-Terre.

HIGHEST POINT: 1,484 m (4,869 ft.), La Soufrière.

LOWEST POINT: Sea level, Caribbean Sea.

TIME ZONE(S): Atlantic Standard.

LANGUAGE: French and Creole.

GOVERNMENT: Overseas Department of France.

UNIT OF CURRENCY: Euro Dollar. $1 U.S. = approx. .78 Euro.

ELECTRICITY: 220 volts, 50 cycles AC.

MINIMUM AGE FOR DRIVERS: 21-25, depending on the rental car agency. U.S. license valid; drive on right.

MINIMUM AGE FOR GAMBLING: 18.

SEAT BELT/CHILD RESTRAINT LAWS: Seat belts are required for all passengers. Children under 12 must ride in the back seat.

HOLIDAYS: Jan. 1; Epiphany, Jan. 6; Easter Monday; Labour Day, May 1; Victory Day, May 8; Ascension Day, May (6th Thurs. after Easter); Whit Monday, May or June (8th Mon. after Easter); Abolition Day, May 27; Bastille Day, July 14; Schoelcher Day, July 21; Feast of the Assumption, Aug. 15; All Saints' Day, Nov. 1; Remembrance Day, Nov. 11; Christmas, Dec. 25.

TAXES: A 10-15 percent service charge is added to most hotel and restaurant bills. Departure tax $20 U.S. (included in plane fare).

IMMIGRATION REQUIREMENTS: A valid passport and return or onward ticket are required for U.S. citizens entering the French West Indies. No visa needed for stays up to 3 months. The U.S. Dept. of Homeland Security requires all U.S. citizens returning from the Caribbean to present a valid passport.

PHONING THE ISLANDS: To call Guadeloupe from the U.S. or Canada, dial 011 + 590 + 590 + the 6-digit local number.

FURTHER INFORMATION FOR VISITORS:

French Government Tourist Office
825 3rd Ave., 29th Floor
New York, NY 10022
(212) 838-7800

Guadeloupe Tourist Office
5 Square de la Banque
Pointe-à-Pitre, Grande-Terre Island
Guadeloupe
(590) 82-09-30

Points of Interest

See map page 133.

Basse-Terre Island (C-2)

The mountainous island of Basse-Terre (boss-TARE) is dominated by 4,869-foot (1,484 m) La Soufrière. The village of St. Claude, noted for its coffee and banana plantations and stately homes, is the starting point for many trips up the volcano. After driving through the East Indian village of Matouba, where such ancient rites as animal sacrifice are still practiced, another road runs through the Bains Jaunes Rain Forest to within a 20-minute climb of the summit.

Southeast of the capital city of Basse-Terre are the engraved rocks at Trois-Rivières, a string of fishing hamlets and Ste. Marie, where Christopher Columbus landed in 1493. Inland from Trois-Rivières are the well-known thermal baths at Ravine Chaude.

BASSE-TERRE (C-2) pop. 12,410

Basse-Terre is the administrative capital of Guadeloupe. Known for its 17th-century Cathedral of Our Lady of Guadeloupe, French provincial atmosphere and colorful port life, this charming city offers fine shops and open-air markets.

ARCHAEOLOGICAL PARK OF ENGRAVED ROCKS (PARC ARCHÉOLOGIQUE DES ROCHES GRAVÉES) is in Trois-Rivières. Deep in a forest grotto, the park protects carvings left by Arawak Indians. A botanical garden is on the grounds. **Tours:** Guided tours are available. **Hours:** Daily 8:30-5. Last entrance 30 minutes before closing. **Cost:** $2.50. **Phone:** (590) 92-91-88.

FORT LOUIS DELGRÈS is near the village of Gourbeyre. The fortification, also known as Fort Saint-Charles, was built about 1650 by Charles Houel, the island governor appointed Marquis de Guadeloupe by Louis XIV. Guarding the approach to Basse-Terre, the fort served in several battles against the British. French officers General Richpance and Admiral Gourbeyre are buried on the premises. **Hours:** Daily 7-5. **Cost:** Free. **Phone:** (590) 81-37-48.

BOUILLANTE (C-2) pop. 7,336

The steep Mamelles mountain range plunges into the sea at the picturesque bay of Bouillante on the western coast. Offshore is Pigeon Island and the Cousteau Marine Reserve, considered one of the best dive sites in the world. Snorkeling, scuba diving and glass-bottom boat tours depart from Malendure Beach.

ZOOLOGICAL AND BOTANTICAL GARDEN OF GUADELOUPE (LE PARC ZOOLOGIQUE ET BOTANIQUE DE GUADELOUPE) is 5.6 mi. (9 km) n.e. The zoo and botanical garden is home to monkeys, raccoons, agoutis, mongooses, turtles, tropical birds and jaguars. A boardwalk canopy tour takes visitors high above the dense forest, and a self-guiding nature walk follows a series of suspension bridges. **Time:** Allow 1 hour minimum. **Hours:** Daily 9-5. **Cost:** $19; $11.50 (ages 8-12); $10 (ages 3-7). **Phone:** (590) 98-83-52.

PETIT-BOURG (C-2) pop. 20,528

DOMAINE DE VALOMBREUSE is on Cabout St. A 9-acre (3.6-hectare) tropical garden contains more than 450 varieties of plants and flowers. Also within the 20-acre (8-hectare) park is a bird sanctuary featuring some 300 species. **Time:** Allow 1 hour minimum. **Hours:** Daily 8-6. Last admission 1 hour before closing. **Cost:** $9.50; $4.50 (ages 0-11). **Phone:** (590) 95-50-50. ⓜ

POINTE NOIRE (C-2) pop. 7,689

Named "Black Point," this small coastal village gets its name from the black volcanic sand on its beaches. Sand paintings are offered at local craft markets.

HOUSE OF COCOA (LA MAISON DU CACAO) is .8 mi. (1 km) s. at the jct. of Route de la Traversée. The history of cocoa and chocolate are represented at this working cocoa plantation, where cocoa is harvested by traditional methods. Tastings are offered. **Time:** Allow 30 minutes minimum. **Hours:** Mon.-Sat. 9:30-5, Sun. 9:30-1; reduced hours Sept. 1-15. **Cost:** $5; $3 (children and senior citizens). **Phone:** (590) 98-25-23. ⓜ

HOUSE OF WOOD (LA MAISON DU BOIS) is on Les Plaines Road. Traditional woodworking and the island's tree varieties are showcased at this house, which is made of local woods and contains permanent exhibits of furniture, boats and musical instruments. **Hours:** Tues.-Sun. 9:30-5, Oct.-July. **Cost:** $12. **Phone:** (590) 98-16-90.

STE. ROSE (C-2) pop. 17,574

LE DOMAINE DE SÉVERIN is just w. of La Boucan traffic circle on road RN2, following signs. Originally called the Bellevue Plantation, this 18th-century sugar estate was purchased by the Marsolle family in 1928. The working rum distillery is operated by a paddlewheel. Tropical gardens and crawfish pools are among the sights on a narrated train tour. Rum tastings are offered, and food is available. **Time:** Allow 1 hour minimum. **Hours:** Mon.-Sat. 8:30-12:30 and 2:30-5:30. Train tours depart at 9:30, 10:45 and 11:30 (also at 2:30 and 3:45, Jan.-Apr.; at 2:30, May-Aug. and Oct.-Dec.). **Cost:** $16; $9 (ages

4-12). **Phone:** (590) 28-91-86 or (590) 28-28-11. [🍴]

MUSÉE DU RHUM is at Belle Vue. The Rum Museum chronicles three centuries of sugar cane history, leading to the distilling of rum. Exhibits include early production equipment, models of trade ships and information about Caribbean customs and daily life. An extensive butterfly and arthropod collection also is displayed. Tastings at the Reimonenq Distillery are offered. **Time:** Allow 2 hours minimum. **Hours:** Mon.-Sat. 9-5. **Cost:** $8.75; $5.85 (ages 10-18); $4.50 (ages 0-9). **Phone:** (590) 28-70-04 or (590) 28-79-92.

VIEUX-HABITANTS (C-2) pop. 7,611

Coffee, vanilla and cocoa flourish on Basse Terre's west-central coast. Vieux-Habitants, the first village on the island, was settled here in 1636. Its name means "old inhabitants." The 18th-century Saint-Joseph Church is noted for its collection of gold and silver relics.

MUSÉE DU CAFÉ is .6 km (.4 mi) n. The museum traces the cultivation of coffee in Guadeloupe from 1721 to the present. Historic exhibits at this working plantation include antique coffee mills and roasters. Visitors may observe the processing of bonifière coffee and taste the finished product. **Time:** Allow 30 minutes minimum. **Hours:** Daily 9-5. **Cost:** $8; $7 (ages 0-12). **Phone:** (590) 98-54-96. [🍴]

Grande-Terre Island (B-3)

Unlike its mountainous sister, Grande-Terre (gron-tare) is characterized by rolling hills, sandy beaches and sugarcane fields. The limestone islet of Gosier, off the coast of the town of the same name, has a white coral beach. Farther east, swimming is delightful at Ste. Anne, Le Moule, Port-Louis and St. François, a fishing village noted for its square and buildings. The coastline is particularly scenic between Le Moule beach and Pointe des Châteaux. A small airport at the Hamak and Kalenda hotels offers charter flights to local islands.

LE MOULE (B-3) pop. 20,827

The former capital of Guadeloupe, Le Moule has a beach that was once the battleground for Carib warriors and French and English soldiers. In the 19th century, nearly all of the sugar and rum produced on Grande-Terre was shipped from Le Moule's harbor.

EDGAR CLERC ARCHEOLOGICAL MUSEUM is 1.2 mi. (2 km) n. at 440 Route de la Rosette in Parc de la Rosette. Two rooms house the permanent collection of archeological artifacts of the Carib and Arawak Indians. The building is surrounded by a tropical garden that overlooks the ocean. **Hours:** Mon.-Wed. 9-5. Closed major holidays. **Cost:** Free. **Phone:** (590) 23-57-57 or (590) 23-57-43.

POINTE-À-PITRE (B-3) pop. 20,948

Pointe-à-Pitre is the commercial capital of Guadeloupe and seat of the sub-prefecture of Grande-Terre. About 40 miles (64 km) northeast of Basse-Terre, Pointe-à-Pitre is reached by either of two bridges from Basse-Terre Island. Colonial and modern buildings complement each other; white bungalows with red roofs are separated by tree-lined parks and a large market square. Place de la Victoire, punctuated by royal palms, shade trees and poincianas, is bordered by attractive wooden houses with balconies.

Guadeloupe Tourist Office: 5 Square de la Banque, Pointe-à-Pitre, Guadeloupe 97163. **Phone:** (590) 82-09-30.

AQUARIUM DE LA GUADELOUPE is .6 mi. (1 km) w. of the marina in Bas du Fort. The facility displays marine life found in the waters around Guadeloupe, including sharks and piranhas. Boat rides to Guadeloupe National Park are available. **Time:** Allow 30 minutes minimum. **Hours:** Daily 9-7. **Cost:** $8; $6 (ages 5-12). **Phone:** (590) 90-92-38. [🍴]

FORT FLEUR D'EPÉE overlooks the bay. The point offers a fine view of the islands of Le Saints and Dominica and the mountains of Basse-Terre. Because of its strategic location, this 18th-century fort was the scene of fierce struggles between the French and English. Today preserved battlements, dungeons with underground passageways, some walls and a small chapel remain. **Hours:** Daily 9-6. **Cost:** Free. **Phone:** (590) 90-94-61.

SCHOELCHER MUSEUM is at 24 rue Peynier behind the market. The museum is dedicated to abolitionist Victor Schoelcher, who is credited with ending slavery in the French West Indies in 1848. Housed in a 19th-century setting, the museum contains some of Schoelcher's personal belongings and traces the island's recent history. **Hours:** Mon.-Fri. 9-5. Closed major holidays. **Cost:** $3; $1.50 (ages 0-12). **Phone:** (590) 82-08-04.

Iles Des Saintes (C-2)

The Saints Islands are a cluster of eight islands considered among the most beautiful in the Caribbean. Their isolation from the plantation system distinguishes them from sister islands and enabled them to maintain a way of life in which fishing is still the main occupation and source of income.

Only two of the islands are inhabited; the fishing village of Bourg is found on Terre-de-Haut. Standing over the bay is Pain de Sucre (Sugar Loaf), a mountain named for its resemblance to a mound of sugar. Terre-de-Haut can be reached by boat from Trois-Rivières or by daily ferry or flights from Pointe-à-Pitre. *Taxis de l'Ile*, or minibuses, provide transportation to the island's points of interest, including Le Fort Napoléon with its modern art gallery and cactus garden. There is a good view of Terre-de-Haut from the old stone watchtower on 1,014-foot Le Chameau, the island's highest point.

Marie-Galante Island (C-3)

On his second voyage to the New World, Columbus named this island after his flagship, the *Maria Galanda*. Fifteen miles (24 km) southeast of Pointe-à-Pitre, Marie-Galante is Guadeloupe's largest dependency. The round, flat island is often called *la*

grande galette, or "the big pancake." More than 100 windmills once dotted the countryside, and many ruins are still visible.

About half of the rural island's 12,500 inhabitants live on the southwest coast at Grand-Bourg, the administrative capital. To the north is the fishing village of Saint-Louis, and to the east is Capesterre, home of the Bielle, Bellevue and Poisson rum distilleries. Transportation to Marie-Galante is available by ferry from Pointe-à-Pitre and St. François or by air.

Dunn's River Falls, Ocho Rios / © Zeid / eStock Photo

Jamaica

A multiracial population and varied scenery are primary components of Jamaica's charm. Most Jamaicans are descendants of African slaves brought to the island between the 17th and 19th centuries, but Chinese, East Indians, Lebanese, Europeans and North Americans as well as nationals from neighboring republics, also have made the island their home. This multiplicity, most evident in the port city of Kingston, reflects a special unity in the country's motto, "Out of many, one people."

Third largest of the Greater Antilles, Jamaica is 550 miles (885 km) south of Florida. About 146 miles (235 km) long and 51 miles (82 km) wide, the landscape is primarily one of contrasts, ranging from misty forest-clad mountains to bare scrubland and fields. The island's diverse terrain also is reflected in its beaches, which vary from fine coral sand in sheltered bays and inlets to black sand along the rugged coastline, where the mountains plunge straight into the sea. Montego Bay, Negril, Ocho Rios and Port Antonio are some of the most popular resort centers. Small towns and mountain villages might lack the comforts of the developed port cities but are rich in island lore and natural

beauty. Blanketed with peach trees and strawberry fields, the summit of 7,402-foot Blue Mountain Peak provides a 90-mile (145-km) panorama on clear days.

History

The Indians in Cuba had told Christopher Columbus of *Xaymaca*, the "land of wood and water." He attempted to land at St. Ann's Bay in May 1494, but was met by hostile Taínos and had to remain offshore. After overcoming lighter resistance, he came ashore at Discovery Bay the next day, then landed at Montego Bay before moving on. Columbus made an inauspicious return in 1503; the last two ships of his fourth voyage were forced to run aground at St.

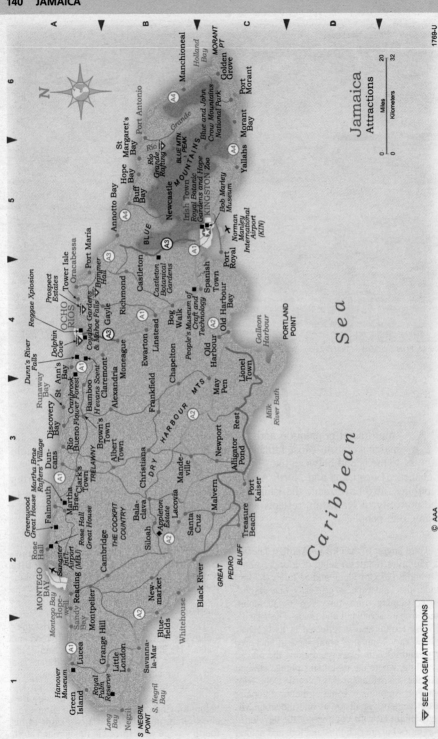

Jamaica
Attractions

Miles 20
Kilometers 32

1769-U

© AAA

▽ SEE AAA GEM ATTRACTIONS

Ann's Bay, and he and his crew were marooned there for more than a year. It wasn't until a small charter could be sent from Hispaniola that Columbus was able to return home, where he died 2 years later.

Diego Columbus, son of the explorer, returned to St. Ann's Bay in 1509 and founded Sevilla Nueva. The marshy site was soon abandoned, however, in favor of Santiago de la Vega (St. James of the Plain) at present-day Spanish Town. Having depleted the Taíno population through overwork and disease, the Spaniards turned to Africa for slaves and in 1517 imported the first of Jamaica's current majority race. The island was never fully developed as a Spanish colony, however, and in 1655 a British expedition literally walked into Spanish Town and took it over. The island was officially ceded to England in 1670 by the Treaty of Madrid.

Also during this time, West Indian buccaneers had made Port Royal their headquarters, giving the city a reputation as a bawdy mecca for the adventurous and the wicked. These were the days when Sir Henry Morgan rose to a commanding position among the privateers who dominated the Caribbean. His widespread successful adventures, however, overlapped the signing of peace with Spain, and he was recalled to England under arrest in 1672. When the Spanish again became a threat, he was knighted by Charles II and returned to Jamaica in 1674 as the deputy governor and the island's only honored pirate.

Kingston, the present capital, was built after an earthquake destroyed Port Royal on June 7, 1692. The flourishing slave trade and sugar and cotton plantations made Jamaica rich during the 18th century.

The cause of the slaves was supported by a group known as the Maroons, slaves freed by the Spanish to harass the English before the Spanish fled the island in 1660. Taking refuge in the hills of the Cockpit Country, these former slaves were joined by other fugitives. Together they successfully waged a guerrilla war against the English, and in 1738 the Maroons were granted self-rule and given title to their lands free of taxes. Descendants of the Maroons still live in this area; they are free of taxation and all government laws, except in the case of murder.

Although the slave trade was finally abolished in 1808, the oppression of this group did not improve. An uprising against the treatment of slaves took place in 1831; Baptist preacher Sam Sharpe led an islandwide revolt that forced the governor to declare martial law. So incensed were members of Britain's Parliament at the government's bloody crackdown, during which Sharpe and thousands more were executed, that

abolition came shortly thereafter. Today Sam Sharpe is a national hero.

As a result of these frequent rebellions, slavery was abolished in 1834. Jamaica's newly freed population underwent years of economic and social hard times. As plantation life came to a gradual end, most workers took to the hills and practiced subsistence farming, a way of life that was to continue for generations. The 20th century, however, brought about sweeping reforms and a national identity. Marcus Garvey engendered racial pride, Alexander Bustamante organized a labor union and Norman Manley a political party. Increasingly, Jamaicans were making a place in the world.

The first civil governor of Jamaica was appointed in 1661, and the island was governed by a representative council until 1866, when a crown-colony government was established by act of Parliament. The island became independent within the British Commonwealth on August 6, 1962. A prime minister heads the government, which has its executive power vested in a cabinet; a governor general represents the British monarch. Legislative functions are assigned to a bicameral house. Sugar, bananas and coffee continue to fluctuate in prominence but are still the chief export crops. Since the 1960s bauxite and alumina exports and tourism have become the main earners of foreign exchange for the island.

Shopping

Jamaica was rich with the plunder of a continent in the days when Capt. Henry Morgan swaggered down the streets of Port Royal. Today the island is rich with merchandise from the four corners of the Earth. Free-port shops in Kingston, Montego Bay, Negril and Ocho Rios have good buys on Swiss watches, cameras, French perfumes, British woolens and cashmeres, imported liquor, silverware, crystal, jewelry and bone china. Boutiques feature Jamaican resort clothes.

Island handicrafts include woodcarvings, inlaid boxes and trays, Jamaican dolls, straw hats, colorful baskets, pottery, shell articles and yard goods with vivid tropical prints. They are sold in specialty shops at the Kingston Crafts Market, north of the cruise ship pier in Kingston, and the Crafts Market at Harbour and Church streets in Montego Bay. Port Antonio has a straw market downtown, and the Ocho Rios Craft Park and the Olde Market are along Main Street in Ocho Rios. At Wassi Art Pottery Works near Fern Gully, visitors can watch potters create ethnic designs from clay.

East of Falmouth, the Caribatik factory produces regionally famous batik paintings and garments. Islanders often set up stalls along the roadside; you should be prepared to barter for good prices. The skill of Jamaican needle-women has made the island's embroidered Irish linen dresses valued throughout the world. Paintings and sculptures by local artists make lasting souvenirs. A pound or so of Jamaica's excellent Blue Mountain Coffee also is a favorite take-home item.

Several shopping centers cover the southern end of Constant Spring Road leading to the Half Way Tree area, Kingston's main shopping district. A shopping complex is on the grounds of Devon House, a 19th-century great house on Hope Road. There also are several shopping malls in the Kingston area. Mall shopping in Montego Bay is available at the Hip Strip (Gloucester Avenue), Fairview Shopping Centre and the town center. In Ocho Rios there are the Island Plaza, Island Village, Little Pub Shopping Complex, Ocean Village Shopping Centre, Soni's Plaza and the Taj Mahal—all on Main Street. Kingston shops are open Mon.-Sat. 9-5, but shops close at noon on Wed. in downtown Kingston and on Thurs. in New Kingston and Montego Bay. In Ocho Rios retail stores also are open Mon.-Sat. 9-5. Banking hours are Mon.-Thurs. 9-2, Fri. 9-4.

Food and Drink

The Jamaican national dish is *ackee* and salt-fish, a dish made from imported salted cod and the fleshy lobes of the seeds of the ackee tree, cooked with onions, tomatoes and pepper in oil. Another staple is boiled rice and peas (red beans). On more exotic menus, gourmets will find goat cooked with Indian curry and served hot with boiled green bananas and rice, baked crab and pepperpot soup, a thick green "hot-pot" made of *callaloo* (a spinach-like vegetable), Indian kale, salted pork, vegetables and pepper. West Indian lobster and red snapper dishes are abundant.

Another peppery-hot island specialty is jerk pork. This was a favorite dish of the Maroons, who roasted wild hogs over a wood fire. The special flavoring is achieved through spices from a rich, peppery marinade and the type of wood used—the pimento (allspice) wood. Jerk pork and jerk chicken are available at roadside stands throughout the island.

Jamaica has a mouthwatering assortment of locally grown fruits and vegetables: mangoes, pawpaws, naseberries, sweetsops, soursops, ortaniques, otaheites, star apples, melons, rose apples, guinep, avocado pears, ugli fruit, tangerines, limes, pineapples, yams, green bananas, plantains, breadfruit, yampie, cocoa,

cho-cho, turnips, pumpkins and beetroot. A delicious ice cream is made from coconut, paw-paw, pineapple and soursop. Another favorite dessert is matrimony, a refreshing dish of oranges and the pulp of the star apple.

Rum is Jamaica's national drink. Consumed in an endless variety of concoctions, it can be mixed with ginger ale or coconut water, brewed with pimento berries to produce Pimento Dram Liqueur, aged with citrus peel, heated to a toddy or blended with coffee to produce Tia Maria Liqueur. Rumona is another rum liqueur. The island's most popular rum-based beverage is Planters Punch. Popular rum brands are Appleton, Myers's and Wray and Nephew's White Overproof.

Jamaica also brews a strong light beer called Red Stripe. Cooling nonalcoholic drinks include homemade ginger beer; sorrel, a Christmas favorite; and fruit punches made with pineapple, banana, orange, melon and tamarind juices and coconut water. Also popular is Ting, a grapefruit-flavored soft drink. Tap water is chlorinated and filtered.

Among eateries offering local cuisine, Montego Bay and Ocho Rios also have their share of Chinese, Italian, French and Continental restaurants. Tips average 15 to 20 percent.

Sports and Amusements

Swimming heads the list of sports and amusements in Jamaica. The most noted beaches with miles of white sand and crystal waters are on the north shore; Doctor's Cave Beach and Cornwall Beach at Montego Bay share an excellent strand. Negril Beach is on the western shore. Good beaches on the south shore include Alligator Pond and Bluefields near Savanna-La-Mar, and the black sand beaches in Kingston and Black River. Outside Kingston Harbour are the white sand beaches of Lime Cay and Maiden Cay. Mineral spas reputed to cure certain rheumatic ailments are Milk River in Clarendon, Rockfort Spa in Kingston and the Bath Fountain in St. Thomas.

Countless water sports opportunities await guests not content to merely lie on the beaches. The offshore islands and cays near Kingston, the coves around Ocho Rios, the offshore reefs at Montego Bay and the waters surrounding Port Antonio and Negril are good diving areas. Diving operators offer both guide services and courses for beginners.

Snorkel and scuba equipment, water skis, jet skis and small sailing craft can be rented from the larger resort hotels and at Turtle Beach in Ocho Rios. Arrangements for sailing can be made through the Morgan's Harbor Hotel in Kingston and the Montego Bay Yacht Club, where colorful regattas are held each winter. The Jamaica Tourist Board maintains a current list of charter companies.

Rafting is popular on the Río Grande, Martha Brae and Great rivers. Less adventuresome visitors can discover the mysteries of the undersea world in a glass-bottom boat.

Mountain streams offer good fishing for mullet; the sea yields marlin, dolphin, tarpon, barracuda, bonefish, snook, wahoo and small tuna. Boats can be chartered for deep-sea fishing for half- or full-day trips at Kingston, Port Antonio, Ocho Rios, Montego Bay, Negril and Whitehouse. A fishing license is not required. Annual fishing tournaments include the Montego Bay and Port Antonio marlin tournaments in early autumn.

You can attend horse racing Wednesday, Saturday and holidays at Caymanas Park, 6 miles (10 km) west of Kingston; pari-mutuel and quinella betting are permitted. Kingston has cricket matches on Saturday afternoons, January through April. Polo matches are held at Caymanas in Kingston, at Chukka Cove near Ocho Rios and at Drax Hall, also near Ocho Rios. Horseback riding is offered at Chukka Cove, the Double A Ranch near Montego Bay and at resort centers.

The island has 11 golf courses as well as tennis and squash courts that are open to hotel and villa guests. Among the major golf tournaments held is the Jamaica Invitational Pro-Am in December.

Most hotels in Jamaica offer after-dinner entertainment, with many doubling as nightclubs and restaurants. Nightclubs and cabarets are available to suit almost every taste. Many clubs offer conventional orchestras; others echo with the distinctive rhythms of calypso and reggae bands. Floor shows are presented regularly in many of the larger clubs.

Jamaica's reggae sound, made world famous by Bob Marley, Peter Tosh and associates, is a prominent fixture in the lives of young Jamaicans. Shows featuring the nation's top performers take place regularly throughout the island. The most popular is Reggae Sumfest, held in late July in Montego Bay.

Winter visitors to Kingston can enjoy a series of local plays, as well as the "Pantomime"—colorful social commentary—at the Ward Theatre (closed for renovations) and The Little Theatre. The National Dance Theatre Company also performs in Kingston. Films are shown in Kingston, Montego Bay, Ocho Rios, Port Antonio and Mandeville. For more information contact the Jamaica Tourist Board, which publishes two calendars of events during the year.

Aqua Sol Theme Park at Montego Bay is the scene of colorful beach parties on selected Fridays at 7 p.m. The Jamaica Tourist Board regularly schedules entertainment programs that include river rafting trips, dances, parties and barbecues, usually set in a secluded area near the major hotels. Inquire at your hotel for more information.

Sightseeing

With more than 7,800 miles (12,550 km) of primary roads and 2,800 miles (4,500 km) of secondary roads linking every village and hamlet, Jamaica is popular for motor tours. Possible itineraries are numerous, the only limitation being the time you can spend.

Beginning and ending at Kingston, a driving tour around the island takes about 2 days. A condensed circle tour of the island out of Kingston might follow Rte. A3 to Ocho Rios and St. Ann's Bay on the north coast and return via A1 by way of Spanish Town, and include such sites as Castleton Botanical Gardens, restored plantations, Dunn's River Falls, Fern Gully, the Ewarton aluminum plant and the Cathedral of St. James.

South and west of Claremont via unimproved roads is the village of Rhoden Hall. Musician Bob Marley was born in Rhoden Hall in 1945 and interred there in 1981. The mausoleum grounds are open to the public; admission is charged.

Rte. A2 heading east from Negril skirts the pristine South Coast and passes through quaint seaside villages, their shores lined with colorful fishing boats. Near Black River roadside vendors tempt visitors with such local delicacies as fresh escovitch fish, bammy and shrimp. A coastal road south leads to the peaceful town of Treasure Beach.

Tour buses offering 3-hour tours of Kingston drive past the historic residences of the prime minister and governor general and through the campus of the University of the West Indies. They also include stops at the National Gallery of Jamaica, Royal Botanical Gardens and Hope Zoo and the Kingston Crafts Market.

The 3-hour Ocho Rios Tour takes in such area highlights as Prospect Estate, Dunn's River Falls, Shaw Park Gardens and Fern Gully. A 3-hour trip from Ocho Rios to Port Maria and Brimmer Hall Plantation also is available. Departing from Montego Bay, the 3- to 4-hour Great Houses Tour includes a complimentary drink at either Rose Hall or Greenwood; reservations can be made through your hotel. Bus tours that include stops at YS Falls, the Black River and Appleton Estate provide lunch, drinks and hotel pickup; inquire at your hotel for information and reservations.

Scheduled morning and sunset cruises are available for tours of Montego Bay; snorkeling cruises also are available. Arrangements can be made through the tour desks at most hotels.

Transportation

Jamaica is easily accessible by air from several North American cities to Kingston's Norman Manley International Airport and Montego Bay's Sangster International Airport. Air service linking Kingston, Port Antonio, Ocho Rios, Negril and Montego Bay is available on Jamaica Air Link or by charter. Ocho Rios and Montego Bay are ports of call for many cruise ships; a few smaller ships also call on Port Antonio.

There are nearly 11,000 miles (17,700 km) of roadway in Jamaica. Since long-distance cab and limousine rides can be expensive, it is recommended that you secure an accommodations package that includes transportation between your hotel and the airport.

Two types of taxis operate on the island: those affiliated with the Jamaica Union of Travellers Association (JUTA) or Jamaica Cooperative Automobile & Limousine (JCAL)—and those that are not. Non-affiliated taxis can be distinguished from private vehicles by their red license plate. Taxis are unmetered; maximum rates are merely suggested by the government, so it is always wise to determine the fare in advance. A typical fare runs around $20 U.S. for

Fast Facts

POPULATION: 2,500,000.

AREA: 10,991 sq km (4,244 sq mi.).

CAPITAL: Kingston.

HIGHEST POINT: 2,256 m (7,402 ft.), Blue Mountain Peak.

LOWEST POINT: Sea level, Caribbean Sea.

TIME ZONE(S): Eastern Standard.

LANGUAGE: English and a local patois.

GOVERNMENT: Independent. Member of the British Commonwealth of Nations.

UNIT OF CURRENCY: Jamaican dollar. $1 U.S. = approx. 88.75 Jamaica dollars. While Jamaican law requires that Jamaican currency be used when paying for all goods and services, this is not enforced. Most hotels, restaurants and attractions accept U.S. dollars, and credit cards may be used. Jamaican currency is available at airport and hotel exchange bureaus and commercial banks. Keep all exchange receipts; you must present them upon departure when you reconvert unspent Jamaican currency.

ELECTRICITY: 110-220 volts, 50 cycles AC, single and three phases; voltage varies with location.

MINIMUM AGE FOR DRIVERS: 21-25, depending on the rental car agency; an underage surcharge may apply. U.S. license valid; drive on left.

SEAT BELT/CHILD RESTRAINT LAWS: Seat belts are required for driver and front-seat passengers.

HELMETS FOR MOTORCYCLISTS: Required.

HOLIDAYS: Jan. 1; Ash Wednesday; Good Friday; Easter Monday; National Labour Day, May 23; Emancipation Day, Aug. 1; Independence Day, Aug. 6; National Heroes Day, Oct. (3rd Mon.); Christmas, Dec. 25; Boxing Day, Dec. 26.

TAXES: A 10-15 percent room tax and a 10 percent service charge are added to most hotel bills. A 16.25 percent government tax is charged on food, beverages, merchandise and rental cars. Departure tax $28 over age 11.

IMMIGRATION REQUIREMENTS: Passport or proof of U.S. citizenship and a return or onward ticket are required. No visa needed for stays up to 6 months. The U.S. Dept. of Homeland Security requires all U.S. citizens returning from the Caribbean to present a valid passport.

PHONING THE ISLANDS: To call Jamaica from the U.S. or Canada, dial 1 + 876 + the 7-digit local number.

FURTHER INFORMATION FOR VISITORS:

Jamaica Tourist Board, United States
5201 Blue Lagoon Drive, Suite 670
Miami, FL 33126
(305) 665-0557
(800) 233-4582

Jamaica Tourist Board, Kingston
64 Knutsford Blvd.
Kingston, Jamaica
(876) 929-9200

every 10 miles; from midnight to 5 a.m. the fare increases by 25 percent.

Cars can be rented by the day or week; a U.S. driver's license is valid for 1 year. Driving in Jamaica is complicated, and, at times, dangerous. Driving on the left side of the road (with the steering wheel on the right side of the vehicle) complicates navigation of narrow, ill-maintained, two-lane roads often found in the interior of the island. Be prepared to relinquish your right-of-way. Though traffic is relatively light in smaller towns, sidewalks are nearly nonexistent, and thus roadways are shared with animals, pedestrians and those on mopeds and bicycles. Maps are often not helpful, as streets may or may not be marked. When driving across the island, allow 40 miles (64 km) to the hour. In larger cities, expect congestion; busy, unmarked intersections; poor road conditions and streets crowded with pedestrians.

If you're not up for a challenge, it is recommended you rent a car with a driver or hire a tour operator. Half- and full-day excursions are available from all the resort areas. Minibuses, inexpensive but usually very crowded, serve all areas of the island.

Points of Interest

See map page 140.

DISCOVERY BAY (A-3)

Christopher Columbus landed at Discovery Bay in 1494. Dedicated to this historic event is 2.75-acre (1-hectare) Columbus Park, 1.5 miles (2.4 km) west of Discovery Bay on Rte. A1. The park is open during daylight hours and provides a fine view of Discovery Bay. Interesting artifacts of early Jamaican life are present on the nicely landscaped grounds. Puerto Seco Beach also is worth visiting.

FALMOUTH (A-2) pop. 7,245

Falmouth is surrounded by sugar estates and cattle land. Once a leading port, the town has excellent examples of 19th-century Georgian architecture along with a faithful restoration of the early 19th-century courthouse destroyed by fire in 1926. Of special interest is the 1796 Falmouth Anglican Church on Rte. A1. Fresh fruit and vegetables are sold along Market Street.

MARTHA BRAE RAFTERS' VILLAGE is 3.5 mi. (5.6 km) s. on Market St., following signs. A relaxing trip down the Martha Brae River is offered aboard a 30-foot bamboo raft. **Time:** Allow 1 hour, 30 minutes minimum. **Hours:** Raft trips are offered daily 9-4. **Cost:** Fare $60 per raft (accommodates two people). Return transportation to Montego Bay can be included in the fare upon request. **Phone:** (876) 952-0889 or (876) 940-7018. Ⓣ

KINGSTON (C-5) pop. 587,798

Kingston was founded in 1692 when survivors of the Port Royal earthquake resettled around a piggery across the harbor. It became Jamaica's capital in 1872 and is today considered the island's cultural center. An earthquake and fire in 1907 destroyed most of the city, but it was immediately rebuilt. On a broad plain beneath the Blue Mountains, Kingston is built around one of the largest natural harbors in the world.

The new Kingston is even busier than the old; suburbs have grown up around residences of officials and wealthy merchants. The town and surrounding districts are well supplied with good hotels, and the Kingston Crafts Market on Port Royal Street is a shopper's mecca. North of downtown is 74-acre (30-hectare) National Heroes Park, where Jamaican leaders Alexander Bustamante, Norman Manley and Marcus Garvey are buried.

King's House on Hope Road was built around 1770 as the official residence for the governor-general. Fire gutted the stately building in 1925; only the facade survives. Surrounding the ruins are 175 acres (71 hectares) of landscaped grounds, which are open by appointment; phone (876) 927-6424.

Hellshire Beach, 14 miles (23 km) southwest of Kingston on the coast, has 200,000-year-old Two Sisters Cave with rare Taíno petroglyphs. Nearby is Fort Clarence Beach, a seaside recreational complex. Both beaches are popular with the locals on weekends.

Jamaica Tourist Board, Kingston: 64 Knutsford Blvd., P.O. Box 360, Kingston, Jamaica. **Phone:** (876) 929-9200.

BLUE AND JOHN CROW MOUNTAINS NATIONAL PARK has three main recreation areas in eastern Jamaica: Portland Gap, which is on the Blue Mountain Peak Trail; Holywell, on the road to Buff Bay; and Millbank, in the Rio Grande Valley.

This pristine preserve, covering nearly 200,000 acres (81,000 hectares), offers mountain vistas, waterfalls, streams, lush rain forests and exotic flora and fauna. The park is the natural habitat for the Giant Swallowtail, the largest butterfly in the Americas. Numerous roads approach the park; however some roads can only be accessed by four-wheel-drive vehicles. Footpaths branch off of the main roads, making hiking a popular way to explore the park.

Mule rides and hiking treks to the top of Blue Mountain offer thrilling views; Cuba is visible on a clear day. At 7,402 feet (2,256 m), this is the highest peak on the island. Cabins are available for rent. **Tours:** Guided tours are available. **Hours:** Park open Tues.-Sun. **Cost:** $5; $2 (ages 4-12). **Phone:** (876) 920-8278.

BOB MARLEY MUSEUM is .5 mi. (.8 km) e. of jct. Waterloo and Hope rds. at 56 Hope Rd. The museum is contained in the former home of Jamaican reggae singer Bob Marley. His life and career are recounted through his personal belongings, tour memorabilia and extensive information about his religion, politics and music. The guided tour also includes an herb garden and meditation area. Photography and tape recording are restricted to certain areas. **Hours:** One-hour tours are offered Mon.-Sat. 9:30-4. **Cost:** $20; $10 (ages 4-12). **Phone:** (876) 927-9152.

CASTLETON BOTANICAL GARDENS is 19 mi. (31 km) n. at Junction Rd. in St. Mary. Many species of tropical plants, including spice and fruit trees and a palm grove, flourish on 15 acres (6 hectares). Swimming is permitted in Wag Water River, which runs through the gardens. **Hours:** Daily 6-6. Closed Labour Day and National Heroes Day. **Cost:** Free. **Phone:** (876) 927-1257.

DEVON HOUSE HERITAGE SITE is at 26 Hope Rd. Following the lines of classical Georgian architecture, Devon House is one of the few buildings left from 19th-century Jamaica where the opulence of the time is preserved in the architecture and the finely crafted antiques and decorations within its walls. The current Devon House property formed part of 600 acres owned by the St. Andrew Parish Church in the 17th and 18th centuries.

George Stiebel, Jamaica's first millionaire of African descent, purchased the rectory and lands from the parish church in 1879 and built Devon House on its foundations in 1881 after amassing wealth from investments in gold mines in Venezuela. Guided 30-minute tours are available. **Time:** Allow 30 minutes minimum. **Hours:** Mon.-Sat. 9:30-4:30. **Cost:** $8; $4 (ages 0-12). **Phone:** (876) 926-0829 or (876) 929-6602. 🍴

INSTITUTE OF JAMAICA is at 10-16 East St. The facility houses an outstanding West Indies reference library, a reading room, an art gallery and a natural history museum that highlights Jamaica's native plants and animals. An herbarium features more than 30,000 specimens. There also are maps and folklore exhibits, including the "shark papers," incriminating journals thrown overboard by a guilty sea captain and found years later in the belly of a shark. **Hours:** Mon.-Thurs. 8:30-4:30, Fri. 8:30-3:30. Natural history museum open Mon.-Fri.

9-4:30. Closed major holidays. **Cost:** $3; $1 (children). **Phone:** (876) 922-0620, (876) 922-0621 for museum, or (876) 967-1526 for library.

KINGSTON PARISH CHURCH is at King St. and South Parade. Founded in 1695, the Church of St. Thomas the Apostle was reconstructed after the 1907 earthquake and contains monuments to prominent Jamaicans. The clock tower honors those killed in World War I. Tombstones in the church graveyard date to the 17th century. **Hours:** Daily. **Phone:** (876) 922-6888 or (876) 948-0065.

NATIONAL GALLERY OF JAMAICA is at 12 Ocean Blvd. in the Kingston Mall on the harborfront. The gallery houses the definitive collection of Jamaican art, tracing its development through different periods and movements. Works represent realism, symbolism, expressionism and surrealism as well as abstract and intuitive styles. The works of Edna Manley are featured prominently. Other artists represented include Carl Abrahams, Henry Daley, John Dunkley, Colin Garland, Albert Huie, Kapo and Namba Roy. Touring exhibitions by foreign artists also are featured. **Tours:** Guided tours are available. **Hours:** Tues.-Thurs. 10-4:30, Fri. 10-4, Sat. 10-3. Closed major holidays. **Cost:** $3.50; $1.75 (ages 65+); free (children and students with ID). Guided tour $30; advance reservations required. **Phone:** (876) 922-1561.

ROYAL BOTANIC GARDENS AND HOPE ZOO is 6 mi. (10 km) n. on Old Hope Rd. More than 150 acres (61 hectares) contain flower beds, lawn areas and a plant nursery as well as butterfly, annual, lily pond and sunken gardens. Also on the grounds are an orchid house and a zoo with a petting area. A 1758 stone aqueduct built on the old Hope sugar estate is still in use. **Hours:** Gardens daily 6-6. Zoo daily 10-4. **Cost:** Gardens free. Zoo $2; $1.25 (ages 3-11). **Phone:** (876) 970-3504 or (876) 970-2459.

UNIVERSITY OF THE WEST INDIES is about 3 mi. (5 km) n. at Mona. The campus features modern architecture and a collection of 18th-century artifacts. The 1799 chapel was moved from its original location on a sugar plantation and meticulously rebuilt. Original stone aqueducts are scattered throughout the campus. The university, established in 1948, is attended by students from all areas of the Caribbean. Visitors may drive through the grounds. **Phone:** (876) 977-5941.

LACOVIA (B-2)

This crossing place on the Black River was the site of a clash between Spanish and English forces in 1655. The town's name is derived from a Spanish word for mahogany, once one of the area's chief exports. Cashew nuts remain a staple of the local economy.

LUCEA (A-1) pop. 6,002

West of Montego Bay, Lucea (pronounced *Lucy*) was the site of Fort Charlotte, one of five 18th-century English forts built to protect the Hanover coast. The 1817 clock atop the courthouse was intended for St. Lucia, but when the timepiece arrived by mistake in Lucea, town fathers raised enough money to keep it.

HANOVER MUSEUM is w. on Rte. A1 to Watson Taylor Dr., just past the library. Centered around a 1776 prison, the museum chronicles the history of Hanover Parish. Displays include official weights and measures; colonial-era artifacts and tools; and exhibits dedicated to Sir Alexander Bustamante, the first Jamaican prime minister, and Capt. William Bligh, owner of the ship *The Bounty*. A small village re-creates the life of Taíno Indians who greeted Columbus in 1494. **Time:** Allow 30 minutes minimum. **Hours:** Mon.-Thurs. 8:30-5, Fri. 8:30-4. Closed major holidays. **Cost:** $2; $1 (ages 0-12). **Phone:** (876) 956-2584.

MANDEVILLE (B-3) pop. 39,430

A quiet elegance pervades the resort of Mandeville, 64 miles (103 km) west of Kingston in the 2,000-foot Manchester Mountains. Resembling a town in the English Midlands, Mandeville exudes backcountry charm with its prim cottages and private gardens, town square and clock tower. The town's avid gardeners compete each May in the Manchester Flower Show, which draws visitors from all over the island; phone (876) 962-2909.

Founded in 1814, Mandeville was named after the Earl of Mandeville, son of the Duke of Manchester—a governor of Jamaica. The town quickly became a retreat for wealthy Jamaican growers drawn by the peaceful setting and cool mountain breezes. Bauxite and alumina mining sustained the area economy beyond the 1940s. Mandeville is now at the heart of the island's citrus industry; the town market overflows with colorful fruits and flowers in season. Dominating Mandeville Square is the 1820 Georgian-style Mandeville Courthouse. Just south is the Parish Church, also built in 1820.

Golf, tennis and sightseeing are enjoyable in the bracing mountain air. Golf and tennis can be played at the Manchester Club on Brumalia Road, the Caribbean's first golf course. Golf Week, Jamaica's oldest tournament, is played on the club's nine-hole course in July. Tennis Week, purportedly the oldest tournament in the Caribbean, is played in August.

A noteworthy attraction is nearby Marshall's Pen, an 18th-century great house on a 300-acre (12-hectare) cattle farm; extensive gardens, a bird sanctuary and hiking trails are on the property. House tours and village tours are offered by appointment; phone (876) 904-5454.

About 20 miles (32 km) west of Mandeville, Rte. A2 enters Bamboo Avenue, a grove of giant bamboo that creates a tropical canopy for about 3 miles (5 km). Paralleling the route southward is Black River. Once the center for crocodile hunting before the sport was prohibited, Black River is the largest navigable river in Jamaica and offers excellent freshwater fishing. Regular boat tours are available.

Only the most courageous sightseers will venture near the edge of Lover's Leap. On the coast about 40 miles (64 km) southwest of Mandeville, the sheer cliff stands about 1,700 feet (518 m) over the sea. The cliff is said to be the spot where two slaves once jumped to avoid separation; this romantic story is re-told daily by interpretive guides. A museum houses area artifacts; phone (876) 965-6634.

About 30 miles (48 km) southeast of town is Milk River Bath. The spring water is a constant 92 degrees Fahrenheit and is purportedly the most radioactive in the world. Bathers are limited to three 15-minute treatments per day; phone (876) 965-6577.

MONTEGO BAY (A-2) pop. 83,446

On the northwest coast 119 miles (191 km) from Kingston, Montego Bay is an exciting, cosmopolitan resort with beautiful beaches and excellent accommodations. The shoreline is dotted with sparkling coves and luxury hotels offering the gamut of water sports. The main resort area is east of the airport in Rose Hall *(see place listing p. 151)*, where such great houses as Greenwood and Rose Hall are open to the public. The ruins of the old British Fort Montego bears further witness to a rich history.

MoBay, as the resort is known locally, was one of Jamaica's original settlements. Christopher Columbus called it *El Golfo de Buen Tiempo,* or "Fair Weather Gulf," back in 1494, but his successors were apparently not as impressed; the current name comes from the Spanish *manteca,* or lard, an early major export. Montego Bay later prospered as a sugar and banana port. Tourism was born in the late 19th century when Dr. Alexander McCatty began attracting wealthy North Americans to the "curative" waters off Doctor's Cave Beach.

At the center of town is busy Sam Sharpe Square, where the slave rebellion leader and hundreds more were hanged in 1832. The colonial government's harsh response to the uprising led England to abolish slavery 2 years later. A monument to Sharpe stands on the site. Northeast on Union Street is the Slave Ring, where slaves were bought, sold and traded.

The strand of MoBay's famous beaches begins just north of town at Aqua Sol Theme Park. Farther north are Doctor's Cave, Cornwall and Chatham beaches. All but Chatham Beach have changing facilities, food and a slight admission charge. More resorts and beaches extend eastward from the airport to Rose Hall. South of town on a man-made peninsula is Freeport, home to the Montego Bay Yacht Club and the Catherine Hall Entertainment Centre. The municipal bus company serves the airport and the hotel strip.

The wild and forbidding Cockpit Country southeast of Montego Bay once harbored the Maroons, slaves who established their own villages after being freed by the Spanish. They were fierce warriors whose relentless guerrilla tactics were successful in frightening the British colonists into riding back-to-back on a single horse whenever they traveled through Maroon territory. Today their descendants welcome travelers to the historic "Land of Look Behind," though some may still warn, "Me no call you, you no come."

About 6 miles (8 km) southwest of Montego Bay on Rte. B8 near Anchovy is the Rocklands Feeding Station, where a wide variety of birds can be observed. Bird feedings take place daily at 3:30; admission is charged. For additional information phone (876) 952-2009. Rafting on the Great River west of the city is offered daily 9-5, with a two-person maximum per raft; consult any tour operator or ask your hotel for information.

Jamaica Tourist Board, Montego Bay: Cornwall Beach at 18 Queens Dr., Montego Bay, Jamaica. **Phone:** (876) 952-4425.

DOCTOR'S CAVE BEACH is off Gloucester Ave. in the hotel area. One of the best beaches in the West Indies was once the property of Jamaican tourism pioneer Dr. Alexander McCatty. The beach now has changing rooms and water sports rentals and is Blue-Flag certified for environmental standards. **Hours:** Daily 8:30-dusk. **Cost:** $5; $2.50 (children). Snorkeling $5 per set. **Phone:** (876) 952-2566. ⅏

ST. JAMES PARISH CHURCH is at Church and King sts. The gray stone cruciform building was dedicated in 1775. Almost destroyed by an earthquake in 1957, the church has been restored. It is considered to be one of the finest churches in Jamaica. The cemetery dates to the late 1700s. **Hours:** Daily dawn-dusk. **Cost:** Donations. **Phone:** (876) 952-5500 or (876) 926-8925.

RECREATIONAL ACTIVITIES

Summer Activities

- **Chukka Caribbean Adventures** includes transportation from local hotels. Rain forest canopy tours feature high-wire traverses across mountain ravines. Other tours include river tube rides, river kayaking safaris, horseback riding trips, Jeep safari rides, and ATV and dune buggy excursions. **Hours:** Trips depart daily. **Phone:** (876) 953-5619 or (877) 424-8552.

NEGRIL (B-1) pop. 1,500

On Jamaica's western tip, Negril (neh-GRILL) is a 90-minute drive down the coast from Montego Bay. Two bays sheltered by coral reefs lie along a 7-mile (11 km) stretch of unbroken shoreline, creating excellent conditions for swimming, snorkeling, scuba diving, sailing, windsurfing, parasailing, water skiing and horseback riding. The longer and more popular beach is at Long Bay. To the north is the more private Bloody Bay—its name dates back to the whaling era. Swimsuits are optional at Bloody Bay.

Pirates knew Negril well during their time. The coastal setting was a favored hideaway of Jamaica's notorious "Calico Jack" Rackham. He was finally apprehended in 1720 while lounging at Bloody Bay with two female mates. Negril remained largely undiscovered, however, until the late 1960s when it

became a haven for young escapists seeking freedom from the modern world. It remains an uncluttered destination; in order to preserve the beauty of the area, an ordinance prohibits the building of any structure taller than the average palm tree.

Given its location at the island's westernmost point, Negril is famous for its spectacular sunsets. Popular vantage points are the numerous cafés at the rock cliffs along West End (also called Lighthouse) Road; Rick's Cafe is one of the most popular. At some cafés locals and visitors can be seen diving off the tall cliffs into the calm sea below. At the end of West End Road is the 100-foot Negril Point Lighthouse. Contact the caretaker for permission to climb to the top.

ROYAL PALM RESERVE is 6 mi. (10 km) e. on Sheffield Rd. (Rte. A1), then n.w. on Springfield Rd., following signs. The reserve protects 300 acres (121 hectares) within the Negril Great Morass. A small museum details native flora and fauna of this wetlands area. A half-mile boardwalk leads to an observation tower. Visitors may glimpse the endangered West Indian whistling duck and 50 other bird species. Guided nature walks and bird-watching tours are offered by appointment.

Time: Allow 45 minutes minimum. **Hours:** Daily 9-6. **Cost:** $15; $7 (ages 0-12). **Phone:** (876) 957-3736. ⅏

OCHO RIOS (A-4) pop. 7,800

Ocho Rios, or Ochi as the locals call it, is on the north shore about 54 miles (87 km) from Kingston. A ballooning tourist industry has reinforced the town's bauxite harvesting, manufacturing and mining industries. The town's antique charm is complemented by its fine hotels, beautiful scenery, good shopping, active nightlife and stable climate. All manner of water sports are available both within the bay and along the coast. Ocho Rios is a popular port of call for private yachts as well as cruise ships.

Some of the island's oldest communities are within a few miles of Ocho Rios. St. Ann's Bay, 7 miles (11 km) west via Rte. A3, is said to be the final resting place of Christopher Columbus' last ships. The ruins of Sevilla Nueva, Jamaica's first settlement, are 9 miles (14 km) west. Laid out by the Spanish in 1509, the site is currently the subject of archeological research.

Popular local tours include an excursion to Dunn's River Falls, a raft trip on the White River and a visit to Shaw Park Botanical Gardens, which has 34 acres (14 hectares) of tropical flora and a waterfall. The gardens are .75 miles (1.2 km) south on Rte. A3 then 1 mile (1.6 km) west, following signs; admission is charged. Visitors can view the pottery-making process at Wassi Art Pottery Works, 1 mile (1.6 km) south on Rte. A1, where glazed earthenware is produced by local artisans. Ocho Rios' central location makes day trips to Kingston, Montego Bay and the interior manageable.

COYABA GARDENS AND MAHOE FALLS is 1.5 mi. (2.4 km) s. on Rte. A3, then w. on Millford Rd. at St. John's Anglican Church to Shaw Park Rd., following signs. Named for the Arawak word meaning "heaven," Coyaba features gardens, ponds, fountains, waterfalls and a raised boardwalk above the Milford mineral springs. A small museum chronicles the island's history. Ysassis Lookout Point offers panoramic views of Ocho Rios Bay. **Time:** Allow 1 hour minimum. **Hours:** Daily 8-5. **Cost:** $10; $5 (ages 0-12). Cash only. **Phone:** (876) 974-6235. ⊓⏐

DOLPHIN COVE is 2 mi. (3.5 km) w. on Belmont Rd. (Rte. A1). Visitors can touch, kiss and swim with these friendly marine mammals at a seaside park. For swimming participants over age 8, two programs offer deep-water encounters in a natural cove: the Swim with two bottlenose dolphins includes play time, a kiss, a foot push, a belly ride and a dorsal pull; and the Encounter offers splashing and dancing with a single dolphin. A program is offered where visitors can rub, hold, and feed sharks as well as snorkel with them.

Children and non-swimmers can enjoy the Touch, which takes place in knee-deep water. Visitors also can interact with stingrays, snorkel, and take miniboat and glass-bottom kayak rides. The park also offers a beach and a jungle trail, where guides encourage interaction with parrots, snakes and iguanas.

Time: Allow 2 hours minimum. **Hours:** Park open daily 8:30-5:30. **Cost:** All-inclusive general admission (includes mini-boat and kayak rides, petting and snorkeling with stingrays, shark show and nature trail adventures) $49.50. Dolphin Swim $214.50, Encounter $141.90, Touch $73.70, shark program $130.90. Dolphin and shark interaction program fees include general admission. Reservations are required. **Phone:** (876) 974-5335. ⊓⏐

DUNN'S RIVER FALLS is 3 mi. (5 km) w. on Rte. A3. The waterfall cascades 600 feet (183 m) through tropical foliage, rushing over layered tiers of smooth rock to the beach. A paved walkway parallels the falls; visitors may also climb to the top with the assistance of guides. Official guides are available only inside the falls' gates.

Aqua shoes or water socks are required; swim wear is recommended. Footholds have been carved in the most difficult places. Personal effects, such as cameras or phones, are not allowed on the climb; guides are not permitted to secure property for guests. Swimming is permitted, and food, lockers and changing rooms are available. **Time:** Allow 1 hour, 30 minutes minimum. **Hours:** Daily 8:30-4:30 (open at 7 a.m. during DST). **Cost:** $15; $12 (ages 2-11). Tipping is optional for the guided climb to the top. Water shoe rental $5. **Phone:** (876) 974-4767 or (954) 974-5944. ⊓⏐

FERN GULLY is along Rte. A3, 1.5 mi. (2.4 km) s. of Rte. A1. The tree-covered canyon features lush growths of ferns and tropical plants. The gorge descends for about 3 miles (5 km), following the course

Bob Marley

Jamaica's distinctive reggae sound found its way onto the world's popular music scene in the early 1970s. Desmond Dekker announced its arrival with his 1969 hit "The Israelites," and in 1972 Johnny Nash popularized the sound with "I Can See Clearly Now," as did Paul Simon with "Mother and Child Reunion." But it was Bob Marley and his group the Wailers, featuring Peter Tosh and Bunny Livingston, and later the back-up vocals of the I-Threes (Rita Marley, Marcia Griffiths and Judy Mowatt), who brought reggae to worldwide prominence.

As his European and American contemporaries did to rock 'n' roll, Bob Marley brought to reggae lyrics of pride and protest. He sang of black unity, in the tradition of national hero Marcus Garvey, and of the tenets of Rastafari, the uniquely Jamaican religion of which he was a devout follower. Bob Marley and the Wailers released nine albums, as well as several compilations, outside of Jamaica. Among his more popular songs are "Get Up Stand Up," "Jamming" and "Is This Love." Eric Clapton recorded Marley's song "I Shot the Sheriff" in 1974, bringing international acclaim to both Marley and the reggae sound.

Bob Marley died from cancer in 1981; he was just 36 years old. During his lifetime, many Jamaicans granted Marley the veneration usually accorded to their political and religious leaders. Shortly before his passing, Marley was awarded the Order of Merit—Jamaica's third highest honor—and he is still spoken of in legendary terms. His birthday, February 6th, is recognized as Bob Marley Day.

of a dry riverbed. Visitors should exercise caution, as the road is narrow and normally damp. Heavy rains can cause floods as well as mudslides and rockslides. There are a limited number of areas wide enough for vehicles to pull off the road. **Cost:** Free.

HARMONY HALL GALLERY is 4 mi. (6.4 km) e. on main road to Oracabessa. Works by renowned Jamaican artists and artisans are featured at this gallery, housed in a restored 19th-century Methodist manse. Monthly exhibitions are held from Thanksgiving through Easter. **Time:** Allow 30 minutes minimum. **Hours:** Tues.-Sun. 10-5:30, Oct.-Aug. Closed Good Friday and Christmas. **Cost:** Free. **Phone:** (876) 975-4222 or (876) 974-2870.

PROSPECT ESTATE is 2 mi. (5 km) e. on Rte. A3, following signs. A comprehensive jitney tour takes visitors through a 1,180-acre (478-hectare) estate, including stops at the White River Gorge and Sir Harold's Viewpoint. Narrators provide the history and background of the various fruits grown on the grounds as well as information about native flora. Highlights of the tour include the Prospect College Chapel with its handmade furnishings, ostrich feedings and views of the great house and gardens. A butterfly aviary also can be toured.

Guided horseback and camel rides are offered; reservations are required. **Time:** Allow 1 hour, 30 minutes minimum. **Hours:** Tours depart Mon.-Sat. at 10:30, 2 and 3:30, Sun. at 11, 1:30 and 3. **Cost:** Estate tour $32; free (ages 0-7). Horseback and camel riding $58. **Phone:** (876) 994-1058. ⅠⅠ

REGGAE XPLOSION is in the Island Village complex on Turtle River Rd. This interactive museum explores the history of reggae music from the 1940s to the present through art, photographs, videos and listening stations. Exhibitions detail the music styles of mento, ska, rock steady, roots rock reggae, 1970s club music and present-day dance hall music. A gallery is dedicated to Bob Marley. **Time:** Allow 1 hour minimum. **Hours:** Mon.-Fri. 9-5, Sat. 10-5. **Cost:** $15; $7.50 (ages 0-12). **Phone:** (876) 675-8895 or (876) 974-8353.

RECREATIONAL ACTIVITIES
Bobsledding
* **Rainforest Adventures Bobsled Jamaica at Mystic Mountain** is just w. of town on Rte. A3. Visitors take an exhilarating bobsled ride through a tropical rain forest. Other activities include ziplining and riding the Sky Explorer. **Hours:** Daily 9-5; reservations are required. **Phone:** (876) 974-3990.

Summer Activities
* **Chukka Caribbean Adventures** offers transportation from local hotels. Activities include a river tubing safari, kayaking safari, a zipline canopy tour, a horseback riding and swimming tour, jeep safari, ATV safari tour, dune buggy tour, dog sled ride and bus tours to Bob Marley's mausoleum. **Hours:** Tours depart daily. Bus tours to mausoleum depart Mon., Wed. and Fri. Phone ahead to

confirm schedule. **Phone:** (876) 972-2506, (876) 972-2727 or (877) 424-8552.

PORT ANTONIO (B-6) pop. 13,246

About 60 miles (97 km) northeast of Kingston on the windward coast, Port Antonio was one of Jamaica's first tourist destinations. Its beautiful twin harbors at the foothills of the lush Blue Mountains lured North America's elite in the early 20th century. Among the likes of William Randolph Hearst, Bette Davis, Ginger Rogers and J.P. Morgan was the irrepressible Errol Flynn, who made Port Antonio his home.

The two harbors, sheltered by Navy Island and Titchfield Peninsula, were largely responsible for the town's early success as a banana port. Since 1729 imposing Fort George has overlooked the harbors, once busy with lines of steamers waiting for their shipments of bananas. Today the docks no longer hum with the rhythm of banana loaders and the colorful refrain "come mister tallyman, tally me banana," but the charm of this port town has survived.

Of interest to sightseers and photographers are the port's ruins of Folly. Built in 1905 by a wealthy American engineer, this extravagant 60-room mansion lay vacant within 30 years, a victim of poor construction and neglect. Its crumbling walls and pillars are all that remain. The Folly Point Lighthouse stands at the end of the peninsula. Dominating the skyline on Bridge Street is the Romanesque Christ Church, built in 1840. Produce and crafts can be had at Musgrave Market on West Harbour east of the ferry dock.

Among the nearby scenic spots is Somerset Falls, about 10 miles (16 km) west, where the Daniels River plunges through a gorge in a series of cascades and pools; admission is charged. Most of the area's beaches extend east of town. Two of the most popular are San San and Boston. Frenchman's Cove and Blue Lagoon also are frequented; admission is $5 for both beaches.

RÍO GRANDE RAFTING departs 5.5 mi. (9 km) w. on Rte. A4. Guests climb aboard a bamboo raft for a 2.5- to 3-hour meandering journey down the slow-moving Rio Grande River, a route popular for transporting bananas from Jamaica's interior. The captain gradually guides the vessel downriver toward sea level, pointing out interesting sites along the way—one feature includes Lovers Rock, a narrow passage wide enough to accommodate the raft. Passengers view the lush valley from the river gorge sandwiched between the Blue and John Crow mountains, encountering banana groves and fluttering swallow tail butterflies, and have the option to swim or enjoy a picnic lunch on the river bank.

Maximum capacity is two adults and one child under 12 per raft. Return transportation is available, or licensed drivers are available on request to transport cars to the journey's end, where they can be picked up by their owners. **Time:** Allow 2 hours, 30 minutes minimum. **Hours:** Daily 9-4. Last trip begins 1 hour before closing. Closed Good Friday and Christmas. **Cost:** Fare $72 per raft. Car transport $15. **Phone:** (876) 913-5434. 🏛

PORT MARIA (A-4) pop. 7,651

Port Maria was an important commercial center during the Spanish era, made possible in large part by its deep natural harbor. Of interest in town is St. Mary Parish Church, built in 1861. Northwest toward Oracabessa are several small, fine beaches, among them Pagee and Murdock's. At Galina is the Galina Point Lighthouse.

On a mountain north of Port Maria is Firefly, the small retreat of Noel Coward, noted English playwright, actor and director. The house, 2.2 miles (3.6 km) north on Rte. A3, then 1 mile (1.6 km) west on Stuart Place track, contains the playwright's possessions; his grave is in the garden. Firefly is open Mon.-Thurs. and Sat. 9-4; admission is charged. Firefly was inspired by Coward's visit to nearby Goldeneye, the home of Ian Fleming, author of the James Bond novels. Goldeneye is not open to the public.

 BRIMMER HALL is 5 mi. (8 km) s., following signs. Pineapple, bananas, coffee, ackee and sugarcane are some of the island staples still produced on this 2,000-acre (809-hectare) working plantation. As passengers ride along in an open-air jitney pulled by a tractor, knowledgeable guides educate them about how these crops are cultivated and point out tropical flora and fauna encountered along the way. Guests may be offered a taste of the sugar cane or some coconut as the jitney bounces along the fields.

The great house, constructed by the plantocracy in 1817 and graced by a breezy wide veranda, is available for touring. Elegant furnishings and antiques adorn the interior rooms, which boast ceilings and floors created from hand-crafted native hardwoods. The former stable stalls now house shops featuring Jamaican crafts like woodcarvings and straw goods. **Hours:** Tours depart Mon.-Fri. at 9, 11, 1:30 and 3:30. **Cost:** $18. Additional fee for house tours. **Phone:** (876) 994-2309.

PORT ROYAL (C-5)

At the tip of a 10-mile (16 km) strip of land called the Palisadoes, Port Royal became the focus of British fortification efforts soon after their takeover in 1655. Construction of Fort Charles began in 1656, and within a few years there were five more forts manned by more than 2,500 soldiers. Port Royal also became headquarters for buccaneers and privateers who preyed on Spanish ships throughout the Caribbean. This era brought Port Royal great wealth and a reputation as one of the wickedest cities in the world.

Shortly before noon on June 7, 1692, as if by divine judgment, an earthquake and tidal wave destroyed 90 percent of the city and claimed more than 2,000 lives; most of the city sank beneath the sea. Attempts were made to rebuild Port Royal, but a 1703 fire and numerous hurricanes thwarted all efforts and the site was eventually abandoned for Kingston across the harbor. Somewhere offshore are the remains of Sir Henry Morgan, who was buried in Port Royal in 1688.

Port Royal is reached by water taxi or bus from Kingston or by a 10-minute drive from Norman Manley International Airport. Boat trips can be arranged to visit the cays offshore from the Palisadoes. Lime Cay is the most popular.

FORT CHARLES is next to the Jamaican Coast Guard headquarters. Built in 1656, the fort was one of few Port Royal structures to survive the 1692 earthquake disaster. Originally named Fort Cromwell, the fort was renamed in 1662 in honor of England's King Charles II. The installation retains many of its old battlements. Horatio Nelson served as a naval lieutenant at Fort Charles in 1779. **Hours:** Fort open daily 9-5. A maritime museum is open daily 10-4. Closed Good Friday and Christmas. **Cost:** $5; $2 (children). **Phone:** (876) 967-8438. 🏛

ST. PETER'S CHURCH is next to the Morgan's Harbour Hotel on Church St. Built in 1725 to replace Christ's Church, which slid into the sea in 1692, this Anglican church houses an 18th-century candelabrum, altar railings, an elaborate organ loft and monuments to a number of distinguished citizens. It also boasts a silver communion plate that was a gift from Sir Henry Morgan. In the churchyard is the tomb of Lewis Galdy, a famous survivor of the Great Earthquake. **Hours:** Mon.-Sat. 9-5. Services on Sun. **Cost:** Donations.

ROSE HALL (A-2)

Montego Bay's resort area, Rose Hall was established in 1750 by George Ash, a wealthy Englishman who named his 6,600-acre (2,670-hectare) sugar plantation after his wife. The estate fell into ruin after the 1831 slave rebellion and was restored in the 1960s. Of the 700 great houses built on Jamaica in the 18th century, Rose Hall and neighboring Greenwood are two of the finest to survive.

GREENWOOD GREAT HOUSE is 4 mi. (6 km) e. on Rte. A1, then 2 mi. (3 km) on a steep, rutted road. The house was built in 1790 by Richard Barrett, a relative of poet Elizabeth Barrett Browning. Having amassed considerable wealth from their sugar plantations, the Barretts presided over an estate that extended about 12 miles (19 km) along the coast from Little River to Falmouth. Antiques include period furniture, family portraits, rare musical instruments and Wedgwood china made exclusively for the Barrett family.

Visitors can see the curvature of the Earth from a 70-foot-long veranda overlooking the Caribbean Sea. **Time:** Allow 1 hour minimum. **Hours:** Guided 45-minute tours are offered daily 9-5:15. **Cost:** $20; $10 (ages 5-12). **Phone:** (876) 953-1077.

ROSE HALL GREAT HOUSE is on Rte. A1 following signs. The original owner named the house after his wife, Rose, who survived him to remarry three times. Rose's fourth husband, John Palmer, completed the Georgian mansion in 1780. Fifty years later, a Palmer descendant married Annee Mae Patterson, the plantation's last mistress. Known as the "White Witch of Rose Hall," she is rumored to have killed three husbands and countless lovers, many of them slaves. Legend says that Annee Palmer, murdered during the 1831 uprising, haunts the house.

Tours: Guided tours are available. **Time:** Allow 45 minutes minimum. **Hours:** Daily 9-6. **Cost:** $20; $10 (ages 4-11). **Phone:** (876) 953-2323.

ST. ANN'S BAY (A-3) pop. 10,518

On the coast west of Ocho Rios, St. Ann's Bay and the surrounding parish were named for Lady Anne Hyde, wife of King James II of England.

CRANBROOK FLOWER FOREST is 1 mi. (1.6 km) w. of Chukka Cove on Rte. A1, then 1 mi. s. on Llandovery Rd. The River Head Adventure Tour follows a hiking trail through a 130-acre (53-hectare) botanical garden along the Little River. Flowering plants and ornamentals include royal palms, ginger lilies, orchids, hibiscus, begonias and bromeliads. Other activities include horseback riding, swimming, mountain biking, pond fishing or visiting a petting zoo.

Comfortable hiking boots and insect repellent are advised. **Time:** Allow 2 hours minimum. **Hours:** Daily 9-5. Closed Good Friday and Christmas. **Cost:** $10; $5 (ages 4-12). **Phone:** (876) 770-8071 or (876) 995-3097. 🛈 🚫 🎢

RECREATIONAL ACTIVITIES

Ziplines

- **H'evans Scent** is at Free Hill off Bamboo Road. Visitors take zip line rides across the valley to enjoy breathtaking scenery. Other activities are offered. **Hours:** Trips depart daily. **Phone:** (876) 427-4866 or (876) 847-5592.

SILOAH (B-2)

At the western end of the Siloah Valley is the rural town of Maggotty, where hydroelectricity is generated by nearly thirty waterfalls on the Black River. Views of the river gorge are offered along Route A2.

APPLETON ESTATE RUM TOUR is 7 mi. (11 km) n. on Rte. A2 to Maggotty, then 3 mi. (5 km) e. The Appleton plantation has been producing sugar, molasses and rum since 1749. The distillery is set in a valley along the Black River. A 90-minute guided tour provides a demonstration of various stages of the production process and a tasting of "wet" sugar. A rum tasting venue is on the premises, and each legal-age visitor receives a complimentary bottle of rum. **Hours:** Mon.-Sat. 9-4. **Cost:** $21; $12 (ages 0-10). **Phone:** (876) 963-9215 or (876) 963-9217.

SPANISH TOWN (C-4) pop. 92,383

First known as Santiago de la Vega (St. James of the Plain), Spanish Town was founded by the Spaniards about 1534 after they abandoned their first city at Sevilla Nueva on the north coast. The British destroyed much of the original town in 1655, but remained to build new structures, many of them fine examples of Georgian architecture. Spanish Town served as capital of Jamaica until 1872, when the capital was moved to Kingston.

The heart of Spanish Town is Emancipation Square with its stately Georgian buildings. Here are the Assembly House, the King's House and the Rodney Memorial. The old courthouse was gutted by fire and has not been restored.

The ruins of 17th-century Colbeck Castle, reached by a slight detour off the road to Old Harbour, are worth visiting. The main facade is more than 100 feet (30 m) high, and the four fortresslike towers are each 40 feet (12 m) high with walls 3 feet (.9 m) thick. The monumental construction hints that this castle was not only a residence but also a bastion against the fierce Maroons.

CATHEDRAL OF ST. JAMES (ST. JAGO DE LA VEGA) is at Barrett and White Church sts. Built by the British in 1662, this is considered the oldest church in the former British colonies. It has served the Church of England for more than 300 years. Many English nobles and islanders are buried in the crypts beneath its floors. **Hours:** Daily 9-4:30. **Cost:** Donations. **Phone:** (876) 984-2535.

JAMAICAN ARCHIVES is at the corner of King and Manchester sts. on Emancipation Square. Records begin with the British occupation of Jamaica in 1655; Spanish records prior to that period did not survive. **Hours:** Mon.-Thurs. 9-4:30, Fri. 9-3:30. **Cost:** Free. **Phone:** (876) 984-2581 or (876) 984-5001.

PEOPLE'S MUSEUM OF CRAFT AND TECHNOLOGY is on the w. side of Emancipation Square. Rebuilt in 1802 following its destruction in 1761, only the Georgian facade remains of the house; the rest burned in 1925. The house was once the official residence of colonial British governors. Early Jamaican relics are displayed in the coach house and stables. **Hours:** Mon.-Fri. 9-4. Closed major holidays. **Cost:** $3; $1 (children). **Phone:** (876) 907-0322 or (876) 929-9200.

RODNEY MEMORIAL is on the n. side of Emancipation Square. This domed building with colonnades honors British admiral George Rodney and his 1782 victory over French forces off the shores of Dominica. His victory assured the safety of Jamaica and other British possessions in the Caribbean. Rodney is portrayed as a Roman emperor in a toga. His 200-ton statue was moved to Kingston in 1872, but outraged Spanish Town citizens reclaimed it in 1889. One stone hand was lost in the process. **Hours:** Daily dawn-dusk. **Cost:** Free.

Near Pointe-du-Bout / © POLYPIX / age fotostock

Martinique

One of the largest islands in the Lesser Antilles, Martinique is 50 miles (80 km) long and 22 miles (35 km) wide. The volcanic Mont Pelée in the north and Les Pitons du Carbet in the central section are the main peaks on this mountainous island.

It is easy to see why the Carib Indians once designated Martinique as the Isle of Flowers—bougainvillea, hibiscus, anthuriums, bamboo and wild orchids deck the woodlands; forests with many varieties of flowering trees rim the hills. Plantation fields with crops containing bananas, pineapples, sugarcane and coffee can be found throughout this fertile island. Martinique's tropical visage is scarred only by the ruins of St. Pierre, the result of an eruption of Mont Pelée in 1902.

History

Christopher Columbus sighted Martinique in 1493 but did not land until his fourth voyage in 1502. Arawak and Carib Indians called the island *Madinina*, the "island of flowers." Because of opposition from the Indians, no settlement took place until 1635, when the French made the island a center for sugar production. France and Britain battled for the island throughout the 17th and 18th centuries until France gained permanent control in 1814.

Like Guadeloupe, Martinique is a department and region of France, represented in the French Parliament by two senators and four deputies. The island is administered by elected general and regional councils as well as by a prefect. The seat of government is Fort-de-France.

Shopping

Martinique offers enough goods and bargains to suit the needs of most shoppers. French perfumes, china, linens, jewelry, crystal and other luxury imports are sold at or below prices in Paris, New York or St. Thomas. The main shopping district is in Fort-de-France along rues Antoine Siger, Victor Hugo and Schoelcher, where shops sell madras cottons, watches, silver and crystal at low prices. Just south of town is La Galleria, billed as the largest shopping center in the West Indies.

Roger Albert's duty-free department store on rue Victor Hugo specializes in French perfume, leather goods, sportswear and crystal, Cadet-Daniel on rue Antoine Siger is known for its jewelry, china, silver and crystal. Most jewelry stores in the district feature handcrafted gold and Creole pieces, including a traditional beaded necklace known as a *collier chou*. Fort-de-France is not truly a "free port," but instead offers a 20 percent discount on purchases paid for with travelers checks or charged to a credit card.

At the Caribbean Arts Center on the seafront, artisans sell their tapestries, Creole dolls, straw baskets, ceramics, handmade jewelry and souvenirs. As on many other Caribbean islands, rum is a popular purchase; Martinique offers 17 varieties. Most distilleries offer free tours and rum tastings.

Shops are open Mon.-Fri. 8:30-6, Sat. 9-noon, and are closed on holidays. Banking hours are Mon.-Fri. 7:30-noon and 2:30-4:30. Stores can give up to 20-percent discounts on some luxury goods purchased with travelers checks or certain credit cards.

Food and Drink

Martinique's cuisine is a mix of classic French and Creole. Local specialties include *colombo,* an Indian curry dish cooked with either beef, pork, chicken, mutton, conch or goat and eaten with rice; *boudin,* a spicy local blood sausage; and *callaloo,* a soup made from greens and West Indian herbs. Typical Creole seafood dishes might include such exotic ingredients as *oursins,* sea urchins; *lambi,* conch; and *langouste,* local rock lobster or crayfish. For dessert, try coconut sorbet or *amour caché,* a traditional pastry made with coconut jam. Local beverages include a potent mix known as "ti punch," bottled rums from a dozen distilleries, and *bière de Lorraine*, the local ale. Didier Water, bottled on the island, is a naturally carbonated mineral water. Tap water and milk are safe to drink.

More than 350 restaurants in Martinique have elevated Creole and French cooking to its highest level of artistic perfection. Most hotels and restaurants include a 15-percent service charge in their prices or add it to the final bill.

Sports and Amusements

Beaches of white, ochre and silver-gray volcanic sand offer unlimited opportunities for

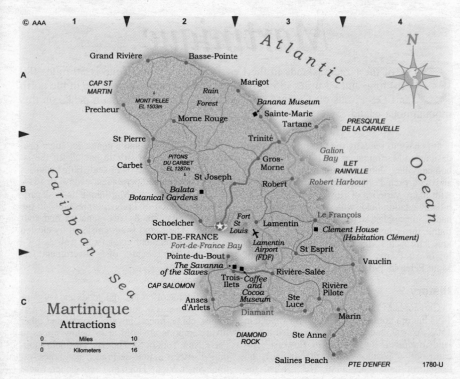

© AAA

Martinique
Attractions

Atlantic

Caribbean Sea

Ocean

Grand Rivière
Basse-Pointe
CAP ST MARTIN
Precheur
MONT PELEE EL 1503m
Rain Forest
Marigot
Morne Rouge
Sainte-Marie
Banana Museum
Tartane
PRESQU'ILE DE LA CARAVELLE
St Pierre
Carbet
PITONS DU CARBET EL 1287m
Trinité
Galion Bay
Gros-Morne
ILET RAINVILLE
St Joseph
Robert
Robert Harbour
Balata
Botanical Gardens
Le François
Schoelcher
Fort St Louis
Lamentin
Clement House (Habitation Clément)
FORT-DE-FRANCE
Fort-de-France Bay
Pointe-du-Bout
Lamentin Airport (FDF)
St Esprit
Vauclin
The Savanna of the Slaves
Rivière-Salée
CAP SALOMON
Trois-Ilets
Coffee and Cocoa Museum
Ste Luce
Rivière Pilote
Anses d'Arlets
Diamant
Marin
DIAMOND ROCK
Ste Anne
Salines Beach
PTE D'ENFER

Miles 0 — 10
Kilometers 0 — 16

1780-U

swimming, skin diving, scuba diving, water skiing and other aquatic sports. Among the island's most popular beaches are Diamant Beach, about 21 miles (34 km) from Fort-de-France on the southwest coast, and the sandy strand at Salines near Ste. Anne. Scuba diving services, including courses for beginners, are available to guests at hotels in the Pointe-du-Bout and Diamant resort areas and elsewhere.

The Pointe-du-Bout area also is a popular spot for sailing. Large boats can be chartered at Pointe-du-Bout and through Moorings, Stardust and several other charter companies at the island's largest marina in Marin. Memberships of most U.S. yacht clubs are honored at the two yacht clubs in Fort-de-France. Most of the larger hotels and the marina at Fort-de-France charter boats for deep-sea fishing.

Other recreational pursuits include horseback riding, hiking, mountain climbing, tennis and golf. An alternative to the resort environment is camping. Campgrounds with showers are found in Ste. Anne, Trois-Ilets and Le Vauclin. Horseback rides through the country and cane fields are conducted through several private clubs and ranches.

A fine 18-hole golf course designed by Robert Trent Jones Sr. is at Trois-Ilets near the Pointe-du-Bout marina-hotel area. Besides the hotel tennis courts, the tennis clubs in Fort-de-France and Lamentin, as well as the Golf Country Club, offer temporary memberships to visiting players. Spectator sports include soccer matches, held every Sunday at the stadium in Fort-de-France.

An annual event that captures the island's mystery and charm is Carnival, a celebration for Vaval, the legendary king of the Carnival. Preparations last for 5 weeks, ending on Ash Wednesday. On Mardi Gras Tuesday, the streets of Fort-de-France are jammed with participants masked and costumed in red to depict the red devils, or *diables rouge.* They perform the *biguine,* a twisting, uninhibited dance that to the Martiniquais is a way of life. On Ash Wednesday, the costumes are black and white and a parade of rhythmic dancing and singing is a wake for Vaval. The parade leads to the waterfront where his funeral pyre is built. When dusk falls, the spectators dance in a frenzy of shadows and flickering flames until Vaval's effigy is burned and Carnival is over for another year.

There is dancing and entertainment in Fort-de-France at Coco Loco, L'Alibi, Le Cheyenne, Le Négresco and Xenakis Club as well as at several major hotels, such as Le Kalenda Resort Hotel, which features a discotheque.

L'Atrium, Fort-de-France's cultural center, features concerts as well as dance and opera performances by internationally known artists. Theater life in Fort-de-France revolves around the Théâtre Municipal. Dance exhibitions performed by the Grands Ballets de la Martinique and other groups are frequently held at the major hotels. Several theaters show French and American films with French soundtracks.

Sightseeing

Good roads, including many four-lane highways, afford pleasant excursions. These include a 5-hour drive to the old capital of St. Pierre, where the historical museum can be visited, and on to Grand Rivière, returning through quaint fishing villages on the eastern coast. A 4-hour trip from Fort-de-France to the southern half of the island includes stops at Trois-Ilets, birthplace of Empress Josephine; Pointe-du-Bout, which offers a fine view of the capital across the bay; and Anses d'Arlets, a small fishing village. Diamant Beach affords a view of Diamond Rock, a giant offshore monolith. Return is through Rivière-Salée.

A half-day drive can be made from Fort-de-France along the island's west coast to St. Pierre, returning the same route. A 5-hour excursion to Ste. Anne might include a stop for a

swim at Ste. Anne Beach or nearby Salines Beach; return via St. Esprit and Ducos.

Fascinating views of the underwater world are offered on glass-bottom boats and 1-hour aquascope excursions.

Transportation

There are Air France flights from Miami and connecting flights from other U.S. cities with Air Caraïbes in Guadeloupe. Air Jamaica offers direct service from New York. Caribbean Airways offer daily service from New York with a LIAT Airline connection in Antigua or Barbados. Air Caraïbes also provides flights to nearby islands; information about schedules is available at local travel agencies. Most major cruise lines include Martinique on their itinerary.

Taxi fare from Martinique Aimé Césaire International Airport in Lamentin to Fort-de-France is $18-$36; fares are 40 percent higher

between 8 p.m. and 6 a.m. Taxis are unmetered so it is wise to determine the fare in advance. Rental cars are available at the airport, Fort-de-France and Pointe-du-Bout; camper-car rentals can be arranged at Anse Mitan.

Collective taxis, private cars or minibuses that serve as jitney buses, will take up to eight passengers to many standard destinations. The name of the final destination is marked on the car. These "group" taxis stop running at 6 p.m. A one-way taxi fare from Fort-de-France to Ste. Anne is approximately $6. Crowded buses, used primarily by islanders, also serve sections of Fort-de-France.

Ferries link Fort-de-France with the main resort areas of Trois-Ilets and Ste. Anne. High-speed passenger ferries operated by Brudey Frères and L'Express des Iles connect Martinique with Dominica, Guadeloupe and St. Lucia.

Fast Facts

POPULATION: 429,510.

AREA: 1,101 sq km (425 sq mi.).

CAPITAL: Fort-de-France.

HIGHEST POINT: 1,397 m (4,584 ft.), Mont Pelée.

LOWEST POINT: Sea level, Caribbean Sea.

TIME ZONE(S): Atlantic Standard.

LANGUAGE: French and Creole.

GOVERNMENT: Overseas Department of France.

UNIT OF CURRENCY: Euro Dollar. $1 U.S. = approx. .78 Euro. U.S. currency is widely accepted.

ELECTRICITY: 220 volts, 50 cycles AC.

MINIMUM AGE FOR DRIVERS: 21-25, depending on the rental car agency. An international driver's license is required; drive on right.

MINIMUM AGE FOR GAMBLING: 18.

SEAT BELT/CHILD RESTRAINT LAWS: Seat belts are required for all passengers. Children under 12 must ride in the back seat.

HOLIDAYS: Jan. 1; Carnival (Mardi Gras and Ash Wednesday); Good Friday; Easter Monday; Labour Day, May 1; Victory Day, May 8; Slavery Abolition Day, May 22; Ascension Day, May (6th Thurs. after Easter); Whit Monday,

May or June (8th Mon. after Easter); Bastille Day, July 14; Assumption Day, Aug. 15; All Saints Day, Nov. 1; Armistice Day, Nov. 11; Christmas, Dec. 25.

TAXES: A 8 percent room tax and 10 percent service charge are added to most hotel bills. Restaurants include a 15 percent service charge.

IMMIGRATION REQUIREMENTS: A valid passport and return or onward ticket are required for U.S. citizens entering the French West Indies. No visa needed for stays up to 3 months. The U.S. Dept. of Homeland Security requires all U.S. citizens returning from the Caribbean to present a valid passport.

PHONING THE ISLANDS: To call Martinique from the U.S. or Canada, dial 011 + 596 + 596 + the 6-digit local number.

FURTHER INFORMATION FOR VISITORS:

French Government Tourist
   Office/Martinique Promotion Bureau
825 3rd Ave., 29th Floor
New York, NY 10022
(212) 838-6887
(212) 838-7800

Martinique Tourist Office (Comité
   Martiniquais du Tourisme)
Immeuble Le Beaupré
Pointe de Jaham
Schoelcher, Martinique 97233
(596) 61-61-77

Points of Interest

See map page 154.

CARBET (B-1) pop. 3,316

Christopher Columbus landed near Carbet (car-BAY) in 1502. Paul Gauguin lived in this village on the scenic coastal route between Fort-de-France and St. Pierre for 5 months in 1887.

CENTRE D'ART MUSÉE PAUL GAUGUIN is at Turin Cove between Carbet and St. Pierre. The museum documents Paul Gauguin's stay on Martinique with copies of manuscripts, letters and a dozen paintings of the island. Art exhibits by local artists also are featured. **Hours:** Daily 9-5. **Cost:** $15.50; $4 (ages 8-15). **Phone:** (596) 78-22-66 or (596) 72-52-49.

FORT-DE-FRANCE (B-2) pop. 134,727

Capital of the "island of flowers," Fort-de-France is stepped like an amphitheater around the celebrated Place de la Savane. This lovely park contains the statue of Pierre Belain D'esnambuc, founder of the French colony here in 1635, the island's first European settlement. Nearby is the marble statue of the Empress Josephine, who was born across the bay near Trois-Ilets. Fort St. Louis dominates the harbor promontory.

The Schoelcher Library, across from La Savane, was designed by French architect Henri Picq for the Paris exposition of 1889, then later disassembled and shipped to the island. The building is named for Victor Schoelcher, a French abolitionist who helped end slavery in Martinique in the mid-1800s. A statue of Schoelcher stands at the entrance to the Court of Justice Building at the corner of rues Schoelcher and Moreau de Jones.

On Rue Schoelcher is the 1895 Saint-Louis Cathedral, a neo-classical church featuring Byzantine décor, stained-glass windows and a massive pipe organ. Built upon the site of six previous churches, the iron structure was designed to withstand fire, earthquake and hurricane. The Sacré-Coeur de Balata basilica is in the suburbs north of Fort-de-France.

BALATA BOTANICAL GARDENS (JARDIN DE BALATA) is 6 mi. (10 km) n. on Route de Balata, following signs. Entered through a restored Creole house furnished in period, the gardens showcase labeled plant varieties including anthuriums, heliconias, begonias, orchids and many others. Ornamental lakes feature water lilies and lotus blossoms. Free-flying hummingbirds are often sighted. A suspended rope bridge and walkways provide a birds-eye view of the landscaped grounds below. **Time:** Allow 1 hour minimum. **Hours:** Daily 9-6. Last admission at 4:30. Phone ahead to confirm schedule in Sept.

Closed major holidays. **Cost:** $17; $9.50 (ages 7-12). **Phone:** (596) 64-48-73. ⓘ

PRE-COLUMBIAN ARCHEOLOGICAL MUSEUM (MUSÉE DÉPARTEMENTAL D'ARCHÉOLOGIE PRÉCOLOMBIENNE) is at 9 rue de la Liberté. The museum, housed in an 1898 military office, features relics from prehistoric Arawak Indian excavations and exhibits about contemporary everyday life. **Hours:** Mon.-Fri. 8-1 and 2-5, Sat. 9-noon. **Cost:** $12; $4 (ages 0-12). **Phone:** (596) 71-57-05.

GAMBLING ESTABLISHMENTS

- **Casino Batelière Plazza** is north of Fort-de-France on Rue des Alizés in Schoelcher. **Hours:** Sun.-Thurs. 10 a.m.-3 a.m., Fri.-Sat. 10 a.m.-4 a.m. **Phone:** (596) 61-73-23.

LE FRANÇOIS (B-3) pop. 18,559

This east coast village was the site of a March 1991 summit meeting between presidents George Bush and François Mitterand to discuss the Middle East peace process. The Atlantic coast at Le François is noted for its breakers and sand bars.

CLEMENT HOUSE (HABITATION CLÉMENT) is at the L'Acajou Estate 1.2 mi. (2 km) w. toward Le St-Esprit. This is home to one of the finest rum distilleries on the island. Visitors can tour the distillery and estate, and free tastings are offered. The 18th-century house of the company's founder evokes plantation life, and an old distillery has been restored as a museum. Tropical gardens are on the grounds. **Time:** Allow 1 hour minimum. **Hours:** Daily 9-5:30, Oct.-Aug. Last admission is 1 hour before closing. **Cost:** $9; $5 (ages 7-18); $22.50

DID YOU KNOW

Josephine, Empress of France, was born in Martinique.

(family, two adults and two children ages 7-18). **Phone:** (596) 54-62-07.

STE. MARIE pop. 20,098

BANANA MUSEUM (MUSÉE DE LA BANANE) is 3 mi. w. in Quartier Fourniols, following signs. The museum, situated on an operating banana plantation, presents information about the fruit's history. Displays outline the banana's origins in India, Asia and Africa; the crop's subsequent migration to the islands; and its worldwide consumption. The adjacent park includes many varieties of banana trees and tropical flowers. **Time:** Allow 1 hour minimum. **Hours:** Daily 9-4. Closed major holidays. **Cost:** $8.50; $5.50 (ages 0-12). **Phone:** (596) 76-27-09.

ST. PIERRE (B-1) pop. 4,453

Sometimes called the Pompeii of the New World, St. Pierre is 20 miles (32 km) northwest of Fort-de-France. Amid this active tropical town are the ruins of the old St. Pierre, which was destroyed by the eruption of Mont Pelée. Now dormant, the volcano roared into life on May 8, 1902, annihilating all but one of St. Pierre's 30,000 inhabitants—a local drunk imprisoned in the basement of the jail. The village was never buried under lava, which bypassed the town on its run to the sea some miles north; it was destroyed within 3 minutes by the exploding volcano's intense heat and gas.

Walls and foundations are all that remain of the magnificent theater that was once the heart of the "Paris of the West Indies." Cars can be driven to within an hour's walk of the summit, and rental vehicles, drivers and guides are available at Morne Rouge, a popular vacation spot for Martiniquais.

MUSÉE VOLCANOLOGIQUE DE FRANCK A. PERRET is on rue Victor Hugo in the center of town. Founded by an American volcanologist, the museum displays items salvaged after the eruption of Mont Pelée along with photographs of the ruins. Photography is not permitted. **Time:** Allow 30 minutes minimum. **Hours:** Daily 9-5. **Cost:** $8; free (ages 0-8). **Phone:** (596) 78-15-16.

TROIS-ILETS (C-2) pop. 5,162

Across the bay from Fort-de-France is Trois-Ilets, named for the three islets floating offshore. Nearby is the birthplace of Marie Josèphe Rose Tascher de la Pagerie, the Creole beauty who later reigned as Napoleon's Empress Josephine. La Pagerie, her partially restored home and the church where she was christened can be visited. The town also contains La Maison de la Canne, a museum featuring exhibits about the sugar industry; phone (596) 68-32-04.

COFFEE AND COCOA MUSEUM (MUSÉE DU CAFÉ ET DU CACAO) is on Route des Trois-Ilets at Domaine Château Gaillard. The museum outlines the history of coffee and cocoa through a collection of memorabilia, including vintage ads and coffee machines, roasters and grinders. A large nursery with exotic plants and a variety of shops and art galleries also are on the grounds. **Time:** Allow 30 minutes minimum. **Hours:** Daily 9-6. Closed major holidays. **Cost:** Free. **Phone:** (596) 68-10-57.

MUSÉE DE LA PAGERIE is near Pointe-du-Bout. Empress Josephine was born here in 1763, the daughter of Joseph Tascher de la Pagerie, a French planter. A museum in the old kitchen quarters of the family home contains mementos of the Empress and of the Napoleonic period. A few of Napoleon's love letters are displayed. A tropical garden is on the grounds of the sugar plantation. **Hours:** Tues.-Fri. 9-5:30, Sat.-Sun. 9:30-1 and 3-5. **Cost:** $15.50; $4 (ages 0-11). **Phone:** (596) 68-38-34 or (596) 68-33-06.

THE SAVANNA OF THE SLAVES (LA SAVANE DES ESCLAVES), e. on Hwy. D7 to Quartier La Ferme, provides a French-narrated guided tour relative to the island's history of slavery. Participants are led through a reproduction of a settlement once inhabited by slaves who escaped plantation life and sought refuge in the swamps. Life in the 1900s village is explored through housing, tools, folk art, everyday goods and medicinal plants. Pamphlets provide some information in English. **Time:** Allow 1 hour, 15 minutes minimum. **Hours:** Daily 9-noon and 2-5:30. Last tour departs 11:30 a.m. before the mid-day break and at 4 p.m. in the afternoon. Closed major holidays. **Cost:** $8.50; $4 (ages 3-12). **Phone:** (596) 68-33-91.

Soufrière Hills Volcano / © Walter Bibikow / awl-images

Montserrat

D uring his second voyage to the New World, Christopher Columbus paid homage to a hill-encircled abbey near Barcelona, Spain, naming a tiny, mountainous island Montserrat after the Spanish landmark. Although the Caribbean land mass 27 miles (43 km) southwest of Antigua outwardly resembles Spain's venerated peak, geologically, it greatly differs from its namesake. The ruggedly beautiful slopes of the "saw-toothed mountain" actually are those of a 3,000-foot (914-meter) volcano, which drew worldwide attention in the 1990s as torrents of hot volcanic debris destroyed its southern portion.

Although the disaster claimed Montserrat's capital and sole airport, the tropical oasis endures today, affording dramatic rock formations, lush vegetation, and secluded, sandy retreats. The government of the overseas British territory now operates out of Brades, with a new $18.5-million airport receiving travelers. In the aftermath of nature's fury, the eruption yielded more fertile soil; healthier and more diverse underwater environments; and an unusual natural attraction—the active Soufrière Hills Volcano.

History

The Arawaks and Caribs resided on *Alliouagana*, "the land of the prickly bush," before

Columbus sailed Montserrat's waters in 1493. Irish-Catholic settlers from St. Kitts arrived in 1632 and were later joined by Irish exiles fleeing Lord Cromwell's troops in Britain. France twice attempted to claim the island, having purchased it from Spain, but Britain maintained control.

Tobacco, sugar and cotton plantations once flourished; the rich, fertile soil produced an abundance of crops. When world markets declined, lime orchards were planted and the juice bottled and exported. In the 1960s, real estate development replaced agricultural pursuits, as Americans, Canadians and Britons flocked to the island to build homes and businesses. Such musicians as Elton John, Stevie Wonder and Eric Clapton also began arriving to record at AIR Studios Montserrat, built by Beatles producer George Martin in 1979.

As the economy became more diversified and with tourism thriving, disaster struck. Hurricane Hugo damaged more than 90 percent of the island's structures, even forcing AIR Studios Montserrat to close. The vital tourist industry was eventually re-established but again crumbled in 1995 when the long-dormant Soufrière Hills Volcano began spewing hot gas and rock. Ash darkened the skies over Plymouth, forcing evacuation to the north as volcanic mudflows buried the capital.

Today, the Exclusion Zone prohibits most entry into the island's southern half. Resilient Monserratians continue to add modern facilities in the north, which also boasts such ecological lures as Runaway Ghaut and Centre Hills.

Shopping

Montserrat is particularly known for its sea island cotton. Long prized for its silky feel, sea island cotton clothing, tablecloths and other items are available through a variety of boutiques and gift shops.

Located in Brades, both the BBC complex and the Ryan buildings feature small clusters of stores. Expeditions can be arranged to shop the scattered studios of local craftsmen selling such handmade items as dolls clad in the plaid green and yellow national dress, leather belts and purses, and stationery.

Bread hot from the oven lures visitors and natives alike to area bakeries, while fresh produce, domestic guava preserves and hot pepper sauces are abundant at several markets.

Food and Drink

Usually found in hotels or in small, colorfully painted wooden buildings with verandahs, a variety of restaurants are found in Montserrat, where the hardest part of ordering is deciding what to drink. The island's wealth of exotic fruits, including mango, guava, tamarind and papaya, can be sampled in juice form while taking in views of the Centre Hills rain forest or Little Bay. Ginger beer also is served, as is sorrel, a seasonal beverage made from a leafy plant of the same name.

Seafood is the heart of many area specialties, with restaurants serving up fresh mahi mahi, shrimp and salted cod. Although chicken frequently appears on local menus, poultry isn't an ingredient in the delicacy mountain chicken. The island favorite actually calls for the legs of a large frog indigenous only to Montserrat and Dominica. Goatwater, on the other hand, does indeed feature goat meat. Eaten with bread, the thick stew is the national dish.

Sports and Amusements

Along Montserrat's west coast, beaches with pearl-grey volcanic sand provide plenty of swimming and water sports opportunities; equipment can be obtained through most local hotels. Snorkeling and scuba diving are popular sports, and the island offers numerous coral reefs for exploration.

Beginners can dive at Lime Kiln Bay, with a maximum depth of 45 feet (14 m). Schools of reef fish dart past swimmers at Northwest Bluff, while Rendezvous Bay cave divers encounter thousands of fruit bats dangling from the chasm's ceiling. High waves make Little Redonda, the Pinnacles and Yellow Hole difficult to reach, although visiting such sights as a sunken 19th-century ship and spectacular undersea rock formations tempt advanced divers.

Little Bay and Woodlands Beach are popular shore sites, with picnic areas and snacks close at hand. For a little privacy, Lime Kiln Beach and Isles Bay Beach are great choices. Furthest north, Rendezvous Beach is the only non-volcanic white sand beach. In the south, the aftereffects of the volcanic eruption are evident at Foxes Bay, where stripped mangrove trees and the ruins of a former bird sanctuary linger. More inspirational is the sight of green, hawksbill and loggerhead turtles nesting on Montserrat's beaches August through September.

Bicycles can be rented on Montserrat either for demanding mountain biking adventures or leisurely tours of the island's charming villages. Arrangements for horseback riding or full- or half-day deep-sea fishing excursions can be made at your hotel. Marlin, wahoo and swordfish are just a few of the fish inhabiting the surrounding waters.

Entertainment and nightlife are found at hotels and at some of the clubs in Salem, St. John's, Cudjoe Head and Little Bay. Locals gather at cozy bars known as rum shops, which have no set closing time and generally offer food and live music as well as the chance to join a friendly game of dominoes.

Several of Montserrat's special events kick up the energy level a few notches. In March, natives commemorate the island's combination of Irish and African heritage with steel drum performances, storytelling, masked street dancers and traditional feasts during St. Patrick's Week. Another major event is Festival, which runs from mid-December through New Year's Day. Monserratians living overseas often return to see the carnival's calypso competitions, costume parades and choral singing shows.

Sightseeing

Built almost exclusively of volcanic rocks, Montserrat is only 12 miles (19 km) long and 7 miles (11 km) wide. Galway's Soufrière, a volcanic crater on the southern half of the island, lies within the Exclusion Zone that covers nearly half the island.

Visitors can view the Soufrière Hills from a safe distance; several companies offer guided tours of accessible areas. Across the Belham Valley, the Daytime Entry Zone affords panoramas of devastating volcanic mudflows. The abandoned capital of Plymouth can be seen from St. George's, Garibaldi and Richmond hills. A viewing facility at Jack Boy Hill includes a platform, picnic areas, a walking trail and a telescope imparting close-ups of Montserrat's destroyed WH Bramble Airport and eastern villages.

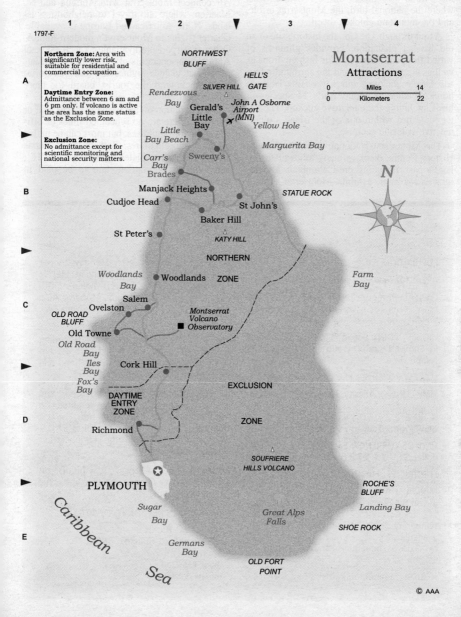

Montserrat Attractions

1797-F

Northern Zone: Area with significantly lower risk, suitable for residential and commercial occupation.

Daytime Entry Zone: Admittance between 6 am and 6 pm only. If volcano is active the area has the same status as the Exclusion Zone.

Exclusion Zone: No admittance except for scientific monitoring and national security matters.

NORTHWEST BLUFF

HELL'S GATE

SILVER HILL

Rendezvous Bay

Gerald's

John A Osborne Airport (MNI)

Little Bay

Yellow Hole

Little Bay Beach

Marguerita Bay

Carr's Bay

Sweeny's

Brades

Manjack Heights

STATUE ROCK

Cudjoe Head

St John's

Baker Hill

St Peter's

KATY HILL

NORTHERN

Woodlands Bay

Woodlands

ZONE

Farm Bay

Salem

Ovelston

OLD ROAD BLUFF

Montserrat Volcano Observatory

Old Towne

Old Road Bay

Iles Bay

Cork Hill

Fox's Bay

EXCLUSION

DAYTIME ENTRY ZONE

ZONE

Richmond

SOUFRIERE HILLS VOLCANO

PLYMOUTH

ROCHE'S BLUFF

Landing Bay

Sugar Bay

Great Alps Falls

SHOE ROCK

Caribbean Sea

Germans Bay

OLD FORT POINT

© AAA

The Montserrat Volcano Observatory provides the best vantage point along with insight into the island's famous, unruly tenant. Scientific staff explain the volcano monitoring program during short tours.

Although the southern portion of the island is uninhabitable, Montserrat remains worthy of the designation "Emerald Isle." The pure, open terrain demands extensive exploration by foot; most trails take hikers through Centre Hills, where the national bird, the Montserrat oriole, and the mountain chicken dwell.

A trail through The Cot, the historic site of an old banana plantation, provides glimpses of varied flora and fauna in their lush environs as well as views of Salem and the surrounding areas. Oriole Walkway and Silver Hills Trail are home to some of Montserrat's 34 species of birds, including the mangrove cuckoo. The latter route lies within one of the island's oldest inactive volcanic centers.

The Montserrat National Trust and Natural History Centre, displays many relics of the island's past, including pre-Columbian, agricultural and volcanic exhibits. Montserrat's senior citizens recount local history through a video display. A small historical library, botanical gardens and the Montserrat Philatelic Bureau, filled with valuable and unusual stamps, also are on site; phone (664) 491-3086 for the history center or (664) 491-2042 for the philatelic bureau.

Transportation

Daily flights aboard FlyMontserrat and SVG Air connect Montserrat with Antigua and St. Maarten, where air travel to neighboring islands, North America and Europe is available. Charter flights to Montserrat's modern John A. Osborne Airport are available as well. Several Antigua tour operators offer day trips to Montserrat that include sightseeing and transportation; check with the tourist board for more information.

Transportation on the island is by car, taxi or minibus. There are no scheduled times or official stops for minibuses, but most can be hailed off main thoroughfares. Both buses and taxis have green license plates beginning with "H"; agree on the appropriate fare to be paid in advance.

Fast Facts

POPULATION: 5,079.

AREA: 102 sq km (39 sq mi.).

CAPITAL: Plymouth (abandoned in 1997 due to volcanic activity; interim government buildings have been built in Brades).

HIGHEST POINT: 930 m (3,051 ft.), Lava Dome in English's Crater (Soufrière Hills volcanic complex).

LOWEST POINT: Sea level, Caribbean Sea.

TIME ZONE(S): Atlantic Standard.

LANGUAGE: English.

GOVERNMENT: British Overseas Territory.

UNIT OF CURRENCY: Eastern Caribbean (E.C.) dollar. $1 U.S. = 2.7 E.C. dollars.

ELECTRICITY: 110-220 volts, 60 cycles AC.

MINIMUM AGE FOR DRIVERS: 21-25, depending on the rental car agency. A valid U.S. driver's license must be presented to obtain a temporary driving permit. The $19 permit is available at port of entry or from Montserrat's police headquarters at Brades or in Salem.

HOLIDAYS: Jan. 1; St. Patrick's Day, March 17; Good Friday; Easter; Easter Monday; Labour Day, May (1st Mon.); Whit Monday, May or June (8th Mon. after Easter); Queen's Birthday, June (2nd Sat.); August Monday, Aug. (1st Mon.); Christmas, Dec. 25; Boxing Day, Dec. 26; Festival Day, Dec. 31.

TAXES: A 7-10 percent room tax (depending on the size of the resort) and a 10 percent service charge are added to most hotel and restaurant bills. Departure tax $21 U.S.

IMMIGRATION REQUIREMENTS: Passport and a return or through ticket are required. No visa needed for stays up to 3 months. The U.S. Dept. of Homeland Security requires all U.S. citizens returning from the Caribbean to present a valid passport.

PHONING THE ISLANDS: To call Montserrat from the U.S. or Canada, dial 1 + 664 + the 7-digit local number.

FURTHER INFORMATION FOR VISITORS:

Montserrat Tourist Board
#7 Farara Plaza, Buildings B&C
Brades, Montserrat
(664) 491-2230
(664) 491-8730

When exploring by rental car, a valid U.S. driver's license must be presented to obtain a temporary driving permit. The permit costs $19 and is available at your port of entry or from Montserrat's police headquarters. Be sure to fill up at one of the two gas stations before maneuvering the island's lengthy roads peppered with twists and steep hills. In addition, driving is on the left and there are no traffic lights; however, names are posted on most streets. If driving seems too challenging, your hotel or the tourist board can provide a road map or a list of local guides.

Points of Interest

See map page 161.

SALEM (C-2)

Just north of the exclusion zone, Salem is a few miles inland on the west coast of the island. Residents were temporarily evacuated in 1997 but returned a year later. On Old Road Beach, souvenir hunters may find bits of pumice and charred wood washed down from the volcano during heavy rains.

MONTSERRAT VOLCANO OBSERVATORY (MVO) is up a steep hill from Salem in Flemmings, following signs. Established soon after the first eruption of the Soufrière Hills volcano on July 18, 1995, the observatory monitors daily seismic activity. An observation deck offers one of the best views of the volcano and the surrounding countryside, including the abandoned capital of Plymouth.

Guided tours include a video presentation of recent eruptions and a description of monitoring techniques and equipment. **Time:** Allow 1 hour minimum. **Hours:** Mon.-Fri. 8:30-4:30. Visitor center Mon.-Thurs. 10-3:30. **Cost:** $3.75. **Phone:** (664) 491-5647.

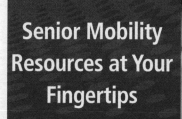

Old San Juan / © Jerry & Marcy Monkman / Danita Delimont Stock Photography

Puerto Rico

A diverse tropical landscape awaits the visitor to the U.S. Commonwealth of Puerto Rico, which boasts more than 300 miles (500 km) of palm-fringed coastline and a lush interior of montage thicket, palm, dwarf and rain forests. The island is a progressive blend of old and new. Nowhere is this more evident than in the capital city of San Juan, with its centuries-old Spanish fortresses and glamorous resort hotels. "Out on the island," as the Puerto Ricans refer to the remainder of the island, the changes are less dramatic but no less important.

Puerto Rico has made great strides economically and today enjoys one of the highest standards of living in the Caribbean. The island is a major banking and business center, and San Juan is the Caribbean's primary air and cruise hub. Complementing this progress, the Commonwealth, with the Institute of Puerto Rican Culture, has fostered an atmosphere in which writers, painters, sculptors, musicians and actors flourish, and has taken steps to preserve the island's crafts, folklore, dances, music and architecture.

History

Originally named *Borikén* (Island of the Brave Lord) by the Taíno Indians, Puerto Rico was discovered by Christopher Columbus in 1493 during his second voyage to the New World. He landed on the northwestern part of the island and named the island San Juan Bautista. The island derived its present name, however, from the exclamation *"¡Qué puerto rico!"* (What a rich port!), said to have been made by *conquistador* Juan Ponce de León upon entering the bay. He established the first settlement at Caparra in 1508 and in 1510 he was appointed the island's first governor by Spain's King Ferdinand. The capital was transferred to its present site and named San Juan Bautista de Puerto Rico in 1521, the year of de León's death.

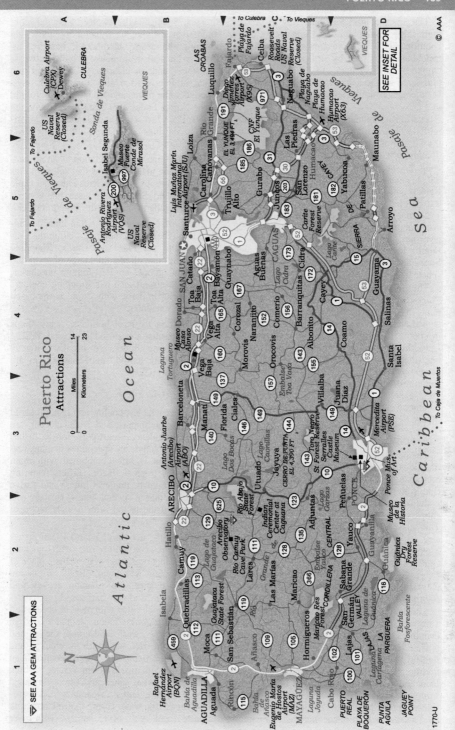

Puerto Rico Attractions

SEE AAA GEM ATTRACTIONS

© AAA

1770-U

The Spanish used San Juan Bay to protect their ships from pirates and attacks by other countries. This strategic area of land was attacked unsuccessfully by Sir Francis Drake, occupied by English forces in 1598, burned and plundered by the Dutch in 1625 and subjected to other sieges until a last attempt by the British in 1797.

Puerto Rico remained a loyal Spanish colony until 1897, when Luis Muñoz Rivera obtained the Charter of Autonomy, which gave the island dominion status. However, before the charter could go into effect, Spain became engaged in the Spanish-American War. In 1898 Puerto Rico became part of the United States by the terms of the Treaty of Paris. The Foraker Act of 1900 enabled the island to establish a civil government under the direction of a U.S.-appointed governor; in 1917 the Jones Act made the Puerto Rican people citizens of the United States and provided for the creation of a local senate.

The first native-born governor was Jesús T. Piñero, appointed by President Harry S. Truman in 1946. The following year Truman signed an act giving Puerto Rico the authority to choose its chief executive by popular vote. Luis Muñoz Marín, the first elected governor, held the office until 1965, when he was succeeded by Roberto Sánchez Vilella. A Congressional resolution signed by President Truman in 1952 elevated Puerto Rico to the status of a commonwealth associated with the United States.

Shopping

The best buys to look for in Puerto Rico are traditional island crafts. Calle Fortaleza in Old San Juan, a 20-minute bus or 10-minute taxi ride from the Condado section of resort hotels, is the center of a large and varied collection of shops selling both local crafts and imports— Thai silks, Spanish furniture and antiques, jewelry and items from the Philippines, India, Mexico and Europe. The tourist information center at La Casita at Pier 1 and the Institute of Puerto Rican Culture in the Ballajá Sector have lists of the numerous craft shops where artisans ply their trade in front of visitors.

Local artisans can be seen at La Casita at Pier 1 every Saturday and Sunday from noon to late evening. On Calle Marina in Old San Juan, opposite Pier 3, is the Plazoleta del Puerto—a delightful collection of shops specializing in traditional crafts. Some of the most notable island crafts include mundillo or bobbin lace; santos, or hand-carved, wooden religious figurines; cuatros, handmade 10-string guitars; festival masks made from coconut husks or papier-mâché; hand-embroidered linens, blouses and dresses; Spanish-style jewelry of copper, gold and silver filigree; hand-painted scarves and clothing; handbags; hammocks; baskets; ceramics; musical instruments; original artwork; and items made of mahogany. Cigars and rum made in Puerto Rico also are popular buys. Though some plants and fruits may be brought to the United States, it is best to check with the USDA Plant Protection and Quarantine Department in San Juan before departure; phone (787) 253-7850 or (787) 771-3611.

Old San Juan has a reputation as an art center, harboring many galleries that sell paintings and sculpture by Puerto Rican artists. Calle Cristo in Old San Juan houses many well-known art galleries such as the Botello Gallery.

The Plaza Las Américas in San Juan, considered to be the largest shopping mall in the Caribbean, and the Plaza del Caribe Shopping Center in Ponce offer a full range of local and continental goods. For last-minute purchases, San Juan's airport also has shopping counters which are open daily, with varied hours based on airline schedules.

In addition to usual holidays, many shops and restaurants are closed on Good Friday. While banking hours are usually Monday through Friday 8:30-4, some banks also are open on Saturday.

Food and Drink

Fruits, vegetables, poultry and fish, prepared with a strong Spanish and island accent, are found in abundance. Roast pork, lobster dishes and seafood platters are specialties in many restaurants. Fruit is often combined with main dishes for a tropical flavor. Buffets featuring American, French, Italian, Chinese and native fare are popular at several hotels. Upscale eateries around the island offer a wide range of cuisines.

Some of the delightful Puerto Rican dishes include arroz con pollo, rice with chicken; pasteles, a local variation of the tamale made of ground plantain with meat, olives, raisins and chickpeas wrapped in plantain leaves and boiled; lechón asado, or barbecued pig; pastelillos, thin dough filled with meat or cheese and deep fried; tostones, green plantains fried in deep fat; jueyes, fresh land crabs, shelled and boiled; paella, rice with saffron, chicken and seafood; and asopao, a traditional Puerto Rican soup made with rice and chicken or shrimp, cooked with wine sauce and often garnished with peas, pimientos, asparagus and hard-boiled eggs. Tap water is safe to drink and milk is pasteurized. A tip of 15 percent, with more for special service, is customary.

Sports and Amusements

The Caribbean, with its clear, warm water, is ideal for both scuba diving and snorkeling. Coral reefs and cays in many areas provide natural harbors for an array of beautiful and exotic sea life—coral, sea horses, starfish and tropical fish.

One of the best diving spots is off the northeastern coast of Puerto Rico around a small chain of islands. Visibility is exceptionally good in these waters, which range in depth from about 15 to 60 feet (5 to 18 m). The southwestern coast near La Parguera and the waters surrounding the eastern islands of Vieques and Culebra, dotted with many reefs, also are excellent spots for diving. Along the northwestern coast, the towns of Rincón and Aguadilla offer diving excursions to Mona and Desecheo islands.

Diving or snorkeling excursions from either the beach or a charter boat can be arranged for an hour, a day or longer; beginners might want to stay along the beach where there is a sheltered cove. There are courses for both beginning and advanced snorkelers and divers. The longer and more expensive advanced courses usually feature night dives or search and recovery expeditions. Major hotels and resorts have information about lessons and packages.

With 272 miles (438 km) of coastline, the island is ringed with good beaches with public facilities, called *balnearios,* which offer lockers, showers and parking for a nominal fee. They are open Tues.-Sun. 8-6 and are closed election days, Good Friday and the Tuesday following Monday holidays. Balneario de Luquillo, east of San Juan near El Yunque, is one of the most beautiful and popular beaches; the scenic bay at Balneario Boquerón near Cabo Rojo is a favorite among islanders.

Like Costa Rica, Panama and many other Central American countries, Puerto Rico is also widely known as a mecca for surfing. Thousands of pro and amateur surfers come here to ride some of the best beach and reef breaks in the Caribbean. The surfing season begins in September and runs through May. Surfing conditions are excellent along the north and west coast. Rincón, on the west coast of the island facing the Mona Passage, is popular with winter surfers, with typical swells delivering 15-foot waves. Surf shops abound in Rincón, as well as throughout the rest of the island.

Steady trade winds provide excellent opportunities for boating and sailing, particularly in San Juan Bay and the waters off Fajardo and La Parguera, which are well protected by coral reefs. Boats and equipment for sailing or deep-sea fishing can be rented from charter operators and marinas in San Juan, Mayagüez, Fajardo, Humacao and other towns. Game fish abound in Puerto Rico's waters, where more than 30 world records have been set, and include marlin, sailfish, mackerel, dolphin fish and wahoo. Snook, grouper, snapper, tarpon and amberjack teem along the southern coast. The International Billfish Tournament usually starts in early September; other fishing tournaments take place throughout the month.

Puerto Rico offers golfers more than 20 courses to play. Most of these are of championship caliber, designed by some of the best-known architects in the golf world and host to local and international tournaments. Landscaped championship golf courses are at the Río Mar Beach Resort in Río Grande, the Hyatt Hacienda del Mar in Dorado, El Conquistador Resort in Fajardo, Palmas del Mar Golf Club in Humacao, Punta Borinquen Golf Club in Aguadilla and Trump International Golf Club in Río Grande. Other golf courses on the island include Aguirre Golf Club in Salinas; Bahía Beach Plantation and Berwind Country Club in Río Grande; Club Deportivo del Oeste in Mayagüez; Coamo Springs and Costa Caribe in Ponce; the Dorado del Mar and Plantation Club in Dorado; El Legado in Guayama; and Bambuas Golf Course in Gurabo.

Tennis courts are available at San Juan Central Park and at many of the hotels in the Condado and Isla Verde areas of San Juan. Hotels out on the island with more than 7 tennis courts are Hyatt Hacienda del Mar in Dorado, El Conquistador Resort in Fajardo and the Palmas del Mar Resort in Humacao. Horseback riding is available at Doral Resort at Palmas del Mar Resort in Humacao, Hacienda Carabalí and Tropical Trail Rides in Isabela.

Spectator sports in Puerto Rico cover a wide range of interests reflecting both Spanish and American cultures. One of the local favorites is basketball; Puerto Ricans eagerly await the beginning of the basketball season in May. Second only to basketball in popularity is baseball, whose season runs from October through February; the game is played at the Hiram Bithorn Stadium (Estadio Hiram Bithorn) in San Juan. Another popular and exciting sport is horse racing; races with pari-mutuel and daily double betting take place at Hipódromo Camarero in Canovanas. Paso Fino horse shows, featuring Puerto Rico's own smooth-gaited breed, take place regularly around the island.

Activities in Puerto Rico do not end at sundown. Supper clubs feature elaborate floor shows, dining and dancing. The Luis A. Ferré Performing Arts Center (Centro de Bellas Artes

Luis A. Ferré) in San Juan regularly presents internationally acclaimed musicians, opera and ballet stars in its three theaters. One of the oldest municipal theaters in the Western Hemisphere, Old San Juan's restored El Tapía Theater offers performances every weekend. Another historic cultural center in Old San Juan is the Puerto Rican Athenaeum (Ateneo Puertorriqueño), which produces all kinds of cultural events throughout the year. The Puerto Rico Symphony Orchestra, a top-ranked ensemble, kicks off its concert season every year at the Luis A. Ferré Performing Arts Center in September and wraps up in May.

Elegant government-regulated casinos are found in most of the large hotels. Various hotels offer a weekly rendition of the Le Lo Lai Festival, sponsored by the Puerto Rico Tourism Co. This colorful extravaganza of Puerto Rican folk songs and dances showcases the European and Afro-Antillean heritage of the island; phone (787) 721-2400 or (800) 866-7827.

In mid-January, internationally acclaimed opera singers, ballet dancers and chamber music artists from around the globe perform at the Luis A. Ferré Performing Arts Center in the Santurce sector of San Juan. In late February is the Pablo Casals Festival, which pays tribute to the life and musical career of the famous Spanish cellist. San Juan Bautista Day is celebrated on June 24, with public parties, bonfires on the beaches, street dances and concerts. Constitution Day on July 25 marks the anniversary of the island's commonwealth status; parades, fireworks and regattas are held throughout the island.

A copy of *QuéPasa!* (What's Happening!) is available at hotel desks and at the Puerto Rico Tourism Co.'s information centers. This quarterly magazine lists events, scenic tours, points of interest, restaurants, nightclubs, shops and visitor information for San Juan and places out on the island.

Sightseeing

With about 3,000 miles (4,800 km) of good roads, Puerto Rico is popular for motor excursions. Though San Juan receives the majority of attention, it is a good idea to venture out on the island to get a true picture of Puerto Rico. Currently, there are 20 forest reserve areas in the island. For detailed information about guided driving tours, consult the Puerto Rico Tourism Co.'s information centers at the International Airport in Isla Verde, Ochoa building near Pier 1 in Old San Juan and the PRTC Headquarters at the La Princesa Building, also in Old San Juan. Self-guiding driving and walking tours are detailed in *QuéPasa!*, the official guide to Puerto Rico.

Many interesting sites are only a short distance from San Juan—famous resorts, craft villages, forests, beaches and scenic areas. For example, a half-day tour from San Juan to the Palo Colorado Recreation Site in the El Yunque National Forest might include a drive through the towns of Río Grande, Luquillo and Loíza, where intricate masks are carved out of coconut shells by descendants of the town's original black plantation slaves.

Another half-day trip from San Juan is a visit to Las Cabezas de San Juan Nature Preserve, a beautiful, ecologically diverse area operated by the Conservation Trust of Puerto Rico. Known locally as El Faro (the lighthouse), the reserve is home to indigenous and endangered species and features each of Puerto Rico's unique ecosystems.

A full day should be allotted for a round-trip drive from San Juan to Arecibo, including stops at Vega Baja, Manatí, the grounds of the Arecibo Observatory and, near Lares, the Río Camuy Cave Park, featuring the world's third largest underground river. Part of the drive follows a scenic coastal road, Rte. 681.

A drive through coffee country from Manatí to Ponce on rtes. 140 and 10, then to San Juan via Rte. 1, might include stops at rock formations and at the ruins of Central Mercedita near Ponce, where sugar was refined.

Longer excursions out on the island are usually worth the extra effort. A 3-day tour from San Juan to Ponce might include overnight stops in Mayagüez and La Parguera, then passing through San Germán and Ponce. Evening boat trips to La Parguera's bioluminescent bay offer an "illuminating" experience. Miniscule marine life known as dinoflagellates produce a glowing chemical light in the water when disturbed on moonless nights.

An interesting attraction in the southwestern area is the Guánica Dry Forest, a scrub and cactus landscape that was the site of the American landing in 1898. For the hardy traveler, a 4-day tour beginning and ending in San Juan and reaching Ponce via Barranquitas can include extensive sightseeing along the highway winding through the Cordillera Central, Puerto Rico's mountain range.

Guided tours provide insight into some of the island's more popular attractions. A 3-hour guided tour of Old San Juan includes visits to the Capitol Building, Fort San Felipe del Morro (El Morro), Fort San Cristóbal, La Iglesia de San José, San Juan Gate, Christ Chapel (Capilla del Cristo) and La Princesa and its paseo. The 4-hour El Yunque Rain Forest Tour explores the rain forest's waterfalls, observation tower and tropical plants; a full-day tour that includes swimming at the beach of Balneario de Luquillo also is available.

Boat and airplane charters to Mona Island, about 50 miles (80 km) west of Puerto Rico and inhabited by a variety of wildlife, are available on the west coast; for information phone the Department of Natural Resources at (787) 999-2200. The islands of Vieques and Culebra off the east coast are reached by plane from San Juan or ferry service from Fajardo.

Transportation

Puerto Rico is accessible by air from most mainland cities including Atlanta, Baltimore, Boston, Charlotte, Chicago, Dallas, Houston, Miami, Newark, New York City, Orlando, Philadelphia and Tampa. There also is air service between San Juan and Mayagüez, Aguadilla, Ponce or Fajardo. American Airlines

provides daily nonstop service from Miami to Ponce. Several U.S. carriers operate out of San Juan's Luis Muñoz Marín International Airport and reach most major U.S. cities. Many of the flights continue to other Caribbean islands. Rafael Hernandez Airport in Aguadilla and Eugenio María de Hostos Airport in Mayagüez serve the west coast of the island.

Having long been a popular port of call, Puerto Rico is one of the largest home-based cruise ship ports in the world. The terminal is in Old San Juan.

Transportation in San Juan includes metered taxicabs at the airport, hotels and other locations throughout the city; taxis can be rented by the hour. Taxis are the fastest way to get to San Juan from the airport. Flat fares from the airport to Isla Verde, to Condado and to Old San Juan are $10, $15 and $19, respectively, aboard Taxis

Fast Facts

POPULATION: 3,806,610.

AREA: 8,897 sq km (3,435 sq mi.).

CAPITAL: San Juan.

HIGHEST POINT: 1,338 m (4,390 ft.), Cerro de Punta.

LOWEST POINT: Sea level, Caribbean Sea.

TIME ZONE(S): Atlantic Standard.

LANGUAGE: Spanish and English.

GOVERNMENT: Commonwealth associated with the United States.

UNIT OF CURRENCY: U.S. dollar.

ELECTRICITY: 110 volts, 60 cycles AC.

MINIMUM AGE FOR DRIVERS: 21-25, depending on the rental car agency; daily surcharge for ages 21-24, $10-$25. U.S. license valid for 4 months; drive on right.

MINIMUM AGE FOR GAMBLING: 18.

SEAT BELT/CHILD RESTRAINT LAWS: Seat belts are required for driver and front-seat passengers. Child restraints required for under age 2; seat belts required for ages 2-12.

HELMETS FOR MOTORCYCLISTS: Required.

HOLIDAYS: Jan. 1; Three Kings Day (Epiphany), Jan. 6; Eugenio María de Hostos' Birthday, Jan. (2nd Mon.); Martin Luther King Jr. Day, Jan. (3rd Mon.); Presidents Day, Feb. (3rd Mon.); Emancipation Day, Mar. 22; Good

Friday; Easter; José de Diego's Birthday, Apr. (3rd Mon.); Memorial Day, May (last Mon.); July 4; Luis Muñoz Rivera's Birthday, July (3rd Mon.); Constitution Day, July 25; José Celso Barbosa's Birthday, July 27; Labor Day, Sept. (1st Mon.); Columbus Day, Oct. (2nd Mon.); Veterans Day, Nov. 11; Discovery of Puerto Rico Day, Nov. 19; Thanksgiving, Nov. (4th Thurs.); Christmas, Dec. 25.

TAXES: A 7-11 percent room tax (depending on the size of the resort) and 10-12 percent service charge are added to most hotel bills.

IMMIGRATION REQUIREMENTS: There are no immigration requirements for U.S. citizens, but a passport is required when travel may involve stops on other Caribbean islands.

PHONING THE ISLANDS: To call Puerto Rico from the U.S. or Canada, dial 1 + area code + the 7-digit local number.

FURTHER INFORMATION FOR VISITORS:

Puerto Rico Tourism Company
135 W. 50th St., 22nd Floor
New York, NY 10103
(212) 586-6262
(800) 223-6530

Puerto Rico Tourism Company, Old San Juan
La Princesa Bldg. #2
Paseo La Princesa
Old San Juan, Puerto Rico 00902
(787) 721-2400
(800) 866-7827

Turísticos. The fare from the piers to Old San Juan or Puerto de Tierra is $10, to Condado $12, to Isla Verde $19. All fares include two pieces of luggage.

The bus system also operates throughout the metropolitan area. Stops are designated by a magenta, orange and white sign bearing the word *Parada*; fare 50c. *Carros Públicos*, public cars that follow established routes between most towns on the island, run during daylight hours. Marked by the letters P or PD following the numbers on their license plate, *públicos* can usually be hailed from the main plaza of a town. *Públicos* are the least expensive transportation available, but prospective riders must wait until the car is full.

Free trolley rides are available within the Old San Juan historic district and along the beachfront in Isla Verde.

Rental cars also are available, as are chauffeur-driven cars. A valid U.S. driver's license is good in Puerto Rico for up to 120 days. Speed limits are posted in miles per hour and are strictly enforced; metric measurements generally are used on distance signs.

Tren Urbano provides fast and reliable mass transit to the municipalities of San Juan, Bayamón and Guyanabo. The "urban train" runs daily from 5:30 a.m. to 11:30 p.m. One-way fare is $1.50; 75c for ages 60-74, students with ID and persons with a disability. For information, phone (787) 765-0927 or (866) 900-1284.

Ferry service provides interesting and inexpensive interisland links. Crossing the bay every 30 minutes, La Lancha de Cataño connects Old San Juan with the municipality of Cataño; fares are very inexpensive. The Fajardo Ferry carries passengers and cars on a triangular route linking Fajardo on the east end of the island with the islands of Vieques and Culebra. Transportation to other Caribbean islands includes America Cruise Ferries, which operates the *Caribbean Fantasy* between Puerto Rico and the Dominican Republic. The eight- to 12-hour overnight crossing operates Monday from Puerto Rico's Pan American terminal and on Wednesday and Friday from Port of Mayagüez; phone (787) 725-2643.

Points of Interest

See maps on pages 165 and 179.

AGUADA (B-1) pop. 42,042, elev. 108'

On the western coast, Aguada (ah-GWAH-da) is traditionally considered the first landing place of Christopher Columbus when he arrived on the island of Puerto Rico in 1493. There is no historical evidence, however, and the nearby town of Aguadilla makes a similar claim. Nevertheless, a 15th-century settlement was established at Aguada, and its port became a stopping point for ships traveling from Spain to South America. The ruins of Ermita Espinar, a chapel built in 1525, are evidence of early attempts to convert Taíno Indians to Christianity.

The Aguada Agricultural Museum (Museo Agricola de Aguada), housed in a former railroad station, displays Taíno and African art, railroad exhibits and artifacts relating to Puerto Rican history.

THE CHURCH OF SAINT FRANCIS OF ASSISI (LA IGLESIA DE SAN FRANCISCO DE ASÍS) is on the central plaza at calles Colón and Paz. Completed in 1936, the Church of Saint Francis of Assisi features two towers standing more than 100 feet high. A series of stained glass windows adorns the interior. Franciscan friars built the first monastery on this site in 1516, but it was destroyed by Carib Indians. A later church was leveled by the earthquake of 1918. **Hours:** Mon.-Fri. 6-11 a.m., Sat. 5-9 p.m.,

Sun. 5:30-9 a.m. and 4-6:30 p.m. Mass held daily. **Cost:** Donations. **Phone:** (787) 868-2630.

AGUADILLA (B-1) pop. 64,685, elev. 301'

On the northwest edge of the island, Aguadilla (ah-gwah-DEE-ya) calls itself "the garden of the Atlantic." With its red-tiled roofs and mountain backdrop, the city is often described as having a Mediterranean feel. Aguadilla was founded in 1775.

Once a fishing village and now a manufacturing center, the city is perhaps best known for its world-class surfing beaches, with colorful names such as Gas Chambers, Survivor and Wilderness. The most popular is Crashboat Beach, prized for its crystal-clear water. Parque de Colón, or Christopher Columbus Park, is on the southernmost beach and features monuments, a boardwalk, a playground and a banyan tree house. A statue of composer Rafael Hernández, who was born in Aguadilla, stands on the town square.

Six miles north at Punta Borinquen, Ramey Air Force Base operated 1939-1971. It boasted one of the longest runways in the Caribbean—more than 2 miles long. Planes flying into the western part of the island now land on this runway at Rafael Hernández Airport. The Punta Borinquen Lighthouse was destroyed by the tidal wave of 1918; ruins are still visible. The Coast Guard light station that replaced it is not open to the public.

LAS CASCADAS WATER PARK is on Hwy. 2. Aquatic features include giant waterslides, a wave pool and the long, winding Crazy River. **Hours:** Daily 10-5, late May to mid-Aug.; Sat.-Sun. 10-5, Mar. 1 to late May and mid-Aug. to early Sept. **Cost:** $19.95; $17.95 (ages 3-12); $10.95 (ages 55-74); free (ages 0-2 and 75+). **Phone:** (787) 819-0950 or (787) 819-1030. [⊤]

ARECIBO (B-2) pop. 100,131, elev. 6′

Arecibo, on the north coast, is the island's largest city in geographical size. It has been called *El Díamante Del Norte*, or "the diamond of the north." The city was settled in 1556. Capt. Antonio Correa and a handful of soldiers repelled a British sea invasion here in 1702 and were later honored for their bravery by King Philip V of Spain.

Cambalache State Forest (Bosque Estatal), midway between Arecibo and Barceloneta on Highway 22, is noted for its plantations of eucalyptus, teak, and mahoe trees. The forest is a popular destination for hiking and mountain biking; a permit is required for camping.

ARECIBO LIGHTHOUSE AND HISTORICAL PARK is off Hwy. 22 exit 71 (Domingo Ruiz), following Rd. 2 to Rds. 681 and 655. The park offers five cultural representations of Puerto Rico's history, from the 1493 Spanish Conquest to the building of the lighthouse in 1898 during the Spanish-American War. Historic replicas include a Taíno Indian village, slave quarters, Blackbeard's pirate ship and the three sailing vessels of Christopher Columbus. Marine artifacts are displayed in the restored lighthouse. The surrounding park on rocky Punta Morillo includes a playground; a small petting zoo; and a pirate's cave containing a saltwater aquarium with sharks, rays and eels.

Hours: Mon.-Fri. 9-6, Sat.-Sun. 10-7. **Cost:** $10; $8 (ages 2-12 and 65+). **Parking:** $2. **Phone:** (787) 880-7540.

ARECIBO OBSERVATORY is at the end of Hwy. 625. The world's largest and most sensitive radio telescope consists of a 1,000-ton, suspended platform that hovers above a 20-acre (8-hectare) dish set in a sinkhole 565 feet (172 m) deep. Built under the direction of Cornell University in 1963, the observatory is the home base for SETI, the Search for Extraterrestrial Life.

The telescope is used by scientists from around the world to study deep-space objects, natural radio emissions, the planets and Earth's atmosphere. Moviegoers have seen the giant reflector dish in such films as "Goldeneye" and "Contact."

The observatory's Ángel Ramos Foundation Visitor Center provides a platform for viewing the telescope and houses a variety of interactive exhibits, audiovisual displays and informative panels. **Time:** Allow 2 hours minimum. **Hours:** Daily 9-4, June-July and Dec. 15-Jan. 15; Wed.-Sun. and major holidays 9-4, rest of year. **Cost:** $6; $4 (ages 3-10 and 65+). **Phone:** (787) 878-2612.

RÍO CAMUY CAVE PARK is 12 mi. (19 km) s. off Hwy. 129. The 250-acre (102-hectare) park's massive cave network encompasses one of the largest underground river systems in the world. Trams transport visitors to the mouth of one of the caves, where guided walking tours begin.

Tours require a moderate level of physical activity that includes climbing stairs; non-slip shoes are recommended. **Tours:** Guided tours are available. **Time:** Allow 3 hours minimum. **Hours:** Two-hour tours depart Wed.-Sun. 8-3 (weather permitting). Visitors should arrive early, as the park reaches maximum capacity quickly. Tram waits may exceed 15 minutes. Phone ahead to confirm schedule. **Cost:** $15; $10 (ages 4-12); $6 (ages 65+). **Parking:** $3-$5. **Phone:** (787) 898-3100. [▲] [⊤] [☂]

ARROYO (D-5) pop. 19,117, elev. 3′

The telegraph was introduced to Puerto Rico and Latin America in 1858 when Samuel F. B. Morse installed the first line at Arroyo. His daughter and son-in-law owned a sugarcane plantation here known as Hacienda La Enriqueta.

On the southeast coast, Arroyo is popular for its beaches, especially Punta Guilarte on the west side of Puerto Patillas bay. The yellow lighthouse at Faro de Punta Figuras has been restored; it offers a striking view of the Caribbean.

MUSEO ANTIGUA ADUANA is on Morse St. next to City Hall. Historical exhibits in this ornate pink building, the former customs house, include memorabilia related to the installation of Puerto Rico's first telegraph line by Samuel F.B. Morse. Taíno artifacts and local artworks also are displayed. **Hours:** Wed.-Sun. 8:30-4:30. **Cost:** Free. **Phone:** (787) 839-8096.

BARRANQUITAS (C-4)
pop. 28,909, elev. 2,063′

Near the center of the island, the mountain town of Barranquitas (bahr-rahn-KEE-tahs) has been called the "cradle of the greats" for the many distinguished Puerto Ricans it has produced. Among them was Luis Muñoz Rivera, who negotiated the island's Charter of Autonomy with the Spanish government in 1897. The small house where he was born, Casa Natal de Luis Muñoz Rivera, has been restored by the Institute of Puerto Rican Culture as a library and museum. The bodies of Rivera and his son, Luis Muñoz Marín—who became Puerto Rico's first elected governor—are entombed at the nearby Maosoleo Luis Muñoz Marín.

Islanders flock to Barranquitas in July for the Feria Nacional de Artesanías, considered the longest-running artisan fair in Puerto Rico and one of its most significant. The fair features food, music and exhibits by some 200 local artists and craftspeople.

South of Barranquitas is the only volcanic rift in Puerto Rico, San Cristóbal Canyon. This rugged and nearly inaccessible gorge is more than 650 feet (198

m) deep, with rushing streams and plunging water-falls along the Río Usabón. Best viewed with a guide, the canyon is an emerging destination for rock climbing and adventure tours.

BAYAMON (B-4) pop. 224,044, elev. 36′

On the northeastern coast, Bayamón (by-ya-MON) is a suburb of San Juan and is the island's second largest city. Founded in 1772, the city's name is derived from *Bayamóngo*, a Taino name for the river running through it. The "city of the traffic jams" lacks a coordinated mass transit and bus system.

Rio Bayamon Golf Course on Laurel Avenue offers nine holes; phone (787) 740-1419. You can enjoy tennis at Honda Tennis Center, which features 16 courts.

LUIS A. FERRÉ SCIENCE PARK (PARQUE DE LAS CIENCIAS LUIS A. FERRÉ) is on Rte. 167, just s. of Diego Expwy. (Hwy. 22). The 42-acre park's extensive facilities include a plaza containing life-size rockets, a planetarium, an art gallery and a small zoo area. Trains, natural science and transportation are just a few of the topics featured at the numerous museum exhibits, where attendants are on hand to provide additional interpretive information. Visitors also can explore a re-created Puerto Rican pueblo or rent paddle boats and cruise a manmade lake. During renovations, some areas might be temporarily closed. **Time:** Allow 2 hours minimum. **Hours:** Wed.-Fri.9-4, Sat.-Sun. 10-6. Last admission 2 hours before closing. Closed major holidays. **Cost:** $5; $2.50 (ages 65-75 and 2-12); free (ages 76+ and 0-2). **Phone:** (787) 740-6878. (T) (A)

CABO ROJO (D-1) pop. 46,911, elev. 62′

On the southwestern coast, the limestone cliffs of Cabo Rojo rise several hundred feet above the Atlantic. The Spanish-style Cabo Robo Lighthouse, or Faro de Los Morillos, was built in 1881 and is now automated. The bay at Boquerón, part of the municipality, extends several miles inland; salt has been mined in the surrounding flats since the time of the Taíno Indians. The public beach at Balneario Boquerón is a long-time favorite of Puerto Ricans for its scenic setting on the bay.

Mona Island, 50 miles (80 km) off the coast, is a unique island preserve in the straits between Puerto Rico and the Dominican Republic. It has often been compared to the Galápagos Islands for its rare species of wildlife, including giant iguanas, sea turtles and red-footed boobies. The iron Isla Mona Lighthouse was designed by Gustave Eiffel. Boat and airplane charters are available; for information phone the Department of Natural Resources at (787) 851-4795 or (787) 999-2200.

CABO ROJO NATIONAL WILDLIFE REFUGE is 3 mi. s. on Hwy. 301 from Hwy. 101 in Boquerón. This bird-watcher's haven in the subtropical dry forest region is home to the endangered yellow-shouldered blackbird.

The Cabo Rojo Salt Flats have been called the single most important point of convergence for migratory shorebirds in Puerto Rico and the U.S. Virgin Islands. The flats are a vital nesting ground for the snowy plover, least tern, peregrine falcon and brown pelican. The refuge features a visitor center, a 2-mile interpretive trail and 12 miles of hiking trails. **Note:** The attraction is undergoing renovation and is currently closed; please call ahead to inquire about opening status. **Hours:** Mon.-Fri. 7:30-4. Salt Flats Wed.-Sun. 8-4:30. **Cost:** Free. **Phone:** (787) 851-7258. (A)

CAGUAS (C-5) pop. 140,502, elev. 229′

MUSEUM OF ART (MUSEO DE ARTE) is at Calle Luis Padial and Segundo Ruiz Belvis. The museum features rotating and permanent exhibits of works by local and regional artists. Mediums include acrylic, oil, mixed media, sculpture and photography. Of special interest is Tradiciones Puertorriqueñas, a 1956 mural by Alfonso Arana, and Paisaje, a signature work by Carlos Osorio. **Time:** Allow 30 minutes minimum. **Hours:** Tues.-Sat. 9-noon and 1-5. **Cost:** Free. **Phone:** (787) 744-8833, ext. 1838.

MUSEUM OF SNUFF (MUSEO DEL TABACO) is at Calle Ramon Emeterio Betances #87, just w. of Plaza Santiago Palmer. Exhibits outline the cultural and economic aspects of tobacco and cigar making in Puerto Rico. Visitors can see a replica of a tobacco drying shed, cigar rollers and other instruments as well as memorabilia of past cigar companies and their various promotions. **Time:** Allow 30 minutes minimum. **Hours:** Tues.-Sat. 9-noon and 1-5. **Cost:** Free. **Phone:** (787) 744-2960.

CANÓVANAS (B-5) pop. 43,335, elev. 29′

East of San Juan in the metropolitan area, *La Cuna de los Indios* (the Indian Cradle) was once home to a large Taíno population and took its name from a local chief. To this day, Canóvanas sports teams are nicknamed the Indios.

In modern times, Canóvanas is known as *La Ciudad de las Carreras* (the Racetrack City) for its famous horse-racing complex, Hipódromo Camarero Race Track. Races are held Monday, Wednesday and Friday through Sunday; phone (787) 641-6060. The annual Clásico del Caribe, or Caribbean Classic, is considered the richest horse race in Latin America; phone (787) 876-2450.

Note: Policies concerning admittance of children to pari-mutuel betting facilities vary. Phone for information.

Casa Jesús T. Piñero, the home of Puerto Rico's first native governor, contains a small museum commemorating Piñero's life. He was appointed to the governor's post in 1946 by President Harry S. Truman; the island's first democratic election was held 2 years later.

COAMO (D-4) pop. 37,597, elev. 511′

One of the oldest settlements on the island, Coamo (ko-AH-mo) is known for its thermal springs, long believed to have therapeutic properties. Local legend says that Juan Ponce de León, who traveled to the New World with Christopher Columbus and colonized Puerto Rico in 1508, mistakenly went off to Florida in search of the Fountain of Youth after hearing natives speak about the Baños de Coamo.

The lovely white Iglesia Católica San Blás de Illesca on the main plaza was established in 1563. Just off the square, the Museo Histórico de Coamo displays archeological artifacts, local exhibits and colonial-style furnishings; phone (787) 803-6716.

CULEBRA (A-6) pop. 1,868, elev. 3'

About 17 miles off the eastern coast, Culebra is the smallest of the inhabited Spanish Virgin Islands. The larger Vieques is 8 miles south. Though a few beach resorts have opened on Culebra in recent years, the island remains largely undeveloped, a laid-back destination for sunning and scuba diving. The pristine Flamenco Beach is considered one of the most stunning beaches in the Caribbean.

Culebra and nearly two dozen islets are part of a national wildlife refuge that protects nesting sea turtles and colonies of endangered sea birds, including nearly 60,000 sooty terns. The abandoned Culebrita Lighthouse was built in 1882 to establish Spanish dominion over the main island. Culebra can be reached by ferry from Fajardo.

DORADO (B-4) pop. 34,017, elev. 13'

West of San Juan on the northern coast, Dorado is home to several beachside golf resorts. The recreation area of El Ojo del Buey is named for a large rock formation resembling the eye of an ox. The public beaches at Sardinera and Cerro Gordo are particularly scenic.

MUSEUM AND CULTURAL CENTER CASA DEL REY (MUSEO Y CENTRO CULTURAL CASA DEL REY) is at Calle Mendez Vigo 292 next to city hall. Once a garrison for Spanish military personnel and later the home of writer Manuel Alonso y Pacheco, this 1823 inn has been restored by the Institute of Puerto Rican Culture. Exhibits chronicle the island's Taíno culture and its Spanish colonization. **Hours:** Mon.-Fri. 8-4:30. **Cost:** Free. **Phone:** (787) 796-5740.

EL YUNQUE NATIONAL FOREST (C-6)

Elevations in the forest range from 1,000 ft. to 3,533 ft. (305 m to 1,077 m) at El Yunque. Refer to AAA maps for additional elevation information.

The El Yunque National Forest is 25 miles (40 km) east of San Juan near the town of Palmer on Hwy. 191. Three other forest roads, rtes. 186, 966 and 988, skirt the western, northern and eastern boundaries. The scenic beach of Balneario Luquillo is off Rte. 3.

The forest, which takes its name from El Yunque (JUNE-kay), a 3,533-foot (1,077-m) peak in the Luquillo Mountains, covers 28,000 acres (11,287 hectares). Proclaimed a forest reserve by Theodore Roosevelt in 1903, El Yunque is the only tropical U.S. National Forest; it is administered by the U.S. Department of Agriculture Forest Service.

The annual rainfall is extremely heavy, and at the high elevations it exceeds 200 inches. Moisture drips from massive trees, dense plants, ferns and moss. Hundreds of streams course down the mountainsides, creating countless falls and pools. The rain forest receives more than 100 billion gallons of rain a year.

Moist, misty and generally cool, the forest supports a dense system of vegetation. Largest are the towering hardwoods, their crowns hung with vines; many trunks or limbs support a fringe of air plants, a large number containing blossoms. Beneath these giants are smaller trees and shrubs that shade flowers, herbs, mosses and tree ferns growing as high as 30 feet (9 m).

The montane thicket covering valleys and slopes above 2,000 feet (610 m) is generally composed of trees and a ground cover of ferns, vines and bromeliads. Extensive stands of sierra palms grow on steep slopes at higher elevations and along streams. The cloud forest, its trees about 12 feet (4 m) high, is found on the highest peaks. In all, the forest harbors more than 240 species of trees, four forest types and dozens of waterfalls. More than 50 of these species of trees are found only in Puerto Rico.

Such resplendent birds as tanagers, woodpeckers, cuckoos, euphonia and the Puerto Rican inhabit the forest. The birds usually remain hidden, but their calls and whistles are heard frequently. The Puerto Rican Parrot, an extremely rare and endangered species, also inhabits the rain forest and is found only in this part of the island. *Coquíes,* tiny inch-long tree frogs, fill the forest with their high-pitched notes, which resemble the singing of their own name.

The forest's main visitor center, El Portal, is just inside the entrance on Hwy. 191 at Km 4.3. Near Km 8 is La Coca Falls, named for 14th-century settler Juan Diego de La Coca. The Yokahú Observation Tower at Km 8.9 offers a magnificent view of the forest and the northeast coast of Puerto Rico. Food and picnic facilities are available at the Sierra Palm Information Center at Km 11.6.

The Palo Colorado Recreation Site, the most visited section of the forest, includes an information center and picnic shelters. In this area around Km 12 are trailheads leading to La Mina Falls, Mt. Britton Lookout Tower and El Toro Peak, the summit of El Yunque. Guided 1-hour interpretive hikes of the recreation area are offered by the Forest Service. In all, the forest contains 24 miles (39 km) of soft and paved hiking trails.

Rain gear and hiking boots are recommended, as trails are often wet and slippery. Park open daily 7:30-6. Information centers are open daily 9:30-5;

closed Christmas. Hiking tours depart daily 10:30-3:30, Feb.-Aug.; based upon guide availability rest of year. Tour tickets are sold at the Palo Colorado Information Center on a first-come, first-served basis. Park admission is free. Hiking tours $5, ages 4-12, $3. Phone (787) 888-1880.

EL PORTAL RAIN FOREST CENTER is on Hwy. 191 at Km 4.3, just inside the El Yunque National Forest entrance. An elevated walkway through the forest canopy takes visitors into the environmental education center, which offers information about the natural features and importance of the El Yunque National Forest and tropical forests worldwide. Noted for its award-winning tropical architecture, the center features four multimedia exhibit pavilions, an orientation film and an interpretive trail through landscaped grounds. **Hours:** Daily 9-4:30. **Cost:** $4; $2 (ages 65+); free (ages 0-15). **Phone:** (787) 888-1880. 🎟

FAJARDO (C-6) pop. 40,712, elev. 29'

On the eastern coast, Fajardo is a major boating center and the departure point for ferry and plane trips to the islands of Vieques and Culebra. With more than 1,000 boat slips, Puerto del Rey Marina is one of the largest marinas in the Caribbean.

The Ceiba Forest stretches from Fajardo to Ceiba along the coast and west to the El Yunque National Forest. It is a subtropical dry woodland, predominantly mangrove.

LAS CABEZAS DE SAN JUAN NATURE PRESERVE is on Hwy. 987. Surrounded on three sides by the Atlantic Ocean, this 321-acre reserve protects a variety of ecological systems, including coral reefs, offshore cays, lagoons, mangroves, a dry forest and a bioluminescent lagoon. The park is accessible only by a 2.5-hour guided tour that combines riding aboard an open-air trolley and walking along boardwalks and nature trails. The last stop is the castle-like lighthouse, Faro de las Cabezas de San Juan, one of the oldest on the island.

Hours: English-language tours depart Wed.-Sun. at 2; three other tours are offered in the morning. The number of visitors is strictly limited to protect the park's fragile ecosystem. **Cost:** $10; $7 (ages 65+ and students with ID). Reservations are required. **Phone:** (787) 722-5882 or (787) 860-2560.

GAMBLING ESTABLISHMENTS

• **El Conquistador Casino** is at 1000 El Conquistador Ave. **Hours:** Mon.-Thurs. 4 p.m.-midnight, Fri.-Sat. 4 p.m.-2 a.m. **Phone:** (787) 863-1000 or (888) 543-1282.

GUÁNICA (D-2) pop. 21,888, elev. 269'

After landing on the northwest tip of the island during his second voyage to the New World, Christopher Columbus founded a settlement at Guánica on the southern coast. During the Spanish-American War, U.S. troops landed here on July 25, 1898, surprising Spain's forces. Fuerte Caprón, which stands

on a hill 450 feet above the bay, was built by American soldiers after the invasion.

Although best known for its mangrove and cactus forest, Guánica is a popular excursion for diving, snorkeling and sunbathing. A small cay off the coast is named Gilligan's Island for its resemblance to the TV show setting. Manatees and endangered hawksbill and leatherback turtles may be found in the crystal blue lagoon at Ballenas Beach.

GUÁNICA DRY FOREST RESERVE (BOSQUE ESTATAL) is off Hwy. 2 on rds. 116, 333 and 334 to the visitor center. One of the largest tropical dry coastal forests in the world, Guánica covers nearly 10,000 acres along the southern coast. This UNESCO Biosphere Reserve, known as *El Bosque Seco,* is home to more than 600 types of rare plants and animals, including 48 endangered species. A population of the supposedly extinct Puerto Rican whippoorwills was discovered here in 1961. One lignum vitae tree is said to be more than 1,000 years old. The ruins of a Spanish lighthouse, El Faro Guánica, are visible.

More than 36 miles of trails lead through the forest, but hiking is recommended only during cool morning hours. Visitors should wear protective clothing and carry drinking water. **Hours:** Daily 8:30-4. **Cost:** Free. **Phone:** (787) 821-5706.

GUAYAMA (D-4) pop. 44,301, elev. 144'

CASA CAUTIÑO MUSEUM is at 1 Palmer St. Visitors tour an elegant 19th-century home designed by renowned architect Manuel Texidor. Features include a collection of Latin, Caribbean and Puerto Rican art, soaring ceilings, hand-blown Murano glass chandeliers, antiques and ornate hand-carved furnishings. Guides provide anecdotal stories of the prominent Cautiño family who lived here and their role in the development of the country's south coast. **Time:** Allow 30 minutes minimum. **Hours:** Tues.-Sat. 9-noon and 1:30-4:30. Closed major holidays. **Cost:** Free. **Phone:** (787) 864-9083.

HUMACAO (C-5) pop. 59,035, elev. 82'

Named for a Taíno chieftain, Humacao (oo-mah-KOU) was once home to a large sugar plantation. This quiet town on the eastern coast is drawing an increasing number of tourists to its resorts, golf courses and beaches.

The Observatorio Astronómico on the campus of the University of Puerto Rico at Humacao is open to the public at 7:30 p.m. the second Thursday of each month during the academic year for viewings of the planets and stars; phone (787) 850-9344.

Just offshore is the island of Cayo Santiago, a field station of the Caribbean Primate Research Center. More than 400 Rhesus monkeys were released here in 1938, and their descendants roam the island today. Access is restricted, but diving and fishing charters provide an offshore glimpse of the colony.

CASA ROIG MUSEUM is at 66 Calle Antonio López. The 1920 home of sugar baron Antonio Roig was designed by architect Antonín Nechodoma, who took his inspiration from Frank Lloyd Wright. Restored by the University of Puerto Rico, the house museum displays regional history exhibits and works of contemporary art. **Hours:** Mon.-Fri. 8:30-4:30. **Cost:** Free. **Phone:** (787) 852-8380.

ISABELA (B-1) pop. 44,444, elev. 200'

On the northwest coast, Isabela was founded by European settlers in 1725. Ruins of the original church and village are visible along the Guajataca River at San Antonio de la Tuna.

GUAJATACA STATE FOREST (BOSQUE ESTATAL) is e. on Rte. 2, then s. on Rte. 446. In the "karst country" of northwest Puerto Rico, where underground limestone dissolves into sinkholes, tunnels and caves, Guajataca (wa-ha-TA-ka) encompasses more than 25 miles of hiking trails through this unusual topography. A walking map is available at the ranger station, and an observation tower provides a scenic view of man-made Guajataca Lake. Cueva de Viento (Wind Cave) features dramatic formations of stalactites and stalagmites. **Hours:** Daily dawn-dusk. **Cost:** Free. **Phone:** (787) 724-3724. 🔼

LA PARGUERA (D-1) pop. 1,141

Settled in 1883, the fishing village of La Parguera has become a modest tourist area centered around the southwest coast's eerie neon waters. Along the coast, dozens of mangrove cays and islets form ornate channels that are popular among kayakers. The Lajas valley is known for its major crop, a large and delicious pineapple called the *Piña Cabezona.*

LA PARGUERA BIOLUMINESCENT BAY is 5 mi. (8 km) s. on the harbor. La Parguera is one of three bioluminescent bays in Puerto Rico; the others are found at Las Cabezas de San Juan Nature Preserve in Fajardo and at Mosquito Bay off the island of Vieques *(see attraction listings).* The eerie blue-green light is produced by microorganisms that cause the water to shimmer and glow when disturbed. **Hours:** Viewing is best on cloudy or moonless nights. Boats leave from the La Parguera dock nightly.

LOÍZA (B-5) pop. 32,537, elev. 9'

East of San Juan on the northern coast, Loíza (loo-EE-zah) has been nicknamed "the capital of traditions." The village was settled by Yoruban slaves in the 1500s and retains one of the highest percentages of African descendants on the island. The week-long Fiesta de Santiago Apóstol in late July is a colorful celebration of Taíno and African culture. Religious processions lead from the 17th-century Iglésia de San Patricio (St. Patrick's Church), considered the island's oldest church in continuous use. The festivities continue with music, food, fireworks and dancing the *bomba.* Loíza's festival masks, made from coconut husks and intricately painted, are highly prized.

MARICAO (C-2) pop. 6,449, elev. 1,525'

High in the central mountain range east of Mayagüez, Maricao (mah-ree-KOU) is one of the island's premier coffee-growing villages. The 3-day Maricao Coffee Festival in February celebrates the annual harvest.

MARICAO FOREST RESERVE (BOSQUE ESTATAL) is on Rte. 20. A prime bird-watching site, the forest has a stone observation tower that provides fine views of the west and south coasts. The elfin woods warbler, the Puerto Rican woodpecker and many other endangered species can be spotted here. Some 25,000 fish, including largemouth bass, channel catfish and Congo perch, are raised yearly at the Maricao Fish Hatchery for release into Puerto Rican rivers and reservoirs. **Hours:** Tues.-Sun. 8-4. **Cost:** Free. **Phone:** (787) 838-1040.

MAYAGÜEZ (C-1) pop. 98,434, elev. 160'

On the west coast, Mayagüez (mah-yah-GWES) is the island's fifth-largest city and an important commercial port for sugar, coffee and fruit as well as one of the world's largest tuna-packing centers. It also is the home of the College of Agricultural Science of the University of Puerto Rico. An elegant plaza dominates the center of the city, which was almost destroyed by an earthquake in 1918. Mayagüez is about 95 miles (153 km) from San Juan; half-hour flights depart frequently.

DR. JUAN A. RIVERO ZOO is 1 mi. (1.6 km) n. off Rte. 108, following signs. The Mayagüez zoo displays tropical plants and animals in their natural settings. More than 340 animal species, including Bengal tigers and Andean condors, have been collected from tropical climates around the world. Walk-through aviaries highlight birds from Central and South America and the Caribbean. All birds, mammals and reptiles are identified in English and Spanish. **Hours:** Wed.-Sun. 8:30-4. **Cost:** $10; $5 (ages 5-11 and 60-74); free (ages 0-4 and 75+). **Parking:** $2 for motorcycles; $3 for cars; $4 for mini vans. **Phone:** (787) 832-6330 or (787) 834-8110. 🍴

TROPICAL AGRICULTURE RESEARCH STATION is on Rte. 65 between rtes. 2 and 108. Since its establishment on an old plantation in 1901, the tropical research center of the U.S. Department of Agriculture has fostered the development of more than 2,000 tropical plant species from around the world. A well-marked self-guiding tour covers most of the important areas. Because of frequent afternoon rains, morning visits are best. **Hours:** Mon.-Fri. 7-4. Closed major holidays. **Cost:** Free. **Phone:** (787) 831-3435.

GAMBLING ESTABLISHMENTS

- **Holiday Inn Mayagüez & Tropical Casino** is at 2701 Ave. Hostos. **Hours:** Daily 24 hours. **Phone:** (787) 833-1100 or (800) 465-4329.
- **The Mayagüez Resort and Casino** is at jct. Hwy. 2 and 104, just n. of Rt. 104 km .3. **Hours:**

Daily 24 hours. Closed Good Friday. **Phone:** (787) 832-3030, ext. 3301 or (888) 689-3030.

MOCA (B-1) pop. 39,697, elev. 249'

The lace center of the island, Moca is famous for its mundillo lace. Woven by hand on a pillow loom with dozens or hundreds of bobbins, the intricate lace can be found in wedding gowns, tapestries, linens and accessories. A bronze statue on the town square, *La tejedora de mundillo*, honors the women who carry on this time-honored tradition. The Festival del Mundillo in November features weaving demonstrations, traditional music and food; phone (787) 818-0105.

PALACETE LOS MOREAU is off Hwy. 2 on Rte. 464 near Isabela. This beautiful two-story manor, once part of a French coffee and sugar plantation, was completed in 1905. One of the first houses on the island built with concrete, it was originally called Castillo Labadie. Novelist Enrique Arturo Laguerre immortalized the estate in his best-known work, "La Llamarada." Newly restored, the yellow mansion features stained-glass windows and period furnishings. **Hours:** Wed.-Sun. 9-5. **Cost:** Free. **Phone:** (787) 830-2540 or (787) 830-4475.

PONCE (D-3) pop. 186,475, elev. 45'

An important commercial port on the south coast, Ponce (PONE-say) is the center of the island's sugar, rum and coffee industries and has some of the largest textile mills in the Caribbean. In its center are two tree-shaded plazas bordering the graceful Cathedral of Our Lady of Guadalupe. The Carnaval Ponceño, which coincides with Mardi Gras celebrations around the world, is famous for its papier-mâché masks and brightly colored costumes.

The Alhambra residential section has more than 125 Spanish-style estates. And throughout the city more than 600 of its 1,000 historic buildings have been restored, particularly on Isabel and Reina streets. A steep hill called *El Vigía* (The Watchman) was once a lookout post. At the top, a 100-foot observation tower in the shape of a cross, La Cruceta del Vigía, offers dramatic views of the city. A visitor information center is located at the base of the tower.

On the corner of avs. Marina and Esquina Aurora, a yellow house known as Casa de la Masacre de Ponce marks a bloody chapter in Puerto Rico's political history. On Easter Sunday 1937, police fired upon Nationalist demonstrators, killing 20 people and injuring hundreds.

CASA PAOLI MUSEUM is at 2648 Mayor St. The childhood home of Puerto Rican opera star Antonio Paolí, known as the "King of Tenors," features exhibits about the singer's life as well as a colorful collection of papier-mâché masks from Ponce's annual carnival. Also displayed are costumes the tenor used in various operas as well as playbills, letters and other memorabilia. **Tours:** Guided tours are available. **Time:** Allow 30 minutes minimum.

Hours: Mon.-Fri. 10-noon and 2-5. **Cost:** Free. **Phone:** (787) 840-4115.

HACIENDA BUENA VISTA is 10 mi. (16 km) n. on SR 10 in Barrio Magüeyes. Considered one of the best surviving examples of a Puerto Rican coffee plantation, this 19th-century estate includes nearly a dozen restored buildings, including a working mill and a two-story hacienda furnished with period antiques. The farm was one of the first to establish a nutrition program for slaves. A scenic waterfall provides power to the coffee mill. Guided 2-hour tours describe the history of the plantation and the cultivation of coffee.

Hours: Tours are offered Sat.-Sun. at 8:30, 10:30, 1:30 and 3:30. **Cost:** $7; $4 (ages 5-8). Reservations are required. **Phone:** (787) 722-5882 or (787) 284-7020.

OLD PONCE FIRE STATION (PARQUE DE BOMBAS) is on Plaza de las Delicias behind the cathedral. Built as the main pavilion for the 1882 Exhibition Trade Fair, this Moorish building with bold red and black stripes is one of the most photographed features on the island. Now a museum, the building houses an antique fire engine and historical exhibits dedicated to Ponce's volunteer fire brigade. **Hours:** Wed.-Mon. 9:30-6. **Cost:** Free. **Phone:** (787) 284-4141, ext. 342 or (787) 284-3338.

PONCE HISTORY MUSEUM (MUSEO DE LA HISTORIA) is on the town square at Isabel and Mayor sts. Ten exhibition halls in two neoclassical buildings contain displays depicting the city's ecology, economy, culture, architecture, government and elements of daily life. Various cultural activities take place on an occasional basis in the Ernesto Ramos Antonini auditorium. A videotape documentary is available in English. **Tours:** Guided tours are available. **Time:** Allow 1 hour minimum. **Hours:** Tues.-Sun. 8:30-5. **Cost:** Free. **Phone:** (787) 844-7071.

PONCE MUSEUM OF ART (MUSEO DE ARTE DE PONCE) is at 2325 Avenue Las Américas opposite Catholic University. Important paintings and sculpture from Europe, Africa and the Americas span the 13th through 20th centuries. Highlights from the permanent collection include works by such artists as Eugène Delacroix, Lord Frederick Leighton, Bartolomé Esteban Murillo, José Ribera, Auguste Rodin, Peter Paul Rubens, Anthony Van Dyck and Diego Velázquez.

The Puerto Rican and Latin American galleries includes pieces by Myrna Báez, José Campeche, Rafael Coronel, López Dirube, Luis Hernández, Carlos Mérida, Francisco Oller and Francisco Rodón. Traveling exhibits also are presented.

The building was designed by Edward Durell Stone, architect of the Kennedy Center in Washington, D.C. The Granada Garden is a replica of the gardens in Spain. **Time:** Allow 1 hour, 30 minutes minimum. **Hours:** Wed.-Mon. 10-6. Last admission 45 minutes before closing. Tours depart at 11 and 2. Closed Jan. 1, Jan. 6, Good Friday, Thanksgiving and Christmas. **Cost:** $6; $3 (ages 0-11, ages 65+

and students with ID). Audio guides $2. **Phone:** (787) 848-0505 or (787) 840-1510.

SERRALLÉS CASTLE (MUSEO CASTILLO SERRALLÉS) is at 17 El Vigía. Guided tours of this Spanish Revival home, built in the 1930s, provide insights into the lifestyle of its owner, a wealthy sugar and rum merchant. Gardens surround the home, and a butterfly house is on the grounds. Scenic city and coastal views are offered from an upstairs terrace. **Hours:** Thurs.-Sun. 9:30-6:30. Last tour departs 1 hour before closing. **Cost:** Museum, gardens and butterfly house $8.50; $4.25 (ages 0-11, ages 60+ and students with ID). **Phone:** (787) 259-1774 or (800) 981-2275.

TIBES INDIGENOUS CEREMONIAL PARK (CENTRO CEREMONIAL INDÍGENA) is on Rte. 503 at km 2.2. The site features seven pre-Taíno ball courts as well as the oldest burial ground yet uncovered in the area. Excavations conducted 1975-1982 revealed 186 human remains believed to belong to an aboriginal Indian population called the Igneris. The center includes a re-created Indian village and a museum with permanent and temporary exhibits.

Hours: Tues.-Sun. 9-4; park opens on Mon. holidays and closes the following day. Closed Jan. 1, Good Friday, Mother's and Father's Days, Thanksgiving and Christmas. **Cost:** $3; $2 (ages 5-12); $1.50 (ages 60-74); free (ages 0-4 and 75+). **Phone:** (787) 840-2255 or (787) 840-5685.

TORO NEGRO STATE FOREST (BOSQUE ESTATAL) is 17 mi. (27 km) n.e. via rtes. 10 and 143. This scenic reserve contains the island's tallest peak, Cerro de Punta, and its highest reservoir, the bamboo-fringed Lake Güineo. Coffee plantations once dotted the mountain's lower elevations. The forest offers hiking trails, an observation tower and picnic, swimming and camping facilities at the Doña Juana Recreational Area. **Hours:** Daily dawn-dusk. **Cost:** Free. **Phone:** (787) 867-3040.

GAMBLING ESTABLISHMENTS

• **Hilton Ponce Golf & Casino Resort** is at 1150 Caribe Ave. **Hours:** Sun.-Thurs. 8 a.m.-4 a.m., Fri.-Sat. 8 a.m.-6 a.m. **Phone:** (787) 259-7676.

• **Holiday Inn Ponce & El Tropical Casino**, 3315 Ponce Bypass. **Hours:** Daily 24 hours. **Phone:** (787) 844-1200.

RINCÓN (C-1) pop. 14,767, elev. 167'

The Atlantic Ocean meets the Caribbean Sea at Rincón (rin-KONE), where 8 miles of reef-lined beaches produce some spectacular waves. This sleepy village on Puerto Rico's west coast—the Porta del Sol, or "Door to the Sun"—has become a winter mecca for experienced surfers. Rincón first gained international attention during the 1968 World Surfing Championship, and many surfers now live here year-round.

Waves during the main season from November to March are generally too rough for swimming, but the surf quiets down the rest of the year for snorkeling, scuba diving and watersports. The largest breaks are at Domes Beach, Playa Marias and Tres Palmas. Most restaurants, hotels and surf shops are clustered around Sandy Beach. More secluded spots include Pools Beach, Antonio's Beach and River Mouth. Tres Palmas Marine Reserve protects an offshore reef of elkhorn coral and other shallow-water varieties. The reserve also is home to hawksbill and leatherback turtles.

Whale watching is popular from January through March, when humpbacks winter in the warm waters of Rincón Bay. The best view is from the park surrounding the Rincón Lighthouse, El Faro Punta Higüero, which was built by the Spanish in 1892 and reconstructed in 1922 after a tsunami.

RÍO GRANDE (B-6) pop. 52,362, elev. 19'

East of San Juan, Río Grande is the closest town to El Yunque National Forest. Several beach and golf resorts have opened here in recent years, drawing new visitors to the northeast coast.

GAMBLING ESTABLISHMENTS

• **Paradisus Puerto Rico Casino** is at 200 Cocoa Beach Blvd. in the Gran Meliá Puerto Rico Golf Resort. **Hours:** 10 a.m.-2 a.m. **Phone:** (787) 657-1051.

• **Wyndham Rio Mar Beach Resort & Casino** is at 6000 Rio Mar Blvd. **Hours:** Daily 10 a.m.-4 a.m. **Phone:** (787) 888-6000.

SAN GERMÁN (D-1) pop. 37,105, elev. 177'

Midway between Mayagüez and Ponce and surrounded by mountains, San Germán (her-MON) has been nicknamed *Ciudad de Las Lomas,* or City of the Hills. This is Puerto Rico's second oldest Spanish village, settled in 1511. It features two plazas with buildings representing a variety of architectural styles. The centerpiece of Parque de Santo Domingo is the famous Porta Coéli Church. Crowning the Plaza Francisco Mariano Quiñones is the Church of San Germán Auxerre, which was founded in 1688 and has undergone countless reconstructions over the centuries. The church features a crystal chandelier and a trompe l'oeil ceiling.

IGLESIA PORTA COÉLI is at Ramas and Dr. Veve sts., overlooking one of San Germán's two plazas, the Parque de Santo Domingo. Built in 1606, Porta Coéli is one of the oldest churches under the American flag. Its name means "gate of heaven."

Restored as a museum, the church has wooden statues, paintings, ornaments and liturgical objects from Puerto Rico's historic churches; images carved by 16th-century *santeros* (saint makers); Spanish mosaics of Biblical scenes; and reproduction paintings by the 18th-century artist José Campeche. **Hours:** Wed.-Sun. 8:30-noon and 1-4:20. Closed major holidays. **Cost:** $3; free (ages 0-11 and 56+). **Phone:** (787) 892-5845.

MUSEO DE ARTE ALFREDO ARELLANO & ROSELL is at 7 Calle Esperanza. This museum contains collections of religious art and objects, including antique altar pieces and vestments worn by Puerto Rico's first cardinal. Taíno artifacts and changing exhibits by local artists also are displayed. **Hours:** Wed.-Sun. 10-noon and 1-3. Closed major holidays. **Cost:** Donations. **Phone:** (787) 892-8870.

SAN JUAN (B-4) pop. 434,374, elev. 13'

One of the oldest capital cities in the Western Hemisphere, San Juan is the principal city of the Commonwealth of Puerto Rico. Enveloped within the metropolitan core are the inner districts of Hato Rey, Río Piedras and Santurce, all bonded to San Juan by the public transportation system. The sprawling urban area also encompasses the municipalities of Bayamón, Carolina, Cataño, Guaynabo and San Juan. The Aqua Express, a daily ferry service, connects Old San Juan at Pier 2 with Cataño and Hato Rey.

Luxury hotels lining Avenida Ashford distinguish the Condado Beach section, known as the Gold Coast. Attractive shops, dining spots, supper clubs, casinos and beachfronts dotted with umbrellas, palm trees and Spanish residences grace this popular resort area.

On Avenida Ponce de León is one of the last buildings to be erected by the Spanish, the General Archive and National Library of Puerto Rico. Built in 1877, it also has functioned as a prison, a cigar factory and a rum plant. Red-tiled floors, stained-glass windows, chandeliers and a chapel make this building interesting.

The 580,000-square-foot Puerto Rico Convention Center, which opened in 2005, is considered the largest and most technologically advanced meeting facility of its kind in the Caribbean. The architectural style is "techno-tropic," and a 113-acre business and entertainment complex is planned for the surrounding peninsula of Isla Grande. The convention center can accommodate up to 10,000 delegates.

Tourism Information Center: Luis Muñoz Marín International Airport, Isla Verde, San Juan, Puerto Rico. **Phone:** (787) 791-1014.

ART MUSEUM OF PUERTO RICO (MUSEO DE ARTE DE PUERTO RICO) is at 299 Ave. de Diego in Santurce. Paintings, sculpture, photography, folk art and other media are housed within an expansive neoclassical building. The collection focuses on Puerto Rico's artistic tradition, with pieces ranging from colonial times to the present. Peppered with sculptures and waterfalls, a nature trail weaves through a verdant setting of native island flora, encircling the center.

Guided tours are available by reservation. **Time:** Allow 1 hour minimum. **Hours:** Tues.-Sat. 10-5 (also Wed. 5-8), Sun. 11-6. Guided tours offered Sat.-Sun. at 2. **Cost:** $6; $3 (ages 5-12, ages 60-74, students with ID and persons with disability); free

(ages 75+ and on Wed. 2-8). **Parking:** $1.87 for first hour, 93c each additional hour. Valet parking $10. **Phone:** (787) 977-6277. 🍴 🅿️

CAPARRA RUINS HISTORICAL MUSEUM AND PARK is 10 mi. (16 km) s. at Km. 6.4 on Hwy. 2 in Guaynabo. The site includes ruins of the ancient fort and settlement founded by explorer Juan Ponce de León in 1508. The small Museum of the Conquest and Colonization of Puerto Rico contains items found during excavations in the area and exhibits about the early colonial period. **Hours:** Mon.-Fri. 8-4:30. **Cost:** Free. **Phone:** (787) 781-4795.

THE CAPITOL (EL CAPITOLIO) is on Ave. Ponce de León. Built of Georgia marble in the Renaissance style, the building is flanked by the commonwealth's legislative offices. The rotunda features an illuminated coat of arms; a pamphlet available on the second floor explains the symbolism of the rotunda's mosaics. Guided tours available by advance reservation. **Hours:** Mon.-Fri. 9-5. **Cost:** Free. **Phone:** (787) 724-2030.

CASA BACARDÍ VISITOR CENTER is 2.5 mi. (4 km) w. on SR 888 at km 2.6 in Cataño. A public ferry connects Old San Juan port and the dock at Cataño, where visitors can take a taxi to the "Cathedral of Rum," said to be the world's largest rum distillery. Displays and samples are offered. **Hours:** One-hour tours of the visitor center are offered Mon.-Sat. 8:30-5:30, Sun. 10-5. Last tour departs 75 minutes before closing. Closed major holidays. **Cost:** Free. **Phone:** (787) 788-1500.

CONTEMPORARY ART MUSEUM OF PUERTO RICO (MUSEO DE ARTE CONTEMPORÁNEO DE PUERTO RICO) is at the corner of Ave. Ponce de León and Ave. Roberto H. Todd in Santurce. The museum features contemporary art works from Latin America, the Caribbean and Puerto Rico. **Hours:** Tues.-Sat. 10-4, Sun. noon-4. **Cost:** Donations. **Phone:** (787) 977-4030.

FUNDACIÓN LUIS MUÑOZ MARÍN is 1.3 mi. s. on Rd. 877, Km 0.4 off Trujillo Alto Expressway in Río Piedras. Luis Muñoz Marín, the island's first democratically elected governor, is known as the "Father of Modern Puerto Rico." After taking office in 1949, he engineered the island's unique commonwealth status with the United States. His 4-acre estate and gardens feature displays of photographs and memorabilia, a library and changing art exhibitions. Guided tours are offered by reservation. **Hours:** Mon.-Fri. 8-5. Guided tours depart Mon.-Fri. at 10 and 2, Sat.-Sun. at 10:30 and 1; reservations required. **Cost:** $6; $3 (ages 0-12 and 60+); free (to all Tues.). **Phone:** (787) 755-7979, ext. 22 or (787) 755-4506.

LUIS MUÑOZ RIVERA NATIONAL PARK (PARQUE NACIONAL LUIS MUÑOZ RIVERA) is on Avenida Luis Muñoz Rivera in Puerta de Tierra. The 27-acre oceanside park honors the statesman and poet who helped Puerto Rico gain its autonomy from Spain in 1897. This land was once a key part

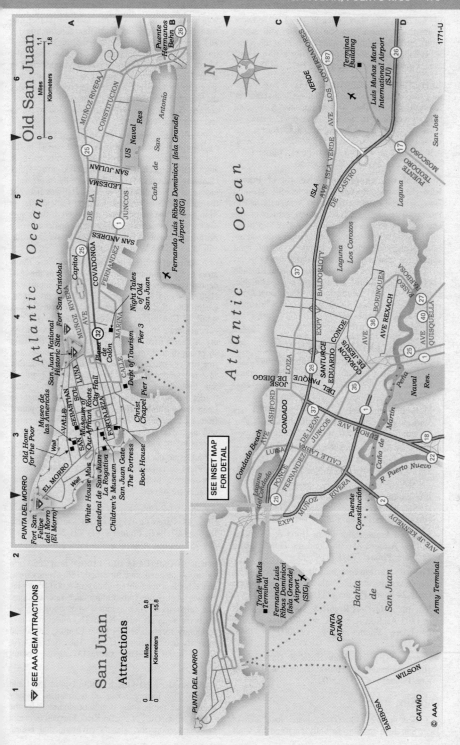

San Juan
Attractions

▽ SEE AAA GEM ATTRACTIONS

Old San Juan

Atlantic Ocean

Atlantic Ocean

Bahía
de
San Juan

© AAA

1771-U

of San Juan's military defense; the 1769 powder house that supplied Fort San Jerónimo still stands on the grounds. Cultural events are held at the open-air Pabellón de la Paz. **Hours:** Daily 8:30-6. **Cost:** Free. **Parking:** $3.25. **Phone:** (787) 721-6133.

UNIVERSITY OF PUERTO RICO is on Ave. Ponce de León in Río Piedras. The university has an enrollment of more than 45,000 students. A museum exhibits paintings by José Campeche and Francisco Oller as well as archeological displays. **Hours:** Museum open Mon.-Wed. and Fri. 9-4:30 (also Wed. 4:30-8:30), Sun. 11:30-3. **Cost:** Free. **Phone:** (787) 764-0000, ext. 2452 for the museum.

Botanical Garden of the University of Puerto Rico (El Jardín Botánico) is at jct. SR 847 and Hwy. 1 at the entrance to Barrio Venezuela in Río Piedras. The 289-acre (117-hectare) garden of the University of Puerto Rico features native and tropical flora, including aquatic and herb gardens and areas devoted to heliconia, bamboo, orchids and palms. The Sculpture Garden features works of art by Leopoldo Maler, Carlos Guzman and Rolando Lopez Dirube. **Tours:** Guided tours are available. **Hours:** Daily 6-6. Closed Jan. 1, Ephiphany, Good Friday, Election Day, Thanksgiving and Christmas. **Cost:** Free. **Phone:** (787) 767-1710 or (787) 758-9957.

GAMBLING ESTABLISHMENTS

- **Condado Plaza Hotel & Casino** is at 999 Ashford Ave. in Condado. **Hours:** Daily 24 hours. **Phone:** (787) 977-4779, ext. 2585 or (787) 721-1000.

- **El San Juan Hotel & Casino** is at 6063 Isla Verde Ave. in Carolina. **Hours:** Daily noon-4 a.m. **Phone:** (787) 791-1000 or (888) 579-2632.

- **Embassy Suites Hotel & Casino San Juan** is at 8000 Tartak St. in Isla Verda. **Hours:** Daily 10 a.m.-4 a.m. Closed Good Friday. **Phone:** (787) 791-0505.

- **Intercontinental San Juan Resort & Casino** is at 5961 Isla Verde Ave. in Carolina. **Hours:** Daily 10 a.m.-4 a.m. **Phone:** (787) 791-6100.

- **Radisson Ambassador Plaza Hotel & Casino** is at 1369 Ashford Ave. in Condado. **Hours:** Daily 24 hours. **Phone:** (787) 721-7300.

- **The Ritz-Carlton San Juan** is at 6961 Avenue of the Governors at Isla Verde in Carolina. **Hours:** Daily 24 hours. **Phone:** (787) 253-1700.

- **San Juan Marriott Resort & Stellaris Casino** is at 1309 Ashford Ave. in Condado. **Hours:** Daily 24 hours. **Phone:** (787) 722-7000 or (888) 817-2033.

- **Sheraton Old San Juan Hotel & Casino** is at 100 Brumbaugh St. **Hours:** Daily 10:30 a.m.-2 a.m. **Phone:** (787) 721-5100.

Old San Juan

Settled in 1521, the seven-square-block area of *Viejo* San Juan remains partially enclosed by walls which once were believed necessary to protect San Juan Harbor. Spain continued this construction for 244 years. By the 19th century the military stronghold, protected by the fortresses of San Felipe del Morro and San Cristóbal, had developed into a quaint residential and commercial community. Restored to its former grandeur, Old San Juan exudes the atmosphere of colonial Spain with its pastel-colored houses, filigreed balconies, hidden plazas and narrow streets.

Paved with *adoquines,* bluish glazed bricks used for ballast in Spanish galleons, some streets in the old quarter are so narrow that the walls on both sides can be touched with outstretched arms. Other charming remnants of early times are the street staircases that scaled this hilly section. Halfway between the cathedral and San Juan Gate on Callejón de las Monjas and one block above it are two of these survivors. A prime example of colonial opulence is *La Fortaleza,* reputedly the oldest executive mansion still in use in the Western Hemisphere.

A series of bridges link the islet with the resort areas of Condado and Isla Verde as well as the residential communities of Santurce and the suburbs of Hato Rey and Río Piedras. The Plaza de Colón, where Old San Juan begins, is dominated by a statue of Christopher Columbus erected in 1893 to commemorate the 400th anniversary of his discovery of Puerto Rico. Today the plaza adjoins the main shopping district on Calle Fortaleza; city buses and free trolleys make frequent stops here. Plaza de San José is bounded by calles San Sebastián, Cristo and San José. Several historic structures and museums border the plaza, where a statue of Juan Ponce de León was fashioned from bronze cannons captured from the British in 1797. Narrow streets and slow-moving traffic make walking the most practical way to explore the old city.

La Casita, the little yellow building near Pier 1 in the Plaza de la Dársena, serves as a visitor information center. Maps, brochures and free daiquiri samples are offered.

Puerto Rico Tourism Company La Princesa Bldg. #2, Paseo La Princesa, Old San Juan, Puerto Rico 00902-3960. **Phone:** (787) 721-2400 or (800) 866-7827.

BOOK HOUSE (CASA DEL LIBRO) is at 255 Calle Cristo. A restored and furnished 18th-century residence holds a specialized library of 4,000 books including many pre-16th-century and rare editions. The emphasis of the museum is upon book arts and the book as an art form. **Note:** The museum is in a temporary location at 199 Calle Capilla; call ahead to verify opening times. **Hours:** Tues.-Sat. 11-4:30. Closed major holidays. **Cost:** Donations. **Phone:** (787) 723-0354.

CASA RAMÓN POWER Y GIRALT is at 155 Calle Tetuán. The former home of a Spanish military commander, the building is now headquarters for the Conservation Trust of Puerto Rico. Interactive media exhibits explore the island's environmental issues.

Hours: Tues.-Sat. 9-4. **Cost:** Free. **Phone:** (787) 722-5834.

CATEDRAL DE SAN JUAN is at 151 Calle Cristo. Built in 1521 and damaged repeatedly by the elements, the present structure is the result of several restorations. The cathedral is a rare example of New World medieval architecture, featuring a circular staircase, vaulted ceilings, 16th-century chalices, the relic of San Pio and a Renaissance madonna. The marble tomb of Juan Ponce de León rests near the transept. **Hours:** Open daily 8-5. Mass is held Mon.-Fri. at 7:25 a.m. and 12:15, Sat. at 7 p.m., Sun. at 9 and 11 a.m. **Cost:** Donations. **Phone:** (787) 723-1895 or (787) 722-0861.

CHILDREN'S MUSEUM (MUSEO DEL NIÑO DE PUERTO RICO) is at 150 Calle Cristo next to El Hotel Convento. The museum features three floors of hands-on exhibits highlighting health, nature, science and society. A re-creation of a town features a grocery store, a shoeshine shop and a plaza for playing hopscotch and dominoes. **Time:** Allow 1 hour minimum. **Hours:** Tues.-Fri. 11-6, Sat.-Sun. noon-6, June-July and 1st week in Aug.; Tues.-Thurs. 9-3:30, Fri. 9-5, Sat.-Sun. 12:30-4:30, rest of year. Last admission 1 hour before closing. Closed major holidays. **Cost:** $7 (ages 1-15); $5 (ages 16+). **Phone:** (787) 722-3791 or (787) 725-7214.

CHRIST CHAPEL (CAPILLA DEL CRISTO) is on Calle Cristo. The tiny chapel, which has room for only some 30 worshipers, was built on the spot where a horse and rider plunged over the 70-foot bluff during a festival race in 1753. One version of the legend says the rider was saved by prayer; another recounts that only his mount survived. The chapel contains an elaborate altar made of silver and gold with antique ornaments and paintings. **Hours:** Tues. 10-4. **Cost:** Free. **Phone:** (787) 723-1895 or (787) 722-0861.

CITY HALL (CASA ALCALDÍA) fronts the Plaza de Armas (Military Square) on Calle San Francisco. Construction began on this building in 1602 and wasn't completed until 1789. The facade is said to have been inspired by the city hall in Madrid, Spain. A small museum chronicles San Juan's history. An information center is near the Calle San Francisco entrance. **Hours:** Mon.-Fri. 8-4. Closed major holidays. **Cost:** Free. **Phone:** (787) 724-7171, ext. 2000.

THE FORTRESS (LA FORTALEZA) is at the foot of Calle Fortaleza. The oldest executive mansion in the Western Hemisphere still in use, the Palacio de Santa Catalina has been the residence of more than 150 governors and the seat of Puerto Rico's government for more than 4 centuries. Tours through the gardens are offered; proper attire is required. **Hours:** Guided 30-minute garden tours in English depart on the hour Mon.-Fri. 9-4 from Fortaleza Street (lobby of Real Audiencia building). Closed major holidays. **Cost:** $3. **Phone:** (787) 721-7000, ext. 2211 or 2323.

LA PRINCESA is on Paseo de la Princesa at 259 Recinto Sur St. The former San Juan Penitentiary, built in 1837, now serves as an art gallery and home to the Puerto Rico Tourism Company. The gallery features contemporary works by island artists, as well as examples of traditional crafts. Elegantly restored and landscaped, the building faces San Juan Bay, overlooking the *Raíces* fountain sculpture. **Hours:** Mon.-Fri. 9-noon and 1-4. **Cost:** Free. **Phone:** (787) 721-2400, ext. 2175.

LA ROGATIVA is just n. of the San Juan Gate on Calle Recinto del Oeste. This striking statue, commissioned for San Juan's 450th anniversary, pays homage to a celebrated legend. During the British siege by Sir Ralph Abercromby's troops in 1797, it is said that the local bishop led his parishioners in a prayer procession through the streets. The enemy, seeing the line of torches, thought Spanish reinforcements had arrived—and fled. The Plazuela de la Rogativa, a little plaza atop the city wall, offers a bird's-eye view of the western harbor and the Paseo del Morro. **Hours:** Daily dawn-dusk. **Cost:** Free.

MUSEO DE ARTE E HISTORIA is at 150 Calle Norzagaray. Puerto Rican art is displayed in the east and west galleries. Concerts and other cultural events take place in the museum's interior patio. Audiovisual shows trace the history of San Juan. **Hours:** Tues.-Fri. 9-4, Sat.-Sun. 10-4. **Cost:** Donations. **Phone:** (787) 724-1875.

MUSEO DE LAS AMÉRICAS is on the second floor of the Cuartel de Ballajá on Calle Norzagaray. Housed in a massive three-story building designed to house Spanish soldiers and their families, the museum presents permanent and temporary exhibits with a concentration on the artwork of the Americas. Displays include archeological artifacts, sculpture, Amazon Indian photographs and objects, folk art, a peasant's house and a replica of a country chapel. A

DID YOU KNOW

Puerto Ricans are U.S. citizens but pay no federal income tax.

permanent exhibit highlights African heritage. Guided tours are available by reservation. **Time:** Allow 30 minutes minimum. **Hours:** Tues.-Sat. 9-noon and 1-4. Closed major holidays. **Cost:** $3; $2 (ages 0-12, ages 65+ and students with ID). **Phone:** (787) 724-5052.

MUSEO PABLO CASALS is at 101 Calle San Sebastián on Plaza de San José. Museum exhibits include memorabilia, manuscripts and photographs of the famous Spanish cellist who lived in Puerto Rico for nearly 20 years. Videotapes of Festival Casals concerts can be viewed upon request. **Hours:** Tues.-Sat. 9:30-4:30. **Cost:** $1; 50c (ages 0-11 and 60+). **Phone:** (787) 723-9185.

MUSEUM OF OUR AFRICAN ROOTS (MUSEO DE NUESTRA RAÍZ AFRICANA) is at 101 Calle San Sebastián on Plaza de San José. The museum is housed in the heavily buttressed building known as Casa de los Contrafuertes, one of the oldest private residences in Viejo San Juan. Exhibits chronicle the history of slavery and the influence of African music, language and culture in Puerto Rico. Photographs, maps, artifacts and musical instruments are labeled in Spanish. **Time:** Allow 30 minutes minimum. **Hours:** Wed.-Sun. 8:30-4:30. **Cost:** $2; $1 (children). **Phone:** (787) 724-4294.

THE NATIONAL GALLERY OF THE INSTITUTE OF PUERTO RICAN CULTURE, formerly known as Convento de los Dominicos, is at 98 Calle Norzagaray. Housed in a former 16th-century convent the museum displays Colonial art and paintings. One room is devoted to the display of wooden *santos*. Cultural activities are regularly presented in the interior patio. A second-floor gallery is closed for renovation with an expected completion date of early 2012; the new exhibits will include Tainos art as well as 21st-century contemporary folk and decorative pieces. **Hours:** Tues.-Sat. 9:30-5. **Cost:** $3; $2 (children and senior citizens). **Phone:** (787) 725-2670 or (787) 725-2671.

NIGHT TALES IN OLD SAN JUAN departs from the flagpole outside the Sheraton Old San Juan Hotel at Pier 3. This guided 2-hour walking tour explores the famous sites of Viejo San Juan, covering approximately 2 miles of the historic district with several rest stops. The tour company, Legends of Puerto Rico, also offers other city and island excursions. Walking tours take place rain or shine. Streets can be slippery; wear comfortable walking shoes. **Hours:** Tours depart Mon. at 7 p.m., Tues.-Sun. at 6 p.m. Closed Jan. 1, Good Friday, Thanksgiving, Christmas Eve, Christmas and Dec. 31. **Cost:** Fee $35; free (ages 0-5). Reservations are required. **Phone:** (787) 605-9060.

OLD HOME FOR THE POOR (ANTIGUO ASILO DE BENEFICENCIA) is off El Morro at 9 Calle Norzagaray. The Home for the Poor, built in the 1840s for the indigent people, now houses the Institute of Puerto Rican Culture. Exhibits include archeological items, rocks, tools, masks and copper geometric figures. The grounds are accented with gardens and courtyards. The Museum of the Indian (Museo del Indio de Puerto Rico) displays artifacts belonging to several Indian cultures that inhabited Puerto Rico and neighboring islands in the pre-Columbian era.

Time: Allow 1 hour minimum. **Hours:** Museum Tues.-Sat. 9-4. Closed major holidays. **Cost:** Free. **Phone:** (787) 724-0700.

SAN JUAN NATIONAL HISTORIC SITE is on the north shore of Old San Juan overlooking the bay. The extensive site contains the fortifications built by the Spanish to protect San Juan and the treasure-laden fleets that sailed past the city en route to Spain. Puerta de San Juan at the foot of Caleta de San Juan is the most impressive and last remaining of six gates of the old city wall. The 1639 structure stands more than 16 feet (5 m) tall.

The site encompasses two large forts and a small inlet fortification, Castillo de San Juan de la Cruz. El Cañuelo, as the smallest fort is known, was built on Isla de Cabras at the entrance to San Juan Harbor, about 1610 as a wooden structure. Destroyed by the Dutch in 1625, it was rebuilt in stone in the 1660s. The tiny fort is closed to the public.

Guided tours of the national historic site are available by reservation. Comfortable walking shoes are recommended. **Tours:** Guided tours are available. **Hours:** Site open daily 9-6. Last admission 1 hour before closing. Closed Jan. 1, Thanksgiving and Christmas. **Cost:** One fort (valid for 24 hours) $3; free (ages 0-15). Both forts (valid for 7 days) $5; free (ages 0-15). **Parking:** free first hour; $2 every hour thereafter. **Phone:** (787) 729-6960.

Fort San Cristóbal stands on a hill at the e. edge of Old San Juan n. of Ave. Muñoz Rivera at San Juan National Historic Site. The 27-acre (11-hectare) fortification was the largest ever built by the Spanish in the New World. Constructed 1635-1783, the castle fort is connected to outworks by a series of tunnels and dry moats. Gunrooms, barracks and officers quarters surround the main courtyard. The fort's powerful artillery repelled British forces attacking from the east in 1797. The first shot of the Spanish-American War in Puerto Rico was fired from the fort in 1898.

Guided tours of the national historic site are available by reservation. Comfortable walking shoes are recommended. **Hours:** Daily 9-6. Last admission 1 hour before closing. Closed Jan. 1, Thanksgiving and Christmas. **Cost:** (good for 24 hours) $3; free (ages 0-15). Combination ticket with Fort San Felipe del Morro (good for 7 days) $5; free (ages 0-15). **Parking:** free first hour; $2 every hour thereafter. **Phone:** (787) 729-6960.

Fort San Felipe del Morro (El Morro) was built on a promontory at the n.w. tip of Old San Juan, now part of San Juan National Historic Site. The grounds are closed to motor vehicles; visitors walk one-quarter mile (.4 km) to the fort from underground parking at Plaza del

Quinto Centenario on Calle Norzagaray.

The most strategic of San Juan's defense systems, El Morro repelled attacks by the British, Dutch and French over the course of 300 years. Six levels of impressive batteries rising 140 feet (43 m) out of the sea afford a beautiful harbor view. A network of ramps and stairways connects the ramparts.

Construction began in 1539 with a simple tower designed to guard the channel to the harbor. Most of the massive earthworks and fortifications were built between 1589 and the 1650s, and the fort was completed by 1787. The fort contains a museum with examples of 16th- and 17th-century armor and weapons, a chapel and audiovisual exhibits. Guided tours of the national historic site are available by reservation. Comfortable walking shoes are recommended. **Hours:** Daily 9-6. Last admission 1 hour before closing. Closed Jan. 1, Thanksgiving and Christmas. **Cost:** (good for 24 hours) $3; free (ages 0-15). Combination ticket with Fort San Cristóbal (good for 7 days) $5; free (ages 0-15). **Parking:** free first hour; $2 every hour thereafter. **Phone:** (787) 729-6960.

WHITE HOUSE MUSEUM (CASA BLANCA) is at 1 Calle San Sebastián above the seawall. A wooden fort on the site burned in 1521, and this fortified mansion was built in its place 2 years later for Juan Ponce de León by his son-in-law. The conquistador died before its completion. His family lived here for 250 years, until the Spanish government acquired it for a military headquarters. Gardens surround the mansion, which is furnished with 16th- and 17th-century antiques.

Time: Allow 30 minutes minimum. **Hours:** Tues.-Sat. 9-noon and 1-4. Closed Jan. 1 and Good Friday. Guided tours are offered by appointment. **Cost:** $3; $2 (children and senior citizens). **Phone:** (787) 725-1454.

AAA Walking Tour

This walking tour of Old San Juan will take 2-4 hours, depending on your pace as well as the number of listed sites you visit. *Those attractions appearing in bold type have detailed listings in the Old San Juan section.* The historic district is small—a seven-square-block area of pastel-colored colonial buildings—but the cobbled streets are often steep and uneven; wear comfortable shoes and walk with care. Don't forget sunscreen, bottled water and a hat in the hottest months.

Begin your walking tour at La Casita, the visitor center of the Puerto Rico Tourism Company. The little yellow building is on the waterfront at Plaza de la Dársena, just west of the first cruise ship pier. Here you can pick up maps, brochures and a free daiquiri sample before venturing into the heart of Old San Juan.

From the visitor center, follow the paved brick walkway west along the port toward El Paseo de La Princesa. The U.S. Customs House with its pink stucco exterior and Moorish details will be on your left; the towering Art Deco edifice of Banco Popular will be on your right across the street. Two orange columns mark the entrance to the Paseo, the tree-lined promenade winding along the ancient city wall and the rocky shore of San Juan Bay. Pocket parks and benches provide resting places along the way. The massive wall, known as "La Muralla," stands 42 feet high and was constructed with parallel sections of sandstone blocks. Sand poured between the sections helped absorb the impact of cannon balls. Completed in 1782, the towering fortification stretches for 3.4 miles and once enclosed the entire colonial capital. *Garitas,* or sentry boxes, crown the wall at prominent points along the bay.

Toward the end of the main promenade is **La Princesa**, the old penitentiary. Now restored, the gray-and-white building houses a visitor center for the Puerto Rico Tourism Company and a gallery for local artists. At the point where the Paseo meets San Juan Bay, the *Raíces* fountain by sculptor Luís Sanguino honors the three cultures—Taíno, Spanish and African—comprising modern Puerto Rico.

Following the walkway into the deep shade of banyan trees, you'll pass the jagged metal spikes of *Crecimiento,* a sculpture by Carmen Inés Blondet. Above the wall are the gardens of La Fortaleza, the governor's mansion.

Rounding a bend in the stone wall, you'll approach the Puerta de San Juan, or San Juan Gate, as seafaring guests approached the city for centuries. The red gate was one of six in the original fortification, and its massive wooden doors were locked at sundown to guard against attack. Disembarking from their ships, visiting dignitaries were greeted here and escorted to the cathedral for an official blessing. The Latin inscription reads, "Blessed is he who comes in the name of the Lord."

From here, the Paseo continues along the wall to the foot of Fort San Felipe del Morro. Future plans call for the trail to access the fort, but for now, it ends below the water battery. Should you decide to walk out to the point and back, you'll see many of Old San Juan's furry residents lazing in the sun; a colony of feral cats is protected by the national park service and fed by a local organization called "Save a Gato."

To continue the walking tour, pass through the gate and take a sharp left to follow the steep walkway up the hill on Calle Recinto del Oeste toward the Plazuela de la Rogativa. This little plaza at the top of the wall is home to La Rogativa, a striking sculpture created by Lindsay Daen to mark San Juan's 450th anniversary. The bronze statue of a bishop and three women bearing torches pays tribute to a beloved local legend: during a British siege in 1797, it is said that the enemy saw the lights of a religious procession and fled, thinking Spanish reinforcements were on the way.

The street splits just above the plaza; follow the lower road through the white gate and into the shade. On your right will be the walled gardens of Casa Blanca, or the White House. On the left, you

1709-E

© AAA

ATLANTIC OCEAN

N

PUNTA DEL MORRO

Fort San Felipe del Morro (El Morro)

Cementerio de San Juan

National Historic Site

Fort San Cristóbal

AVE MUÑOZ RIVERA

CONSTITUCION

PASEO DE COVANDONGA

GILBERTO CONCEPCION GRACIA

Pier 4

Caño de San Antonio

To San Juan

Pier 3

Pier 2

To Cataño

Pier 1

Antiguo Casino

AVE DE LA

Teatro Tapia

Plaza de Colón

CALLE O'DONELL

CALLE LUNA

Iglesia de San Francisco

CALLE SAN FRANCISCO

TANCA

CALLE LA MARINA

OIC

COMERCIO

FORTALEZA

TETUAN

CALLE SUR

La Casita

START TOUR

CALLE LA

CALLE DE SAN JUSTO

San Juan

NORZAGARAY

SAN SEBASTIAN

SOL

CALLE DE SAN

Museum of Our African Roots

JUAN BLVD

CALLE

DE

SAN

CALLE

DEL

CALLE

DE

CRUZ

Plaza de Armas

City Hall

San Jose

Plaza de San Juan

Casa Ramón Power y Giralt

RECINTO

PRINCESA

LA PUNTILLA

CALLE

PRESIDIO

La Princesa

PASEO DE LA

Book House

Christ Chapel

Catedral de San Juan

Hotel El Convento

Children's Museum

Antiguo Hospital de la Concepción

CRISTO

CALLE

CALLE

CALLE

SAN JOSE

OESTE

RECINTO

LAS MONJAS

CALLE SAN JUAN

San Juan Gate The Fortress

SAN JUAN GATE

La Rogativa

Iglesia San José

Museo Pablo Casals

Convento de Los Dominicos

Plaza del Quinto Centenario

Museo de las Americas

Cuartel de Ballajá

Plaza de Ballajá

Plaza San José

SAN

CALLE BENEFICENCIA

CALLE MOROVIS

MORRO

White House Museum

Old Home for the Poor

Casa Rosa

CALLE DEL

Bahía de San Juan

Old San Juan
Walking Tour

Miles   0   0.4
Kilometers 0   0.6

WALK TOUR
CITY WALL
FOOT PATH
LIGHTHOUSE
GEM ATTRACTION
PARKING

will pass Casa Rosada, the Pink House, a former Spanish barracks and now a day-care center. Follow the long walls of the Institute of Puerto Rican Culture and the Academy of Fine Arts to the top of the hill, where you will face the low citadel of **Fort San Felipe del Morro (El Morro)**. It's a quarter-mile across the field; the grounds are closed to motor traffic. On weekends, you'll often see families flying kites and picnicking on the grass. The fortification is part of San Juan National Historic Site, and admission to its sister fort, San Cristóbal, can also be purchased here (good for 7 days). Water fountains and restrooms are available at both sites.

Built on a promontory high above the harbor, El Morro repelled attacks by the British, Dutch and French over the course of three centuries. Construction began in 1539 and continued until 1787. Surrounded by a dry moat, it covers six levels—from the water battery to the upper bastions—and includes kitchens, barracks, a chapel, gun batteries, dungeons, secret tunnels and a lighthouse. Looking west from the battlements you can see El Cañuelo, smallest of the three forts built to defend the harbor. The first wooden fort, San Juan de la Cruz, was built on La Isla de Cabras (Goat Island) about 1610. Destroyed by the Dutch, it was reconstructed in stone in the 1670s.

To the east, you have a bird's-eye view of the beautiful Cementerío de San Juan with its pink-domed chapel dedicated to Santa Maria Magdalena de Pazzis. The colorful neighborhood beyond the cemetery, La Perla, is picturesque from a distance but should not be explored on foot—it's one of few places in Old San Juan deemed unsafe for tourists.

Leaving the fort, follow the main walkway across the field and through the traffic intersection on Calle Norzagaray into the Plaza de Ballajá. This was once the city's hospital center. The first building on the right, the 1858 Antiguo Manicomio, housed the mentally ill. It now contains classrooms for the Puerto Rican Academy of Fine Arts. Next is the stately **Old Home for the Poor (Antiguo Asilo de Beneficencia)**, or indigents' hospital. The buff-colored building with green ironwork contains museum displays of the Institute of Puerto Rican Culture.

Across the plaza, the three-story Cuartel de Ballajá was a barracks for 19th-century Spanish soldiers and their families. With its massive inner courtyard, the building covers nearly 3 acres. Take time to walk upstairs to the second floor, where the **Museo de las Américas** displays archeological artifacts and colorful examples of folk art.

Leaving Cuartel de Ballajá, walk to the top of the plaza; on the right is the **White House Museum (Casa Blanca)**. This fortified mansion was built in 1523 for Juan Ponce de León by his son-in-law. The conquistador died before its completion, but his family lived here for 250 years until the Spanish government acquired it for a military headquarters. Three centuries' worth of antiques decorate the museum home, and the gardens are a shady spot to rest.

Leaving Casa Blanca, cross the plaza to face the statue honoring Eugenio Maria de Hostos, a 19th-century educator who advocated an independent confederation between Puerto Rico, the Dominican Republic and Cuba. Follow the street leading east between the Cuartel de Ballajá and its yellow counterpart, the Antiguo Hospital de la Concepción, toward the white Church of San José.

On the left, you will enter the top terrace of the Plaza del Quinto Centenario, commemorating the 500th anniversary of Columbus' arrival in the New World. The giant stone pillar, *Tótem Telúrico*, was created by sculptor Jaime Suárez as a symbol of Caribbean Indian cultures.

Beneath the monument is a parking garage, and the busy street of Calle Cristo emerges from under the terrace into Old San Juan. Watch for fast-moving taxis and trucks as you return to the walking route. The street will jog toward the right, bringing you into Plaza San José.

The statue of Ponce de León at the center of this square was created by melting down British cannons. It's a popular gathering place for local residents. The plaza's heart is La Iglesia de San José, the second-oldest church in the Western Hemisphere. Dominican friars began building the original chapel in 1532. The interior features vaulted Gothic ceilings, a collection of religious paintings and frescoes, Ponce de León's family coat of arms and a figure of Christ on the cross that may date to the mid-16th century. **The National Gallery of the Institute of Puerto Rican Culture** houses Colonial art and a chapel museum.

In the northern corner of the plaza, the **Museo Pablo Casals** honors the famous Spanish cellist who lived in Puerto Rico for nearly 20 years. Adjoining it is the Casa de los Contrafuertes, one of the oldest private residences in the city. The salmon-colored building with buttressed walls now contains an artisans' shop and the **Museum of Our African Roots (Museo de Nuestra Raíz Africana)**.

Follow the steep, cobbled street of Calle Cristo as it leads downhill from Plaza San José toward the port. On the right, you'll pass the 1842 Seminario Concilar and the 17th-century El Convento Hotel, a former Carmelite convent. The hotel faces the shaded Plaza de la Catedral and the graceful **Catedral de San Juan**. This rare example of Caribbean medieval architecture features a circular staircase, vaulted ceilings and venerated relics. The marble tomb of Juan Ponce de León stands near the transept. On the western edge of the plaza is the **Children's Museum (Museo del Niño de Puerto Rico)** with three floors of hands-on exhibits.

Continue south on Calle Cristo past the designer shops and T-shirt stores to Calle Fortaleza. One block to your right is the oldest executive mansion still in use in the Western Hemisphere, **The Fortress (La Fortaleza)**. Also known as El Palacio de Santa Catalina, the blue-and-white building has been the residence of Puerto Rico's governors and the seat of government for more than 4 centuries.

Guided tours of the gardens are offered in English; proper attire is required.

Calle Cristo ends at the gated **Christ Chapel (Capilla del Cristo)**, a small stone chapel built in honor of a fabled miracle. Legend says that a horse and rider plunged off this cliff during a festival race in 1753, but prayers saved the rider's life. (Some versions of the story say he died but his mount survived.) Nevertheless, this tiny chapel was erected in thanksgiving. The building is only open to the public on Tuesdays, when the glass doors are unlocked to reveal a golden altar and painted icons. The Parque de las Palomas atop the city wall offers a good view of the port. Keep your camera handy—when a visitor buys a bag of dried corn to feed the pigeons, it can look like a scene from Hitchcock's "The Birds."

Also within the cul-de-sac at the end of Calle Cristo are the **Book House (Casa del Libro)**, a restored and furnished 18th-century residence holding a specialized library of 4,000 antique books; and the Centro Nacional de Artes Populares y Artesanías, a popular place to shop for handcrafted souvenirs.

To end the tour early and take a shortcut back to the waterfront, walk behind the chapel and follow Calle Tetuán east, passing **Casa Ramón Power y Giralt**—the former home of a Spanish military hero and now headquarters of the Conservation Trust of Puerto Rico—and the pink Iglesia de Santa Ana. Turn right on Calle San Justo to finish your tour at the cruise ship piers.

To continue the full walking tour, return north on Calle Cristo to Calle Fortaleza and turn right. Take a left at the next corner onto Calle de San José to reach Old San Juan's main square, Plaza de Armas. The statues on the fountain represent the four seasons. The former Spanish treasury on the left, La Intendencia, is headquarters of the Puerto Rico Department of State. **City Hall (Casa Alcaldía)** fronts the plaza on Calle San Francisco. The building's façade was said to have been inspired by the city hall in Madrid.

There are two drug stores on the northeast corner if you need to pick up any supplies. Continue past them on Calle San Francisco. On the left, you'll come to La Bombonera, a local cafe famous for its fresh-baked pastries. A little farther on is the Plaza de Salvador Brau with its seated statue of the 19th-century Puerto Rican writer. Adjoining the plaza is the 1756 Franciscan Chapel.

The street will open onto Plaza de Colón (Columbus Square), where a statue of the explorer stands on the stone column above a fountain. A two-sided sign with maps of the island and Old San Juan will help you get your bearings. At the bottom of the plaza is El Teatro Tapía, one of Puerto Rico's most cherished cultural monuments. Built in 1832, the restored theater is one of the oldest still in use in the Western Hemisphere. To the east, the gray-and-white Antiguo Casino is an opulent example of French Second Empire architecture, now used for state functions.

The walls of **Fort San Cristóbal** dominate the northeast corner. From Plaza de Colón, follow the street up the hill to the gate of the city's main defense against land attacks. The 27-acre (11-hectare) fortification was the largest ever built by the Spanish in the New World. Visitors can climb the ramparts and wander a maze of tunnels inside this UNESCO World Heritage Site, which remains a monument to military engineering. Take time to explore the museum exhibits of armor and weaponry.

From Fort San Cristóbal it's a short walk back down to the waterfront. If you're ready for a break, hop aboard the free trolley (although it may be crowded if cruise ships are in port).

On foot, walk back through Plaza de Colón and follow Recinto Sur; El Teatro Tapía will be on your left. At the intersection of Recinto Sur and Calle Tetuán, you'll pass a triangular plaza and a statue of Arturo Somohano, composer and director of the San Juan Symphony Orchestra. International restaurants along Recinto Sur offer everything from sushi to Italian to Transylvanian cuisine. Passing the six-story Galeria, you'll see the U.S. Post Office and Courthouse with its Moorish roof. Turn left on Calle Tanca to come full circle on your walking tour of Old San Juan.

UTUADO (C-3) pop. 35,336, elev. 610'

In the Cordillera Central Mountain Range, Utuado (oo-too-AH-do) is a departure point for trips to Río Abajo State Forest. Nearby off Rte. 10 is manmade Lago Dos Bocas, a long, winding hydroelectric reservoir. One- or 2-hour launch trips on the lake, including stops at several mountain villages, depart from the wharf several times daily.

The Indian Ceremonial Center at Caguana, 7.5 miles (12 km) west of Utuado on Rte. 111, was constructed by Taíno Indians more than 700 years ago. A soccer-like game was played here on dozens of ritual courts, or *bateyes*; many are lined with inscribed monoliths. The park is open Wednesday through Sunday; phone (787) 894-7325.

RÍO ABAJO STATE FOREST (BOSQUE ESTATAL) is reached via Rte. 10 to Rte. 621. Teak and mahogany trees cover the oddly shaped karst hills of the 5,730-acre (2,319-hectare) forest, which contains a recreation area and offers exploring possibilities in dozens of mountain caves and ruined sugar mills. **Hours:** Daily dawn-dusk. **Cost:** Free. **Phone:** (787) 880-6557 or (787) 999-2200, ext. 5158. ⊠

VEGA BAJA (B-3) pop. 61,929, elev. 49'

MUSEO CASA ALONSO is at Calle Betances 34. A guided tour of the 1776 Neoclassic-Criollo structure includes the music room, library, kitchens and bedrooms. Furnishings from the 18th- through 20th-centuries are on display. Guides discuss the various families that owned the house and their influence on

Puerto Rico's history. **Time:** Allow 1 hour minimum. **Hours:** Mon.-Sat. 9-3. Closed major holidays. **Cost:** $2; $1 (senior citizens and ages 0-12). **Phone:** (787) 855-1364.

VIEQUES (B-6, D-6) pop. 9,106, elev. 131'

Long a missile range for the U.S. Navy, Vieques (vee-AY-kays) finally saw an end to the bombing in May 2003. The military had purchased part of the island in the 1940s to use for weapons testing. After many years of protest, the base was finally turned over to the government of Puerto Rico, which is working to reclaim the land. Only the eastern tip of the island remains restricted. The Vieques National Wildlife Refuge has been established on nearly 18,000 acres on both ends of the island to protect such endangered animals as the brown pelican, the Antillean manatee and four species of sea turtles.

With its quiet beaches, coral reefs and bioluminescent bay, Vieques has become a popular destination for eco-tourism. The Punta Mulas Lighthouse, known as Morropó, has been protecting the port town of Isabel Segunda since 1893. Vieques lies about 8 miles off the eastern shore of Puerto Rico; daily ferries run from Fajardo and San Juan, and air flights are available from Luis Muñoz Marin International Airport.

BAHÍA MOSQUITO BIOLUMINESCENT BAY TOURS depart from the Biobay Eco-Center on Rte. 996 at Km 4.5, just west of Esperanza. The waters literally glow in the dark at Mosquito Bay, one of the brightest bioluminescent bays in the world. Tiny microorganisms called dinoflagellates create the mysterious blue-green light, which is best viewed on cloudy or moonless nights. Narrated 2.5-hour trips to the bay include a star and planet lecture and a chance to swim in the glowing waters. Electric pontoon boats prevent pollution of the fragile ecosystem.

Passengers who wish to swim should wear bathing suits under their clothes and refrain from using insect repellent or skin lotion. **Hours:** Trips depart nightly when the moon is not in full phase. **Cost:** Fare $32.10; $16.05 (ages 3-12). **Phone:** (787) 741-0720.

MUSEO FUERTE CONDE DE MIRASOL is in the Barriada Fuerte sector of Isabel Segunda. Built 1845-1855 by order of the governor of Puerto Rico, the fort was one of the last Spanish military structures to be erected in the New World. The restored fort displays local artwork and exhibits about the island's archeology, slavery, sugar production, colonial influences and military presence. **Hours:** Wed.-Sun. 10-4. **Cost:** Donations. **Phone:** (787) 741-1717.

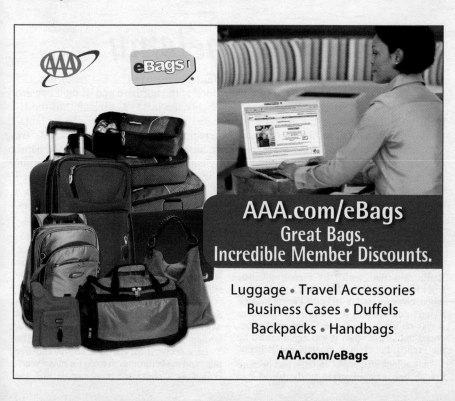

Gustavia / © SIME / eStock Photo

St. Barthélemy

Affectionately called St. Barths, St. Barthélemy (bar-TELL-a-mee) lies 125 miles (200 km) northwest of Guadeloupe at the northern end of the Leeward Islands. St. Barths' residents are probably the least "Caribbean" of the islands' people. Because the island's rocky, arid soil supported few slave plantations—and due to an unlikely 100-year ownership by Sweden—most residents are fair-skinned. Remnants of the Swedish ownership remain, most notably in the name of the capital, Gustavia. A trip around the tiny island, however, reveals scenes reminiscent of 17th-century France, a legacy of the island's original settlers maintained by today's reserved and self-sufficient residents. A quiet island with more than a dozen white sand beaches, St. Barths also has rocky hillsides and lush green valleys.

History

Discovered by Christopher Columbus in 1493 and named for his brother Bartolomeo, St. Barths was first settled by French colonists from nearby St. Kitts in 1648. The settlement failed, however, and in 1651 the French sold the island to the Knights of Malta. Five years later it was raided by the fierce Caribs, then abandoned until 1673 when it was again settled by the French, but from Normandy and Brittany.

This colony succeeded, in large part because French buccaneers brought to the island vast quantities of plunder from Spanish galleons. One such pirate, Monbars the Exterminator, reputedly maintained his headquarters on St. Barths, and his treasure is said to be hidden among the coves and buried in the island sands.

Except for a brief British takeover in 1758, St. Barths remained in French hands until 1784 when it was ceded to Sweden in exchange for trading rights in Gothenburg, Sweden. The Swedes declared St. Barths a neutral and free port, and made fortunes in trade for many years. Following a protracted economic decline, the

Swedish people voted to sell the island back to France. France agreed to repurchase the island and maintained its free-port status. After being a dependency of Guadeloupe, a department and region of France, St. Barths became a Overseas Collectivity of France in 2007.

The people of St. Barths are industrious, spiritual and soft-mannered. Some work in the expanding tourist trade, but these private people return quietly to their homes at the end of the day. Lacking significant agricultural and industrial opportunities, the men have taken to the sea and are considered superb sailors and fishermen. Many women have become skilled at weaving straw hats, baskets and similar items to sell to tourists. Sailboats and yachts fill the harbor, but St. Barths doesn't promote itself as a cruise destination. Government officials hope to control growth on the island, thus preserving its reputation as a chic hideaway for the rich and famous.

Shopping

St. Barths is a duty-free port; therefore, perfumes, cosmetics, china, crystal, watches, imported jewelry, resort wear, liquor and tobacco sell at bargain prices. Some selections are limited, but there are enough bargains to warrant setting aside time for shopping, particularly for "name" merchandise. Besides duty-free items, there is delicately woven reed work unique to St. Barths as well as bonnets, seashells, pottery and island artwork. The village of Corossol is known for its straw goods.

Downtown Gustavia is a center for boutiques and duty-free shops. Shopping centers include La Villa Créole and Pelican Plage in St. Jean and La Savane Commercial Center opposite the airport. An array of lotions and cosmetics is produced in Lorient.

Most shops are open daily 9-noon and 2-6, although some close for the day at noon on Saturday. Banking hours are Mon.-Fri. 8-noon and 2-3:30; a bank at Les Galeries du Commerce in St. Jean is open Tues.-Sat. until 5. The currency exchange office in downtown Gustavia is open Mon.-Fri. 8:30-noon and 2:30-5, Sat. 8:30-noon. Banks are closed on holidays and some afternoons preceding holidays. U.S. dollars are accepted everywhere, and prices are often quoted in dollars. Major credit cards are usually accepted.

Food and Drink

Dining on St. Barths can be a memorable experience. Young chefs who have trained in some of France's greatest restaurants enjoy plying their trade on the island. Combining local fruits and spices with classical French traditions, they have created a Caribbean showcase of French cuisine.

Most restaurants are small, but each is different either in food, setting or atmosphere. Some are beach cafes featuring fresh lobster and charcoal-grilled steaks; some specialize in seafood; and some, particularly in the finer hotels, present traditional French cuisine and international menus.

In Gustavia some of the restaurants are housed in quaint little buildings dating back to the Swedes and early French settlers. La Rotisserie is a deluxe French deli offering picnic fare and afternoon gourmet treats. Another popular

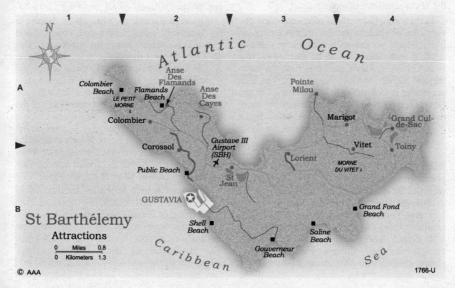

daytime eatery is Cheeseburger in Paradise, next to Le Select. Restaurants are required by law to add a 10-15 percent service charge (service compris) to their prices. Reservations are always a good idea. Some hotels and restaurants might be closed in the fall for refurbishing or due to their owners' vacations.

St. Barths offers the usual Caribbean fare in the way of beer and potent rum punch. The wine connoisseur, however, will appreciate the island's wine cellars, where more than a million bottles of France's best vintages are kept under strictly controlled conditions.

Sports and Amusements

For many the attraction to St. Barths is its quiet, leisurely pace. There are no casinos, large resorts or organized activities and few nightclubs. You won't find a single golf course on the island, though there is a driving range, and only a few tennis courts. Instead the emphasis is on sand and surf. Opportunities abound for swimming, yachting and sailing, windsurfing, deep-sea fishing, scuba diving and snorkeling.

The gleaming white sand beaches are all public and free; most are never crowded, and complete privacy is often readily available. Swimming and sunbathing au naturel are prohibited, and the law is enforced by local police. The beaches of Grand Cul de Sac, on the northeast shore, and St. Jean are both in the vicinity of hotels, restaurants and water sports outlets. Flamands, to the northwest of St. Jean, is a classic stretch of white sand fringed with palm trees. Favored by island families on Sundays, the secluded beaches at Marigot and Lorient on the north shore are otherwise quiet.

In the south, Gouverneur offers complete privacy; Saline, just to the east, is more popular. Shell Beach, so named because it is partially covered with seashells, can be reached on foot from Gustavia. Public Beach is near the commercial pier on the other side of town. The least accessible is Colombier in the northwest. It can be reached by boat from Gustavia or by car to the villages of Colombier or Flamands, then a 20-minute hike down a scenic path.

Lying about midway between the major yachting centers of Antigua and Virgin Gorda Island, St. Barths is naturally a popular yachting destination. Gustavia's harbor has docking facilities for about 40 yachts, and there also are anchorages at nearby Public, Corossol, Colombier and Fourchue; mooring instructions are available from the Marine Reserve at Colombier. Shipchandler du Port Franc in Gustavia carries yachting supplies and accessories; phone (590) 27-86-29. Sailing information is available from the Office du Tourisme on the harborfront in Gustavia. A full-day round-trip sail from Gustavia to Ile Fourchue, an uninhabited island, and Colombier is available. Other charter trips also can be arranged.

Windsurfing is perhaps the most popular sport on the island; the colorful, billowing sails are a common offshore sight. Rentals and lessons are available at outlets in St. Jean and Grand Cul de Sac. Sailing enthusiasts can rent Hobie Cats in St. Jean. Carib Waterplay in St. Jean offers specialized instruction.

The waters around St. Barths abound in tazard, wahoo, dolphin, bonito, barracuda and marlin. Fishing is prohibited in several offshore zones protected by the St. Barthélemy Marine Reserve; information about deep-sea fishing expeditions is available through Ocean Must Marine Service, Masterski Pilou and Yannis Marine.

Licensed, accredited divemasters at West Indies Dive-Marine Service in Gustavia conduct dive schools and have all the necessary gear available; phone (590) 27-70-34. Other scuba clubs in Gustavia include La Bulle-Ocean Must, (590) 27-62-25; Plongée Caraïbes, (590) 27-55-94 or (690) 54-66-14; St. Barth Plongée, (590) 27-54-44; Big Blue, (590) 27-83-74; and Splash, (590) 29-64-23 or (690) 56-90-24. Diving equipment and lessons also are available at Ouanalao Dive in Grand Cul de Sac, (690) 63-74-34. Snorkeling is good in many areas off the beaches and islets; the waters off Gouverneur, St. Jean and Grand Cul de Sac are usually the calmest. Gear is sold in Gustavia and St. Jean.

The landlubber might enjoy horseback riding on the island. Ranch des Flamands offers 2-hour rides and instruction for beginning riders; phone (690) 39-87-01 or (590) 27-13-87.

Although limited, nightlife on St. Barths is not totally lacking. Sailors and young locals gather at Le Select, across the street at the Bar de l'Oubli or at the BAZ Bar (Le Bête A Z'Ailes) in Gustavia. The lounges at the upscale Hotel Carl Gustaf and the Mandala Restaurant, both overlooking the harbor, are popular with visiting yachtsmen. During the winter season, live jazz is on the menu at some spots. St. Barth Magazine, Le Journal de St. Barth, Le News and St Barth Weekly contain information about current entertainment. Published regularly during the winter season, they are distributed free all over the island.

With its Carnival festivities kicking off in early January and continuing through Ash Wednesday, St. Barthélemy is one of few countries in the world not to end its celebration on the traditional "Fat Tuesday" of Mardi Gras. The St. Barthélemy Music Festival in mid-January features world-renowned classical and jazz musicians. The St. Barths Bucket Regatta is a 3-day mega-yacht race held in late March. At the St. Barthélémy Caribbean Film Festival during the last week in April, all films are presented in French. The St. Barthélémy Theater Festival follows in the first week of May.

The year's most important event is the annual Festival of St. Barthélemy, celebrated on the weekends before and after August 24—feast day of the island's patron saint. Colorful booths line the streets of Gustavia, giving it the look and feel of a French country fair. July and August events featuring regattas, live music and fireworks also are held in the villages of Corossol at the St. Louis Festival and Lorient at the Fête du Vent.

Sightseeing

Just four or five roads meander around St. Barths, so it's nearly impossible to get off the beaten path; you can drive all around the island in about an hour. An island map can be obtained in Gustavia at the Office du Tourisme on the harborfront. Gustavia also is a good place to get an introduction to island life; this quaint little harbor town can be explored on foot. At about

11 a.m., sleek catamarans start arriving with day trippers from St. Maarten, filling the streets and shops with visitors. From Monday afternoon through Thursday morning, visitors can mingle with the locals at a small public market on rue du Roi Oscar II.

Northwest of Gustavia is the village of Corossol, where colorful fishing boats bob at anchor in the harbor and women at roadside stands weave palm fronds into baskets. Even while displaying their wares, villagers are camera shy and do not like to be photographed. Similar scenes can be found in the nearby village of Colombier.

From Colombier you can continue north to the secluded beach where an easy hike takes you to viewpoint at Grande Roche. Here you can see the uninhabited offshore islands to the north and Pointe Milou to the east.

Another possible trip is through the busy resort town of St. Jean, east through Lorient, along the north shore to Pointe Milou and Marigot, then south to the rocky coast of Grand Fond. The hilly vicinity of Vitet is just a short

Fast Facts

POPULATION: 8,732.

AREA: 21 sq km (8 sq mi.).

CAPITAL: Gustavia.

HIGHEST POINT: 286 m (938 ft.), Morne du Vitet.

LOWEST POINT: Sea level, Caribbean Sea.

TIME ZONE(S): Atlantic Standard.

LANGUAGE: French and English.

GOVERNMENT: Overseas Collectivity of France.

UNIT OF CURRENCY: Euro Dollar. $1 U.S. = approx. .78 Euro. U.S. currency is widely accepted.

ELECTRICITY: 220 volts, 60 cycles AC.

MINIMUM AGE FOR DRIVERS: 18-25, depending on the rental car agency. An international driving permit is advised; drive on right.

HOLIDAYS: Jan. 1; Epiphany, Jan. 6; Mardi Gras (day before Ash Wednesday); Easter Monday; Labour Day, May 1; Victory Day, May 8; Ascension Day, May (6th Thurs. after Easter); Bastille Day, July 14; Festival of St. Barthélemy, Aug. 24; All Saints Day, Nov. 1;

All Souls Day, Nov. 2; Armistice Day, Nov. 11; Assumption Day and St. Barths' Pitea Day, Nov. 16; Christmas, Dec. 25.

TAXES: A 5 percent room tax and a 10-15 percent service charge are added to most hotel and restaurant bills. Departure tax $6 U.S.

IMMIGRATION REQUIREMENTS: A valid passport and return or onward ticket are required for U.S. citizens entering the French West Indies. No visa needed for stays up to 3 months. The U.S. Dept. of Homeland Security requires all U.S. citizens returning from the Caribbean to present a valid passport.

PHONING THE ISLANDS: To call St. Barthélemy from the U.S. or Canada, dial 011 + 590 + 590 + the 6-digit local number.

FURTHER INFORMATION FOR VISITORS:

French Government Tourist Office
825 3rd Ave., 29th Floor
New York, NY 10022
(212) 838-7800

Office du Tourisme
Quai du Général de Gaulle
BP 113
Gustavia, St. Barthélemy 97133
(590) 27-87-27

drive from Marigot. The volcanic Morne du Vitet, at 938 feet (286 m), is the highest peak on the island. From Grand Fond the road turns inland and back to Lorient, St. Jean and Gustavia.

Island tours are available for up to eight people by minibus or taxi, and there are a number of tour operators.

Transportation

St. Jean's Gustave III Airport has a short landing strip able to handle nothing larger than 20-seat STOL (Short Take-Off and Landing) aircraft, and it is not equipped for night landings. The steep landing approach tests the nerves of even veteran air travelers. From the United States, the principal gateway to St. Barths is St. Maarten, where Air Caraïbes and Windward Island Airways (Winair) fly in from Princess Juliana International Airport. St. Barth Commuter also flies from Esperance Airport on the French side in St. Martin. These flights take about 15 minutes.

Other flights are available from San Juan, Guadeloupe and Antigua. Most carriers offer several flights daily. St. Barths also is a port of call for some cruise ships.

Taxis are available at the airport; the minimum fare is around $12, and the fare to most hotels is about $30. Fares increase by 50 percent Mon.-Sat.

from 8 p.m. to 6 a.m. and all day Sun. and holidays. Rates are not fixed, so it is always a good idea to agree upon the fare in advance. There are just two taxi stands on St. Barths: at the airport, (590) 27-75-81, and on the Rue de la République harborfront in Gustavia, (590) 27-66-31.

Several major and local car rental agencies operate from the airport. Rates are about $75 per day and include unlimited mileage, collision damage insurance and free delivery and pickup; rates are discounted in the summer. A U.S. driver's license is valid. Small sport utility vehicles are replacing the familiar gurgels, minimokes and other jeeplike conveyances for traveling the island's narrow, hilly roads.

Car rental plans can sometimes be made in advance through your hotel. Reservations are required during peak season. Motorbikes also are available for rent at about $60 per day with a $100 deposit; a valid driver's license is required. Helmets are required on the island when operating two-wheeled vehicles.

Edge Catamaran departs for Simpson Bay, St. Maarten, Tuesday through Saturday. This is a 1-day round-trip excursion, but the skippers will take one-way passengers on a space-available basis for about $50. The ferry *Voyager* travels between Gustavia and Marigot or Oyster Pond, St. Martin, four times daily; phone (590) 87-10-68.

Points of Interest

See map page 189.

COROSSOL (B-2)

In the "straw village" of Corossol, women carry on the tradition of weaving palm fronds into baskets, hats and handbags. Past generations in this tiny fishing hamlet wore modest, long-sleeved dresses and shoulder-length bonnets called *quichenottes* or "kiss-me-nots," vestiges of their French provincial origins. The bonnets offered protection from the sun but also thwarted the unwanted advances of suitors. Visitors may still see these traditional costumes during celebrations, most notably the St. Louis Festival on Aug. 25.

INTER OCEANS MUSEUM is on the waterfront. A private collector amassed this eclectic display of some 9,000 seashells from around the world, including more than a thousand pieces from Caribbean waters and examples of sand from far-flung beaches. **Hours:** Tues.-Sat. 9-12:30 and 3-5. **Cost:** $4. **Phone:** (590) 27-62-97.

GUSTAVIA (B-2) pop. 6,825

St. Barths' harbor town and capital, Gustavia was called Carénage by the French for the shelter it provided to damaged ships. The present name dates

back to 1784, which marked the beginning of the island's Swedish era. The Anglican Episcopal Church on the harborfront was completed in 1855.

Three forts built in the mid- to late 17th century protected the harbor. The sites of Fort Karl, overlooking Shell Beach south of town, and Fort Gustave, at the base of the Gustavia Lighthouse to the north, reward hikers with idyllic panoramas. Fort Oscar, at the tip of Gustavia Peninsula, houses the National Police.

Office du Tourisme: Quai du Général de Gaulle, BP 113, Gustavia, St. Barthélemy F.W.I. **Phone:** (590) 27-87-27.

WALL HOUSE MUSEUM is on rue de Pitea. Dating from the Swedish period 1785-1878, this restored building houses a variety of exhibits pertaining to the island's history and culture. Traditional costumes, farming tools and old documents are of special interest. **Time:** Allow 30 minutes minimum. **Hours:** Mon.-Tues. and Thurs.-Fri. 8:30-12:30 and 2:30-6, Wed. 8:30-12:30, Sat. 9-12:30. Closed major holidays. **Cost:** $3. **Phone:** (590) 29-71-55.

Fort Oranje, Oranjestad, St. Eustatius / © Helene Rogers / age fotostock

St. Eustatius and Saba

Quiet and tiny, with an area of merely 11.8 square miles (31 sq km), St. Eustatius (also called Statia) consists of two dormant volcanoes linked by a central plain. While the northern volcano has been eroded to a cluster of hills, the southern one, known as the Quill, is perfectly formed and rises precipitously to nearly 2,000 feet (610 m). Home to some 58 species of birds and 18 species of orchids, the Quill derived its name from English settlers because they could not pronounce the Dutch word *Kuil.*

Climatic conditions vary strikingly for such a small island: The Atlantic side has strong winds and low vegetation; the Caribbean side is calm with tall coconut, almond, cotton and mango trees.

Even smaller is Saba (SAY-ba), only 5 square miles (13 sq km) and located just north of Statia. Saba is unusual among Caribbean islands—its steep volcanic cliffs rise straight out of the water, leaving no room for beaches. What it lacks in sand, the island makes up for in breathtaking views of the sea.

Along with St. Maarten, Statia and Saba form the Windward Islands of the Dutch Caribbean.

History

Christopher Columbus first sighted St. Eustatius on his second voyage in 1493. Never settled by Spain, the island was first colonized by France in 1629, then by Holland in 1636. St. Eustatius changed hands 22 times between the French and Dutch—and the English in 1665—before Dutch possession finally became permanent in 1816.

During its early years St. Eustatius developed into a prosperous center for the slave trade and mercantile exchange of the eastern Caribbean, earning the nickname "The Golden Rock." It also was a vital depot for supplies shipped from Europe to the American Revolutionaries. In 1776 St. Eustatius became the first foreign government to officially recognize the United States by firing a salute from Fort Oranje to the American brig *Andrew Doria*. But the Dutch settlers' pro-American sympathies ultimately led to the sacking of St. Eustatius by George Bridges Rodney, a British admiral based in St. Lucia. Rodney arrived in St. Eustatius with a fleet of 15 ships and a crew of 3,000 men on Feb. 3, 1781, an event that marked the end of the tiny island's prosperity.

Shopping

Saba's local specialties are Saba lace, including handcrafted blouses, handkerchiefs and linens, and Saba Spice, an aromatic blend of 150 proof cask rum, brown sugar, fennel seed, cinnamon, nutmeg and cloves. The Windwardside is an ideal place to purchase these and one-of-a-kind handmade glass beads, jewelry, folk art

and original paintings by local artisans and artists.

Food and Drink

Spiny lobster in garlic sauce, whelk stew, bread baked in stone ovens and various shrimp and goat dishes are popular on St. Eustatius. Local restaurants serve such specialties as tripe, bullfoot soup, conch soup and curried vegetables.

Fare on Saba includes gourmet seafood and duck dishes as well as Caribbean and Creole meals.

Sports and Amusements

Reef and wreck diving is popular in St. Eustatius. Several vendors offer PADI certification, dive packages and equipment rental, including Golden Rock Dive Center, (599) 318-2964 or (800) 311-6658, and Scubaqua, (599) 318-5450. In Saba, various dive packages

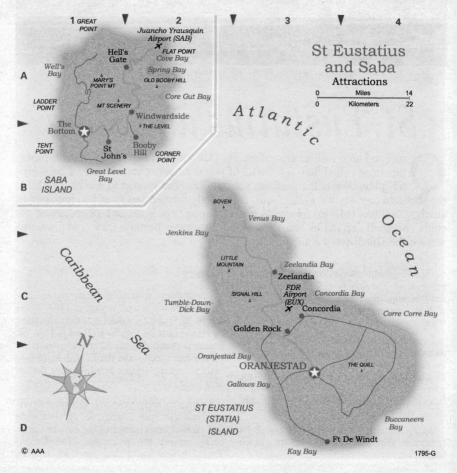

© AAA

1795-G

are offered by Saba Deep Dive Center, (599) 416-3347; Saba Divers, (599) 416-2740 or (866) 656-7222; and Sea Saba Dive Center, (599) 416-2246.

The St. Eustatius Marine Park offers more than 30 sites where divers can view pristine coral reefs, drop-offs, walls, pinnacles, canyons and historical wrecks with an abundance of fish, lobster and sea turtles. The park covers more than 10 square miles (27.5 sq km), encompassing the entire coast. Sites range from Gallows Bay to the White Wall area and from Jenkins Bay to North Point and Oranjebaai. No boat anchoring is permitted in the park. Fee $4 per dive, annual pass $20.

The Saba Marine Park, which encircles the entire island, has marked dive sites and snorkeling trails. Surrounded by waters with a visibility up to 200 feet (60 m), Saba is ideal for divers.

Sightseeing

Sightseeing is concentrated near Fort Oranje in Oranjestad, the capital of St. Eustatius. The fort was built in 1629 by the French and enlarged in 1636 by the Dutch to include bigger cannons from Amsterdam. Maps for walking tours past many 17th-, 18th- and 19th-century buildings are available at the St. Eustatius Historical Foundation Museum in Upper Town. Three Widows' Corner near the fort features an 18th-century townhouse and a 19th-century Victorian home in a charming tropical courtyard.

In addition to a few shops and inns, the town also contains the historic Government's Guest House, where government is headquartered; the Dutch Reformed Church, a 1755 structure with a 75-foot tower; the ruins of the 1739 Honen Dalim Synagogue, one of the oldest Jewish synagogues in the Western Hemisphere; and a

---

Fast Facts

POPULATION: St. Eustatius: 3,183. Saba: 1,500.

AREA: St. Eustatius: 31 sq km (11.8 sq mi.). Saba: 13 sq km (5 sq mi.).

CAPITAL: St. Eustatius: Oranjestad. Saba: The Bottom.

HIGHEST POINT: 862 m (2,828 ft.), Mount Scenery, Saba.

LOWEST POINT: Sea level, Caribbean Sea.

TIME ZONE(S): Atlantic Standard.

LANGUAGE: Dutch, English, Spanish and Papiamentu.

GOVERNMENT: Autonomous special municipalities of the Kingdom of the Netherlands.

UNIT OF CURRENCY: U.S. Dollar

ELECTRICITY: 110 volts, 60 cycles AC.

MINIMUM AGE FOR DRIVERS: 18; a valid license is required; drive on right.

SEAT BELT/CHILD RESTRAINT LAWS: Seat belts are required for all passengers. Child restraints required for under age 4; children under 12 must ride in the back seat.

HELMETS FOR MOTORCYCLISTS: Required.

HOLIDAYS: Jan. 1; Good Friday; Easter Monday; Queen's Birthday, Apr. 30; Labour Day, May 1; Ascension Day, May (6th Thurs. after Easter); Carnival Monday, July; Antillean Day,

Oct. 21; Statia/America Day, Nov. 16; Christmas, Dec. 25; Boxing Day, Dec. 26.

TAXES: A 7 percent room tax and 10-15 percent service charge are added to most hotel bills. In lieu of a gratuity, restaurants may add a 15 percent service charge on food and beverage items. Departure tax $22 U.S.; Dutch interisland tax $6.80.

IMMIGRATION REQUIREMENTS: Passport or proof of U.S. citizenship and a return or onward ticket are required. No visa needed for stays up to 2 weeks. The U.S. Dept. of Homeland Security requires all U.S. citizens returning from the Caribbean to present a valid passport.

PHONING THE ISLANDS: To call St. Eustatius and Saba from the U.S. or Canada, dial 011 + 599 + the 7-digit local number.

FURTHER INFORMATION FOR VISITORS:

St. Eustatius Tourist Office
Fort Oranje
Oranjestad, St. Eustatius
St. Eustatius and Saba
(599) 318-2433

Saba Tourist Bureau
P.O. Box 527
Windwardside, Saba
St. Eustatius and Saba
(599) 416-2231
(599) 416-2322

library. The St. Eustatius Historical Foundation Museum contains exhibits about the pre-Columbian and Colonial periods.

Fort de Windt, built in the mid-18th century presumably under the command of Jan de Windt, lies at the southern tip of the island, offering breathtaking views of St. Kitts. Fort de Windt and Fort Oranje are the only two forts that are restored out of 19 surrounding the island. On the island's northeastern side is Lynch Plantation Museum, also known as Berkel Family Plantation, which features an impressive collection of domestic artifacts and antiques.

The tourist office has information about tours, history, cruises, swimming, kayaking, snorkeling and scuba diving. Guides lead hikes to the top of The Quill, an extinct volcano whose cone rises 2,000 feet (610 m); the crater contains a lush tropical rain forest. Near the Quill is the Miriam C. Schmidt Botanical Garden, which includes floral collections, walking paths and a variety of uncommon plants and tea bush along with a breathtaking view of St. Kitts, St. Barths and St. Maarten.

Day trips from St. Eustatius to Saba are possible. Possibly the only island in the Caribbean without a beach, Saba is a tiny volcanic island draped with lush vegetation. The rocky shoreline of the island contains tide pools home to numerous sealife.

A rain forest exists some 3,000 feet (915 m) above sea level; a constant cloud of moisture surrounds the area. Various trails lead hikers into the rain forest where 15 species of wild orchids live along with such other tropical foliage as ferns, giant elephant ears and banana and mango trees. Here 1,064 steps chiseled from vertical rock connect the village of Windwardside with The Bottom, the island's capital. These steps were the island's only thoroughfare until a twisting road was built by hand in the 1940s. At 1,900 feet (580 m), Windwardside offers a superb view of the Caribbean. Trail maps and information can be obtained from The Trail Shop, Windwardside, Saba.

The Saba Museum is housed in an 1840s sea captain's cottage; contact the tourist bureau for more information. Descend by jeep to The Bottom, 1,000 feet (305 m) below, and head for the Saba Artisans' Foundation for locally designed fashions.

Transportation

St. Eustatius' Franklin Delano Roosevelt Airport has daily flights to St. Maarten via Windward Islands Airways (Winair) as well as flights to Saba's Juancho E. Yrausquin Airport and St. Kitts. Windjammer cruises call here twice monthly. Car rental information can be obtained at the airport information desk.

Points of Interest

See map page 194.

St. Eustatius

Discovered in 1493, the diminutive island known as Statia changed hands at least 22 times before the Dutch took possession in 1636. St. Eustatius was a major arms supplier to the American colonies during the Revolutionary War.

ORANJESTAD (D-3)

The capital city of Oranjestad was considered the first foreign port to acknowledge the sovereignty of the United States. On Nov. 16, 1776, an American ship flying the stars and stripes entered Statia's harbor and fired a salute; the guns at Fort Oranje returned the greeting. A plaque presented by Pres. Franklin D. Roosevelt in 1939 commemorates the event.

Oranjestad is divided by coastal cliffs into two sections. Traditionally, Lower Town was the base for mercantile operations, while residents built their homes in Upper Town.

St. Eustatius Tourist Office: Fort Oranje, Oranjestad, St. Eustatius, St. Eustatius and Saba. **Phone:** (599) 318-2433.

ST. EUSTATIUS HISTORICAL FOUNDATION MUSEUM is across from Fort Oranje at Wilhelminaweg #3 in Upper Town. The museum chronicles the island's pre-Columbian and colonial history. Special exhibits depict sugar production, shipping and commerce. Built by prominent merchant Simon Doncker, the house served as headquarters for Admiral George Rodney after he invaded the island in 1781. A walking tour of Oranjestad departs from the museum; advance reservations are required. **Time:** Allow 30 minutes minimum. **Hours:** Mon.-Thurs. 9-5, Fri. 9-3:30, Sat.-Sun. 9-noon. **Cost:** $3; $1 (ages 3-18). **Phone:** (599) 318-2288.

Brimstone Hill Fortress National Park, near Basseterre, St. Kitts / © Richard Cummins / SuperStock

St. Kitts and Nevis

S eparated by a mere 2 miles (3.2 km), St. Kitts and Nevis (NEE-vis) constitute one of the world's tiniest nations. Their beauty and charm, however, are not proportional to their size. Dominated by 3,792-foot (1,156-m) Mount Liamuiga, mountainous St. Kitts contains some of the islands' finest beaches. Nevis embraces a single peak rising from the sea to a cloud-shrouded height of 3,232 feet (985 m). Beaches of coral sand are found along its shores. Missing from St. Kitts and Nevis is the profusion of towering resorts found on many of the bigger, more developed islands, as by law no building can be taller than the palm trees. Its visitors can still enjoy the rustic atmosphere and slow-paced "island time" that some say makes for real relaxation.

History

When Christopher Columbus discovered the two sister islands in 1493, the cloud-encircled volcanic peak of the smaller island inspired him to call it *Las Nieves,* meaning "the snows." Over the years the island's name has evolved into simply Nevis. The larger island is said to be named St. Christopher after the explorer, but the British adopted the diminution St. Kitts after Sir Thomas Warner established a settlement, the first English colony in the West Indies, at Old Road Town in 1623. The next year the

French also established a colony, and the Anglo-French rivalry for control of the islands was to last for the next 160 years.

After changing hands several times, the islands fell under British rule in 1783 through the Treaty of Versailles. Evidence of their turbulent history remains in the battlegrounds and ruined forts on St. Kitts. Today inhabitants pursue the more peaceful activities of accommodating tourists and growing the island's agriculture and other industries.

The two islands became an Associated British State in 1967. On Sept. 19, 1983, the British

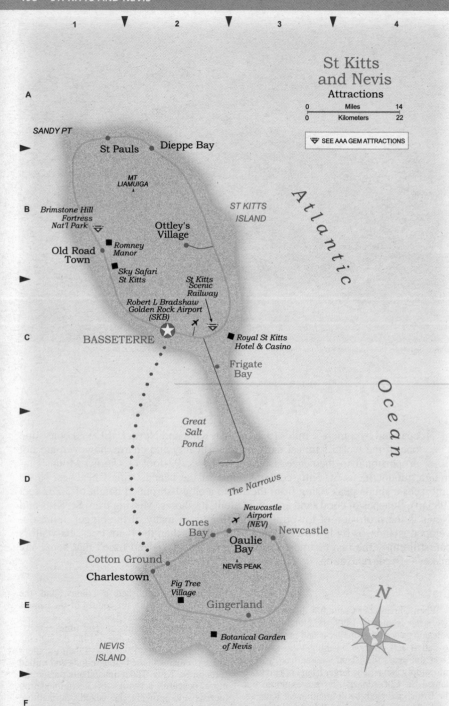

1 2 3 4

A

St Kitts and Nevis
Attractions

| 0 | Miles | 14 |
| 0 | Kilometers | 22 |

SEE AAA GEM ATTRACTIONS

SANDY PT

St Pauls Dieppe Bay

MT LIAMUIGA

B

ST KITTS ISLAND

Brimstone Hill Fortress Nat'l Park

Ottley's Village

Romney Manor

Old Road Town

Sky Safari St Kitts

St Kitts Scenic Railway

Robert L Bradshaw Golden Rock Airport (SKB)

C

BASSETERRE

Royal St Kitts Hotel & Casino

Frigate Bay

Great Salt Pond

D

The Narrows

Newcastle Airport (NEV)

Jones Bay

Oaulie Bay

Newcastle

NEVIS PEAK

Cotton Ground

Charlestown

Fig Tree Village

Gingerland

E

Botanical Garden of Nevis

NEVIS ISLAND

N

F

© AAA

1792-G

Atlantic

Ocean

Union Jack was replaced by the green, red, yellow and black flag of the newly independent nation of St. Kitts and Nevis. The governmental structure includes a prime minister, governor-general and legislature for St. Kitts and an Island Assembly with a premier and deputy governor-general for Nevis.

Shopping

Shopping activity on the islands centers on Basseterre, the capital of St. Kitts. Clusters of modern shops surrounding "The Circus," the town's main square at Fort Street and Liverpool Row, provide local crafts, souvenirs and some duty-free imports. Two blocks east near the ferry dock the Pelican Mall offers several duty-free shops in a pleasant indoor setting of traditional Kittitian facades and pastel colors. Port Zante offers such shops as the Caribbean Gift & Liquors, Diamonds International, International Concepts Jewelry, Kay's Fine Jewelry and Piranha Joe's.

A favorite take-home item is a hand-dyed tropical fashion from Caribelle Batik. These colorful cotton garments can be purchased in Basseterre and Charlestown, Nevis, but visitors to their factory at Romney Manor west of Old Road Town on St. Kitts also can witness the batik process. Stamp collectors will appreciate visits to the St. Kitts Philatelic Bureau in Basseterre and the Nevis Philatelic Bureau in Charlestown.

The Eva Wilkin Gallery at Clay Ghaut, Gingerland, features prints by the artist known for her sketches and paintings of Nevis. Well-known Kittitian artist Kate Spencer features prints and original works showcasing life on St. Kitts in her gallery, "Kate Design," on Bank Street in Basseterre, located on a side street off The Circus. For original pottery creations that have a distinct Caribbean flair, visit Potter's House Art Gallery and Studio on St. Kitts' North Independence Square.

Store hours are generally Mon.-Wed. and Fri.-Sat. 8-noon and 1-4, Thurs. 8-noon. Banking hours are Mon.-Fri. 8-2 (also Fri. 2-4).

Food and Drink

The cuisine of St. Kitts and Nevis is highlighted with exotic Caribbean and continental flavors. Beef, chicken, pork and seafood all are complemented by homegrown fruit and vegetables. Such favorite native dishes as Creole red bean soup, conch chowder, goat water (a soup) and boiled saltfish stew are served in several local restaurants. Conch fritters and saltfish balls make good appetizers.

St. Kitts' own Carib Beer or Brinley Gold Rum are good complements to a hearty West Indian meal. Two other local products—Ting, a grapefruit-based soft drink, and CSR (Cane Spirit Rothschild), distilled from fresh cane juice—make a fine blend.

Sports and Amusements

Besides those along Frigate Bay, good beaches are found along the south coast, at Dieppe Bay in the north and along the southeast peninsula. From the white sands of the peninsula's Turtle Beach, Sandy Bank Bay and Cockleshell Bay, visitors can get fine views of Nevis. Pinney's Beach and Oualie Beach on Nevis offer excellent swimming.

The waters between St. Kitts and Nevis are the final resting place for more than 400 ships sunk 1492-1825, yet only about a dozen sites have been identified thus far. Experienced divers can explore many of the sites. Arrangements for dive trips can be made through most hotels. For a fee, local anglers will take you deep-sea fishing. A favorite spot for experienced divers is "The Caves," a series of coral grottoes on Nevis' west coast.

Water sports at various island establishments include scuba diving, snorkeling, windsurfing and sailing. PADI certification courses, full- and half-day charters and underwater camera and video camera rentals also are available. Free transportation to Turtle Beach is provided for guests of the Ocean Terrace Inn.

The Royal St. Kitts 18-hole golf course at Frigate Bay lies on the narrowest portion of the island, between the Caribbean Sea and the Atlantic Ocean. Evening entertainment is provided by many of the area hotels and local beach bars.

Most hotels on Nevis have tennis courts and will make arrangements for guests to go deep-sea fishing and horseback riding. The Four Seasons Resort Nevis has an 18-hole golf course that winds up the slope of Mount Nevis. Hiking to the top of Mount Nevis adds to the recreational activities available on the island. Nevis also offers isolated beaches and unspoiled, uncluttered countryside.

Special events on the islands start with National Carnival in late December. Highlights of the 10-day event include a beauty and talent pageant, calypso contests, parades, a masqued gala and musical entertainment. The St. Kitts and Nevis Triathlon, in mid-March, starts with a 2.5-mile (4-km) ocean swim and is followed by a 45-mile (72 km) mountain bicycle race and a 14-mile (23-km) run. The St. Kitts Music Festival is held in June and features an eclectic mix of local and international artists.

Sightseeing

Excursions on St. Kitts can be breathtaking—both aesthetically and physically. Climbing Mount Liamuiga (lee-a-MWEE-ga) is an all-day affair; the crater, 1,192 feet (363 m) below the peak, is the usual stopping point. Hikers can explore the tropical rain forest, which abounds with monkeys, birds, butterflies, fruits and flowers, while enjoying a coastal view of the sea. The monkeys, left behind by the French who kept them as pets, now outnumber the human population by a ratio of approximately 2.5-to-1.

Other sites worth investigating are Brimstone Hill Fortress National Park, a UNESCO World Heritage site, positioned approximately 800 feet (244 m) atop a rock cliff; the Carib Indian petroglyphs at Old Road; Bloody Point near Challengers village, the site of a Carib Indian massacre in 1626; Montravers House, a former sugar plantation; and Caribelle Batik, housed at Romney Manor, a 17th-century great house set above Old Road Town. In a churchyard at Middle Island is the tomb of Sir Thomas Warner, the British founder of St. Kitts.

Fun-loving seafarers will enjoy an all-day cruise aboard the catamaran *Spirit of St. Kitts*. The day includes a beach barbecue and snorkeling. For information and reservations phone (869) 465-7474.

St. Kitts' scenic southeast peninsula is accessible via the Dr. Kennedy A. Simmonds Highway, a modern roadway completed in 1990. The 6-mile (10-km) highway leads from Frigate Bay east of Basseterre to Major's Bay, just 2 miles (3.2 km) from Nevis. The peninsula's mountainous terrain affords spectacular views of the sea and offshore islands.

Fast Facts

POPULATION: St. Kitts: 38,756. Nevis: 11,000

AREA: St. Kitts: 176 sq km (68 sq mi.). Nevis: 93 sq km (36 sq mi.).

CAPITAL: St. Kitts: Basseterre. Nevis: Charlestown.

HIGHEST POINT: 1,156 m (3,792 ft.), Mount Liamuiga, St. Kitts.

LOWEST POINT: Sea level, Caribbean Sea.

TIME ZONE(S): Atlantic Standard.

LANGUAGE: English.

GOVERNMENT: Independent. Member of the British Commonwealth of Nations.

UNIT OF CURRENCY: Eastern Caribbean (E.C.) dollar. $1 U.S. = 2.7 E.C. dollars.

ELECTRICITY: 230 volts, 60 cycles AC.

MINIMUM AGE FOR DRIVERS: 21-25, depending on the rental car agency. Local license ($25) required; drive on left.

MINIMUM AGE FOR GAMBLING: 21.

HOLIDAYS: Jan. 1; Carnival, Jan. 2; Good Friday; Easter Monday; Labour Day, May (1st Mon.); Whit Monday, May or June (8th Mon. after Easter); Queen's Birthday, June (2nd Sat.); August Monday, Aug. (1st Mon.); Culturama Last Lap, Aug. (1st Tues.); National Heroes Day, Sept. 16; Independence Day, Sept. 19; Christmas, Dec. 25; Boxing Day, Dec. 26.

TAXES: A 7-10 percent room tax and 10-15 percent service charge are added to most hotel bills. Departure tax $22 U.S.; a tourism enhancement tax of $1.50 also is charged.

IMMIGRATION REQUIREMENTS: Passport and a return or onward ticket are required. No visa needed for stays up to 1 month. The U.S. Dept. of Homeland Security requires all U.S. citizens returning from the Caribbean to present a valid passport.

PHONING THE ISLANDS: To call St. Kitts and Nevis from the U.S. or Canada, dial 1 + 869 + the 7-digit local number.

FURTHER INFORMATION FOR VISITORS:

St. Kitts Tourism Authority New York
414 E. 75th St., Suite 5
New York, NY 10021
(212) 535-1234
(800) 582-6208

St. Kitts Tourism Office, Basseterre
Pelican Mall, Bay Road
Basseterre, St. Kitts
St. Kitts and Nevis
(869) 465-4040

Nevis Tourism Authority
Main Street
Charlestown, Nevis
St. Kitts and Nevis
(869) 469-7550
(866) 556-3847
(407) 287-5204 in the U.S.

Transportation

Non-stop service to St. Kitts' Robert L. Bradshaw International Airport is available from Charlotte aboard U.S. Airways. American Airlines offers non-stop flights from Miami and New York's JFK International Airport. Delta Airlines offers non-stop flights from Atlanta. American Eagle and LIAT provide flights and connections from Antigua, San Juan and St. Maarten. Port Zante in St. Kitts is a leading port of call for cruise ships.

Taxis are readily available. An approximate fare from Robert L. Bradshaw International Airport to Basseterre is $8. An additional 50%

surcharge is added 10 p.m. to 6 a.m. A taxi tour around St. Kitts takes about 4 hours. Minimokes are also a fun way to get around. Car rentals also are available. A local driver's license is required to drive on the islands and can be obtained for about $20 at the Police Traffic Department in Basseterre.

Nevis is accessible from Puerto Rico and St. Kitts via a brief flight to Vance W. Amory International Airport or regular ferry trips from St. Kitts aboard the *Caribe Queen*, *Sea Hustler*, *Caribe Breeze/Surf* and *Mark Twain*. Direct flights to St. Kitts are available from New York, Miami, Atlanta and Charlotte.

Points of Interest

See map page 198.

Nevis

Nevis is a volcanic island surrounded by coral reefs. Forested slopes rise from palm-lined beaches to the island's cloud-shrouded summit. Relatively untouched by tourism, Nevis attracts those in search of a quiet escape. Except for the Four Seasons Resort Nevis, lodging consists mostly of small family-run businesses—guest cottages, hotels and a few sugar plantations converted to inns, many of which are nestled among the foothills of Nevis Peak.

As on many of the Caribbean isles, the use of slave labor at sugar plantations on Nevis created a wealthy upper class. During the 19th century the islands, including Nevis, quickly became the haunt of the elite of British society, who frequented the island's mineral baths and hot springs at the Bath Hotel, considered one of the most ambitious structures built in the West Indies in 1778.

Jamestown, the former capital that fell prey to an earthquake and tidal wave in 1680, is accessible by the main road that circles Nevis. Snorkelers and scuba divers frequent the area.

Among the historic figures associated with Nevis is Alexander Hamilton, the American author and statesman, who was born here in 1757. When he was a captain, Horatio Nelson courted and married Fanny Nisbet in Nevis. Montpelier Plantation was the site of their 1787 marriage, in which the future King William IV of England acted as best man. Their marriage certificate was recorded at St. John's Church in Fig Tree Village.

CHARLESTOWN (E-1) pop. 1,820

During the Spanish Inquisition many Jews fled South America to the Caribbean to escape persecution. The Jewish community on Nevis can be traced

to the early 17th century with a tombstone in the Nevis Jewish Cemetery dated 1658. Visitors to Charlestown can view the Nevis Synagogue archeological dig taking place at an old stone building in partial ruin. The site, adjacent to the government administration building, is believed to be one of the Caribbean's oldest synagogues.

ALEXANDER HAMILTON MUSEUM is .2 mi. (.3 km) n. on Low St. Housed in a reconstruction of Alexander Hamilton's birthplace, the museum features a series of small exhibits related to both Hamilton and the history of Nevis. Of interest is a bronze plaque commemorating the visit made by a group of 144 Englishmen in 1607 who landed on the island, spent 6 days and went on to found Jamestown, Virginia, the first permanent English settlement. **Hours:** Mon.-Fri. 9-4, Sat. 9-noon. Closed major holidays. **Cost:** $5; $2 (ages 0-11). **Phone:** (869) 469-5786.

THE BOTANICAL GARDENS OF NEVIS is 3 mi. (5 km) s. at the Montpelier Estate in Gingerland. Orchids, bromeliads, rare palms, flowering vines and fruit trees are among the hundreds of species at this 7-acre (3-hectare) tropical hillside haven, which features fountains, waterfalls, lily pools, a bee and honey farm and a rain forest conservatory with a butterfly garden. The garden also features a large collection of Asian stone sculptures. The estate offers striking views of Nevis and St. Kitts. **Time:** Allow 2 hours minimum. **Hours:** Mon.-Sat. 9-5, mid-Oct. to mid-Aug. Closed some major holidays. Phone ahead to confirm schedule. **Cost:** $15; $7 (ages 6-12). **Phone:** (869) 469-3509 or (869) 469-2673.

MUSEUM OF NEVIS HISTORY is .5 mi. (.8 km) s. behind the Bath Hotel. A large collection of memorabilia associated with Adm. Horatio Nelson, a frequent visitor to Nevis, includes glassware, ceramics, paintings, prints and ship models. Permanent and changing exhibits chronicle the history of Nevis and its people. **Time:** Allow 30 minutes minimum. **Hours:** Mon.-Fri. 9-4, Sat. 9-noon. Closed major holidays. **Cost:** $5; $2 (ages 0-11). **Phone:** (869) 469-0408.

St. Kitts

While it retains its charm as an off-the-beaten-track destination, St. Kitts is welcoming an ever-increasing number of tourists. Accommodations on the island range from grand beach-front resorts to intimate plantation inns, and activities range from sightseeing and shopping to deep-sea fishing and water sports. Beaches are quiet and secluded, with sands of volcanic black, gold or powder white.

BASSETERRE (C-1) pop. 13,220

Bordering a harbor on the island's southern end, Basseterre (boss-tare) is the principal city and capital of St. Kitts. The town has preserved many early examples of West Indian and Georgian architecture; a good example of the former is the Treasury building on the waterfront. But the architectural legacy of British colonialism can best be seen in Independence Square, originally the slave market. This park of manicured lawns and shade trees includes the Catholic church and several 18th-century homes. Another landmark is the ornate Victorian clock in "The "Circus," a roundabout in the town's main square that was modeled after Piccadilly Circus in London.

St. Kitts Tourism Authority Office: Pelican Mall, Bay Road, Basseterre, St. Kitts, W.I. **Phone:** (869) 465-4040.

GREG'S SAFARIS offers Land Rover tours with pickup service from local hotels, the airport and cruise-ship dock. The half-day Plantation Tour takes in some of the island's sugar plantations. The half-day Windward Coast Rainforest Safari features a nature walk through the lush rain forest. The physically challenging full-day Volcano Tour involves a 1,600-foot (488-m) hike to the rim of Mount Liamuiga; lunch is included. Inquire about other tours. **Hours:** Tours are available daily. **Cost:** Half-day tours $65. Full-day tours $95. **Phone:** (869) 465-4121 or (869) 663-6008.

ST. KITTS SCENIC RAILWAY departs from Needsmust Station on Bay Rd., just e. of the airport. The narrow gauge railway, once used to transport sugar cane, has been converted for double-deck sightseeing cars. Given seats on both levels, passengers are free to move between the lower air-conditioned compartment and the open-air upper deck. Each trip includes colorful narration, live musical entertainment and complimentary refreshments.

The 3-hour scenic rail tour makes a complete circuit around the island, providing views of old sugar estates, villages and farms, cane fields, rain forests and the volcanic cone of Mt. Liamuiga. Historic sites include St. Paul, home of the prime minister; Old Road Town, where Thomas Jefferson's great grandfather is buried; and Brimstone Hill Fortress *(see place listing)*.

Time: Allow 3 hours, 30 minutes minimum. **Hours:** Trains depart Mon. at 1 and Wed. at 9:30, May-Oct.; based upon cruise ship arrivals rest of year. Phone ahead to confirm schedule. **Cost:** Scenic tour $89; $44.50 (ages 3-11). **Phone:** (869) 465-7263.

GAMBLING ESTABLISHMENTS

- **Royal Beach Casino at St. Kitts Marriott Resort** is at 858 Frigate Bay Rd. **Phone:** (869) 466-1200 or (866) 302-9870.

- **Royal St. Kitts Hotel & Casino** is at Frigate Bay. **Hours:** Open daily 4 p.m.-1 a.m. **Phone:** (869) 465-2186, (869) 465-8651 or (866) 806-6242.

BRIMSTONE HILL FORTRESS NATIONAL PARK (B-1)

Nine miles (14 km) west of Basseterre, this massive British fortress on a hill 800 feet (244 m) above the sea was built by slaves over a 100-year period beginning in the late 1600s. Once known as "The Gibraltar of the West Indies," Brimstone Hill was so intimidating that ship captains often changed course rather than come within range of its powerful guns. The British believed the fort to be impregnable, but the French proved them quite wrong in 1782. Despite the French victory, the British regained the fort a year later through the Treaty of Versailles.

Today visitors can explore the fortress, look out over the now dormant cannons and enjoy the panoramic view that inspired Her Majesty, Queen Elizabeth II, to declare Brimstone Hill a national monument. The UNESCO World Heritage Site covers 38 acres (15 hectares). A visitor center in the Commissariat features a 10-minute film orientation and audio tours for rental; all presentations are available in four languages. At the citadel museum, artifacts, paintings and exhibits chronicle the history of the fortress and the struggle between the British and French for control of the islands during the 1700s.

Food is available. Allow 1 hour minimum. Daily 9:30-5:30; closed Good Friday and Christmas. Last admission 30 minutes before closing. Admission $8; $4 (ages 0-16). Audio tour rental $5. Phone (869) 465-2609 or (869) 465-6771.

OLD ROAD TOWN (B-1)

Founded in 1623 by Sir Thomas Warner, Old Road Town was the first permanent English colony in the West Indies. English and French troops banded together in 1626 to attack the native Carib Indians at a spot known as Bloody Point. Here, some 2,000 Caribs were massacred. Near Romney Manor is a cluster of large boulders carved with petroglyphs, bearing mute witness to the island's original inhabitants.

ROMNEY MANOR is on Old Road. On the grounds of this 17th-century plantation are lush botanical gardens, sugar mill ruins, a 350-year-old saman tree, Carib Indian rock drawings and a rain forest. The adjoining estate, Wingfield, is said to have belonged to an ancestor of Thomas Jefferson. The Earls of Romney owned the property 1713-1819. Wild tobacco grows in the ruins, though the plant hasn't been cultivated in 400 years. At Caribelle Batik, situated in the remains of the Romney great house, visitors can watch the production of wax-dyed cotton fabric. **Time:** Allow 30 minutes minimum.

Hours: Mon.-Fri. 8:30-4. Closed major holidays. **Cost:** Free. **Phone:** (869) 465-6253.

RECREATIONAL ACTIVITIES
Ziplines

- **Sky Safari St. Kitts** is at Wingfield Estate. From the various ziplines, visitors have unobstructed views of Brimstone Hill Fortress National Park and the "Valley of the Giants," a large river basin. **Hours:** Daily, year-round. **Phone:** (869) 466-4259 or (869) 465-4347.

KEEP YOUR CHILDREN SAFE IN THE CAR

AAA and the timeless characters of Richard Scarry, one of the best-selling children's authors of all time, have partnered to promote child passenger safety. To keep your child safe, use the right car seat and follow the guidelines at **AAA.com/SafeSeats4Kids**. To install your car safety seat correctly, call an expert at **866-SEAT-CHECK(732-8243)** or visit **seatcheck.org**. Remember, car seats save lives!

Gros and Petit Pitons, Soufrière / © Brent Winebrenner / Lonely Planet Images

St. Lucia

Lush greenery, endless banana plantations, wooded mountains and fertile valleys are just some of the elements that harmonize to make St. Lucia (LOO-sha) "the Helen of the West Indies." This tropical paradise, which is 27 miles (43 km) long and 14 miles (23 km) wide, contains 19,000 acres (7,689 hectares) of rain forest. Quaint fishing villages and enticing beaches provide a backdrop that complements the diverse landscape of the interior. Gros and Petit Pitons, regal twin peaks separated by a picturesque bay, are prominent landmarks.

History

The first settlers were the peace-loving Arawak Indians, who probably came to St. Lucia to escape the warlike Caribs. However, the Arawaks did not endure—the Caribs eventually followed and succeeded in driving them off the island by A.D. 800.

Although it has not been established whether Christopher Columbus or Juan de la Cosa discovered St. Lucia, the first European to settle on the island was pirate François de Clerc. In 1550, de Clerc attacked passing Spanish ships from his base on Pigeon Island.

The English attempted to settle the island in 1605 and 1639, but the fierce Caribs thwarted their efforts on both occasions. In 1650 the French finally established the first permanent settlement; a treaty with the Caribs was signed in 1660. About this time, a bitter dispute originated in which each country claimed ownership of the territory.

A 150-year-long struggle for control ensued, as St. Lucia changed hands between the feuding French and British 14 times. The island was ultimately ceded to the British in 1814 and became one of the Windward Islands in 1838.

Sugar plantations flourished from the mid-1700s to the mid-1800s. With African slaves providing free labor, the industry thrived. Once slavery was abolished in 1834, a labor shortage ensued that contributed to the industry's decline. Such epidemics as smallpox and cholera also impeded prosperity during the remainder of the 19th century. The economy improved in the early 20th century, as a greater emphasis was placed on the cultivation of bananas and cocoa. Although the sugar industry briefly resurged, production eventually ceased in the 1960s.

As a provision of the West Indies Act of 1967, St. Lucia became entirely self-governing in internal affairs. The United Kingdom retained authority in regard to defense and external matters. On Feb. 22, 1979, the island obtained full independence. That same year, St. Lucia became a member of the British Commonwealth of Nations.

The country remains a stable parliamentary democracy, with a governor-general designated by Queen Elizabeth II. Agriculture and tourism are economic mainstays, accounting for about 80 percent of total economic revenue.

Shopping

Local goods available on St. Lucia include batik fabrics, perfumes, straw works, unglazed pottery, and handicrafts produced from wood and shell. The island is particularly known for its cane furniture and batik designs. These items can be found in duty-free shopping complexes at La Place Carenage in Castries and at Pointe Seraphine on the north side of the bay on Vigie Peninsula; both places are expanding to meet cruise ship demand.

Gemstone jewelry; fine china, crystal, figurines, perfume, international apparel and colorful silk-screened clothing are among choice buys. Local straw work is sold at two large open-air markets, the Vendor's Arcade and the Castries Market. For a dollar fare, water taxis provide transportation across the bay.

Several shops and restaurants can be found at the Rodney Bay Marina, near Gros Islet at the north end of the island. While browsing in boutiques offering beachwear, local crafts, electronics and island souvenirs, visitors can enjoy splendid views of the bay and of gleaming yachts docked in the marina.

Downtown Castries also provides shopping opportunities such as those at the Castries Market Arcade. William Peter Boulevard, lined with department stores, souvenir shops and banks, is the city's center of shopping activity. A multitude of street vendors make their home on the boulevard as well as on many other streets in the downtown area. Gablewoods is a small shopping complex just north of Castries off the Castries-Gros Islet Highway.

Eudovic Art Studio is about 15 minutes south of Castries off the road that snakes up the slopes of Morne Fortune. Woodcarvings fashioned from mahogany, teak and cedar are exhibited in a small gallery; works available for purchase at the adjacent shop include whisk-broom dolls in traditional madras costumes.

Also on Morne Fortune is Caribelle Batik, situated in Hewelton House on Old Victoria Road. Clothing enhanced by unique colors and patterns is available for purchase, and the dye-resistant method incorporated by the batik process is demonstrated by workers as they create freehand designs. On the terrace at the rear of the facility, shoppers can sip a refreshing drink and relish the view of Castries.

Another Morne Fortune landmark is Bagshaw Studios, which features clothing, place mats, tablecloths, wall hangings and other fabrics hand painted with cheery island motifs. Workers create brightly colored designs from a stenciled pattern during the silk-screening process, which can be observed in the print shop. Caribbean Perfumes, also on the Morne, creates exotic fragrances from herbs and tropical flowers found throughout St. Lucia.

Choiseul, a small coastal village in the southwest portion of the island, is the site of the Choiseul Art and Craft Center. Artists produce

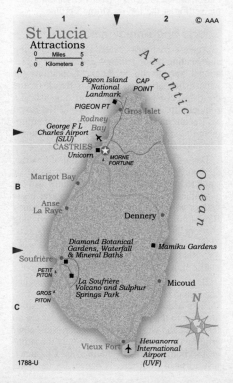

St Lucia Attractions

traditional Carib Indian crafts, including clay pottery and handwoven baskets constructed from straw and wicker.

In addition, St. Lucia's major resorts usually have shops on the premises. Shopping hours throughout the island are generally Mon.-Fri. 8:30-12:30 and 1:30-4:30, Sat. 8:30-12:30. Shopping malls are usually open until 6.

Food and Drink

Restaurants on St. Lucia are concentrated in Castries and Gros Islet. Many specialize in Creole cuisine, while others offer Italian, Chinese and Continental food. The national dish is "green fig," boiled green bananas usually served with saltfish. Other local specialties include lobster, snapper, dolphin, kingfish, swordfish, *callaloo* soup, breadfruit, plantain and pumpkin soufflé. Hearty pepperpot stew and spicy curries also are popular.

Fresh juices—including tamarind, guava, passion fruit, mango and grapefruit—accompany most meals. Bounty Rum is distilled near Roseau in the Cul-de-Sac Valley. The local Piton beer is often mixed with fruit juice for a lighter taste. Restaurants providing native fare include The Still, an establishment in Soufrière that was once a rum distillery, and the Green Parrot, which presents Creole delights in a scenic setting at the top of Morne Fortune.

Sports and Amusements

Aquatic pastimes—water skiing, snorkeling and boating among them—are popular recreational pursuits on St. Lucia. Conditions for windsurfing are good at Reduit Beach on the northwest coast and at Vieux Fort at the island's southern tip; The Rex St. Lucian and The Royal St. Lucian hotels on Reduit Beach rent equipment to the public. The Rex St. Lucian also offers parasailing.

Day or sunset cruises operate out of Castries Harbour; longer excursions to Martinique or south to St. Vincent and the Grenadines also are available. Sailing enthusiasts can charter boats with or without a crew at Marigot Bay, Rodney Bay Marina and Vigie Marina. Deep-sea fishing charters are provided by Mako Watersports, (758) 452-0412, and Captain Mike's, (758) 452-7044. The main catches are barracuda, blue marlin, kingfish, tuna, swordfish and wahoo.

Because of St. Lucia's volcanic origins, black sand is found on many beaches. All of St. Lucia's beaches, even those fronted by resorts, are open to the public. The most popular are on the north and west coasts; waves are very powerful on the Atlantic side, where only the strongest swimmers should venture. Anse Chastanet, just north of Soufrière, is named for the hotel

that graces its shores. The beach area, accented by a hilly panorama, is flanked by a restaurant and dive shop. Water taxis provide transportation to Anse Chastanet and the hideaway beach of Anse Mamim; be sure to reserve a ride for the return trip.

Farther north, the quaint fishing village of Anse la Raye boasts a picturesque beach with a wealth of graceful palms. South of Castries, Marigot Bay is a charming tropical cove peppered with colorful yachts. Visitors can just relax and sip a refreshing drink in the shade, or take a swim in the cove's tranquil waters where the original "Dr. Doolittle" was filmed. Yachts anchor offshore at the little beach at Soufrière, which is perfect for sunning and a leisurely lunch.

Although the beige-sand beach at La Toc Bay, south of Castries, is a great place to soak up the sun and enjoy the view, swimming is not advised due to occasional strong currents. Choc Bay, north of Castries in the vicinity of several major resorts, has calm waters ideal for swimming. Windsurfing is popular at Vieux Fort in the south and Cas-en-Bas in the north; beginners prefer the calmer waters of the resort area of Reduit Beach, where a variety of watersports rental equipment is available.

Sun worshipers will revel in the fine selection of secluded white-sand beaches at Pigeon Point; the area is connected to the island by a man-made causeway. Conditions are excellent for swimming, and a nearby restaurant provides refreshment. At the extreme southern tip of the island, Vieux Fort consists of miles of white-sand beaches against a backdrop of coconut palms. From this expanse of land, the contrast between the deep blue Caribbean waters and the murky hues of the Atlantic is apparent. The island also possesses several isolated stretches of beach accessible only by boat.

Scuba St. Lucia offers diving courses geared toward certification as well as daytime and evening diving expeditions; locations include the Anse Chastanet Hotel in Soufrière, (758) 459-7755, and the St. Lucian Hotel in Rodney Bay, (758) 452-8009. Also at Rodney Bay is Buddies Scuba, (758) 450-8406. Marigot Beach Club & Dive Resort, (758) 451-4974 or (758) 458-3323, offers PADI training facilities with dives at several sites around St Lucia.

Divers can experience a spectacular sampling of steep underwater drop-offs and unspoiled marine life. The waters off the west coast provide the best opportunities for diving, with most of the sites concentrated between Marigot Bay and Choiseul. *Lesleen M.*, a 165-foot vessel south of Marigot Bay that was deliberately sunk in the 1980s, has several compartments that can be explored. For the less adventurous, *Volga* is an easy 20-foot wreck dive near Castries.

Anse Chastanet Reef contains a colorful display of coral and a 150-foot-deep wall; this reef also is home to a large school of squid. Keyhole Pinnacles is another popular dive site just south of Anse Chastanet. Piton Wall, a site that features a vibrant assortment of coral and sponges, begins at about 30 feet and plunges to a depth of 1,300 feet.

Horseback riding, an excellent way to tour St. Lucia, can be arranged through Trim's National Riding Stables, (758) 450-8273, at Casen-Bas in Gros Islet; Country Saddles, (758) 450-5467 or (758) 450-0197, east of Castries in Babonneau; and the Fox Grove Inn, (758) 454-0281, on the east coast.

St. Lucia Golf and Country Club's 18-hole course, the island's only public golf course, is scenically situated on the northern end of the island at Cap Estate. Reservations are advised; phone (758) 450-8523. Sandals La Toc Resort, (758) 452-3081, ext. 6054, has nine holes for guests. Tennis courts are open to non-guests at the Rex St. Lucian and Windjammer Landing, as well as at the St. Lucia Racquet Club. The St. Lucia Golf and Country Club and the St. Lucia Yacht Club offer squash courts. Legacies of the island's English heritage are the popular spectator sports of soccer and cricket. Cricket matches can be observed on Sunday near the Choc Bay War Memorial in the northwestern portion of the island.

Two villages host Friday night street parties, known locally as "jump-ups." The most popular of these is held in Gros Islet, a small fishing town in northern St. Lucia. Locals and tourists alike enjoy the carnival atmosphere, where the pulsating beat of reggae and soca music permeates the air. Food vendors stationed on the sidewalk grill spicy Caribbean delights as merrymakers dance to the latest soca tunes. Many hotels arrange round-trip bus transportation to the Gros Islet "jump-up."

Seafood Friday, the second "jump-up," is held weekly in the fishing village of Anse la Raye on the west coast. Vendors sell a variety of prepared seafood, much like they do in Gros Islet. The popular event draws locals from all over the island for its fried mackerel, dorado and tuna, as well as lambi (conch), lobster, octopus and the national dish, green fig and saltfish.

Island nightlife centers on the hotels, where steel bands perform folk music, calypso and reggae. The island also plays host to a number of cultural events.

The St. Lucia Jazz Festival, now one of the world's top jazz events, draws international acts—and their fans—for two weeks in early May. Free lunchtime and evening concerts are held at Derek Walcott Square in Castries. Many hotels also host shows in conjunction with official jazz events. A day-long concert known as Jazz in the South, held at the Balembouche Estate south of Choiseul, is popular with locals.

Masquerade bands take to the streets during the annual Carnival celebration held the third Monday and Tuesday in July; a multitude of activities takes place in the days preceding these holidays, among the island's biggest events. The festivals of La Rose and La Marguerite occur on Aug. 30 and Oct. 17, and St. Lucia's Day on Dec. 13. October is Creole Heritage Month, featuring a series of cultural activities leading up to International Creole Day, or *Jounen Kweyol*, celebrated by Creole-speaking people around the world.

Sightseeing

Those exploring St. Lucia's interior will be rewarded with views of the island's lush greenery. Drivers will often encounter roosters and other farm animals during their travels and may have to stop and wait patiently while a stray cow or goat wanders slowly across the road.

It is not unusual to see natives diligently walking with a huge display of bananas perched precariously on their heads. Sightseers will be overwhelmed by the seemingly endless maze of banana plants, sometimes wrapped in peculiar plastic bags which serve as protection against insects. Colorful rum shops, often ramshackle in appearance, serve as neighborhood meeting spots where locals exchange the latest news.

Pigeon Island off the northwestern coast is named for Admiral Rodney's carrier pigeons, which were once housed at the ruined fort. Joined to the main island by a causeway, the area is now a national park which contains Arawak remnants, lookouts, gun batteries and barracks set amid tropical plant life. Union Agricultural Station, also in the northern portion of the island, is the headquarters of the Forestry Division. The station has a small zoo with animals native to St. Lucia, a medicinal herb garden and a nature trail; phone (758) 450-2078.

Just north of Castries, Rodney Bay Village is being developed as a yachting center and resort area. Marigot Bay, a popular yacht harbor with an inviting beach, is a half-hour coastal drive south of Castries. Nearby, at the colorful fishing village of Anse la Raye, fishermen continue to craft their vessels out of logs. Also south of Castries is Soufrière, which can be reached by a long but scenic drive or by boat, which also provides an oceangoing view of *Les Pitons.* Soufrière's volcano acts as a safety valve; it releases small amounts of pressure, forestalling a major volcanic eruption.

From Soufrière the road toward Fond St. Jacques penetrates the island's rain forest, which can be seen by organized tour. Hikers may spot the endangered St. Lucia parrot and are rewarded with views such as orchids and anthuriums growing wild, and agoutis and manicous playing. The rain forest also can be toured by arranging a guide through the Forestry and Lands Division; phone (758) 468-5649. Visitors are cautioned to dress appropriately, as the forest can be extremely muddy in areas.

Flora-loving travelers may tour the Diamond Botanical Gardens in Soufrière, Mamiku Gardens off the East Coast Highway, Tropica Gardens on the northern end of the island and La Sikwi Sugar Mill and Gardens at Anse La Raye.

Excursions also can be made to two of the island's working banana plantations: Marquis Estate in the northern part of the island and Errard Plantation in the Dennery area. The Marquis tour provides a trip down the unspoiled Marquis River. Practical footwear and clothing are advised, as grounds are often muddy. The rise and fall of St. Lucia's once-thriving sugar industry is the subject of an organized tour at Invergoil Estate; a restored sugar mill is on the grounds. Excursions to the Cap Moule à Chique Lighthouse also are available.

Most boat excursions sail from Castries to Soufrière and include bus tours of Sulphur Springs and Diamond Falls. Tours usually include lunch and time for snorkeling.

Dramatic views of St. Lucia's rugged terrain and lush rain forest are possible by helicopter. Flights glide past such sites as the inspiring twin Pitons and the 18th-century fortifications on Morne Fortune. Narrated tours are offered by St. Lucia Helicopters, (758) 453-6950, and SunLink Tours, (758) 456-9100.

Transportation

Non-stop flights arrive at Hewanorra International Airport from Miami aboard American

Fast Facts

POPULATION: 158,178.

AREA: 616 sq km (238 sq mi.).

CAPITAL: Castries.

HIGHEST POINT: 950 m (3,117 ft.), Mount Gimie.

LOWEST POINT: Sea level, Caribbean Sea.

TIME ZONE(S): Atlantic Standard.

LANGUAGE: English and Kwéyòl.

GOVERNMENT: Independent. Member of the British Commonwealth of Nations.

UNIT OF CURRENCY: Eastern Caribbean (E.C.) dollar. $1 U.S. = 2.7 E.C. dollars.

ELECTRICITY: 220 volts, 50 cycles AC.

MINIMUM AGE FOR DRIVERS: 21-25, depending on the rental car agency. Local license ($20) required, valid for 3 months; drive on left.

SEAT BELT/CHILD RESTRAINT LAWS: Seat belts are required for all passengers.

HELMETS FOR MOTORCYCLISTS: Required.

HOLIDAYS: Jan. 1; Carnival, Jan. 2; Independence Day, Feb. 22; Good Friday; Easter; Easter Monday; Labour Day, May (1st Mon.); Whit Monday, May or June (8th Mon. after Easter); Feast of Corpus Christi, May or June (9th Thurs. after Easter); Carnival, July; Emancipation Day, Aug. 1; Thanksgiving, Oct.; St. Lucia Day, Dec. 13; Christmas, Dec. 25; Boxing Day, Dec. 26.

TAXES: An 8 percent room tax and 10-15 percent service charge are added to most hotel bills. Departure tax $26 U.S. over age 12.

IMMIGRATION REQUIREMENTS: Passport and a return or onward ticket are required. No visa needed for stays up to 6 months. The U.S. Dept. of Homeland Security requires all U.S. citizens returning from the Caribbean to present a valid passport.

PHONING THE ISLANDS: To call St. Lucia from the U.S. or Canada, dial 1 + 758 + the 7-digit local number.

FURTHER INFORMATION FOR VISITORS:

St. Lucia Tourist Board
800 Second Ave., Suite 910
New York, NY 10017
(212) 867-2950
(800) 456-3984

St. Lucia Tourist Board, Castries
Pointe Seraphine
Castries, St. Lucia
(758) 452-4094

Airlines, Charlotte and Philadelphia via US Airways, New York aboard JetBlue and Atlanta via Delta Airlines. George F.L. Charles Airport, just outside of Castries, services on-island charters and interisland flights to and from Barbados, Trinidad, Antigua and several other islands; flights also arrive from Puerto Rico aboard American Eagle. Most resorts in the northern end of the island furnish complimentary transportation to guests flying into Hewanorra; the trip usually takes about an hour.

While there is no organized public bus system in St. Lucia, minibuses do run frequently between Castries and such points as Vigie, Gros Islet and Vieux Fort. There is no set schedule, and buses are often crowded, but they stop at designated sites about every half hour, and the longest trip costs no more than $5. Service between Castries and some outlying villages may be limited to once a day. Taxis are available but relatively expensive; establish the fare before your ride. The cab rate for sightseeing tours is usually around $25 per hour. Cars can be rented; a temporary license, which costs $20 and is valid for 3 months, is required. Hertz, with outlets at both airports and Rodney Bay Marina, offers discounts to AAA members; phone (758) 452-0679 or (800) 654-3080.

Water taxis provide one of the quickest routes between Castries and Soufrière. Expect to pay around $25 per person, depending on the boat or yacht. Service also is available north to Anse Chastanet and points along the coast. High-speed passenger ferries operated by Caribbean Express and L'Express des Iles connect St. Lucia with Dominica, Guadeloupe and Martinique. Channel Shuttles also travels between St. Lucia and Martinique.

Points of Interest

See map page 205.

CASTRIES (B-1) pop. 64,344

St. Lucia's capital, Castries (CASS-trees) is a bustling harbor town surrounded by rolling hills. Only a few historic landmarks stand; since its founding by the French in the 18th century, Castries has been destroyed by fire four times.

The town's colorful downtown market on Jeremie Street has been in existence since 1895; it is open Monday through Saturday 6-6. Saturday is the best time to visit the market, which is renowned for its lush tropical fruits, fresh vegetables, exotic spices, wicker furniture, wood carvings and handicrafts. Boutiques in town sell European perfumes, jewelry, clothes and fabric. Some shops sell handmade cane furniture and batik clothing, for which the island is noted.

Bordered by Peynier, Laborie and Micoud streets, the 1890s Cathedral of the Immaculate Conception reveals impressive murals by St. Lucian artist Dunstan St. Omer. Derek Walcott Square, next to the cathedral, is named for the island's Nobel prizewinning poet. The square contains a 400-year-old samaan tree and a monument to the St. Lucians who died in World Wars I and II. An antique map collection focusing on St. Lucia and the Caribbean Sea can be found at the Central Library on Bourbon Street.

Morne Fortune, or "hill of good fortune," is on the southern side of Castries. The 845-foot-high hill offers a striking view of Castries Harbour, Vigie Peninsula and the northern portion of the island. The road winds past Government House, a Victorian-style residence occupied by the governor-general. At the top of the Morne are the remains of Fort Charlotte, which changed hands between British and French forces during the 18th and 19th centuries. A monument marks the site of a battle fought in 1796. Many of the structures have been restored to house the University of the West Indies.

St. Lucia Tourist Board: Pointe Seraphine, Vide Boutielle, Castries, St. Lucia, W.I. **Phone:** (758) 452-4094.

THE BRIG *UNICORN* docks at Rodney Bay Marina. The working sailing ship is a 140-foot replica of a 19th-century brig. The impressive vessel, with its billowing white sails, appeared in the television series "Roots" and the film "Pirates of the Caribbean." Passengers depart for a land-based tour of Soufrière's volcano and waterfall at Rodney Bay. On the return boat trip, visitors can take a swim at Anse Cochon. Farther north, *Unicorn* sails through picturesque Marigot Bay. Sunset cruises also are offered.

Hours: Eight-hour trips depart Mon. and Fri. at 8:30. **Cost:** Fare $110; $50 (ages 2-12). Fare includes lunch, beverages and transfers. **Phone:** (758) 452-8644.

PIGEON ISLAND NATIONAL LANDMARK is 7 mi. (11 km) n. via a man-made causeway. The 44-acre (18-hectare) park preserves the crumbling barracks, magazines and ramparts of Fort Rodney, built in the late 1700s and named for British Adm. George Rodney. From the fort's excellent vantage points, Rodney monitored the French fleet in Martinique. A hike to the top of the fort will reward visitors with a contrasting view of the lush landscape of the Caribbean side of St. Lucia and the rugged terrain of the east coast.

The Pigeon Island Interpretive Centre is devoted to the historical significance of the park's stone-and-brick military ruins. Visitors can interact with the exhibits by listening to narratives through headphones and participating in other hands-on exercises. Hiking trails and two private beaches are on the premises. **Hours:** Daily 9-5. **Cost:** $5; $1 (ages 2-12). **Phone:** (758) 453-7656 or (758) 450-0603. ⊞

MICOUD (C-2) pop. 16,041

Baron de Micoud, former governor of St. Lucia, acquired this estate on the island's east coast in 1766. The Creole plantation came to be known as "Mamiku" after the baron's wife, Madame de Micoud. Later a British military post under Gen. John Moore, the estate house was destroyed in 1796 and stood abandoned for 200 years. Mamiku is now a working plantation again.

MAMIKU GARDENS is off the East Coast Hwy. A haven of tropical flowers, fruits and birds, the 15-acre (6-hectare) botanical garden includes a banana plantation, forest trails, a medicinal herb garden and an archeological dig. The Mystic Garden features wild and cultivated orchids. On the grounds is the site of a battle between British and French forces in 1796. At the gate house, visitors may borrow plant guidebooks, maps and walking sticks. **Time:** Allow 1 hour minimum. **Hours:** Daily 9-5. Guided tours are offered at 10 and 1. Closed Good Friday and Christmas. **Cost:** $6; $4 (ages 5-16). Guided tours $7.50. **Phone:** (758) 455-3729. ⊞

SOUFRIÈRE (C-1) pop. 7,656

Established by the French in 1746, the quaint west coast village of Soufrière (soo-free-AIR) is actually a low-lying volcanic crater. The town derived its name from the bubbling pits of sulphur at the nearby volcano and sulphur springs. Once the flourishing French capital, Soufrière is now a sleepy fishing village characterized by traces of French Colonial architecture and black sand beaches.

Soufrière is perhaps most renowned as the home of the towering twin Pitons, volcanic peaks that spring forth majestically from the ocean to a height of more than a half-mile (.8 km). Gros Piton (2,619 ft./798 m) can be climbed by experienced hikers; Petit Piton (2,438 ft./743 m) is not considered safe to climb. Anse des Pitons, a picturesque bay, separates the Pitons.

The town's marketplace, especially active on Saturday, can be recognized by its charming gingerbread trim. Situated near the waterfront on Bay Street, the market offers fresh fruits and vegetables, spices and island crafts. Le Toc Battery, built in 1888, overlooks Castries Harbor. The military installation includes cartridge and shell stores, underground tunnels and an original 18-ton cannon.

DIAMOND BOTANICAL GARDENS, WATERFALL AND MINERAL BATHS is about 1.5 mi. (2.4 km) s.e. on Diamond Rd. King Louis XVI of France had bathhouses built for his troops at this site just prior to the French Revolution. Visitors can bathe in the mineral-rich pools. The exotic tropical garden is filled with colorful flora and fauna. A path that winds through landscaped grounds leads to a magnificent waterfall; the unique coloration of the rocks is due to mineral deposits left by the streaming water. A nature trail takes visitors past a restored sugar mill and water wheel. **Hours:** Mon.-Sat. 10-5, Sun. and holidays 10-3. **Cost:** $5; bathing in outdoor pools $4; bathing in private baths $6. **Phone:** (758) 459-7565 or (758) 452-4759. ⊞

LA SOUFRIÈRE VOLCANO AND SULPHUR SPRINGS PARK is 2 mi. (3.2 km) s.e. The 25-acre (10-hectare) park contains a high-temperature geothermal system that last erupted in 1766. A road winds alongside hot pools that bubble and steam with sulphurous gases, and cars were once allowed to enter the crater—hence the park's nickname, "the world's only drive-in volcano." An interpretive center features information about the volcano that erupted and collapsed here some 40,000 years ago, forming a crater 8 miles (13 km) wide. Guided 30-minute tours are offered. **Hours:** Daily 9-5. **Cost:** (including guided tour) $8. **Phone:** (758) 459-7686 or (758) 459-5726.

MORNE COUBARIL ESTATE is 1 mi. (6 km) s. on West Coast Road. Costumed guides conduct 90-minute tours of this working cocoa plantation, the first major estate on the island. The 250-acre site includes the ruins of an 18th-century sugar mill, a renovated great house and a re-created Carib workers' village. **Hours:** Daily 10-4. **Cost:** $6. Reservations are recommended. **Phone:** (758) 459-7340. ⊞

DID YOU KNOW

Great Britain went to war with France 14 times to gain control of St. Lucia.

Philipsburg, St. Maarten / © Dennis MacDonald / age fotostock

St. Martin/St. Maarten

S hared between France and the Netherlands, St. Martin/St. Maarten is the smallest territory in the world governed by two sovereign states. Until a few years ago the island was a largely undiscovered hideaway; today modern tourist accommodations are plentiful. Philipsburg, the capital of St. Maarten, is on a sandbar between Great Bay and the Great Salt Pond. Marigot, the quintessentially French capital of St. Martin, is known for its fine shopping and as a haven for yachts, as are Oyster Pond and Great Bay in St. Maarten.

History

The Arawaks were the first to inhabit the island in pre-Columbian times. The Caribs, who eventually replaced their peace-loving predecessors, called the island *Soualiga,* meaning "land of salt," due to its numerous salt ponds. When Christopher Columbus discovered the island during his second voyage in 1493, he named it after St. Martin of Tours.

Spanish colonization didn't come until about 1640; until then they battled with the Dutch and French for the island's coveted anchorages and valuable salt ponds. In 1634 a Spanish battery went up at Pointe Blanche, southeast of present-day Philipsburg, and on the peninsula where the

ruins of Fort Amsterdam can now be found, and the island was defended successfully until the Spanish finally abandoned it in 1648. The island was then settled by French and Dutch prisoners and their countrymen from nearby St. Kitts and St. Eustatius.

The two remaining contestants decided to divide the island, and local legend holds that they defined the border through a walking contest. A Frenchman and a Dutchman started in the same spot, walked around the island in opposite directions and drew the boundary line where they met. In reality, though, the 1648 Treaty of Concordia granted France the greater portion of the island because its navy could offer greater protection. Though claims to the territory remained in some dispute for another 170 years, the settlers' idea of harmonious coexistence has lasted. In 1948 the islanders, who by this time considered themselves one people, erected a monument commemorating their 300 years as neighbors.

The salt ponds remained important economically through the 19th century. Sugar cane and tobacco, however, brought only brief prosperity; slaves were imported to work the plantations in the late 1700s, but following abolition in 1848 most of the plantations fell to ruin. A devastating hurricane followed by an earthquake in 1819 foreshadowed the island's economic decline. It was not until 1939 when the island declared itself a free port that the economy began to turn around. An airport was built in the late 1950s, and the tourism industry was born.

Since 1845, Dutch St. Maarten was part of the Netherlands Antilles; it became an autonomous country within the Kingdom of the Netherlands in 2010 when the Netherlands Antilles was dissolved. In 1946, French St. Martin became a dependency of the French overseas department of Guadeloupe, ultimately becoming a French Overseas Collectivity in 2007.

Shopping

The two capitals of Philipsburg and Marigot are a treasureland for shoppers. Duty-free luxury imports include Dutch and French silver, crystal, Delftware, cameras, French perfume, china, fashions, jewelry, Italian leather and electronics. Inexpensive souvenirs are available among such plentiful island wares as hand-drawn and embroidered linens, ceramics, woodcarvings, straw goods, original paintings, St. Martin music and books, cane furniture and *pareu,* a length of fabric that is twisted and turned depending on how it is worn.

The island's shopping mecca is Philipsburg's Frontstreet, where more than 100 shops line the mile-long (1.6 km-long) thoroughfare. Hidden behind Frontstreet are numerous shops along Backstreet and Cannegieter Street—all connected by *steegjes,* or alleyways. Island handicrafts are for sale along the pier and in nearby Wathey Square. Other shopping opportunities are available west of town in the Simpson Bay and Maho Bay areas as well as the Blue Mall in Cupecoy.

In Marigot the shops center on Port la Royale on the marina and across the street along rue Général de Gaulle and rue de la Liberté. Rue de la République, the road leading to the ferry pier,

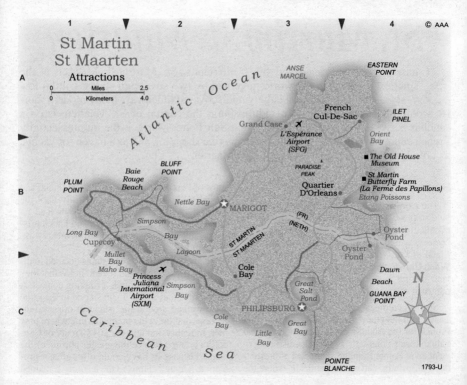

also has several fine shops. Boutiques in Marigot specialize in European designer fashions and tropical clothing. Wednesday and Saturday mornings Market Square on the harbor bustles with the activity of locals selling fresh food and handicrafts.

Shopping hours on the Dutch side are generally Mon.-Sat. 8-noon and 2-6, and on the French side Mon.-Sat. 9-12:30 and 3-7. Banking hours in Philipsburg are Mon.-Fri. 8:30-3. In Marigot banking hours are Mon.-Fri. 8:30-4.

Food and Drink

Few experienced travelers would disagree that St. Martin/St. Maarten offers some of the best dining in the Caribbean. The dual nationality of the island adds a dimension of culinary variety, and there are more than 375 restaurants to choose from. French and West Indian menus predominate, though Italian and American also are popular.

As expected of a former French colony, St. Martin is especially renowned for its cuisine, both in its classic version and its Creole cousin. Northeast of Marigot is the tiny village of Grand Case, considered the island's gourmet capital; some of the island's best French and West Indian restaurants can be found here. In Marigot there are several Gallic restaurants as well as those offering other cuisines. Marigot also features several French-style sidewalk cafes.

The restaurants in Philipsburg and elsewhere in St. Maarten offer greater variety. In addition to French, the finest in West Indian, Italian, American, Mexican, Thai, sushi, Argentinean, Indonesian and even Chinese cuisines can be found. Restaurants add a 10- to 15-percent service charge to the bill.

St. Maarten's own Guavaberry Island Folk Liqueur makes a good take-home item. Six bittersweet flavors are available and can be sampled at a tasting house at the east end of Frontstreet in Philipsburg. The island's tap water is purified; bottled water also is widely available.

Sports and Amusements

Most daytime activities on the island are water oriented and take place on white sand beaches and in secluded coves. The island is fringed with some three dozen beaches. Great Bay and Little Bay beaches are the most accessible from Philipsburg. To the west are Simpson Bay Beach, replete with water sports outlets; Mullet Bay Beach, with convenient facilities; and secluded Cupecoy Beach. Scenic Dawn Beach on the east coast also is good for snorkeling. Tiny but popular Maho Beach offers an unusually close view of jets landing at Princess Juliana International Airport.

On the French side west of Simpson Bay Lagoon are the unspoiled beaches of Baie Longue and intimate Baie Rouge. Mile-long (1.6 km) Grand Case Beach on the northwest shore has calm, clear waters. Orient Beach on the northeast shore is the island's most popular. Topless bathing is common on the French side; bathing *au naturel* is possible at Orient.

Such water sports concessions as scuba diving, snorkeling, windsurfing, parasailing, water skiing and jet skiing are concentrated around Grand Case Beach, Anse Marcel and Orient Beach in St. Martin and Great Bay, Little Bay and Simpson Bay in St. Maarten. Ocean Explorers at Simpson Bay offers the Sea Walk, in which participants don specially made bell helmets for a walk on the sea floor; swimming is not required.

The island's coral reefs teem with marine life, and its waters allow for visibility of up to 200 feet. Experienced divers have many interesting diving spots to choose from, including the Alleys, bound by cliffs and ledges; Green Key; Flat Island; and Hen and Chick, small islands with beautiful elkhorn coral reefs. Outside Great Bay is the 1801 wreck of the British warship HMS *Proselyte*.

Several firms offer scuba diving lessons lasting about 3 hours. Picnic sails and snorkeling trips to such nearby deserted islands as Tintamarre (Flat Island) and Pinel or Prickly Pear islands also are available. Arrangements for diving and snorkeling trips and lessons can be made through all the island's marinas and major hotels. Deep-sea fishing charters can be arranged at Bobby's Marina and Great Bay Marina in Philipsburg, Port la Royale in Marigot and Port Lonvilliers in Anse Marcel. Dolphin, kingfish, sailfish, blue marlin and wahoo are the main catches.

But those seeking land-based activities need not feel so out of the swim of things. Horseback riding is available at Crazy Acres Riding Center in Cole Bay, St. Maarten, and Caid & Isa in Anse Marcel, St. Martin; guided excursions are available. Tennis courts can be found at most hotels and resorts, and many are lighted. Le Privilège, a sports and spa complex in Anse Marcel, has four lighted courts as well as exercise equipment, squash courts and a pool. An 18-hole golf course is available on the Dutch side at Mullet Bay.

The island is definitely not lacking in nighttime diversions. Evening entertainment takes place primarily at 13 hotel casinos, all on the Dutch side, and the resorts, where carnival shows and Caribbean music are on tap. St.

Maarten's club scene centers on the Maho area, where Cheri's Cafe and Tantra attract youthful revelers.

The first weekend in March, the St. Maarten Heineken Regatta includes yacht races and soirees. A popular event is Carnival, held around Shrove Tuesday and Ash Wednesday in St. Martin and for two weeks beginning in late April in St. Maarten.

Sightseeing

The island is easily toured by car, but caution should be exercised—many side roads are rough and narrow, and wandering livestock are common, especially on the French side. Steep roads should not be attempted following rains. The border between the Dutch and French sides can be traversed freely. Road maps are available at the airport, car rental agencies located at the airport and the tourist offices in Philipsburg and Marigot.

On a peninsula between Great Bay and Little Bay is Fort Amsterdam, built by the Dutch in 1631 but occupied by the Spanish 1633-48. Peter Stuyvesant, eventual governor of America's New Netherlands colony, lost his right leg here while battling the Spanish in 1644. The unimproved site is accessible via the Divi Little Bay Beach Resort. Due north atop Fort Hill are the ruins of Fort William, which dates to 1801. A steep hike to the top rewards the adventurous with a spectacular panorama; driving is not recommended.

Another excellent vantage point is the roadside lookout a few miles west on Cole Bay Hill. Several neighboring islands can be seen, including on a clear day St. Kitts and Nevis—about 45 miles (72 km) southeast. Union Road, the route north from Cole Bay Hill, is the quickest way to Marigot; at the halfway point stands the Border Monument, erected in 1948 to commemorate the islanders' 300 years as neighbors. A longer but worthwhile route proceeds west past the airport and through the island's lowlands, circling Simpson Bay Lagoon. En route are some of the island's finest resorts.

From Philipsburg the especially scenic east coast of St. Maarten is accessible via Sucker Garden Road. The first turnoff leads to Guana Bay Point and the second to Dawn Beach and Oyster Pond. Both paved routes are steep and meandering, but the vistas to be enjoyed are worth the effort. Most noticeable among the numerous offshore landmarks is the French island of St. Barthélemy, about 14 miles (23 km) offshore. Picturesque Oyster Pond, reminiscent of the French Riviera, is a favorite anchorage of Caribbean boaters.

North of Oyster Pond is the rural area of Orléans, seemingly untouched by time and tourism, and the large Etang aux Poissons, or Fish Lake. Farther north along the coast are popular Orient Beach and several smaller, more secluded spots. Off the eastern shore of rural French Cul de Sac is uninhabited Pinel Island, a favorite day-sail destination where water sports and facilities are available.

From French Cul de Sac the road turns westward through Grand Case. This charming former fishing village has earned its reputation as the island's gourmet capital. The Creole-style structures along the main road house some of the island's best restaurants. And at numerous roadside food stands, or *lolos*, barbecued lobster, chicken and ribs and such Caribbean specialties as plantains and johnnycakes are sold.

The road south passes Paradise Peak; at 1,391 feet (424 m) it is the highest point on the island. On clear days the view encompasses both capitals and the island's patchwork of blue and green. The road to the inland village of Colombier, south of Paradise Peak, is lined on the north by lush tropical flora and on the south by rolling green hills decorated with long, meandering stone walls.

Glass-bottom boat trips, picnic sails and luncheon, sunset and moonlight yacht cruises are available out of the marinas at Philipsburg, Simpson Bay, Cole Bay, Marigot, Anse Marcel and Oyster Pond. Day trips to nearby Anguilla, St. Barthélemy, Saba, St. Eustatius and St. Kitts and Nevis also can be arranged.

Transportation

Princess Juliana International Airport has direct flights from San Juan, Atlanta, Boston, Fort

DID YOU KNOW

St. Martin/St. Maarten is the smallest territory in the world shared by two countries.

Lauderdale, Miami and New York. LIAT offers service from Antigua, St. Croix, St. Kitts and Tortola; and Windward Islands Airways (Winair) from Anguilla, Nevis, St. Barthélemy, St. Eustatius and Saba. Dutch Antilles Express provides daily service between Aruba, Bonaire, Curaçao and St. Maarten. Air Caraïbes has daily flights from Guadeloupe. In addition to Juliana Airport, Air Caraïbes flies into L'Espérance Airport, a small domestic airstrip

in Grand Case. Philipsburg is a port of call for many cruise ships. Smaller ships dock at Marigot.

Automobiles rented from companies with outlets at Princess Juliana International Airport cannot be picked up at the airport; courtesy shuttles transport visitors to the rental car lots. Automobiles rented from outlets not near the airport are delivered free to hotels, and many hotels have car rental offices on the premises.

Fast Facts

POPULATION: St. Martin: 29,888. St. Maarten: 38,876.

AREA: 96 sq km (37 sq mi.)

CAPITAL: St. Martin: Marigot. St. Maarten: Philipsburg.

HIGHEST POINT: 424 m (1,391 ft.), Pic du Paradis (Paradise Peak), St. Martin.

LOWEST POINT: Sea level, Caribbean Sea.

TIME ZONE(S): Atlantic Standard.

LANGUAGE: St. Martin: French and English. St. Maarten: Dutch, English and a local patois.

GOVERNMENT: St. Martin: French Overseas Collectivity. St. Maarten: Autonomous country within the Kingdom of the Netherlands.

UNIT OF CURRENCY: St. Martin: Euro Dollar. $1 U.S. = approx. .78 Euro. U.S. currency is widely accepted. St. Maarten: U.S. Dollar.

ELECTRICITY: St. Martin: 220 volts, 60 cycles AC. St. Maarten: 110 volts, 60 cycles AC.

MINIMUM AGE FOR DRIVERS: 25; maximum age 65-70. U.S. license valid; drive on right.

MINIMUM AGE FOR GAMBLING: 18.

SEAT BELT/CHILD RESTRAINT LAWS: Seat belts are required for all passengers. Child restraints required for under age 4; children under 12 must ride in the back seat.

HELMETS FOR MOTORCYCLISTS: Required.

HOLIDAYS: St. Martin: Jan. 1; Epiphany, Jan. 6; Mardi Gras; Good Friday; Easter; Easter Monday; Queen's Birthday, Apr. 30; Labour Day, May 1; Ascension Day, May (6th Thurs. after Easter); Whit Monday, May or June (8th Mon. after Easter); Bastille Day, July 14; Schoelcher Day, July 21; Feast of the Assumption, Aug. 15; All Saints Day, Nov. 1; Concordia Day/Armistice Day, Nov. 11; Christmas, Dec. 25; Boxing Day, Dec. 26. **St. Maarten:**

Jan. 1; Good Friday; Easter; Easter Monday; Queen's Birthday, Apr. 30; Labour Day, May 1; Day after Carnival, early May; Antillean Day, Oct. 21; St. Maarten's Day, Nov. 11; Christmas, Dec. 25; Boxing Day, Dec. 26.

TAXES: St. Martin: A 5 percent room tax and 10-15 percent service charge are added to most hotel bills. Departure tax $20 U.S.; interisland tax $5 U.S. St. Maarten: A 5-8 percent room tax and 10-15 percent service charge are added to most hotel bills. Departure tax $30 U.S., ages 2 and up; interisland tax $10 U.S.

IMMIGRATION REQUIREMENTS: St. Martin: A valid passport and return or onward ticket are required for U.S. citizens entering the French West Indies. No visa needed for stays up to 3 months. St. Maarten: Passport and return or onward ticket are required. No visa needed for stays up to 2 weeks. The U.S. Dept. of Homeland Security requires all U.S. citizens returning from the Caribbean to present a valid passport.

PHONING THE ISLANDS: St. Martin: From the U.S. or Canada, dial 011 + 590 + 590 + the 6-digit local number. St. Maarten: Dial 011 + 599 + the 7-digit local number.

FURTHER INFORMATION FOR VISITORS:

St. Martin/St. Maarten Tourist Office
675 Third Ave., Suites 1806-7
New York, NY 10017
(646) 227-9440 (St. Martin)
(800) 786-2278 (St. Maarten)
(212) 953-2084 (St. Maarten)

St. Martin Tourist Office
Route de Sandy Ground
Marigot, St. Martin 97150
(590) 87-57-21

St. Maarten Tourist Bureau
W.G. Buncamper Rd. #33
Philipsburg, St. Maarten
(599) 542-2337

Most cars have automatic transmissions and air conditioning. Motor scooters also are available; caution is advised due to rough roads and steep hills. Major credit cards are accepted.

Taxis are abundant on both the Dutch and French sides. Taxi rates are regulated, but it is always wise to agree on the fare in advance. Rates increase by 25 percent from 10 p.m. to midnight and by 50 percent from midnight to 6 a.m. Each additional passenger over two is an extra $5. The rates from Princess Juliana Airport are posted at the taxi stand outside. Tipping is customary. The two capitals of Philipsburg and Marigot are connected by inexpensive public buses that operate from 6 a.m. to 10 p.m.

The islands of Anguilla, St. Barthélemy, Saba and St. Eustatius are accessible by any one of several boats operating out of Philipsburg in St. Maarten. High-speed ferries can make the trip in 40 minutes. Several ferries to St. Barthélemy and Anguilla operate out of Marigot in St. Martin.

Points of Interest

See map page 212.

St. Maarten

Covering 16 square miles (41 sq km) on the southern half of the island, the Dutch dependency of St. Maarten is characterized by rolling hills and white sand beaches. Arawak Indians harvested salt from the many lagoons and salt lakes in the area.

CUPECOY (B-1)

The last Dutch beach on the western end of the island, picturesque Cupecoy Beach was once a series of coves running along the sandstone cliffs and caves. Time and the sea have washed away most of the sand, and a single cove remains. The beach is clothing-optional and was once fairly secluded; condo development has changed the landscape in recent years.

GAMBLING ESTABLISHMENTS
• **Atlantis World Casino** is at 106 Rhine Rd. **Hours:** Daily 24 hours. **Phone:** (599) 545-4601.

MAHO BAY (C-1)

The island's largest resort area, Mayo Bay is famous for a tiny stretch of sand at the end of the airport runway. Jumbo jets roar overhead at Maho Beach, and signs warn about the danger of engine blasts. Even so, many thrillseekers come here for the chance to be blown off their feet by incoming aircraft.

GAMBLING ESTABLISHMENTS
• **Casino Royale at Sonesta Maho Beach Resort** is at 1 Rhine Rd. **Hours:** Daily 1 p.m.-4 a.m. **Phone:** (599) 545-2115 or (800) 766-3782.

PHILIPSBURG (C-3)

Philipsburg is the busy Dutch capital. Its three main thoroughfares are usually crammed with shoppers browsing through stores stocked with duty-free luxuries. Among the jumble of shops, restaurants and modern buildings are remnants of an earlier Philipsburg. One of the most notable of the town's historic buildings is the 18th-century Philipsburg Courthouse. The courthouse borders Wathey Square, the town center of activity. Fort Amsterdam, built in 1631 on a peninsula between Great Bay and Little Bay, was the first Dutch military outpost in the Caribbean.

St. Maarten Tourist Bureau: W.G. Buncamper Rd. #33, Philipsburg, St. Maarten. **Phone:** (599) 542-2337.

LORD SHEFFIELD TALL SHIP ADVENTURES departs from Dock Maarten adjacent to Great Bay Marina. Trips aboard this square-rigged brigantine include anchors at a swimming beach, snorkeling and jumping from the bowsprit. Barbecue ribs and rum punch are served aboard the pirate ship. **Time:** Allow 3 hours minimum. **Hours:** Three-hour cruise daily at 9 and 1 when cruise ships are in port. Four-and-a-half-hour cruise Mon.-Fri. at 11, Sun. at 2. Three-hour sunset cocktail cruises are offered Tues.-Fri. at 4:30. **Cost:** Fare $55-$80; $44-$62 (ages 3-12). Reservations are recommended. **Phone:** (599) 552-0875. ⊞

ST. MAARTEN NATIONAL HERITAGE FOUNDATION & MUSEUM is at 7 Frontstreet. Revolving exhibits depict the island's history and culture. Among the items displayed are pre-Columbian artifacts; old maps and photos; and articles from the island's forts and plantations, including an 18th-century Chinese porcelain dinner service. Exhibits related to nature, environment and geology also are featured. A reference library is on the premises. **Hours:** Mon.-Fri. 10-4. **Cost:** Donations. **Phone:** (599) 542-4917.

ST. MAARTEN PARK is on the n. side of Great Salt Pond on Arch Rd. More than 80 species at this tropical garden zoo include parrots, monkeys, ocelots, golden lion tamarins and capybaras. On the grounds are a walk-through aviary, a reptile house, a bat cave exhibit and a petting zoo. **Time:** Allow 1 hour minimum. **Hours:** Daily 9-5. **Cost:** $10; $5 (ages 3-11). **Phone:** (599) 543-2030. [¶]

ST. MAARTEN'S 12 METRE CHALLENGE departs from Bobby's Marina downtown at Front St. and Yrausquin Blvd. Participants experience the thrill of riding aboard multi-million-dollar America's Cup race boats. Crew members can grind, winch, trim sails or sit back and relax aboard Dennis Conner's *Stars & Stripes, Canada II* or *True North*. Prior sailing experience is not necessary. **Time:** Allow 3 hours minimum. **Hours:** Departures daily at 8:30, 10, 11:45 and 1:30. Closed Christmas. Phone ahead to confirm schedule. **Cost:** Fare $80. Not recommended for children under 12. **Phone:** (599) 542-0045 or (599) 542-0046.

SEAWORLD EXPLORER **CORAL REEF TOUR** departs from the Atlantis dock on Grand Case Blvd. This 51-foot-long semi-submarine cruises to Creole Rock for excellent views above deck of French Grand Case and British Anguilla, and below deck of marine life and coral formations. **Hours:** Morning and afternoon trips depart daily, based upon cruise ship demand. Closed major holidays. **Cost:** Fare $39; $25 (ages 2-12). Reservations are required. **Phone:** (599) 542-4078.

GAMBLING ESTABLISHMENTS

- **Casino Rouge et Noir** is at 66 Front St. **Hours:** Daily 9 a.m.-4 a.m. **Phone:** (599) 542-3222.

- **Coliseum Casino** is at 74 Front St. **Hours:** Daily 10 a.m.-2 a.m. **Phone:** (599) 543-2101.

- **Diamond Casino** is in the StreetKaanal Bldg. at 1 Front St. **Hours:** Thurs.-Mon. 11 a.m.-3 a.m., Tues.-Wed. 9 a.m.-3 a.m. **Phone:** (599) 543-2583.

- **Jump Up Casino** is at the end of Front Street at 1 Emmaplein. **Hours:** Daily 10 a.m.-4 a.m. **Phone:** (599) 542-0862.

- **Princess Casino at Port de Plaisance Resort** is at 155 Union Rd. **Hours:** Daily 2 p.m.-4 a.m. **Phone:** (599) 544-4311 or (866) 786-2278.

- **Tropicana Casino** is at Cole Bay at 34 Welfare Rd. **Hours:** Daily 2 p.m.-4 a.m. **Phone:** (599) 544-5654.

SIMPSON BAY (C-2)

One of the largest landlocked bodies of water in the Caribbean, Simpson Bay Lagoon sprawls across the western end of the island. The saltwater bay is popular for yachting and watersports, including jet-skiing, waterskiing and parasailing. Rental equipment is available at several outlets along Simpson Bay Beach.

GAMBLING ESTABLISHMENTS

- **Hollywood Casino** is at the Pelican Resort at 37 Billy Folly Rd. **Phone:** (599) 544-4463.

St. Martin

Occupying 21 square miles (54 sq km) on the northern half of the island, the French dependency of St. Martin is known for its secluded beaches and resort areas.

ANSE MARCEL (A-3)

On the northern tip of the island, the pleasant family beach at Anse Marcel is prized for its white sands, shallow waters and shady coves. The resort Le Meridien L'Habitation was the site of a summit meeting between United States President George Bush and French President François Mitterand in 1989.

PLANTATION MONT VERNON is just e. of jct. Anse Marcel Rd. and Main Rd., following signs. Visitors take a walking tour of this 1786 plantation while listening to a personal audio narration of the history of St. Martin and the cultivation of coffee, cotton, indigo and sugar cane. Free samples are available at coffee and rum distillery exhibits. **Time:**

Allow 1 hour minimum. **Hours:** Daily 9-5. **Cost:** $16; $7 (ages 3-12). **Phone:** (590) 29-50-62.

GRAND CASE (A-3)

Considered the island's gourmet capital, Grand Case is home to some of the island's best French and West Indian restaurants. The tiny village is also known for the elaborate gingerbread trim on its pastel-colored houses.

LOTERIE FARM is on the road to Pic Paradis, following signs. On the site of a former sugar plantation, the nature reserve features interesting rock formations and caves, thriving vegetation and the ruins of a historic mill and distillery. Such species as the yellow-, black- and white-colored sugarbird can be spotted in the island's sole tropical humid forest. Marked trails that vary in degree of difficulty are available for hikers and nature enthusiasts. Zipline activities also are available.

Comfortable walking shoes are recommended. **Tours:** Guided tours are available. **Time:** Allow 1 hour minimum. **Hours:** Tues.-Sun. 9-4:30. **Cost:** $7. **Phone:** (590) 87-86-16 from the U.S. or (599) 57-28-55. [Ⅱ]

MARIGOT (B-3) pop. 29,078

The quaint harbor town of Marigot (MAR-ee-go) is thoroughly French. The traditional architecture of wrought-iron balconies and fretwork trim is visible along its busy streets and residential roads, and a stroll among the shops and sidewalk cafes of Port la Royale transports visitors to the French Riviera. The restored ruins of 18th-century Fort St. Louis overlook Marigot's harbor, providing an excellent view; the fort can be reached on foot via the steps behind the Sous-Préfecture off rue de L'Hôpital.

Adding to the quaintness, a tree-lined promenade borders the water's edge and a series of pleasure boat slips. At the far end of the boulevard is the town marketplace.

St. Martin Tourist Office: Route de Sandy Ground, Marigot, St. Martin, Guadeloupe. **Phone:** (590) 87-57-21.

ST. MARTIN MUSEUM is at Sandy Ground just outside the city center on the waterfront. "On the Trail of the Arawaks" is a permanent collection of pre-Columbian pottery and artifacts depicting the cultures of the island's first inhabitants. Early island photographs also are displayed. **Hours:** Mon.-Sat. 9-1 and 3-5. **Cost:** $6; $4 (ages 0-11). **Phone:** (590) 29-22-84 or (590) 29-48-36.

QUARTIER D'ORLEANS (B-3)

Some of the original 17th-century structures of the island's first French settlement are preserved at Quartier d'Orleans, or the French Quarter. This quaint village is a mile south of clothing-optional Orient Beach, one of the island's most popular stretches of sand.

THE OLD HOUSE MUSEUM is on the main road between Orient Beach and Quartier d'Orleans. Preserved as a historic site, this Creole house contains artifacts from the 1800s to the present. Farm implements from the sugar plantation's history also are displayed. A separate display depicts the history of rum making in the area. **Tours:** Guided tours are available. **Time:** Allow 30 minutes minimum. **Hours:** Tues.-Fri. and Sun. 10-4. **Cost:** $5.50; free (ages 0-10). **Phone:** (590) 87-32-67.

ST. MARTIN BUTTERFLY FARM (LA FERME DES PAPILLONS) is on Galion Beach Rd. More than 40 butterfly species from around the world are housed in a tropical garden, where tour guides provide information about butterfly names, characteristics and life cycles. Brightly colored clothing and perfume will attract these colorful insects. Visitors can learn how to gently handle the butterflies as well as caterpillars. **Time:** Allow 30 minutes minimum. **Hours:** Daily 9-3:30. **Cost:** (good for 7 days) $14; $7 (ages 4-12); free (ages 0-4). **Phone:** (590) 87-31-21.

Port Elizabeth, Bequia / © Paul Thompson / Danita Delimont Stock Photography

St. Vincent and The Grenadines

The barefoot life of a traditional West Indian island is readily available on St. Vincent, 18 miles (29 km) long and 11 miles (18 km) wide. Relatively unknown to tourists until recently, St. Vincent is one of the most picturesque of the Windwards, with quaint fishing villages, coconut and arrowroot plantations and palm-fringed coves of black volcanic sand. St. Vincent and its string of Grenadine islands, which reach south to Grenada, offer some of the best sailing, swimming, diving and snorkeling in the Caribbean. Complementing these pleasures are the small comfortable inns that provide much of the guest accommodations on St. Vincent and its sun-swept satellite islands, which include Bequia (beck-way), Mayreau (my-row), Mustique (mus-teek), Canouan (can-no-wan), Petit St. Vincent, Palm, Union and Young islands.

History

Generations before Christopher Columbus sighted the area in 1498, fierce Carib Indians from the South American mainland had annihilated St. Vincent's population of gentle Arawaks. St. Vincent was left relatively undisturbed until the 18th century when, despite the hostility of the Caribs, the French, Dutch and British began to vie for settlement. Near the close of the 18th century the Caribs were deported to the Bay of Honduras. By the Treaty of Paris in 1763, France ceded the island to Britain but recaptured it in 1779. Britain gained final possession in 1783 by the Treaty of Versailles.

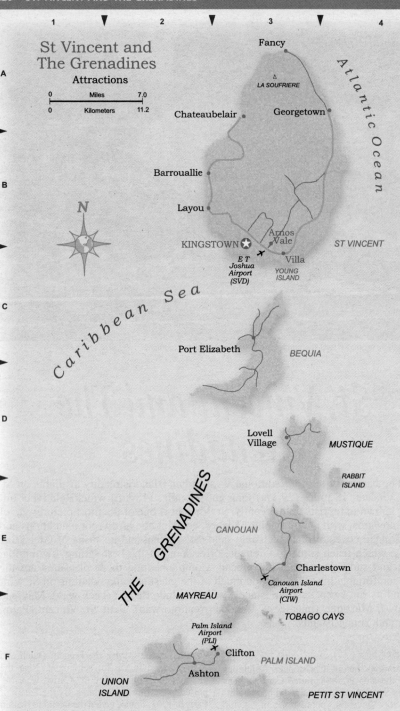

St Vincent and
The Grenadines
Attractions

Miles 0 — 7.0
Kilometers 0 — 11.2

N

Fancy

△ LA SOUFRIERE

Chateaubelair

Georgetown

Atlantic Ocean

Barrouallie

Layou

Arnos Vale

KINGSTOWN

ST VINCENT

E T Joshua Airport (SVD)

Villa

YOUNG ISLAND

Caribbean Sea

Port Elizabeth

BEQUIA

Lovell Village

MUSTIQUE

RABBIT ISLAND

THE GRENADINES

CANOUAN

Charlestown

Canouan Island Airport (CIW)

MAYREAU

TOBAGO CAYS

Palm Island Airport (PLI)

Clifton

PALM ISLAND

Ashton

UNION ISLAND

PETIT ST VINCENT

1789-U

© AAA

Independence from Britain was finally granted in 1979.

That same year La Soufrière, the 4,048-foot volcano in the north, erupted, spewing ash that filtered all the way to Barbados, 100 miles (160 km) east. While necessitating the evacuation of Carib descendants living on the volcano's slopes, the eruption posed no threat to the capital of Kingstown, 30 miles (48 km) south.

Sharing the characteristics of the other Windward Islands, St. Vincent relies on tourism and agriculture as its main sources of income. Cut flowers have become St. Vincent's newest export. Green mountains and productive valleys cover the island. The rural Mesopotamia Valley, also called Marriaqua Valley, is the focus of much agricultural activity. Besides breadfruit, introduced from Tahiti by Captain Bligh of "Mutiny on the Bounty" fame, bananas, coconuts and arrowroot constitute the principal crops.

Shopping

Kingstown's main street has several interesting shops, a few selling clothing with island motifs. Sea island cotton with screened designs is available at the cruise ship terminal. Local artisans offer a large variety of macramé items, jewelry and straw handicrafts, some made on the spot. A cluster of shops is tucked in the courtyard of the Cobblestone Inn, inland from the main waterfront road. The dockside Market Square comes alive on Friday and Saturday mornings when vendors and anglers gather to sell their goods; the weekly loading of the banana boats enhances this vibrant scene.

Shopping hours are generally Mon.-Fri. 8-noon and 1-4, Sat. 8-noon, though some stores are open Mon.-Fri. 8-4. Banking hours are Mon.-Thurs. 8-2, Fri. 8-5.

Food and Drink

Traditional West Indian cuisine—local fish, island produce and thick soups—as well as international flavors are available at hotels. Wilkie's, in the Grand View Beach Hotel at Villa Point, 10 minutes southeast of Kingstown, offers a typical island meal. Other hotel restaurants worth investigating are in the Cobblestone Inn, Mariners Hotel and Grenadine House. Hotel kitchens often use the bountiful produce from the native market at the far end of the main street.

Sports and Amusements

The beaches at Villa Bay, Indian Bay and in the Grenadines are excellent for swimming, sunning, snorkeling and scuba diving. Sailing, boating, fishing and diving equipment can be rented for either half- or full-days. Cumberland Bay on the leeward coast is a secluded beach, ideal for snorkeling and diving. Just minutes from Port Elizabeth in Bequia, Princess Margaret is a tree-lined stretch of soft sand, named after the princess who enjoyed a dip there in 1958. Casuarina is a white-sand beach that runs the entire length of Palm Island. Boating enthusiasts consider Saltwhistle Bay in Mayreau to be one of the Grenadines' most stunning; sailors favor this bay due to its calm waters. Macaroni Bay, on Mustique's east coast, is one of the island's most popular beaches and includes a covered picnic area. The main dive centers are on St. Vincent, Bequia, Mustique, Canouan and Union Island.

Hotels offer evening entertainment—local steel or string bands play live music. Grenadine House, Sunset Shores Beach Hotel, Grand View Beach Hotel and Young Island Resort are some of the properties that host performances, usually on Friday and Saturday.

Sightseeing

A hike to La Soufrière involves a full day and requires good physical conditioning. The trip to the still-active volcano begins by car along the coast and crosses the Yurumein/Taiwan bridge, then proceeds on foot through the Bamboo Forest and straight up the 4,048-foot summit for an unparalleled view. The Vermont Nature Trail and Trinity Falls also provide scenic outlooks. Dark View Falls, two majestic falls set in the forest-clad Richmond Valley on the island's northwest side, can be reached via a natural bamboo bridge spanning across a tumbling river. Elevations rise up to 229 feet.

Day trips also can be made on island schooners and motorized mailboats to Bequia and other islands of the Grenadines. Bequia, Union Island and Canouan are accessible by plane. Port Elizabeth's harbor area has colorful shops along the waterfront as well as lodgings, restaurants and water sports facilities. The production of hand-carved wooden sailboats is a prosperous industry on Bequia.

If you have less time you can take a half-day drive through the Mesopotamia Valley, which includes hillsides covered with banana and arrowroot crops and the craggy windward shore. On the leeward shore the quaint fishing village of Layou boasts the Carib Stones, huge sacrificial altars with carved heads and petroglyphs from pre-Columbian, Arawak and Carib

Indians. Farther north lies the traditional fishing village of Barrouallie, which has remained unchanged for centuries. Close to Kingstown, Dorsetshire Hill and Mount Saint Andrew offer pleasant climbs.

Transportation

Air connections to St. Vincent's E.T. Joshua Airport are via Barbados, Grenada, Martinique, St. Lucia, Puerto Rico, and Trinidad. Public buses operate in Kingstown and throughout St. Vincent; rental cars are available with or without driver. Of the 600 miles (960 km) of roads on the island, about 360 miles (580 km) are paved. The other 31 islands that constitute the Grenadines are accessible via small boats or planes. LIAT operates three flights per week from Grenada to Canouan; flights also are available from St. Vincent via Grenadine Airways. Several resorts offer air limousine service

from Barbados, Grenada, Martinique and St. Lucia. Bequia airport is 4 miles (6 km) south of Port Elizabeth and can accommodate small capacity propeller aircraft.

Two large ferries, the MV *Barracuda* and the MV *Gem Star*, make two and three weekly runs to Union Island, with stops in Canouan and Mayreau; phone (784) 456-5073 and (784) 457-1531, respectively. The *Bequia Express* and *Admiralty Transport* make daily trips between St. Vincent and Bequia; phone (784) 458-3472 and (784) 458-3348, respectively.

These islands possess a natural, unspoiled beauty that is fading from some of the more commercially developed Caribbean islands. A few of the Grenadines are owned exclusively by one resort or hotel; reservations for these secluded accommodations are often required a year in advance.

Fast Facts

POPULATION: 110,000.

AREA: 344 sq km (133 sq mi.).

CAPITAL: Kingstown.

HIGHEST POINT: 1,234 m (4,048 ft.), La Soufrière.

LOWEST POINT: Sea level, Caribbean Sea.

TIME ZONE(S): Atlantic Standard.

LANGUAGE: English and French patois.

GOVERNMENT: Independent (parliamentary democracy). Member of the British Commonwealth of Nations.

UNIT OF CURRENCY: Eastern Caribbean (E.C.) dollar. $1 U.S. = 2.7 E.C. dollars.

ELECTRICITY: 220 volts, 50 cycles AC (except for Petit St. Vincent and Palm Island, which have 110 volts, 60 cycles).

MINIMUM AGE FOR DRIVERS: 21-25, depending on the rental car agency. A valid U.S. or international driver's license must be presented to obtain a temporary local license ($37). Drive on left.

MINIMUM AGE FOR GAMBLING: 18.

HOLIDAYS: Jan. 1; National Heroes Day, Mar. 14; Good Friday; Easter Monday; Labour Day, May (1st Mon.); Whit Monday, May or June (8th Mon. after Easter); Carnival, July (2nd Mon. and Tues.); August Monday, Aug. (1st

Mon.); Independence Day, Oct. 27 (or Mon., Oct. 28, if holiday falls on a Sun.); Christmas, Dec. 25; Boxing Day, Dec. 26.

TAXES: A 10 percent service tax, 10 percent VAT on hotel room, and 15 percent tax on food and other purchased items; service and VAT are often combined at hotels, with a total of 10 percent charged for the two. Departure tax $15 U.S.

IMMIGRATION REQUIREMENTS: Passport and return or onward ticket are required. No visa needed for stays up to 6 months for U.S. citizens. The U.S. Dept. of Homeland Security requires all U.S. citizens returning from the Caribbean to present a valid passport.

PHONING THE ISLANDS: To call St. Vincent and the Grenadines from the U.S. or Canada, dial 1 + 784 + the 7-digit local number.

FURTHER INFORMATION FOR VISITORS:

St. Vincent and The Grenadines Tourism Office, United States
801 Second Ave., 1st Floor
New York, NY 10017
(212) 687-4981
(800) 729-1726

St. Vincent and The Grenadines Tourism Authority
NIS Building, Floor 2
Kingstown, St. Vincent
St. Vincent and The Grenadines
(784) 456-6222

Points of Interest

See map page 220.

CANOUAN (E-3)

Named "turtle island" by the Carib Indians, this once deserted sugar plantation and whaling outpost is now home to the 300-acre Raffles Resort and luxury villas and estate properties developed by Donald Trump. The 18-hole course at the Trump International Golf Club was designed by Jim Fazio; phone (784) 458-8000. An extensive coral reef offers excellent snorkeling and scuba diving.

GAMBLING ESTABLISHMENTS
- **Casino at Trump Club Privée** is at the Raffles Resort. **Phone:** (784) 458-8000.

KINGSTOWN (B-2) pop. 13,212

The capital city of Kingstown is an enjoyable place to explore, with its mixture of English and French architectural styles, exemplified by 19th-century houses and such historic buildings as Wesleyan Hall and St. George's Anglican Cathedral.

St. Mary's Catholic Cathedral is an architectural wonder incorporating a variety of styles; it has Roman arches, Gothic spires and a myriad of balconies, turrets, battlements and courtyards.

St. Vincent and The Grenadines Tourism Authority: NIS Building, Floor 2, Kingstown, St. Vincent. **Phone:** (784) 456-6222.

FORT CHARLOTTE is on Berkshire Hill west of town. Completed by the British in 1806, the fortification perches 600 feet (183 m) above the city. The fort ruins afford a commanding view of the harbor and the Grenadines. Mounted guns face inland, not out to sea, evidence of the struggle for possession among the British, French and Carib Indians. Paintings that trace the island's history are in the old officers' quarters, now a museum. **Hours:** Daily 6 a.m.-6 p.m. **Cost:** Free. **Phone:** (784) 456-1165.

ST. VINCENT BOTANICAL GARDENS is just s. of Fort Charlotte. Founded in 1762, the 20-acre (8-hectare) gardens are considered the oldest in the Western Hemisphere. Lush with tropical palms, lilies, hibiscus and bougainvillea, the gardens are home to Captain Bligh's breadfruit tree, grown from the original plant, along with such unusual trees as the flowering cannonball and the sealing wax palm. Also at the gardens is an aviary housing the rare St. Vincent parrot, and an archeology museum.

Time: Allow 30 minutes minimum. **Hours:** Daily 8-4. **Cost:** The gardens are free, and plants are labeled in English for self-guiding tours. Local guides offer their services for $4-$6 per hour; be sure to negotiate a rate in advance. **Phone:** (784) 457-1003.

GAMBLING ESTABLISHMENTS
- **Emerald Valley Resort & Casino** is 7 mi. (11 km) outside of Kingstown in Penniston Valley. **Hours:** Daily 9 p.m.-3 a.m. **Phone:** (784) 430-9296.

Royal Botanic Gardens, Queen's Park Savannah, Port of Spain, Trinidad / © Paul Thompson Images / Alamy

Trinidad and Tobago

T rinidad is the southernmost island of the West Indies. It was once an extension of the northern coast of Venezuela, but the lowlands were washed away by the Orinoco River centuries ago; at the closest point only 7 miles (11 km) of sea separate Trinidad and Venezuela. Port of Spain, the capital, is one of the Caribbean's most cosmopolitan cities. People from Africa, China, Britain, India, France, Holland, Portugal, Spain and many other countries make their home here along with descendants of the Arawak and Carib Indians. The architecture is as varied, with ornate mansions, Spanish patios and tiled roofs, French grillwork, cathedrals, mosques and temples.

Christopher Columbus is said to have encountered the island of Trinidad on July 31, 1498, naming it after the Holy Trinity. Many Trinidadians leave the hustle and bustle of their island to vacation on subdued Tobago, some 20 miles (32 km) away. Columbus reported seeing Tobago, which he named Bella Forma, but did not land on the island. Tobago's present name may be derived from the Spanish word for tobacco, but exactly when and how the island was named is unknown. It is believed that Tobago was the inspiration for the shipwreck tales of the Swiss Family Robinson and Robinson Crusoe. Today's visitors will find wide, white beaches and small contemporary hotels.

History

Trinidad was originally inhabited by several Amerindian tribes, including the Caribs, who called the island *Iere,* meaning "land of the hummingbird." However, Christopher Columbus was inspired by three mountain peaks when he sighted land in 1498, and he called the island La Trinidad, a confirmation of his vow to name his next discovery after the Holy Trinity. He claimed it for Spain, but a permanent settlement, San Jose de Oruña, was not established until 1577 by Don José de Oruña. Now known as St. Joseph, the town was named as the capital in 1592 upon the arrival of the Spanish governor to Trinidad and Guyana, Don Antonio de Berrio y Oruña,

The 1600s saw raids by the Dutch and French, but the Spanish retained control. Crop failures kept the island poor until 1783, when a Spanish proclamation offered land grants to immigrants willing to develop agriculture and commerce. In 1797, attracted by the resulting prosperity, the British sent an expedition that gained control of the island. Trinidad was formally ceded to Great Britain by the Treaty of Amiens in 1802.

Inhabited by Caribs when first sighted by Columbus, Tobago was subsequently coveted

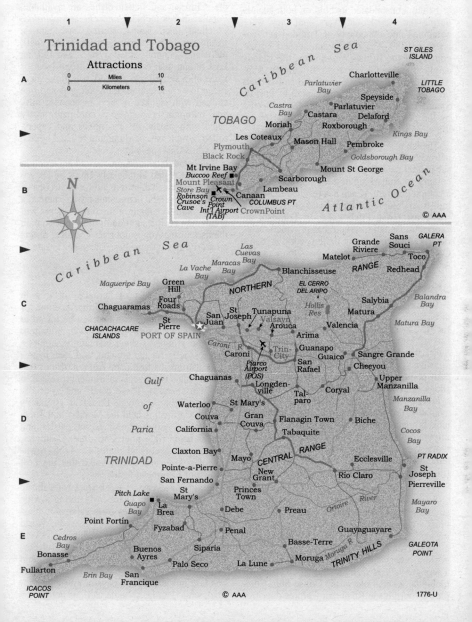

Trinidad and Tobago

Attractions

as a strategic position by every major power operating in the Caribbean. As a result the island changed hands more than any other in the West Indies; during the 17th and 18th centuries it was taken and retaken by France, Britain, Holland and Spain. In accordance with an agreement in 1749, the island was left unmolested for 13 years, but the struggle began anew when the reprieve ran out. Tobago finally became a crown colony of the Windward Island group in 1814.

Britain consolidated its hold on both islands during the Napoleonic Wars, and they were combined into the colony of Trinidad and Tobago in 1889. The richest and second largest country of the British West Indies, the islands acquired independence from Britain on Aug. 31, 1962. In March 1976, Trinidad and Tobago became a republic, with the capital at Port of Spain, Trinidad. The prime minister is elected by the people, and the president is chosen by the electoral college.

The islands' principal exports are petroleum, petrochemicals and sugar. The discovery of substantial natural gas reserves has enabled the country to embark upon a revitalized industrialization program, which has resulted in a large industrial complex at Point Lisas off Trinidad's southwest coast. Pitch Lake on Trinidad, an enormous asphalt reservoir, has provided material for surfacing many of the world's roads. Cocoa, coffee and—increasingly—tourism also are important economically.

Shopping

Frederick Street in Port of Spain is known throughout the Caribbean and South America for its fascinating shops and merchandise. Luxury imports include French perfumes, Swiss watches, jewelry, china, porcelain, crystal, silver, cameras, leather handbags, beads and petit point. Modern department stores and gift shops offer English tweeds and worsteds and synthetic fibers. Irish linens and fine silks are available; dresses, suits and sports and evening jackets are custom tailored on short notice from imported materials. The Oriental shops feature ivory carvings, brassware, saris, richly patterned silks, carved curios and furniture, native filigree jewelry, embroidered slippers and silk apparel.

Such local crafts as hand-carved articles, straw and sisal goods, imaginative ceramics and tiles, vivid paintings, hand-embroidered clothing and gold, silver and copper jewelry make good souvenirs. Trinidad's fine rums and Angostura bitters are available at bargain prices. There are several malls in and around the city, including a small one at the Cruise Ship Complex on Wrightson Road that features duty free stores, clothing boutiques and souvenir shops. Stores on Frederick Street are open Mon.-Fri. 8-4; some are open until 5, on Fri. until 6 and on Sat. until noon. Malls are open daily 10-6. Banking hours are Mon.-Thurs. 9-2 and Fri. 9-1 and 3-5 at banks and daily 10-6 at malls.

Food and Drink

The food on Trinidad is as cosmopolitan as the island; British, American, Continental, Creole, Chinese and Indian dishes are available. Popular dishes include *sancoche* and *callaloo,* excellent thick soups; stuffed cascadura, a freshwater fish; crabmeat served in the shell; the island's famous small oysters; and *roti,* an East Indian dish consisting of curried meat or vegetables stuffed into a rolled, soft, flour shell. *Pelau* is a combination of pigeon peas and rice cooked with chicken or beef in coconut milk and pumpkin. *Pastelles,* a cornmeal pastry filled with meats, raisins, olives and capers, rolled in fig leaves or aluminum foil and boiled, is a Christmas specialty.

Angostura bitters originated and are made in Trinidad. Created in the early 1800s by Dr. Johann Siegert as a digestive aid for the troops of Simon Bolivar, the ingredients have remained a secret. Said to contain a mixture of herbs and spices, the recipe supposedly does not contain the bark of the Angostura tree. The local rum is a favorite in fruit punches. The water is safe to drink.

Sports and Amusements

The islands' African heritage surfaces in three art forms: calypso, a lilting medium for political and social satire that can be traced to the arrival of the first African slaves brought to work on Trinidad's sugar plantations; limbo, a dance strictly for the athletic; and steel bands, with instruments fashioned from oil drums (reputedly the only musical instrument invented in the 20th century). These bands are especially popular during Carnival. Based in Trinidad's capital, Carnival is held the Monday and Tuesday before Ash Wednesday, but parties and dances begin right after Christmas. Costumes, calypso and steel-band contests and the crowning of a king and queen make this the best known of Caribbean festivals.

In alternate years, 3-week steel band music festivals are held in October, featuring a wide variety of musical styles from calypso to classical: In odd-numbered years it is the World Steelband Music Festival, while in even-numbered years it is the Pan is Beautiful Festival. The SteelPan and Jazz Festival is held every October, bringing together pan drummers and jazz musicians for 3 days of music in Trinidad, while Pan Jazz "in de yard" is held every

April in Tobago. Yearly, the Best Village Folk Festival in late November offers displays of traditional skills, dance and drama combined with tastes of local cuisine. The islands also are the scene of Hindu and Muslim festivals.

Beautiful beaches line the coast of Trinidad and none is less than an hour's drive from Port of Spain. Maracas Beach, with its white sand, limpid water and coconut palms, is considered one of the world's most beautiful beaches. Trinidad's efforts to develop the natural beauty of the coastland are focused on Maracas and Las Cuevas bays northwest of Port of Spain and Manzanilla and Mayaro beaches on the east coast.

Good fishing in the Gulf of Paria and adjacent waters is available all year, but the best fishing is from June through September. Boats, guides and equipment are available for hire. Yachting is best during hurricane season, usually falling between July and November; the Trinidad Yacht Club will arrange sailing parties.

Inland activities on Trinidad include golf, hunting and some lively spectator sports. Eighteen-hole golf is played at St. Andrew's (Moka) Golf Club and Pointe-à-Pierre Golf Course. Near the airport at Sunrise Park Trincity is Millennium Lakes Golf & Country Club, with a PGA-designed 18-hole par 71 championship course. On the sister island of Tobago, golfers can choose from Mt. Irvine Golf Club or the Tobago Plantations Golf and Country Club. Large hotels usually have facilities catering to tennis buffs. Hunting season in Trinidad runs October through February.

Horse racing takes place at the Santa Rosa Racing Track in Arima during late May, July and August. For spectators and players alike Trinidad offers such popular sports as cricket, January through April; field hockey, January through June; and soccer, which generally runs July through December.

The calypso singers, steel bands and Port of Spain's long history as a sailor's town have earned the island a reputation for its own raucous, gaudy, exciting brand of nightlife. Clubs throughout town vibrate with the beat of Trinidadian dance and music, and stay open until the wee hours of the morning. Hotels also have entertainment, but it is geared toward those with more conservative tastes.

Recreation on Tobago centers on the sea. The island's many inlets, bays, shoals and reefs are excellent for fishing with line or spear; boats, guides and equipment are available for hire. Scuba diving and snorkeling are excellent at Buccoo Reef, and there is bathing at the Nylon Pool, 2 miles (3.2 km) out in the Caribbean.

Sightseeing

Lovely drives around Port of Spain enable visitors to relish the island's tropical beauty. Lady Chancellor Road affords a panorama of the city, the Gulf of Paria and San Fernando Hill. Lady Young Road also offers fine views of the city and the hills. Excellent views of the countryside, Venezuela and the sea are available from the Shrine of Our Lady of Fatima in Laventille and from Fort George, both a short distance from Port of Spain.

The North Coast Road to Las Cuevas Bay is spectacular; most of it is between 500 and 1,500 feet (150-450 m) above sea level and overlooks La Vache and Balata bays. This 34-mile (55-km) round trip from Port of Spain is the most popular shore excursion with Caribbean cruise passengers, as it highlights Trinidad's great scenic variety. Also high in Trinidad's northern mountain range at 1,200 feet (365 m) is the very secluded Asa Wright Nature Center. Tours can be arranged out of Port of Spain to the center, which has a former estate house and day- and week-long nature programs; phone (868) 667-5162.

The northwest coast road to Carenage and Chaguaramas also is particularly scenic. This area includes the islands of Monos and Gaspar Grande (described by the locals as "down the islands"), the latter containing an interesting group of caves on its southern end. The Gasparee Caves are entered by a long winding staircase to the bottom, where stalactites and stalagmites can be seen. A nature trail on Gaspar Grande leads to mounted guns left from World War II and offers a panoramic view of the sea and surrounding islands.

The driving tour from Port of Spain to the Maraval Valley passes through the San Juan cocoa plantations and the Santa Cruz Valley, where planters' houses of French and Spanish colonial days and the great samaan trees still stand. Maracas Bay and Maracas Beach climax the drive from Port of Spain along the Saddle Road.

From Port of Spain the trip to Pitch Lake travels along the Uriah Butler Highway through Chaguanas, noted for its East Indian jewelry; Pointe-à-Pierre, the site of a large oil refinery and the Wildfowl Trust; and San Fernando. Circle tours of Trinidad, lasting 7 hours, travel past the Gulf of Paria, across the central plains, through Pointe-à-Pierre and San Fernando, continue past sugarcane and coconut plantations to Mayaro Beach and return via Manzanilla Beach. Lunch and swimming are included.

An excursion on Tobago might include a tour of Old Fort King George, the Botanical Gardens and the shopping district in Scarborough, combined with a drive past coconut plantations and beaches to Store Bay and Plymouth. A cruise to the Coral Gardens and the Natural Aquarium at Buccoo Reef provides an opportunity for snorkeling and swimming. Both of these excursions take about a half day.

A pleasant full-day drive on Tobago follows Windward Road along the Atlantic coast from Scarborough to Charlotteville. Visitors can take a pleasant detour off Windward Road, traveling northwest from Roxborough to Parlatuvier. The well-maintained, two-lane Roxborough-Parlatuvier Road climbs across the spine of the island, passing through forest and cultivated land. As the road descends to Parlatuvier, it provides a fine view of the Caribbean side of the island.

Boats depart from Speyside to Little Tobago, where guides conduct walks through a 450-acre (182-hectare) bird sanctuary.

Transportation

Daily direct flights to Trinidad's Piarco International Airport leave New York, Orlando, Houston, Newark, Fort Lauderdale and Miami; other flights from New York and Miami stop at San Juan, Barbados and other intermediate islands. There is regular and frequent air service between Trinidad and the other Caribbean islands and nearby Venezuela. Trinidad also is a port of call for some cruise lines. Cars can be rented by the day or week; driving is on the left. Trinidad's 4,600 miles (7,400 km) of asphalt highways are among the best in the Caribbean. City and island sightseeing tours with a driver-guide are available in Port of Spain. Taxis are abundant.

Fast Facts

POPULATION: 1,305,000.

AREA: Trinidad: 4,828 sq km (1,864 sq mi.). Tobago: 300 sq km (116 sq mi.).

CAPITAL: Port of Spain, Trinidad.

HIGHEST POINT: 940 m (3,084 ft.), El Cerro del Aripo, Trinidad.

LOWEST POINT: Sea level, Caribbean Sea.

TIME ZONE(S): Atlantic Standard.

LANGUAGE: English.

GOVERNMENT: Independent (parliamentary democracy). Member of the British Commonwealth of Nations.

UNIT OF CURRENCY: Trinidad and Tobago dollar. $1 U.S. = approx. 6 Trinidad/Tobago dollars.

ELECTRICITY: 110-230 volts, 60 cycles AC; voltage varies with location.

MINIMUM AGE FOR DRIVERS: 21-25, depending on the rental car agency. U.S. license valid for 3 months; drive on left.

SEAT BELT/CHILD RESTRAINT LAWS: Seat belts are required for driver and front-seat passengers.

HOLIDAYS: Jan. 1; Spiritual Baptist Shouter Liberation Day, Mar. 30; Good Friday; Easter Monday; Indian Arrival Day, May 30; Feast of Corpus Christi, May or June (9th Thurs. after Easter); Labour Day, June 19; Emancipation

Day, Aug. 1; Independence Day, Aug. 31; Eid-ul-Fitr (Muslim Holy Day), Sept. 11; Republic Day, Sept. 24; Divali, Nov. 12; Christmas, Dec. 25; Boxing Day, Dec. 26.

TAXES: A 10 percent room tax and 10-15 percent service charge are added to most hotel bills. Many restaurants include a 10-15 percent service charge. A 15 percent VAT (value-added tax) is added to most consumer goods. Departure tax $17 U.S.

IMMIGRATION REQUIREMENTS: A valid passport and return or onward ticket are required. No visa needed for stays up to 90 days. The U.S. Dept. of Homeland Security requires all U.S. citizens returning from the Caribbean to present a valid passport.

PHONING THE ISLANDS: To call Trinidad and Tobago from the U.S. or Canada, dial 1 + 868 + the 7-digit local number.

FURTHER INFORMATION FOR VISITORS:

Trinidad and Tobago Tourism Development Co.
Maritime Centre, 29 Tenth Ave.
P.O. Box 222
Barataria, Trinidad
Trinidad and Tobago
(868) 675-7034

Tobago Department of Tourism
12 Sangster Hill
Scarborough, Tobago
Trinidad and Tobago
(868) 639-2125
(868) 639-4636

Twenty-minute flights between Piarco International Airport and Tobago's Crown Point International Airport are available several times a day. There are two ways visitors can travel on ferry between Trinidad and Tobago—fast ferry or conventional. Fast ferry sailing time is under 2 hours. The conventional ferry takes 5 1/2

hours; these car/passenger ferries have dining rooms and bars. For additional information, phone (868) 625-3055. Cars can be rented on Tobago, which has about 220 miles (354 km) of good roads. Public buses traverse the island several times daily and charge very reasonable rates.

Points of Interest

See map page 225.

Tobago

The island of Tobago, 21 miles (34 km) northeast of Trinidad, covers 116 square miles (300 sq km). A low mountain ridge divides the island, which is a sanctuary for hummingbirds, green parrots, jacamars, motmots and nightjars.

Robinson's Crusoe's Cave, 10 miles (16 km) west of Scarborough, is named for Daniel Defoe's fictional castaway. The subterranean cave traverses Crown Point and Store Bay. The ruins of Fort James are nearby at Plymouth; a powder magazine on the grounds has been restored.

SCARBOROUGH (B-3) pop. 15,830

Scarborough, the main town and administrative center of Tobago, is on Rockley Bay on the island's southern shore. Its native market is most active Friday and Saturday. The Coral Gardens on Buccoo Reef is a popular spot for both snorkelers and divers.

The ruins of Fort King George overlook the city at its highest point. Built 1784-87, the fort originally was named Fort Castries by the French. When the British took over, they renamed the fort after their king. Within the fort is the Tobago Museum, where exhibits include prehistoric Amerindian artifacts, historical maps and documents and local history displays. The Rockery Vale sugar estate, parceled out in the late 1800s, now is home to a 17-acre (7-hectare) botanic garden and the Welbeck House.

Trinidad

Just 7 miles (11 km) off the coast of Venezuela, Trinidad is the southernmost island in the Caribbean archipelago. Trinidad covers 1,864 square miles (4,828 sq km), roughly the size of Rhode Island. Three mountain ranges cross the island; at 3,085 feet (940 m), El Cerro del Aripo is the highest point. Half of the island is forest, and mangrove swamps provide wildlife habitats on both the east and west coasts.

The Pitch Lake at San Fernando prompted interest in Trinidad's petrochemical resources; the first oil well was drilled here in 1857. By the early 20th century, oil had replaced sugar as the island's chief export. A surplus of Navy oil drums led to the invention of Trinidad's famed steel drums.

The church of Notre Dame de Montserrat in Tortuga contains the statue of the Black Virgin. The wooden figure is said to have been brought from Spain by Capuchin monks. In nearby Carapichaima stands the 85-foot-tall Hanuman Murti, reputed to be the tallest Hindu statue of its kind outside India. The brightly-colored effigy of a monkey-faced god is east of the Waterloo Temple, also known as the Temple-in-the-Sea. A laborer built this shrine in the Gulf of Paria after he was forbidden from using sugar land.

PORT OF SPAIN (C-2) pop. 49,031

Busy markets, exotic houses of worship and modern buildings give Port of Spain a cosmopolitan atmosphere. The city has been the capital of Trinidad since 1757 and the capital of both Trinidad and Tobago since they were united in 1899. From the hills north of the city, the coast of Venezuela can be seen across the Gulf of Paria.

Just outside of Port of Spain on the Eastern Main Road in Laventille is the House of Angostura, maker of several varieties of rum and its signature, Angostura aromatic bitters. The distillery features a museum, art gallery and butterfly collection; factory tours are available by reservation. Phone (868) 623-1841.

CARONI SWAMP AND BIRD SANCTUARY is 7 mi. (11 km) s. on the Uriah Butler Hwy. This 15,000-acre (6,000-hectare) mangrove swamp is nesting ground to the scarlet ibis, now threatened by pollution and poachers. At sunset, thousands of the brilliantly colored birds return to roost in the mangrove trees, offering a spectacular sight. Guided 2.5-hour boat trips are offered by Nanan's Bird Sanctuary Tours. An observation tower, viewing platform and boardwalk provide visitors with an up-close view of the roosting birds.

Insect repellent and binoculars are advised; boats do not disturb the birds by approaching closely. **Hours:** Tours depart daily at 4; passengers should arrive at the sanctuary 15 minutes before departure. Closed Christmas. **Cost:** Fare $10; $5 (children); free (ages 0-4). Reservations are required. **Phone:** (868) 645-1305.

CATHEDRAL OF THE HOLY TRINITY faces the southern side of Woodford Square on Abercromby St. and is entered from Queen St. This Anglican church was built 1816-18; a 1908 fire destroyed the original building and the church was subsequently rebuilt. The Georgian and Gothic structure has a mahogany ceiling patterned after the one in London's Westminster Hall. The altar and choir stalls also are noteworthy. **Hours:** Daily 6-6. **Cost:** Donations. **Phone:** (868) 623-7271.

CATHEDRAL OF THE IMMACULATE CONCEPTION is at Independence Square. Begun in 1816, this Catholic cathedral with dual towers was consecrated in 1851. **Hours:** Daily 9-5. **Cost:** Donations. **Phone:** (868) 623-5232.

NATIONAL MUSEUM AND ART GALLERY is on the s.w. corner of Queen's Park Savannah at 117 Frederick St. Guarded by Spanish cannons that date from 1797, the museum houses an anchor that Columbus lost in Trinidad. Displays relate to natural history, industry, geology and archeology. Of special note are elaborate costumes worn during Carnival Week celebrations as well as a gallery of folk art and crafts. **Time:** Allow 1 hour minimum. **Hours:** Tues.-Sat. 10-6, Sun. 2-6. **Cost:** Free. **Phone:** (868) 623-5941.

QUEEN'S PARK SAVANNAH is in the center of the fashionable residential district. The park covers nearly 200 grassland acres (81 hectares). The Stollmeyer House in the eastern section was built in 1904 as a copy of a wing of Balmoral Castle in Scotland; other excellent examples of Grand Colonial Architecture surround the park. Cricket, football and rugby events are held here. The Emperor Valley Zoo and the Royal Botanic Gardens *(see attraction listing)*, laid out in 1820, face the northern side of the park; Memorial Square and the National Museum are on the park's east side.

Food is available inside the zoo. **Hours:** Park open daily 24 hours. Zoo open Wed.-Mon. 9-6; closed Christmas and Carnival Monday and Tuesday. **Cost:** Park and botanic gardens free. Zoo $2; $1 (ages 3-12). **Phone:** (868) 622-3530 for the zoo. ▯

RED HOUSE is on Abercromby Street opposite Woodford Square. The handsome building once housed the legislative council and other government agencies and now serves as the seat of the nation's parliament. The main chamber is noted for its ornate gesso ceiling, which was created in England, shipped in panels and installed by an Italian craftsman in 1906. An eternal flame symbolizing "the need to be ever vigilant in the protection of democracy" burns on the eastern lawn atop a marble cenotaph. Guided tours are offered by appointment. **Hours:** Daily 8-4. **Cost:** Free. **Phone:** (868) 624-7275.

ROYAL BOTANIC GARDENS adjoins the president's house at Queen's Park Savannah. Tropical plants and trees, including lotus lilies, monkey pods and Ceylon willows, grow on about 70 acres (28 hectares). Evening band concerts occasionally take place. Guided tours are available by appointment. **Hours:** Daily 6-6. **Cost:** Free. **Phone:** (868) 622-4221.

SAN FERNANDO (D-2) pop. 55,419

San Fernando, Trinidad's second largest city, is built on a hill on the Gulf of Paria. Sugar estates and factories are nearby; oil fields lie to the southeast.

PITCH LAKE is s.w. at La Brea. One of three natural asphalt lakes in the world, the tar pit covers 100 barren acres (40 hectares). Its hard surface will bear foot traffic—with caution. About 165,000 tons of asphalt are excavated yearly. Local legend attributes the origin of this lake to the Great Spirit, anguished by the Chayma Indians' sacrifice of the sacred hummingbird. In retribution, the Great Spirit caused the earth to swallow up the guilty, leaving the lake as a reminder. **Cost:** Free.

Provo Golf Club, Providenciales / © Timothy O'Keefe / Photolibrary

Turks and Caicos Islands

The tiny islands of Turks and Caicos (KAY-kos) lie southeast of The Bahamas and north of the Dominican Republic and Haiti. The Turks and Caicos are comprised of eight major islands and some 40 smaller cays, most of which remain uninhabited. Grand Turk and Salt Cay are in the Turks, and North, Middle (also known as Grand), South, East and West Caicos and Providenciales (also known as Provo) are in the Caicos. The two groups are separated by the Turks Island Passage. Of the Atlantic group, these beautiful islands resemble those found farther south, with dazzling white or gold sand and sparkling waters. Most of the resorts are on Provo and Grand Turk; more intimate accommodations are available on the other islands. The islands' business, banking and government center is Cockburn Town on Grand Turk.

History

The Turks and Caicos might have been among the islands mentioned in Christopher Columbus' 1492 diary, but there is no official record of discovery until Juan Ponce de León arrived in 1512. The native inhabitants were the Arawak Indians, whose population was almost destroyed by the French and Spanish. The British finally took control of the islands under the Treaty of Madrid, and during the American Revolution they were the territory of Loyalists and pirates. At the end of the war the Loyalists and settlers from Bermuda began producing salt and set up cotton and sisal plantations, ventures that eventually supported the islands for many years. Tourism is now the mainstay of the economy. The Turks are named for the Turk's Head Cactus, while Caicos is a derivation of *cayos*, the Spanish word for "small island."

Shopping, Food and Drink

Compared with some other islands, shopping opportunities are limited. Shoppers commonly

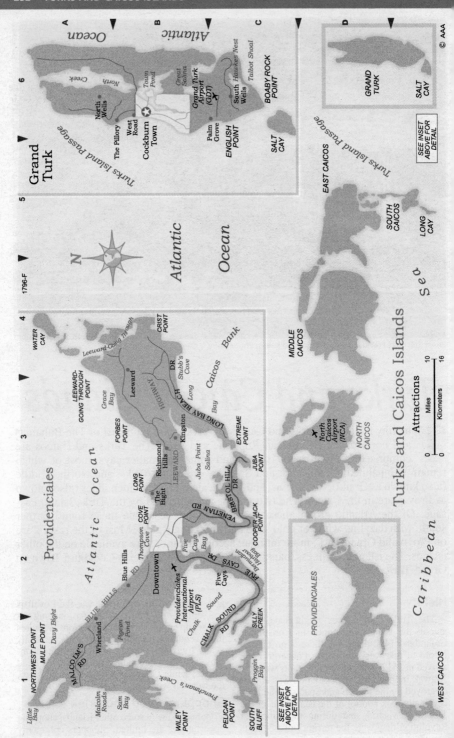

Turks and Caicos Islands

purchase stamps and coins and souvenirs crafted from straw or seashells. Liquor and tobacco are available at duty-free prices. Dining options are plentiful, with local restaurants serving such seafood delicacies as conch stew, spiny lobster, grouper, turtle and wahoo. Other restaurants serve French, Italian, Chinese, German and Mexican dishes. Some of the islands' fruit and rum libations are popular aperitifs.

Sports and Amusements

The focal point for recreation in the Turks and Caicos is the nearly 230 miles (370 km) of beaches. North Caicos and Provo each claim a 12-mile (19-km) stretch of sand; North Caicos also boasts a 5-mile (8-km) strand at Sandy Point. Swimming, snorkeling and scuba diving are understandably popular activities at most resorts. The scuba diving is said to be among the best in the world, especially off Provo and Grand Turk. Dive operators based at resorts on Grand Turk, North and South Caicos, Provo and Salt Cay provide rentals for scuba diving as well as the services of a divemaster. Along the north shore of Provo, Grace Bay is the location of Princess Alexandra Marine Park.

The annual migration of the humpback whale takes place in the winter. These eastern Atlantic whales travel through the Turks Island passage to the Mouchoir and Silver banks to the south; they mate and give birth to their young in these waters. The whales can be observed from the shore south of Grand Turk and Salt Cay, and whale-watching charters also can be arranged.

Fishing is a favorite pastime throughout the islands; the Caicos are noted for bonefishing. Pine Cay has a freshwater lake, and South, Middle and North Caicos, Pine Cay and Provo offer guides who can predict where the best catch will be. Deep-sea fishing can be arranged at North Caicos, Provo, Grand Turk and South Caicos. Boat rentals for sailing are available at Provo, Pine Cay, South Caicos and at most hotels.

Tennis courts are available to guests of hotels on North Caicos, Pine Cay and Provo. The

Fast Facts

POPULATION: 18,122.

AREA: 430 sq km (166 sq mi.).

CAPITAL: Grand Turk.

HIGHEST POINT: 49 m (161 ft.), Blue Hills, Providenciales.

LOWEST POINT: Sea level, Atlantic Ocean.

TIME ZONE(S): Eastern Standard. DST.

LANGUAGE: English.

GOVERNMENT: British Overseas Territory.

UNIT OF CURRENCY: U.S. dollar.

ELECTRICITY: 110-120 volts, 60 cycles AC.

MINIMUM AGE FOR DRIVERS: 21-25, depending on the rental car agency. U.S. license valid for 30 days; drive on left.

MINIMUM AGE FOR GAMBLING: 18.

SEAT BELT/CHILD RESTRAINT LAWS: Seat belts are required for all passengers.

HOLIDAYS: Jan. 1; Commonwealth Day, Mar. (2nd Mon.); Good Friday; Easter Monday; National Heroes Day, May 26; Queen's Birthday, June (3rd weekend); Emancipation Day, Aug. (1st Mon.); Constitution Day, Aug. 30; National Youth Day, Sept. 30; Columbus Day, Oct. 13; International Human Rights Day, Oct. 24; Christmas, Dec. 25; Boxing Day, Dec. 26.

TAXES: A 7-9 percent room tax and 10-15 percent service charge are added to most hotel bills. Many restaurants include a 10 percent service charge. Departure tax $45 U.S.

IMMIGRATION REQUIREMENTS: Passport and a return or onward ticket are required. No visa needed for stays up to 30 days. The U.S. Dept. of Homeland Security requires all U.S. citizens returning from the Caribbean to present a valid passport.

PHONING THE ISLANDS: To call the Turks and Caicos Islands from the U.S. or Canada, dial 1 + 649 + the 7-digit local number.

FURTHER INFORMATION FOR VISITORS:

Turks and Caicos Tourist Board, United States
The Lincoln Building
60 E. 42nd St., Suite 2817
New York, NY 10165
(646) 375-8830
(800) 241-0824

Turks and Caicos Tourist Board, Grand Turk
Front Street
Grand Turk
Turks and Caicos Islands
(649) 946-2321

Provo Golf Club offers an 18-hole championship course. Hotels offer information about sightseeing. Some interesting sites include old churches, the 19th-century Bermudian Great White House (open by appointment) on Salt Cay, caves on Middle Caicos, the herd of wild horses roaming outside an 1820 house called Highlands on South Caicos, and ruins of the salt industry. Hotels also offer some nightlife in the way of after-dinner dancing and pubs.

A short boat ride from Provo, Little Water Cay has become a sanctuary for the endangered rock iguana. The Little Water Cay Nature Trail is a system of boardwalks that allows visitors to observe these creatures without endangering their habitat. Observation towers along the trail offer views of the island's interior and the azure waters surrounding it.

Boats from many towns participate in the annual regatta at South Caicos in May. Carnival is celebrated in September with the coronation of the queen and the parade in which each island is represented. Junkanoo, a street party celebrating the island's rich culture and history, is held on December 26 (Boxing Day) and January 1.

Transportation

Providenciales International Airport can be reached by air from Atlanta aboard Delta flights, from Charlotte via US Airways, and Dallas, New York and Miami with American Airlines. Bahamasair offers connecting flights from Provo to Grand Turk Airport. Island-hopping flights stop at Grand Turk, South Caicos, North Caicos, Salt Cay and Provo. Arrangements also can be made for flights to The Bahamas and the Dominican Republic.

A new $45-million cruise ship terminal opened on the southern end of Grand Turk in 2005, bringing a new wave of tourists to the island.

Bicycles, mopeds and automobiles can be rented on Grand Turk and Provo. A valid driver's license from your home country is required for rentals, and vehicles are driven on the left side of the road. Chartering a boat is an excellent way to see a wide variety of islands while you enjoy the sun and sea.

Points of Interest

See map page 232.

Grand Turk (B-6)

Grand Turk island, 6 miles (9.7 km) long, is noted for its beaches and scuba-diving. Flat and dry, the island was used as a salt-making station in the 1600s. Cockburn Town, the nation's administrative capital, features Bermuda-style architecture in many of its 18th- and 19th-century buildings.

The Grand Turk Lighthouse at the north end was constructed in 1852, though its whale-oil lamps failed to prevent shipwrecks until the addition of a Fresnel lens and kerosene lights in 1943. Now electrified, the lighthouse remains in service.

TURKS AND CAICOS NATIONAL MUSEUM is in Guinep House on Front Street. The building, constructed in the mid-1800s of native stone, houses artifacts from the Molasses Reef shipwreck, said to be the oldest European wreck discovered in the Western Hemisphere. Several exhibits portray the culture and natural history of the islands. A 7-minute film is presented. Artifacts from what is thought to be the oldest Lucayan Indian site in the Bahamian archipelago, dating to 750 A.D., also are displayed. Behind-the-Scenes and dive tours are offered.

Time: Allow 1 hour minimum. **Hours:** Mon.-Tues. and Thurs.-Sat. 9-1, Wed. 1-5. Closed major holidays. **Cost:** $7. **Phone:** (649) 946-2160.

Providenciales (B-2)

Larger in size than Bermuda, Providenciales (known as Provo) has become the Turks and Caicos Islands' tourism center. Not a single wheeled vehicle was in use on the island until 1965; it now has miles of good roads and a variety of fine accommodations and restaurants. On a hilltop overlooking Sapodilla Bay, stones bear the inscriptions of 18th-century sailors.

CAICOS CONCH FARM is on the n.e. tip of the island at Leeward. Guided 20-minute tours educate visitors about the queen conch (pronounced *konk*), which is raised here for food and pearl production. The 5-acre (2-hectare) working farm includes a hatchery, nursery ponds, sea pens and a processing facility. Two "trained" conches are introduced during the tour. **Hours:** Mon.-Fri. 9-4, Sat. 9-2. Last tour departs 20 minutes before closing. Closed major holidays. **Cost:** $10; $5 (ages 0-11). **Phone:** (649) 232-5119 or (649) 946-5643.

Cane Garden Bay, Tortola Island / © SIME / eStock Photo

Virgin Islands, British

Islands tinged with the warm colors of a Paul Gauguin painting and white sand beaches cooled by refreshing breezes characterize the Virgin Islands. About 60 miles (97 km) east of Puerto Rico, the archipelago lies directly in the path of the trade winds and enjoys a pleasant climate with moderate rainfall and maximum sunlight. The principal British islands are Tortola, Virgin Gorda, Anegada (ah-nee-GAH-da) and Jost Van Dyke; except for the flat coral island of Anegada, both the U.S. and British Virgins are volcanic in origin.

Though not as developed as their U.S. sisters, the British Virgin Islands have a distinctive appeal. Tortola has the capital, Road Town, with its serene harbor and rugged 1,709-foot (521-m) Mount Sage. Virgin Gorda Island has an untamed natural beauty, and uninhabited Norman Island is reputed to be the "Treasure Island" of Robert Louis Stevenson fame. Some of the smaller, secluded islands are privately owned and offer the ultimate in escapist vacations.

History

The British Virgin Islands saw their first Europeans when Christopher Columbus arrived in 1493. Except for some copper on Virgin Gorda, the Spanish found little of interest on the islands and eventually lost them to the British in 1628. However, it was the Dutch who settled Tortola and initiated the lucrative sugar trade, which sparked the envy of other countries. Yet, despite battles between the French, Spanish, Dutch, Danes and various pirates, Britain regained the islands in 1666 and has held them ever since. Today the islands constitute a territory, administered by a queen-appointed governor and a locally elected government headed by a Chief Minister. While livestock raising is still important, offshore banking and tourism and its related industries dominate the islands' economy.

Shopping

Most of the retail shops in the islands are found along Main Street in Road Town or along the harbor in Virgin Gorda. Because there is no duty on British imports, bargains can be found on some English china, fabrics and foods. Among other bargains are rum, whiskey and gin as well as intricate straw goods, island crafts, jewelry and fabric designs. One popular shopping area in Road Town is Main Street, which has shops offering souvenirs, spices, jewelry and china. Such native spices as Tortola's rum, pepper sauce and BVI Caribbean seasoning are found at the retail outlets of Tortola's two spice factories. Locations include Main Street, Crafts Alive Market, Soper's Hole Marina and the Beef Island Airport.

Local stamps are unique in that they are the only stamps in the British Commonwealth sold in a denomination of U.S. currency, official tender in the British Virgins. Stamps are available in Road Town or at the small post office at West End on Tortola. Major credit cards and travelers checks are accepted at most hotels and restaurants.

Food and Drink

Except for seafood, mutton, beef or home-grown vegetables and fruit, all food is imported. Tortola and Virgin Gorda have the largest selection of restaurants. On other inhabited islands a small hotel or inn is often the only establishment. Hotels usually serve three meals a day and have wine lists as well as a wide assortment of liquors and fruit drinks. Island cuisine is characterized by fish or seafood dishes, the most popular being *fungee*. This type of Caribbean polenta is made from corn meal, mixed with onions, sweet peppers and okra, boiled into cakes and served with boiled fish and green vegetables.

Sports and Amusements

The islands' most popular activity and biggest drawing card is sailing. Their reputation as a mecca for yachting enthusiasts, though long known by advocates of the sport, has been discovered by amateur sailors and tourists. As a result hundreds of yachts are available for charter. The more than 40 islands and cays are ripe for exploring.

Many half- or full-day cruises include a picnic lunch, snorkeling, swimming or tours of such sites as Virgin Gorda's Baths—gigantic boulders forming a labyrinth of grottoes and beaches. The best equipped marinas are on Tortola, Virgin Gorda and Peter Island. You should make reservations for longer sailing excursions during the peak season, December through February.

Deep-sea fishing is another popular activity in the British Virgin Islands, where record catches of blue marlin, tuna and wahoo have been made. Special competitions take place June through November.

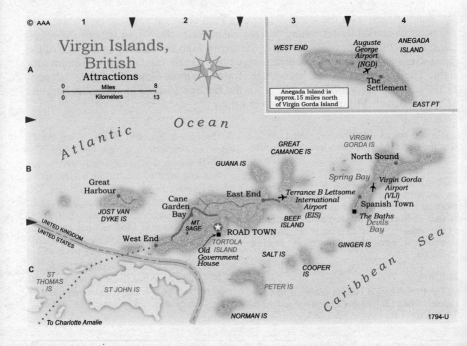

The clarity of the waters off these islands creates superb scuba and snorkeling conditions. Especially notable is the wreck of the RMS *Rhone* located off Salt Island; this wreck is ranked as one of the top-rated sites by several diving publications. Expert guides are available, and arrangements can be made through any of the islands' many dive shops or hotels. Caribbean Images and Rainbow Visions in Tortola rent cameras and offer courses on underwater photography.

The variety of birds, including pink flamingos, inhabiting the flat island of Anegada also make a visit worthwhile. Some 154 species of birds are found throughout the British Virgin Islands. Tennis courts can be found at hotels on Virgin Gorda, Tortola and Peter Island.

The appeal of the British Virgin Islands is tranquility, which means few dance clubs and no high-rises, jets or mammoth cruise ships. Evening diversions, therefore, are minimal. Moonlight cruises, listening to a steel band or dancing to after-dinner music at one of the hotels constitute most of the organized activities. Tortola's Festival, held the last week in July through the first weekend in August, incorporates the Emancipation Day Parade; Virgin Gorda's Festival celebrations take place Easter weekend. The festivities, popular with visitors and residents alike, include parades, dances, food fairs, beauty contests and band competitions.

The Welcome, the bimonthly tourist news magazine available free throughout the islands, provides up-to-date information. *The Limin' Times* is a good source for news about entertainment and activities. The British Virgin Islands Tourist Board maintains an office in Road Town and at the yacht harbor on Virgin Gorda Island.

Transportation

Tortola's Terrance B. Lettsome International Airport can be reached by plane from St. Thomas, St. Maarten, St. Croix, Antigua, St. Kitts or San Juan via Air Sunshine, American

Fast Facts

POPULATION: 19,100.

AREA: 153 sq km (59 sq mi.).

CAPITAL: Road Town, Tortola.

HIGHEST POINT: 521 m (1,709 ft.), Mount Sage, Tortola.

LOWEST POINT: Sea level, Caribbean Sea.

TIME ZONE(S): Atlantic Standard.

LANGUAGE: English.

GOVERNMENT: British Overseas Territory.

UNIT OF CURRENCY: U.S. dollar.

ELECTRICITY: 110-120 volts, 60 cycles AC; voltage varies with location.

MINIMUM AGE FOR DRIVERS: 25. Local license ($10) required, valid for 3 months; drive on left.

SEAT BELT/CHILD RESTRAINT LAWS: Seat belts are required for all passengers.

HOLIDAYS: Jan. 1; H.L. Stoutt's Birthday, Mar. (1st Mon.); Commonwealth Day, Mar. (2nd Mon.); Good Friday; Easter; Easter Monday; Whit Monday, May or June (8th Mon. after Easter); Sovereign's Birthday, June (2nd Sat.); Territory Day, July 2; Festival Days, Aug. (1st Mon., Tues. and Wed.); St. Ursula's Day, Oct. 18; Prince of Wales' Birthday, Nov. 14; Christmas, Dec. 25; Boxing Day, Dec. 26.

TAXES: An 8 percent room tax and 10-15 percent service charge are added to most hotel bills. Departure tax is $20 U.S. by air, $7 by cruise ship, $5 by ferry.

IMMIGRATION REQUIREMENTS: Passport and return or onward ticket are required. No visa needed for stays up to 30 days. The U.S. Dept. of Homeland Security requires all U.S. citizens returning from the Caribbean to present a valid passport.

PHONING THE ISLANDS: To call the British Virgin Islands from the U.S. or Canada, dial 1 + 284 + the 7-digit local number.

FURTHER INFORMATION FOR VISITORS:

British Virgin Islands Tourist Board, United States
1 West 34th Street, Suite 302
New York, NY 10001
(212) 563-3117
(800) 835-8530

British Virgin Islands Tourist Board, Road Town
DeCastro Street
2nd Floor, AKARA Building
Road Town, Tortola Island
Virgin Islands, British
(284) 494-3134

Eagle, Cape Air or LIAT. Virgin Gorda has frequent connections with St. Thomas and San Juan. Frequent interisland flights link Tortola with Anegada. Charter flights are available through Fly BVI and Clair Aero.

While inland transportation is fairly limited, taxis are available on Tortola, Virgin Gorda, Anegada and Jost Van Dyke; all offer island tours. Rental cars can be hired on Tortola, Virgin Gorda and Anegada, and with limited availability on Jost Van Dyke; a local driver's license good for 90 days is required and can be obtained at car rental agencies or the traffic licensing office.

Ferries operate daily between both Charlotte Amalie and Red Hook, St. Thomas in the U.S. Virgin Islands, and West End, Tortola. Trips take 30-50 minutes. A 90-minute ferry runs to Road Town, Tortola. Phone (284) 495-4617, (284) 494-2323 or (284) 495-4495 for fares and schedules. Within the British Virgin Islands, ferry service operates daily from Road Town, Tortola, to Virgin Gorda and Peter Island. A ferry also connects West End, Tortola, with Jost Van Dyke. Phone Jost Van Dyke Ferry, (284) 495-2000; New Horizon Ferry, (284) 495-9278; Peter Island Ferry, (284) 495-2000; Smith's Tortola Fast Ferry, (284) 495-4495; or Speedy's Ferry (284) 495-5240. North Sound Express operates a ferry between Beef Island and North Sound, Virgin Gorda, with stops in the valley; phone (284) 495-2138. Some of the more remote islands can only be reached by sailboat or motorboat out of Tortola and Virgin Gorda.

Points of Interest

See map page 236.

Tortola Island (B-2)

Its name meaning "turtledove" in Spanish, 24-square-mile (62-sq-km) Tortola is the largest of the British Virgin Islands. It rests in the shadow of 1,709-foot Mount Sage, where traces of a primeval rain forest can still be found. Settled first by the Dutch and then the English in 1666, Tortola was granted its charter in 1773.

Road Town is the business center and seat of government. Fishing, scuba diving, snorkeling, sailing, swimming, windsurfing, kayaking, hiking, bicycling and horseback riding are popular diversions that can be enjoyed island-wide. Cane Garden Bay is one of the island's most popular beaches; others include Brewer's Bay Beach, Smuggler's Cove and Lambert Bay.

OLD GOVERNMENT HOUSE is on Waterfront Dr. in Road Town. This elegant house for the Commissioner of the British Virgin Islands was built in 1926 after the original was destroyed by a hurricane. The first floor and gardens are open to the public; historical exhibits include period furniture, cannonballs and glass bottles recovered during excavation of the grounds. Murals in the dining room depicting 19th-century island life were painted by the governor's wife. **Hours:** Mon.-Fri. 9-4. **Cost:** $3. Guided tours are offered for a fee. **Phone:** (284) 494-4091.

DID YOU KNOW

The British Virgin Islands inspired Robert Louis Stevenson's "Treasure Island."

Virgin Gorda Island (B-4)

Expanses of unspoiled beaches characterize Virgin Gorda (The Fat Virgin). Ten miles (16 km) long and almost 2 miles (3.2 km) wide in some places, the 8-square-mile (21-sq-km) island is the third largest of the British group and commands the Anegada Passage. Settled by the English in the late 1600s, Virgin Gorda was developed into agricultural estates. With the abolition of slavery in 1834, the population—once more than 8,000—dwindled to about 3,000.

Excursions on Virgin Gorda include trips to serene Spring Bay, Valley Trunk Bay, North Sound, Gorda Peak National Park, Devil's Bay, the boulder-strewn labyrinth of grottoes and beaches known as The Baths, and the ruins of a 19th-century Cornish mine at Copper Mine National Park.

BAHIA BEACH
PUERTO RICO

CANCUN

THE WESTIN RESORT & CASINO, ARUBA

This beachfront resort is situated on a perfect spot on famous Palm Beach; enjoy the calm breezes and breathtaking views from under our beach Palapas or from your private balcony offered in all guestrooms and suites. All this is enhanced by our multiple restaurants, lounges, casino, full-service spa, upscale boutiques, supervised Westin Kids Club and all the Heavenly amenities that only a Westin can offer.

THE WESTIN RESORT & SPA, CANCUN

This stunning resort, uniquely located between the breathtaking Caribbean Sea and the Nichupte Lagoon offers the serenity of a private white sand beach. Pamper yourself at the luxurious Heavenly Spa, experience the Temazcal Ancient Mayan ritual, or enjoy great snorkeling at the "Palancar" reef within walking distance. A great selection of bars and restaurants, all rooms offering ocean or lagoon views will create a renewal experience.

THE WESTIN ST. JOHN RESORT & VILLAS

A 47-acre tropical retreat, located along the palm lined shores of Great Cruz Bay, St. John, with 1,200 feet of private beach, just minutes from the pristine U.S. Virgin Islands National Park. Travel to the resort on a private vessel. Nestled among colorful hibiscus & bougainvillea choose from guestrooms, suites, studios, and two or three bedroom deluxe villas all with Signature Westin Heavenly Bed & Bath. An array of dining options and a variety of amenities including tennis, daily activities for all ages at The Westin Kids Club & Teen Center, Westin Workout, spa services, and quarter acre pool with poolside cabanas.

THE WESTIN CASUARINA RESORT & SPA, GRAND CAYMAN

Nestled in the warm sands of the famous Seven Mile Beach, this resort offers easy access to all of Grand Cayman's attractions, as well as a swim-up pool bar and a nearby 18-hole golf course. Explore some of the world's best scuba-diving spots with gear from the on-site dive shop or get pampered at the full-service spa. Luxurious guest rooms feature balconies ideal for relaxing in the year-round sunshine and breathtaking views of Grand Cayman. As the sun sets, don't miss a blend of Cuban and Caribbean cuisine at the open-air, oceanfront Casa Havana restaurant.

W RETREAT AND SPA, VIEQUES ISLAND

Escape to an undiscovered destination nestled on the unspoiled island of Vieques, just eight miles off the coast of Puerto Rico. No passport is required to be whisked away to this island respite from any U.S. Port of Origin. All rooms are a personal retreat, each with patios and balconies, surrounded by two pristine beaches. The exclusive SPA CHAKRA is a full-service oceanfront luxury spa offering a signature line of products. Guests will also discover an Alain Ducasse food experience.

SHERATON PUERTO RICO HOTEL & CASINO

San Juan's newest urban resort provides a superb location minutes from the airport, the cruise terminals and Old San Juan. A comfortable and contemporary design, an impressive 57,000 square feet of pool and sun deck, the largest casino on the island and chic shops and quaint cafes make this a true urban resort.

THE ST. REGIS BAHIA BEACH RESORT

In the romantic setting of a Caribbean coconut plantation nestled between a lush rainforest and the sparkling sea, embrace elegant tropical luxury perfected at the new St. Regis Bahía Beach Resort. Pleasure is a daily mantra when you tee off at the challenging Robert Trent Jones, Jr. golf course, succumb to exclusive Remède® Spa pampering, savor Jean-Georges' acclaimed cuisine, lounge at the pool esplanade or bask on our pristine sandy beach.

SHERATON NASSAU BEACH RESORT,

Ideally situated on a beautiful stretch of Nassau's spectacular Cable Beach, with all 694 guestrooms and suites boasting a large private balcony or patio with inspiring views of the Atlantic Ocean and seven acres of dazzling waterscape with three pools, cascading waterfalls and oversized whirlpools. In addition to the fantastic range of activities on-site, the hotel is also within a short distance of golf and an adjoining casino. Offering high standards of comfort and luxury with warm bright interiors and friendly Bahamian service.

St. Thomas Skyride, Charlotte Amalie, St. Thomas Island / © Fyne Photos / eStock Photo

Virgin Islands, U.S.

Taken together, all three U.S. Virgin Islands—St. Thomas, St. Croix and St. John—create the ideal West Indies vacation package. Charlotte Amalie (a-MAL-ya), capital of the islands, typifies the Caribbean town with its delightful shops and patios, winding streets and Old World, Continental flavor. Its picturesque harbor is among the busiest cruise ports in the Caribbean. Varied nightlife and a resort atmosphere make St. Thomas the liveliest of the U.S. Virgins. The largest of the islands, St. Croix is dotted with the ruins of plantation great houses and secluded beaches. St. Croix also offers shopping and amusement opportunities, but at a slower, less hectic pace. For those seeking peace, quiet and natural beauty, St. John is the archetype of the remote and undeveloped Caribbean isle. The beautiful Virgin Islands National Park covers two-thirds of the island.

History

Christopher Columbus discovered the Virgin Islands during his second voyage in 1493. His fleet of 17 ships first anchored off the north coast of Santa Cruz, or St. Croix as the French would later call it, then sailed off to the chain of smaller islands on their northern horizon. Columbus named the chain in honor of the 11,000 virgins who in legend were martyred with St. Ursula in a battle with a pagan ruler in the third century.

The English and French attempted to colonize St. Croix as early as 1625; the Dutch and Spanish made later appearances. After changing hands several times, St. Croix was ceded to the Knights of Malta in 1653, then sold to the French. The Danish West India & Guinea Co., permanently chartered in 1671, established Denmark's first settlement in the West Indies on St. Thomas under Gov. Georg Jorgen Iversen. St. John was acquired in 1684, St. Croix in 1733.

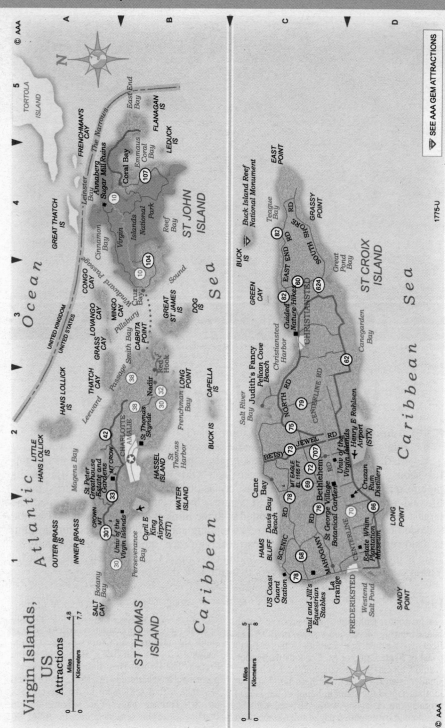

Virgin Islands, US
Attractions

SEE AAA GEM ATTRACTIONS

1775-U

Denmark ruled these islands for nearly 250 years, with the exception of two brief periods of British administration in the early 19th century. The Danish West Indies became the U.S. Virgin Islands in 1917, when Denmark sold them to the United States. The American government, which desired a naval base in the Caribbean and proximity to the Panama Canal, purchased the islands for $25 million in gold. Many of Charlotte Amalie's thoroughfares still bear Danish names.

Tourism to the U.S. Virgin Islands began to boom in the 1960s partly because of the closing of Cuba to tourists from the United States. The number of visitors quickly escalated from about 100,000 per year to more than 2 million. At the same time tourism was rising, the islands' population tripled. Other islanders were attracted by the relative economic security.

Today the U.S. Virgin Islands is an unincorporated territory of the United States, and its people are American citizens. The islands were administered by a governor appointed by the president until 1970, when the first gubernatorial election was held.

Shopping

Among the bargains in the U.S. Virgin Islands are imported liqueurs and local rums. In some instances, considerable savings are possible on Royal Copenhagen, Limoges, Wedgwood, Bing and Grondahl china; Baccarat, Waterford, Lalique, Daum and Val St. Lambert crystal; Swiss watches; island wearing apparel; jewelry and precious gems; English doeskin products; cashmere sweaters from Scotland; and designer fashions from Europe. Silver bracelets, earrings, cuff links, table settings, fine perfumes and Danish silver also can be found. Handicrafts include basketry, hats, handbags, dolls and embroideries.

Hundreds of tiny shops crowd the narrow streets of Charlotte Amalie; at its center is Royal Dane Mall, a group of shops housed in former warehouses for trading goods and rum. Havensight Mall, at the cruise ship dock, has more than 100 stores, restaurants and businesses. Atop St. Peter Mountain in the center of St. Thomas, Mountain Top offers a spectacular view of the north coast in addition to shopping opportunities. Also in St. Thomas, Tillett Gardens was once a Dutch farm and now is a marketplace for local arts and crafts. In St. Croix, King, Strand and Company streets in Christiansted are lined with shops and arcades, as is Frederiksted's waterfront; King's Alley Walk offers stores, restaurants and hotel suites. Shopping on St. John centers around Mongoose Junction, Wharfside Village and The Marketplace in Cruz Bay, which feature specialty shops, restaurants and water sports outlets.

St. Thomas shopping hours are Mon.-Sat. 9-5; Havensight Mall is open Mon.-Sat. 8-6, Sun. 9-1. Banking hours are Mon.-Thurs. 9-2:30 and Fri. 9-2 and 3:30-5. On St. Croix, most shops in Christiansted are open Mon.-Sat. 10-6, and banks are open Mon.-Thurs. 9-3, Fri. 9-4.

Food and Drink

Restaurants serve a variety of cuisine, including West Indian and Danish dishes as well as American, French, Mexican, Italian, Asian and Middle Eastern; seafood is especially popular. Many hotels also have individual specialties.

The Virgin Islands' tropical climate produces an abundance of exotic culinary favorites, including papayas, mangoes, avocados, passion fruit and bananas. Leaves of wild herbs and plants, combined with meat, fish, okra and other native ingredients, make the most truly native of all dishes, a thick island soup called *kallaloo*. Cornmeal and okra are combined to make *fungee*, a common side dish.

Ripe soursop is used as a fruit and in ice cream; it also is made into a refreshing nonalcoholic drink, as is tamarind. Desserts include tarts made with pineapple, coconut, guava and guavaberry. It is said that the banana daiquiri was perfected at the U.S. Army base on Signal Hill in the 1940s; to date, more than 6 million of these sweet concoctions have been served at Mountain Top.

Drinking water, obtained by the desalinization of seawater or from rainwater cisterns, is safe in hotels and restaurants. Tipping customs are the same as in the United States.

Sports and Amusements

All of the U.S. Virgin Islands are havens of lovely beaches and pools, providing excellent scuba diving and snorkeling. Buck Island Reef, 6 miles (10 km) northeast of Christiansted, St. Croix, is the only underwater U.S. national monument. Beginning divers enjoy investigating the more than 300 reefs around the islands; the experienced usually head for spots in Drake's Passage northwest of St. John. In a protected cove near Buck Island off the south shore of St. Thomas is the 190-foot World War I cargo vessel *Cartenser Sr.* On St. Thomas and St. John, dive shops operating through major hotels offer equipment rental, diving excursions and lessons; there are independent shops as well. The National Park Service offers similar services at Cinnamon Bay in St. John. Independent and resort dive shops in St. Croix are located near dive sites in Cane Bay, Christiansted, Frederiksted and Salt River.

For swimming and sunbathing, Magens Bay on the north coast of St. Thomas is considered one of the top 10 beaches in the world, as is Trunk Bay on St. John. On St. Croix, some of the out-of-the-way inns and hotels have superb beaches and plenty of privacy. Popular beaches include Half Penny, Cramer's Park and Jack's and Isaac's Bays. For sailors, and landlubbers with binoculars, there is the Rolex Regatta in late March.

Deep-sea fishing is popular. The most important gamefish are blue marlin, sailfish, dolphin, kingfish, tuna and wahoo. The USVI Open/Atlantic Blue Marlin Tournament is held in August. Fishing boats are available for charter on all three islands. Sailboats and yachts also can be chartered on all three islands; private cruises are available around the Virgin Islands to Puerto Rico.

For those who prefer land-based pastimes, St. Croix has an 18-hole championship golf course at the Carambola Beach Resort & Spa, an 18-hole course at The Buccaneer and a 9-hole course at The Reef Condominiums at Teague Bay. St. Thomas also sports an 18-hole championship course at the Mahogany Run Golf Course. You can play tennis at hotels and on public courts. St. Croix has many magnificent trails for horseback riding. Horse races are held on holidays at Clinton Phipps Race Track on St. Thomas and Randall "Doc" James Racetrack on St. Croix. Softball and baseball are played during the season on both St. Thomas and St. Croix, and some locals gather for cricket matches on Sunday.

Though sea, sun and sand are the islands' main attractions, there are enough evening pastimes to keep the spirit alive well after sunset. Dinner dancing, jazz, calypso music, limbo dancing and native acts are featured in many hotels and nightclubs. There are dance clubs on all three islands and movie theaters on St. Croix and St. Thomas.

DID YOU KNOW

St. Croix is the
easternmost U.S.
territory in the
Western Hemisphere.

Island Center, a cultural complex on Peppertree Hill on St. Croix, presents plays, musicals and other performances by well-known artists from the United States and neighboring islands. Similar fare is offered at the Reichhold Center for the Arts, an amphitheater on St. Thomas. The St. John School of the Arts and the Cinnamon Bay Amphitheater periodically host vocal, instrumental and theatrical performances. Check with *St. Thomas/St John This Week* and *St. Croix This Week* magazines to find out what's happening and where.

Sightseeing

Island tours are most easily arranged through your hotel activities desk. A 2-hour tour of St. Thomas stops at Drake's Seat and Mountain Top. Visitors to the island's eastern end will find beach clubs and fishing centers. Sunset and harbor cruises are available from Charlotte Amalie.

A scenic trip to Magens Bay for swimming also departs from Charlotte Amalie; sailboats and beach equipment can be rented. A 2-hour tour to the island's western end passes a World War II submarine base, the University of the Virgin Islands and Brewer's Bay on the way to Crown Mountain. The return trip includes a stop at the old sugar mill at Estate Contant; admission is included. Safari bus tours of the island are often less expensive than taxi tours.

Perhaps the best of the many excellent scenic vantage points in Charlotte Amalie is Paradise Point atop Flag Hill. Southeast of Havensight Mall via a steep roadway, the site is especially popular at sunset. St. Thomas Skyride transports visitors to the hilltop. West of the harbor is the fishing village of Frenchtown, where the descendants of settlers from St. Barths continue to live off the sea.

Popular excursions on St. Croix include 3-hour glass-bottom boat or catamaran trips to Buck Island Reef National Monument for snorkeling. Beach barbecues are available with some all-day sails. Arrangements can be made at local dive shops in Christiansted Harbor. Full- and half-day tours of local highlights are available, including the rain forest and Salt River, where Columbus landed. In February the St. Croix Landmarks Society conducts house tours that include restored sugar mills, great houses and elegant mansions.

You can hire one of several safari guides for exploring St. John. A popular day tour includes excursions to the Virgin Islands National Park, Annaberg Sugar Mill ruins and lunch and swimming at Trunk Bay. For those more interested in aquatic sports, boat trips to St. John are available and include 2 hours in Francis Bay for swimming and snorkeling.

Transportation

Direct jet service is available from the U.S. mainland via several airlines. Commuter airlines fly between Puerto Rico, St. Thomas' Cyril E. King Airport and St. Croix's Henry E. Rohlsen Airport. Many cruise ships call at Charlotte Amalie and Frederiksted.

The Vitran bus service on St. Croix, St. John and St. Thomas is mainly for local traffic. Taxi service on St. Thomas and on St. Croix is good, and you also can rent cars on all three islands. Taxi rates are set in advance and apply per passenger. It is always wise to agree on the fare in advance. Parking is usually very scarce in Charlotte Amalie; a public lot east of Fort Christian costs $1 per hour ($5 per day). Taxi service is available on St. John as well, and jeeps can be rented by the day or week. A U.S. driver's license is valid.

Daily ferry service to Cruz Bay, St. John, is offered from two St. Thomas ports: Red Hook, a 20-minute trip, and Charlotte Amalie, a 45-minute trip. Daily ferry service connects both Charlotte Amalie and St. John with the British Virgin Islands of Jost Van Dyke, Tortola and Virgin Gorda; proof of citizenship is required. Service providers include Island Boat Service, (340) 776-6597, and Native Sons, (340) 744-8685.

Fast Facts

POPULATION: 108,612.

AREA: 344 sq km (133 sq mi.).

CAPITAL: Charlotte Amalie, St. Thomas.

HIGHEST POINT: 474 m (1,555 ft.), Crown Mountain, St. Thomas.

LOWEST POINT: Sea level, Caribbean Sea.

TIME ZONE(S): Atlantic Standard.

LANGUAGE: English; Spanish or Spanish creole; French or French creole.

GOVERNMENT: Unincorporated U.S. territory.

UNIT OF CURRENCY: U.S. dollar.

ELECTRICITY: 110-120 volts, 60 cycles AC.

MINIMUM AGE FOR DRIVERS: 21-25, depending on the rental car agency. U.S. license valid; drive on left.

SEAT BELT/CHILD RESTRAINT LAWS: Seat belts are required for driver and front-seat passengers. Child restraints required for under age 3; seat belts required for ages 3-5.

HELMETS FOR MOTORCYCLISTS: Required.

HOLIDAYS: Jan. 1; Three Kings Day, Jan. 6; Martin Luther King Jr. Day, Jan. (3rd Mon.); Presidents Day, Feb. (3rd Mon.); Holy Thursday; Good Friday; Easter Monday; Transfer Day, Mar. 31; Memorial Day, May (last Mon.); Organic Act Day, June (3rd Mon.); VI Emancipation Day/Danish West Indies Emancipation Day, July 3; U.S. Independence Day, July 4; Hurricane Supplication Day, July (4th Mon.); Labor Day, Sept. (1st Mon.); Columbus/Puerto Rico Friendship Day, Oct. (2nd Mon.); Hurricane Thanksgiving, Oct. (3rd Mon.); D. Hamilton Jackson Day, Nov. 1; Veterans Day, Nov. 11; U.S. Thanksgiving, Nov. (4th Thurs.); Christmas, Dec. 25; Boxing Day, Dec. 26.

TAXES: An 8 percent room tax and 10-15 percent service charge are added to most hotel bills. Departure fee is $3 U.S. by air.

IMMIGRATION REQUIREMENTS: Proof of U.S. citizenship is not needed to enter the U.S. Virgin Islands, but it is required to reenter the United States. A valid passport or birth certificate accompanied by a photo ID is accepted. A passport is required when travel involves stops on other Caribbean islands.

PHONING THE ISLANDS: To call the U.S. Virgin Islands from the U.S. or Canada, dial 1 + 340 + the 7-digit local number.

FURTHER INFORMATION FOR VISITORS:
U.S. Virgin Islands Department of Tourism, St. Thomas
78 Contant 1-2-3
Charlotte Amalie, St. Thomas Island 00804
Virgin Islands, U.S.
(340) 774-8784
(800) 372-8784

U.S. Virgin Islands Department of Tourism, St. Croix
P.O. Box 4538
Christiansted, St. Croix Island 00822
Virgin Islands, U.S.
(340) 772-0357
(800) 372-8784

Points of Interest

See map page 240.

St. Croix Island

Old Danish towns rising above the Caribbean characterize the lovely island of St. Croix. Santa Cruz, as it was known by Christopher Columbus, rivaled Barbados as the leading sugar producer in the West Indies; great plantation houses recall these days of wealth on the 84-square-mile island. Modern St. Croix, the easternmost point in the United States territories, is the agricultural and industrial center of the U.S. Virgin Islands as well as a major tourist destination.

Self-guiding tours: The U.S. Virgin Islands Department of Tourism provides a walking/driving tour brochure covering Christiansted and Frederiksted.

BUCK ISLAND REEF NATIONAL MONUMENT (C-4)

About 6 miles (10 km) off the northeast coast of St. Croix, Buck Island Reef offers snorkeling, swimming, picnicking, bird-watching and exploring. The foremost attraction of the national monument—one of only a few underwater parks in the U.S. national park system—is the fine barrier reef. Buck Island, which covers 176 acres (71 hectares), is the only dry land in the park. The remaining 18,800 acres (7,600 hectares) comprise "one of the finest marine gardens in the Caribbean sea." Underwater trails offer excellent opportunities for snorkeling; markers identify the reef's fauna and flora.

Full- and half-day trips to Buck Island from St. Croix can be arranged with licensed concession boats at Christiansted Wharf or Green Cay Marina; snorkeling equipment and instruction are available. Park open daily dawn-dusk. Park admission free. Full-day boat trips (including meals) $80-$98; $60-$78 (ages 6-12); $25 (ages 0-5). Half-day trip $55-$68; $45-$50 (ages 6-12); $20 (ages 0-5). Phone (340) 773-1460 for the park office.

CHRISTIANSTED (C-3) pop. 2,637

Christiansted has preserved the 18th-century buildings of its Danish settlers. Solid stone buildings in pastel colors with bright red tile roofs line the cobblestone sidewalks, adding a touch of European charm. The town's symmetry, with streets running at right angles to the waterfront, makes it popular for walking tours. The shopping area centers on King, Strand and Company streets, next to Christiansted National Historic Site.

CHRISTIANSTED NATIONAL HISTORIC SITE covers three city blocks along the waterfront and town square. The 7-acre (3-hectare) site includes such landmarks of the Danish colonial period as Fort Christiansvaern (1738), the best preserved of the five remaining Danish forts in the Virgin Islands; the Old Scalehouse; the Old Danish Customs House; the Danish West India & Guinea Co. Warehouse; and the Government House, once capitol of the Danish West Indies.

The Steeple Building, St. Croix's first Lutheran church, houses a museum with Arawak and Carib Indian relics. A self-guiding tour brochure is available from the National Park Service headquarters; caution is advised on the area's uneven sidewalks and stairs. **Hours:** Site open daily 8-4:45. Museum open Mon.-Fri. 8-4:45, Sat.-Sun. 9-4:45. Closed Thanksgiving and Christmas. **Cost:** $3; free (ages 0-15 with adult). **Parking:** $1 per hour ($5 maximum per day). **Phone:** (340) 773-1460.

FREDERIKSTED (D-1) pop. 732

The emancipation of slaves was proclaimed on July 3, 1848, at Fort Frederik on the waterfront at the northern edge of Frederiksted. Destroyed by a fire in 1878, Frederiksted was restored during the Victorian era, as reflected in the town's architecture.

Modern Frederiksted operates at a slower pace than Christiansted, except when cruise ships dock in Frederiksted's deepwater port. Visitor information is available at the entry to the pier. Fort Frederik houses art and cultural exhibits, including a police museum which details the history of the town.

Of historical interest are the palatial ruins of Judith's Fancy, the former residence of the governor of the Knights of Malta. Set on an estate of several hundred acres, it has a view of the site where Christopher Columbus anchored at Salt River in 1493. Due to the greeting he received from the Carib Indians, Columbus named it the Cape of the Arrows.

CRUZAN RUM DISTILLERY, on West Airport Rd. at 3A Estate Diamond, is the world's only facility where this rum is produced. Tours and rum tastings are offered at the Estate Diamond visitor's pavilion. **Hours:** Mon.-Fri. 9-4. Closed major holidays. **Cost:** $5; $1 (ages 6-18). **Phone:** (340) 692-2280.

ESTATE WHIM PLANTATION MUSEUM is 1.5 mi. (2.4 km) e. on Queen Mary Hwy. The restored three-room plantation house is furnished with antiques, china, paintings and silver. A museum in the cookhouse contains sugar- and rum-making equipment, household and military articles and reproductions of old engravings. A restored stone sugar mill with large grinding mechanisms typical of those used in the late 18th century also is on the grounds.

Hours: Guided tours depart every 30 minutes Mon.-Sat. 10-4. **Cost:** $10; $5 (senior citizens); $4 (ages 6-12). **Phone:** (340) 772-0598.

LAWAETZ MUSEUM is n. on Rte. 63, then 1.5 mi. e. on Mahogany Rd. (Rte. 76). The 19th-century house of a prominent Danish-Crucian family has been restored at Little La Grange, a working plantation since the 1750s. The West Indian great house contains handcrafted furniture, antiques, photographs and memorabilia. Guided tours reflect rural life during the first half of the 20th century.

Hours: Tues., Thurs. and Sat. 10-4, Nov.-Apr.; Tues., Thurs. and Sat. 10-3, rest of year. **Cost:** $10; $5 (ages 65+); $4 (ages 6-12). **Phone:** (340) 772-1539 or (340) 772-0598.

ST. GEORGE VILLAGE BOTANICAL GARDEN is 4 mi. (6 km) e. at 127 Estate St., just n. of Centerline Rd. This 16-acre (6-hectare) tropical garden surrounds the ruins of a 19th-century workers' village and restored buildings. Royal Poinciana trees burst into flamboyant bloom in summer; hibiscus unfold all year. Housed in a restored worker's cottage, a museum details the village's history through artifacts and photographs. A botanical library also is on the grounds. **Hours:** Grounds open daily 9-5. Museum open Mon.-Fri. 9-5 (also Sat.-Sun. when cruise ship is in port). Library open Tues. 1-4 or by appointment. Closed Christmas. **Cost:** $8; $6 (ages 60+); $1 (ages 0-11). **Phone:** (340) 692-2874.

RECREATIONAL ACTIVITIES

Horseback Riding

• **Paul and Jill's Equestrian Stables** is off Rte. 58. Guided horseback rides are offered; riding lessons are provided. Weight limit is 230 pounds for men, 200 pounds for women. **Hours:** Tours depart Mon.-Sat. **Phone:** (340) 772-2880 or (340) 332-0417.

St. John Island

St. John owes its reputation as a quiet, largely undeveloped haven to the generosity of Laurance Rockefeller. His love of the island's beauty moved Rockefeller in the 1950s to purchase as much of St. John as he could acquire, then to donate most of it to the United States for the creation of a national park, ensuring that "this thing of beauty will be a joy forever." Rockefeller saw his wish fulfilled in 1956 with the dedication of Virgin Islands National Park.

Smaller than Manhattan Island, 19-square-mile (49-sq-km) St. John is scalloped by lovely bays rimmed with white sand beaches of pristine beauty. The most famous is Trunk Bay, where the National Park Service maintains an underwater snorkel trail. Bordeaux Mountain, at 1,277 feet (390 m), dominates the island's rugged topography, and the lush forests conceal ruins of forts and plantation houses and traces of the Arawak and Carib Indians, the island's pre-Columbian inhabitants. Small museums at Cruz Bay exhibit relics of these peoples; their cryptic petroglyphs can be seen on rocks at Reef Bay, along Reef Bay Trail and other places.

The subdued atmosphere of Cruz Bay, the island's main town, conceals a history as a bustling center for the cotton, sugar and rum trade in the days when plantations thrived on St. John. A slave revolt occurred in 1733; the rebels held St. John for 6 months against the Danes and the British before the French finally overran them. Prosperous plantation farming continued through the mid-1830s and limited production continued until 1916, lasting through the emancipation of slaves in 1848.

Accommodations on St. John range from rustic to rich. Platform campsites front the beach at Cinnamon and Maho bays, while Caneel Bay, the world-renowned luxury resort developed by Laurance Rockefeller, occupies the site of an 18th-century sugar estate.

VIRGIN ISLANDS NATIONAL PARK (B-4)

Virgin Islands National Park covers about two-thirds of St. John and most of Hassel Island in St. Thomas Harbor off Charlotte Amalie. Encompassing nearly 15,000 acres (6,000 hectares), including 5,600 acres (2,300 hectares) of offshore waters, the park protects tropical forests, white-sand beaches and coral reefs. Pre-Columbian petroglyphs and the ruins of Danish sugar plantations also are found within its borders. The Cruz Bay Visitor Center, north of the ferry dock, offers park information and exhibits.

Swimming, snorkeling and boating are popular at the park; equipment can be rented. To protect the coral reefs and seagrass beds, moorings have been installed in many areas. Boaters are encouraged to contact the park for information related to safe boating.

Hiking trails lead to scenic overlooks and into deep valleys such as Reef Bay. Park programs range from guided hiking and snorkeling trips to illustrated evening programs at the campground amphitheater.

Annaberg Sugar Mill, built in 1718, is one of the island's best preserved examples of colonial sugar production. A self-guiding walking trail leads through the factory ruins, including a windmill and slave quarters; guided tours are offered by park rangers.

Camping is permitted at Cinnamon Bay, 4 miles (6 km) northeast of Cruz Bay, where accommodations include cottages, tents and tent sites. Maho Bay Campground, on privately-owned land within park boundaries 6 miles (10 km) northeast of Cruz Bay, features canvas cottages connected by wooden walkways that meander through the thickly wooded hillside. Supplies and water sports equipment are available at both sites. Reservations must be made well in advance, often up to a year before the desired date.

The park is open daily 24 hours. Cruz Bay Visitor Center open daily 8-4:30; closed Dec. 25. Ferry service from Red Hook, St. Thomas, to St. John departs hourly 6 a.m.-midnight. Park admission is free. A $4 user fee is charged at Annaberg Ruins and Trunk Bay; under 17 free. For park information, phone (340) 776-6201, ext. 238. For camping reservations, phone Cinnamon Bay at (340) 776-6330 or (800) 539-9998; or Maho Bay at (340) 715-0501 or (800) 392-9004.

St. Thomas Island

Settled by Danes in 1672, St. Thomas covers 32 square miles (83 sq km) of hilly terrain about 40 miles (64 km) east of Puerto Rico. Crown Mountain, at 1,555 feet (472 m), and Signal Hill, at 1,505 feet (460 m), are the highest points. From the road that cuts through the mountain range, both sides of the island can be seen. Near the top of the range is Drake's Seat, from which Sir Francis Drake is supposed to have charted the course of the channel now bearing his name. From this point there is a fine view of Magens Bay, many islands and the Atlantic Ocean.

In the days of piracy, St. Thomas was a favorite hideout for Captain Kidd, Bluebeard and Blackbeard. The towers from which buccaneers are said to have searched the sea for potential victims are now hotels.

St. Thomas' checkered past has left the landscape dotted with contrasting architectural styles. Pastel houses line narrow cobblestone streets and alleys, where the doors reflect the Dutch heritage and the red tile roofs, the Danish. The elaborate iron grill-work was left by the French, and the patios lend a Spanish accent.

Tourism is the chief means of livelihood on St. Thomas. Tennis, golf, boating, swimming and fishing are available; spear fishing and snorkeling are excellent near the coral reefs around the island. Magens Bay on the north coast has a beautiful heart-shaped sand beach.

CHARLOTTE AMALIE (B-2) pop. 11,004

The only town on St. Thomas, Charlotte Amalie is the territorial capital of the U.S. Virgin Islands. This town, climbing up the steep sides of Mafolie Mountain, Frenchman's Hill and Solberg, once served as the home port for such unsavory characters as Captain Kidd, Bluebeard and Blackbeard. Sir Francis Drake employed the port's favorable location to descend upon the gold-laden galleons that sailed through the Anegada Passage en route to Spain.

Under the Danish colonial government the port accommodated one of the world's biggest slave trade operations, routing slaves from Africa to other areas in the Caribbean and on the mainland. From Emancipation Garden, the city's central square, slaves heard the proclamation giving them freedom in 1848.

Valdemar Hill Drive offers a panoramic view of Charlotte Amalie and its deepwater harbor, usually busy with several major cruise ships, container ships, island sloops and yachts. The 17th-century warehouses now house shops and restaurants that accommodate the tourist trade. Distinctive among the city's old buildings is the governor's office, the Government House, furnished with antiques and paintings by native impressionist Camille Pissarro.

At the base of the nearby "Ninety-Nine Steps," one of the few remaining stair-streets that once helped residents traverse the hilly town, is Government Hill, a wealthy residential community of the 18th century. Crown House, a national historic landmark, is a fine example of how wealthy Danish planters lived during the sugar heyday.

Historically significant churches include the Dutch Reformed Church, one of the first outside New York's Dutch colony; and the Frederick Lutheran Church, where silver equipment more than 2 centuries old is still in use. The Jewish Synagogue is one of the oldest in the Western Hemisphere and still has sand on its floor to symbolize the Jews' flight from Egypt through the desert. The New Herrnhut Moravian Church, about 2.5 miles (4 km) east of town, was built by missionaries in 1738.

U.S. Virgin Islands Department of Tourism, St. Thomas: P.O. Box 6400, Charlotte Amalie, St. Thomas, Virgin Islands 00804. **Phone:** (340) 774-8784 or (800) 372-8784.

CORAL WORLD OCEAN PARK is 7.5 mi. (12 km) n.e. at 6450 Coki Point. This 5-acre (2-hectare) marine park features exotic aquariums, outdoor pools, nature trails and the Undersea Observatory. Visitors can pet sharks and feed the stingrays and iguanas during feeding shows. Additional activities include the Sea Trek helmet dive; sea lion swim; sea lion, turtle and shark encounter programs; parasailing; snuba dives; and a semi-submarine ride.

Food, lockers and fresh-water showers are available. **Time:** Allow 1 hour minimum. **Hours:** Daily 9-4. Last admission 1 hour before closing. Hours may vary May-Oct.; phone ahead. **Cost:** $19 (not including special activities or water sports); $10 (ages 3-12); $60 (family, two adults and four children). Coral World and Sea Trek helmet dive $77; $68 (ages 8-12); under age 8 or under 80 pounds not permitted. Coral World and sea lion swim $124; $115 (ages 5-12); under age 5 or under 50 pounds not permitted, under age 12 must be accompanied by adult swimmer. Coral World and sea lion encounter $84; $75 (ages 5-12); under age 12 must be accompanied by adult swimmer. Coral World and turtle or shark encounter $51; $42 (48 inches tall to 12 years); under 48 inches not permitted. Coral World and snuba dive $71; $62 (ages 3-12). Coral World and semi-submarine $39; $30 (ages 3-12). Reservations are recommended for all activities. **Phone:** (340) 775-1555, ext. 233, or (888) 695-2073. [Ⅱ]

FORT CHRISTIAN VIRGIN ISLAND MUSEUM stands on the waterfront near Emancipation Garden Park. The red masonry structure once housed the entire St. Thomas colony. Built by the Danes in 1672, it has been reconstructed several times. Several cells display a collection of Arawak and Carib artifacts and items relating to the early Danish settlers. Under renovation, portions of the fort may close temporarily; phone ahead to confirm schedule. **Hours:** Mon.-Fri. 9-4:30. Closed major holidays. **Cost:** Donations. **Parking:** $1 per hour; $5 per day. **Phone:** (340) 776-4566.

ST. PETER GREATHOUSE ESTATE AND GARDENS is at 6A St. Peter Mountain Rd. Part of a French plantation built in the 1800s, the restored manor is surrounded by 11 acres (4.5 hectares) of landscaped botanical gardens with an elevated nature trail. An observation deck 1,000 feet (305 m) above sea level provides a panoramic view of more than 20 islands. Caribbean artwork is displayed throughout the house.

Mountain Top, the highest point on the island, offers duty-free shopping and banana daiquiris, the signature drink said to have been invented here in the 1940s. **Hours:** Estate open daily 9-4:30. **Cost:** $10; $5 (ages 0-11). **Phone:** (340) 774-4999.

ST. THOMAS SKYRIDE is across from Havensight Mall and the cruise ship dock. Aerial gondolas transport passengers 700 feet (213 m) up a mountainside to Paradise Point. The 15-minute round trip offers views of the harbor and Charlotte Amalie. At the top, tropical bird shows are presented, and a nature trail and shops are available. **Hours:** Daily 9-5 (also Tues. 5-8 and Wed. 5-9) when cruise ships are in port. Bird shows are offered at 10:30 and 1:30. Phone ahead to confirm schedule. **Cost:** Day pass $21; $10.50 (ages 6-12). **Phone:** (340) 774-9809.

AAA Travel Information
In Print, Online and On The Go

**Get AAA's reliable travel information
just the way you want it.**

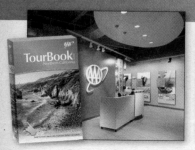
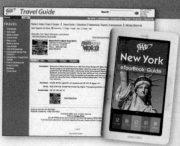

- **TourBook® Guides** - Printed guidebooks available at AAA/CAA offices
- **Travel Guides** - Online destination content available at AAA.com and CAA.ca
- **eTourBook℠ Guides** - eReader travel guides available at AAA.com/ebooks

Create and save trips online with TripTik® Travel Planner and
use them on the go with the TripTik Mobile app.

- **TripTik Travel Planner** - Online trip planning at AAA.com and CAA.ca
- **TripTik Mobile** - Travel app details at AAA.com/mobile

Caribbean

Elbow Cay, Hope Town,
Great Abaco Island,
The Bahamas
© Larry Ulrich

ANGUILLA

This index helps you "spot" where approved hotels and restaurants are located on the corresponding detailed maps. Hotel daily rate range is for comparison only and show the property's high season. Restaurant rate range is a combination of lunch and/or dinner. Turn to the listing page for more detailed rate information and consult display ads for special promotions.

MEADS BAY

Map Page	Hotel	Diamond Rated	High Season	Page
❶ p. 251	Malliouhana Hotel & Spa	◆◆◆	$430-$1590	253

Map Page	Restaurant	Diamond Rated	Cuisine	Meal Range	Page
① p. 251	The Michel Rostang at Malliouhana Restaurant	◆◆◆	International	$20-$60	253

SHOAL BAY EAST

Map Page	Hotel	Diamond Rated	High Season	Page
❸ p. 251	Ku'	◆◆◆	$180-$420	254

RENDEZVOUS BAY

Map Page	Hotels	Diamond Rated	High Season	Page
❹ p. 251	Anguilla Great House Beach Resort (See ad p. 253.)	◆◆	$210-$340	253
❺ p. 251	**CuisinArt Resort & Spa**	◆◆◆◆	$440-$3300 (SAVE)	253

Map Page	Restaurant	Diamond Rated	Cuisine	Meal Range	Page
⑯ p. 251	**Santorini**	◆◆◆◆	Mediterranean	$28-$54	254

COVE BAY

Map Page	Hotel	Diamond Rated	High Season	Page
❽ p. 251	**Paradise Cove Resort**	◆◆◆	$195-$480 (SAVE)	251

MAUNDAYS BAY

Map Page	Hotels	Diamond Rated	High Season	Page
❿ p. 251	Sheriva Luxury Villas & Suites (See ad p. 252.)	◆◆◆◆	$800-$1500	252
⓬ p. 251	**Cap Juluca**	◆◆◆◆	$425-$1675 (SAVE)	252

Map Page	Restaurant	Diamond Rated	Cuisine	Meal Range	Page
④ p. 251	Pimms	◆◆◆	International	$38-$52	252

SHOAL BAY WEST

Map Page	Hotel	Diamond Rated	High Season	Page
⓮ p. 251	Cove Castles	◆◆◆	$595-$2695	254

WEST END

Map Page	Hotel	Diamond Rated	High Season	Page
⓰ p. 251	Viceroy Anguilla Resort & Residences	◆◆◆◆	$495-$1695	254

ISLAND HARBOUR

Map Page	Restaurant	Diamond Rated	Cuisine	Meal Range	Page
⑥ p. 251	Cote Mer Seaside Restaurant	◆◆	French	$22-$36	251

THE VALLEY

Map Page	Restaurant	Diamond Rated	Cuisine	Meal Range	Page
⑭ p. 251	KoalKeel	◆◆◆	International	$32-$52	254

Enjoy great savings on hotel rates
at AAA.com or CAA.ca

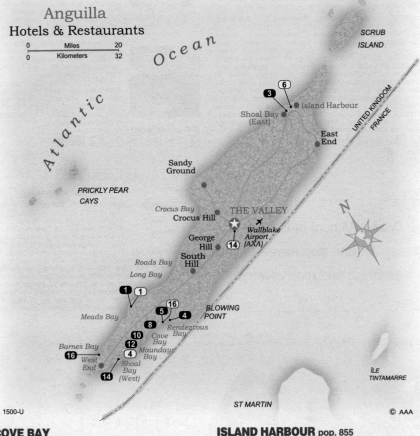

Anguilla
Hotels & Restaurants

0	Miles	20
0	Kilometers	32

Atlantic Ocean

SCRUB ISLAND

Island Harbour

Shoal Bay (East)

East End

UNITED KINGDOM
FRANCE

Sandy Ground

PRICKLY PEAR CAYS

Crocus Bay
Crocus Hill

THE VALLEY

Wallblake Airport (AXA)

George Hill

South Hill

Roads Bay

Long Bay

BLOWING POINT

Meads Bay

Rendezvous Bay

Cove Bay

Maundays Bay

Barnes Bay

West End

Shoal Bay (West)

ÎLE TINTAMARRE

ST MARTIN

1500-U

© AAA

COVE BAY
• Hotels & Restaurants index & map p. 250

PARADISE COVE RESORT   Phone: (264)497-6603   **8**

Boutique Hotel
$195-$480

Address: Paradise Dr AI2640
Location: Just w of ferry dock; center.
Facility: A few blocks from the beach, this locally owned property offers a variety of well-appointed guest rooms and apartment-style units. Meets AAA guest room security requirements. 29 units, some two bedrooms, efficiencies and kitchens. 2-3 stories (no elevator), interior/exterior corridors. **Terms:** office hours 6 am-11 pm, 60 day cancellation notice, 30 day off season. **Amenities:** safes. **Pool(s):** outdoor. **Activities:** whirlpools, beach access, snorkeling, exercise room. **Guest Services:** valet and coin laundry, area transportation-beach. **Free Special Amenities:** continental breakfast and high-speed Internet.

ISLAND HARBOUR pop. 855
• Hotels & Restaurants index & map p. 250

COTE MER SEASIDE RESTAURANT
Phone: 264/498-2683   **6**

French
$22-$36

AAA Inspector Notes: The chef at this al fresco restaurant utilizes a variety of imported and local ingredients to create sumptuous fare with a French-Caribbean flair along with some Mediterranean influences. Appetizers include escargot in puff pastry and fish carpaccio. Entrées range from a selection of such fresh fish as mahi mahi and red snapper to beef tenderloin and veal steak imported from Auge Valley. Homemade desserts are a treat. Friday night is fish grill night while Sunday offers live steel pan music. **Bar:** full bar. **Reservations:** suggested. **Address:** Island Harbour Rd **Location:** Just w of center.

Safety tip: Keep a current AAA/CAA
Road Atlas in every vehicle

MAUNDAYS BAY
• Hotels & Restaurants index & map p. 250

CAP JULUCA
Phone: (264)497-6666 **12**

Resort Hotel
$425–$1675

Address: Maundays Bay **Location:** Oceanfront. 10 mi (16 km) sw of Wallblake International Airport; situated on the southwest coast.
Facility: This high-end resort, which has earned a stellar reputation, offers all ocean-view units in Moorish-style villas. 98 units, some two bedrooms and kitchens. 2 stories (no elevator), exterior corridors. **Terms:** 30 day cancellation notice-fee imposed. **Amenities:** safes, honor bars. **Dining:** 2 restaurants, also, Pimms, see separate listing, entertainment. **Pool(s):** outdoor. **Activities:** sailboats, windsurfing, waterskiing, snorkeling, miniature golf, 3 tennis courts (2 lighted). **Fee:** bicycles, massage. **Guest Services:** valet laundry. **Free Special Amenities:** continental breakfast and high-speed Internet.

[SAVE] [icons] / SOME UNITS [P]

SHERIVA LUXURY VILLAS & SUITES
Phone: (264)498-9898 **10**

Vacation Rental House
$800–$1500

Location: 9.7 mi (15.7 km) sw of Wallblake International Airport; near West End. **Facility:** Spacious villas are well appointed with upscale comforts, including a personal housekeeper and chef assigned to each unit. 7 houses. 2 stories (no elevator), interior/exterior corridors. **Terms:** office hours 7 am-10 pm, 3 night minimum stay, 30 day cancellation notice-fee imposed. **Amenities:** high-speed Internet, safes. **Activities:** whirlpools, game room, exercise room. **Fee:** bicycles, massage. **Guest Services:** complimentary laundry.

(See ad this page.)

[icons]

WHERE TO EAT

PIMMS
Phone: 264/497-6666 **4**

International
$38–$52

AAA Inspector Notes: The talented chef at this fine dining eatery proposes an eclectic menu served al fresco with casual service. Carpaccio of tuna, pheasant soup and the patta negra ham with figs make great starters. The varied and often-changing entree selections may include veal with juniper emulsion, black grouper with macadamia nut butter or the sea bass with wild mushroom ravioli. The tempting desserts include souffles, chocolate and peanut butter terrine along with banana bavarois and warm banana fritters. **Bar:** full bar. **Reservations:** required. **Address:** Maundays Bay **Location:** 10 mi (16 km) sw of Wallblake International Airport; situated on the southwest coast; in Cap Juluca. [D] [icons]

▼ See AAA listing this page ▼

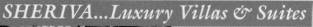

MEADS BAY
• Hotels & Restaurants index & map p. 250

MALLIOUHANA HOTEL & SPA
Phone: 264/497-6111

Vintage Resort Hotel
$430-$1590

Address: Meads Bay Rd **Location:** Oceanfront. 7 mi (11.2 km) w of Wallblake International Airport. **Facility:** Spacious Mediterranean-style units and villas are set on a terraced hillside overlooking a white-sand beach; staff is well trained and personable. 55 units, some two bedrooms. 3 stories (no elevator), exterior corridors. **Terms:** open 12/1-9/1 & 11/1-11/30, 30 day cancellation notice-fee imposed. **Amenities:** high-speed Internet (fee), safes, honor bars. **Dining:** 2 restaurants, also, The Michel Rostang at Malliouhana Restaurant, see separate listing, entertainment. **Pool(s):** 4 outdoor. **Activities:** saunas, whirlpools, steamrooms, waterslide, boating, sailboats, windsurfing, waterskiing, snorkeling, fishing, 4 lighted tennis courts, playground, basketball, volleyball, spa. **Guest Services:** valet laundry.

WHERE TO EAT

THE MICHEL ROSTANG AT MALLIOUHANA RESTAURANT
Phone: 264/497-6111 (1)

International
$20-$60

AAA Inspector Notes: At the Malliouhana Resort Anguilla, this romantic open-air restaurant features candlelit tables facing the sea. The sophisticated setting is perfect for a leisurely dining experience. The menu features a fine mix of international dishes prepared with a Caribbean influence. **Bar:** full bar. **Reservations:** required. **Address:** Meads Bay Rd **Location:** 7 mi (11.2 km) w of Wallblake International Airport; in Malliouhana Hotel & Spa.

B L D

RENDEZVOUS BAY
• Restaurants p. 254
• Hotels & Restaurants index & map p. 250

ANGUILLA GREAT HOUSE BEACH RESORT
Phone: 264/497-6062 (4)

Hotel
$210-$340

Address: Rendezvous Bay Rd **Location:** Oceanfront. 5 mi (8 km) sw of Wallblake International Airport. **Facility:** 31 units. 1-2 stories (no elevator), exterior corridors. *Bath:* shower only. **Terms:** office hours 7 am-11 pm, 30 day cancellation notice, 14 day in season-fee imposed. **Pool(s):** outdoor. **Activities:** snorkeling equipment rental. *Fee:* sailboats. **Guest Services:** valet laundry. *(See ad this page.)*

CUISINART RESORT & SPA Phone: 264/498-2000 (5)

Resort Hotel
$440-$3300

Address: Rendezvous Bay Rd **Location:** Oceanfront. 8 mi (12.8 km) sw of Wallblake International Airport. **Facility:** This distinctive resort with architecture reminiscent of the Greek Isle of Mykonos is on a white-sand beach. The well-appointed rooms are spacious. Meets AAA guest room security requirements. 102 units, some two bedrooms, three bedrooms and houses. 1-3 stories (no elevator), interior/exterior corridors. **Parking:** on-site and valet. **Terms:** 30 day cancellation notice-fee imposed. **Amenities:** high-speed Internet, safes, honor bars. **Dining:** 2 restaurants, also, Santorini, see separate listing, entertainment. **Pool(s):** outdoor. **Activities:** whirlpool, sailboats, windsurfing, snorkeling, 3 lighted tennis courts, recreation programs, playground, volleyball, spa. *Fee:* saunas, steamrooms, bicycles. **Guest Services:** valet laundry.

▼ See AAA listing this page ▼

(See index & map p. 250.)

WHERE TO EAT

SANTORINI

Phone: 264-498-2000 16

Mediterranean
$28-$54

AAA Inspector Notes: Choose from air-conditioned interior dining or al fresco with a pool view at this eatery. The attentive service leaves nothing to chance. Much of the menu centers around the on-site, hydroponically-grown fruits, vegetables and herbs. **Bar:** full bar. **Reservations:** required. **Address:** Rendezvous Bay AI 2640 **Location:** 8 mi (12.8 km) sw of Wallblake International Airport; in CuisinArt Resort & Spa. **Parking:** on-site and valet. D

SHOAL BAY EAST
• Hotels & Restaurants index & map p. 250

KU'

Phone: 264-497-2011 3

Hotel
$180-$420

Address: Shoal Bay E **Location:** Oceanfront. Northwest coast; just s of Island Harbour. **Facility:** 27 kitchen units, some two bedrooms. 1-3 stories (no elevator), exterior corridors. *Bath:* shower only. **Terms:** office hours 7 am-11 pm, 30 day cancellation notice, 21 day off season-fee imposed. **Amenities:** high-speed Internet (fee), safes. **Pool(s):** outdoor. **Activities:** volleyball, exercise room. *Fee:* sailboats, windsurfing, scuba diving, snorkeling, massage. **Guest Services:** valet laundry.

SHOAL BAY WEST
• Hotels & Restaurants index & map p. 250

COVE CASTLES

Phone: 264-497-6801 14

Vacation Rental House
$595-$2695

Location: Oceanfront. West end of island, follow signs. **Facility:** Dotted along a secluded beach are Mediterranean-style villas that have won architectural awards. 16 houses. 1-2 stories (no elevator), exterior corridors. **Terms:** open 12/1-8/31 & 10/31-11/30, office hours 8 am-11 pm, 61 day cancellation notice, 31 day off season. **Amenities:** safes. **Activities:** snorkeling, lighted tennis court, bicycles, exercise room. **Guest Services:** valet laundry.

THE VALLEY (B-2) pop. 1,169
• Hotels & Restaurants index & map p. 250

KOALKEEL

Phone: 264-497-2930 14

International
$32-$52

AAA Inspector Notes: On the site of an old sugar and cotton mill plantation, this pleasant dining room reflects on the history of days gone by. The menu features a wonderful mix of international fare and tandoori specialties. Candlelit tables lend to the romantic feel. Main courses arrive under silver dome covers to add a sense of drama to the meal. All of the not-to-be-missed desserts are prepared fresh to order. Complimentary shuttle service is offered from many island hotels. **Bar:** full bar. **Reservations:** suggested. **Address:** Coronation Ave **Location:** Center. **Historic** D AC

WEST END pop. 736
• Hotels & Restaurants index & map p. 250

VICEROY ANGUILLA RESORT & RESIDENCES

Phone: (264)497-7000 16

Contemporary Resort Hotel
$495-$1695

Address: Meads Bay Rd **Location:** Oceanfront. Main Road to West End; between Barnes Bay and Meads Bay. **Facility:** Perched on a bluff above sugar-sand beaches, this chic and contemporary opulent hotel offers huge guest units and bathrooms that scream luxury. Meets AAA guest room security requirements. 166 units, some two bedrooms, three bedrooms, efficiencies, kitchens and houses. 1-4 stories, interior/exterior corridors. **Terms:** 30 day cancellation notice, 7 day off season-fee imposed. **Amenities:** high-speed Internet, safes, honor bars. **Dining:** 5 restaurants. **Pool(s):** 3 outdoor. **Activities:** paddleboats, sailboats, windsurfing, snorkeling, 3 lighted tennis courts, recreation programs, bicycles, playground, basketball, volleyball, spa. **Guest Services:** valet laundry, area transportation (fee)-ferry dock.

Discover mobile travel solutions at
AAA.com/mobile and CAA.ca/mobile

ANTIGUA AND BARBUDA

This index helps you "spot" where approved hotels and restaurants are located on the corresponding detailed maps. Hotel daily rate range is for comparison only and show the property's high season. Restaurant rate range is a combination of lunch and/or dinner. Turn to the listing page for more detailed rate information and consult display ads for special promotions.

CEDAR GROVE

Map Page	Hotel	Diamond Rated	High Season	Page
1 p. 257	Blue Waters Antigua	◆◆◆	$362-$2715	258

Map Page	Restaurant	Diamond Rated	Cuisine	Meal Range	Page
① p. 257	Le Bistro	◆◆◆	French	$35-$56	258

DICKENSON BAY

Map Page	Hotels	Diamond Rated	High Season	Page
2 p. 257	Buccaneer Beach Club	◆◆	$165-$450	258
3 p. 257	Dickenson Bay Cottages	◆◆	$137-$155	258
4 p. 257	Siboney Beach Club	◆◆	$150-$325	258
5 p. 257	Sandals Grande Antigua Resort & Spa *(See ad on insert.)*	◆◆◆◆	$1416-$3294	258

Map Page	Restaurants	Diamond Rated	Cuisine	Meal Range	Page
② p. 257	Bay House Restaurant	◆◆	International	$15-$40	258
③ p. 257	Opus Restaurant	◆◆◆	International	$18-$32	258
④ p. 257	The Beach	◆◆	International	$17-$42	258
⑥ p. 257	Warri Pier	◆◆	International	$29-$40	259
⑧ p. 257	Ristorante La Bussola	◆◆	Italian	$20-$45	259

JUMBY BAY (Long Island)

Map Page	Hotel	Diamond Rated	High Season	Page
6 p. 257	Jumby Bay, A Rosewood Resort	◆◆◆◆	$975-$3200	260

FIVE ISLANDS

Map Page	Hotels	Diamond Rated	High Season	Page
7 p. 257	Coconut Beach Club	◆	$135-$350	259
9 p. 257	**Galley Bay Resort & Spa**	◆◆◆	$990-$1200 [SAVE]	259

WILLIKIES

Map Page	Hotel	Diamond Rated	High Season	Page
13 p. 257	**The Verandah Resort & Spa**	◆◆◆	$690-$1300 [SAVE]	260

BOLANS

Map Page	Hotel	Diamond Rated	High Season	Page
16 p. 257	Jolly Beach Resort Antigua & Spa	◆	$345-$508	258

ST. MARY'S

Map Page	Hotel	Diamond Rated	High Season	Page
19 p. 257	**Carlisle Bay**	◆◆◆◆	$555-$1150 [SAVE]	260

Map Page	Restaurant	Diamond Rated	Cuisine	Meal Range	Page
⑯ p. 257	East	◆◆◆	Asian	$24-$38	260

RUNAWAY BAY

Map Page	Restaurant	Diamond Rated	Cuisine	Meal Range	Page
⑩ p. 257	Russell's Bar & Seafood Restaurant	▽	Caribbean	$19-$34	260

ENGLISH HARBOUR

Map Page	Restaurants	Diamond Rated	Cuisine	Meal Range	Page
⑫ p. 257	Pizza by Le Cap Horn	▽	Pizza	$13-$21	259
⑭ p. 257	The Admiral's Inn Restaurant	▽ ▽	International	$18-$36	259
⑮ p. 257	The Terrace Restaurant	▽ ▽ ▽	International	$22-$32	259

ST. JOHN'S

Map Page	Restaurant	Diamond Rated	Cuisine	Meal Range	Page
⑱ p. 257	Hemingways Caribbean Cafe	▽ ▽	Caribbean	$20-$34	260

Antigua and Barbuda
Hotels & Restaurants

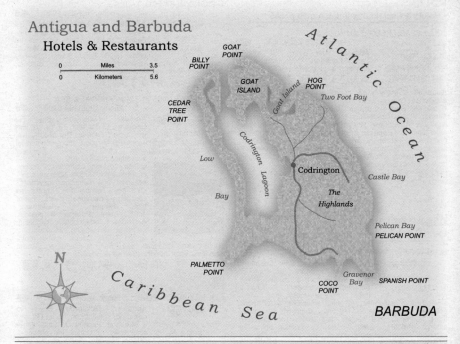

© AAA

1501-U

BOLANS pop. 1,447
• Hotels & Restaurants index & map p. 255

JOLLY BEACH RESORT ANTIGUA & SPA
Phone: (268)462-0061 **16**

Resort Hotel
$345-$508

Address: Jolly Beach, St. Mary's Parish **Location:** Oceanfront. 6 mi (9.6 km) s of downtown St. John's; 12.3 mi (19.7 km) se of airport. **Facility:** The expansive, oceanfront resort offers many water sports activities and five room categories ranging from compact super-savers to junior suites. 464 units. 1-4 stories (no elevator), exterior corridors. **Terms:** 7 day cancellation notice, 3 day off season-fee imposed. **Amenities:** safes (fee). **Dining:** 5 restaurants, entertainment. **Pool(s):** 2 outdoor. **Activities:** canoeing, paddleboats, sailboats, windsurfing, recreation programs, playground, basketball, game room, shuffleboard, volleyball, exercise room, spa. *Fee:* scuba diving, 4 lighted tennis courts. **Guest Services:** valet laundry.

[icons: 🍴 🍸 🏋 🏊 BIZ 🛜 / SOME UNITS 📶 💻]

CEDAR GROVE
• Hotels & Restaurants index & map p. 255

BLUE WATERS ANTIGUA Phone: 268/462-0290 **1**

Resort Hotel
$362-$2715

Address: Soldiers Bay **Location:** Oceanfront. On north coast; 4.4 mi (7 km) nw of airport; at Soldiers Point. **Facility:** The oceanfront resort has a large, open-air lobby and offers several room categories with extra amenities; water sports activities also are offered. 110 units, some two bedrooms, three bedrooms and houses. 2-3 stories (no elevator), exterior corridors. **Terms:** 28 day cancellation notice-fee imposed. **Amenities:** safes, honor bars. *Some:* high-speed Internet. **Dining:** 3 restaurants, entertainment. **Pool(s):** 3 outdoor. **Activities:** whirlpool, paddleboats, sailboats, windsurfing, snorkeling, lighted tennis court, game room, exercise room. *Fee:* massage. **Guest Services:** valet laundry. [icons: 🍴 🍸 🏋 SD 🏊 BIZ 🛜 💻]

WHERE TO EAT

LE BISTRO Phone: 268/462-3881 **1**

French
$35-$56

AAA Inspector Notes: Diners enjoy a spacious, candlelit dining room and a menu of traditional French cuisine prepared with an island flair. Fresh fish and Caribbean lobster are favorites. **Bar:** full bar. **Reservations:** required. **Address:** Hodges Bay **Location:** In Hodges Bay; 5 mi (8 km) e of downtown; 2 mi (3.2 km) n of airport.

[icons: D AC 🚭]

DICKENSON BAY
• Hotels & Restaurants index & map p. 255

BUCCANEER BEACH CLUB
Phone: 268/562-6785 **2**

Motel
$165-$450

Address: Dickenson Bay Rd **Location:** Oceanfront. Center. **Facility:** 18 units, some efficiencies, kitchens and cottages. 1-2 stories (no elevator), exterior corridors. *Bath:* shower only. **Terms:** office hours 7:30 am-10 pm, 14 day cancellation notice. **Amenities:** high-speed Internet, safes. **Pool(s):** outdoor. **Activities:** *Fee:* snorkeling, bicycles. **Guest Services:** complimentary laundry.

[icons: 📶 SD 🏊 🛜 📶 💻]

DICKENSON BAY COTTAGES
Phone: 268/462-4940 **3**

Motel
$137-$155

Address: Dickenson Bay Rd **Location:** Just n of Dickenson Bay. **Facility:** 14 kitchen units. 2 stories (no elevator), exterior corridors. **Terms:** office hours 8 am-8 pm, 21 day cancellation notice. **Amenities:** safes. **Pool(s):** outdoor. **Guest Services:** valet laundry.

[icons: 📶 SD 🏊 🛜 📶 💻 💻]

SANDALS GRANDE ANTIGUA RESORT & SPA
Phone: (268)484-0100 **5**

Resort Hotel
$1416-$3294 12/1-3/31
$1348-$3294 4/1-11/30

Address: Dickenson Bay Rd **Location:** Oceanfront. 7.5 mi (12 km) w of airport. **Facility:** This all-inclusive, couples-only resort offers economical units and more grandeur accommodations. 373 units. 2-7 stories, exterior corridors. **Terms:** check-in 4 pm, 3 night minimum stay - seasonal, age restrictions may apply, 45 day cancellation notice-fee imposed. **Amenities:** safes, honor bars. **Dining:** 9 restaurants, entertainment. **Pool(s):** 8 outdoor. **Activities:** whirlpools, canoeing, sailboats, windsurfing, snorkeling, 2 lighted tennis courts, game room, shuffleboard, volleyball, spa. *Fee:* scuba diving. **Guest Services:** valet laundry. *(See ad on insert.)*

[icons: ✈ 🍴 🍸 SD 🏊 FEE 📶 BIZ 🛜 ✕ 📶 💻]

SIBONEY BEACH CLUB Phone: 268/462-0806 **4**

Motel
$150-$325

Address: Dickenson Bay Rd **Location:** Oceanfront. 7.5 mi (12 km) w of airport. **Facility:** 13 units, some efficiencies. 3 stories (no elevator), exterior corridors. *Bath:* shower only. **Terms:** office hours 7 am-11 pm, 7 night minimum stay - seasonal, 21 day cancellation notice-fee imposed. **Amenities:** safes. **Pool(s):** outdoor.

[icons: 🍴 🍸 🏋 🏊 🛜 📶 💻 💻]

WHERE TO EAT

BAY HOUSE RESTAURANT
Phone: 268/462-1223 **2**

International
$15-$40

AAA Inspector Notes: Perched on a hill with panoramic views, this restaurant offers touches of island elegance in an al fresco setting. Tasty coconut shrimp are a great beginning. Lamb, numerous fresh fish dishes and a variety of pasta creations are among hearty entrees. Crème brûlée and panna cotta are tempting finales. **Bar:** full bar. **Reservations:** suggested, for dinner. **Address:** Dickenson Bay **Location:** 6.7 mi (10.7 km) w of airport; 4 mi (6.5 km) n of downtown St. John's; in Tradewinds Hotel.

[icons: B L D AC 🚭]

THE BEACH Phone: 268/480-6940 **4**

International
$17-$42

AAA Inspector Notes: The beachside al fresco restaurant presents a broad menu of pizza, burgers, lamb, pasta and fresh seafood. Preparation styles span the culinary world. Service is languid and easygoing at the popular spot. Top off the meal with tiramisu or a lemon-lime tart. **Bar:** full bar. **Reservations:** suggested, for dinner. **Address:** Dickenson Bay **Location:** 7.3 mi (11.7 km) w of airport; in Antigua Village. [icons: L D AC 🚭]

OPUS RESTAURANT Phone: 268/462-1501 **3**

International
$18-$32

AAA Inspector Notes: This charming restaurant offers a varied menu which includes salmon, red snapper, duck and lamb preparations, as well as a gourmet pizza menu. **Bar:** full bar. **Address:** Dickenson Bay Rd **Location:** At Trade Winds. [icons: D AC]

(See index & map p. 255.)

RISTORANTE LA BUSSOLA

Phone: 268/726-5559   8

Italian
$20-$45

AAA Inspector Notes: Many visitors to Antigua point their internal compass here for an upscale Italian dining experience created by a hands-on Italian family. The award-winning chef offers a variety of dishes combining French, Italian and Mediterranean cooking techniques. Diners can start with the popular seafood antipasto. The range of main courses include veal shank osso buco, lobster Thermidor and lamb cutlets. The not-to-be-missed desserts include creme brûlée, tiramisu and fruit crepes. **Bar:** full bar. **Reservations:** suggested. **Address:** Runaway Beach **Location:** 7.8 mi (12.5 km) w of airport.

WARRI PIER

Phone: 268/462-0256   6

International
$29-$40

AAA Inspector Notes: At the end of a wooden pier overlooking the sea, this open-air restaurant is a romantic choice for dinner. Peaceful sea breezes wash over the dining room, which is appointed in pleasant island decor. The menu focuses on international fare, including fresh fish, steak and lamb, as well as a nice selection of tasty desserts. **Bar:** full bar. **Reservations:** required. **Address:** Dickenson Bay **Location:** 7 mi (11.2 km) w of airport; 4 mi (6.4 km) e of St. John's; in Halcyon Cove by Rex Resorts.

ENGLISH HARBOUR (F-2) pop. 614
• Hotels & Restaurants index & map p. 255

THE ADMIRAL'S INN RESTAURANT

Phone: 268/460-1027   14

International
$18-$36

AAA Inspector Notes: This restaurant is an ideal stop for lunch or dinner while touring the historic Nelson Dockyard. The blackboard menu changes frequently but always features seafood and meats often prepared utilizing French cooking techniques with a West Indies twist. Fresh local seafood, fish and vegetables from nearby farms are used throughout the menu. The staff is laid-back. **Bar:** full bar. **Address:** Nelson's Dockyard **Location:** 15 mi (24 km) s of St. John's; on south coast; in Nelson's Dockyard National Park overlooking Falmouth Harbour.

Historic

PIZZA BY LE CAP HORN   **Phone:** 268/460-1194   12

Pizza
$13-$21

AAA Inspector Notes: This charming pizzeria offers a small selection of thin-crust pizza with gourmet toppings and then baked in a wood-burning oven. Besides pizza, diners may order goat-cheese salad or one of the entrees from the blackboard menu which includes a catch-of-the-day as well as a butcher's choice. **Bar:** full bar. **Address:** English Harbour Rd **Location:** Center of village. **Parking:** street only.

THE TERRACE RESTAURANT

Phone: 268/460-1014   15

International
$22-$32

AAA Inspector Notes: High on a hill overlooking English Harbour, this restaurant offers open-air and terrace dining and a romantic ambience. Tables are candlelit, and diners enjoy gazing at the stars and the twinkling lights of the harbor below as they feast on fine international cuisine. The menu is ever-changing, with a focus on fresh local and regional ingredients. Sophisticated, attentive servers exude warm island hospitality. **Bar:** full bar. **Reservations:** required. **Address:** Shirley Heights Rd **Location:** In Dockyard National Park on road to Shirley Heights; 16 mi (25.6 km) s of airport; in The Inn at English Harbour.

FIVE ISLANDS
• Hotels & Restaurants index & map p. 255

COCONUT BEACH CLUB   **Phone:** 268/462-3239   7

Motel
$135-$350

Address: Five Islands Rd **Location:** Oceanfront. At entrance to Five Islands, follow signs. **Facility:** 38 units, some efficiencies. 3 stories (no elevator), exterior corridors. **Terms:** office hours 7 am-11 pm, age restrictions may apply, 21 day cancellation notice, in winter-fee imposed. **Amenities:** safes. **Pool(s):** outdoor. **Activities:** sailboats, snorkeling, 2 tennis courts, volleyball. Fee: massage. **Guest Services:** valet laundry.

GALLEY BAY RESORT & SPA

Phone: (268)462-0302   9

Resort Hotel
$990-$1200 12/1-4/14
$940-$1060 4/15-11/30

Address: Galley Bay **Location:** Oceanfront. 4 mi (6.4 km) w of St. John's Harbor via New Rd to Five Islands, follow signs. **Facility:** This luxurious romantic hideaway has rooms that vary from junior suites to Polynesian-style cottages; some units feature a private plunge pool. 100 units, some cottages. 1-2 stories (no elevator), exterior corridors. **Terms:** 5 night minimum stay, 14 day cancellation notice-fee imposed. **Amenities:** safes. **Dining:** 3 restaurants, entertainment. **Pool(s):** outdoor. **Activities:** sailboats, windsurfing, snorkeling, fishing, tennis court, bicycles, jogging, exercise room, spa. **Guest Services:** valet laundry. **Free Special Amenities:** early check-in/late check-out.

Long Island

JUMBY BAY

• Hotels & Restaurants index & map p. 255

JUMBY BAY, A ROSEWOOD RESORT

Phone: (268)462-6000   **6**

Resort Hotel
$975–$3200

Address: Long Island **Location:** Oceanfront. Private island 2 mi (3.2 km) ne of airport; accessed by boat launch on the hour between 7 am and midnight; behind Beach Comber Hotel.
Facility: Set on 300 acres, this private island resort boasts three beaches; guest rooms include soft bedding and a flat-panel television with a DVD player. 58 units, some three bedrooms and houses. 1-2 stories (no elevator), exterior corridors. **Parking:** no self-parking. **Terms:** 45 day cancellation notice, 30 day off season. **Amenities:** safes, honor bars. **Dining:** 3 restaurants, entertainment. **Pool(s):** 2 outdoor. **Activities:** paddleboats, sailboats, windsurfing, boat dock, waterskiing, snorkeling, putting green, 3 tennis courts (2 lighted), recreation programs, bicycles, playground, exercise room, spa. *Fee:* scuba diving. **Guest Services:** valet laundry.

This ends listings for Long Island.
The following resumes the alphabetical listings of cities in Antigua and Barbuda.

RUNAWAY BAY

• Hotels & Restaurants index & map p. 255

RUSSELL'S BAR & SEAFOOD RESTAURANT

Phone: 268/462-5479   **10**

Caribbean
$19–$34

AAA Inspector Notes: Situated in the oceanfront, historic Fort James, this eatery offers a simple menu of Caribbean-inspired cuisine including fresh fish, chicken and beef. Affable owner Russell makes a point to visit each and every table. **Bar:** full bar. **Address:** Fort James **Location:** At Fort James.

ST. JOHN'S (D-2) pop. 22,342

• Hotels & Restaurants index & map p. 255

HEMINGWAYS CARIBBEAN CAFE

Phone: 268/462-2763   **18**

Caribbean
$20–$34

AAA Inspector Notes: Upstairs in a historical building overlooking downtown, the restaurant offers fresh fish, lobster, steaks, lamb and some pasta dishes, all made fresh with the use of local herbs and spices. **Bar:** full bar. **Reservations:** suggested. **Address:** St. Mary's St **Location:** Downtown; at Heritage Quay. **Parking:** street only. **Historic**

ST. MARY'S pop. 10,000

• Hotels & Restaurants index & map p. 255

CARLISLE BAY

Phone: (268)484-0000   **19**

Resort Hotel
$555–$1150

Address: Old Rd **Location:** Oceanfront. Carlisle Bay; on south coast. **Facility:** Enter the chic lobby by crossing a moat but don't expect the uniqueness to end there as the property also features a 50-seat indoor movie theater. 82 units, some three bedrooms. 2-3 stories (no elevator), exterior corridors. **Parking:** on-site and valet. **Terms:** open 12/1-8/27 & 10/16-11/30, 28 day cancellation notice-fee imposed. **Amenities:** high-speed Internet, safes, honor bars. **Dining:** East, see separate listing. **Pool(s):** outdoor. **Activities:** saunas, beach access, sailboats, windsurfing, boat dock, snorkeling, 9 tennis courts (4 lighted), recreation programs, bicycles, playground, basketball, exercise room, spa. *Fee:* waterskiing, scuba diving. **Guest Services:** valet laundry. **Free Special Amenities:** high-speed Internet and children's activities.

WHERE TO EAT

EAST

Phone: 268/484-0000   **16**

Asian
$24–$38

AAA Inspector Notes: This is a sleek, refined restaurant with Asian-minimalist decor. The menu is a mix of Chinese, Thai and Japanese influences converging in seafood dishes centered on shrimp, sea bass and crab and flavored with delicate sauces. The duck is especially succulent. Portions are not overbearing so as to encourage the sampling of several different dishes. The service is polished and attentive. **Bar:** full bar. **Reservations:** suggested. **Address:** Old Rd **Location:** Carlisle Bay; on south coast; in Carlisle Bay.   **D**

WILLIKIES pop. 1,042

• Hotels & Restaurants index & map p. 255

THE VERANDAH RESORT & SPA

Phone: (268)562-6848   **13**

Resort Hotel
$690–$1300 12/1-4/14
$590–$1200 4/15-11/30

Address: Dian Bay **Location:** Oceanfront. At Dian Bay; 12.8 mi (20.5 km) e of St. John's; follow signs; 2.3 mi (3.7 km) e of town; on east coast. **Facility:** Nestled on a bluff, the resort offers cottage-like units with varied amenities, rattan-style furniture, a wet bar and an LCD TV. 180 units. 1 story, exterior corridors. **Terms:** 14 day cancellation notice-fee imposed. **Amenities:** safes. **Dining:** 3 restaurants, entertainment. **Pool(s):** 3 outdoor. **Activities:** canoeing, paddleboats, sailboats, windsurfing, snorkeling, 2 lighted tennis courts, recreation programs, playground, horseshoes, shuffleboard, volleyball, exercise room, spa. *Fee:* sauna. **Guest Services:** valet laundry. **Free Special Amenities:** early check-in/late check-out.

GRAND PINEAPPLE BEACH RESORT

Phone: 268/463-2006

fyi Not evaluated. **Address:** Long Bay **Location:** Oceanfront. 11.8 mi (18.9 km) e of St. John's; 1.3 mi (2.1 km) e of town; on northeast coast, follow signs. Facilities, services, and decor characterize a mid-scale property.

Create complete trip routings and custom maps
with the TripTik® Travel Planner on AAA.com or CAA.ca

Vacation with Peace of Mind

Experience an incredible vacation with amazing value on select *AAA Vacations*® tour and cruise departures. Includes our **Best Price Guarantee** and **24/7 Member Care** for a worry-free vacation.

arashi beach

ARUBA
One happy island

My happy
place gets
5,000
visitors
a day,
most with
gills

find your happy @
aruba.com

ARUBA

Aruba

This index helps you "spot" where approved hotels and restaurants are located on the corresponding detailed maps. Hotel daily rate range is for comparison only and show the property's high season. Restaurant rate range is a combination of lunch and/or dinner. Turn to the listing page for more detailed rate information and consult display ads for special promotions.

PALM BEACH

Map Page	Hotels	Diamond Rated	High Season	Page
2 p. 265	Riu Palace Aruba	▽▽▽	$236-$670	275
3 p. 265	Marriott's Aruba Surf Club	▽▽▽	$251-$626	275
4 p. 265	Hyatt Regency Aruba Resort & Casino *(See ad p. 270.)*	▽▽▽▽	$255-$765 SAVE	275
5 p. 265	Aruba Marriott Resort & Stellaris Casino *(See ad on insert.)*	▽▽▽▽	$359-$809 SAVE	274
8 p. 265	Holiday Inn SunSpree Resort Aruba *(See ad p. 274.)*	▽▽▽	$189-$245	274
9 p. 265	Radisson Aruba Resort, Casino & Spa *(See ad p. 276, p. 52.)*	▽▽▽▽	$275-$769 SAVE	275
10 p. 265	The Westin Resort & Casino, Aruba *(See ad p. 272, on insert, p. 52.)*	▽▽▽▽	$269-$999 SAVE	275
12 p. 265	Divi Aruba Phoenix Beach Resort	▽▽▽	$179-$432 SAVE	274

Map Page	Restaurants	Diamond Rated	Cuisine	Meal Range	Page
1 p. 265	Papillon Restaurant	▽▽▽	French	$25-$40	277
2 p. 265	Taste of Belgium	▽▽	International	$8-$25	278
3 p. 265	Tango Argentine Grill	▽▽	Argentine	$24-$37	278
4 p. 265	Hostaria da' Vittorio	▽▽	Italian	$23-$39	277
5 p. 265	Amazonia Churrascaria	▽▽	Brazilian	$28-$45	277
6 p. 265	Casa Tua Mediterranee	▽▽	Mediterranean	$15-$32	277
7 p. 265	Daniel's Steak & Chop	▽▽▽	Steak	$25-$45	277
8 p. 265	Gianni's Ristorante Italiano	▽▽▽	Italian	$17-$38	277
10 p. 265	Pago Pago	▽▽▽	Steak	$29-$45	277
11 p. 265	Cafe Japengo	▽▽▽	Asian	$24-$45	277
12 p. 265	Las Ruinas del Mar	▽▽▽	Spanish	$28-$46	277
13 p. 265	Sunset Grille *(See ad p. 276.)*	▽▽▽▽	Steak	$30-$58	278
14 p. 265	Aqua Grill	▽▽▽	International	$24-$46	277
15 p. 265	Tandoor Indian Grill House	▽▽	Indian	$12-$23	278
16 p. 265	Texas de Brazil	▽▽▽	Brazilian	$30-$45	278

BUBALI

Map Page	Hotels	Diamond Rated	High Season	Page
16 p. 265	Bucuti & Tara Beach Resorts	▽▽▽	$263-$562 SAVE	266
17 p. 265	Divi Golf and Beach Resort/Divi Village All Inclusive Villas *(See ad p. 268.)*	▽▽▽	$275-$475 SAVE	266

BUBALI (cont'd)

Map Page	Hotels (cont'd)	Diamond Rated	High Season	Page
18 p. 265	**Divi Aruba All Inclusive Beach Resort** *(See ad p. 269.)*	▽▽▽	$438-$626 SAVE	266
19 p. 265	Aruba Beach Club	▽▽	$177-$370	266
21 p. 265	**Tamarijn Aruba All Inclusive Beach Resort**	▽▽	$362-$488 SAVE	266
24 p. 265	**Amsterdam Manor Beach Resort** *(See ad p. 268.)*	▽▽▽	$179-$435 SAVE	265
26 p. 265	Paradise Beach Villas	▽▽	$90-$221	266

Map Page	Restaurants	Diamond Rated	Cuisine	Meal Range	Page
18 p. 265	Chalet Suisse Restaurant	▽▽▽	International	$24-$38	266
20 p. 265	**French Steakhouse Restaurant**	▽▽	Steak	$24-$38	267

ORANJESTAD

Map Page	Hotel	Diamond Rated	High Season	Page
30 p. 265	**Renaissance Aruba Resort & Casino** *(See ad p. 271, on insert, p. 52.)*	▽▽▽▽	$227-$449 SAVE	267

Map Page	Restaurants	Diamond Rated	Cuisine	Meal Range	Page
26 p. 265	Casa Tua Barcelona	▽▽	Mediterranean	$12-$36	273
27 p. 265	Sushi-Ya	▽▽	Japanese	$15-$38	273
28 p. 265	**Iguana Joe's Caribbean Bar & Grill**	▽	International	$11-$24	273
29 p. 265	Driftwood Restaurant	▽▽	Caribbean	$27-$42	273
31 p. 265	L.G. Smith's Steak & Chop House	▽▽▽	Steak	$24-$38	273
32 p. 265	Cuba's Cookin	▽▽	Cuban	$20-$33	273
33 p. 265	CILO, City Lounge	▽▽	International	$12-$25	273
35 p. 265	El Gaucho Argentine Grill	▽▽▽	Argentine	$15-$38	273
36 p. 265	Yemanja Woodfired Grill	▽▽▽	International	$24-$39	273

NOORD

Map Page	Restaurants	Diamond Rated	Cuisine	Meal Range	Page
21 p. 265	Sawasdee Thai Restaurant	▽▽	Thai	$13-$24	267
23 p. 265	Madame Janette	▽▽▽	International	$20-$32	267
25 p. 265	**Buccaneer Restaurant**	▽▽	Continental	$17-$30	267

ARASHI

Map Page	Restaurant	Diamond Rated	Cuisine	Meal Range	Page
38 p. 265	La Trattoria El Faro Blanco	▽▽	Italian	$15-$33	265

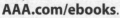

© AAA

Arashi

Malmok

Palm Beach

Noord

Bushiribana

Bubali

Paradera

PUNTA BRABO

Atlantis
Submarine
Expedition

Andicuri

ORANJESTAD

Santa Cruz

Queen Beatrix
International
Airport
(AUA)

Fontein

Balashi

YAMANOTA

Savaneta

Aruba
Hotels & Restaurants

| 0 | Miles | 12 |
| 0 | Kilometers | 20 |

▽ SEE AAA GEM ATTRACTIONS

San Nicolas

Seroe Colorado

COLORADO POINT

1502-U

ARASHI
• Hotels & Restaurants index & map p. 263

LA TRATTORIA EL FARO BLANCO

Italian
$15-$33

Phone: 297/586-0786   ③⑧

AAA Inspector Notes: Adjacent to the California Lighthouse, the windswept area provides stunning views of the breathtaking sunsets and scenery. Those who enter the former home of the lighthouse keeper can choose to dine on the spacious terrace or inside with rustic decor depicting the pirate era of the 1600s. Seafood selections include striped sea bass and lobster linguine. Osso buco and filet mignon with porcini mushrooms are sure to please patrons with hearty appetites. Gourmet pizza is another option. **Bar:** full bar. **Reservations:** required, for dinner. **Address:** California Lighthouse Dr **Location:** Northern tip of island; at California Lighthouse.

B L D 🖊

Learn about AAA/CAA Diamond Ratings at AAA.com/Diamonds

BUBALI
• Restaurants p. 266
• Hotels & Restaurants index & map p. 263

AMSTERDAM MANOR BEACH RESORT
Phone: (297)527-1100   ㉔

Boutique Hotel
$179-$435

Address: JE Irausquin Blvd 252 **Location:** 6.2 mi (9.9 km) nw of airport; 3.5 mi (5.6 km) nw of downtown; across from English Beach. **Facility:** The Dutch Colonial architecture stands out at this intimate hotel just across from the beach. 72 units, some two bedrooms, efficiencies and kitchens. 1-3 stories (no elevator), exterior corridors. **Terms:** check-in 4 pm. **Amenities:** high-speed Internet, safes. **Dining:** 2 restaurants. **Pool(s):** outdoor. **Activities:** beach access, volleyball. *Fee:* snorkeling, bicycles. **Guest Services:** valet and coin laundry. **Free Special Amenities:** high-speed Internet and manager's reception.
(See ad p. 268.)

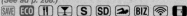

(See index & map p. 263.)

ARUBA BEACH CLUB — Phone: 297/582-3000 [19]

◇◇◇
Condominium
$177-$370

Address: JE Irausquin Blvd 53 **Location:** Oceanfront. Punto Bravo; 4.9 mi (7.8 km) nw of airport; 2.2 mi (3.5 km) nw of downtown. **Facility:** Meets AAA guest room requirements. 131 condominiums. 2-3 stories, interior corridors. *Bath:* shower only. **Terms:** check-in 4 pm, cancellation fee imposed. **Amenities:** safes. **Dining:** entertainment. **Pool(s):** outdoor. **Activities:** recreation programs, playground. *Fee:* 2 lighted tennis courts, massage. **Guest Services:** valet and coin laundry.

[icons]

BUCUTI & TARA BEACH RESORTS — Phone: (297)583-1100 [16]

◇◇◇
Boutique Hotel
$263-$562

Address: L.G. Smith Blvd 55B **Location:** Oceanfront. 5.1 mi (8.1 km) nw of airport; 2.4 mi (3.8 km) nw of downtown; at Eagle Beach. Located behind Alhambra Casino Complex. **Facility:** Located on a gorgeous beach, this award-winning, adults-only hotel is small enough to provide personalized service and an intimate experience. Meets AAA guest room security requirements. 104 units, some efficiencies. 1-4 stories, interior/exterior corridors. **Terms:** 5-7 night minimum stay - seasonal, age restrictions may apply, 45 day cancellation notice, 21 day off season-fee imposed. **Amenities:** safes, honor bars. **Dining:** entertainment. **Pool(s):** outdoor. **Activities:** whirlpool, exercise room. *Fee:* massage. **Guest Services:** valet and coin laundry. **Free Special Amenities:** full breakfast and high-speed Internet.

[icons]

DIVI ARUBA ALL INCLUSIVE BEACH RESORT — Phone: (297)525-5200 [18]

◇◇◇
Resort Hotel
$438-$626

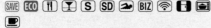

Address: JE Irausquin Blvd 45 **Location:** Oceanfront. 4.7 mi (7.5 km) nw of airport; 2 mi (3.2 km) nw of downtown; adjacent to Punto Bravo Beach. Across from Alhambra Casino Complex. **Facility:** This resort shares facilities with Tamarijn Aruba All Inclusive Beach Resort; all units have a balcony or patio with ocean views and Caribbean-style décor. 203 units. 1-3 stories (no elevator), interior/exterior corridors. **Terms:** 5 night minimum stay, 30 day cancellation notice-fee imposed. **Amenities:** safes (fee). **Dining:** 4 restaurants, entertainment. **Pool(s):** 3 outdoor. **Activities:** whirlpool, canoeing, sailboats, windsurfing, snorkeling, 2 lighted tennis courts, recreation programs, bicycles, shuffleboard, volleyball, exercise room, spa. **Guest Services:** valet laundry.
(See ad p. 269.)

[icons]

DIVI GOLF AND BEACH RESORT/DIVI VILLAGE ALL INCLUSIVE VILLAS — Phone: (297)583-5000 [17]

◇◇◇
Resort
Condominium
$275-$475

Address: JE Irausquin Blvd #93 **Location:** L.G. Smith Blvd, exit JE Irausquin Blvd. **Facility:** Guest units range from luxurious to well appointed at this expansive property. 471 condominiums. 2-5 stories, interior/exterior corridors. **Terms:** check-in 4 pm, 3 night minimum stay, 30 day cancellation notice-fee imposed. **Amenities:** safes. **Dining:** 6 restaurants, entertainment. **Pool(s):** 7 outdoor. **Activities:** whirlpools, beach access, 3 lighted tennis courts. **Guest Services:** valet and coin laundry.

(See ad p. 268.)

[icons] / SOME UNITS [icons]

PARADISE BEACH VILLAS — Phone: 297/587-4000 [26]

◇◇◇
Vacation Rental
Condominium
$90-$221

Address: JE Irausquin Blvd 64 **Location:** Oceanfront. 5.8 mi (9.3 km) nw of airport; 3.1 mi (4.9 km) nw of downtown. **Facility:** Designed for long-term stays, this condo-style lodging across from Eagle Beach is distinguished by its architectural Spanish-Dutch influences. Meets AAA guest room security requirements. 80 condominiums. 3-4 stories, interior/exterior corridors. **Terms:** office hours 6:30 am-10 pm, check-in 4 pm, 7 day cancellation notice-fee imposed. **Amenities:** safes. **Dining:** 2 restaurants. **Pool(s):** 2 outdoor. **Activities:** whirlpools, shuffleboard, exercise room. **Guest Services:** coin laundry.

[icons]

TAMARIJN ARUBA ALL INCLUSIVE BEACH RESORT — Phone: (297)525-5200 [21]

◇◇◇
Resort Hotel
$362-$488

Address: JE Irausquin Blvd 41 **Location:** Oceanfront. 4.5 mi (7.2 km) nw of airport; 1.8 mi (2.9 km) nw of downtown. **Facility:** This all-inclusive resort with a contemporary lobby features an expansive gym, theme restaurants, a rock climbing wall and rooms with tropical décor. 236 units. 2 stories (no elevator), exterior corridors. **Terms:** 5 night minimum stay, 30 day cancellation notice-fee imposed. **Amenities:** safes (fee). **Dining:** 4 restaurants, entertainment. **Pool(s):** outdoor. **Activities:** canoeing, sailboats, windsurfing, snorkeling, 2 lighted tennis courts, recreation programs, bicycles, game room, shuffleboard, volleyball, exercise room. **Guest Services:** valet laundry.

[icons]

WHERE TO EAT

CHALET SUISSE RESTAURANT — Phone: 297/587-5054 [18]

◇◇◇
International
$24-$38

AAA Inspector Notes: The restaurant has earned a solid reputation since it opened in 1988. International and Continental flavors influence the French-trained chef's preparations, which include dishes made from prime cuts of meat and fresh seafood. Portions are ample. Swiss-style architecture and decor characterizes the bustling dining room, where diners often linger over the decadent chocolate fondue. Repeat guests often favor the early-bird specials. **Bar:** full bar. **Reservations:** required. **Address:** JE Irausquin Blvd 246 **Location:** 3.1 mi (4.9 km) nw of downtown; across from Eagle Beach. [D]

(See index & map p. 263.)

FRENCH STEAKHOUSE RESTAURANT

Menu on AAA.com   **Phone:** 297/582-3444   **20**

▼▼ ▼▼
Steak
$24-$38

AAA Inspector Notes: The restaurant specializes in beef and seafood. The French decor touches accent a dining room comfortable for casual dining or a special occasion. An extensive wine list is offered. **Bar:** full bar. **Reservations:** required. **Address:** JE Irausquin Blvd 55 **Location:** 5 mi (8 km) nw of airport; 2.3 mi (3.7 km) nw of downtown at Punto Bravo; in Manchebo Beach Resort & Spa. D

NOORD
• **Hotels & Restaurants index & map p. 263**

BUCCANEER RESTAURANT

Phone: 297/586-6172   **25**

▼▼ ▼▼
Continental
$17-$30

AAA Inspector Notes: The popular, casual spot might make diners feel as though they are eating in a ship's cabin; windows display saltwater aquariums, and two bars are made from old ships. Patrons should stop in early for a good table, as reservations are not accepted. Seafood, beef and European specialties, all served in large portions, line the menu. **Bar:** full bar. **Address:** Gasparito 11-C **Location:** 0.3 mi (0.5 km) e from Palm Beach, 0.3 mi (0.5 km) s, follow signs. D

MADAME JANETTE

Phone: 297/587-0184   **23**

▼▼ ▼▼
International
$20-$32

AAA Inspector Notes: The restaurant is a perennial favorite with repeat tourists and locals alike. Guests can savor the international flavors of Caribbean-influenced cuisine in the al fresco garden courtyard. Rich rock lobster a la creme in a puff pastry and crab cakes with spicy island remoulade are great beginnings. Among offerings in a sea of fresh fish are snapper, grouper, mahi mahi and sea bass. Carnivores might try the veal chop with marinara sauce or beef stroganoff. **Bar:** full bar. **Reservations:** suggested. **Address:** Cunucu Abao 37 **Location:** 3.5 mi (5.6 km) n of downtown; just e of L.G. Smith Blvd; in front of Blue Village Apartments. D 🅐 🗡

SAWASDEE THAI RESTAURANT

Phone: 297/586-8071   **21**

▼▼ ▼▼
Thai
$13-$24

AAA Inspector Notes: A complete Thai meal can be had at this restaurant where the owners-hosts are quite congenial. An array of curry dishes, pad Thai, beef, chicken and seafood are offered. The soups are very flavorful and the dishes are cooked to order so guests can select how spicy they desire the dish. **Bar:** full bar. **Reservations:** suggested. **Address:** Palm Beach, #186B **Location:** Corner of Sasaki and Palm Beach rds. D

ORANJESTAD (A-1) pop. 26,355
• **Restaurants p. 273**
• **Hotels & Restaurants index & map p. 263**

RENAISSANCE ARUBA RESORT & CASINO

Phone: (297)583-6000   **30**

▼▼ ▼▼ ▼▼
Resort Hotel
$227-$449

R
RENAISSANCE®
HOTELS & RESORTS

AAA Benefit: AAA hotel discounts of 5% or more.

Address: L.G. Smith Blvd 82 **Location:** Oceanfront. 2.7 mi (4.3 km) nw of airport; downtown. Part of Seaport Village Complex. **Facility:** The marina tower is ideal for singles or couples with its cool, chic ambiance whereas the beach tower is ideal for families and long-term guests. 556 units, some condominiums. 5-6 stories, interior corridors. **Parking:** on-site and valet. **Terms:** check-in 4 pm, 3 day cancellation notice. **Amenities:** high-speed Internet (fee), safes. **Dining:** 22 restaurants, also, CILO, City Lounge, L.G. Smith's Steak & Chop House, Sushi-Ya, see separate listings, entertainment. **Pool(s):** 3 outdoor. **Activities:** marina, 2 lighted tennis courts, recreation programs, basketball, game room, volleyball, spa. *Fee:* steamrooms, boats, canoes, paddleboats, sailboats, windsurfing, scuba diving, snorkeling, charter fishing. **Guest Services:** valet and coin laundry.
(See ad p. 271, on Insert, p. 52.)

SAVE 🔥 🍴 🏊 🎣 S SD 🛄 👨‍👩‍👧 BIZ
📶 ✕ 🔋 🖥 / SOME UNITS 🧳

(See index & map p. 263.)

Share a New View on Travel at
AAATravelViews.com

Read stories, tips and trends from AAA insiders.
Post comments and get your questions answered by our
travel experts.

(See index & map p. 263.)

Explore the Travel Guides on
AAA.com/Travel or CAA.ca/Travel

(See index & map p. 263.)

▼ *See AAA listing p. 275* ▼

Download eTourBook guides for ereaders and
smartphones at AAA.com/ebooks

▼ See AAA listing p. 267 ▼

WHERE RELAXATION AND RECREATION COMBINE IN ONE REMARKABLE RESORT.

When you arrive at Renaissance Aruba Resort, you are walking into your own personal paradise. Immerse yourself in our world of culture, excitement and did we mention Aruba's only private beaches? Unwinding will be easy, choosing what to experience first may take some time.

For reservations please call **1-800-421-8188** and ask for our AAA preferred rate or visit **www.renaissancearuba.com** and use promotional code AAA.

R
RENAISSANCE®
ARUBA RESORT & CASINO

Indulge in a tropical escape
from $169 a night**

Westin gives you lots of ways to make the most of family time no matter what size your family is. Now you can spend more time together—for less.

Come for reviving sunshine, deliciously wholesome menus, pampering treatments, blissful relaxation and the excitement of our newly renovated Palm Beach Casino. At the Westin Resort & Casino Aruba, we have just what you need for a delightful family vacation.

TO VIEW YOUR SPECIAL AAA OFFERS GO TO WESTINARUBA.COM/AUTODEAL OR TO MAKE A RESERVATION CALL 1.877.822.2222.

THE WESTIN
RESORT & CASINO
ARUBA

Scan this tag on your
smartphone & start
saving today!

Get the free mobile app at
http://gettag.mobi

(See index & map p. 263.)

WHERE TO EAT

CASA TUA BARCELONA Phone: 297/588-5695 **26**

Mediterranean
$12-$36

AAA Inspector Notes: Situated downtown, this Spanish-Mediterranean-influenced restaurant offers a gourmet pizza menu, pasta and an array of tapas. On Friday there is a special paella menu as well as a live flamenco dancing show. **Bar:** full bar. **Address:** Havenstraat #4 **Location:** Downtown; upstairs of Aventura Mall; behind Renaissance Aruba Resort & Casino. **Parking:** street only.

CILO, CITY LOUNGE Phone: 297/588-7996 **33**

International
$12-$25

AAA Inspector Notes: This eatery, adjacent to the downtown marina, is a great place for people watching. Diners can start the day with one of the full English, American or Dutch breakfast options. Lunch features a variety of sandwiches and wraps with a wide choice of breads and fillings including parma ham, steak tartar and crab salad. Full-course dinner entrées include pork medallions with a Cognac sauce and a salmon filet in a creamy herb-spinach sauce. Attentive service and wine-by-the-glass choices are offered. **Bar:** full bar. **Address:** L.G. Smith Blvd 28 **Location:** 2.7 mi (4.3 km) nw of airport; downtown; in Renaissance Aruba Resort & Casino.

CUBA'S COOKIN Phone: 297/588-0627 **32**

Cuban
$20-$33

AAA Inspector Notes: With captivating original Cuban art on the walls, this rustic, intimate interior reflects the ambience of old Havana. Effervescent servers dish up hearty portions of Cuban-inspired cuisine including lechon (roast pork), ropa vieja (skirt steak), churrasco Cubano and lobster enchiladas are satisfying. Among side dishes are yuca and plantains. Live music is featured nightly. **Bar:** full bar. **Reservations:** required. **Address:** Wilhelminastraat #27 **Location:** Downtown; just se of Seaport Village; across from police station.

DRIFTWOOD RESTAURANT Phone: 297/583-2515 **29**

Caribbean
$27-$42

AAA Inspector Notes: For almost 20 years the owner of this restaurant has been catching the fish for this downtown restaurant daily. Meals are served in the rustic ambience of a natural driftwood dining room. The chefs prepare a wide variety of fish and seafood dishes Arubian style. All meals come with pan bati, a type of cornbread. **Bar:** full bar. **Reservations:** suggested. **Address:** Klipstraat 12 **Location:** Just s; corner of Rifstraat and Klipstraat sts; downtown. **Parking:** street only. **D**

EL GAUCHO ARGENTINE GRILL Phone: 297/582-3677 **35**

Argentine
$15-$38

AAA Inspector Notes: Serving the area since 1977, this Argentine steakhouse has been serving prime Argentine beef, imported lamb, veal chops and Aruban seafood in a tastefully rustic ambience with refined service. Diners with kids in tow may enjoy the fact there is a kids' playroom in a separate area from the dining rooms. Weekends feature strolling guitarists. **Bar:** full bar. **Reservations:** suggested. **Address:** Wilhelminastraat 80 **Location:** 3 mi (4.5 km) nw of airport; downtown; just s of Renaissance Aruba Resort & Casino. **Parking:** on-site and street. **L** **D**

IGUANA JOE'S CARIBBEAN BAR & GRILL Phone: 297/583-9373 **28**

International
$11-$24

AAA Inspector Notes: This fun, festive grill has an open-air terrace upstairs overlooking the gallery of downtown shops. The easy-to-spot restaurant is not far from the cruise ship docks. Burgers, barbecue, quesadillas and fajitas are favorites. Sangria is refreshing on a hot day. **Bar:** full bar. **Address:** Royal Plaza Mall, Suite 302 **Location:** Downtown; across from cruise ship docks; upstairs in Royal Plaza Mall. **Parking:** street only.

L.G. SMITH'S STEAK & CHOP HOUSE Phone: 297/523-6195 **31**

Steak
$24-$38

AAA Inspector Notes: A popular spot on the Aruba dining scene, this contemporary steakhouse serves certified aged Angus beef in a hip, stylish atmosphere. Steak choices range from the 8-ounce petit filet mignon to a whopping 22-ounce porterhouse. Live music is featured Wednesday through Monday. **Bar:** full bar. **Reservations:** suggested. **Address:** L.G. Smith Blvd 82 **Location:** 2.7 mi (4.3 km) nw of airport; downtown; in Renaissance Aruba Resort & Casino. **Parking:** on-site and valet. **D**

SUSHI-YA Phone: 297/583-9982 **27**

Japanese
$15-$38

AAA Inspector Notes: Located in the Renaissance Seaport Marketplace, this sushi-bar restaurant offers indoor tatami seating or al fresco dining on the patio. Besides a wide array of sushi, sashimi and tempura, the eatery offers a large sake menu and traditional Japanese-inspired dinners. **Bar:** full bar. **Address:** L.G. Smith Blvd z/n **Location:** 2.7 mi (4.3 km) nw of airport; downtown; in Renaissance Marketplace. **L** **D** **N**

YEMANJA WOODFIRED GRILL Phone: 297/588-4711 **36**

International
$24-$39

AAA Inspector Notes: Situated in two Dutch-Colonial buildings, this restaurant is distinguished by the use of wood-fired grill preparations utilizing mesquite and hickory wood. For starters there are an array of salads including one with scallops as well as carpaccio fish and beef. Entrées include wood-fire grilled grouper, tuna, chicken, lamb and prime cuts of beef. Enjoy the casual dining ambience with attentive service. **Bar:** full bar. **Reservations:** suggested. **Address:** Wilhelminastraat 2 **Location:** Downtown; behind Renaissance Aruba Resort & Casino. **Parking:** street only. **D** **N**

PALM BEACH (A-1)
- **Restaurants p. 277**
- **Hotels & Restaurants index & map p. 263**

ARUBA MARRIOTT RESORT & STELLARIS CASINO
Phone: (297)586-9000

Resort Hotel
$359-$809

AAA Benefit: AAA hotel discounts of 5% or more.

Address: L.G. Smith Blvd 101 **Location:** Oceanfront. 8.6 mi (13.7 km) nw of airport; 6.9 mi (11 km) nw of downtown; north end of town. **Facility:** A renovation resulted in very contemporary décor throughout the sprawling oceanfront resort with a free-form lagoon-style pool. Meets AAA guest room security requirements. 411 units. 8 stories, interior corridors. **Terms:** check-in 4 pm, 7 day cancellation notice. **Amenities:** high-speed Internet (fee), safes. **Dining:** 7 restaurants, entertainment. **Pool(s):** outdoor. **Activities:** saunas, whirlpool, 2 lighted tennis courts, recreation programs, playground, basketball, game room, volleyball, spa. *Fee:* scuba diving, snorkeling. **Guest Services:** valet laundry. *(See ad on insert.)*

DIVI ARUBA PHOENIX BEACH RESORT
Phone: 297/586-6066

Resort
Condominium
$179-$432

Address: JE Irausquin Blvd 75 **Location:** Oceanfront. 6.9 mi (11 km) nw of airport; 4.2 mi (6.7 km) nw of downtown. **Facility:** A variety of room types are available to choose from, all with contemporary decor, as well as well-appointed public areas. Meets AAA guest room security requirements. 240 condominiums. 4-14 stories, interior/exterior corridors. **Terms:** check-in 4 pm, 7 day cancellation notice-fee imposed. **Amenities:** safes. **Dining:** 3 restaurants, entertainment. **Pool(s):** 3 outdoor. **Activities:** sauna, whirlpools, lighted tennis court, racquetball court, recreation programs, volleyball. *Fee:* massage. **Guest Services:** valet and coin laundry.

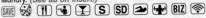

HOLIDAY INN SUNSPREE RESORT ARUBA
Phone: (297)586-3600

Resort Hotel
$189-$245 12/1-4/9
$129-$149 4/10-11/30

Address: JE Irausquin Blvd 230 **Location:** Oceanfront. 8 mi (12.8 km) nw of downtown. **Facility:** Meets AAA guest room security requirements. 600 units, some two bedrooms. 6-7 stories, interior corridors. **Terms:** check-in 4 pm, 2 night minimum stay - weekends, 7 day cancellation notice-fee imposed. **Amenities:** safes. **Dining:** 4 restaurants, entertainment. **Pool(s):** 2 outdoor. **Activities:** saunas, whirlpools, rental paddleboats, rental sailboats, boat dock, snorkeling equipment rental, 2 lighted tennis courts, recreation programs, playground, basketball, volleyball, exercise room, spa. *Fee:* waterskiing, scuba diving, game room. **Guest Services:** valet and coin laundry. *(See ad this page.)*

 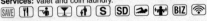

Plan. Map. Go.
TripTik® Travel Planner

Where premier mapping technology meets complete travel information. Only on AAA.com and CAA.ca.

(See index & map p. 263.)

HYATT REGENCY ARUBA RESORT & CASINO
Phone: (297)586-1234 **4**

Resort Hotel
$255-$765

AAA Benefit: Members save 10% or more everyday.

Address: JE Irausquin Blvd 85 **Location:** Oceanfront. 7.4 mi (11.8 km) nw of airport; 5.7 mi (9.1 km) nw of downtown. **Facility:** Well-appointed rooms and extensive, tropically landscaped grounds enhance this beachfront high-rise resort with popular nightlife and refined service. Meets AAA guest room security requirements. 357 units. 9 stories, interior corridors. **Parking:** on-site and valet. **Terms:** check-in 4 pm, 14 day cancellation notice-fee imposed. **Amenities:** safes, honor bars. **Dining:** 4 restaurants, also, Cafe Japengo, Las Ruinas del Mar, see separate listings, entertainment. **Pool(s):** 2 outdoor. **Activities:** sauna, whirlpools, steamroom, waterslide, rental boats, rental paddleboats, rental sailboats, rental sailboards, fishing, 2 lighted tennis courts, recreation programs, playground, basketball, game room, shuffleboard, volleyball, exercise room, spa. **Fee:** waterskiing, scuba diving, snorkeling, charter fishing. **Guest Services:** valet laundry. (See ad p. 270.)

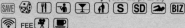

MARRIOTT'S ARUBA SURF CLUB
Phone: (297)586-9000 **3**

Resort Condominium
$251-$626

AAA Benefit: AAA hotel discounts of 5% or more.

Address: L.G. Smith Blvd 103 **Location:** 8.6 mi (13.7 km) nw of airport; 6.9 mi (11 km) nw of downtown; north end of Palm Beach. **Facility:** Handsome rooms and a fine beach are offered at this service-oriented property, which also features expansive, tropical public areas. Meets AAA guest room security requirements. 900 condominiums. 14 stories, interior corridors. **Terms:** off-site registration, check-in 4 pm, 7 day cancellation notice. **Amenities:** high-speed Internet (fee), safes. **Dining:** entertainment. **Pool(s):** 2 outdoor. **Activities:** saunas, whirlpools, steamrooms, waterslide, 2 lighted tennis courts, playground, basketball, game room, horseshoes, shuffleboard, volleyball. **Guest Services:** valet and coin laundry.

Simply Reliable

The Diamond Ratings in this TourBook guide are backed by our expert, in-person evaluations, whether the hotel or restaurant is no-frills, moderate or upscale.

Learn more at **AAA.com/Diamonds**

RADISSON ARUBA RESORT, CASINO & SPA
Phone: (297)586-6555 **9**

Resort Hotel
$275-$769

Address: Oceanfront. 7.6 mi (12.1 km) nw of airport; 4.9 mi (7.8 km) nw of downtown. **Facility:** The property features spectacular landscaping, a superlative beachfront location along with guest rooms boasting rich, tropical décor and furnishings. 355 units. 4-8 stories, interior corridors. **Terms:** check-in 4 pm, 21 day cancellation notice, 14 day off season. **Amenities:** high-speed Internet, safes. **Dining:** 2 restaurants, also, Sunset Grille, see separate listing, entertainment. **Pool(s):** 2 outdoor. **Activities:** whirlpools, rental boats, rental canoes, rental paddleboats, rental sailboats, rental sailboards, recreation programs, playground, game room, volleyball, spa. **Fee:** saunas, steamrooms, waterskiing, scuba diving, snorkeling, charter fishing. **Guest Services:** valet laundry. **Free Special Amenities:** high-speed Internet and manager's reception.
(See ad p. 276, p. 52.)

RIU PALACE ARUBA
Phone: 297/586-3900 **2**

Resort Hotel

$236-$670 12/1-4/30
$236-$480 5/1-11/30

Address: JE Irausquin Blvd #79 **Location:** Oceanfront. 7.3 mi (11.7 km) nw at Palm Beach; downtown. **Facility:** Guest rooms at this large all-inclusive resort are well equipped and feature a European flair; recreational facilities abound. 450 units. 8-10 stories, interior/exterior corridors. **Terms:** 7 day cancellation notice-fee imposed. **Amenities:** safes, honor bars. **Dining:** 6 restaurants, entertainment. **Pool(s):** 2 outdoor. **Activities:** saunas, whirlpools, recreation programs, game room, volleyball, spa. **Guest Services:** valet laundry.

THE WESTIN RESORT & CASINO, ARUBA
Phone: (297)586-4466 **10**

Resort Hotel
$269-$999 12/1-4/12
$279-$689 4/13-11/30

WESTIN HOTELS & RESORTS **AAA Benefit:** Enjoy up to 15% off your next stay, plus Starwood Preferred Guest® bonuses.

Address: JE Irausquin Blvd 77 **Location:** Oceanfront. 7.2 mi (11.5 km) nw of airport; 4.5 mi (7.2 km) nw of downtown. **Facility:** Comprehensive resort facilities with a variety of restaurants featured and new spa facilities. The spacious guest rooms provide numerous updates. 481 units. 18 stories, interior corridors. **Parking:** on-site and valet. **Terms:** check-in 4 pm, 3 day cancellation notice-fee imposed. **Amenities:** high-speed Internet, safes. **Dining:** 4 restaurants, also, Pago Pago, see separate listing, entertainment. **Pool(s):** outdoor. **Activities:** steamrooms, rental paddleboats, snorkeling & rental equipment, recreation programs, playground, volleyball, spa. **Fee:** waterskiing, scuba diving. **Guest Services:** valet laundry. (See ad p. 272, on insert, p. 52.)

▼ See AAA listing p. 275 ▼

(See index & map p. 263.)

WHERE TO EAT

AMAZONIA CHURRASCARIA

Phone: 297/586-4444 (5)

Brazilian
$28-$45

AAA Inspector Notes: This memorable dining experience is nirvana for the indisputable carnivore. Besides the extensive selection of Brazilian hot dishes and salad bar fixings, there are specialized carvers who, on command, bring cuts of rodizio charcoal-grilled beef, lamb, pork and chicken to the table. Try a refreshing Brazilian caipirinha to wash everything down. **Bar:** full bar. **Reservations:** required. **Address:** JE Irausquin Blvd 374 **Location:** 7.8 mi (12.5 km) nw of town at Palm Beach; across from Hyatt Regency Aruba Resort & Casino.

D CALL M

AQUA GRILL

Phone: 297/586-5900 (14)

International
$24-$46

AAA Inspector Notes: Swimming in a sea of restaurants, this eatery continues to make a big splash with repeat clientele. It serves not only freshly-caught, local seafood and fish but also other seafood and fish that is flown in daily. August is lobster month. The attentive and engaging staff serves meals in stylish dining rooms. **Bar:** full bar. **Reservations:** required. **Address:** JE Irausquin Blvd 374 **Location:** 7.8 mi (12.5 km) nw of town at Palm Beach; across from Hyatt Regency Aruba Resort & Casino.

D

CAFE JAPENGO

Phone: 297/586-1234 (11)

Asian
$24-$45

AAA Inspector Notes: Crisp, attentive service awaits diners at this distinctly Asian restaurant. Among at least six catches of the day are ahi tuna, Chilean sea bass and grouper. Fish can be broiled, blackened or pan-fried, and three signature sauces accompany each. Other specialties include char-su duck, seared ginger beef and cashew chicken. Patrons also can order from a full sushi menu. **Bar:** full bar. **Reservations:** required. **Address:** JE Irausquin Blvd 85 **Location:** 7.4 mi (11.8 km) nw of airport; 5.7 mi (9.1 km) nw of downtown; in Hyatt Regency Aruba Resort & Casino. D

CASA TUA MEDITERRANEE

Phone: 297/586-8275 (6)

Mediterranean
$15-$32

AAA Inspector Notes: Mediterranean cuisine prepared with Greek, Spanish, Arab and Moroccan influences bring guests to this lively pedestrian mall eatery featuring beautiful and entertaining belly dancers. Patrons can enjoy eggplant moussaka, lamb chops, couscous and gourmet thin-crust pizza as well as satisfying shrimp tagine cooked in a special clay pot. **Bar:** full bar. **Reservations:** suggested. **Address:** L.G. Smith 95 **Location:** At Palm Beach Plaza Mall. L D

DANIEL'S STEAK & CHOP

Phone: 297/586-1144 (7)

Steak
$25-$45

AAA Inspector Notes: A small, intimate restaurant with attentive service that specializes in steaks and chops with a few grilled fish dishes as well. Start with the escargot or the French onion soup. A variety of succulent steaks, pork chops, lamb and veal are grilled to perfection. Guests can choose to sit inside the refined dining area or outside in a courtyard setting. **Bar:** full bar. **Reservations:** suggested. **Address:** JE Irausquin Blvd 348 **Location:** Across from Radisson Aruba Resort, Casino & Spa; next to Gianni's Ristorante Italiano. D

GIANNI'S RISTORANTE ITALIANO

Phone: 297/586-7794 (8)

Italian
$17-$38

AAA Inspector Notes: This popular restaurant offers outside seating for great people watching opportunities and indoor dining with the cool, well-appointed interior. A varied menu of pasta dishes include spaghetti with octopus, pasta puttanesca-style, linguini's with mussels and for the real seafood lover the frutti di mar. There are various preparations of gnocchi, polenta, veal and chicken as well as live Maine lobster. Attentive service and a lively ambience are offered. **Bar:** full bar. **Reservations:** suggested. **Address:** JE Irausquin Blvd 348-B **Location:** Center; across from Radisson Aruba Resort, Casino & Spa.

D

HOSTARIA DA' VITTORIO

Phone: 297/586-3838 (4)

Italian
$23-$39

AAA Inspector Notes: The menu is lined with authentic Italian cuisine, in which guests can choose from starters such as a beef carpaccio or a zuppa di minestrone. Varied pastas are prepared using an array of ingredients. Veal, lamb, pork and a fresh selection of fish are well prepared. The staff provides somewhat attentive service. **Bar:** full bar. **Reservations:** required. **Address:** L.G. Smith Blvd #380 **Location:** 6.1 mi (9.7 km) nw of downtown; just e of Hyatt Regency Aruba Resort & Casino.

L D

LAS RUINAS DEL MAR

Phone: 297/586-1234 (12)

Spanish
$28-$46

AAA Inspector Notes: Continental cuisine incorporates Mediterranean influences in this establishment, which replicates the 19th-century ruins of Bushiribana Gold Mill. Guests can request indoor or patio seating in a romantic setting overlooking a pond of water with black swans. **Bar:** full bar. **Reservations:** required. **Address:** JE Irausquin Blvd 85 **Location:** 7.4 mi (11.8 km) nw of airport; 5.7 mi (9.1 km) nw of downtown; in Hyatt Regency Aruba Resort & Casino. B D

PAGO PAGO

Phone: 297/586-4466 (10)

Steak
$29-$45

AAA Inspector Notes: Enjoy prime cuts of American aged beef and chops as well as fresh seafood in a sophisticated, romantic setting. The finely tuned service is pleasantly accommodating. **Bar:** full bar. **Reservations:** suggested. **Address:** JE Irausquin Blvd 77 **Location:** 7.2 mi (11.5 km) nw of airport; 4.5 mi (7.2 km) nw of downtown; in The Westin Resort & Casino, Aruba.

D

PAPILLON RESTAURANT

Phone: 297/586-5400 (1)

French
$25-$40

AAA Inspector Notes: This restaurant, offering relaxed fine dining, is named for Frenchman Henri Charriére-known as Papillon for the butterfly tattoo on his chest-who was imprisoned for 13 years and was the first convict to escape Devil's Island. Besides daily specials, the menu reflects the Frenchman's journey to freedom with French dishes with a Caribbean flair and includes such well-prepared entrees as duck a la orange, veal with crispy sweetbreads and apple compote as well as filet mignon with a creamy truffle sauce. **Bar:** full bar. **Reservations:** required. **Address:** JE Irausquin 348-A **Location:** 7.6 mi (12.1 km) nw of airport; 4.9 mi (7.8 km) nw of downtown; across from Radisson Aruba Resort, Casino & Spa. D

(See index & map p. 263.)

SUNSET GRILLE   Phone: 297/586-6555   ⑬

Steak
$30-$58

AAA Inspector Notes: This upscale restaurant offers indoor and outdoor seating in an atmosphere that remains casually elegant. The menu lists Angus steaks, lamb, pork, chicken and assorted seafood from around the world prepared in the open grill area. Although the emphasis is on hearty meat portions, the spectacular desserts are no letdown. Oysters Rockefeller, escargot, the monster seafood appetizer for two and assorted bread offerings make it hard to push back from the table. **Bar:** full bar. **Reservations:** required. **Address:** JE Irausquin Blvd 81 **Location:** 7.6 mi (12.1 km) nw of airport; 4.9 mi (7.8 km) nw of downtown; in Radisson Aruba Resort, Casino & Spa. *(See ad p. 276.)*

D ⃠

TANDOOR INDIAN GRILL HOUSE
     Phone: 297/586-0944   ⑮

Indian
$12-$23

AAA Inspector Notes: Mostly known for marinated chicken, lamb, fish and shrimp cooked in a special oven that seals in the flavor the menu at this casual spot also features dishes made with basmati rice, skewered meats and vegetarian specialties. Dining patrons can choose to sit al fresco on the second-story terrace or inside the dining room decorated with an Indian motif. **Bar:** full bar. **Reservations:** suggested. **Address:** South Beach Center **Location:** Center; in High Rise Hotel area.

L D ⃠

TANGO ARGENTINE GRILL
     Phone: 297/586-8600   ③

Argentine
$24-$37

AAA Inspector Notes: South American memorabilia enhances the spacious dining room, where patrons with hearty appetites can try the mixed grill-an array of sausages, cuts of beef, pork and chicken. Indoor and outdoor dining is available. **Bar:** full bar. **Reservations:** suggested. **Address:** JE Irausquin Blvd #370 **Location:** 5.1 mi (8.1 km) nw of downtown; across from Palm Beach; in Arawak Garden Shopping Plaza. D ⃠

TASTE OF BELGIUM   Phone: 297/586-6388   ②

International
$8-$25

AAA Inspector Notes: Located in Paseo Herencia, this courtyard eatery offers an attractive backdrop and tasty French-Belgium-Mediterranean-inspired cuisine. Choose from one of their many sandwiches, entree-size salads and a range of seafood, beef and pasta dishes. Save room for one of their scrumptious desserts-anything chocolate is a house specialty. There is a wide selection of Belgium beer and there are nightly waltzing fountain and light shows in the main courtyard. Early bird specials are from 5-7 pm. **Bar:** full bar. **Address:** JE Irausquin Blvd 382 **Location:** Paseo Herencia Mall; opposite Holiday Inn Sunpree Resort Aruba. **Parking:** on-site (fee).

B L D ⃠

TEXAS DE BRAZIL   Phone: 297/586-4686   ⑯

Brazilian
$30-$45

AAA Inspector Notes: "Gauchos" bring skewered meat selections directly to the table at the Brazilian-style steakhouse, and diners use a small colored coaster to let the server know when they are ready for another selection of beef, chicken, pork or lamb. The extensive salad bar gets meals off to the right start. Desserts are worthy of serious consideration. **Bar:** full bar. **Reservations:** required. **Address:** JE Irausquin Blvd 382 **Location:** 5.1 mi (8.1 km) nw of downtown; in Palm Beach area; at Hacienda Mall. **Parking:** on-site (fee). D ⃠

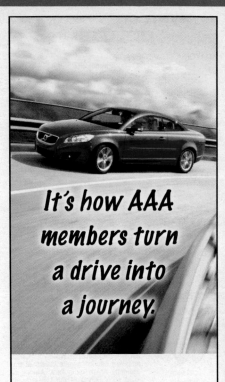

THE BAHAMAS

This index helps you "spot" where approved hotels and restaurants are located on the corresponding detailed maps. Hotel daily rate range is for comparison only and show the property's high season. Restaurant rate range is a combination of lunch and/or dinner. Turn to the listing page for more detailed rate information and consult display ads for special promotions.

LUCAYA (Grand Bahama Island)

Map Page	Hotels	Diamond Rated	High Season	Page
3 p. 281	Taino Beach Resorts & Club	◆◆	$125-$375	283
7 p. 281	Grand Lucayan, a Radisson Resort (See ad p. 283.)	◆◆◆◆	$139-$269 SAVE	283

Map Page	Restaurants	Diamond Rated	Cuisine	Meal Range	Page
1 p. 281	Pisces Seafood Restaurant	◆◆	International	$14-$32	284
2 p. 281	Cappuccino's Italian Restaurant	◆◆◆	Italian	$15-$30	283
3 p. 281	China Beach	◆◆	Chinese	$18-$35	283
4 p. 281	Giovanni's Cafe	◆◆	Italian	$14-$33	283
6 p. 281	Zorba's Greek Cuisine	◆	Greek	$9-$26	284
15 p. 281	Luciano's	◆◆◆	Continental	$26-$36	284

FREEPORT (Grand Bahama Island)

Map Page	Hotel	Diamond Rated	High Season	Page
8 p. 281	Castaways Resort & Suites	◆◆	$105-$155	282

Map Page	Restaurant	Diamond Rated	Cuisine	Meal Range	Page
33 p. 281	Ruby Swiss European Restaurant	◆◆	International	$8-$30	282

TREASURE CAY (Great Abaco Island)

Map Page	Hotel	Diamond Rated	High Season	Page
10 p. 281	Treasure Cay Hotel Resort & Marina	◆◆	$150-$350	286

GREEN TURTLE CAY (Great Abaco Island)

Map Page	Hotels	Diamond Rated	High Season	Page
13 p. 281	Green Turtle Club and Marina	◆◆◆	$99-$695	284
14 p. 281	Coco Bay Cottages	◆◆	$275-$700	284

Map Page	Restaurant	Diamond Rated	Cuisine	Meal Range	Page
38 p. 281	Laura's Kitchen	◆	American	$10-$21	284

MARSH HARBOUR (Great Abaco Island)

Map Page	Hotels	Diamond Rated	High Season	Page
18 p. 281	Conch Inn Hotel & Marina	◆◆	$120-$160	285
19 p. 281	Abaco Beach Resort at Boat Harbour	◆◆◆	$290-$1700 SAVE	285

Map Page	Restaurants	Diamond Rated	Cuisine	Meal Range	Page
16 p. 281	Curly Tails Restaurant and Bar	◆◆◆	Seafood	$18-$34	286
17 p. 281	Snappas Grill and Chill	◆	American	$8-$22	286
19 p. 281	Wally's	◆◆	Caribbean	$10-$29	286
20 p. 281	Angler's Restaurant	◆◆◆	International	$11-$32	285
22 p. 281	Mangoes Restaurant	◆◆◆	Caribbean	$12-$32	286

HOPE TOWN (Great Abaco Island)

Map Page	Hotels	Diamond Rated	High Season	Page
23 p. 281	Hope Town Hideaways	◆◆◆	$400-$2500	285

HOPE TOWN (Great Abaco Island) (cont'd)

Map Page	Hotels (cont'd)		Diamond Rated	High Season	Page
26 p. 281	**Sea Spray Resort & Marina**		◆◆	$1235-$3900 [SAVE]	285

Map Page	Restaurants	Diamond Rated	Cuisine	Meal Range	Page
23 p. 281	Harbour's Edge Restaurant	◆	Caribbean	$10-$26	285
24 p. 281	Cap'N Jacks	◆	American	$8-$19	285
25 p. 281	Abaco Inn Dining Room	◆◆	International	$12-$33	285
26 p. 281	Boat House Restaurant	◆◆	International	$11-$40	285

HARBOUR ISLAND (Harbour Island)

Map Page	Hotel		Diamond Rated	High Season	Page
31 p. 281	Pink Sands		◆◆◆◆	$750-$4500	287

Map Page	Restaurants	Diamond Rated	Cuisine	Meal Range	Page
28 p. 281	Garden Terrace Restaurant	◆◆◆	American	$34-$45	287
29 p. 281	The Landing Restaurant	◆◆◆	International	$39-$46	287

GOVERNOR'S HARBOUR (Eleuthera Island)

Map Page	Hotel	Diamond Rated	High Season	Page
34 p. 281	Cigatoo Inn Resort	◆◆	$109-$119	282

CAT ISLAND (Cat Island)

Map Page	Hotels	Diamond Rated	High Season	Page
35 p. 281	Sammy T's Beach Resort	◆◆	$135-$255	282
36 p. 281	The Bridge Inn	◆	$90-$200	282
37 p. 281	Greenwood Beach Resort	◆	$110-$130	282

LONG ISLAND (Long Island)

Map Page	Hotel	Diamond Rated	High Season	Page
41 p. 281	Cape Santa Maria Beach Resort	◆◆◆	$235-$795	287

GEORGE TOWN (Great Exuma Island)

Map Page	Hotels	Diamond Rated	High Season	Page
42 p. 281	The Exuma Palms at Three Sisters Resort Ltd	◆◆	$120-$200	286
43 p. 281	**Grand Isle Resort and Spa**	◆◆◆	$350-$3000 [SAVE]	286
44 p. 281	Sandals Emerald Bay, Great Exuma, Bahamas (See ad on insert.)	◆◆◆◆	$1540-$4978	286
45 p. 281	Hideaways at Palm Bay	◆◆◆	$160-$500	286

Map Page	Restaurant	Diamond Rated	Cuisine	Meal Range	Page
31 p. 281	Coconut Cove	◆◆	American	$15-$35	287

ANDROS ISLAND (Andros Island)

Map Page	Hotels	Diamond Rated	High Season	Page
51 p. 281	Small Hope Bay Lodge	◆	$235-$260	282
54 p. 281	Emerald Palms	◆◆◆	$159-$645	282

Map Page	Restaurant	Diamond Rated	Cuisine	Meal Range	Page
43 p. 281	Dining Room at Emerald Palms	◆◆	Caribbean	$10-$28	282

Discover mobile travel solutions at
AAA.com/mobile and CAA.ca/mobile

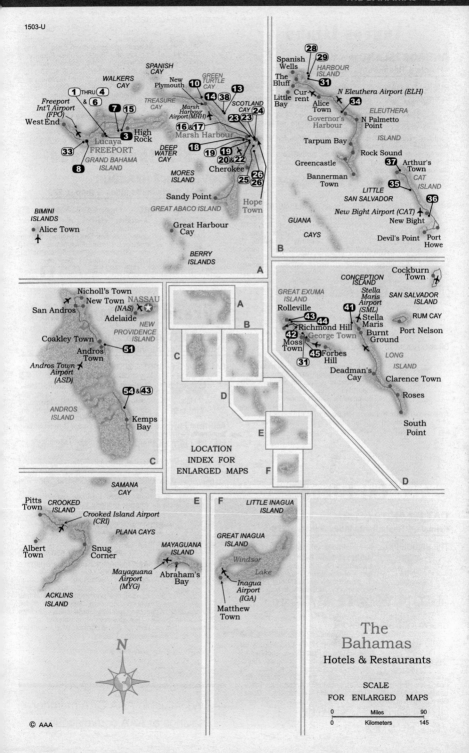

1503-U

WALKERS CAY

SPANISH CAY

GREEN TURTLE CAY

TREASURE CAY

Freeport Int'l Airport (FPO)

West End

Lucaya

FREEPORT

GRAND BAHAMA ISLAND

New Plymouth

Marsh Harbour Airport (MHH)

Marsh Harbour

High Rock

DEEP WATER CAY

SCOTLAND CAY

MORES ISLAND

Cherokee

Sandy Point

GREAT ABACO ISLAND

Hope Town

BIMINI ISLANDS

Alice Town

Great Harbour Cay

BERRY ISLANDS

Spanish Wells

The Bluff

Little Bay

Current

Alice Town

Governor's Harbour

HARBOUR ISLAND

N Eleuthera Airport (ELH)

ELEUTHERA ISLAND

N Palmetto Point

Tarpum Bay

Rock Sound

Greencastle

Bannerman Town

Arthur's Town

CAT ISLAND

LITTLE SAN SALVADOR

New Bight Airport (CAT)

New Bight

GUANA CAYS

Devil's Point

Port Howe

Nicholl's Town

New Town

NASSAU (NAS)

San Andros

Adelaide

NEW PROVIDENCE ISLAND

Coakley Town

Andros Town

Andros Town Airport (ASD)

ANDROS ISLAND

Kemps Bay

Cockburn Town

CONCEPTION ISLAND

GREAT EXUMA ISLAND

Stella Maris Airport (SML)

SAN SALVADOR ISLAND

Rolleville

Richmond Hill

George Town

Stella Maris

RUM CAY

Port Nelson

Moss Town

Burnt Ground

Forbes Hill

Deadman's Cay

LONG ISLAND

Clarence Town

Roses

South Point

LOCATION INDEX FOR ENLARGED MAPS

A
B
C
D
E
F

SAMANA CAY

Pitts Town

CROOKED ISLAND

Crooked Island Airport (CRI)

PLANA CAYS

Albert Town

Snug Corner

MAYAGUANA ISLAND

Mayaguana Airport (MYG)

Abraham's Bay

ACKLINS ISLAND

LITTLE INAGUA ISLAND

GREAT INAGUA ISLAND

Windsor Lake

Inagua Airport (IGA)

Matthew Town

N

The Bahamas

Hotels & Restaurants

SCALE FOR ENLARGED MAPS

Miles
0   90
Kilometers
0   145

© AAA

Andros Island

ANDROS ISLAND pop. 7,686
• Hotels & Restaurants index & map p. 279

EMERALD PALMS   Phone: 242-369-2713 [54]
Hotel
$159-$645

Address: South Andros **Location:** Oceanfront. In Driggs Hill; 3 mi (4.8 km) n of airport, s of ferry dock. **Facility:** 32 units, some two bedrooms and efficiencies. 1 story, exterior corridors. **Terms:** 30 day cancellation notice-fee imposed. **Amenities:** safes. **Dining:** Dining Room at Emerald Palms, see separate listing. **Pool(s):** outdoor. **Activities:** snorkeling, bicycles. **Fee:** fishing, charter fishing, massage. **Guest Services:** valet laundry.

SMALL HOPE BAY LODGE   Phone: 242-368-2014 [51]
Cabin
$235-$260

Address: Queens Hwy **Location:** Oceanfront. In Small Hope Bay; 3 mi (4.8 km) n of Fresh Creek (Andros Town) Airport. **Facility:** 21 cabins. 1 story, exterior corridors. *Bath:* some shared. **Terms:** open 12/1-9/9 & 10/15-11/30, cancellation fee imposed. **Activities:** whirlpool, beach access, boating, sailboats, windsurfing, boat dock, snorkeling, bicycles. **Fee:** scuba diving, fishing, charter fishing, massage.

WHERE TO EAT

DINING ROOM AT EMERALD PALMS   Phone: 242-369-2713 [43]
Caribbean
$10-$28

AAA Inspector Notes: Friendly staff serve such scrumptious items as fresh fish, meat or vegetarian creations with locally produced vegetables as much as possible. Lunch ranges from wraps and quesadillas to pizza. **Bar:** full bar. **Address:** The Bluff, Driggs Hill **Location:** In Driggs Hill; 3 mi (4.8 km) n of airport, s of ferry dock; in Emerald Palms.

Cat Island

CAT ISLAND pop. 1,647
• Hotels & Restaurants index & map p. 279

THE BRIDGE INN   Phone: 242-342-3013 [36]
Hotel
$90-$200

Address: New Bight Gen'l Delivery **Location:** Fly into New Bight Airport, just s of downtown. **Facility:** 12 units. 1 story, exterior corridors. *Bath:* shower only. **Activities:** fishing.

GREENWOOD BEACH RESORT   Phone: (242)342-3053 [37]
Hotel
$110-$130

Address: Port Howe **Location:** 4 mi (6.4 km) ne of Port Howe. **Facility:** 15 units. 1 story, exterior corridors. *Bath:* shower only. **Terms:** office hours 7:30 am-9:30 pm, 14 day cancellation notice-fee imposed. **Pool(s):** outdoor. **Activities:** limited beach access. **Fee:** scuba diving, snorkeling. **Guest Services:** valet laundry.

SAMMY T'S BEACH RESORT
Phone: 242-354-6009 [35]
Cottage
$135-$255

Address: Bennett's Harbour **Location:** Oceanfront. 5 mi (8 km) s of Arthur's Town Airport. **Facility:** 7 cottages. 1 story, exterior corridors. **Terms:** open 12/1-8/31 & 10/15-11/30, office hours 8 am-6 pm, check-in 4 pm, 3 night minimum stay, age restrictions may apply, 30 day cancellation notice. **Activities:** paddleboats, windsurfing, snorkeling, bicycles, volleyball. **Fee:** fishing.

Eleuthera Island

GOVERNOR'S HARBOUR
• Hotels & Restaurants index & map p. 279

CIGATOO INN RESORT   Phone: 242-332-3060 [34]
Hotel
$109-$119

Address: Haynes Ave **Location:** Downtown; at top of hill. **Facility:** 22 units. 2 stories (no elevator), exterior corridors. **Terms:** office hours 7 am-10 pm, 3 day cancellation notice. **Pool(s):** outdoor. **Activities:** tennis court. **Guest Services:** valet laundry.

Grand Bahama Island

FREEPORT (B-1) pop. 26,910
• Hotels & Restaurants index & map p. 279

CASTAWAYS RESORT & SUITES
Phone: (242)352-6682 [8]
Hotel
$105-$155

Address: E Mall Dr **Location:** Center. **Facility:** 118 units. 4 stories, interior/exterior corridors. **Terms:** 3 day cancellation notice. **Amenities:** safes (fee). **Pool(s):** outdoor. **Activities:** playground, exercise room. **Guest Services:** coin laundry, area transportation-beach.

VIVA WYNDHAM FORTUNA BEACH
Phone: 242-373-4000
[fyi] Not evaluated. **Address:** Churchill Dr with Doubloon Rd **Location:** Jct Churchill Dr and Doubloon Rd; at Fortuna Beach. Facilities, services, and decor characterize a mid-scale property.

WHERE TO EAT

RUBY SWISS EUROPEAN RESTAURANT
Phone: 242-352-8507 [33]
International
$8-$30

AAA Inspector Notes: The extensive menu caters to all tastes and appetites. Selections range from lighter fare such as burgers, sandwiches and salads, to full entrée dishes including lobster thermidor, pork chops, rack of lamb and grouper. Some diners enjoy the all-you-can-eat pasta. The atmosphere is relaxed with a yesteryear ambience. **Bar:** full bar. **Address:** W Sunrise Hwy **Location:** Next to International Bazaar.

Find valuable AAA/CAA member savings at AAA.com/discounts

LUCAYA (B-1) pop. 9,924
• Hotels & Restaurants index & map p. 279

GRAND LUCAYAN, A RADISSON RESORT
Phone: (242)373-1333

Resort Hotel
$139-$269

Address: Sea Horse Ln **Location:** Oceanfront. 6 mi (9.6 km) se of Freeport on Lucaya Beach; opposite Port Lucaya Marketplace. **Facility:** This full-scale resort offers an array of leisure activities as well as several room categories, all tastefully furnished and well equipped. 740 units, some two and three bedrooms. 2-10 stories, interior/exterior corridors. **Parking:** on-site and valet. **Terms:** 3 day cancellation notice-fee imposed. **Amenities:** *Some:* high-speed Internet, safes, honor bars. **Dining:** 12 restaurants, also, China Beach, see separate listing, nightclub. **Pool(s):** 6 outdoor. **Activities:** saunas, whirlpools, steamrooms, waterslide, rental boats, rental paddleboats, rental sailboats, rental sailboards, recreation programs, playground, basketball, shuffleboard, volleyball, spa. *Fee:* snorkeling, charter fishing, golf-36 holes, 4 lighted tennis courts. **Guest Services:** valet laundry. **Free Special Amenities:** high-speed Internet and manager's reception.
(See ad this page.)

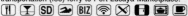

TAINO BEACH RESORTS & CLUB
Phone: 242/373-4682 **3**

Condominium
$125-$375

Address: Jolly Rodger Rd **Location:** Oceanfront. Just e of Port Lucaya. **Facility:** 157 condominiums. 4 stories, exterior corridors. **Terms:** office hours 7 am-11 pm, check-in 4 pm. **Amenities:** safes. **Pool(s):** outdoor. **Activities:** whirlpool, waterslide, marina, tennis court, playground, shuffleboard, volleyball. *Fee:* boats, sailboats, snorkeling, charter fishing, bicycles, massage. **Guest Services:** coin laundry, area transportation (fee)-ferry to Port Lucaya Marketplace.

▼ See AAA listing this page ▼

CAPPUCCINO'S ITALIAN RESTAURANT
Phone: 242/373-1584 **2**

Italian
$15-$30

AAA Inspector Notes: This quaint eatery serves a wide selection of homemade Italian fare and seafood in an intimate setting. Diners can kick back on the outdoor patio or in the cozy air-conditioned dining room. In addition to tasty pasta, the chef also prepares grilled meats and seafood, including excellent broiled island lobster. Early-bird specials appeal to tourists. **Bar:** full bar. **Reservations:** suggested. **Address:** Port Lucaya Marketplace **Location:** 6 mi (9.6 km) se of Freeport; at Port Lucaya Marketplace.

CHINA BEACH
Phone: 242/373-1333 **3**

Chinese
$18-$35

AAA Inspector Notes: Diners can sit indoors or on the patio to explore the menu of tasty Chinese food. The oceanfront setting offers a visual distraction outside, while the kitchen view of chefs at work entertains inside. Among offerings of Asian fare are traditional spring rolls, won ton soup and stir-fries. The chef also incorporates many seafood items into the dishes. **Bar:** full bar. **Reservations:** suggested. **Address:** Sea Horse Ln **Location:** 6 mi (9.6 km) se of Freeport on Lucaya Beach; in Radisson Our Lucaya Resort, Grand Bahama Island. **Parking:** on-site and valet.

GIOVANNI'S CAFE
Phone: 242/373-9107 **4**

Italian
$14-$33

AAA Inspector Notes: This quaint eatery is very popular with the family market due to its good value and hearty portions of freshly prepared Italian fare. Guests can choose from the cozy indoor dining area with a distinct European decor or the popular outdoor patio. In addition to the extensive selections of pasta, also featured are steak, seafood and grilled meat. **Bar:** full bar. **Address:** Port Lucaya Marketplace **Location:** 6 mi (9.6 km) se of Freeport; at Port Lucaya Marketplace. **Parking:** street only.

(See index & map p. 279.)

LUCIANO'S   Phone: 242/373-9100   ⑮

Continental
$26-$36

AAA Inspector Notes: On the waterfront, this second-floor location offers marina and bandstand views from its outdoor patio. Blending French and Continental cuisine, this restaurant's menu is ably complemented by the island's most extensive wine list. **Bar:** full bar. **Reservations:** required. **Address:** Seahorse Rd at Port Lucaya **Location:** In Port Lucaya Marketplace.

D ⟍

PISCES SEAFOOD RESTAURANT
          Phone: 242/373-5192   ①

International
$14-$32

AAA Inspector Notes: A nautical motif punctuates the Port Lucaya Marketplace restaurant, which offers cozy seating indoors or on the sidewalk. Patrons are often swayed to ordering from the huge selection of gourmet pizza, many with seafood toppings, but seafood pasta dishes, veal and chicken parmigiana, entrée-size salads and curry dishes also merit a look. **Bar:** full bar. **Reservations:** suggested. **Address:** Port Lucaya Marketplace **Location:** At Port Lucaya Marketplace.

D ⟍

ZORBA'S GREEK CUISINE   Phone: 242/373-6137   ⑥

Greek
$9-$26

AAA Inspector Notes: Popular for take-out gyros, this eatery also is nice for a quick bite on the wraparound porch. Patrons with hearty appetites might try the Greek platter, which includes moussaka, lamb, Greek lasagna, dolmades and tzatziki sauce. Hearty breakfast fare includes local souse made with fish, chicken or pig's feet. **Bar:** full bar. **Address:** Sea Horse Rd **Location:** 6 mi (9.6 km) se of Freeport; in Port Lucaya Marketplace.

B L D ⟍

Great Abaco Island

GREEN TURTLE CAY
• Hotels & Restaurants index & map p. 279

COCO BAY COTTAGES   Phone: 561/202-8149   ⑭

Cottage
$275-$700

Address: North End of Green Turtle Cay **Location:** Fly into Treasure Cay Airport, taxi to Green Turtle Cay Ferry; Green Turtle Cay Ferry dock is 25 mi (40 km) n of Marsh Harbour. **Facility:** 6 cottages. 1 story, exterior corridors. **Terms:** 4 night minimum stay, cancellation fee imposed. **Activities:** boat dock. **Guest Services:** valet laundry.

SD 🛜 ✕ 🍴 🖼 ▭

GREEN TURTLE CLUB AND MARINA
          Phone: 242/365-4271   ⑬

Hotel
$99-$695

Address: White Sound Harbour **Location:** Oceanfront. Treasure Cay Airport, taxi to Green Turtle Cay Ferry; Green Turtle Cay Ferry dock is 25 mi (40 km) n of Marsh Harbour. **Facility:** 33 units, some two bedrooms and cottages. 1 story, exterior corridors. **Terms:** open 12/1-9/4 & 10/27-11/30, office hours 7:45 am-6:30 pm, 14 day cancellation notice-fee imposed. **Pool(s):** outdoor. **Activities:** fishing. *Fee:* marina, scuba diving, snorkeling, massage. **Guest Services:** coin laundry.

🍴 🍸 SD 🏊 🛜 ✕ 🅿 🍴 ▭
/ SOME UNITS �W 🖼

 WHERE TO EAT

LAURA'S KITCHEN   Phone: 242/365-4287   ㊳

American
$10-$21

AAA Inspector Notes: Located in downtown New Plymouth, this eatery is within easy walking distance from the town dock. Simple decor and informal service are apparent. Ample portions of island and American dishes are served including fried chicken and pork chops but there are such Bahamian preparations as conch steak, grouper and conch chowder. **Bar:** beer & wine. **Address:** King St **Location:** Just above Town Dock; in New Plymouth.

L D

HOPE TOWN (B-2)
• Hotels & Restaurants index & map p. 279

HOPE TOWN HIDEAWAYS   Phone: 242/366-0224

Cottage
$400-$2500

Address: 1 Purple Porpoise Pl **Location:** Oceanfront. On Elbow Cay; accessed from Marsh Harbour by ferry boat. **Facility:** Set across from Hope Town and reached only by boat, this property boasts privacy in a lush tropical garden setting; cottages are equipped with boats. 4 cottages. 1 story, exterior corridors. **Terms:** office hours 9 am-5 pm, check-out 9 am, 3 night minimum stay, 30 day cancellation notice-fee imposed. **Pool(s):** outdoor. **Activities:** beach access, boating. *Fee:* marina. **Guest Services:** coin laundry, area transportation-beach & restaurants.

SEA SPRAY RESORT & MARINA
Phone: 242/366-0065   26

Cottage
$1235-$3900

Address: White Sound, Elbow Cay **Location:** 3.5 mi (5.6 km) s of village; on White Sound. Located in a secluded area. **Facility:** 7 cottages. 1 story, exterior corridors. **Terms:** office hours 8 am-5 pm, 3 night minimum stay - seasonal, 30 day cancellation notice-fee imposed. **Dining:** Boat House Restaurant, see separate listing. **Pool(s):** outdoor. **Activities:** snorkeling equipment rental. *Fee:* marina. **Guest Services:** valet laundry. **Free Special Amenities:** early check-in/late check-out and local transportation.

/ SOME UNITS

⬤ WHERE TO EAT

ABACO INN DINING ROOM
Phone: 242/366-0133   25

International
$12-$33

AAA Inspector Notes: Patio and inside tables afford spectacular daylight views of the Atlantic Ocean. Included in dishes of delicious, well-prepared island and American cuisine are some vegetarian preparations. A comfortable and relaxed atmosphere prevails. A popular Sunday breakfast/brunch buffet is offered. **Bar:** full bar. **Reservations:** suggested, for dinner. **Address:** Elbow Cay **Location:** 2.5 mi (4 km) s of village; on White Sound; in Abaco Inn. B L D

BOAT HOUSE RESTAURANT
Phone: 242/366-0359   26

International
$11-$40

AAA Inspector Notes: On the dock in picturesque White Sound, this simple, relaxed eatery is known for serving hearty and filling portions of island cuisine. Indoor and patio seating in the simple, unadorned setting overlooks the marina. Complimentary transportation is available from anywhere on the island. **Bar:** full bar. **Reservations:** required, for dinner. **Address:** White Sound, Elbow Cay **Location:** 3.5 mi (5.6 km) s of village; on White Sound; in Sea Spray Resort & Marina. B L D

CAP'N JACKS
Phone: 242/366-0247   24

American
$8-$19

AAA Inspector Notes: This waterfront restaurant is wholly informal, from the atmosphere to the service. Diners who sit indoors or on the outside deck at the plastic tables can tackle hearty portions of burgers, pasta, sandwiches, seafood and nightly changing specials. Service, while nonchalant, is somewhat dispassionate but that is part of the easygoing island attitude. **Bar:** full bar. **Address:** Queens Hwy **Location:** Harbourfront. **Parking:** street only.

L D

HARBOUR'S EDGE RESTAURANT
Phone: 242/366-0292   23

Caribbean
$10-$26

AAA Inspector Notes: Great for keeping an eye on the harbor activity, the open-air deck overlooks Hope Town Harbor and sets the tone for a casual mood. Local specialties of simply prepared and presented island and American cuisine line an often-changing menu. **Bar:** full bar. **Address:** Main Rd **Location:** In center of village; adjacent to town dock. L D

MARSH HARBOUR pop. 4,700
• Hotels & Restaurants index & map p. 279

ABACO BEACH RESORT AT BOAT HARBOUR
Phone: 242/367-2158   19

Hotel
$290-$1700

Address: Marsh Harbour **Location:** 3.5 mi (5.6 km) n from airport. **Facility:** Meets AAA guest room security requirements. 86 units, some efficiencies, cottages and condominiums. 3-4 stories (no elevator), exterior corridors. **Terms:** 14 day cancellation notice-fee imposed. **Amenities:** safes. **Dining:** Angler's Restaurant, see separate listing, entertainment. **Pool(s):** 2 heated outdoor. **Activities:** limited beach access, rental boats, canoeing, snorkeling, 2 lighted tennis courts, recreation programs, playground, horseshoes, volleyball, exercise room. *Fee:* marina, charter fishing. **Guest Services:** valet and coin laundry.

  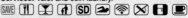

/ SOME UNITS FEE

CONCH INN HOTEL & MARINA
Phone: 242/367-4000   18

Motel
$120-$160

Address: E Bay St **Location:** 3 mi (4.8 km) n from airport. Located at marina. **Facility:** 9 units. 1 story, exterior corridors. **Terms:** office hours 7:30 am-7 pm, cancellation fee imposed. **Dining:** Curly Tails Restaurant and Bar, see separate listing. **Pool(s):** outdoor. **Activities:** rental boats, rental sailboats, scuba equipment rental. *Fee:* marina. **Guest Services:** valet laundry.

⬤ WHERE TO EAT

ANGLER'S RESTAURANT   Phone: 242/367-2158   20

International
$11-$32

AAA Inspector Notes: The dining room of this eatery affords a lovely view of the ocean, beach and marina. The full menu specializes in fresh local seafood but also offers a selection of meat entrees. Servers are pleasant and attentive. **Bar:** full bar. **Reservations:** suggested. **Address:** Queen Elizabeth Dr **Location:** 3.5 mi (5.6 km) n from airport; in Abaco Beach Resort at Boat Harbour.

B L D

(See index & map p. 279.)

CURLY TAILS RESTAURANT AND BAR
Phone: 242/367-4444 (16)

Seafood
$18-$34

AAA Inspector Notes: This popular waterfront eatery offers a choice of an outdoor open-air patio or indoor air conditioned dining. The menu features an innovative mix of island and international seafood. Entrées may include local lobster, cracked conch, blackened fresh fish, lemon butter chicken over mushroom ravioli or classic New York strip. The upstairs lounge offers a limited menu of such hearty bar fare as nachos, grouper fingers, wings and burgers. Smoking is permitted in the bar and on the dockside patio. **Bar:** full bar. **Reservations:** suggested. **Address:** E Bay St **Location:** 3 mi (4.8 km) n from airport; in Conch Inn Hotel & Marina. L D LATE

MANGOES RESTAURANT **Phone:** 242/367-2366 (22)

Caribbean
$12-$32

AAA Inspector Notes: This attractive waterfront dining room borders an active marina and offers guests complimentary use of the dock. The menu lists well-prepared local seafood and meat entrées. **Bar:** full bar. **Address:** Bay St **Location:** Center.
B L D

SNAPPAS GRILL AND CHILL
Phone: 242/367-2278 (17)

American
$8-$22

AAA Inspector Notes: A popular local hangout and great place to grab casual fare in a relaxed setting, this eatery offers waterfront, semi-open dining. The daily happy hour is popular with tourists and locals alike. **Bar:** full bar. **Address:** E Bay St **Location:** 3 mi (4.8 km) n from airport. L D

WALLY'S **Phone:** 242/367-2074 (19)

Caribbean
$10-$29

AAA Inspector Notes: Close to the harbor, this restaurant lures diners with its open-air setting and pleasant service. Local specialties are highlighted on a daily changing menu of Caribbean and American cuisine. Freshly prepared food is dished up in hearty portions. A cozy bar is inside. **Bar:** full bar. **Address:** Bay St **Location:** On waterfront; center. L D

TREASURE CAY

• Hotels & Restaurants index & map p. 279

TREASURE CAY HOTEL RESORT & MARINA
Phone: (242)365-8801 (10)

Resort Hotel
$150-$350

Address: Treasure Cay Rd **Location:** 7 mi (11.2 km) s from Treasure Cay Airport. **Facility:** This resort offers many varied guest units with marina views and easy access to the beach located across the street. 96 units, some kitchens. 2 stories (no elevator), exterior corridors. **Terms:** office hours 7 am-9 pm, 30 day cancellation notice-fee imposed. **Amenities:** high-speed Internet. **Dining:** 2 restaurants. **Pool(s):** outdoor. **Activities:** beach access, rental boats, rental paddleboats, rental sailboats, rental bicycles, volleyball. *Fee:* marina, scuba diving, snorkeling, fishing, charter fishing, golf-18 holes, 6 tennis courts. **Guest Services:** valet and coin laundry.
SD

Great Exuma Island

GEORGE TOWN (C-3)

• Hotels & Restaurants index & map p. 279

THE EXUMA PALMS AT THREE SISTERS RESORT LTD
Phone: 242/358-4040 (42)

Motel
$120-$200

Address: Queens Hwy **Location:** Oceanfront. 3.7 mi (6.1 km) nw of Exuma International Airport. **Facility:** 11 units. 2 stories (no elevator), exterior corridors. *Bath:* shower only. **Terms:** office hours 9 am-5 pm.
SD

GRAND ISLE RESORT AND SPA
Phone: (242)358-5000 (43)

Condominium
$350-$3000

Address: Emerald Bay **Location:** Oceanfront. 6.5 mi (10.4 km) nw of Exuma International Airport; 15.6 mi (24.9 km) nw of town. **Facility:** This new, upscale condo complex is located near a marina; spacious units include upgraded appliances and a 50-inch flat-screen TV. 57 condominiums. 2-3 stories, exterior corridors. **Terms:** office hours 7 am-11 pm, check-in 4 pm, 30 day cancellation notice-fee imposed. **Amenities:** high-speed Internet, safes. **Pool(s):** heated outdoor. **Activities:** whirlpool, snorkeling, recreation programs in winter, exercise room, spa. *Fee:* fishing. **Guest Services:** complimentary laundry. **Free Special Amenities: high-speed Internet and manager's reception.**
SAVE SD

HIDEAWAYS AT PALM BAY
Phone: (242)336-2787 (45)

Hotel
$160-$500

Address: Queens Hwy **Location:** Oceanfront. 7.5 mi (12 km) se of Exuma International Airport; 1.6 mi (2.6 km) nw of town. **Facility:** 69 units, some two bedrooms, kitchens and cottages. 1-2 stories, exterior corridors. **Terms:** office hours 8 am-9 pm, cancellation fee imposed. **Amenities:** safes. **Pool(s):** 2 outdoor. **Activities:** paddleboats, snorkeling equipment rental, volleyball. *Fee:* fishing. **Guest Services:** area transportation-town.
SD
/ SOME UNITS FEE

SANDALS EMERALD BAY, GREAT EXUMA, BAHAMAS
Phone: (242)336-6800 (44)

Resort Hotel
$1540-$4978

Address: Queens Hwy **Location:** 6.5 mi (10.4 km) nw of Exuma International Airport; 15.6 mi (24.9 km) nw of town. **Facility:** Situated on a quiet island, rooms at this luxury, all-inclusive resort are spacious; staff is attentive. 246 units. 3 stories, interior corridors. **Terms:** 3 night minimum stay - seasonal, 45 day cancellation notice-fee imposed. **Amenities:** high-speed Internet (fee), safes, honor bars. **Dining:** 5 restaurants. **Pool(s):** 2 heated outdoor. **Activities:** saunas, whirlpools, steamrooms, lifeguard on duty, paddleboats, sailboats, windsurfing, scuba diving, snorkeling, 6 lighted tennis courts, recreation programs, game room, shuffleboard, volleyball, spa. *Fee:* marina, golf-18 holes. **Guest Services:** valet laundry. ***(See ad on insert.)***
S SD BIZ

(See index & map p. 279.)

Long Island

LONG ISLAND pop. 2,992
• Hotels & Restaurants index & map p. 279

WHERE TO EAT

COCONUT COVE

American
$15-$35

Phone: 242-336-2659   **31**

AAA Inspector Notes: The unassuming, low-key eatery prepares lamb, lobster, seafood and curry dishes. Laid-back service and healthy portions are the norm. **Bar:** full bar. **Reservations:** suggested. **Address:** Queens Hwy **Location:** 7.5 mi (12 km) se of Exuma International Airport; 1.6 mi (2.6 km) nw of town.

B D ✎

Harbour Island

HARBOUR ISLAND pop. 1,639
• Hotels & Restaurants index & map p. 279

PINK SANDS

Resort Cottage
$750-$4500

Phone: (242)333-2030   **31**

Address: Chapel St **Location:** Oceanfront. From Government ferry dock, just e on Church St, just n on Dunmore St, then just e. **Facility:** These spacious cottages feature a distinctive blend of East Indian and Moroccan décor, and range in size from one to four bedrooms with secluded patios offering ocean or garden views. 27 cottages, some kitchens. 1 story, exterior corridors. **Terms:** 3 night minimum stay, 30 day cancellation notice-fee imposed. **Amenities:** safes, honor bars. **Dining:** 2 restaurants. **Pool(s):** heated outdoor. **Activities:** limited beach access, snorkeling, 2 tennis courts (1 lighted), rental bicycles, exercise room. *Fee:* fishing, charter fishing, massage. **Guest Services:** valet laundry.

🍴 🍸 🏋 SD 🏊 📶 🖥

WHERE TO EAT

GARDEN TERRACE RESTAURANT
American
$34-$45

Phone: 242/333-2030   **28**

AAA Inspector Notes: Choose from seating al fresco in the tropical garden or air-conditioned seating in the attractive dining room at this restaurant. A creative menu with Caribbean twists features spicy conch picatta or spinach salad and blue cheese fondue with warm ice-wine dressing for starters. Then follow it up with a walnut-crusted, free-range chicken or the local seafood pepper pot. Save room for such delicious desserts as coconut bread pudding with rum cream sauce. Fine friendly service caps off the evening. **Bar:** full bar. **Reservations:** suggested. **Address:** Chapel St **Location:** From N Eleuthera Airport via taxi and ferry; from Fast Ferry from Nassau 2 hours one way; in Pink Sands. D ✎

THE LANDING RESTAURANT
International
$39-$46

Phone: 242/333-2707   **29**

AAA Inspector Notes: Located across from the waterfront, this charming dining room offers both indoor and patio seating, along with a diverse menu of Mediterranean, Bahamian and American flavors using lamb, chicken, beef and fresh local seafood. Breakfast features such treats as toasted coconut bread, French toast, and homemade pastries. Friendly, attentive servers nurture the relaxed atmosphere. **Bar:** full bar. **Reservations:** suggested. **Address:** Bay St **Location:** Just above Town Dock; overlooking harbor. **Parking:** street only. **Historic**

B D

CAPE SANTA MARIA BEACH RESORT
Cottage
$235-$795

Phone: 242-338-5273   **41**

Address: Northwest Coast **Location:** Oceanfront. 6 mi (9.6 km) n from Stella Maris Airport at Cape Santa Maria. **Facility:** A superb beach and attractive cottages dot the shoreline of this isolated popular getaway for anglers and romantics alike. 35 units, some houses and cottages. 1-2 stories (no elevator), exterior corridors. **Terms:** open 12/1-8/29 & 11/1-11/30, office hours 7 am-10 pm, 30 day cancellation notice. **Amenities:** safes. *Some:* high-speed Internet. **Activities:** bicycles, exercise room. *Fee:* scuba diving, snorkeling, fishing, charter fishing, massage. **Guest Services:** complimentary laundry.

🍴 🍸 🏋 SD 📶 🚫 📞 🖥
/ SOME UNITS 🛒 🅿 🍳

Safety tip: Keep a current
AAA/CAA Road Atlas
in every vehicle

New Providence Island and Nassau

This index helps you "spot" where approved hotels and restaurants are located on the corresponding detailed maps. Hotel daily rate range is for comparison only and show the property's high season. Restaurant rate range is a combination of lunch and/or dinner. Turn to the listing page for more detailed rate information and consult display ads for special promotions.

CABLE BEACH (New Providence Island)

Map Page	Hotels	Diamond Rated	High Season	Page
1 p. 289	Wyndham Nassau Resort	◆◆◆	$155-$215	290
2 p. 289	**Sheraton Nassau Beach Resort** (See ad on insert, p. 293.)	◆◆◆	$129-$399 SAVE	290
3 p. 289	Sandals Royal Bahamian Resort Spa & Offshore Island (See ad on insert.)	◆◆◆◆	$1370-$3052	290
4 p. 289	Blue Water Resort	◆◆	$99-$397	290

Map Page	Restaurants	Diamond Rated	Cuisine	Meal Range	Page
② p. 289	The Poop Deck Sandyport	◆◆	Caribbean	$15-$55	290
④ p. 289	Capriccio Ristorante	◆◆	Italian	$12-$28	290

GAMBIER VILLAGE (New Providence Island)

Map Page	Hotel	Diamond Rated	High Season	Page
6 p. 289	Compass Point Beach Resort	◆◆◆	$350-$560	290

Map Page	Restaurant	Diamond Rated	Cuisine	Meal Range	Page
⑧ p. 289	Compass Point Restaurant	◆◆	Caribbean	$10-$39	291

NASSAU (New Providence Island)

Map Page	Hotels	Diamond Rated	High Season	Page
12 p. 289	**British Colonial Hilton Nassau** (See ad p. 292, opposite title page.)	◆◆◆◆	$189-$449 SAVE	291
14 p. 289	**Graycliff Hotel**	◆◆◆	$325-$700 SAVE	291

Map Page	Restaurants	Diamond Rated	Cuisine	Meal Range	Page
⑫ p. 289	Twin Brothers Seafood & Steakhouse	◆◆	Caribbean	$9-$28	294
⑬ p. 289	Cricket Club Restaurant and Lounge	◆	British	$10-$20	294
⑭ p. 289	**Aqua Restaurant**	◆◆◆	American	$14-$36	291
⑮ p. 289	Ichiban Restaurant	◆◆◆	Asian	$11-$45	294
⑯ p. 289	Clay Oven	◆◆	Indian	$12-$24	294
⑰ p. 289	Hard Rock Cafe	◆◆	American	$12-$24 SAVE	294
⑱ p. 289	Cafe Matisse	◆◆◆	Italian	$15-$32	291
⑲ p. 289	Luciano's of Chicago	◆◆◆	Italian	$16-$49	294
⑳ p. 289	**Graycliff**	◆◆◆◆	International	$27-$66	294
㉑ p. 289	Humidor Churrascaria Restaurant	◆◆◆	Brazilian	$40	294
㉔ p. 289	The Poop Deck Yacht Haven Marina	◆◆	Seafood	$13-$36	294
㉕ p. 289	East Villa Restaurant	◆◆	Chinese	$10-$28	294

PARADISE ISLAND (New Providence Island)

Map Page	Hotels	Diamond Rated	High Season	Page
20 p. 289	Atlantis Paradise Island	◆◆◆◆	$260-$590	295
21 p. 289	Riu Palace Paradise Island	◆◆◆	$273-$584	298
22 p. 289	One & Only Ocean Club	◆◆◆◆	$515-$3300	298
24 p. 289	Club Land'Or Resort	◆◆	$265-$399	295
25 p. 289	**Comfort Suites Paradise Island** (See ad starting on p. 296.)	◆◆◆	$279-$414 SAVE	296
26 p. 289	Paradise Island Harbour Resort	◆◆◆	$330-$550	298

PARADISE ISLAND (New Providence Island) (cont'd)

Map Page	Hotels (cont'd)	Diamond Rated		High Season	Page
28 this page	**Best Western Plus Bay View Suites** *(See ad p. 295.)*	▽▽▽		$210-$280 SAVE	295

Map Page	Restaurants	Diamond Rated	Cuisine	Meal Range	Page
30 this page	Bahamian Club	▽▽▽	Steak	$30-$46	298
31 this page	Seafire Steakhouse	▽▽▽	International	$39-$56	298
33 this page	Casa D'Angelo	▽▽▽	Italian	$32-$60	298
34 this page	Nobu	▽▽▽	Asian	$18-$46	298
35 this page	Cafe Martinique	▽▽▽	International	$38-$65	298
38 this page	Dune	▽▽▽▽	French	$24-$59	298
40 this page	The Green Parrot	▽	International	$9-$24	298
42 this page	Anthony's Grill	▽▽	International	$13-$36	298

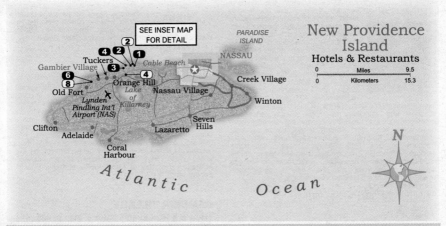

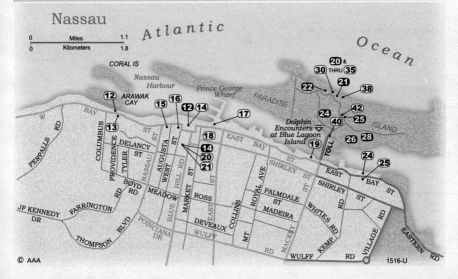

CABLE BEACH
• **Hotels & Restaurants index & map p. 288**

BLUE WATER RESORT   Phone: (242)327-7568   [4]

Vacation Rental Condominium
$99-$397

Address: West Bay St **Location:** Oceanfront. 5.5 mi (8.8 km) w of Rawson Square; 3 mi (4.8 km) e of airport. **Facility:** Three-story units feature bedrooms on the upper two floors and a kitchen and living room on the main floor; a small, secluded beach is available. 35 condominiums. 3 stories (no elevator), exterior corridors. **Terms:** office hours 9 am-7 pm, check-in 4 pm, 7 day cancellation notice. **Amenities:** safes. **Dining:** entertainment. **Pool(s):** heated outdoor. **Activities:** tennis court, recreation programs. **Guest Services:** complimentary and valet laundry.

SANDALS ROYAL BAHAMIAN RESORT SPA & OFFSHORE ISLAND   Phone: (242)327-6400   [3]

Resort Hotel
$1370-$3052 3/9-11/30
$1244-$2950 12/1-3/8

Address: West Bay St **Location:** 5 mi (8 km) w of Rawson Square; at west end of Cable Beach. **Facility:** Greco-Roman statuary adorns the expansive common areas of this couples-only resort, which offers accommodations in a manor house and garden suites. Located west of downtown in the fashionable Cable Beach area, the property offers an array of ethnic theme restaurants to choose from (try Italian, French, Japanese and Caribbean) and a full service spa provides a variety of treatments. Meets AAA guest room security requirements. 403 units. 2-6 stories, interior/exterior corridors. **Terms:** 3 night minimum stay - seasonal, age restrictions may apply, 45 day cancellation notice-fee imposed. **Amenities:** Some: high-speed Internet (fee), safes, honor bars. **Dining:** 9 restaurants, nightclub, entertainment. **Pool(s):** 6 outdoor. **Activities:** whirlpools, lifeguard on duty, limited beach access, paddleboats, sailboats, windsurfing, snorkeling, 2 lighted tennis courts, recreation programs, basketball, game room, horseshoes, shuffleboard, volleyball, spa. Fee: saunas, steamrooms, scuba diving. **Guest Services:** valet laundry.
(See ad on insert.)

SHERATON NASSAU BEACH RESORT
Phone: (242)327-6000   [2]

Resort Hotel
$129-$399

AAA Benefit: Members get up to 15% off, plus Starwood Preferred Guest® bonuses.

Address: West Bay St **Location:** 5 mi (8 km) w of Rawson Square; 3.5 mi (5.6 km) e of airport. **Facility:** On the ocean, this renovated hotel boasts both a beach and a 25,000-square-foot lagoon-style swimming pool surrounded by lush landscaping. 694 units. 9 stories, interior corridors. **Parking:** on-site and valet. **Terms:** 7 day cancellation notice-fee imposed. **Amenities:** video games (fee), high-speed Internet, safes. **Dining:** 4 restaurants, entertainment. **Pool(s):** 3 outdoor. **Activities:** whirlpools, lifeguard on duty, canoeing, paddleboats, snorkeling, recreation programs, playground, basketball, volleyball, exercise room, spa. Fee: golf-18 holes. **Guest Services:** valet laundry. *(See ad on insert, p. 293.)*

WYNDHAM NASSAU RESORT
Phone: (242)327-6200   [1]

Resort Hotel
$155-$215

Address: West Bay St **Location:** Oceanfront. On Cable Beach; 5 mi (8 km) w of Rawson Square; 4.2 mi (6.7 km) e of airport. Located in a developed commercial and residential area. **Facility:** This large resort designed to resemble a cruise ship offers many activities and a variety of views. Guest rooms are renovated and upgraded. 559 units. 11-15 stories, interior corridors. **Parking:** on-site and valet. **Terms:** check-in 4 pm, 3 day cancellation notice. **Amenities:** safes. **Dining:** 8 restaurants, entertainment. **Pool(s):** outdoor. **Activities:** saunas, whirlpools, waterslide, lifeguard on duty, rental paddleboats, recreation programs, playground, volleyball, exercise room, spa. **Guest Services:** valet laundry.

WHERE TO EAT

CAPRICCIO RISTORANTE   Phone: 242/327-8547   [4]

Italian
$12-$28

AAA Inspector Notes: A local favorite, this restaurant lets patrons choose to dine inside or outside on the terrace. Italian dishes are prepared to order with the diner's preferred pasta and sauces. **Bar:** full bar. **Address:** West Bay St **Location:** At west end of Cable Beach.

THE POOP DECK SANDYPORT
Phone: 242/327-3325   [2]

Caribbean
$15-$55

AAA Inspector Notes: The raw bar at this casual spot serves conch ceviche, raw oysters, sushi and sashimi. Mouthwatering appetizer standouts are blue mussels, soft-shell crab and escargot. Expertly prepared entrées range from the fisherman's platter to hog snapper, Angus beef and seafood bouillabaisse. Guests can sit in the air-conditioned dining room or enjoy balmy breezes on the al fresco deck. **Bar:** full bar. **Reservations:** suggested. **Address:** West Bay St **Location:** W of Cable Beach; at Sandyport.

GAMBIER VILLAGE
• **Hotels & Restaurants index & map p. 288**

COMPASS POINT BEACH RESORT
Phone: (242)327-4500   [6]

Cottage
$350-$560

Address: West Bay St, Gambier **Location:** Oceanfront. Adjacent to Love Beach; 10 mi (16 km) w of Rawson Square; 1.5 mi (2.4 km) w of airport on John F Kennedy Dr. **Facility:** The brightly colored cottages and cabanas face the sea and include a private deck; an upbeat, chic atmosphere prevails. 18 cottages. 1-2 stories (no elevator), exterior corridors. Bath: shower only. **Terms:** 3 night minimum stay, 45 day cancellation notice. **Amenities:** safes. **Dining:** Compass Point Restaurant, see separate listing. **Pool(s):** outdoor. **Activities:** whirlpool, limited beach access, spa.

(See index & map p. 288.)

WHERE TO EAT

COMPASS POINT RESTAURANT

Phone: 242/327-4500 (8)

Caribbean
$10-$39

AAA Inspector Notes: A tropical feeling prevails at this eatery, thanks to bright, island decor and pretty ocean views. Talented chefs utilize ingredients from the sea to create Caribbean and Bahamian culinary treats. The friendly staff, attired in brightly colored island shirts, makes guests feel at home. **Bar:** full bar. **Reservations:** suggested, for dinner. **Address:** West Bay St **Location:** Adjacent to Love Beach; 10 mi (16 km) w of Rawson Square; 1.5 mi (2.4 km) w of airport on John F Kennedy Dr; in Compass Point Beach Resort.

B L D ✎

NASSAU (C-2) pop. 210,832
• Hotels & Restaurants index & map p. 288

BRITISH COLONIAL HILTON NASSAU
Phone: (242)322-3301 (12)

Historic Hotel
$189-$449

Hilton

AAA Benefit: Members save 5% or more everyday!

Address: No 1 Bay St **Location:** Just w of Rawson Square. Located in the downtown commercial and financial district. **Facility:** In the heart of the downtown shopping area, this Spanish Colonial-style hotel offers modern amenities and a cabana bar spilling out to the beach. Meets AAA guest room security requirements. 288 units. 7 stories, interior corridors. **Parking:** on-site (fee) and valet. **Terms:** 1-7 night minimum stay, cancellation fee imposed. **Amenities:** high-speed Internet (fee), safes. **Dining:** 2 restaurants, also, Aqua Restaurant, see separate listing, name entertainment. **Pool(s):** heated outdoor. **Activities:** lifeguard on duty, limited beach access, paddleboats, boat dock, volleyball, exercise room. *Fee:* scuba diving, snorkeling. **Guest Services:** valet laundry.
(See ad p. 292, opposite title page.)

SAVE ▮ ▮ S SD �》 BIZ 🖢 ✕ ▮ ▮

GRAYCLIFF HOTEL

Phone: (242)302-9150 (14)

Classic Historic
Country Inn
$325-$700

Address: 8-12 West Hill St **Location:** Downtown; opposite Government House. **Facility:** This downtown 18th-century mansion has elegantly furnished rooms and suites as well as meticulously tended grounds. A cigar factory is on the premises. 20 units. 2 stories (no elevator), interior/exterior corridors. **Terms:** office hours 7:30 am-11:30 pm, 3 night minimum stay - seasonal, 7 day cancellation notice. **Amenities:** high-speed Internet, safes, honor bars. **Dining:** Graycliff, Humidor Churrascaria Restaurant, see separate listings, entertainment. **Pool(s):** 2 outdoor. **Activities:** exercise room, spa. **Guest Services:** valet laundry. **Free Special Amenities:** local telephone calls and high-speed Internet.

SAVE ▮ ▮ SD �》 🖢

WHERE TO EAT

AQUA RESTAURANT

Phone: 242/322-3301 (14)

American
$14-$36

AAA Inspector Notes: The casual air and bright contemporary decor at this restaurant is complimented by a tasty menu with such appetizers as lobster Wellington, chicken satay and a conch sampler. Some of the entrees include thyme-and-sage-crusted chicken with black trumpet and field mushroom jus, baby lamb with guava chutney and seared salmon with green pea puree and pimento coulis. A breakfast and lunch buffet is available along with a less extensive a la carte menu. **Bar:** full bar. **Reservations:** suggested. **Address:** No 1 Bay St **Location:** Just w of Rawson Square; in British Colonial Hilton Nassau. **Parking:** on-site (fee) and valet.

B L D

CAFE MATISSE

Phone: 242/356-7012 (18)

Italian
$15-$32

AAA Inspector Notes: Enjoy homemade pasta, seafood and Mediterranean and Bahamian dishes on the terrace or in the quaint European-theme dining room at this bustling restaurant. **Bar:** full bar. **Reservations:** required. **Address:** Bank Ln **Location:** Across from courthouse; behind Parliament Square; just off Bay St; downtown. **Parking:** valet and street only. **Historic**

L D ✎

Learn about
AAA/CAA Diamond Ratings
at AAA.com/Diamonds

▼ See AAA listing p. 291 ▼

HHONORS
HILTON WORLDWIDE

Exquisite Accommodations

Our beautifully designed hotel boasts 288 exquisite rooms and suites featuring contemporary décor and sweeping island and harbour views. From sunrise to sunset, you will be refreshed by the comfort and beauty of your accommodations. Each room is individually climate-controlled and includes Cable TV, an ergonomic desk and chair with modem outlet and Internet access, voice mail system and an electronic safety deposit box. Welcome to a truly relaxing and enjoyable Caribbean getaway that offers you the luxury for which Hilton has long been known.

For more information, call (242) 322.3301

Visit our website: www.hiltoncaribbean.com/nassau
Facebook: www.facebook.com/hiltonnassau

British Colonial Hilton Nassau
No. 1 Bay Street, Nassau, The Bahamas

British Colonial Hilton
Nassau

▼ See AAA listing p. 290 ▼

(See index & map p. 288.)

CLAY OVEN
Phone: 242/325-2525 ⑯

Indian
$12-$24

AAA Inspector Notes: The distinctive marrying of specific herbs and spices in the cuisine creates a sensuous tasting experience. Samosa starters feature either seasoned diced vegetables or diced seasoned lamb and vegetables stuffed in a pastry shell, then deep-fried and served with tamarind chutney. Entrée choices include curry specialties made with tender lamb, grouper fillets, jumbo shrimp or boneless chicken. Obvious favor is given to tandoori meals, which are cooked to perfection in a clay oven. **Bar:** full bar. **Address:** 100 W Bay St **Location:** Center of downtown. **Parking:** street only.

CRICKET CLUB RESTAURANT AND LOUNGE
Phone: 242/326-4720 ⑬

British
$10-$20

AAA Inspector Notes: A favorite gathering spot, this friendly, casual club's open-air dining balcony overlooks the cricket grounds. British pub fare is prepared with a Bahamian twist. **Bar:** full bar. **Address:** West Bay St **Location:** At Haynes Oval; just w of downtown.

EAST VILLA RESTAURANT
Phone: 242/393-3377 ㉕

Chinese
$10-$28

AAA Inspector Notes: Popular with locals and tourists alike, this restaurant prepares mainly Chinese cuisine but also offers some Continental specialties. With more than 50 items, the menu lists something for every palate. House favorites include pineapple duck, Szechuan lobster and mu shu pork, as well as classic preparations of shrimp scampi, chicken parmigiana and broiled rack of lamb. After-dinner coffee concoctions are laced with rum or liqueur and a pianist plays on the weekend. **Bar:** full bar. **Reservations:** suggested. **Address:** East Bay St **Location:** 1 mi (1.6 km) e of downtown. **Parking:** on-site and valet.

GRAYCLIFF
Phone: 242/322-2796 ⑳

International
$27-$66

AAA Inspector Notes: In an elegant 18th-century Bahamian plantation mansion, this upscale dining room boasts a wine cellar of 175,000 rare and vintage wines, as well as an excellent choice of ports and Armagnacs. At an on-site cigar factory, Cuban-born workers roll the reputed house-blend cigars. The cuisine focus is on classically prepared dishes such as Chateaubriand, roasted Colorado baby rack of lamb, scampi and a savory bouillabaisse. Many guests order one of the many dessert souffles in advance. Semi-formal attire. **Bar:** full bar. **Reservations:** required. **Address:** 8-12 West Hill St **Location:** Downtown; opposite Government House; in Graycliff Hotel. **Parking:** valet and street only. **Historic**

HARD ROCK CAFE
Phone: 242/325-7625 ⑰

American
$12-$24

AAA Inspector Notes: Rock 'n' roll memorabilia decorates the walls of the popular theme restaurant. Live music on the weekends contributes to the bustling atmosphere. On the menu is a wide variety of American cuisine-- from burgers and sandwiches to seafood, steaks and pasta. **Bar:** full bar. **Address:** Charlotte St N **Location:** Corner of Bay and Charlotte sts; downtown. **Parking:** street only.

HUMIDOR CHURRASCARIA RESTAURANT
Phone: 242/322-2796 ㉑

Brazilian
$40

AAA Inspector Notes: This upscale Brazilian steakhouse allows diners to begin with a buffet of well-prepared appetizers before moving on to the main course: more than 20 cuts of meat, including beef, ribs, pork, chicken and lamb, carved at the table by the roving, well-attired staff. **Reservations:** suggested. **Address:** 8-12 W Hill St **Location:** Downtown; opposite Government House; in Graycliff Hotel. **Parking:** street only. **Historic**

ICHIBAN RESTAURANT
Phone: 242/326-7224 ⑮

Asian
$11-$45

AAA Inspector Notes: Offering a warm and comfortable ambience, this restaurant covers all the bases by featuring a selection of Thai, Chinese, Japanese and even some familiar Continental dishes. Menu favorites include rack of lamb, shrimp curry and a wide array of sushi rolls. **Bar:** full bar. **Reservations:** suggested. **Address:** W Bay St **Location:** Just w of downtown center; across from Western Esplanade; between Cunningham Ln and Nassau St. **Parking:** on-site and valet.

LUCIANO'S OF CHICAGO
Phone: 242/323-7770 ⑲

Italian
$16-$49

AAA Inspector Notes: This popular restaurant, located in a waterfront mansion, offers captivating views of Atlantis. Skillful Chef Martinez prepares a wide range of Tuscan Italian dishes along with some Bahamian specialties. An array of pasta dishes with various sauces include seafood pasta fruti di mar and penne di Lucca made with sausage. Full size entrées, such as osso buco made with veal shank and Nassau grouper with lemon butter, are sure to please. The signature chocolate rum raisin bread pudding is delicious. **Bar:** full bar. **Reservations:** suggested. **Address:** East Bay St **Location:** Just w of Paradise Island Bridge. **Parking:** valet only.

THE POOP DECK YACHT HAVEN MARINA
Phone: 242/393-8175 ㉔

Seafood
$13-$36

AAA Inspector Notes: This popular casual eatery and pub offers guests a full view of the active marina. On the menu are fresh local seafood, including some traditional dishes, and various comfort foods, such as sandwiches, burgers and fish and chips. **Bar:** full bar. **Address:** East Bay St **Location:** At Nassau Yacht Haven Marina; just e of Paradise Island Bridge.

SENOR FROG'S
Phone: 242/323-1777

Tex-Mex
$9-$21

AAA Inspector Notes: Part of the chain of Mexican restaurants that also includes Carlos 'n Charlie's, the fun and festive eatery is a great place to eat with the family or rendezvous with friends. The menu is lined with Tex-Mex, American and Mexican favorites, such as chicken wings, quesadillas, fajitas and burritos. After hours, a bar atmosphere prevails. **Bar:** full bar. **Address:** Woodes Rogers Walk **Location:** At British Colonial Centre of Commerce; waterfront downtown. **Parking:** street only.

TWIN BROTHERS SEAFOOD & STEAKHOUSE
Phone: 242/328-5033 ⑫

Caribbean
$9-$28

AAA Inspector Notes: Located in always busy Arawak Cay, be prepared to wait for a table as this place draws a crowd with its authentic spin on Bahamian food served hot. The focus is beef and fresh seafood. **Bar:** full bar. **Address:** Arawak Cay **Location:** West of downtown.

PARADISE ISLAND

- Restaurants p. 298
- Hotels & Restaurants index & map p. 288

ATLANTIS PARADISE ISLAND

Phone: (242)363-3000 **20**

Resort Hotel
$260-$590

Address: Casino Dr **Location:** Reached by toll bridge from Nassau. **Facility:** Stocked lagoons, underwater viewing tunnels, a water park, a lazy river, entertainment and extensive shops complete this property. 3419 units, some two bedrooms and condominiums. 2-24 stories, interior/exterior corridors. **Parking:** valet only. **Terms:** 14 day cancellation notice-fee imposed. **Amenities:** high-speed Internet (fee), safes, honor bars. **Dining:** 34 restaurants, also, Bahamian Club, Cafe Martinique, Casa D'Angelo, Nobu, Seafire Steakhouse, see separate listings, nightclub, entertainment. **Pool(s):** 13 heated outdoor. **Activities:** whirlpools, waterslide, lifeguard on duty, beach access, rental canoes, rental paddleboats, rental sailboats, recreation programs, playground, basketball, shuffleboard, volleyball, spa. **Fee:** sauna, marina, scuba diving, snorkeling, fishing, charter fishing, golf-18 holes, 6 lighted tennis courts, game room. **Guest Services:** valet laundry, area transportation-One & Only Ocean Club, Harbourside Towers & golf course. Affiliated with A Preferred Hotel.

Check out
our travel blog at
AAATravelViews.com

BEST WESTERN PLUS BAY VIEW SUITES

Phone: (242)363-2555 **28**

 Condominium
$210-$280

 AAA Benefit: Members save up to 20%, plus 10% bonus points with Best Western Rewards®.

Address: Bay View Dr **Location:** Reached by toll bridge from Nassau. **Facility:** Spacious one- and two-bedroom suites, townhouses and villas are set in a peaceful, tropical setting with a public beach within walking distance. 25 condominiums. 1-2 stories (no elevator), exterior corridors. **Terms:** office hours 8:30 am-10 pm, 7 day cancellation notice-fee imposed. **Amenities:** high-speed Internet, safes. **Pool(s):** 3 outdoor. **Activities:** lighted tennis court, playground. **Guest Services:** coin laundry. **Free Special Amenities:** high-speed Internet. *(See ad this page.)*

CLUB LAND'OR RESORT **Phone:** 242/363-2400 **24**

Condominium
$265-$399

Address: Marina Dr **Location:** Reached by toll bridge from Nassau. **Facility:** Meets AAA guest room security requirements. 72 condominiums. 3 stories (no elevator), interior/exterior corridors. *Bath:* shower only. **Terms:** check-in 4 pm, 3 day cancellation notice-fee imposed. **Amenities:** safes. **Dining:** name entertainment. **Pool(s):** outdoor. **Activities:** whirlpool, exercise room. **Guest Services:** complimentary and valet laundry.

▼ See AAA listing this page ▼

(See index & map p. 288.)

▼ *See AAA listing this page* ▼

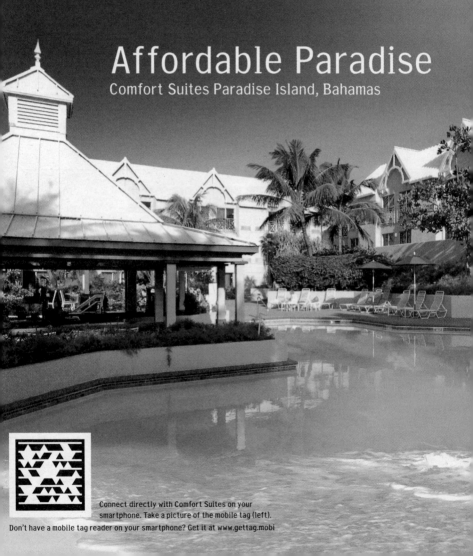

(See index & map p. 288.)

(See index & map p. 288.)

ONE & ONLY OCEAN CLUB

Phone: (242)363-2501 ㉒

Resort Hotel
$515-$3300

Address: One Casino Dr **Location:** Oceanfront. Reached by toll bridge from Nassau. **Facility:** Highlights include luxurious accommodations with 24-hour butler service, a spa and the use of recreational facilities at Atlantis Paradise Island. 105 units, some houses and cottages. 1-2 stories, exterior corridors. **Parking:** valet only. **Terms:** 2 night minimum stay, 14 day cancellation notice-fee imposed. **Amenities:** video games (fee), high-speed Internet, safes, honor bars. **Dining:** 2 restaurants, also, Dune, see separate listing. **Pool(s):** 2 outdoor. **Activities:** steamrooms, lifeguard on duty, snorkeling, 6 lighted tennis courts, bicycles, jogging, spa. **Fee:** golf-18 holes. **Guest Services:** valet laundry, area transportation-golf course & Atlantis Paradise Island.

PARADISE ISLAND HARBOUR RESORT

Phone: 242/363-2561 ㉖

Hotel
$330-$550

Address: Harbour Dr **Location:** Oceanfront. Reached by toll bridge from Nassau. **Facility:** Meets AAA guest room security requirements. 246 units. 12 stories, interior corridors. **Terms:** check-in 4 pm, 3 day cancellation notice-fee imposed. **Amenities:** safes. **Fee:** video games, high-speed Internet. **Dining:** 3 restaurants, entertainment. **Pool(s):** outdoor. **Activities:** whirlpool, 2 lighted tennis courts, recreation programs, basketball, horseshoes, volleyball, exercise room. **Fee:** game room, massage. **Guest Services:** valet and coin laundry.

RIU PALACE PARADISE ISLAND

Phone: (242)363-3500 ㉑

Resort Hotel
$273-$584

Address: Casino Dr **Location:** Oceanfront. Reached by toll bridge from Nassau. **Facility:** Well suited for families, the expansive property boasts multiple recreational opportunities; units are comfortable. Meets AAA guest room security requirements. 379 units. 15 stories, interior corridors. **Terms:** 7 day cancellation notice-fee imposed. **Amenities:** safes, honor bars. **Dining:** 5 restaurants, entertainment. **Pool(s):** outdoor. **Activities:** saunas, whirlpools, lifeguard on duty, recreation programs, volleyball, exercise room, spa. **Fee:** scuba diving. **Guest Services:** valet laundry.

WHERE TO EAT

ANTHONY'S GRILL

Phone: 242/363-3152 ㊷

International
$13-$36

AAA Inspector Notes: Enjoy bright tropical decor, Casablanca fans and lively music playing in the background at this decidedly Caribbean grill. An array of island-inspired dishes and American favorites line the menu including steak, local fish, seafood platters, conch, baby back ribs and gourmet burgers. There is Key lime pie for dessert, and try one of the limbering potent libations. **Bar:** full bar. **Address:** Casino Dr **Location:** Across from Atlantis Paradise Island; in Paradise Village Shopping Center. **Parking:** on-site (fee). B L D

BAHAMIAN CLUB

Phone: 242/363-3000 ㉚

Steak
$30-$46

AAA Inspector Notes: The mood is elegant and sophisticated, yet relaxed, at this upscale restaurant. Specialties include Chateaubriand for two, steak and grilled seafood. Some dishes are prepared tableside. Semi-formal attire. **Bar:** full bar. **Reservations:** required. **Address:** Casino Dr **Location:** On Paradise Island; reached by toll bridge from Nassau; in Atlantis Paradise Island. **Parking:** on-site (fee) and valet. D

CAFE MARTINIQUE

Phone: 242/363-3000 ㉟

International
$38-$65

AAA Inspector Notes: Elegant, posh and decadent are just a few words to describe the ambience at this upscale restaurant. Guests are dressed for the night. Sophisticated servers expertly provide tableside preparation and pampering attention, and diners are entertained with live music throughout the night. The menu lists a wonderful selection of grilled meats and fresh regional seafood, as well as fine international fare. **Bar:** full bar. **Reservations:** required. **Address:** Casino Dr **Location:** On Paradise Island; reached by toll bridge; in Atlantis Paradise Island. **Parking:** on-site and valet. D CALL

CASA D'ANGELO

Phone: 242/363-3000 ㉝

Italian
$32-$60

AAA Inspector Notes: Classic Italian cuisine as well as fine meat and veal offerings make this eatery a perfect spot for an upscale dining experience. Set in the Atlantis Paradise Resort, diners can enjoy the chic and elegant ambience and the gracious formal service. Seating for guests with children under the age of 6 is permitted at 5:30 pm and 5:45 pm. Semi-formal attire. **Bar:** full bar. **Reservations:** required. **Address:** Casino Dr **Location:** Reached by toll bridge from Nassau; in Atlantis Paradise Island. **Parking:** on-site (fee) and valet. D

DUNE

Phone: 242/363-2501 ㊳

French
$24-$59

AAA Inspector Notes: Developed by famed celebrity chef and restaurateur Jean Georges Vongerichten, this oceanfront restaurant takes Paradise Island dining to new heights. Herbs from an on-site garden punch up the flavor in dishes that draw on Asian and French inspiration. Well-rehearsed and attentive team service and a congenial atmosphere enhance the dining experience. **Bar:** full bar. **Reservations:** required, for dinner. **Address:** Paradise Island **Location:** On Paradise Island; in One & Only Ocean Club. B L D

THE GREEN PARROT

Phone: 242/363-3633 ㊵

International
$9-$24

AAA Inspector Notes: Good comfort food awaits at this casual marina bar where locals and tourists interact. Patrons can order their food at the bar and then head to a table to watch the passing boats and marina life outside. **Bar:** full bar. **Address:** Hurricane Hole Marina **Location:** On Paradise Island; reached by toll bridge from Nassau; at Hurricane Hole Marina. L D

NOBU

Phone: 242/363-3000 ㉞

Asian
$18-$46

AAA Inspector Notes: Well-known Chef Nobu Matsuhisa and actor Robert De Niro join forces to create a sleek, modern and hip dining venue. Combining the flavors and techniques of Japanese cuisine with South American Peruvian ingredients, the menu features such favorites as baby abalone, Arctic char and halibut cheeks with wasabi pepper sauce. To satisfy the sweet tooth, the bento box includes warm Valrhona chocolate souffle cake, shiso syrup, white chocolate sauce and a green tea ice cream. Children under 6 years old are not permitted. Semi-formal attire. **Bar:** full bar. **Reservations:** required. **Address:** Casino Dr **Location:** On Paradise Island; reached by toll bridge from Nassau; in Atlantis Paradise Island. **Parking:** valet only. D

SEAFIRE STEAKHOUSE

Phone: 242/363-3000 ㉛

International
$39-$56

AAA Inspector Notes: A popular dining spot for the boaters moored at the Atlantis Marina, this is a great place for people watching and biting into a huge cut of beef. The bustling hot spot is trendy and hip. Diners enjoy the menu of fine wines and huge cuts of fresh prime beef as well as fresh seafood specialties. **Bar:** full bar. **Reservations:** required. **Address:** Casino Dr **Location:** On Paradise Island; reached by toll bridge; at Marina Village; in Atlantis Paradise Island. **Parking:** valet only. D

BARBADOS

This index helps you "spot" where approved hotels and restaurants are located on the corresponding detailed maps. Hotel daily rate range is for comparison only and show the property's high season. Restaurant rate range is a combination of lunch and/or dinner. Turn to the listing page for more detailed rate information and consult display ads for special promotions.

SHERMANS (St. Lucy Parish)

Map Page	Hotel	Diamond Rated	High Season	Page
1 p. 303	Little Good Harbour Hotel	▼▼▼	$249-$940	316

SPEIGHTSTOWN (St. Peter Parish)

Map Page	Hotels	Diamond Rated	High Season	Page
3 p. 303	**Almond Beach Village**	▼▼▼	$340-$875 SAVE	318
4 p. 303	Cobblers Cove	▼▼▼	$465-$895	318
5 p. 303	Sunset Sands Beach Apartments	▼	$85-$110	318

Map Page	Restaurant	Diamond Rated	Cuisine	Meal Range	Page
1 p. 303	Mango's by the Sea	▼▼▼	International	$25-$50	318

MAYNARDS (Christ Church Parish)

Map Page	Hotel	Diamond Rated	High Season	Page
6 p. 303	**Sugar Cane Club Hotel & Spa**	▼▼▼	$205-$455 SAVE	308

MULLINS BAY (St. Peter Parish)

Map Page	Hotel	Diamond Rated	High Season	Page
8 p. 303	Bayfield House	▼▼	$155-$350	318

Map Page	Restaurant	Diamond Rated	Cuisine	Meal Range	Page
35 p. 303	Mullins Restaurant & Cocktail Bar	▼▼▼	International	$14-$52	318

THE GARDEN (St. James Parish)

Map Page	Hotel	Diamond Rated	High Season	Page
10 p. 303	Cove Spring	▼▼▼	$714-$1000	315

PORTERS (St. James Parish)

Map Page	Hotels	Diamond Rated	High Season	Page
12 p. 303	Lone Star Restaurant & Hotel	▼▼▼	$500-$900	315
13 p. 303	The Fairmont Royal Pavilion	▼▼▼▼	$449-$1759	315
15 p. 303	**Colony Club Hotel**	▼▼▼▼	$430-$1460 SAVE	314
16 p. 303	Coral Reef Club	▼▼▼▼	$245-$2610	315

Map Page	Restaurants	Diamond Rated	Cuisine	Meal Range	Page
2 p. 303	Lone Star Restaurant	▼▼▼	International	$24-$40	315
19 p. 303	Palm Terrace Restaurant	▼▼▼	International	$35-$49	315

HOLETOWN (St. James Parish)

Map Page	Hotels	Diamond Rated	High Season	Page
17 p. 303	Sunswept Beach Hotel	▼	$125-$185	313
18 p. 303	The Sandpiper	▼▼▼	$310-$2610	311
19 p. 303	All Seasons Resort - Europa	▼▼	$91-$180	311
20 p. 303	**Settlers Beach Hotel** *(See ad p. 313.)*	▼▼▼	$294-$1220 SAVE	313
21 p. 303	**Mango Bay**	▼▼▼	$385-$725 SAVE	311
23 p. 303	Almond Beach Club & Spa	▼▼	$637-$1456	311
24 p. 303	**Sandy Lane Hotel** *(See ad p. 312.)*	▼▼▼▼▼	$1050-$5460 SAVE	311

Map Page	Restaurants	Diamond Rated	Cuisine	Meal Range	Page
③ p. 303	The Mews Restaurant	▼▼	International	$21-$38	313
⑤ p. 303	The Tides Restaurant	▼▼▼	International	$13-$35	314
⑥ p. 303	The Sandpiper Dining Room	▼▼▼	International	$35-$45	314
⑦ p. 303	Spago Restaurant & Bar	▼▼	Italian	$14-$28	314
⑧ p. 303	The Beach House Bar & Restaurant	▼▼▼	International	$27-$45	313

WESTMORELAND (St. James Parish)

Map Page	Hotel	Diamond Rated	High Season	Page
26 p. 303	Royal Westmoreland	▼▼▼	$350-$3000	316

PAYNES BAY (St. James Parish)

Map Page	Hotels	Diamond Rated	High Season	Page
28 p. 303	Beach View	▼▼▼	$200-$750	314
29 p. 303	Shades	▼▼	$165-$245	314
30 p. 303	**Treasure Beach Hotel**	▼▼▼	$315-$1900 [SAVE]	314

Map Page	Restaurants	Diamond Rated	Cuisine	Meal Range	Page
⑨ p. 303	Daphne's	▼▼▼	New Italian	$27-$60	314
⑩ p. 303	**Kathy's**	▼▼▼	International	$18-$73	314
⑪ p. 303	Scarlet	▼▼	International	$23-$29	314

APPLEBY (St. James Parish)

Map Page	Hotel	Diamond Rated	High Season	Page
38 p. 303	**Crystal Cove Hotel**	▼▼▼	$405-$1179 [SAVE]	310

PROSPECT (St. James Parish)

Map Page	Hotel	Diamond Rated	High Season	Page
39 p. 303	**Best E Villas**	▼	$110-$216 [SAVE]	315

Map Page	Restaurant	Diamond Rated	Cuisine	Meal Range	Page
⑬ p. 303	Il Tempio Restaurant & Bar	▼▼	Italian	$17-$50	315

BRIDGETOWN (St. Michael Parish)

Map Page	Hotel	Diamond Rated	High Season	Page
44 p. 303	**Hilton Barbados** (See ad opposite title page, p. 317.)	▼▼▼▼	$369-$529 [SAVE]	316

Map Page	Restaurants	Diamond Rated	Cuisine	Meal Range	Page
⑮ p. 303	The Grille	▼▼▼	Fusion	$27-$42	316
⑯ p. 303	**Brown Sugar Restaurant**	▼▼	Caribbean	$18-$45	316

BATHSHEBA (St. Joseph Parish)

Map Page	Hotel	Diamond Rated	High Season	Page
46 p. 303	Sea-U Guest House	▼	$119-$219	316

ST. PHILIP PARISH (St. Philip Parish)

Map Page	Hotel	Diamond Rated	High Season	Page
52 p. 303	**The Crane Residential Resort** (See ad p. 319.)	▼▼▼▼	$150-$850 [SAVE]	319

Map Page	Restaurant	Diamond Rated	Cuisine	Meal Range	Page
42 p. 303	Zen	▼▼▼	Asian	$27-$46	319

HASTINGS (Christ Church Parish)

Map Page	Hotels	Diamond Rated	High Season	Page
55 p. 303	The Savannah Hotel Barbados	▼▼▼	$246-$562	305
56 p. 303	**Courtyard by Marriott Bridgetown** (See ad p. 305.)	▼▼▼	$123-$309 [SAVE]	304

HASTINGS (Christ Church Parish) (cont'd)

Map Page	Hotels (cont'd)	Diamond Rated	High Season	Page
57 p. 303	Hotel PomMarine	◆◆	$106-$186	304
58 p. 303	Pirate's Inn	◆	$90-$120	305

Map Page	Restaurants	Diamond Rated	Cuisine	Meal Range	Page
⑰ p. 303	Bistro Monet	◆◆	International	$21-$44	305
⑱ p. 303	Black Pearl Seafood, Steakhouse & Wine Bar	◆◆	International	$33-$49	305

WORTHING (Christ Church Parish)

Map Page	Hotels	Diamond Rated	High Season	Page
64 p. 303	**Accra Beach Hotel & Spa** (See ad p. 309.)	◆◆◆	$175-$571 [SAVE]	309
66 p. 303	Blue Orchids Beach Hotel	◆◆	$123-$320	309
67 p. 303	Coral Mist Beach Hotel	◆◆	$123-$320	310
68 p. 303	Sea Foam Haciendas	◆	$130-$240	310
72 p. 303	Rockley Plumtree Club	◆◆	$110-$255	310
73 p. 303	**South Beach Resort and Vacation Club**	◆◆◆	$188-$285 [SAVE]	310

Map Page	Restaurants	Diamond Rated	Cuisine	Meal Range	Page
⑳ p. 303	Champers Wine Bar & Restaurant	◆◆◆	International	$25-$50	310
㉑ p. 303	Lucky Horseshoe Steakhouse	◆	American	$10-$25	310
㉒ p. 303	Bert's Bar	◆◆	International	$12-$28	310
㉓ p. 303	Fusion Restaurant & Lounge	◆◆◆	Asian	$15-$42	310
㉕ p. 303	**Bubba's Sports Bar & Restaurant**	◆	American	$20-$45	310

ST. LAWRENCE (Christ Church Parish)

Map Page	Hotels	Diamond Rated	High Season	Page
74 p. 303	**Little Bay Hotel**	◆	$105-$165 [SAVE]	308
75 p. 303	Maresol Beach Condominiums	◆	$98-$331	308
77 p. 303	Mistle Cove Condos	◆◆◆	$220-$600	308
80 p. 303	Southern Palms Beach Club	◆◆	$193-$520	308

Map Page	Restaurants	Diamond Rated	Cuisine	Meal Range	Page
㉖ p. 303	Bellini's Trattoria	◆◆◆	Italian	$17-$32	308
㉚ p. 303	David's Place by the Sea	◆◆	Caribbean	$23-$43	308
㉛ p. 303	Harlequin Restaurant	◆◆	International	$20-$35	308
㉜ p. 303	Sweet Potatoes	◆	Caribbean	$19-$26	308
㉝ p. 303	Josef's	◆◆◆	International	$50-$60	308

DOVER (Christ Church Parish)

Map Page	Hotels	Diamond Rated	High Season	Page
82 p. 303	**Dover Beach Apartment Hotel**	◆	$120-$200 [SAVE]	302
84 p. 303	Turtle Beach Resort	◆◆◆	$428-$1260	302
85 p. 303	Almond Casuarina Beach Resort	◆◆◆	$637-$1261	302

Map Page	Restaurant	Diamond Rated	Cuisine	Meal Range	Page
㊳ p. 303	Luigi's Ristorante Italiano	◆◆	Italian	$18-$35	303

MAXWELL (Christ Church Parish)

Map Page	Hotels	Diamond Rated	High Season	Page
86 p. 303	**Bougainvillea Beach Resort** (See ad p. 307.)	◆◆◆	$178-$688 [SAVE]	306

MAXWELL (Christ Church Parish) (cont'd)

Map Page	Hotels (cont'd)	Diamond Rated	High Season	Page
88 p. 303	**Sea Breeze Beach Hotel**	▽▽▽	$340-$512 [SAVE]	306
89 p. 303	**Sunbay Hotel** *(See ad p. 306.)*	▽	$88-$220 [SAVE]	306
90 p. 303	Butterfly Beach Hotel	▽▽	$90-$330	306

ENTERPRISE (Christ Church Parish)

Map Page	Hotel	Diamond Rated	High Season	Page
92 p. 303	**Little Arches Hotel**	▽▽▽	$205-$590 [SAVE]	303

Map Page	Restaurant	Diamond Rated	Cuisine	Meal Range	Page
40 p. 303	Cafe Luna	▽▽▽	Mediterranean	$28-$43	304

SILVER SANDS (Christ Church Parish)

Map Page	Hotel	Diamond Rated	High Season	Page
94 p. 303	Inchcape Seaside Villas	▽▽	$85-$215	309

INCH MARLOWE (Christ Church Parish)

Map Page	Hotel	Diamond Rated	High Season	Page
98 p. 303	Peach and Quiet Inn	▽▽	$109-$119	306

OISTINS (Christ Church Parish)

Map Page	Hotel	Diamond Rated	High Season	Page
99 p. 303	**Cumber's Tropical Apartment Complex**	▽	$90-$130 [SAVE]	308

DERRICKS (St. James Parish)

Map Page	Restaurant	Diamond Rated	Cuisine	Meal Range	Page
14 p. 303	The Cliff	▽▽▽▽	International	$124-$144	310

BAGATELLE (St. Thomas Parish)

Map Page	Restaurant	Diamond Rated	Cuisine	Meal Range	Page
34 p. 303	Paulo's Churrasco Do Brasil	▽▽	Brazilian	$35-$50	319

Christ Church Parish

DOVER

• Hotels & Restaurants index & map p. 299

ALMOND CASUARINA BEACH RESORT
Phone: (246)620-3600　85

▽▽▽
Resort Hotel
$637-$1261

Address: Dover Rd **Location:** Oceanfront. Just s of St. Lawrence Gap; center. **Facility:** This resort features more than eight different room categories which differ in size and location but include an LCD TV and well-appointed bathroom. 280 units. 3-5 stories, interior/exterior corridors. **Terms:** 3 night minimum stay, 3 day cancellation notice-fee imposed. **Amenities:** high-speed Internet (fee), safes. **Dining:** 3 restaurants, entertainment. **Pool(s):** 3 outdoor. **Activities:** sailboats, snorkeling, 2 lighted tennis courts, recreation programs, exercise room, spa. **Guest Services:** valet laundry, area transportation-Almond properties.

    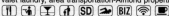

DOVER BEACH APARTMENT HOTEL
Phone: (246)428-8076　82

▽
Motel
$120-$200

Address: St. Lawrence Gap Rd BB15026 **Location:** Oceanfront. South end of St. Lawrence Gap. **Facility:** 59 units, some efficiencies. 2-3 stories (no elevator), interior/exterior corridors. **Terms:** office hours 7 am-10 pm, check-in 4 pm, 21 day cancellation notice, 7 day off season-fee imposed. **Amenities:** safes (fee). **Pool(s):** outdoor. **Activities:** exercise room. *Fee:* bicycles. **Guest Services:** valet and coin laundry. **Free Special Amenities: continental breakfast and local telephone calls.**

[SAVE] [ECO] [TI] [DOG] [Y] [A] [SD] [SPA] [BIZ] [WIFI] [X] [ACC] / SOME UNITS [REFRIG]

TURTLE BEACH RESORT Phone: (246)428-7131　84

▽▽▽
Resort Hotel
$428-$1260

Address: Dover, Christ Church **Location:** Oceanfront. South end of St. Lawrence Gap. **Facility:** This resort with a multi-tiered lobby area surrounded by restaurants and gift shops features varying room types. Meets AAA guest room security requirements. 164 units. 2-4 stories, exterior corridors. **Terms:** 5 night minimum stay - seasonal, 21 day cancellation notice, 7 day-fee imposed. **Amenities:** high-speed Internet (fee), safes. **Dining:** 3 restaurants, entertainment. **Pool(s):** 3 outdoor. **Activities:** whirlpool, sailboats, windsurfing, snorkeling, 2 lighted tennis courts, recreation programs, playground, volleyball, exercise room. *Fee:* massage. **Guest Services:** valet laundry.

[TI] [DOG] [Y] [A] [SD] [SPA] [BIZ] [WIFI] [X] [ACC] [REFRIG]

SEE AAA GEM ATTRACTIONS

NORTH POINT

ST LUCY PARISH

HARRISON POINT

CUCKOLD POINT

Barbados
Hotels & Restaurants

| 0 | Miles | 4.1 |
| 0 | Kilometers | 6.6 |

Atlantic Ocean

15   Fairfield

10

Shermans

1   Coleton   6   Portland

3   Maynards   ST ANDREW PARISH

5   Speightstown   Greenland
                    St Andrew's Church

4   Mullins Bay   Barbados Wildlife Reserve, Grenade Hall Forest and Signal Station

1   1   35

19 12 2   8   Chalky Mount   CHALKY MT

13   10   Westmoreland   ST JOSEPH PARISH

18 15   2A   MT HILLABY   46   Bathsheba   ST JOHN PARISH

6   16   The Garden

20   Porters   34   Welchman Hall   3A   3

21   8 17   Holetown   7

5   19   1A   Newcastle   Consett Bay

11   26   Blackmans

23   3   28 29

24   9   3B   CULPEPPER IS

30   Derricks Bagatel   Todds   RAGGED POINT

10 13   Appleby   ST THOMAS PARISH   4   Three Houses

ST JAMES PARISH   14   39   Prospect   Locust Hall   Sandford   Bottom Bay

38   Lazaretto   GUN HILL   ST GEORGE PARISH   Long Bay

1   4B   5A   Marchfield

ST MICHAEL PARISH   3   4   5

Atlantis Submarine Expedition   BRIDGETOWN   Carlisle Bay   52 42

44 15   6   Highgate   72 73   6   ST PHILIP PARISH

16   25   57   21 THRU 23   Bannatyne

55   Hastings   66 67   85   80 THRU 84

58 & 17   18   56   Dover   Balls   99   Chancery Lane   Grantley Adams International Airport (BGI)

64   20   74   75   86   40   Incb Marlowe

© AAA   Worthing   68   St Lawrence   38   90   92   98

77 26 THRU 33   Enterprise   Silver Sands

1504-U

(See index & map p. 299.)

WHERE TO EAT

LUIGI'S RISTORANTE ITALIANO   Phone: 246/428-9218   (38)

Italian
$18-$35

AAA Inspector Notes: In business at the same location for more than 40 years, this restaurant serves authentic Italy-inspired cuisine in a large house setting with a wrap-around porch. The extensive menu includes seven soups, six salads, personal-size pizza and more than two dozen pasta dishes. Silky panna cotta is a tempting way to conclude the meal. **Bar:** full bar. **Reservations:** suggested. **Address:** Dover Woods **Location:** South end of St. Lawrence Gap, follow signs. (D) (AC)

ENTERPRISE
• Restaurants p. 304
• Hotels & Restaurants index & map p. 299

LITTLE ARCHES HOTEL   Phone: (246)420-4689   (92)

Boutique Country Inn
$205-$590

Address: Enterprise Beach Rd **Location:** Oceanfront. Just s of Oistins, follow signs; opposite Enterprise Beach. **Facility:** Originally a mansion-villa, this stylish Mediterranean property with Caribbean influences boasts a range of individually decorated room categories and floor plans. 10 units, some efficiencies and kitchens. 3 stories (no elevator), exterior corridors. *Bath:* shower only. **Terms:** office hours 7 am-10 pm, 3-7 night minimum stay - seasonal, age restrictions may apply, 30 day cancellation notice, 15 day off season-fee imposed. **Amenities:** safes. **Dining:** Cafe Luna, see separate listing. **Pool(s):** outdoor. **Activities:** bicycles. *Fee:* massage. **Guest Services:** valet laundry.

(See index & map p. 299.)

WHERE TO EAT

CAFE LUNA   Phone: 246/428-6172   40

Mediterranean
$28-$43

AAA Inspector Notes: Located on the rooftop of a former mansion turned boutique hotel, this casual eatery offers an eclectic menu combining the best attributes of several cuisines. Starters include baked brie in phyllo dough and Canadian mussels. Entrées range from New Zealand rack of lamb with a Dijon-rosemary demi-glaze to Scottish salmon with a Chablis butter sauce and a hearty seafood bouillabaisse. A fantastic dessert selection is offered. Thursdays and Fridays are sushi nights. **Bar:** full bar. **Reservations:** required. **Address:** Enterprise Main Rd **Location:** Just s of Oistins, follow signs; opposite Enterprise Beach; in Little Arches Hotel. **Parking:** on-site and street.

Safety tip: Keep a current
AAA/CAA Road Atlas
in every vehicle

• Hotels & Restaurants index & map p. 299

HASTINGS

COURTYARD BY MARRIOTT BRIDGETOWN
Phone: (246)625-0000   56

Hotel
$123-$309

AAA Benefit: AAA hotel discounts of 5% or more.

Address: The Garrison Historic Area **Location:** Center of Hastings; at The Garrison. **Facility:** Meets AAA guest room security requirements. 118 units. 4 stories, interior corridors. **Amenities:** high-speed Internet, safes. **Pool(s):** outdoor. **Activities:** exercise room. **Guest Services:** valet and coin laundry. **Free Special Amenities:** local telephone calls and high-speed Internet. (See ad p. 305.)

HOTEL POMMARINE   Phone: 246/228-0900   57

Hotel
$106-$186

Address: Marine Gardens **Location:** Just e of Hastings Main Rd; at Hospitality Institute. **Facility:** 21 units, some kitchens. 3 stories, interior/exterior corridors. **Terms:** 14 day cancellation notice. **Amenities:** safes. **Dining:** 2 restaurants. **Pool(s):** outdoor. **Activities:** lighted tennis court. **Guest Services:** valet laundry.

(See index & map p. 299.)

PIRATE'S INN
Phone: 246-426-6273 **58**

Motel
$90-$120

Address: Browne's Gap **Location:** Just w of Hastings Main Rd; at Browne's Gap, just e of Hastings Plaza. **Facility:** 22 kitchen units. 2 stories (no elevator), exterior corridors. *Bath:* shower only. **Terms:** cancellation fee imposed. **Amenities:** safes. **Pool(s):** outdoor. **Guest Services:** valet laundry.

THE SAVANNAH HOTEL BARBADOS
Phone: (246)228-3800 **55**

Hotel
$246-$562

Address: Hastings Main Rd **Location:** Oceanfront. 11.3 mi (18.1 km) w of international airport; 1.8 mi (2.9 km) s of downtown Bridgetown. **Facility:** Meets AAA guest room security requirements. 92 units. 4 stories, exterior corridors. **Terms:** 14 day cancellation notice, 7 days off season. **Amenities:** safes, honor bars. **Dining:** 2 restaurants. **Pool(s):** 2 outdoor. **Activities:** spa. **Guest Services:** valet laundry, area transportation-Rockley Beach.

▼ See AAA listing p. 304 ▼

BISTRO MONET
Phone: 246-435-9389 **17**

International
$21-$44

AAA Inspector Notes: In a cottage-style building with French cafe decor, this bistro gives diners the choice of indoor or outdoor seating. The menu offers a lot of variety, with French, Continental, West Indies and American fare. Menu items include local fish cakes, Greek salad, escargot, seafood gumbo and create-your-own pasta dishes. A favorite option is shrimp and lobster coquille. **Bar:** full bar. **Reservations:** suggested. **Address:** Hastings Main Rd **Location:** 2.6 mi (4.1 km) s of Bridgetown; on South Coast. **L D**

BLACK PEARL SEAFOOD, STEAKHOUSE & WINE BAR
Phone: 246/435-1234 **18**

International
$33-$49

AAA Inspector Notes: Situated along the new boardwalk is this beachside eatery featuring fresh seafood and steaks and chops. There is a romantic outdoor seating area and a large lounge area inside. **Bar:** full bar. **Reservations:** required. **Address:** Main Rd **Location:** In Shak Shak Complex. **D**

Create complete trip routings and custom maps
with the TripTik® Travel Planner on AAA.com or CAA.ca

INCH MARLOWE
• Hotels & Restaurants index & map p. 299

PEACH AND QUIET INN   Phone: 246/428-5682   98

Country Inn
$109-$119

Address: Inch Marlowe Rd **Location:** Oceanfront. 4 mi (6.4 km) sw of airport; next to Surfer's Point. **Facility:** 22 units. 2 stories (no elevator), exterior corridors. **Bath:** shower only. **Terms:** open 12/1-4/26 & 11/9-11/30, office hours 6:30 am-10 pm, age restrictions may apply, 45 day cancellation notice-fee imposed. **Amenities:** safes. **Pool(s):** outdoor. **Activities:** snorkeling. *Fee:* massage. **Guest Services:** valet laundry.

MAXWELL
• Hotels & Restaurants index & map p. 299

BOUGAINVILLEA BEACH RESORT
Phone: (246)418-0990   86

Resort Hotel
$178-$688

Address: Maxwell Coast Rd, Christ Church Rd **Location:** Oceanfront. 8.6 mi (13.7 km) w of international airport; 1.5 mi (2.4 km) nw of Oistins. **Facility:** The small scale-resort has a free-form cascading pool and bright, colorful guest room decor that matches the tropical ambience. Meets AAA guest room security requirements. 138 units, some two bedrooms, efficiencies and kitchens. 3-4 stories (no elevator), exterior corridors. **Terms:** check-in 4 pm, 28 day cancellation notice-fee imposed. **Amenities:** safes. **Dining:** 2 restaurants, entertainment. **Pool(s):** 3 outdoor. **Activities:** snorkeling, lighted tennis court, game room, shuffleboard, volleyball. *Fee:* sailboats, windsurfing, waterskiing, massage. **Guest Services:** valet laundry. **Free Special Amenities:** high-speed Internet and manager's reception. *(See ad p. 307.)*

BUTTERFLY BEACH HOTEL
Phone: (246)428-9095   90

Hotel
$90-$330

Address: Maxwell Main Rd **Location:** Oceanfront. Center. **Facility:** 93 units, some two bedrooms, efficiencies and kitchens. 2-5 stories, interior/exterior corridors. **Terms:** 21 day cancellation notice, 14 day off season-fee imposed. **Amenities:** high-speed Internet, safes (fee). **Pool(s):** outdoor. **Activities:** whirlpools. **Guest Services:** coin laundry.

SEA BREEZE BEACH HOTEL
Phone: 246/428-2825   88

Hotel
$340-$512

Address: Maxwell Coast Rd **Location:** Oceanfront. Center. **Facility:** 78 units, some two bedrooms. 3 stories (no elevator), exterior corridors. **Terms:** 3 day cancellation notice-fee imposed. **Amenities:** high-speed Internet (fee), safes. **Dining:** 3 restaurants, entertainment. **Pool(s):** 2 outdoor. **Activities:** whirlpools, sailboats, windsurfing, snorkeling, recreation programs, basketball, volleyball, exercise room. *Fee:* massage. **Guest Services:** coin laundry. **Free Special Amenities:** local telephone calls and high-speed Internet.

SUNBAY HOTEL
Phone: (246)428-9900   89

Hotel
$88-$220

Address: Maxwell Coast Rd BB15031 **Location:** 8.4 mi (13.4 km) w of international airport; 1.3 mi (2.1 km) nw of Oistins. **Facility:** 103 units. 4 stories, interior/exterior corridors. **Terms:** cancellation fee imposed. **Amenities:** safes. **Pool(s):** outdoor. **Activities:** limited beach access. *Fee:* massage. **Guest Services:** valet laundry. **Free Special Amenities:** continental breakfast and high-speed Internet. *(See ad this page.)*

▼ See AAA listing this page ▼

(See index & map p. 299.)

▼ See AAA listing p. 306 ▼

Your Journey
Ends Here.

Bougainvillea
BEACH RESORT
"Beachfront Suites"

Imagine a getaway that combines the beauty of Barbados with the comfort, elegance and charm of an award winning resort. Spacious suites and an inviting atmosphere of laidback luxury awaits, where you can do as much or as little as you like.

For more information contact
Tel: (246) 418 0990 Fax: (246) 428 2524
or email res@bougainvillearesort.com

www.bougainvillearesort.com

MAYNARDS
• Hotels & Restaurants index & map p. 299

SUGAR CANE CLUB HOTEL & SPA
Phone: 246/422-5026   **6**

Hotel
$205-$455

Address: Maynards Main Rd **Location:** Just n of Speightstown, then just e, follow signs. **Facility:** 45 units, some two bedrooms, efficiencies and kitchens. 2-3 stories (no elevator), exterior corridors. **Terms:** office hours 7 am-10 pm, age restrictions may apply, 21 day cancellation notice, 14 day off season. **Amenities:** high-speed Internet (fee), safes. **Pool(s):** 2 outdoor. **Activities:** canoeing, snorkeling, racquetball court, bicycles, hiking trails, exercise room, spa. **Guest Services:** coin laundry, area transportation-beach house facilities & Speightstown. **Free Special Amenities:** local telephone calls and high-speed Internet.

SAVE | ⏸ | ⌁ | SD | ⋙ | BIZ | ⚡ | ✕ | ⬛ | ⬜

OISTINS (D-2)
• Hotels & Restaurants index & map p. 299

CUMBER'S TROPICAL APARTMENT COMPLEX
Phone: 246/418-9957   **99**

Condominium
$90-$130

Address: Oistins Main Rd **Location:** Just s of town center; in Pegwell Gardens. **Facility:** 8 condominiums. 3 stories (no elevator), exterior corridors. *Bath:* shower only. **Terms:** office hours 9 am-5 pm, 21 day cancellation notice. **Guest Services:** complimentary laundry. **Free Special Amenities: high-speed Internet and use of on-premises laundry facilities.**

SAVE | ⚡ | ⬛ | ⬜ | ⬜

ST. LAWRENCE
• Hotels & Restaurants index & map p. 299

LITTLE BAY HOTEL
Phone: 246/420-7587   **74**

Motel
$105-$165

Address: St. Lawrence Gap Rd **Location:** Oceanfront. At entrance to St. Lawrence Gap. **Facility:** 10 efficiencies. 3 stories (no elevator), interior corridors. **Terms:** office hours 9 am-5 pm, 2 night minimum stay, 14 day cancellation notice-fee imposed. **Dining:** Bellini's Trattoria, see separate listing. **Guest Services:** valet laundry. **Free Special Amenities:** local telephone calls.

SAVE | ⏸ | SD | ⚡ | ✕ | ⬛ | ⬜

MARESOL BEACH CONDOMINIUMS
Phone: 246/428-9300   **75**

Condominium
$98-$331

Address: St. Lawrence Gap Rd **Location:** Oceanfront. Center. **Facility:** 13 condominiums. 1-2 stories (no elevator), exterior corridors. **Terms:** office hours 8:30 am-5 pm, 3 night minimum stay, 60 day cancellation notice-fee imposed. **Amenities:** *Some:* safes. **Guest Services:** complimentary laundry.

⏸ | SD | ⚡ | ⬛ | ⬜ | / SOME UNITS | W

MISTLE COVE CONDOS
Phone: 246/420-3727   **77**

Condominium
$220-$600

Address: St. Lawrence Gap Rd **Location:** Oceanfront. Middle of St. Lawrence Gap; center. **Facility:** Each of the well-appointed, spacious units are individually decorated and furnished; bathrooms are spacious, many with a spa shower and separate tub. Meets AAA guest room security requirements. 12 condominiums. 5 stories, exterior corridors. **Terms:** office hours 8 am-4 pm, 7 night minimum stay - seasonal, 60 day cancellation notice, 45 day off season. **Amenities:** safes. **Pool(s):** outdoor. **Guest Services:** complimentary laundry.

⏸ | SD | ⋙ | ⚡ | ✕ | ⬛ | ⬜

SOUTHERN PALMS BEACH CLUB
Phone: (246)428-7171   **80**

Hotel
$193-$520

Address: St. Lawrence Gap **Location:** Oceanfront. Center. **Facility:** 92 units, some efficiencies. 1-3 stories (no elevator), exterior corridors. **Amenities:** safes (fee).
Pool(s): 2 outdoor. **Activities:** windsurfing, snorkeling, miniature golf, 2 lighted tennis courts, shuffleboard, volleyball, limited exercise equipment. *Fee:* massage. **Guest Services:** valet and coin laundry.

ECO | ⏸ | ⌁ | ⬆ | SD | ⋙ | ⚡ | ⬛

WHERE TO EAT

BELLINI'S TRATTORIA
Phone: 246/420-7587   **26**

Italian
$17-$32

AAA Inspector Notes: This distinctly Caribbean open-air eatery offers a wonderful setting overlooking the sea. The varied menu brings together freshly prepared pasta dishes, seafood and grilled items. Warm hospitality emanates from the personable staff. **Bar:** full bar. **Reservations:** suggested. **Address:** St. Lawrence Gap **Location:** At entrance to St. Lawrence Gap; in Little Bay Hotel. D | ⌥

DAVID'S PLACE BY THE SEA
Phone: 246/435-9755   **30**

Caribbean
$23-$43

AAA Inspector Notes: A very popular oceanfront dining spot owned by cheerful David; well-rounded menu with everything from steak to local seafood, curry dishes, lamb, rabbit and goat is served by an attentive staff. **Bar:** full bar. **Reservations:** suggested. **Address:** St. Lawrence Main Rd **Location:** Entrance to St. Lawrence Gap. D | ⌥

HARLEQUIN RESTAURANT
Phone: 246/420-7677   **31**

International
$20-$35

AAA Inspector Notes: In the heart of the entertainment and dining district of St. Lawrence Gap, the Baja-style chattel house presents an international menu that represents offerings from the Caribbean, Asia and the Mediterranean. Among entree choices are tuna with tropical fruit salsa, duck breast with raspberry au jus and nut-crusted salmon. Tempting desserts include piña colada cheesecake, bread and butter pudding and hot apple pie. **Bar:** full bar. **Reservations:** suggested. **Address:** St. Lawrence Gap Rd **Location:** Center at St. Lawrence Gap; adjacent to Rostrevor Hotel; across from Ship's Inn. **Parking:** on-site (fee) and street. D | ⌥

JOSEF'S
Phone: 246/435-8245   **33**

International
$50-$60

AAA Inspector Notes: Enjoy a unique brand of international haute cuisine blended with elements of Asian and Caribbean influences at this oceanfront seaside restaurant. **Bar:** full bar. **Reservations:** required. **Address:** Waverly House **Location:** In St. Lawrence Gap; 7.5 mi (12 km) w of international airport; 4 mi (6.4 km) s of downtown Bridgetown. **Parking:** street only. D | ⌥

SWEET POTATOES
Phone: 246/435-9638   **32**

Caribbean
$19-$26

AAA Inspector Notes: This down-home Bajan eatery is located in hip St. Lawrence Gap, in a converted home with veranda-style dining. There are many items to choose from, but some favorites include the vegetable stuffed flying fish and jerked pork. The large drink menu offers some very creative concoctions. Save room for the moist bread pudding with rum sauce. **Bar:** full bar. **Address:** St. Lawrence Gap, Christ Church **Location:** In St. Lawrence Gap; 7.3 mi (11.7 km) w of international airport; 3.8 mi (4.8 km) s of downtown Bridgetown. **Parking:** on-site (fee) and street. L | D | ⌥ | ◲

SILVER SANDS
• Hotels & Restaurants index & map p. 299

INCHCAPE SEASIDE VILLAS
Phone: 246/428-7006 **94**

Vacation Rental House
$85-$215

Location: Oceanfront. Center; follow signs. **Facility:** Nestled on a bluff, these cottages and villas provide comfortable, homey accommodations near several beaches. 13 units, some two bedrooms, efficiencies, houses and cottages. 1-2 stories, exterior corridors. **Terms:** office hours 8 am-5 pm, check-in 4 pm, cancellation fee imposed. **Amenities:** safes. **Guest Services:** valet laundry.

Share a New View on Travel at AAATravelViews.com

Read stories, tips and trends from AAA insiders. Post comments and get your questions answered by our travel experts.

WORTHING
• Restaurants p. 310
• Hotels & Restaurants index & map p. 299

ACCRA BEACH HOTEL & SPA
Phone: (246)435-8920 **64**

Hotel
$175-$571

Address: Rockley, Christ Church BB15139 **Location:** Oceanfront. 7.7 mi (12.3 km) w of international airport; 2 mi (3.2 km) s of downtown. **Facility:** 224 units, some two bedrooms. 3-4 stories, interior corridors. **Terms:** 14 day cancellation notice, 7 day off season-fee imposed. **Amenities:** high-speed Internet, safes. **Dining:** 3 restaurants, entertainment. **Pool(s):** 2 outdoor. **Activities:** snorkeling, game room, volleyball, exercise room, spa. **Guest Services:** valet laundry. **Free Special Amenities:** high-speed Internet and manager's reception. (See ad this page.)

BLUE ORCHIDS BEACH HOTEL
Phone: 246/435-8057 **66**

Hotel
$123-$320

Address: 18 Worthing Rd **Location:** Oceanfront. Center. **Facility:** 31 units, some two bedrooms, efficiencies and kitchens. 2-4 stories, exterior corridors. **Terms:** 21 day cancellation notice-fee imposed. **Pool(s):** outdoor. **Activities:** snorkeling, game room, volleyball, exercise room. **Guest Services:** valet laundry.

▼ See AAA listing this page ▼

An Oasis of Tranquility

Breathtaking setting on the ocean
Located on a pristine, south coast beach
3 miles from the capital and 7 miles from the airport
Enjoy one of two swimming pools and
cocktails at the swim up bar
Surrender yourself to the embrace of the Chakra Spa

Accra Beach Hotel & Spa
Rockley, Christ Church • Barbados
246-435-8920 • Toll Free: 1-888-712-2272
www.accrabeachhotel.com

(See index & map p. 299.)

CORAL MIST BEACH HOTEL
Phone: 246/435-7712 [67]

Hotel
$123-$320

Address: Worthing, Christ Church **Location:** Oceanfront. Center. **Facility:** 32 efficiencies, some two bedrooms. 4 stories, exterior corridors. **Terms:** 21 day cancellation notice, 14 day-fee imposed. **Pool(s):** outdoor. **Activities:** snorkeling, recreation programs, exercise room. **Guest Services:** valet laundry.

ROCKLEY PLUMTREE CLUB
Phone: 246/435-7606 [72]

Condominium
$110-$255

Address: Plumtree Cluster Golf Club Rd **Location:** 10.2 mi (16.3 km) n of international airport; 2.8 mi (4.5 km) s of downtown Bridgetown; in Club Rockley. **Facility:** 40 condominiums. 2 stories (no elevator), exterior corridors. **Terms:** office hours 9 am-5 pm, 21 day cancellation notice-fee imposed. **Amenities:** safes. **Pool(s):** outdoor. **Activities:** Fee: golf-9 holes, 4 lighted tennis courts, massage. **Guest Services:** valet and coin laundry, area transportation-Rockley Beach.

SEA FOAM HACIENDAS
Phone: 246/435-7380 [68]

Condominium
$130-$240

Address: Worthing Main Rd **Location:** Center; just s of Rockley Beach. **Facility:** 10 condominiums. 3 stories (no elevator), exterior corridors. **Bath:** shower only. **Terms:** office hours 8:30 am-6 pm, 3 night minimum stay, 21 day cancellation notice-fee imposed. **Amenities:** safes. **Guest Services:** valet laundry.

SOUTH BEACH RESORT AND VACATION CLUB
Phone: (246)435-8561 [73]

Hotel
$188-$285

Address: Rockley Beach, Christ Church **Location:** In Rockley Beach; 7.7 mi (9.3 km) w of international airport; 2.1 mi (3.3 km) s of downtown Bridgetown. 49 units, some efficiencies and kitchens. 5 stories, interior/exterior corridors. **Parking:** street only. **Terms:** 3 night minimum stay - seasonal, 14 day cancellation notice-fee imposed. **Amenities:** safes. **Dining:** Fusion Restaurant & Lounge, see separate listing. **Pool(s):** outdoor. **Activities:** beach access. **Guest Services:** valet and coin laundry, area transportation-Bridgetown.

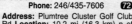

WHERE TO EAT

BERT'S BAR
[22]

International
$12-$28

AAA Inspector Notes: Dine al fresco while being surrounded by pools of fish. Large bar area is great for sports fans to unwind with a beer and some pizza. The dinner menu offers something for everyone including local specialties like flying fish, pizza, burgers and entrée size salads. **Bar:** full bar. **Address:** Rockley Main Rd **Location:** 2.7 mi (4.3 km) s of Bridgetown on Hwy 7; 10 mi (16 km) w of international airport. L D

BUBBA'S SPORTS BAR & RESTAURANT
Phone: 246/435-8731 [25]

American
$20-$45

AAA Inspector Notes: Diners can escape the heat inside the air-conditioned restaurant and enjoy live satellite sporting events while imbibing and noshing on a freshly prepared meal. For a warm-up, try fish fingers, chicken wings or coconut shrimp. Main-event entrees range from shrimp Provencal to flying fish, kebabs, fajitas and porterhouse steak. Also popular are satisfying burgers and a good selection of sandwiches all served with a jacket potato. **Bar:** full bar. **Address:** Rockley Main Rd **Location:** 2.4 mi (3.9 km) s of Bridgetown on Hwy 7; 10.3 mi (16.6 km) w of international airport. L D CALL

CHAMPERS WINE BAR & RESTAURANT
Phone: 246/434-3463 [20]

International
$25-$50

AAA Inspector Notes: The dining room excels in comfort and service; the menu has been refined with many gourmet selections including the variety of fish that are among the most popular choices; also available is lamb, chicken, duck dishes, all cooked to perfection. **Bar:** full bar. **Reservations:** required. **Address:** Torrington Skeete's Hill, Rockley Christ Church **Location:** 2.3 mi (3.7 km) s of downtown Bridgetown; at Rockley Beach. L D

FUSION RESTAURANT & LOUNGE
Phone: 246/436-1538 [23]

Asian
$15-$42

AAA Inspector Notes: Cool and chic surroundings epitomize this Asian-style restaurant with a variety of seating options. The cuisine runs the gamut of Chinese, Japanese, Vietnamese and Thai favorites. Besides the extensive sushi menu and designer drinks there are noodle and rice dishes as well as curry dishes. Save room for such delicious desserts as the lemongrass crème brûlée. **Bar:** full bar. **Reservations:** suggested. **Address:** Rockley Beach **Location:** 7.7 mi (9.3 km) w of international airport; 2.1 mi (3.3 km) s of downtown Bridgetown; in South Beach Resort and Vacation Club. L D LATE

LUCKY HORSESHOE STEAKHOUSE
Phone: 246/435-5825 [21]

American
$10-$25

AAA Inspector Notes: With an International and American menu, there is something for everyone at this 24-hour eatery including a wide selection of sandwiches, hamburgers, beef and fish. **Bar:** full bar. **Address:** Worthing Main Rd **Location:** Center; across from beach. B L D 24

St. James Parish

APPLEBY
• Hotels & Restaurants index & map p. 299

CRYSTAL COVE HOTEL
Phone: 246/432-2683 [38]

Boutique Resort Hotel
$405-$1179

Address: Main Rd **Location:** Oceanfront. 15.5 mi (24.8 km) nw of international airport; 5.3 mi (8.5 km) n of downtown Bridgetown. **Facility:** Multi-level, meandering pools with a grotto-like cave bar are distinct features of this all-inclusive resort. Room categories are based on location. 88 units. 2-3 stories (no elevator), exterior corridors. **Terms:** 7 night minimum stay - seasonal, 21 day cancellation notice, 7 day off season-fee imposed. **Amenities:** high-speed Internet (fee), safes. **Dining:** 2 restaurants, entertainment. **Pool(s):** 3 outdoor. **Activities:** sailboats, windsurfing, waterskiing, snorkeling, 2 lighted tennis courts, exercise room. **Guest Services:** valet laundry, area transportation-water taxi.

DERRICKS
• Hotels & Restaurants index & map p. 299

THE CLIFF
Phone: 246/432-1922 [14]

International
$124-$144

AAA Inspector Notes: Located on top of a coral cliff, this open-air, tiered dining room offers a varied international, Thai and Caribbean menu featuring creative and innovative entrées. Flavorful food and delectable desserts are served in a setting of candlelight and art. **Bar:** full bar. **Reservations:** required. **Address:** Hwy 1, Derricks **Location:** 5 mi (8 km) n of Bridgetown. **Parking:** valet only. D

HOLETOWN (C-1)
- Restaurants p. 313
- Hotels & Restaurants index & map p. 299

ALL SEASONS RESORT - EUROPA
Phone: (246)432-5046 **19**

Cottage
$91-$180

Address: Palm Ave **Location:** Just e of town; just e at Sunset Crest Laforet entrance, just s, then just e, follow signs. **Facility:** 48 cottages. 1 story, exterior corridors. *Bath:* shower only. **Terms:** office hours 7 am-10 pm, 2 night minimum stay, 7 day cancellation notice, 3 day off season. **Amenities:** safes (fee). **Pool(s):** outdoor. **Guest Services:** valet laundry, area transportation-within 3 mi & beach.

ALMOND BEACH CLUB & SPA
Phone: (246)432-7840 **23**

Resort Hotel
$637-$1456

Address: Vauxhall, St. James **Location:** Oceanfront. In Vauxhall; 17.4 mi (27.8 km) nw of international airport; 7.1 mi (11.3 km) n of downtown Bridgetown. **Facility:** On the popular Gold Coast surrounded by attractively landscaped grounds, the resort offers a bountiful supply of pools and water-oriented activities. 161 units. 3-4 stories (no elevator), exterior corridors. **Terms:** 3 night minimum stay, age restrictions may apply, 21 day cancellation notice-fee imposed. **Amenities:** high-speed Internet (fee), safes. **Dining:** 3 restaurants, entertainment. **Pool(s):** 3 outdoor. **Activities:** saunas, whirlpool, steamrooms, boating, sailboats, windsurfing, waterskiing, snorkeling, fishing, lighted tennis court, recreation programs, volleyball, spa. **Guest Services:** valet laundry, area transportation-Almond properties & Bridgetown.

MANGO BAY
Phone: (246)432-1384 **21**

Hotel
$385-$725

Address: 2nd St **Location:** Oceanfront. 17.2 mi (27.5 km) nw of international airport; 7.7 mi (12.3 km) n of downtown Bridgetown. **Facility:** 67 units. 3-4 stories, exterior corridors. **Terms:** 45 day cancellation notice, 14 day off season. **Amenities:** safes. **Dining:** entertainment. **Pool(s):** outdoor. **Activities:** paddleboats, sailboats, waterskiing, snorkeling, volleyball, exercise room. *Fee:* massage. **Guest Services:** valet laundry.

THE SANDPIPER
Phone: 246/422-2251 **18**

Hotel
$310-$2610

Address: Hwy 1, St. James **Location:** Oceanfront. 17.7 mi (28.3 km) nw of international airport; 8 mi (12.8 km) n of downtown Bridgetown. **Facility:** 48 units, some efficiencies and houses. 2-3 stories (no elevator), exterior corridors. **Terms:** open 12/1-8/15 & 10/8-11/30, 7 night minimum stay - seasonal, age restrictions may apply, 28 day cancellation notice, 14 day off season. **Amenities:** safes. **Dining:** The Sandpiper Dining Room, see separate listing, entertainment. **Pool(s):** outdoor. **Activities:** sailboats, waterskiing, snorkeling, 2 lighted tennis courts, exercise room. **Guest Services:** valet laundry, area transportation-Coral Reef Club & Bridgetown.

SANDY LANE HOTEL
Phone: (246)444-2000 **24**

Resort Hotel
$1050-$5460

Address: St. James BB 24024 **Location:** Oceanfront. 17.2 mi (27.5 km) nw of international airport; 6.9 mi (11 km) n of downtown Bridgetown. **Facility:** Boutiques, Bentleys and the beach await at this luxurious property offering state-of-the-art amenities, gourmet dining and a fully appointed spa. Meets AAA guest room security requirements. 113 units, some two bedrooms and houses. 4 stories, interior corridors. **Parking:** valet only. **Terms:** check-in 4 pm, 28 day cancellation notice-fee imposed. **Amenities:** high-speed Internet, safes, honor bars. **Dining:** 5 restaurants, entertainment. **Pool(s):** outdoor. **Activities:** sauna, whirlpools, steamroom, boating, paddleboats, sailboats, windsurfing, snorkeling, 9 lighted tennis courts, recreation programs, jogging, playground, basketball, game room, volleyball, spa. *Fee:* waterskiing, golf-45 holes, bicycles. **Guest Services:** valet laundry, area transportation-country club & golf course. **Free Special Amenities:** full breakfast and high-speed Internet. Affiliated with A Preferred Hotel. *(See ad p. 312.)*

Visit AAA.com or CAA.ca for one-stop
travel planning and reservations

(See index & map p. 299.)

SETTLERS BEACH HOTEL
Phone: 246/422-3052 [20]

Cottage
$294-$1220 12/1-8/31
$147-$814 10/1-11/30

Address: Trents **Location:** Oceanfront. 17.8 mi (28.5 km) nw of international airport; 8.1 mi (13 km) n of downtown Bridgetown. **Facility:** The stylish and spacious cottages are situated in a peaceful, tranquil setting on world-famous Platinum coast. 23 cottages. 1-2 stories (no elevator), exterior corridors. **Terms:** open 12/1-8/31 & 10/1-11/30, office hours 8 am-10 pm, 14 day cancellation notice-fee imposed. **Amenities:** safes. **Pool(s):** outdoor. **Activities:** Fee: massage. **Guest Services:** valet and coin laundry. **Free Special Amenities:** high-speed Internet and manager's reception.
(See ad this page.)

SUNSWEPT BEACH HOTEL
Phone: 246/432-2715 [17]

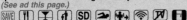

Motel
$125-$185

Address: Main Rd **Location:** Oceanfront. Center; in Tropical Sunset Complex. **Facility:** 23 efficiencies. 3 stories (no elevator), interior corridors. **Terms:** 3 night minimum stay, 21 day cancellation notice-fee imposed. **Amenities:** safes (fee). **Pool(s):** outdoor. **Guest Services:** valet laundry.

WHERE TO EAT

THE BEACH HOUSE BAR & RESTAURANT
Phone: 246/432-1163 [8]

International
$27-$45

AAA Inspector Notes: A romantic, oceanfront setting with gentle breezes wafting through the air, this popular eatery offers such great starters as crab cakes garnished with spiced apple and mango chutney or homemade chicken liver pate. Main courses range from jerk pork loin, Cajun snapper filet and lamb loin with a mint-rosemary sauce. Featured desserts include toffee pudding, crème brûlée and bread pudding. There is a chic lounge area ideal for relaxing before or after dinner. **Bar:** full bar. **Reservations:** required. **Address:** Holetown Main Rd **Location:** Center; at Sunset Crest.

THE MEWS RESTAURANT
Phone: 246/432-1122 [3]

International
$21-$38

AAA Inspector Notes: On the restaurant row of Holetown is this jewel of a restaurant. While the service can be deficient at times, the cuisine hits the mark. Many guests enjoy the blend of international and Caribbean dishes with the occasional Asian influence mixed in. Choose from either the more popular upstairs dining area, offering a comfortable decorative ambience with tables tightly tucked together, or the downstairs lounge/dining area. **Bar:** full bar. **Reservations:** suggested. **Address:** 2nd St **Location:** In 2nd St Restaurant Row. **Parking:** street only. D

Download eTourBook guides for ereaders and smartphones at AAA.com/ebooks

(See index & map p. 299.)

THE SANDPIPER DINING ROOM

Phone: 246/422-2251 [6]

International
$35-$45

AAA Inspector Notes: At this popular, elegant spot, twice a week guests can take advantage of a specialty buffet dinner in lieu of the a la carte menu. Dim lighting and candlelit tables lend to the romantic feel of the covered open-air dining room, where high ceiling fans create a refreshing breeze. The chef changes the menu daily to feature the freshest local and international ingredients, which combine with global cooking influences and island flair. **Bar:** full bar. **Reservations:** required. **Address:** Hwy 1, St. James **Location:** 17.7 mi (28.3 km) nw of international airport; 8 mi (12.9 km) n of downtown Bridgetown; in The Sandpiper.

[B] [L] [D] [AC]

SPAGO RESTAURANT & BAR

Phone: 246/432-7394 [7]

Italian
$14-$28

AAA Inspector Notes: In the city's restaurant row area, this cute Bajan chattel-style cottage restaurant lets patrons relax indoors or on the porch over plates of Italy-influenced fare, including varied pasta dishes, gourmet pizza, entree salads and the catch of the day. **Bar:** full bar. **Reservations:** suggested. **Address:** 2nd St **Location:** 17.2 mi (27.5 km) nw of international airport; 7.7 mi (12.3 km) n of downtown Bridgetown; just n of Holetown Center. **Parking:** street only. [D] [AC]

THE TIDES RESTAURANT

Phone: 246/432-8356 [5]

International
$13-$35

AAA Inspector Notes: Set directly on the edge of the mesmerizing azure sea. The proprietor creates memorable meals incorporating culinary techniques, ingredients and flavors that span the globe in order to suit any palate. The chef's talent showcases his special preparations of lamb, shrimp, scallops, beef, pork and duck. **Bar:** full bar. **Reservations:** required. **Address:** Queens Hwy **Location:** 16.8 mi (26.9 km) nw of international airport; 7.5 mi (12 km) n of downtown Bridgetown; in St. James. **Parking:** valet only. [D] [AC]

PAYNES BAY

• Hotels & Restaurants index & map p. 299

BEACH VIEW

Phone: 246/432-2300 [28]

Vacation Rental Condominium
$200-$750

Address: Paynes Bay Rd **Location:** Center. **Facility:** These contemporary, fully equipped residential-style condominiums are situated across the street from the sea; the pool area is attractive. Meets AAA guest room security requirements. 36 condominiums. 3 stories, exterior corridors. **Terms:** office hours 8 am-5 pm, 14 day cancellation notice, 7 day off season-fee imposed. **Amenities:** safes. **Pool(s):** 2 outdoor. **Guest Services:** complimentary laundry.

[icons]

SHADES

Phone: 246/432-6697 [29]

Motel
$165-$245

Address: Laynes Rd **Location:** Just e of town. **Facility:** 7 kitchen units, some two bedrooms. 2 stories (no elevator), exterior corridors. **Bath:** shower only. **Terms:** 42 day cancellation notice. **Amenities:** safes. **Pool(s):** outdoor. **Activities:** exercise room. **Guest Services:** coin laundry.

[icons] / SOME UNITS

Enjoy great savings on hotel rates at AAA.com or CAA.ca

TREASURE BEACH HOTEL

Phone: (246)419-4200 [30]

Hotel
$315-$1900

Address: Paynes Bay **Location:** Oceanfront. Center. **Facility:** 35 units. 2-3 stories (no elevator), exterior corridors. **Terms:** open 12/1-8/29 & 10/10-11/30, age restrictions may apply, 28 day cancellation notice, 14 day off season-fee imposed. **Amenities:** safes. **Dining:** see separate listing, entertainment. **Pool(s):** outdoor. **Activities:** snorkeling, exercise room. *Fee:* massage. **Guest Services:** valet laundry. **Free Special Amenities:** high-speed Internet and manager's reception.

[icons]

WHERE TO EAT

DAPHNE'S

Phone: 246/432-2731 [9]

New Italian
$27-$60

AAA Inspector Notes: A chic oasis on the Platinum Coast, the elegantly rustic al fresco dining area sustains a romantic air and has muslin sheets draped from the ceiling. The sophisticated menu lines up such selections as carpaccio marlin, sashimi-grade tuna and lamb cutlets, as well as a range of Italian-inspired pasta dishes, including tagliatelle, rigatoni and linguine; potato dumpling gnocchi; and risotto. **Bar:** full bar. **Reservations:** suggested. **Address:** Payne's Bay Rd **Location:** 20.3 mi (32.5 km) nw of international airport; 7.5 mi (12 km) n of Bridgetown; in The House at Tamarind Cove. **Parking:** on-site and valet.

[L] [D] [AC]

KATHY'S

Phone: 246/432-1346 [10]

International
$18-$73

AAA Inspector Notes: This elegant dining room offers a sophisticated yet relaxed dining experience in a covered open-air setting. The well-trained staff provides fine service, while the chef prepares fine international fare. During the day, guests enjoy nice views of the surrounding gardens, while at night, the atmosphere is more romantic. A daily changing two, three or four course men is available. **Bar:** full bar. **Reservations:** suggested. **Address:** Paynes Bay, St. James **Location:** Center; in Treasure Beach Hotel.

[B] [L] [D] [AC] [N]

SCARLET

Phone: 246/432-3663 [11]

International
$23-$29

AAA Inspector Notes: The chic surroundings and avante-garde menu along with the cozy tables and cool music set the tone for a different kind of evening at this sleek eatery. The menu ranges from chicken liver pate and gourmet burgers to Thai beef salad and grilled salmon. A variety of adventurous cocktails compliment the meal. **Bar:** full bar. **Reservations:** required. **Address:** Paynes Bay Main Rd **Location:** Center; across from ocean. [D]

PORTERS

• Hotels & Restaurants index & map p. 299

COLONY CLUB HOTEL

Phone: (246)422-2335 [15]

Boutique Resort Hotel
$430-$1460

Address: Porters **Location:** Oceanfront. 18 mi (28.8 km) nw of international airport; 8.3 mi (13.3 km) n of downtown Bridgetown. **Facility:** Swimming pools with waterfalls characterize the tropical garden setting found at this beachfront property. Several room categories are available. 96 units. 1-3 stories (no elevator), exterior corridors. **Terms:** 7 night minimum stay - seasonal, age restrictions may apply, 21 day cancellation notice, 7 day off season-fee imposed. **Amenities:** high-speed Internet (fee), safes, honor bars. **Dining:** 2 restaurants, entertainment. **Pool(s):** 4 outdoor. **Activities:** sailboats, windsurfing, waterskiing, snorkeling, 2 lighted tennis courts, recreation programs in season, exercise room. *Fee:* massage. **Guest Services:** valet laundry, area transportation-water taxi to sister hotels.

[icons]

(See index & map p. 299.)

CORAL REEF CLUB
Phone: 246/422-2372 **16**

Hotel
$245-$2610

Address: Hwy 1 **Location:** Oceanfront. 17.9 mi (28.6 km) n of international airport; 8.2 mi (13.1 km) n of downtown Bridgetown. **Facility:** Varied room categories are offered at this family-operated beachfront property, which features a real country club atmosphere. 88 units, some efficiencies and cottages. 1-3 stories (no elevator), exterior corridors. **Parking:** on-site and valet. **Terms:** open 12/1-5/20 & 7/21-11/30, 7-14 night minimum stay - seasonal, age restrictions may apply, 28 day cancellation notice-fee imposed. **Amenities:** safes. **Dining:** entertainment. **Pool(s):** 2 outdoor. **Activities:** paddleboats, sailboats, windsurfing, snorkeling, 2 lighted tennis courts, playground, exercise room, spa. *Fee:* waterskiing. **Guest Services:** valet laundry, area transportation-Bridgetown.

THE FAIRMONT ROYAL PAVILION
Phone: (246)422-5555 **13**

Hotel
$449-$1759

Address: Porters **Location:** Oceanfront. 18.5 mi (29.6 km) nw of international airport; 8.8 mi (14.1 km) n of downtown Bridgetown. **Facility:** The well-appointed guest rooms feature furnished, ocean-facing balconies at this picturesque beachfront resort with a tranquil ambiance. Meets AAA guest room security requirements. 75 units, some houses. 2-3 stories, exterior corridors. **Parking:** on-site and valet. **Terms:** check-in 4 pm, age restrictions may apply, 30 day cancellation notice, 14 day off season-fee imposed. **Amenities:** high-speed Internet, safes, honor bars. **Dining:** Palm Terrace Restaurant, see separate listing, entertainment. **Pool(s):** outdoor. **Activities:** whirlpool, paddleboats, sailboats, windsurfing, snorkeling, 2 lighted tennis courts, recreation programs in summer, exercise room. *Fee:* scuba diving, massage. **Guest Services:** valet laundry.

LONE STAR RESTAURANT & HOTEL
Phone: 246/419-0599 **12**

Bed & Breakfast
$500-$900

Address: Mount Standfast **Location:** Oceanfront. 22.2 mi (35.5 km) nw of international airport; 9.4 mi (15 km) n of Bridgetown. **Facility:** Units are spacious with large balconies facing the ocean, giving the property a retreat-like ambiance. 4 units. 2 stories (no elevator), exterior corridors. *Bath:* shower only. **Terms:** office hours 8 am-11 pm, 90 day cancellation notice-fee imposed. **Amenities:** high-speed Internet, safes. **Dining:** restaurant, see separate listing. **Activities:** snorkeling. **Guest Services:** valet laundry.

 WHERE TO EAT

LONE STAR RESTAURANT
Phone: 246/419-0599 **2**

International
$24-$40

AAA Inspector Notes: Attached to a hotel by the same name, the oceanfront al fresco dining room reflects a romantic ambiance. Well-presented cuisine incorporates Asian and Mediterranean influences. The meze plate appetizer--which includes baba ghanoush, hummus, goat cheese truffles and kalamata olives--is ideal for sharing. Savory main plates range from lamb cutlets and duck to mahi mahi and lobster. A real favorite is tuna nicoise. **Bar:** full bar. **Reservations:** required, in winter. **Address:** Mount Standfast **Location:** 22.2 mi (35.5 km) nw of international airport; 9.4 mi (15 km) n of Bridgetown; in Lone Star Restaurant & Hotel. L D

PALM TERRACE RESTAURANT
Phone: 246/422-5555 **19**

International
$35-$49

AAA Inspector Notes: In refined surroundings, guests are recommended to reserve early at this elegant eatery for an oceanfront table. The exquisite menu offers such appetizers as warm spinach salad with bacon and egg dressing and candied ginger and seared foie gras. Entrées include a variety of such fish as tuna, grouper and sea bass in red curry coconut broth as well as a rack of lamb with mint pesto. Decadent desserts include a molten chocolate cake with pecan whiskey ice cream. **Bar:** full bar. **Reservations:** required. **Address:** Porters Main Rd **Location:** 18.5 mi (29.6 km) nw of international airport; 8.8 mi (14.1 km) n of downtown Bridgetown; in The Fairmont Royal Pavilion. D

PROSPECT
• Hotels & Restaurants index & map p. 299

BEST E VILLAS
Phone: 246/425-9751 **39**

Condominium
$110-$216

Address: Crusher Site Rd **Location:** Center; at Green Ridge, follow signs. **Facility:** 5 condominiums. 2 stories (no elevator), exterior corridors. **Terms:** office hours 8 am-4:30 pm, 3 night minimum stay, 21 day cancellation notice. **Amenities:** safes. **Pool(s):** outdoor. **Guest Services:** complimentary laundry. **Free Special Amenities:** local telephone calls and high-speed Internet.

 **WHERE TO EAT**

IL TEMPIO RESTAURANT & BAR
Phone: 246/417-0057 **13**

Italian
$17-$50

AAA Inspector Notes: The casual, oceanfront restaurant offers refined overtones and a beachfront bar. Diners can choose from savory pasta dishes as well as veal, beef, chicken and seafood entrées. The tortellini stuffed with lamb is a favorite. A broad selection of appetizers-such as beef carpaccio, and salads, including caprese-whets the appetite. **Bar:** full bar. **Reservations:** required, for dinner. **Address:** Fitts Village, St. James **Location:** At Fitts Village; 5 mi (8 km) n of downtown Bridgetown; 14.7 mi (23.5 km) nw of international airport. L D

THE GARDEN
• Hotels & Restaurants index & map p. 299

COVE SPRING
Phone: 246/422-3166 **10**

Vacation Rental House
$714-$1000

Location: Oceanfront. Center; on main road. **Facility:** Guests at this well-appointed, luxury home can rent one room or all ten; a private chef is available to design meals according to guests' preferences. 10 units. 2 stories (no elevator), interior corridors. **Terms:** 7 night minimum stay, 5 day cancellation notice. **Amenities:** *Some:* safes. **Pool(s):** outdoor. **Activities:** whirlpool, snorkeling, exercise room. *Fee:* massage. **Guest Services:** complimentary laundry.

Safety tip: Keep a current
AAA/CAA Road Atlas
in every vehicle

WESTMORELAND
• Hotels & Restaurants index & map p. 299

ROYAL WESTMORELAND Phone: 246/422-4653 **26**

Vacation Rental House
$350-$3000

Location: Just e of Reads Bay and Porters, follow signs. **Facility:** Located inland, this residential-style resort community is an ideal home away from home for large families or groups. 33 houses. 2 stories (no elevator), exterior corridors. **Terms:** office hours 9 am-6 pm, 3 night minimum stay, 60 day cancellation notice-fee imposed. **Amenities:** safes. *Some:* high-speed Internet. **Dining:** 4 restaurants. **Pool(s):** 3 outdoor. **Activities:** whirlpool, 2 lighted tennis courts, recreation programs, basketball, spa. *Fee:* golf-18 holes. **Guest Services:** complimentary laundry, area transportation-Mullins Beach.

St. Joseph Parish

BATHSHEBA (B-3)
• Hotels & Restaurants index & map p. 299

SEA-U GUEST HOUSE Phone: (246)433-9450 **46**

Bed & Breakfast
$119-$219

Address: Tent Bay **Location:** Just s of center, follow signs. **Facility:** 9 units, some kitchens. 1-2 stories (no elevator), exterior corridors. **Terms:** office hours 8 am-7 pm, age restrictions may apply, 28 day cancellation notice, 21 day off season-fee imposed. **Amenities:** safes. **Activities:** beach access.

St. Lucy Parish

SHERMANS
• Hotels & Restaurants index & map p. 299

LITTLE GOOD HARBOUR HOTEL
Phone: (246)439-3000 **1**

Extended Stay Hotel
$249-$940

Address: Fort Rupert **Location:** 23.4 mi (37.5 km) nw of airport; 13.2 mi (21.2 km) n of downtown Bridgetown. **Facility:** Meets AAA guest room security requirements. 21 kitchen units, some two and three bedrooms. 1-2 stories (no elevator), exterior corridors. **Terms:** open 12/1-9/1 & 10/14-11/30, office hours 7 am-7 pm, 3-7 night minimum stay, 28 day cancellation notice, 14 day in summer-fee imposed. **Amenities:** safes. **Pool(s):** 2 outdoor. **Activities:** limited beach access, canoeing, snorkeling, spa. **Guest Services:** valet and coin laundry.

St. Michael Parish

BRIDGETOWN (D-1) pop. 7,500
• Hotels & Restaurants index & map p. 299

HILTON BARBADOS Phone: (246)426-0200 **44**

Hotel
$369-$529 12/1-4/15
$209-$309 4/16-11/30

AAA Benefit: Members save 5% or more everyday!

Address: Needham's Point **Location:** Oceanfront. 1.5 mi (2.4 km) s of downtown, 0.4 mi (0.6 km) w at Aquatic Gap turn off. **Facility:** This hotel is nestled between the Caribbean Sea and Carlisle Bay on the site of Old Fort Charles; the modern guest units are well equipped. 350 units. 6-8 stories, interior corridors. **Terms:** 1-7 night minimum stay, cancellation fee imposed. **Amenities:** high-speed Internet (fee), safes, honor bars. **Dining:** 3 restaurants, also, The Grille, see separate listing, entertainment. **Pool(s):** 2 outdoor. **Activities:** whirlpool, snorkeling, 4 lighted tennis courts, recreation programs, volleyball, exercise room. *Fee:* scuba diving, massage. **Guest Services:** valet laundry. **Free Special Amenities:** manager's reception and children's activities.
(See ad opposite title page, p. 317.)

WHERE TO EAT

BROWN SUGAR RESTAURANT
Menu on AAA.com Phone: 246/426-7684 **16**

Caribbean
$18-$45

AAA Inspector Notes: Located in Aquatic Gap, this rebuilt and now rediscovered restaurant offers the best in Bajan and Caribbean cuisine. The very popular lunch buffet has an wide variety of selections to choose from. Multiple dining rooms offer something for everyone. Flying fish and stewed and curried dishes keep guests coming back here time after time. Live jazz is offered on the weekends. Monday nights feature local music and an extravagant local Bajan buffet. **Bar:** full bar. **Reservations:** suggested. **Address:** Aquatic Gap, Bay St **Location:** At Aquatic Gap turnoff; 1.2 mi (1.9 km) s of downtown.

THE GRILLE Phone: 246/426-0200 **15**

Fusion
$27-$42

AAA Inspector Notes: This fine-dining establishment envelops patrons in plush, comfortable surroundings characterized by rich decor. Seafood and steak pair with choices from an excellent wine list prepared to impress the true connoisseur. The adjacent lounge offers live music most nights. Semi-formal attire. **Bar:** full bar. **Reservations:** required. **Address:** Needham's Point **Location:** 1.5 mi (2.4 km) s of downtown, 0.4 mi (0.6 km) w at Aquatic Gap turn off; in Hilton Barbados.

Learn about AAA/CAA Diamond Ratings
at AAA.com/Diamonds

A World Of Possibilities

Hilton Barbados is an unforgettable getaway nestled in the lush tropical peninsula of Needham's Point. Explore historic Bridgetown. Snorkel in turquoise waters among some of the world's most beautiful coral reefs. Catch your breath in a place that will forever take it away.

For reservations and information on Hilton Barbados, visit **hiltoncaribbean.com/barbados** or call **877 GO HILTON.**

Hilton Barbados
Needham's Point, St. Michael, Barbados

© Hilton Worldwide 2011.

St. Peter Parish

MULLINS BAY
• Hotels & Restaurants index & map p. 299

BAYFIELD HOUSE　　**Phone:** 246/419-0497　**8**

Bed & Breakfast
$155-$350

Address: Mullins Rd **Location:** Just e of Mullins Beach. **Facility:** 10 units. 2 stories (no elevator), exterior corridors. *Bath:* shower only. **Terms:** office hours 6:30 am-6 pm, 3 night minimum stay, age restrictions may apply, 21 day cancellation notice, 14 day in summer. **Amenities:** safes. **Pool(s):** outdoor. **Guest Services:** valet laundry.

WHERE TO EAT

MULLINS RESTAURANT & COCKTAIL BAR
　　Phone: 246-422-2044　**35**

International
$14-$52

AAA Inspector Notes: Situated on a deck above a sugary-white beach is this well-regarded eatery providing attentive service and an inviting lounge area. The varied menu offers such items as hoisin sauce pork ribs and herb-crusted lamb loin as well as grilled local barracuda and kingfish, pan-seared scallops and seared yellowfin tuna. To cap off the meal, the warm bread-and-butter pudding with rum-soaked currants and vanilla sauce is delightful. **Bar:** full bar. **Reservations:** required. **Address:** Gibbs Main Rd **Location:** Center. **Parking:** on-site and valet.

SPEIGHTSTOWN (B-1)
• Hotels & Restaurants index & map p. 299

ALMOND BEACH VILLAGE　**Phone:** (246)422-4900　**3**

Resort Hotel
$340-$875

Address: Hwy 1 Heywoods-St. Peter **Location:** Oceanfront. 12.5 mi (20 km) n of Bridgetown on Hwy 1; 1.2 mi (1.9 km) n of town. **Facility:** The former sugar plantation is on 30 acres of landscaped grounds; all units have a patio or balcony, some with garden, pool or ocean views. Meets AAA guest room security requirements. 395 units. 2-5 stories (no elevator), exterior corridors. **Terms:** 3 night minimum stay, 21 day cancellation notice-fee imposed. **Amenities:** safes. **Dining:** 5 restaurants, nightclub, entertainment. **Pool(s):** 11 outdoor. **Activities:** whirlpools, paddleboats, sailboats, windsurfing, waterskiing, snorkeling, fishing, golf-9 holes, 4 lighted tennis courts, racquetball courts, recreation programs, playground, game room, shuffleboard, volleyball, exercise room. *Fee:* massage. **Guest Services:** valet and coin laundry, area transportation-sister property Almond Beach Club & Spa, Almond Casuarina Beach.

COBBLERS COVE　　**Phone:** 246/422-2291　**4**

Boutique Country Inn
$465-$895

Address: Road View, St. Peter **Location:** Oceanfront. 22.2 mi (35.5 km) nw of international airport; 11.9 mi (19 km) n of downtown Bridgetown; 1 mi (1.6 km) s of town. **Facility:** Lush foliage accent the courtyard of this beachfront resort; units include a living room, bedrooms and a private balcony or patio. 40 units, some two bedrooms. 2 stories (no elevator), exterior corridors. **Terms:** open 12/1-8/3 & 10/4-11/30, age restrictions may apply, 30 day cancellation notice, 14 day off season-fee imposed. **Amenities:** safes, honor bars. **Dining:** entertainment. **Pool(s):** outdoor. **Activities:** sailboats, windsurfing, waterskiing, snorkeling, lighted tennis court, recreation programs in summer, exercise room. *Fee:* massage. **Guest Services:** valet laundry.

SUNSET SANDS BEACH APARTMENTS
　　Phone: 246-438-1096　**5**

Vacation Rental Condominium
$85-$110

Address: Sand St **Location:** Center of downtown. **Facility:** These apartment-style guest units with rattan furnishings are located in the center of town across from the waterfront. 4 condominiums. 2 stories (no elevator), interior corridors. **Parking:** street only. **Terms:** office hours 9 am-4 pm. **Amenities:** safes. **Guest Services:** coin laundry.

WHERE TO EAT

MANGO'S BY THE SEA　**Phone:** 246/422-0704　**1**

International
$25-$50

AAA Inspector Notes: In an outstanding location overlooking the sea, this second-level island eatery entices diners with its covered open-air setting and fine views. The small dining room has a distinct island feel in both its decor and its menu offerings, which include homemade chicken pate, grilled meats and fresh fish and other seafood prepared with island spices. Tempting passion fruit cheesecake exemplifies the lush desserts that also reflect the island. **Bar:** full bar. **Reservations:** suggested. **Address:** West End #2 Queen St **Location:** Center; waterfront.

Check out our travel blog at
AAATravelViews.com

St. Philip Parish

ST. PHILIP PARISH (D-4)
• Hotels & Restaurants index & map p. 299

THE CRANE RESIDENTIAL RESORT
Phone: (246)423-6220 52

Resort Hotel
$150-$850

Address: Crane Beach, St. Philip BB11098 **Location:** Oceanfront. In Crane; 4.8 mi (7.7 km) se of international airport; 17.6 mi (28.1 km) se of downtown Bridgetown. **Facility:** Reputed to be the oldest continuous operating resort in the Caribbean, the property is in a stunning location built around a former plantation. 230 units, some two bedrooms, three bedrooms, efficiencies and kitchens. 2-5 stories, exterior corridors. **Parking:** on-site and valet. **Terms:** check-in 4 pm, 3-7 night minimum stay - seasonal, 30 day cancellation notice, 15 day off season. **Amenities:** high-speed Internet, safes. **Dining:** 3 restaurants, also, Zen, see separate listing, entertainment. **Pool(s):** 5 outdoor. **Activities:** whirlpool, 2 lighted tennis courts, exercise room, spa. **Guest Services:** valet and coin laundry, area transportation-Bridgetown. **Free Special Amenities:** local telephone calls and high-speed Internet.
(See ad this page.)

WHERE TO EAT

ZEN
Phone: 246/423-6220 42

Asian
$27-$46

AAA Inspector Notes: Diners at this casual spot can select preparations from a fine menu of freshly prepared Thai and Japanese cuisine, which can be ordered a la carte or via full tasting menus. Japanese elements, including a large sushi bar and tatami room, enhance the dining room. **Bar:** full bar. **Reservations:** required. **Address:** Crane Beach, St. Philip **Location:** In Crane; 4.8 mi (7.7 km) se of international airport; 17.6 mi (28.1 km) se of downtown Bridgetown; in The Crane Residential Resort. D

St. Thomas Parish

BAGATELLE
• Hotels & Restaurants index & map p. 299

PAULO'S CHURRASCO DO BRASIL
Phone: 246/421-6767 34

Brazilian
$35-$50

AAA Inspector Notes: Located in the Bagatelle Great House which dates to 1645, this Brazilian steak-house features a buffet with a variety of starters, salads and appetizers as well as a dessert bar. Gaucho dressed carvers or passadors continuously circulate the dining room with skewers of beef, ribs, pork loin, chicken, sausage and rabbit. **Bar:** full bar. **Reservations:** required. **Address:** Bagatelle Great House **Location:** At Bagatelle Great House, follow signs; between D'Arcy Scott Roundabout and Lawrence Johnson Roundabout; behind Sandy Lane Golf Course. D

▼ See AAA listing this page ▼

BERMUDA

This index helps you "spot" where approved hotels and restaurants are located on the corresponding detailed maps. Hotel daily rate range is for comparison only and show the property's high season. Restaurant rate range is a combination of lunch and/or dinner. Turn to the listing page for more detailed rate information and consult display ads for special promotions.

HAMILTON (Pembroke Parish)

Map Page	Hotels	Diamond Rated	High Season	Page
1 p. 322	**Royal Palms Hotel**	◆◆◆	$279-$410 SAVE	327
3 p. 322	The Oxford House	◆◆	$224-$246	326
4 p. 322	Rosemont Guest Suites	◆◆	$198-$242	326
5 p. 322	Edgehill Manor Guest House	◆◆	$172-$240	326
6 p. 322	Rosedon Hotel	◆◆◆	$212-$418 SAVE	326
7 p. 322	**The Fairmont Hamilton Princess** (See ad on insert, p. 332.)	◆◆◆◆	$299-$499 SAVE	326
10 p. 322	Robin's Nest	◆◆	$150	326

Map Page	Restaurants	Diamond Rated	Cuisine	Meal Range	Page
① p. 322	**House of India**	◆◆	Indian	$16-$22	327
② p. 322	Harley's Bistro (See ad on insert.)	◆◆◆	Continental	$27-$39	327
③ p. 322	La Trattoria	◆◆	Italian	$10-$32	327
④ p. 322	Ascots Restaurant at Royal Palms	◆◆◆	Mediterranean	$17-$49	327
⑤ p. 322	The Lobster Pot Restaurant & Boathouse Bar	◆◆	Continental	$11-$32	328
⑥ p. 322	The Red Carpet	◆◆	Continental	$17-$36	328
⑦ p. 322	L'Oriental	◆◆◆	Asian	$16-$48	328
⑧ p. 322	The Little Venice	◆◆◆	Italian	$22-$40	328
⑩ p. 322	Portofino	◆◆	Italian	$12-$29	328
⑪ p. 322	The Harbourfront Restaurant & Komodaru Sushi Lounge	◆◆◆	International	$17-$39	327
⑫ p. 322	Port O' Call Restaurant	◆◆◆	Seafood	$14-$38	328
⑬ p. 322	Hog Penny Restaurant & Pub	◆◆	English	$16-$34	327
⑭ p. 322	Barracuda Grill	◆◆◆	Seafood	$15-$55	327
⑮ p. 322	Silk Thai Cuisine	◆◆	Thai	$12-$23	328
⑯ p. 322	The Robin Hood Pub & Restaurant	◆	English	$12-$28	328
⑰ p. 322	Cafe Cairo Restaurant & Bar	◆◆◆	Middle Eastern	$18-$30	327
⑱ p. 322	The Spot Restaurant	◆	Comfort Food	$7-$18	328
⑳ p. 322	Bolero Brasserie	◆◆◆	French	$18-$42	327
㉒ p. 322	Latin	◆◆	Latin American	$13-$39	327

SMITH'S PARISH (Smith's Parish)

Map Page	Hotel	Diamond Rated	High Season	Page
13 p. 322	Pink Beach Club & Cottages	◆◆◆	$460-$995	331

Map Page	Restaurants	Diamond Rated	Cuisine	Meal Range	Page
㊶ p. 322	Speciality Inn	◆	International	$10-$21	331
㊷ p. 322	North Rock Brewing Company	◆◆	English	$15-$39	331

ST. GEORGE'S (St. George's Parish)

Map Page	Hotel	Diamond Rated	High Season	Page
16 p. 322	The St. George's Club	◆◆	$179-$460	328

SANDY'S PARISH (Sandy's Parish)

Map Page	Hotels	Diamond Rated	High Season	Page
20 p. 322	**Cambridge Beaches Resort & Spa** *(See ad p. 330, p. 87.)*	◆◆◆◆	$295-$1690 SAVE	329
21 p. 322	9 Beaches	fyi	$190-$600	329

Map Page	Restaurant	Diamond Rated	Cuisine	Meal Range	Page
29 p. 322	The Frog & Onion Pub	◆	English	$12-$25	331

SOUTHAMPTON PARISH (Southampton Parish)

Map Page	Hotels	Diamond Rated	High Season	Page
25 p. 322	Pompano Beach Club	◆◆◆	$220-$540	331
28 p. 322	The Reefs	◆◆◆	$410-$1099	331
30 p. 322	**The Fairmont Southampton** *(See ad on insert, p. 332.)*	◆◆◆◆	$229-$499 SAVE	331

Map Page	Restaurants	Diamond Rated	Cuisine	Meal Range	Page
32 p. 322	**The Waterlot Inn Steakhouse**	◆◆◆	Steak	$30-$68	333
33 p. 322	The Dining Room	◆◆	International	$14-$30	333
35 p. 322	**Bacci**	◆◆◆	Italian	$15-$38	333
37 p. 322	Tio Pepe	◆◆	Italian	$16-$32	333

PAGET PARISH (Paget Parish)

Map Page	Hotels	Diamond Rated	High Season	Page
35 p. 322	Greenbank & Cottages	◆◆	$145-$400	325
36 p. 322	Salt Kettle House	◆	$150-$190	325
39 p. 322	Fourways Inn Cottage Colony	◆◆◆	$245-$525	325
41 p. 322	Little Pomander Guest House	◆	$110-$150	325
42 p. 322	**Elbow Beach Bermuda, A Mandarin Oriental Hotel**	◆◆◆◆	$355-$595 SAVE	325
44 p. 322	Coco Reef Resort	◆◆	$179-$479	325

Map Page	Restaurants	Diamond Rated	Cuisine	Meal Range	Page
42 p. 322	Beau Rivage	◆◆	French	$13-$39	325
44 p. 322	**Fourways Inn Restaurant**	◆◆◆	International	$30-$42	325
48 p. 322	Lido Restaurant	◆◆◆	International	$24-$45	325

WARWICK PARISH (Warwick Parish)

Map Page	Hotels	Diamond Rated	High Season	Page
43 p. 322	Granaway Guest House & Cottage	◆◆	$120-$230	333
47 p. 322	Surf Side Beach Club	◆◆	$180-$550	333
48 p. 322	Clairfont Apartments	◆◆	$150-$175	333

HAMILTON PARISH (Hamilton Parish)

Map Page	Hotels	Diamond Rated	High Season	Page
49 p. 322	Grotto Bay Beach Resort	◆◆◆	$199-$359	323
50 p. 322	Rosewood Tucker's Point *(See ad p. 324.)*	◆◆◆◆	$450-$1780	323

Map Page	Restaurants	Diamond Rated	Cuisine	Meal Range	Page
50 p. 322	The Point	◆◆◆	New American	$21-$40	323
52 p. 322	Hibiscus Room	◆◆◆	Continental	$20-$29	323
53 p. 322	Swizzle Inn Pub & Restaurant	◆	English	$15-$29	323
54 p. 322	**Tom Moore's Tavern**	◆◆◆◆	International	$29-$40	323

ST. DAVID'S ISLAND (St. George's Parish)

Map Page	Restaurant	Diamond Rated	Cuisine	Meal Range	Page
55 p. 322	The Black Horse Tavern	◆	English	$17-$37	328

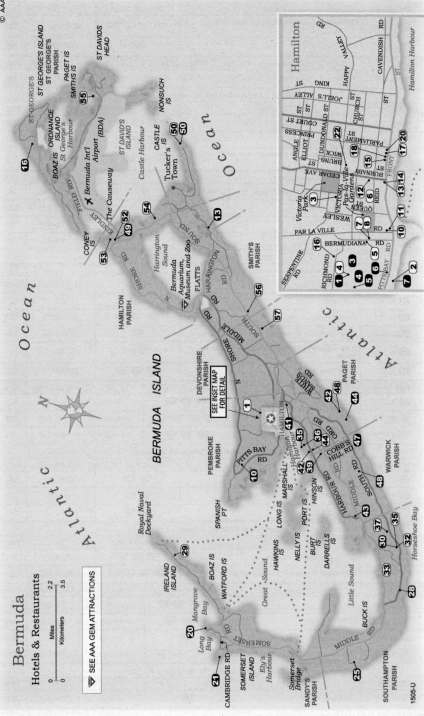

Bermuda
Hotels & Restaurants

SEE AAA GEM ATTRACTIONS

Hamilton Parish

HAMILTON PARISH (B-4) pop. 5,270
• Hotels & Restaurants index & map p. 320

GROTTO BAY BEACH RESORT
Phone: (441)293-8333 [49]

Resort Hotel
$199-$359

Address: 11 Blue Hole Hill **Location:** Oceanfront. On Bailey's Bay; just w of the causeway bridge. **Facility:** Situated on a lovely hillside overlooking Bailey's Bay and 21 acres of landscaped grounds, all guest rooms have bay views from private balconies. 201 units. 3 stories (no elevator), exterior corridors. **Terms:** 2 night minimum stay, 14 day cancellation notice-fee imposed. **Amenities:** safes. **Dining:** 3 restaurants, also, Hibiscus Room, see separate listing. **Pool(s):** heated outdoor. **Activities:** whirlpool, rental boats, rental paddleboats, rental sailboats, rental sailboards, recreation programs, rental bicycles, playground, shuffleboard, exercise room. *Fee:* scuba diving, snorkeling, 4 tennis courts (2 lighted). **Guest Services:** valet and coin laundry.

ROSEWOOD TUCKER'S POINT
Phone: (441)298-4000 [50]

Resort Hotel
$450-$1780

Address: 60 Tucker's Point Dr **Location:** Oceanfront. Just n of South Shore Rd. **Facility:** Fine art and upscale decorative pieces enhance the property throughout. The large upscale suites and villas feature an oversize tub. Meets AAA guest room security requirements. 88 units, some two bedrooms. 2-5 stories, interior/exterior corridors. **Terms:** 2 night minimum stay - seasonal and/or weekends, 14 day cancellation notice-fee imposed. **Amenities:** high-speed Internet, safes, honor bars. **Dining:** 3 restaurants, also, The Point, see separate listing. **Pool(s):** 2 outdoor, 2 heated outdoor. **Activities:** saunas, rental boats, rental paddleboats, rental sailboats, recreation programs in summer, rental bicycles, shuffleboard, volleyball, spa. *Fee:* marina, waterskiing, scuba diving, snorkeling, charter fishing, golf-18 holes, 4 lighted tennis courts. **Guest Services:** valet laundry, area transportation-within property & beach club. Affiliated with A Preferred Hotel. *(See ad p. 324.)*

WHERE TO EAT

HIBISCUS ROOM
Phone: 441/293-8333 [52]

Continental
$20-$29

AAA Inspector Notes: This contemporary dining room with a tropical theme presents a daily changing menu with a mix of European and Bermudian influences. Guests might start the day with the all-inclusive breakfast buffet or wrap it up with a la carte service at dinner. Outdoor terrace seating is an option. Semi-formal attire. **Bar:** full bar. **Reservations:** suggested, for dinner. **Address:** 11 Blue Hole Hill **Location:** On Bailey's Bay; just w of causeway bridge; in Grotto Bay Beach Resort.

THE POINT
Phone: 441/298-4000 [50]

New American
$21-$40

AAA Inspector Notes: Decorated with the original Pan Am murals, this opulent restaurant offers fine cuisine crafted from the freshest ingredients. For starters, guests can enjoy pumpkin and ricotta cheese ravioli with tomato coulis or lobster and champagne bisque. Attentive servers deliver such entrées as Wadson Farm chicken filled with pine nuts and chanterelle mushrooms and truffle jus, Long Island duck marinated in Galliano and pink peppercorns or braised short-ribs and Angus sirloin with red wine reduction. Semi-formal attire. **Bar:** full bar. **Reservations:** required. **Address:** 60 Tucker's Point Dr **Location:** Just n of South Shore Rd; in Rosewood Tucker's Point.

SWIZZLE INN PUB & RESTAURANT
Phone: 441/293-1854 [53]

English
$15-$29

AAA Inspector Notes: Legend has it that the historic pub is the birthplace of the rum swizzle. Patrons' business cards cover the walls and ceiling. Alfresco seating is available. The menu centers on English pub fare: sandwiches to full meals. Portions are hearty. Live entertainment is lined up in the summer. **Bar:** full bar. **Address:** 3 Blue Hole Hill **Location:** On Blue Hole Hill; in Bailey's Bay. **Historic**

TOM MOORE'S TAVERN
Phone: 441/293-8020 [54]

International
$29-$40

AAA Inspector Notes: Considered to be Bermuda's oldest restaurant, the carefully restored mid-17th-century home occupies a lovely, peaceful setting. Contributing to the graceful atmosphere are handsome table settings, original woodwork and antiques. The cadre of servers is pampering and attentive. Continental cuisine with Bermudian influences is skillfully prepared, delicious and visually appealing. Semi-formal attire. **Bar:** full bar. **Reservations:** required. **Address:** 7 Walsingham Ln **Location:** Walsingham Bay; off Harrington Sound Rd. **Historic**

▼ See AAA listing p. 323 ▼

Paget Parish

PAGET PARISH (D-3) pop. 5,088

• **Hotels & Restaurants index & map p. 320**

COCO REEF RESORT

Phone: (441)236-5416

▼▼▼▼
Hotel
$179-$479

Address: 3 Stonington Cir PG04 **Location:** Oceanfront. Off South Shore Rd; on Elbow Beach. **Facility:** 64 units. 2 stories (no elevator), exterior corridors. **Terms:** 3 day cancellation notice-fee imposed. **Amenities:** safes. **Pool(s):** heated outdoor. **Activities:** 2 tennis courts. **Guest Services:** valet laundry.

🍽 🍸 🏋 SD 🏊 📶 ✕ 🛅 💻 / SOME UNITS 🐾 🖼

ELBOW BEACH BERMUDA, A MANDARIN ORIENTAL HOTEL

Phone: (441)236-3535   42

▼▼▼▼▼
Hotel
$355-$595

Address: 60 South Shore Rd PG04 **Location:** Oceanfront. At Elbow Beach; on south coast. **Facility:** This refined property offers a variety of spacious units hosted in separate buildings on 50 landscaped acres sloping down to a pink-sand beach. 98 units, some cottages. 1-2 stories, interior/exterior corridors. **Terms:** 4 night minimum stay - seasonal and/or weekends, 14 day cancellation notice-fee imposed. **Amenities:** high-speed Internet (fee), safes, honor bars. **Dining:** 3 restaurants, also, Lido Restaurant, see separate listing, entertainment. **Pool(s):** heated outdoor. **Activities:** whirlpool, snorkeling & rental equipment, putting green, recreation programs in summer, volleyball, spa. *Fee:* scuba diving, 5 tennis courts (2 lighted), bicycles. **Guest Services:** valet laundry. **Free Special Amenities:** newspaper.

SAVE 🍽 🛎 🍸 🏋 S SD 🏊 📶 BIZ 📶 ✕ 💻

FOURWAYS INN COTTAGE COLONY

Phone: (441)236-6517   39

▼▼▼
Cottage
$245-$525 12/1-3/31
$195-$375 4/1-11/30

Address: 1 Middle Rd **Location:** Jct Cobbs Hill and Middle rds. Located in a quiet, secluded area. **Facility:** Luxurious units in refined cottage setting. 11 cottages. 2 stories (no elevator), exterior corridors. **Terms:** office hours 7 am-midnight, 21 day cancellation notice-fee imposed. **Amenities:** safes. **Dining:** Fourways Inn Restaurant, see separate listing. **Pool(s):** outdoor.

🍽 🍸 🏋 SD 🏊 📶 ✕ 🛅 🖼 💻

GREENBANK & COTTAGES

Phone: 441/236-3615   35

▼▼
Historic Cottage
$145-$400

Address: 17 Salt Kettle Rd **Location:** Oceanfront. On Salt Kettle Peninsula; off Harbour Rd. Located in a secluded area. **Facility:** Quaint cottages surround a small main house at this complex located on a picturesque peninsula across the bay from Hamilton. 11 units, some cottages. 1 story, exterior corridors. **Terms:** office hours 9 am-5 pm, 3 night minimum stay, 30 day cancellation notice-fee imposed. **Amenities:** safes. **Activities:** boat dock.

🏋 SD 📶 ✕ 🛅 💻 / SOME UNITS 🅦 🖼

LITTLE POMANDER GUEST HOUSE

Phone: 441-236-7635   41

◆
Bed & Breakfast
$110-$150

Address: 16 Pomander Rd **Location:** Jct The Lane, just w. **Facility:** 6 units. 2 stories (no elevator), interior/exterior corridors. **Terms:** office hours 9 am-5 pm, 5 night minimum stay - seasonal, 21 day cancellation notice-fee imposed.

SD 📶 ✕ 🛅 🖼

SALT KETTLE HOUSE

Phone: 441/236-0407   36

◆
Historic Bed & Breakfast
$150-$190

Address: 10 Salt Kettle Rd **Location:** Oceanfront. On Salt Kettle Peninsula; off Harbour Rd. Located in a secluded area. **Facility:** On Hamilton Harbour, this charming rustic inn has guest rooms in the main house as well as some converted cottages with homey decorative touches. 8 units, some cottages. 1 story, exterior corridors. **Terms:** office hours 8 am-8 pm. **Amenities:** safes. **Guest Services:** complimentary laundry.

SD 📶 ✕ / SOME UNITS 🅦 🇿 🛅 🖼

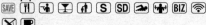

WHERE TO EAT

BEAU RIVAGE

Phone: 441/232-8686   42

▼▼▼
French
$13-$39

AAA Inspector Notes: Professional and friendly service is the norm at this striking restaurant offering stunning views of the harbor. The menu features classic dishes but the chef keeps it up to date. Starters might include crab vichyssoise, Bermuda quiche or frog legs with tarragon sauce and such entrees as coquilles St. Jacques with truffle cream, coq au vin or veal with wild mushroom cream and leeks. **Bar:** full bar. **Reservations:** suggested. **Address:** 27 Harbour Rd **Location:** At Belmont Ferry; in Newstead Belmont Hills Golf Resort & Spa.

B L D

FOURWAYS INN RESTAURANT

Phone: 441/236-6517   44

▼▼▼
International
$30-$42

AAA Inspector Notes: The 1727 Georgian-style Bermuda manor house, now handsomely restored, is a picture of charming elegance. Service is outstanding, and even the most sophisticated palate will be pleased by the exceptional menu of haute cuisine. Try the signature dish: foie gras prepared with caramelized pineapple and apple quenelles laced with fig essence. The entrées range from Chateaubriand to Arctic char. Indulge in a souffle du jour for dessert. **Bar:** full bar. **Reservations:** required. **Address:** 1 Middle Rd **Location:** Jct Cobbs Hill and Middle rds; in Fourways Inn Cottage Colony. **Historic** D

LIDO RESTAURANT

Phone: 441/236-3535   48

▼▼▼
International
$24-$45

AAA Inspector Notes: Patrons can relax in an elegant ocean setting with marvelous views of the water. Some starter offerings might include Bermuda fish chowder, Angus tenderloin marinated in herbs and Jerez vinegar or half orders of pasta and risotto dishes. Entrées feature fresh seafood with Bermuda lobster Thermidor or tuna steak seared in peppercorns as well as such meat dishes as lamb chops with couscous, feta cheese and yogurt jus. The desserts are simply too tempting to pass up. **Bar:** full bar. **Reservations:** required. **Address:** 60 South Shore Rd **Location:** At Elbow Beach; on south coast; in Elbow Beach Bermuda, A Mandarin Oriental Hotel.

B L D

Explore the Travel Guides on
AAA.com/Travel or CAA.ca/Travel

Pembroke Parish

HAMILTON (C-3) pop. 969
• Hotels & Restaurants index & map p. 320

EDGEHILL MANOR GUEST HOUSE
Phone: 441/295-7124 **5**

Bed & Breakfast
$172-$240

Address: 36 Rosemont Ave **Location:** Just w on Pitts Bay Rd, 0.5 mi (0.8 km) n. **Facility:** 14 units, some kitchens. 2 stories (no elevator), interior/exterior corridors. **Terms:** 7 day cancellation notice-fee imposed. **Amenities:** safes. *Some:* high-speed Internet. **Pool(s):** outdoor.

THE FAIRMONT HAMILTON PRINCESS
Phone: (441)295-3000 **7**

Hotel
$299-$499

Address: 76 Pitts Bay Rd **Location:** Oceanfront. **Facility:** On the edge of downtown overlooking the harbor, the renovated property offers varied facilities and services; many units include a balcony. Meets AAA guest room security requirements. 410 units. 3-7 stories, interior corridors. **Terms:** 3 day cancellation notice. **Amenities:** high-speed Internet (fee), safes, honor bars. **Dining:** Harley's Bistro, see separate listing. **Pool(s):** outdoor, heated outdoor. **Activities:** putting green, recreation programs in summer, rental bicycles, exercise room, spa. *Fee:* sailboats, boat dock. **Guest Services:** valet laundry, area transportation-ferry service to beach club at The Fairmont Southampton. *(See ad on insert, p. 332.)*

THE OXFORD HOUSE
Phone: 441/295-0503 **3**

Bed & Breakfast
$224-$246

Address: 20 Woodbourne Ave **Location:** Between Pitts Bay and Richmond rds. **Facility:** 12 units. 2 stories (no elevator), interior/exterior corridors. **Parking:** street only. **Terms:** office hours 7 am-6 pm, 14 day cancellation notice-fee imposed. **Amenities:** high-speed Internet. **Guest Services:** valet laundry.

ROBIN'S NEST
Phone: 441/292-4347 **10**

Motel
$150

Address: 37 Mount View Rd **Location:** Jct St. John's Rd, just n. **Facility:** 8 kitchen units. 2 stories (no elevator), exterior corridors. **Terms:** 3 night minimum stay, age restrictions may apply, 14 day cancellation notice. **Amenities:** safes. **Pool(s):** outdoor.

ROSEDON HOTEL
Phone: (441)295-1640 **6**

Bed & Breakfast
$212-$418

Address: 61 Pitts Bay Rd HM 06 **Location:** Downtown; across from waterfront. **Facility:** The Victorian-style mansion houses modern rooms which look out onto a lush garden courtyard and pool. 39 units. 2 stories (no elevator), interior/exterior corridors. **Terms:** office hours 7 am-8 pm, 14 day cancellation notice-fee imposed. **Amenities:** safes. **Pool(s):** heated outdoor. **Guest Services:** valet laundry.

ROSEMONT GUEST SUITES
Phone: (441)292-1055 **4**

Motel
$198-$242

Address: 41- Rosemont Ave **Location:** 0.5 mi (0.8 km) w of downtown; just w on Pitts Bay Rd, then just n. **Facility:** 47 efficiencies. 3 stories, exterior corridors. **Terms:** office hours 8 am-8 pm, 14 day cancellation notice-fee imposed. **Amenities:** safes. **Pool(s):** outdoor. **Guest Services:** valet and coin laundry.

(See index & map p. 320.)

ROYAL PALMS HOTEL
Phone: (441)292-1854 **❶**

Country Inn
$279-$410

Address: 24 Rosemont Ave **Location:** Just w on Pitts Bay Rd, 0.8 mi (1.3 km) n. Located in a quiet residential area. **Facility:** This small, charming inn has an ambience recalling Bermuda in an earlier time; restored residences house richly furnished lodgings. 32 units. 2 stories (no elevator), interior/exterior corridors. **Terms:** office hours 7:30 am-9 pm, 7 day cancellation notice-fee imposed. **Amenities:** high-speed Internet, safes. **Dining:** Ascots Restaurant at Royal Palms, see separate listing. **Pool(s):** outdoor. **Guest Services:** valet laundry. **Free Special Amenities: expanded continental breakfast and high-speed Internet.**

WHERE TO EAT

ASCOTS RESTAURANT AT ROYAL PALMS
Phone: 441/295-9644 **④**

Mediterranean
$17-$49

AAA Inspector Notes: The former Bermuda home boasts a gracious Victorian-style dining room and a charming veranda. The cedar-lined bar's pleasant atmosphere is fitting for relaxing before or after dinner. The chef/owner prepares creative cuisine with an international flair, and the four-course chef's surprise menu changes daily. **Bar:** full bar. **Reservations:** required. **Address:** 24 Rosemont Ave **Location:** Just w on Pitts Bay Rd, 0.8 mi (1.3 km) n; in Royal Palms Hotel. L D

BARRACUDA GRILL
Phone: 441/292-1609 **⑭**

Seafood
$15-$55

AAA Inspector Notes: A very cool and contemporary-style restaurant with dark mahogany furnishings. Fresh, creatively prepared seafood and chops are served in a friendly, crisp manner. Over fifteen wines by the glass are featured. **Bar:** full bar. **Reservations:** suggested. **Address:** 5 Burnaby Hill **Location:** Just off Front St; downtown; above Hog Penny Restaurant & Pub. **Parking:** street only. L D

BOLERO BRASSERIE
Phone: 441/292-4507 **⑳**

French
$18-$42

AAA Inspector Notes: Opposite the Hamilton waterfront, this charming, second-floor bistro has a veranda that overlooks the busy Front Street action. The owner/chef offers classic dishes with fresh innovative twists. Highlights include snails Francoise, cassoulet appetizers and such entrées as beef a la bourguignonne and balsamic glazed veal sweetbreads along with a variety of beef, lamb and fresh seafood dishes. A French-inspired dessert and cheese selection as well as a good wine list is offered. **Bar:** full bar. **Reservations:** suggested. **Address:** 95 Front St **Location:** Down Bermuda House Ln between Parliament St and Chancery Ln. **Parking:** street only. L D

CAFE CAIRO RESTAURANT & BAR
Phone: 441/295-5155 **⑰**

Middle Eastern
$18-$30

AAA Inspector Notes: One of the latest and most unique restaurants on the Bermuda dining scene, the authentic Middle Eastern restaurant combines the best elements of Egyptian, Lebanese and Moroccan cuisine with a decorative motif in three distinct dining areas. Some of the favorite dishes include the stuffed grape leaves and the moussaka. Also offered are a mixed cold appetizer platter as well as a hot appetizer platter--both are great for sharing. Belly dancing is featured on some nights. **Bar:** full bar. **Reservations:** suggested. **Address:** 93 Front St **Location:** Downtown; on waterfront. **Parking:** street only.
D

THE HARBOURFRONT RESTAURANT & KOMODARU SUSHI LOUNGE
Phone: 441/295-4207 **⑪**

International
$17-$39

AAA Inspector Notes: The menu at this award-winning eatery sports well-prepared Mediterranean and Asian cuisines like duck breast with orange anise sauce, veal Oscar with shiitake mushroom sauce and a bento box with an array of sushi, sashimi, black cod and tempura shrimp. Escargot or salmon and tuna carpaccio are excellent starters while the chocolate truffle with coconut ice cream ends the dining experience on a fine note. **Bar:** full bar. **Reservations:** suggested. **Address:** 40 Crow Ln **Location:** Just e of downtown Hamilton; on E Broadway; in Bermuda Underwater Exploration Institute. L D

HARLEY'S BISTRO
Phone: 441/295-3000 **②**

Continental
$27-$39

AAA Inspector Notes: Overlooking Hamilton Harbor, the tastefully appointed dining room offers a relaxed dining experience. A varied menu features such international favorites as swordfish, rack of lamb and seafood cioppino. The fish chowder, Bermuda onion bisque, surf and turf carpaccio or coconut milk marinated fried calamari is a great way to start the meal. Popular for a lingering breakfast and Sunday brunch. Semi-formal attire. **Bar:** full bar. **Reservations:** required. **Address:** 76 Pitts Bay Rd **Location:** Downtown; in The Fairmont Hamilton Princess. *(See ad on insert.)* B L D

HOG PENNY RESTAURANT & PUB
Phone: 441/292-2534 **⑬**

English
$16-$34

AAA Inspector Notes: One of the oldest pubs in Bermuda, this cozy, informal spot prepares traditional pub fare such as fish and chips, steak and kidney pie and bangers and mash, as well as Indian curry selections, sandwiches and burgers. The staff is cheerful and unpretentious. **Bar:** full bar. **Reservations:** suggested. **Address:** 5 Burnaby Hill **Location:** Just off Front St; downtown. **Parking:** street only. **Historic** L D

HOUSE OF INDIA
Phone: 441/295-6450 **①**

Indian
$16-$22

AAA Inspector Notes: This little hole-in-the-wall operation across from the Salvation Army barracks in an area of Hamilton known locally as Back of Town offers Indian and Pakistani dishes that come highly recommended by locals. Diners will find an excellent selection of breads, meats, seafood and vegetarian delights. A buffet-only lunch makes way for a much wider, a la carte selection for dinner. **Bar:** beer & wine. **Reservations:** suggested. **Address:** 57 North St **Location:** Just e of north end of Court St; in Park View Plaza. **Parking:** street only. L D

LATIN
Phone: 441/296-5050 **㉒**

Latin American
$13-$39

AAA Inspector Notes: This popular eatery offers such appetizers as corn-cheese cakes topped with braised beef, achiote pork and shrimp chicharrones, and a variety of seviche and raw bar items. Entrees range from yellow fin tuna with quinoa risotto and coconut-apple chutney to maple-glazed beef tenderloin with short-rib potato empanadas and molasses demi-glace. Guacamole for two is prepared tableside and in-house desserts are rich and yummy. A rum bar downstairs creates some lively noise levels. **Bar:** full bar. **Reservations:** suggested. **Address:** 29 Victoria St **Location:** Centre; between Cedar Ave and Brunswick St. **Parking:** street only. L D CALL Ⓜ

LA TRATTORIA
Phone: 441/295-1877 **③**

Italian
$10-$32

AAA Inspector Notes: Guests can follow their nose to the aroma of garlic. Checkered tablecloths and a bustling, upbeat atmosphere make for a cozy, informal experience. The all-Italian staff serves authentic food. **Bar:** full bar. **Reservations:** suggested, for dinner. **Address:** 22 Washington Ln **Location:** Between Reid and Church sts; downtown; adjacent to Washington Mall. L D

(See index & map p. 320.)

THE LITTLE VENICE **Phone:** 441/295-3503 ⑧

Italian
$22-$40

AAA Inspector Notes: This restaurant is popular with locals and out-of-towners alike. The antipasto, carpaccio or calamari are great beginnings to a fine meal. For pasta lovers there are savory preparations of gnocchi, risotto, penne, ravioli, lasagna and pappardelle to choose from. Salmon, clams, sea bass and scallops top the seafood portion of the menu while meats include rack of lamb, veal tenderloin, free-range chicken and Barberry duck breast. Fabulous desserts round off the menu. **Bar:** full bar. **Reservations:** required. **Address:** 32 Bermudiana Rd **Location:** Between Church and Front sts; downtown. **Parking:** street only. L D

THE LOBSTER POT RESTAURANT & BOATHOUSE BAR **Phone:** 441/292-6898 ⑤

Continental
$11-$32

AAA Inspector Notes: A popular spot with locals and tourists alike, the casual eatery sports nautical decor and sustains a bustling atmosphere. Traditional and island seafood dishes are prepared in a number of ways. Tempting meat and poultry selections appeal to landlubbers. **Bar:** full bar. **Reservations:** suggested. **Address:** 6 Bermudiana Rd **Location:** Just off Front St; center of downtown. **Parking:** street only. L D

L'ORIENTAL **Phone:** 441/296-4477 ⑦

Asian
$16-$48

AAA Inspector Notes: The bustling dining room features Teppanyaki tables and two sushi bars. Fusion cuisine is served here blending the finest elements of Asian and Mediterranean cooking. An array of sushi, sashimi and tempura dishes are offered. Main course offerings may include grilled pork chop with oriental five spice, Thai beef curry or giant scallops with mushroom pasta and smoked tomato concasse. Don't neglect dessert with such temptations as orange infused creme caramel or Asian peach tart. Semi-formal attire. **Bar:** full bar. **Reservations:** required. **Address:** 32 Bermudiana Rd **Location:** Between Church and Front sts; downtown. **Parking:** street only. L D

PORT O' CALL RESTAURANT **Phone:** 441/295-5373 ⑫

Seafood
$14-$38

AAA Inspector Notes: Located across from the waterfront, this popular dining spot offers fresh seafood and well-prepared steak in a casual upscale setting. Enjoy dining al fresco at sidewalk tables in the warmer weather. An award-winning, lengthy wine list is featured. **Bar:** full bar. **Reservations:** suggested. **Address:** 87 Front St **Location:** Downtown; on waterfront. **Parking:** street only. L D

PORTOFINO **Phone:** 441/292-2375 ⑩

Italian
$12-$29

AAA Inspector Notes: Pasta, pizza and creative daily specials tempt diners at the lively eatery, which is in the hub of activity. **Bar:** full bar. **Address:** 48 Bermudiana Rd **Location:** Corner of Front St; west side of downtown. L D

THE RED CARPET **Phone:** 441/292-6195 ⑥

Continental
$17-$36

AAA Inspector Notes: Popular with local businesspeople, the comfortable dining room incorporates copious amounts of red into the decor. Well-prepared cuisine blends Continental, Italian and German elements. **Bar:** full bar. **Reservations:** suggested. **Address:** 37 Reid St **Location:** In Armory Building. **Parking:** street only. L D

THE ROBIN HOOD PUB & RESTAURANT **Phone:** 441/295-3314 ⑯

English
$12-$28

AAA Inspector Notes: This boisterous tavern draws a mixed crowd of locals, tourists and sports enthusiasts who watch the flat screen TVs. Those who like to imbibe a favorite brew will find pleasure here, as well. Straightforward service matches well with the large portions of comfort food. Besides the familiar pub fare, menu items include bangers and mash, fish and chips and hearty chowders. Hours may vary during significant game days. **Bar:** full bar. **Address:** 25 Richmond Rd **Location:** Between Pitts Bay Rd and Woodbourne Ave; downtown. B L D

SILK THAI CUISINE **Phone:** 441/295-0449 ⑮

Thai
$12-$23

AAA Inspector Notes: The island's only Thai restaurant, the award-winning spot has earned international accolades. Well-planned decor transports guests to far-off Thailand. Among dishes are red, green and yellow curries combined with seafood, chicken, pork or beef, in addition to four delicately prepared soups. After a savory meal, such desserts as chocolate and banana custard cake are a great finale. **Bar:** full bar. **Reservations:** suggested. **Address:** 55 Front St **Location:** Downtown; across from waterfront; in Masters Building. **Parking:** street only. L D

THE SPOT RESTAURANT **Phone:** 441/292-6293 ⑱

Comfort Food
$7-$18

AAA Inspector Notes: Popular with the locals and tourists for more than 65 years for their down-home favorites with a Bermudian twist. Roast turkey, fried chicken, and a daily vegetable selection are just a few samples from the lengthy menu that also offers sandwiches, wraps and seafood. **Address:** 6 Burnaby Hill **Location:** Jct Front St, 2 blks n. **Parking:** street only. B L D

St. George's Parish

ST. DAVID'S ISLAND (A-6)

• **Hotels & Restaurants index & map p. 320**

THE BLACK HORSE TAVERN **Phone:** 441/297-1991 (55)

English
$17-$37

AAA Inspector Notes: The simple restaurant is known for fresh seafood. Visitors to St. David's Lighthouse often stop in for lunch. Hearty fish chowder and English-style fish and chips are favorites. **Bar:** full bar. **Address:** 34 Great Bay Rd **Location:** Beside St. David's Post Office; overlooking Great Bay. L D AC

ST. GEORGE'S (A-6) pop. 1,752

• **Hotels & Restaurants index & map p. 320**

THE ST. GEORGE'S CLUB **Phone:** 441/297-1200 ⑯

Condominium
$179-$460

Address: 6 Rose Hill St **Location:** Just n of York St. **Facility:** 71 condominiums. 1-2 stories, exterior corridors. **Terms:** check-in 4 pm, 2 night minimum stay, 21 day cancellation notice. **Amenities:** safes. **Dining:** 2 restaurants. **Pool(s):** 2 outdoor, heated outdoor. **Activities:** beach access, 3 lighted tennis courts, exercise room. **Guest Services:** coin laundry.

SD

Sandy's Parish

SANDY'S PARISH (C-1) pop. 7,275
- Restaurants p. 331
- Hotels & Restaurants index & map p. 320

9 BEACHES
[fyi]
Cottage
$190-$600

Phone: 441/232-6655 [21]
Under major renovation, scheduled to be completed December 2012. **Last Rated:** ▼▼▼ **Address:** 4 Daniel's Head Ln **Location:** Oceanfront. On Daniel's Head Beach. **Facility:** A large resort on the water, its over-the-sea cabanas have canvas interior walls and a section of glass floor so guests can look into the ocean. 84 cottages. 1 story, exterior corridors. *Bath:* shower only. **Terms:** open 4/1-11/30, 21 day cancellation notice, in season-fee imposed. **Amenities:** safes. **Dining:** 2 restaurants. **Pool(s):** outdoor. **Activities:** rental paddleboats, rental sailboats, tennis court, rental bicycles, playground, volleyball, exercise room. **Guest Services:** coin laundry.

CAMBRIDGE BEACHES RESORT & SPA
Phone: (441)234-0331 [20]
▼▼▼ ▼▼▼
Hotel
$295-$1690

Address: 30 Kings Point Rd **Location:** Oceanfront. Kings Point west side of island. **Facility:** This multi-award winning, luxurious cottage colony is located on a 25-acre peninsula surrounded by five beaches. 94 units, some two bedrooms. 1-2 stories (no elevator), exterior corridors. **Terms:** office hours 7 am-11 pm, age restrictions may apply, 21 day cancellation notice-fee imposed. **Amenities:** high-speed Internet (fee), safes. **Dining:** 3 restaurants, entertainment. **Pool(s):** outdoor, heated indoor. **Activities:** whirlpool, rental boats, rental sailboats, putting green, 3 tennis courts, recreation programs, rental bicycles, hiking trails, jogging, horseshoes, exercise room, spa. *Fee:* saunas, steamroom, marina, snorkeling. **Guest Services:** valet laundry. **Free Special Amenities: full breakfast and high-speed Internet.** Affiliated with A Preferred Hotel.
(See ad p. 330, p. 87.)

Create complete trip routings and custom maps with the TripTik® Travel Planner on AAA.com or CAA.ca

▼ See AAA listing p. 329 ▼

(See index & map p. 320.)

(See index & map p. 320.)

WHERE TO EAT

THE FROG & ONION PUB   Phone: 441/234-2900   (29)

English
$12-$25

AAA Inspector Notes: The English-style pub exhibits a fine display of nautical artifacts. Representative of traditional pub fare are sausage and mash, shepherd's pie and fish and chips. Seasonal entertainment and a large game room keep guests amused. **Bar:** full bar. **Address:** Royal Naval Dockyard **Location:** Within the walls of Royal Naval Dockyard. **Historic** [L] [D]

Smith's Parish

SMITH'S PARISH (C-4) pop. 5,658
• Hotels & Restaurants index & map p. 320

PINK BEACH CLUB & COTTAGES
Phone: (441)293-1666   (13)

Hotel
$460-$995

Address: 116 South Shore Rd **Location:** Oceanfront. Jct South Shore Rd and Devil's Hole Hill, just e. **Facility:** 94 units. 1-2 stories (no elevator), exterior corridors. **Terms:** open 12/1-12/15 & 3/15-11/30, 4 night minimum stay, 21 day cancellation notice-fee imposed. **Amenities:** safes. **Dining:** 2 restaurants. **Pool(s):** heated outdoor. **Activities:** limited beach access, snorkeling, 2 tennis courts, playground, exercise room. **Fee:** massage. **Guest Services:** valet laundry.

/ SOME UNITS

WHERE TO EAT

NORTH ROCK BREWING COMPANY
Phone: (441)236-6633   (57)

English
$15-$39

AAA Inspector Notes: Bermuda's only microbrewery features such hand-crafted brews as Blackwatch stout, India Pale Ale and Porter. The broad menu lists traditional English fare, including fish and chips, cottage pie and steak and ale pie. Tempting desserts range from prune Armagnac mousse to raspberry creme brulee to chocolate truffle cake. **Bar:** full bar. **Reservations:** suggested. **Address:** 10 South Shore Rd **Location:** Jct South Shore and Collectors Hill rds. [L] [D]

SPECIALITY INN   Phone: 441/236-3133   (56)

International
$10-$21

AAA Inspector Notes: This eatery offers the island's idea of comfort food which includes burgers, sandwiches, pasta, pizza and, of all things, a sushi bar. Do not forget to check out the daily specials on the menu board before ordering. Seafood is most popular with Bermudians, but do not be afraid to experiment. **Address:** 4 South Shore Rd **Location:** Jct Collectors Hill Rd. [B] [L] [D]

Southampton Parish

SOUTHAMPTON PARISH (D-1) pop. 6,117
• Restaurants p. 333
• Hotels & Restaurants index & map p. 320

THE FAIRMONT SOUTHAMPTON
Phone: (441)238-8000   (30)

Resort Hotel
$229-$499

Address: 101 South Shore Rd **Location:** Oceanfront. Between Middle and South Shore rds. **Facility:** In an impressive hilltop setting buffered by manicured grounds, the well-appointed property offers a spa and luxurious guest rooms. Meets AAA guest room security requirements. 593 units, some two bedrooms. 6 stories, interior corridors. **Terms:** check-in 4 pm, 3 day cancellation notice-fee imposed. **Amenities:** high-speed Internet (fee), safes, honor bars. **Dining:** 4 restaurants, also, Bacci, The Waterlot Inn Steakhouse, see separate listings, entertainment. **Pool(s):** heated outdoor, heated indoor. **Activities:** whirlpools, recreation programs, rental bicycles, jogging, volleyball, spa. **Fee:** saunas, steamrooms, scuba diving, snorkeling, golf-18 holes, 6 tennis courts (3 lighted), game room. **Guest Services:** valet laundry, area transportation-dock & Hamilton. *(See ad on insert, p. 332.)*

POMPANO BEACH CLUB   Phone: (441)234-0222   (25)

Hotel
$220-$540

Address: 36 Pompano Beach Rd **Location:** Oceanfront. Off Middle Rd, 0.5 mi (0.8 km) w via Pompano Beach Rd; adjacent to Port Royal Golf Club. **Facility:** 75 units, some condominiums. 1-2 stories, exterior corridors. **Terms:** office hours 6 am-midnight, 4 night minimum stay - seasonal, 21 day cancellation notice-fee imposed. **Amenities:** safes. **Dining:** 3 restaurants, entertainment. **Pool(s):** heated outdoor. **Activities:** whirlpools, rental paddleboats, rental sailboats, rental sailboards, boat dock, fishing, 5 tennis courts (3 lighted), game room, exercise room, spa. **Fee:** snorkeling, golf-18 holes. **Guest Services:** valet and coin laundry, area transportation-golf course, bus stop & ferry.

THE REEFS   Phone: (441)238-0222   (28)

Hotel
$410-$1099

Address: 56 South Shore Rd **Location:** Oceanfront. At Christian Bay. **Facility:** 64 units, some cottages and condominiums. 2 stories, interior/exterior corridors. **Terms:** 5 night minimum stay - seasonal, 28 day cancellation notice-fee imposed. **Amenities:** safes. **Dining:** 3 restaurants, entertainment. **Pool(s):** heated outdoor. **Activities:** whirlpool, snorkeling, 2 tennis courts, recreation programs in summer, shuffleboard, exercise room, spa. **Guest Services:** valet laundry.

/ SOME UNITS

Learn about AAA/CAA Diamond Ratings

at AAA.com/Diamonds

(See index & map p. 320.)

WHERE TO EAT

BACCI
Phone: 441/238-8000   (35)

Italian
$15-$38

AAA Inspector Notes: Refined surroundings and a sumptuous antipasti bar are hallmarks of the popular resort restaurant. Lining the menu are many pasta, ravioli, gnocchi and risotto dishes, in addition to such heartier entrees as osso buco alla milanese, grilled veal chop and striped sea bass. Popular as well are create-your-own individual gourmet pizzas. Irresistible desserts range from chocolate fudge cake to classic tiramisu. Diners can count on precision service. **Bar:** full bar. **Reservations:** required. **Address:** 101 South Shore Rd **Location:** Between Middle and South Shore rds; in The Fairmont Southampton.
D

THE DINING ROOM
Phone: 441/238-8679   (33)

International
$14-$30

AAA Inspector Notes: Located at the Gibbs Hill Lighthouse, this appealing dining room offers a condensed menu that is well-prepared with local produce and good quality ingredients. There is something for everyone starting with such appetizers as crab samosas, fish chowder or a spinach and Gorgonzola salad with sour cherries. Entrees run the gamut from gourmet thin-crust pizza to Indonesian coconut chicken, mussels with a choice of sauces or steak with arugula and horseradish sauce. **Bar:** full bar. **Reservations:** required, for dinner. **Address:** 68 St. Anne's Rd **Location:** Jct South Shore Rd, just n on Lighthouse Rd, then just w; at Gibbs Hill Lighthouse.   L D ☒

TIO PEPE
Phone: 441/238-1897   (37)

Italian
$16-$32

AAA Inspector Notes: The menu includes basic, home-style Italian food and some Spanish dishes. Seafood linguine is a local favorite. Nine-inch thin-crust pizzas are cooked in a brick oven. Guests can order from the lunch menu until 5 pm When the weather is nice, the terrace is a nice spot for seating. **Bar:** full bar. **Reservations:** suggested. **Address:** 117 South Rd **Location:** 0.5 mi (0.8 km) e of The Fairmont Southampton.   L D

THE WATERLOT INN STEAKHOUSE

Menu on AAA.com   Phone: 441/238-8000   (32)

Steak
$30-$68

AAA Inspector Notes: Located in a historic cottage with beautifully landscaped grounds and a delightful view, this traditional American steakhouse offers aged steaks and chops as well as an assortment of seafood entrées. A selection of fine wines, spirits and Cuban cigars also is available. **Bar:** full bar. **Reservations:** required. **Address:** 101 South Shore Rd **Location:** Between Middle and South Shore rds; in The Fairmont Southampton.
Historic   D

THE NEWPORT ROOM
Phone: 441/238-8000

(fyi)   Not evaluated. Modern and classic cuisine is served in a luxurious dining room designed after the grand salon of an ocean yacht. Uniformed in formal nautical attire, waitstaff is befitting of the atmosphere. Jackets are required. Semi-formal attire. **Address:** 101 South Shore Rd **Location:** Between Middle and South Shore rds; in The Fairmont Southampton. *(See ad on insert.)*

Warwick Parish

WARWICK PARISH pop. 8,587
• Hotels & Restaurants index & map p. 320

CLAIRFONT APARTMENTS
Phone: 441/238-3577   (48)

Extended Stay Motel
$150-$175

Address: 6 Warwickshire Rd **Location:** Jct South Shore Rd, just n. **Facility:** 8 units, some efficiencies and kitchens. 2 stories (no elevator), exterior corridors. **Terms:** office hours 10 am-4 pm, 2 night minimum stay, 14 day cancellation notice. **Amenities:** high-speed Internet, safes. **Pool(s):** outdoor. **Guest Services:** valet laundry.
S SD ⊠ 🖨 🖼

GRANAWAY GUEST HOUSE & COTTAGE
Phone: 441/236-3747   (43)

Bed & Breakfast
$120-$230

Address: 1 Longford Rd **Location:** Belmont Ferry dock, just w on Harbour Rd. **Facility:** 5 units, some cottages. 2 stories (no elevator), interior/exterior corridors. **Terms:** office hours 9 am-6 pm, 3 night minimum stay, 30 day cancellation notice-fee imposed. **Pool(s):** heated outdoor. **Guest Services:** valet laundry.   SD ⊠ 🛜 ☒ 🖨 🖼

SURF SIDE BEACH CLUB   Phone: (441)236-7100   (47)

Motel
$180-$550

Address: 90 South Shore Rd **Location:** Oceanfront. Corner of Cobbs Hill and South Shore rds. **Facility:** 38 units, some two bedrooms, kitchens and cottages. 1-2 stories (no elevator), exterior corridors. **Terms:** office hours 8 am-10 pm, 14 day cancellation notice-fee imposed. **Amenities:** safes. **Pool(s):** outdoor. **Activities:** *Fee:* snorkeling, massage. **Guest Services:** coin laundry.
🏋 🛜 🖨 🖵 / SOME UNITS 🐕 🖼

BONAIRE

✈ Airport Accommodations

Map Page	BONAIRE, NETHERLAND ANTILLES - FLAMINGO FIELD	Diamond Rated	High Season	Page
5 p. 335	Bellafonte Chateau de la Mer, just s of airport	▽▽ ▽▽	$125-$495	334
1 p. 335	Divi Flamingo Beach Resort & Casino, 0.8 mi (1.3 km) n of terminal	▽▽ ▽▽	$156-$270 [SAVE]	334

Bonaire

This index helps you "spot" where approved hotels and restaurants are located on the corresponding detailed maps. Hotel daily rate range is for comparison only and show the property's high season. Restaurant rate range is a combination of lunch and/or dinner. Turn to the listing page for more detailed rate information and consult display ads for special promotions.

KRALENDIJK

Map Page	Hotels	Diamond Rated	High Season	Page
1 p. 335	**Divi Flamingo Beach Resort & Casino**	▽▽ ▽▽	$156-$270 [SAVE]	334
2 p. 335	Den Laman Condominiums	▽▽ ▽▽	$120-$300	334
5 p. 335	Bellafonte Chateau de la Mer	▽▽ ▽▽	$125-$495	334

Map Page	Restaurants	Diamond Rated	Cuisine	Meal Range	Page
③ p. 335	It Rains Fishes	▽▽ ▽▽	International	$15-$23	335
⑥ p. 335	Casablanca Argentinian Grill	▽▽	Argentine	$15-$26	334
⑧ p. 335	**Chibi Chibi**	▽▽ ▽▽	International	$9-$24	335

KRALENDIJK (B-1) pop. 2,000
• Hotels & Restaurants index & map p. 334

BELLAFONTE CHATEAU DE LA MER
      Phone: 599/717-3333 **5**

▽▽ ▽▽
Condominium
$125-$495

Address: EEG Boulevard 10 **Location:** Oceanfront. Just s of airport. **Facility:** 22 condominiums. 4 stories, exterior corridors. *Bath:* shower only. **Terms:** office hours 8 am-5 pm, 30 day cancellation notice-fee imposed. **Amenities:** safes. **Activities:** whirlpool, boat dock, snorkeling. *Fee:* massage. **Guest Services:** valet laundry.

🏋 📶 🍴 📷 📺

DEN LAMAN CONDOMINIUMS
      Phone: (599)717-1700 **2**

▽▽ ▽▽
Condominium
$120-$300

Address: Kaya Gobernador N Debrot 77 **Location:** 0.8 mi (1.3 km) n of downtown. **Facility:** 16 condominiums. 3 stories (no elevator), interior corridors. *Bath:* shower only. **Terms:** office hours 8 am-5 pm, off-site registration, 45 day cancellation notice-fee imposed. **Amenities:** high-speed Internet (fee), safes. **Activities:** boat dock. *Fee:* scuba diving, snorkeling. **Guest Services:** valet and coin laundry.

🍴 🍸 SD 📶 ✕ 🛁 📷

DIVI FLAMINGO BEACH RESORT & CASINO
      Phone: (599)717-8285 **1**

▽▽ ▽▽
Resort Hotel
$156-$270

Address: JA Abraham Blvd #40 **Location:** Oceanfront. 0.8 mi (1.3 km) s of town; 1.4 mi (2.2 km) n of airport. **Facility:** 129 units, some condominiums. 2 stories (no elevator), exterior corridors. **Terms:** 7 day cancellation notice-fee imposed. **Amenities:** safes (fee). **Dining:** 2 restaurants, also, Chibi Chibi, see separate listing. **Pool(s):** 2 outdoor. **Activities:** boat dock, recreation programs, shuffleboard, exercise room, spa. *Fee:* scuba diving, snorkeling. **Guest Services:** valet laundry.

[SAVE] 🐾 🍴 🍸 🏋 SD 🌊 BIZ 📶 ✕ 🛁
📺 / SOME UNITS 📷

WHERE TO EAT

CASABLANCA ARGENTINIAN GRILL
      Phone: 599/717-4433 **6**

▽▽
Argentine
$15-$26

AAA Inspector Notes: Within walking distance of downtown, this restaurant lets guests enjoy al fresco meals on the veranda or in the rear courtyard. Menu selections include various cuts of Argentinean beef, various sausages, pork ribs and chicken. One night a week is all-you-can-eat night and a lunch buffet is offered daily. **Bar:** full bar. **Address:** JA Abraham Blvd #6 **Location:** Just s of downtown center. L D ✎

Check out our travel blog at
AAATravelViews.com

© AAA

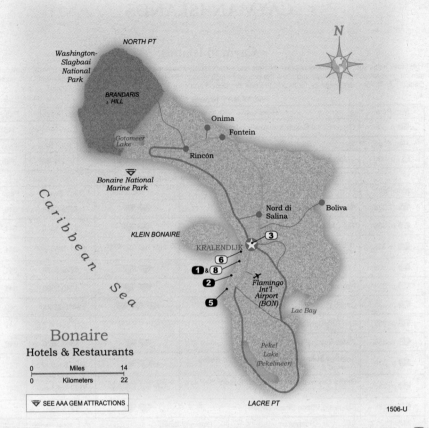

N

NORTH PT

Washington-
Slagbaai
National
Park

BRANDARIS
HILL

Onima

Fontein

Gotomeer
Lake

Rincón

Bonaire National
Marine Park

Nord di
Salina

Boliva

KLEIN BONAIRE

KRALENDIJK ★   3

6

1 & 8

2

5

Flamingo
Int'l
Airport
(BON)

Lac Bay

Pekel
Lake
(Pekelmeer)

Caribbean Sea

Bonaire
Hotels & Restaurants

| 0 | Miles | 14 |
| 0 | Kilometers | 22 |

▽ SEE AAA GEM ATTRACTIONS

LACRE PT

1506-U

(See index & map p. 334.)

CHIBI CHIBI   Phone: 599/717-8285   8

International
$9-$24

AAA Inspector Notes: Named after a local sweet bird, this over-the-water restaurant offers captivating views and also features a beach entrance. The bright and colorful restaurant offers a complete and varied international menu. The menu consists of fresh local fish, pasta, steak and a variety of entrée-size salads. An international award-winning bartender serves up a cocktail menu of more than 30 fresh fruit concoctions. **Bar:** full bar. **Reservations:** suggested. **Address:** JA Abraham Blvd #40 **Location:** 0.8 mi (1.3 km) s of town; 1.4 mi (2.2 km) n of airport; in Divi Flamingo Beach Resort & Casino.

B L D 🄰 🚬

IT RAINS FISHES   Phone: 599/717-8780   3

International
$15-$23

AAA Inspector Notes: Great waterfront location for people watching in a casual atmosphere. Mostly a seafood centered menu focusing on local fish and fresh lobster but the barbecue ribs are a favorite here as well. **Bar:** full bar. **Reservations:** required. **Address:** Kaya Jan NE Crane #24 **Location:** Waterfront; downtown. **Parking:** street only.   B L D 🄰 🚬

Explore the Travel Guides on
AAA.com/Travel or CAA.ca/Travel

CAYMAN ISLANDS

Cayman Islands

This index helps you "spot" where approved hotels and restaurants are located on the corresponding detailed maps. Hotel daily rate range is for comparison only and show the property's high season. Restaurant rate range is a combination of lunch and/or dinner. Turn to the listing page for more detailed rate information and consult display ads for special promotions.

WEST BAY (Grand Cayman)

Map Page	Hotel	Diamond Rated	High Season	Page
1 p. 338	Cobalt Coast Resort & Suites	◆◆◆	$195-$495	346

Map Page	Restaurant	Diamond Rated	Cuisine	Meal Range	Page
3 p. 338	Cracked Conch by the Sea	◆◆	Caribbean	$12-$37	346

SEVEN MILE BEACH (Grand Cayman)

Map Page	Hotels	Diamond Rated	High Season	Page
3 p. 338	Aqua Bay Club Condos	◆◆	$275-$625	340
4 p. 338	The Christopher Columbus Condos	◆◆	$210-$540	341
5 p. 338	**Westin Casuarina Resort & Spa-Grand Cayman** (See ad on insert, p. 343, p. 102.)	◆◆◆◆	$161-$865 [SAVE]	344
8 p. 338	Tamarind Bay	◆◆	$299-$550	341
10 p. 338	Plantana Condominiums	◆◆	$240-$680	341
12 p. 338	Caribbean Club	◆◆◆	$610-$2500	340
13 p. 338	**The Ritz-Carlton, Grand Cayman**	◆◆◆◆◆	$549-$8000 [SAVE]	341
14 p. 338	7 Mile Beach Resort & Club	◆◆	$300-$675	340
16 p. 338	**Comfort Suites & Resort, Seven Mile Beach** (See ad p. 342.)	◆◆	$120-$240 [SAVE]	341
18 p. 338	**Grand Cayman Marriott Beach Resort** (See ad on insert.)	◆◆◆◆	$192-$563 [SAVE]	341
20 p. 338	Plantation Village Beach Resort	◆◆	$215-$600	341

Map Page	Restaurants	Diamond Rated	Cuisine	Meal Range	Page
4 p. 338	**Casa Havana** (See ad p. 343.)	◆◆◆◆	International	$29-$44	344
5 p. 338	Yoshi Sushi	◆◆	Japanese	$11-$30	346
6 p. 338	Abacus	◆◆◆	International	$15-$48	344
8 p. 338	Edoardo's Fine Italian Cuisine	◆◆◆	Italian	$17-$35	345
9 p. 338	Prime Brazilian Steak House	◆◆◆	Brazilian	$24-$47	345
10 p. 338	Deckers Bistro & Grill	◆◆	International	$24-$48	345
11 p. 338	Aqua Beach Restaurant & Bar	◆◆	International	$13-$20	344
12 p. 338	**7 Prime Cuts and Sunsets**	◆◆◆◆	International	$18-$63	344
13 p. 338	Copper Falls Steakhouse	◆◆◆	Steak	$26-$75	345
14 p. 338	Gateway of India	◆◆	Indian	$19-$38	345
15 p. 338	Ristorante Ragazzi	◆◆	Italian	$14-$44	346
16 p. 338	Chicken! Chicken!	◆	Caribbean	$8-$16	344
18 p. 338	Cimboco, A Caribbean Cafe	◆	International	$12-$20	344
19 p. 338	Coconut Joe's Beachouse Bar & Grill	◆	International	$13-$26	345

Map Page	Restaurants (cont'd)	Diamond Rated	Cuisine	Meal Range	Page
⑳ p. 338	Agua Restaurant & Lounge	◆◆◆	International	$11-$34	344
㉒ p. 338	Bamboo Lounge	◆◆◆	Japanese	$27-$58	344
㉓ p. 338	Hemingway's Beach Club Restaurant	◆◆◆	Continental	$15-$45	345
㉔ p. 338	**Blue**	◆◆◆◆◆	International	$103-$156	344
㉕ p. 338	Luca	◆◆◆	Italian	$28-$48	345
㉖ p. 338	**Solana on Seven Mile Beach**	◆◆◆	International	$15-$45	346
㉘ p. 338	Thai Orchid	◆◆	Asian	$14-$32	346
㉚ p. 338	The Reef Grill at the Royal Palms	◆◆◆	International	$18-$40	345
㉜ p. 338	Fidel Murphy's	◆◆	Irish	$14-$28	345

COLLIERS (Grand Cayman)

Map Page	Hotel	Diamond Rated	High Season	Page
㉕ p. 338	**The Reef Resort** *(See ad p. 339.)*	◆◆◆	$175-$705 SAVE	339

CAYMAN BRAC (Cayman Brac)

Map Page	Hotel	Diamond Rated	High Season	Page
㉚ p. 338	Brac Reef Beach Resort	◆◆◆	$140-$195	339

Map Page	Restaurant	Diamond Rated	Cuisine	Meal Range	Page
(52) p. 338	Captain's Table	◆◆	International	$7-$35	339

LITTLE CAYMAN (Little Cayman)

Map Page	Hotels	Diamond Rated	High Season	Page
㉜ p. 338	Little Cayman Beach Resort	◆◆◆	$151-$191	346
㉞ p. 338	Paradise Villas	◆◆	$175-$200	347
㉟ p. 338	The Club at Little Cayman	◆◆◆	$249-$550	346
㊲ p. 338	Southern Cross Club	◆◆◆	$278-$329	347

Map Page	Restaurant	Diamond Rated	Cuisine	Meal Range	Page
(56) p. 338	Hungry Iguana	◆	American	$14-$28	347

GEORGE TOWN (Grand Cayman)

Map Page	Restaurants	Diamond Rated	Cuisine	Meal Range	Page
㉞ p. 338	The Wharf Restaurant	◆◆	International	$30-$45	340
㉟ p. 338	Casanova Restaurant by the Sea	◆◆◆	Italian	$14-$44	340
㊱ p. 338	Hard Rock Cafe	◆◆	American	$12-$24 SAVE	340
㊲ p. 338	Breezes by the Bay	◆	International	$13-$24	340
㊳ p. 338	Grand Old House	◆◆◆	International	$18-$48	340
㊵ p. 338	Guy Harvey Island Grill Restaurant & Bar	◆◆	International	$13-$43	340
㊷ p. 338	**The Brasserie**	◆◆◆	International	$15-$38	340

BREAKERS (Grand Cayman)

Map Page	Restaurant	Diamond Rated	Cuisine	Meal Range	Page
㊺ p. 338	The Lighthouse Restaurant at the Breakers	◆◆	International	$11-$46	339

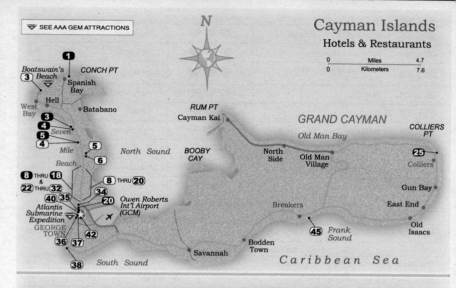

SEE AAA GEM ATTRACTIONS

N

Cayman Islands
Hotels & Restaurants

| 0 | Miles | 4.7 |
| 0 | Kilometers | 7.6 |

1

Boatswain's Beach
3

CONCH PT

Spanish Bay

West Bay

Hell

3

Batabano

4
5
4

Seven

5

Mile

6

Beach

North Sound

RUM PT
Cayman Kai

BOOBY CAY

North Side

Old Man Bay

Old Man Village

GRAND CAYMAN

COLLIERS PT

25

Colliers

Gun Bay

East End

Old Isaacs

8 THRU **18**
22 THRU **32**
40 **35**

Atlantis Submarine Expedition
GEORGE TOWN

36 **37**

38

8 THRU **20**

34

20

Owen Roberts Int'l Airport (GCM)

42

South Sound

Savannah

Bodden Town

Breakers

45

Frank Sound

Caribbean Sea

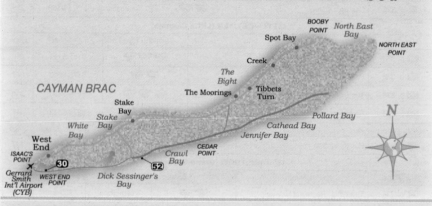

Caribbean Sea

CAYMAN BRAC

West End

ISAAC'S POINT

Gerrard Smith Int'l Airport (CYB)

WEST END POINT

30

White Bay

Stake Bay

Stake Bay

52

Crawl Bay

CEDAR POINT

Dick Sessinger's Bay

Spot Bay

Creek

The Bight

The Moorings

Tibbets Turn

BOOBY POINT

North East Bay

NORTH EAST POINT

Pollard Bay

Cathead Bay

Jennifer Bay

N

LITTLE CAYMAN

Bloody Bay

Spot Bay

Edward Bodden Airfield (LYB)

WEST END POINT

34 **56**

South Town

Tarpon Lake

32 **35**

The Bight

37

Mary's Bay

Wearis Bay

SNIPE POINT

EAST POINT

SANDY POINT

Caribbean Sea

N

© AAA

1511-U

Cayman Brac

CAYMAN BRAC pop. 1,822
• Hotels & Restaurants index & map p. 336

BRAC REEF BEACH RESORT   **Phone:** 345/948-1323   **30**

Hotel
$140-$195

Address: 383 South Side Rd **Location:** Oceanfront. 2.6 mi (4.1 km) se of airport. **Facility:** 40 units. 2 stories (no elevator), exterior corridors. **Terms:** office hours 7 am-9 pm. **Amenities:** high-speed Internet. *Some:* safes. **Dining:** 2 restaurants. **Pool(s):** outdoor. **Activities:** limited beach access, lighted tennis court, bicycles, basketball, volleyball, exercise room, spa. *Fee:* scuba diving, snorkeling, fishing. **Guest Services:** valet and coin laundry.

WHERE TO EAT

CAPTAIN'S TABLE   **Phone:** 345/948-1418   **52**

International
$7-$35

AAA Inspector Notes: Local seafood, fish and chicken curries, jerk chicken and homemade burgers are among the items served in this simply decorated island-casual restaurant. All desserts are made in house. Diners can sit in the air-conditioned interior or on the deck by the pool, which is cooled by refreshing breezes. **Bar:** full bar. **Reservations:** suggested. **Address:** Stake Bay **Location:** 2.4 mi (3.8 km) se of airport; in Carib Sands and Brac Caribbean Beach Village. L D

Find valuable AAA/CAA
member savings
at AAA.com/discounts

Grand Cayman

BREAKERS
• Hotels & Restaurants index & map p. 336

THE LIGHTHOUSE RESTAURANT AT THE BREAKERS
    Phone: 345/948-2047   **45**

International
$11-$46

AAA Inspector Notes: The building of this eatery resembles a lighthouse and has a relaxed and classic seafaring theme. The varied menu lists an extensive selection of seafood and Italian dishes. Luncheon choices center on lighter fare. Both indoor and patio seating overlook the ocean. **Bar:** full bar. **Reservations:** suggested. **Address:** Queens Hwy **Location:** Just s of Bodden. L D

COLLIERS
• Hotels & Restaurants index & map p. 336

THE REEF RESORT   **Phone:** (345)947-3100   **25**

Hotel
$175-$705 12/1-9/15
$99-$595 9/22-11/30

Address: 2221 Queens Hwy **Location:** Oceanfront. At Colliers Bay; 24 mi (38.4 km) e of George Town; 23 mi (36.8 km) e of Owen Roberts International Airport. **Facility:** 151 units, some two bedrooms and kitchens. 2-3 stories, exterior corridors. **Terms:** open 12/1-9/15 & 9/22-11/30, office hours 7 am-11 pm, check-in 4 pm, 14 day cancellation notice-fee imposed. **Amenities:** high-speed Internet (fee), safes. **Dining:** 3 restaurants, entertainment. **Pool(s):** 3 outdoor. **Activities:** whirlpools, lighted tennis court, recreation programs, bicycles, basketball, volleyball, exercise room, spa. *Fee:* paddleboats, sailboats, windsurfing, scuba diving, snorkeling, charter fishing. **Guest Services:** coin laundry. *(See ad this page.)*

▼ See AAA listing this page ▼

GEORGE TOWN (B-1) pop. 20,626
• Hotels & Restaurants index & map p. 336

THE BRASSERIE
Phone: 345/945-1815   **42**

▼▼▼

International
$15-$38

AAA Inspector Notes: A slightly hidden downtown gem, this cool, swanky restaurant is well worth searching out. An on-site bakery creates a wonderful array of breads and desserts. For starters, try the cedar plank baked brie or seviche. Roasted sea bass, duck and lamb are just a few of the notable entrees. Those with lighter appetites might order from the tapas or shared plates menu. For dessert, Key lime pie made with coconut rum and the pumpkin cheesecake receive rave reviews. There is a large selection of wines by the glass. **Bar:** full bar. **Reservations:** suggested. **Address:** Elgin Ave **Location:** Just s of downtown; in Cricket Square. [L] [D]

BREEZES BY THE BAY
Phone: 345/943-8439   **37**

▼

International
$13-$24

AAA Inspector Notes: The downtown restaurant-bar affords views of the bay and puts forth a pirate-nautical-beach theme. Examples of perfect-for-sharing contemporary Caribbean and international dishes include conch fritters and ceviche. Among main courses are whole fish escovitch, jerk glazed pork chops and rasta pasta. Popular as well are the array of rum drink concoctions. **Bar:** full bar. **Address:** Harbour Dr **Location:** Downtown; on waterfront. **Parking:** street only. [B] [L] [D]

CASANOVA RESTAURANT BY THE SEA
Phone: 345/949-7633   **35**

▼▼▼

Italian
$14-$44

AAA Inspector Notes: Whether you dine al fresco on the deck overlooking the bay or in the cozy dining room accented with red table cloths and Italian-inspired wall murals, you'll savor expertly-prepared cuisine such as ceviche, salmon, filet mignon and Chateaubriand as well as an array of pasta dishes. The tiramisu and crème brûlée are a very tempting finale. The well rehearsed service includes waiters using a sprinkling of Italian words to add to the authenticity. **Bar:** full bar. **Reservations:** suggested. **Address:** 65 N Church St **Location:** Downtown; on waterfront. [L] [D] [N]

GRAND OLD HOUSE
Phone: 345/949-9333   **38**

▼▼▼▼

International
$18-$48

AAA Inspector Notes: On the sea's edge, the circa 1900 residence now is home to a restaurant where guests unwind on the seaside veranda or inside dining rooms. The fine menu selection includes a wide variety of seafood, island cuisine and international specialties. The wine list is outstanding. **Bar:** full bar. **Reservations:** required. **Address:** 648 S Church St **Location:** 1.5 mi (2.4 km) s of town. **Historic** [L] [D]

GUY HARVEY ISLAND GRILL RESTAURANT & BAR
Phone: 345/946-9000   **40**

▼▼▼

International
$13-$43

AAA Inspector Notes: Popular for sunsets and sea views this casual restaurant offers international cuisine with French influences all served in a nautical ambience decorated by the artwork of Guy Harvey. Some popular items include the seafood bouillabaisse and crusted rack of lamb. Bargain nightly specials include fish and chips night or curry night. A bar atmosphere prevails after dinner hours. **Bar:** full bar. **Reservations:** suggested. **Address:** 55 S Church St **Location:** Center of downtown; across from cruise ship docks; at Aquaworld Duty Free Mall.

[B] [L] [D]

HARD ROCK CAFE
Phone: 345/945-2020   **36**

▼▼

American
$12-$24

AAA Inspector Notes: Rock 'n' roll memorabilia decorates the walls of the popular theme restaurant. Live music on the weekends contributes to the bustling atmosphere. On the menu is a wide variety of American cuisine--from burgers and sandwiches to seafood, steaks and pasta. **Bar:** full bar. **Address:** 43 S Church St **Location:** Center; on waterfront, just s of cruise ship docks. [SAVE] [L] [D]

THE WHARF RESTAURANT
Phone: 345/949-2231   **34**

▼▼▼

International
$30-$45

AAA Inspector Notes: Sophisticated yet relaxed, this waterfront location boasts a large outdoor terrace with cozy, candlelit tables. A highlight here is the tarpon feeding off the dock every evening at 9 pm. On the menu is island and international cuisine. Tuesday night is salsa dance night. **Bar:** full bar. **Reservations:** suggested. **Address:** West Bay Rd #43 **Location:** 1 mi (1.6 km) n of town. [D] [N]

SEVEN MILE BEACH
• Restaurants p. 344
• Hotels & Restaurants index & map p. 336

7 MILE BEACH RESORT & CLUB
Phone: (345)949-0332   **14**

▼▼▼

Vacation Rental
Condominium
$300-$675

Address: 19 D Piper Ln **Location:** 1.4 mi (2.2 km) n of town; 2.6 mi (4.1 km) n of Owen Roberts International Airport. **Facility:** Originally built in 1991, the property's units feature two full-size bathrooms, two bedrooms, well-equipped kitchens and a patio or balcony. 36 condominiums. 3 stories (no elevator), exterior corridors. **Terms:** office hours 9 am-6 pm, check-in 4 pm, 30 day cancellation notice. **Amenities:** high-speed Internet, safes. **Pool(s):** outdoor. **Activities:** whirlpool, recreation programs. **Fee:** scuba diving, snorkeling. **Guest Services:** complimentary laundry.

[icons]

AQUA BAY CLUB CONDOS
Phone: 345/945-4728   **3**

▼▼

Condominium
$275-$625

Address: 2093 West Bay Rd **Location:** Oceanfront. West end of Seven Mile Beach. **Facility:** 20 condominiums. 3 stories (no elevator), exterior corridors. **Terms:** office hours 9 am-5 pm, 3 night minimum stay, 30 day cancellation notice, 90 day in season. **Amenities:** high-speed Internet, safes. **Pool(s):** outdoor. **Activities:** whirlpool. **Guest Services:** coin laundry. [SD] [icons]

CARIBBEAN CLUB
Phone: (345)623-4500   **12**

▼▼▼▼

Condominium
$610-$2500

Address: 871 West Bay Rd **Location:** Oceanfront. Center. **Facility:** Situated oceanfront, the property offers residential-style units with features like granite countertops, LCD televisions and plush bedding. Meets AAA guest room security requirements. 23 condominiums. 7 stories, interior/exterior corridors. **Terms:** check-in 4 pm, 60 day cancellation notice, 30 day off season-fee imposed. **Amenities:** high-speed Internet, safes. **Pool(s):** outdoor. **Activities:** exercise room. **Guest Services:** complimentary laundry.

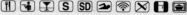

(See index & map p. 336.)

THE CHRISTOPHER COLUMBUS CONDOS
Phone: (345)945-4354 **4**

Vacation Rental
Condominium
$210-$540

Address: 2013 West Bay Rd **Location:** Oceanfront. West end of Seven Mile Beach. **Facility:** The property's two- and three-bedroom units feature residential-style décor. 30 condominiums. 3 stories (no elevator), exterior corridors. **Terms:** office hours 9 am-5 pm, 7 night minimum stay - seasonal, 45 day cancellation notice-fee imposed. **Amenities:** high-speed Internet. **Pool(s):** outdoor. **Activities:** 2 lighted tennis courts. **Guest Services:** coin laundry.

COMFORT SUITES & RESORT, SEVEN MILE BEACH
Phone: (345)945-7300 **16**

Hotel
$120-$240

Address: 22 Piper Way KY1 1201 **Location:** 1.5 mi (2.4 km) n of town; 2.5 mi (4 km) n of Owen Roberts International Airport; at Seven Mile Beach. **Facility:** Meets AAA guest room security requirements. 107 units, some two bedrooms and efficiencies. 5 stories, interior corridors. **Terms:** 3 day cancellation notice-fee imposed. **Amenities:** safes (fee). **Dining:** entertainment. **Pool(s):** outdoor. **Activities:** whirlpool, beach access, scuba diving & rental equipment, snorkeling & rental equipment, limited exercise equipment. *Fee:* massage. **Guest Services:** valet and coin laundry. **Free Special Amenities: expanded continental breakfast and high-speed Internet.**
(See ad p. 342.)

 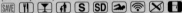

GRAND CAYMAN MARRIOTT BEACH RESORT
Phone: (345)949-0088 **18**

Resort Hotel
$192-$563

Marriott **AAA Benefit:** AAA
HOTELS & RESORTS hotel discounts of 5% or more.

Address: 389 West Bay Rd **Location:** Oceanfront. 1.8 mi (2.9 km) n of town; 2.8 mi (4.5 km) n of Owen Roberts International Airport. **Facility:** On the south end of Seven Mile Beach, the property offers a large reception area as well as spacious guest units with contemporary décor. 295 units. 5 stories, interior corridors. **Terms:** check-in 4 pm, 3 day cancellation notice. **Amenities:** high-speed Internet (fee), safes. **Dining:** 2 restaurants, also, Solana on Seven Mile Beach, see separate listing, entertainment. **Pool(s):** outdoor. **Activities:** whirlpool, rental paddleboats, rental sailboards, rental sailboards, recreation programs, exercise room, spa. *Fee:* waterskiing, scuba diving, snorkeling. **Guest Services:** valet laundry. **Free Special Amenities: early check-in/late check-out and manager's reception.**
(See ad on insert.)

PLANTANA CONDOMINIUMS
Phone: 345/945-4430 **10**

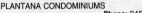
Vacation Rental
Condominium
$240-$680

Address: 1293 West Bay Rd **Location:** Center. **Facility:** These comfortable two-bedroom units, which vary in décor, feature two bathrooms and a fully furnished screened patio or balcony. 35 condominiums. 3 stories (no elevator), exterior corridors. **Terms:** office hours 8:30 am-4:30 pm, 3-5 night minimum stay - seasonal, 60 day cancellation notice, 30 day 4/15-11/15. **Amenities:** high-speed Internet, safes. **Pool(s):** outdoor. **Guest Services:** complimentary laundry.

PLANTATION VILLAGE BEACH RESORT
Phone: (345)949-4199 **20**

Vacation Rental
Condominium
$215-$600

Address: 323 West Bay Rd **Location:** Oceanfront. Center; east end of Seven Mile Beach. **Facility:** A seaside condominium-style operation with guest units that can be variable in decor depending on the taste of the owner. Meets AAA guest room security requirements. 20 condominiums. 3 stories (no elevator), exterior corridors. **Terms:** office hours 8:30 am-5 pm, 30 day cancellation notice-fee imposed. **Amenities:** high-speed Internet, safes. **Pool(s):** 2 outdoor. **Activities:** lighted tennis court, bicycles. **Guest Services:** coin laundry.

THE RITZ-CARLTON, GRAND CAYMAN
Phone: (345)943-9000 **13**

Resort Hotel
$549-$8000

THE RITZ-CARLTON® **AAA Benefit:** Unequaled service at Special Member Savings.

Address: West Bay Rd **Location:** Oceanfront. 4 mi (6.4 km) n of town; 5 mi (8 km) n of Owen Roberts International Airport. **Facility:** The epitome of a tropical island location, this crown jewel property offers spacious guest units with either an island or ocean view. Meets AAA guest room security requirements. 365 units, some two and three bedrooms. 3-8 stories, interior corridors. **Parking:** valet only. **Terms:** 7 day cancellation notice-fee imposed. **Amenities:** video games, high-speed Internet (fee), safes, honor bars. **Dining:** 4 restaurants, also, 7 Prime Cuts and Sunsets, Blue, see separate listings, entertainment. **Pool(s):** 2 outdoor. **Activities:** saunas, whirlpools, steamrooms, rental paddleboats, rental sailboats, rental sailboats, snorkeling & rental equipment, recreation programs, playground, basketball, horseshoes, volleyball, spa. *Fee:* scuba diving, charter fishing, golf-9 holes, 4 lighted tennis courts. **Guest Services:** valet laundry.

TAMARIND BAY
Phone: 345/949-4593 **8**

Condominium
$299-$550

Address: 37 Piper Way **Location:** Oceanfront. Center. **Facility:** Meets AAA guest room security requirements. 6 condominiums. 3 stories (no elevator), exterior corridors. **Terms:** office hours 9 am-5 pm, 21 day cancellation notice-fee imposed. **Amenities:** high-speed Internet, safes. **Pool(s):** outdoor. **Guest Services:** complimentary laundry.

(See index & map p. 336.)

▼ See AAA listing p. 341 ▼

All-suites hotel steps from Seven Mile Beach

The Comfort Suites® Seven Mile Beach is nestled in the heart of elegant "hotel row" in Grand Cayman

- Complimentary breakfast
- Complimentary wireless internet access

- Sundeck, outdoor pool and hot tub
- Onsite Stingers Restaurant and Bar
- Onsite Dive Shop and Spa
- Easy access to duty free shopping, dining and night clubs

COMFORT SUITES®

BY CHOICE HOTELS

For special AAA member rates, call 888.9.SUNFUN or visit choicecaribbean.com

RELAX
AND REJUVENATE

Get away and get back to your best self. Indulge in blissful pampering treatment at the luxurious Hibiscus Spa, enjoy mouthwatering cuisine while overlooking breath-taking ocean views and delight in the adventure of a lifetime through our dive shop. We have just what you need to escape the everyday.

FOR MORE INFORMATION OR TO MAKE A RESERVATION, VISIT WESTIN.COM/ CAYMANSPECIALS OR CALL 800.937.8461

THE WESTIN
CASUARINA
RESORT & SPA
GRAND CAYMAN

Get the free mobile app at
http://gettag.mobi

(See index & map p. 336.)

WESTIN CASUARINA RESORT & SPA-GRAND CAYMAN

Phone: (345)945-3800 [5]

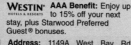

Resort Hotel
$161-$865

WESTIN HOTELS & RESORTS

AAA Benefit: Enjoy up to 15% off your next stay, plus Starwood Preferred Guest® bonuses.

Address: 1149A West Bay Rd **Location:** Oceanfront. 3.2 mi (5.1 km) n of town; 4.2 mi (6.7 km) n of Owen Roberts International Airport; on Seven Mile Beach. **Facility:** Named for the stately casuarina tree, the resort is on Seven Mile Beach; find a large pool area, a spa and well-appointed guest rooms. Meets AAA guest room security requirements. 343 units. 5 stories, interior corridors. **Terms:** 15 day cancellation notice-fee imposed. **Amenities:** high-speed Internet (fee), safes, honor bars. **Dining:** 3 restaurants, also, Casa Havana, see separate listing, entertainment. **Pool(s):** outdoor. **Activities:** whirlpools, rental sailboards, recreation programs, volleyball, exercise room, spa. **Fee:** sailboats, waterskiing, scuba diving, snorkeling, fishing, charter fishing. **Guest Services:** valet laundry.
(See ad on insert, p. 343, p. 102.)

[SAVE] [❡❡] [👤] [🏊] [🐾] [S] [SD] [🖊] [BIZ] [📶] [✕] [▭]

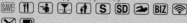

WHERE TO EAT

7 PRIME CUTS AND SUNSETS

Phone: 345-943-9000 [12]

International
$18-$63

AAA Inspector Notes: Diners enjoy upscale, refined dining either outdoors with direct views of the beach and ocean, or in the cool indoors amid elegant surroundings. Experienced servers are very knowledgeable and assist in exploring the menu. Numerous beef cuts include U.S. prime beef, Angus and Kobe. Besides beef, there are some fish and seafood dishes, and the desserts are heavenly. **Bar:** full bar. **Reservations:** required. **Address:** West Bay Rd **Location:** Oceanside, 4 mi (6.4 km) n of town; 5 mi (8 km) n of Owen Roberts International Airport; in The Ritz-Carlton, Grand Cayman. [L] [D]

ABACUS

Phone: 345-623-8282 [6]

International
$15-$48

AAA Inspector Notes: This hip and contemporary restaurant offers menu items that range from ahi tuna and pork tenderloin with tamarind essence to rack of lamb and Asian-style frog legs. Entrées pair nicely with the extensive wine list. An open kitchen and al fresco seating add to the bistro atmosphere. Live music is offered on some nights. **Bar:** full bar. **Reservations:** suggested. **Address:** 45 Market St **Location:** In Camana Bay. [L] [D]

AGUA RESTAURANT & LOUNGE

Phone: 345-949-2482 [20]

International
$11-$34

AAA Inspector Notes: This appealing bistro-style restaurant focuses heavily on fresh seafood with a smattering of meat dishes and features a variety of seviches and tiraditos. The menu runs the gamut with such great appetizers as lobster crepes with ragout or goat cheese phyllo baskets with honey and caramelized pears. Entrées include wahoo Mediterranean with sun-dried tomatoes and spicy plum tomato puree and coq au vin. The lunch menu features casual entrees. **Bar:** full bar. **Reservations:** suggested. **Address:** West Bay Rd **Location:** 2.4 mi (3.8 km) n of town; 3.4 mi (5.4 km) n of Owen Roberts International Airport; in Galleria Plaza at Seven Mile Beach. [L] [D] [LATE]

AQUA BEACH RESTAURANT & BAR

Phone: 345/949-8498 [11]

International
$13-$20

AAA Inspector Notes: Picnic tables and private, thatched-roof cabanas offer al fresco dining in a relaxed, beach-themed atmosphere. The menu boasts such comfort foods as a chicken and rib barbecue platter, a variety of wraps, salmon, double-cut pork chop, pecan grouper as well as pastas and entrée salads. **Bar:** full bar. **Address:** 426 West Bay Rd **Location:** Center; across from Grand Cayman Marriott Beach Resort.

[L] [D] [LATE] [⬚]

BAMBOO LOUNGE

Phone: 345/949-1234 [22]

Japanese
$27-$58

AAA Inspector Notes: Sleek, chic surroundings epitomize the sushi bar at this eatery. The considerable menu lists an assortment of sushi rolls, sashimi and tempura, as well as some designer martinis. Unobtrusive service allows for a relaxing evening most weekday nights, but expect large crowds on the weekends as the locals arrive to imbibe and dine. **Bar:** full bar. **Address:** West Bay Rd **Location:** 2.5 mi (4 km) n of town; 3.5 mi (5.6 km) n of Owen Roberts International Airport at Seven Mile Beach; Grand Cayman Beach Suite Hotel. [D] [LATE]

BLUE

Phone: 345/815-6100 [24]

International
$103-$156

AAA Inspector Notes: Celebrity chef Eric Ripert originated this restaurant concept, which centers on artistically presented offerings of creative and bold fish and other seafood. Those interested in exploring flavors in depth should consider the chef's tasting menu. Blue hues and blue roses lend to the water-inspired theme, and the experienced, international waitstaff carries out world-class service with grace and charm. **Bar:** full bar. **Reservations:** required. **Address:** West Bay Rd **Location:** 4 mi (6.4 km) n of town; in The Ritz-Carlton, Grand Cayman. **Parking:** valet only.

[D]

CASA HAVANA

Phone: 345/945-3800 [4]

International
$29-$44

AAA Inspector Notes: Creative menu selections center on Cuban and Caribbean specialties. Indoor and outdoor tables in this oceanfront restaurant lend an air of upscale elegance. Good food choices include certified Angus beef, rack of lamb and some innovative seafood dishes. The menu borrows from many culinary traditions to please the palate with such delightful tapas as foie gras with roasted mango-apple tart. **Bar:** full bar. **Reservations:** required. **Address:** West Bay Rd **Location:** 3.2 mi (5.1 km) n of town; 4.2 mi (6.7 km) n of Owen Roberts International Airport; on Seven Mile Beach; in Westin Casuarina Resort & Spa-Grand Cayman. *(See ad p. 343.)*

[D]

CHICKEN! CHICKEN!

Phone: 345/945-2290 [16]

Caribbean
$8-$16

AAA Inspector Notes: For a quick, value-priced and nutritious meal, this is the place for dining in or take-out. Wood-roasted chicken comes Caribbean-style or in citrus- or herb-marinated versions. Guests can choose from a whole, half or quarter bird. Among the many side options are mashed potatoes, rice and beans, jicama coleslaw or garlic- and herb-roasted potatoes. **Bar:** beer & wine. **Address:** West Shore Center SMB **Location:** 3.2 mi (5.1 km) n of town; in West Shore Shopping Center.

[L] [D]

CIMBOCO, A CARIBBEAN CAFE

Phone: 345/947-2782 [18]

International
$12-$20

AAA Inspector Notes: Dine in festively decorated surroundings or choose to take-away a meal. Individual wood-fired gourmet pizzas and some creative pasta dishes are the specialties here. **Bar:** full bar. **Address:** Harquail Bypass **Location:** 2 mi (3.2 km) n of town; at The Marque.

[B] [L] [D]

(See index & map p. 336.)

COCONUT JOE'S BEACHOUSE BAR & GRILL
Phone: 345/943-5637　19

International
$13-$26

AAA Inspector Notes: Across from Seven Mile Beach, the restaurant with al fresco seating shaded by a grove of trees has a prevailing beach and surfer theme. The menu features familiar fare such as quesadillas, wings, wraps, nachos and Greek salad. New to the menu are Asian rice bowls, which come with a choice of beef, chicken, shrimp or veggies. A party atmosphere heightens later in the evening. **Bar:** full bar. **Address:** West Bay Rd **Location:** Center; across from Comfort Suites & Resort, Seven Mile Beach. B L D 🍸

COPPER FALLS STEAKHOUSE
Phone: 345/945-4755　13

Steak
$26-$75

AAA Inspector Notes: This well-appointed restaurant is popular for its U.S. grade beef, available in a variety of cuts including rib-eye, porterhouse, New York strip and filet mignon. The menu also includes a few fish entrées including tuna, salmon and sea bass. Choice of a complimentary martini, highball or beer is included with all steak dishes. Sunday and Monday night is prime rib dinner night. Friday and Saturday is barbecue night. **Bar:** full bar. **Reservations:** suggested. **Address:** 43 Canal Point Rd **Location:** Across from Strand Shopping Plaza. D

DECKERS BISTRO & GRILL
Phone: 345/945-6600　10

International
$24-$48

AAA Inspector Notes: This distinctive bar, in the hub of Seven Mile Beach, is built in an original London double-decker bus, setting the comfortable restaurant apart. Among creative menu selections are Caribbean, pasta and seafood specialties including pine nut basil pesto fettuccine and steak au poivre. Guests can sit indoors or on the patio and enjoy the entertainment. **Bar:** full bar. **Reservations:** suggested. **Address:** West Bay Rd **Location:** 2.5 mi (4 km) n of town; across from Seven Mile Beach; across from Grand Cayman Beach Suite Hotel. D

EDOARDO'S FINE ITALIAN CUISINE
Phone: 345/945-4408　8

Italian
$17-$35

AAA Inspector Notes: This restaurant has an Old World rustic charm. Outstanding well-prepared Italian cuisine includes such signature dishes as cannelloni Venezia with veal, beef, spinach and ricotta cheese and arugula salad with Gorgonzola cheese and grapes. The chef uses select ingredients, including Angus beef, snapper, veal and baked grouper. Prepared-in-house pasta dishes range from farfalle and cannelloni to penne and lasagna. Among tempting desserts are banana toffee pie, cannoli and heavenly tiramisu. **Bar:** full bar. **Reservations:** suggested. **Address:** West Bay Rd **Location:** 3.1 mi (4.9 km) n of town; 4.1 mi (6.5 km) w from airport; in Coconut Place Shopping Center. L D

FIDEL MURPHY'S
Phone: 345/949-5189　32

Irish
$14-$28

AAA Inspector Notes: Dark woods, stained and frosted glass and an Irish pride and sports motif set the tone at the pub, which is a popular place to meet and watch sporting events. Those who don't go for the create-your-own-sandwich menu might try a pasta or seafood dish or maybe a traditional Irish choice, such as fish and chips, shepherd's pie and cannelloni to penne and lasagna. **Address:** West Bay Rd **Location:** 1.2 mi (1.9 km) n of town; in Queen's Court Shopping Plaza. B L D

GATEWAY OF INDIA
Phone: 345/946-2815　14

Indian
$19-$38

AAA Inspector Notes: Close-fitting tables nurture a cozy feel in a dining room neatly adorned with East Indian art and curios. The descriptive menu details varied curries made with a choice of lamb, beef, chicken and seafood, in addition to tandoori specialties, which are slow-cooked in a clay oven. A bountiful lunch buffet is the highlight of weekday afternoons. **Bar:** full bar. **Reservations:** suggested, for dinner. **Address:** Canal Point Rd **Location:** 3 mi (4.8 km) n of town; across from Strand Shopping Center. L D

HEMINGWAY'S BEACH CLUB RESTAURANT
Phone: 345/945-5700　23

Continental
$15-$45

AAA Inspector Notes: Handsome tropical decor characterizes this charming and sophisticated dining room and outdoor patio, which overlook the beach. The attentive staff serves well-prepared regional and Continental cuisine, which is ably complemented by the good wine list. Candlelit tables make the setting romantic. Although parking is limited, additional spaces can be found across the street. **Bar:** full bar. **Reservations:** required. **Address:** West Bay Rd **Location:** 2.5 mi (4 km) n of town; 3.5 mi (5.6 km) n of Owen Roberts International Airport at Seven Mile Beach; in Grand Cayman Beach Suite Hotel. B L D

LUCA
Phone: 345/623-4550　25

Italian
$28-$48

AAA Inspector Notes: Dine in a sleek and contemporary stylish ambience with dapper, attentive servers. The homemade pasta prepared with a variety of creative sauces is popular. Besides pasta the menu features Hudson Valley foie gras, a chilled cucumber soup and pumpkin ravioli as well as filet mignon with green peppercorn brandy sauce. The chef also features a six-course tasting menu. **Bar:** full bar. **Reservations:** suggested. **Address:** 871 West Bay Rd **Location:** Center; in Caribbean Club. L D

PRIME BRAZILIAN STEAK HOUSE
Phone: 345/623-7272　9

Brazilian
$24-$47

AAA Inspector Notes: Polished wood, elegant window treatments and decorative light fixtures lend to a rich and upscale backdrop for the Brazilian rodizio experience, believed to be the first of its kind in the Cayman Islands. For starters, the restaurant offers a fabulous buffet to whet the appetite. Afterward, the real fun begins as carvers circulate the dining room with skewers of grilled and roasted meat such as suckling pig, jerk pork, leg of lamb and steak. **Bar:** full bar. **Reservations:** suggested. **Address:** Governor's Square **Location:** In Governor's Square. L D

THE REEF GRILL AT THE ROYAL PALMS
Phone: 345/945-6358　30

International
$18-$40

AAA Inspector Notes: Examples of American and island cuisine-such as lobster ravioli, seared tuna with Asian slaw or beef tenderloin-line this restaurant's innovative menu. The modern dining room offers indoor or patio dining in a tropical garden setting. **Bar:** full bar. **Reservations:** suggested. **Address:** 537 West Bay Rd **Location:** 2.1 mi (3.3 km) n of town; on Seven Mile Beach; in Royal Palms Beach Club. D

(See index & map p. 336.)

RISTORANTE RAGAZZI   Phone: 345/945-3484   (15)

▽▽▽▽
Italian
$14-$44

AAA Inspector Notes: This voguish trattoria employs Italian and international servers. The extensive menu includes skillfully prepared pasta dishes-ranging from tortellini to lasagna to gnocchi-as well as such tempting grilled meat plates as marinated pork tenderloin and Marsala chicken. Also popular are traditional thin-crusted pizza with a plethora of topping combinations. **Bar:** full bar. **Reservations:** suggested. **Address:** West Bay Rd **Location:** 2.4 mi (3.8 km) n of town; across from Seven Mile Beach; in Buckingham Square. [L] [D]

SOLANA ON SEVEN MILE BEACH
                    Phone: 345/949-0088   (26)

▽▽▽▽
International
$15-$45

AAA Inspector Notes: Diners at this eatery have a choice of indoor or outdoor patio dining overlooking the ocean. The decor is simple, but the pretty presentations of well-prepared food is the real attraction. The chef prepares an international menu utilizing fresh island produce and ingredients creating such delicious items as arugula and octopus salad or jerk chicken with orange spice sauce. **Bar:** full bar. **Reservations:** suggested. **Address:** 389 W Bay Rd **Location:** 1.8 mi (2.9 km) n of town; 2.8 mi (4.5 km) n of Owen Roberts International Airport; in Grand Cayman Marriott Beach Resort. [L] [D] CALL ⑤M 🅺

Gourmet cuisine, oceanfront dining & spectacular views.

THAI ORCHID   Phone: 345/949-7955   (28)

▽▽▽
Asian
$14-$32

AAA Inspector Notes: Chefs prepare an extensive selection of savory cuisine. The menu's focus is primarily Thai cuisine with an extensive array of sushi, sashimi and tempura dishes as well as a few Indonesian specialties. Meals are made a la minute so the diner's taste and preferences are taken into account. The staff is cordial and attentive. The owner is an accomplished artist, and the decor is distinguished by her intriguing work on the walls. **Bar:** full bar. **Address:** West Bay Rd **Location:** 1.1 mi (1.7 km) n of town; in Queens Court Plaza. [L] [D]

YOSHI SUSHI   Phone: 345/943-9674   (5)

▽▽▽
Japanese
$11-$30

AAA Inspector Notes: Limited seating at this popular restaurant makes reservations a must. The sleek and modern setting includes a tatami section, and attentive service adds to the dining experience. A large assortment of sashimi and sushi rolls, many prepared with a creative twist, is offered. In addition, diners can order complete dinners, such as the robato dinner (shish kebab skewers) or hibachi dinner with chargrilled tuna, beef, salmon or tofu. **Bar:** full bar. **Reservations:** suggested. **Address:** West Bay Rd **Location:** In The Falls Plaza; across from Westin Casuarina Resort & Spa Grand Cayman. [L] [D]

Safety tip: Keep a current
AAA/CAA Road Atlas
in every vehicle

WEST BAY pop. 8,243
• Hotels & Restaurants index & map p. 336

COBALT COAST RESORT & SUITES
                    Phone: (345)946-5656   ❶

▽▽▽▽
Country Inn
$195-$495

Address: 18A Sea Fan Dr **Location:** Oceanfront. 7 mi (11.2 km) n of George Town to West Bay four-way stop, 2.5 mi (4 km) n, follow signs. **Facility:** A diver's paradise, this plantation-style country inn is far enough from Seven Mile Beach to ensure tranquility but near enough for a quick visit. Meets AAA guest room security requirements. 18 units, some two bedrooms and cottages. 2 stories (no elevator), exterior corridors. **Terms:** office hours 7 am-11 pm, 14 day cancellation notice-fee imposed. **Amenities:** safes. **Pool(s):** outdoor. **Activities:** whirlpool, snorkeling equipment rental. **Fee:** scuba diving, massage. **Guest Services:** valet laundry.

WHERE TO EAT

CRACKED CONCH BY THE SEA
                    Phone: 345/945-5217   (3)

▽▽ ▽▽
Caribbean
$12-$37

AAA Inspector Notes: The casual setting incorporates an oceanfront patio and an indoor dining room appointed with nautical decor. In addition to a wide selection of seafood, the menu includes pasta, burgers and lighter fare. Be sure to visit the tiki bar. **Bar:** full bar. **Reservations:** suggested. **Address:** NW Point Rd **Location:** 8 mi (12.8 km) n of George Town; 9 mi (14.4 km) n of Owen Roberts International Airport; adjacent to Turtle Farm. [L] [D]

Little Cayman

LITTLE CAYMAN pop. 115
• Hotels & Restaurants index & map p. 336

THE CLUB AT LITTLE CAYMAN
                    Phone: (345)948-1033   ㉟

▽▽▽▽
Condominium
$249-$550

Address: Guy Banks Rd KY3-2501 **Location:** Oceanfront. 0.4 mi (0.7 km) e of airstrip. **Facility:** Spacious condos feature upscale, residential-quality appointments. Meets AAA guest room security requirements. 5 condominiums. 2 stories (no elevator), exterior corridors. **Terms:** office hours 7 am-8 pm, off-site registration, 31 day cancellation notice-fee imposed. **Pool(s):** outdoor. **Activities:** whirlpool, boat dock. **Fee:** bicycles. **Guest Services:** complimentary laundry.

LITTLE CAYMAN BEACH RESORT
                    Phone: 345/948-1033   ㉜

▽▽▽▽
Hotel
$151-$191

Address: 1128 Guy Banks Rd **Location:** Oceanfront. 0.5 mi (0.8 km) e of airstrip. **Facility:** 40 units. 2 stories (no elevator), exterior corridors. **Terms:** office hours 7 am-8 pm, 21 day cancellation notice. **Amenities:** safes. **Pool(s):** outdoor. **Activities:** whirlpools, boat dock, exercise room. **Fee:** scuba diving, snorkeling, fishing, charter fishing, massage. **Guest Services:** valet laundry, area transportation (fee)-island tour.

(See index & map p. 336.)

PARADISE VILLAS Phone: (345)948-0001 **34**

Cottage
$175-$200

Address: Guy Banks Rd **Location:** Oceanfront. Just e of airstrip. **Facility:** 12 cottages. 1 story, exterior corridors. **Terms:** open 12/1-9/4 & 10/25-11/30, office hours 9 am-5 pm, 2 night minimum stay, 30 day cancellation notice-fee imposed. **Dining:** Hungry Iguana, see separate listing. **Pool(s):** outdoor. **Activities:** Fee: scuba diving, snorkeling, bicycles.

SOUTHERN CROSS CLUB Phone: 345/948-1099 **37**

Cottage
$278-$329

Address: Guy Banks Rd **Location:** Oceanfront. 0.7 mi (1.1 km) e of airstrip. **Facility:** Popular with divers, these well-equipped, charming cottages are spaced along an enchanting stretch of beach; diving and fishing options are offered. 12 cottages. 1 story, exterior corridors. Bath: shower only. **Terms:** open 12/1-8/15 & 10/15-11/30, office hours 7 am-8:30 pm, 5 night minimum stay - seasonal, 45 day cancellation notice-fee imposed. **Pool(s):** outdoor. **Activities:** boat dock, snorkeling & rental equipment, bicycles. Fee: scuba diving, fishing, charter fishing. **Guest Services:** valet laundry, area transportation-within the island.

WHERE TO EAT

HUNGRY IGUANA Phone: 345/948-0007 **56**

American
$14-$28

AAA Inspector Notes: Near the airport, this inviting restaurant has a resident retinue of iguanas. The familiar menu features American and island-inspired dishes. Daily lunch specials range from stewed conch and meatloaf to barbecue chicken and spaghetti with meatballs. Monday is pizza night. **Bar:** full bar. **Address:** Guy Banks Rd **Location:** Just e of airstrip; in Paradise Villas.

CURAÇAO

✈ Airport Accommodations				
Map Page	**CURAÇAO AEROPUERTO HATO**	Diamond Rated	High Season	Page
❶ p. 349	Blue Bay Curacao, 1.9 mi (3 km) s of airport	💎💎💎	$300-$400	352

Curaçao

This index helps you "spot" where approved hotels and restaurants are located on the corresponding detailed maps. Hotel daily rate range is for comparison only and show the property's high season. Restaurant rate range is a combination of lunch and/or dinner. Turn to the listing page for more detailed rate information and consult display ads for special promotions.

WILLEMSTAD

Map Page	Hotels	Diamond Rated	High Season	Page
❶ p. 349	Blue Bay Curacao	💎💎💎	$300-$400	352
❷ p. 349	Hotel Kura Hulanda Spa & Casino	💎💎💎💎	$260-$840	352
❸ p. 349	Hilton Curacao *(See ad opposite title page.)*	💎💎💎	$130-$480	352
❹ p. 349	**Marriott Curacao Resort** *(See ad on insert.)*	💎💎💎	$119-$512 SAVE	352
❺ p. 349	**Renaissance Curacao Resort & Casino** *(See ad p. 354, p. 109.)*	💎💎💎💎	$128-$434 SAVE	352
❼ p. 349	Clarion Hotel & Suites Curacao *(See ad p. 353.)*	💎💎	$145-$280	352
⓫ p. 349	Avila Hotel	💎💎💎	$220-$430	352

Map Page	Restaurants	Diamond Rated	Cuisine	Meal Range	Page
① p. 349	Fort Nassau Restaurant	💎💎	International	$12-$32	355
⑦ p. 349	The Ribs Factory	💎	Barbecue	$14-$24	355
⑩ p. 349	**Craving Sushi**	💎💎	Japanese	$15-$28	355
⑪ p. 349	Ema-Tei	💎💎	Japanese	$22-$30	355
⑫ p. 349	**Bistro Le Clochard**	💎💎💎	French	$17-$44	355
⑬ p. 349	La Pergola	💎💎	Italian	$12-$31	355
⑰ p. 349	Blue's Restaurant	💎💎	International	$16-$24	355
⑱ p. 349	Belle Terrace	💎💎💎	International	$18-$34	355

WESTPUNT

Map Page	Hotel	Diamond Rated	High Season	Page
⓯ p. 349	Lodge Kura Hulanda & Beach Club	💎💎💎	$135-$550	351

NIEUWPOORT

Map Page	Hotel	Diamond Rated	High Season	Page
⓲ p. 349	**Hyatt Regency Curacao Golf Resort, Spa and Marina** *(See ad p. 350.)*	💎💎💎💎	$139-$539 SAVE	349

Map Page	Restaurant	Diamond Rated	Cuisine	Meal Range	Page
⑳ p. 349	Shor American Seafood Grill	💎💎💎	International	$13-$45	351

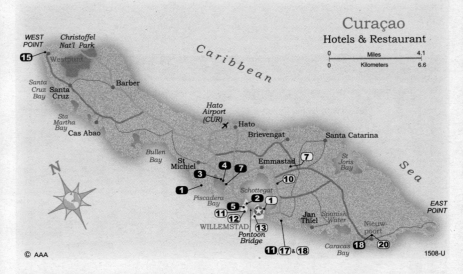

Curaçao
Hotels & Restaurant

© AAA

1508-U

NIEUWPOORT
• Restaurants p. 351
• Hotels & Restaurants index & map p. 348

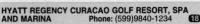

HYATT REGENCY CURACAO GOLF RESORT, SPA AND MARINA
Phone: (599)9840-1234   (18)

Resort Hotel
$139-$539

HYATT
HOTELS & RESORTS

AAA Benefit: Members save 10% or more everyday.

Address: Porta Blancu **Location:** Oceanfront. 18 mi (28.9 km) se from Curacao Hato Airport; on Santa Barbara Plantation. **Facility:** This property offers contemporary guest units and a plethora of activities. Meets AAA guest room security requirements. 350 units. 4 stories, interior/exterior corridors. **Parking:** on-site and valet. **Terms:** check-in 4 pm, 3 day cancellation notice-fee imposed. **Amenities:** high-speed Internet (fee), safes. **Dining:** 3 restaurants, also, Shor American Seafood Grill, see separate listing, entertainment. **Pool(s):** 2 outdoor. **Activities:** snorkeling & rental equipment, 4 lighted tennis courts, recreation programs, exercise room, spa. *Fee:* sailboats, windsurfing, marina, scuba diving, golf-18 holes. **Guest Services:** valet laundry. *(See ad p. 350.)*

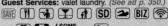
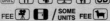

Create complete trip routings and custom maps
with the TripTik® Travel Planner on AAA.com or CAA.ca

(See index & map p. 348.)

▼ See AAA listing p. 349 ▼

Learn about AAA/CAA Diamond Ratings
at AAA.com/Diamonds

(See index & map p. 348.)

WHERE TO EAT

SHOR AMERICAN SEAFOOD GRILL
Phone: 599/9840-4785 (20)

◆◆◆◆
International
$13-$45

AAA Inspector Notes: This oceanfront restaurant has an accommodating and congenial staff that assists guests in navigating the menu with the many seafood and grilled meat offerings. A tasty starter is the tuna poke made from raw tuna or the New England-style seafood chowder. Guests can choose their own seasoning and sauce for the grilled mahi mahi, salmon and grouper. For lunch, a gourmet burger bar includes a cedar plank salmon burger and a seared blue crab burger. Friday night is martini night. **Bar:** full bar. **Reservations:** suggested. **Address:** Portu Blancu **Location:** 18 mi (28.9 km) se of Curacao Hato Airport; on Santa Barbara Plantation; in the Hyatt Regency Curacao Golf Resort, Spa and Marina.

L D CALL ⬛M ⬛

WESTPUNT
• Hotels & Restaurants index & map p. 348

LODGE KURA HULANDA & BEACH CLUB
Phone: (599)9839-3600 (15)

◆◆◆◆
Boutique Resort
Hotel
$135-$550

Address: Playa Kalki 1 **Location:** Oceanfront. 18 mi (28.8 km) w of Willemstad. **Facility:** On sprawling grounds, the property offers comfortable accommodations providing rustic sophistication in several different room categories. Meets AAA guest room security requirements. 74 units, some efficiencies. 2 stories (no elevator), interior/exterior corridors. **Terms:** 3 day cancellation notice-fee imposed. **Amenities:** safes. **Dining:** 3 restaurants. **Pool(s):** outdoor. **Activities:** exercise room. *Fee:* paddleboats, sailboats, scuba diving, snorkeling, lighted tennis court, massage. **Guest Services:** coin laundry, area transportation-Willemstad.

WILLEMSTAD (B-2) pop. 43,550

- **Restaurants p. 355**
- **Hotels & Restaurants index & map p. 348**

AVILA HOTEL
Phone: (599)9461-4377 **11**

▼▼▼ ▼▼▼
Boutique Hotel
$220-$430

Address: Penstraat 130 **Location:** Oceanfront. 0.9 mi (1.4 km) e from Punda side of downtown. **Facility:** This very popular hotel features a historic building, a pier restaurant, a beachfront bar and several room categories. 152 units, some efficiencies and kitchens. 2-4 stories, interior/exterior corridors. **Terms:** check-in 4 pm, 7 day cancellation notice, 21 day in season-fee imposed. **Amenities:** high-speed Internet, safes, honor bars. **Dining:** 2 restaurants, also, Belle Terrace, Blue's Restaurant, see separate listings, entertainment. **Pool(s):** outdoor. **Activities:** saunas, whirlpool, steamrooms, lighted tennis court, spa. **Guest Services:** valet laundry, area transportation-Punda side & Willemstad.

🍴 🍷 SD 🏊 ♿ BIZ 📶 🔌 📺
/ SOME UNITS 🖥️

BLUE BAY CURACAO
Phone: 599/9888-8800 **1**

▼▼▼ ▼▼▼
Vacation Rental House
$300-$400

Location: 1.9 mi (3 km) s of airport, 3.1 mi (5 km) w of downtown, follow signs. **Facility:** Inside a gated community and a short stroll of a premium beach, these villas feature a wrap-around veranda, large living room and complete kitchen. 35 houses. 1-2 stories (no elevator), exterior corridors. *Bath:* shower only. **Terms:** office hours 8 am-10 pm, 30 day cancellation notice-fee imposed. **Amenities:** high-speed Internet, safes. **Pool(s):** 2 outdoor. **Activities:** lighted tennis court, recreation programs, playground, exercise room. **Fee:** scuba diving, snorkeling, golf-18 holes, massage. **Guest Services:** complimentary laundry. 🍴 🍷 SD 🏊 BIZ 🔌 🖥️ 📺

CLARION HOTEL & SUITES CURACAO
Phone: (599)9433-6666 **7**

▼▼▼ ▼▼
Hotel
$145-$280

Address: John F Kennedy Blvd **Location:** Piscadera Bay; 3.1 mi (5 km) w of Otrobanda side of town; 5.5 mi (8.9 km) s of airport. **Facility:** 97 units, some efficiencies. 4 stories, interior corridors. **Terms:** check-in 4 pm. **Amenities:** high-speed Internet, safes. **Pool(s):** outdoor. **Activities:** limited beach access, playground. **Guest Services:** valet laundry. *(See ad p. 353.)*

🍴 🍷 SD 🏊 ♿ BIZ 📶
❌ 🔌 📺 / SOME UNITS 🖥️

HILTON CURACAO
Phone: (599)9462-5000 **3**

▼▼▼ ▼▼▼
Resort Hotel
$130-$480 12/1-4/10
$130-$350 4/11-11/30

AAA Benefit: Members save 5% or more everyday!

Address: John F Kennedy Blvd **Location:** Oceanfront. Piscadera Bay; 3.1 mi (5 km) w of Otrobanda side of town; 5.5 mi (8.9 km) s of airport. **Facility:** This high-rise resort features nice facilities, including a free-form lagoon-style pool, sprawling grounds and a theme dinner restaurant. 196 units. 5 stories, interior corridors. **Terms:** 1-7 night minimum stay, cancellation fee imposed. **Amenities:** high-speed Internet (fee), safes. **Dining:** 3 restaurants, entertainment. **Pool(s):** 2 outdoor. **Activities:** sauna, steamroom, miniature golf, playground, spa. **Fee:** paddleboats, sailboats, scuba diving, snorkeling, 2 lighted tennis courts. **Guest Services:** valet laundry. *(See ad opposite title page.)*

🌐 🍴 ♿ 🍷 SD 🏊 ♿ BIZ 📶 📺

HOTEL KURA HULANDA SPA & CASINO
Phone: (599)9434-7700 **2**

▼▼▼ ▼▼▼
Historic Hotel
$260-$840

Address: Langestraat 8 **Location:** Center of downtown; on the Otrobanda. **Facility:** A re-created Dutch Colonial village in the heart of town, the hotel features winding streets, an open-air café, an eco-friendly pool and charming units. Meets AAA guest room security requirements. 82 units. 1-2 stories (no elevator), interior/exterior corridors. **Terms:** 3 day cancellation notice. **Amenities:** high-speed Internet, safes. **Dining:** 3 restaurants, entertainment. **Pool(s):** 2 outdoor. **Activities:** sauna, whirlpool, steamroom, exercise room, spa. **Guest Services:** valet laundry, area transportation-Blue Bay Beach Club.

🍴 🍷 SD 🏊 BIZ 📶 🔌

MARRIOTT CURACAO RESORT
Phone: (599)9736-8800 **4**

▼▼ ▼▼
Resort Hotel
$119-$512

Marriott HOTELS & RESORTS

AAA Benefit: AAA hotel discounts of 5% or more.

Address: John F Kennedy Blvd **Location:** Oceanfront. 3.1 mi (5 km) w of Otrobanda side of town; 5.5 mi (8.9 km) s of airport. **Facility:** Located on Piscadera Bay, this resort offers large, well-appointed facilities, including an upscale casino. Many units offer ocean views. Meets AAA guest room security requirements. 247 units. 3 stories, exterior corridors. **Terms:** check-in 4 pm, 3 day cancellation notice. **Amenities:** high-speed Internet (fee), safes. **Dining:** 5 restaurants. **Pool(s):** outdoor. **Activities:** saunas, whirlpools, steamrooms, playground, volleyball, exercise room. **Fee:** sailboats, scuba diving, snorkeling, massage. **Guest Services:** valet laundry. *(See ad on insert.)*

SAVE 🎮 🍴 🍷 ♿ SD 🏊 BIZ ❌ 📺
/ SOME UNITS 🔌

RENAISSANCE CURACAO RESORT & CASINO
Phone: (599)9435-5000 **5**

▼▼▼ ▼▼▼
Contemporary Hotel
$128-$434

R RENAISSANCE* HOTELS & RESORTS

AAA Benefit: AAA hotel discounts of 5% or more.

Address: Baden Powellweg #1 **Location:** Oceanfront. On waterfront adjacent to Rif Fort; downtown. **Facility:** Within walking distance of the historic Rif Fort complex, the flamboyantly chic property boasts a well-defined, man-made beach and infinity pool. Meets AAA guest room security requirements. 237 units. 4 stories, interior corridors. **Terms:** check-in 4 pm, 3 day cancellation notice. **Amenities:** high-speed Internet (fee), safes. **Dining:** 2 restaurants, entertainment. **Pool(s):** 2 outdoor. **Activities:** exercise room. **Fee:** massage. **Guest Services:** valet laundry. *(See ad p. 354, p. 109.)*

SAVE 🎮 🍴 ♿ 🍷 🏋️ S SD 🏊 BIZ
📶 ❌ 🔌 📺

(See index & map p. 348.)

▼ See AAA listing p. 352 ▼

Full service value minutes from Curacao's shopping district

This full-service hotel is located on the World Trade Center complex, only a fifteen minute drive from Hato International Airport and a short drive to colorful Willemstad shopping and tourist center.
- Free continental breakfast
- Free Internet access

- Outdoor swimming pool with poolside bar and sauna
- Fitness center
- Modern convention facility and business center
- Conveniently located near Kura Hulanda Museum, Curacao Maritime Museum and more

Clarion
Hotel & Suites
BY CHOICE HOTELS

For special AAA member rates, call 888.9.SUNFUN or visit choicecaribbean.com

Explore the Travel Guides on
AAA.com/Travel or CAA.ca/Travel

▼ See AAA listing p. 352 ▼

(See index & map p. 348.)

WHERE TO EAT

BELLE TERRACE Phone: 599/9461-4377 18

International
$18-$34

AAA Inspector Notes: An open-air dining room at this casual eatery is just steps away from the beach. Such items as baked butterfish coated with macadamia nuts and rack of lamb with rosemary sauce are representative of the fare. On Wednesday nights, the chef creates an Antillean-themed menu, while Saturday is Caribbean grill night with live music. **Bar:** full bar. **Reservations:** suggested, for dinner. **Address:** Penstraat 130 **Location:** 0.9 mi (1.4 km) e from Punda side of downtown; in Avila Hotel.

B L D

BISTRO LE CLOCHARD Phone: 599/9462-5666 12

French
$17-$44

AAA Inspector Notes: In a picturesque setting at the mouth of a ship channel, this restaurant is known for its savory French and Swiss cuisine and attentive service. Well-prepared and attractively presented dishes employ fresh seafood, lamb, duck and veal and on occasion, a special wild game menu including rabbit, venison and wild boar. Friday and Saturday evenings feature live music. **Bar:** full bar. **Reservations:** required, for dinner. **Address:** Riffort Village **Location:** Downtown; in Riffort Village; Otrobanda side of town; at entrance to ship channel near Queen Emma Pontoon Bridge. **Parking:** on-site and street. **Historic** L D

BLUE'S RESTAURANT Phone: 599/9461-4377 17

International
$16-$24

AAA Inspector Notes: Waves lap beneath the pier as rhythm-and-blues recordings play in the background. Tempting, skillfully prepared dishes include grilled wahoo with goat cheese ravioli, marinated veal on tarragon risotto and baked grouper a la Parmesan with gnocchi. A vegetarian plate du jour also is available. Guests should stay for the encore of exotic desserts. The menu changes periodically. The youthful staff is pleasantly accommodating. Happy hour lures locals and tourists alike. **Bar:** full bar. **Reservations:** suggested. **Address:** Penstraat 130 **Location:** 0.9 mi (1.4 km) e from Punda side of downtown; in Avila Hotel. D

CRAVING SUSHI Phone: 599/9736-6711 10

Japanese
$15-$28

AAA Inspector Notes: Located in a shopping mall area, this decoratively enhanced restaurant offers one of the island's only complete sushi bar as well as an array of well-prepared Japanese dishes. **Bar:** full bar. **Reservations:** suggested. **Address:** Promenade Shopping Center **Location:** 3 mi (4.8 km) e. L D

EMA-TEI Phone: 599/9465-5890 11

Japanese
$22-$30

AAA Inspector Notes: This Japanese restaurant in Curacao is situated in the historical Rif Fort along the ocean's edge. An array of sushi rolls are offered with tuna and eel among the favorites. Besides sushi there is sashimi, tempura, teriyaki and noodle dishes available. **Bar:** full bar. **Reservations:** suggested. **Address:** Rif Fort Village 432 **Location:** Downtown; in Rif Fort Village Otrobanda. **Parking:** on-site (fee). **Historic** L D

FORT NASSAU RESTAURANT Phone: 599/9461-3450 1

International
$12-$32

AAA Inspector Notes: Ponder choices not only of Continental fare but also of the Dutch and Caribbean variety at this charming spot that gets its name from its location within the walls of a historic fort. A reasonably priced prix fixe menu also is available. The location on a hill above Willemstad means guests can expect some spectacular views. **Bar:** full bar. **Reservations:** suggested. **Address:** Seru Fort Nassau **Location:** At historical Fort Nassau; just n of downtown on Sablica Hill. **Historic** L D

LA PERGOLA Phone: 599/9461-3482 13

Italian
$12-$31

AAA Inspector Notes: Within the walls of an old fort, this restaurant is in a historic waterfront location affording fine ocean views. Well-prepared Italian dishes include many made from fresh seafood. Diners have a choice of indoor seating or dining al fresco in the terrace which is ideal for people-watching. The service is island-casual and the multilingual staff is friendly. **Bar:** full bar. **Reservations:** suggested. **Address:** Waterfront Arches #12 **Location:** On Punda side of downtown; east side of Queen Emma Pontoon Bridge. **Parking:** street only. **Historic** D

THE RIBS FACTORY Phone: 599/9461-0440 7

Barbecue
$14-$24

AAA Inspector Notes: This hole-in-the-wall barbecue joint offers ribs and chicken but also some Mexican fare including nachos, quesadillas and fajitas. **Bar:** full bar. **Address:** Caracasbaaiweg 54 **Location:** 2 mi (3.2 km) s of downtown. L D

DOMINICA

This index helps you "spot" where approved hotels and restaurants are located on the corresponding detailed maps. Hotel daily rate range is for comparison only and show the property's high season. Restaurant rate range is a combination of lunch and/or dinner. Turn to the listing page for more detailed rate information and consult display ads for special promotions.

ROSEAU

Map Page	Hotels	Diamond Rated	High Season	Page
5 p. 357	The Garraway Hotel	▼	$100-$200	358
6 p. 357	Fort Young Hotel (See ad p. 359.)	▼▼	$85-$255	358
7 p. 357	Papillote Wilderness Retreat and Nature Sanctuary	▼▼	$115-$130	359

Map Page	Restaurants	Diamond Rated	Cuisine	Meal Range	Page
① p. 357	Fort Young Waterfront Restaurant	▼▼▼	Caribbean	$12-$36	359
④ p. 357	Port of Call Restaurant & Bar	▼	Caribbean	$15-$26	359

FOND ST. JEAN

Map Page	Hotel	Diamond Rated	High Season	Page
10 p. 357	Zandoli Inn, Roche Cassee-Stowe	▼▼	$145	358

DELICES

Map Page	Hotel	Diamond Rated	High Season	Page
12 p. 357	Jungle Bay Resort & Spa	▼▼▼	$169-$199	357

Map Page	Restaurant	Diamond Rated	Cuisine	Meal Range	Page
⑩ p. 357	The Pavilion	▼▼	Caribbean	$20-$28	358

HATTON GARDEN

Map Page	Hotel	Diamond Rated	High Season	Page
16 p. 357	Silks Luxury Boutique Hotel	▼▼▼	$135-$220	358

CANEFIELD

Map Page	Restaurant	Diamond Rated	Cuisine	Meal Range	Page
⑦ p. 357	The Cove	▼	International	$5-$24	357

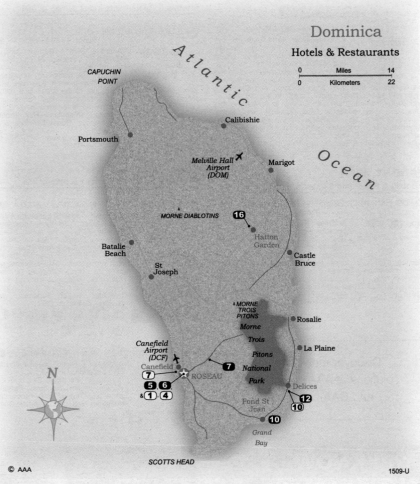

Dominica

Hotels & Restaurants

0	Miles	14
0	Kilometers	22

CAPUCHIN POINT

Atlantic

Calibishie

Portsmouth

Melville Hall Airport (DOM) ✈

Marigot

Ocean

▲ MORNE DIABLOTINS

16

Hatton Garden

Batalie Beach

Castle Bruce

St Joseph

▲ MORNE TROIS PITONS

Morne

Rosalie

Trois

La Plaine

Pitons

Canefield Airport (DCF)
Canefield ✈

7

National

☆ ROSEAU

Park

7

Delices

5 **6**

12

& **1** **4**

Fond St Jean

10

10

Grand Bay

SCOTTS HEAD

© AAA

1509-U

CANEFIELD

• Hotels & Restaurants index & map p. 356

THE COVE ◇ International $5-$24

Phone: 767/440-2683 **7**

AAA Inspector Notes: Prepared with Caribbean characteristics, patrons enjoy a nice mix of barbecue ribs, chicken, steak, wings, entree salads and the catch of the day while gazing upon the black-sand beach located just steps away. Music adds a lively touch to the atmosphere. **Bar:** full bar. **Address:** The Fisherman's Cove, Rockaway **Location:** 1.9 mi (3 km) n of Roseau; just s of Canefield Airport.

DELICES

• Restaurants p. 358
• Hotels & Restaurants index & map p. 356

JUNGLE BAY RESORT & SPA

Phone: 767/446-1789 **12**

◇◇◇ Cottage $169-$199

Address: Pointe Mulatre **Location:** Oceanfront. 1.9 mi (3 km) s of Delices; on the southeast coast. **Facility:** Jungle-themed cottages at this eco-friendly resort provide the perfect retreat for privacy, comfort and relaxation while offering beautiful views. 35 cottages. 1 story, exterior corridors. *Bath:* shower only. **Terms:** open 12/1-9/5 & 9/20-11/30, office hours 6 am-10 pm, 14 day cancellation notice-fee imposed. **Dining:** The Pavilion, see separate listing. **Pool(s):** outdoor. **Activities:** beach access, game room, spa. *Fee:* snorkeling. **Guest Services:** valet laundry, area transportation (fee)-ferry terminal.

(See index & map p. 356.)

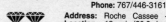

THE PAVILION

Caribbean
$20-$28

Phone: 767/446-1789 ⑩

AAA Inspector Notes: Although the menu is limited, it does change frequently. Generally, a starter, entrée and dessert are offered for a set price. The entrées usually center around the selection of one chicken, one fish and one vegetarian dish most often prepared with Caribbean herbs and spices. Don't expect, though, to find red meat or pork on the menu as there is an aversion to serving it at this restaurant. The congenial staff enhance the dining experience with their Caribbean charm. **Bar:** full bar. **Reservations:** suggested. **Address:** Pointe Mulatre **Location:** 1.9 mi (3 km) s of town; on southeast coast; in Jungle Bay Resort & Spa. ⒷⓁⒹ🅧

FOND ST. JEAN
• Hotels & Restaurants index & map p. 356

ZANDOLI INN, ROCHE CASSEE-STOWE

Bed & Breakfast
$145

Phone: 767/446-3161 ⑩

Address: Roche Cassee - Stowe **Location:** 13 mi (20.8 km) se of Roseau towards Loubiere, e to Stowe; property is on south side of road before reaching Fond St Jean. **Facility:** 5 units. 3 stories (no elevator), exterior corridors. *Bath:* shower only. **Terms:** office hours 7 am-9 pm, 2 night minimum stay, 30 day cancellation notice-fee imposed. **Pool(s):** outdoor. **Guest Services:** valet laundry.

🍽 SD 🏊 🛜 🅧 🕅 🗲

HATTON GARDEN
• Hotels & Restaurants index & map p. 356

SILKS LUXURY BOUTIQUE HOTEL

Country Inn
$135-$220

Phone: 767/445-8846 ⑯

Address: Hatton Garden Junction, Marigot Rd **Location:** 24.5 mi (39 km) nw of Roseau; in Pagua Valley. **Facility:** This completely refurbished hotel offers modern amenities while blending the history and culture of the island in a natural setting. 5 units. 1-2 stories, exterior corridors. **Terms:** open 12/1-7/31 & 9/1-11/30, office hours 8 am-4 pm, 30 day cancellation notice-fee imposed. **Amenities:** safes. **Pool(s):** outdoor. **Activities:** *Fee:* massage. **Guest Services:** valet laundry.

🍽 🍸 SD 🏊 🛜 🅦 🗲 / SOME UNITS 🐾

ROSEAU (C-1) pop. 16,535
• Hotels & Restaurants index & map p. 356

FORT YOUNG HOTEL

Hotel
$85-$255

Phone: 767/448-5000 ⑥

Address: Victoria St **Location:** Across from cruise ship port; downtown. **Facility:** 71 units. 1-4 stories, exterior corridors. **Terms:** 7 day cancellation notice-fee imposed. **Amenities:** safes. *Some:* high-speed Internet. **Dining:** Fort Young Waterfront Restaurant, see separate listing. **Pool(s):** outdoor. **Activities:** whirlpools, exercise room. *Fee:* scuba diving, snorkeling, massage. **Guest Services:** valet laundry. *(See ad p. 359.)*

🍽 🍸 SD 🏊 BIZ 🛜 📶
📠 / SOME UNITS 📺

THE GARRAWAY HOTEL

Hotel
$100-$200

Phone: 767/449-8800 ⑤

Address: 1 Dame Eugenia Charles Blvd **Location:** On bayfront; center of downtown. **Facility:** 31 units. 5 stories, interior corridors. **Parking:** street only. **Terms:** 8 day cancellation notice-fee imposed. **Amenities:** high-speed Internet. **Guest Services:** valet laundry.

🍽 🍸 BIZ 📶 / SOME UNITS 📺

(See index & map p. 356.)

PAPILLOTE WILDERNESS RETREAT AND NATURE SANCTUARY Phone: 767/448-2287

Country Inn
$115-$130

Address: Trafalgar Rd **Location:** On Trafalgar Falls Rd, 6.5 mi (10.4 km) ne of downtown. **Facility:** 7 units. 2 stories (no elevator), exterior corridors. **Bath:** shower only. **Terms:** open 12/1-8/31 & 11/1-11/30, office hours 8 am-10:30 pm, 30 day cancellation notice-fee imposed. **Activities:** hiking trails. **Guest Services:** valet laundry.

FEE 🛬 🍴 🍸 📶 ⚫ 📺 🌀 / SOME UNITS 🛗

PORT OF CALL RESTAURANT & BAR
Phone: 767/448-2910 ④

Caribbean
$15-$26

AAA Inspector Notes: The simple eatery is popular for take-out or dine-in meals. Quick fixes for the hungry, choices include an array of sandwiches, burgers, chicken wings, fish, pork chops and even a T-bone steak. **Bar:** full bar. **Address:** 3 Kennedy Ave **Location:** Center of downtown; just e of waterfront. **Parking:** street only. [L] [D] ⚫ ⬛

WHERE TO EAT

FORT YOUNG WATERFRONT RESTAURANT
Phone: 767/448-5000 ①

Caribbean
$12-$36

AAA Inspector Notes: Enjoy the vista of the harbor while feasting on Caribbean-inspired cuisine at this eatery. The mouthwatering appetizers include escargot, baked mussels in a turmeric cheese sauce and smoked salmon stuffed with crab meat. The versatile chef serves up entrees such as Long Island duckling with balsamic honey sauce or marlin wrapped in a banana leaf. The staff is cordial. **Bar:** full bar. **Reservations:** suggested. **Address:** Victoria St **Location:** Across from cruise ship port; downtown; in Fort Young Hotel. [B] [L] [D] ⬛

▼ See AAA listing p. 358 ▼

DOMINICAN REPUBLIC

✈ Airport Accommodations

Map Page	SANTO DOMINGO - LAS AMERICAS INTERNATIONAL AIRPORT	Diamond Rated	High Season	Page
42 p. 362	Quality Hotel Real Aeropuerto Santo Domingo, 1.2 mi (1.9 km) w of airport	▽▽▽	$84-$135 SAVE	376

✈ Airport Accommodations

Map Page	PUNTA CANA INTERNATIONAL AIRPORT	Diamond Rated	High Season	Page
17 p. 362	Tortuga Bay Punta Cana Resort & Club, 1 mi (1.6 km) w of airport	▽▽▽▽▽	$709-$950 SAVE	372

Dominican Republic and Haiti

This index helps you "spot" where approved hotels and restaurants are located on the corresponding detailed maps. Hotel daily rate range is for comparison only and show the property's high season. Restaurant rate range is a combination of lunch and/or dinner. Turn to the listing page for more detailed rate information and consult display ads for special promotions.

PUERTO PLATA

Map Page	Hotels	Diamond Rated	High Season	Page
2 p. 362	Club Hotel Riu Bachata	▽▽	$87-$226	364
6 p. 362	Casa Colonial Beach & Spa Hotel (See ad p. 364.)	▽▽▽▽	$286-$1200 SAVE	364

Map Page	Restaurants	Diamond Rated	Cuisine	Meal Range	Page
1 p. 362	Lucia Restaurant	▽▽▽▽	International	$20-$57	365
2 p. 362	Cariatides Restaurant & Bar	▽▽	International	$6-$27	365

PUNTA CANA

Map Page	Hotels	Diamond Rated	High Season	Page
7 p. 362	Hard Rock Hotel & Casino Punta Cana (See ad p. 368.)	▽▽▽▽	$254-$762 SAVE	367
8 p. 362	Dreams Palm Beach Punta Cana (See ad on insert.)	▽▽▽▽	$348-$1404 SAVE	366
9 p. 362	Dreams Punta Cana	▽▽▽▽	$466-$984 SAVE	366
10 p. 362	Melia Caribe Tropical (See ad p. 369.)	▽▽▽	$380-$800 SAVE	367
11 p. 362	Paradisus Punta Cana (See ad p. 371.)	▽▽▽▽	$590-$1000 SAVE	367
13 p. 362	Catalonia Bavaro Beach, Golf & Casino Resort (See ad p. 366.)	▽▽▽	$168-$248 SAVE	366
14 p. 362	Hotel Riu Palace Punta Cana	▽▽▽	$195-$497	367
15 p. 362	Be Live Grand Bavaro	▽▽▽	$294-$521	365
16 p. 362	Catalonia Royal Bavaro (See ad p. 366.)	▽▽▽▽	$200-$658 SAVE	366
17 p. 362	Tortuga Bay Punta Cana Resort & Club (See ad p. 374.)	▽▽▽▽▽	$709-$950 SAVE	372
19 p. 362	Sivory Punta Cana Boutique Hotel (See ad p. 373.)	▽▽▽▽	$350-$540 SAVE	372
21 p. 362	Paradisus Palma Real (See ad p. 370.)	▽▽▽▽	$364-$821 SAVE	367

Map Page	Restaurants	Diamond Rated	Cuisine	Meal Range	Page
5 p. 362	Hard Rock Cafe	▽▽	American	$12-$24 SAVE	375
35 p. 362	Gourmond Restaurant	▽▽▽▽	International	$38-$48	375
36 p. 362	Laveranda Restaurant	▽▽▽	Mediterranean	$14-$32	375
37 p. 362	Tau Restaurant	▽▽▽	Asian	$24-$45	375
42 p. 362	Bamboo	▽▽▽	International	$15-$85	375

SANTO DOMINGO

Map Page	Hotels	Diamond Rated	High Season	Page
32 p. 362	**Hilton Santo Domingo** *(See ad opposite title page.)*	◆◆◆	$94-$218 [SAVE]	376
34 p. 362	Courtyard by Marriott Santo Domingo	◆◆◆	$75-$189	375
42 p. 362	**Quality Hotel Real Aeropuerto Santo Domingo** *(See ad p. 376.)*	◆◆◆	$84-$135 [SAVE]	376
46 p. 362	Hotel Santo Domingo	◆◆	$106-$188	376
48 p. 362	**InterContinental V Centenario**	◆◆◆	$119-$169 [SAVE]	376

Map Page	Restaurants	Diamond Rated	Cuisine	Meal Range	Page
12 p. 362	El Conuco	◆◆	Dominican	$9-$18	377
13 p. 362	La Residence	◆◆◆	International	$16-$32	377
16 p. 362	Pat'e Palo European Brasserie	◆◆◆	International	$19-$30	378
17 p. 362	Le Patio	◆◆◆	International	$14-$26	377
18 p. 362	Museo del Jamon	◆◆	Spanish	$10-$28	377
20 p. 362	Hard Rock Cafe	◆◆	American	$12-$24 [SAVE]	377
21 p. 362	La Briciola Ristorante	◆◆	Italian	$12-$35	377
23 p. 362	Restaurante Cantabrico	◆◆	Spanish	$15-$32	378
27 p. 362	El Meson de la Cava	◆◆◆	International	$16-$34	377
29 p. 362	Vesuvio del Malecon	◆◆◆	Italian	$17-$30	378

BAYAHIBE

Map Page	Hotel	Diamond Rated	High Season	Page
60 p. 362	Iberostar Hacienda Dominicus	◆◆◆	Rates not provided	363

CABRERA

Map Page	Hotel	Diamond Rated	High Season	Page
67 p. 362	La Catalina	◆◆	$98-$168	363

CABARETE

Map Page	Hotel	Diamond Rated	High Season	Page
68 p. 362	Viva Wyndham Tangerine	◆◆	$195-$340	363

LAS GALERAS

Map Page	Hotel	Diamond Rated	High Season	Page
69 p. 362	Villa Serena Hotel	◆◆	$110-$120	364

LAS TERRENAS

Map Page	Hotel	Diamond Rated	High Season	Page
71 p. 362	Las Palmas Residence	◆◆	$70-$99	364

JUAN DOLIO

Map Page	Restaurants	Diamond Rated	Cuisine	Meal Range	Page
31 p. 362	El Sueno Ristorante	◆	Italian	$9-$20	363
32 p. 362	El Concon Restaurante	◆◆	International	$8-$22	363

BOCA CHICA

Map Page	Restaurant	Diamond Rated	Cuisine	Meal Range	Page
38 p. 362	Neptuno's Club	◆◆◆	Seafood	$12-$32	363

Find valuable AAA/CAA member savings
at AAA.com/discounts

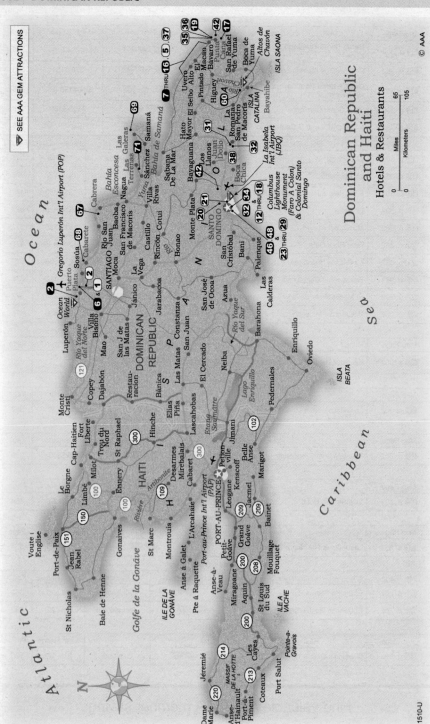

Dominican Republic and Haiti
Hotels & Restaurants

Miles
0 — 65
Kilometers
0 — 105

© AAA

1510-U

BAYAHIBE
• Hotels & Restaurants index & map p. 360

IBEROSTAR HACIENDA DOMINICUS
Phone: 809/688-3600

Resort Hotel
Rates not provided
Address: Playa Bayahibe **Location:** Oceanfront. 15 mi (24 km) e of La Romana International Airport. **Facility:** Offered at this oceanfront resort are well-appointed guest units and numerous dining options. 498 units. 3 stories (no elevator), exterior corridors. **Amenities:** safes (fee), honor bars. **Dining:** 5 restaurants, nightclub, entertainment. **Pool(s):** 3 outdoor. **Activities:** whirlpool, paddleboats, sailboats, windsurfing, snorkeling, recreation programs, volleyball, exercise room, spa. *Fee:* scuba diving. **Guest Services:** valet laundry.

VIVA WYNDHAM DOMINICUS BEACH
Phone: 809/686-5658

[fyi]   Not evaluated. **Address:** Bayahibe Rd **Location:** Oceanfront. At Playa Dominicus; 10.5 mi (16.8 km) e of La Romana International Airport; center of downtown. Facilities, services, and decor characterize a mid-scale property.

VIVA WYNDHAM DOMINICUS PALACE
Phone: 809/686-5658

[fyi]   Not evaluated. **Address:** Bayahibe Rd **Location:** Oceanfront. Center; at Playa Dominicus; 10.5 mi (16.8 km) e of La Romana International Airport. Facilities, services, and decor characterize a mid-scale property.

BOCA CHICA (C-5) pop. 46,385
• Hotels & Restaurants index & map p. 360

NEPTUNO'S CLUB
Phone: 809/523-4703   (38)

Seafood
$12-$32
AAA Inspector Notes: Sleek and chic, this restaurant is built over the water's edge of Boca Chica. The suave servers deliver well-prepared cuisine with Asian and Mediterranean influences. **Bar:** full bar. **Reservations:** suggested. **Address:** Duarte # 12 **Location:** Waterfront of Boca Chica; center, follow signs; adjacent to Oasis Hamaca Beach Resort Spa and Casino.

CABARETE (A-5)
• Hotels & Restaurants index & map p. 360

VIVA WYNDHAM TANGERINE
Phone: (809)571-0402   (68)

Resort Hotel
$195-$340
Address: Carretera Sosua-Cabarete **Location:** Oceanfront. Just w of center. **Facility:** This all-inclusive resort features a performance theatre for nightly entertainment; guest units vary in size but all are equipped for basic comfort. Meets AAA guest room security requirements. 273 units. 3 stories (no elevator), interior/exterior corridors. **Terms:** cancellation fee imposed. **Amenities:** *Fee:* high-speed Internet, safes. **Dining:** 3 restaurants, nightclub, entertainment. **Pool(s):** 2 outdoor. **Activities:** whirlpool, sailboats, windsurfing, lighted tennis court, recreation programs, playground, basketball, game room, volleyball, exercise room, spa. *Fee:* sauna, steamroom, snorkeling. **Guest Services:** valet laundry.

WHERE TO EAT

RESTAURANTE LA CASITA DE DON ALFREDO PAPI

[fyi]   Not evaluated. This popular beachfront restaurant is known for its shrimp dishes. **Address:** Carretera Principal

CABRERA
• Hotels & Restaurants index & map p. 360

LA CATALINA
Phone: 809/589-7700   (67)

Hotel
$98-$168
Address: Las Farollones Nagua MTS Rd **Location:** 1.1 mi (1.7 km) n of town, then just e, follow signs. **Facility:** 33 units, some two bedrooms and kitchens. 2 stories (no elevator), exterior corridors. **Terms:** office hours 7:30 am-11 pm, 30 day cancellation notice-fee imposed. **Amenities:** honor bars. *Some.* safes. **Pool(s):** 2 outdoor. **Activities:** lighted tennis court. *Fee:* massage. **Guest Services:** valet laundry, area transportation (fee)-beaches & golf course.

JARABACOA pop. 27,370

HOTEL GRAN JIMENOA
Phone: 809/574-6304

[fyi]   Not evaluated. **Address:** Main Rd **Location:** Center. Facilities, services, and decor characterize a mid-scale property.

HOTEL PINAR DORADO
Phone: 809/574-2820

[fyi]   Not evaluated. **Address:** Main Rd **Location:** Center; at Rio Yaque del Norte. Facilities, services, and decor characterize a mid-scale property.

RANCHO BAIGUATE
Phone: 809/574-6890

[fyi]   Not evaluated. **Address:** Jarabacao Rd **Location:** Center. Facilities, services, and decor characterize a mid-scale property.

JUAN DOLIO
• Hotels & Restaurants index & map p. 360

EL CONCON RESTAURANTE
Phone: 809/526-2652   (32)

International
$8-$22
AAA Inspector Notes: This covered outdoor restaurant offers a wide variety of options. There is a brick-oven for baking pizza and a paradilla (wood-fired grill) for grilling meats and some Italian and Continental specialties. Escalloped pork, shrimp rellenos, Creole-style goat and chicken cordon bleu are just a few of the dishes found at this restaurant. **Bar:** full bar. **Address:** Calle Buleval 1 Miramar **Location:** Center; at Villas del Mar.

EL SUENO RISTORANTE
Phone: 809/526-3903   (31)

Italian
$9-$20
AAA Inspector Notes: Across from the ocean on the mini-malecon is this Italian-owned and -operated eatery. Fresh seafood dishes ranging from calamari and shrimp to fish and octopus are popular. Lackadaisical service prevails, so relax with a cold beer or glass of wine and savor the moment while the meal is prepared. **Bar:** full bar. **Address:** Calle Principal **Location:** Center; on Malecon. **Parking:** street only.

LA ROMANA (C-6) pop. 191,303

CASA DE CAMPO
Phone: 809/523-3333

[fyi]   Not evaluated. **Address:** Casa de Campo Rd **Location:** 5.6 mi (9 km) s of La Romana Airport. Facilities, services, and decor characterize a mid-scale property.

LAS GALERAS
• Hotels & Restaurants index & map p. 360

VILLA SERENA HOTEL   Phone: 809/538-0000   [69]

Country Inn
$110-$120
Address: Las Galeras Beach **Location:** Oceanfront. On Samana Peninsula; near downtown. **Facility:** 21 units. 2 stories (no elevator), interior corridors. **Terms:** office hours 8 am-9 pm, 14 day cancellation notice-fee imposed. **Amenities:** safes. **Pool(s):** outdoor. **Activities:** snorkeling, bicycles. *Fee:* massage. **Guest Services:** valet laundry.

LAS TERRENAS
• Hotels & Restaurants index & map p. 360

LAS PALMAS RESIDENCE   Phone: 809/240-6436   [71]
Cottage
$70-$99
Address: Calle Esq Benelux #1 **Location:** Just e of commercial center; across from Playa Las Terrenas. **Facility:** 17 cottages. 2 stories (no elevator), exterior corridors. *Bath:* shower only. **Terms:** office hours 8 am-7 pm, 2-7 night minimum stay - seasonal and/or weekends, 14 day cancellation notice. **Amenities:** high-speed Internet, safes.

PUERTO PLATA (A-4) pop. 112,036
• Hotels & Restaurants index & map p. 360

CASA COLONIAL BEACH & SPA HOTEL
Phone: (809)320-3232   [6]

Boutique Resort Hotel
$286-$1200
Address: Playa Dorada Complex **Location:** Oceanfront. 8.1 mi (13 km) w of Puerto Plata Airport; in Playa Dorada Beach Complex. **Facility:** Guest rooms at the boutique-style, oceanfront resort are spacious and well appointed with fine furnishings and plenty of amenities. 50 units. 4 stories, interior/exterior corridors. **Parking:** on-site and valet. **Amenities:** safes, honor bars. **Dining:** 2 restaurants, also, Lucia Restaurant, see separate listing. **Pool(s):** outdoor. **Activities:** saunas, whirlpools, steamrooms, rental paddleboats, rental sailboats, rental sailboards, 2 lighted tennis courts, spa. **Guest Services:** valet laundry. **Free Special Amenities:** full breakfast and early check-in/late check-out. *(See ad this page.)*
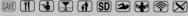

CLUB HOTEL RIU BACHATA
Phone: (809)320-1010   [2]
Resort Hotel
$87-$226
Address: Bahia de Maimon **Location:** Oceanfront. 4.4 mi (7 km) w of town; 17.5 mi (28 km) w of Puerto Plata Airport. **Facility:** 610 units. 2-3 stories (no elevator), interior corridors. **Terms:** 3 night minimum stay, 7 day cancellation notice-fee imposed. **Amenities:** safes, honor bars. **Dining:** 2 restaurants, nightclub, entertainment. **Pool(s):** 2 outdoor. **Activities:** whirlpool, paddleboats, sailboats, windsurfing, snorkeling, 2 lighted tennis courts, recreation programs, playground, sports court, game room, volleyball, exercise room, spa. *Fee:* sauna, scuba diving. **Guest Services:** valet laundry.

▼ *See AAA listing this page* ▼

(See index & map p. 360.)

BARCELO PUERTO PLATA   Phone: 809/320-5084

 Not evaluated. **Address:** Compejo Playa Dorada **Location:** Oceanfront. 11 mi (18 km) w of Puerto Plata International Airport. Facilities, services, and decor characterize a mid-scale property.

WHERE TO EAT

CARIATIDES RESTAURANT & BAR
                              Phone: 809/320-1410

International
$6-$27

AAA Inspector Notes: Patrons enjoy a "semi-al fresco" experience at the inviting eatery, which has a background waterfall in its garden setting. The international menu lists at least six soups, varied pasta dishes, pork chops, lamb and paella, in addition to eight tempting desserts. **Bar:** full bar. **Reservations:** suggested. **Address:** Plaza el Doral **Location:** Just e of downtown; in Plaza el Doral. B L D

LUCIA RESTAURANT   Phone: 809/320-3232   1

International
$20-$57

AAA Inspector Notes: This restaurant features refined surroundings and attentive service. The chef combines the best elements of Dominican, Italian and Asian cuisine. Starter options include Thai or Caesar salad, ceviche and foie gras. The well-prepared entrees range from Caribbean lobster and venison to curried goat and Chilean sea bass. After dinner, there are many tempting desserts available. **Bar:** full bar. **Reservations:** required. **Address:** Playa Dorada Complex **Location:** 8.1 mi (13 km) w of Puerto Plata Airport; in Playa Dorada Beach Complex; in Casa Colonial Beach & Spa Hotel. **Parking:** valet only. D

PUNTA CANA (B-6)
- **Restaurants p. 375**
- **Hotels & Restaurants index & map p. 360**

BE LIVE GRAND BAVARO
                              Phone: (809)686-9898   **15**

Resort Hotel
$294-$521

Address: Carretera Cabeza de Toro, KM 7 **Location:** Oceanfront. 14 mi (22 km) e of Punta Cana International Airport. **Facility:** This attractive, contemporary all-inclusive property offers added services and is ideal for families, couples or a business getaway meeting. Located along a white sugar sand beach with crystal clear water this complete resort also features a free form swimming pool with a swim-up bar and expanded fitness room facilities. 248 units. 3 stories, exterior corridors. **Terms:** 3 day cancellation notice-fee imposed. **Amenities:** safes (fee). *Some:* high-speed Internet (fee). **Dining:** entertainment. **Pool(s):** 4 outdoor. **Activities:** paddleboats, sailboats, windsurfing, snorkeling, recreation programs, bicycles, playground, game room, volleyball, exercise room, spa. *Fee:* waterskiing, scuba diving, 2 lighted tennis courts, horseback riding. **Guest Services:** valet laundry.

Safety tip: Keep a current
AAA/CAA Road Atlas
in every vehicle

(See index & map p. 360.)

CATALONIA BAVARO BEACH, GOLF & CASINO RESORT
Phone: 809/412-0000 **13**

Resort Hotel
$168-$248

Address: Cabeza de Toro **Location:** Oceanfront. 10.4 mi (16.7 km) ne of Punta Cana Airport; follow signs; in Bavaro area. **Facility:** This all-inclusive beachside resort offers an abundance of dining and recreational opportunities; a variety of guest units are available. 711 units, some two and three bedrooms. 3 stories (no elevator), exterior corridors. **Parking:** on-site and valet. **Terms:** cancellation fee imposed. **Amenities:** safes, honor bars. **Dining:** 9 restaurants, nightclub, entertainment. **Pool(s):** 2 outdoor. **Activities:** sauna, whirlpool, steamroom, paddleboats, sailboats, windsurfing, snorkeling, racquetball court, recreation programs, bicycles, jogging, playground, sports court, basketball, horseshoes, volleyball, exercise room, spa. *Fee:* scuba diving, golf-27 holes, 2 lighted tennis courts. **Guest Services:** valet laundry. *(See ad this page.)*

CATALONIA ROYAL BAVARO
Phone: 809/412-0011 **16**

Resort Hotel
$200-$658

Address: Cabeza de Toro **Location:** Oceanfront. 10.4 mi (16.7 km) ne of Punta Cana Airport, follow signs; in Bavaro area. **Facility:** This chic adults-only property offers spacious well-appointed guest units with all the extra comforts and pampering needed for a relaxing getaway. 255 units, some two bedrooms. 2-3 stories (no elevator), exterior corridors. **Parking:** on-site and valet. **Terms:** age restrictions may apply, cancellation fee imposed. **Amenities:** safes, honor bars. **Dining:** 3 restaurants, entertainment. **Pool(s):** 2 outdoor. **Activities:** sauna, whirlpools, steamroom, paddleboats, sailboats, windsurfing, snorkeling, recreation programs, bicycles, jogging, sports court, basketball, horseshoes, shuffleboard, volleyball, exercise room, spa. *Fee:* scuba diving, golf-27 holes, 2 lighted tennis courts. **Guest Services:** valet laundry. *(See ad this page.)*

DREAMS PALM BEACH PUNTA CANA
Phone: (809)552-6000 **8**

Resort Hotel
$348-$1404

Address: Cabeza de Toro **Location:** Oceanfront. At Cabeza de Toro; 14.2 mi (22.7 km) e of Punta Cana International Airport. **Facility:** This all-inclusive oceanfront resort with lush landscaping and a variety of theme restaurants offers eight room categories, some with a whirlpool tub. 500 units. 3 stories, interior corridors. **Parking:** on-site and valet. **Terms:** 3 day cancellation notice-fee imposed. **Amenities:** high-speed Internet (fee), safes, honor bars. **Dining:** 7 restaurants, nightclub, entertainment. **Pool(s):** 3 outdoor. **Activities:** paddleboats, sailboats, windsurfing, snorkeling, 2 lighted tennis courts, recreation programs, playground, basketball, game room, shuffleboard, volleyball, exercise room, spa. *Fee:* saunas, whirlpools, steamroom, scuba diving. **Guest Services:** valet laundry. *(See ad on insert.)*

DREAMS PUNTA CANA
Phone: 809/682-0404 **9**

Resort Hotel
$466-$984

Address: Playa De Uvero Alto **Location:** Oceanfront. 22 mi (35.2 km) n of Punta Cana International Airport; in Uvero Alto. **Facility:** Featured are well-appointed units, comprehensive resort facilities and multiple recreation and dining options. Meets AAA guest room security requirements. 620 units. 3 stories (no elevator), interior corridors. **Parking:** on-site and valet. **Terms:** 7 day cancellation notice-fee imposed. **Amenities:** high-speed Internet (fee), safes, honor bars. **Dining:** 6 restaurants, nightclub, entertainment. **Pool(s):** outdoor. **Activities:** whirlpool, lifeguard on duty, canoeing, paddleboats, sailboats, windsurfing, snorkeling, 2 lighted tennis courts, recreation programs, playground, sports court, basketball, game room, volleyball, spa. *Fee:* saunas, steamrooms, scuba diving. **Guest Services:** valet laundry.

Visit AAA.com or CAA.ca
for one-stop travel
planning and reservations

(See index & map p. 360.)

HARD ROCK HOTEL & CASINO PUNTA CANA
Phone: (809)731-0099 **7**

Resort Hotel
$254-$762

Address: Blvd Turistico Del Este KM 28 Parc 74 23000 **Location:** Oceanfront. 17.5 mi (28 km) from Punta Cana International Airport; in Macao. **Facility:** This mega all-inclusive oceanfront resort features extensive facilities, very spacious guest rooms loaded with amenities, numerous dining options and a world-class spa. Meets AAA guest room security requirements. 1790 units. 3-4 stories, interior corridors. **Parking:** on-site and valet. **Terms:** 3 night minimum stay, 3 day cancellation notice-fee imposed. **Amenities:** video games (fee), high-speed Internet, safes. **Dining:** 9 restaurants, nightclub, entertainment. **Pool(s):** 13 outdoor. **Activities:** waterslide, lifeguard on duty, miniature golf, 2 lighted tennis courts, recreation programs, bicycles, playground, basketball, game room, volleyball, spa. *Fee:* saunas, whirlpools, steamrooms, paddleboats, sailboats, windsurfing, scuba diving, snorkeling, golf-18 holes. **Guest Services:** valet laundry. **Free Special Amenities: early check-in/late check-out and high-speed Internet.**
(See ad p. 368.)

HOTEL RIU PALACE PUNTA CANA
Phone: (809)687-4242 **14**

Resort Hotel
$195-$497 5/1-11/30
$156-$265 12/1-4/30

Address: Arena Gorda **Location:** Oceanfront. 19 mi (30 km) ne from Punta Cana Airport. **Facility:** The property features grand public areas, lots of recreational opportunities and multiple dining outlets; guest units are modest but comfortable. 612 units. 4 stories, interior/exterior corridors. **Terms:** 3 night minimum stay, 7 day cancellation notice-fee imposed. **Amenities:** safes, honor bars. **Dining:** 6 restaurants, entertainment. **Pool(s):** outdoor. **Activities:** whirlpool, paddleboats, sailboats, windsurfing, snorkeling, 2 lighted tennis courts, recreation programs, playground, game room, volleyball, exercise room, spa. *Fee:* saunas, scuba diving. **Guest Services:** valet laundry.

MELIA CARIBE TROPICAL
Phone: (809)221-1290 **10**

Resort Hotel
$380-$800

Address: Playa de Bavaro **Location:** Oceanfront. Northeast of airport. **Facility:** This sprawling, all-inclusive mega-resort boasts 13 theme restaurants, a live performance theater, multiple swimming pools and junior suite-style rooms. 1128 units, some efficiencies. 2 stories (no elevator), exterior corridors. **Terms:** 3 day cancellation notice. **Amenities:** safes. *Some:* video games. **Dining:** 14 restaurants, nightclub, entertainment. **Pool(s):** 6 outdoor. **Activities:** saunas, whirlpools, steamrooms, lifeguard on duty, canoeing, paddleboats, sailboats, windsurfing, snorkeling, 8 lighted tennis courts, recreation programs, playground, sports court, basketball, game room, volleyball, spa. *Fee:* scuba diving, golf-27 holes. **Guest Services:** valet laundry. **Free Special Amenities: children's activities.** *(See ad p. 369.)*

   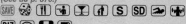
PARAD...

Res...
$3...

Activities: whirlpools, paddleboats, sailboats, windsurfing, scuba diving, snorkeling, 3 lighted tennis courts, recreation programs, bicycles, horseback riding, playground, game room, horseshoes, volleyball, spa. *Fee:* saunas, steamrooms, charter fishing, golf-27 holes. **Guest Services:** valet laundry. **Free Special Amenities: room upgrade (subject to availability with advance reservations).**
(See ad p. 370.)

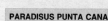

PARADISUS PUNTA CANA
Phone: (809)687-9923 **11**

Resort Hotel
$590-$1000

Address: Playa de Bavaro **Location:** Oceanfront. 13.5 mi (21.6 km) n from Punta Cana Airport; just off Punta Cana Higuey Rd. **Facility:** This is truly a complete resort, with a plethora of leisure and recreational activities; find spacious, junior suite-size units and a pleasant staff. 689 units, some two bedrooms. 2-3 stories (no elevator), exterior corridors. **Terms:** 3 day cancellation notice-fee imposed. **Amenities:** safes, honor bars. **Dining:** 12 restaurants, nightclub, entertainment. **Pool(s):** 8 outdoor. **Activities:** whirlpools, canoeing, paddleboats, sailboats, windsurfing, scuba diving, snorkeling, golf-27 holes, 4 lighted tennis courts, recreation programs, bicycles, jogging, horseback riding, playground, basketball, game room, volleyball, exercise room, spa. *Fee:* saunas, steamrooms. **Guest Services:** valet laundry. **Free Special Amenities: early check-in/late check-out and room upgrade (subject to availability with advance reservations).**
(See ad p. 371.)

ALL-INCLUSIVE CARIBBEAN HOTEL & CASINO **PUNTA CANA**

LUXURIOUS ACCOMMODATIONS. CASINO. ROCK SPA®. NICKLAUS DESIGN GOLF COURSE.
9 RESTAURANTS. 15 BARS. 15 POOLS.

$**1,500** RESORT CREDIT

BOOK NOW AND RECEIVE $1,500 RESORT CREDIT*

Vacation like a rock star with $1,500 of spa treatments, golf, casino gaming, Dominican tours, even one of our Precious Wedding Collection™ packages.

Punta Cana, Dominican Republic
888-ROCK-002. hardrockhotelpuntacana.com

▼ *See AAA listing p. 367* ▼

Paradisus

PALMA REAL RESORT
DOMINICAN REPUBLIC

Experience the wonders of Paradisus Palma Real, where stunning Mediterranean architecture is framed by an endless Caribbean shoreline. Relaxation is our beachfront free-form swimming pool, championship golf, or horseback riding along the coast. Savor seven diverse dining experiences. Rejuvenate and reinvigorate at YHI Spa. Royal Service is a private, romantic getaway exclusively for adults. Family Concierge is personal, dedicated, and liberating.

The Pure Freedom to Just Be

Contact your travel specialist, call **888.741.5600** or visit **WWW.PARADISUS.COM**

COSTA RICA | DOMINICAN REPUBLIC | MEXICO

A Sol Meliá Hotels & Resorts Brand.

Paradisus

PUNTA CANA RESORT
DOMINICAN REPUBLIC

Experience the beauty of Paradisus Punta Cana, where lush tropical gardens brush an immaculate Caribbean shore. Where international cuisine reigns. Where glimmering pools lead the way to the Spa and white-sand beaches. The Reserve offers the finest in all-suite residential accommodations with its own special pools, restaurants, and private beach. Royal Service is a private, romantic getaway exclusively for adults. Family Concierge is personal, dedicated, and liberating.

The Pure Freedom to Just Be

Contact your travel specialist, call **888.741.5600** or visit **WWW.PARADISUS.COM**

COSTA RICA | DOMINICAN REPUBLIC | MEXICO

A Sol Meliá Hotels & Resorts Brand.

(See index & map p. 360.)

SIVORY PUNTA CANA BOUTIQUE HOTEL
Phone: 809/333-0500 **19**

Boutique Hotel
$350-$540

Address: Uvero Alto, Main Rd **Location:** Oceanfront. 25 mi (40 km) n of Punta Cana International Airport. **Facility:** These bungalow-style units are spaced apart in natural garden areas, some with ocean views; an attentive staff caters to the details. 55 units, some two bedrooms. 2 stories (no elevator), exterior corridors. **Parking:** on-site and valet. **Terms:** cancellation fee imposed. **Amenities:** high-speed Internet, safes, honor bars. **Dining:** Gourmond Restaurant, Laveranda Restaurant, Tau Restaurant, see separate listings, entertainment. **Pool(s):** outdoor. **Activities:** sauna, whirlpool, steamroom, sailboats, windsurfing, snorkeling, tennis court, exercise room, spa. **Guest Services:** valet laundry. **Free Special Amenities:** full breakfast and high-speed Internet.
(See ad p. 373.)

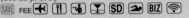

TORTUGA BAY PUNTA CANA RESORT & CLUB
Phone: 809-959-2269 **17**

Boutique Resort Hotel
$709-$950

Address: Punta Cana Main Rd **Location:** Oceanfront. 1 mi (1.6 km) w of airport. **Facility:** Located in a gated community, these spacious, luxurious residential-style guest units feature every conceivable amenity. 30 units, some two bedrooms. 2 stories (no elevator), exterior corridors. **Terms:** 21 day cancellation notice-fee imposed. **Amenities:** high-speed Internet, safes, honor bars. **Dining:** 2 restaurants, also, Bamboo, see separate listing, entertainment. **Pool(s):** 2 outdoor. **Activities:** saunas, whirlpool, steamrooms, fishing, 3 lighted tennis courts, recreation programs, bicycles, horseback riding, exercise room, spa. *Fee:* scuba diving, snorkeling, charter fishing, golf-36 holes. **Guest Services:** valet laundry. **Free Special Amenities:** full breakfast and high-speed Internet.
(See ad p. 374.)

BARCELO BAVARO PALACE DELUXE
Phone: 809/686-5797

fyi Not evaluated. **Address:** Barcelo Bavaro Complex **Location:** Oceanfront. 12.5 mi (20 km) n of the Punta Cana International Airport; in Bavaro area. Facilities, services, and decor characterize a mid-scale property.

IBEROSTAR BAVARO
Phone: 809/221-6500

fyi Not evaluated. **Address:** Carretera Arena Gorda **Location:** Oceanfront. Center of Bavaro. Facilities, services, and decor characterize a mid-scale property.

Learn about
AAA/CAA Diamond Ratings
at AAA.com/Diamonds

▼ *See AAA listing p. 372* ▼

SIVORY PUNTA CANA BOUTIQUE HOTEL

This welcoming AAA 4 Diamond awarded sandy beach resort is high on style and comfort. East Asian influences are seen throughout combining the natural beauty of the eastern Caribbean with the style of a traditional Polynesian paradise. Each of the beautifully designed rooms features the finest furnishings and has a private balcony or patio.

There are 3 unique restaurants including the AAA 4 Diamond awarded Gourmand restaurant, a cigar lounge and an extensive wine library housing an impressive selection of 8,000 bottles of the world's finest wine to enjoy. And the Aquarea Spa & Wellness Center, situated within 4,300 sq. ft. of lush tropical gardens, will help you achieve the maximum level of relaxation during your stay. Whether walking the pristine beach, lounging by the infinity pool or experiencing Caribbean-infused cuisine, you are guaranteed personalized service and exceptional luxury.

PLAYA SIVORY, UVERO ALTO/PUNTA CANA
+1.855.748.6790
www.sivorypuntacana.com

Get the free mobile app at
http://gettag.mobi

Authentically Dominican
Uniquely PUNTACANA

30 Suites designed by Oscar de la Renta
36 Holes Of Championship Golf On Two Courses
Designed By Tom Fazio & P.B. Dye
5 Miles Of Private Beach
Six Senses Spa

THE LEADING HOTELS
OF THE WORLD®

TORTUGA BAY

AAA
Five Diamond
Award

www.puntacana.com | info@puntacana.com | 888.442.2262

(See index & map p. 360.)

IBEROSTAR GRAND HOTEL BAVARO
Phone: 809/221-6500

fyi Not evaluated. **Address:** Carretera Arena Gorda **Location:** Oceanfront. Center of Bavaro. Facilities, services, and decor characterize a mid-scale property. ***(See ad on insert.)***

IBEROSTAR PUNTA CANA & DOMINICANA
Phone: 809/221-6500

fyi Not evaluated. **Address:** Carr Arena Gorda **Location:** Oceanfront. Center of Bavaro. Facilities, services, and decor characterize a mid-scale property.

RIU BAMBU HOTEL **Phone:** 809/221-7575

fyi Not evaluated. **Address:** Playa Arena Gorda **Location:** Oceanfront. 19 mi (30.4 km) n from Punta Cana Airport. Facilities, services, and decor characterize a mid-scale property.

RIU NAIBOA HOTEL **Phone:** 809/221-7515

fyi Not evaluated. **Address:** Playa Arena Gorda Higuey Rd **Location:** Oceanfront. 19 mi (30.4 km) n from Punta Cana Airport. Facilities, services, and decor characterize a mid-scale property.

RIU PALACE MACAO HOTEL **Phone:** 809/221-7171

fyi Not evaluated. **Address:** 109 Playa Arena Gorda, Higuey Rd **Location:** Oceanfront. 19 mi (30.4 km) n from Punta Cana Airport. Facilities, services, and decor characterize a mid-scale property.

RIU TAINO HOTEL **Phone:** 809/221-2290

fyi Not evaluated. **Address:** Playa Arena Gorda, Higuey Rd **Location:** Oceanfront. 19 mi (30.4 km) n from Punta Cana Airport. Facilities, services, and decor characterize a mid-scale property.

WHERE TO EAT

BAMBOO **Phone:** 809/959-2269 (42)

International
$15-$85

AAA Inspector Notes: Located on the posh grounds of a residential-inspired resort is this somewhat casual and child-friendly restaurant that offers exquisite cuisine. The talented chef prepares a variety of comfort-food and such Dominican dishes as goat stew and sancocho. Other highlights include New Zealand lamb loin, Kurobuta pork, Atlantic salmon and Chilean sea bass with an eggplant compote. Also featured are a well-rounded wine list, a caviar menu for the true gourmand and an extensive cigar and cordial menu. **Bar:** full bar. **Reservations:** required. **Address:** Punta Cana Main Rd **Location:** 1 mi (1.6 km) w of airport; in Tortuga Bay Punta Cana Resort & Club. **Parking:** on-site and valet. B L D

GOURMOND RESTAURANT
Phone: 809/333-0500 (35)

International
$38-$48

AAA Inspector Notes: Start with foie gras mixed with apples and crab or celery velouté poured over tartar lobster quenelle. For the main course, choose from such favorites as grilled sea bass over creamy pumpkin risotto or confit of lamb served with dried fruit pilaf. The well-presented dessert selection varies from coconut mousse wrapped in a rice noodle nest and chocolate and carrot sponge served over pumpkin gelee and blackberries topped with cinnamon meringue. A cup of their premium coffee is the perfect ending. **Bar:** full bar. **Reservations:** required. **Address:** Uvero Alto, Main Rd **Location:** 25 mi (40 km) n of Punta Cana International Airport; in Sivory Punta Cana. **Parking:** on-site and valet. D

HARD ROCK CAFE **Phone:** 809/552-0594 (5)

American
$12-$24

AAA Inspector Notes: Rock 'n' roll memorabilia decorates the walls of the popular theme restaurant. Live music on the weekends contributes to the bustling atmosphere. On the menu is a wide variety of American cuisine--from burgers and sandwiches to seafood, steaks and pasta. **Bar:** full bar. **Address:** Plaza Palma Real **Location:** Center; adjacent to Paradisus Palma Real Resort.
SAVE L D

LAVERANDA RESTAURANT
Phone: 809/333-0500 (36)

Mediterranean
$14-$32

AAA Inspector Notes: Situated near the ocean and alongside an attractive designer pool, the restaurant provides professional, attentive service. Recommended starters include the fish ceviche or lobster bisque. A main plate favorite is the seafood hot pot which includes clams, shrimp, lobster and fish simmered in a saffron-coconut ginger broth. **Bar:** full bar. **Reservations:** suggested. **Address:** Uvero Alto, Main Rd **Location:** 25 mi (40 km) n of Punta Cana International Airport; in Sivory Punta Cana. **Parking:** on-site and valet. B L D

TAU RESTAURANT **Phone:** 809/333-0500 (37)

Asian
$24-$45

AAA Inspector Notes: This restaurant offers an attractive Zen-style dining area and a kitchen that prepares exquisite Pan-Asian cuisine. **Bar:** full bar. **Reservations:** required. **Address:** Uvero Alto, Main Rd **Location:** 25 mi (40 km) n of Punta Cana International Airport; in Sivory Punta Cana. **Parking:** on-site and valet.
D

HURACAN CAFE **Phone:** 809/221-6643

fyi Not evaluated. This chic oceanfront eatery offers a menu with influences ranging from Italian to Tex-Mex. **Address:** Main Rd **Location:** Center of Punta Cana.

LA YOLA **Phone:** 809/959-2262

fyi Not evaluated. Al fresco waterfront dining featuring Caribbean cuisine with Mediterranean influences at this casual spot. **Address:** Punta Cana Main Rd **Location:** 1 mi (1.6 km) w of airport; inside Tortuga Bay Punta Cana Resort & Club.

RESTAURANTE PULPO COJO

fyi Not evaluated. This popular seaside restaurant serves up large portions of grilled and fried seafood. **Address:** Playa Cortecito **Location:** In Bavaro area at Playa Cortecito.

SANTO DOMINGO (C-5) pop. 1,887,586

- **Restaurants p. 377**
- **Hotels & Restaurants index & map p. 360**

COURTYARD BY MARRIOTT SANTO DOMINGO
Phone: (809)685-1010 (34)

Hotel
$75-$189

AAA Benefit:
AAA hotel discounts of 5% or more.

Address: 50 A Maximo Gomez Ave **Location:** Center of downtown; 12.5 mi (20 km) w of Las Americas International Airport. **Facility:** Meets AAA guest room security requirements. 143 units. 5 stories, interior corridors. **Amenities:** video games (fee), high-speed Internet, safes. **Pool(s):** outdoor. **Activities:** exercise room. **Guest Services:** valet and coin laundry.
S SD BIZ FEE / SOME UNITS

(See index & map p. 360.)

HILTON SANTO DOMINGO

Phone: (809)685-0000 **32**

Hotel
$94-$218

AAA Benefit: Members save 5% or more everyday!

Address: 500 Ave George Washington **Location:** Center; on Malecon; at Malecon Center. **Facility:** Adjacent to the Malecon Shopping Center, the high-rise hotel offers contemporary, stylish guest rooms; a rooftop pool grants nice views. 228 units. 21 stories, interior corridors. **Terms:** 1-7 night minimum stay, cancellation fee imposed. **Amenities:** high-speed Internet (fee), safes, honor bars. **Pool(s):** outdoor. **Activities:** exercise room. *Fee:* massage. **Guest Services:** valet laundry. *(See ad opposite title page.)*

SAVE 🛎 🍴 🛜 🍸 S SD 🏊 BIZ 🛜 ▣ / SOME UNITS 🖥

HOTEL SANTO DOMINGO

Phone: (809)221-1511 **46**

Hotel
$106-$188

Address: Ave Independencia Abraham Lincoln 2122 **Location:** Corner of Independencia and Abraham Lincoln aves. **Facility:** 215 units. 3 stories, interior corridors.
Parking: on-site and valet. **Terms:** cancellation fee imposed. **Amenities:** high-speed Internet, safes, honor bars. **Dining:** 2 restaurants, entertainment. **Pool(s):** outdoor. **Activities:** saunas, 3 lighted tennis courts, exercise room, massage. **Guest Services:** valet laundry.

🍴 🍸 SD 🏊 BIZ 🛜

INTERCONTINENTAL V CENTENARIO

Phone: (809)221-0000 **48**

Hotel
$119-$169

Address: 218 Ave George Washington **Location:** Downtown; on Malecon. **Facility:** This hotel promises guests sweeping views and comprehensive public areas; several executive concierge units are available with personalized service. 196 units. 15 stories, interior corridors. **Amenities:** video games, high-speed Internet, safes, honor bars. **Dining:** 2 restaurants, name entertainment. **Pool(s):** outdoor. **Activities:** whirlpool, lighted tennis court, exercise room, spa. *Fee:* saunas. **Guest Services:** valet laundry. **Free Special Amenities:** room upgrade (subject to availability with advance reservations) and high-speed Internet.

SAVE 🛎 🍴 🛜 🍸 S SD 🏊 BIZ 🛜

FEE 🎬

QUALITY HOTEL REAL AEROPUERTO SANTO DOMINGO

Phone: (809)549-2525 **42**

Hotel
$84-$135

Address: KM 22 Autopista Las Americas **Location:** 11.2 mi (18 km) e of downtown; 1.2 mi (1.9 km) w of Las Americas International Airport. **Facility:** Meets AAA guest room security requirements. 124 units. 4 stories, interior corridors. **Terms:** cancellation fee imposed. **Pool(s):** outdoor. **Activities:** exercise room, spa. **Guest Services:** valet and coin laundry. **Free Special Amenities:** full breakfast and high-speed Internet.
(See ad this page.)

SAVE 🍴 🛜 🍸 CALL 🚹M

S SD 🏊 BIZ 🛜 ▣ / SOME UNITS 🖥

▼ *See AAA listing this page* ▼

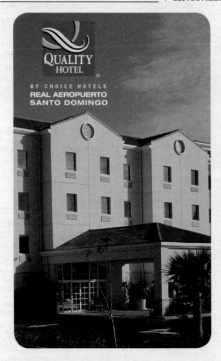

(See index & map p. 360.)

COCO BOUTIQUE HOTEL Phone: 809/685-8467
fyi Not evaluated. **Address:** 7 Arzobispo Porte **Location:** Center of Colonial City; between Calle Las Damas and Isabel la Catolica. Facilities, services, and decor characterize a mid-scale property.

EL BEATERIO Phone: 809/687-8657
fyi Not evaluated. **Address:** 8 Calle Duarte **Location:** In Colonial City; between Arzobispo Nouel and Padre Billini sts. Facilities, services, and decor characterize a mid-scale property.

EUROPA HOTEL BOUTIQUE Phone: 809/285-0005
fyi Not evaluated. **Address:** Arzobispo Merino #109 **Location:** Corner of Arzobispo Merino and Emiliano Tejera. Facilities, services, and decor characterize a mid-scale property.

HODELPA CARIBE COLONIAL Phone: 809/688-7799
fyi Not evaluated. **Address:** 159 Isabel La Catolica **Location:** Center of Colonial City. Facilities, services, and decor characterize a mid-scale property.

HOSTAL NOMADAS Phone: 809/689-0057
fyi Not evaluated. **Address:** 299 Calle Hostos **Location:** Corner of Hostos and Las Mercedes calles; across from La Altagracia Church; in Colonial City. Facilities, services, and decor characterize a mid-scale property.

HOTEL ATARAZANA Phone: 809/688-3693
fyi Not evaluated. **Address:** 19 Calle Duarte **Location:** Center of Colonial City. Facilities, services, and decor characterize a mid-scale property.

HOTEL DONA ELVIRA Phone: 809/221-7415
fyi Not evaluated. **Address:** 207 Padre Billini St **Location:** Center of Colonial City. Facilities, services, and decor characterize a mid-scale property.

HOTEL FRANCES SANTO DOMINGO Phone: 809/685-9331
fyi Not evaluated. **Address:** Calle Las Mercedes est. Arzobispo Merino **Location:** Center of Colonial City. Facilities, services, and decor characterize a mid-scale property.

HOTEL RESIDENCIA Phone: 809/412-7298
fyi Not evaluated. **Address:** 62 Calle Danae **Location:** In Gazcua. Facilities, services, and decor characterize a mid-scale property.

HOTEL VILLA COLONIAL Phone: 809/221-1049
fyi Not evaluated. **Address:** 157 Sanchez St **Location:** Center of Colonial City. Facilities, services, and decor characterize a mid-scale property.

WHERE TO EAT

EL CONUCO Phone: 809/686-0129 (12)
Dominican
$9-$18

AAA Inspector Notes: Under several festively decorated bohios, the semi-al fresco and decidedly Dominican eatery provides not only island cuisine but also nightly Dominican-style entertainment. Besides the sancocho, an obligatory national dish, diners are in for a treat with such signature dishes as tostones, platanos, yuca and chicharrones (deep-fried chicken and pork). **Bar:** full bar. **Reservations:** suggested. **Address:** Casimiro de Moya 152 **Location:** In Sector Gazcue; next to Iglesia San Antonio. **Parking:** street only.

EL MESON DE LA CAVA Phone: 809/533-2818 (27)
International
$16-$34

AAA Inspector Notes: This spectacular restaurant is built in a natural cavern 40 feet underground. Service is formal. Flavorful cuisine is well-presented and served in sizable portions. **Bar:** full bar. **Reservations:** suggested. **Address:** Ave Mirador Sur, #1 **Location:** Near southeast end of Paseo de los Indios; 0.6 mi (1 km) w of jct Jimenez Nova and Mirador Sur aves. **Parking:** on-site and valet. L D

HARD ROCK CAFE Phone: 809/686-7771 (20)
American
$12-$24

AAA Inspector Notes: Rock 'n' roll memorabilia decorates the walls of the popular theme restaurant. Live music on the weekends contributes to the bustling atmosphere. On the menu is a wide variety of American cuisine-- from burgers and sandwiches to seafood, steaks and pasta. **Bar:** full bar. **Address:** El Conde 103, Colonial City District **Location:** Center of historical district along pedestrian promenade. **Parking:** valet and street only.
SAVE L D LATE

LA BRICIOLA RISTORANTE Phone: 809/688-5055 (21)
Italian
$12-$35

AAA Inspector Notes: The restaurant offers dining in a refined setting but is challenged by the mediocre service and cuisine descriptions that sound better than what is actually delivered. Various beef, chicken and pasta dishes are featured. **Bar:** full bar. **Reservations:** suggested. **Address:** 152 A Arzobispo Merino **Location:** Corner of Calle Padre Bellini and Arzobispo Merino; across from Plaza Colon in Colonial City District. **Parking:** on-site (fee) and street. Historic L D

LA RESIDENCE Phone: 809/685-9955 (13)
International
$16-$32

AAA Inspector Notes: In a restored 15th-century mansion is the exquisite restaurant, which presents a menu of gourmet meals enhanced by plate presentations. Dapper servers exude congenial hospitality. The broad menu lists expertly prepared roasted duck breast, veal cutlet, steamed sea bream in a banana leaf and hand-made ravioli stuffed with prawns and wild mushrooms. One house-favorite dessert is the warm chocolate cake with mint-cinnamon ice cream. **Bar:** full bar. **Reservations:** required. **Address:** Calle Las Damas **Location:** Entrance to Colonial City District; in Nicolas de Ovando Santo Domingo. Historic
B L D LATE

LE PATIO Phone: 809/685-9331 (17)
International
$14-$26

AAA Inspector Notes: In a renovated 16th-century mansion, this restaurant offers indoor air-conditioned seating as well as spots in the romantic garden courtyard. Well-prepared cuisine shows off the skills of an experienced chef, especially the foie gras or escargot appetizer. Red snapper fish in creamy sauce with mussels is a winner. Also tempting are other French-Spanish-inspired preparations of veal, chicken and lechon. **Bar:** full bar. **Reservations:** suggested. **Address:** Calle Las Mercedes **Location:** Center of Colonial City District; corner of Las Mercedes and Arzobispo Merino sts; in Hotel Frances Santo Domingo. Historic L D

MUSEO DEL JAMON Phone: 809/688-9644 (18)
Spanish
$10-$28

AAA Inspector Notes: In the restaurant row area of Zona Colonial this historic restaurant features seating al fresco or indoors where hams are suspended from the ceiling. Besides the famed Serrano ham, the Spanish menu features such items as rabbit, mussels, pork loin and chicken dishes as well as Dominican specialties. Thursday through Sunday features live flamenco dancing and music. **Bar:** full bar. **Address:** Calle Atarazana 17 **Location:** Colonial City District; at Atarazana across from Alcazar de Colon; between General Cabral and Vincent C Duarte sts. **Parking:** on-site (fee) and street. Historic
 L D

(See index & map p. 360.)

PAT'E PALO EUROPEAN BRASSERIE
Phone: 809/687-8089 (16)

International
$19-$30

AAA Inspector Notes: Pat'e Palo translates to peg leg, hence the charming pirate-clad waiters. The broad menu features such starters as tuna carpaccio, ceviche, frog legs and a range of pates. Among entrée choices are seafood preparations-including dorado, sea bass and red snapper-and the double-cut pork chop. Most dishes go well with a pitcher of sangria. Indoor seating reflects the Spanish decor of the street-side courtyard and offers views of the oldest city in the New World. **Bar:** full bar. **Reservations:** suggested. **Address:** La Atarazana #25 **Location:** Colonial City District; across from Plaza Colon; at Atarazana. **Parking:** street only. **Historic** [L] [D] [N]

RESTAURANTE CANTABRICO
Phone: 809/687-5101 (23)

Spanish
$15-$32

AAA Inspector Notes: Attractively presented and flavorful seafood and Dominican specialties are served in a European atmosphere. Impressive works by local artists decorate the Spanish-style restaurant. The courteous staff provides attentive service. **Bar:** full bar. **Reservations:** suggested. **Address:** Ave Independencia 54 **Location:** On Ave Independencia; adjacent to Cemetery and just w of Independence Park. [L] [D]

VESUVIO DEL MALECON
Phone: 809/221-1954 (29)

Italian
$17-$30

AAA Inspector Notes: Since 1954, this landmark restaurant's dapper staff has been serving Spanish- and Italian-inspired meals in well-appointed surroundings. Entrées include deft preparations of lamb, chicken, beef and veal. The finale is when the dessert cart is rolled around, and the temptation for one more indulgence is too great. **Bar:** full bar. **Reservations:** suggested. **Address:** 521 Ave George Washington **Location:** On Malecon; facing Caribbean Sea. **Parking:** valet only. [L] [D] [N]

ADRIAN TROPICAL DEL MALECON
Phone: 809/221-1764

[fyi] Not evaluated. For more than 30 years this chain restaurant has been pleasing customers with grilled seafood, a local dish called sancocho(a hearty stew) and mofongo made from mashed plantains. **Address:** George Washington Ave **Location:** On the Malecon.

CAFETERIA EL CONDE
Phone: 809/682-6944

[fyi] Not evaluated. Guest can sample a mix of Italian and international cuisine all served in a comfortable atmosphere. **Address:** Corner of El Conde and Arzobispo Mirino; Colonial City.

MESON DE BARI
Phone: 809/687-4091

[fyi] Not evaluated. This popular restaurant focuses on upmarket Dominican cuisine. **Address:** 302 Hostos **Location:** Corner of Eriquillo and Hostos sts; center of Colonial City.

More choices. Bigger savings.
Easier booking.

AAA.com

It all clicks at AAA.com/Travel

GRENADA

This index helps you "spot" where approved hotels and restaurants are located on the corresponding detailed maps. Hotel daily rate range is for comparison only and show the property's high season. Restaurant rate range is a combination of lunch and/or dinner. Turn to the listing page for more detailed rate information and consult display ads for special promotions.

ST. GEORGE'S (St. George Parish)

Map Page	Hotels	Diamond Rated	High Season	Page
❶ p. 380	Mount Cinnamon Beach Resort	▽▽▽	$345-$720	381
❷ p. 380	Spice Island Beach Resort	▽▽▽▽	$860-$2313 SAVE	381
❹ p. 380	Coyaba Beach Resort	▽▽	$240-$365	381
❺ p. 380	Blue Horizons Garden Resort	▽▽	$155-$230	381
❽ p. 380	Laluna	▽▽▽	$415-$1550	381

Map Page	Restaurants	Diamond Rated	Cuisine	Meal Range	Page
④ p. 380	BB's Crabback Caribbean Restaurant	▽▽	Caribbean	$12-$32	381
⑦ p. 380	Coconut Beach Restaurant	▽	Caribbean	$18-$36	382
⑧ p. 380	La Belle Creole	▽▽▽	Caribbean	$18-$33	382
⑨ p. 380	Laluna	▽▽▽	Italian	$24-$36	382
⑩ p. 380	The Beach House Restaurant & Bar	▽▽▽	International	$18-$38	382
⑫ p. 380	The Aquarium Restaurant	▽▽	Caribbean	$18-$39	381

L'ANSE AUX EPINES (St. George Parish)

Map Page	Hotels	Diamond Rated	High Season	Page
⑫ p. 380	The Calabash Hotel	▽▽▽	$295-$1000	380
⑭ p. 380	Lance Aux Epines Cottages	▽▽	$110-$365	380
⑮ p. 380	Coral Cove	▽	$90-$190	380

Map Page	Restaurants	Diamond Rated	Cuisine	Meal Range	Page
⑯ p. 380	Rhodes Restaurant	▽▽▽	International	$31-$39	381
⑰ p. 380	The Red Crab	▽▽	International	$12-$40	381

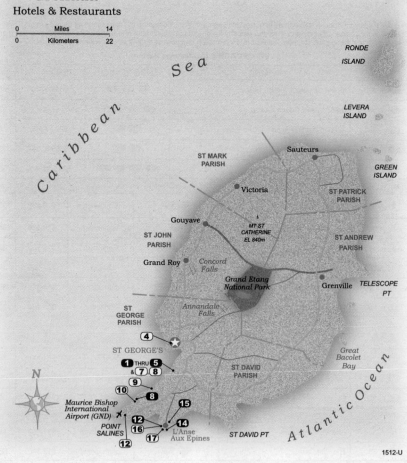

Grenada
Hotels & Restaurants

| 0 | Miles | 14 |
| 0 | Kilometers | 22 |

Caribbean Sea

RONDE ISLAND

LEVERA ISLAND

GREEN ISLAND

ST MARK PARISH

Sauteurs

Victoria

ST PATRICK PARISH

Gouyave

▲ MT ST CATHERINE EL 840m

ST JOHN PARISH

ST ANDREW PARISH

Grand Roy

Concord Falls

Grand Etang National Park

Grenville   TELESCOPE PT

ST GEORGE PARISH

Annandale Falls

ST GEORGE'S ★

Great Bacolet Bay

❶ THRU ❺ & ❼ ❽

ST DAVID PARISH

❾

❿   ❽

Atlantic Ocean

Maurice Bishop International Airport (GND) ✈

❶❺

POINT SALINES

❶❷ ❶❹

❶❻   L'Anse Aux Epines

❶❼   ST DAVID PT

❶❷

N

1512-U

St. George Parish

L'ANSE AUX EPINES
• Hotels & Restaurants index & map p. 379

THE CALABASH HOTEL   **Phone:** (473)444-4334   ❶❷
Hotel
$295-$1000
Address: L'Anse aux Epines **Location:** Oceanfront. 5 mi (8 km) s of town; 3.3 mi (5.3 km) ne of airport. **Facility:** These duplex cottages and two-story apartments face a secluded cove of Prickly Bay; the décor is fresh and inviting. 30 units, some houses. 2 stories (no elevator), exterior corridors. **Terms:** open 12/1-8/12 & 10/6-11/30, office hours 7 am-11 pm, age restrictions may apply, 30 day cancellation notice, 14 day off season. **Amenities:** safes, honor bars. **Dining:** Rhodes Restaurant, see separate listing, entertainment. **Pool(s):** outdoor. **Activities:** sailboats, snorkeling, lighted tennis court, shuffleboard, exercise room, spa. *Fee:* scuba diving. **Guest Services:** valet laundry.

CORAL COVE   **Phone:** 473/444-4422   ❶❺
Cottage
$90-$190
Address: L'Anse aux Epines **Location:** Oceanfront. 5.2 mi (8.3 km) s of town; 4 mi (6.4 km) nw of airport. **Facility:** 11 cottages. 1 story, exterior corridors. *Bath:* shower only. **Terms:** office hours 8 am-1 pm, 3 night minimum stay - seasonal and/or weekends, 21 day cancellation notice-fee imposed. **Pool(s):** outdoor. **Activities:** snorkeling, tennis court. **Guest Services:** valet laundry.

🏊 📶 🛗 🖥 / SOME UNITS Ⓚ

LANCE AUX EPINES COTTAGES
Phone: 473/444-4565   ❶❹
Cottage
$110-$365
Address: L'Anse aux Epines **Location:** Oceanfront. 5.2 mi (8.3 km) s of town; 3.5 mi (13.3 km) ne of airport; on south coast. **Facility:** 11 cottages. 1-2 stories (no elevator), exterior corridors. *Bath:* shower only. **Terms:** office hours 8:30 am-4 pm, 3-7 night minimum stay - seasonal, 60 day cancellation notice, 30 day off season-fee imposed. **Amenities:** high-speed Internet, safes. **Activities:** paddleboats, sailboats, game room. **Guest Services:** complimentary laundry.

(See index & map p. 379.)

WHERE TO EAT

THE RED CRAB
Phone: 473/444-4424 (17)

International
$12-$40

AAA Inspector Notes: Both indoors and outdoors, the restaurant sustains a relaxed English pub atmosphere. Guests can choose from a selection of local seafood dishes and house specialties as well as lighter meals and sandwiches. **Bar:** full bar. **Address:** L'Anse aux Epines **Location:** 8 mi (12.8 km) s of town; 4 mi (6.4 km) ne of airport. L D D X

RHODES RESTAURANT
Phone: 473/444-4334 (16)

International
$31-$39

AAA Inspector Notes: This elegant restaurant nurtures an upscale feel in its covered open-air setting, where diners enjoy pleasant Caribbean-style entertainment as they sample the chef's highly innovative fare. The freshest regional ingredients mingle with island spices and exotic fruits in preparations such as chilled gazpacho with melon balls to start and Caribbean spiced steak with green peppercorn sauce or many fresh fish and other seafood selections as entrées. **Bar:** full bar. **Reservations:** required. **Address:** L'Anse aux Epines **Location:** 5 mi (8 km) s of town; 3.3 mi (5.3 km) ne of airport; in The Calabash Hotel. D X

ST. GEORGE'S (C-1) pop. 37,000
• Hotels & Restaurants index & map p. 379

BLUE HORIZONS GARDEN RESORT
Phone: (473)444-4316 5

Hotel
$155-$230

Address: Morne Rouge **Location:** 5.5 mi (8.8 km) s of town; 3.8 mi (6 km) nw of airport. **Facility:** 32 units, some efficiencies. 1 story, exterior corridors. **Terms:** office hours 7 am-10:30 pm, 7 night minimum stay - seasonal, 30 day cancellation notice, 7 day in summer-fee imposed. **Amenities:** safes. **Dining:** La Belle Creole, see separate listing. **Pool(s):** outdoor. **Activities:** playground. **Guest Services:** valet laundry.

COYABA BEACH RESORT
Phone: (473)444-4129 4

Hotel
$240-$365

Address: Grand Anse **Location:** Oceanfront. 5.4 mi (8.6 km) s of town; 3.9 mi (6.2 km) nw of airport. **Facility:** 80 units. 2 stories (no elevator), exterior corridors. **Terms:** 2-3 night minimum stay - seasonal, 21 day cancellation notice, 14 day off season-fee imposed. **Amenities:** safes. **Dining:** 2 restaurants. **Pool(s):** outdoor. **Activities:** canoeing, sailboats, windsurfing, snorkeling, lighted tennis court, recreation programs, shuffleboard, exercise room. **Fee:** scuba diving, massage. **Guest Services:** valet laundry.

LALUNA
Phone: (473)439-0001 8

Cottage
$415-$1550

Address: Morne Rouge **Location:** Oceanfront. 7.1 mi (11.3 km) s of town; 5.5 mi (8.8 km) from airport. Located on ten acres in secluded area. **Facility:** Well-equipped cottages include an LCD TV, four-poster Balinese hand-carved beds with Italian linens and a private plunge pool. 16 cottages. 1 story, exterior corridors. **Bath:** shower only. **Terms:** office hours 7 am-11 pm, 3 night minimum stay, age restrictions may apply, 30 day cancellation notice-fee imposed. **Amenities:** safes, honor bars. **Dining:** restaurant, see separate listing. **Pool(s):** outdoor. **Activities:** sailboats, snorkeling, bicycles, exercise room, spa. **Guest Services:** valet laundry.

MOUNT CINNAMON BEACH RESORT
Phone: 473/439-9900 1

Vacation Rental Condominium
$345-$720

Address: Morne Rouge **Location:** 6 mi (9.6 km) s of town; 3.3 mi (5.3 km) nw of airport. **Facility:** Perched on a hillside with spectacular views, these individually decorated residential-style units reflect stylistic decor and many comforts. Meets AAA guest room security requirements. 21 condominiums. 1-2 stories (no elevator), exterior corridors. **Terms:** 30 day cancellation notice. **Amenities:** high-speed Internet, safes. **Dining:** 2 restaurants, entertainment. **Pool(s):** outdoor. **Activities:** limited beach access, sailboats, windsurfing, snorkeling, tennis court, recreation programs, horseback riding, volleyball, exercise room. **Fee:** massage. **Guest Services:** valet and coin laundry, area transportation-within 4 mi.

SPICE ISLAND BEACH RESORT
Phone: 473/444-4258 2

Resort Hotel
$860-$2313

Address: Grand Anse Beach **Location:** Oceanfront. 5.5 mi (8.8 km) s of town; 4 mi (6.4 km) nw of airport. **Facility:** Offering attractively decorated accommodations with furnished balconies or terraces, the beachfront property affords nice views. 64 units. 1-2 stories (no elevator), exterior corridors. **Terms:** 7-10 night minimum stay - seasonal, 30 day cancellation notice, 14 days off season-fee imposed. **Amenities:** high-speed Internet, safes, honor bars. **Dining:** 2 restaurants, entertainment. **Pool(s):** outdoor. **Activities:** sailboats, snorkeling, lighted tennis court, bicycles, exercise room, spa. **Fee:** sauna, scuba diving. **Guest Services:** valet laundry. **Free Special Amenities:** preferred room (subject to availability with advance reservations) and high-speed Internet.

WHERE TO EAT

THE AQUARIUM RESTAURANT
Phone: 473/444-1410 (12)

Caribbean
$18-$39

AAA Inspector Notes: Situated in a dramatic setting with an exposed cliff and white sand beach, this roomy al fresco restaurant features seafood, lobster, pasta and lamb dishes. Surrounded by the captivating seductive artwork of the owner-artist, many patrons enjoy an appetizer of seared scallops, callaloo cannelloni or crab cushions before moving on to an entrée. Sweet treats include hot apple crumb pie, crème caramel or death by chocolate. Sunday is beach barbecue day with live reggae and steel-pan music. **Bar:** full bar. **Reservations:** required. **Address:** Aquarium Beach, Point Salines **Location:** Just s of airport, follow signs; in Maca Bana. L D X

BB'S CRABBACK CARIBBEAN RESTAURANT
Phone: 473/435-7058 4

Caribbean
$12-$32

AAA Inspector Notes: BB has returned home to the Caribbean after numerous years as an award-winning London chef. While the decor of this eatery is simplistic, diners come here for the view and the savory Caribbean-inspired cuisine. The popular crabback (stuffed and baked land crab) starter leads into house signature dishes including jerk pork and curried goat. Fish lovers can choose from a wide variety, including parrot fish, red mullet, sea brim, red snapper and barracuda. Wednesday is special priced curry night. **Bar:** full bar. **Address:** Progress House **Location:** On north side of The Carenage; downtown.

(See index & map p. 379.)

THE BEACH HOUSE RESTAURANT & BAR
Phone: 473/444-4455

International
$18-$38

AAA Inspector Notes: Enjoy open-air dining at this fine, beachfront eatery. Colorful artwork, live plants and the background sounds of the ocean create a relaxed yet sophisticated atmosphere. With a varying degree of complexity and creativeness, menu offerings include lamb, duck and cuts of beef as well as seafood selections of scallops, tuna, snapper, marlin and lobster in season. **Bar:** full bar. **Reservations:** suggested. **Location:** 0.5 mi (0.8 km) n of airport; 9.3 mi (14.9 km) s of town, follow signs.

L D 🄷

COCONUT BEACH RESTAURANT
Phone: 473/444-4644 (7)

Caribbean
$18-$36

AAA Inspector Notes: Situated on the beach, patrons have a seating choice at umbrella-covered tables on the sand or inside the festive Creole-Caribbean-style shack. Lobster, available in season, is prepared six different ways. Also lining the menu is a seafood platter, lambi (conch) calypso, pepper steak and fish such as marlin, swordfish and mahi mahi. The sweet coconut pie or local-made ice cream are nice finishing touches to a tasty meal. **Bar:** full bar. **Address:** Grand Anse Beach **Location:** 3.1 mi (5 km) s of downtown; 1.6 mi (2.5 km) n of Grand Anse Beach roundabout. L D 🄷 🄽

LA BELLE CREOLE
Phone: 473/444-4316 (8)

Caribbean
$18-$33

AAA Inspector Notes: A subtle, elegant atmosphere prevails in this open-air dining room set up on a hill with views of the distant waterfront and city below. The table d'hote menu combines Continental and island recipes, all created with market-fresh ingredients. Candlelit tables and lovely night views add to the eatery's relaxed ambience. **Bar:** full bar. **Reservations:** required. **Address:** Morne Rouge **Location:** 5.5 mi (8.8 km) s of town; 3.8 mi (6 km) nw of airport; in Blue Horizons Garden Resort.

B D 🄷 🄽

LALUNA
Phone: 473/439-0001 (9)

Italian
$24-$36

AAA Inspector Notes: In a remote and romantic location high on a hill, this covered open-air dining room incorporates contemporary flair into its Caribbean atmosphere, which includes candlelit tables and upbeat background music. The menu features an innovative mix of island-influenced Italian and international cuisine, including the grilled catch of the day in pineapple citrus salsa, Sicilian-style shrimp, grilled meats and freshly prepared pasta dishes. **Bar:** full bar. **Reservations:** suggested. **Address:** Morne Rouge **Location:** 7.1 mi (11.3 km) s of town; 5.5 mi (8.8 km) from airport. B L D 🄷 🄽

Learn about AAA/CAA Diamond Ratings
at AAA.com/Diamonds

GUADELOUPE

This index helps you "spot" where approved hotels and restaurants are located on the corresponding detailed maps. Hotel daily rate range is for comparison only and show the property's high season. Restaurant rate range is a combination of lunch and/or dinner. Turn to the listing page for more detailed rate information and consult display ads for special promotions.

GOSIER (Grande-Terre Island)

Map Page	Hotel		Diamond Rated	High Season	Page
3 p. 384	Auberge de la Vieille Tour		◆◆◆	$253-$700	384

Map Page	Restaurants	Diamond Rated	Cuisine	Meal Range	Page
2 p. 384	Restaurant Les Langoustes	◆◆	Creole	$20-$46	385
4 p. 384	Ristorante Rosini	◆◆	Italian	$20-$42	385
6 p. 384	Auberge de la Vieille Tour	◆◆◆	Continental	$50-$71	385
15 p. 384	L'Agouba Restaurant Dampierre Grill	◆	Barbecue	$12-$22	385

SAINTE ANNE (Grande-Terre Island)

Map Page	Hotel		Diamond Rated	High Season	Page
8 p. 384	Hotel La Toubana		◆◆◆	$239-$477	385

Map Page	Restaurant	Diamond Rated	Cuisine	Meal Range	Page
18 p. 384	Kote Sud Le Restaurant	◆◆◆	French	$18-$34	386

TROIS-RIVIERES (Basse-Terre Island)

Map Page	Hotel		Diamond Rated	High Season	Page
15 p. 384	Le Jardin Malanga		◆◆◆	$359-$378	384

ST. LOUIS (Marie-Galante Island)

Map Page	Hotel		Diamond Rated	High Season	Page
19 p. 384	Kawann Beach Hotel		◆◆	$137-$206	386

ST. FRANCOIS (Grande-Terre Island)

Map Page	Restaurants	Diamond Rated	Cuisine	Meal Range	Page
26 p. 384	Chez Man Michel	◆	Creole	$21-$33	385
27 p. 384	Resto des Artistes	◆◆	Creole	$15-$30	385

POINTE-À-PITRE (Grande-Terre Island)

Map Page	Restaurants	Diamond Rated	Cuisine	Meal Range	Page
37 p. 384	La Mandala	◆◆	International	$28-$49	385
40 p. 384	Cote du Boeuf	◆◆	Steak	$26-$44	385
41 p. 384	Cote Jardin	◆◆◆	French	$16-$38	385

BOUILLANTE (Basse-Terre Island)

Map Page	Restaurant	Diamond Rated	Cuisine	Meal Range	Page
46 p. 384	Restaurant La Touna	◆◆	Creole	$22-$37	384

Check out our travel blog at
AAATravelViews.com

© AAA

Guadeloupe
Hotels & Restaurants

| 0 | Miles | 14 |
| 0 | Kilometers | 23 |

1513-U

Basse-Terre Island

BOUILLANTE (C-2) pop. 7,336
• Hotels & Restaurants index & map p. 383

RESTAURANT LA TOUNA

Phone: 590/590-98-70-10 **46**

Creole
$22-$37

AAA Inspector Notes: Near the Jacques Cousteau Marine Reserve, this oceanfront restaurant has a subtle nautical theme that incorporates madras tablecloths and live lobster tanks. The extensive menu of Antillean and French gastronomic preparations lists everything from duck and stingray to kangaroo and ostrich, including at least six types of fish. The wide selection of appetizers and homemade desserts round out a fine meal. **Bar:** full bar. **Address:** Pigeon Galet 97132 **Location:** On Rt de Malendure; on waterfront; 2.5 mi (4 km) n of Bouillante.

Explore the Travel Guides
on AAA.com/Travel or
CAA.ca/Travel

TROIS-RIVIERES pop. 8,738
• Hotels & Restaurants index & map p. 383

LE JARDIN MALANGA

Phone: (590)590-92-67-57 **15**

Country Inn
$359-$378

Address: La Rue Hermitage 60 97114 **Location:** Basse Terre side of Guadeloupe south coast; from southern highway, just s at Hermitage turn off, follow signs. **Facility:** Situated on six acres of a former circa 1927 banana plantation, this charming inn features mahogany furnishings and stunning views of Les Saintes. 9 units. 1-2 stories (no elevator), interior/exterior corridors. **Terms:** open 12/1-6/1 & 10/17-11/30, 14 day cancellation notice-fee imposed. **Amenities:** safes. **Pool(s):** outdoor.

Grande-Terre Island

GOSIER pop. 25,360
• Hotels & Restaurants index & map p. 383

AUBERGE DE LA VIEILLE TOUR

Phone: (590)590-84-23-23 **3**

Hotel
$253-$700

Address: Montauban 97190 **Location:** Oceanfront. 3.7 mi (5.9 km) se of Pointe-a-Pitre Airport. **Facility:** 103 units. 1-3 stories (no elevator), interior/exterior corridors. **Terms:** 30 day cancellation notice. **Amenities:** high-speed Internet (fee), safes, honor bars. **Dining:** restaurant, see separate listing, entertainment. **Pool(s):** outdoor. **Activities:** snorkeling, lighted tennis court. **Fee:** massage. **Guest Services:** valet laundry.

(See index & map p. 383.)

WHERE TO EAT

AUBERGE DE LA VIEILLE TOUR
Phone: 590/590-84-23-23

Continental
$50-$71

AAA Inspector Notes: In a restored sugar mill at the hotel of the same name, the restaurant nurtures a refined atmosphere with an island flair. Diners often arrive early to enjoy a tropical cocktail or glass of wine before noshing on a meal in the open-air verandah. Fine Continental and French cuisine is listed on a la carte and prix fixe menus. **Bar:** full bar. **Reservations:** required. **Address:** Montauban 97190 **Location:** 3.7 mi (5.9 km) se of Pointe-a-Pitre Airport.

[B] [L] [D]

L'AGOUBA RESTAURANT DAMPIERRE GRILL
Phone: 590/590-68-14-50 (15)

Barbecue
$12-$22

AAA Inspector Notes: A perennial favorite, this roadside grill barbecues tasty chicken, ribs, lobster and fish. Affordable-priced dishes are great for take-out or dine-in. All plates come with French fries or salad. **Bar:** full bar. **Address:** Route de Dampierre 97190 **Location:** Just e of town. [L] [D]

RESTAURANT LES LANGOUSTES
Phone: 590/590-90-85-43 (2)

Creole
$20-$46

AAA Inspector Notes: Lobster tanks fill the room of this rustic, nautical-theme eatery. Enjoy flavorful Creole dishes with a broad selection from an extensive menu including more than five types of fish prepared various ways, conch, lobster, accras, crab farci and boudin. The service is casual, prompt and efficient. **Bar:** full bar. **Address:** 92 imp. Bas du Fort 97190 **Location:** At Bas du Fort; next to Hotel Novotel. [L] [D]

RISTORANTE ROSINI
Phone: 590/590-90-87-81 (4)

Italian
$20-$42

AAA Inspector Notes: Near tourist hotels in the Bas du Fort area, the restaurant tempts diners with freshly prepared Italian cuisine, including a wide selection of homemade pasta, pizza and meat. **Bar:** full bar. **Reservations:** suggested. **Address:** La Porte des Caraibes 97190 **Location:** In Bas du Fort. [L] [D]

POINTE-À-PITRE (B-3) pop. 20,948
• Hotels & Restaurants index & map p. 383

COTE DU BOEUF
Phone: 590/590-21-23-59 (40)

Steak
$26-$44

AAA Inspector Notes: Outdoor seats afford the best views of the marina, but if a controlled climate is a higher priority, the air-conditioned indoor seats meet that need. The menu focuses mainly on various beef dishes but also lists pork, chicken and local and imported seafood. **Bar:** full bar. **Reservations:** suggested, weekends. **Address:** La Marina Pointe-a-Pitre 97190 **Location:** At Marina de Pointe-a-Pitre. [L] [D]

COTE JARDIN
Phone: 590/590-90-91-28 (41)

French
$16-$38

AAA Inspector Notes: Tucked in a quiet corner of the busy Pointe-a-Pitre Marina, the restaurant treats guests to an exceptional menu of fine French cuisine. Sophistication-in the form of rich sauces and specialty ingredients-marks each made-to-order course. Charming French country appointments lend character to the quaint dining room, where diners can hear chefs assembling their creations from the open-concept kitchen. The menus are in French, but will be translated upon request by the professional servers. **Bar:** full bar. **Reservations:** suggested. **Address:** La Marina, Pointe-a-Pitre 97190 **Location:** At Marina de Pointe-a-Pitre. **Parking:** street only. [L] [D]

LA MANDALA
Phone: 590/590-20-39-87 (37)

International
$28-$49

AAA Inspector Notes: On the ever-popular marina restaurant row, this waterfront eatery offers an Asian interior motif dominated by a huge Buddha statue or al fresco seating. The menu centers on Asian and French cuisine including a full sushi-sashimi menu, beef tartare, fresh fish and duck. Each dish has an artistically detailed presentation. For dessert, it is worth savoring the warm chocolate fondant. **Bar:** full bar. **Reservations:** suggested. **Address:** La Marina Gosier 9 Quai 97110 **Location:** At Marina de Pointe-a-Pitre/Gosier. **Parking:** street only. [L] [D]

ST. FRANCOIS pop. 10,659
• Hotels & Restaurants index & map p. 383

CHEZ MAN MICHEL
Phone: 590/590-88-72-79 (26)

Creole
$21-$33

AAA Inspector Notes: Just a short walk from the beach is the rustic al fresco eatery, which serves home-style Creole cuisine. Fish blaff, court-bouillon fish and conch, as well as goat and chicken Colombo, are house specialties. A selection of salads, accras and crab farci accompanies the entrees. The broad choice of ice creams cools the after-dinner palate. Friday night features local Zouk music and dancing along with a special seafood menu which includes grilled lobster. **Bar:** full bar. **Address:** Plage de Tarare 97118 **Location:** 1.3 mi (2 km) w of Pointe des Chateaux; Plage de Tarare; east coast of island.

[L] [D]

RESTO DES ARTISTES
Phone: 590/590-88-75-44 (27)

Creole
$15-$30

AAA Inspector Notes: Laid-back servers circulate through the cozy, familiar marina-front al fresco restaurant. Large entrée-size salads are dressed with duck, seafood, chicken or beef, and seafood dishes can be steamed, grilled or sauteed. A local dish especially worth trying is Colombo de porc, a Creole curry dish. **Bar:** full bar. **Address:** Marina Golf 97118 **Location:** 0.6 mi (1 km) from town; at Marina Golf. **Parking:** street only. [L] [D]

SAINTE ANNE pop. 20,410
• Restaurants p. 386
• Hotels & Restaurants index & map p. 383

HOTEL LA TOUBANA
Phone: (590)590-88-25-78 (8)

Cottage
$239-$477

Address: Fonds Thezan **Location:** Oceanfront. 1 mi (1.6 km) w of town village, then just s, follow signs. **Facility:** Perched on a hillside overlooking the beach, this property offers individually decorated garden or ocean-view cottages with a terrace. 33 cottages. 1 story, exterior corridors. **Terms:** 7 day cancellation notice-fee imposed. **Amenities:** safes. **Dining:** 2 restaurants. **Pool(s):** outdoor. **Activities:** whirlpool, snorkeling, exercise room, spa. **Guest Services:** valet laundry.

(See index & map p. 383.)

(See index & map p. 383.)

WHERE TO EAT

Marie-Galante Island

KOTE SUD LE RESTAURANT
Phone: 590/590-88-17-31 ⑱

French
$18-$34

AAA Inspector Notes: The popular restaurant earns rave reviews from locals and tourists alike. The Creole-style home's covered porch creates a casual ambience for al fresco dining. Food is the highlight here. Choices from the ever-changing menu might include ostrich, Tahitian-style fish, brochette of conch and grilled red snapper with fennel emulsion. **Bar:** full bar. **Reservations:** suggested. **Address:** 16 Lot Dore Durivage 97180 **Location:** 0.8 mi (1.2 km) w of town; just s, follow signs; on Route de Rotabas-Durivage. **Parking:** street only. Ⓓ 🍴 ➘

ST. LOUIS pop. 2,995
• Hotels & Restaurants index & map p. 383

KAWANN BEACH HOTEL
Phone: (590)590-97-50-50 ⑲

Hotel
$137-$206

Address: Cocoyer 97112 **Location:** Oceanfront. Just s of town; at Folle Anse; 3.8 mi (6 km) e of Grand-Bourg; 5.4 mi (9 km) from airport. **Facility:** 100 units, some kitchens. 1-2 stories (no elevator), exterior corridors. *Bath:* shower only. **Terms:** open 12/1-9/1 & 10/1-11/30, office hours 6 am-10 pm, 7 day cancellation notice-fee imposed. **Pool(s):** outdoor. **Activities:** 2 tennis courts (Fee: 2 lighted), rental bicycles, volleyball. *Fee:* massage.

🍴 🍸 🛗 🐎 📶 ⊠ / SOME UNITS 🐕 🗂

JAMAICA

✈ Airport Accommodations

Map Page	SANGSTER INTERNATIONAL AIRPORT	Diamond Rated	High Season	Page
15 p. 390	Hotel Riu Montego Bay, 1.7 mi (2.7 km) e of airport	▼▼▼	$160-$355	392

✈ Airport Accommodations

Map Page	NEGRIL AIRPORT	Diamond Rated	High Season	Page
45 p. 390	Couples Swept Away, 2.3 mi (3.6 km) s of airport	▼▼▼	$593-$928	396

Jamaica

This index helps you "spot" where approved hotels and restaurants are located on the corresponding detailed maps. Hotel daily rate range is for comparison only and show the property's high season. Restaurant rate range is a combination of lunch and/or dinner. Turn to the listing page for more detailed rate information and consult display ads for special promotions.

KINGSTON

Map Page	Hotels	Diamond Rated	High Season	Page
2 p. 390	The Jamaica Pegasus Hotel	▼▼	$180-$300	391
3 p. 390	Spanish Court Hotel	▼▼	$124-$195	391
7 p. 390	**The Courtleigh Hotel & Suites**	▼▼▼	$145-$400 [SAVE]	391

Map Page	Restaurants	Diamond Rated	Cuisine	Meal Range	Page
① p. 390	Norma's on the Terrace	▼▼▼	Jamaican	$14-$35	391
② p. 390	Redbones-The Blues Cafe	▼▼	New Caribbean	$11-$30	391
④ p. 390	Heather's Garden Restaurant and Bar	▼	International	$7-$23	391
⑥ p. 390	Jade Garden Restaurant	▼▼	Chinese	$12-$40	391

HOPEWELL

Map Page	Hotel	Diamond Rated	High Season	Page
8 p. 390	Round Hill Hotel and Villas	▼▼▼▼	$410-$2000	391

MONTEGO BAY

Map Page	Hotels	Diamond Rated	High Season	Page
10 p. 390	Sunset Beach Resort Spa and Waterpark *(See ad p. 394.)*	▼▼	$290-$820	394
11 p. 390	**Secrets St. James Montego Bay** *(See ad on insert.)*	▼▼▼▼	$546-$984 [SAVE]	394
12 p. 390	Holiday Inn SunSpree Resort Montego Bay *(See ad p. 392.)*	▼▼	$429-$567	392
13 p. 390	Sandals Carlyle *(See ad on insert.)*	▼▼▼	$682-$1396	392
14 p. 390	Sandals Royal Caribbean Resort & Private Island *(See ad on insert.)*	▼▼▼▼	$1134-$3246	394
15 p. 390	Hotel Riu Montego Bay	▼▼▼	$160-$355	392
16 p. 390	Coyaba Beach Resort & Club	▼▼▼	$230-$440	392
17 p. 390	**Secrets Wild Orchid Montego Bay Jamaica** *(See ad on insert.)*	▼▼▼▼	$573-$1035 [SAVE]	394

Map Page	Restaurants	Diamond Rated	Cuisine	Meal Range	Page
⑧ p. 390	The Houseboat Grill	▼▼	Fusion	$14-$32	395
⑪ p. 390	Marguerites Seafood by the Sea	▼▼▼	Caribbean	$28-$54	395
⑬ p. 390	Pelican Grill	▼	Jamaican	$10-$30	396
⑮ p. 390	The Native Restaurant & Bar	▼▼	Jamaican	$9-$30	395

Map Page	Restaurants (cont'd)	Diamond Rated	Cuisine	Meal Range	Page
⑰ p. 390	Akbar and Thai Garden Restaurant	◆◆	Asian	$12-$35	395

ROSE HALL

Map Page	Hotels	Diamond Rated	High Season	Page
⑱ p. 390	**Hilton Rose Hall Resort & Spa**	◆◆◆	$119-$449 [SAVE]	400
⑲ p. 390	**The Ritz-Carlton Golf & Spa Resort, Rose Hall, Jamaica**	◆◆◆◆◆	$279-$1100 [SAVE]	400
⑳ p. 390	**Half Moon, A RockResort** *(See ad p. 393.)*	◆◆◆◆	$250-$1680 [SAVE]	400

Map Page	Restaurant	Diamond Rated	Cuisine	Meal Range	Page
⑱ p. 390	Sugar Mill Restaurant	◆◆◆	International	$19-$35	400

OCHO RIOS

Map Page	Hotels	Diamond Rated	High Season	Page
㉒ p. 390	Sandals Royal Plantation Ocho Rios, Jamaica	◆◆◆◆	$1774-$4898	399
㉔ p. 390	Beaches Boscobel Resort & Golf Club *(See ad on insert.)*	◆◆◆	$924-$2542	398
㉖ p. 390	**Jamaica Inn**	◆◆◆	$315-$1935 [SAVE]	398
㉚ p. 390	Sandals Grande Riviera Beach & Villa Golf Resort	◆◆◆◆	$1102-$3128	399

Map Page	Restaurants	Diamond Rated	Cuisine	Meal Range	Page
㉙ p. 390	**Evita's**	◆◆	Italian	$13-$26	399
㉜ p. 390	Jamaica Inn Dining Room	◆◆◆	International	$14-$38	399
㊱ p. 390	Passage to India	◆◆	Indian	$11-$27	399
㊳ p. 390	Toscanini Italian Restaurant	◆◆◆	Italian	$15-$29	399

NEGRIL

Map Page	Hotels	Diamond Rated	High Season	Page
㊳ p. 390	Riu Club Hotel	◆◆	$115-$420	397
㊵ p. 390	Hotel Riu Palace Tropical Bay	◆◆◆	$268-$550	397
㊷ p. 390	**Breezes Grand Resort and Spa Negril**	◆◆◆	$335-$908 [SAVE]	396
㊸ p. 390	Rondel Village	◆◆	$75-$440	397
㊹ p. 390	Sandals Negril Beach Resort & Spa *(See ad on insert.)*	◆◆◆◆	$1044-$3742	397
㊺ p. 390	Couples Swept Away	◆◆◆	$593-$928	396
㊻ p. 390	Couples Negril	◆◆◆	$635-$977	396
㊼ p. 390	Beaches Sandy Bay *(See ad on insert.)*	◆◆◆	$748-$1556	396
㊾ p. 390	Beaches Negril Resort & Spa *(See ad on insert.)*	◆◆◆	$1036-$5926	396
㊿ p. 390	The Caves	◆◆◆	$608-$710	396

Map Page	Restaurants	Diamond Rated	Cuisine	Meal Range	Page
㊴ p. 390	Cosmo's Seafood Restaurant	◆	Jamaican	$6-$22	397
㊵ p. 390	**Norma's Restaurant on the Beach at Sea Splash Resort**	◆◆◆	Jamaican	$12-$35	397
㊷ p. 390	Kuyaba on the Beach	◆◆	Jamaican	$16-$32	397
㊺ p. 390	Sweet Spice Restaurant	◆	Jamaican	$10-$20	398
㊾ p. 390	Rock House Restaurant	◆◆	Jamaican	$11-$22	398
㊿ p. 390	Rick's Cafe	◆◆	Caribbean	$8-$24	397

Map Page	Restaurants (cont'd)	Diamond Rated	Cuisine	Meal Range	Page
52 p. 390	Xtabi On The Cliff	◤◤	Jamaican	$11-$28	398

PORT ANTONIO

Map Page	Hotel	Diamond Rated	High Season	Page
55 p. 390	The Jamaica Palace Hotel	◤◤	$170-$190	399

Map Page	Restaurant	Diamond Rated	Cuisine	Meal Range	Page
54 p. 390	Panorama Restaurant and Lounge	◤	Caribbean	$12-$27	400

SANDY BAY

Map Page	Hotel	Diamond Rated	High Season	Page
57 p. 390	**The Tryall Club**	◤◤◤◤	$400-$1570 [SAVE]	401

IRISH TOWN

Map Page	Hotel	Diamond Rated	High Season	Page
59 p. 390	Strawberry Hill	◤◤◤	$230-$775	391

RUNAWAY BAY

Map Page	Hotel	Diamond Rated	High Season	Page
63 p. 390	Breezes Resort, Spa & Golf Club Runaway Bay	◤◤◤	$240-$450	400

WHITEHOUSE

Map Page	Hotel	Diamond Rated	High Season	Page
66 p. 390	Sandals Whitehouse European Village & Spa *(See ad on insert.)*	◤◤◤◤	$876-$3138	401

N

Manchioneal

Holland
Bay

MORANT
PT.

Golden
Grove

Port
Morant

54

Port Antonio

55

Rio Grande

Blue and John
Crow Mountains
National Park

St.
Margaret's
Bay

Hope
Bay

Rio
Grande

Rio
Grande
Rafting

BLUE MTN.
PEAK

2 3 7

1 THRU **6**

Morant
Bay

Buff
Bay

A4

Newcastle

MOUNTAINS

Irish Town

Yallahs

A4

Annotto Bay

BLUE

A4

59

KINGSTON

Port
Royal

Norman
Manley
International
Airport
(KIN)

Port Maria

Castleton

A3

A3

Spanish
Town

Old Harbour
Bay

Galleon
Harbour

PORTLAND
POINT

Tower
Isle Oracabessa

Brimmer
Hall

Gayle

Richmond

Bog
Walk

Old Harbour

A2

Prospect
Plantation

30

36

38

Linstead

Ewarton

Chapelton

May
Pen

Lionel
Town

22 THRU **32**

Dolphin
Cove

OCHO
RIOS

29

Moneague

Claremont

Frankfield

A3

A1

Newport

Alligator
Rest

Milk
River Bath

St Ann's
Bay

33

Brown's
Town

Bamboo

Alexandria

HARBOUR

A2

Runaway
Bay

Discovery
Bay

Rio
Bueno

Dun-
cans

Clark's
Town

Albert
Town

Christiana

DRY

MTS.

Mandeville

Falmouth

Martha
Brae

TRELAWNY

Bala-
clava

Malvern

Port
Kaiser

A1

THE COCKPIT
COUNTRY

Siloah

Lacovia

Santa
Cruz

Treasure
Beach

GREAT

PEDRO

BLUFF

Cambridge

Montpelier

A2

Rose
Hall

11 THRU **20**

18

15

Sangster
Int'l
Airport
(MBJ)

10

8

8

Reading

Hope-
well

MONTEGO
BAY

11 THRU **15**

Sandy
Montego Bay
Bay

A1

Grange Hill

57

Lucea

Green Island

Little
London

49 THRU **39**

42

45

40

Negril

51 THRU **52**

S. Negril
Bay

Long
Bay

New-
market

66

Blue-
fields

Whitehouse

Black River

Savanna-
la-Mar

A2

Caribbean

Sea

Jamaica
Hotels & Restaurants

Miles   20
Kilometers 32

▽ SEE AAA GEM ATTRACTIONS

© AAA

1514-U

HOPEWELL
• Hotels & Restaurants index & map p. 387

ROUND HILL HOTEL AND VILLAS
Phone: (876)956-7050   **8**

▼▼▼▼
Classic Resort Hotel
$410-$2000

Address: John Pringle Dr **Location:** Oceanfront. 1.1 mi (1.7 km) e of town. Located in a quiet secluded location. **Facility:** This beachfront setting offers a scenic hillside location; guests may choose between a traditional hotel unit or an upscale villa. 127 units, some two bedrooms, three bedrooms, houses and cottages. 1-2 stories (no elevator), exterior corridors. **Terms:** open 12/1-9/4 & 10/6-11/30, 30 day cancellation notice, 14 day off season-fee imposed. **Amenities:** high-speed Internet, safes. **Dining:** 2 restaurants, entertainment. **Pool(s):** 2 outdoor. **Activities:** paddleboats, sailboats, windsurfing, 5 tennis courts (2 lighted), recreation programs, jogging, basketball, exercise room, spa. **Fee:** waterskiing, scuba diving, snorkeling. **Guest Services:** valet laundry, area transportation-Montego Bay Shopping & Tryall Golf Course.

ECO ❙ ❙ ❙ SD ❙ BIZ ❙ ❙ ❙ / SOME UNITS ❙

IRISH TOWN
• Hotels & Restaurants index & map p. 387

STRAWBERRY HILL
Phone: 876/944-8400   **59**

▼▼▼▼
Cottage
$230-$775

Address: Irish Town Rd **Location:** N of Kingston (B1), 6 mi (9.6 km) s of Newcastle. **Facility:** Set in the scenic Blue Mountains, 3,100 feet above Kingston, this stylish, rustic-chic property offers well-appointed cottages and common areas. 13 cottages. 1-2 stories (no elevator), exterior corridors. **Terms:** office hours 7 am-11 pm, 3 night minimum stay - seasonal, 14 day cancellation notice. **Amenities:** safes, honor bars. **Pool(s):** outdoor. **Activities:** spa.

❙ ❙ ❙ SD ❙ ❙ ❙ ❙

KINGSTON (C-5) pop. 587,798
• Hotels & Restaurants index & map p. 387

THE COURTLEIGH HOTEL & SUITES
Phone: (876)929-9000   **7**

▼▼▼▼
Hotel
$145-$400

Address: 85 Knutsford Blvd **Location:** In New Kingston; 14 mi (22.4 km) from airport; between Trafalgar and Oxford rds. **Facility:** 128 units, some two bedrooms and efficiencies. 2-10 stories, interior/exterior corridors. **Amenities:** safes. **Dining:** 3 restaurants. **Pool(s):** outdoor. **Activities:** exercise room. **Guest Services:** valet and coin laundry. **Free Special Amenities:** full breakfast and high-speed Internet.

SAVE ❙ ❙ ❙ SD ❙ BIZ ❙ ❙ ❙ / SOME UNITS ❙

THE JAMAICA PEGASUS HOTEL
Phone: (876)926-3691   **2**

▼▼▼ ▼▼▼
Hotel
$180-$300

Address: 81 Knutsford Blvd **Location:** In New Kingston; 14 mi (22.4 km) from airport; between Trafalgar and Oxford rds. Located in downtown business district. **Facility:** 300 units, some two bedrooms. 17 stories, interior corridors. **Amenities:** high-speed Internet, safes. **Dining:** 3 restaurants. **Pool(s):** outdoor. **Activities:** jogging, exercise room, massage. **Fee:** 2 lighted tennis courts. **Guest Services:** valet laundry.

❙ ❙ ❙ ❙ SD ❙ BIZ ❙ ❙ ❙

SPANISH COURT HOTEL   **Phone:** (876)926-0000   **3**

▼▼▼▼
Boutique Hotel
$124-$195

Address: 1 St. Lucia Ave **Location:** Center of New Kingston. **Facility:** The well-appointed guest units feature Jamaican-made fabrics and furniture as well as oversize tubs. Meets AAA guest room security requirements. 107 units. 3 stories, interior corridors. **Amenities:** high-speed Internet, safes. **Pool(s):** outdoor. **Activities:** exercise room. **Guest Services:** valet laundry.

❙ ❙ ❙ S SD ❙ ❙ ❙ ❙ ❙

WHERE TO EAT

HEATHER'S GARDEN RESTAURANT AND BAR
Phone: 876/926-2826   **4**

▼
International
$7-$23

AAA Inspector Notes: Jamaican and Chinese cuisine dominate the menu along with a few Lebanese dishes at this popular dining spot. Many Americans and other expatriates in Kingston frequent the pleasant, informal restaurant bar. The covered garden-view terrace is kept cool by ceiling fans and is a popular dining spot. **Bar:** full bar. **Address:** 9 Haining Rd **Location:** In New Kingston; on Haining Rd off Oxford Rd. L D ❙ ❙

JADE GARDEN RESTAURANT
Phone: 876/978-3476   **6**

▼▼
Chinese
$12-$40

AAA Inspector Notes: On the second floor of a shopping center near a movie theater, this pleasant, cool and comfortable restaurant presents an extensive menu of Chinese fare. The well-attired waitstaff provides formalized, attentive service. **Bar:** full bar. **Address:** 106 Hope Rd **Location:** Corner of Hope and Barbican rds; in Sovereign Shopping Center. L D ❙

NORMA'S ON THE TERRACE
Phone: 876/968-5488   **1**

▼▼▼▼
Jamaican
$14-$35

AAA Inspector Notes: Located on the verandah of the mansion of the first native Jamaican millionaire is the restaurant of celebrity chef Norma Shirley. The menu utilizes many fresh local ingredients. Try the smoked marlin as an appetizer, or the flavorful island salad. **Bar:** full bar. **Reservations:** suggested. **Address:** 26 Hope Rd **Location:** Just n of New Kingston; corner of Hope and Waterloo rds; in Devon House. **Historic** L D ❙ ❙

REDBONES-THE BLUES CAFE
Phone: 876/978-8262   **2**

▼▼▼
New Caribbean
$11-$30

AAA Inspector Notes: This vibrantly decorated restaurant offers a jazz-inspired theme. The husband and wife owners designed the restaurant to create an ambience to complement the nouvelle Jamaican cuisine. The menu changes frequently but the uptown comfort food may include such dishes as the grilled baby lamb chops with glazed guava or grilled fish in a caper-lime sauce. Save room for the sweet potato pudding. **Bar:** full bar. **Reservations:** suggested. **Address:** 1 Argyle Rd **Location:** Center of New Kingston; off Braemar Ave. L D ❙ ❙

MONTEGO BAY (A-2) pop. 83,446
• Restaurants p. 395
• Hotels & Restaurants index & map p. 387

COYABA BEACH RESORT & CLUB
Phone: 876/953-9150   **16**

Hotel
$230-$440

Address: Mahoe Bay, Rosehall **Location:** Oceanfront. 6.3 mi (10 km) e on Rt A1; 4.2 mi (6.7 km) e of airport. **Facility:** Meets AAA guest room security requirements. 50 units. 3 stories (no elevator), interior/exterior corridors. **Terms:** age restrictions may apply, 14 day cancellation notice. **Amenities:** safes. **Dining:** 3 restaurants, entertainment. **Pool(s):** outdoor. **Activities:** whirlpool, paddleboats, sailboats, windsurfing, boat dock, snorkeling, playground, game room, exercise room. **Fee:** lighted tennis court, massage. **Guest Services:** valet laundry.

HOLIDAY INN SUNSPREE RESORT MONTEGO BAY
Phone: 876/953-2485   **12**

Resort Hotel
$429-$567 1/2-11/30
$408-$567 12/1-1/1

Address: Queens Hwy (Rt A1), Rose Hall **Location:** Oceanfront. 6.8 mi (10.8 km) e; 4.7 mi (7.5 km) e of airport. **Facility:** Built in the 1960s, this renovated family-oriented beachfront resort offers large rooms and spacious suites, all with a balcony or patio. Meets AAA guest room security requirements. 518 units. 4 stories, interior/exterior corridors. **Terms:** 2 night minimum stay - seasonal and/or weekends, 7 day cancellation notice-fee imposed. **Amenities:** *Some:* safes. **Dining:** 6 restaurants, entertainment. **Pool(s):** 2 outdoor. **Activities:** whirlpools, paddleboats, sailboats, snorkeling, miniature golf, 4 tennis courts, recreation programs, playground, basketball, shuffleboard, volleyball, exercise room, spa. **Fee:** scuba diving, game room. **Guest Services:** valet and coin laundry. *(See ad this page.)*

HOTEL RIU MONTEGO BAY
Phone: (876)940-8010   **15**

Resort Hotel
$160-$355

Address: Queens Hwy **Location:** Oceanfront. 2.8 mi (4.5 km) e of downtown; 1.7 mi (2.7 km) e of Montego Bay Airport; at Mahoe Bay. **Facility:** Well-appointed public areas exemplify the oceanfront property; comfortable guest units and spacious marble bathrooms are featured. 681 units. 3-4 stories, interior corridors. **Terms:** 3 night minimum stay, 7 day cancellation notice-fee imposed. **Amenities:** safes, honor bars. **Dining:** 6 restaurants, nightclub, entertainment. **Pool(s):** outdoor. **Activities:** saunas, whirlpools, steamrooms, paddleboats, sailboats, windsurfing, snorkeling, 2 lighted tennis courts, recreation programs, playground, game room, volleyball, spa. **Fee:** scuba diving. **Guest Services:** valet laundry.

SANDALS CARLYLE
Phone: (876)952-4140   **13**

Hotel
$682-$1396 12/1-3/31
$670-$1370 4/1-11/30

Address: Kent Ave **Location:** 2 mi (3.2 km) w of airport; just ne of "Hip Strip". **Facility:** 52 units. 3 stories (no elevator), interior/exterior corridors. **Terms:** 3 night minimum stay - seasonal, age restrictions may apply, 45 day cancellation notice-fee imposed. **Amenities:** safes. **Dining:** 3 restaurants, entertainment. **Pool(s):** outdoor. **Activities:** saunas, whirlpool, limited beach access, lighted tennis court, recreation programs, basketball, shuffleboard, volleyball, exercise room. **Fee:** massage. **Guest Services:** valet laundry, area transportation-other Sandals in Montego Bay. *(See ad on insert.)*

Find valuable AAA/CAA
member savings
at AAA.com/discounts

(See index & map p. 387.)

▼ See AAA listing p. 400 ▼

Half Moon, A RockResort

Half Moon, a AAA Four Diamond Award-winning hotel, is a 400-acre luxury resort featuring 197 guest rooms and suites, 33 private four-seven bedroom Royal Villas, the renowned 68,000-square-foot Fern Tree Spa, an 18-hole signature golf course and more. A combination of Old World charm and elegant modern touches, Half Moon is truly paradise found.

AAA Members earn a complimentary upgrade and welcome amenity!

HALF MOON
ROSE HALL, JAMAICA
A ROCKRESORT

HALFMOON.COM
877-956-ROCK (7625)

Enjoy great savings on hotel rates

at AAA.com or CAA.ca

(See index & map p. 387.)

SANDALS ROYAL CARIBBEAN RESORT & PRIVATE ISLAND
Phone: (876)953-2231 **14**

Resort Hotel
$1134-$3246 12/1-3/31
$1030-$3246 4/1-11/30

Address: Mahoe Bay **Location:** Oceanfront. 5.5 mi (8.8 km) e on Rt A1; 4 mi (6.4 km) e of airport. **Facility:** The all-inclusive, couples-only, luxury beach resort offers well-appointed guest rooms and extensive recreational facilities. 197 units. 2-3 stories, interior/exterior corridors. **Terms:** 3 night minimum stay - seasonal, 45 day cancellation notice-fee imposed. **Amenities:** high-speed Internet (fee). Some: safes, honor bars. **Dining:** 4 restaurants, entertainment. **Pool(s):** 4 outdoor. **Activities:** saunas, whirlpools, lifeguard on duty, paddleboats, sailboats, windsurfing, boat dock, snorkeling, 3 tennis courts (2 lighted), recreation programs, basketball, shuffleboard, volleyball, exercise room. Fee: scuba diving, charter fishing, massage. **Guest Services:** valet laundry, area transportation-other Montego Bay Sandals.
(See ad on insert.)

SECRETS ST. JAMES MONTEGO BAY
Phone: (876)953-6601 **11**

Resort Hotel
$546-$984

Address: Lot A59 Freeport **Location:** Oceanfront. 2 mi (3.2 km) sw of Montego Bay's "Hip" Strip; 4.2 mi (6.7 km) sw of airport. Near the "Freeport" cruise ship docks. **Facility:** This luxury adult property offers very spacious guest units featuring a host of amenities as well as plenty of recreation and dining opportunities. 350 units. 4-5 stories, exterior corridors. **Terms:** 3 night minimum stay, 3 day cancellation notice-fee imposed. **Amenities:** high-speed Internet, safes, honor bars. **Dining:** 8 restaurants, nightclub, entertainment. **Pool(s):** 3 outdoor, heated outdoor. **Activities:** whirlpools, lifeguard on duty, paddleboats, sailboats, windsurfing, boat dock, snorkeling & rental equipment, recreation programs, bicycles, basketball, game room, horseshoes, shuffleboard, volleyball, spa. Fee: scuba diving. **Guest Services:** valet laundry.
(See ad on insert.)

SECRETS WILD ORCHID MONTEGO BAY JAMAICA
Phone: (876)953-6600 **17**

Resort Hotel
$573-$1035

Address: Lot A59 Freeport **Location:** Oceanfront. 2 mi (3.2 km) sw of Montego Bay's "Hip" Strip; 4.2 mi (6.7 km) sw of airport. Near the "Freeport" cruise ship docks. **Facility:** The well-appointed property offers spacious guest units, numerous recreational opportunities and various dining options. 350 units. 4-5 stories, exterior corridors. **Terms:** 3 night minimum stay, 3 day cancellation notice-fee imposed. **Amenities:** high-speed Internet, safes, honor bars. **Dining:** 8 restaurants, nightclub, entertainment. **Pool(s):** 3 outdoor. **Activities:** whirlpools, lifeguard on duty, paddleboats, sailboats, windsurfing, boat dock, snorkeling & rental equipment, lighted tennis court, recreation programs, bicycles, basketball, game room, horseshoes, shuffleboard, volleyball, spa. Fee: scuba diving. **Guest Services:** valet laundry. **Free Special Amenities:** full breakfast and manager's reception.
(See ad on insert.)

SUNSET BEACH RESORT SPA AND WATERPARK
Phone: (876)979-8800 **10**

Resort Hotel
$290-$820

Address: Sunset Dr **Location:** Oceanfront. 2.2 mi (3.6 km) sw of Montego Bay's "Hip Strip"; 4.4 mi (7 km) sw of airport. Near the "Freeport" cruise ship docks. **Facility:** The comprehensive oceanfront resort with theme restaurants offers guest units with tropical décor. 430 units. 2-10 stories, exterior corridors. **Terms:** 3 night minimum stay - seasonal, 30 day cancellation notice-fee imposed. **Amenities:** safes (fee). **Dining:** 5 restaurants, nightclub, entertainment. **Pool(s):** 4 outdoor. **Activities:** whirlpools, waterslide, lifeguard on duty, paddleboats, sailboats, windsurfing, snorkeling, miniature golf, 4 lighted tennis courts, recreation programs, playground, basketball, game room, horseshoes, shuffleboard, volleyball, spa. Fee: saunas, steamrooms. **Guest Services:** valet and coin laundry. *(See ad this page.)*

▼ *See AAA listing this page* ▼

(See index & map p. 387.)

SANDALS MONTEGO BAY   Phone: 876/952-5510

fyi Not evaluated. **Address:** 100 Kent Ave **Location:** 1.7 mi (2.7 km) e of airport; 0.5 mi (0.8 km) w, follow signs. Facilities, services, and decor characterize a mid-scale property. **(See ad on insert.)**

WHERE TO EAT

AKBAR AND THAI GARDEN RESTAURANT
Phone: 876/953-8240   (17)

Asian
$12-$35

AAA Inspector Notes: The menu lists both Indian and Thai dishes, which are prepared exquisitely with spiciness adjusted for the more timid and served on copper-plated dinnerware. Efficient servers circulate in the exotic Asian-decorated dining room. Complimentary transportation is provided to and from local hotels. **Bar:** full bar. **Address:** Half Moon Shopping Village **Location:** 7.6 mi (12 km) e on Rt A1; 5.1 mi (8 km) w of airport; in Half Moon Shopping Village.

L D CALL M

THE HOUSEBOAT GRILL   Phone: 876/979-8845   (8)

Fusion
$14-$32

AAA Inspector Notes: True to its name, this restaurant is truly a houseboat in the water. Guests are ferried across on a small barge to enjoy well-prepared cuisine. Examples of the types of dishes on the menu, which changes every three weeks, include smoked marlin dip and New Zealand mussels starters, fresh fish entrées, blue cheese-encrusted beef fillet and potato gnocchi in apple-hazelnut creme sauce. Warm banana cake with sabayon sauce is not to be missed. **Bar:** full bar. **Reservations:** required. **Address:** Southern Cross Blvd **Location:** 2 mi (3.2 km) w of town; in Montego Freeport District.

D K

JIMMY BUFFETT'S MARGARITAVILLE
Phone: 876/952-4777

Caribbean
$12-$28

AAA Inspector Notes: Amenities at this lively bayfront bar and grill include a waterslide, floating trampolines and a terrace with a hot tub. Among Caribbean-style specialties are jerk chicken, mango snapper, conch, Jamaican pizza and lobster tail, all complemented by an impressive array of 52 varieties of margaritas. Musicians perform most nights. **Bar:** full bar. **Address:** Glouster Ave **Location:** 2 mi (3.2 km) se of airport; just s of Doctor's Cave Beach; center of "Hip Strip". L D K

MARGUERITES SEAFOOD BY THE SEA
Phone: 876/952-4777   (11)

Caribbean
$28-$54

AAA Inspector Notes: Overlooking the bay, this pleasant dining room affords beautiful sunset views. Since 1995 this restaurant has received praise from international celebrities. Menu offerings include preparations of regional fresh fish and seafood, such as lobster, shrimp, sea bass, tuna and grouper, as well as pasta, chicken piccata and filet mignon. The signature dish is reef snapper wrapped in callaloo and plantains simmered in coconut milk. A complimentary shuttle is available in the Montego Bay area. **Bar:** full bar. **Reservations:** suggested. **Address:** Gloucester Ave **Location:** 2 mi (3.2 km) se of airport; just s of Doctor's Cave Beach; center of "Hip Strip". **Parking:** on-site and valet. D K

THE NATIVE RESTAURANT & BAR
Phone: 876/979-2769   (15)

Jamaican
$9-$30

AAA Inspector Notes: This well-established restaurant is perched on a terrace above the streets of the Hip Strip with views of the ocean. Smartly attired servers provide island-friendly service in the al fresco eatery adorned with Jamaican art. The extensive menu offers many Jamaican specialties including ackee, codfish fritters, stuffed crab back, oxtail stew and of course escovitch fish. **Bar:** full bar. **Reservations:** suggested. **Address:** 29 Gloucester Ave **Location:** Center of "Hip Strip". B L D K

(See index & map p. 387.)

PELICAN GRILL Phone: 876/952-3171 (13)

Jamaican
$10-$30

AAA Inspector Notes: Hearty, home-style meals are served in a Jamaican-style diner. Favorite selections include curried chicken and goat, escovitch fish and callaloo soup. Be sure to try the lofty and luscious banana-rum cream pie. **Bar:** full bar. **Address:** Gloucester Ave **Location:** In "Hip Strip"; downtown. [B] [L] [D]

NEGRIL (B-1) pop. 1,500
• Hotels & Restaurants index & map p. 387

BEACHES NEGRIL RESORT & SPA
Phone: 876/957-9270 (49)

Resort Hotel
$1036-$5926

Address: Norman Manley Blvd **Location:** Oceanfront. 1.2 mi (1.9 km) s of Negril Airport; 1.5 mi (2.4 km) n of downtown. **Facility:** Dining and recreational facilities are featured at this all-inclusive, family-friendly resort on beachfront grounds; numerous room options are available. 210 units, some two bedrooms. 3 stories (no elevator), exterior corridors. **Terms:** 3 night minimum stay - seasonal, 45 day cancellation notice-fee imposed. **Amenities:** high-speed Internet (fee), safes. Some: honor bars. **Dining:** 5 restaurants, nightclub, entertainment. **Pool(s):** 2 outdoor. **Activities:** saunas, whirlpools, waterslide, lifeguard on duty, boating, paddleboats, sailboats, windsurfing, waterskiing, snorkeling, miniature golf, 2 lighted tennis courts, recreation programs, playground, game room, horseshoes, shuffleboard, volleyball, spa. **Fee:** scuba diving. **Guest Services:** valet and coin laundry, area transportation-Beaches Sandy Bay. *(See ad on insert.)*

BEACHES SANDY BAY Phone: (876)957-5100 (47)

Resort Hotel
$748-$1556

Address: Norman Manley Blvd **Location:** Oceanfront. 0.5 mi (0.8 km) s of Negril Airport; 2.3 mi (3.7 km) n of downtown. **Facility:** Boasting 1,000 feet of beach and six acres of tropical lushness, this resort offers seven room categories. 128 units, some two bedrooms. 3 stories (no elevator), exterior corridors. **Terms:** 3 night minimum stay - seasonal, 45 day cancellation notice-fee imposed. **Amenities:** safes. **Dining:** 4 restaurants, nightclub, entertainment. **Pool(s):** 2 outdoor. **Activities:** whirlpool, lifeguard on duty, canoeing, paddleboats, sailboats, windsurfing, waterskiing, scuba diving, snorkeling, 2 lighted tennis courts, recreation programs, playground, basketball, game room, shuffleboard, volleyball. **Fee:** massage. **Guest Services:** valet and coin laundry, area transportation-Beaches Negril Resort. *(See ad on insert.)*

Safety tip: Keep a current
AAA/CAA Road Atlas
in every vehicle

BREEZES GRAND RESORT AND SPA NEGRIL
Phone: (876)957-5010 (42)

Resort Hotel
$335-$908

Address: Norman Manley Blvd **Location:** Oceanfront. Just s of Negril Airport; 4.4 mi (7.1 km) n of downtown. **Facility:** This popular all-inclusive resort sits on a magnificent stretch of beach along Bloody Bay and offers extensive recreational facilities. 210 units. 2 stories (no elevator), exterior corridors. **Terms:** age restrictions may apply, 22 day cancellation notice-fee imposed. **Amenities:** high-speed Internet (fee), safes, honor bars. **Dining:** 6 restaurants, nightclub, entertainment. **Pool(s):** 2 outdoor. **Activities:** sauna, whirlpools, steamroom, lifeguard on duty, paddleboats, sailboats, windsurfing, waterskiing, scuba diving, snorkeling, 4 tennis courts (2 lighted), recreation programs, game room, volleyball, exercise room, spa. **Guest Services:** valet laundry. **Free Special Amenities:** full breakfast and airport transportation.

THE CAVES Phone: 876/957-0270 (51)

Cottage
$608-$710 12/1-9/15
$445-$520 10/7-11/30

Address: Light House Rd **Location:** Oceanfront. 5 mi (8 km) s of Negril Airport via West End Rd; 2.1 mi (3.4 km) w of downtown. **Facility:** Stylish cliffside wooden cottages perched above grotto caves and honeycombed cliffs give this ocean-view property the ambience of a tropical oasis. 12 units, some houses. 1-2 stories, exterior corridors. **Terms:** open 12/1-9/15 & 10/7-11/30, office hours 8:30 am-8 pm, age restrictions may apply, 30 day cancellation notice-fee imposed. **Amenities:** safes, honor bars. **Dining:** 2 restaurants. **Pool(s):** outdoor. **Activities:** sauna, whirlpools, snorkeling, bicycles. **Fee:** massage.

COUPLES NEGRIL Phone: (876)957-5960 (46)

Resort Hotel
$635-$977

Address: Norman Manley Blvd **Location:** Oceanfront. Just n of Negril Airport; 4.8 mi (7.7 km) n of downtown. **Facility:** Built for romance, this couples-only resort is an idyllic escape. The spacious guest rooms are stylishly chic with a bright color scheme. 234 units. 3 stories (no elevator), exterior corridors. **Terms:** check-in 4 pm, 3 night minimum stay, age restrictions may apply, 30 day cancellation notice-fee imposed. **Amenities:** safes, honor bars. **Dining:** 4 restaurants, nightclub, entertainment. **Pool(s):** outdoor. **Activities:** whirlpools, boating, paddleboats, sailboats, windsurfing, waterskiing, scuba diving, snorkeling, golf-18 holes, 4 tennis courts (2 lighted), recreation programs, basketball, game room, horseshoes, shuffleboard, volleyball, exercise room, spa. **Guest Services:** valet laundry.

COUPLES SWEPT AWAY Phone: 876/957-4062 (45)

Resort Hotel
$593-$928

Address: Norman Manley Blvd **Location:** Oceanfront. 2.3 mi (3.6 km) s of Negril Airport; 2.4 mi (3.9 km) n of downtown. **Facility:** This all-inclusive beachfront resort has an elaborate sports complex; each of the villa-style units feature a large balcony or patio. 312 units. 2-3 stories (no elevator), exterior corridors. **Terms:** 3 night minimum stay, age restrictions may apply, 30 day cancellation notice-fee imposed. **Amenities:** safes. Some: honor bars. **Dining:** 6 restaurants, entertainment. **Pool(s):** 3 outdoor. **Activities:** saunas, whirlpools, steamrooms, paddleboats, sailboats, windsurfing, waterskiing, scuba diving, snorkeling, 10 lighted tennis courts, racquetball courts, recreation programs, jogging, sports court, basketball, volleyball, spa. **Fee:** charter fishing. **Guest Services:** valet laundry.

(See index & map p. 387.)

HOTEL RIU PALACE TROPICAL BAY
Phone: (876)957-5900 **40**

Resort Hotel
$268-$550 12/1-4/30
$208-$350 5/1-11/30

Address: Norman Manley Blvd **Location:** Oceanfront. 4.2 mi (6.7 km) n of Negril; 48.3 mi (77 km) w of Montego Bay. **Facility:** The hotel features well-appointed public areas and comfortable guest rooms with extra amenities; several on-premise activities are available. 416 units. 3 stories (no elevator), exterior corridors. **Terms:** 3 night minimum stay, 7 day cancellation notice-fee imposed. **Amenities:** safes, honor bars. **Dining:** 8 restaurants, entertainment. **Pool(s):** 2 outdoor. **Activities:** saunas, whirlpools, paddleboats, windsurfing, 2 lighted tennis courts, recreation programs, playground, volleyball, exercise room, spa. *Fee:* scuba diving, snorkeling. **Guest Services:** valet laundry.

RIU CLUB HOTEL
Phone: (876)957-5700 **38**

Resort Hotel
$115-$420 12/1-4/30
$151-$290 5/1-11/30

Address: Norman Manley Blvd **Location:** Oceanfront. 1.2 mi (1.8 km) n of Negril Airport; 5.9 mi (9.4 km) n of downtown. **Facility:** Featuring lavish, elegantly appointed public areas, this all-inclusive mega resort is ideal for families, couples or singles. 420 units. 3 stories (no elevator), interior/exterior corridors. **Terms:** 7 day cancellation notice-fee imposed. **Amenities:** safes, honor bars. **Dining:** 4 restaurants, nightclub, entertainment. **Pool(s):** 2 outdoor. **Activities:** saunas, whirlpools, paddleboats, sailboats, windsurfing, 2 lighted tennis courts, recreation programs, playground, volleyball, exercise room, spa. *Fee:* scuba diving, snorkeling. **Guest Services:** valet laundry.

RONDEL VILLAGE
Phone: (876)957-4413 **43**

Hotel
$75-$440

Address: Norman Manley Blvd **Location:** Oceanfront. 3.2 mi (5.1 km) s of Negril Airport; 1.4 mi (2.2 km) n of downtown. **Facility:** 40 units, some two bedrooms and kitchens. 1-3 stories (no elevator), exterior corridors. **Terms:** office hours 7 am-9:30 pm, 3-7 night minimum stay - seasonal, 22 day cancellation notice-fee imposed. **Amenities:** safes (fee). **Pool(s):** 2 outdoor. **Activities:** whirlpools. **Guest Services:** valet laundry.

SANDALS NEGRIL BEACH RESORT & SPA
Phone: (876)957-5216 **44**

Resort Hotel
$1044-$3742 12/1-3/31
$990-$3742 4/1-11/30

Address: Norman Manley Blvd **Location:** Oceanfront. 4.5 mi (7.2 km) e of downtown. **Facility:** Manicured grounds surround this couples-only, all-inclusive beachfront resort. Extensive recreational facilities are offered. 222 units. 2-3 stories, exterior corridors. **Terms:** 3 night minimum stay - seasonal, age restrictions may apply, 45 day cancellation notice-fee imposed. **Amenities:** *Some:* high-speed Internet (fee), safes, honor bars. **Dining:** 6 restaurants, entertainment. **Pool(s):** 3 outdoor. **Activities:** saunas, whirlpools, steamrooms, lifeguard on duty, canoeing, paddleboats, sailboats, windsurfing, waterskiing, scuba diving, snorkeling, 4 tennis courts (2 lighted), recreation programs, sports court, horseshoes, shuffleboard, volleyball, spa. **Guest Services:** valet laundry.
(See ad on insert.)

WHERE TO EAT

COSMO'S SEAFOOD RESTAURANT
Phone: 876/957-4784 **39**

Jamaican
$6-$22

AAA Inspector Notes: Native Jamaican cuisine is served at covered and open tables in a casual beachside setting. Try bammy--a fried cassava cake--or red pea soup with dumplings. The more daring might order escovitch fish prepared with vinegar, onions and hot peppers. **Bar:** full bar. **Address:** Norman Manley Blvd **Location:** 1 mi (1.6 km) s of Negril Airport; 1.7 mi (2.7 km) n of downtown.

JIMMY BUFFETT'S MARGARITAVILLE
Phone: 876/957-4467

Caribbean
$12-$28

AAA Inspector Notes: This is a "no prude zone" type of place to kick back, relax, listen to music and enjoy some great island-inspired fare. Begin with one of the refreshing libations while perusing a menu of choices as colorful and whimsical as the festive decor. Favorites are peel-and-eat shrimp, conch chowder and whole fish served escovitched style. The menu also abounds with fajitas, jerks, pizzas, pastas and cheeseburgers--in paradise, of course. **Bar:** full bar. **Address:** Norman Manley Blvd **Location:** 1.6 mi (2.5 km) s of Negril Airport; 1.1 mi (1.7 km) n of downtown.

KUYABA ON THE BEACH
Phone: 876/957-4318 **42**

Jamaican
$16-$32

AAA Inspector Notes: Facing the beach is this charming restaurant with a series of thatched-roof decks. Serving Jamaican comfort food, guests can expect a meal loaded with flavor. The jerk sausage and red pea soup and the ackee and salt-fish crepe are ideal starters. Entrées include several Jamaican-inspired pasta dishes with lobster and conch as well as crab and pumpkin cakes, coconut curried conch and snapper filet with orange sauce. For dessert, the peanut butter pie and mango cheesecake are tempting. **Bar:** full bar. **Reservations:** suggested. **Address:** Norman Manley Blvd **Location:** 2.8 mi (4.5 km) s of Negril Airport; 1.9 mi (3 km) n of downtown; in Kuyaba Negril.

NORMA'S RESTAURANT ON THE BEACH AT SEA SPLASH RESORT
Phone: 876/957-4041 **40**

Jamaican
$12-$35

AAA Inspector Notes: Associated with well-regarded chef Norma Shirley's, the restaurant features oceanfront seating, where you can enjoy lobster tail, coconut chicken or rasta pasta for lunch. All dinner entrées are available after 2 pm and include such dishes as pork loin chop marinated in ginger and beer, filet au poivre and filet of red snapper. An array of desserts also are available. **Bar:** full bar. **Reservations:** suggested. **Address:** Norman Manley Blvd **Location:** 2.5 mi (4 km) s of Negril Airport; 2.1 mi (3.3 km) n of downtown; in Sea Splash.

RICK'S CAFE
Phone: 876/957-0380 **51**

Caribbean
$8-$24

AAA Inspector Notes: This restaurant-bar is well known for the view at sunset from the rocky oceanfront cliff and for the amazing locals who dare to dive from the cliffs and plunge into the clear grotto waters below. For those not interested in the plunge from the cliff there is a swimming pool. The menu features Caribbean and international-inspired preparations of fresh fish, lobster, pasta and chicken. Live music from reggae to steel band is featured most nights. **Bar:** full bar. **Address:** Lighthouse Rd **Location:** 3 mi (4.8 km) w on West End Rd (Lighthouse Rd).

(See index & map p. 387.)

ROCK HOUSE RESTAURANT
Phone: 876/957-4373   49

Jamaican
$11-$22

AAA Inspector Notes: Tucked away along the lush cliffs of this chic boutique-style hotel is this relaxing restaurant. Enjoy some traditional Jamaican cuisine with an updated twist. Favorites are the pepperpot soup and the escovitch fish that is tantalizingly spicy. The coconut cream pie is luscious. **Bar:** full bar. **Address:** West End Rd **Location:** 4.2 mi (6.7 km) s of Negril Airport; 1.1 mi (1.7 km) w of downtown via West End Rd; in Rock House Hotel. Ⓑ Ⓛ Ⓓ Ⓚ ▧

SWEET SPICE RESTAURANT
Phone: 876/957-4621   45

Jamaican
$10-$20

AAA Inspector Notes: A favorite among both locals and tourists, this simple, unpretentious diner uses fresh fruit in all-natural drinks and milkshakes. Depending on the season, lobster, shrimp and curried conch are offered along with Jamaican preparations of chicken, goat and oxtail. Filet of snapper is a favorite. **Address:** 1 White Hall Rd **Location:** 0.5 mi (0.8 km) e on Rt A2, jct Whitehall Rd. **Parking:** street only. Ⓑ Ⓛ Ⓓ

XTABI ON THE CLIFF
Phone: 876/957-0121   52

Jamaican
$11-$28

AAA Inspector Notes: A fun place to relax and hang out or enjoy an evening cocktail as the sun sets over the ocean, this eatery is perfectly situated over the cliffs for breathtaking views as guests can listen to gentle music and enjoy simple island dishes. **Bar:** full bar. **Address:** West End Rd **Location:** 1.7 mi (2.8 km) w on West End Rd (Lighthouse Rd). Ⓑ Ⓛ Ⓓ Ⓚ ▧

OCHO RIOS (A-4) pop. 7,800
• Hotels & Restaurants index & map p. 387

BEACHES BOSCOBEL RESORT & GOLF CLUB
Phone: (876)975-7777   24

Resort Hotel
$924-$2542 12/1-4/15
$856-$2542 4/16-11/30

Address: Hwy A3 **Location:** Oceanfront. Just w of Boscobel Airport. **Facility:** This ultra all-inclusive resort sets on 22 acres and offers 10 room categories, five at the concierge level. 223 units. 3-5 stories, exterior corridors. **Terms:** 3 night minimum stay - seasonal, 45 day cancellation notice-fee imposed. **Amenities:** safes. **Dining:** 5 restaurants, nightclub, entertainment. **Pool(s):** 4 outdoor. **Activities:** sauna, whirlpools, steamroom, waterslide, lifeguard on duty, canoeing, paddleboats, sailboats, windsurfing, boat dock, scuba diving, snorkeling, golf-18 holes, 4 tennis courts (2 lighted), recreation programs, basketball, game room, shuffleboard, volleyball, spa. *Fee:* charter fishing. **Guest Services:** valet and coin laundry. *(See ad on insert.)*

✈ 🍽 🍸 🏃 SD 🏊 📶 🔌 🖥

JAMAICA INN
Phone: (876)974-2514   26

Hotel
$315-$1935

Address: 1 Old Rd **Location:** Oceanfront. 1.7 mi (2.7 km) e on Rt A3, just n of road to Shaw Park. **Facility:** 51 units, some cottages. 1-2 stories (no elevator), exterior corridors. **Terms:** open 12/1-9/1 & 10/10-11/30, age restrictions may apply, 30 day cancellation notice, 14 day off season-fee imposed. **Amenities:** *Some:* safes. **Dining:** restaurant, see separate listing, entertainment. **Pool(s):** outdoor. **Activities:** sailboats, snorkeling, exercise room, spa. **Guest Services:** valet laundry.

SAVE FEE ✈ 🍽 🍸 SD 🏊 📶 Ⓦ / SOME UNITS 🔌 🖥

▼ *See AAA listing p. 399* ▼

Visit AAA.com or CAA.ca for one-stop
travel planning and reservations

(See index & map p. 387.)

SANDALS GRANDE RIVIERA BEACH & VILLA GOLF RESORT
Phone: (876)974-5691 **30**

Resort Hotel
$1102-$3128 12/1-3/31
$1078-$3128 4/1-11/30

Address: Main St **Location:** Oceanfront. 1 mi (1.6 km) e of downtown. **Facility:** This upscale adults-only resort boasts extensive recreational facilities and a beautiful beachfront location. 529 units, some two bedrooms and kitchens. 1-5 stories, interior/exterior corridors. **Terms:** 3 night minimum stay - seasonal, age restrictions may apply, 45 day cancellation notice-fee imposed. **Amenities:** high-speed Internet (fee), safes, honor bars. **Dining:** 11 restaurants, nightclub, entertainment. **Pool(s):** 7 outdoor. **Activities:** saunas, whirlpools, steamrooms, lifeguard on duty, canoeing, paddleboats, sailboats, windsurfing, boat dock, scuba diving, snorkeling, fishing, golf-18 holes, 4 lighted tennis courts, racquetball court, recreation programs, sports court, basketball, game room, horseshoes, shuffleboard, volleyball, spa. **Fee:** charter fishing. **Guest Services:** valet laundry.

SANDALS ROYAL PLANTATION OCHO RIOS, JAMAICA
Phone: (876)974-5601 **22**

Resort Hotel
$1774-$4898 12/1-3/31
$1726-$4752 4/1-11/30

Address: Main St **Location:** Oceanfront. 1.5 mi (2.4 km) e of downtown. **Facility:** On a bluff overlooking the sea, the property has spacious luxury accommodations and refined, discreet service; all guests must be over age 18. Meets AAA guest room security requirements. 74 units, some houses. 3 stories (no elevator), exterior corridors. **Terms:** 3 night minimum stay - seasonal, age restrictions may apply, 45 day cancellation notice-fee imposed. **Amenities:** high-speed Internet (fee), safes, honor bars. **Dining:** 3 restaurants, entertainment. **Pool(s):** heated outdoor. **Activities:** saunas, whirlpool, steamrooms, paddleboats, sailboats, windsurfing, boat dock, snorkeling, golf-18 holes, 2 lighted tennis courts, recreation programs, exercise room, spa. **Fee:** scuba diving. **Guest Services:** valet laundry, area transportation-golf course.

THE JEWEL DUNN'S RIVER BEACH RESORT & SPA
Phone: 876/972-7400

fyi Not evaluated. **Address:** Mammee Bay **Location:** 65 mi (104 km) e of Montego Bay International Airport. Facilities, services, and decor characterize a mid-scale property. **(See ad p. 398.)**

RIU OCHO RIOS HOTEL
Phone: 876/972-2200

fyi Not evaluated. **Address:** Mammee Bay St. Ann **Location:** Oceanfront. 4.6 mi (7.3 km) w of town. Facilities, services, and decor characterize a mid-scale property.

WHERE TO EAT

EVITA'S
Menu on AAA.com
Phone: 876/974-2333 **29**

Italian
$13-$26

AAA Inspector Notes: The charming converted 1860 gingerbread house sits high on a hillside overlooking the town and bay. Well-prepared Italian food, made with fresh pasta, and some Jamaican specialties make up the diverse menu. Guests should reserve early for one of the popular veranda tables. Some nights feature live music. **Bar:** full bar. **Reservations:** required. **Address:** Eden Bower Rd **Location:** Jct Rt A1, just s. **Historic**

JAMAICA INN DINING ROOM
Phone: 876/974-2514 **32**

International
$14-$38

AAA Inspector Notes: Well-trained servers move around the romantic terrace dining room, which offers views of the beach and sea. An international wine list complements preparations of excellent Continental, French and island cuisine. Most nights feature live music. **Bar:** full bar. **Reservations:** required, for dinner. **Address:** Old Road **Location:** 1.7 mi (2.7 km) e on Rt A3, just n of road to Shaw Park; in Jamaica Inn.

JIMMY BUFFETT'S MARGARITAVILLE
Phone: 876/675-8800

Caribbean
$12-$28

AAA Inspector Notes: Adjacent to the cruise ship docks is the restaurant opened by famed singer and songwriter Jimmy Buffett. More than a restaurant, the facility also includes a rooftop hot tub, 100-foot-long waterslide and three bars, including a swim-up pool bar. Caribbean decor complements island-inspired fare, such as jerk pork and chicken, conch chowder and, of course, the cheeseburger in paradise. Copious margaritas, beer and a variety of "boat drinks" leave patrons saying, "Irie, mon!". **Bar:** full bar. **Address:** Island Village Shopping Mall **Location:** Just w of town center; in Island Village Complex.

PASSAGE TO INDIA
Phone: 876/795-3182 **36**

Indian
$11-$27

AAA Inspector Notes: Patrons can sample tandoori and North Indian dishes at the rooftop restaurant in Soni's Plaza. Palate-teasers include kebabs and tikka, fish or meat marinated in spices then baked in a tandoor oven. Main-event entrees include mutton, fish and chicken simmered in various sauces, including vindaloo, masala and begum bahar sauce: a tomato-and-cashew-nut gravy. **Bar:** full bar. **Reservations:** suggested. **Address:** 50 Main St **Location:** Center; at Soni's Plaza; across from Sunset Jamaica Grande.

TOSCANINI ITALIAN RESTAURANT
Phone: 876/975-4785 **38**

Italian
$15-$29

AAA Inspector Notes: Patrons are treated to al fresco dining on the veranda of this gingerbread mansion. Italian dishes, served in large portions, incorporate a hint of island influences and are nicely matched with the selection of imported wines. Take time to tour the art collection. **Bar:** full bar. **Reservations:** required. **Address:** Oracabessa Main Rd **Location:** 4.5 mi (7.2 km) e on Rt A3; at Harmony Hall; Tower Isle. **Historic**

PORT ANTONIO (B-6) pop. 13,246
- **Restaurants p. 400**
- **Hotels & Restaurants index & map p. 387**

THE JAMAICA PALACE HOTEL
Phone: (876)993-7720 **55**

Hotel
$170-$190

Address: Williamsfield **Location:** 5 mi (8 km) e of town. **Facility:** 80 units. 2 stories (no elevator), exterior corridors. **Terms:** 30 day cancellation notice-fee imposed. **Amenities:** safes (fee). **Pool(s):** outdoor. **Guest Services:** valet laundry.

(See index & map p. 387.)

WHERE TO EAT

PANORAMA RESTAURANT AND LOUNGE
Phone: 876/993-7374 (54)

Caribbean
$12-$27

AAA Inspector Notes: On the outskirts of town, this restaurant is nestled high in the hills overlooking the ocean. The covered al fresco dining room provides spectacular views. Choices on the Jamaican-West Indies-influenced menu range from rich red pea soup and jerked meats to oxtail stew and curried chicken. **Bar:** full bar. **Address:** Fern Hill **Location:** 5.5 mi (8.8 km) e on Rt A4; in Fern Hill Hotel and Villa Resort.

[B] [L] [D] [✗] [◻]

ROSE HALL (A-2)
• Hotels & Restaurants index & map p. 387

HALF MOON, A ROCKRESORT
Phone: 876/953-2211 (20)

Resort Hotel
$250-$1680

Address: Rt A1 **Location:** Oceanfront. 7.6 mi (12.1 km) e on Rt A1; 5.1 mi (8.1 km) e of airport. Located in a gated area. **Facility:** This oceanfront resort offers mostly spacious guest rooms and suites as well as staffed villas; the recreational facilities are extensive. 398 units, some two bedrooms and houses. 1-2 stories (no elevator), interior/exterior corridors. **Terms:** 5 day cancellation notice, 3 day off season-fee imposed. **Amenities:** high-speed Internet, safes, honor bars. **Dining:** 6 restaurants, see separate listing, entertainment. **Pool(s):** 3 outdoor. **Activities:** whirlpools, rental sailboats, miniature golf, 13 lighted tennis courts, recreation programs, rental bicycles, hiking trails, jogging, playground, basketball, game room, shuffleboard, volleyball, spa. *Fee:* saunas, steamrooms, paddleboats, windsurfing, waterskiing, scuba diving, snorkeling, fishing, golf-18 holes, horseback riding. **Guest Services:** valet laundry. *(See ad p. 393.)*

[SAVE] [ECO] FEE [✦] [⊪] [⊡] [Y] [⋔] [SD] [⇲]
[⇔] [BIZ] [⊚] [▭] / SOME UNITS [⊟] [⬚]

HILTON ROSE HALL RESORT & SPA
Phone: (876)953-2650 (18)

Resort Hotel
$119-$449

Hilton

AAA Benefit: Members save 5% or more everyday!

Address: Rose Hall, Montego Bay **Location:** Oceanfront. 9.7 mi (15.5 km) e on Rt A1; 7.7 mi (12.3 km) e of airport. **Facility:** The property offers a mini water park as well as manicured grounds, a golf course and a fine beach; guest rooms feature contemporary touches. Meets AAA guest room security requirements. 488 units. 7 stories, interior corridors. **Terms:** check-in 4 pm, 3 day cancellation notice-fee imposed. **Amenities:** high-speed Internet (fee), safes. **Dining:** 5 restaurants, nightclub, entertainment. **Pool(s):** 2 outdoor. **Activities:** whirlpools, waterslide, lifeguard on duty, canoeing, sailboats, windsurfing, snorkeling, recreation programs, jogging, playground, basketball, game room, horseshoes, volleyball, exercise room, spa. *Fee:* waterskiing, scuba diving, golf-18 holes, 6 lighted tennis courts. **Guest Services:** valet laundry.

[SAVE] [⊪] [Y] [⋔] [S] [SD] [⇲] [BIZ] [⊚] [⊟] [▭]

THE RITZ-CARLTON GOLF & SPA RESORT, ROSE HALL, JAMAICA
Phone: (876)953-2800 (19)

Resort Hotel
$279-$1100

AAA Benefit: Unequaled service at Special Member Savings.

Address: 1 Ritz-Carlton Dr **Location:** Oceanfront. 8.6 mi (13.7 km) e on Rt A1; 6.1 mi (9.7 km) e of airport. **Facility:** A modern spa, golf courses and other recreational facilities combine with luxury lodgings to give this upscale resort a refined, world-class ambiance. 427 units. 5 stories, interior corridors. **Parking:** valet only. **Terms:** 21 day cancellation notice-fee imposed. **Amenities:** high-speed Internet, safes, honor bars. **Dining:** 3 restaurants, entertainment. **Pool(s):** outdoor. **Activities:** saunas, whirlpool, steamrooms, lifeguard on duty, sailboats, windsurfing, 2 lighted tennis courts, recreation programs, jogging, playground, basketball, horseshoes, volleyball, spa. *Fee:* scuba diving, snorkeling, golf-18 holes. **Guest Services:** valet laundry, area transportation-within 1 mi. **Free Special Amenities:** high-speed Internet and manager's reception.

[SAVE] FEE [✦] [⊪] [⊡] [Y] [⋔] CALL [⌘M] [S] [SD]
[⇲] [⇔] [BIZ] [⊚] [✗] [▭] / SOME UNITS [⊟] [⬚]

IBEROSTAR GRAND HOTEL ROSE HALL
Phone: 876/680-0000

(fyi) Not evaluated. **Address:** Rose Hall Main Rd **Location:** Center. Facilities, services, and decor characterize a mid-scale property. *(See ad on insert.)*

IBEROSTAR ROSE HALL BEACH
Phone: 876/680-0000

(fyi) Not evaluated. **Address:** Rose Hall Main Rd **Location:** Oceanfront. Center. Facilities, services, and decor characterize a mid-scale property.

IBEROSTAR ROSE HALL SUITES
Phone: 876/680-0000

(fyi) Not evaluated. **Address:** Rose Hall Main Rd **Location:** Center. Facilities, services, and decor characterize a mid-scale property.

WHERE TO EAT

SUGAR MILL RESTAURANT
Phone: 876/953-2314 (18)

International
$19-$35

AAA Inspector Notes: European and Caribbean dishes intertwine at this restaurant overlooking a golf course and the sea with an original 17th century sugar mill as a backdrop. The innovative menu features such tasty dishes as coconut-encrusted chicken breast with a fruit chutney. Numerous wines are available from the wine cellar. **Bar:** full bar. **Reservations:** required. **Address:** Rt A1 **Location:** 7.6 mi (12.1 km) e on Rt A1; 5.1 mi (8.1 km) e of airport; in Half Moon, A RockResort. **Historic**

[D] [✗] [◻]

RUNAWAY BAY
• Hotels & Restaurants index & map p. 387

BREEZES RESORT, SPA & GOLF CLUB RUNAWAY BAY
Phone: (876)973-6099 (63)

Resort Hotel
$240-$450

Address: Rt A1 **Location:** Oceanfront. On Rt A1; between Montego Bay and Ocho Rios. **Facility:** The all-inclusive resort caters to guests 14 years and older with a variety of activities and recreation as well as a good beach. 266 units. 2-3 stories (no elevator), interior corridors. **Terms:** 3 night minimum stay, age restrictions may apply, 21 day cancellation notice-fee imposed. **Amenities:** high-speed Internet (fee), safes. *Some:* honor bars. **Dining:** 5 restaurants, nightclub, entertainment. **Pool(s):** 3 outdoor. **Activities:** whirlpools, lifeguard on duty, paddleboats, sailboats, windsurfing, scuba diving, snorkeling, golf-18 holes, 4 lighted tennis courts, recreation programs, basketball, game room, shuffleboard, volleyball, exercise room, spa. **Guest Services:** valet laundry.

[✦] [⊪] [Y] [SD] [⇲] [⊚] [⊟] [▭] / SOME UNITS [⊟]

SANDY BAY
• Hotels & Restaurants index & map p. 387

THE TRYALL CLUB   Phone: 876/956-5660

Vacation Rental House
$400-$1570

Location: Oceanfront. Between Hopewell and Lucea; 12 mi (19.2 km) w of Montego Bay Airport. **Facility:** A 2200-acre property, this resort evokes the gentile atmosphere of yesteryear. Each elegantly appointed villa comes with a cook and a maid. 85 units, some two bedrooms, houses and condominiums. 1 story, exterior corridors. **Terms:** 7 night minimum stay - seasonal, 60 day cancellation notice, 30 day off season-fee imposed. **Amenities:** high-speed Internet, safes. **Dining:** 2 restaurants, entertainment. **Pool(s):** outdoor. **Activities:** sailboats, snorkeling, 9 tennis courts (4 lighted), recreation programs, jogging, playground, basketball, volleyball. *Fee:* golf-18 holes, massage. **Guest Services:** complimentary laundry. **Free Special Amenities:** manager's reception.

WHITEHOUSE
• Hotels & Restaurants index & map p. 387

SANDALS WHITEHOUSE EUROPEAN VILLAGE & SPA
                    Phone: (876)640-3000

Resort Hotel
$876-$3138 12/1-3/31
$844-$3138 4/1-11/30

Address: Whitehouse **Location:** Oceanfront. On the south coast. **Facility:** In a remote area, the resort offers extensive recreational facilities, include a signature spa and a tri-level theatre with live entertainment. 360 units. 4 stories, exterior corridors. **Terms:** 3 night minimum stay - seasonal, age restrictions may apply, 45 day cancellation notice-fee imposed. **Amenities:** high-speed Internet (fee), safes, honor bars. **Dining:** 7 restaurants, nightclub, entertainment. **Pool(s):** 5 outdoor. **Activities:** saunas, whirlpools, steamrooms, lifeguard on duty, paddleboats, sailboats, windsurfing, scuba diving & rental equipment, snorkeling, 4 lighted tennis courts, racquetball courts, recreation programs, basketball, shuffleboard, volleyball, spa. **Guest Services:** valet laundry. *(See ad on insert.)*

MARTINIQUE

This index helps you "spot" where approved hotels and restaurants are located on the corresponding detailed maps. Hotel daily rate range is for comparison only and show the property's high season. Restaurant rate range is a combination of lunch and/or dinner. Turn to the listing page for more detailed rate information and consult display ads for special promotions.

DIAMANT

Map Page	Hotel	Diamond Rated	High Season	Page
1 this page	Hotel Diamond Rock	▼▼ ▼▼	Rates not provided	402

LE FRANÇOIS

Map Page	Hotel	Diamond Rated	High Season	Page
4 this page	Fregate Bleue Inn	▼▼ ▼▼	$160-$640	402

DIAMANT pop. 3,958
• Hotels & Restaurants index & map this page

HOTEL DIAMOND ROCK   **Phone:** 596/76-42-42   **1**
▼▼ ▼▼
Hotel
Rates not provided
Address: Pointe de la Cherry **Location:** Oceanfront. Le Diamant, 2 mi (3.2 km) e on D7, 0.7 mi (1 km) s; at la Cherry. **Facility:** 181 units. 2 stories (no elevator), interior corridors. **Amenities:** safes. **Pool(s):** outdoor. **Activities:** paddleboats, windsurfing, 2 lighted tennis courts, recreation programs, volleyball. *Fee:* scuba diving, fishing. **Guest Services:** valet laundry. 🍴 🍽 🏊 📶 ✖

LE FRANÇOIS (B-3) pop. 18,559
• Hotels & Restaurants index & map this page

FREGATE BLEUE INN   **Phone:** 596/54-54-66   **4**
▼▼ ▼▼
Country Inn
$160-$640
Address: Fregate Est 4 97240 **Location:** 2.5 mi (4 km) se of town towards Vauclin; on Hwy N6, just s of Ravine Fregate, follow signs on Fregate East 4; in Dostaly. **Facility:** 10 units, some two bedrooms. 1-2 stories (no elevator), exterior corridors. **Pool(s):** outdoor. **Guest Services:** coin laundry. 🍴 🏊 📶 ✖ 🅿 📵 / SOME UNITS 📺

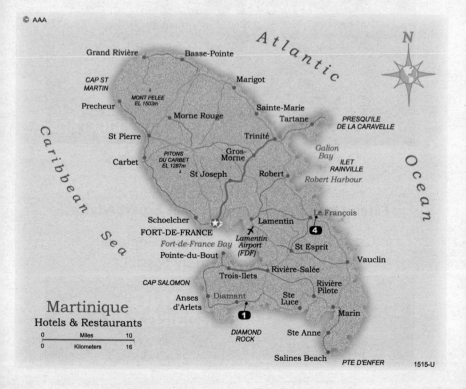

© AAA

Atlantic

N

Grand Rivière   Basse-Pointe

CAP ST MARTIN

MONT PELEE EL 1503m

Precheur   Marigot

Morne Rouge   Sainte-Marie   PRESQU'ILE DE LA CARAVELLE

St Pierre   Tartane

Trinité

Carbet   PITONS DU CARBET EL 1287m   Gros-Morne   *Galion Bay*   ILET RAINVILLE

St Joseph   Robert   *Robert Harbour*

Caribbean Sea

Ocean

Schoelcher   Lamentin   Le François

FORT-DE-FRANCE   **4**

Fort-de-France Bay   Lamentin Airport (FDF)   St Esprit

Pointe-du-Bout

Rivière-Salée   Vauclin

Trois-Ilets

CAP SALOMON   Rivière Pilote

Anses d'Arlets   *Diamant*   Ste Luce   Marin

Martinique
Hotels & Restaurants

| 0 | Miles | 10 |
| 0 | Kilometers | 16 |

1

DIAMOND ROCK   Ste Anne

Salines Beach   PTE D'ENFER   1515-U

MONTSERRAT

This index helps you "spot" where approved hotels and restaurants are located on the corresponding detailed maps. Hotel daily rate range is for comparison only and show the property's high season. Restaurant rate range is a combination of lunch and/or dinner. Turn to the listing page for more detailed rate information and consult display ads for special promotions.

SWEENEY'S

Map Page	Hotel	Diamond Rated	High Season	Page
1 p. 404	Tropical Mansion Suites	◈◈	$129-$160	403

BRADES

Map Page	Restaurant	Diamond Rated	Cuisine	Meal Range	Page
3 p. 404	Tina's Restaurant	◈	Caribbean	$9-$20	403

BRADES
• **Hotels & Restaurants index & map this page**

TINA'S RESTAURANT   **Phone:** 664/491-3538   **3**

Caribbean
$9-$20

AAA Inspector Notes: This popular restaurant with locals and tourists is located in a former house. Guests can order off an ever-changing blackboard menu with such choices as baked chicken, curry dishes, oxtail stew and local fish. For a meal-ender, guests can choose from several confections located in the dessert case. **Bar:** full bar. **Reservations:** suggested. **Address:** Brades Main Rd **Location:** Center. [L] [D]

SWEENEY'S
• **Hotels & Restaurants index & map this page**

TROPICAL MANSION SUITES
   Phone: (664)491-8767   **1**

Motel
$129-$160

Address: 404 Sweeney's **Location:** Just w of airport. **Facility:** 18 units, some efficiencies. 3 stories (no elevator), exterior corridors. **Terms:** office hours 6:30 am-10 pm. **Amenities:** high-speed Internet. **Pool(s):** outdoor. **Guest Services:** valet laundry.

1528-F

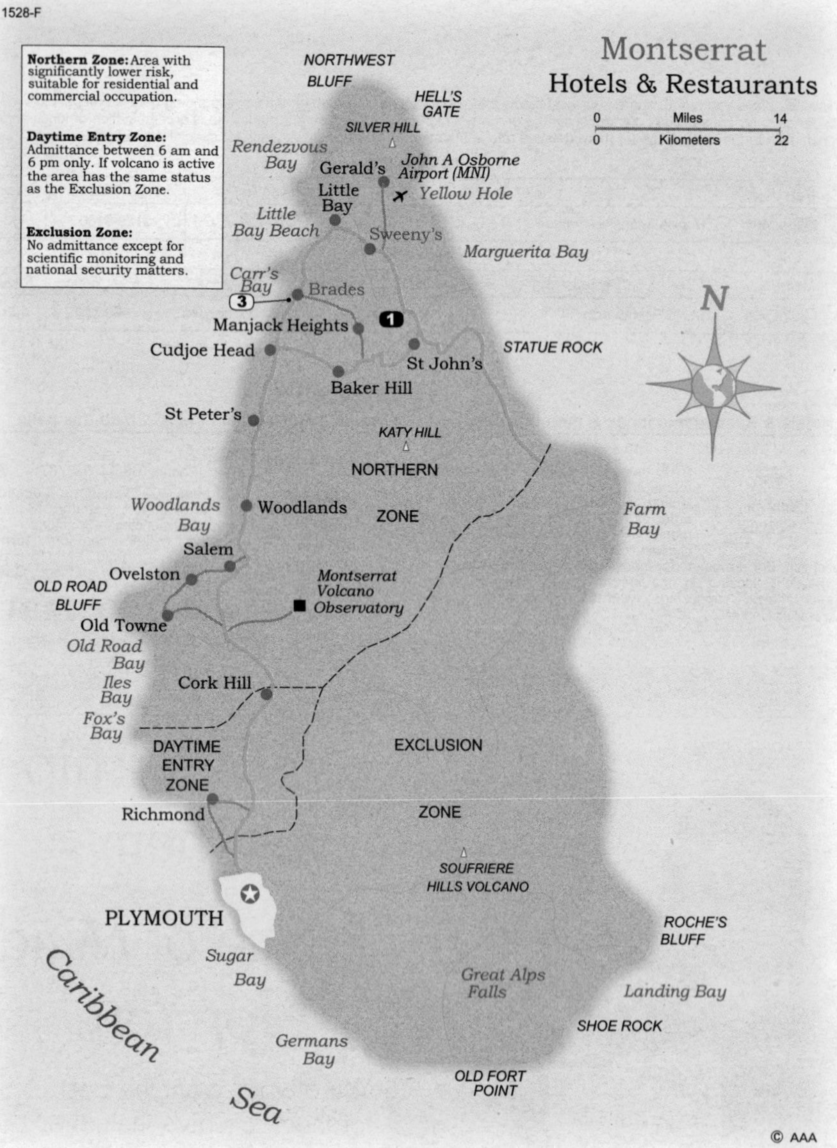

Montserrat
Hotels & Restaurants

Northern Zone: Area with significantly lower risk, suitable for residential and commercial occupation.

Daytime Entry Zone: Admittance between 6 am and 6 pm only. If volcano is active the area has the same status as the Exclusion Zone.

Exclusion Zone: No admittance except for scientific monitoring and national security matters.

NORTHWEST BLUFF

HELL'S GATE

SILVER HILL

Rendezvous Bay

Gerald's

John A Osborne Airport (MNI)

Yellow Hole

Little Bay

Little Bay Beach

Sweeny's

Marguerita Bay

Carr's Bay

Brades

3

Manjack Heights

1

Cudjoe Head

St John's

STATUE ROCK

Baker Hill

St Peter's

KATY HILL

NORTHERN

Woodlands Bay

Woodlands

ZONE

Farm Bay

Salem

Ovelston

OLD ROAD BLUFF

Montserrat Volcano Observatory

Old Towne

Old Road Bay

Iles Bay

Cork Hill

Fox's Bay

EXCLUSION

DAYTIME ENTRY ZONE

Richmond

ZONE

SOUFRIERE HILLS VOLCANO

PLYMOUTH

ROCHE'S BLUFF

Sugar Bay

Great Alps Falls

Landing Bay

SHOE ROCK

Caribbean

Germans Bay

OLD FORT POINT

Sea

© AAA

| 0 | Miles | 14 |
| 0 | Kilometers | 22 |

N

Learn about AAA/CAA Diamond Ratings

at AAA.com/Diamonds

PUERTO RICO

This index helps you "spot" where approved hotels and restaurants are located on the corresponding detailed maps. Hotel daily rate range is for comparison only and show the property's high season. Restaurant rate range is a combination of lunch and/or dinner. Turn to the listing page for more detailed rate information and consult display ads for special promotions.

DORADO

Map Page	Hotel	Diamond Rated	High Season	Page
① p. 407	Embassy Suites Dorado del Mar Beach & Golf Resort	◈◈◈	$149-$209	412

RÍO GRANDE

Map Page	Hotels	Diamond Rated	High Season	Page
② p. 407	**Gran Melia Puerto Rico Golf Resort** *(See ad p. 424.)*	◈◈◈◈	$150-$475 [SAVE]	424
③ p. 407	**Rio Mar Beach Resort & Spa - A Wyndham Grand Resort** *(See ad p. 425.)*	◈◈◈	$130-$300 [SAVE]	424

Map Page	Restaurant	Diamond Rated	Cuisine	Meal Range	Page
② p. 407	Palio	◈◈◈	Italian	$30-$45	425

HATILLO

Map Page	Hotel	Diamond Rated	High Season	Page
④ p. 407	Hotel Rosa del Mar	◈◈◈	$119-$149	416

RINCÓN

Map Page	Hotels	Diamond Rated	High Season	Page
⑦ p. 407	The Lazy Parrot Inn & Restaurant	◈◈	$125-$165	423
⑨ p. 407	Villa Cofresi Hotel & Restaurant	◈◈	$95-$170	423

ANASCO

Map Page	Hotel	Diamond Rated	High Season	Page
⑩ p. 407	**Rincon Beach Resort** *(See ad p. 423.)*	◈◈◈	$190-$630 [SAVE]	411

FAJARDO

Map Page	Hotels	Diamond Rated	High Season	Page
⑫ p. 407	**El Conquistador Resort and Las Casitas Village, A Waldorf Astoria Resort** *(See ad p. 413, p. 414.)*	◈◈◈◈	$199-$869 [SAVE]	413
⑭ p. 407	The Fajardo Inn	◈◈	$110-$300	414

HUMACAO

Map Page	Hotel	Diamond Rated	High Season	Page
⑯ p. 407	**Wyndham Garden Hotel & Casino at Palmas Del Mar** *(See ad p. 417.)*	◈◈◈	$165-$225 [SAVE]	417

Map Page	Restaurant	Diamond Rated	Cuisine	Meal Range	Page
⑤ p. 407	Chez Daniel	◈◈◈	French	$27-$37	417

PONCE

Map Page	Hotels	Diamond Rated	High Season	Page
⑲ p. 407	**Holiday Inn Ponce & El Tropical Casino** *(See ad p. 419.)*	◈◈	$146-$187 [SAVE]	419
⑳ p. 407	**Hilton Ponce Golf & Casino Resort** *(See ad opposite title page, p. 434.)*	◈◈◈	$149-$209 [SAVE]	418
㉑ p. 407	**Howard Johnson Hotel Ponce** *(See ad p. 420.)*	◈◈	$119-$160 [SAVE]	419
㉒ p. 407	Quality Inn El Tuque *(See ad p. 421.)*	◈	$100-$280	419

Map Page	Restaurants	Diamond Rated	Cuisine	Meal Range	Page
⑨ p. 407	Cabuqui Restaurant Bar & Cava	◈◈	International	$10-$32	422
⑪ p. 407	La Cava Restaurant	◈◈◈	International	$29-$35	422

Map Page	Restaurants (cont'd)	Diamond Rated	Cuisine	Meal Range	Page
(13) p. 407	Restaurant Rincon Argentino Bar & Tapas	◆	Argentine	$14-$33	422

GUÁNICA

Map Page	Hotel	Diamond Rated	High Season	Page
(24) p. 407	Copamarina Beach Resort & Spa (See ad p. 415.)	◆◆◆	$195-$235 SAVE	415

VIEQUES

Map Page	Hotels	Diamond Rated	High Season	Page
(29) p. 407	W Retreat & Spa Vieques Island (See ad on insert, p. 452.)	◆◆◆◆	$389-$1200 SAVE	451
(30) p. 407	Hacienda Tamarindo	◆◆◆	$135-$275	451

CAGUAS

Map Page	Hotel	Diamond Rated	High Season	Page
(32) p. 407	Four Points by Sheraton Caguas Real (See ad p. 411.)	◆◆◆	$225-$405 SAVE	411

MAYAGÜEZ

Map Page	Hotel	Diamond Rated	High Season	Page
(35) p. 407	Holiday Inn of Mayaguez & Tropical Casino (See ad p. 418.)	◆◆◆	$135-$250 SAVE	418

GUAYANILLA

Map Page	Hotel	Diamond Rated	High Season	Page
(38) p. 407	Pichi's Hotel, Convention Center & Casino (See ad p. 416.)	◆◆◆	$130-$155 SAVE	416

ISABELA

Map Page	Restaurant	Diamond Rated	Cuisine	Meal Range	Page
(20) p. 407	Eclipse Restaurant	◆◆	International	$9-$26	417

CABO ROJO

Map Page	Restaurant	Diamond Rated	Cuisine	Meal Range	Page
(24) p. 407	Tino's Restaurant	◆	Puerto Rican	$12-$28	411

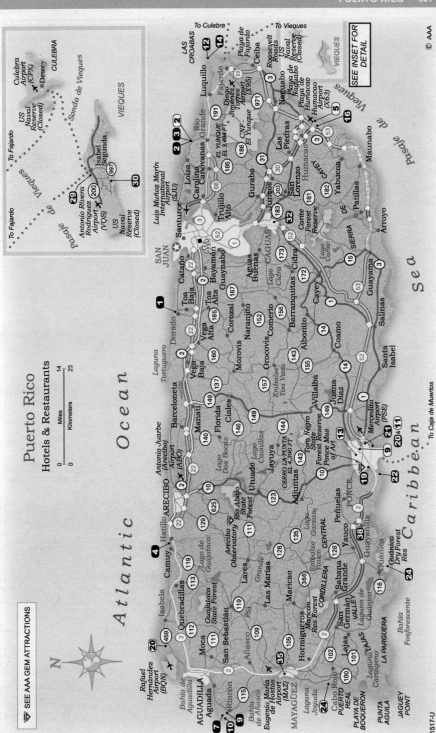

Puerto Rico

Hotels & Restaurants

SEE AAA GEM ATTRACTIONS

© AAA

SEE INSET FOR DETAIL

1517-U

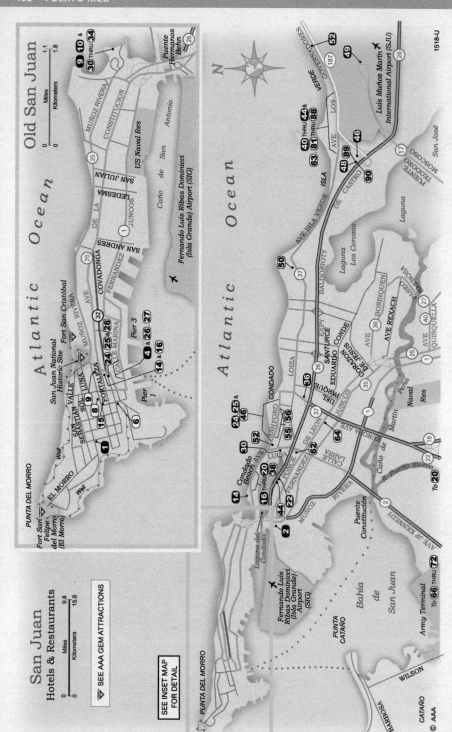

San Juan
Hotels & Restaurants

Old San Juan

SEE AAA GEM ATTRACTIONS

SEE INSET MAP FOR DETAIL

© AAA

1518-U

✈ Airport Accommodations

Map Page	LUIS MUNOZ MARIN INTERNATIONAL AIRPORT	Diamond Rated	High Season	Page
㊾ p. 408	Best Western San Juan Airport Hotel, in airport	◈◈	$125-$148 [SAVE]	426
㊼ p. 408	Courtyard by Marriott-Isla Verde Beach Resort, 0.3 mi (0.5 km) n of airport	◈◈◈	$135-$275 [SAVE]	429
㊶ p. 408	El San Juan Hotel & Casino, 2 mi (3.2 km) nw of airport	◈◈◈	$159-$759 [SAVE]	432
㊻ p. 408	Embassy Suites Hotel & Casino San Juan, 1.5 mi (2.4 km) w of airport	◈◈◈	$155-$195 [SAVE]	432
㊸ p. 408	Hampton Inn & Suites-San Juan, 2 mi (3.2 km) nw of airport	◈◈◈	$159-$299	434
㊵ p. 408	InterContinental San Juan Resort & Casino, 2.1 mi (3.3 km) e of airport	◈◈◈	$199-$659 [SAVE]	437
㊹ p. 408	The Ritz-Carlton San Juan Hotel, Spa & Casino, 1 mi (1.6 km) n of airport	◈◈◈◈	$299-$899	442
㊽ p. 408	Verdanza Hotel, 1.6 mi (2.5 km) w of airport	◈◈◈	$170-$250	446

San Juan

This index helps you "spot" where approved hotels and restaurants are located on the corresponding detailed maps. Hotel daily rate range is for comparison only and show the property's high season. Restaurant rate range is a combination of lunch and/or dinner. Turn to the listing page for more detailed rate information and consult display ads for special promotions.

SAN JUAN

Map Page	Hotels	Diamond Rated	High Season	Page
❶ p. 408	Hotel El Convento *(See ad p. 437.)*	◈◈◈◈	$185-$365 [SAVE]	437
❷ p. 408	Sheraton Puerto Rico Hotel & Casino *(See ad on insert.)*	◈◈◈◈	$119-$489 [SAVE]	443
❹ p. 408	Sheraton Old San Juan Hotel *(See ad p. 446.)*	◈◈◈	$149-$399 [SAVE]	443
❾ p. 408	Condado Lagoon Villas at Caribe Hilton *(See ad opposite title page, p. 428.)*	◈◈◈	$179-$399 [SAVE]	428
❿ p. 408	Caribe Hilton *(See ad opposite title page, p. 426.)*	◈◈◈	$179-$399 [SAVE]	426
⓮ p. 408	Conrad San Juan Condado Plaza *(See ad p. 429.)*	◈◈◈	$179-$409 [SAVE]	429
⓰ p. 408	Holiday Inn Express *(See ad p. 435.)*	◈◈	$119-$139 [SAVE]	434
⓱ p. 408	Comfort Inn San Juan *(See ad p. 427.)*	◈	$89-$140 [SAVE]	428
⓳ p. 408	La Concha, A Renaissance Resort *(See ad p. 440.)*	◈◈◈	$118-$399 [SAVE]	440
⓴ p. 408	El Canario by the Lagoon	◈	$70-$155 [SAVE]	431
㉒ p. 408	Courtyard by Marriott San Juan Miramar *(See ad p. 430.)*	◈◈	$109-$199	430
㉔ p. 408	San Juan Marriott Resort & Stellaris Casino *(See ad starting on p. 444.)*	◈◈◈	$159-$324 [SAVE]	443
㉕ p. 408	Radisson Ambassador Plaza Hotel & Casino *(See ad p. 442.)*	◈◈	$239-$279 [SAVE]	442
㉚ p. 408	Quality Inn El Portal *(See ad p. 441.)*	◈	$95-$155 [SAVE]	440
㊱ p. 408	DoubleTree by Hilton San Juan *(See ad p. 431.)*	◈◈◈	$169-$209	431
㊵ p. 408	InterContinental San Juan Resort & Casino *(See ad starting on p. 438.)*	◈◈◈	$199-$659 [SAVE]	437
㊶ p. 408	El San Juan Hotel & Casino *(See ad p. 432.)*	◈◈◈	$159-$759 [SAVE]	432
㊸ p. 408	Hampton Inn & Suites-San Juan	◈◈◈	$159-$299	434
㊹ p. 408	The Ritz-Carlton San Juan Hotel, Spa & Casino	◈◈◈◈	$299-$899	442
㊻ p. 408	Embassy Suites Hotel & Casino San Juan *(See ad p. 433.)*	◈◈◈	$155-$195 [SAVE]	432
㊽ p. 408	Verdanza Hotel *(See ad p. 443.)*	◈◈◈	$170-$250	446
㊾ p. 408	Best Western San Juan Airport Hotel	◈◈	$125-$148 [SAVE]	426

SAN JUAN (cont'd)

Map Page	Hotels (cont'd)	Diamond Rated	High Season	Page
52 p. 408	**Courtyard by Marriott-Isla Verde Beach Resort** (See ad p. 430.)	◊◊◊	$135-$275 SAVE	429

Map Page	Restaurants	Diamond Rated	Cuisine	Meal Range	Page
6 p. 408	Old Harbor Brewery Steak & Lobster House	◊◊	International	$12-$38	449
8 p. 408	Sofia Italian Kitchen & Wine Bar	◊◊◊	Italian	$14-$27	450
9 p. 408	The Parrot Club	◊◊	New Latin American	$13-$37	449
14 p. 408	Tantra Indo-Latino Cuisine	◊◊	Indian	$16-$28	450
15 p. 408	Dragonfly	◊◊	New Latin American	$12-$25	448
16 p. 408	Aguaviva Seaside Latino Cuisine	◊◊	New Latin American	$22-$42	447
20 p. 408	El Alcazar Marisqueria y Tasca Espanola	◊◊◊	Spanish	$15-$33	448
24 p. 408	Al Dente Ristorante and Wine Bar	◊◊	Italian	$15-$35	447
25 p. 408	J-Taste	◊◊◊	Japanese	$12-$40	448
26 p. 408	Chicago Burger	◊	Burgers	$7-$11	447
27 p. 408	Palio, A Tuscan Chophouse	◊◊◊	Italian	$18-$42	449
28 p. 408	Panza Restaurant at Chateau Cervantes	◊◊◊	International	$17-$29	449
30 p. 408	Morton's The Steakhouse	◊◊◊	American	$29-$50	449
32 p. 408	Restaurante Escambron Beach Club	◊	Puerto Rican	$12-$26	450
34 p. 408	Lemon Grass	◊◊◊	New Asian	$27-$33	449
38 p. 408	Jose Jose Restaurant	◊◊◊	International	$24-$33	448
44 p. 408	Augusto's Cuisine	◊◊◊	Continental	$24-$45	447
46 p. 408	Ropa Vieja Grill	◊◊	Cuban	$16-$34	450
50 p. 408	Che's Restaurant Argentino	◊◊	Argentine	$14-$29	447
52 p. 408	Buenos Ayres Bar & Grill	◊	Argentine	$17-$33	447
55 p. 408	Tijuana's Bar & Grill	◊	Mexican	$10-$25	450
56 p. 408	Latin Star Restaurant	◊	Puerto Rican	$9-$32	449
62 p. 408	Bodega Compostela	◊◊◊	Spanish	$15-$45	447
63 p. 408	BLT Steak	◊◊◊◊	Steak	$28-$55	447
64 p. 408	La Casona Restaurante	◊◊◊	Spanish	$19-$37	448
66 p. 408	Restaurante Los Chavales	◊◊◊	Spanish	$14-$34	450
67 p. 408	Tierra Santa Restaurant	◊◊	Arabic	$11-$23	450
68 p. 408	Tierra del Fuego	◊◊	Argentine	$12-$30	450
72 p. 408	El Zipperle Restaurante	◊◊	International	$17-$32	448
81 p. 408	Momoyama	◊	Japanese	$18-$41	449
82 p. 408	Ruth's Chris Steak House	◊◊◊	Steak	$28-$46	450
84 p. 408	La Piccola Fontana	◊◊◊	Italian	$22-$42	449
85 p. 408	Platos Restaurant	◊◊	Puerto Rican	$18-$38	450
86 p. 408	Metropol Restaurant	◊	Cuban	$9-$35	449
87 p. 408	Il Mulino	◊◊◊	Italian	$24-$65	448
88 p. 408	Alfredo Restaurant	◊◊◊	Italian	$18-$38	447
89 p. 408	Eighty20 Bistro	◊◊	International	$12-$28	448
90 p. 408	J.H. Yee's Asian Bistro	◊◊	Asian	$17-$29	448

ANASCO pop. 28,348
• Hotels & Restaurants index & map p. 405

RINCON BEACH RESORT
Phone: (787)589-9000   **10**

Hotel
$190-$630

Address: Carr 115, KM 5.8 00610 **Location:** Oceanfront. 5.4 mi (8.6 km) s of Rincon; just n of jct Hwy 429 and 115. **Facility:** Meets AAA guest room security requirements. 112 units, some two bedrooms and kitchens. 4-6 stories, exterior corridors. **Terms:** 2-3 night minimum stay - weekends, 3 day cancellation notice-fee imposed. **Amenities:** safes. **Dining:** 2 restaurants. **Pool(s):** outdoor. **Activities:** whirlpool, playground, volleyball, exercise room. *Fee:* paddleboats, massage. **Guest Services:** valet laundry. **Free Special Amenities: early check-in/late check-out and high-speed Internet.** Affiliated with A Preferred Hotel. *(See ad p. 423.)*

 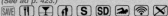
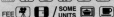

CABO ROJO (D-1) pop. 46,911, elev. 62'
• Hotels & Restaurants index & map p. 405

TINO'S RESTAURANT
Phone: 787/851-2976   **24**

Puerto Rican
$12-$28

AAA Inspector Notes: The casual restaurant nurtures a family atmosphere. Puerto Rican seafood specialties--such as mofongo relleno con mariscos, which is loaded with fish, octopus and shrimp inside a mashed fried plantain shell--line the menu. **Bar:** full bar. **Address:** Rd 102, KM 13.6 **Location:** In Joyuda's Beach; Hwy 2 or 52 to Cabo Rojo, 4 mi (6.4 km) s on Hwy 100, 3.4 mi (5.4 km) w on Hwy 102 at KM 13.6.

CAGUAS (C-5) pop. 140,502, elev. 229'
• Hotels & Restaurants index & map p. 405

FOUR POINTS BY SHERATON CAGUAS REAL
Phone: (787)653-1111   **32**

Hotel
$225-$405

FOUR POINTS **AAA Benefit:** Members get up to 15% off, plus Starwood Preferred Guest® bonuses.

Address: 500 Alhambra & Granada Blvd 00725 **Location:** 22 mi (35.2 km) s of airport; Hwy 52 exit 22 northbound; exit 23 southbound. **Facility:** Comfortable guest units feature up-to-date amenities, and noteworthy facilities include a courtyard pool area and a large casino. Meets AAA guest room security requirements. 126 units. 4 stories, interior corridors. **Parking:** on-site (fee) and valet. **Terms:** 3 day cancellation notice-fee imposed. **Amenities:** video games (fee), high-speed Internet. *Some:* safes. **Pool(s):** outdoor. **Activities:** whirlpool, exercise room. **Guest Services:** valet and coin laundry. **Free Special Amenities: high-speed Internet.** *(See ad this page.)*

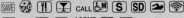

WHERE TO EAT

FACCIO PIZZA
Phone: 787/746-4185

Italian
$7-$18

AAA Inspector Notes: Family owned and operated for many decades, this popular eatery serves outstanding thin crust pizza and a variety of pastas and other Italian dishes. All moderately priced, it is difficult to choose from the varied menu selections including lasagna, ravioli, manicotti and seafood. **Bar:** full bar. **Address:** Ave Luis Munoz Marin, #AB-10 00725 **Location:** In Urb Caguas Norte.

DORADO (B-4) pop. 34,017, elev. 13'
• Hotels & Restaurants index & map p. 405

EMBASSY SUITES DORADO DEL MAR BEACH & GOLF
RESORT   Phone: (787)796-6125

Resort Hotel
$149-$209 12/1-4/15
$129-$209 4/16-11/30

AAA Benefit:
Members save 5% or more
everyday!

Address: 201 Dorado del Mar Blvd 00646 **Location:**
Oceanfront. From San Juan, 25 mi (40 km) w on Hwy 22 to
exit 22 (Dorado), 2 mi (3.2 km) n on Hwy 165; 3.5 mi (5.6
km) w on Hwy 693/6165. **Facility:** Spacious, well-equipped
units at this contemporary resort-hotel are on the beach and
adjacent to the golf course. Meets AAA guest room security
requirements. 174 units. 7 stories, interior corridors.
Parking: on-site (fee) and valet. **Terms:** check-in 4 pm, 1-7
night minimum stay, cancellation fee imposed. **Amenities:**
video games (fee), high-speed Internet, safes. **Dining:** 2
restaurants, entertainment. **Pool(s):** outdoor. **Activities:**
whirlpool, snorkeling equipment rental, recreation programs,
playground, volleyball, exercise room. **Fee:** paddleboats,
golf-18 holes, 2 lighted tennis courts, game room, massage.
Guest Services: valet and coin laundry.

Check out
our travel blog at
AAATravelViews.com

FAJARDO (C-6) pop. 40,712, elev. 29'

- Restaurants p. 414
- Hotels & Restaurants index & map p. 405

EL CONQUISTADOR RESORT AND LAS CASITAS VILLAGE, A WALDORF ASTORIA RESORT

Phone: (787)863-1000

Resort Hotel
$199-$869 12/1-4/30
$149-$419 5/1-11/30

AAA Benefit:
Unparalleled hospitality at a special Member rate.

Address: 1000 El Conquistador Ave 00738 **Location:** 31 mi (49.6 km) e of Luis Muñoz Marin International Airport; Hwy 3 to Avenida Conquistador, n then e, follow signs. **Facility:** Situated on a 300-foot cliff along the northeast coast, this resort has a private off-shore island and large, well-equipped guest units. Meets AAA guest room security requirements. 951 units, some two bedrooms, three bedrooms, efficiencies, kitchens and condominiums. 2-6 stories, interior/exterior corridors. **Parking:** on-site (fee) and valet. **Terms:** check-in 4 pm, 1-7 night minimum stay, cancellation fee imposed. **Amenities:** safes. **Dining:** 18 restaurants, also, Strip House, see separate listing, nightclub. **Pool(s):** 7 outdoor. **Activities:** whirlpools, rental boats, rental paddleboats, rental sailboats, rental sailboards, marina, snorkeling & rental equipment, fishing, 7 tennis courts (4 lighted), recreation programs, game room, volleyball, spa. *Fee:* steamrooms, waterslide, scuba diving, charter fishing, golf-18 holes, horseback riding. **Guest Services:** valet laundry, area transportation-water taxi to Palomino Island. **Free Special Amenities:** local telephone calls and high-speed Internet. *(See ad this page, p. 414.)*

     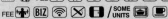

▼ See AAA listing this page ▼

(See index & map p. 405.)

THE FAJARDO INN

Hotel
$110-$300

Phone: (787)860-6000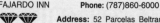

Address: 52 Parcelas Beltran 00740 **Location:** Just e of jct Rd 987 and 195; just w of ferry docks. **Facility:** 118 units, some two bedrooms, three bedrooms and kitchens. 2-3 stories, interior/exterior corridors. *Bath:* shower only. **Terms:** check-in 4 pm, 3 day cancellation notice. **Amenities:** safes. **Dining:** 4 restaurants. **Pool(s):** 2 outdoor. **Activities:** whirlpool, lighted tennis court, playground, basketball. *Fee:* miniature golf. **Guest Services:** coin laundry.

WHERE TO EAT

STRIP HOUSE

Steak
$24-$44

Phone: 787/863-6789

AAA Inspector Notes: One of the hottest new steakhouse concepts from New York City has reached the shores of Puerto Rico. Tastefully done burlesque decor sets a sexy mood for dining on thick Choice steak, veal, lamb and fish, such as salmon and tuna. Large portions make the side dishes and appetizers great for sharing. The well-trained staff is attentive to many details. **Bar:** full bar. **Reservations:** required. **Address:** 1000 El Conquistador Ave 00738 **Location:** 31 mi (49.6 km) e of Luis Muñoz Marin International Airport; in El Conquistador Resort and Las Casitas Village, A Waldorf Astoria Resort. **Parking:** on-site (fee) and valet. D

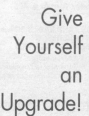

▼ See AAA listing p. 413 ▼

GUÁNICA (D-2) pop. 21,888, elev. 269'
• Hotels & Restaurants index & map p. 405

COPAMARINA BEACH RESORT & SPA
Phone: (787)821-0505 (24)

Resort Hotel
$195-$235

Address: Rt 333, KM 6.5 00653
Location: Oceanfront. Hwy 2 exit 194 (SR 16), 2.4 mi (3.8 km) s, then 3.8 mi (6.1 km) e on SR 333, follow signs to Cana Gorda. **Facility:** The beachfront resort on 20 landscaped acres provides a laid-back alternative to the frenetic pace of the cities. 106 units, some three bedrooms and kitchens. 1-2 stories (no elevator), exterior corridors. **Terms:** 3 night minimum stay - weekends, 7 day cancellation notice-fee imposed. **Amenities:** safes. **Dining:** 2 restaurants. **Pool(s):** 2 outdoor. **Activities:** whirlpools, steamrooms, rental boats, rental paddleboats, rental sailboats, boat dock, 2 lighted tennis courts, recreation programs, hiking trails, playground, game room, volleyball, exercise room, spa. *Fee:* scuba diving, snorkeling. **Guest Services:** coin laundry. **Free Special Amenities: local telephone calls and high-speed Internet.**
(See ad this page.)

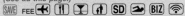

Vacation with Peace of Mind

Experience an incredible vacation with amazing value on select *AAA Vacations*® tour and cruise departures. Includes our **Best Price Guarantee** and **24/7 Member Care** for a worry-free vacation.

Explore the Travel Guides on AAA.com/Travel or CAA.ca/Travel

Contact your local AAA Travel Professional or visit AAA.com/Travel for full details.
Terms and conditions apply

▼ See AAA listing this page ▼

Live the blue...

• Spacious Rooms
• Adult and kid's Pools
• Fitness Center
• Two Tennis Courts
• Children's Playground
• Volleyball
• Free Parking

• Water Sports Activities
• "Bodyderm Spa"
• Onsite Restaurants
• Banquet & Meeting Facilities
• Free Wireless Network Connection

"Ask for our All Inclusive and Romance Packages"

Route 333 Km. 6.5, Guánica, Puerto Rico • 787-821-0505 • 1-800-468-4553
reservations@copamarina.com • www.copamarina.com

GUAYANILLA pop. 23,072
• Hotels & Restaurants map & index p. 407

PICHI'S HOTEL, CONVENTION CENTER & CASINO

Hotel
$130-$155

Phone: (787)835-3335　[38]

Address: Exit 205, Rd 127, KM 8.6 **Location:** Hwy 2 exit 205. **Facility:** This well-appointed property features a stylish casino and live music on weekends. Guest units have a trendy and modern appeal. Meets AAA guest room security requirements. 136 units. 7 stories, interior corridors. **Terms:** 5 day cancellation notice. **Amenities:** high-speed Internet, safes. **Dining:** 2 restaurants, entertainment. **Pool(s):** outdoor. **Activities:** exercise room. **Guest Services:** valet laundry. **Free Special Amenities:** full breakfast and newspaper.
(See ad this page.)

  FEE   BIZ

GUAYNABO pop. 100,053

FACCIO PIZZA

Italian
$7-$18

Phone: 787/731-6566

AAA Inspector Notes: Family owned and operated for many decades, this popular eatery serves outstanding thin crust pizza and a variety of pastas and other Italian dishes. All moderately priced, it is difficult to choose from the varied menu selections including lasagna, ravioli, manicotti and seafood. **Bar:** full bar. **Address:** Ave Esmeralda **Location:** Urb Muñoz Rivera. [L] [D]

HATILLO pop. 38,925
• Hotels & Restaurants index & map p. 405

HOTEL ROSA DEL MAR　　　Phone: 787/262-1515　[4]

Hotel
$119-$149

Address: Carr 2 KM 86.6 00659 **Location:** Center. **Facility:** 30 units. 4 stories, interior corridors. **Terms:** 3 day cancellation notice. **Amenities:** safes. **Pool(s):** outdoor.

HUMACAO (C-5) pop. 59,035, elev. 82'
• Hotels & Restaurants index & map p. 405

WYNDHAM GARDEN HOTEL & CASINO AT PALMAS DEL MAR 16

Hotel
$165-$225

Address: Candelero Dr, #170 Palmas del Mar 00791 **Location:** 2 mi (3.2 km) s off Hwy 53 on Hwy 906 exit 35B; in Palmas del Mar residential resort. **Facility:** Guests can select from several spacious room categories at this hotel in a sprawling residential resort community. 107 units. 3 stories (no elevator), exterior corridors. **Parking:** on-site (fee) and valet. **Terms:** 3 day cancellation notice-fee imposed. **Amenities:** video games (fee), high-speed Internet, safes. **Pool(s):** outdoor. **Activities:** whirlpool, game room, exercise room. **Guest Services:** valet and coin laundry. **Free Special Amenities:** newspaper and high-speed Internet.
(See ad this page.)

SAVE 🐕 🍴 🍷 S SD 🏊 📶 ✕ FEE 🎥
📱 💻

WHERE TO EAT

CHEZ DANIEL   **Phone:** 787/850-3838   5

French
$27-$37

AAA Inspector Notes: Owner-chef Daniel Vasse has treated local and tourist clientele for more than 25 years at this marina restaurant. The authentic French cuisine features duck, lamb venison, halibut and seafood bouillabaisse as well as exotic dishes utilizing frog legs, pheasant and quail. For starters the frog legs and escargot are distinctive offerings. Sunday brunch is very popular. **Bar:** full bar. **Reservations:** suggested. **Address:** 110 Harbour Dr, Suite 5 00791 **Location:** 2 mi (3.2 km) s off Hwy 53 on Hwy 906 exit 35B to Palmas del Mar; at Palmas del Mar Marina. D

ISABELA (B-1) pop. 44,444, elev. 200'
• Hotels & Restaurants index & map p. 405

ECLIPSE RESTAURANT   **Phone:** 787/872-9554   20

International
$9-$26

AAA Inspector Notes: This somewhat chic, oceanside restaurant offers such inspiring dishes as five-spice-crusted calamari, curry-marinated duck breast, pan-roasted tilapia and chimichurri-marinated lamb chops with goat cheese and tamarind sauce. Tempting desserts, such as the baked Bosc pear tart and bourbon pecan pie, are difficult to pass up. **Bar:** full bar. **Reservations:** suggested. **Address:** Carr 4466 KM 1.9, Interior 00662 **Location:** SR 2 exit Hwy 110, 4.1 mi (6.5 km) n to Rt 4466, then 1.2 mi (1.9 km) toward Playa Jobo S; follow signs to Villa Montana Beach Resort.

B L D AC

Simply Reliable

The Diamond Ratings in this TourBook guide are backed by our expert, in-person evaluations, whether the hotel or restaurant is no-frills, moderate or upscale.

Learn more at **AAA.com/Diamonds**

▼ *See AAA listing this page* ▼

Extend your weekend, buy 3 nights and get the 4th night free! Wyndham Garden Hotel and Casino at Palmas Del Mar is a lovely property just steps from the beach and only 45 minutes from San Juan. Access to golf, spa, tennis, beach club, shopping, cafes, restaurants and other amenities. Golf and spa packages available.

WEEKEND ESCAPE

WYNDHAM GARDEN
Hotel and Casino at
Palmas del Mar

**WYNDHAM GARDEN HOTEL & CASINO AT PALMAS DEL MAR
CALL 787-850-6000
1-800-WYNDHAM
OR VISIT WYNDHAM.COM**

Get the free mobile app at
http://gettag.mobi

MAYAGÜEZ (C-1) pop. 98,434, elev. 160'
- Hotels & Restaurants index & map p. 405

HOLIDAY INN OF MAYAGUEZ & TROPICAL CASINO
Phone: (787)833-1100 ③⑤

Hotel
$135-$250

Address: 2701 Hwy 2 00682 **Location:** Hwy 2, n of downtown; 1.2 mi (2 km) from Mayaguez Airport; at KM 149.9. **Facility:** Located north of the city center, the hotel offers modern units with up-to-date décor and contemporary amenities. Meets AAA guest room security requirements. 141 units. 6 stories, interior corridors. **Terms:** cancellation fee imposed. **Amenities:** safes. **Pool(s):** outdoor. **Activities:** basketball, volleyball, exercise room. *Fee:* game room. **Guest Services:** valet and coin laundry. **Free Special Amenities:** high-speed Internet. *(See ad this page.)*

[SAVE] [icons] CALL [icons] [S] [SD] [icons] [wifi]
[icons] /SOME UNITS [icon]

PONCE (D-3) pop. 186,475, elev. 45'
- Restaurants p. 422
- Hotels & Restaurants index & map p. 405

HILTON PONCE GOLF & CASINO RESORT
Phone: (787)259-7676 ②⓪

Resort Hotel
$149-$209

Hilton **AAA Benefit:** Members save 5% or more everyday!

Address: 1150 Caribe Ave 00716 **Location:** Oceanfront. Hwy 52 exit 104B; 1 mi (1.6 km) s on Hwy 12, then 0.5 mi (0.8 km) e, follow signs. **Facility:** Surrounded by lush tropical landscaping, the property's tasteful rooms have a private balcony; a golf course and clubhouse rounds out the offerings. 255 units, some two bedrooms. 4-5 stories, exterior corridors. **Parking:** on-site (fee) and valet. **Terms:** 1-7 night minimum stay, cancellation fee imposed. **Amenities:** high-speed Internet, safes. **Dining:** 6 restaurants, also, La Cava Restaurant, see separate listing. **Pool(s):** 2 outdoor. **Activities:** saunas, whirlpools, steamrooms, miniature golf, 4 lighted tennis courts, bicycles, playground, basketball, game room, volleyball. *Fee:* sailboats, golf-27 holes, massage. **Guest Services:** valet laundry. *(See ad opposite title page, p. 434.)*

[SAVE] [icons] CALL [icons] [S] [SD] [icons]
[icons] [BIZ] [wifi] [X] FEE [icons] [icon] [icon]

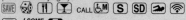

(See index & map p. 405.)

HOLIDAY INN PONCE & EL TROPICAL CASINO
Phone: (787)844-1200 **19**

Hotel
$146-$187

Address: 3315 Ponce Bypass 00728 **Location:** Just off Hwy 2, 1.9 mi (3 km) e at end of Hwy 52 (autopista); in sector El Tuque. **Facility:** Just west of the city center, this well-known chain hotel is situated on a hill above the freeway. There is a lively casino and large pool area. Meets AAA guest room security requirements. 116 units. 5 stories, interior corridors. **Pool(s):** outdoor. **Activities:** limited exercise equipment. *Fee:* game room. **Guest Services:** valet and coin laundry. **Free Special Amenities:** newspaper and high-speed Internet.
(See ad this page.)

HOWARD JOHNSON HOTEL PONCE
Phone: (787)841-1000 **21**

Hotel
$119-$160

Address: Turpo Industrial Park, #103 00715 **Location:** Hwy 52 exit 99A/99B, just s. **Facility:** Meets AAA guest room security requirements. 120 units. 2 stories (no elevator), interior corridors. **Amenities:** high-speed Internet, safes (fee). *Some:* video games. **Pool(s):** outdoor. **Activities:** whirlpool, exercise room. *Fee:* game room. **Guest Services:** valet and coin laundry.
(See ad p. 420.)

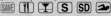   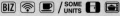

QUALITY INN EL TUQUE   Phone: (787)290-2000 **22**

Motel
$100-$280

Address: 3330 Ponce ByPass, El Tuque 00728 **Location:** Just w of town; at Ponce International Speedway Park; Hwy 2 at KM 220.1; in El Tuque. **Facility:** 99 units. 1-2 stories (no elevator), exterior corridors. **Terms:** office hours 7 am-11 pm, cancellation fee imposed. **Amenities:** high-speed Internet. **Pool(s):** outdoor. **Activities:** basketball. **Guest Services:** valet and coin laundry.
(See ad p. 421.)

Discover mobile travel solutions at AAA.com/mobile and CAA.ca/mobile

▼ See AAA listing this page ▼

A landmark in southern Puerto Rico, Ponce Holiday Inn, with its awesome view of the city and the Caribbean Sea, has it all: fantastic facilities, great food and a lively casino. Located within a short drive to all the good things Ponce has to offer.

For reservations call: tel. 787-844-1200 • Toll Free 1-800-HOLIDAY
3315 Ponce By Pass Ponce, 00728-1502 Puerto Rico www.holidayinn.com/ponce • email: lrodriguez@hitcponce.com

(See index & map p. 405.)

▼ *See AAA listing p. 419* ▼

Great Value and Convenience in Ponce

This charming garden-style hotel offers easy access to miles of sandy beaches along the Caribbean Sea.

- Free deluxe continental breakfast
- Free high-speed Internet access

- Outdoor pool with sundeck
- Conveniently located near Ponce International Speedway and Speed and Splash Waterpark
- Nearby Paseo Tablado La Guancha boardwalk with sidewalk cafes

QUALITY INN

BY CHOICE HOTELS

For special AAA member rates, call 888.9.SUNFUN or visit choicecaribbean.com

TourBook Comments

Are we meeting your travel needs?

If your visit to an establishment listed in a AAA TourBook guide doesn't meet your expectations, tell us about it.

Complete an easy online form at **AAA.com/TourBookComments.**

(See index & map p. 405.)

WHERE TO EAT

CABUQUI RESTAURANT BAR & CAVA
                          Phone: 787/984-5696   ⑨

International
$10-$32

AAA Inspector Notes: Near the historic district, in an ornate house, this restaurant offers indoor dining and outdoor garden seating. The menu has a range of appetizers and soups. Several pasta dishes, barbecue ribs, churrasco steak, surf and turf and crab cakes are just some of the favorite dishes. Lunch is served only on Thursday and Friday. **Bar:** full bar. **Reservations:** suggested. **Address:** Calle Isabel #32 00728 **Location:** Corner of Calle Isabel and Calle Salud; just e of Plaza de los Bomberos. ⓓ

LA CAVA RESTAURANT   **Phone:** 787/259-7676   ⑪

International
$29-$35

AAA Inspector Notes: Inside the Hilton resort, this refined restaurant features upscale appointments. Dapper waiters provide attentive service. The restaurant boasts an extensive wine list to complement a creative menu of both complex and simple dishes, including appetizers of escargot, beef carpaccio and duck foie gras and main courses of Australian lamb chops, Kobe beef short ribs, Maine lobster and duck breast. **Bar:** full bar. **Reservations:** required. **Address:** 1150 Caribe Ave, Suite 201 00716 **Location:** Hwy 52 exit 104B; 1 mi (1.6 km) s on Hwy 12, then 0.5 mi (0.8 km) e, follow signs; in Hilton Ponce Golf & Casino Resort. **Parking:** on-site (fee) and valet. ⓓ

RESTAURANT RINCON ARGENTINO BAR & TAPAS
                          Phone: 787/284-1762   ⑬

Argentine
$14-$33

AAA Inspector Notes: In the heart of the Ponce historic district, this Argentino parrilla-style restaurant offers outdoor patio seating or interior seating in a home-like atmosphere. Beef is king here, grilled to perfection but also available are a variety of sausages, pork and chicken. A few nights there is live music in the cozy bar. **Bar:** full bar. **Address:** 67/69 Salud esq Isabel 00728 **Location:** Just n of Central Plaza de los Bomberos. **Parking:** street only. Ⓛ ⓓ

Share a New View on Travel at AAATravelViews.com

Read stories, tips and trends from AAA insiders. Post comments and get your questions answered by our travel experts.

RINCÓN (C-1) pop. 14,767, elev. 167'
- Hotels & Restaurants index & map p. 405

THE LAZY PARROT INN & RESTAURANT

Phone: (787)823-5654   **7**

Country Inn
$125-$165

Address: Rd 413 KM 4.1, Puntas Sector 00677 **Location:** On Hwy 413, 2.9 mi (4.6 km) n of downtown, just above El Faro Lighthouse. **Facility:** 21 units. 2-3 stories (no elevator), interior/exterior corridors. **Terms:** office hours 8 am-5 pm, 3-4 night minimum stay - seasonal, 7 day cancellation notice-fee imposed. **Dining:** 2 restaurants. **Pool(s):** outdoor. **Activities:** whirlpool. *Fee:* miniature golf. **Guest Services:** valet laundry.

VILLA COFRESI HOTEL & RESTAURANT
Phone: (787)823-2450   **9**

Hotel
$95-$170

Address: Carr 115 KM 12.0 00677 **Location:** Oceanfront. Just s of downtown, follow signs. **Facility:** 86 units, some two bedrooms, efficiencies and kitchens. 3 stories (no elevator), interior/exterior corridors. **Terms:** office hours 7 am-11 pm, 2 night minimum stay - weekends, 3 day cancellation notice-fee imposed. **Amenities:** safes. **Dining:** 2 restaurants. **Pool(s):** outdoor. **Activities:** game room. *Fee:* boats, canoes, sailboats, massage.

▼ See AAA listing p. 411 ▼

RÍO GRANDE (B-6) pop. 52,362, elev. 19'
• Hotels & Restaurants index & map p. 405

GRAN MELIA PUERTO RICO GOLF RESORT
Phone: (787)657-1026 **2**

Resort Hotel
$150-$475

Address: 200 Coco Beach Blvd 00745 **Location:** Oceanfront. 18.5 mi (29.6 km) e of Luis Muñoz Marin International Airport, 3 mi (4.8 km) n, follow signs. **Facility:** This well-regarded oceanfront resort has spacious, attractively appointed guest rooms that feature many comforts and extra amenities. Meets AAA guest room security requirements. 486 units. 1-2 stories (no elevator), exterior corridors. **Parking:** on-site (fee) and valet. **Terms:** 3 day cancellation notice-fee imposed. **Amenities:** safes, honor bars. **Fee:** video games, high-speed Internet. **Dining:** 4 restaurants, entertainment. **Pool(s):** 2 outdoor. **Activities:** whirlpools, rental paddleboats, rental sailboats, rental sailboards, 3 lighted tennis courts, recreation programs, playground, basketball, volleyball, spa. **Fee:** saunas, steamrooms, snorkeling, golf-36 holes, bicycles. **Guest Services:** valet laundry.
(See ad this page.)

RIO MAR BEACH RESORT & SPA - A WYNDHAM GRAND RESORT
Phone: (787)888-6000 **3**

Resort Hotel
$130-$300

Address: 6000 Rio Mar Blvd 00745 **Location:** Oceanfront. 19 mi (30.4 km) e of Luis Muñoz Marin International Airport; jct Hwy 3 and 968, 0.8 mi (1.3 km) n on Hwy 968. **Facility:** Extensive beach, tennis and golf facilities are available at this well-equipped resort built in the mid-1990s; guest rooms are well appointed. Meets AAA guest room security requirements. 600 units. 7 stories, interior corridors. **Parking:** on-site (fee) and valet. **Terms:** check-in 4 pm, 3 day cancellation notice-fee imposed. **Amenities:** safes. **Fee:** video games, high-speed Internet. **Dining:** 11 restaurants, also, Palio, see separate listing, entertainment. **Pool(s):** 2 outdoor, whirlpools, steamrooms, waterslide, lifeguard on duty, rental boats, rental sailboats, rental sailboards, fishing, recreation programs, jogging, playground, sports court, basketball, volleyball, spa. **Fee:** charter fishing, golf-36 holes, 13 lighted tennis courts. **Guest Services:** valet laundry, area transportation-resort facilities.
(See ad p. 425.)

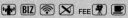

Find valuable AAA/CAA member savings
at AAA.com/discounts

(See index & map p. 405.)

ST. REGIS BAHIA BEACH   **Phone:** 787/809-8000
[fyi]   **AAA Benefit:** Legendary stays at a
preferred rate.

Not evaluated. **Address:** SR 187, KM 4.2 00745 **Location:**
SR 187, KM 4.2. Facilities, services, and decor characterize
an upscale property. **(See ad on insert.)**

**Enjoy great savings on hotel
rates at AAA.com or CAA.ca**

PALIO   **Phone:** 787/888-6000   ②
Italian   **AAA Inspector Notes:** This signature
$30-$45   restaurant features classic Italian
cuisine, including freshly prepared
pasta dishes, veal and choice cuts of
beef as well as select seafood.
Contemporary and elegant high
ceilings, graceful arches and marble floors combine to
provide an upscale setting. Semi-formal attire. **Bar:** full bar.
Reservations: required. **Address:** 6000 Rio Mar Blvd 00745
Location: 19 mi (30.4 km) e of Luis Muñoz International
Airport; jct Hwy 3 and 968, 0.8 mi (1.3 km) n on Hwy 968; in
Rio Mar Beach Resort & Spa-A Wyndham Grand Resort.
Parking: on-site (fee) and valet. [D] CALL [&][M]

▼ See AAA listing p. 424 ▼

SAN JUAN (B-4) pop. 434,374, elev. 13'

- Restaurants p. 447
- Hotels & Restaurants map & index p. 408

BEST WESTERN SAN JUAN AIRPORT HOTEL
Phone: (787)791-1700   **49**

Hotel
$125-$148

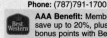
AAA Benefit: Members save up to 20%, plus 10% bonus points with Best Western Rewards®.

Address: Airport Rd 00937 **Location:** At Luis Muñoz Marin International Airport. **Facility:** Meets AAA guest room security requirements. 125 units. 6 stories, interior corridors. **Parking:** on-site (fee). **Amenities:** high-speed Internet, safes. **Activities:** whirlpools, exercise room. **Guest Services:** complimentary laundry. **Free Special Amenities:** local telephone calls and high-speed Internet.

/ SOME UNITS FEE

Safety tip: Keep a current AAA/CAA Road Atlas in every vehicle

---

CARIBE HILTON
Phone: (787)721-0303   **10**

Resort Hotel
$179-$399 12/1-4/30
$139-$329 5/1-11/30

AAA Benefit: Members save 5% or more everyday!

Address: San Geronimo Grounds Calle 1 00902 **Location:** Oceanfront. Between Condado and Old San Juan; off Muñoz Rivera Ave. **Facility:** Featuring a private beach and a bird sanctuary, this luxury hotel is situated on 17 acres next to 16th-century Fort San Geronimo. Meets AAA guest room security requirements. 646 units. 8-20 stories, interior corridors. **Parking:** on-site (fee) and valet. **Terms:** check-in 4 pm, 1-7 night minimum stay, cancellation fee imposed. **Amenities:** high-speed Internet (fee), safes. **Dining:** 6 restaurants, also, Lemon Grass, Morton's The Steakhouse, see separate listings, entertainment. **Pool(s):** 2 outdoor. **Activities:** whirlpools, snorkeling & rental equipment, miniature golf, 3 lighted tennis courts, recreation programs in summer, playground, sports court, shuffleboard, volleyball, spa. *Fee:* saunas, steamrooms, paddleboats, scuba diving, game room. **Guest Services:** valet laundry.
(See ad opposite title page, this page.)

▼ *See AAA listing this page* ▼

Get Away from the Everyday at Caribe Hilton

Stay with Caribe Hilton and enjoy world-renowned hospitality and service, a convenient location and great amenities. Customize your stay with Hilton Fitness by Precor® and Hilton Breakfast, designed to help you create a personalized travel experience.

San Geronimo Grounds Calle 1, San Juan, PR 00902 | 1-877-GO-HILTON
www.caribehilton.com

Four Diamond Award

Caribe Hilton
San Juan
©2010 Hilton Worldwide

HHONORS
HILTON WORLDWIDE

Save Money in Your Sleep

Members get the best available room rates with AAA/CAA preferred lodging partners.

Visit over 1,100 AAA/CAA Offices   **Click** AAA.com/CAA.ca
Call 1-866-AAA-SAVE (222-7283)

Show Your Card & Save®
Preferred Hotels

(See map & index p. 408.)

▼ See AAA listing p. 428 ▼

Relax and Unwind
in the Heart of Condado

This San Juan hotel offers updated rooms within walking distance to the Atlantic Ocean and minutes from the picturesque cobblestone streets of historic Old San Juan.

- Free continental breakfast
- Free high-speed Internet
- Conveniently located near Ashford Avenue with casinos, nightclubs and restaurants

Comfort INN

BY CHOICE HOTELS

For special AAA member rates, call 888.9.SUNFUN or visit choicecaribbean.com

(See map & index p. 408.)

COMFORT INN SAN JUAN
Phone: (787)721-0170

Motel
$89-$140

Address: 6 Clemenceau St 00907 **Location:** In Condado; corner of Clemenceau and Mariano Ramirez Bages sts. **Facility:** Meets AAA guest room security requirements. 56 units. 7 stories, interior corridors. **Parking:** on-site (fee). **Terms:** cancellation fee imposed. **Amenities:** high-speed Internet, safes. **Pool(s):** outdoor. **Guest Services:** valet laundry. **Free Special Amenities: continental breakfast and high-speed Internet.** (See ad p. 427.)

/ SOME UNITS

Visit AAA.com or CAA.ca
for one-stop travel
planning and reservations

CONDADO LAGOON VILLAS AT CARIBE HILTON
Phone: (787)721-0303   9

Resort
Condominium
$179-$399 12/1-4/30
$139-$329 5/1-11/30

AAA Benefit: Members save 5% or more everyday!

Address: One Los Rosales St 00901 **Location:** Oceanfront. Between Condado and Old San Juan; off Munoz Rivera. **Facility:** Recently built, this property offers residential-like studios and one- to two-bedroom condo-style units with shared resort facilities. Meets AAA guest room security requirements. 264 condominiums. 8-10 stories, interior corridors. **Parking:** on-site (fee) and valet. **Terms:** check-in 4 pm, 1-7 night minimum stay, cancellation fee imposed. **Amenities:** high-speed Internet (fee), safes. **Dining:** 6 restaurants, also, Lemon Grass, Morton's The Steakhouse, see separate listings, entertainment. **Pool(s):** 2 outdoor. **Activities:** whirlpools, snorkeling & rental equipment, miniature golf, 3 lighted tennis courts, recreation programs in summer, playground, sports court, shuffleboard, volleyball, spa. *Fee:* saunas, steamrooms, paddleboats, scuba diving, game room. **Guest Services:** valet laundry. *(See ad opposite title page, this page.)*

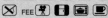

▼ See AAA listing this page ▼

Condado Lagoon Villas

- Ocean Front, Lagoon or
  San Geronimo Fort Views
- Fully Equipped Kitchens
- One or Two Bedroom Villas
- Swimming Pool
- Exclusive Access to
  Caribe Hilton Facilities

One Los Rosales Street, San Juan, PR 00901
1-877-GO-Hilton
www.condadolagoonvillas.com • info.caribe@hilton.com

AAA
Approved
▼▼▼

Condado Lagoon Villas
at Caribe Hilton
San Juan, Puerto Rico

Discover mobile travel solutions at
AAA.com/mobile and CAA.ca/mobile

(See map & index p. 408.)

CONRAD SAN JUAN CONDADO PLAZA
Phone: (787)721-1000 **14**

Hotel
$179-$409 12/1-4/30
$149-$279 5/1-11/30

AAA Benefit: Contemporary luxury at a special Member rate.

Address: 999 Ashford Ave 00907 **Location:** Oceanfront. West end of Ashford Ave. **Facility:** Reflecting a contemporary ambiance, the property is comprised of two mid-rise towers that face the ocean and a lagoon. Meets AAA guest room security requirements. 570 units. 10 stories, interior corridors. **Parking:** on-site (fee) and valet. **Terms:** check-in 4 pm, 1-7 night minimum stay, cancellation fee imposed. **Amenities:** video games (fee), high-speed Internet, safes. **Dining:** 6 restaurants, entertainment. **Pool(s):** 3 outdoor. **Activities:** sauna, whirlpools, steamroom, waterslide, rental paddleboats, 2 lighted tennis courts, recreation programs, rental bicycles, volleyball. *Fee:* snorkeling, game room, massage. **Guest Services:** valet and coin laundry. **Free Special Amenities: local telephone calls and high-speed Internet.** *(See ad this page.)*

SAVE ⊗ ❮ 〒 ⓕ S SD ⟲ 👶 BIZ
📶 ✕ FEE 🎮 🔌 🖥 SOME/UNITS 🖨

COURTYARD BY MARRIOTT-ISLA VERDE BEACH RESORT
Phone: (787)791-0404 **52**

Hotel
$135-$275

AAA Benefit: AAA hotel discounts of 5% or more.

Address: 7012 Boca de Cangrejos Ave 00914 **Location:** Oceanfront. Just e of jct Hwy 187 and 37; east end of Isla Verde. **Facility:** This popular, award-winning hotel is located on a very attractive stretch of beach; guest units are upscale and spacious with extra amenities. Meets AAA guest room security requirements. 260 units. 12 stories, interior corridors. **Parking:** on-site (fee) and valet. **Terms:** 3 day cancellation notice. **Amenities:** high-speed Internet, safes. **Dining:** 4 restaurants, entertainment. **Pool(s):** outdoor. **Activities:** whirlpool, playground, game room, volleyball, exercise room. *Fee:* massage. **Guest Services:** valet and coin laundry. **Free Special Amenities: local telephone calls and high-speed Internet.** *(See ad p. 430.)*

SAVE ⊗ ❮ 〒 ⓕ CALL 🄼 S SD ⟲
BIZ 📶 ✕ FEE 🎮 🔌 ☕

▼ *See AAA listing this page* ▼

BE YOURSELF.
EVERYONE ELSE IS TAKEN

Offering breathtaking views, this is the only luxury hotel in Puerto Rico overlooking the Atlantic Ocean and Condado Lagoon. The hotel is energized with chic décor, restaurants and lounges, a 24-hour casino, and is within walking distance to area boutiques and bars.

THE LUXURY OF BEING YOURSELF

For more information and AAA discounts, call 888-722-1276, or visit CondadoPlaza.com.

CONRAD
SAN JUAN
CONDADO PLAZA

Create complete trip routings and custom maps
with the TripTik® Travel Planner on AAA.com or CAA.ca

(See map & index p. 408.)

COURTYARD BY MARRIOTT SAN JUAN MIRAMAR
Phone: (787)721-7400 **22**

Hotel
$109-$199

AAA Benefit:
AAA hotel discounts of 5% or more.

Address: 801 Ponce de Leon Ave 00907 **Location:** 5 mi (8 km) w of airport; Ponce de Leon and Calle Trigo. **Facility:** Meets AAA guest room security requirements. 134 units. 10 stories, interior corridors. **Parking:** valet only. **Terms:** 3 day cancellation notice. **Amenities:** *Some:* high-speed Internet, safes. **Dining:** Augusto's Cuisine, see separate listing. **Pool(s):** outdoor. **Activities:** exercise room. **Guest Services:** valet and coin laundry. ***(See ad this page.)***

S SD BIZ / SOME UNITS

Learn about
AAA/CAA Diamond Ratings
at AAA.com/Diamonds

▼ *See AAA listing p. 429* ▼

▼ ***See AAA listing this page*** ▼

(See map & index p. 408.)

DOUBLETREE BY HILTON SAN JUAN
Phone: (787)721-1200 **36**

Contemporary Hotel
$169-$209

AAA Benefit:
Members save 5% or more everyday!

Address: 105 de Diego Ave 00911 **Location:** Near Condado District; 0.3 mi (0.5 km) n of Hwy 26. **Facility:** Meets AAA guest room security requirements. 184 units. 3-8 stories, interior corridors. **Parking:** on-site (fee) and valet. **Terms:** 1-7 night minimum stay, cancellation fee imposed. **Amenities:** high-speed Internet, safes. **Dining:** 4 restaurants. **Pool(s):** outdoor. **Activities:** whirlpool, exercise room. *Fee:* massage. **Guest Services:** valet and coin laundry. *(See ad this page.)*

EL CANARIO BY THE LAGOON
Phone: (787)722-5058 **20**

Motel
$70-$155

Address: 4 Calle Clemenceau 00907 **Location:** Just s of Ashford Ave at Joffrey St; overlooking Condado Lagoon. **Facility:** Meets AAA guest room security requirements. 44 units. 5 stories, interior corridors. *Bath:* shower only. **Terms:** 4 day cancellation notice-fee imposed. **Amenities:** safes (fee). **Guest Services:** coin laundry. **Free Special Amenities:** expanded continental breakfast and newspaper.

A moderately priced small European-style hotel centrally located in Condado, San Juan.

TourBook Comments

Are we meeting your travel needs?

If your visit to an establishment listed in a AAA TourBook guide doesn't meet your expectations, tell us about it.

Complete an easy online form at **AAA.com/TourBookComments**.

(See map & index p. 408.)

EL SAN JUAN HOTEL & CASINO
Phone: (787)791-1000

Resort Hotel
$159-$759 12/1-4/30
$169-$399 5/1-11/30

Hilton **AAA Benefit:** Members save 5% or more everyday!

Address: 6063 Isla Verde Ave 00901 **Location:** Oceanfront. 2 mi (3.2 km) nw of airport; in Isla Verde. **Facility:** This centerpiece of Isla Verde features an extravagant world-class lobby, rooftop restaurant, lagoon-style pool and several guest room categories. 382 units, some kitchens. 2-10 stories, interior/exterior corridors. **Parking:** on-site (fee) and valet. **Terms:** check-in 4 pm, 1-7 night minimum stay, cancellation fee imposed. **Amenities:** high-speed Internet (fee), safes, honor bars. **Dining:** 7 restaurants, also, La Piccola Fontana, see separate listing, nightclub, entertainment. **Pool(s):** 3 outdoor. **Activities:** whirlpools, recreation programs, volleyball, exercise room, spa. *Fee:* lighted tennis court. **Guest Services:** valet laundry. **Free Special Amenities: local telephone calls and high-speed Internet.** Affiliated with A Hilton Hotel. *(See ad this page.)*

EMBASSY SUITES HOTEL & CASINO SAN JUAN
Phone: (787)791-0505

Hotel
$155-$195 12/1-4/19
$135-$155 4/20-11/30

AAA Benefit: Members save 5% or more everyday!

Address: 8000 Tartak St, Isla Verde 00979 **Location:** Jct Isla Verde Ave, just s; Hwy 187 exit Tartak St. Located in a commercial area. **Facility:** The hotel is popular with business travelers during the week and local and foreign leisure travelers on weekends. Meets AAA guest room security requirements. 299 units. 8 stories, interior corridors. **Parking:** on-site (fee) and valet. **Terms:** check-in 4 pm, 1-7 night minimum stay, cancellation fee imposed. **Amenities:** video games (fee), high-speed Internet, safes. **Dining:** 4 restaurants. **Pool(s):** outdoor. **Activities:** whirlpool, game room, exercise room. *Fee:* massage. **Guest Services:** valet and coin laundry. **Free Special Amenities: full breakfast and manager's reception.** *(See ad p. 433.)*

▼ See AAA listing this page ▼

One Life to Live, Live it Here.

Located in the hip Isla Verde district, El San Juan Resort & Casino is a lush Caribbean oasis that sits on the most beautiful beach in Puerto Rico. With an electrifying nightlife and scintillating pool complex, this completely renovated resort supports a lavish lifestyle, and offers close proximity to Old San Juan. For more information and AAA discounts, call 888.579.2635, or visit ElSanJuanResort.com.

©2011 Hilton Worldwide

El San Juan Resort & Casino
6063 Isla Verde Avenue
Carolina, P.R. 00979

Check out our travel blog at AAATravelViews.com

(See map & index p. 408.)

▼ See AAA listing p. 432 ▼

Explore the Travel Guides on

AAA.com/Travel or CAA.ca/Travel

(See map & index p. 408.)

HAMPTON INN & SUITES-SAN JUAN
Phone: (787)791-8777 **43**

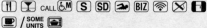

Hotel
$159-$299 12/1-4/30
$149-$299 5/1-11/30

AAA Benefit:
Members save up to 10%
everyday!

Address: 6530 Isla Verde Ave 00979 **Location:** 2 mi (3.2 km) nw of airport; in Isla Verde area, close to intersection with Hwy 187. Located on edge of busy commercial area. **Facility:** Meets AAA guest room security requirements. 201 units. 4-5 stories, interior corridors. **Parking:** on-site (fee). **Terms:** 1-7 night minimum stay, cancellation fee imposed. **Amenities:** high-speed Internet, safes. **Pool(s):** outdoor. **Activities:** whirlpool, exercise room. **Guest Services:** valet and coin laundry.

HOLIDAY INN EXPRESS
Phone: (787)724-4160 **16**

Motel
$119-$139

Address: 1 Mariano Ramirez Bages St 00907 **Location:** In Condado; corner of Mariano Ramirez Bages and Clemenceau sts. **Facility:** Meets AAA guest room security requirements. 115 units. 7 stories, interior corridors. **Parking:** on-site (fee). **Terms:** check-in 4 pm, 3 day cancellation notice-fee imposed. **Amenities:** safes. **Pool(s):** outdoor. **Activities:** whirlpool, limited exercise equipment. **Guest Services:** valet laundry. **Free Special Amenities:** expanded continental breakfast and high-speed Internet.
(See ad p. 435.)

▼ See AAA listing p. 418 ▼

(See map & index p. 408.)

See AAA listing p. 434

Everything at Holiday Inn Express® is designed so that you can relax. Because we know all you really need on the road is a place to be yourself. That's what Holiday Inn Express was built for. Now, that's smart.

- **Great AAA Discounts**
- **Free Hot Breakfast Bar**
- **Free Local and 1-800 calls**
- **Free High-Speed Internet**

Holiday Inn Express San Juan
1 Mariano Ramirez Bages St.
San Juan, 00907
1-800-HOLIDAY
hiexpress.com

Plan. Map. Go.

TripTik® Travel Planner

Where premier mapping technology meets complete travel information. Only on AAA.com and CAA.ca.

Vacation with Peace of Mind

Experience an incredible vacation with amazing value on select *AAA Vacations®* tour and cruise departures. Includes our **Best Price Guarantee** and **24/7 Member Care** for a worry-free vacation.

Contact your local AAA Travel Professional or visit **AAA.com/Travel** for full details on these exclusive *AAA Vacations®* benefits.

Terms and conditions apply

(See map & index p. 408.)

HOTEL EL CONVENTO   Phone: (787)723-9020   ❶

Historic Hotel
$185-$365

Address: 100 Calle Cristo 00901 **Location:** Center of Old San Juan; across from San Juan Cathedral. **Facility:** Built in 1651 as a Carmelite convent, the small elegant inn offers distinctive, cozy accommodations and a large courtyard. 72 units. 5 stories, interior corridors. **Parking:** valet only. **Terms:** 2 night minimum stay - seasonal and/or weekends, 3 day cancellation notice. **Amenities:** high-speed Internet, safes. **Dining:** 3 restaurants. **Pool(s):** outdoor. **Activities:** whirlpool, exercise room. *Fee:* massage. **Guest Services:** valet laundry. **Free Special Amenities:** high-speed Internet and manager's reception.
(See ad this page.)

INTERCONTINENTAL SAN JUAN RESORT & CASINO   Phone: (787)791-6100   ❹⓿

Hotel
$199-$659

Address: 5961 Isla Verde Ave 00979 **Location:** Oceanfront. 2.1 mi (3.3 km) e of airport. **Facility:** Situated in lively Isla Verde, the hotel offers comfort, style and a host of amenities. Meets AAA guest room security requirements. 398 units. 2-16 stories, interior corridors. **Parking:** on-site (fee) and valet. **Terms:** check-in 4 pm, cancellation fee imposed. **Amenities:** video games (fee), safes. **Dining:** 3 restaurants, also, Alfredo Restaurant, Momoyama, Ruth's Chris Steak House, see separate listings, entertainment. **Pool(s):** outdoor. **Activities:** sauna, whirlpool, steamroom, recreation programs, playground, volleyball, spa. **Guest Services:** valet laundry.
(See ad starting on p. 438.)

Simply Reliable

The Diamond Ratings in this TourBook guide are backed by our expert, in-person evaluations, whether the hotel or restaurant is no-frills, moderate or upscale.

Learn more at **AAA.com/Diamonds**

(See map & index p. 408.)

▼ See AAA listing p. 437 ▼

(See map & index p. 408.)

HOW MEMORABLE YOUR VACATION IS DEPENDS ON WHERE YOU SPEND IT.

There's no better place to spend your vacation than at InterContinental San Juan. To help you get the most from your destination, we'll share our expert local knowledge so you can discover authentic experiences to make your stay truly memorable.

Do you live an InterContinental life?

For more information or to make a reservation, please call 1-800-443-2009 or visit www.icsanjuanresort.com

INTERCONTINENTAL
SAN JUAN RESORT & CASINO

In over 170 locations across the globe including HONG KONG • LONDON • NEW YORK • PARIS

(See map & index p. 408.)

LA CONCHA, A RENAISSANCE RESORT

Phone: (787)721-7500 **19**

Contemporary Hotel
$118-$399

RENAISSANCE
HOTELS & RESORTS

AAA Benefit: AAA hotel discounts of 5% or more.

Address: 1077 Ashford Ave 00907 **Location:** Oceanfront. Center of Condado. **Facility:** Chic and modern best describe this hotel with its added trendy techno music piped throughout. Meets AAA guest room security requirements. 483 units. 11-12 stories, interior/exterior corridors. **Parking:** on-site (fee) and valet. **Terms:** check-in 4 pm. **Amenities:** high-speed Internet, safes. **Dining:** 5 restaurants, entertainment. **Pool(s):** 3 outdoor. **Activities:** whirlpools. **Guest Services:** valet laundry. **Free Special Amenities:** newspaper and high-speed Internet. *(See ad this page.)*

 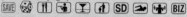 

QUALITY INN EL PORTAL

Phone: (787)721-9010 **30**

Motel
$95-$155

Address: 76 Condado Ave 00907 **Location:** At entrance to Condado Central. **Facility:** 47 units. 6 stories, interior corridors. *Bath:* shower only. **Parking:** on-site and street. **Terms:** cancellation fee imposed. **Amenities:** high-speed Internet, safes. **Guest Services:** valet laundry. **Free Special Amenities:** expanded continental breakfast and high-speed Internet. *(See ad p. 441.)*

▼ See AAA listing this page ▼

Flirt with Life...
and see where it takes you.

La Concha
A RENAISSANCE RESORT
San Juan, Puerto Rico

Four Diamond Award

For reservations call toll free 877 | **LCH.RSRT**
                                         524.7778
or visit us at www.LaConchaResort.com

(See map & index p. 408.)

▼ See AAA listing p. 440 ▼

Great value, steps from
Condado's best dining and shopping

Quality Inn® El Portal, a San Juan hotel in the trendy Condado Beach area is one-half mile from the beautiful Atlantic Ocean with easy access to popular island attractions and points of interest.

• Free rooftop continental breakfast

• Free wireless high-speed Internet access
• On-site Bulgao Seafood Bistro
• Conveniently located to Old San Juan, San Juan Cruise Port and museums

For special AAA member rates, call
888.9.SUNFUN or visit choicecaribbean.com

Visit AAA.com or CAA.ca for one-stop
travel planning and reservations

(See map & index p. 408.)

RADISSON AMBASSADOR PLAZA HOTEL & CASINO
Phone: (787)721-7300   **25**

Hotel
$239-$279

Address: 1369 Ashford Ave 00907 **Location:** Center of Condado. **Facility:** Located in the Condado area, this older casino-hotel's informal atmosphere is popular with locals and tourists alike. Meets AAA guest room security requirements. 233 units. 8 stories, interior corridors. **Parking:** on-site (fee) and valet. **Amenities:** video games (fee), high-speed Internet, safes. **Dining:** entertainment. **Pool(s):** outdoor. **Activities:** exercise room. *Fee:* massage. **Guest Services:** valet laundry. **Free Special Amenities:** local telephone calls and high-speed Internet.
(See ad this page.)

 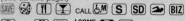 

THE RITZ-CARLTON SAN JUAN HOTEL, SPA & CASINO
Phone: (787)253-1700   **44**

Resort Hotel
$299-$899

AAA Benefit: Unequaled service at Special Member Savings.

Address: 6961 Avenue of the Governors 00979 **Location:** Oceanfront. 1 mi (1.6 km) n of Luis Muñoz Marin International Airport; on Isla Verde Ave (Hwy 187). **Facility:** On the beach, this service-oriented hotel is the epitome of luxury, featuring upscale spa facilities and well-landscaped grounds and pool area. 416 units. 10 stories, interior corridors. **Parking:** on-site (fee) and valet. **Terms:** check-in 4 pm, cancellation fee imposed. **Amenities:** high-speed Internet, safes, honor bars. **Dining:** 3 restaurants, also, BLT Steak, Il Mulino, see separate listings, entertainment. **Pool(s):** outdoor. **Activities:** sauna, whirlpools, steamrooms, snorkeling, 2 lighted tennis courts, recreation programs, volleyball, spa. **Guest Services:** valet laundry.

▼ *See AAA listing this page* ▼

Explore the Travel Guides on
AAA.com/Travel or CAA.ca/Travel

(See map & index p. 408.)

SAN JUAN MARRIOTT RESORT & STELLARIS CASINO
Phone: (787)722-7000 **24**

▼▼▼ ▼▼▼
Resort Hotel
$159-$324

Marriott. HOTELS & RESORTS

AAA Benefit: AAA hotel discounts of 5% or more.

Address: 1309 Ashford Ave 00907 **Location:** Oceanfront. In Condado; corner of Calle Caribe and Ashford Ave. **Facility:** A high-rise in the Condado area, the resort offers luxury services, many ocean-facing units and an upscale lobby. Meets AAA guest room security requirements. 525 units. 9-21 stories, interior corridors. **Parking:** on-site (fee) and valet. **Terms:** check-in 4 pm. **Amenities:** safes. *Some:* high-speed Internet (fee). **Dining:** 5 restaurants, entertainment. **Pool(s):** 2 outdoor. **Activities:** saunas, whirlpool, waterslide, recreation programs, volleyball, spa. *Fee:* 2 lighted tennis courts. **Guest Services:** valet and coin laundry.
(See ad starting on p. 444.)

SAVE 🐾 🍽 🍸 🏃 CALL 🔊M S SD 🏊
📶 BIZ 📶 ✕ FEE 📹 🖥 💻

Share a New View on Travel at AAATravelViews.com

Read stories, tips and trends from AAA insiders. Post comments and get your questions answered by our travel experts.

SHERATON OLD SAN JUAN HOTEL
Phone: (787)721-5100 **4**

▼▼▼ ▼▼▼
Hotel
$149-$399

Ⓢ **Sheraton** HOTELS & RESORTS

AAA Benefit: Members get up to 15% off, plus Starwood Preferred Guest® bonuses.

Address: 100 Brumbaugh St 00901 **Location:** In Old San Juan; across from cruise ship terminal. **Facility:** This hotel overlooks the cruise-ship terminals and is convenient to shops and restaurants; the casino features live music some nights. Meets AAA guest room security requirements. 240 units. 9 stories, interior corridors. **Parking:** valet only. **Terms:** 3 day cancellation notice-fee imposed. **Amenities:** high-speed Internet (fee), safes. **Dining:** Chicago Burger, Palio, A Tuscan Chophouse, see separate listings, entertainment. **Pool(s):** outdoor. **Activities:** whirlpool, exercise room. **Guest Services:** valet laundry. **Free Special Amenities:** newspaper. *(See ad p. 446.)*

SAVE 🐾 🍽 🍸 CALL 🔊M S SD 🏊 BIZ
📶 ✕ 💻 / SOME UNITS FEE 🖥

SHERATON PUERTO RICO HOTEL & CASINO
Phone: (787)993-3500 **2**

▼▼▼ ▼▼▼
Contemporary Resort Hotel
$119-$489

Ⓢ **Sheraton** HOTELS & RESORTS

AAA Benefit: Members get up to 15% off, plus Starwood Preferred Guest® bonuses.

Address: 200 Convention Center Blvd 00907 **Location:** In San Juan Convention Center District; in Miramar. **Facility:** The property is impressive with its designer infinity pool, hip bar, tastefully appointed rooms and Puerto Rico's largest casino. Meets AAA guest room security requirements. 503 units. 12 stories, interior corridors. **Parking:** on-site (fee) and valet. **Terms:** cancellation fee imposed. **Amenities:** high-speed Internet, safes. **Dining:** 5 restaurants, entertainment. **Pool(s):** outdoor. **Activities:** whirlpool, exercise room, spa. *Fee:* saunas, steamrooms. **Guest Services:** valet laundry. *(See ad on insert.)*

SAVE 🐾 🍽 🍸 S SD 🏊 BIZ 📶 ✕
💻 / SOME UNITS 🐕 🖥

▼ See AAA listing p. 446 ▼

SAN JUAN
RESORT & STELLARIS® CASINO

Marriott.

To check availability and make reservations log onto:
www.marriottsanjuan.com
Or call 1-800-228-9290

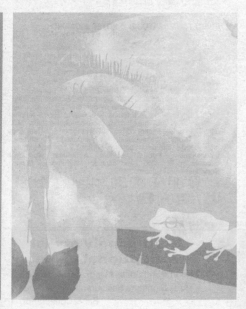

LOSE YOURSELF IN AN ENCHANTED WORLD.
We live in a cosmopolitan city of lush foliage,
endless beaches and dark late-night bars pulsating with the
sounds of the tropics.
Service you expect. A style that surprises.

(See map & index p. 408.)

VERDANZA HOTEL

Hotel
$170-$250

Phone: (787)253-9000 **48**
Address: 8020 Tartak St 00979
Location: Jct Isla Verde Ave, just s; 1.6 mi (2.5 km) w of airport at Tartak St exit, off Hwy 187. **Facility:** Meets AAA guest room security requirements. 222 units, some cottages. 3-8 stories, interior corridors. **Parking:** on-site (fee) and valet. **Amenities:** video games (fee), high-speed Internet, safes. **Dining:** 2 restaurants, also, Eighty20 Bistro, J.H. Yee's Asian Bistro, see separate listings. **Pool(s):** outdoor. **Activities:** whirlpool, jogging, exercise room. **Guest Services:** valet laundry. Affiliated with A Preferred Hotel. *(See ad p. 443.)*

[🍴] [🍸] [S] [SD] [🛏] [BIZ] [📶] [✖] FEE [📹] [🔌]
[💻] / SOME UNITS FEE [🐕]

▼ See AAA listing p. 443 ▼

(See map & index p. 408.)

WHERE TO EAT

AGUAVIVA SEASIDE LATINO CUISINE
Phone: 787/722-0665 (16)

New Latin American
$22-$42

AAA Inspector Notes: One of the favorite hot spots on the block in the SOFO area of old San Juan. The vivacity and conviviality among the diners and staff set the mood to enjoy the total Latino-inspired seafood. Snuggle up to the ceviche bar to enjoy marinated pulpo, tuna, red snapper, scallops and shrimp. The Spanglish menu offers a sea of opportunity to enjoy flavorful wild salmon or the seared dorado with coconut poached yuca and smoky shrimp salsa. Chilled or fried seafood towers are great for sharing. **Bar:** full bar. **Address:** 364 Calle Fortaleza 00901 **Location:** Center of Old San Juan; just n of cruise ship docks. **Parking:** on-site (fee) and street. **Historic** [D]

AL DENTE RISTORANTE AND WINE BAR
Phone: 787/723-7303 (24)

Italian
$15-$35

AAA Inspector Notes: This charming restaurant in the heart of town for some 20 years, presents a menu of varied pasta dishes, including gnocchi. Among other entrées are Italian-inspired preparations of fresh fish, lamb and veal. Any of the tempting homemade desserts, such as crème brûlée and tiramisu complete a fine meal. **Bar:** full bar. **Reservations:** suggested. **Address:** 309 Recinto Sur 00901 **Location:** Center of Old San Juan; near cruise ship docks; across from Doña Fela parking garage. **Parking:** on-site (fee) and street. **Historic** [L] [D]

ALFREDO RESTAURANT
Phone: 787/791-6100 (88)

Italian
$18-$38

AAA Inspector Notes: At arrival, the attentive staff brings a complementary flute of Champagne and an amuse-bouche; at departure, a lemoncello digestif. In addition to a well-rounded menu, a seasonally changing chef's tasting menu is available. Starters include spicy, steamed clams and chilled gazpacho with crab meat. Homemade pasta can be found in the traditional lasagna and seafood spaghetti. Other hearty main courses include veal osso buco, grilled lamb chops and halibut with a lemon caper sauce. **Bar:** full bar. **Reservations:** suggested. **Address:** 5961 Isla Verde Ave 00979 **Location:** 2.1 mi (3.3 km) e of airport; in InterContinental San Juan Resort & Casino. **Parking:** on-site (fee) and valet. [B] [D] CALL [&M]

AUGUSTO'S CUISINE
Phone: 787/725-7700 (44)

Continental
$24-$45

AAA Inspector Notes: International, classical cuisine exhibits regional influences. Among menu favorites are foie gras terrine, wild salmon tartar with wasabi flying fish roe, Colorado lamb duo, crispy Muscovy duck breast and Angus filet mignon with black truffle sauce. For dessert, try the chocolate souffle with Grand Marnier anglaise sauce. Because the restaurant caters to an adult crowd, children under 12 are not allowed. **Bar:** full bar. **Reservations:** suggested. **Address:** 801 Ponce de Leon Ave 00907 **Location:** 5 mi (8 km) w of airport; Ponce de Leon and Calle Trigo; in Courtyard by Marriott San Juan Miramar. **Parking:** valet only. [L] [D]

BLT STEAK
Phone: 787/253-1700 (63)

Steak
$28-$55

AAA Inspector Notes: This cutting-edge steaks, chops and seafood restaurant from New York City provides flawless service in a refined yet lively atmosphere. Lining the sumptuous menu are West Coast/East Coast oysters, Alaskan king crab, Kobe and Black Angus beef, Dover sole and Maine lobster. To end a memorable dining experience here, many indulge in American artisan cheese, warm coconut bread pudding with rum raisin ice cream or peanut butter mousse pie with banana ice cream. **Bar:** full bar. **Reservations:** required. **Address:** 6961 Ave of the Governors 00979 **Location:** 1 mi (1.6 km) n of Luis Muñoz Marin International Airport; on Isla Verde Ave (Hwy 187); in The Ritz-Carlton San Juan Hotel, Spa & Casino. **Parking:** on-site (fee) and valet. [D]

BODEGA COMPOSTELA
Phone: 787/724-6088 (62)

Spanish
$15-$45

AAA Inspector Notes: This restaurant offers chic surroundings and suave service. The 10-course degustation menu offers an assortment of tastes including codfish tempura, stuffed lamb shank and angel hair pasta with sausage, rabbit and veal. An extensive tapas menu with such savory treats as octopus gallega-style, escargot with shiitake mushrooms and Serrano ham as well as veal tripe. The wine cellar has a stellar selection of wine by the glass and by the bottle. **Bar:** full bar. **Reservations:** suggested. **Address:** 106 Condado Ave 00907 **Location:** In Santurce: jct Calle Labra and Condado Ave; just s of Hwy 2. **Parking:** valet only. [L] [D]

BUENOS AYRES BAR & GRILL
Phone: 787/725-1818 (52)

Argentine
$17-$33

AAA Inspector Notes: This attractive corner neighborhood churrascaria offers quick friendly service in a relaxed ambience. Grilled beef, pork, chicken and seafood, including lobster and fish, line the menu. The large pictures of sangria are great for sharing. The tres leches cake is a must order. **Bar:** full bar. **Address:** 56 Condado Ave 00907 **Location:** Corner of Condado and Magdalena aves; in Condado just s of Ashford Ave. **Parking:** valet only. [L] [D]

CHE'S RESTAURANT ARGENTINO
Phone: 787/726-7202 (50)

Argentine
$14-$29

AAA Inspector Notes: Locals frequent the modestly decorated restaurant for snappy service and simply presented meals with good flavor. Entrees range from steak, veal and pork to chicken and pasta dishes. Good starters include several soups, salad or flaky empanadas. Flan or a dish of ice cream is a sweet finish. **Bar:** full bar. **Address:** 35 Coaba St 00907 **Location:** Jct Laurel St and Isla Verde Ave; between Isla Verde and Condado aves; at Punta Las Marias. **Parking:** on-site and valet. [L] [D]

CHICAGO BURGER
Phone: 787/721-5100 (26)

Burgers
$7-$11

AAA Inspector Notes: Lining the menu at this quasi-fast food eatery are Angus beef, ahi tuna and veggie burgers. Seating is available in the contemporary dining room and on the outdoor patio where patrons enjoy watching the docked cruise ships. **Bar:** full bar. **Address:** 100 Brumbaugh St 00901 **Location:** In Old San Juan; adjacent to cruise ship terminal; in Sheraton Old San Juan Hotel. **Parking:** on-site (fee). [L] [D]

(See map & index p. 408.)

DRAGONFLY
Phone: 787/977-3886 (15)

New Latin American
$12-$25

AAA Inspector Notes: Along the SoFo restaurant row of Old San Juan is the cozy eatery specializing in Asian-Latino cuisine. Patrons sit at communal tables while enjoying the chef's adventurous creations. Service comes with hip pizzazz. **Bar:** full bar. **Address:** 364 Fortaleza St 00979 **Location:** Center Old San Juan; just n of cruise ship docks. **Parking:** street only. **Historic**

L D

EIGHTY20 BISTRO
Phone: 787/253-9000 (89)

International
$12-$28

AAA Inspector Notes: Tucked away and adjacent to the pool of the Verdanza Hotel is this consistent eatery offering a unique blend of cuisines presented with a flair. Diners can sit inside in the chic surroundings or dine al fresco. A variety of tapas, sandwiches and full-size entrées and salads are available. The breakfast and lunch buffet is popular with tourists and locals alike. **Bar:** full bar. **Address:** 8020 Tartak 00979 **Location:** Jct Isla Verde Ave, just s; 1.6 mi (2.5 km) w of airport at Tartak St exit, off Hwy 187; in Verdanza Hotel. B L D

EL ALCAZAR MARISQUERIA Y TASCA ESPANOLA
Phone: 787/707-0102 (20)

Spanish
$15-$33

AAA Inspector Notes: Authentic Spanish restaurant with dapper, attentive servers. The rustically rich decor is very comfortable. Paellas are worth the wait; other entrees ranging from beef, chicken and fish are also very satisfying. The flan de coco is a popular dessert. **Bar:** full bar. **Reservations:** suggested. **Address:** 1013 Roosevelt Ave 00920 **Location:** In Puerto Nuevo; just w of Plaza Las Americas. **Parking:** valet only. L D

EL ZIPPERLE RESTAURANTE
Phone: 787/763-1636 (72)

International
$17-$32

AAA Inspector Notes: With chalet-style decor, murals on the wall and decorative sconce lighting, the dining room evokes the ambience of yesteryear fine dining. The menu lists an interesting mix of German, Spanish and Puerto Rican cuisine. Decision-making can be arduous due to the dizzying array of choices, including nine soups and salads, paella, lobster prepared five ways and Chateaubriand for two. The tableside arrival of the dessert trolley marks the meal's finale. **Bar:** full bar. **Reservations:** required. **Address:** Ave Roosevelt #352 00979 **Location:** In Hato Rey; just w of Plaza Las Americas. **Parking:** valet only. L D

FACCIO PIZZA
Phone: 787/268-7755

Italian
$7-$18

AAA Inspector Notes: Family owned and operated for many decades, this popular eatery serves outstanding thin crust pizza and a variety of pastas and other Italian dishes. All moderately priced, it is difficult to choose from the varied menu selections including lasagna, ravioli, manicotti and seafood. **Bar:** full bar. **Address:** 4820 Ave Isla Verde 00979 **Location:** In Isla Verde; in Howard Johnson Hotel. **Parking:** on-site (fee). L D

FACCIO PIZZA
Phone: 787/755-5415

Italian
$6-$18

AAA Inspector Notes: Family owned and operated for many decades, this popular eatery serves outstanding thin crust pizza and a variety of pastas and other Italian dishes. All moderately priced, it is difficult to choose from the varied menu selections including lasagna, ravioli, manicotti and seafood. **Bar:** full bar. **Address:** Carretera 176 00918 **Location:** 7 mi (11.2 km) s on SR 18 exit SR 21, follow signs to Cupey 1.5 mi (2.4 km); just s of jct SR 176 and 845; Urb Sagrado Corazon. L D

IL MULINO
Phone: 787/791-8632 (87)

Italian
$24-$65

AAA Inspector Notes: The famous New York eatery comes to San Juan, bringing its tradition of fine Italian cuisine with fresh pasta, seafood, lamb and more into a cozy, bustling dining room. **Bar:** full bar. **Reservations:** required. **Address:** 6961 Ave of the Governors 00979 **Location:** 1 mi (1.6 km) n of Luis Muñoz Marin International Airport; on Isla Verde Ave (Hwy 187); in The Ritz-Carlton San Juan Hotel, Spa & Casino. **Parking:** on-site (fee) and valet. D

J.H. YEE'S ASIAN BISTRO
Phone: 787/793-8300 (90)

Asian
$17-$29

AAA Inspector Notes: Pan-Asian cuisine is served in a soothing dining room by well-groomed, uniformed staff. Menu offerings show influences of Japanese, Chinese, Vietnamese and Thai cuisine. Start the meal off with a refreshing seaweed salad or one of the many satisfying soups. A variety of entrées include Tahitian pineapple chicken, Cantonese orange beef, tempura, sushi and Peking duck. **Bar:** full bar. **Address:** 8020 Tartak St 00979 **Location:** Jct Isla Verde Ave, just s; 1.6 mi (2.5 km) w of airport at Tartak St exit, off Hwy 187; in Verdanza Hotel. **Parking:** on-site (fee). L D

JOSE JOSE RESTAURANT
Phone: 787/725-8496 (38)

International
$24-$33

AAA Inspector Notes: The slightly hidden gem is well worth the effort to find. Classically decorated dining rooms reflect an elegant atmosphere. Dapper, poised servers provide refined help. The extensive menu often features specialty dishes of ostrich, rabbit, goat and suckling pig. Whole baked red snapper is satisfying, and duck a l'Orange is succulently sweet. Save room for a decadent souffle. The comprehensive wine list includes a good concentration of Spanish wines. **Bar:** full bar. **Reservations:** required. **Address:** 1110 Magdalena Ave 00901 **Location:** Just e of jct Ashford and Magdalena aves; in center of Condado section; next to post office. **Parking:** valet only.

L D

J-TASTE
Phone: 787/724-2003 (25)

Japanese
$12-$40

AAA Inspector Notes: Upscale, chic decor and artfully presented Japanese dishes are offered at this eatery. Besides the many sushi rolls and sashimi available this swanky restaurant also offers teppanyaki cooking, yakitori, tempura and noodle dishes. The broiled eel is especially tasty. **Bar:** full bar. **Reservations:** suggested. **Address:** 307 Recinto Sur 00901 **Location:** In Old San Juan; just w of cruise ship docks. **Parking:** on-site (fee). L D

LA CASONA RESTAURANTE
Phone: 787/727-2717 (64)

Spanish
$19-$37

AAA Inspector Notes: The chef/owner, originally from Spain, brings the techniques and recipes of Spanish cuisine here with some Puerto Rican specialties. Housed in a stately mansion, this fine dining establishment has been pleasing the palate of guests in an atmosphere of elegance and refinement since 1971. An Andalusia guitarist has been entertaining guests here for more than two decades. **Bar:** full bar. **Reservations:** required. **Address:** 609 San Jorge St 00909 **Location:** In Santurce; corner of San Jorge St and Ave Fernandez Juncos. **Parking:** valet only. **Historic** L D

(See map & index p. 408.)

LA PICCOLA FONTANA
Phone: 787/791-1000 (84)

Italian
$22-$42

AAA Inspector Notes: Diners can enjoy the bustling atmosphere in this cozy yet elegant dining room, where tuxedo-clad staff members whisk by them throughout the night. Lending to the fine European decor are hand-painted murals and lovely chandeliers. The menu lists a good mix of sophisticated Italian fare, including a wide range of freshly prepared pasta, veal, meat and seafood offerings. Semi-formal attire. **Bar:** full bar. **Reservations:** required. **Address:** 6063 Isla Verde Ave 00902 **Location:** 2 mi (3.2 km) nw of airport; in Isla Verde; in El San Juan Hotel & Casino. **Parking:** valet only. (D)

LATIN STAR RESTAURANT
Phone: 787/724-8141 (56)

Puerto Rican
$9-$32

AAA Inspector Notes: The proximity of nightlife hot spots and casinos contributes to this 24-hour eatery staying busy at all hours. Specializing in Latino and Puerto Rican comfort food, the huge menu features everything from lechon (pork), filet mignon, T-bone steaks, churrasco and pork chops to seafood, including conch, lobster, shrimp and octopus. Local favorites include goat stew, asopao, rice-like gruel with a choice of meat and mofongo made with mashed plantains. **Bar:** full bar. **Address:** 1128 Ashford Ave 00907 **Location:** In Condado.

(B) (L) (D) (24)

LEMON GRASS
Phone: 787/724-5888 (34)

New Asian
$27-$33

AAA Inspector Notes: This upscale and refined restaurant puts forth a Pacific Island-Polynesian motif. Team-style service is attentive and engaging. Fusion dishes combine the best techniques and ingredients of both Latino and Asian cuisine in an avant-garde style, with healthful aspects in mind. The menu items are sized to encourage grazing, sampling and sharing. **Bar:** full bar. **Reservations:** required. **Address:** San Geronimo Fort, Los Rosales St 00901 **Location:** Between Condado and Old San Juan; off Munoz Rivera; on grounds of Caribe Hilton Hotel & Condado Lagoon Villas at Caribe Hilton. **Parking:** on-site (fee) and valet. (D)

METROPOL RESTAURANT
Phone: 787/791-5585 (86)

Cuban
$9-$35

AAA Inspector Notes: Adjacent to the cock fighting arena and in business since 1965, this bustling eatery serves up substantial portions of Puerto Rican and Cuban cuisine. The staff provides matter-of-fact service at the diner-style restaurant, which is popular with locals and tourists alike. Varied items are freshly prepared, and most come with rice, beans and plantains. **Bar:** full bar. **Address:** Boca Cangrejos Rd 00907 **Location:** 2 mi (3.2 km) nw of airport; just w of jct Hwy 187; off Isla Verde Ave.

(L) (D)

MOMOYAMA
Phone: 787/791-8883 (81)

Japanese
$18-$41

AAA Inspector Notes: Japanese chefs design beautifully presented sushi and sashimi platters. Less adventuresome diners might try teriyaki or tempura dishes. **Bar:** full bar. **Reservations:** suggested. **Address:** 5961 Isla Verde Ave 00907 **Location:** 2.1 mi (3.3 km) e of airport; in InterContinental San Juan Resort & Casino. **Parking:** on-site (fee) and valet. (L) (D)

MORTON'S THE STEAKHOUSE
Phone: 787/977-6262 (30)

American
$29-$50

AAA Inspector Notes: Patrons should make sure to reserve ahead for the popular, well-known steakhouse. Large portions, including huge cuts of fine beef and plentiful seafood, are the norm. Even the vegetables are oversized, with baked potatoes big enough for sharing. **Bar:** full bar. **Reservations:** suggested. **Address:** 1 Calle San Geronimo Grounds 00901 **Location:** Between Condado and Old San Juan; off Munoz Rivera; in Condado Lagoon Villas at Caribe Hilton. **Parking:** on-site (fee) and valet. (D)

OLD HARBOR BREWERY STEAK & LOBSTER HOUSE
Phone: 787/721-2100 (6)

International
$12-$38

AAA Inspector Notes: The only known microbrewery in Puerto Rico, this place boasts a casual side and a more refined side with an exhibition kitchen in the same setting. The varied menu includes salmon, several pasta dishes, escargot, gourmet burgers, Kobe and Angus beef and live Caribbean lobsters taken straight from the tank. **Bar:** full bar. **Reservations:** suggested, Thurs-Sun. **Address:** 202 Tizol St 00901 **Location:** In Old San Juan; corner of Tizol and Recinto Sur sts. **Parking:** on-site (fee). (L) (D)

PALIO, A TUSCAN CHOPHOUSE
Phone: 787/721-5100 (27)

Italian
$18-$42

AAA Inspector Notes: An upscale ambience and gourmet Italian cuisine is served by an accommodating, suave staff in formal attire. Antipasti and tuna tartare are great starters. Pasta dishes include lasagna and seafood linguine. Among other favorites are veal Marsala and chicken parmigiana. Luscious desserts merit the indulgence. **Bar:** full bar. **Reservations:** suggested. **Address:** 100 Brumbaugh St 00901 **Location:** In Old San Juan; adjacent to cruise ship terminal; in Sheraton Old San Juan Hotel. **Parking:** on-site (fee) and valet. (D)

PANZA RESTAURANT AT CHATEAU CERVANTES
Phone: 787/724-7722 (28)

International
$17-$29

AAA Inspector Notes: Located in the discreet and chic boutique hotel Chateau Cervantes, this restaurant is sure to please the epicurean of fine cuisine. The creative chef blends the best ingredients and techniques of many cultures to create his own signature cuisine. Starters may include a truffle cream soup. The often changing entrées feature such selections as oven-roasted lamb chops or shrimp and chorizo risotto. A nice ending is the artisan cheese and fruit plate. An attentive waitstaff are smartly attired. **Bar:** full bar. **Reservations:** required. **Address:** 329 Recinto Sur 00901 **Location:** Center; Old San Juan. **Parking:** street only. **Historic** (D)

THE PARROT CLUB
Phone: 787/725-7370 (9)

New Latin American
$13-$37

AAA Inspector Notes: This ever popular hot spot is a place of continual celebrations in an island vibrant, urban hip atmosphere, and is always brimming with diners. Specializing in Nuevo Latino cuisine, the meals are fun, tasty and creative. Begin with one of the many designer martinis. Enjoy one of the ceviches as an appetizer. Try the tamarind glazed baby back ribs, sashimi grade tuna or smoked chicken for a main course. All meals are served with side accompaniments including plantains and yucca. **Bar:** full bar. **Reservations:** suggested. **Address:** 363 Fortaleza St 00901 **Location:** Center of Old San Juan; just n of cruise ship docks. **Parking:** on-site (fee) and street. **Historic** (L) (D)

(See map & index p. 408.)

PLATOS RESTAURANT Phone: 787/791-7474 (85)

Puerto Rican
$18-$38

AAA Inspector Notes: This casual eatery features a contemporary decor and a creative menu of freshly prepared cuisine. Rich sauces and fresh island ingredients enhance the bold flavor and texture in the extensive selection of choices, which make up hearty courses ideal for sharing. Starters such as fried cheese with coconut dipping sauce lead up to entrées of fresh seafood, in addition to meats and pork cooked in varied ways. Closed on Wednesday in the summer and fall. **Bar:** full bar. **Reservations:** suggested. **Address:** Calle Rosa #2, Isla Verde 00979 **Location:** 2 mi (3.2 km) nw of airport in Isla Verde area; close to intersection with Hwy 187; in Coral by the Sea Hotel. **Parking:** no self-parking. [D]

RESTAURANTE ESCAMBRON BEACH CLUB Phone: 787/724-3344 (32)

Puerto Rican
$12-$26

AAA Inspector Notes: When the weather permits, diners can enjoy great views of the beach and water from the large outdoor patio of this restaurant, which is well lit at night. Or they can relax in the air-conditioned comfort of the casual yet contemporary indoor dining area. A distinctive Puerto Rican flair punctuates the creative island menu, which focuses on fresh local fare, including a section dedicated exclusively to stuffed mashed plantains. Other popular items include local fish and other seafood and grilled meats. **Bar:** full bar. **Address:** Ave Muñoz Rivera 00979 **Location:** At Parque del Tercer Milenio. [L] [D]

RESTAURANTE LOS CHAVALES Phone: 787/767-5017 (66)

Spanish
$14-$34

AAA Inspector Notes: Paella is the house favorite while other well-prepared dishes include hearts of palm salad, a hearty Spanish soup called caldo gallego and escargots; the extensive entree menu features lamb osso buco, sea bass, shrimp empanadas and beef Wellington. **Bar:** full bar. **Reservations:** suggested. **Address:** 253 Ave FD Roosevelt 00918 **Location:** In Hato Rey; 0.4 mi (0.6 km) e of Plaza Las Americas. **Parking:** valet only. [L] [D]

ROPA VIEJA GRILL Phone: 787/725-2665 (46)

Cuban
$16-$34

AAA Inspector Notes: Part of the pulse of the Condado area is the designer eatery, which whips up some tasty Cuban Criollo fare. Lechon and mofongo are favorites. For a lighter dish, try steamed bacalao, a type of cod. Indulge in one of the refreshing Mojito cocktails. Save space to try one of the silky smooth flans; several flavors are available. **Bar:** full bar. **Reservations:** suggested. **Address:** 1025 Ashford Ave 00901 **Location:** In Condado; west end of Ashford Ave. **Parking:** valet only. [L] [D]

RUTH'S CHRIS STEAK HOUSE Phone: 787/253-1717 (82)

Steak
$28-$46

AAA Inspector Notes: The main fare is steak, which is prepared from several cuts of prime beef and cooked to perfection, but the menu also lists lamb, chicken and seafood dishes. Guests should come hungry because the side dishes, which are among the a la carte offerings, could make a meal in themselves. **Reservations:** required. **Address:** 5961 Isla Verde Ave 00979 **Location:** 2.1 mi (3.3 km) e of airport; in InterContinental San Juan Resort & Casino. **Parking:** valet only. [D]

SOFIA ITALIAN KITCHEN & WINE BAR Phone: 787/721-0396 (8)

Italian
$14-$27

AAA Inspector Notes: Within the historical walls of this establishment, guests will be pleased with the attentive, pleasant staff and the sumptuous Italian-inspired dishes. Diners can choose to start with a tuna or beef carpaccio or one of the several salads. Entrées range from roast lamb shank to grouper wih goat cheese gnocchi as well as gourmet pizza and an array of pasta dishes. A great wine selection and in-house prepared desserts round out the experience. **Bar:** full bar. **Reservations:** required. **Address:** 355 Calle San Francisco 00901 **Location:** Center of Old San Juan. **Parking:** on-site (fee) and street. **Historic** [L] [D]

TANTRA INDO-LATINO CUISINE Phone: 787/977-8141 (14)

Indian
$16-$28

AAA Inspector Notes: A well-established favorite to the Old San Juan dining scene, this casual spot features Chef Ramesh Pillai, who whips up delicious Indo-Latino cuisine. Starters include ceviche, empanadas and mofongo with curry sauce. Such main course temptations as Marsala-crusted lamb chops and spiced duck breast, awaken the senses. The decor has soothing, contemplative qualities and Hindu and Buddhist elements. Exotic belly dancing performances are featured on Friday and Saturday nights. **Bar:** full bar. **Address:** 356 Calle Fortaleza 00901 **Location:** Center of Old San Juan; just n of cruise ship docks. **Parking:** on-site (fee) and street. **Historic** [L] [D] [LATE]

TIERRA DEL FUEGO Phone: 787/294-7018 (68)

Argentine
$12-$30

AAA Inspector Notes: Located in a shopping mall is this popular casual dining experience. The spry waitstaff, dressed in gaucho uniforms provide amiable service. The decor reflects the ambience of Argentinean life on the Pampas. Lining the menu is practically every cut of beef imaginable as well as pork, chicken and a few fish entrées. The Churrasco or marinated flank steak is a favorite. For the true carnivore the hearty mix-grill is a must. Desserts include creme caramel and a variety of flan. **Bar:** full bar. **Address:** #601 Tercer Nivel Plaza Las Americas 00918 **Location:** Hato Rey; in Plaza Las Americas, 3rd Floor. [L] [D]

TIERRA SANTA RESTAURANT Phone: 787/754-6865 (67)

Arabic
$11-$23

AAA Inspector Notes: The locals flock here for the lunch buffet, which offers a good value. At night, there is an array of Middle Eastern dishes to select including preparations with lamb, chicken, beef and vegetarian dishes. The sampler platter affords patrons the opportunity to explore a variety of tastes. It can get crowded on Friday and Saturday night when live belly dancing shows are offered. **Bar:** full bar. **Reservations:** suggested. **Address:** 284 Roosevelt Ave 00918 **Location:** In Hato Rey; 0.3 mi (0.5 km) e of Plaza Las Americas. **Parking:** on-site and valet. [L] [D]

TIJUANA'S BAR & GRILL Phone: 787/723-3939 (55)

Mexican
$10-$25

AAA Inspector Notes: A popular hole in the wall in the Condado area, this restaurant affords patrons a choice of indoor seating in an area dominated by the bar or outside, where al fresco meals come with plenty of good people-watching. The food is typical Mexican fare: burritos, enchiladas, nachos and quesadillas. **Bar:** full bar. **Address:** 1512 Ashford Ave 00901 **Location:** In Condado. **Parking:** on-site (fee). [L] [D]

VIEQUES (B-6, D-6) pop. 9,106, elev. 131'

• Hotels & Restaurants map & index p. 405

HACIENDA TAMARINDO   **Phone:** 787/741-8525   **30**

Bed & Breakfast
$135-$275

Address: Rt 996, 4.5 KM 00765 **Location:** 5 mi (8 km) s of airport; 0.8 mi (1.3 km) w of Esperanza. **Facility:** A large tamarind tree rises through the center of the lobby atrium of this charming inn. Each room is creatively decorated and tastefully appointed. 17 units, some houses. 2 stories (no elevator), interior/exterior corridors. **Terms:** office hours 8:30 am-6:30 pm, age restrictions may apply, 30 day cancellation notice-fee imposed. **Pool(s):** outdoor. **Activities:** *Fee:* massage. **Guest Services:** valet laundry.

 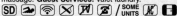

W RETREAT & SPA VIEQUES ISLAND
Phone: (787)741-4100   **29**

Resort Hotel
$389-$1200 12/1-8/14
$289-$599 8/15-11/30

W
HOTELS

AAA Benefit: Special member room rates, plus Starwood Preferred Guest® bonuses.

Address: SR 200; KM 3.2 HC1 00765 **Location:** Oceanfront. Reached by ferry from Fajardo or commuter plane from San Juan. **Facility:** Located on a chic outpost, this resort hotel offers luxurious accommodations with an avant-garde flair, a weekly beach party and a restaurant featuring a renowned chef. 157 units, some houses. 2 stories (no elevator), exterior corridors. **Terms:** 15 day cancellation notice-fee imposed. **Amenities:** video games (fee), safes, honor bars. **Dining:** 3 restaurants. **Pool(s):** 2 outdoor. **Activities:** snorkeling & rental equipment, 2 lighted tennis courts, recreation programs, basketball, spa. *Fee:* sailboats, scuba diving, bicycles. **Guest Services:** valet laundry, area transportation. **Free Special Amenities:** early check-in/late check-out and preferred room (subject to availability with advance reservations). *(See ad on Insert, p. 452.)*

   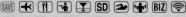 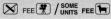

Check out our travel blog at AAATravelViews.com

▼ See AAA listing p. 451 ▼

ST. BARTHÉLEMY

Map Page	ST BARTHELEMY AIRPORT	Diamond Rated	High Season	Page
❶ p. 454	Hotel St. Barth Isle de France, 2.5 mi (4 km) w	▽▽▽	$563-$4118	455

St. Barthélemy

This index helps you "spot" where approved hotels and restaurants are located on the corresponding detailed maps. Hotel daily rate range is for comparison only and show the property's high season. Restaurant rate range is a combination of lunch and/or dinner. Turn to the listing page for more detailed rate information and consult display ads for special promotions.

ANSE DES FLAMANDS

Map Page	Hotel	Diamond Rated	High Season	Page
❶ p. 454	Hotel St. Barth Isle de France	▽▽▽	$563-$4118	455

ANSE DES CAYES

Map Page	Hotel	Diamond Rated	High Season	Page
❷ p. 454	Hotel Manapany Cottages and Spa	▽▽▽	$219-$3625	455

Map Page	Restaurant	Diamond Rated	Cuisine	Meal Range	Page
③ p. 454	Fellini	▽▽▽	International	$19-$48	455

POINTE MILOU

Map Page	Hotel	Diamond Rated	High Season	Page
❹ p. 454	Christopher St. Barth	▽▽▽	$294-$2043	457

GRAND CUL-DE-SAC

Map Page	Hotels	Diamond Rated	High Season	Page
❺ p. 454	**Hotel Guanahani & Spa**	▽▽▽▽	$533-$3522 [SAVE]	455
❻ p. 454	Le Sereno	▽▽▽▽	$648-$3145	455

Map Page	Restaurant	Diamond Rated	Cuisine	Meal Range	Page
⑤ p. 454	Bartolomeo	▽▽▽▽	French	$50-$65	455

LORIENT

Map Page	Hotel	Diamond Rated	High Season	Page
❼ p. 454	La Banane	▽▽▽	$519-$1812	456

GUSTAVIA

Map Page	Hotel	Diamond Rated	High Season	Page
❾ p. 454	**Carl Gustaf Hotel & Spa**	▽▽▽▽	$604-$2362 [SAVE]	455

Map Page	Restaurants	Diamond Rated	Cuisine	Meal Range	Page
⑥ p. 454	Victoria's Restaurant	▽▽▽	French	$38-$65	456
⑦ p. 454	Pipiri Palace	▽▽	Creole	$33-$46	456
⑧ p. 454	Wall House Restaurant	▽▽▽	French	$28-$83	456
⑪ p. 454	Do Brazil	▽▽	International	$12-$56	456
⑫ p. 454	Le Repaire	▽▽	Creole	$27-$40	456
⑬ p. 454	Baz Bar	▽▽	Asian	$19-$39	456
⑭ p. 454	L'Isola Ristorante	▽▽▽	Italian	$39-$62	456
⑮ p. 454	Harbour's Saladerie	▽▽	International	$28-$42	456
⑯ p. 454	La Route des Boucaniers	▽▽▽	French	$22-$70	456

TOINY

Map Page	Hotel	Diamond Rated	High Season	Page
11 this page	Hotel Le Toiny	▼▼▼	$803-$2686	457

Map Page	Restaurant	Diamond Rated	Cuisine	Meal Range	Page
22 this page	Le Gaiac	▼▼▼▼	French	$33-$68	457

ST. JEAN

Map Page	Hotels	Diamond Rated	High Season	Page
13 this page	Hotel Le Village Saint Jean	▼▼	$198-$737	457
14 this page	Eden Rock-St. Barths	▼▼▼▼	$662-$3139	457

Map Page	Restaurant	Diamond Rated	Cuisine	Meal Range	Page
20 this page	On the Rocks	▼▼▼▼	French	$56-$70	457

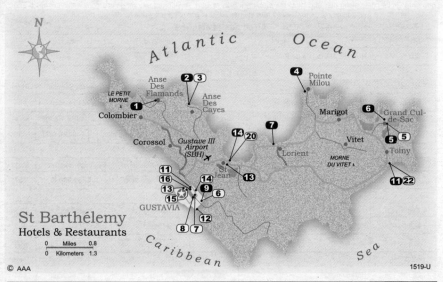

St Barthélemy
Hotels & Restaurants

© AAA   1519-U

It's how AAA members turn a drive into a journey.

ANSE DES CAYES
• **Hotels & Restaurants index & map p. 453**

HOTEL MANAPANY COTTAGES AND SPA
Phone: (590)590-27-66-55　**2**

▼▼▼ ▼▼▼
Cottage
$219-$3625

Address: Anse des Cayes 97133 **Location:** Oceanfront. 1.2 mi (1.9 km) w of airport. **Facility:** A 600-foot private beach fronts these spacious, upscale cottages; some are waterfront while others afford nice sea views. 41 cottages. 1 story, exterior corridors. **Terms:** 14 day cancellation notice-fee imposed. **Amenities:** safes, honor bars. *Some:* high-speed Internet (fee). **Dining:** Fellini, see separate listing. **Pool(s):** outdoor. **Activities:** lighted tennis court, exercise room, spa. **Guest Services:** valet laundry.

WHERE TO EAT

FELLINI
Phone: 590/590-27-66-55　**3**

▼▼▼ ▼▼▼
International
$19-$48

AAA Inspector Notes: French, Italian and Caribbean influences are represented in the wide selection of seafood, pasta, beef, chicken and salad dishes. Colorful presentations add to the appeal. The decor is pleasant and the service cordial. **Bar:** full bar. **Reservations:** suggested. **Address:** Anse des Cayes 97133 **Location:** 1.2 mi (1.9 km) w of airport; in Hotel Manapany Cottages and Spa. B L D 🍷 ✎

ANSE DES FLAMANDS
• **Hotels & Restaurants index & map p. 453**

HOTEL ST. BARTH ISLE DE FRANCE
Phone: (590)590-27-61-81　**1**

▼▼▼ ▼▼▼
Boutique Hotel
$563-$4118

Address: Baie des Flamands 97133 **Location:** Oceanfront. 2.5 mi (4 km) w of airport; 3.7 mi (5.9 km) n of Gustavia. **Facility:** The luxury hotel on an extraordinary beach offers beach rooms, junior suites and various bungalows and cottages. 1-2 stories, exterior corridors. **Terms:** open 12/1-8/31 & 10/15-11/30, age restrictions may apply, 60 day cancellation notice, 30 day off season-fee imposed. **Amenities:** high-speed Internet, safes, honor bars. **Pool(s):** outdoor. **Activities:** snorkeling, exercise room. *Fee:* steamroom. **Guest Services:** valet laundry.

🎿 🚐 BIZ 🛜 ✕ 🖵
/ SOME UNITS 🍽 🔲 📷

Complete Vacation Planning

AAA.com/Travel and **CAA.ca/Travel** – everything you need to plan and book your vacations, backed by the travel experts at local AAA/CAA offices.

GRAND CUL-DE-SAC
• **Hotels & Restaurants index & map p. 453**

HOTEL GUANAHANI & SPA
Phone: (590)590-27-66-60　**5**

▼▼▼ ▼▼▼
Resort Hotel
$533-$3522

Address: Anse de Grand Cul de Sac 97133 **Location:** Oceanfront. 5 mi (8.1 km) ne of Gustavia; 3.8 mi (6.1 km) ne of airport. **Facility:** On a 16-acre peninsula, upgraded property offers eight room categories ranging from 290 to 540 square feet. 67 units, some two bedrooms, three bedrooms and kitchens. 1 story, exterior corridors. **Terms:** 3 night minimum stay - seasonal, 30 day cancellation notice, 14 day off season. **Amenities:** safes, honor bars. **Dining:** 2 restaurants, also, Bartolomeo, see separate listing. **Pool(s):** 2 outdoor. **Activities:** whirlpool, steamroom, canoeing, paddleboats, sailboats, windsurfing, snorkeling, 2 lighted tennis courts, recreation programs, volleyball, exercise room, spa. *Fee:* waterskiing, scuba diving. **Guest Services:** valet laundry, area transportation-Gustavia Harbour. **Free Special Amenities:** full breakfast and high-speed Internet.

SAVE 🎿 🍴 🛗 🍷 🎿 BIZ 🛜
/ SOME UNITS 🍽 🖵

LE SERENO
Phone: (590)590-29-83-00　**6**

▼▼▼ ▼▼▼
Boutique Hotel
$648-$3145

Address: Grand Cul-de-Sac Beach Main Rd 97133 **Location:** Oceanfront. 5 mi (8 km) ne of Gustavia; 3.7 mi (5.9 km) e of airport. **Facility:** This oceanfront hotel features large guest rooms and exquisite villas created by renowned Parisian designer Christian Liaigre. 39 units, some houses. 1-2 stories (no elevator), exterior corridors. **Terms:** open 12/1-9/1 & 11/1-11/30, 30 day cancellation notice, 15 day off season-fee imposed. **Amenities:** high-speed Internet, safes, honor bars. **Pool(s):** outdoor. **Activities:** snorkeling, 2 lighted tennis courts, exercise room. *Fee:* massage. **Guest Services:** valet laundry, area transportation-Gustavia Ferry Dock.

🎿 🍴 🛗 🍷 🎿 🚐 🛜 🖵 / SOME UNITS 🍽

WHERE TO EAT

BARTOLOMEO
Phone: 590/590-52-90-12　**5**

▼▼▼ ▼▼▼
French
$50-$65

AAA Inspector Notes: Surrounded by soothing gardens, diners have numerous choices from a gourmet menu. Main courses include thyme lamb, beef filet with truffle salad and stuffed rabbit with spinach casserole. The dapper servers provide exquisite service. **Bar:** full bar. **Reservations:** required. **Address:** Marigot Bay 97133 **Location:** 5 mi (8.1 km) ne of Gustavia; 3.8 mi (6.1 km) ne of airport; in Hotel Guanahani & Spa. D 🍷 ✎

GUSTAVIA (B-2) pop. 6,825
• **Restaurants p. 456**
• **Hotels & Restaurants index & map p. 453**

CARL GUSTAF HOTEL & SPA
Phone: (590)590-29-79-00　**9**

▼▼▼ ▼▼▼
Boutique Contemporary Hotel
$604-$2362

Address: Rue des Normands 97099 **Location:** Just n of downtown. **Facility:** Upscale cottage suites, each with a plunge pool, are perched above Gustavia and afford tremendous views; the multilingual staff is service oriented. 14 units, some two bedrooms, three bedrooms, efficiencies and kitchens. 1-2 stories, exterior corridors. **Terms:** open 12/1-9/1 & 11/3-11/30, 30 day cancellation notice, 15 day off season-fee imposed. **Amenities:** safes, honor bars. *Some:* high-speed Internet. **Dining:** Victoria's Restaurant, see separate listing. **Activities:** beach access, snorkeling, exercise room, spa. *Fee:* whirlpool, steamroom. **Guest Services:** valet laundry, area transportation-Gustavia Ferry Dock. **Free Special Amenities:** newspaper and high-speed Internet. Affiliated with A Preferred Hotel.

SAVE 🎿 🍴 🛗 🍷 🎿 CALL 🅖🅜 BIZ 🛜 ✕
🔲 📷 🖵 / SOME UNITS 🍽

(See index & map p. 453.)

WHERE TO EAT

BAZ BAR
Phone: 590/590-29-74-09   13

Asian
$19-$39

AAA Inspector Notes: This is an intimate sushi bar situated in Gustavia Harbor. A variety of sushi rolls, sashimi, salads and tempura are offered. Late-night live music is offered frequently. **Bar:** full bar. **Reservations:** suggested. **Address:** La Rue 97133 **Location:** Center of downtown; on the waterfront Gustavia Harbor; next to post office. **Parking:** street only.

D   ☒

DO BRAZIL
Phone: 590/590-29-06-66   11

International
$12-$56

AAA Inspector Notes: This beachfront restaurant affords a fantastic view of Shell Beach. Creative, well-prepared dishes blend French, Asian and Creole techniques and ingredients. Additional service is available on the beach with complimentary lounge chairs. **Bar:** full bar. **Reservations:** suggested. **Address:** Shell Beach 97133 **Location:** Just se of downtown.

B   L   D   ☒   ☒

HARBOUR'S SALADERIE
Phone: 590/590-29-52-24   15

International
$28-$42

AAA Inspector Notes: This harbor-side restaurant features mostly gourmet pizza but also entrée-size salads prepared with ahi tuna or duck. In addition, there are a few pasta as well as steak and fish dishes. **Bar:** full bar. **Address:** La Rue 97133 **Location:** Gustavia Harbor; just past the post office. **Parking:** street only.

L   D   ☒   ☒

LA ROUTE DES BOUCANIERS
Phone: 590/590-27-73-00   16

French
$22-$70

AAA Inspector Notes: Francis Delage-author, chef and television personality--has created this casual restaurant with upscale French-Creole cuisine situated on the picturesque marina of Gustavia. Popular starters are the foie gras or the cappuccino-style lobster bisque. Decisions are difficult when it comes to the broad selection of entrées including sea scallop and shrimp risotto, marinated fall-off-the-bone-ribs, ahi tuna and steak tartar. There is a Creole platter great for sharing. **Bar:** full bar. **Reservations:** suggested. **Address:** Rue du Bord de Mer 97133 **Location:** At Gustavia Harbor. **Parking:** street only.

L   D   LATE   ☒   ☒

LE REPAIRE
Phone: 590/590-27-72-48   12

Creole
$27-$40

AAA Inspector Notes: Downtown on the waterfront, this restaurant presents an extensive menu of French bistro-style cuisine mixed with some French-Creole influences. Ever-changing daily specials will not disappoint. Plentiful portions appeal to big appetites. **Bar:** full bar. **Reservations:** suggested. **Address:** Rue de la Republique 97133 **Location:** Center of downtown waterfront. **Parking:** street only.

B   L   D   ☒

L'ISOLA RISTORANTE
Phone: 590/590-51-00-05   14

Italian
$39-$62

AAA Inspector Notes: Multiple dining areas offer chic, sleek surroundings. Attentive team service is offered by an amiable staff and management circulates to ensure all is tutto bene. The exceptionally well-prepared cuisine is presented with artistic flair. Veal, imported and local fish and a wide selection of homemade pasta line the menu. **Bar:** full bar. **Reservations:** required. **Address:** Rue du roi Oscar II 97133 **Location:** Center of downtown. **Parking:** street only. D

PIPIRI PALACE
Phone: 590/590-27-53-20   7

Creole
$33-$46

AAA Inspector Notes: A truly talented chef deftly combines choice flavors and ingredients into scintillating meals within a Creole-style house veranda. Such soups as gazpacho, cold watermelon with prosciutto, onion au gratin and lobster bisque line the menu. Warm walnut-crusted goat cheese salad, crab cake and fish carpaccio are appetizers to whet the appetite. For an unforgettable seafood dish, try the skate. Meat preparations range from duck and lamb to baby back ribs and fillet of beef flambé with cognac. **Bar:** full bar. **Reservations:** suggested. **Address:** Rue du General de Gaulle 97133 **Location:** Center; just n of Gustavia Harbour. **Parking:** street only.

D   ☒

VICTORIA'S RESTAURANT
Phone: 590/590-29-79-00   6

French
$38-$65

AAA Inspector Notes: With sweeping and stunning views of Gustavia, this restaurant offers a French-Caribbean influenced menu featuring such starters as foie gras and tuna tartar as well as a caviar menu. The chef's trilogy menu is a popular option as is such savory dishes as rack of lamb with goat cheese ravioli. Tempting desserts include a trio of crème brûlée and a hot chocolate fondant. The extensive menu offers grappa, aged rums and armagnacs as well as a cigar menu. **Bar:** full bar. **Reservations:** required. **Address:** BP 700 Rues des Normands 97099 **Location:** Just n of downtown, follow signs; in Carl Gustaf Hotel & Spa. D

WALL HOUSE RESTAURANT
Phone: 590/590-27-71-83   8

French
$28-$83

AAA Inspector Notes: Well-presented fine dining cuisine is served in a bistro-style setting with a bevy of attentive waiters. The trio of chilled soups, escargot or leek salad are great starters. The extensive menu includes duck foie gras with rhubarb compote, rack of lamb and spit-roasted squab as well as grouper, crab and sea scallops. Sweet delicacies from the dessert trolley are very tempting. **Bar:** full bar. **Reservations:** suggested. **Address:** La Pointe 97133 **Location:** Corner of Rue de le Presou'lle and Rue de Pitea; across from Hotel de la Collectivite. **Parking:** street only. L   D   ☒   ☒

LORIENT

• Hotels & Restaurants index & map p. 453

LA BANANE
Phone: (590)590-52-03-00   7

Cottage
$519-$1812

Address: Baie de Lorient **Location:** 2 mi (3.2 km) ne of airport; 3 mi (4.8 km) ne of Gustavia. **Facility:** Guest rooms at this hip, chic and intimate hotel feature high-quality fabrics and splashes of Creole colors. Some units have an open-air bathroom. 9 cottages. 1 story, exterior corridors. **Bath:** shower only. **Terms:** open 12/1-9/1 & 10/25-11/30, office hours 7 am-9 pm, 2-3 night minimum stay, age restrictions may apply, 60 day cancellation notice, 30 day off season-fee imposed. **Amenities:** safes, honor bars. **Pool(s):** 2 outdoor. **Activities:** snorkeling. **Fee:** massage. **Guest Services:** valet laundry, area transportation-Gustavia Ferry Dock.

✈   🍽   🍸   🛏   BIZ   🛜   / SOME UNITS   ▣

Learn about
AAA/CAA Diamond Ratings
at AAA.com/Diamonds

POINTE MILOU
• Hotels & Restaurants index & map p. 453

CHRISTOPHER ST. BARTH

▼▼▼ ▼▼▼
Boutique Hotel
$294-$2043

Phone: (590)590-27-63-63 **4**
Address: Pointe Milou 97133 **Location:** Center; follow signs. **Facility:** This lifestyle property is situated on rugged coastline; two types of well-appointed guest units are offered. 38 units, some two bedrooms. 1-2 stories (no elevator), exterior corridors. **Terms:** open 12/1-8/26 & 10/27-11/30, 3 night minimum stay, 30 day cancellation notice, 21 day off season-fee imposed. **Amenities:** safes, honor bars. **Dining:** 2 restaurants. **Pool(s):** outdoor. **Activities:** *Fee:* massage. **Guest Services:** valet laundry, area transportation (fee)-Gustavia Ferry.

FEE 🛫 🍴 🛁 🍸 🏧 SD 🏊 BIZ 🛜 ✕
📠 / SOME UNITS 🐾

ST. JEAN
• Hotels & Restaurants index & map p. 453

EDEN ROCK-ST. BARTHS

▼▼▼ ▼▼▼
Boutique Hotel
$662-$3139

Phone: (590)590-29-79-99 **14**
Address: Baie de St. Jean 97133 **Location:** Oceanfront. 0.9 mi (1.4 km) e of airport; on St. Jean Bay; center. **Facility:** Situated along St. Jean Beach, the hotel offers well-appointed, stylish theme guest rooms with oversize bathrooms. 34 units, some houses. 1-2 stories (no elevator), exterior corridors. **Terms:** open 12/1-8/29 & 10/15-11/30, 3 night minimum stay, 30 day cancellation notice-fee imposed. **Amenities:** safes, honor bars. **Dining:** On the Rocks, see separate listing. **Activities:** snorkeling, exercise room. *Fee:* massage. **Guest Services:** valet laundry, area transportation-Gustavia Ferry Dock.

🛫 🍴 🛁 🍸 🏧 BIZ 🛜 ✕ 📠
/ SOME UNITS 🐾

HOTEL LE VILLAGE SAINT JEAN

▼▼ ▼▼
Cottage
$198-$737

Phone: 590/590-27-61-39 **13**
Address: Rue de St. Jean **Location:** Center; just above St. Jean Bay; 1 mi (1.6 km) e of airport. **Facility:** 27 units, some houses and cottages. 1 story, exterior corridors. *Bath:* shower only. **Terms:** office hours 7:30 am-8 pm, 45 day cancellation notice, 30 day off season-fee imposed. **Amenities:** safes. **Pool(s):** outdoor. **Activities:** whirlpool, exercise room. *Fee:* massage. **Guest Services:** valet laundry.

🏊 🛜 🔌 / SOME UNITS 🅦

WHERE TO EAT

ON THE ROCKS

▼▼▼ ▼▼▼
French
$56-$70

Phone: 590/590-29-79-99 **20**
AAA Inspector Notes: Dramatically positioned on a precipice jutting over the ocean, this multitiered dining room breathes a tropical essence. The waitstaff provides solid team service to the lively and well-heeled clientele. Chefs fuse Asian and French ingredients and techniques to create scintillating flavors. Some favorites include shrimp ravioli and sauteed sweetbreads with trumpet mushroom sauce, monkfish and seared foie gras with roasted fig. **Bar:** full bar. **Reservations:** required. **Address:** Baie de St. Jean 97133 **Location:** 0.9 mi (1.4 km) e of St. Barths Airport; center on St. Jean Bay; in Eden Rock-St. Barths.

D 🎿 📶

TOINY
• Hotels & Restaurants index & map p. 453

HOTEL LE TOINY

▼▼▼ ▼▼▼
Cottage
$803-$2686

Phone: (590)590-27-88-88 **11**
Address: Anse de Toiny 97133 **Location:** 4.4 mi (7 km) e of airport; 5.5 mi (8.8 km) ne from downtown Gustavia. **Facility:** A true refuge from the rest of the world; each lavishly decorated and exceptionally equipped cottage has a private pool. 15 cottages. 1 story, exterior corridors. **Terms:** open 12/1-6/1 & 9/1-11/30, 60 day cancellation notice, 30 day off season-fee imposed. **Amenities:** high-speed Internet, safes, honor bars. **Dining:** Le Gaiac, see separate listing. **Pool(s):** outdoor. **Activities:** snorkeling, exercise room. *Fee:* massage. **Guest Services:** valet laundry, area transportation-Gustavia Ferry Dock.

🛫 🍴 🛁 🍸 🏧 🏊 🛜 🔌 🗄 📠
/ SOME UNITS FEE 🐾

WHERE TO EAT

LE GAIAC

▼▼▼ ▼▼▼
French
$33-$68

Phone: 590/590-29-77-47 **22**
AAA Inspector Notes: Perched on a hillside overlooking the nearby sea, this al fresco dining room sustains a romantic ambience. An unpretentious waitstaff hails mostly from France. The changing menu is a showcase for the chef's skill and knowledge of blending fine ingredients into superb dishes. Lamb always is a favorite, as is the local seafood. Tuesday is fish market night where a prix fixe menu is offered featuring local seafood. Save room for one of the decadent soufflés. **Bar:** full bar. **Reservations:** required. **Address:** Anse de Toiny 97133 **Location:** 4.4 mi (7 km) e of airport; 5.5 mi (8.8 km) ne from downtown Gustavia; in Hotel Le Toiny.

B L D 🎿 📶

ST. EUSTATIUS AND SABA

St. Eustatius and Saba

This index helps you "spot" where approved hotels and restaurants are located on the corresponding detailed maps. Hotel daily rate range is for comparison only and show the property's high season. Restaurant rate range is a combination of lunch and/or dinner. Turn to the listing page for more detailed rate information and consult display ads for special promotions.

WINDWARDSIDE (Saba)

Map Page	Hotel	Diamond Rated	High Season	Page
1 p. 459	Juliana's Hotel	▼	$95-$280	458

Map Page	Restaurants	Diamond Rated	Cuisine	Meal Range	Page
② p. 459	Saba's Treasure	▼	American	$9-$24	458
③ p. 459	Scout's Place Restaurant & Bar	▼	International	$10-$29	458
④ p. 459	Swinging Doors	▼	American	$15-$20	459

THE BOTTOM (Saba)

Map Page	Hotel	Diamond Rated	High Season	Page
3 p. 459	**Queen's Gardens Resort - A Hampshire Classic**	▼▼▼	$250-$400 [SAVE]	458

BOOBY HILL (Saba)

Map Page	Hotel	Diamond Rated	High Season	Page
5 p. 459	Shearwater Resort	▼▼▼	$175-$275	458

ORANJESTAD (St. Eustatius)

Map Page	Restaurant	Diamond Rated	Cuisine	Meal Range	Page
⑨ p. 459	Smoke Alley Bar & Grill	▼	International	$9-$28	459

Saba

BOOBY HILL
• **Hotels & Restaurants index & map p. 458**

SHEARWATER RESORT   Phone: 599/416-2498   **5**
▼▼▼
Country Inn
$175-$275

Address: Booby Hill **Location:** 4 mi (6.5 km) s of airport. **Facility:** These spacious rooms offer upscale décor, luxury bedding, and balconies with amazing panoramic views of the Caribbean Sea and the cliffs below. 8 units, some kitchens. 2 stories (no elevator), exterior corridors. **Terms:** 30 day cancellation notice-fee imposed. **Amenities:** safes. **Pool(s):** outdoor. **Activities:** whirlpool, tennis court, bicycles, exercise room. **Guest Services:** valet laundry.

THE BOTTOM
• **Hotels & Restaurants index & map p. 458**

QUEEN'S GARDENS RESORT - A HAMPSHIRE CLASSIC
Phone: 599/416-3494   **3**
▼▼▼
Country Inn
$250-$400

Address: 1 Troy Hill Dr **Location:** 7.5 mi (12 km) se of airport; 0.5 mi (0.8 km) n. **Facility:** This inn is perched on a steep hill above The Bottoms and offers apartment-style guest units featuring Indonesian furnishings and panoramic views. 11 units. 1-4 stories (no elevator), exterior corridors. *Bath:* shower only. **Terms:** office hours 7 am-10 pm, check-in 4 pm, 30 day cancellation notice-fee imposed. **Amenities:** safes, honor bars. **Pool(s):** outdoor. **Activities:** hiking trails, exercise room. *Fee:* massage. **Guest Services:** valet laundry. **Free Special Amenities:** early check-in/late check-out and high-speed Internet.

WINDWARDSIDE
• **Hotels & Restaurants index & map p. 458**

JULIANA'S HOTEL   Phone: 599/416-2269   **1**
▼
Bed & Breakfast
$95-$280

Address: Park Ln **Location:** 3.5 mi (5.6 km) s of airport; center. **Facility:** 13 units, some efficiencies and cottages. 2 stories (no elevator), exterior corridors. *Bath:* shower only. **Terms:** office hours 7 am-6 pm, 30 day cancellation notice-fee imposed. **Pool(s):** outdoor. **Activities:** whirlpool. **Guest Services:** valet laundry.

WHERE TO EAT

SABA'S TREASURE   Phone: 599/416-2819   ②
▼
American
$9-$24

AAA Inspector Notes: This open-air bar and grill is known for their stone-baked pizza. The menu also includes burgers, steak and seafood. **Bar:** full bar. **Address:** Main St **Location:** 3.7 mi (5.9 km) s of airport; center. **Parking:** street only.   B L D [K] [\]

SCOUT'S PLACE RESTAURANT & BAR
Phone: 599/416-2740   ③
▼
International
$10-$29

AAA Inspector Notes: A popular spot for the diving, tourist and local crowds alike, this restaurant offers a good variety of breakfast options including European, American, French or Spanish style breakfast specials. Every night is a different theme night including fajita Mondays, chicken Tuesdays and Thursdays, gyro Wednesdays and soul food Fridays. **Bar:** full bar. **Address:** Main St **Location:** Center; in Scouts Place.

B L D [K] [\]

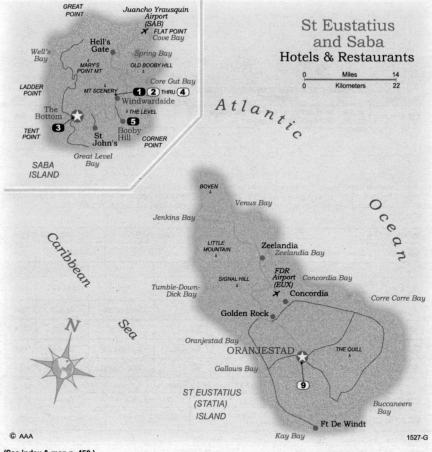

St Eustatius
and Saba
Hotels & Restaurants

Miles		14
Kilometers		22

© AAA

1527-G

(See index & map p. 458.)

St. Eustatius

SWINGING DOORS   **Phone:** 599/416-2506   ④

♦♦♦
American
$15-$20

AAA Inspector Notes: In the center of town, this Texas western-themed restaurant with rustic decor serves dinner on Tuesday, Friday and Sunday nights when they only offer one meat choice and one vegetarian platter per night. Some nights, guests have the option of grilling their own meat. No credit cards are accepted, so bring cash. **Bar:** full bar. **Reservations:** suggested. **Address:** Main St **Location:** 3.7 mi (5.9 km) s of airport; center. **Parking:** street only.

ORANJESTAD (D-3)
• Hotels & Restaurants index & map p. 458

SMOKE ALLEY BAR & GRILL

Phone: 599/318-2002   ⑨

♦♦♦
International
$9-$28

AAA Inspector Notes: In lower Oranjestad, this open-air waterfront eatery offers a menu of familiar items, including fajitas, fish and chips, tacos, New York strip steak and shrimp scampi. Various toppings flavor the wide variety of hamburgers. Check the daily specials and soup du jour. Lunch is served weekdays only. **Bar:** full bar. **Address:** Lower Town **Location:** 2.2 mi (3.5 km) sw of airport; in Lower Town. L D 🏧 🚫

ST. KITTS AND NEVIS

✈ Airport Accommodations

Map Page	ROBERT L BRADSHAW INTERNATIONAL AIRPORT	Diamond Rated	High Season	Page
6 p. 462	St. Kitts Marriott Resort & the Royal Beach Casino, 2.5 mi (4 km) se of airport	💎💎💎💎	$405-$799 SAVE	464

St. Kitts and Nevis

This index helps you "spot" where approved hotels and restaurants are located on the corresponding detailed maps. Hotel daily rate range is for comparison only and show the property's high season. Restaurant rate range is a combination of lunch and/or dinner. Turn to the listing page for more detailed rate information and consult display ads for special promotions.

BASSETERRE (St. Kitts)

Map Page	Hotel	Diamond Rated	High Season	Page
1 p. 462	Ocean Terrace Inn	💎💎	$165-$460 SAVE	464

Map Page	Restaurants	Diamond Rated	Cuisine	Meal Range	Page
① p. 462	**Serendipity Restaurant & Lounge Bar**	💎💎💎	Fusion	$12-$35	464
④ p. 462	The Ballahoo	💎	International	$6-$28	464
⑥ p. 462	**Fisherman's Wharf**	💎	Seafood	$26-$36	464
⑧ p. 462	**Waterfalls Restaurant**	💎💎💎	International	$20-$33	464
⑨ p. 462	Circus Grill Bar & Restaurant	💎	International	$8-$40	464

FRIGATE BAY (St. Kitts)

Map Page	Hotel	Diamond Rated	High Season	Page
6 p. 462	St. Kitts Marriott Resort & the Royal Beach Casino *(See ad p. 465, on insert.)*	💎💎💎💎	$405-$799 SAVE	464

Map Page	Restaurants	Diamond Rated	Cuisine	Meal Range	Page
⑩ p. 462	**Marshall's**	💎💎💎	International	$25-$48	466
⑪ p. 462	La Cucina	💎💎💎	Italian	$18-$32	466
⑬ p. 462	**La Belle Vie**	💎💎💎	French	$22-$36	466
⑭ p. 462	Royal Grille Steakhouse	💎💎💎	Steak	$24-$45	466
⑮ p. 462	**Rock Lobster Bar & Restaurant**	💎💎	International	$14-$48	466
⑰ p. 462	Ciao Ristorante Italiano	💎💎	Italian	$16-$40	465

NEWCASTLE (Nevis)

Map Page	Hotels	Diamond Rated	High Season	Page
7 p. 462	The Mount Nevis Hotel & Beach Club	💎💎💎	$250-$450	463
8 p. 462	**Nisbet Plantation Beach Club**	💎💎💎💎	$295-$795 SAVE	463

Map Page	Restaurants	Diamond Rated	Cuisine	Meal Range	Page
㉖ p. 462	The Mount Nevis Restaurant	💎💎💎	International	$15-$60	464
㉘ p. 462	**The Great House Dining Room**	💎💎💎💎	International	$60-$65	463

GINGERLAND (Nevis)

Map Page	Hotel	Diamond Rated	High Season	Page
13 p. 462	**Montpelier Plantation and Beach**	💎💎💎💎	$320-$1280 SAVE	463

Map Page	Restaurant	Diamond Rated	Cuisine	Meal Range	Page
(24) p. 462	**750**	♦♦♦♦	International	$75	463

COTTON GROUND (Nevis)

Map Page	Restaurant	Diamond Rated	Cuisine	Meal Range	Page
(30) p. 462	Coconut Grove Restaurant and Wine Lounge	♦♦♦	International	$21-$27	463

JONES BAY (Nevis)

Map Page	Restaurant	Diamond Rated	Cuisine	Meal Range	Page
(33) p. 462	Miss June's Cuisine	♦♦♦	International	$80	463

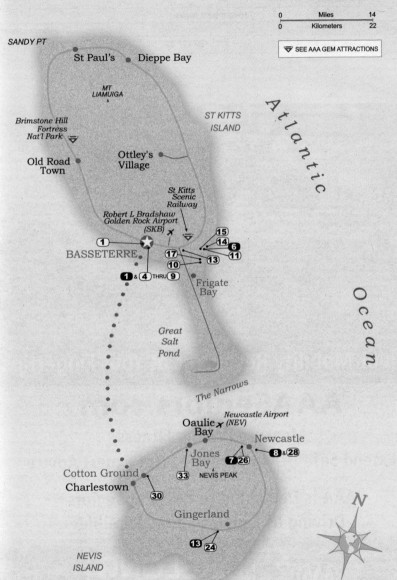

St Kitts and Nevis
Hotels & Restaurants

0	Miles	14
0	Kilometers	22

▽ SEE AAA GEM ATTRACTIONS

SANDY PT

St Paul's   Dieppe Bay

MT
LIAMUIGA
▲

*ST KITTS
ISLAND*

*Brimstone Hill
Fortress
Nat'l Park* ▽

Old Road
Town

Ottley's
Village

*St Kitts
Scenic
Railway*

*Robert L Bradshaw
Golden Rock Airport
(SKB)* ✈   ▽

1

BASSETERRE

15
14
6
17
11
13
10
1 & **4** THRU **9**

*Frigate
Bay*

*Great
Salt
Pond*

The Narrows

*Newcastle Airport
(NEV)* ✈
Oaulie
Bay

Newcastle

Jones
Bay   **7** **26**   **8** & **28**

33   NEVIS PEAK
▲

Cotton Ground
Charlestown
30

Gingerland

13 **24**

*NEVIS
ISLAND*

Atlantic

Ocean

N

© AAA

1520-G

Nevis

COTTON GROUND
• Hotels & Restaurants index & map p. 460

COCONUT GROVE RESTAURANT AND WINE LOUNGE
Phone: 869/469-1020 (30)

International
$21-$27

AAA Inspector Notes: One of the area's popular eateries, this distinctively designed open-air spot abuts a comfortable wine bar. The continually evolving menu comprises classic dishes made from the freshest ingredients and incorporating Asian and Caribbean influences. Gary, the affable host and owner, provides the savoir faire and attention to detail expected at a fine-dining establishment. A seaside swimming pool offers a place to gather for lunch or drinks. A boutique with beachwear and gifts is on the property. **Bar:** full bar. **Reservations:** suggested. **Address:** Main Island Rd **Location:** Just e of town; at Cotton Ground, Clifton Estate.

GINGERLAND
• Hotels & Restaurants index & map p. 460

MONTPELIER PLANTATION AND BEACH
Phone: (869)469-3462 (13)

Cottage
$320-$1280

Address: Cole Hill **Location:** 3.5 mi (5.6 km) e of Charlestown; 1 mi (1.6 km) s, follow signs. **Facility:** On 60 acres set 750 feet above sea level, this restored 17th-century sugar plantation evokes the charm of days gone by. 19 cottages. 1 story, exterior corridors. **Terms:** open 12/1-8/1 & 10/1-11/30, office hours 7 am-7 pm, age restrictions may apply, 30 day cancellation notice-fee imposed. **Amenities:** safes. **Dining:** 2 restaurants, also, 750, see separate listing. **Pool(s):** outdoor. **Activities:** snorkeling, tennis court, bicycles. **Fee:** massage. **Guest Services:** valet laundry, area transportation-beach. **Free Special Amenities: full breakfast and high-speed Internet.**

/ SOME UNITS

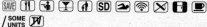

750
Phone: 869/469-3462 (24)

International
$75

AAA Inspector Notes: Dinner at this historic sugar plantation begins with drinks, canapes and conversation in the Great Room. Guests then adjourn to the terrace, overlooking floodlit gardens, to enjoy a leisurely three-course, prix fixe choice menu. Caribbean influences are woven into the menu of classical cuisine and the wine list features 74 wines from seven countries. A fish barbecue is offered Friday nights accompanied by soup, an assortment of fresh salads and tasty desserts. Child restrictions apply. **Bar:** full bar. **Reservations:** required. **Address:** Cole Hill **Location:** 3.5 mi (5.6 km) e of Charlestown; 1 mi (1.6 km) s, follow signs; in Montpelier Plantation and Beach.

JONES BAY
• Hotels & Restaurants index & map p. 460

MISS JUNE'S CUISINE
Phone: 869/469-5330 (33)

International
$80

AAA Inspector Notes: At this fine dining spot guests can enjoy a distinctive event as the Trinidadian hostess/chef welcomes visitors into her home in a dinner party atmosphere. The six-course meal is partially a buffet of Asian and West Indian specialties. The price includes service, tax and all beverages. **Bar:** full bar. **Reservations:** required. **Address:** Jones Bay **Location:** 4 mi (6.4 km) nw of Charlestown.

NEWCASTLE
• Hotels & Restaurants index & map p. 460

THE MOUNT NEVIS HOTEL & BEACH CLUB
Phone: (869)469-9373 (7)

Hotel
$250-$450

Address: Shaws Rd/Cottle Church Rd **Location:** 6.7 mi (10.7 km) ne of Charlestown; just n, then 1 mi (1.6 km) e of airport, follow signs. **Facility:** 55 units, some two bedrooms, three bedrooms, efficiencies, kitchens and houses. 2 stories (no elevator), exterior corridors. **Terms:** office hours 8 am-6 pm, 28 day cancellation notice, 14 day off season-fee imposed. **Amenities:** high-speed Internet, safes. **Dining:** 3 restaurants, also, The Mount Nevis Restaurant, see separate listing. **Pool(s):** outdoor. **Activities:** whirlpool, exercise room. **Guest Services:** valet laundry, area transportation-beach.

/ SOME UNITS

NISBET PLANTATION BEACH CLUB
Phone: (869)469-9325 (8)

Historic Cottage
$295-$795

Address: Nisbet Beach, St. James Parish **Location:** Oceanfront. 1 mi (1.6 km) e of Newcastle Airport; 7.6 mi (12.2 km) ne of Charlestown. **Facility:** Set amid coconut palms and fringed by a long stretch of beach, this 1778 sugar plantation offers a retreat-like atmosphere. Refined service prevails. 36 cottages. 1-2 stories (no elevator), exterior corridors. **Terms:** open 12/1-8/11 & 10/6-11/30, office hours 6 am-10 pm, 28 day cancellation notice, 14 day off season-fee imposed. **Amenities:** safes, honor bars. **Dining:** 3 restaurants, also, The Great House Dining Room, see separate listing, entertainment. **Pool(s):** outdoor. **Activities:** whirlpool, snorkeling, tennis court, exercise room, spa. **Fee:** windsurfing, bicycles. **Guest Services:** valet laundry. **Free Special Amenities: full breakfast and early check-in/late check-out.**

THE GREAT HOUSE DINING ROOM
Phone: 869/469-9325 (28)

International
$60-$65

AAA Inspector Notes: Housed in a historic plantation home, this elegantly candlelit dining room is a popular favorite. Island influences punctuate offerings of Continental food on the ever-changing menu. Highlights include such options as smoked salmon, carpaccio of beef tenderloin and crab cakes. The well-prepared entrée selections range from grouper over basil linguine to red wine braised veal osso buco and maple mustard-glazed duck breast with an orange grenadine sauce. Save room for tempting desserts. **Bar:** full bar. **Reservations:** required. **Address:** St. James Parish **Location:** 1 mi (1.6 km) e of Newcastle Airport; 7.6 mi (12.1 km) ne of Charlestown; in Nisbet Plantation Beach Club. **Historic** (D)

(See index & map p. 460.)

THE MOUNT NEVIS RESTAURANT
Phone: 869/469-9373 〔26〕

▼▼▼▼ ◆◆
International
$15-$60

AAA Inspector Notes: The locals frequent this open-air restaurant, set high on a hill and offering spectacular views of the mountains, ocean and tropical countryside. Chefs pride themselves in an ever-changing international menu that takes regular theme nights into account. Professional service is expected. **Bar:** full bar. **Reservations:** required, for dinner. **Address:** Shaws Rd **Location:** 6.7 mi (10.7 km) ne of Charlestown; just n, then 1 mi (1.6 km) e of airport, follow signs; in The Mount Nevis Hotel & Beach Club. 〔B〕〔L〕〔D〕〔🅐🅒〕〔◥〕

St. Kitts

BASSETERRE (C-1) pop. 13,220
• Hotels & Restaurants index & map p. 460

OCEAN TERRACE INN
Phone: (869)465-2754 〔1〕

▼▼ ▼▼
Hotel
$165-$460

Address: Wigley Ave **Location:** At west end of town, 3.7 mi (6 km) ne of Robert L. Bradshaw International Airport; at Fortlands. **Facility:** 64 units, some efficiencies and kitchens. 2-3 stories (no elevator), exterior corridors. **Parking:** street only. **Terms:** 3 day cancellation notice-fee imposed. **Amenities:** safes (fee). **Dining:** Fisherman's Wharf, Waterfalls Restaurant, see separate listings. **Pool(s):** 3 outdoor. **Activities:** exercise room. *Fee:* scuba diving, snorkeling, massage. **Guest Services:** valet laundry, area transportation-beaches. **Free Special Amenities:** early check-in/late check-out and room upgrade (subject to availability with advance reservations).

 〔SAVE〕〔🍴〕〔🛗〕〔🍸〕〔🏋〕〔SD〕〔🏊〕〔📶〕〔✕〕〔📷〕〔💻〕 / SOME UNITS 〔🖨〕

WHERE TO EAT

THE BALLAHOO
Phone: 869/465-4197 〔4〕

▼ ◆◆
International
$6-$28

AAA Inspector Notes: Splashed in bright, tropical decor, this second-story, open-air dining room overlooks the town center. On the menu is a good selection of appetizers, as well as burgers, chicken, pasta, salads, fish, lobster and traditional Caribbean fare. **Bar:** full bar. **Address:** The Circus **Location:** Center of town; at The Circus overlooking the clock tower. **Parking:** street only. 〔B〕〔L〕〔D〕〔🅐🅒〕〔◥〕

CIRCUS GRILL BAR & RESTAURANT
Phone: 869/465-0143 〔9〕

▼ ◆◆
International
$8-$40

AAA Inspector Notes: In the hub of Basseterre activity, the second-story open-air restaurant presents a varied menu with a focus on West Indies cuisine. Notable choices include roti, curried goat and the well-seasoned fresh local fish, which taste great after a delicious beginning of callaloo soup or crab back. Guests can sit at the large verandah bar to watch the world go by. **Bar:** full bar. **Address:** Bay Rd **Location:** Center; at The Circus, overlooking the clock tower. **Parking:** street only. **Historic** 〔B〕〔L〕〔D〕〔🅐🅒〕〔◥〕

FISHERMAN'S WHARF
Phone: 869/465-2754 〔6〕

▼▼▼▼ ◆◆
Seafood
$26-$36

AAA Inspector Notes: The rustic, nautical-themed restaurant was built over the water. At least six types of fish are cooked according to specifications. The Caribbean-style buffet of fixings that accompanies each meal includes eggplant casserole, peas and rice, potatoes au gratin and such steamed vegetables as broccoli, carrots, cauliflower and chayote. **Bar:** full bar. **Address:** Wigley Ave **Location:** At west end; 1.8 mi (2.9 km) w of downtown; at Fortlands; just below Ocean Terrace Inn. 〔D〕〔🅐🅒〕

SERENDIPITY RESTAURANT & LOUNGE BAR
Phone: 869/465-9999 〔1〕

▼▼▼ ◆◆
Fusion
$12-$35

AAA Inspector Notes: This well-regarded restaurant on the gourmet dining scene is in a converted house with interior and terrace dining. Native-born French-trained Chef Alexander-with experience preparing meals for the Pope, Nelson Mandela and Queen Elizabeth-prepares savory, creatively inspired and eye-appealing dishes that include lamb loin, duck and such favorite fish as grouper and red snapper with a fusion of Caribbean and European flavors. Scallops, shrimp and crayfish in Jacqueline sauce is a favorite. **Bar:** full bar. **Reservations:** required. **Address:** 3 Wigley Ave **Location:** Just w of downtown; at Fortlands; adjacent to Ocean Terrace Inn. **Parking:** street only. 〔L〕〔D〕

WATERFALLS RESTAURANT
Phone: 869/465-2754 〔8〕

▼▼▼ ◆◆
International
$20-$33

AAA Inspector Notes: A tropical waterfall and interesting hand-painted murals depicting local scenes and wildlife greet guests on entry to the dining room. There is a choice of seating in the elegant covered open-air patio or in the sophisticated dining room with upscale artwork. The chef's extensive and innovative international menu offers traditional fine cuisine as well as options with a distinct Caribbean flair. The decadent Sunday buffet brunch has a loyal following. **Bar:** full bar. **Reservations:** suggested. **Address:** Wigley Ave **Location:** At west end of town; 3.7 mi (6 km) ne of Robert L. Bradshaw International Airport; in Ocean Terrace Inn. **Parking:** street only. 〔B〕〔L〕〔D〕〔🅐🅒〕

FRIGATE BAY
• Hotels & Restaurants index & map p. 460

ST. KITTS MARRIOTT RESORT & THE ROYAL BEACH CASINO
Phone: (869)466-1200 〔6〕

▼▼▼▼ ◆◆
Resort Hotel
$405-$799

Marriott HOTELS & RESORTS
AAA Benefit: AAA hotel discounts of 5% or more.

Address: 858 Frigate Bay Rd **Location:** Oceanfront. 2.5 mi (4 km) se of Robert L. Bradshaw International Airport. **Facility:** Said to be the largest resort in St. Kitts, this property has earned a reputation for upscale comfort and attentive service. Meets AAA guest room security requirements. 393 units. 3-5 stories, interior/exterior corridors. **Terms:** check-in 4 pm, 3 day cancellation notice. **Amenities:** high-speed Internet, safes. **Dining:** 8 restaurants, also, La Cucina, Royal Grille Steakhouse, see separate listings, entertainment. **Pool(s):** 3 outdoor. **Activities:** saunas, whirlpools, steamrooms, 4 lighted tennis courts, recreation programs, game room, volleyball, exercise room, spa. *Fee:* paddleboats, scuba diving, snorkeling, golf-18 holes. **Guest Services:** valet and coin laundry. **Free Special Amenities: room upgrade (subject to availability with advance reservations).**
(See ad p. 465, on insert.)

 〔SAVE〕〔🏌〕〔🍴〕〔🛗〕〔S〕〔SD〕〔🏊〕〔BIZ〕〔📶〕〔✕〕 FEE〔🐾〕〔📷〕〔💻〕

(See index & map p. 460.)

WHERE TO EAT

CIAO RISTORANTE ITALIANO

Phone: 869/466-3735 (17)

Italian
$16-$40

AAA Inspector Notes: Owned and operated by an Italian couple, the eatery has a delectable menu of choices that include a fabulous osso buco made with a veal shank, fresh fish like snapper and grouper as well as gnocchi, ravioli and lasagna. Start with one of the three soups or beef carpaccio and end with the silky smooth panna cotta. An Italian wine list is available. **Bar:** full bar. **Address:** Frigate Bay Rd **Location:** In St. Christopher Club.

L D ✎

▼ See AAA listing p. 464 ▼

(See index & map p. 460.)

LA BELLE VIE

French
$22-$36

Phone: 869/764-6035 ⑬

AAA Inspector Notes: At this casual spot, exquisite classical French cuisine is served up with an occasional local enhancement utilizing mostly local produce, fish and seafood. For starters, try the earth and sea salad or the tasty escargot. The entrées include rack of lamb, savory rabbit and the signature dish of filet of red snapper prepared with a white butter and aniseed sauce. The chocolate fondant served with coconut ice cream and the mango crème brûlée are difficult to pass up. Attentive service is offered. **Bar:** full bar. **Reservations:** required. **Address:** 19 Gulf View Dr **Location:** At entrance to Frigate Bay; at first roundabout. **Parking:** street only. D AC

Fine French cuisine, romantic atmosphere in Frigate Bay

LA CUCINA

Italian
$18-$32

Phone: 869/466-1200 ⑪

AAA Inspector Notes: Relax in the casually elegant dining room while enjoying traditional Italian cuisine. Specialties include osso buco and chicken parmigiana, as well as pasta and risotto dishes. An extensive wine list is featured, as is an antipasto buffet. **Bar:** full bar. **Reservations:** suggested. **Address:** 858 Frigate Bay Rd **Location:** 2.5 mi (4 km) se of Robert L. Bradshaw International Airport; in St. Kitts Marriott Resort & The Royal Beach Casino. D

MARSHALL'S
Menu on AAA.com

International
$25-$48

Phone: 869/466-8245 ⑩

AAA Inspector Notes: This well-regarded restaurant offers some refined elements in service. The al fresco dining area is cooled by the constant trade winds. Some highlights of the menu are the Angus beef, lobster, Chilean sea bass, seafood coquille and the duck. Competent meal preparations of mostly tried-and-tested recipes utilize a variety of ingredients. **Bar:** full bar. **Reservations:** required. **Address:** Frigate Bay **Location:** On hill above Frigate Bay; at Horizons Villa Resort; Fort Tyson Rise. D AC

ROCK LOBSTER BAR & RESTAURANT

International
$14-$48

Phone: 869/466-1092 ⑮

AAA Inspector Notes: Diners can choose from al fresco porch seating or interior air conditioned dining. The not too complex menu includes a selection of seafood, steak and chicken as well as a tapas menu which offers the opportunity to share a variety of savory dishes. **Bar:** full bar. **Reservations:** suggested. **Address:** Zenway Blvd **Location:** Center; in St. Christopher Club. D

ROYAL GRILLE STEAKHOUSE

Steak
$24-$45

Phone: 869/465-7802 ⑭

AAA Inspector Notes: For mouth-watering steaks and chops served in a refined ambience, this restaurant is sure to please. A variety of sizes and cuts of steak as well as grilled seafood, lamb and veal are prepared in an exhibition kitchen. **Bar:** full bar. **Reservations:** suggested. **Address:** 858 Frigate Bay Rd **Location:** 2.5 mi (4 km) se of Robert L. Bradshaw International Airport; in St. Kitts Marriott Resort & The Royal Beach Casino.

D AC

ST. LUCIA

✈ Airport Accommodations

Map Page	GEORGE F.L. CHARLES AIRPORT	Diamond Rated	High Season	Page
17 p. 469	East Winds Inn, 2.3 mi (3.6 km) n of airport	◆◆◆	$470-$1200	469
15 p. 469	Almond Morgan Bay, 2 mi (3.2 km) n of airport	◆◆◆	$429-$897	471
13 p. 469	**Windjammer Landing Villa Beach Resort & Spa, 2.5 mi (4 km) n of airport**	◆◆◆	$239-$831 [SAVE]	472

✈ Airport Accommodations

Map Page	HEWANORRA INTERNATIONAL AIRPORT	Diamond Rated	High Season	Page
36 p. 469	**Coconut Bay Beach Resort & Spa, 0.3 mi (0.5 km) s of airport**	◆◆◆	$190-$371 [SAVE]	477

St. Lucia

This index helps you "spot" where approved hotels and restaurants are located on the corresponding detailed maps. Hotel daily rate range is for comparison only and show the property's high season. Restaurant rate range is a combination of lunch and/or dinner. Turn to the listing page for more detailed rate information and consult display ads for special promotions.

RODNEY BAY

Map Page	Hotels	Diamond Rated	High Season	Page
1 p. 469	Harmony Suites	◆◆	$100-$200	473
3 p. 469	**Bay Gardens Hotel**	◆◆	$100-$275 [SAVE]	473
6 p. 469	**Bay Gardens Beach Resort**	◆◆◆	$157-$430 [SAVE]	473
9 p. 469	Coco Palm	◆◆◆	$125-$340	473

Map Page	Restaurants	Diamond Rated	Cuisine	Meal Range	Page
4 p. 469	Key Largo	◆	Pizza	$10-$17	474
5 p. 469	Memories of Hong Kong	◆◆	Chinese	$15-$24	474
6 p. 469	Charthouse Restaurant & Bar	◆◆	Steak	$20-$44	474
7 p. 469	Fire Grill & Lounge Bar	◆◆	Steak	$7-$26	474
8 p. 469	Razmataz Tandoori Restaurant & Bar	◆◆	Indian	$14-$23	474
9 p. 469	Buzz Seafood & Grill	◆◆	International	$17-$35	473
10 p. 469	Ku De Ta	◆◆◆	Thai	$14-$26	474
12 p. 469	Tequila Joe's	◆◆	Tex-Mex	$15-$38	474
15 p. 469	The Edge	◆◆◆	International	$12-$34	474

GROS ISLET

Map Page	Hotels	Diamond Rated	High Season	Page
10 p. 469	Sandals Grande St. Lucian Spa & Beach Resort *(See ad on insert.)*	◆◆◆◆	$1218-$3714	472
11 p. 469	**The Landings, St. Lucia, A RockResort** *(See ad p. 470.)*	◆◆◆◆	$99-$1900 [SAVE]	471
12 p. 469	Habitat Terrace	◆◆	$85-$140	471
13 p. 469	**Windjammer Landing Villa Beach Resort & Spa** *(See ad p. 472.)*	◆◆◆	$239-$831 [SAVE]	472
15 p. 469	Almond Morgan Bay	◆◆◆	$429-$897	471

Map Page	Restaurant	Diamond Rated	Cuisine	Meal Range	Page
2 p. 469	**Tao Restaurant**	◆◆◆	Asian	$20-$32	473

CASTRIES

Map Page	Hotels	Diamond Rated	High Season	Page
17 p. 469	East Winds Inn	◆◆◆	$470-$1200	469
18 p. 469	Sandals Halcyon Beach St. Lucia *(See ad on insert.)*	◆◆◆	$1082-$2384	471
20 p. 469	Sandals La Toc Golf Resort & Spa in St. Lucia *(See ad on insert.)*	◆◆◆	$1164-$4458	471

Map Page	Restaurants	Diamond Rated	Cuisine	Meal Range	Page
22 p. 469	Coal Pot Restaurant	◆◆	Creole	$12-$32	471
23 p. 469	Jacques Waterfront Dining	◆◆	French	$17-$37	471

MARIGOT BAY

Map Page	Hotel	Diamond Rated	High Season	Page
24 p. 469	**Discovery Marigot Bay Hotel**	◆◆◆◆	$355-$2790 [SAVE]	473

Map Page	Restaurants	Diamond Rated	Cuisine	Meal Range	Page
25 p. 469	Chateau Mygo	◆◆	Creole	$12-$28	473
26 p. 469	Boudreau Restaurant	◆◆◆	International	$28-$39	473

SOUFRIÈRE

Map Page	Hotels	Diamond Rated	High Season	Page
28 p. 469	Ladera Resort	◆◆◆◆	$380-$1025	477
29 p. 469	**Anse Chastanet Resort** *(See ad p. 475.)*	◆◆◆◆	$330-$915 [SAVE]	474
30 p. 469	**Jade Mountain Resort** *(See ad p. 476.)*	◆◆◆◆◆	$900-$2430 [SAVE]	477
31 p. 469	**Stonefield Estate Villa Resort & Spa**	◆◆◆	$250-$1000 [SAVE]	477
32 p. 469	**Fond Doux Holiday Plantation**	◆◆◆	$150-$500 [SAVE]	474
34 p. 469	**The Jalousie Plantation**	◆◆◆◆	$270-$990 [SAVE]	477

Map Page	Restaurant	Diamond Rated	Cuisine	Meal Range	Page
34 p. 469	The Great Room	◆◆◆	International	$28-$42	477

VIEUX FORT

Map Page	Hotel	Diamond Rated	High Season	Page
36 p. 469	**Coconut Bay Beach Resort & Spa**	◆◆◆	$190-$371 [SAVE]	477

ANSE LA RAYE

Map Page	Hotel	Diamond Rated	High Season	Page
37 p. 469	Ti Kaye Village Resort	◆◆◆	$220-$540	469

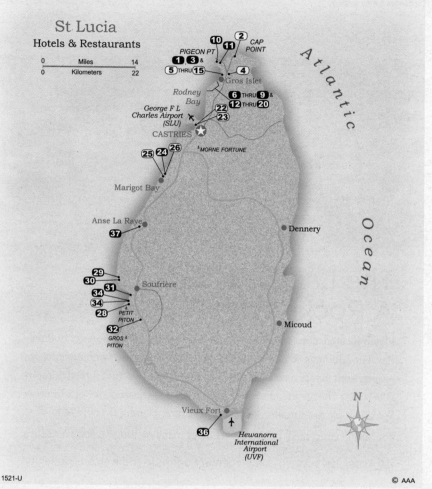

St Lucia
Hotels & Restaurants

Miles	
0	14
0	22
Kilometers	

PIGEON PT

10 **2** CAP
11   POINT
1 **3** &
5 THRU **15**   **4**
Gros Islet

Rodney Bay

6 THRU **9** &
12 THRU **20**

George F L Charles Airport (SLU) ✈
22
23
CASTRIES ★

▲ *MORNE FORTUNE*

25 **24** **26**

Marigot Bay

Anse La Raye
37

● *Dennery*

A t l a n t i c

O c e a n

29
30
34 **31**
34   ● *Soufrière*
28 ▲
PETIT PITON
32
GROS ▲
PITON

● *Micoud*

Vieux Fort
✈
36
Hewanorra International Airport (UVF)

N

1521-U

© AAA

ANSE LA RAYE
• **Hotels & Restaurants index & map p. 467**

TI KAYE VILLAGE RESORT

Cottage
$220-$540

Phone: (758)456-8101 **37**

Address: Anse Cochon **Location:** Oceanfront. 2 mi (3.2 km) s of town, then 1.9 mi (3 km) w on unimproved road, follow signs. **Facility:** On a hillside overlooking Anse Cochon, this mini resort is in a spectacular setting. The West Indies-style cottages have verandas and open-air showers. 33 cottages. 1 story, exterior corridors. *Bath:* shower only. **Terms:** office hours 7 am-11 pm, 4 night minimum stay - seasonal, age restrictions may apply, 30 day cancellation notice. **Amenities:** safes. **Dining:** 2 restaurants. **Pool(s):** outdoor. **Activities:** volleyball, exercise room, spa. *Fee:* scuba diving, snorkeling.

🍴 🍸 ⓈⒹ 🏊 📶 🅦 🛄 💻

CASTRIES (B-1) pop. 64,344
• **Restaurants p. 471**
• **Hotels & Restaurants index & map p. 467**

EAST WINDS INN

Cottage
$470-$1200

Phone: 758/452-8212 **17**

Address: La Brelotte Bay **Location:** Oceanfront. 2.3 mi (3.7 km) n of George F.L. Charles Airport, 1 mi (1.6 km) w via signs. **Facility:** Find tastefully furnished units in single-story cottages at this all-inclusive property on eight acres of tropical gardens on La Brelotte Bay Beach. 30 cottages. 1 story, exterior corridors. *Bath:* shower only. **Terms:** 3 night minimum stay, age restrictions may apply, 7 day cancellation notice-fee imposed. **Amenities:** safes, honor bars. **Dining:** entertainment. **Pool(s):** outdoor. **Activities:** paddleboats, snorkeling. *Fee:* massage. **Guest Services:** valet laundry.

🍴 🍸 🚤 📶 ✕ 💻 / ⓈⓄⓂⒺ ⓊⓃⒾⓉⓈ 🅚 🅦

(See index & map p. 467.)

▼ See AAA listing p. 471 ▼

The Landings St. Lucia, A RockResort

Ideally located along 800-feet of white-sand beach on the shores of Rodney Bay, The Landings St. Lucia, a AAA Four Diamond Award-winning hotel, is a waterfront luxury resort featuring spacious one-, two- and three-bedroom villa suites. The resort's amenities include a 7,000-square-foot RockResorts Spa*, multiple restaurants, private yacht harbor, swimming pools, tennis courts and convenient access to St. Lucia's many exciting vacation activities.

AAA Members earn a complimentary upgrade and welcome amenity!

THE
LANDINGS
ST. LUCIA

A ROCKRESORT

LANDINGSSTLUCIA.COM
877-657-ROCK (7625)

Download eTourBook guides for ereaders and smartphones at AAA.com/ebooks

(See index & map p. 467.)

SANDALS HALCYON BEACH ST. LUCIA
Phone: (758)453-0222

Resort Hotel
$1082-$2384 12/1-3/31
$1050-$2384 4/1-11/30

Address: Choc Bay **Location:** Oceanfront. 1 mi (1.6 km) n of George F.L. Charles Airport; 36 mi (57.6 km) n of Hewanorra International Airport. **Facility:** This couples-only, all-inclusive resort provides numerous dining and recreational options; variety of guest room categories available. 169 units. 1-2 stories (no elevator), exterior corridors. **Terms:** 3 night minimum stay - seasonal, age restrictions may apply, 45 day cancellation notice-fee imposed. **Amenities:** high-speed Internet (fee), safes. *Some:* honor bars. **Dining:** 3 restaurants, nightclub, entertainment. **Pool(s):** 3 outdoor. **Activities:** saunas, whirlpools, steamrooms, lifeguard on duty, beach access, paddleboats, sailboats, windsurfing, waterskiing, scuba diving, snorkeling, 2 lighted tennis courts, recreation programs, basketball, horseshoes, shuffleboard, volleyball. *Fee:* massage. **Guest Services:** valet laundry, area transportation-Sandals Grande St. Lucian Spa & Beach Resort and Sandals La Toc Golf Resort & Spa in St. Lucia. **(See ad on insert.)**

SANDALS LA TOC GOLF RESORT & SPA IN ST. LUCIA
Phone: (758)452-3081

Resort Hotel
$1164-$4458 12/1-3/31
$1118-$4458 4/1-11/30

Address: La Toc **Location:** Oceanfront. 3 mi (4.8 km) s of George F.L. Charles Airport; 32 mi (51.2 km) n of Hewanorra International Airport. **Facility:** This 220-acre, all-inclusive, couples-only resort on a bluff overlooking the beach offers 19 room categories, including some with private plunge pools. 331 units. 1-7 stories, interior/exterior corridors. **Terms:** 3 night minimum stay - seasonal, age restrictions may apply, 45 day cancellation notice-fee imposed. **Amenities:** high-speed Internet (fee), safes, honor bars. **Dining:** 8 restaurants, entertainment. **Pool(s):** 4 outdoor. **Activities:** saunas, whirlpools, lifeguard on duty, beach access, canoeing, paddleboats, sailboats, windsurfing, scuba diving, snorkeling, golf-9 holes, 5 lighted tennis courts, recreation programs, basketball, game room, horseshoes, shuffleboard, spa. **Guest Services:** valet laundry, area transportation-Sandals Halcyon Beach St. Lucia & Sandals Grande St. Lucian Spa & Beach Resort. **(See ad on insert.)**

WHERE TO EAT

COAL POT RESTAURANT   **Phone: 758/452-5566**

Creole
$12-$32

AAA Inspector Notes: A longstanding favorite on Castries Bay, this idyllic open-air waterfront setting in rustic surroundings sets a calm mood for relaxation. The talented chef combines West Indies cuisine with a dash of French influence. Included in the large fish selection are such offerings as salmon, tuna, red snapper, kingfish and bar. Stuffed crab back is a tasty treat to whet the appetite. Diners can expect casual, easygoing service. **Bar:** full bar. **Reservations:** suggested. **Address:** Vigie Marina **Location:** At Vigie Cove; across from airport.

JACQUES WATERFRONT DINING
Phone: 758/458-1900

French
$17-$37

AAA Inspector Notes: Chef Jacques creates a fusion of Caribbean and French cuisine at the waterfront restaurant. Appetizers include mussels cooked in white wine and garlic and baked herb-crusted crab back. Chilled tomato and green peppercorn soup is refreshing. Deftly prepared entrees range from lamb chops to pan-seared scallops to duck breast in honey, lime and ginger sauce. Desserts--such as lime meringue pie, baked banana pie and coconut creme brulee--are too tempting to pass up. **Bar:** full bar. **Reservations:** required. **Address:** Vigie Cove **Location:** Access road opposite airport; just w of John Compton Hwy, follow signs.

GROS ISLET pop. 20,872

ALMOND MORGAN BAY   **Phone: (758)457-3700**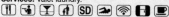

Resort Hotel
$429-$897

Address: Choc Bay **Location:** Oceanfront. 2 mi (3.2 km) n of George F.L. Charles Airport; 37 mi (59.2 km) n of Hewanorra International Airport. **Facility:** Nestled on 22 acres with a palm-fringed sugar-sand beach, the all-inclusive resort offers contemporary guest units and is well suited for families. Meets AAA guest room security requirements. 340 units. 3-4 stories, exterior corridors. **Terms:** 3 day cancellation notice-fee imposed. **Amenities:** safes. **Dining:** 5 restaurants, entertainment. **Pool(s):** 4 outdoor. **Activities:** paddleboats, sailboats, windsurfing, waterskiing, snorkeling, 4 tennis courts (2 lighted), recreation programs, playground, basketball, game room, horseshoes, exercise room, spa. **Guest Services:** valet laundry.

HABITAT TERRACE   **Phone: 758/452-0822**

Bed & Breakfast
$85-$140

Address: Old Military Rd & Habitat Dr **Location:** Just n of Rodney Bay, just e at Bonneterre turnoff, then just s on Old Military Rd. **Facility:** 11 units, some two bedrooms and kitchens. 2 stories (no elevator), interior/exterior corridors. *Bath:* shower only. **Terms:** 4 day cancellation notice. **Amenities:** safes. **Pool(s):** outdoor. **Guest Services:** valet laundry.

THE LANDINGS, ST. LUCIA, A ROCKRESORT
Phone: (758)458-7300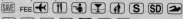

Resort Hotel
$99-$1900

Address: Rodney Bay **Location:** Oceanfront. Northern end of island; near Cap Estates; 7.7 mi (12.3 km) n of George F.L. Charles Airport. **Facility:** Guest rooms at this well-appointed resort with 800 feet of beach frontage are spacious and residential in style. Meets AAA guest room security requirements. 122 kitchen units, some two and three bedrooms. 3-4 stories, exterior corridors. **Terms:** 7 day cancellation notice-fee imposed. **Amenities:** high-speed Internet, safes. **Dining:** 2 restaurants, entertainment. **Pool(s):** 3 outdoor. **Activities:** whirlpools, steamrooms, paddleboats, sailboats, windsurfing, 2 lighted tennis courts, spa. **Guest Services:** complimentary laundry, area transportation-shopping mall. *(See ad p. 470.)*

(See index & map p. 467.)

SANDALS GRANDE ST. LUCIAN SPA & BEACH RESORT
Phone: (758)455-2000 **10**

Resort Hotel

$1218-$3714 12/1-3/31
$1186-$3714 4/1-11/30

Address: Pigeon Island Cswy **Location:** Oceanfront. Northern end of island near Cap Estates; 8 mi (12.8 km) n of George F.L. Charles Airport. **Facility:** The all-inclusive, couples-only resort overlooks Rodney Bay and the Caribbean Sea with Pigeon Island as a backdrop; find high-level service. 301 units, some two bedrooms and cottages. 1-3 stories, exterior corridors. **Terms:** 3 night minimum stay - seasonal, age restrictions may apply, 45 day cancellation notice-fee imposed. **Amenities:** high-speed Internet (fee), safes. *Some:* honor bars. **Dining:** 6 restaurants, entertainment. **Pool(s):** 5 outdoor. **Activities:** saunas, whirlpools, steamrooms, lifeguard on duty, boating, canoeing, paddleboats, sailboats, windsurfing, waterskiing, scuba diving, snorkeling, 2 lighted tennis courts, recreation programs, hiking trails, game room, horseshoes, shuffleboard, volleyball, spa. **Guest Services:** valet laundry, area transportation-Sandals La Toc Golf Resort & Spa in St. Lucia & Sandals Halcyon Beach. *(See ad on insert.)*

WINDJAMMER LANDING VILLA BEACH RESORT & SPA
Phone: (758)456-9000 **13**

Resort Hotel

$239-$831

Address: Labrelotte Bay **Location:** Oceanfront. 2.5 mi (4 km) n of George F.L. Charles Airport, 1 mi (1.6 km) w via signs; 38 mi (60.8 km) n of Hewanorra International Airport. Located in a secluded area. **Facility:** Casually sophisticated, this village resort boasts 55 acres and a 1,000-foot stretch of beach; varied rooms, many with private plunge pool. 161 units, some two bedrooms, kitchens and houses. 2 stories (no elevator), exterior corridors. **Terms:** 3 night minimum stay, 14 day cancellation notice, 21 day in season-fee imposed. **Amenities:** high-speed Internet, safes. **Dining:** 5 restaurants, entertainment. **Pool(s):** 6 outdoor. **Activities:** whirlpool, steamroom, paddleboats, sailboats, windsurfing, boat dock, 2 lighted tennis courts, recreation programs, playground, basketball, game room, volleyball, exercise room, spa. *Fee:* waterskiing, scuba diving, snorkeling. **Guest Services:** valet and coin laundry. **Free Special Amenities:** high-speed Internet and manager's reception. *(See ad this page.)*

(See index & map p. 467.)

WHERE TO EAT

TAO RESTAURANT
Phone: 758/457-7800   (2)

Asian
$20-$32

AAA Inspector Notes: This restaurant occupies an open-air veranda in a health spa. Attentive servers bring out exquisite cuisine that blends the culinary traditions and ingredients of East and West. For starters, gazpacho soup refreshes and the distinctive foie gras bursts with flavor. Entrees run the gamut from char-sui salmon and banga mary (a local fish) to lamb, twice-cooked duck and tandoori chicken. **Bar:** full bar. **Reservations:** required. **Address:** Cariblue Beach **Location:** 9.5 mi (15.2 km) n of Castries; Cap Estates; in LeSport Body Holiday Resort & Spa.

MARIGOT BAY

• Hotels & Restaurants index & map p. 467

DISCOVERY MARIGOT BAY HOTEL
Phone: (758)458-5300   (24)

Hotel
$355-$2790

Address: Marigot Bay **Location:** Oceanfront. At Marigot Bay. **Facility:** Overlooking Marigot Bay, the hotel offers nicely appointed units with all the expected comforts and amenities. Meets AAA guest room security requirements. 122 units, some kitchens. 2-4 stories (no elevator), exterior corridors. **Terms:** check-in 4 pm, 14 day cancellation notice, 7 day off season-fee imposed. **Amenities:** high-speed Internet, safes. **Dining:** 2 restaurants, also, Boudreau Restaurant, see separate listing. **Pool(s):** 2 outdoor. **Activities:** whirlpools, limited beach access, paddleboats, sailboats, marina, snorkeling, exercise room, spa. **Guest Services:** valet and coin laundry. **Free Special Amenities: continental breakfast and high-speed Internet.**

WHERE TO EAT

BOUDREAU RESTAURANT
Phone: 758/458-5300   (26)

International
$28-$39

AAA Inspector Notes: This restaurant offers fine dining on Marigot Bay with views of the marina and world class yachts. Some guests start with the refreshing chilled-pea soup or the savory beef carpaccio. The entrées range from slow-braised leg of lamb to mahi mahi with polenta gnocchi. Sweet endings include a dark-chocolate tart with coffee sauce and the creme brulee. Attentive and refined service is well-executed. **Bar:** full bar. **Reservations:** suggested. **Address:** Marigot Bay **Location:** At Marigot Bay; in Discovery Marigot Bay Hotel.

CHATEAU MYGO
Phone: 758/451-4772   (25)

Creole
$12-$28

AAA Inspector Notes: Patrons look out over Marigot Bay from this eatery's open-air dining deck. The varied menu combines West Indies cuisine with Creole family recipes. In addition to pizza and barbecue pork chops, it lists curried lamb, fish with mango-raisin sauce, roast duck with plum sauce and local lobster. **Bar:** full bar. **Reservations:** suggested. **Address:** Main Rd Marigot Bay **Location:** Waterfront Marigot Bay.

RODNEY BAY

• Hotels & Restaurants index & map p. 467

BAY GARDENS BEACH RESORT
Phone: (758)457-8500   (6)

Hotel
$157-$430

Address: Rodney Bay Village **Location:** Oceanfront. 6.3 mi (10.1 km) n of George F.L. Charles Airport; 41.8 mi (66.9 km) n of Hewanorra International Airport; at Reduit Beach. **Facility:** Meets AAA guest room security requirements. 75 units, some kitchens. 3 stories (no elevator), exterior corridors. **Terms:** check-in 4 pm, 14 day cancellation notice. **Amenities:** high-speed Internet, safes. **Dining:** 2 restaurants. **Pool(s):** outdoor. **Activities:** whirlpool, recreation programs, basketball, volleyball, exercise room, spa. **Fee:** boats, sailboats, windsurfing, scuba diving, snorkeling. **Guest Services:** valet and coin laundry.

BAY GARDENS HOTEL
Phone: (758)452-8060   (3)

Hotel
$100-$275

Address: Rodney Bay Village **Location:** 5.5 mi (8.8 km) n of George F.L. Charles Airport; 41 mi (65.6 km) n of Hewanorra International Airport. **Facility:** 87 units, some two bedrooms and efficiencies. 2 stories (no elevator), exterior corridors. **Terms:** 14 day cancellation notice, 7 day off season-fee imposed. **Amenities:** safes. **Pool(s):** 2 outdoor. **Activities:** whirlpool. **Guest Services:** valet laundry.

COCO PALM
Phone: 758/456-2800   (9)

Boutique Hotel
$125-$340

Address: Rodney Bay Blvd **Location:** 5 mi (8 km) n of George F.L. Charles Airport; center; Rodney Bay Village. **Facility:** Guests can select from units with upgraded appointments in the main section or cozy rooms with Caribbean Creole accents in the annex section. 101 units. 2-4 stories, interior corridors. **Terms:** 21 day cancellation notice-fee imposed. **Amenities:** safes. **Pool(s):** outdoor. **Activities:** limited beach access, limited exercise equipment. **Fee:** massage. **Guest Services:** valet laundry, area transportation-Reduit Beach.

HARMONY SUITES
Phone: 758/452-8756   (1)

Hotel
$100-$200

Address: Flamboyant Dr **Location:** 5.3 mi (8.5 km) n of George F.L. Charles Airport on Rodney Bay; 41 mi (65.6 km) n of Hewanorra International Airport; in Rodney Bay Village. Located in a quiet residential area. **Facility:** 30 units, some efficiencies. 2 stories (no elevator), exterior corridors. **Terms:** office hours 7 am-11 pm, age restrictions may apply, 14 day cancellation notice. **Amenities:** safes. **Dining:** The Edge, see separate listing. **Pool(s):** outdoor. **Fee:** scuba diving, snorkeling, massage. **Guest Services:** valet laundry.

WHERE TO EAT

BUZZ SEAFOOD & GRILL
Phone: 758/458-0450   (9)

International
$17-$35

AAA Inspector Notes: Longtime St. Lucian restaurateur Pat Bowden has created another Rodney Bay favorite. The cuisine mixes French, Mediterranean and Caribbean influences. Such seafood specialties as seared yellowfin tuna, seafood Creole and potato-crusted snapper are sumptuous. Other savory entrees include barbecue baby back ribs, Moroccan spiced lamb shanks and West Indian pepper pot made with chicken, lamb and beef. Nightly happy hour and summertime value specials are provided. **Bar:** full bar. **Reservations:** suggested. **Address:** Rodney Bay Village **Location:** 5.8 mi (9.3 km) n of downtown Castries; opposite The Royal St. Lucian Hotel. **Parking:** street only.

(See index & map p. 467.)

CHARTHOUSE RESTAURANT & BAR
Phone: 758-452-8115 ⑥

Steak
$20-$44

AAA Inspector Notes: On Rodney Bay, this restaurant has deck seating that overlooks the waterfront. Specialties include steak, ribs and seafood. **Bar:** full bar. **Reservations:** suggested. **Address:** Rodney Bay Village **Location:** Center; follow signs. Ⓓ Ⓚ Ⓝ

THE EDGE
Phone: 758-450-3343 ⑮

International
$12-$34

AAA Inspector Notes: A mix of Asian and New World cuisine is served along the shores of Rodney Bay. Besides an attractive dining area there is an enclosed, air-conditioned sushi bar. The trio of seviche is a great starter and for an entrée, the tuna is cooked to perfection. Sushi specials are offered on Tuesday night. **Bar:** full bar. **Reservations:** required. **Address:** Flamboyant Dr **Location:** Waterfront on Rodney Bay; in Harmony Suites. Ⓑ Ⓛ Ⓓ Ⓚ

FIRE GRILL & LOUNGE BAR
Phone: 758-451-4745 ⑦

Steak
$7-$26

AAA Inspector Notes: This modern, casual restaurant offers more than just steak-king fish ceviche and seafood as well as duck, barbecue ribs and lamb are featured. The lounge with leather sofas and a tempting cocktail menu is inviting. **Bar:** full bar. **Reservations:** suggested. **Address:** Rodney Bay Village **Location:** Center.

KEY LARGO
Phone: 758-452-0282 ④

◆
Pizza
$10-$17

AAA Inspector Notes: Across from Rodney Bay Marina, the casual restaurant welcomes families. On the menu are thin-crust pizzas baked in a wood-fired brick oven, as well as a wide selection of entree-size salads and pasta dishes. **Bar:** full bar. **Address:** Gros Islet Hwy **Location:** Just n of town. Ⓛ Ⓓ Ⓚ Ⓝ

KU DE TA
Phone: 758-458-4968 ⑩

Thai
$14-$26

AAA Inspector Notes: St. Lucia's only Thai restaurant affords a fine-dining experience. The professional decor is artfully tasteful, and seating is offered in an air-conditioned section or around the herb garden. The trained staff is attentive and accommodating. Skilled chefs prepare delectable dishes centered on duck, local fish, lamb, chicken and pork in an array of rich sauces. Lemon grass creme brulee is an interesting indulgence. **Bar:** full bar. **Reservations:** suggested. **Address:** Rodney Bay Village **Location:** Near entrance to Rodney Bay area.
Ⓛ Ⓓ Ⓝ

MEMORIES OF HONG KONG
Phone: 758-452-8218 ⑤

Chinese
$15-$24

AAA Inspector Notes: Brightly decorated in Chinese fashion complete with a pagoda-style roof, this restaurant offers exceptional fare. Fresh seafood, beef, chicken and pork dishes are prepared in a myriad of ways. Congenial servers and an extensive cocktail menu round out the experience. **Bar:** full bar. **Reservations:** suggested. **Address:** Rodney Bay Village **Location:** Across from Reduit Beach; 5.5 mi (8.8 km) n of Castries; at Rodney Bay. **Parking:** street only. Ⓓ Ⓚ Ⓝ

RAZMATAZ TANDOORI RESTAURANT & BAR
Phone: 758-452-9800 ⑧

◆◆◆
Indian
$14-$23

AAA Inspector Notes: Authentic Indian cuisine is served in the airiness of a Caribbean-style house with a large verandah. Specializing in Tandoori and Balti cuisine, the menu offers such appetizers as samosas, papadums, and shish kebab. Fragrant and exotic spices are used to flavor such entrée dishes as vindaloo, tikka masala, rogan josh and tandoori, most of which can be prepared with either chicken, lamb, beef, vegetable, fish or shrimp. A bevy of side dishes, rice preparations and various naan complete the meal. **Bar:** full bar. **Address:** Rodney Bay Village **Location:** Across from Reduit Beach. **Parking:** street only.
Ⓓ Ⓚ Ⓝ

TEQUILA JOE'S
Phone: 758-453-7469 ⑫

◆◆
Tex-Mex
$15-$38

AAA Inspector Notes: Three floors of food, fun, music and dancing are offered at this Mexican-themed restaurant. Features include 14 flat screen TVs with nonstop sports viewing, an interactive and engaging house band that plays 3 to 5 nights a week and Tex-Mex style cuisine including hefty burritos, quesadillas and tacos and an array of creative tequila-vodka based concoctions. **Bar:** full bar. **Address:** Rodney Bay Village **Location:** Center. Ⓛ Ⓓ Ⓚ Ⓝ

SOUFRIÈRE (C-1) pop. 7,656
• Restaurants p. 477
• Hotels & Restaurants index & map p. 467

ANSE CHASTANET RESORT
Phone: (758)459-7000 ㉙

Resort Cottage
$330-$915

Address: Old French Rd **Location:** 2 mi (3.2 km) n of town; 30 mi (48 km) s of Castries via West Coast Rd; 20 mi (32 km) n of Hewanorra International Airport. Located in a secluded area. **Facility:** To take advantage of the stunning, wondrous views of the Pitons, the cottages were designed with only three walls at this award-winning resort. 49 cottages. 1 story, exterior corridors. **Bath:** shower only. **Terms:** office hours 7 am-11 pm, 3 night minimum stay - seasonal, age restrictions may apply, 3 day cancellation notice-fee imposed. **Amenities:** safes. **Dining:** 4 restaurants, entertainment. **Activities:** limited beach access, sailboats, windsurfing, boat dock, snorkeling, tennis court, recreation programs, bicycle trails, hiking trails, jogging, spa. **Fee:** scuba diving, charter fishing. **Guest Services:** valet laundry, area transportation-water taxi & shuttle within resort.
(See ad p. 475.)
ⓈⒶⓋⒺ 🍴 🍸 ♿ BIZ 🛜 🅿 ☎ 🗄 🖥
/ SOME UNITS Ⓚ

FOND DOUX HOLIDAY PLANTATION
Phone: (758)459-7545 ㉜

◆◆◆
Historic Cottage
$150-$500

Address: Estangs **Location:** 3 mi (4.8 km) s of town; 17 mi (27.2 km) n of Hewanorra International Airport. **Facility:** Situated on a 250-year-old continuously working cocoa plantation, the hotel features private Creole-style cottages spaced out over 135 acres. 10 cottages. 1-2 stories (no elevator), exterior corridors. **Bath:** shower only. **Terms:** 14 day cancellation notice. **Amenities:** safes. **Dining:** 2 restaurants. **Pool(s):** 3 outdoor. **Activities:** whirlpool, hiking trails. **Fee:** massage. **Guest Services:** valet laundry. **Free Special Amenities: continental breakfast and early check-in/late check-out.**
ⓈⒶⓋⒺ 🍴 🍸 ♿ 🛶 🛜 Ⓚ 🅿 🗄
/ SOME UNITS 📺 🖥

Discover mobile travel solutions at
AAA.com/mobile and CAA.ca/mobile

(See index & map p. 467.)

JADE MOUNTAIN RESORT

Phone: (758)459-4000 30

Boutique
Contemporary Hotel
$900-$2430

Address: Old French Rd, Anse Chastanet **Location:** 2 mi (3.2 km) n of town; 30 mi (48 km) s of Castries via West Coast Rd; 20 mi (32 km) n of Hewanorra International Airport. **Facility:** Each guest unit, known here as a sanctuary, is decorated differently but they each have a large private plunge pool that faces the Pitons. 29 units. 8 stories (no elevator), exterior corridors. **Terms:** 2-3 night minimum stay - seasonal, age restrictions may apply, 21 day cancellation notice, 14 day off season-fee imposed. **Amenities:** safes. *Some:* honor bars. **Dining:** entertainment. **Pool(s):** outdoor. **Activities:** limited beach access, snorkeling, recreation programs, exercise room, spa. *Fee:* scuba diving, charter fishing. **Guest Services:** valet laundry. *(See ad p. 476.)*

THE JALOUSIE PLANTATION

Phone: 758/456-8000 34

Resort Hotel
$270-$990

Address: Forbidden Beach, Eden Bay **Location:** Oceanfront. 3 mi (4.8 km) s of town center, just w, follow signs. **Facility:** Between the Piton peaks, this full-service resort encompasses more than 100 acres of lush grounds; sugar mill and villa-style units with plunge pools are offered. 53 units, some two bedrooms and cottages. 1-2 stories (no elevator), exterior corridors. **Terms:** 21 day cancellation notice-fee imposed. **Amenities:** safes. **Dining:** 2 restaurants, also, The Great Room, see separate listing, entertainment. **Pool(s):** outdoor. **Activities:** sauna, paddleboats, sailboats, windsurfing, scuba diving & rental equipment, snorkeling, 3 lighted tennis courts, recreation programs, jogging, playground, volleyball, exercise room, spa. **Guest Services:** valet laundry.

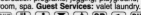

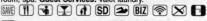

Simply Reliable

The Diamond Ratings in this TourBook guide are backed by our expert, in-person evaluations, whether the hotel or restaurant is no-frills, moderate or upscale.

Learn more at **AAA.com/Diamonds**

LADERA RESORT

Phone: 758/459-7323 28

Cottage
$380-$1025

Address: Rabot Estate **Location:** 2 mi (3.2 km) s of town; 32 mi (51.2 km) s of Castries via West Coast Rd; 18 mi (28.8 km) n of Hewanorra International Airport. **Facility:** With a spectacular location, each of the unique guest units feature a plunge pool with open views of the ocean and surrounding Pitons. 32 cottages. 1-2 stories (no elevator), exterior corridors. **Bath:** shower only. **Terms:** open 12/1-8/28 & 10/1-11/30, 3 night minimum stay, age restrictions may apply, 21 day cancellation notice, 14 day off season-fee imposed. **Amenities:** safes, honor bars. **Dining:** entertainment. **Pool(s):** outdoor. **Activities:** snorkeling, hiking trails, exercise room, spa. **Guest Services:** valet laundry, area transportation-boat launch & beaches.

STONEFIELD ESTATE VILLA RESORT & SPA

Phone: (758)459-7037 31

Vacation Rental
Cottage
$250-$1000

Address: Stonefield Estate Rd **Location:** Just s of town, then just w, follow signs. **Facility:** Thoughtful appointments and fully equipped conveniences make this villa resort ideal for both families and couples. 18 units, some houses and cottages. 1 story, exterior corridors. **Bath:** shower only. **Terms:** office hours 7 am-11 pm, age restrictions may apply, 30 day cancellation notice-fee imposed. **Amenities:** safes, honor bars. **Pool(s):** outdoor. **Activities:** snorkeling, exercise room, spa. **Guest Services:** valet laundry, area transportation-beach. **Free Special Amenities:** full breakfast and high-speed Internet.

WHERE TO EAT

THE GREAT ROOM

Phone: 758/456-8000 34

International
$28-$42

AAA Inspector Notes: Romantic and sophisticated dining on a terrace of a re-created plantation great house. Diners enjoy the mix of Caribbean and International cuisine which includes hearts of palm soup, sashimi and such entrees as rack of lamb, duck and local seafood including mahi mahi, tuna and yellow-tail snapper. **Bar:** full bar. **Reservations:** required. **Address:** Forbidden Beach, Eden Bay **Location:** 3 mi (4.8 km) s of town center, just w, follow signs; in The Jalousie Plantation. D

VIEUX FORT pop. 14,754

• Hotels & Restaurants index & map p. 467

COCONUT BAY BEACH RESORT & SPA

Phone: (758)459-6000 36

Resort Hotel
$190-$371

Address: Bean Field **Location:** Oceanfront. Just s of Hewanorra International Airport. **Facility:** Guest rooms at the oceanfront, all-inclusive resort are well equipped; recreational facilities include a water slide, tennis courts and pools. 250 units. 4 stories, exterior corridors. **Bath:** shower only. **Terms:** 3 day cancellation notice-fee imposed. **Amenities:** high-speed Internet (fee), safes. **Dining:** 4 restaurants, entertainment. **Pool(s):** 3 outdoor. **Activities:** whirlpool, waterslide, 4 lighted tennis courts, recreation programs, playground, basketball, game room, volleyball, exercise room, spa. *Fee:* saunas, steamrooms. **Guest Services:** valet and coin laundry.

ST. MARTIN/ST. MAARTEN

This index helps you "spot" where approved hotels and restaurants are located on the corresponding detailed maps. Hotel daily rate range is for comparison only and show the property's high season. Restaurant rate range is a combination of lunch and/or dinner. Turn to the listing page for more detailed rate information and consult display ads for special promotions.

GRAND CASE (St. Martin)

Map Page	Hotels	Diamond Rated	High Season	Page
1 p. 480	Hotel L'Esplanade	▽▽▽	$245-$595	485
5 p. 480	Le Petit Hotel	▽▽	$265-$625	485

Map Page	Restaurants	Diamond Rated	Cuisine	Meal Range	Page
③ p. 480	Le Tastevin	▽▽▽	French	$26-$56	485
⑤ p. 480	Il Nettuno	▽▽	Italian	$25-$52	485
⑦ p. 480	L'Auberge Gourmande	▽▽▽	French	$22-$34	485
⑧ p. 480	L'Escapade	▽▽▽	French	$33-$52	485
⑨ p. 480	La California	▽▽	International	$16-$41	485
⑩ p. 480	Spiga Restaurant	▽▽▽	New Italian	$27-$43	485
⑪ p. 480	The Blue Martini Restaurant, Bar and Tropical Garden	▽▽▽	French	$24-$45	485
⑬ p. 480	Le Pressoir	▽▽▽	French	$38-$55	485

ORIENT BAY (St. Martin)

Map Page	Hotels	Diamond Rated	High Season	Page
15 p. 480	La Plantation	▽▽	$200-$355	487
17 p. 480	Palm Court Hotel	▽▽▽	$260-$400	487

MARIGOT (St. Martin)

Map Page	Hotels	Diamond Rated	High Season	Page
18 p. 480	Hotel La Samanna	▽▽▽▽	$395-$5275	486
19 p. 480	Mercure St. Martin & Marina	▽▽	$108-$187	486

Map Page	Restaurants	Diamond Rated	Cuisine	Meal Range	Page
㉑ p. 480	Le Bistro de la Mer	▽	French	$14-$32	486
㉒ p. 480	La Main a la Pate	▽▽	Mediterranean	$18-$29	486
㉓ p. 480	Don Camillo Restaurant	▽▽▽	Italian	$24-$39	486
㉖ p. 480	Mario's Bistro	▽▽▽	French	$31-$42	486
㉙ p. 480	Le Santal by the Sea	▽▽▽▽	French	$33-$49	486
㉛ p. 480	The Restaurant at La Samanna	▽▽▽▽	International	$48-$54	486
㉟ p. 480	Le Chanteclair	▽▽▽	French	$32-$39	486
㉛ p. 480	Restaurant Les Boucaniers	▽▽	Creole	$15-$29	486

OYSTER POND (St. Martin)

Map Page	Hotel	Diamond Rated	High Season	Page
26 p. 480	Captain Oliver's Resort and Marina	▽▽	$140-$335	487

Map Page	Restaurant	Diamond Rated	Cuisine	Meal Range	Page
㊹ p. 480	Captain Oliver's	▽▽	Creole	$12-$27	487

OYSTER POND (St. Maarten)

Map Page	Hotel	Diamond Rated	High Season	Page
27 p. 480	The Westin St. Maarten Dawn Beach Resort & Spa *(See ad p. 482, p. 217.)*	▽▽▽▽	$397-$666 [SAVE]	481

Map Page	Restaurant	Diamond Rated	Cuisine	Meal Range	Page
(42) p. 480	Aura	▽▽▽	Steak	$33-$45	483

LITTLE BAY (St. Maarten)

Map Page	Hotels	Diamond Rated	High Season	Page
30 p. 480	Belair Beach Hotel	▽▽	$259-$429	480
31 p. 480	Divi Little Bay Beach Resort	▽▽▽	$208-$812 [SAVE]	481

MAHO BAY (St. Maarten)

Map Page	Hotel	Diamond Rated	High Season	Page
34 p. 480	Sonesta Maho Beach Resort & Casino	▽▽	$190-$700	481

ANSE MARCEL (St. Martin)

Map Page	Hotels	Diamond Rated	High Season	Page
36 p. 480	The Radisson Blu St. Martin Resort Marina and Spa *(See ad p. 484, p. 218.)*	▽▽▽▽	$266-$1269 [SAVE]	483
38 p. 480	Marquis Boutique Hotel & Spa	▽▽▽	$335-$1115	483

CUPECOY (St. Maarten)

Map Page	Restaurants	Diamond Rated	Cuisine	Meal Range	Page
(50) p. 480	Dare to be...Rare	▽▽▽	Steak	$29-$54	480
(52) p. 480	Le Montmartre	▽▽▽	French	$26-$50	480
(54) p. 480	La Gondola Ristorante	▽▽▽	Italian	$19-$39	480

PHILIPSBURG (St. Maarten)

Map Page	Restaurants	Diamond Rated	Cuisine	Meal Range	Page
(75) p. 480	Antoine by the Sea	▽▽	International	$11-$38	483
(77) p. 480	Shiv Sagar Bar & Restaurant	▽▽	Indian	$10-$22	483
(78) p. 480	The Greenhouse Bar and Restaurant	▽▽	International	$10-$28	483

SIMPSON BAY (St. Maarten)

Map Page	Restaurants	Diamond Rated	Cuisine	Meal Range	Page
(80) p. 480	Skip Jack's Seafood Grill, Bar & Fish Market	▽▽	Seafood	$17-$28	483
(85) p. 480	Top Carrot	▽	Natural/Organic	$8-$15	483

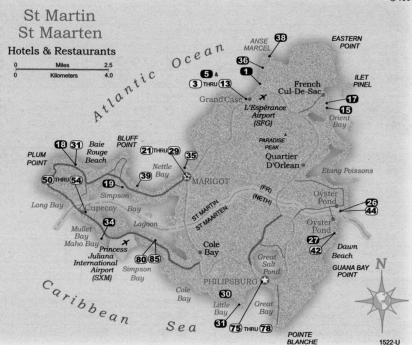

St Martin
St Maarten

Hotels & Restaurants

© AAA

St. Maarten

CUPECOY (B-1)

• Hotels & Restaurants index & map p. 478

DARE TO BE...RARE   Phone: 599/545-5714   (50)

Steak
$29-$54

AAA Inspector Notes: The sleek, urban and hip spot is matched by superlative service. Several cuts of wet- and dry-aged beef, Kobe beef and veal prove to be most popular. Tantalizing sauces accompany most steaks, and the selection of martinis is extensive. **Bar:** full bar. **Reservations:** suggested. **Address:** 103 Rhine Rd **Location:** West side of island; just w of Mullet Bay Golf Course; at Atlantis World Casino. (D)

LA GONDOLA RISTORANTE

Phone: 599/545-3938   (54)

Italian
$19-$39

AAA Inspector Notes: Patrons have a choice of seating in the bistro's intimate, air-conditioned dining room or on the small street side patio. Friendly, attentive servers in sharp attire carry around plates of homemade pasta and other traditional fare along the lines of lobster ravioli or beef tenderloin in a light Gorgonzola sauce. **Bar:** full bar. **Reservations:** required. **Address:** The Lowlands **Location:** Just w of Mullet Bay Golf Course; at Atlantis World Casino. **Parking:** on-site and valet.

(D)

LE MONTMARTRE   Phone: 599/545-3939   (52)

French
$26-$50

AAA Inspector Notes: Patrons can splurge on a real slice of French ambience and cuisine on the Dutch side of the island. Servers deftly perform filleting. The chefs prepare such temptations as sea bass with Provencal sauce. Fresh, artistic presentations of delectable tiramisu, creme brulee and profiteroles complete a memorable meal. **Bar:** full bar. **Reservations:** required. **Address:** Atlantis World Casino **Location:** Southwest corner of island; just e of French/Dutch border; at Atlantis World Casino. **Parking:** on-site and valet. (D) (N)

LITTLE BAY

• Hotels & Restaurants index & map p. 478

BELAIR BEACH HOTEL   Phone: 599/542-3362   (30)

Condominium
$259-$429

Address: Welgelen Rd, #70 **Location:** Oceanfront. 3 mi (4.8 km) w of Philipsburg; 4.5 mi (7.2 km) e of airport, 3.1 mi (5 km) se. **Facility:** Meets AAA guest room security requirements. 71 condominiums. 4 stories, exterior corridors. **Terms:** check-in 4 pm, 3 night minimum stay - seasonal, 21 day cancellation notice, 14 day off season-fee imposed. **Amenities:** safes. **Pool(s):** outdoor. **Activities:** rental paddleboats, rental sailboards, tennis court. Fee: scuba diving, snorkeling, massage. **Guest Services:** valet and coin laundry.

(See map & index p. 480.)

DIVI LITTLE BAY BEACH RESORT

Phone: (599)542-2333 **31**

Resort Hotel
$208-$812

Address: Little Bay Rd **Location:** Oceanfront. 2.7 mi (4.3 km) w of Philipsburg. **Facility:** Offering hotel and condo-style units, the resort is superbly located on a peninsula surrounded by a white-sand beach with views of Philipsburg. 210 units, some two bedrooms and kitchens. 1-3 stories (no elevator), exterior corridors. **Terms:** check-in 4 pm, 3 night minimum stay, cancellation fee imposed. **Amenities:** safes. **Dining:** 3 restaurants. **Pool(s):** 3 outdoor. **Activities:** whirlpools, rental boats, rental canoes, lighted tennis court, recreation programs, volleyball, exercise room, spa. **Fee:** scuba diving, snorkeling. **Guest Services:** valet and coin laundry.

MAHO BAY (C-1)
• Hotels & Restaurants index & map p. 478

SONESTA MAHO BEACH RESORT & CASINO

Phone: (599)545-2115 **34**

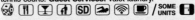
Resort Hotel
$190-$700

Address: Maho Bay **Location:** Oceanfront. 0.4 mi (0.6 km) w of Princess Juliana International Airport. **Facility:** 537 units. 6-10 stories, interior corridors. **Parking:** on-site (fee). **Terms:** 8 day cancellation notice-fee imposed. **Amenities:** safes. **Dining:** 3 restaurants, entertainment. **Pool(s):** 2 outdoor. **Activities:** snorkeling, recreation programs, volleyball, exercise room, spa. **Fee:** 4 lighted tennis courts. **Guest Services:** valet laundry.

OYSTER POND (ST. MAARTEN)
• Restaurants p. 483
• Hotels & Restaurants index & map p. 478

THE WESTIN ST. MAARTEN DAWN BEACH RESORT & SPA

Phone: (599)543-6700 **27**

Resort Hotel
$397-$666

WESTIN HOTELS & RESORTS

AAA Benefit: Enjoy up to 15% off your next stay, plus Starwood Preferred Guest® bonuses.

Address: 144 Oyster Pond Rd **Location:** Oceanfront. 5.9 mi (9.4 km) e of Princess Juliana International Airport. **Facility:** Situated on Dawn Beach, the full-service resort features well-appointed accommodations. Meets AAA guest room security requirements. 317 units, some two bedrooms. 3 stories, interior corridors. **Parking:** on-site and valet. **Terms:** 90 day cancellation notice, 15 day off season. **Amenities:** high-speed Internet (fee), safes, honor bars. **Dining:** 2 restaurants, also, Aura, see separate listing, entertainment. **Pool(s):** outdoor. **Activities:** saunas, whirlpool, steamrooms, recreation programs, playground, volleyball, exercise room, spa. **Fee:** scuba diving, snorkeling. **Guest Services:** valet laundry. **Free Special Amenities:** local telephone calls and newspaper.
(See ad p. 482, p. 217.)

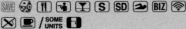

▼ See AAA listing p. 481 ▼

Embrace Calm.

Unkink your body. Soothe your spirit. Book your next vacation getaway at the Westin St. Maarten Dawn Beach Resort & Spa, where the mind and body are always renewed. Conveniently located in a tropical paradise in close proximity to the ambiance of the French side and the energy of the Dutch side.

- Renew your spirit in the luxurious Hibiscus Spa
- Enjoy breathtaking views in one of our exquisite restaurants, including AAA Four Diamond rated Aura Steak House
- Try your luck in the on-site casino

For more information, please call 1-800-937-8461 or visit westin.com/stmaartenspecials.

THE WESTIN

ST. MAARTEN DAWN BEACH
RESORT & SPA

(See map & index p. 480.)

WHERE TO EAT

AURA Phone: 599/543-6700 42

Steak
$33-$45

AAA Inspector Notes: This upscale steakhouse with a refined ambience offers a 21-day dry aged Angus beef that is succulent and flavorful. Recommended starters are the escargot with foie gras and the jumbo shrimp cocktail. Other highlights include Colorado lamb, veal, salmon and a variety of beef cuts. The side dishes are great for sharing. **Bar:** full bar. **Reservations:** suggested. **Address:** 144 Oyster Pond Rd **Location:** 5.9 mi (9.4 km) e of Princess Juliana International Airport; In The Westin St. Maarten Dawn Beach Resort & Spa. **Parking:** on-site and valet. D

PHILIPSBURG (C-3)

• **Hotels & Restaurants index & map p. 478**

ANTOINE BY THE SEA Phone: 599/542-2964 75

International
$11-$38

AAA Inspector Notes: The restaurant has been impressing patrons since 1978. Chef Jean-Pierre combines traditional French cuisine with some Italian influences. Escargots, homemade pate and vichyssoise are great beginnings. Seafood specialties include red snapper, tuna steak, baked salmon and shrimp scampi, and duck Montmorency is another rich and flavorful choice. The attractively priced three-course menu also is worth a look. **Bar:** full bar. **Reservations:** suggested. **Address:** 119 Front St **Location:** Downtown; on waterfront boardwalk. **Parking:** valet and street only. L D

THE GREENHOUSE BAR AND RESTAURANT Phone: 599/542-2941 78

International
$10-$28

AAA Inspector Notes: For more than 25 years this restaurant has been a consistent favorite among island visitors and locals alike. Located at Bobby's Marina with views of Great Bay, the casual eatery has a fun loving staff offering an array of whimsically named drinks. The varied menu includes conch fritters, nachos, chicken wings and jalapeno poppers for starters. Offered are a variety of entrée size salads, ribs, pasta and seafood as well as such sandwiches as the classic Reuben and Philly cheesesteak. **Bar:** full bar. **Address:** Bobby's Marina **Location:** Just e of downtown; on boardwalk; at Bobby's Marina, Great Bay.

L D

SHIV SAGAR BAR & RESTAURANT Phone: 599/542-2299 77

Indian
$10-$22

AAA Inspector Notes: Just upstairs from the hustle and bustle of the shops on Front Street is an oasis for fine Indian dining. Pleasant uniformed staffers offer many suggestions from the extensive menu, including well-prepared and exotically spiced dishes, curries and tandoori selections. **Bar:** full bar. **Address:** 20 Front St **Location:** Center of downtown. **Parking:** street only.

L D

Enjoy great savings
on hotel rates at
AAA.com or CAA.ca

SIMPSON BAY (C-2)

• **Hotels & Restaurants index & map p. 478**

SKIP JACK'S SEAFOOD GRILL, BAR & FISH MARKET Phone: 599/544-2313 80

Seafood
$17-$28

AAA Inspector Notes: The popular restaurant prepares numerous grilled and seared cuts of meat and fish. The superb lunch spot serves gourmet burgers and entree-size salads. Diners might start a meal with peel-and-eat shrimp or crab cakes or enjoy a libation in the sunken bar area designed to resemble a boat. The good-humored staff provides island-friendly and mostly efficient service. **Bar:** full bar. **Address:** Airport Rd **Location:** 0.4 mi (0.6 km) e of Princess Juliana International Airport.

L D

TOP CARROT Phone: 599/544-3381 85

Natural/Organic
$8-$15

AAA Inspector Notes: A good place for a quick breakfast or lunch, the eatery focuses on vegetarian and Middle East-inspired sandwiches and dishes. Popular as well are nutrition drinks that blend such ingredients as carrot juice, wheatgrass and ginger. Ethnic craft displays lend to the decor. **Address:** Airport Rd **Location:** 1.2 mi (1.9 km) of Princess Juliana International Airport; in Plaza del Lago.

B L

St. Martin

ANSE MARCEL (A-3)

• **Hotels & Restaurants index & map p. 478**

MARQUIS BOUTIQUE HOTEL & SPA Phone: (590)590-29-42-30 38

Boutique Hotel
$335-$1115

Address: Pigeon Pea Hill 97150 **Location:** Above Anse Marcel Beach, follow signs; north coast of island. **Facility:** The charming boutique hotel is perched on a hill overlooking Marcel Bay and boasts an intimate European ambience. 17 units. 2 stories (no elevator), exterior corridors. **Terms:** office hours 7:30 am-10:30 pm, check-in 4 pm, 21 day cancellation notice, 14 day off season. **Amenities:** safes, honor bars. **Pool(s):** outdoor. **Activities:** 4 lighted tennis courts. **Fee:** massage. **Guest Services:** valet laundry, area transportation-Anse Marcel Beach.

THE RADISSON BLU ST. MARTIN RESORT MARINA AND SPA Phone: (590)590-87-67-00 36

Hotel
$266-$1269

Address: BP 581 Anse Marcel 97056 St Martin CEDEX 97150 **Location:** Oceanfront. North coast of island. **Facility:** This renovated and upgraded bayfront property offers picturesque views; guest rooms are well appointed. 253 units. 2-3 stories, interior/exterior corridors. **Terms:** 21 day cancellation notice, 7 day off season-fee imposed. **Amenities:** high-speed Internet, safes, honor bars. **Dining:** 2 restaurants. **Pool(s):** outdoor. **Activities:** whirlpool, paddleboats, recreation programs, playground, volleyball, exercise room, spa. **Fee:** marina, scuba diving, snorkeling. **Guest Services:** valet laundry. **Free Special Amenities:** high-speed Internet. (See ad p. 484, p. 218.)

▼ See AAA listing p. 483 ▼

GRAND CASE (A-3)
• Hotels & Restaurants index & map p. 478

HOTEL L'ESPLANADE
Phone: 590/590-87-06-55

Motel
$245-$595

Address: On the Hill 97150 **Location:** Just ne of downtown; just n of Grand Case Airport. **Facility:** 24 units, some efficiencies and kitchens. 2 stories (no elevator), exterior corridors. **Terms:** open 12/1-9/1 & 10/1-11/30, office hours 7:30 am-9 pm, check-in 4 pm, 45 day cancellation notice, 21 day off season-fee imposed. **Amenities:** high-speed Internet, safes. **Pool(s):** outdoor. **Activities:** *Fee:* massage. **Guest Services:** valet laundry.

LE PETIT HOTEL
Phone: 590/590-29-09-65

Motel
$265-$625

Address: 248 Blvd de Grand Case 97150 **Location:** Oceanfront. 0.9 mi (1.5 km) from Grand Case Airport; 9.7 mi (15.5 km) from Princess Juliana International Airport; west end of Grand Case Village. **Facility:** 10 efficiencies. 3 stories (no elevator), exterior corridors. **Terms:** open 12/1-9/13 & 9/30-11/30, office hours 9 am-5 pm, 45 day cancellation notice, 21 day off season-fee imposed. **Amenities:** high-speed Internet, safes. **Guest Services:** valet laundry.

WHERE TO EAT

THE BLUE MARTINI RESTAURANT, BAR AND TROPICAL GARDEN
Phone: 590/590-29-27-93 ⑪

French
$24-$45

AAA Inspector Notes: Veteran restaurateur Pascal has created another chic eatery in downtown Grand Case. The bold red interior is in a Creole house, reputed to be the oldest in town. The varied menu offers French-based cuisine with Mediterranean and Asian influences. Entree-size salads, pasta and gourmet pizza line the menu as well as escargot, beef carpaccio, foie gras and a variety of tasty grilled kebabs. For the truly famished an all-you-can-eat foie gras and charcuterie can be enjoyed. **Bar:** full bar. **Reservations:** suggested. **Address:** 63 Blvd de Grand Case 97150 **Location:** Center of village. **Parking:** on-site (fee) and street. ⏴

IL NETTUNO
Phone: 590/590-87-77-38 ⑤

Italian
$25-$52

AAA Inspector Notes: Open-air tables offer a view of the waterfront on Grand Case Bay. A good wine list accompanies such fine quality and attractively presented dishes as the house specialty linguine frutti di mare. Servers are knowledgeable and personable. **Bar:** full bar. **Reservations:** required. **Address:** 70 Blvd de Grand Case 97150 **Location:** Center of village. **Parking:** on-site (fee) and street.

LA CALIFORNIA
Phone: 590/590-87-55-57 ⑨

International
$16-$41

AAA Inspector Notes: On the waterfront of the former fishing village of Grand Case, the gourmet restaurant presents a menu of exquisitely prepared meals, including frog's legs, crab cakes and foie gras pate appetizers and such popular entrees as lamb chops with baked goat cheese, pork tenderloin with fig sauce, gourmet pizzas and delicately prepared seafood. **Bar:** full bar. **Reservations:** suggested. **Address:** 134 Blvd de Grand Case 97150 **Location:** Center of village. **Parking:** on-site (fee) and street.

L'AUBERGE GOURMANDE
Phone: 590/590-87-73-37 ⑦

French
$22-$34

AAA Inspector Notes: In a historic Creole home with a street view, this small, candlelit dining room is a cozy, charmingly decorated spot for classic French cuisine. Homemade desserts are excellent, and the wine selection is good. Flavorful cuisine takes into account texture and color. Service is formal yet friendly. **Bar:** full bar. **Reservations:** suggested. **Address:** 89 Blvd de Grand Case 97150 **Location:** Center of village. **Parking:** on-site (fee) and street.

LE PRESSOIR
Phone: 590/590-87-76-62 ⑬

French
$38-$55

AAA Inspector Notes: The highly regarded restaurant in the "gourmet capital" of the Caribbean occupies a restored Creole cottage dating back to 1886. The chef shows his talents in lovingly preparing inspired dishes with exquisite sauces, specialized ingredients and artistic presentations. The suave wait staff complement the romantic dining experience with a casual elegance. **Bar:** full bar. **Reservations:** required. **Address:** 30 Blvd de Grand Case 97150 **Location:** Center of village. **Parking:** on-site (fee) and street. **Historic**

L'ESCAPADE
Phone: 590/590-87-75-04 ⑧

French
$33-$52

AAA Inspector Notes: In a French-Creole-style home, the restaurant prepares sumptuous fare for the discriminating palate. Among favorite dishes are Anguillan lobster, tuna tartare, veal sweetbreads, rack of lamb and mussels risotto. Service is casual. **Bar:** full bar. **Reservations:** required. **Address:** 94 Blvd de Grand Case 97150 **Location:** On waterfront; center of downtown. **Parking:** on-site (fee) and street.

LE TASTEVIN
Phone: 590/590-87-55-45 ③

French
$26-$56

AAA Inspector Notes: Diners can unwind on the open-balcony dining room on the bay while sampling lobster and other seafood specialties. Nouvelle creations are the kitchen's hallmark. The dining room sustains a relaxed, country-tropical charm. **Bar:** full bar. **Reservations:** required, for dinner. **Address:** 86 Blvd de Grand Case 97150 **Location:** Center of village. **Parking:** street only. **Historic**

SPIGA RESTAURANT
Phone: 590/590-52-47-83 ⑩

New Italian
$27-$43

AAA Inspector Notes: Creative Italian-inspired cuisine is served at this traditional French-Creole house with indoor or outdoor seating. The chef deftly prepares an array of dishes including daily specials. Favorites may include Colorado lamb with eggplant mousse, pappardelle pasta with braised beef, monkfish stuffed with shrimp and seafood risotto. Be sure to save room for dessert with such offerings as creme brulee, raspberry panna cotta and lemon ricotta cake with chocolate cannoli. **Bar:** full bar. **Reservations:** required. **Address:** 4 Route de L'Esperance 97150 **Location:** North end of Grand Case village; corner of Esperance Rd and Blvd de Grand Case. **Parking:** on-site (fee) and street.

MARIGOT (B-3) pop. 29,078
• **Hotels & Restaurants index & map p. 478**

HOTEL LA SAMANNA
Phone: (590)590-87-64-00 **18**

Resort Hotel
$395-$5275

Address: Baie Longue, Lowlands 97064 **Location:** Oceanfront. On Long Bay. **Facility:** An outstanding white-sand beach fronts this upscale property, where lodgings include individual Mediterranean-style villas, cottages and hotel rooms. 83 units, some two bedrooms and efficiencies. 2-4 stories (no elevator), interior/exterior corridors. **Terms:** open 12/1-9/1 & 11/1-11/30, 30 day cancellation notice, 14 day off season. **Amenities:** safes. **Dining:** 2 restaurants, also, The Restaurant at La Samanna, see separate listing, entertainment. **Pool(s):** 2 outdoor. **Activities:** sailboats, snorkeling, 3 lighted tennis courts, recreation programs, exercise room, spa. **Fee:** waterskiing, scuba diving. **Guest Services:** valet laundry.

MERCURE ST. MARTIN & MARINA
Phone: (590)590-87-54-54 **19**

Hotel
$108-$187

Address: Baie Nettle 97150 **Location:** Oceanfront. At Baie Nettle-Simson Beach; just s of downtown. **Facility:** 169 units. 3 stories (no elevator), exterior corridors. *Bath:* shower only. **Amenities:** safes. **Dining:** entertainment. **Pool(s):** outdoor. **Activities:** whirlpool, lighted tennis court, recreation programs, volleyball, exercise room, spa. *Fee:* paddleboats, scuba diving, snorkeling. **Guest Services:** valet laundry.

WHERE TO EAT

DON CAMILLO RESTAURANT
Phone: 590/590-87-52-88 **23**

Italian
$24-$39

AAA Inspector Notes: For more than 25 years, the restaurant has received rave reviews from diners, many of whom return year after year. Italian-Mediterranean cuisine focuses on the freshest available ingredients, including fish, lobster, calamari, octopus, beef, chicken, pork and shrimp. Dishes display the presentation and preparation skills of the chef. The waiter, John, shows true finesse in providing refined, detail-oriented service. **Bar:** full bar. **Reservations:** suggested. **Address:** 68 La Frigate **Location:** At Marina Port La Royale. **Parking:** street only.

LA MAIN A LA PATE
Phone: 590/590-87-71-19 **22**

Mediterranean
$18-$29

AAA Inspector Notes: In the Marigot Marina, where al fresco eateries abound, is this special gem. Gregarious servers are an appealing aspect, as is the menu, which lists gourmet pizza, varied pasta dishes and nearly a dozen entrée-size salads. Tempting desserts include creme brulee and tiramisu. **Bar:** full bar. **Reservations:** suggested. **Address:** Marina Port La Royale 97150 **Location:** Center; at Marina Port La Royale.

LE BISTRO DE LA MER
Phone: 590/590-29-57-44 **21**

French
$14-$32

AAA Inspector Notes: A projection screen shows music videos at the lively cafe, where patrons sit at sidewalk tables and can watch the activity in the lobster tank. Service is casual and deliberate, and the cuisine is the hallmark. The varied menu lists entrée-size salads, gourmet pizza, bouillabaisse, rib steak and pork ribs, as well as panini, burgers and sandwiches. **Bar:** full bar. **Address:** Blvd de France Philippe Laude 97150 **Location:** Front de la Mer; center of waterfront. **Parking:** street only.

LE CHANTECLAIR
Phone: 590/590-87-94-60 **35**

French
$32-$39

AAA Inspector Notes: A husband and wife team from Normandy offer original and fine French cuisine. Many daily specials employ the freshest specialty and seasonal ingredients. Offerings include foie gras preparations, lamb, duck and Caribbean shrimp. Not-to-be-missed desserts include stewed pineapple and fresh custard, as well as the famous no name dessert. Bon appetit! **Bar:** full bar. **Reservations:** suggested. **Address:** 19 Marina Port La Royale 97150 **Location:** Center; at Marina Port La Royale.

LE SANTAL BY THE SEA
Phone: 590/590-87-53-48 **29**

French
$33-$49

AAA Inspector Notes: The award-winning, long-established oceanfront restaurant pampers guests with refined, well-honed service in a romantic atmosphere. Exquisitely prepared cuisine is artistically presented. Among courses prepared tableside are Chateaubriand and flambeed dishes. The marriage of tantalizing flavors and complex cooking techniques showcases the chef's talents. Heavenly souffles in four flavors are a fine finish to an extraordinary dining experience. **Bar:** full bar. **Reservations:** required. **Address:** 40 rue Lady Fish 97150 **Location:** At Sandy Ground. **Parking:** on-site and valet.

MARIO'S BISTRO
Phone: 590/590-87-06-36 **26**

French
$31-$42

AAA Inspector Notes: Outstanding contemporary French cuisine reflects global and regional influences. The bright, colorful, open-air dining room overlooks the water. Service is well-executed, and dishes are prepared with quality ingredients and presented in an aesthetically attractive manner. **Bar:** full bar. **Reservations:** required. **Address:** Sandy Ground Bridge 44 Mornerond 97150 **Location:** Just w of Sandy Ground Bridge, 0.6 mi (1 km) w of center.

THE RESTAURANT AT LA SAMANNA
Phone: 590/590-87-64-00 **31**

International
$48-$54

AAA Inspector Notes: Enjoy a memorable dinner in this elegant open-air dining room overlooking beautiful Baie Longue. The cuisine is a fusion of French and Creole with Asian influences. The wine cellar boasts an extensive collection. Popular items include the French foie gras with pearls of ginger and rich lobster bisque flavored with local rum and star anise. Creative entrees include rack of lamb, braised veal cheeks and braised Chilean sea bass. Save room for the tempting desserts. **Bar:** full bar. **Reservations:** required. **Address:** Baie Longue, Lowlands 97064 **Location:** 5 mi (8 km) w on Long Bay; 1.5 mi (2.4 km) e of Princess Juliana International Airport; in Hotel La Samanna.

RESTAURANT LES BOUCANIERS
Phone: 590/590-29-21-75 **39**

Creole
$15-$29

AAA Inspector Notes: The husband and wife duo managing the restaurant exude warm hospitality in the dining room and talent in the kitchen. The chef, formerly of Le Chanteclair, excels in delivering original French and Creole cuisine. For starters try the "boudins Creole" or the "salade de la Mer." Besides nightly specials the menu features fish, seafood, duck and pork. **Bar:** full bar. **Address:** Lot 501 Nettle Bay Beach Club 97150 **Location:** 1.6 mi (2.5 km) w from Marigot Center; across from Baie Nettle.

ORIENT BAY
• **Hotels & Restaurants index & map p. 478**

LA PLANTATION
Boutique Hotel
$200-$355
Phone: (590)590-29-58-00 **15**
Address: C5 Orient Bay 97150 **Location:** Northeast corner of island at Orient Bay. **Facility:** Colonial-style villas on seven acres are near world-renowned Orient Bay Beach; units boast huge, fully furnished terraces and tasteful Caribbean décor. 52 units, some efficiencies and kitchens. 1 story, exterior corridors. *Bath:* shower only. **Terms:** open 12/1-9/1 & 10/15-11/30, office hours 8 am-9 pm, 30 day cancellation notice, 7 day off season-fee imposed. **Amenities:** safes. **Pool(s):** outdoor. **Activities:** limited beach access, 2 lighted tennis courts. **Fee:** massage. **Guest Services:** valet laundry.

PALM COURT HOTEL   **Phone:** (590)590-87-41-94   **17**
Motel
$260-$400
Address: Parc de la Baie Orientale 97150 **Location:** Northeast corner of island; at Orient Beach. **Facility:** 24 units. 3 stories (no elevator), exterior corridors. *Bath:* shower only. **Terms:** office hours 9 am-7 pm, 3 night minimum stay, 30 day cancellation notice-fee imposed. **Amenities:** safes. **Pool(s):** outdoor. **Activities:** limited beach access. **Guest Services:** area transportation.

Safety tip: Keep a current
AAA/CAA Road Atlas
in every vehicle

OYSTER POND (ST. MARTIN)
• **Hotels & Restaurants index & map p. 478**

CAPTAIN OLIVER'S RESORT AND MARINA
Hotel
$140-$335
Phone: (590)590-87-40-26   **26**
Address: Oyster Pond 97150 **Location:** Oceanfront. 7.5 mi (12 km) e of Princess Juliana International Airport. **Facility:** 37 units. 1 story, exterior corridors. *Bath:* shower only. **Terms:** office hours 7 am-10:30 pm, 3 night minimum stay - seasonal, 14 day cancellation notice, 7 day off season. **Amenities:** safes, honor bars. **Dining:** Captain Oliver's, see separate listing. **Pool(s):** outdoor. **Activities:** rental boats, rental sailboats, marina. **Fee:** scuba diving, snorkeling, charter fishing. **Guest Services:** valet laundry. Affiliated with A Preferred Hotel.

WHERE TO EAT

CAPTAIN OLIVER'S
Creole
$12-$27
Phone: 590/590-87-30-00   **44**
AAA Inspector Notes: The deck, which overlooks Oyster Pond and a marina, is a cozy spot for sampling fresh seafood with French and Creole influences. Other good choices include offerings from the barbecue grill. Live entertainment is offered six nights a week. **Bar:** full bar. **Reservations:** suggested. **Address:** Oyster Pond **Location:** 7.5 mi (11.2 km) e of Princess Juliana International Airport; in Captain Oliver's Resort and Marina.

ST. VINCENT AND THE GRENADINES

This index helps you "spot" where approved hotels and restaurants are located on the corresponding detailed maps. Hotel daily rate range is for comparison only and show the property's high season. Restaurant rate range is a combination of lunch and/or dinner. Turn to the listing page for more detailed rate information and consult display ads for special promotions.

ARNOS VALE

Map Page	Hotel	Diamond Rated	High Season	Page
❶ p. 489	Villa Lodge Hotel and Breezeville Apartments	▽▽	$115-$150	490

YOUNG ISLAND

Map Page	Hotel	Diamond Rated	High Season	Page
❸ p. 489	Young Island Resort	▽▽	$448-$1222	491

VILLA

Map Page	Hotel	Diamond Rated	High Season	Page
❹ p. 489	Beachcombers Hotel and Restaurant	▽	$90-$275	491

BEQUIA

Map Page	Hotels	Diamond Rated	High Season	Page
❻ p. 489	Firefly Bequia	▽▽▽	$525-$575	490
❼ p. 489	Sugar Apple Inn	▽▽	$96-$132	490

Map Page	Restaurant	Diamond Rated	Cuisine	Meal Range	Page
⑧ p. 489	Maria's French Terrace	▽▽	French	$9-$26	490

CANOUAN

Map Page	Hotels	Diamond Rated	High Season	Page
❽ p. 489	**Canouan Resort at Carenage Bay-The Grenadines** (See ad p. 490.)	▽▽▽▽	$850-$4085 [SAVE]	490
❾ p. 489	Tamarind Beach Hotel & Yacht Club	▽▽▽	$260-$750	491

PALM ISLAND

Map Page	Hotel	Diamond Rated	High Season	Page
⓬ p. 489	**Palm Island Resort**	▽▽▽	$855-$1285 [SAVE]	491

KINGSTOWN

Map Page	Restaurants	Diamond Rated	Cuisine	Meal Range	Page
② p. 489	Basil's Bar & Restaurant	▽	International	$10-$26	491
③ p. 489	Grenadine House	▽▽▽	Creole	$18-$30	491

© AAA

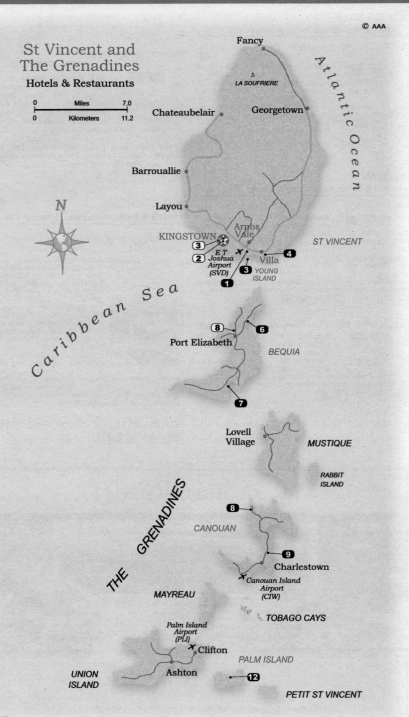

St Vincent and
The Grenadines
Hotels & Restaurants

| 0 | Miles | 7.0 |
| 0 | Kilometers | 11.2 |

N

Fancy

△
LA SOUFRIERE

Chateaubelair

Georgetown

Atlantic Ocean

Barrouallie

Layou

Arnos
Vale

KINGSTOWN

ST VINCENT

③

E T
② Joshua
Airport
(SVD)

✈

③

Villa

④

① YOUNG
ISLAND

Caribbean Sea

⑧

⑥

Port Elizabeth

BEQUIA

⑦

Lovell
Village

MUSTIQUE

*RABBIT
ISLAND*

THE GRENADINES

⑧

CANOUAN

⑨

Charlestown

✈ Canouan Island
Airport
(CIW)

MAYREAU

TOBAGO CAYS

Palm Island
Airport
(PLI)

✈ Clifton

PALM ISLAND

*UNION
ISLAND*

Ashton

⑫

PETIT ST VINCENT

1523-H

ARNOS VALE
• Hotels & Restaurants index & map p. 488

VILLA LODGE HOTEL AND BREEZEVILLE APARTMENTS
Phone: 784/458-4641

Motel
$115-$150

Address: Indian Bay **Location:** 3 mi (4.8 km) se of airport. **Facility:** 9 kitchen units, some two bedrooms. 2 stories (no elevator), interior/exterior corridors. **Terms:** office hours 7 am-11 pm, 14 day cancellation notice. **Amenities:** safes. **Pool(s):** outdoor. **Guest Services:** valet laundry.

BEQUIA
• Hotels & Restaurants index & map p. 488

FIREFLY BEQUIA
Phone: 784/458-3414

Country Inn
$525-$575

Address: Spring Bay Rd **Location:** 1 mi (1.6 km) e of airport. **Facility:** Situated on a 30-acre working plantation, this intimate inn offers luxury comforts to create the ideal getaway. 4 units. 1-2 stories, exterior corridors. *Bath:* shower only. **Terms:** open 12/1-9/1 & 10/1-11/30, age restrictions may apply, 45 day cancellation notice-fee imposed. **Amenities:** safes, honor bars. **Pool(s):** outdoor. **Activities:** snorkeling. *Fee:* massage. **Guest Services:** valet laundry.

SUGAR APPLE INN
Phone: 784/457-3148

Motel
$96-$132

Address: Friendship Bay Rd **Location:** 1.5 mi (2.4 km) s of airport; 1.5 mi (2.4 km) e of ferry dock; at Friendship Bay. **Facility:** 8 kitchen units. 2 stories (no elevator), exterior corridors. *Bath:* shower only. **Terms:** 2 night minimum stay, 14 day cancellation notice. **Pool(s):** outdoor.

WHERE TO EAT

MARIA'S FRENCH TERRACE
Phone: 784/458-3337

French
$9-$26

AAA Inspector Notes: Located on the waterfront in a gingerbread-style house is this casual dining spot serving French cuisine with Caribbean and American influences, including a variety of sandwiches as well as entrée-size salads and pasta. Sunday evening features live music from 6:30-10 pm. Two-for-one sunset happy hour is offered Wednesday, Friday and Sunday. **Bar:** full bar. **Address:** Front St **Location:** At the waterfront; across from ferry docks. **Parking:** street only.

CANOUAN (E-3)
• Hotels & Restaurants index & map p. 488

CANOUAN RESORT AT CARENAGE BAY-THE GRENADINES
Phone: 784/458-8000

Resort Hotel
$850-$4085

Address: Canouan, The Grenadines **Location:** Oceanfront. North side of island. **Facility:** On a secluded island, the world-class resort features two beaches, a golf course, a 17th-century church, spa, fine dining restaurants and a casino. 88 units, some two bedrooms and houses. 1 story, exterior corridors. **Terms:** 30 day cancellation notice. **Amenities:** safes, honor bars. **Dining:** 4 restaurants, entertainment. **Pool(s):** outdoor. **Activities:** sailboats, windsurfing, snorkeling, recreation programs, bicycles, hiking trails, playground, volleyball, spa. *Fee:* golf-18 holes, putting green. **Guest Services:** valet laundry, area transportation (fee). **Free Special Amenities:** full breakfast and high-speed Internet. *(See ad this page.)*

▼ See AAA listing this page ▼

(See index & map p. 488.)

TAMARIND BEACH HOTEL & YACHT CLUB
Phone: 784/458-8044
Hotel
$260-$750
Address: Main Rd **Location:** Oceanfront. Just n of Grand Bay. **Facility:** 39 units, some efficiencies. 2 stories (no elevator), exterior corridors. **Terms:** 21 day cancellation notice, 14 day off season. **Amenities:** safes, honor bars. **Dining:** 2 restaurants. **Activities:** paddleboats, sailboats, windsurfing. **Fee:** scuba diving, golf-18 holes, massage. **Guest Services:** valet laundry.

KINGSTOWN (B-2) pop. 13,212
• Hotels & Restaurants index & map p. 488

BASIL'S BAR & RESTAURANT
Phone: 784/457-2713 (2)
International
$10-$26
AAA Inspector Notes: Convenient to businesses, shopping and the ferry dock, the downtown restaurant is in the historic Cobblestone Inn. Guests can stop in for the daily lunch buffet. Regional dishes reflect international influences. **Bar:** full bar. **Address:** Upper Bay St **Location:** Downtown; in Cobblestone Inn. **Parking:** street only.
B L D

Visit AAA.com or CAA.ca
for one-stop travel
planning and reservations

GRENADINE HOUSE **Phone: 784/493-1120** (3)
Creole
$18-$30
AAA Inspector Notes: Located in the lower level of an historical mid-18th-century home, this restaurant specializes in Creole and Western cuisine using fresh and local ingredients such as conch chowder, seared tuna and peppered sirloin steak. Desserts may include Key lime pie and coconut cake. Exposed stone walls, lovely tropical decor and linen topped tables add to the romantic appeal. Servers are professional and provide personal attention. **Bar:** full bar. **Location:** 1.2 mi (2 km) n of center. **Historic** D

PALM ISLAND
• Hotels & Restaurants index & map p. 488

PALM ISLAND RESORT **Phone: (784)458-8824** (12)
Resort Cottage
$855-$1285 12/1-4/14
$725-$1155 4/15-11/30
Address: Palm Island **Location:** Oceanfront. 1 mi (1.6 km) e of Union Island, accessed via property boat launch. **Facility:** This cabana-village resort on a secluded private tropical island boasts a beautiful white sand beach; cottages feature private indoor/outdoor showers. 43 units, some cottages. 1 story, exterior corridors. **Parking:** no self-parking. **Terms:** 30 day cancellation notice-fee imposed. **Amenities:** safes, honor bars. **Dining:** 2 restaurants, entertainment. **Pool(s):** outdoor. **Activities:** sailboats, windsurfing, boat dock, snorkeling, fishing, tennis court, bicycles, hiking trails, horseshoes, limited exercise equipment. **Fee:** charter fishing, massage. **Free Special Amenities:** early check-in/late check-out.

VILLA
• Hotels & Restaurants index & map p. 488

BEACHCOMBERS HOTEL AND RESTAURANT **Phone: 784/458-4283** (4)
Hotel
$90-$275
Address: Villa Main Rd **Location:** 3.5 mi (5.6 km) s of airport; center. **Facility:** 32 units, some efficiencies. 1-3 stories (no elevator), exterior corridors. **Bath:** shower only. **Terms:** office hours 7 am-10:30 pm, 14 day cancellation notice. **Amenities:** Some: safes. **Pool(s):** outdoor. **Activities:** sauna. **Guest Services:** valet laundry.

YOUNG ISLAND
• Hotels & Restaurants index & map p. 488

YOUNG ISLAND RESORT **Phone: 784/458-4826** (3)
Cottage
$448-$1222
Address: South Coast **Location:** Oceanfront. 4 mi (6.4 km) s of airport to Young Island Ferry Landing; call box at landing. Located on private island just off the coast of St. Vincent. **Facility:** 29 cottages. 1 story, exterior corridors. **Bath:** shower only. **Parking:** no self-parking. **Terms:** office hours 6:30 am-10 pm, 30 day cancellation notice-fee imposed. **Amenities:** safes. **Pool(s):** outdoor. **Activities:** paddleboats, sailboats, windsurfing, boat dock, snorkeling, lighted tennis court. **Fee:** massage. **Guest Services:** valet laundry, area transportation-St. Vincent & Young Island.

TRINIDAD AND TOBAGO

✈ Airport Accommodations				
Map Page	**PIARCO INTERNATIONAL AIRPORT**	Diamond Rated	High Season	Page
18 p. 494	Holiday Inn Express Hotel & Suites Trincity Trinidad Airport, 1 mi (1.5 km) n of airport	◆◆◆	$180-$300	499

✈ Airport Accommodations				
Map Page	**TOBAGO CROWN POINT AIRPORT**	Diamond Rated	High Season	Page
8 p. 494	Coco Reef Resort & Spa, 0.5 mi (0.8 km) n of airport	◆◆◆	$326-$1102	495

Trinidad and Tobago

This index helps you "spot" where approved hotels and restaurants are located on the corresponding detailed maps. Hotel daily rate range is for comparison only and show the property's high season. Restaurant rate range is a combination of lunch and/or dinner. Turn to the listing page for more detailed rate information and consult display ads for special promotions.

PLYMOUTH (Tobago)

Map Page	Hotel	Diamond Rated	High Season	Page
2 p. 494	Turtle Beach by Rex Resorts	◆◆	$300-$400	496

BLACK ROCK (Tobago)

Map Page	Hotel	Diamond Rated	High Season	Page
4 p. 494	Plantation Beach Villas	◆◆	$250-$710	495

CROWN POINT (Tobago)

Map Page	Hotel	Diamond Rated	High Season	Page
8 p. 494	Coco Reef Resort & Spa	◆◆◆	$326-$1102	495

Map Page	Restaurants	Diamond Rated	Cuisine	Meal Range	Page
22 p. 494	Bonkers Restaurant	◆◆	Caribbean	$12-$36	495
23 p. 494	Kariwak Village Restaurant	◆◆	Caribbean	$12-$41	495
24 p. 494	Café Iguana	◆	International	$10-$26	495
26 p. 494	Cafe Coco	◆◆	International	$10-$25	495
27 p. 494	Dillon's Seafood Restaurant	◆	Caribbean	$14-$33	495

PORT OF SPAIN (Trinidad)

Map Page	Hotels	Diamond Rated	High Season	Page
10 p. 494	The Carlton-Savannah (See ad p. 496.)	◆◆◆◆	$149-$199 [SAVE]	496
12 p. 494	Hyatt Regency Trinidad (See ad p. 497.)	◆◆◆◆	$149-$409 [SAVE]	498
13 p. 494	Courtyard by Marriott Port of Spain (See ad p. 497.)	◆◆◆	$148-$188 [SAVE]	496
14 p. 494	Hilton Trinidad & Conference Centre (See ad opposite title page.)	◆◆◆	$159-$189	496
15 p. 494	Kapok Hotel	◆◆	$176-$248	498
16 p. 494	Crowne Plaza Trinidad	◆◆◆	$165-$350	496

Map Page	Restaurants	Diamond Rated	Cuisine	Meal Range	Page
1 p. 494	Sweet Lime	◆	Caribbean	$19-$45	498
2 p. 494	Ca-Sa	◆◆◆◆	International	$39-$50	498
3 p. 494	Apsara	◆◆	Indian	$15-$52	498
5 p. 494	Il Colosseo Restaurant	◆◆	Italian	$12-$35	498
6 p. 494	Waterfront Restaurant	◆◆◆	International	$20-$40	499

Map Page	Restaurants (cont'd)	Diamond Rated	Cuisine	Meal Range	Page
⑦ p. 494	Joseph's	▼▼▼	International	$20-$66	498
⑧ p. 494	Angelo's Italian Restaurant	▼▼▼	Italian	$18-$52	498
⑨ p. 494	Battimamzelle Restaurant	▼▼▼	International	$17-$42	498
⑩ p. 494	Tiki Village Restaurant	▼▼▼	Asian	$12-$33	498
⑪ p. 494	Trotters	▼▼	International	$10-$58	499
⑫ p. 494	Woodford Cafe	▼▼	International	$17-$35	499
⑬ p. 494	Zanzibar	▼▼	International	$18-$56	499

TRINCITY (Trinidad)

Map Page	Hotel	Diamond Rated	High Season	Page
⑱ p. 494	Holiday Inn Express Hotel & Suites Trincity Trinidad Airport	▼▼▼	$180-$300	499

Map Page	Restaurant	Diamond Rated	Cuisine	Meal Range	Page
⑱ p. 494	Muscovado Restaurant	▼▼	International	$10-$25	499

VALSAYN

Map Page	Restaurants	Diamond Rated	Cuisine	Meal Range	Page
⑮ p. 494	Valpark Chinese Restaurant	▼▼	Chinese	$8-$24	499
⑯ p. 494	Rasam Authentic Indian Restaurant	▼▼	Indian	$17-$34	499

MOUNT PLEASANT (Tobago)

Map Page	Restaurants	Diamond Rated	Cuisine	Meal Range	Page
㉚ p. 494	Cafe Melange	▼▼	International	$16-$41	495
㉛ p. 494	Shirvan Watermill	▼▼▼	International	$20-$37	496
㉜ p. 494	MeShells	▼▼	Caribbean	$19-$47	495
㉞ p. 494	Patino's Restaurant	▼▼	International	$22-$41	495

Trinidad and Tobago

Hotels & Restaurants

Miles 0 — 10
Kilometers 0 — 16

St Giles Island

TOBAGO

Charlotteville
Parlatuvier Bay
Speyside
LITTLE TOBAGO
Castra Bay
Castara
Parlatuvier
Delaford
Moriah
Roxborough
Kings Bay
Les Coteaux
Pembroke
Plymouth
2
Mason Hall
Goldsborough Bay
Black Rock
4
Mt Irvine Bay
31 **32** &
Scarborough
Mount St George
22
34
Lambeau
Mount Pleasant
30
Store Bay
8
Canaan
26 & **27**
Atlantic Ocean
23
COLUMBUS PT
24
Crown Point
Crown Point Int'l Airport (TAB)

Miles 0 — 22
Kilometers 0 — 35

© AAA

Caribbean Sea

Grande Riviere
Sans Souci
GALERA PT
Matelot
Toco
Las Cuevas Bay
Blanchisseuse
RANGE
Redhead
La Vache Bay
Maracas Bay
EL CERRO DEL ARIPO
Green Hill
1
2
NORTHERN
Salybia
Balandra Bay
Four Roads
Tunapuna
Matura
Chaguaramas
10
15
Hollis Res
St Pierre
St Joseph
Valencia
Matura Bay
CHACACHACARE ISLANDS
San Juan
Valsayn
Arouca
PORT OF SPAIN
16
18
Arima
12 THRU **16**
Caroni R
18
Guanapo
Sangre Grande
3 THRU **13**
Caroni
Trin city
San Rafael
Guaico
Cheeyou
Chaguanas
Piarco Airport (POS)
Longdenville
Upper Manzanilla
Gulf of Paria
Waterloo
St Mary's
Tal-paro
Coryal
Manzanilla Bay
Couva
Gran Couva
Flanagin Town
Biche
California
Tabaquite
Cocos Bay
TRINIDAD
Claxton Bay
CENTRAL RANGE
Ecclesville
PT RADIX
Mayo
Pointe-a-Pierre
New Grant
Rio Claro
St Joseph Pierreville
San Fernando
Princes Town
River
Mayaro Bay
St Mary's
Guapo Bay
La Brea
Debe
Preau
Ortoire
Point Fortin
Fyzabad
Penal
Guayaguayare
Cedros Bay
Siparia
Basse-Terre
GALEOTA POINT
Bonasse
Buenos Ayres
Palo Seco
Moruga
TRINITY HILLS
Fullarton
Erin Bay
San Francique
La Lune
Moruga R
ICACOS POINT

© AAA
1524-U

Are we meeting your travel needs?

If your visit to an establishment listed in a AAA TourBook guide doesn't meet your expectations, tell us about it.

Complete an easy online form at
AAA.com/TourBookComments.

Tobago

BLACK ROCK
• Hotels & Restaurants index & map p. 492

PLANTATION BEACH VILLAS
Phone: 868/639-9377 **4**

◆◆ ◆◆
Vacation Rental House
$250-$710

Location: 7.5 mi (12 km) n of airport; on west coast. **Facility:** On a hill across a street from the beach, three-bedroom, three-bath villas offer large verandas with ocean views; only bedrooms have air-conditioning. 6 houses. 2 stories (no elevator), exterior corridors. *Bath:* shower only. **Terms:** office hours 8 am-6 pm, 3 night minimum stay, 45 day cancellation notice-fee imposed. **Amenities:** safes. **Pool(s):** outdoor. **Activities:** volleyball. **Guest Services:** complimentary laundry.

[icons]

CROWN POINT
• Hotels & Restaurants index & map p. 492

COCO REEF RESORT & SPA
Phone: (868)639-8571 **8**

◆◆◆
Resort Hotel
$326-$1102

Address: Lower Milford Rd **Location:** Oceanfront. 0.5 mi (0.8 km) e of Crown Point Airport; on Coconut Bay. **Facility:** Lush tropical foliage and a sugar-sand beach envelope this award-winning resort, where an attentive staff offers warm, Tobagonian hospitality. 138 units, some two bedrooms and kitchens. 2-3 stories (no elevator), interior/exterior corridors. **Terms:** 14 day cancellation notice, 7 day off season-fee imposed. **Amenities:** safes. *Some:* honor bars. **Dining:** 2 restaurants, entertainment. **Pool(s):** outdoor. **Activities:** sauna, canoeing, paddleboats, sailboats, windsurfing, snorkeling, 2 lighted tennis courts, exercise room. *Fee:* scuba diving, bicycles, massage. **Guest Services:** valet laundry.

[icons]

WHERE TO EAT

BONKERS RESTAURANT
Phone: 868/639-7173 **22**

◆◆ ◆◆
Caribbean
$12-$36

AAA Inspector Notes: An open-air restaurant in an unusual octagon shaped building, patrons can enjoy live music most night in the center-stage bar. The menu reflects Caribbean and West Indies culinary influences with dishes such as curry lamb, mojo chicken and tom tom tuna topped with green peppercorns, corn relish and ginger butter sauce. **Bar:** full bar. **Address:** Store Bay Local Rd **Location:** Just e of airport; in Toucan Inn & Bonkers.

[icons]

CAFE COCO
Phone: 868/639-0996 **26**

◆◆ ◆◆
International
$10-$25

AAA Inspector Notes: Fun Caribbean atmosphere offering open air dining in modern art gallery type setting. Unique table tops are a centerpiece on their own. Good menu variety featuring a spicy blend of Island, Mexican and vegetarian specialties. Fresh ingredients. **Reservations:** suggested. **Address:** Pigeon Point Rd **Location:** 0.8 mi (1.3 km) e of Crown Point Airport. **Parking:** street only. [icons]

CAFÉ IGUANA
Phone: 868/631-8205 **24**

◆◆
International
$10-$26

AAA Inspector Notes: Adjacent to the airport and the center of Crown Point, this al fresco eatery carries out a bluesy jazz theme in its decor. The menu consists of many local favorites, including fish, baked chicken and curried dishes. **Bar:** full bar. **Address:** Store Bay Local Rd **Location:** Just e of Crown Point Airport. **Parking:** street only. [icons]

DILLON'S SEAFOOD RESTAURANT
Phone: 868/639-8765 **27**

◆
Caribbean
$14-$33

AAA Inspector Notes: A favorite with the locals, this eatery with a plain exterior and Spartan dining room offers basic service. A typical selection of fresh seafood is presented daily in a casual and relaxed atmosphere. **Bar:** full bar. **Address:** Main Rd **Location:** Center. **Parking:** street only. [icons]

KARIWAK VILLAGE RESTAURANT
Phone: 868/639-8442 **23**

◆◆ ◆◆
Caribbean
$12-$41

AAA Inspector Notes: Well-prepared and presented West Indian cuisine is served amid attractive island decor. The accent is on fresh, grown-on-the-premises herbs. Open-air seating contributes to the relaxing tropical atmosphere. Full-course set meals are offered at dinner, while the lunch menu centers on lighter selections, such as salads and sandwiches. **Bar:** full bar. **Reservations:** suggested. **Address:** Store Bay Local Rd **Location:** Just outside Crown Point Airport; in Kariwak Village Hotel.

[icons]

MOUNT PLEASANT
• Hotels & Restaurants index & map p. 492

CAFE MELANGE
Phone: 868/631-0121 **30**

◆◆ ◆◆
International
$16-$41

AAA Inspector Notes: In a Creole-style house, this casual restaurant exhibits some hints of fine dining. Seating is mostly al fresco on the expanded porch. The eclectic menu is a showcase for the chef's talents and versatility. **Bar:** full bar. **Reservations:** suggested. **Address:** 133 Shirvan Rd **Location:** 3.8 mi (6.1 km) ne of Crown Point Airport. [icons]

MESHELLS
Phone: 868/631-0353 **32**

◆◆ ◆◆
Caribbean
$19-$47

AAA Inspector Notes: Most diners expect a seafood-only menu but, while seafood does steal center stage, there are steaks, pork chops and salads available. **Bar:** full bar. **Reservations:** suggested. **Address:** Old Buccoo Rd **Location:** Corner of Shirvan and Buccoo rds. [icons]

PATINO'S RESTAURANT
Phone: 868/639-9481 **34**

◆◆ ◆◆
International
$22-$41

AAA Inspector Notes: Offering a refreshing menu served in a garden-like ambiance, this restaurant features steaks, seafood, fish and a few pasta dishes are well prepared. **Bar:** full bar. **Reservations:** suggested. **Address:** 198-202 Shirvan Rd **Location:** Corner of Shirvan and Buccoo rds; in Buccoo; in Enchanted Waters. [icons]

(See index & map p. 492.)

SHIRVAN WATERMILL   Phone: 868/639-0000   31

▼▼▼

International

$20-$37

AAA Inspector Notes: In a restored sugar mill, the restaurant fills a peaceful, open-air setting. Candlelit tables, an attractive fountain and a fish pond lend to an elegant, yet relaxed, atmosphere. Creative regional selections center on seafood, duck, chicken and beef. **Bar:** full bar. **Reservations:** suggested, in season. **Address:** Shirvan Rd **Location:** 3.5 mi (5.6 km) e of Crown Point Airport, just n. D ◎

PLYMOUTH
• Hotels & Restaurants index & map p. 492

TURTLE BEACH BY REX RESORTS
                            Phone: (868)639-2851   2

▼▼▼

Hotel

$300-$400

Address: Plymouth Main Rd **Location:** Oceanfront. Just s of town; Courland Bay. **Facility:** 125 units. 2-3 stories (no elevator), exterior corridors. **Terms:** 30 day cancellation notice. **Amenities:** safes. **Dining:** entertainment. **Pool(s):** outdoor. **Activities:** whirlpool, rental canoes, tennis court, playground. **Fee:** paddleboats, windsurfing, snorkeling, massage. **Guest Services:** valet laundry.

Trinidad

PORT OF SPAIN (C-2) pop. 49,031
• Restaurants p. 498
• Hotels & Restaurants index & map p. 492

THE CARLTON-SAVANNAH   Phone: (868)621-5000   10

▼▼▼ ▼▼▼

Boutique
Contemporary Hotel

$149-$199

Address: 2-4 Coblentz Ave **Location:** Just off the Savannah; at St. Anne exit. **Facility:** Just off Queen's Park Savannah, the chic and stylish urban boutique hotel offers oversize guest units with contemporary comforts and conveniences. 165 units. 12 stories, interior corridors. **Parking:** on-site and valet. **Amenities:** high-speed Internet, safes. **Dining:** 2 restaurants, also, Ca-Sa, see separate listing. **Pool(s):** outdoor. **Activities:** exercise room. **Guest Services:** valet laundry. **Free Special Amenities:** newspaper and high-speed Internet. Affiliated with A Preferred Hotel. *(See ad this page.)*

COURTYARD BY MARRIOTT PORT OF SPAIN
                            Phone: (868)627-5555   13

▼▼▼

Hotel

$148-$188

AAA Benefit: AAA hotel discounts of 5% or more.

Address: Audrey Jeffers Hwy **Location:** At Invaders Bay; 1.7 mi (2.7 km) n of downtown; across from H Crawford Stadium and adjacent to Movie Town. **Facility:** Meets AAA guest room security requirements. 119 units. 4 stories, interior corridors. **Amenities:** high-speed Internet, safes. **Pool(s):** outdoor. **Activities:** exercise room. **Guest Services:** valet and coin laundry. *(See ad p. 497.)*

CROWNE PLAZA TRINIDAD
                            Phone: (868)625-3366   16

▼▼▼

Hotel

$165-$350

Address: 1017 Wrightson Rd **Location:** Center of downtown; 15 mi (24.1 km) nw of Piarco International Airport. **Facility:** Meets AAA guest room security requirements. 243 units. 15 stories, interior corridors. **Amenities:** safes. *Some:* high-speed Internet. **Dining:** 2 restaurants. **Pool(s):** outdoor. **Activities:** exercise room. **Fee:** massage. **Guest Services:** valet laundry.

HILTON TRINIDAD & CONFERENCE CENTRE
                            Phone: (868)624-3211   14

▼▼▼

Hotel

$159-$189

AAA Benefit:
Members save 5% or more everyday!

Address: 1B Lady Young Rd **Location:** On Belmont Hill; off Lady Young and Circular rds overlooking Queen's Park Savannah. **Facility:** 416 units, some kitchens. 6-9 stories, interior corridors. **Terms:** 1-7 night minimum stay, cancellation fee imposed. **Amenities:** high-speed Internet (fee), safes. **Dining:** 2 restaurants. **Pool(s):** outdoor. **Activities:** sauna, 2 lighted tennis courts, exercise room. **Fee:** massage. **Guest Services:** valet laundry. *(See ad opposite title page.)*

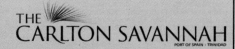

(See index & map p. 492.)

(See index & map p. 492.)

HYATT REGENCY TRINIDAD

Phone: (868)623-2222   **12**

Contemporary Hotel
$149-$409

HYATT HOTELS & RESORTS

AAA Benefit: Members save 10% or more everyday.

Address: 1 Wrightson Rd **Location:** On waterfront; downtown. **Facility:** Spacious guest units are appointed with luxury touches. The hotel features a gourmet restaurant and a rooftop pool with nice views. Meets AAA guest room security requirements. 428 units. 22 stories, interior corridors. **Terms:** 3 day cancellation notice-fee imposed. **Amenities:** high-speed Internet (fee), safes. **Dining:** 4 restaurants, also, Waterfront Restaurant, see separate listing, entertainment. **Pool(s):** outdoor. **Activities:** whirlpool, exercise room, spa. **Guest Services:** valet laundry. **Free Special Amenities:** newspaper. (See ad p. 497.)

[SAVE] [⏐⏐] [🛏] [Y] [S] [SD] [≈] [BIZ] [📶] [✕]
[🔒] [▣]

KAPOK HOTEL

Phone: (868)622-5765   **15**

Hotel
$176-$248

Address: 16-18 Cotton Hill, St. Clair **Location:** Just n of jct Circular and Maraval rds; north end of Queen's Park Savannah. **Facility:** 94 units, some efficiencies. 10 stories, interior corridors. **Terms:** 3 day cancellation notice-fee imposed. **Amenities:** high-speed Internet, safes. **Dining:** Tiki Village Restaurant, see separate listing. **Pool(s):** outdoor. **Activities:** exercise room. **Guest Services:** valet and coin laundry.

[⏐⏐] [🛏] [Y] [🏋] [SD] [≈] [BIZ] [📶] [✕] [🔒] [▣]
[/SOME UNITS] [▣]

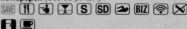

WHERE TO EAT

ANGELO'S ITALIAN RESTAURANT

Phone: 868/628-5551   **8**

Italian
$18-$52

AAA Inspector Notes: Native Italian-born chef Angelo is touted to be the most important Italian chef in Trinidad. This charming restaurant is housed in an Old World-style home with an enclosed piazza as well as elegant interior dining rooms that reflect an intimate, romantic ambience. Complimentary marinated olives help whet the appetite for well-prepared cuisine that includes a seafood fettuccine dish, veal tenderloin and gnocchi. **Bar:** full bar. **Reservations:** suggested. **Address:** 38 Ariapita Ave **Location:** Between Cornelio and Murray sts; in Ariapita Avenue entertainment strip. **Parking:** valet and street only.

[L] [D] [AC]

APSARA

Phone: 868/623-7659   **3**

Indian
$15-$52

AAA Inspector Notes: In one of the mansions that grace the streets of Queen's Savannah, the fine Indian restaurant prepares curries, tandoori and a variety of naans that please the palate. Servers in authentic Indian attire grace the well-appointed dining room. **Bar:** full bar. **Reservations:** required, for dinner. **Address:** 13 Queen's Park E **Location:** Downtown; east side of Queen's Park Savannah. **Historic** [L] [D]

BATTIMAMZELLE RESTAURANT

Phone: 868/621-0541   **9**

International
$17-$42

AAA Inspector Notes: An intimate dining area, with the choice of indoor or outdoor garden seating, offers detailed service and an award-winning wine list. The cuisine is nouvelle West Indian created by a talented chef. **Bar:** full bar. **Reservations:** required. **Address:** 44 Coblentz Ave **Location:** In Cascade section of downtown; in Coblentz Inn.

[B] [L] [D]

CA-SA

Phone: 868/621-5000   **2**

International
$39-$50

AAA Inspector Notes: Avant-garde cuisine can be found at this new urban boutique hotel. With a chic decor and deft service, guests are treated to an array of creative cuisine options. The geera shrimp with braised pig tails and the lamb panko with aubergine choka are two house favorites. In addition there are preparations of rabbit loin and curry duck. For a fantastic ending try the panna cotta or the tamarind cheesecake with Scotch bonnet sorbet. **Bar:** full bar. **Reservations:** suggested. **Address:** 2-4 Coblentz Ave **Location:** Just off the Savannah at St. Ann exit; in The Carlton-Savannah. **Parking:** on-site and valet. [D]

IL COLOSSEO RESTAURANT

Phone: 868/628-1494   **5**

Italian
$12-$35

AAA Inspector Notes: Refined decor with attentive service enrich the dining experience at this restaurant. The menu lists Southern and Northern Italian preparations of veal, beef, chicken and seafood, as well as a range of skillfully prepared pasta dishes. To finish the evening meal, take a look at the dessert trolley, which is a showcase of no fewer than 10 sweet treats. **Bar:** full bar. **Reservations:** suggested. **Address:** 16 Rust St **Location:** Downtown; in St. Clair sector. **Parking:** on-site and street. [L] [D]

JOSEPH'S

Phone: 868/622-5557   **7**

International
$20-$66

AAA Inspector Notes: The cuisine at this eatery ranges from Continental and West Indies to Middle Eastern. Some items to consider include escargots, tabbouleh, frog's legs, kibbeh and lamb specialties. **Bar:** full bar. **Reservations:** suggested. **Address:** 3A Rookery Nook Ave **Location:** Maraval section of Port of Spain; in Rookery Nook. [L] [D] [⬦]

SWEET LIME

Phone: 868/624-9983   **1**

Caribbean
$19-$45

AAA Inspector Notes: A popular gathering place for ex-pats, locals and tourists, this open-air eatery is adjacent to a casino and nightclub. Besides an array of tempting libations, the varied appetizer menu offers stuffed crab, Cajun wings and shark nuggets. Main courses include a variety of entree-size salads, burgers and sandwiches in addition to dishes such as lobster Taino, Yara Bay king fish and jerk rib-eye steak. **Bar:** full bar. **Address:** 19-23 Ariapita Ave **Location:** Corner of French St and Ariapita Ave; downtown. **Parking:** on-site and valet.

[L] [D] [LATE] [AC] [⬦]

TIKI VILLAGE RESTAURANT

Phone: 868/622-5765   **10**

Asian
$12-$33

AAA Inspector Notes: Chef Peter from Beijing brings his culinary talents to this rooftop restaurant with views of Port of Spain. The extensive menu ranges from sizzling fire pot dishes made with shrimp, beef and tofu to sesame fish, curried chicken and Mongolian-style beef. While the menu has a Polynesian flair dishes from around Asia can be found including Chinese pot stickers, spicy scallops in chili sauce and seafood noodles. **Bar:** full bar. **Reservations:** suggested. **Address:** 16-18 Cotton Hill Rd **Location:** Just n of jct Circular and Maraval rds; north end of Queen's Park Savannah; in Kapok Hotel. [B] [L] [D]

(See index & map p. 492.)

TROTTERS
Phone: 868/628-6461   (11)

International
$10-$58

AAA Inspector Notes: This restaurant, with a sports bar atmosphere, pays homage to sports, media and other cultural icons in a vivacious atmosphere offering a wide range of familiar dishes often with a signature twist. Lining the extensive menu are various burgers, gourmet pizza and entrée-size salads including Chinese chicken, Thai beef and Cobb. Other full size dishes include deep-fried chicken, shrimp and crab fettuccine and baby back ribs. For the health conscious there are some guilt-free options. **Bar:** full bar. **Address:** Maraval Rd **Location:** Corner of Maraval and Sweet Briar rds; just w of Queen's Park Savannah; in St. Clair sector. **Parking:** street only. [L] [D]

WATERFRONT RESTAURANT
Phone: 868/623-2222   (6)

International
$20-$40

AAA Inspector Notes: A combination of cooking styles is delivered from the exhibition kitchen. Start with the shrimp ceviche or the Trinidadian frito mixto which includes accras, eggplant and cassava. Main courses range from Chilean sea bass, lamb chops and seafood linguine. **Bar:** full bar. **Reservations:** suggested. **Address:** 1 Wrightson Rd **Location:** On waterfront; downtown; in Hyatt Regency Trinidad. [B] [L] [D]

WOODFORD CAFE
Phone: 868/627-2233   (12)

International
$17-$35

AAA Inspector Notes: Hearty portions of local and international cuisine is served in a vibrant and lively ambience. Favorites include entrée size salads, stewed pig tails, gourmet burgers and sandwiches as well as steak and salmon. Unplugged Tuesday features live entertainment. Kids eat free on Sunday. **Bar:** full bar. **Address:** Fiesta Plaza, Invaders Bay **Location:** At Invaders Bay; in Movie Towne Shopping Plaza. [L] [D]

ZANZIBAR
Phone: 868/627-0752   (13)

International
$18-$56

AAA Inspector Notes: Bright, stylish decor compliments the eclectic menu of offerings at this pub. Such starters as ceviche and stuffed portobello mushrooms help whet the appetite for the hearty main courses ranging from roasted rack of lamb and pork osso buco to honey and pineapple teriyaki salmon. The pyramid-shaped chocolate eruption cake with a caramel liquid center is a sweet ending. **Bar:** full bar. **Address:** Shop 54, Fiesta Plaza **Location:** At Invaders Bay; in Movie Towne Shopping Plaza.

[L] [D] [K]

TRINCITY
• Hotels & Restaurants index & map p. 492

HOLIDAY INN EXPRESS HOTEL & SUITES TRINCITY TRINIDAD AIRPORT
Phone: (868)669-6209   (18)

Hotel
$180-$300

Address: 1 Exposition Dr **Location:** 1 mi (1.5 km) n of airport. **Facility:** 82 units. 3 stories, interior corridors. **Amenities:** high-speed Internet, safes. **Pool(s):** outdoor. **Activities:** exercise room. **Guest Services:** area transportation-Trincity Mall & Muscovado Restaurant.

[⊞] [S] [SD] [⤴] [BIZ] [🛜] [✕] [▭]
/ SOME UNITS [🯄] [▣]

MUSCOVADO RESTAURANT
Phone: 868/640-9259   (18)

International
$10-$25

AAA Inspector Notes: Part of a country club golf course that is open to the public, this refined eatery employs a young, eager staff that serves international and West Indies cuisine. Grilled fish, meats and curries line the menu. **Bar:** full bar. **Reservations:** suggested. **Address:** Sunrise Loop Rd **Location:** At Millennium Lakes Golf & Country Club. [L] [D] [◪]

VALSAYN
• Hotels & Restaurants index & map p. 492

RASAM AUTHENTIC INDIAN RESTAURANT
Phone: 868/645-0994   (16)

Indian
$17-$34

AAA Inspector Notes: Rich Indian decor and well-prepared cuisine await guests dining here. Meals begin with a selection of chutneys and poppadom (wafer-thin bread). The chef prepares rich sauces made from a variety of spices and nuts with some items prepared in a tandoori oven. All items go wonderfully with the naan bread and basmati rice. The yogurt-based lassi drinks come in a number of flavors and cool the palate after such a spicy indulgence. **Reservations:** suggested. **Address:** City of Grand Bazaar **Location:** In City of Grand Bazaar Shopping Plaza. [L] [D]

VALPARK CHINESE RESTAURANT
Phone: 868/662-4540   (15)

Chinese
$8-$24

AAA Inspector Notes: This long standing restaurant is situated above a shopping center where locals flock most nights. Matter of fact service is provided by servers attired in traditional Chinese dress. Wednesdays and Sundays are buffet nights with an array of items including spare ribs, roast pork and pepper squid. Other nights the menu is a la carte featuring many Cantonese specialties. **Bar:** full bar. **Reservations:** suggested. **Address:** Morequito Ave **Location:** Center; in Valpark Shopping Plaza. [L] [D]

TURKS AND CAICOS ISLANDS

This index helps you "spot" where approved hotels and restaurants are located on the corresponding detailed maps. Hotel daily rate range is for comparison only and show the property's high season. Restaurant rate range is a combination of lunch and/or dinner. Turn to the listing page for more detailed rate information and consult display ads for special promotions.

NORTH CAICOS

Map Page	Hotel	Diamond Rated	High Season	Page
● p. 501	Parrot Cay Resort & Como Shambhala Retreat	▽▽▽	$696-$4574	502

PROVIDENCIALES

Map Page	Hotels	Diamond Rated	High Season	Page
● p. 501	**Villa del Mar**	▽▽▽	$225-$750 [SAVE]	505
● p. 501	**The Regent Grand Resort and Spa** (See ad p. 505.)	▽▽▽▽	$375-$3100 [SAVE]	504
● p. 501	The Tuscany	▽▽▽	$525-$1425	505
● p. 501	**Grace Bay Club**	▽▽▽▽	$550-$2200 [SAVE]	502
● p. 501	Ocean Club Resorts Ocean Club and Ocean Club West	▽▽▽	$179-$720	502
● p. 501	Royal West Indies Resort	▽▽▽	$180-$845	505
● p. 501	Villa Renaissance	▽▽▽	$510-$990	506
● p. 501	**Le Vele**	▽▽▽	$348-$1448 [SAVE]	502
● p. 501	**Point Grace** (See ad p. 504.)	▽▽▽	$425-$3281 [SAVE]	504
● p. 501	**The Regent Palms Turks and Caicos**	▽▽▽▽	$450-$3150 [SAVE]	505
● p. 501	**Comfort Suites-Turks and Caicos** (See ad p. 503.)	▽▽	$129-$234 [SAVE]	502
● p. 501	Beaches Turks & Caicos Resort Villages & Spa (See ad on insert.)	▽▽▽▽	$1120-$6890	502

Map Page	Restaurants	Diamond Rated	Cuisine	Meal Range	Page
② p. 501	Opus Wine Bar & Grill	▽▽▽	International	$21-$36	507
④ p. 501	Yoshi's Sushi Bar & Japanese Restaurant	▽▽	Japanese	$18-$39	507
⑤ p. 501	Mango Reef Restaurant	▽▽	International	$9-$34	507
⑥ p. 501	Calico Jacks Bar and Restaurant	▽▽	International	$9-$22	506
⑦ p. 501	Anacaona	▽▽▽▽	International	$30-$42	506
⑧ p. 501	**Grace's Cottage**	▽▽▽	International	$43-$54	507
⑨ p. 501	Hemingway's on the Beach	▽▽	International	$11-$33	507
⑩ p. 501	Bay Bistro	▽▽	International	$14-$32	506
⑪ p. 501	**Parallel23**	▽▽▽▽	International	$26-$37	507
⑬ p. 501	Caicos Cafe Bar & Grill	▽▽	Mediterranean	$11-$32	506
⑭ p. 501	Coco Bistro	▽▽▽	International	$28-$39	506
⑰ p. 501	Bella Luna Ristorante	▽▽▽	Regional Italian	$16-$32	506
⑱ p. 501	Danny Buoys Irish Pub and Restaurant	▽▽	International	$11-$28	506
⑳ p. 501	Saltmills Cafe & Diner	▽	Breakfast	$11-$19	507
㉔ p. 501	Magnolia Wine Bar & Restaurant	▽▽▽	International	$24-$38	507
㉗ p. 501	Coyaba	▽▽▽	New Caribbean	$32-$42	506
㉘ p. 501	Baci Ristorante	▽▽	Italian	$12-$28	506
㉚ p. 501	The Tiki Hut-Cabana Bar and Grill	▽▽	International	$10-$26	507

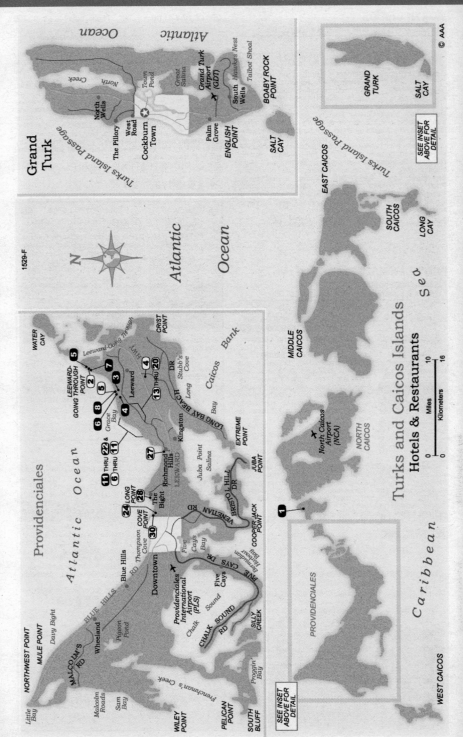

Turks and Caicos Islands
Hotels & Restaurants

NORTH CAICOS
• **Hotels & Restaurants index & map p. 500**

PARROT CAY RESORT & COMO SHAMBHALA RETREAT
Phone: (649)946-7788 **1**

Resort Hotel
$696-$4574

Address: Parrot Cay **Location:** Oceanfront. In Parrot Cay; private island off northwest coast of North Caicos Island; reached by boat launch from Providenciales. **Facility:** The world-renowned, award-winning resort is set on a private island and offers large units with upscale amenities, a luxury spa and attentive service. Meets AAA guest room security requirements. 65 units, some two bedrooms, three bedrooms, efficiencies, kitchens and houses. 1-2 stories (no elevator), exterior corridors. **Parking:** no self-parking. **Terms:** 3-10 night minimum stay, 30 day cancellation notice, 14 day off season. **Amenities:** safes, honor bars. **Dining:** 2 restaurants. **Pool(s):** 2 outdoor. **Activities:** saunas, whirlpools, steamrooms, canoeing, sailboats, windsurfing, snorkeling, 2 lighted tennis courts, exercise room, spa. **Guest Services:** valet laundry.

PROVIDENCIALES (B-2) pop. 15,000
• **Restaurants p. 506**
• **Hotels & Restaurants index & map p. 500**

BEACHES TURKS & CAICOS RESORT VILLAGES & SPA
Phone: (649)946-8000 **22**

Resort Hotel
$1120-$6890 12/1-4/15
$1082-$6890 4/16-11/30

Address: Lower Bight Rd **Location:** Oceanfront. From airport, 7 mi (11.2 km); on north coast. **Facility:** The resort's extensive facilities and elegantly equipped units and villa suites are set in tropical gardens; the French and Italian villages are notable. 614 units, some two bedrooms, three bedrooms and efficiencies. 1-3 stories, interior/exterior corridors. **Terms:** 3 night minimum stay - seasonal, 45 day cancellation notice-fee imposed. **Amenities:** safes. *Some:* honor bars. **Dining:** 10 restaurants, nightclub, entertainment. **Pool(s):** 3 outdoor, 4 heated outdoor. **Activities:** saunas, whirlpools, steamrooms, waterslide, lifeguard on duty, boating, paddleboats, sailboats, windsurfing, scuba diving, snorkeling, 4 lighted tennis courts, recreation programs, playground, basketball, game room, shuffleboard, volleyball, spa. *Fee:* charter fishing. **Guest Services:** valet and coin laundry. *(See ad on insert.)*

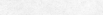

COMFORT SUITES-TURKS AND CAICOS
Phone: (649)946-8888 **17**

Motel
$129-$234

Address: Grace Bay Rd **Location:** North coast at Grace Bay; 8 mi (12.8 km) from airport. Adjacent to Ports of Call Shopping and Dining Complex. **Facility:** Meets AAA guest room security requirements. 98 units. 3 stories (no elevator), interior/exterior corridors. **Terms:** cancellation fee imposed. **Amenities:** safes. **Pool(s):** outdoor. **Guest Services:** valet laundry. **Free Special Amenities:** continental breakfast and high-speed Internet. *(See ad p. 503.)*

GRACE BAY CLUB
Phone: 649/946-5050 **6**

Boutique Resort Hotel
$550-$2200

Address: Inner Grace Bay Cir **Location:** Oceanfront. Grace Bay; 8.7 mi (13.9 km) e of airport. **Facility:** On Grace Bay, the oceanfront property offers spacious one-room units to three-bedroom condominiums, adult and family-friendly pools and a spa. 132 units, some two bedrooms, three bedrooms and kitchens. 3-6 stories, exterior corridors. **Terms:** open 12/1-9/4 & 10/4-11/30, 5 night minimum stay - seasonal, 30 day cancellation notice. **Amenities:** safes. **Dining:** 3 restaurants, also, Anacaona, see separate listing, entertainment. **Pool(s):** 3 outdoor. **Activities:** whirlpools, steamrooms, sailboats, windsurfing, snorkeling, 2 lighted tennis courts, bicycles, exercise room, spa. **Guest Services:** valet laundry, area transportation-within Grace Bay. **Free Special Amenities:** full breakfast and high-speed Internet.

LE VELE
Phone: (649)941-8800 **12**

Condominium
$348-$1448

Address: Grace Bay Rd **Location:** Oceanfront. Grace Bay; 6 mi (9.9 km) e of airport. Located in Princess Alexander Park. **Facility:** An Italian-inspired design, spacious guest units with solid wood furnishings and a 30-foot balcony with bay views identify this property. Meets AAA guest room security requirements. 9 condominiums. 5 stories, interior/exterior corridors. **Terms:** 21 day cancellation notice-fee imposed. **Amenities:** safes. **Pool(s):** outdoor. **Activities:** bicycles, exercise room. **Guest Services:** complimentary laundry. **Free Special Amenities:** continental breakfast and high-speed Internet.

The turquoise water and the white powdery sand of Grace Bay await you for this special occasion!

OCEAN CLUB RESORTS OCEAN CLUB AND OCEAN CLUB WEST
Phone: 649/946-5880 **7**

Condominium
$179-$720

Address: Grace Bay Rd **Location:** Oceanfront. North coast at Grace Bay; 9.7 mi (15.5 km) e of airport. **Facility:** These two different properties one mile apart offer varied studio and one-, two- and three-bedroom, condominium-style units. Meets AAA guest room security requirements. 164 condominiums. 3 stories (no elevator), interior/exterior corridors. **Terms:** office hours 6 am-11 pm, check-in 4 pm, 21 day cancellation notice-fee imposed. **Amenities:** safes. **Dining:** 2 restaurants. **Pool(s):** 3 outdoor. **Activities:** rental boats, rental canoes, rental sailboats, rental sailboards, 3 lighted tennis courts, bicycles, exercise room. *Fee:* scuba diving, snorkeling, massage. **Guest Services:** complimentary laundry, area transportation-between Ocean Club & Ocean Club West.

Learn about AAA/CAA Diamond Ratings at AAA.com/Diamonds

(See map & index p. 501.)

▼ See AAA listing p. 502 ▼

An inviting oasis steps from Grace Bay Beach

Located on the island of Providenciales, the hotel is surrounded by lush tropical gardens, just across the street from Grace Bay Beach and adjacent to the Ports of Call Shopping Village with a variety of restaurants, bars and shops.
- Free continental breakfast
- Free WiFi

- Palm shaded pool deck and bar
- 100% smoke free
- Walking distance to Grace Bay Beach with shades and lounges
- Conveniently located near: snorkeling, scuba diving, deep sea fishing and the championship 18-hole Provo Golf Club

COMFORT SUITES

BY CHOICE HOTELS

For special AAA member rates, call 888.9.SUNFUN or visit choicecaribbean.com

Create complete trip routings and custom maps with the TripTik® Travel Planner on AAA.com or CAA.ca

(See map & index p. 501.)

POINT GRACE

Boutique Hotel
$425-$3281

Phone: (649)946-5096 **13**

Address: Grace Bay Rd **Location:** Oceanfront. 7.6 mi (12.1 km) e of airport; Grace Bay. Located in Princess Alexander Park, a marine reserve. **Facility:** Exquisite property for those with discriminating tastes; the spacious, equipped to the hilt suites feature Indonesian furniture and exotic fabrics. 28 kitchen units, some two and three bedrooms. 4 stories, exterior corridors. **Terms:** open 12/1-9/1 & 10/1-11/30, 30 day cancellation notice-fee imposed. **Amenities:** safes. **Dining:** Grace's Cottage, see separate listing. **Pool(s):** outdoor. **Activities:** whirlpool, sailboats, windsurfing, snorkeling, bicycles. *Fee:* massage. **Guest Services:** valet and coin laundry, area transportation-golf course, fitness center, tennis facilities. **Free Special Amenities:** continental breakfast and high-speed Internet.
(See ad this page.)

 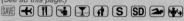

THE REGENT GRAND RESORT AND SPA

Condominium
$375-$3100

Phone: (649)941-7770 **4**

Address: Regent St **Location:** Oceanfront. 8.1 mi (13 km) e of airport; at Grace Bay. **Facility:** This well-appointed residential, luxury-style property is welcoming. Meets AAA guest room security requirements. 22 condominiums. 2-7 stories, interior/exterior corridors. **Terms:** check-in 4 pm, 30 day cancellation notice-fee imposed. **Amenities:** safes. **Pool(s):** heated outdoor. **Activities:** whirlpools, lighted tennis court, bicycles, exercise room. *Fee:* massage. **Guest Services:** complimentary laundry. **Free Special Amenities:** manager's reception and airport transportation.
(See ad p. 505.)

  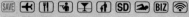

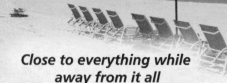

Learn about AAA/CAA Diamond Ratings
at AAA.com/Diamonds

(See map & index p. 501.)

THE REGENT PALMS TURKS AND CAICOS
Phone: (649)946-8666

Boutique Resort Hotel
$450-$3150

Address: 16 Princess Dr **Location:** Oceanfront. Grace Bay; 6.9 mi (11.1 km) e of airport. **Facility:** The upscale resort promises attentive service and spacious island-style units with the finest comforts and luxuries. Meets AAA guest room security requirements. 164 units, some two bedrooms, three bedrooms and kitchens. 5 stories, interior corridors. **Parking:** on-site and valet. **Terms:** 21 day cancellation notice, 7 day off season-fee imposed. **Amenities:** high-speed Internet, safes. **Dining:** Parallel23, see separate listing. **Pool(s):** outdoor. **Activities:** saunas, whirlpool, steamrooms, sailboats, windsurfing, snorkeling, lighted tennis court, spa. **Guest Services:** valet and coin laundry. **Free Special Amenities: expanded continental breakfast and high-speed Internet.**

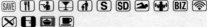

ROYAL WEST INDIES RESORT
Phone: (649)946-5004 8

Condominium
$180-$845

Address: Grace Bay Rd **Location:** Oceanfront. 8.8 mi (14.1 km) e of airport. **Facility:** Well landscaped grounds buffet the gorgeous strand of beach. The rooms are smartly designed and handsomely decorated in colonial Caribbean decor. 95 condominiums. 3 stories (no elevator), exterior corridors. **Terms:** office hours 6 am-11 pm, 3-5 night minimum stay - seasonal, 21 day cancellation notice. **Amenities:** safes. **Dining:** Mango Reef Restaurant, see separate listing. **Pool(s):** 2 outdoor. **Activities:** whirlpool, sailboats, snorkeling, bicycles. **Guest Services:** complimentary laundry.

THE TUSCANY
Phone: 649/941-4667

Condominium
$525-$1425

Address: Grace Bay Rd **Location:** Oceanfront. North coast at Grace Bay, 9.5 mi (15.2 km) from airport. **Facility:** Upscale design and décor provide the ultimate in luxurious comfort; a cell phone with island-wide coverage is provided with each unit. 14 condominiums. 5 stories, exterior corridors. **Terms:** office hours 9 am-5 pm, 60 day cancellation notice, 30 day off season-fee imposed. **Amenities:** safes. **Pool(s):** outdoor. **Activities:** whirlpool, lighted tennis court, bicycles, exercise room. **Fee:** massage. **Guest Services:** complimentary laundry.

VILLA DEL MAR
Phone: 649/941-5160 3

Condominium
$225-$750

Address: 1 Crescent Dr **Location:** 8.7 mi (13.9 km) e of airport. **Facility:** Modern accommodations incorporate enhanced beds, flat-screen TVs and kitchen facilities or wet bars. Guests can lounge around the saltwater pool. Meets AAA guest room security requirements. 42 condominiums. 4 stories, exterior corridors. **Terms:** office hours 7 am-11 pm, 61 day cancellation notice, 30 day off season. **Amenities:** high-speed Internet, safes. **Pool(s):** 2 outdoor. **Activities:** whirlpool, beach access, bicycles, limited exercise equipment. **Guest Services:** complimentary laundry. **Free Special Amenities: expanded continental breakfast and high-speed Internet.**

▼ See AAA listing p. 504 ▼

(See map & index p. 501.)

VILLA RENAISSANCE
Phone: (649)941-5300 **11**

WWW WWW WWW
Condominium
$510-$990

Address: Ventura Dr, Grace Bay Rd **Location:** Oceanfront. 8 mi (12.9 km) e of airport; Grace Bay. **Facility:** Spacious, well-appointed units feature marble floors and British Colonial-style furnishings. Meets AAA guest room security requirements. 17 condominiums. 4 stories, interior/exterior corridors. **Terms:** office hours 7 am-10 pm, 21 day cancellation notice-fee imposed. **Amenities:** safes. **Pool(s):** outdoor. **Activities:** whirlpool, lighted tennis court, bicycles, exercise room. *Fee:* massage. **Guest Services:** complimentary laundry.

[icons]

WHERE TO EAT

ANACAONA
Phone: 649/946-5050 **7**

WWW WWW WWW
International
$30-$42

AAA Inspector Notes: Regarded as one of the top spots in Provo for the cuisine and location, this restaurant's al fresco dining room, under a huge bohio, is in one of Grace Bay's most elegant hotels. The talented chef uses such high-quality ingredients as rack of lamb, grouper, ahi tuna, veal tenderloin and local rock lobster and prepares tantalizing dishes with flair. A good beginning is with one of the chilled soups or bisques. The adjacent bar is great for reflecting before or after dinner. **Bar:** full bar. **Reservations:** required. **Address:** Inner Grace Bay Cir **Location:** Grace Bay; 8.7 mi (13.9 km) e of airport; in Grace Bay Club.

[icons]

BACI RISTORANTE
Phone: 649/941-3044 **28**

WWW WWW
Italian
$12-$28

AAA Inspector Notes: At Turtle Cove, this delightful eatery features both indoor and outdoor patio seating. Patrons unwind amid the casual European atmosphere for a meal of Italian fare, including daily lunch specials, entrée-size salads, hearty pasta dishes and pizza baked in a brick oven. **Bar:** full bar. **Reservations:** suggested. **Address:** Harbour Towne at Turtle Cove **Location:** Harbour Towne at Turtle Cove.

[icons]

BAY BISTRO
Phone: 649/946-5396 **10**

WWW WWW
International
$14-$32

AAA Inspector Notes: In a boutique-style hotel, this restaurant employs servers who make an effort to ensure an enjoyable evening. The menu centers on seafood, including creative preparations of tuna, grouper, lobster and snapper. In addition to seafood, diners can order lamb, steak and a few vegetarian dishes. All desserts are made in-house. **Bar:** full bar. **Reservations:** suggested. **Address:** The Bight **Location:** Northeast coast at Grace Bay; 7 mi (11.2 km) e of airport; in Sibonne Beach Hotel.

[icons]

BELLA LUNA RISTORANTE
Phone: 649/946-5214 **17**

WWW WWW
Regional Italian
$16-$32

AAA Inspector Notes: An open, elevated deck and indoor dining area with colorful wall and ceiling murals invite diners to relax. The creative menu incorporates selections of fresh pasta and seafood blanketed in rich, tasty sauces. Portions are ample. **Bar:** full bar. **Reservations:** suggested. **Address:** Grace Bay Rd **Location:** North coast at Grace Bay; 7.5 mi (12 km) e of airport; in Glass House.

[icons]

CAICOS CAFE BAR & GRILL
Phone: 649-946-5278 **13**

WWW WWW
Mediterranean
$11-$32

AAA Inspector Notes: Listed on the daily changing menu at this spot are grilled fresh seafood and meat prepared with Caribbean, Mediterranean and French influences. The atmosphere is friendly and laid back. **Bar:** full bar. **Reservations:** suggested. **Address:** Governor's Rd **Location:** North coast at Grace Bay; 8 mi (12.8 km) e of airport.

[icons]

CALICO JACKS BAR AND RESTAURANT
Phone: 649/946-5129 **6**

WWW WW
International
$9-$22

AAA Inspector Notes: Both locals and tourists enjoy this casual spot, where tasty fare includes tempting finger foods along the lines of wings, conch fritters and rings, as well as hearty burgers, fish and chips, pasta and grilled meats. The feel on the patio is relaxed. **Bar:** full bar. **Address:** Grace Bay Rd **Location:** In Ports of Call Shopping Plaza.

[icons]

COCO BISTRO
Phone: 649/946-5369 **14**

WWW WWW WWW
International
$28-$39

AAA Inspector Notes: The chef/owner has elevated the dining experience in this romantic al fresco setting enveloped by a thick grove of palm trees, tiki torches and delightful background music. The chef's creative talent emerges in delectable dishes such as Colorado rack of lamb with pomegranate molasses and macadamia nut crust, conch potato soup with Gruyere cheese, soft-shell crab with jalapeno salsa and Kurobuta pork. **Bar:** full bar. **Reservations:** required. **Address:** Grace Bay Rd **Location:** 8.9 mi (14.2 km) e of airport; Grace Bay.

[icons]

COYABA
Phone: 649/946-5186 **27**

WWW WWW WWW
New Caribbean
$32-$42

AAA Inspector Notes: At this al fresco dining room, set in a lush tropical garden, the chef comes to the table to explain all that he has created. Some signature dishes include pan-fried fillet of grouper with an ackee and callaloo souffle or a rack of lamb with sun-dried tomato pesto and rosemary au jus. Each evening features an array of specials. True gourmands favor the sumptuous seven-course tasting menu. **Bar:** full bar. **Reservations:** suggested. **Address:** Grace Bay Rd **Location:** North coast at Grace Bay; 9 mi (14.4 km) e of airport.

[icons]

DANNY BUOYS IRISH PUB AND RESTAURANT
Phone: 649/946-5921 **18**

WWW WW
International
$11-$28

AAA Inspector Notes: A great watering hole for locals, divers and tourist alike. Guests can watch sporting events on large-screen satellite TVs in the handsome bar area. Among the many menu options are such Irish favorites as fish and chips, chicken pot pie and potato-leek soup. Some other house specialties include pot of nachos, buffalo wings and bacon-wrapped scallops. Brunch is served from 10 am-4 pm on weekends. DJ music is offered on Friday and Saturday night as well as karaoke on Tuesday. **Bar:** full bar. **Address:** Grace Bay Rd **Location:** Grace Bay; across from Regent Grand; adjacent to The Saltmills.

(See map & index p. 501.)

GRACE'S COTTAGE
Phone: 649/946-5096 [8]

International
$43-$54

AAA Inspector Notes: Romantically set al fresco around a gingerbread-style cottage. The chef visits each table to explain the frequently changing menu in great detail, which may feature starters like red snapper ceviche and entrees like grilled wahoo with pineapple salsa or braised lamb shank with rosemary risotto. Dessert is the piece de resistance with choices like mango souffle, tempura bananas with rum butter scotch sauce and roasted pumpkin ginger cheesecake with whiskey and walnut sauce. **Bar:** full bar. **Reservations:** required. **Address:** Grace Bay Rd **Location:** 6 mi (9.6 km) e of airport; Grace Bay; in Point Grace. [D] CALL [&] [🖋] [🛇]

HEMINGWAY'S ON THE BEACH
Phone: 649/941-8408 [9]

International
$11-$33

AAA Inspector Notes: The casual restaurant allows for oceanfront dining in a covered area or on a patio terrace overlooking the sea. Candlelit tables set the scene for a romantic evening. The varied menu blends light finger foods and sandwiches at lunch with full meat, seafood and pasta specialties at dinner. **Bar:** full bar. **Reservations:** suggested. **Address:** Grace Bay **Location:** North coast at Grace Bay; 7.5 mi (12 km) e of airport; in The Sands at Grace Bay. [B] [L] [D] [🖋] [🛇]

MAGNOLIA WINE BAR & RESTAURANT
Phone: 649/941-5108 [24]

International
$24-$38

AAA Inspector Notes: On a hill, the refined and romantic restaurant offers views of the ocean and marina. Well-attired servers are quick to make recommendations from the varied menu, which includes escargots, tempura shrimp and tuna tartare as appetizers. Main course choices range from seafood bouillabaisse to black Angus beef to rack of lamb with mint-rosemary jus. Molten chocolate cake served warm is luscious. The wine bar is a popular spot for sunsets. **Bar:** full bar. **Reservations:** suggested. **Address:** Miramar Resort **Location:** At Miramar Resort; just sw of Turtle Cove Marina; overlooking the marina. [D] [🖋] [🛇]

MANGO REEF RESTAURANT
Phone: 649/946-8200 [5]

International
$9-$34

AAA Inspector Notes: Diners can choose seating indoors or outside on the porch. The Caribbean staff is cheerful. Pineapple and conch fritters with chipotle mayonnaise and rock shrimp tostada are popular choices. Entrée-size salads can be topped with seared tuna, jerk chicken or coconut shrimp. Caribbean flavors burst forth from such dishes as island ribs with guava glaze and red snapper Caribe. For lunch, there is a selection of gourmet burgers and sandwiches, including panini. **Bar:** full bar. **Address:** Grace Bay Rd **Location:** 8.8 mi (14.1 km) e of airport; in Royal West Indies Resort. [B] [L] [D] [🖋] [🛇]

OPUS WINE BAR & GRILL
Phone: 649/946-5885 [2]

International
$21-$36

AAA Inspector Notes: This contemporary restaurant offers diners the option for al fresco garden terrace seating or interior air-conditioned seating. Tempting appetizers range from cherry-stone clams to conch seviche. The menu features an array of tapas that are great for sharing. Besides red snapper and salmon, other entrees include steak and lamb. An extensive wine list is available. **Bar:** full bar. **Reservations:** suggested. **Address:** Grace Bay Rd **Location:** Ocean Club Plaza; adjacent to Ocean Club East; across from Provo Golf Course. [D] [🛇]

PARALLEL23
Phone: 649/946-8666 [11]

International
$26-$37

AAA Inspector Notes: This sophisticated restaurant's gourmet menu combines the best of culinary techniques and ingredients from the East and West. Starters include grouper tostada, beef yakitori and salad of citrus-cured duck confit. For entrees, the chef prepares such items as wood-roasted pork chops, roasted organic chicken, cote du boeuf and poached reef snapper. An extensive seafood menu is offered. The attentive islander staff presents dishes with flair. **Bar:** full bar. **Reservations:** suggested. **Address:** Grace Bay Rd **Location:** 6.9 mi (11.1 km) e of airport; in The Regent Palms Turks and Caicos. [B] [D]

SALTMILLS CAFE & DINER
Phone: 649/941-8148 [20]

Breakfast
$11-$19

AAA Inspector Notes: Submarine sandwiches, panini sandwiches, wraps and burgers in addition to entrée-size salads topped with grilled beef or chicken are served in this casual family friendly eatery across from Grace Bay. This spot also is popular for breakfast. **Bar:** full bar. **Address:** Grace Bay Rd **Location:** At The Saltmills across from Grace Bay. [B] [L]

THE TIKI HUT-CABANA BAR AND GRILL
Phone: 649/941-5341 [30]

International
$10-$26

AAA Inspector Notes: A local hangout at Turtle Cove Marina, the bustling eatery nurtures a relaxed island atmosphere. Guests can sit in the covered open-air dining room or at the large casual bar. The menu lists a mix of great island and American dishes. Lending to the ambience are friendly servers who often can be heard singing. **Bar:** full bar. **Address:** Turtle Cove Marina **Location:** At Turtle Cove Marina. [L] [D] [🖋] [🛇]

YOSHI'S SUSHI BAR & JAPANESE RESTAURANT
Phone: 649/941-3374 [4]

Japanese
$18-$39

AAA Inspector Notes: This eatery offers an expansive menu of sushi, sashimi, tempura and teriyaki dishes. The tasteful surroundings and spacious bar create the perfect spot to meet friends and colleagues. **Bar:** full bar. **Reservations:** suggested. **Address:** Grace Bay Rd **Location:** In Salt Mills Plaza. [L] [D] [🛇]

VIRGIN ISLANDS, BRITISH

This index helps you "spot" where approved hotels and restaurants are located on the corresponding detailed maps. Hotel daily rate range is for comparison only and show the property's high season. Restaurant rate range is a combination of lunch and/or dinner. Turn to the listing page for more detailed rate information and consult display ads for special promotions.

VIRGIN GORDA ISLAND

Map Page	Hotels	Diamond Rated	High Season	Page
1 this page	Nail Bay Resort	▼▼▼	$185-$1800	510
3 this page	Mango Bay Resort	▼▼	$150-$595	510

Map Page	Restaurant	Diamond Rated	Cuisine	Meal Range	Page
① this page	The Rock Cafe	▼▼	Italian	$20-$38	510

TORTOLA ISLAND

Map Page	Hotels	Diamond Rated	High Season	Page
7 this page	Sugar Mill Hotel	▼▼	$255-$695	509
8 this page	**Long Bay Beach Resort**	▼▼	$290-$810 SAVE	509
10 this page	Treasure Isle Hotel	▼▼	$170-$270	509

Map Page	Restaurants	Diamond Rated	Cuisine	Meal Range	Page
⑤ this page	Sugar Mill Restaurant	▼▼▼	International	$27-$32	510
⑧ this page	Capriccio di Mare	▼	Italian	$7-$16	509
⑨ this page	Brandywine Bay	▼▼▼	International	$22-$60	509
⑫ this page	Myett's Garden & Grille Restaurant	▼▼	Caribbean	$12-$28	509
⑯ this page	Kong Ming Asian Terrace	▼▼	Chinese	$9-$22	509

PETER ISLAND

Map Page	Hotel	Diamond Rated	High Season	Page
12 this page	**Peter Island Resort & Spa**	▼▼▼▼	$675-$1375 SAVE	509

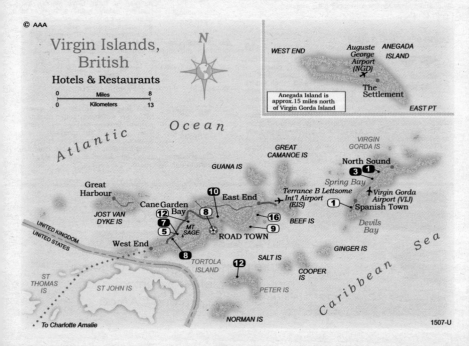

© AAA

Virgin Islands, British
Hotels & Restaurants

Miles 0 — 8
Kilometers 0 — 13

1507-U

PETER ISLAND
• Hotels & Restaurants index & map p. 508

PETER ISLAND RESORT & SPA
Phone: 284/495-2000 **12**

Resort Hotel
$675-$1375

Address: Peter Island **Location:** Oceanfront. Taxi and ferry service from Beef Island Airport, Tortola. **Facility:** This upscale private-island resort features five pristine beaches and 1,800 acres to roam; afternoon tea is served between 4 and 5 pm. 55 units, some houses. 2 stories (no elevator), exterior corridors. **Parking:** no self-parking. **Terms:** 5-10 night minimum stay - seasonal, 30 day cancellation notice. **Amenities:** safes. **Dining:** 2 restaurants, entertainment. **Pool(s):** 2 outdoor. **Activities:** boating, sailboats, windsurfing, snorkeling, fishing, 4 tennis courts (2 lighted), bicycles, hiking trails, jogging, sports court, basketball, volleyball, exercise room, spa. *Fee:* marina, scuba diving, charter fishing. **Guest Services:** valet laundry, area transportation-Tortola Ferry. **Free Special Amenities:** early check-in/late check-out and high-speed Internet. Affiliated with A Preferred Hotel.

TORTOLA ISLAND (B-2) pop. 16,630
• Hotels & Restaurants index & map p. 508

LONG BAY BEACH RESORT
Phone: 284/495-4252 **8**

Resort Hotel
$290-$810 12/1-4/15
$250-$730 4/16-11/30

Address: Long Bay **Location:** Oceanfront. 11 mi (17.6 km) nw of Road Town. **Facility:** Units at the full-service resort range from deluxe beachfront to standard hillside accommodations, many offering water views. 123 units, some houses. 2-3 stories (no elevator), exterior corridors. **Terms:** 14 day cancellation notice-fee imposed. **Amenities:** safes (fee). **Dining:** 3 restaurants. **Pool(s):** outdoor. **Activities:** whirlpool, exercise room, spa. *Fee:* scuba diving, snorkeling, 2 lighted tennis courts. **Guest Services:** valet laundry. **Free Special Amenities:** early check-in/late check-out.

SUGAR MILL HOTEL
Phone: (284)495-4355 **7**

Country Inn
$255-$695

Address: Little Apple Bay **Location:** 11 mi (17.6 km) nw of Road Town; on north shore in west end. Located in a secluded area. **Facility:** 23 units, some two bedrooms and kitchens. 1-2 stories (no elevator), exterior corridors. **Terms:** open 12/1-7/28 & 10/1-11/30, office hours 7 am-11 pm, 3 night minimum stay - seasonal, age restrictions may apply, 30 day cancellation notice-fee imposed. **Dining:** Sugar Mill Restaurant, see separate listing. **Pool(s):** outdoor. **Activities:** beach access, snorkeling. **Guest Services:** valet laundry.

TREASURE ISLE HOTEL
Phone: 284/494-2501 **10**

Hotel
$170-$270

Address: Pasea Estate **Location:** 0.5 mi (0.8 km) e of Road Town. **Facility:** 65 units. 2 stories (no elevator), exterior corridors. **Terms:** office hours 7 am-11 pm, 14 day cancellation notice. **Amenities:** high-speed Internet. **Pool(s):** outdoor. **Guest Services:** valet laundry.

BRANDYWINE BAY
Phone: 284/495-2301 **9**

International
$22-$60

AAA Inspector Notes: On a breeze-swept hillside overlooking the sea, this historic gunnery's open-air stone terrace makes for an intriguing dining spot. The Italian-born owner creates a daily-changing menu of creative and traditional dishes. House specials include homemade pasta, roast duck and whole fish. **Bar:** full bar. **Reservations:** suggested. **Address:** Brandywine Estate **Location:** 3 mi (4.8 km) e of Road Town.

CAPRICCIO DI MARE
Phone: 284/494-5369 **8**

Italian
$7-$16

AAA Inspector Notes: On a covered sidewalk patio, the casual setting invites diners to unwind while noshing on gourmet pizza, pasta, large salads and panini sandwiches. Also tempting are the great desserts, cappuccino and espresso. **Bar:** full bar. **Address:** Abbot Bldg, Waterfront Dr **Location:** Center Road Town; near ferry terminal. **Parking:** street only.

KONG MING ASIAN TERRACE
Phone: 284/495-1174 **16**

Chinese
$9-$22

AAA Inspector Notes: Patrons enjoy upstairs views on the verandah or air-conditioned comfort in the Asia-themed interior dining room. The typically broad Chinese menu lists many soups, as well as entrees centered on ingredients ranging from duck, lamb and spare ribs to prawns and fish. Two popular methods of preparation are Manchurian and Szechuan style. **Bar:** full bar. **Reservations:** suggested. **Address:** Harbour View Marina **Location:** 6.5 mi (10.5 km) e of Road Town; at Harbor View Marina.

MYETT'S GARDEN & GRILLE RESTAURANT
Phone: 284/495-9649 **12**

Caribbean
$12-$28

AAA Inspector Notes: Chef Stone from Jamaica prepares Caribbean-inspired cuisine at this spot, where patrons soak up the garden atmosphere as they take in partial views of the beach and ocean. Al fresco meals center on steak, the catch of the day, jerk chicken, roasted duck with tamarind glaze and grilled rack of lamb, as well as more than half a dozen pasta dishes. Favorite starters are conch chowder or pepperpot soup. Dessert temptations include mango cheesecake, Key lime pie and chocolate ecstasy cake. **Bar:** full bar. **Reservations:** suggested. **Address:** Cane Garden Bay Rd **Location:** In Cane Garden Bay; oceanside.

PUSSER'S MARINA CAY
Phone: 284/495-4554

International
$15-$32

AAA Inspector Notes: The eatery's ideal marina location attracts a varied crowd of locals, seafaring folks and land-excursion tourists. Nautical and whimsical appointments foster a casual mood that recalls Jimmy Buffett songs. Among well-prepared favorites are baby back ribs, jerk chicken and fish—either escabéche or with coconut curry sauce. Mouthwatering starters include peel-and-eat shrimp, crab cakes and Prince Edward Island mussels. Tempting desserts and creative libations also merit strong consideration. **Bar:** full bar. **Reservations:** suggested. **Address:** Soper's Hole Marina **Location:** At Soper's Hole Marina; west end.

(See map & index p. 508.)

PUSSER'S ROAD TOWN PUB & COMPANY STORE
Phone: 284/494-3897

International
$10-$24

AAA Inspector Notes: Enjoy a wide variety of Caribbean, English and American fare at this popular gathering spot overlooking the harbor. The menu includes jerk pork and chicken, shepherd's pie and fish and chips, as well as burgers, sandwiches, salads and pizza. Dine on the porch or inside the air-conditioned Victorian bar. **Bar:** full bar. **Address:** Waterfront Rd **Location:** In Road Town; across from ferry dock. [L] [D]

SUGAR MILL RESTAURANT
Phone: 284/495-4355 [5]

International
$27-$32

AAA Inspector Notes: Plentiful artwork created by the owner adorns the walls of the rustic setting. Award-winning four-course dinners reflect local and international influences. Although the service has a formal edge, the atmosphere remains casual. **Bar:** full bar. **Reservations:** required. **Address:** Little Apple Bay **Location:** 11 mi (17.6 km) nw of Road Town; on north shore in west end; in Sugar Mill Hotel. **Historic**

[B] [D] [K]

VIRGIN GORDA ISLAND pop. 3,063
• Hotels & Restaurants index & map p. 508

MANGO BAY RESORT
Phone: 284/495-5672 [3]

Cottage
$150-$595

Address: Plum Tree Rd **Location:** Oceanfront. 2.2 mi (3.5 km) n of ferry dock and airport, follow signs. **Facility:** 22 cottages. 1-2 stories (no elevator), exterior corridors. **Terms:** open 12/1-9/1 & 9/30-11/30, office hours 9 am-5 pm, 3-5 night minimum stay - seasonal, 45 day cancellation notice-fee imposed. **Amenities:** safes. **Activities:** snorkeling.

[icons]

NAIL BAY RESORT
Phone: (284)494-8000 [1]

Vacation Rental
Condominium
$185-$1800

Address: Nail Bay **Location:** 4 mi (6.4 km) n of ferry dock and airport, follow signs. **Facility:** Situated on 150 acres, this property offers a fine assortment of individually decorated accommodations, some with a private pool. 25 units, some two bedrooms, kitchens and houses. 1-2 stories (no elevator), exterior corridors. **Terms:** office hours 8 am-7 pm, 3-10 night minimum stay, 61 day cancellation notice. **Amenities:** safes. **Pool(s):** outdoor. **Activities:** whirlpool, snorkeling, lighted tennis court, spa. **Guest Services:** complimentary laundry.

[icons]

WHERE TO EAT

THE ROCK CAFE
Phone: 284/495-5482 [1]

Italian
$20-$38

AAA Inspector Notes: This restaurant is popular for its food and setting. Conch fritters make great munchies before moving on to such pasta dishes as penne Caprese or one of the many local fish dishes. The al fresco dining area is built around boulders and rock outcroppings. The creme caramel has a rich, creamy texture. Sam's Piano bar is popular before and after dinner. **Bar:** full bar. **Reservations:** required. **Address:** Tower Rd **Location:** Just s of Spanish Town; between The Baths and Spanish Town; at The Valley. [D]

VIRGIN ISLANDS, U.S.

Map Page	ST THOMAS - CYRIL E KING INTERNATIONAL	Diamond Rated	High Season	Page
1 p. 513	Best Western Carib Beach Resort, just n of airport	◈◈	$150-$210 SAVE	518
2 p. 513	Best Western Plus Emerald Beach Resort, 0.6 mi (1 km) s of airport	◈◈◈	$179-$309 SAVE	520

Virgin Islands, U.S.

This index helps you "spot" where approved hotels and restaurants are located on the corresponding detailed maps. Hotel daily rate range is for comparison only and show the property's high season. Restaurant rate range is a combination of lunch and/or dinner. Turn to the listing page for more detailed rate information and consult display ads for special promotions.

CHARLOTTE AMALIE (St. Thomas Island)

Map Page	Hotels	Diamond Rated	High Season	Page
1 p. 513	Best Western Carib Beach Resort	◈◈	$150-$210 SAVE	518
2 p. 513	Best Western Plus Emerald Beach Resort (See ad p. 518.)	◈◈◈	$179-$309 SAVE	520

Map Page	Restaurants	Diamond Rated	Cuisine	Meal Range	Page
① p. 513	Sib's on the Mountain	◈	American	$12-$28	521
③ p. 513	Thirteen Restaurant	◈◈◈	International	$19-$29	521
⑦ p. 513	Old Stone Farmhouse	◈◈◈◈	Continental	$29-$54	520
⑧ p. 513	Mafolie	◈◈◈	Continental	$21-$48	520
⑩ p. 513	Virgilio's	◈◈◈	Northern Italian	$13-$48	521
⑫ p. 513	Tavern on the Waterfront	◈◈◈	Continental	$10-$48	521
⑬ p. 513	Cuzzin's Caribbean Restaurant	◈	Caribbean	$12-$23	520
⑭ p. 513	Cafe Amici	◈◈	Italian	$12-$18	520
⑱ p. 513	Oceana Restaurant and Wine Bar	◈◈◈	Seafood	$29-$65	520
⑲ p. 513	Amalia Cafe	◈◈◈	Spanish	$15-$32	520
⑳ p. 513	Gladys' Cafe	◈◈	Caribbean	$10-$21	520
㉑ p. 513	Hook, Line, & Sinker Bar and Restaurant	◈◈	International	$10-$28	520
㉒ p. 513	Calico Jack's	◈◈	Pizza	$13-$17	520
㉔ p. 513	The Greenhouse Restaurant St. Thomas	◈◈	International	$12-$28	520
㉘ p. 513	Shipwreck Tavern	◈	American	$8-$29	521

FRENCHMAN BAY (St. Thomas Island)

Map Page	Hotel	Diamond Rated	High Season	Page
5 p. 513	Frenchman's Reef & Morning Star Marriott Beach Resort (See ad p. 519, on insert.)	◈◈◈	$387-$780 SAVE	521

Map Page	Restaurant	Diamond Rated	Cuisine	Meal Range	Page
⑨ p. 513	Havana Blue	◈◈◈	Latin American	$32-$48	521

RED HOOK (St. Thomas Island)

Map Page	Hotels	Diamond Rated	High Season	Page
11 p. 513	Secret Harbour Beach Resort (See ad p. 522.)	◈◈	$185-$725 SAVE	522
13 p. 513	The Ritz-Carlton, St. Thomas	◈◈◈◈	$269-$999	522

Map Page	Restaurants	Diamond Rated	Cuisine	Meal Range	Page
⑭ p. 513	Bleuwater	◈◈◈◈	Creole	$30-$48	523

Map Page	Restaurants (cont'd)	Diamond Rated	Cuisine	Meal Range	Page
32 p. 513	The Agave Terrace	◆◆◆	International	$25-$47	523
33 p. 513	The Cellar	◆◆◆	New American	$26-$36	523
36 p. 513	Molly Molones	◆	American	$10-$29	523
37 p. 513	Fish Tails	◆◆	Seafood	$10-$45	523
38 p. 513	Duffy's Love Shack	◆	International	$10-$20	523

SMITH BAY (St. Thomas Island)

Map Page	Hotel	Diamond Rated	High Season	Page
15 p. 513	**Wyndham Sugar Bay Resort & Spa**	◆◆◆	$187-$646 SAVE	523

Map Page	Restaurant	Diamond Rated	Cuisine	Meal Range	Page
30 p. 513	Romano's Restaurant & Art Gallery	◆◆◆	Northern Italian	$24-$38	523

VIRGIN ISLANDS NATIONAL PARK (St. John Island)

Map Page	Hotel	Diamond Rated	High Season	Page
25 p. 513	Caneel Bay, A Rosewood Resort	◆◆◆◆	$450-$1700	518

CRUZ BAY (St. John Island)

Map Page	Hotels	Diamond Rated	High Season	Page
26 p. 513	Estate Lindholm	◆◆◆	$170-$380	516
27 p. 513	Garden by the Sea B&B	◆◆	$160-$275	517
28 p. 513	**Gallows Point Resort**	◆◆◆	$265-$395 SAVE	516
29 p. 513	**The Westin St. John Resort & Villas** *(See ad on insert, p. 517.)*	◆◆◆◆	$169-$2715 SAVE	517

Map Page	Restaurants	Diamond Rated	Cuisine	Meal Range	Page
42 p. 513	Asolare	◆◆◆	Asian	$25-$38	517
43 p. 513	St. John Waterfront Bistro	◆◆	French	$10-$39	517
45 p. 513	Deli Grotto	◆	Deli	$6-$10	517
46 p. 513	Morgan's Mango	◆◆	Caribbean	$15-$28	517

CHRISTIANSTED (St. Croix Island)

Map Page	Hotels	Diamond Rated	High Season	Page
31 p. 513	The Buccaneer *(See ad p. 514.)*	◆◆◆	$265-$995	514
32 p. 513	Chenay Bay Beach Resort	◆◆	$309-$799	514
33 p. 513	**Hotel Caravelle**	◆	$130-$170 SAVE	515
34 p. 513	Holger Danske Hotel *(See ad p. 515.)*	◆	$110-$165	514
35 p. 513	**Divi Carina Bay Resort & Casino** *(See ad p. 515.)*	◆◆◆	$210-$626 SAVE	514
38 p. 513	**Tamarind Reef Hotel**	◆◆	$200-$400 SAVE	515

Map Page	Restaurants	Diamond Rated	Cuisine	Meal Range	Page
54 p. 513	RumRunners	◆◆	American	$9-$26	516
55 p. 513	Cheeseburgers in America's Paradise	◆	American	$9-$19	516
58 p. 513	Tutto Bene	◆◆	Italian	$16-$31	516
60 p. 513	Kendrick's	◆◆	Continental	$25-$39	516
61 p. 513	Bacchus	◆◆◆	American	$22-$36	516
62 p. 513	Dashi	◆◆	Asian	$7-$32	516

FREDERIKSTED (St. Croix Island)

Map Page	Hotel	Diamond Rated	High Season	Page
37 p. 513	Sand Castle on the Beach Hotel & Restaurant	◆◆	$109-$349	516

Map Page	Restaurant	Diamond Rated	Cuisine	Meal Range	Page
64 p. 513	Beachside Cafe	◆◆	Continental	$10-$27	516

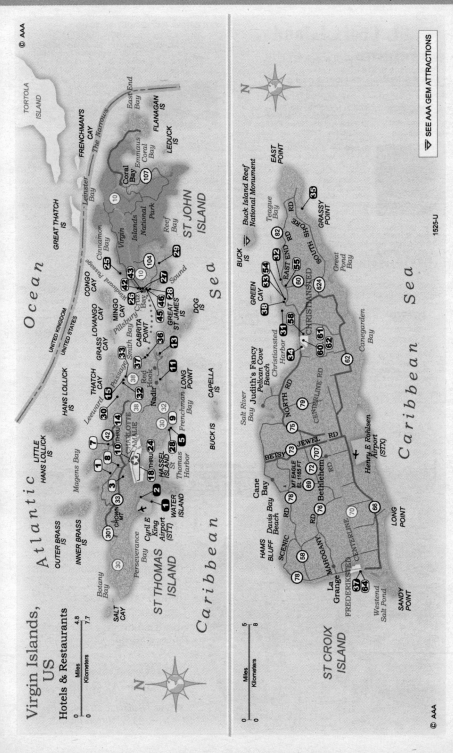

Virgin Islands, US

Hotels & Restaurants

SEE AAA GEM ATTRACTIONS

1525-U

St. Croix Island

CHRISTIANSTED (C-3) pop. 2,637

- **Restaurants p. 516**
- **Hotels & Restaurants index & map p. 511**

THE BUCCANEER

Resort Hotel
$265-$995

Phone: (340)712-2100   **31**

Address: 5007 Estate Shoys, Lot #7 00824 **Location:** Oceanfront. 1.8 mi (2.9 km) e of downtown. **Facility:** Golf and tennis facilities enhance this sprawling resort that has been family-owned for generations; most guest rooms feature luxurious appointments. 138 units, some two bedrooms. 1-2 stories (no elevator), interior/exterior corridors. **Terms:** 21 day cancellation notice, 7 day off season. **Amenities:** safes. **Dining:** 3 restaurants, entertainment. **Pool(s):** 2 outdoor. **Activities:** boat dock, snorkeling, recreation programs, hiking trails, jogging, basketball, volleyball, exercise room, spa. *Fee:* golf-18 holes, 8 tennis courts (2 lighted). **Guest Services:** valet and coin laundry, area transportation (fee)-town. **(See ad this page.)**

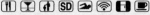

CHENAY BAY BEACH RESORT

Cottage
$309-$799

Phone: (340)718-2918   **32**

Address: Rt 82 East End Quarter 00820 **Location:** Oceanfront. 3.6 mi (5.7 km) e of downtown. **Facility:** 50 cottages. 1 story, exterior corridors. **Terms:** office hours 8 am-10 pm, check-in 4 pm, 3 day cancellation notice-fee imposed. **Dining:** entertainment. **Pool(s):** outdoor. **Activities:** whirlpool, sailboats, snorkeling, 2 tennis courts, playground, basketball, volleyball. *Fee:* scuba diving. **Guest Services:** coin laundry.

DIVI CARINA BAY RESORT & CASINO

Phone: (340)773-9700   **35**

Resort Hotel
$210-$626

Address: 25 Estate Turner Hole 00820 **Location:** Oceanfront. 10.4 mi (16.6 km) se of downtown from either north side road or south shore road. **Facility:** In a somewhat remote area, this resort has numerous recreational opportunities; many oceanfront units are spacious and include a wet bar. Meets AAA guest room security requirements. 200 units. 3 stories, exterior corridors. **Terms:** 3-7 night minimum stay - seasonal, 7 day cancellation notice-fee imposed. **Amenities:** high-speed Internet, safes. **Dining:** 4 restaurants, entertainment. **Pool(s):** 2 outdoor. **Activities:** whirlpools, rental paddleboats, rental sailboats, rental sailboards, snorkeling equipment rental, recreation programs, game room, horseshoes, shuffleboard, volleyball, exercise room, spa. *Fee:* scuba diving, 2 lighted tennis courts. **Guest Services:** valet and coin laundry.
(See ad p. 515.)

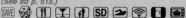

HOLGER DANSKE HOTEL

Phone: (340)773-3600   **34**

Motel
$110-$165

Address: 1200 King Cross St 00820 **Location:** Oceanfront. Downtown on waterfront. **Facility:** Meets AAA guest room security requirements. 42 units, some efficiencies. 3 stories (no elevator), exterior corridors. **Amenities:** high-speed Internet. **Pool(s):** outdoor. **Guest Services:** coin laundry. *(See ad p. 515.)*

(See index & map p. 511.)

HOTEL CARAVELLE   Phone: (340)773-0687   **33**

Hotel
$130-$170

Address: 44A Queen Cross St 00820 **Location:** Oceanfront. Historic downtown. **Facility:** 44 units. 3 stories (no elevator), exterior corridors. *Bath:* shower only. **Terms:** 21 day cancellation notice, 7 day in summer-fee imposed. **Amenities:** safes. **Dining:** RumRunners, see separate listing. **Pool(s):** outdoor. **Activities:** *Fee:* scuba diving. **Guest Services:** valet laundry. **Free Special Amenities: local telephone calls and high-speed Internet.**

TAMARIND REEF HOTEL   Phone: 340/718-4455   **38**

Motel
$200-$400

Address: 5001 Tamarind Reef 00820 **Location:** Oceanfront. Just e of town. **Facility:** Meets AAA guest room security requirements. 39 units, some efficiencies. 2 stories (no elevator), exterior corridors. *Bath:* shower only. **Terms:** 21 day cancellation notice-fee imposed. **Amenities:** safes. **Dining:** 2 restaurants. **Pool(s):** outdoor. **Activities:** snorkeling. *Fee:* 2 lighted tennis courts. **Guest Services:** coin laundry. **Free Special Amenities: newspaper and high-speed Internet.**

▼ *See AAA listing p. 514* ▼

▼ *See AAA listing p. 514* ▼

(See index & map p. 511.)

WHERE TO EAT

BACCHUS   Phone: 340/692-9922   [61]

American
$22-$36

AAA Inspector Notes: Food is served in the cozy atmosphere of a historic townhouse by gregarious servers. For starters try the roasted beets and Gorgonzola or the smoked duck chili. Entrées range from pork prime rib to beef stroganoff to the seafood stew, which is a savory meal of mussels, clams, scallops, shrimp and fish simmered in a white wine herb broth served over spaghetti. An award-winning wine list and very tempting dessert offerings are available. **Bar:** full bar. **Reservations:** required, in season. **Address:** 52 Queen Cross St 00820 **Location:** Between Strand and King sts; downtown. **Parking:** street only.

[D]

CHEESEBURGERS IN AMERICA'S PARADISE
                               Phone: 340/773-1119   [55]

American
$9-$19

AAA Inspector Notes: Under a tent tarp, the fun, open-air spot mostly serves burgers, burritos, nachos and daily specials. Live entertainment is offered Thursday through Sunday. **Bar:** full bar. **Address:** East End Rd (Rt 82) 00840 **Location:** 3.5 mi (5.6 km) e of town.

DASHI   Phone: 340/773-6911   [62]

Asian
$7-$32

AAA Inspector Notes: Enjoy a variety of Asian fare, including a lengthy list of sushi, amid the casual setting of a twinkle light-draped courtyard or in the air-conditioned comfort of the modern red and black dining room. Dishes feature the flavors of China, Japan, Thailand and occasionally India. Entrées include such options as Asian fish tacos, pad thai and General Tso's wahoo stir fry. **Bar:** full bar. **Address:** 1104 Strand St, Suites 8 & 9 00820 **Location:** Historic downtown; in Caravelle Arcade. **Parking:** street only.

[D]

KENDRICK'S   Phone: 340/773-9199   [60]

Continental
$25-$39

AAA Inspector Notes: Enjoy creatively prepared fare with French influences in a charming courtyard setting at this family-owned restaurant. Entrées include a daily changing duck preparation, as well as seafood, beef, pork, chicken and pasta. Specialties include herb-crusted rack of lamb, seared tuna and filet mignon. The homemade desserts make a sweet ending to the meal. **Bar:** full bar. **Reservations:** suggested. **Address:** 2132 Company St 00820 **Location:** Downtown; jct Company and King Cross sts. **Parking:** street only. [D]

RUMRUNNERS   Phone: 340/773-6585   [54]

American
$9-$26

AAA Inspector Notes: This open-air restaurant features a relaxed setting directly overlooking the town boardwalk and waterfront. Diners can choose from a wide selection of tasty lighter fare, well-prepared full entrées and daily specials of fresh local seafood, all served with a distinct island flair. All dishes are prepared to order, and the desserts are homemade. **Bar:** full bar. **Address:** 44A Queen Cross St 00820 **Location:** Historic district; on waterfront; in Hotel Caravelle. **Parking:** street only.

[B] [L] [D]

TUTTO BENE   Phone: 340/773-5229   [58]

Italian
$16-$31

AAA Inspector Notes: This restaurant continues to live up to its well-earned reputation for excellent Italian cuisine and skilled service. In addition to an array of pasta dishes, the menu lists entrées of salmon, veal, rack of lamb and filet mignon. Lunch is popular with take-away dishes. **Bar:** full bar. **Reservations:** suggested. **Address:** 2006 Eastern Suburb, Suite One 00820 **Location:** Just e of town. [L] [D]

FREDERIKSTED (D-1) pop. 732
• Hotels & Restaurants index & map p. 511

SAND CASTLE ON THE BEACH HOTEL & RESTAURANT
                               Phone: (340)772-1205   [37]

Hotel
$109-$349

Address: 127 Estate Smithfield 00840 **Location:** Oceanfront. 0.5 mi (0.8 km) s of Freetown. **Facility:** 22 units, some two bedrooms and efficiencies. 1-2 stories (no elevator), exterior corridors. *Bath:* shower only. **Terms:** office hours 9 am-9 pm, age restrictions may apply, 60 day cancellation notice-fee imposed. **Amenities:** safes. **Dining:** Beachside Cafe, see separate listing. **Pool(s):** 2 outdoor. **Activities:** exercise room. *Fee:* scuba diving, snorkeling, massage. **Guest Services:** coin laundry.

 / SOME UNITS FEE

WHERE TO EAT

BEACHSIDE CAFE   Phone: 340/772-1266   [64]

Continental
$10-$27

AAA Inspector Notes: Enjoy oceanfront dining in an al fresco restaurant with captivating sunsets, nightly specials and a menu of fresh seafood, steak and pasta. Entrées include classic lasagna, stuffed lobster and braised lamb shank. Lighter fare is offered at lunch and includes salads, sandwiches, seasoned fish tacos and a pulled-pork barbecue sandwich. Live music is featured on Saturday nights. **Bar:** full bar. **Reservations:** suggested. **Address:** 127 Estate Smithfield **Location:** 0.5 mi (0.8 km) s of Freetown; in Sand Castle on the Beach Hotel & Restaurant. [L] [D]

St. John Island

CRUZ BAY pop. 2,743
• Hotels & Restaurants index & map p. 511

ESTATE LINDHOLM   Phone: 340/776-6121   [26]

Bed & Breakfast
$170-$380

Address: Parcel 6 Estate Caneel Bay 00830 **Location:** 0.5 mi (0.8 km) n of town. **Facility:** On a hillside within the national park, the property overlooks Cruz Bay and distant islands; the lodging buildings are surrounded by lush landscaping. 14 units. 2 stories (no elevator), exterior corridors. *Bath:* shower only. **Terms:** 3 night minimum stay, age restrictions may apply, 30 day cancellation notice-fee imposed. **Amenities:** safes. **Pool(s):** outdoor. **Activities:** hiking trails, exercise room.

GALLOWS POINT RESORT   Phone: (340)776-6434   [28]

Condominium
$265-$395

Address: 3AAA Gallows Point Rd 00831 **Location:** Oceanfront. 0.3 mi (0.5 km) s of ferry dock. **Facility:** On a small peninsula, all of these spacious one-bedroom and bi-level loft units feature Caribbean décor and offer harbor or sea views. Meets AAA guest room security requirements. 60 condominiums. 1-2 stories, exterior corridors. *Bath:* shower only. **Terms:** 3 night minimum stay, age restrictions may apply, 30 day cancellation notice-fee imposed. **Amenities:** safes. **Pool(s):** outdoor. **Activities:** whirlpool. *Fee:* snorkeling. **Guest Services:** coin laundry, area transportation-Cruz Bay Ferry Dock. **Free Special Amenities:** newspaper and high-speed Internet.

(See index & map p. 511.)

GARDEN BY THE SEA B&B
Phone: 340/779-4731 27

Bed & Breakfast
$160-$275

Address: 203 Contant & Enighed 00831 **Location:** At Contant and Enighed. Adjacent to bird sanctuary. **Facility:** 3 units. 3 stories (no elevator), exterior corridors. *Bath:* shower only. **Terms:** office hours 9 am-6 pm, 45 day cancellation notice-fee imposed.

THE WESTIN ST. JOHN RESORT & VILLAS
Phone: (340)693-8000 29

Resort Hotel
$169-$2715

WESTIN HOTELS & RESORTS **AAA Benefit:** Enjoy up to 15% off your next stay, plus Starwood Preferred Guest® bonuses.

Address: Great Cruz Bay 00831 **Location:** Oceanfront. 2 mi (3.2 km) se of town on Hwy 104. **Facility:** This sprawling resort, with a large pool area and sugar-sand beach, offers fully equipped, condo-style units as well as some tastefully appointed hotel rooms. Meets AAA guest room security requirements. 321 units, some two bedrooms, kitchens and condominiums. 2-3 stories, exterior corridors. **Terms:** 15 day cancellation notice-fee imposed. **Amenities:** safes. *Fee:* video games, high-speed Internet. **Dining:** 4 restaurants, entertainment. **Pool(s):** 3 outdoor. **Activities:** saunas, whirlpools, rental boats, paddleboats, sailboats, windsurfing, boat dock, 6 lighted tennis courts, recreation programs, jogging, playground, sports court, game room, shuffleboard, volleyball, spa. *Fee:* scuba diving, snorkeling, charter fishing. **Guest Services:** valet laundry.
(See ad on insert, this page.)

[icons]

WHERE TO EAT

ASOLARE
Phone: 340/779-4747 42

Asian
$25-$38

AAA Inspector Notes: The terrace of this old stone home above Cruz Bay affords sweeping views of breathtaking sunsets. Imaginative dishes use fresh ingredients and blend Asian with tropical and Southern influences. **Bar:** full bar. **Reservations:** suggested. **Address:** North Shore Rd 00831 **Location:** Just n of town. [D] [M] [N]

DELI GROTTO
Phone: 340/777-3061 45

Deli
$6-$10

AAA Inspector Notes: Tucked into a corner of the quaint shops of Mongoose Junction, this tiny deli offers an air-conditioned oasis to enjoy gourmet sandwiches, salads, fresh cakes and cookies, or a specialty coffee. The display case presents a tantalizing array of prepared dishes and salads that can be packed to-go for picnicking at the beach. Internet kiosks are located at the rear of the cafe. No credit cards are accepted. **Bar:** beer only. **Address:** 507 Mongoose Junction 00830 **Location:** Just n of ferry dock; in Mongoose Junction. **Parking:** no self-parking. [B] [L]

MORGAN'S MANGO
Phone: 340/693-8141 46

Caribbean
$15-$28

AAA Inspector Notes: On the second floor of a West Indies-style verandah, this restaurant offers a boisterous atmosphere most nights due to its popularity with locals and tourists alike since 1993. The menu is a trip around the Caribbean islands with a few of the favorites being the voodoo snapper, the seafood brochette and the flying fish. The Brie quesadilla or the lobster cakes are savory appetizers to whet the appetite. Live music is featured on some nights. **Bar:** full bar. **Reservations:** suggested. **Address:** Main Rd 00831 **Location:** Center; near ferry dock; across from National Park Visitors Center. **Parking:** street only. [D] [M] [N]

ST. JOHN WATERFRONT BISTRO
Phone: 340/777-7755 43

French
$10-$39

AAA Inspector Notes: This bistro offers relaxed, casual dining in an open-air covered waterside location. Classic French cuisine with some Caribbean influences is served as well as lighter fare of soups, salad and sandwiches during lunch. **Bar:** full bar. **Address:** Wharfside Village 00830 **Location:** Just s of passenger ferry terminal. **Parking:** street only. [L] [D] CALL [&M] [M]

▼ See AAA listing this page ▼

VIRGIN ISLANDS NATIONAL PARK (B-4)
• Hotels & Restaurants index & map p. 511

CANEEL BAY, A ROSEWOOD RESORT
Phase: (340)776-6111   25

▼▼▼▼ ▼▼▼▼
Resort Hotel
$450-$1700

Address: North Shore Dr **Location:** Oceanfront. On Caneel Bay; accessible by ferry from Charlotte Amalie waterfront or Red Hook ferry terminal. Located in Virgin Islands National Park. **Facility:** On 170 acres of an old sugar plantation, the resort is surrounded by a national park; widely dispersed lodgings add to the feeling of seclusion. 166 units, some two bedrooms. 1-2 stories (no elevator), exterior corridors. **Terms:** open 12/1-9/4 & 10/27-11/30, office hours 6 am-11 pm, 28 day cancellation notice, 14 day off season-fee imposed. **Amenities:** safes, honor bars. **Dining:** 4 restaurants, entertainment. **Pool(s):** outdoor. **Activities:** boating, sailboats, windsurfing, boat dock, snorkeling, 11 tennis courts, recreation programs, hiking trails, playground. *Fee:* scuba diving, charter fishing, massage. **Guest Services:** valet laundry, area transportation (fee)-Charlotte Amalie.

FEE ⊞ ¶¶ ⟙ ⋔ SD ⇖ ✠ BIZ 🛜 ⊠
🅦 ✂ ▣

St. Thomas Island

CHARLOTTE AMALIE (B-2) pop. 11,004
• Restaurants p. 520
• Hotels & Restaurants index & map p. 511

BEST WESTERN CARIB BEACH RESORT
Phone: (340)774-2525   1

▼▼▼ ▼▼
Motel
$150-$210

AAA Benefit: Members save up to 20%, plus 10% bonus points with Best Western Rewards®.

Address: 8070 Lindbergh Bay 00802 **Location:** Oceanfront. Just n of St Thomas-Cyril E King International Airport. **Facility:** 51 units. 2-3 stories (no elevator), interior/exterior corridors. **Terms:** check-in 4 pm, cancellation fee imposed. **Amenities:** safes (fee). **Pool(s):** outdoor. **Guest Services:** valet laundry. **Free Special Amenities:** room upgrade (subject to availability with advance reservations) and high-speed Internet.

SAVE ¶¶ SD ⇖ 🛜 ⊠ ▣ / SOME UNITS FEE 🛏

▼ See AAA listing p. 520 ▼

Best Western PLUS
Emerald Beach Resort
Saint Thomas, Virgin Islands

Beachfront Accommodations
Group Rates
All Inclusive Packages
Receptions
Beach Weddings
Honeymoons

Emerald Beach Resort
8070 Lindbergh Bay, St. Thomas, USVI 00802
Phone: 340-777-8800   Toll Free: 800-233-4936
Fax: 340-776-3426   reservations@emeraldbeach.com
www.emeraldbeach.com

(See index & map p. 511.)

▼ See AAA listing p. 521 ▼

Discover mobile travel solutions at
AAA.com/mobile and CAA.ca/mobile

(See index & map p. 511.)

BEST WESTERN PLUS EMERALD BEACH RESORT
Phone: (340)777-8800   **2**

Hotel
$179-$309

AAA Benefit: Members save up to 20%, plus 10% bonus points with Best Western Rewards®.

Address: 8070 Lindbergh Bay 00802 **Location:** Oceanfront. 2.5 mi (4 km) w of town, on Lindbergh Bay; 0.6 mi (1 km) from airport. **Facility:** Meets AAA guest room security requirements. 90 units. 3 stories (no elevator), exterior corridors. **Terms:** check-in 4 pm, 3 day cancellation notice-fee imposed. **Amenities:** high-speed Internet, safes (fee). **Pool(s):** outdoor. **Activities:** tennis court, exercise room. **Guest Services:** valet laundry. **Free Special Amenities:** high-speed Internet and manager's reception. *(See ad p. 518.)*

WHERE TO EAT

AMALIA CAFE
Phone: 340/714-7373   **19**

Spanish
$15-$32

AAA Inspector Notes: Visitors can enjoy a delightful and relaxing meal at this casual cafe. Start with the gambos Santa Fe cafe, a dish of crab meat-stuffed jumbo shrimp in a herb butter, followed by the entrecote Madrid-Barcelona, a Spanish version of the American favorite steak and eggs. The curried lobster bisque is an excellent choice. Tapas, seafood, beef, lamb and duck also highlight a vibrant menu. Finish off the meal with a creme catalana. **Bar:** full bar. **Address:** 24 Palm Passage 00803 **Location:** Downtown; in Palm Passage. **Parking:** street only.

CAFE AMICI
Phone: 340/714-7704   **14**

Italian
$12-$18

AAA Inspector Notes: This cafe offers covered-patio dining in the heart of the shopping district. The menu features salads, excellent homemade soups and many Italian favorites all served in a relaxed atmosphere. **Bar:** full bar. **Address:** 36-37 Dronningens Gade 00802 **Location:** Downtown; in A.H. Riise Mall. **Parking:** street only.

CALICO JACK'S
Phone: 340/775-0500   **22**

Pizza
$13-$17

AAA Inspector Notes: I really enjoyed the laid-back atmosphere while eating a great pizza in this really fun restaurant located in the downtown shopping district. **Bar:** full bar. **Address:** 34-35 Dronningens Gade 00802 **Location:** Downtown; in Hibiscus Alley. **Parking:** street only.

CUZZIN'S CARIBBEAN RESTAURANT
Phone: 340/777-4711   **13**

Caribbean
$12-$23

AAA Inspector Notes: In the heart of Charlotte Amalie's bustling shopping district is the ever-popular restaurant, which offers West Indian fare. On the menu are preparations of fresh local fish and conch, curry dishes and traditional sides such as fungi, a familiar island favorite similar to polenta. **Bar:** full bar. **Address:** 7 Back St 00802 **Location:** Jct Trompeter Gade; downtown. **Parking:** street only.

GLADYS' CAFE
Phone: 340/774-6604   **20**

Caribbean
$10-$21

AAA Inspector Notes: Located in the heart of the shopping district, this cozy restaurant offers a choice between a light fare of salads, burgers and sandwiches as well as full lunches of chicken, pork chops and seafood with a Caribbean flair. **Bar:** full bar. **Address:** Royal Dane Mall W 00803 **Location:** Downtown; in Royal Dane Mall. **Parking:** street only.

THE GREENHOUSE RESTAURANT ST. THOMAS
Phone: 340/774-7998   **24**

International
$12-$28

AAA Inspector Notes: Popular with locals and tourists like, this island-centric restaurant, which schedules dining and entertainment theme nights, overlooks the harbor. Mouth-watering steaks, barbecue and fresh seafood line the menu. In addition there are a wide range of entrée-size salads including Greek salad, taco salad and a grilled mahi mahi salad. Seafood ranges from Alaskan king crab legs and Creole shrimp to salmon and baked stuffed swordfish. **Bar:** full bar. **Address:** Veterans Dr 00802 **Location:** Jct Veterans Dr and Storetvaer Gade. **Parking:** street only.

HOOK, LINE, & SINKER BAR AND RESTAURANT
Phone: 340/776-9708   **21**

International
$10-$28

AAA Inspector Notes: Located at the marina, this casual eatery's menu features burgers, sandwiches and salads for lunch. Dinner options include escargot or mussels as starters and stuffed yellow-tail tuna, pepper-crusted duck with a berry demi glace as well as a variety of pasta dishes and a filet mignon wrapped in bacon. **Bar:** full bar. **Reservations:** suggested. **Address:** 6200 Honduras 00802 **Location:** SR 30 at Frenchtown Yacht Harbor.

MAFOLIE
Phone: 340/774-2790   **8**

Continental
$21-$48

AAA Inspector Notes: Spectacular views from the tiered dining room of this fine dining spot include wonderful sunsets, boats and cruise ships in the harbor and the twinkling lights of downtown. The food is just as fabulous. Specialties range from shrimp and scallop Newburg and filet mignon to Caribbean lobster and bouillabaisse. **Bar:** full bar. **Reservations:** suggested. **Address:** 7091 Estate Mafolie 00802 **Location:** Rt 35, 1 mi (1.7 km) n, follow signs. **Parking:** street only.

OCEANA RESTAURANT AND WINE BAR
Phone: 340/774-4262   **18**

Seafood
$29-$65

AAA Inspector Notes: This restaurant at the water's edge offers wonderful upscale dining. Guests can partake in a tasting-table as well as delicious entrées of seafood, steak, lamb and other selected delicacies. **Bar:** full bar. **Reservations:** suggested. **Address:** Waters Edge at Villa Olga 00803 **Location:** 1 mi (1.7 km) w; at Frenchtown Harbor.

OLD STONE FARMHOUSE
Phone: 340/777-6277   **7**

Continental
$29-$54

AAA Inspector Notes: Visitors can enjoy an evening of elegant fare served in a 250-year-old stone-and-ship ballast farm house while tasting inventive courses comprised of the finest ingredients. Sample the poached jumbo shrimp cocktail in a calamari ceviche followed by a Tasmanian rib-eye. Other favorites on the changing menu include veal osso buco with gremolata-seasoned calamari, beef short rib with butter poached lobster and beef Wellington. Guests can visit the kitchen to meet the chef. Semi-formal attire. **Bar:** full bar. **Reservations:** suggested. **Address:** Mahogany Run Rd 00802 **Location:** Jct Rt 35 and 42, 2 blks e. **Parking:** valet only. **Classic**

(See index & map p. 511.)

SHIPWRECK TAVERN   Phone: 340/777-1293   28

American
$8-$29

AAA Inspector Notes: This tavern is a local favorite that provides late-night hours where patrons can enjoy menu choices ranging from over-sized specialty burgers to full steak dinners. Set in a nautically themed decor, diners can watch sporting events on the many well-placed TVs. **Bar:** full bar. **Address:** 9718 Estate Thomas 00802 **Location:** 1.5 mi e; in Al Cohen Mall at Havensight.

 L D LATE

SIB'S ON THE MOUNTAIN   Phone: 340/774-8967   1

American
$12-$28

AAA Inspector Notes: Perched on the side of the mountain, this longtime local favorite features chicken and seafood dishes, as well as pasta, stir-fries, sandwiches and wraps. Guests can opt to dine in the modest dining room or outside. **Bar:** full bar. **Address:** 33-5 Estate Elizabeth 00802 **Location:** North of town, halfway up mountain top; at Estate Elizabeth; jct Hwy 37 and 33. **Parking:** on-site and street. D LATE

TAVERN ON THE WATERFRONT
Phone: 340/776-4328   12

Continental
$10-$48

AAA Inspector Notes: This eatery offers wonderful views of the harbor as well as a great variety of menu offerings with something that will please everyone. Inventive dinners range from fresh seafood to juicy steaks. Lighter fare is available during lunch. Jazz is featured on Friday nights. **Bar:** full bar. **Reservations:** suggested. **Address:** 30 Dronningens Gade 00802 **Location:** Downtown; on the waterfront. **Parking:** street only.

L D ⬎

THIRTEEN RESTAURANT   Phone: 340/774-6800   3

International
$19-$29

AAA Inspector Notes: With a Northern view from the top of the island, this eatery offers the best traditions of fine dining. Guests can choose from a selection of steaks, duck, rack of lamb, Cornish hens or fresh seafood. **Bar:** full bar. **Reservations:** required. **Address:** 13A Estate Dorothea 00802 **Location:** Jct Rt 33 and 40 (Four Corners), 1 mi (1.7 km) w. **Parking:** street only. D

VIRGILIO'S   Phone: 340/776-4920   10

Northern Italian
$13-$48

AAA Inspector Notes: Fine dining in the Northern Italian tradition can be enjoyed at this eatery. Upscale presentations of seafood, chicken, veal, lamb, steaks and inventive pasta entrées are featured. For lunch, a lighter fare of pasta and sandwiches is offered. **Bar:** full bar. **Reservations:** suggested. **Address:** 18 Dronningens Gade 00802 **Location:** 2 blks n of the waterfront; downtown. **Parking:** street only. L D

FRENCHMAN BAY
• Hotels & Restaurants index & map p. 511

FRENCHMAN'S REEF & MORNING STAR MARRIOTT BEACH RESORT   Phone: (340)776-8500   5

Resort Hotel
$387-$780

Marriott
HOTELS & RESORTS

AAA Benefit: AAA hotel discounts of 5% or more.

Address: 5 Estate Bakkeroe 00801 **Location:** Oceanfront. 1 mi (1.6 km) e of town on Frenchman Bay Rd. **Facility:** On the edge of a cliff overlooking the water, this resort offers many service options and food outlets. 478 units. 2-8 stories, interior/exterior corridors. **Terms:** check-in 4 pm, 7 day cancellation notice-fee imposed. **Amenities:** safes. **Dining:** 4 restaurants, also, Havana Blue, see separate listing, entertainment. **Pool(s):** 3 outdoor. **Activities:** rental boats, rental sailboats, rental sailboards, boat dock, snorkeling equipment rental, recreation programs, game room, volleyball, massage. *Fee:* 2 lighted tennis courts. **Guest Services:** valet laundry, area transportation-water taxi to Charlotte Amalie. **Free Special Amenities:** preferred room (subject to availability with advance reservations) and manager's reception. *(See ad p. 519, on insert.)*

SAVE ⅋ Y CALL ⅋M S SD ⟲ ⤬ BIZ
🛜 ✕ 📱 💻 / SOME UNITS 🖥

WHERE TO EAT

HAVANA BLUE   Phone: 340/715-2583   9

Latin American
$32-$48

AAA Inspector Notes: One of the more trendy restaurants on the island, the dining room offers a chic design. Inspired young servers energize the floor. The tastefully presented dishes integrate Caribbean, Cuban and Asian culinary influences. Choose from Angus beef, duck breast and lamb as well as select seafood and fish dishes. The designer cocktails are especially tempting. **Bar:** full bar. **Reservations:** suggested. **Address:** 5 Estate Bakkeroe 00802 **Location:** 1 mi (1.6 km) e of town on Frenchman Bay Rd; in Frenchman's Reef & Morning Star Marriott Beach Resort. D

RED HOOK
• Hotels & Restaurants index & map p. 511

THE RITZ-CARLTON, ST. THOMAS
Phone: (340)775-3333 [13]

Resort Hotel
$269-$999

AAA Benefit:
Unequaled service at Special Member Savings.

Address: 6900 Great Bay 00802 **Location:** Oceanfront. 3 mi (4.8 km) e of Charlotte Amalie; Hwy 38 to jct Hwy 32, 3.5 mi (5.6 km) e to jct Hwy 322, then 2 mi (3.2 km) se. **Facility:** The resort's main building resembles an Italian-Mediterranean villa with an open-air courtyard; a newly built extension also is featured. Meets AAA guest room security requirements. 180 units. 3-5 stories, exterior corridors. **Parking:** on-site and valet. **Terms:** check-in 4 pm, 14 day cancellation notice-fee imposed. **Amenities:** high-speed Internet, safes, honor bars. **Dining:** 3 restaurants, also, Bleuwater, see separate listing, entertainment. **Pool(s):** outdoor, 2 heated outdoor. **Activities:** whirlpools, steamrooms, boating, sailboats, windsurfing, snorkeling, 2 lighted tennis courts, recreation programs, game room, volleyball, spa. *Fee:* scuba diving, charter fishing. **Guest Services:** valet laundry.

[icons] FEE [icons] / SOME UNITS [icons]

SECRET HARBOUR BEACH RESORT
Phone: (340)775-6550 [11]

Address: 6280 Estate Nazareth 00802 **Location:** Oceanfront. 3 mi (4.8 km) e of Charlotte Amalie; on Hwy 38 to jct Hwy 32, 3.5 mi (5.6 km) e to jct Hwy 322, 1 mi (1.6 km) se. **Facility:** Meets AAA guest room security requirements. 72 condominiums. 2-3 stories (no elevator), exterior corridors. **Terms:** 14 day cancellation notice, 7 day off season-fee imposed. **Amenities:** safes. *Some:* high-speed Internet. **Pool(s):** outdoor. **Activities:** boat dock, 3 tennis courts, exercise room. *Fee:* scuba diving, snorkeling, massage. **Guest Services:** coin laundry. **Free Special Amenities:** high-speed Internet and manager's reception.
(See ad this page.)

Condominium
$185-$725

[icons] CALL [icons]
[icons]

▼ *See AAA listing this page* ▼

Where Tranquility Meets the Beach!

73 Unit All Suite Boutique Resort
Ocean View & Beachfront Accommodations
Seaside Dining ♦ Dive Shop ♦ Water Sports
Weddings ♦ Family Reunions ♦ Retreats

www.secretharbourvi.com ♦ 6280 Estate Nazareth, US Virgin Islands 00802 ♦ (340) 775-6550

Find valuable AAA/CAA member savings
at AAA.com/discounts

(See index & map p. 511.)

WHERE TO EAT

THE AGAVE TERRACE   Phone: 340/775-4142   (32)

International
$25-$47

AAA Inspector Notes: Situated on a cliff, the open-air dining room of this eatery offers breath-taking views of the sea. On the menu are distinctive preparations of the freshest local seafood. Tempting starters include lobster bisque and seared-tuna. Entrees range from seared-duck breast with tamarind Barolo glaze to seafood carnival-a pasta dish with lobster, shrimp, conch and snapper. Desserts include mango chocolate bread pudding and coconut rum crème brulée. Live music is offered on most nights. **Bar:** full bar. **Reservations:** suggested. **Address:** 6600 Estate Smith Bay, #4 00802 **Location:** 8 mi (12.8 km) e of Charlotte Amalie; on north coast Hwy 38; in Point Pleasant Resort and Villas. D ⓚ

BLEUWATER   Phone: 340/775-3333   (14)

Creole
$30-$48

AAA Inspector Notes: Enjoy a menu by notable local chef David Benjamin that puts a spin on Creole fare, using many local ingredients including plantains and native lobster. The intimate seaside bistro is casually upscale, but always welcoming, accommodating with ease the fickle tastes of children. Patio seating is a popular choice. Mid-August through mid-December, the restaurant is closed on Mondays-Tuesdays, but hotel guests can make arrangements for dinner on the beach. **Bar:** full bar. **Reservations:** suggested. **Address:** 6900 Great Bay 00802 **Location:** 3 mi (4.8 km) e of Charlotte Amalie; Hwy 38 to jct Hwy 32, 3.5 mi (5.6 km) e to jct Hwy 322, then 2 mi (3.2 km) se; in The Ritz-Carlton, St. Thomas. **Parking:** on-site and valet. D CALL ⓛⓜ

THE CELLAR   Phone: 340/715-1442   (33)

New American
$26-$36

AAA Inspector Notes: Progressive American cuisine is served in a stylish ambience at this spot. Besides the soup of the day, there are several tempting appetizers on the eclectic menu such as the pan-seared Hudson Valley foie gras and Kobe beef tartar. A broad range of entrées reflect the skills of the chef and include such meats as New Zealand elk, Texas wild boar, Angus beef Wellington and buffalo. There also is live Maine lobster, local snapper and yellow fin tuna. Desserts include bread pudding and rum cake. **Bar:** full bar. **Reservations:** required. **Address:** Red Hook Plaza 00802 **Location:** At America Yacht Harbor. D ⓚ

DUFFY'S LOVE SHACK   Phone: 340/779-2080   (38)

International
$10-$20

AAA Inspector Notes: This small, open-air spot is known for its nightlife and fun. The interesting eclectic menu incorporates Asian, Mexican and Caribbean specialties. Many of the outrageous tropical drinks come in souvenir glasses. **Bar:** full bar. **Address:** 6500 Red Hook Plaza 00802 **Location:** East end in Red Hook Plaza; opposite St. John Ferry Dock. L D LATE ⓚ ⓢ

FISH TAILS   Phone: 340/714-3188   (37)

Seafood
$10-$45

AAA Inspector Notes: Located next to the ferry launch at the marina, patrons can sit waterside in a covered, open-air dining room while enjoying beverages and the nice offerings from the menu. Entrées include seafood, steak, pasta, sandwiches and salads. **Bar:** full bar. **Address:** 6501 Red Hook Plaza, Suite 201 00802 **Location:** Downtown; adjacent to ferry launch. **Parking:** on-site (fee) and street. B L D LATE ⓚ

MOLLY MOLONES   Phone: 340/775-1270   (36)

American
$10-$29

AAA Inspector Notes: This pub-style eatery, not far from the ferry docks, offers lunch options which include thick delicatessen sandwiches, gourmet burgers and Philly cheesesteaks, while the full dinner menu is lined with such starters as wings and conch fritters and entrées such as shepherd's pie, Irish stew, Angus steaks and fresh catches of the day. **Bar:** full bar. **Address:** 6100 Red Hooks Quarters 00802 **Location:** Center; at American Yacht Harbour. B L D ⓚ ⓢ

SMITH BAY
• Hotels & Restaurants index & map p. 511

WYNDHAM SUGAR BAY RESORT & SPA
Phone: (340)777-7100   (15)

Resort Hotel
$187-$646

Address: 6500 Estate Smith Bay 00802 **Location:** Oceanfront. 8.5 mi (13.6 km) e of Charlotte Amalie; on Hwy 38. **Facility:** The resort is on a bluff and all units feature patios with sweeping views of Smith Bay or St. John; a variety of activities are available. Meets AAA guest room security requirements. 294 units. 3-4 stories, exterior corridors. **Terms:** 3 night minimum stay - seasonal and/or weekends, cancellation fee imposed. **Amenities:** Some: video games (fee), safes. **Dining:** 6 restaurants, nightclub, entertainment. **Pool(s):** 3 outdoor. **Activities:** whirlpools, snorkeling & rental equipment, 4 lighted tennis courts, recreation programs, jogging, basketball, volleyball, spa. Fee: saunas, steamrooms, sailboats, windsurfing, scuba diving, miniature golf, game room. **Guest Services:** valet laundry. **Free Special Amenities:** manager's reception and children's activities.

SAVE 🍴 🍸 S SD 🏊 🛅 BIZ 🛜 FEE 🎱
/ SOME UNITS 🛏 🍽

WHERE TO EAT

ROMANO'S RESTAURANT & ART GALLERY
Phone: 340/775-0045   (30)

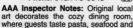
Northern Italian
$24-$38

AAA Inspector Notes: Original local art decorates the cozy dining room, where guests taste pasta, seafood and veal prepared in a nouvelle Italian fashion. Nightly specials are worth a try, as are the sinful raspberry or banana Napoleons. **Bar:** full bar. **Reservations:** suggested. **Address:** 6697 Smith Bay 00802 **Location:** On Coral World Rd, just n of jct Hwy 38. D

More choices.
Bigger savings.
Easier booking.

- Hotel discounts up to 35%
- 24/7 access to live support
- AAA Diamond ratings
- Discounts and benefits from Hertz

It all clicks at AAA.com/Travel

Caribbean Club Contacts

AAA Auto Club South has an office in San Juan, Puerto Rico, to serve visiting AAA/CAA members. The branch office provides auto travel services, including maps, TourBook guides and on-demand TripTik® routings, as well as travel agency services. The office is at 654 Avenida Muñoz Rivera, Lobby Level, Suites 103-1119, approximately 6 miles from Old San Juan's cruise ship piers in the suburb of Hato Rey. Office hours are Monday through Friday 9-6 (Atlantic Standard Time). For more information, phone (787) 620-7805.

Language Tips

ON THE FOLLOWING PAGES are listed some of the words and phrases that are most useful to English-speaking travelers in the Caribbean. Expressions are given in Dutch, French and Spanish, the three languages most commonly spoken in addition to English.

Although not essential, knowledge of basic terms—particularly "please" and "thank you"—is helpful. Most islanders who deal with tourists speak at least some English, and those who don't will be only too glad to assist you in your attempts at a foreign language.

General Expressions

Dutch

Please	Alstublief
Thank you	Dank u zeer
Excuse me	Neemt u mij niet kwalijk
Yes	Ja
No	Neen
Good day (hello)	Goedendag
Good evening	Goedenavond
Good night	Goedenacht
Good-bye	Tot ziens
Do you speak English?	Spreekt u Engels?
I do not understand	Ik begrijp niet
Please repeat	Zegt u het nog eens
Sir	Mijnheer
Madam	Mevrouw
Miss	Juffrouw

French

Please	S'il vous plaît
Thank you	Merci
Excuse me	Excusez-moi
Yes	Oui
No	Non
Good day (hello)	Bonjour
Good evening	Bonsoir
Good night	Bonne nuit
Good-bye	Au revoir
Do you speak English?	Parlez-vous anglais?
I do not understand	Je ne comprends pas
Please repeat	Répétez, s'il vous plaît
Sir	Monsieur
Madam	Madame
Miss	Mademoiselle

Spanish

Please	Por favor
Thank you	Gracias
Excuse me	Discúlpeme usted
Yes	Si
No	No
Good day (hello)	Buenos días
Good evening	Buenas tardes
Good night	Buenas noches
Good-bye	Adiós
Do you speak English?	¿Habla usted inglés?
I do not understand	No entiendo
Please repeat	Repita, por favor
Sir	Señor
Madam	Señora
Miss	Señorita

On The Road

English

1. Please show me the road to ____.
2. I want to go to ____.
3. Are we far from ____?
4. Where are we?
5. May I park here?
6. Go straight ahead.
7. To the right.
8. To the left.
9. How far is

a. a garage?
b. a gas station?
c. a doctor?
d. a police station?
e. a telephone?
f. a post office?
g. a hotel?
h. a restaurant?

Dutch

1. Wilt u mij de weg naar ____wijzen.
2. Ik wil naar ____.
3. Zijn we ver van ____?
4. Waar zijn we?
5. Mag ik hier stoppen?
6. Rijdt u rechtdoor?
7. Rechts.
8. Links.
9. Hoe ver hier vandaan is
   a. een garage?
   b. een benzinestation?
   c. een doktor?
   d. een politie-bureau?
   e. een telefooncel?
   f. een postkantoor?
   g. een hotel?
   h. een restaurant?

French

1. Veuillez m'indiquer la route a ____.
2. Je desire aller a ____.
3. Sommes-nous loins de ____?
4. Ou sommes nous?
5. Puis-je m'arreter ici?
6. Roulez tout droit.
7. À droit

8. À gauche
9. À quelle distance se trouve
   a. un garage?
   b. un poste a essence?
   c. un medecin?
   d. un poste de police?
   e. une cabine?
   f. la poste?
   g. un hotel?
   h. un restaurant?

Spanish

1. Sirvase indicarme el camino para ____.
2. Quiero ir a ____?
3. ¿Estamos lejos de ____?
4. ¿Dónde estamos?
5. ¿Puedo detenerme aquí?
6. Siga el camino recto.
7. A la derecha
8. A la izquierda
9. ¿A que distancia está
   a. un garaje?
   b. una estación de gasolina?
   c. un médico?
   d. una estación de policia?
   e. una cabina telefónica?
   f. la oficina de correos?
   g. un hotel?
   h. un restaurante?

At The Restaurant

Dutch

Water	Water
Coffee	Koffie
Tea	Thee
Milk	Melk
Beer	Bier
Wine	Wijn
Cider	Appelwijn
Lemonade	Citroenlimonade
Hors d'oeuvres	Hors d'oeuvres
Bread	Brood
Soup	Soep
Eggs	Eiren
Fish	Vis
Lobster	Kreeftesla
Meat	Vlees
Beef	Rundvlees
Beefsteak	Biefstuk
Pork	Varkenvlees
Ham	Ham
Mutton	Schapevlees
Venison	Wild
Veal	Kalfvlees
Chicken	Kip
Rice	Rijst
Potatoes	Aardappelen
Vegetables	Groenten
Salad	Salade
Tomatoes	Tomaten
Cabbage	Kool
Green peas	Doperwten
Green beans	Princesseboontjes
Cauliflower	Bloemkool
Mushrooms	Champignons
Cheese	Kaas
Fruit	Fruit
Pastries	Gebak
Ice cream	Ijs
Cookies	Beschult
Orange	Sinaasappel
Apple	Appel
Banana	Banaan
Grapes	Druiven
Pear	Peer
Cherries	Kersen
Strawberries	Aardbeien
Sugar	Suiker
Cream	Room
Salt	Zout
Pepper	Peper
Oil	Olie
Vinegar	Azijn
Mustard	Mosterd
Garlic	Knoflook
Butter	Boter
Jam	Jam
Knife	Mes
Fork	Vork
Spoon	Lepel
Bottle	Fles
Glass	Glas
Cup	Kopje
Plate	Bord
Napkin	Servet
Rare	Half rauw
Medium	Gaar
Well done	Gebakken
Warm	Warm
Iced, cold	Gekoeld
Give me the menu.	Geeft u mij het menu
I should like.	Ik sou willen.
How much is the meal?	Hoeveel kost de maaltijd?
Is service included?	Is de bediening inbegrepen?
The bill, please.	De rekening, alstublift.
Breakfast	Ontbijt
Lunch	Lunch
Dinner	Diner

French

Water	Eau
Coffee	Cafe
Tea	The

Milk	Lait	Tea	Té
Beer	Biere	Milk	Leche
Wine	Vin	Beer	Cerveza
Cider	Cidre	Wine	Vino
Lemonade	Citronnade	Cider	Sidra
Hors d'oeuvres	Hors d'oeuvres	Lemonade	Limonada
Bread	Pain	Hors d'oeuvres	Entremeses
Soup	Soupe	Bread	Pan
Egg	Oeuf	Soup	Sopa
Omelette	Omelette	Eggs	Huevos
Fish	Poisson	Omelette	Tortilla
Lobster	Homard	Fish	Pescado
Shrimp	Crevette	Lobster	Langosta
Oyster	Huitre	Shrimp, prawn	Langostino
Clam	Moule	Oyster	Ostra
Meat	Viande	Clam	Almeja
Beef	Boeuf	Meat	Carne
Beefsteak	Bifteck	Beef	Vaca
Pork	Porc	Beefsteak	Bistec
Ham	Jambon	Pork	Cerdo
Mutton	Mouton	Ham	Jamón
Lamb	Agneau	Mutton	Cordero
Veal	Veau	Lamb	Cordero
Chicken	Poulet	Veal	Ternera
Rice	Riz	Chicken	Pollo
Potatoes	Pommes de terre	Rice	Arroz
Vegetables	Legumes	Potatoes	Papas
Salad	Salade	Vegetables	Legumbres
Tomatoes	Tomates	Salad	Ensalada
Lettuce	Laitue	Tomatoes	Tomates
Green peas	Petits pois	Lettuce	Lechuga
Beans	Haricots	Peas	Guisantes
Asparagus	Asperges	Beans	Habichuelas
Carrots	Carottes	Asparagus	Esparrago
Mushrooms	Champignons	Carrots	Zanahorias
Cheeses	Fromages	Mushrooms	Hongos
Fruits	Fruits	Cheese	Queso
Pastries	Patisseries	Fruits	Frutas
Ice cream	Glace	Pastries	Pastelería
Cookies	Biscuits	Ice cream	Helados
Orange	Orange	Cookies	Galletas
Apple	Pomme	Orange	Naranja
Banana	Banane	Apple	Manzana
Strawberries	Fraises	Banana	Güineo
Sugar	Sucre	Strawberries	Fresas
Cream	Creme	Sugar	Azúcar
Salt	Sel	Cream	Crema
Pepper	Poivre	Salt	Sal
Butter	Beurre	Pepper	Pimienta
Oil	Huile	Butter	Mantequilla
Vinegar	Vinaigre	Oil	Aceite
Mustard	Moutarde	Vinegar	Vinagre
Gravy, sauce	Sauce	Mustard	Mostaza
Garlic	Ail	Sauce, gravy	Salsa
Jam	Confiture	Garlic	Ajo
Knife	Couteau	Jelly	Jalea
Fork	Fourchette	Knife	Cuchillo
Spoon	Cuiller	Fork	Tenedor
Bottle	Bouteille	Spoon	Cuchara
Glass	Verre	Bottle	Botella
Cup	Tasse	Glass	Vaso
Plate	Assiette	Cup	Taza
Napkin	Serviette	Plate	Plato
Roasted	Roti	Napkin	Servilleta
Fried	Frit	Roasted	Asado
Rare	Saignant	Fried	Frito
Medium	A point	Rare	Poco cocido
Well done	Cuit	Medium	A punto
Warm	Chaud	Well done	Bien cocido
Iced	Glace	Warm	Tibio
Show me the menu	Montrez-moi le menu.	Frozen	Congelado
I should like	Je voudrais.	Show me the menu	Muestreme el menú.
What is the price of the meal?	Quel est le prix du repas?	I want	Yo quiero.
Is service included?	Le service est-il compris?	How much is the meal?	Cuánto cuesta la comida?
The bill, please	L'addition, s'il vous plaît.	Is service included?	Está incluido el servicio?
Breakfast	Petit dejeuner	The bill, please	La cuenta, por favor.
Lunch	Dejeuner	Breakfast	Desayuno
Dinner	Diner	Lunch	Almuerzo

Spanish

Water	Agua	Dinner	Cena
Coffee	Café		

Metric Equivalents Chart

TEMPERATURE

To convert Fahrenheit to Celsius, subtract 32 from the Fahrenheit temperature, multiply by 5 and divide by 9.
To convert Celsius to Fahrenheit, multiply by 9, divide by 5 and add 32.

ACRES

1 acre = 0.4 hectare (ha)	1 hectare = 2.47 acres

MILES AND KILOMETERS

Note: A kilometer is approximately 5/8 or 0.6 of a mile.
To convert kilometers to miles multiply by 0.6.

Miles/Kilometers		Kilometers/Miles	
15	24.1	30	18.6
20	32.2	35	21.7
25	40.2	40	24.8
30	48.3	45	27.9
35	56.3	50	31.0
40	64.4	55	34.1
45	72.4	60	37.2
50	80.5	65	40.3
55	88.5	70	43.4
60	96.6	75	46.6
65	104.6	80	49.7
70	112.7	85	52.8
75	120.7	90	55.9
80	128.7	95	59.0
85	136.8	100	62.1
90	144.8	105	65.2
95	152.9	110	68.3
100	160.9	115	71.4

Celsius °		Fahrenheit °
100	BOILING	212
37		100
35		95
32		90
29		85
27		80
24		75
21		70
18		65
16		60
13		55
10		50
7		45
4		40
2		35
0	FREEZING	32
-4		25
-7		20
-9		15
-12		10
-15		5
-18		0
-21		-5
-24		-10
-27		-15

LINEAR MEASURE

Customary	Metric
1 inch = 2.54 centimeters	1 centimeter = 0.4 inches
1 foot = 30 centimeters	1 meter = 3.3 feet
1 yard = 0.91 meters	1 meter = 1.09 yards
1 mile = 1.6 kilometers	1 kilometer = .62 miles

LIQUID MEASURE

Customary	Metric
1 fluid ounce = 30 milliliters	1 milliliter = .03 fluid ounces
1 cup = .24 liters	1 liter = 2.1 pints
1 pint = .47 liters	1 liter = 1.06 quarts
1 quart = .95 liters	1 liter = .26 gallons
1 gallon = 3.8 liters	

WEIGHT

If You Know:	Multiply By:	To Find:
Ounces	28	Grams
Pounds	0.45	Kilograms
Grams	0.035	Ounces
Kilograms	2.2	Pounds

PRESSURE

Air pressure in automobile tires is expressed in kilopascals. Multiply pound-force per square inch (psi) by 6.89 to find kilopascals (kPa).

24 psi = 165 kPa	28 psi = 193 kPa
26 psi = 179 kPa	30 psi = 207 kPa

GALLONS AND LITERS

Gallons/Liters				Liters/Gallons			
5	19.0	12	45.6	10	2.6	40	10.4
6	22.8	14	53.2	15	3.9	50	13.0
7	26.6	16	60.8	20	5.2	60	15.6
8	30.4	18	68.4	25	6.5	70	18.2
9	34.2	20	76.0	30	7.8	80	20.8
10	38.0	25	95.0	35	9.1	90	23.4

Caribbean Customs Information

Each Caribbean nation has its own immigration requirements; these are summarized in the *Fast Facts* boxes. The U.S. Dept. of Homeland Security requires all citizens traveling by air between the United States and the Caribbean to present a valid passport, NEXUS card, U.S. military ID with travel orders or U.S. Coast Guard Merchant Mariner document to reenter the United States. Citizens traveling by land or sea also are required to present a valid passport or other documents that comply with the Western Hemisphere Travel Initiative (WHTI). AAA recommends carrying a passport when traveling anywhere outside the United States, both to expedite your way through customs and to provide identification in case of an emergency. AAA travel agents can assist you with the passport application procedure.

Before you leave, make two color copies of your passport's identification page, keeping one at home and carrying the other with you separately. Should you lose your passport, go to the nearest American Embassy or Consulate, or contact the National Passport Information Center at (877) 487-2778 or TTY (888) 874-7793 for information about obtaining an emergency passport. A U.S. driver's license and a copy of the original passport will save time in applying for a replacement.

Pets taken to the islands are subject to each island's public health department's regulations, and pets taken out of the United States are subject to U.S. Public Health and Department of Agriculture requirements on return. Also check with state, county and municipal authorities about restrictions on importing pets, and make arrangements well in advance. Consult the Pets and Wildlife Licensing and Health Requirements publication (# 0000-0509) online at www.cbp.gov or by writing to U.S. Customs and Border Protection, 1300 Pennsylvania Ave. NW, Washington, D.C. 20229; phone (877) 227-5511 or TTY (866) 880-6582.

If you plan to carry more than $10,000 in currency or negotiable instruments in or out of the United States, you must file a Report of International Transportation of Currency or Monetary Instruments (FinCEN Form 105) with Customs and Border Protection (CBP) at the port of exit or at the port of entry. Forms are available online or from your local CBP office. They also can be obtained at U.S. international airports and all other ports of entry.

Note: Due to heightened security, travel regulations may change without notice. For the most current information about passports, duties and taxes and federal restrictions, contact U.S. Customs and Border Protection at (877) 227-5511, or visit their web site at www.cbp.gov. The brochure "Know Before You Go" (publication 0000-00512) provides comprehensive information for U.S. citizens traveling abroad.

RETURNING TO THE UNITED STATES

EXEMPTIONS: Any articles you acquire abroad and bring back to the United States must be declared. This requirement includes any repairs made to articles taken abroad and any gifts, such as wedding or birthday presents, you received while abroad.

It is wise to register foreign-made possessions—such as laptop computers, cameras, watches and CD players—at any CBP office *before* leaving the United States in order to avoid being charged duty on them when you return. Only items with serial numbers or other clearly identifiable marks may be registered. If you are traveling with unnumbered items such as expensive jewelry, a sales receipt, insurance policy or appraisal will be sufficient proof that the items were in your possession before you left the U.S. You may register items at the airport prior to departure or take them to a CBP office in advance. Inspectors must *see* the items being registered; keep your documentation for future trips.

Returning U.S. residents are allowed a duty-free exemption for articles they carry with them. If you are arriving from anywhere other than a U.S. insular possession (the U.S. Virgin Islands, American Samoa or Guam), your personal exemption is $800; there are limits on the amount of alcohol, cigarettes, cigars and other tobacco products you may include *(see Alcohol and Tobacco)*. If you travel to the U.S. Virgin Islands, your duty-free allowance is $1,600, of which no more than $800 may have been acquired elsewhere in the Caribbean.

To receive the duty-free exemption, you must have been out of the country a minimum of 48 hours and have not used the exemption within the preceding 30-day period. The 48-hour minimum does not apply to U.S. residents returning from the U.S. Virgin Islands.

The exemption, based on fair retail value, applies to articles for your personal or household use or intended to be given as bona fide gifts *(see Gifts)*. Returning residents who do not meet the 48-hour or 30-day time requirements may bring back up to $200 worth of items for personal or household use free of duty and tax. Antiques at least 100 years old and fine art may enter the country duty-free.

High-quality merchandise from all over the world is usually featured in most duty-free shops. Prices are generally about the same as you would expect to pay in the country of origin. Do not be misled, however, by the words "duty free." This simply means that the local merchant has been exempted from his own country's taxes. All duty-free goods that return with you to the United States must be declared and are subject to U.S. import duties if you exceed your personal exemption.

DUTIES: A flat rate duty of 3 percent is applied to the next $1,000 worth of merchandise in excess of the maximum customs duty-free exemption. Items purchased in the U.S. Virgin Islands are assessed at a rate of 1.5 percent. The flat-rate provision and duty-free exemptions may not be exercised more than once every 30 days. Assessment of merchandise is based on the fair retail value in the country of origin; remember to retain sales slips for proof of value. Keeping purchases and sales slips in a carry-on bag speeds the customs declaration procedure.

Members of a family residing in the same household and traveling together can make a joint declaration, combining their individual articles for application of the flat-rate duty. Any merchandise that exceeds the flat-rate duty on $1,000 worth of goods is dutiable at the various rates that apply to particular articles.

The United States and the following countries have entered into an agreement called the Caribbean Basin Initiative (CBI). These countries include Antigua and Barbuda, Aruba, The Bahamas, Barbados, the British Virgin Islands, Dominica, Grenada, Jamaica, Montserrat, the Netherlands Antilles, St. Kitts and Nevis, St. Lucia, St. Vincent and the Grenadines, and Trinidad and Tobago. Some articles made in and purchased in these countries are accorded a free rate of duty and are not counted against your exemption or flat rate.

Articles acquired abroad and sent home by you or by the store where you purchased them do not qualify as accompanied baggage and are subject to duty and taxes. You do not have to declare these items, as they cannot be included on the customs exemption; duty may be waived on articles not exceeding $200 in total value.

However, articles you purchase and send home from CBI countries or the U.S. Virgin Islands may be duty-free under your personal exemption if the items are properly declared and processed. The CBP form 255 (Declaration of Unaccompanied Articles) must be affixed to each mailed package; merchants can usually supply this form. All shipped items should be indicated on your customs declaration form.

If requested, you must present all sales receipts to Customs upon returning to the United States. *Do not* accept the friendly shopkeeper's offer to give you a sales slip showing a price lower than that actually paid. Customs inspectors are experts at spotting fraudulent receipts. If you understate an article's value or misrepresent an article on your declaration, you might have to pay a penalty in addition to the duty. Under certain circumstances the article might be seized and forfeited. Keep a record of what you spend for merchandise as you spend it.

If you owe duty, it must be paid when you arrive in the United States. Acceptable forms of payment include U.S. currency, personal checks, money orders, travelers checks (value not exceeding $50 of the amount due), and in some locations, MasterCard or Visa.

GIFTS: Gifts worth up to $100 in total fair retail value where acquired may be sent duty free to friends and relatives in the United States, provided only one such package is received by the same person in one day. The dollar value for gifts sent from the U.S. Virgin Islands increases to $200. Gifts for more than one person may be mailed in the same package, provided each gift is individually wrapped and labeled with the name of the recipient. If any article in the consolidated gift package is subject to duty and tax, or if the total value of all articles exceeds the gift allowance, no article will be exempt from duty and tax. Duty cannot be prepaid; it is collected by the United States Postal Service when the package is delivered.

You may not send gifts to yourself, nor may persons traveling together send gifts to each other. The gift allowance does not include alcoholic beverages, tobacco products or perfume valued at more than $5 if it contains alcohol. All parcels must be marked *Unsolicited Gift,* and the nature of the gift and its estimated fair retail value must be noted on the outside wrapper.

RESTRICTED ARTICLES: To prevent the introduction of plant and animal pests and diseases into the United States, an agricultural quarantine bans importation of most fruits, vegetables, plants, livestock, poultry and meats. For details refer to the Department of Agriculture's Animal Products and Fruit and Vegetable manuals online at www.aphis.usda.gov.

Endangered animal or plant species, and products made from them, generally cannot be exported or imported. This includes products made from elephant ivory, although articles made from antique ivory may be imported, provided they can be documented as being at least 100 years old. If you wish to purchase and bring back to the United States any articles made from whalebone, ivory, tortoise shell, animal skins or fur, or products manufactured wholly or in part of any type of wildlife, contact the U.S. Fish and Wildlife Service at (800) 358-2104 to make sure items are admissible.

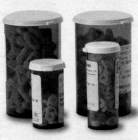

Certain articles considered injurious or detrimental to the United States also are prohibited; these include absinthe, firearms, biological specimens, meat products and narcotics. There are stringent import restrictions on firearms and ammunition as well; consult the Bureau of Alcohol, Tobacco, Firearms and Explosives. Products originating in Angola, Iran, Liberia, Myanmar, North Korea, Serbia and Montenegro, Sudan and Cuba—and all items containing Cuban components—are subject to restriction and require a license. Cuban cigars are expressly forbidden. For further information consult the Office of Foreign Assets Control, Department of the Treasury, 1500 Pennsylvania Ave. N.W., Washington, DC 20220, phone (800) 540-6322, or visit their web site at www.treas.gov/ofac.

If you require medicines containing habit-forming drugs or narcotics, keep them in their original containers and bring an authorizing prescription to avoid potential customs problems upon return to the United States. It is wise to pack medicines in your carry-on luggage.

The distribution rights for many trademarked items are protected by law, and those items may not be brought into the U.S. by unlicensed entities. Residents returning with foreign-made articles bearing a protected trademark are allowed one exemption per type of article; for example, one Chanel handbag and one Polo shirt. The goods must be intended for personal use and must not be sold within 1 year of importation. Articles bearing a counterfeit mark or an inappropriately used federally registered trademark are subject to seizure and forfeiture.

ALCOHOL AND TOBACCO: A returning resident 21 years or older entitled to the $800 duty-free exemption may include 2 liters of alcoholic beverages—provided 1 liter was produced in a CBI country. Additional quantities are subject to duty and taxes. Travelers 21 years and older returning from the U.S. Virgin Islands may bring back 5 liters of alcoholic beverages, provided that 1 liter was produced there. Liquor cannot be mailed to the United States.

There are no federal age restrictions for persons returning with tobacco products. However, the laws of each state where an entry port is located are enforced, and tobacco products may be confiscated if the holder is under the state's minimum age for purchase of tobacco. Persons who meet age requirements may bring back up to 100 cigars and 200 cigarettes. Travelers returning from the U.S. Virgin Islands also may include in their exemption 1,000 cigarettes, provided no more than 200 were acquired elsewhere, and 100 cigars. It is illegal to bring cigars and tobacco products of Cuban origin into the United States.

Travelers may import previously exported tobacco products in quantities not exceeding their eligible exemptions. These items are usually stamped "Tax Exempt: For Use Outside the United States." Amounts exceeding your exemption will be seized and destroyed. Under this regulation, you may bring home 200 previously exported cigarettes plus an additional quantity of foreign-made cigarettes, paying duty and taxes only on the second group.

Laws concerning the importation of cigarettes and alcohol vary from state to state; check the importation requirements of your state of residence, as well as the state of entry.

AUTOMOBILES: Automobiles taken out of the country may be brought back duty free as long as they accompany you upon your return and meet EPA standards. Unleaded fuel is sometimes not available in the Caribbean; if leaded fuel is used, catalytic converters on late-model cars will become inoperative and in most cases will fail to meet emission standards, requiring replacement in order to obtain entry back into the United States. For details visit the EPA's website at www.epa.gov/otaq/imports or contact the agency directly: Environmental Protection Agency, Ariel Ross Bldg., Investigation/Import Section, 1200 Pennsylvania Ave. N.W., Washington, DC 20460; phone (734) 214-4100.

Points of Interest Index

Index Legend

NB............................national battlefield	NR...............................national river	
NBP.....................national battlefield park	NS.............................national seashore	
NC..............................national cemetery	NWR.....................national wildlife refuge	
NF................................national forest	PHP...................provincial historic(al) park	
NHM...............national historic(al) monument	PHS....................provincial historic(al) site	
NHP..................national historic(al) park	PP................................provincial park	
NHS...................national historic(al) site	SF..................................state forest	
NL...............................national lakeshore	SHM...............state historic(al) monument	
NME............................national memorial	SHP...................state historic(al) park	
NMO............................national monument	SHS....................state historic(al) site	
NMP..........................national military park	SME................................state memorial	
NP................................national park	SP....................................state park	
NRA........................national recreation area	SRA.........................state recreation area	

▼ GEM: Points of Interest Offering a *Great Experience for Members*®

MUSIC HALLS & OPERA HOUSES

NATURAL BRIDGES

NATURAL PHENOMENA

NATURE CENTERS

NATURE TRAILS

NAUTICAL TOURS

OBSERVATORIES

PARKS, CITY; STATE; PROVINCIAL

PARKS, NATIONAL

Bed & Breakfast Hotels Index

Some bed and breakfasts listed below might have historical significance.
Those properties are also referenced in the Historical index.

Country Inns Index

Some of the following country inns can also be considered as bed-and-breakfast operations.

Historical Hotels & Restaurants Index

Some of the following historical hotels can also be considered as bed-and-breakfast operations.

Resorts Index

Many establishments are located in resort areas; however, the following
places have extensive on-premises recreational facilities:

Resorts (cont'd)

Resorts (cont'd)

Comprehensive City Index

Here is an alphabetical list of all cities appearing in this TourBook® guide. Cities are presented by state/province. Page numbers under the POI column indicate where points of interest text begins. Page numbers under the L&R column indicate where hotel and restaurant listings begin.

Comprehensive City Index (cont'd)

Comprehensive City Index (cont'd)

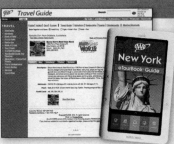

Vacation with Peace of Mind

Experience an incredible vacation with amazing value on select *AAA Vacations*® tour and cruise departures. Includes our **Best Price Guarantee** and **24/7 Member Care** for a worry-free vacation.

Contact your local AAA Travel Professional or visit **AAA.com/Travel** for full details on these exclusive *AAA Vacations*® benefits.

Terms and conditions apply

It's how AAA members turn a drive into a journey.

AAA members get exclusive values on Hertz rentals in every car class ... ensuring ideal wheels for every trip!

For offers and complete terms, visit AAA.com/hertz or Hertz.com.

Visit: Over 1,100 AAA Offices
Click: AAA.com/hertz
Call: 800-654-3080

KEEP YOUR CHILDREN
SAFE IN THE CAR

AAA and the timeless characters of Richard Scarry, one of the
best-selling children's authors of all time, have partnered to promote
child passenger safety. To keep your child safe, use the right car seat
and follow the guidelines at **AAA.com/SafeSeats4Kids.**
To install your car safety seat correctly, call an expert at
866-SEAT-CHECK(732-8243) or visit seatcheck.org.

Remember, car seats save lives!

Get Involved and Keep Teens Safe

TeenDriving.AAA.com

Exploring the countryside or visiting a nearby city can be perfect opportunities for your teen to gain important driving experience. AAA can help you teach good habits and the rules of the road — before and after your teen learns to drive.

Find valuable resources at TeenDriving.AAA.com:

- Information about your state's licensing process
- Tools to help your teen improve driving skills
- Tips for teens to avoid distracted driving
- Downloadable parent-teen driving agreement

Plus, check out the free StartSmart teen driving program, developed by AAA and the National Institutes of Health.

Visit **TeenDriving.AAA.com** today. Get involved. Keep teens safe.

Bringing Everyone CLOSER TOGETHER

BOOK **5** ROOMS
OR MORE WITH FAMILY AND FRIENDS AND YOU'LL ALSO GET...

- Family Picnic
- Family Private Dinner▲
- Family Reunion Activities
- 15-minute Family Portrait Session
- 5 X 7 Group Photo◆
- Farewell Cake
- Family Reunion Concierge

How do you get the entire family together and keep them happy? A Family Reunion at Beaches Resorts...giving you quality time as a family and something everyone will love to do. There's *The Caribbean Adventure with Sesame Street*® for little ones and the Xbox 360® Game Garage, Scratch DJ Academy® and tons of cool hangouts for tweens & teens. Adults can enjoy the Red Lane® Spa*, play golf, go scuba diving◆, or just relax. Plus, for family bonding time, there's endless fun on the best beaches, exciting water sports, gourmet dining, and exclusive reunion activities. Beaches is the perfect getaway to get closer together.

Call Your AAA Travel Professional

Beaches
Resorts for Everyone · by Sandals

▲One group dinner gathering included. ◆One 5x7 photo per room. *Spa additional. ◆Included for certified divers. For non-certified divers, resort dive course is available for a nominal fee. Family Reunion offer not combinable with any other group program or promotion.

TURKS & CAICOS · JAMAICA